MUSIC SURVEY
NEW SERIES
1949-1952

MUSIC SURVEY

NEW SERIES
1949-1952

EDITED BY
DONALD MITCHELL
AND
HANS KELLER

FABER MUSIC
in association with
FABER & FABER
London

This Collected Edition © Donald Mitchell and Hans Keller, 1981
First published in this Collected Edition, 1981
by Faber Music Ltd in association with Faber and Faber Ltd
3 Queen Square London WC1N 3AU
Reproduced from the original numbers
Jacket design by Berthold Wolpe
Printed in England by Whitstable Litho Ltd

British Library Cataloguing in Publication Data
Music survey new series, 1949–1952
1. Music – Periodicals
I. Mitchell, Donald   II. Keller, Hans
780'.5   ML5
ISBN 0–571–10040–6

50 Willow Road, Hampstead:
the editors editing, c. 1950
D.M.   H.K.

Oil painting by MILEIN COSMAN
77 × 52 cm

Contents

Illustrations

Frontispiece: The editors editing (by Milein Cosman)

Preface

in the form of a dialogue

DONALD MITCHELL and HANS KELLER

PC* Why was your magazine necessary? What did you want to do that you felt was missing from the tone or style of the other musical journalism published at the time?

HK Everything was missing at the time; perhaps with the single exception of *The Music Review*, which was open-minded and even allowed itself to publish articles by musicians, there was hardly a musical journal around which published articles of interest to musicians. Up to a point this is still true today. There is hardly a practising musician who reads journals like *The Musical Times*, or even *The Musical Quarterly*, unless he is being reviewed there. So what one was aiming at was a *musical* music journal which – with the partial exception of *The Music Review* – did not exist. Would you agree?

DM I think the musicality of the responses in *Music Survey* was a central point of the intention of the journal, in so far as it could be said to have a consistent intention. The other day I was re-reading the issue [October, 1951] that contained a symposium of reactions to Schoenberg's death. Do you remember, Hans, we published a whole series, a whole sequence of obituaries! What I liked about re-reading them was the warmth and musicality of the responses that came from exceptionally diverse quarters. In short, we chose our writers...

HK Wisely...

DM ...with care; and I think on looking through the journal as a whole, it is that extraordinarily positive, *musical* response to music that emerges as an outstanding feature. That was genuinely part of the style of running the journal. However, *Music Survey* did not start out quite as it developed to be, after you joined me as co-editor, Hans. That was obviously a crucial moment in the history of the periodical. For six issues I edited *Music Survey* alone, and I should be nonplussed if anybody asked me why in fact I started the paper.

HK But that is interesting.

PC It is. Can I help by putting this question into perspective? Was it something in particular that you were angry about? Or was it simply that there was a huge blank which you wanted to attempt to fill?

DM The anger, I think, came in later, though I don't know whether 'anger' is the right word: 'righteous indignation', rather. The polemical character of the paper belonged to the New Series – was a manifestation, if you like, of the new editorial set-up.

PC You embarked, you said, on your own in the first place?

DM I think my policy in the early issues was not uninteresting and indeed sat very comfortably alongside the new ideas that Hans brought to

*Our interlocutor was Patrick Carnegy.

the paper when he joined me as co-editor. What really worried me as a young man was the awful parochialism of English musical life, the complacent provinciality of the opinion-makers. I wanted to oppose all that; and if you look at the first six issues of *Music Survey*, you'll find there, for example, two really admirable articles on Pfitzner by Harold Truscott, still a highly interesting and important contribution to a very small literature in English. There were unpublished letters of Max Reger, and two very important articles by Dika Newlin about Schoenberg's compositions from his American period.

HK Actually, I think these were important articles because, if I'm not mistaken, this was the first time Dika Newlin introduced the concepts of 'progressive' and 'concentric tonality', which meanwhile have become classical terms.

DM I think that's correct. There were other flags run up too – for example, Mahler was a distinct presence. I'm mentioning these signals because they suggest that whereas I may not have developed an identifiable platform or programme, nonetheless those early issues of *Music Survey* bear witness to my attempt to bring to the notice of readers those composers who I felt were neglected or cold-shouldered in England, or to whom the English were indifferent. I had already a sense of certain causes that I was anxious to try to fight, and saw no prospect of winning those battles in established periodicals, at least not in the late 1940s. The solution was to start a periodical of my own which could put forward reasoned arguments for those composers about whom I felt passionately at the time. It was a pretty catholic list when you look at it: Pfitzner, Reger, Schoenberg, Mahler – and alongside them, Roussel, Sibelius, Mendelssohn, Searle, Haydn....Perhaps an indiscriminate taste in some ways, but also unconventional.

PC They were your enthusiasms at the time?

DM As a young man; and for some of those composers my enthusiasm has in no way diminished – for Mahler, above all.

PC How old were you?

DM Twenty-two. And I think that unorthodox choice of topics was one of the things about those early issues that may have encouraged Hans's interest in the proposal that we should jointly edit *Music Survey*.

PC Were you in fact writing music articles, criticism, call it what you like, elsewhere before you published the journal?

DM I think we both were, before, during and after. I wrote everywhere – in places probable and improbable, wherever I could get an opening.

PC Did you feel a sense of constraint from the editors of those journals in whose pages you then wrote, or would have liked to write?

DM I certainly felt that many – most – journals and newspapers took up aesthetic attitudes, or showed attitudes to certain composers, with which I was totally out of sympathy. Therefore I didn't expect to find much of a market for my particular interests. As it happens, though, the very first broadcast I ever made for the BBC was on Max Reger, with illustrations at the piano by Harold Truscott, who was later to contribute to *Music Survey*, as I've already mentioned. That was a pioneering event when you think of the date – 1945 or '46, very early days. But I want to round off this bit of our conversation with an account of how it was that I encountered Hans. It wasn't, initially, through a meeting but through reading his reviews in *The Music Review*, a quarterly review, still appearing intermittently today but then edited by the late Geoffrey Sharp. There were two things about his reviews that caught my attention at the time: first of all the combative manner of the criticism, and then the detailed information that backed it up, which often included an array of footnotes. I thought that anybody who could mount a serious critical assault or for that matter a serious critical appraisal on a given work or composer and reinforce it with a bibliography – this was something I found entirely gripping. Then – a curious coincidence – we found that we both were living in South London, only a mile or two apart. I think it was out of my response to something very special embodied in Hans's critical work that a meeting finally emerged; and out of that meeting developed our partnership as editors of *Music Survey*.

PC Launching a magazine is a difficult and expensive operation. How did you set about funding the journal and distributing it?

DM I was working as a schoolmaster in a prep school in South London, and we were very fortunate in persuading the headmaster of the school to be a generous patron. He put up the money for our enterprise and I am glad to have the chance of warmly acknowledging W. W. Livingston's support. Whether he realized altogether what precisely he was supporting, or whether he always approved of what the editors did with his money, I'm not sure, but he paid the printer's bills, and without that help we would have found it very hard – indeed, impossible – to keep going. As for distribution, it was all done by ourselves. I can remember addressing envelopes, sticking on stamps and delivering the new issue to the local Post Office. That, I think, was entirely done with some help from outside – friends, relatives, and so on.

PC Did you rely on subscriptions, or was it possible to get the thing through the conventional distributors?

DM On the contrary. In those days you could buy *Music Survey* on W. H. Smith's railway-station bookstalls and some people did so. There was in fact a rather rough and ready distribution system, but our main support came from our regular subscribers – including some libraries at home and overseas. However, I doubt if there were more than about a hundred or a hundred and fifty subscribers altogether.

PC What was the print run?

HK I seem to remember that the maximum was a thousand and the minimum around five hundred.

DM I think that the paper's reputation was out of all proportion to the actual number of copies sold. There was always a certain number of people eagerly awaiting the appearance of a new issue, who would be first out on the streets to try to secure a copy. Among them, inevitably, were some upon whom we had launched our latest critical attack. I remember hearing about one senior critic, seen walking down the Charing Cross Road with his face buried in the current issue – and I daresay emerging, metaphorically speaking, with a black eye.

PC Were you actually reviewed by the music critics?

DM Before we get on to that, may we look at this moment of change when we began editing in harness? I've said how it was that it came about, that I'd been very much gripped by what I'd read of Hans's criticism and then found that we were neighbours in South London. As a result of Hans coming in as joint editor I think *Music Survey* did develop a policy, with rather more definition and edge to it than had been the case before. Perhaps Hans might have something to say about that?

HK Well, first of all, I think I ought to answer your question about the constraint which we might have felt in other journals and which might have prompted us to do that in *Music Survey* which we couldn't do elsewhere. As far as I'm concerned, I can't agree that I felt under constraint at the time. As Donald said, I chiefly wrote for *The Music Review*, where I had total freedom, though it must be admitted that there were certain issues, above all that of Britten, where this freedom was not altogether total – so that my essay on 'Britten and Mozart' was refused by *The Music Review* and subsequently accepted by *Music and Letters*; but this was an exceptional instance. On the whole I should say that I did not feel frustrated, and that no such negative feeling was responsible for my enthusiasm for *Music Survey*. In spite of the polemical nature of the journal, the aims I had in mind were entirely positive, and they were closely related to Donald's, except that they were not conceived of in national terms. They were, simply, defence of great or substantial composers whom our musical world neglected. Such defence, of course, inevitably took polemical shape, since one fought people who said that those composers were no good or were not composers at all. Don't forget that this was the time when *the* Music Critic of *The Times*, Frank Howes, published an extended article in which he demonstrated that Schoenberg wasn't a composer at all. Ineluctably, therefore, when one wrote about Schoenberg one's tone was slightly polemical, in view of such official statements.

But behind all such polemics was something which had nothing to do with aggression, which was sheer enthusiasm, musical enthusiasm for great composers who were not yet recognized as being great. And our range was trans-school, which is to say that since there was Schoenberg on the one hand and, shall we say, Britten on the other, there could not have been the slightest suspicion that we subscribed to any current school of compositorial thought. I think we rather commendably concentrated on musical substance – even if it did not betray downright genius, so that composers like Benjamin Frankel and quite a few others were taken up again and again for this simple reason, that there was a great deal of underestimation; I mention Frankel because at the moment, his music is suffering a parallel stretch of underestimation. If I may summarize at this stage, then, it's important to realize that much of the aggression which shows in *Music Survey* is positive; that is to say, it sprang from the spirit of defence of great music. In fact, come to think of it, there was no other aggression. All those who felt attacked had attacked in the first place: we only attacked attackers. It's my recollection that we did not devote much energy to the destruction of rubbish.

DM There was the *occasional* review which did just that: an act of demolition, very often achieved in one sentence. We aimed in particular to deflate the bogus and the pretentious. Proper targets, surely?

HK The bogus, I quite agree.

DM For the rest, Hans is absolutely right. Our attacks were born out of our commitment to the composers in whom we believed. Also, I think, they were generated by a belief I still hold to this day that the best criticism is founded in an enthusiasm for – and thereby, in my view, a comprehension of – the music, or the artist about whom one is writing. We were very much against the philosophy which teaches that criticism means being sceptical or negative, a view which is disseminated still in all too many academic institutions. Many of our colleagues seemed surprised to discover that this was a view we did not share. And, if I can add one further thing to what Hans has said so interestingly, and return for a moment to Schoenberg, only the other day I was reading an article by Arnold Whittall about Schoenberg in England, where he happens to make a very revealing comment: that if somebody wanted to find out – from a historical point of view – how the English regarded Schoenberg, and that person read the obituary summings-up published in *Music and Letters* – I don't know if you recall them, but I do very well – then the unavoidable conclusion would be that attitudes to Schoenberg in England in the 1950s were almost exclusively unsympathetic, hostile or negative in tone. But, as Whittall says, that would be a misleading impression because, if our hypothetical researcher then turned to *Music Survey* – Whittall kindly describes us as 'a short-lived but stimulating periodical', or something of the sort – and read *our* anthology of Schoenberg obituaries, he or she would find radically different attitudes, radically contrasting points of view. In that particular context, I think *Music Survey* can be said to have stood for something that was historically very important, something which went against the tide of received opinion.

　　If I can just make one other point, I think that while it's absolutely true that neither of us felt, as a critic or writer, under any particular constraint, and contributed widely to a whole range of specialist and minority publications, both good and bad, I doubt if we should have found it easy – in any case, we weren't asked – to have joined the music staff of, say, *The Times* or *The Daily Telegraph*. In other words, the mass media, including the BBC of course, did not hasten to open their doors to us during those years. I'm not suggesting that one was suppressed or censored; but one was not encouraged.

PC May I remind you, Donald, of one instance indicative of the strange cultural climate of thirty years ago? You had begun to write as a freelance critic for *The Times*, and were just off to review a concert including the Schoenberg First Chamber Symphony, when Frank Howes, 'Our Music Critic', took you on one side to say, 'Well, you know, we have a policy about him', as if the paper had made up its mind about the composer – as indeed it had about its attitude to Europe, Iceland, or whatever – and was going to stick to it.

DM That is correct. I don't want to criticize Frank Howes so long after his death; he was, in fact, very kind to me as a young man. But certainly, although not saying: 'You've got to write x, y or z about Schoenberg, about the Chamber Symphony', he *did* make it perfectly clear that *The Times* had pronounced its verdict and therefore what *I* should write should not in any way contradict 'official' opinion. *The Times* had spoken. It was not for me to *un*speak it. I think I got round it by talking about the performance, and I'm sure that anybody who read my notice would certainly have got the message that I thought the First Chamber Symphony was a pretty good piece. But I couldn't have written: 'This great work by Schoenberg'; and that in turn reminds me of that extraordinary remark Eric Blom once made to me, when he said: 'Mitchell,' – or 'Donald', or whatever he called me at the time – 'the fact of the matter is we just don't want Mahler here', which is yet further evidence of that continuity of negative opinion to which you referred in connection with *The Times*. 'We just don't want him here': Blom said that without qualification or reservation and in absolute confidence of the rightness of his judgement. Well, that's a view that has experienced a singular reversal.

PC To what extent did you yourselves revalue your opinions even as you wrote them?

HK I've got three answers to your question. First, so far as revaluation is concerned – and I'm speaking for myself now – I don't think that any revaluation took place at any stage, because when there was music that I hated, disliked and therefore probably did not understand, I hadn't written about it in the first place: I kept off such music, so any revaluation that may have taken place had taken place in private and not in public. Now comes answer number two. So far as one's attitude to tradition was concerned – again I can only speak for myself for the moment – I did not think in terms of tradition, ever – so that, when I was confronted with a traditional attitude, an attitude that insisted on a certain tradition (as indeed Frank Howes did, within the context of Vaughan Williams for instance), what took place was what Donald calls 'demolition': I tried to demolish all *evaluation in terms of style* in favour of *evaluation in terms of substance*. This brings me to my third answer: the problem which I think you want to raise did not exist at all so far as my own mind was concerned. There was no problem. There was great music which I understood: that I wrote about. There was lousy music which I thought I understood: that I sometimes wrote about too. There was a lot of great music I did not understand, which I never touched upon, and still don't. And there was even lousy music which I could not trust myself to understand – which, likewise, I did not touch upon. In terms of tradition, I reiterate, I never did think, and still do not, with the sole and well-definable exception of the development of composition: if you are saying that there is a tradition of twelve-tone technique, inasmuch as this technique has developed within its life-span, yes, that I was interested in – the history of the technique. But my concern with tradition never went beyond such technical aspects. I trust these three answers satisfy your question.

PC   You printed articles, you printed correspondence. Did you also print concert reviews?

HK   Indeed. We wrote them, yes.

PC   How did you choose your writers?

HK   We chose people whose musicality we trusted, and whose understanding of that particular music we trusted.

DM   Yes, we certainly tried to match our reviewers to musical events with which we knew they would be sympathetic and about which they would be knowledgeable and thus competent.

HK   We were never scared of overestimation. We were only scared of underestimation. After all, from a certain level upwards, there is no such thing as overestimation, and I'm sure that even now there might be plenty of people who would regard some of the reviews in *Music Survey* as overrating the composers or performers in question. I don't think that problem ever bothered us. On the contrary, other things being equal, we always picked the deepest enthusiasts.

PC   How did you work with your contributors? Did you edit them? And, if so, was this largely a matter of cutting?

HK   *Edit* them? To put it mildly. God!

DM   We worked immensely hard at editing our contributors, a major consequence, I'm sure, of Hans joining the paper, who introduced an entirely new set of standards into the editorial process. This was not solely a consequence, in my view, of Hans's personality and idiosyncratic editorial techniques. I think there was more to it than that. I don't at all apologize for the Old Series of *Music Survey* which, as I've said, broke quite a lot of new ground in a quiet way – even in a discernibly un-English way in their choice of topic. On the other hand, given my own education and a tradition of writing about music in English – elegant, bland, complacent and above all *empty* – which was the only tradition I was familiar with, I doubt if I should have arrived on my own account at the editorial style that came to characterize *Music Survey*. Hans, remember, came from another culture and quite another intellectual tradition. His astonishing linguistic ability enabled him to look at English from the outside and perceive potentialities not immediately apparent to those whose mother-tongue English was. It was a linguistic confrontation I found entirely fascinating. Then there were two other rather un-English qualities I believe Hans brought to our editing – discipline and rigour. This meant that everything had to be considered at the deepest level, from the content of a contribution to the distinction between commas Roman and italicized, a fine typographical point I've worried about ever since. It almost constituted a symbolic embodiment of the passion we brought to our editing.

PC Karl Kraus said that if all the commas were in the right place there'd be no more wars.

DM I learnt an enormous amount from the methodology I've just outlined. I believe those were qualities that we tried to make characteristic of the paper as a whole and which we also tried to encourage our contributors to develop in or for themselves. When they were absent, I suppose we tried to write them in.

HK Indeed, and joyfully so. Since you ask this question about editing, we spent immeasurably more time – correct me if I'm wrong – on editing other people's pieces than on our own writing. In fact, quite often we virtually had to rewrite entire pieces. That was the hardest part of the job, I should think.

PC You sent them proofs, obviously?

DM O yes, certainly. But the editing was a tremendous chore, an enormous job. So too was the proof-reading. Of course, in those days one was much younger and much less busy, so one had the energy and the time. Our frontispiece – I hope to use Milein's painting of us both at Hampstead – will show us hard at work. When the weather allowed, we sat on the terrace at 50 Willow Road, outside the kitchen, with Milein feeding us coffee and other things, and corrected the proofs. I remember that very vividly.

PC Did your contributors go along with your editing? Were there any protests?

DM I think the contributors who felt closely allied to the policy of the paper sustained their loyalty through thick and thin, though I don't doubt they had misgivings from time to time. On the other hand, the changing composition of the editorial board tells its own story. We did bring in various friends and acquaintances to function as a kind of consultative body, even if our consultative process never went very far. But every so often one or other member of the board would send us a letter of resignation. Either we'd trodden on a particularly sensitive toe, or, more likely, written something rude about the institution where the board member worked, or wanted to work. People kept on retiring, or retreating, so you find the editorial board – which we finally gave up altogether, I think, because it was impossible to keep a coherent body of people with us – in a constant state of flux. Some toes we trod on emitted a sharp cry of protest. I still recall Ernest Chapman's postcard, in which he threatened to appear with a loaded revolver and shoot the editors if we printed one further review with a qualifying editorial footnote attached to it. The correspondence section, indeed, includes cries from those whose toes had been trodden on by others than ourselves. There's Peter Pears's postcard, for example – do you remember? – from Germany. In it, the Music Critic of *The Times* was assured that, although he'd buried both Schoenberg and Stravinsky in a recent article, Stravinsky in fact was alive and well – and rehearsing *Oedipus Rex* with Pears in Cologne. The hapless Howes received his own funeral tribute from the great singer – 'Grand Undertaker of Music', or something of the sort.

PC You've put a lot of stress on passionate advocacy of the things you believed in, and yet you also offended and insulted people.

HK The 'and yet' is wrong. One flowed from the other. The insults flowed from the passion. The insults were confined to attacks on attacks, and the attacks which we attacked were attacks on great music we felt passionate about.

DM I think, Hans, that there were two crucial, one might almost say classic examples of this particular aspect of the paper's work. One was your famous article, 'Schoenberg and the Men of the Press', and the other, my piece on *Billy Budd* – 'More Off than On *Billy Budd*'. I think each in its own way admirably documents this particular mode of attacking the attackers.

HK They are perfect illustrations, I quite agree, of the attackers attacking attacks. Nor did we, as could be seen from those two pieces, attack people as people. We attacked their attacks, directly, and confined ourselves to their attacks when we attacked, though it is true to say that in the case of critics who habitually manifested their non-understanding aggression towards certain great composers, we allowed ourselves to talk about their work as a whole as being destructive of music. But in principle, the attacks were always confined to the things which most clearly show up in the two pieces Donald mentions: there it can be seen that we concentrated on the actual music, showed where these people failed when they talked about the music, showed what the music meant in reality, how it worked technically. The best and most factual proof of the success of our venture was the spontaneous gratitude of the composers. Schoenberg's gratitude for my strictly musical assault was explosive.

DM And in the case of Britten it was almost the only article of mine I wrote about him that he actually admitted to having read. I was much moved, years after – it must have been at least twenty years after the event – when he told me how much it had meant to him at the time, reading that particular piece on *Budd*.

HK At the same time one accumulated so much goodwill amongst composers that way that when it came to rather critical stages such as the publication of Schoenberg's last piece against Thomas Mann, one was treated with friendly understanding. On that occasion, I was really frightened to begin with. Schoenberg had written the article in German, and I translated it. Some of it, however, was clearly libellous. So I had to rewrite little bits in order to keep just within the law of libel and, knowing of Schoenberg's personality, I expected an outburst. But no, he was so happy about us by that stage that when I sent him this rewritten piece he immediately returned it with a postcard which said, 'Okay, fine': an unusual reaction from Schoenberg, which showed the amount of goodwill in our credit account.
    Briefly, we were liked by composers and hated by critics.

DM Schoenberg's article on Thomas Mann's *Dr Faustus*: I can very vividly remember it arriving and our looking at it together and coming across Schoenberg's description of Mann as a 'Tagschreiber' [journalist]; and I remember thinking somewhat uneasily that, although one had a lot of sympathy with what Schoenberg was saying, that show of contempt was carrying it a shade too far – an unease that was intensified when 'tapeworms' were introduced as an image of Mann's sentence structure. I think you had to find some way round of dropping those particular gems.

HK Precisely, yes.

DM One of the few reviews the periodical got was from Frank Howes. He wrote that the editors of *Music Survey* may have had interesting ideas, though less than elegantly expressed, but that the important lesson they had not yet learned was that dog does not eat dog. Do you remember that?

HK Ah yes, indeed I do.

DM And of course *Music Survey* in this particular area took the contrary view: that dog – when necessary – should eat dog. We didn't accept that unwritten but widely observed code of behaviour, and in so far as we felt we succeeded in demonstrating how much of the dismissal of what we considered to be great music was based, at best, on defective, and, at worst, on incompetent reviewing, we felt wholly justified in attacking much of the criticism that was manifest in the forties and fifties. We probably did make quite a dent in how people regarded critics and criticism, and perhaps the standard may have risen a bit as a result.

PC Apart from outraged dogs wanting to get back at you, presumably there must have been some colleagues who saw the point of what you were doing, and when there was a new number of *Music Survey* went out of their way to draw their readers' attention to it?

HK On one or two occasions.

DM You're quite right. Desmond Shawe-Taylor, for example, although I don't think one could describe him as having been an enthusiastic *Music Survey* reader, none the less seemed to see that we were serious and had an intelligent and intelligible point of view. For the rest, I don't think people fell over themselves to try to acquaint a wider public with an influence that they thought to be subversive and with opinions with which they were out of sympathy.

HK There were quarter-hearted, silent supporters, such as William Mann. And there were, of course, Deryck Cooke and H.C. Robbins Landon. For the rest, you are really implying that there were such people as musical music critics or musical musicologists – whereas what we did, I think, was to offer a lonely platform for musical music criticism and musical musicology. It virtually did not exist elsewhere.

PC Can I now take you quite a long way back, because you said that the existing so-called music journals didn't get through to the musicians, i.e. the musical musicians, the musical musicologists? Was *Music Survey* read by people who spent their lives thinking about music, and perhaps writing music? Did you get through to lots of conductors and performers?

HK I would say very occasionally, and the reason why it was only occasionally was that so far as the negative part of our activities was concerned, we concentrated a great deal on the mutilation of great music by performers: long pieces on performances were usually black lists, very detailed and concrete, specifying lists of what people had done wrong, thus preventing the music from getting across. There were also highly positive pieces on people like Furtwängler; but of necessity, they were in the minority, because there aren't all that many great performances in the world and, in any case, we did not, as a journal, concentrate on performance. So I would say the answer to your question is, very occasionally: we certainly didn't 'get through to lots'!

PC As a result of your endeavours, do you think you managed to get more of the music you were interested in published and performed?

HK In the long run, yes. In the short run, no. Only now perhaps can the effect of our then endeavours be felt. You can't overestimate the degree to which we were regarded as outcasts. Early on, there was no question of any publisher being stimulated by us towards printing something he had not wanted to print. That happened very, very gradually, and I should say the chief effect of *Music Survey* in this respect really manifested itself after its own demise.

PC In that sense, 'O brave pioneers!'

HK 'Brave'? I'm not sure…. Pioneers, yes, but courage? What did we risk? Courage you can only measure in terms of risk.

PC But neither of you was earning your living from journalism?

HK When I started with Donald, I think that was almost precisely the point at which I had switched over, as far as my living was concerned, from playing to writing – when I earned my living through writing. Mind you, you can't imagine what I wrote. I mean, my chief living came from contributions to *National Entertainment Monthly, The Stage* – to twenty-odd awful publications.

PC Donald, I believe you were a prepschool master when you began *Music Survey*. At what point did you join *The Daily Telegraph*?

DM Oh, my *Telegraph* job was later, years later. When I was asked to join the *Telegraph* music staff there had been a long enough passage of time for the memory of *Music Survey* to have faded from the scene – I doubt if my association with *Music Survey* would have been thought to have been a recommendation.

PC Can I ask a word or two about the contributors? How did you choose them?

DM I don't think we went searching, because that implies we had a map, which we didn't have. I think we just used our noses, our hunches….

PC What about contributors from abroad?

HK Dika Newlin, she's the only foreigner I can remember.

DM But there were Schoenberg and Dallapiccola; and perhaps one or two others, René Leibowitz, for example. However, most of the contributors and the contributions – there were many reviews as well as articles, and also a lively correspondence section – most of them came from a fairly small band of friends and acquaintances. I don't think there was ever a coterie: it was a small circle of people, sympathetic with what the paper stood for. And often people like Robert Simpson and Harold Truscott...

HK Two very good examples...

DM ...both of whom were very old friends of mine from my youth, would offer – or be conscripted – to write for us.

HK And they show that one went for musicians in the first place. Robert Simpson is, of course, a marvellous writer, but quite often we had to rewrite things, when they came from sheer musicians.

DM And a frequent contributor like Paul Hamburger, I'm sure, Hans, came through your friendship with him. Hans Redlich, I can't quite remember.

HK I had played with him – in chamber music recitals.

DM He contributed very substantially, as did Denis Stevens. I was surprised, indeed, on looking through the issues to see how many contributions there were from Denis. It shows that the historical scope of *Music Survey* was broader than I had remembered it to be.

HK Our contributors certainly didn't choose themselves. We were the choosers, and our criteria were pretty rigid: in the first place, we absolutely insisted on total musical competence. Our literary requirements we sometimes had to postpone until – and meet at – the editing stage.

PC What kind of relationship, if any, did you have with the so-called academic world – people like Professor Westrup and others?

DM We had very few contacts, I think, in or with the academic world....

HK Redlich.

DM Yes, there was Redlich. In those days, if I remember correctly, he was an extra-mural studies man, somewhere in the home counties. I don't think the academic world impinged on us much, and I'm not sure whether we impinged on it. There was, of course, our notorious confrontation with Professor Westrup, which is immortalized in the pages of *Music Survey*. Denis Stevens had jokingly – though, it turned out to be, imprudently – remarked that if Westrup's ambitions as conductor of the University Opera Club continued, then he would have to consider closing down the University Music Faculty altogether. The professor didn't take at all kindly to this suggestion. We received a very stiff letter from his lawyers and had to publish a retraction and an apology – and pay the professor's costs, which we could ill afford. That was about the only crossing of paths with academia that occurred to my knowledge during the life of the paper – more of a collision than a colloquy.

HK We regarded the academic world, quite rightly, as pretty sterile. So we showed proportionately little interest; after all, this is still true to a considerable extent, though far less so.

PC Did you have any fellow spirits among BBC producers?

HK Bob Simpson was the only one. Had he joined...?

DM I don't think Bob was yet with the BBC. Moreover, our feelings about the BBC were not all that positive at the time.

HK There was that editorial I wrote, 'A Bedside Editorial for the BBC'....

DM That was about Schoenberg – a pretty sharp editorial.

HK At the appointments board for my first BBC job, although I was chosen, I was reliably informed that the then Head of Music, Maurice Johnstone, was the first to speak after I had left the room: 'In view of what *Music Survey* has done to us, only over my dead body.'

PC But it *was* over him, if not over his dead body?

HK Indeed, and later on we became friends: after a few months, having written an enthusiastic report about me, he took me to lunch in order to tell me that he had been mistaken.

DM I think it's rather difficult in the 1980s to realize quite what musical opinions were current in the BBC in the late forties and early fifties. I know from my own experience that, despite my early and unusual start at the BBC with a programme about Reger, it was by no means easy to champion musicians to whom the BBC in those days – the musical bureaucrats, I suspect, rather than the producers – had developed a resistance, to put it as politely and as mildly as possible. I can recall a programme I did on Britten in the early years of the Third Programme, not what I said so much as the awful atmosphere that surrounded the talk and its aftermath – a mixture of disbelief and disapprobation, a dislike, certainly, for my particular views which was intensified by distrust of their enthusiastic expression and doubt about the value of the composer's work. In short, taking Britten with such a degree of seriousness gave offence.

I had the same sort of experience in quite another field of study – Furtwängler as a Beethoven interpreter. Here the anti-Britten complex was perversely transformed into an anti-Continental complex. Thus the odours were various but mostly ill, and when allied with the famous bad taste and uncouth manners of *Music Survey*, small wonder that, though not exactly proscribed, one was all the same not invited to broadcast, which is how the system worked in those days. I'm not, by the way, making myself out to be a martyr in any sense, but there is no doubt that the kind of opinions we advanced and stood for didn't make us much loved by the BBC of more than twenty-five years ago.

PC Subsequently, both of you and many of your contributors actually went on to exercise great influence on the BBC and on other institutions, did you not?

HK Decades later.

DM When William Glock arrived at the BBC, it was entirely different.

But I think many of the views and attitudes that we launched in *Music Survey* took a good ten or fifteen years before they started to be influential.

HK I would say between ten and twenty years.

DM I can still remember – which now may seem very extraordinary – I can remember Britten's publishers in the 1950s, Boosey & Hawkes, actually telling me what harm we'd done to Britten by putting together the symposium* and compiling the Britten issue of *Music Survey* – harm, because our enthusiasm for his music had aroused...

HK ...had brought him into ill-repute...

DM ...had aroused feelings of envy, or whatever the feelings were supposed to be which would have remained benignly dormant if it hadn't been for our passionate advocacy upsetting the apple cart. That was the kind of *Alice in Wonderland* world in which one lived at that time. However, it was all enormous fun, quite apart from everything one learned from it as an experience. I certainly learned an immense amount from it, and from working with Hans during those years.

HK Through the development of that collaboration such things as our Britten symposium happened: it was really an extension of *Music Survey*, and wouldn't have happened without it. One need, I think, we were always conscious of – not to be exclusively topical. If and when the occasion on or for which we wrote seemed topical, we were anxious to say things which would be of interest in future years. That purpose one was always acutely conscious of in the case of a musical quarterly: both of us were alive to it in both *Music Survey* and *The Music Review*, which we thus regarded as a bit of a sister journal.

DM That's right, yes.

PC You came out more often...?

DM No, we came out quarterly, and in rather irregular quarters, I fear. The journal was printed by a very small firm in the south of London, a family business I'd known since my childhood. I think the type was virtually set by hand on antiquated machinery, while the average age of the printers must have been well over seventy – it wasn't, of course, but so it seemed to me. Somehow, however, we got our issues out.

   If you note the topics we chose to have articles written about, the composers we championed, bear in mind our concept of attacking the attacks, our policy of striving for alternative critical standards, of trying to achieve improved critical competence, our emphasis on musicality – then it seems to me that whatever demerits the journal may be said to have had fade away into relative insignificance. And there's still one quality I haven't mentioned – a certain prescience, an instinct not only for what was topical but what would become so. I still cannot help feeling a certain sense of gratification after all these

Benjamin Britten: A Commentary on his works from a group of specialists, ed. Mitchell and Keller, London 1952.

years when I read Redlich's admirable obituary of Kurt Weill. It must have been, in those days, probably the only journal in the English-speaking world that took the opportunity seriously to assess Weill's importance as a composer. In that kind of editorial act I think the value of *Music Survey* resided and continues to reside.

PC Why did this wonderful enterprise come to an end?

HK It was purely external, extraneous, incidental circumstances.

DM I think the patterns of our lives changed radically, though in different ways.

HK Did it not have to do with money, in other words that for some reason or other the flow of money ceased? I'm not sure, but I have some such vague recollection.

PC But you couldn't possibly have had any sense that you had accomplished your purpose?

DM I don't think it was that. We both started to be even busier, and you must remember too that this was an unpaid job.

PC The contributors weren't paid either?

DM We did pay our contributors, notional sums, I dare say, but at least something. We didn't pay ourselves anything. It was entirely unpaid, the editorial part of it.

HK One practical, factual criterion it is interesting to apply: this morning I had an extended look at *Music Survey* and found absolutely nothing in it that's out of date, with the sole exception of things having been positively revalued meanwhile, so that it's no longer necessary to fight for them. But that revaluation in itself shows how relevant the original articles were. There's nothing that gives you the feeling of out-of-dateness from the point of view of today's cultured musician. Would you not agree?

DM Yes, I think *Music Survey* wears well. Some things are still uproariously funny. For example, I think the exchange of letters about our use of the umlaut, in which Bill Mann sought to give you lessons in German, remains a uniquely comic contribution which I hope will find, like much else in the journal, a whole generation of new readers.

London,
December, 1980

MUSIC SURVEY

A Quarterly Review

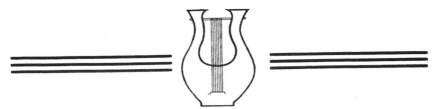

Vol. II.   No. 1.   1949

2s. 6d.

MUSIC . SURVEY

(KATHLEEN LIVINGSTON. WILLIAM W. LIVINGSTON. DONALD MITCHELL)

EDITORIAL BOARD :

E. D. MACKERNESS   H. B. RAYNOR   RALPH W. WOOD

C. H. STEPAN   DENIS W. STEVENS   ROBERT DONINGTON

EDITORS :

DONALD MITCHELL

HANS KELLER

CONTENTS

Published for MUSIC-SURVEY by NEWMAN WOLSEY, Publishers, 244, HIGH HOLBORN, W.C.1.

EDITORIAL CORRRESPONDENCE should be addressed to the EDITORS, MUSIC-SURVEY, OAKFIELD SCHOOL, WEST DULWICH, S.E.21.

All enquiries relating to advertising space in this journal should be made to : THE ALDRIDGE PRESS, LTD., 15, CHARTERHOUSE STREET, HOLBORN CIRCUS, LONDON, E.C.1.

Editorial: On Musical Understanding

Nihil est ab omni parte beatum.

Horace.

TO describe musical understanding to the musical is unnecessary ; to explain it to the unmusical is impossible. But it is desirable to reflect on the when and why of its absence—questions which each of us must decide in his own mind before he can claim the right to criticise. Two of the three chief enemies of musical understanding are (a) lack of technical knowledge, (b) technical knowledge. The third obstacle in the way of our understanding something is our understanding of something else.

To stress the need for technical knowledge at this time of the day is luxurious. Nowadays only music critics do without it. They represent the public ; hence their duty is to represent ignorance. Good music, however, unlike a pudding, is the result of a revelation which necessarily creates much of its own technique. What is more, while there is no technique left once the pudding is on the table, music develops a good deal of its technique each time it is played or imagined ; technique and result overlap. The technique of a good pudding and of bad music is of course of little interest to the consumer—the former because it is satisfactory, the latter because it isn't. But it will not do to neglect an inspired technique. Since, however, the good composer does not arrive at what he has to say via his technique, we don't either. Technical studies must be inspired by an understanding of the revelation which inspired his technique. Without technical knowledge we cease to understand when the composer's inspiration leaves us. With technical knowledge, we then begin to understand, and to write highly competent, unfavourable reviews. Misunderstanding can be an enjoyable activity, but from it there is a longer way to understanding than from lack of understanding.

How, then, should one try to understand the composer's revelation? One shouldn't. " *Wenn ihr's nicht fühlt, ihr werdet's nicht erjagen* " (Goethe, *Faust I.*) The grasping of inspiration, like inspiration itself, has nothing to do with effort or expertness. Wherefrom some will deduce their own pet view that good music is there to be understood by Everybody rather than by the Expert, a view fashionable nowadays among those who base their scientific investigations into the position of art in society on their complete ignorance of the science of the mind. The truth is that given money, time, inclination, and a sufficient dose of unconscious guilt for making him enjoy hard, futile work, more or less everybody can become what among other everybodies is known as an expert. But only few get anywhere near understanding the full, terrific meaning of, for instance, what I have shown to be Mozart's inter-operatic Leitmodulations*, and some of them may neither know nor care what I wish to convey by this term. In a word, only a small minority of us is musical through and through, and the understanding of great art is at the time of writing limited to a spiritual aristocracy. How far this regrettable state of affairs may be improved through changes in early upbringing remains to be seen ; that it cannot be improved by adult education is obvious from the established fact that character formation is determined in childhood.

THE MUSIC REVIEW, May 1948, p. 110 f., and November 1948, p. 298 ff.

And how are we to know if and when we belong to the few who really understand ? If and when we belong, we know. But we do not always know if and when we don't belong. An example from my own experience: I had been passionately in love with *Figaro* since my childhood. I had always been delighted with, indeed intensely moved by the sextet. I had every wrong reason to believe that I understood this piece completely, for I knew it inside out. Until one day I discovered that what I had known inside out was not much more than its outside. It had been an exhausting day ; I arrived at the opera later in the evening, and on the verge of going to sleep. When I entered, the sextet was just starting, and now, for the first time, I heard everything it revealed and concealed. Its cogency, its universality, the heavenly resignation underlying this understatement of all that moves, divides and unites the world, the easy victory over deep tragedy that is its humour—it all overwhelmed me and, to be frank, I cried. From then onwards, I was convinced that the sextet was *Figaro's* best number, and when some time later I read that Mozart himself thought so, my belief that I understood Mozart received a confirmation it did not need.

Now it is my understanding of, for instance, Mozart which gives me a standard by which I judge what I understand and what I don't. I think that nobody should talk or write about music unless he has developed such a standard. That there is no further standard by which one can objectively ascertain the existence of one's criterion of understanding is unfortunate, but does not get us round the need for it. Doubtless the composer(s) on whose understanding our standard is based must be part of our lives. One trouble here is that one meets and reads people who have made a composer part of their lives while showing a none too exhaustive understanding of his music.

The other trouble is that once you have lived yourself into the music of one composer, your understanding of other composers may suffer, especially of those whose artistic tendencies are in some way opposed to the individual traits of your favourite. This risk does not simply stand in inverse relation to your musicality, but depends to a great extent on your character. The strongly original and revolutionary genius shows less broad an understanding for other composers than the more conservative and eclectic genius ; otherwise, indeed, the former could not be revolutionary, nor the latter eclectic. Similar with the listener, according to whether or how far he tends to be single—or many-minded.

The greatest danger to music is mindless, seeming many-mindedness, a danger that has become acute since there are more composers, musicians, critics, and music-lovers than musical people. I do not deny the beneficial aspects of the Music-for-the-Masses (and -by-the-Masses) policy, but I marvel at the naiveté with which its adherents overlook the fact that while not every bad thing has a good side, every good thing has a bad one, which in this case happens to be pretty awful. It is they who deplore the present-day cleft between the composer and the public, but instead of blaming the public they blame the composer, and ask him to climb down to the greatest and uncommonly common measure of idiocy which is the inevitable consequence of bringing music to the unmusical.

The public always, and the composer and executant artist rarely get the critics they merit, for it is the public who pay for the critics, and it is the artists and the few able critics who, being after all human, are far too cowardly to pronounce openly what a racket the greater part of musical criticism is—as each of them will gladly tell you in private. Since at the present time the majority of audiences lack even the faintest criterion by which to measure their understanding, they welcome everything from a critic as long as it makes nonsense, giving particular preference to factually wrong criticism. One or the other reader may remember the controversy I recently had with one of our leading critics in one of our weeklies. He had written an extremely unfavourable review of Britten's *Beggar's Opera*, basing his irrelevant criticisms of the composer's harmonies on verifiably wrong observations, e.g. the imputation of keylessness. While I had not at that time seen the score (a fact which I pointed out), I enumerated the keys of, *inter alia*, the numbers which showed strong chromatic intensification, In his reply to my stressedly factual protest this critic had not the courage to admit that he had been, simply and provably, wrong. Instead, beside discharging an undue amount of hostility, he suggested that the proof of the pudding lay in the eating, a retort which in this case was more than usually absurd since I, too, knew the work only from hearing.

The point I wish to make is that a leading critic can, without an uproar on the part of the musical public, criticise *harmonies* without (among other blunders) noticing the presence of *keys ;* and that, when one points this out, he is still allowed to believe that he sufficiently understands the stuff to criticise it. The gravity of such a symptomatic incident can hardly be overestimated, once we are agreed that wherever the proof of the music is to be found, it does not lie in the ear of the deaf.

H.K.

Paul Hindemith—I

BY ARNOLD COOKE.

IT is over twenty years since Hindemith came forward as one of the leading names in contemporary music. The appearance of his opera *Cardillac* in 1926 established his fame, but already for some years previously he had been hailed by discerning musicians as the leader of the younger generation of German composers, the creator of a new style of music, the prototype of the new musician of the time. By the end of the 1920's he had a considerable following both in his own country and outside. Since then his reputation has steadily grown, but this is not to say that his music has become at all popular. Even amongst musicians, especially perhaps in this country, only few have a wide knowledge of his large output, and his music has not been performed frequently enough for the general public to have become familiar with his style. Opposition was at first strong and persistent, but gradually his music has won adherents, and it is only a question of time before it will receive more performances and win more general recognition. Initial opposition or indifference to a new style is quite the usual experience. Generally speaking, the newer and more original the style, the more difficulty it has in winning acceptance and establishing itself, though there are often other causes of neglect.

Before discussing Hindemith's music in general, I should like to deal with one or two prevalent misconceptions of it. One of them concerns this question of his relation to the ordinary music-lover. About this time (the 1920's) a movement was started by a number of younger German musicians for the creation and propagation of a type of music outside the ordinary concert business, which was termed "Gebrauchsmusik." This rather cumbersome title is misleading if directly translated into English as "Utility Music." As in many other instances, such a general term, which covers a variety of meanings, is better translated by several different terms. The nearest English equivalent would be Music for Amateurs, and under this heading we would include, Music for Schools, Music for the Home, Music for Children, etc. There is obviously no question here of substituting "utility" music for real music as we nowadays have utility furniture and clothing in place of the better and more expensive articles because of the shortage of materials. The object of the Gebrauchsmusik was to provide music in a new idiom, which should yet be simple enough for average amateur musicians to play or sing, most modern music being beyond their technical capacity. For this purpose Hindemith produced a number of works of a comparatively easy technical standard, including pieces for string instruments to be played in the first position. For him this was not merely a technical problem but also one of communication, of making himself intelligible to the ordinary person ; which is not the same as making a bid for popularity.

It was an opportunity, too, of establishing contact with the youth movements, whose musical activities lay outside the ordinary concert world. In writing this music, Hindemith did not change his style ; he simplified it. No doubt these works are not of great artistic importance in themselves, and they are not intended for ordinary concert performance, but they are at least far more interesting and stimulating than masses of insipid stuff turned out for a similar purpose. They also have an interest for the study of Hindemith's development, and the simplification of style and technique involved had a profound influence on his subsequent work. One of these works for instance, Das Lehrstück, to words by Bert Brecht, shows the beginnings of a new choral style, which he developed more fully later in the Oratorio Das Unaufhörliche.

It is important to see this question of Gebrauchsmusik in its proper perspective, because some writers have tended to draw too much attention to it and give the impression that Hindemith's whole creative activity and outlook are governed by considerations of practical utility, which exclude emotional and expressive elements from his work. It is true that he does not believe in composing at random without any purpose or without a potential public in mind, but this is also true of most genuine composers, certainly of the greater ones. It is surely obvious that Bach's Wohltemperiertes Klavier, his cantatas and organ works, Mozart's operas and concertos, Chopin's Waltzes and Mazurkas were written just as much for a definite purpose and public, and were influenced just as much by their social environment, as are Hindemith's works, quite apart from the specific purpose of the Gebrauchsmusik. And surely it is absurd to suggest that a composer who has written three full scale operas, two of them of a deeply serious nature, and the other a gay satire on contemporary life, has no interest in the emotional and human side of his art.

Another mistaken idea which is probably less prevalent now than some years ago, is that Hindemith writes or has written atonal music. Although some of his works are certainly complex both in texture and structure, tonality is always clearly defined. Neither in theory nor in practice has Hindemith ever been an atonalist, for the simple reason that he does not believe in the existence of atonality. In his masterly theoretical work, *The Craft of Composition* (*Unterweisung im Tonsatz*), he shows that tonality is fundamental to music, as gravity is a fundamental force in the material world. Tonality arises out of the very nature of the tones themselves. What is often regarded as atonality is simply obscured tonality, resulting partly from the frequent and perhaps also unco-ordinated shifting of key centres and partly from the continuous use of the extremer dissonances which render tonality difficult to detect aurally. But a so-called atonal piece can be just as clearly analysed by Hindemith's method as a classical piece, and its tonal structure laid bare. The twelve-note technique on the other hand is a method of composition, not a system of harmony. In making use of all twelve notes of the chromatic scale in a fixed series or tone row throughout a piece of music, the method no doubt has the advantage of logic and consistency as its adherents claim, but often at the expense of clear tonality. Hindemith believes that it is better to try to understand the true nature and properties of musical tones and their relationships to one another, and to found one's practice and theories accordingly, rather than to introduce an arbitrary logic, which may satisfy some musical requirements but neglect others equally important. This he has attempted in the book mentioned. Whether he is entirely successful or not, and no doubt there is some debatable ground here, the work is certainly a new and valuable contribution to musical theory, and a great advance on previous theories of harmony.

I do not here propose to discuss Hindemith's theories and researches, which can be studied in detail in this book. The above references to this side of his activities and to *Gebrauchsmusik* indicate his general attitude towards music, and also suggest reasons why he he has not as yet achieved wider acceptance among the general public. Like most other composers of his generation, Hindemith reacted strongly against the overblown romanticism and luxuriance of the period which ended with the first World War. As on the technical side romanticism expressed itself chiefly in a great increase in harmonic resource and colour, so it is not surprising to find in Hindemith the emphasis laid on linear development, on counterpoint and formal design, with an absence of colouristic attractions and a freer use of dissonance. The resulting style in his first mature works could hardly be immediately ingratiating to ears attuned to the luxuriance and sweetness of late romantic music. It has been the same with Stravinsky once he abandoned the colourful style of his early works. There is always a considerable time lag before a new style and a new outlook can become absorbed and digested by the general public. This is particularly true of our own time, where a revolution in taste has been going on in all the arts since early in this century, namely, the reaction against romanticism and the revival of interest in classical and pre-classical art, in line and form and strictness of style. It has its counterpart in the social revolutions of this century, and these together with the revolution in taste, account very largely for the cleavage between many of the leading creative artists and the masses. In periods when there is a settled form of society, and consequently a more stable attitude to art, there is no great gap between the artist and the public, such as there is liable to be in a transitional period like our own.

Hindemith has been in the forefront of this revolution which looks forward to the future, and at the same time backward for its sustenance to classical and pre-classical times. Hence we find in his work, along with modernism and neo-classicism, an interest in mediævalism and folk song. He uses folk tunes extensively in his teaching, and the treatise on *Two Part Writing* (*The Craft of Composition*, Part II) contains a collection of German folk songs which serve as melodic models for two part settings. He considers this material the most suitable for the purpose, because, as he says, " the melody develops in the full freshness of unrestrained pleasure in linear design, without being hampered by overstressed harmonic considerations in the scheme of definite cadences and marked symmetrical phrase structure which later determines the form. These old songs thus give rich possibilities to a polyphonic treatment ; above all, they are the ideal material for two part settings."

There are a number of examples in his own works of the use of folk song, e.g. in the opera *Mathis der Mahler* and the Viola Concerto *Der Schwanendreher*. Hindemith does not, however, approach these old melodies in any archaic spirit, nor does he attempt to base a musical style upon them. He weaves them into the fabric of his own polyphony. Similarly in the exercises in two parts there is no attempt at modalism nor at imitating the musical style of the times when these tunes came into existence. The extended possibilities of modern writing in the chromatic scale are accepted from the beginning, though naturally with severe restrictions and regulations for the purpose of this elementary study. Thus the student is not obliged at first to learn an archaic style of a particular period, as in the studies of 16th-century strict counterpoint, or of the four-part system of harmony invented by Rameau, which are still the basis of teaching at colleges and academies. These studies, particularly of strict counterpoint, are of course still of value in a general musical training, and to some extent for the study of the periods they represent ; but beyond this they are of little use to the budding composer, who must learn to master the rich and varied possibilities of the musical material as it is to-day. He can make a beginning in this with Hindemith's exercises, as they are not based on any pre-conceived style, and thus leave him free to form his own.

The tendency to look backwards to mediæval music shows itself in Hindemith more in certain technical aspects than in the actual use of musical material of that period, though in one of his most attractive works, the music to the ballet *Nobilissima Visione*, he uses for the introduction a charming Troubadour melody, harmonized simply and effectively. Even in this simple treatment we can observe a practice derived ultimately from early mediæval music, the use of parallel fourths and fifths. We are of course quite accustomed to this by now in modern music, the practice having been introduced by Debussy and others already before the turn of the century, but it is very important for the beginnings of modern harmony. As all know who have studied harmony at all, the progressions are not permissible in classical harmony, parallel fifths being entirely forbidden and parallel fourths being allowed only when occurring as the upper parts of chords, not when occurring with the bass. One need not go into the historical and technical reasons for this, but it is clear to any musician that these parallels are foreign to the classical system and to the polyphonic period preceding it. Thus the early mediæval practice of organum, which was discarded as polyphony developed, is reintroduced as a a means to open the way to greater harmonic freedom at the end of the nineteenth century. At the same time the increasing use of dissonances without the strict classical resolutions freed music from the cadential formulæ by which phraseology was largely determined in classical and romantic music, and from the leading note principle and appogiature which assume such an important part in late romantic music. *Tristan* is the climax of the use of the appogiatura as a means of expression and of musical continuity. In some later romantic music whole melodies may be constructed of practically nothing but appogiature and leading notes. Melody had become entirely dependent on harmony, and music had to be freed from the domination of these devices and formulæ before melody could regain its independence, and before a full use of the chromatic material was possible. This freedom was achieved by the second decade of this century, when composers were able to use every conceivable combination and progression within the chromatic scale. But with the dissolution of the classical system came the pressing need for a new system to give order and stability to music, and new theories to interpret the new sound material. Quite apart from questions of style and taste, musical material has its own natural laws which have to be understood in order to be mastered. The classical system in music may be likened to the Newtonian in physics. It was complete and satisfactory in view of the facts known at that time, but appears inadequate in the light of modern discoveries ; similarly new theories are required to interpret fully the whole universe of musical sounds. This universe is for us contained in the twelve notes of the chromatic scale. There may be other systems possible beyond this, based on quarter tones, sixth tones, etc. but with these we can have no contact, because our physical laws do not permit it, and we cannot get beyond our closed space. Our tonal universe appears to be finite though unbounded.

Now Bach exploited the tonal universe as fully as the classical system would allow. The use of all the keys on the keyboard was possible to him through the invention of equal temperament, a possibility of which he took full advantage in *Das Wohltemperierte Klavier*. In one of his more recent compositions, *Ludas Tonalis*, Hindemith has approached the same sort of problem from a modern standpoint. Bach, while able to use every key, was fundamentally diatonic in each, obeying the rules of classical harmony. Hindemith is able to be fully chromatic in every key with a free use of all intervals and harmonic combinations. This is simply a measure of the extension of musical material since Bach's time. Apart from its technical interest, *Ludus Tonalis* is one of Hindemith's best works and deserves the closest study. Composed in 1942, it is a fully mature example of his style, and has also the advantage for practical study of being written for the piano, and of bringing together a large number of short pieces of varified character in one unified work. Its scheme differs in several respects from that of the ' 48.' There is also a fugue in each key, but instead of preludes Hindemith uses Interludes, which serve the purpose of contrast and of transition from one fugue to the next. Thus after the first fugue in C there is an Interlude which begins in C but ends in G, the key of the second fugue. After the fugue in F the Interlude starts in F, but ends on E, the dominant of the next key A. Also, the sequence of keys is different. Bach proceeds semitonally up the scale, whereas Hindemith arranges his keys in accordance with his theory of tonal relationships. The sequence is C, G, F, A, E♭, A♭, D, B♭, D♭, B and F♯, the last being tonally the farthest removed from C. There is no distinction between major and minor, as it is the chromatic scale which Hindemith uses, not the diatonic major and minor as in Bach. To round off the whole, the work opens with a Prelude in free improvisatory style, beginning in C and moving to F♯. After the final fugue in F♯ the Prelude is repeated backwards and inverted as the Postlude which thus proceeds from F♯ back to C. This is not only an ingenious and happy use of a device which is often regarded as purely cerebral and of mere paper value, but the music itself is remarkably free and expressive and thoroughly pianistic. There are other examples of such devices in the work. Fugue No. 3 divides in the middle and repeats backwards, No. 10 in D flat repeats from the middle in inversion, and No. 11 in B is a strict canon ; but in each case the technical device is justified by its musical results. There is no reason why a composer should not be as clever as he likes, provided the result is musical. All the fugues are in three parts. The composer probably felt that more than three would result in too great a complexity in this idiom, and that the music would become unmanageable for two hands. Even as it stands it is often difficult enough to play and in any case the Interludes provide ample contrast and variety of texture.

There are many characteristic things throughout this long series of pieces. Fugue No. 2 in G for instance, with its repeated notes and leaps of fourths in 5/8 time is very typical, as are the 4th fugue in A and the *moto perpetuo* Interlude which follows it. Then there is the excellent March after the 6th fugue in E♭. Hindemith has always had a pre-dilection for marches. They appear in different sorts of works through-out his whole output, in concertos, sonatas, cantatas and piano works. Quite personal in character, they are a natural expression of his strong rhythmical sense. He does not often go in for the unusual and distorted types of rhythm favoured by some modern composers, particularly of course Stravinsky ; but it does not follow that his rhythm is uninteresting or monotonous. His handling of normal rhythms is usually dynamic and vital, and his occasional use of syncopation and rhythmical displacement entirely convincing and natural. One very good example of the latter is in the second movement of his Sonata for Piano Duet. Of the slow movements in *Ludus Tonalis*, the Interlude after the A♭ fugue is the most imposing, with its broad lines and rich harmonisation. Fugue No. 9 in B♭ is an exquisite piece of musical jugglery, while the succeeding Interlude breathes an intense calm suggestive of late Beethoven. Perhaps the most beautiful and expressive fugue is the last in F sharp. It has a certain strangeness in keeping with the key, and its character is epitomised in the remote beauty of its cadential phrase, which is heard first in the dominant half way through and in the tonic at the end. Here we have reached the farther side of the tonal universe after our long journey through the keys. The Postlude follows immediately, and one of the most extraordinary things about the whole work is the moving effect of this final piece, as it unfolds in reverse direction to the Prelude and brings us back to our starting point. I should think that nowhere has Hindemith achieved a more perfect fusion of thought, feeling and technique than in *Ludus Tonalis*.

(The conclusion of this article follows in our next issue—Eds.)

Bruckner's Forgotten Symphony ' No. 0 '

BY HANS F. REDLICH

IT is less than a truism to speak glibly of the mystical number " Nine " in connection with the symphonies of the Vienna Classics—it is something of an inaccuracy, as the much contested existence of works like Beethoven's " Jena " Symphony, Schubert's ghostly " Gastein," and the tantalizing fragment of Mahler's " Tenth " go to show. It certainly is a palpable mistake in the case of Anton Bruckner, who left to posterity (quite apart from the numerous different versions in which his middle Symphonies continue to exist) 10 symphonic scores of undeniable completeness, to which—by a *consensus omnium*— the magnificent torso of Symphony No. IX should be added. Of the two works which in any reliable account of Bruckner's symphonic work must needs be mentioned alongside the traditional " nine," one is admittedly more in the nature of an apprentice work : the so-called " Studiensymphonie " in F minor. It was composed from February to May 1863 in Linz as a " set piece " of schoolwork, suggested by Otto Kitzler, Bruckner's tutor in practical composition and orchestration, causing teacher and pupil but little satisfaction. Soon afterwards it was laid aside as an unsuccessful attempt to master the problems of traditional Symphony*).

Very different, however, is the case of the other Symphony, frequently mentioned together with the one in F minor as an immature " Jugendwerk " and as having been written at approximately the same early date in Bruckner's creative life, i.e. well *before* the conception of the three great Masses and Symphony No. I (C minor)—works which within the short period of four years (1864/68) firmly established Bruckner's claim to greatness. The wrong evaluation of this second symphonic essay—commonly called " Die Nullte " (' No. O ' Symphony)—chiefly resulting from a wrong assessment of its date of origin, has hitherto led to its almost universal neglect. This is all the more regrettable as this work (even more than the Symphony No. I in C minor) represents the original blueprint for the general type of Bruckner's Symphony, revealing for the first time the unmistakable features of his symphonic individuality. For a deeper understanding

No full score of this work is available up to date. But an arrangement for Piano for two hands was published in Goellerich's Bruckner Biography (ed. M. Auer), Vol. III/2, 1932.

of Bruckner the symphonist, a thorough knowledge of this work is all the more indispensable as Bruckner used it later on as a quarry for the thematic material of some of his most important later Symphonies‖.

Before discussing this Symphony's claim for admittance into the hallowed precincts of the " Nine," the work itself should be re-dated, whence its thematic material and its significance for Bruckner's symphonic development will be seen in a new light.

Among Bruckner's biographers No. 0 is something of a bone of contention. It receives but grudging praise from Max Auer*, who places the date of its presumable genesis in the winter 1863/64, thus relegating the composition to the end of Bruckner's protracted period of gestation and creative immaturity†. In contradiction to him J. v. Woess‡ and Prof. Franz Moissl§ believe that the bulk of the score was actually written as late as 1869 and that it should be valued as a composition of the mature Bruckner, the creator of the monumental Mass in F minor (1867/68) and of the revolutionary Symphony No. 1 in C minor (1865/66). While older biographers like E. Decsey (1919)** and Max Auer (in the first edition of his Bruckner biography, Zuerich, 1923) omit the symphony altogether, J. v. Woess asserts that its score was known to him as far back as 1914††. This lack of agreement is the natural result of Bruckner's ambiguous attitude towards his own creation. In 1895, before his removal to the flat in the " Belvedere," the manuscript turned up suddenly. Bruckner‡‡ described then the score to his pupil Goellerich as a product of his " Linz period " (which came to an end with his Vienna appointment of Oct. 1, 1868) and wrote on its cover :

" Symphony ' O,' quite invalid (only an attempt)."

But (and this seems to point to his real feelings) he refrained from burning the manuscript (as he did with may musical manuscripts before his removal) and bequeathed it in his last will to the " Ober-Oesterreichische Landesmuseum " at Linz.

‖It is a pity that the B.B.C. omitted No. 0 from its recent Bruckner cycle. The work should have found its rightful place (as this article is trying to prove) between the broadcasts of the two C minor Symphonies No. I and No. II as the first remarkable essay in the eloquent key of D minor, the key of Beethoven's " Ninth " as well as of Bruckner's own most daring works : the first Mass, the " Wagner " Symphony No. III and the unfinished Symphony No. IX. No. O was also ignored in the introductory talks and articles which accompanied the early broadcasts of this most welcome series.

*Max Auer " Anton Bruckner—sein Leben und Werk," Musikwissenschaftlicher Verlag. Wien, 1934.

†Other writers, E. Buecken in his " Handbuch der Musikwissenschaft " (" Musik des 19. Jahrhunderts bis zur Moderne," Potsdam, 1928) among them, have changed this date quite arbitrarily to the succeeding winter of 1864/65, an obvious impossibility, as will be shown later on in this article.

‡The editor of its first publication, Universal Edition, Vienna, 1924.

§The conductor of its first complete performance, at Klosterneuburg near Vienna, on October 12, 1924.

**Decsey merely mentions the existence of No. 0 and refers the reader to F. Graeflinger, one of the very first Bruckner biographers.

††The present writer found many years ago an article in " Die Musik " (Schuster & Loeffler, Berlin) year 1902, containing a complete account of No. 0 and quoting its main themes. He has so far been unable to retrace the number of the issue.

‡‡Cf. M. Auer, op. cit. pag. 93 et passim.

According to the dates in this MS., the Symphony was written between January 24 and September 12, 1869. The claim to its early genesis rests entirely on supposition, on Bruckner's cryptic remark about its connection with the " Linz period " and on the " internal evidence " of its alleged immaturity of style. But the MS. itself speaks a clear language. The first movement was completed last, i.e. on Sept. 12, 1869, the second movement on August 21, 1869. The Scherzo alone bears no date in the MS. It is the movement most likely to represent an earlier stratum of style, with its terse thematic lay-out and its shortwinded continuation. But the " Trio " (which for sheer melodic beauty bears comparison with the famous " Trio " in the Scherzo of Symphony No. VII) was definitely composed on July 16, 1869 and the Finale was completed on August 19, 1869. Further proof for the late date of the actual composition may be gathered from Bruckner's letters.* In a letter to his friend Moriz v. Mayfeld in Linz, Bruckner writes on July 15, 1869 (i.e. one day before *composing* the " Trio " of No. 0) : ". . . On the Symphony† much work is being done. You will be surprised how I have followed your advice in the Andante. The whole middle section is new . . ."‡.

This letter proves unmistakably that a large portion of the second movement (probably from cue number 30 to 100 and again in the recapitulation from cue number 115 to 135) was composed during July, 1869. The movement represents a very mature standard of composition and shows Bruckner's typical stylistic features—such as rapid harmonic successions in the quaver motion of the strings, off-setting a daring two-part counterpoint between oboe and horn, and between oboe and clarinet, comparable to the " Et incarnatus " section in the Mass in F minor.

Bruckner's letters, however, contain further proof. In a letter of Jan. 26, 1865 (addressed to his friend R. Weinwurm in Linz) he refers to " the score of my Symphony." This can only be the " Studiensymphonie " in F minor, whose completion Bruckner had announced to Weinwurm in a letter of Sept. 1, 1863. Three days later, on Jan. 29, 1865, Bruckner tells the same friend : ". . . I am just working on a C minor Symphony (No. 2) . . .," which M. Auer quite correctly identifies as the later Symphony No. 1 in C minor. If Bruckner had sketched another symphonic work meantime—i.e. between the completion of the " Studien " Symphony in F minor (Sept. 1863) and the start of this new Symphony in C minor— he would certainly have mentioned it to Weinwurm and would not have referred to the new work as " No. 2 " only 3 days after having alluded to the full score of his earlier F minor Symphony. It is of course possible, technically as well as psychologically, that Bruckner worked on portions of No. 0 some time during the winter of 1863/64. He had completed Psalm 112 and the " Germanenzug " by September, 1863, and presumably did not embark on the first Mass in D minor before the later spring of 1864. But again, would he in such a case call the new Symphony of January 1865 expressly ," No. 2 " ?

*" *Bruckner's Briefe, Neue Folge*," *ed. M. Auer, 1924.*
†*M. Auer adds an explanatory footnote : No. " 0," D minor.*
‡*op. cit. No. 75, pag. 107.*

Between Spring, 1864, and September, 1868, Bruckner composed the three Masses in D, E and F minor, and the Symphony No. 1 in C minor. It is more than unlikely that he found any time for No. 0 within that period of Herculean creative labour. Further, a great part of the winter and spring of 1866/67—i.e. between the completion of the Mass in E and the beginning of the Mass in F—were lost to composition because of a serious nervous breakdown.

All this evidence goes to show that the decisive creative effort for No. 0 must have occurred between January and September 1869—that is to say, well after the disheartening experience of the first performance of Symphony No. 1 (May 1868, Linz) and as an unmistakable psychological reaction to it. Additional proof for the present writer's assertion that No. 0 represents an *advanced* stage in Bruckner's symphonic development rather than the opposite, may be found in the fact that Bruckner performed part of it in Vienna in the presence of Otto Dessoff, the influential, first conductor of the " Hofoper," who after having listened to the first movement, asked candidly : " Where is the principal theme ? " That question clinched the matter and the score was definitely laid aside*. Bruckner would certainly not have presented an immature work to Dessoff, on whose good-will he counted at the start of his own activities in Vienna.

Surely the best proof for the true value of this neglected Symphony No. 0 must lie in the fact that its first theme (exactly the one which Dessoff could not or would not recognise) supplied the thematic backcloth for the glorious trumpet theme of Symphony No. 3 in D minor (composed 1872, revised later on and first performed in 1877) dedicated to Richard Wagner because of the latter's partiality for this tune.

Here are both themes in their clear derivation from one common source : the beginning of Beethoven's Ninth, which must have acted as a catalyst in Bruckner's creative imagination.

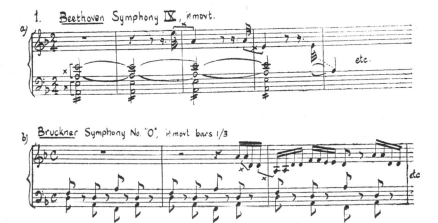

*Cf. M. Auer, op. cit. pag. 94.

c) Bruckner Symphony No. III, 1st movt. bars 1/3

The root-motif of the descending 5th and 4th is identical with the intitial motif of Beethoven's Ninth. The similarity even includes the accessory feature of the dronelike pedal on an open 5th, in bars 1-30 of Bruckner's Third and bars 1-4 of Beethoven's Ninth.

The same idea of the initial, indeed primordial, bare 5th which slowly generates a melodic complex as it gathers momentum, reveals itself at the beginning of Bruckner's Ninth.

2. Bruckner Symphony No. IX, 1st movt. bars 4/10

(Horns)

Another motif from Beethoven's Ninth (1st mov., coda, bars 513 ff.) provides Bruckner with a kind of permanent coda motif, first employed in No. 0 (1st mov., bars 298 ff.) and re-used, with striking effect, in the 1st movement of his 3rd Symphony (one bar after letter X) at the same structural juncture.

3) Beethoven Symphony Nr. IX. 1st movt. (Coda)

Bruckner's Ninth Symphony and its architectural peculiarities assume canonical importance for Bruckner the symphonist. The quotation of the themes of the preceding movements at the beginning of the finale (shortly before the first appearance of the " Joy " melody) finds its counterpart in the finale of Bruckner's 5th Symphony at exactly the same stage in its exposition. The principal themes of earlier movements, moreover, are frequently requoted at the last climaxes of Bruckner's monumental finales (cf. in particular the finales of Symphonies No. 5 and 7). Already E. Buecken has drawn

attention to the likeness in type between the principal themes in the
Scherzos of Beethoven's Ninth and Bruckner's No. 0.*

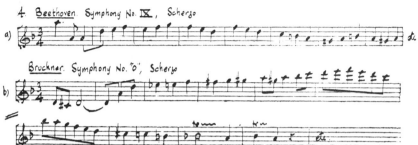

Many motifs of No. 0 have been re-employed in later Symphonies
(quite apart from the most striking case of Exx. 1 and 3). The beginning
of the Coda in the 1st mov. of No. 0 reappears in the finale of Symphony
No. 6,

while the continuation motif in its own finale constitutes a most
important element in the first subject-group of the 1st movement of
Symphony No. 3.

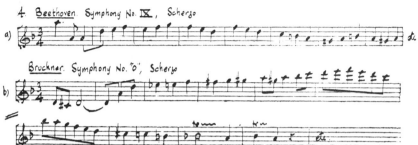

Perhaps the most convincing proof (purely by internal evidence) of
No. 0's late origin is the twice-repeated quotation in the Andante of
No. 0 of a mournful motif, sung to the words " *qui tollis peccata
mundi* " in the " Gloria " of the Mass in E minor (composed 1866).
Such deliberate self-quotations—especially from the major liturgical
works in later symphonies—are not frequent with Bruckner, but they
are of great psychological significance whenever they do occur. They
invariably appear in symphonies planned and written at about the same
time as the religious works from which they are taken. The most
striking cases (as far as the present writer is aware) are the quotation

cf. op. cit. pp. 270 ff.

of (1) the " Benedictus " theme from the Mass in F minor (1867/68, perf. 1871) in the Adagio of Symphony No. 2 in C minor (comp. 1871/72, perf. 1873) and of (2) the " *Non confundar in aeternum* " theme from the " Tedeum " (comp. 1883/84, perf. 1885) in the Adagio of Symphony No. 7 (comp. 1881/83, perf. 1884). To these should now be added the above-mentioned quotation from the main liturgical work of 1866, which would lose all significance if merely anticipated in an early sketch of 1863, but would emphasize the emotional import of this passage, if understood as the outcome of Bruckner's spiritual crisis during 1866/67. For the present writer this final juxtaposition

clinches the matter. He believes Symphony No. 0 to be the work of a mature master, the first dawn of a new characteristically Brucknerian type of Symphony.

Thomas Mann's " Dr. Faustus "*:
A Contribution to the Philosophy of Music
By PAUL HAMBURGER.

It must be a peculiar people who can produce a Thomas Mann, the greatest living prose-writer and humanist, and an Adrian Leverkuehn, the fictitious, though truly German hero of " Dr. Faustus." The Germans have always theorized about genius, classifying artists into " apollonic " and " dionysic " ones. Leverkuehn, the composer of genius, cannot be said to begin his career under the tutelage of Apollo and the harmonious muses ; but he certainly becomes initiated in early manhood into the mysteries of Dionysus, the Devil. It is an open question whether any creative artist, including Goethe and Thomas Mann himself, is ever untouched by influences from " down below." Mann, hiding as he may behind the humanist's cloak of Dr. Zeitblom, the horrified witness of the story, is also in Leverkuehn, by virtue of his uneasy sympathy with him, and indeed his ability to create this figure.

*DR. FAUSTUS—*THE LIFE OF THE GERMAN COMPOSER ADRIAN LEVERKUEHN, AS TOLD BY A FRIEND. Trans. H. T. Lowe-Porter.* Pp. 510. Secker & Warburg, 15s.

Mann is painfully aware that there " dwell two souls in the bosom " of all Germans, and demonstrates the German's ambivalence towards Good and Evil, towards the Beautiful and the Ugly, in the realms of politics and music. We are here only concerned with the latter—yet how to separate them clearly if music is to be seen historically ? A nation that cannot make history save by fits and starts acquires in its more contemplative intellects a very keen sense of the currents of the time, of what is old and outlived, and what is up and coming. This goes for the history of art, too. It had to be shown through a *German* composer how the " historical view " of the 19th century, the study of occidental music from the Greeks onwards, would come to a head and turn itself against the creative artist. Historicity turned against History, Critique against Creation—this is the dilemma in which the modern artist finds himself. It becomes acute in a German who is weighed down by the great musical tradition of his country, its social instability, and by his own cool, critical, far too clever head. And since he happens to be a musical genius, only the devil can help him.

But before we come to that personage, let us look at Leverkuehn's character in which traits favourable and unfavourable to a composer's life are strangely mixed. He comes from old peasant stock, and while having the peasant's pride, industry, and the frugality of a Haydn, has not the latter's naïveté, good humour, nor simple belief. His father already dabbles in natural science, " speculates the elements " ; and Leverkuehn himself grows up in the medieval atmosphere of Kaisersaschern, an old, small town, far from the pulse of modern life. Hence his bent for science in its old and new form, such as alchemy and astrophysics ; hence also his deep, but equivocal religiosity, his quite medieval awareness of having a soul, the centre of the universe, in which God and the Devil wage their war, while he himself gives both their due. He studies theology and philosophy at the old Lutheran university of Halle, seemingly in order to come nearer to God, but in reality to seek out the other one, the " great religiosus," whom he promptly encounters in the guise of a professor lecturing on demonology. As with many German composers, music to Leverkuehn is a theological and philosophical discipline. The physical cosmos seems to be given over to the devil, and after his pact with him, the devil, as in Goethe's Faust, has to show him the " great world." From his expeditions to the deep sea, and to the Milky Way and the outer nebulæ, Leverkuehn brings back the symphony called" The Marvels of the Universe " whose mock-pathetic name indicates the " bizarre and unpleasant character of the work . . . which is grotesque in a solemn, formal, mathematical way." On the other hand—and how German this is—he sets Klopstock's Ode of Praise, " Spring Festival," for baritone, organ and string-orchestra, as a plea to God, a work of attrition.

Leverkuehn's repressed, two-sided emotionalism which makes for an uncanny, parodistic, and again deadly serious style of composing, is also present in his sexuality. He has the chastity-mania of a saint, which, under the temptation of the devil, is for once abandoned in such folly that the rest of his life is perforce spent in continence.

21

Beethoven's idealised sensuality, and Brahms' melancholy bachelor-hood are mirrored in him ; also Schubert's and Wolf's venereal infections and the latter's schizophrenia. It is characteristic that Hungary should be the place of his fatal adventure, as well as the home-land of an influential lady-admirer (who remains unseen, like Tchaikovsky's Madame v. Meck). For him, for Brahms and Liszt, Hungary and the East are the lands of counterpoint-less licence (see Leverkuehn's violin-concerto) ; whereas Italy, as to all German artists from Dürer on, is the land of innocent sensuality and classical beauty. Yet while in Italy, Leverkuehn refuses to look at the country—he always refuses to be drawn, to be deflected from his purpose (he has very few real friends, people being overawed by him).

The tensions within his ego are so strong that only in strictest seclusion can he keep balanced. His composing is, as it were, the electrical exchange between the poles of his split personality ; a risky business that has to be transacted cautiously in the solitude of the Bavarian village where he lives for 20 years, writing his major works. The Devil, with whom he " held plenteous parley " before settling there (Leverkuehn always speaks old German in embarrassing situations), is not the Romantic devil of Reason, Rebellion, and Freedom mentioned in Mann's " Magic Mountain " ; this devil does not make life bright for him. He is the German devil of heaviness, claustrophobia, primitive brutality. He sells time to Leverkuehn, 24 years, in which the " incipient drunkenness " of Leverkuehn's diseased body and mind may lift him above mere reason, beyond the scruples of his cool intellect, and may let him experience archaic, primeval inspiration, the " divine raptus." More the devil cannot do, he cannot compose for him ; the actual work, the gestation of Leverkuehn's technically enormously complicated compositions has to be born by the composer himself, during alternations of rapture and despair. There is no place for the " world " in such a life. When Leverkuehn's fame spreads, a Jewish-French impresario comes from Paris to captivate him for the " civilized West." Naturally, he fails, but he has very intelligent things to say about music in Germany and elsewhere. Amongst other things, he notices Leverkuehn's German ambivalence towards Western Europe, towards what he imagines to be the " sphere of the valse brillante " ; an attitude made up of arrogance and a sense of inferiority. On the other hand, Leverkuehn, like every great German, ridicules his own people, and is, from a distance, cosmopolitan. Like Beethoven, he has a high regard for the English, and writes an opera (in English) on " Love's Labour Lost," as well as songs on poems by Keats and Blake.

But we have not come to the end of the contradictions of this soul. Related to the ambivalence of his national sympathies are his views about the exclusiveness, or else the popularity, of art. His own work, in its proud and difficult isolation, is, of course, at least in his lifetime, only the concern of a *coterie*. But he dreams of the day when music will shed her ambitions, when " a new innocence, yes, harmlessness " will be hers, and she will go out among the people. This antithesis becomes clearest in Leverkuehn's settings of the " Gesta Romanorum " (a medieval book of legends) for the puppet-stage, with chamber-orchestra and singers. Here, the naïve, fabulous, thoroughly popular

22

tone of the stories is partly matched by naïve music, partly set off by the most intricate, modernistic, parody of styles. Again, there is Leverkuehn's ambivalence to the traditional in music, and indeed to musical form, which he deeply respects, and ironizes. We touch here on a complex in Leverkuehn's thinking which has been prepared by his erstwhile teacher in composition. That remarkable man, in his lectures, postulated the difference of cult epochs (" polyphonic objectivity ") and cultural epochs (" homophonic subjectivity "), implying the superiority of the former.* He also holds that music, of all arts, has a secret tendency to return to its primitive, unorganised state (illustrating this by oddly simple, tonic-dominant pieces by the great masters, and also by modern repetitive primitiveness). But he shows in another lecture how, on the other hand, the masters reached the peak of abstraction when they secretly nested in their writings things that are only meant for the reading eye, like the crab-fugues of the Flemish School. This points to a certain asceticism in music, a wish " not to be heard," which, when compared with the modern lush, but spiritually primitive orchestral-sound, makes music appear to be a " penitent in the garb of a seductress," like Kundry. These theories exert a life-long influence on Leverkuehn. Since " expression " and " sentiment " are music's tribute to a " cultural," bourgeois epoch (a view of the devil to which Leverkuehn readily agrees), the New Music must, when not parodizing old styles, be primitive or abstract. Its realm must extend from the howl, the sliding scale, to the mathematical formula. This concept becomes apparent in Leverkuehn's *magnum opus*, the " *Apocalypsis cum figuris*," an oratorio for large orchestra (including some sub-orchestras, with saxophones, for the description of hell), soloists (including the evangelist, a high tenor, who has to report, in a chilly crow, the " Latest News of World Destruction ") and several choirs. There are lengthy, shrieking *glissandi* for the choir, and the trombones also, with the opening of the apocalyptic seals. There are speaking choruses here that turn through antiphonal speech and humming into the most abstract polyphonic music. There is also the laughter of hell, ending the first part of the " Apocalypse," which starts with the chuckle of a single voice, and swells into a fortissimo-*tutti* of yelling and howling. It comes again, re-shaped and re-orchestrated, but note for note the same, as the " icily clear, glassily transparent " chorus of angels that begins the second part. This is Leverkuehn's idea of strict style and the significance of his music.

Perhaps these few examples will suffice to send the reader hunting for parallels in the history of contemporary music. The public reaction to the " Apocalypse," as indeed similar to specimens of " real " music, is one of abhorrence and fascination, both of which, after a dictum of Goethe, are incited when the absurd is represented with taste. But at the same time, the difficulties of modern art, which the Devil so gladly expounds, are obvious : " Form " has become questionable to all but the Folklorists and Neo-classicists. The ruthless demand for compression, for " strict style," for the identity of material, works against Time, the dimension of music. With the censure of the formula, the traditional phrase, and the ornament,

Why are the best parts of these lectures cut in the English translation ? This should be amended in the next edition.

23

" pretence and play," the self-sufficiency of Form, have also disappeared. In Harmony, " every composer of the better sort carries within himself a canon of the forbidden, the self-forbidding, which by degrees includes all the possibilities of tonality." The technical *niveau* is so high that not only has the dissonance—consonance norm become utterly precarious, but the material of a composition, once established, makes the severest demands of correct treatment on the composer. His activity has to exhaust itself in the execution of these demands,— " a composing before composition."

Though much of this is true one has to remember that these are the devil's arguments. With his help, as we have seen, Leverkuehn succeeds in overcoming his paralysing scruples, and in forging critique into an instrument of production. But how can he get further, how can he regain for his work the human content, the " espressivo " ? Yet he succeeds in this too, in his last work, " The Lamentation of Dr. Faustus," which is in strictest style, built throughout on a 12-tone motif, and thus curiously freeing Leverkuehn's expressiveness. To be sure, his expressiveness cannot be anything but lament, the pathos of the rejected soul. In this oratorio, based on the old Faust book, he goes back in spirit to Monteverdi and the Madrigalists, to the time when music " conscious of itself as expression, became lament and ' *lasciatemi morire*,' the lament of Ariadne, to the softly echoing plaintive song of nymphs." The plaintive echo-effects of the Baroque are here employed in a deeper, more mournful context. This work, the lament of the German soul, is written with an eye on Beethoven's Ninth, " as its counterpart in a most melancholy sense of the word." With it, the Ninth symphony is revoked ; at its end, the chorus subsides, the liberating word is finally negated by a long, dying-away orchestral postlude—" Then nothing more : silence, and night." " Silence and night " in Germany, as in Leverkuehn. His time being over, he is taken by the devil ; that is, his schizophrenia breaks out and he has to be interned.

If Mann thinks that this tragic book is the revocation of *his* Ninth symphony (the *Joseph* books), one hopes that he may be wrong. He, and also Germany, could yet give us an 11th symphony.

Hans Pfitzner (1869-1949) :
An Unpublished Letter

PFITZNER is dead. So seems, for many, his music. Not because they have seen it die, but because they have never heard it live.

For the reasons for the neglect of Pfitzner we have to look into those little brains and empty hearts which have been confused by an anti-romantic revolution they do not understand. At the same time they continue, of course, to admire post-romanticism as long as it is not deep. The truth is that Pfitzner made a uniquely successful stand against History herself. She had no doubt intended him to be crushed by Wagner's inevitable influence, to be but an ephemeral epigone. Instead there came, *inter alia*, *Palestrina*, great and deep, a strongly individual opera that is not indebted to Wagner's art because it is worthy of it. Indeed, according to a recent, cosmopolitan opinion, the work is " among the most magnificent, spiritual accomplishments of mankind*."

We here print a letter from Pfitzner to Mr. Rudolf Kömpfner, now of Oxford, to whom we express our thanks for his permission to translate and publish the document. The translation is the present writer's.

Prof. Dr. HANS PFITZNER.

München 27,
Wasserburgerstrasse 21,
Telefon 481 008.

11th February, 1935.

DEAR Mr. Kömpfner (thus at least I read your name),

Accept my heart-felt thanks for your kind letter of February 8th. It comforted me greatly, for of course the biography†, too‡, is very frequently being attacked. When throughout a life-span all newspapers and journals write that *I* am a problematic figure who exists only for a few people, but that another one, and always the same one, is indisputably the world's greatest composer‖, then this is accepted as a mere matter of course. But when, for once, there appears one§ who says according to his conviction that this place belongs to *me*, then there is no end of indignation. By such letters as yours one must, again and again, take one's bearings ; and, thank Heaven, your letter is not the only one of this kind, and I am receiving more than a few of such unreserved affirmations.

Once more, many thanks,

With my best respects,
Yours,
HANS PFITZNER.

Pfitzner's Palestrina, with whom the composer identifies himself, says : " The world's innermost is loneliness." (*Das Innerste der Welt ist Einsamkeit.*) The innermost of Pfitzner's art is a loneliness which all who can should share. Furtwängler or Bruno Walter, both of whom have an intimate knowledge of the score of *Palestrina*, ought as soon as possible to be asked to perform the work.

H.K.

* *Graf, M.,* FROM BEETHOVEN TO SHOSTAKOVICH : THE PSYCHOLOGY OF THE COMPOSING PROCESS, *New York, 1947.*
† *Abendroth, W.,* HANS PFITZNER, *Munich, 1935.*
‡ *Like Pfitzner himself.*
‖ *Obviously Strauss.*
§ *Walter Abendroth. See* (†).

[*Trans.*].

Film Music—The Question of Quotation

ART arises where the abitrary and the predictable are superseded by unpredictable inevitability. Musical quotations in not purely musical works often suffer from lack of art, for their extra-musical determinants tend to make them extra-musically predictable and musically arbitrary. This frequent absence of an artistic *raison d'être*, however, is not the only reason for their frequency. They can splendidly serve the mind's most beloved secret activity, i.e. the covert expression of simultaneous love and hate towards a parent figure—the quoted composer*. They are, moreover, finely suited for

* *See my observations on the psychology of musical quotation, imitation and caricature in* THE MUSIC REVIEW, *vol. IX, No. 2, May, 1948, pp. 114 f.*

assuaging some of a man's guilt over the rubbish he has written. Similarly as in literature a quotation serves to authorise a wrong statement, so a musical quotation may answer the quoter's need for parental approbation ; he feels that by thus honouring, and identifying himself with, daddy's holy words, he sanctifies his own. A rose thrown into a midden, however, does not improve the latter's smell, but rather starts to stink itself. One would therefore suppose that the human minority of cinema-goers will not easily tolerate the majority of film-musical quotations. However, they will. In fact the quotes offer them pleasure almost as intense as the thrill which the ordinary cinema-goer (*sus domesticus*) gets out of the stench. At any point during the film, that is to say, the spectator-listener holds a certain amount of psychic energy (tension) in preparation for grasping what the next moment is to bring. If a quotation of something known ensues, the prepared amount of energy suddenly turns out to be too big, and the surplus is discharged†. Relief of tension—hence pleasure. Add to this the kick of being in the know : Surrounded by ignoramuses, our human cinema-goer belongs to the initiated who know that this is " the Tchaikovsky Concerto " ; its first movement is in fact among his selection of gramophone records. His satisfaction here derives again, indeed doubly, from the parent complex. Not only does he partake of superior and therefore parental knowledge, but the very object of his knowledge, the " good," " superior," classical " composer has for him (as for the film composer or musical director) parental significance.

Whereas, however, until recently " classical " was for Hollywood a synonym for Romantic, their musicological department has now discovered that a few guys wrote usable music before the Romantic era. Not usable in its original form and scoring, to be sure. Mr. Lionel Newman, Musical Director of *Apartment for Peggy*, has struck upon Mozarts' clarinet quintet, struck off the clarinet, and stuck on, so as to be dead wrong, flute and harp. It seems that the selfsame musicological department's researches have also unearthed Mozart's concerto for flute and harp, whence the arranger of the clarinet quintet came to choose the two instruments which Mozart disliked throughout his life. This, of course, is not all. The form of the second trio, for instance, is improved upon by a contraction ; a full orchestral version, in A instead of D, of part of the second movement aptly serves as suicide-motive ; the minuet appears at one point as background music in A flat (though it is of course played, as distinct from reproduced, in A) and triumphs finally, in its turn fully orchestrated, as coda to the film. The reader will absolve me from the task of going into the various unbelievable details of the arrangements ; suffice it to say that of the innumerable cinematic misuses of good music known to me this is so far the most scandalous. Every musician, and nobody else, should hear it.

† *For Aristotle, joy at recognition was the basis of the pleasure we gain from art. Groos* (DIE SPIELE DER MENSCHEN, *1899*) *pointed out that Aristotle exaggerated the indubitably great importance of this principle. Freud* (DER WITZ UND SEINE BEZIEHUNG ZUM UNBEWUSSTEN, *1905*) *was the first to give a clear indication of what determines such joy. My reflection is founded on Freud.*

When I arrived at the Press Show of the British picture *Fools Rush In*, and saw from the synopsis that the central event would be the calling off of a wedding, I prayed : " Neither of the wedding marches, please!" They came both. The composer, Mr. Wilfred Burns, a name new to me, treats the Lohengrin one in his title music, and as the family of Pam or whoever it is return home from the unwedding with the wedding cake, he duly distorts the Mendelssohn. At this juncture I retired, because I felt sure that the wedding marches wouldn't. Criticism : The composer does nothing to make his quotations musically inevitable, inevitable though they are when you know about the story and about film music. It might be said that you aren't supposed to know about the story, and that the overture cleverly announces the theme of the film. A musical announcement, however, must be as musical as it is an announcement: it must stand repeated hearing. Nowise a treat, Mr. Burns' treatments of the marches are as predictable as the marches themselves. They simply translate, anticipatorily in the case of the Wagner. All good descriptive music transforms ; all musical translation is superfluous. And art apart, the superiority feeling to be derived from being in the know is not in this case overwhelming either, for even *sus domesticus* knows the wedding marches. As for the pleasure gain from the save-up of psychic expenditure, bless them who were not expecting the Mendelssohn and, if they knew about the film from the papers, the Wagner. In addition to being inartistic, then, the wedding march quotations are inane.

There is a third, smallish class of film-musical quotations that are neither beneath criticism as our first, nor as silly as the second. Though not actually artistic, they could be agreeable if—. Many readers will remember Alexander Korda's *Lady Hamilton*, which features " La ci darem la mano " from *Don Giovanni*. The duettino is relatively well recorded, its context not absurd. But far from being given as a whole, it is cut before the upbeat in bar 16. You can always foresee the typical, musically arbitrary cinematic cut, which will never fall on a full close, even though this be, as in the present instance, just one further bar along the road. And why cut at the precise point where, for structural reasons, the ensuing feeling of incompleteness will be strongest ? Because such is the cinema's idea of maintaining movement. Never, however, has one art gained by infringing upon another.

A fourth group, the (near) artistic quotations, are so far pretty quiescent. One example, the use of Bach's Weimar Organ Prelude in A minor (*Bachgesellschaft* (Breitkopf & Härtel) XV, No. 13) in *La Symphonie Pastorale*, I have discussed elsewhere‡. There would be more of them if film musicians would care to keep our opening oracle in mind.   HANS KELLER.

‡ THE NEED FOR COMPETENT FILM MUSIC CRITICISM (*British Film Institute*, 1947), *pp. 16 f.*

Music by Radio

THE BRUCKNER SYMPHONIES.
Undoubtedly the Third Programme is the conscience of the B.B.C. Like all consciences it is sometimes amenable to euphemism, especially when it is being merely dutiful. Such a euphemism was the promise

that all nine of Bruckner's symphonies were to be broadcast. What actually emerged from the speaker ? Surely those tinnily tremulous, long-protracted noises of a band in the bathroom were not intended to represent the symphonies of Bruckner ? If good recordings are not possible, none so miserable as those from Munich should have been foisted : the tragedy was that Hans Rosbaud's performances were of a very high order indeed, as anyone knowing the music and having the scores could tell. We were allowed to ' do ' the Bruckner symphonies much as a tourist ' does ' a country through dirty motor coach windows. At this time of writing the first eight have been transmitted.*

With ill-concealed testiness, I give the following facts :—

No. 1 (*Linz version*) (Munich Phil. Orch., c. Hans Rosbaud). This was faded in at bar 23 : someone suddenly realised that the motor coach blinds were down.

No. 2 (*first version*) (same performers). The blind fell down before the end of the slow movement.

No. 3 (*revised version*) (London Phil. Orch., c. van Beinum) (studio performance).

No. 4 (*first version*) (Munich—Rosbaud). As if the recording were not dim enough in itself, it was run too slowly, so that the symphony sounded in D major instead of E flat, with all its tempi correspondingly dragged. The effect was appalling.

No. 5 (*first version*) (B.B.C. Orch., c. Boult) (studio performances).

No. 6 (*first version*) (Munich—Rosbaud).

No. 7 (*revised version*) (Concertgebouw Orkest—v. Beinum) (Decca records).

No. 8 (*first version*) (Munich—Rosbaud).

The Linz version of No. 1 is the earliest score, which was drastically revised by Bruckner himself 25 years later in 1890-1. The later edition should have been used, since it constitutes the composer's own final score, beside which the *Linzer Fassung* appears a mere sketch. The very fine performance was marred, like all those from Munich, by the distorted recording which, made in an acoustically dead studio with equipment that imparted palsy to the orchestra, reduced the richest sonorities to a nasal clangour. The Second Symphony sounded better : the recording was an improvement on all the other Munich ones, and Rosbaud's grip on the music was unfailing. He is a superb Brucknerian and one of the blessed few who, in performing the original versions, do not superimpose on them the Wagnerian *tempo* marks of the revisions, most of which are as uncharacteristic as they are unattested. In No. 2 both the first and last movements gain enormously from a steady speed : this work, less often played than most, is very easy to enjoy and might well be the best introduction to Bruckner. It was once nicknamed the ' Pause ' Symphony because of its frequent use of sudden silences. To deride this kind of thing is to show one's blind

*Since, the Ninth Symphony has been broadcast in a recording by the Frankfurt Radio Orchestra under Winfried Zillig. This recording, while not ideal, was far better than those from Munich, and the performance was excellent, especially in the *Adagio*. The conductor made one or two *accelerandi* in the first movement that resulted in a loss of space and dignity, and the trio seemed a little lame at his rather slow pace. But in the slow movement, the orchestra's strings distinguished themselves.

faith in Wagner's slick and superficial dictum that the art of composition is the art of transition, a remark which has had its *reductio ad absurdum* in those murky atonalists whose works are all transition and no composition. An honest gap is often a better transition than all the ' logic ' on earth, for music is neither philosophy nor argument, and Bruckner is able to space his masses and voids according to his own wish, free from language-bound preconceptions. In this he stands apart from the all too verbal Nineteenth Century in which he lived. Nor is it of any use to say that this view confuses a time-art with a space-art, for it takes time to perceive anything : the chief difference between a cathedral and a Bruckner symphony is that in the first case one has a general impression before beginning to absorb the details (a time-process), while in the musical experience the general impression depends entirely on the co-ordinating power of the memory. Ultimately both cases resolve similarly, for the complete image of a building exists in the mind only after one's legs have carried one through and round the whole structure: no object, in fact, can be seen in a *coup d'oeil*, any more than a piece of music can be heard instantaneously ; the difference is chiefly one of degree. Language is in different case, for it is unintelligible if it is not either descriptive or logical, i.e. transitional : the Nineteenth Century was tyrannised by the literary mind and most of its musicians shared its bias. That is why Bruckner was out of his time, and why his methods seem obtuse to nine-tenths of his critics, whose inclinations are moulded by the habits of the older generation. Bruckner's style might be regarded as a great expansion of the work begun by Giovanni Gabrieli. He demands a reorientation of the mind.

The revision of the Third Symphony was given a fair deal by the the L.P.O. under van Beinum, though the usual insufficiency of this orchestra's strings did little to cushion the more than sufficient noise of the trombones—Mr. Maxted's tone was often dangerously like that of rending corrugated iron. But the playing had plenty of life and the conductor's (at times rather Wagnerian) conviction carried the work successfully. No 3 marks the start of Bruckner's real maturity ; yet it not so even in quality as No. 2 in spite of its greater impressiveness. Perhaps the original version, which does not seem to have been published yet, will have greater cohesion. This symphony and the Fourth are transitional works, leading from the first-period group to the monumental last five. Rosbaud's performance of the Fourth was, so far as one's cruelly taxed imagination could divine, as good as one had by now come to expect, though the finest performance under the best conditions would have difficulty in rescuing the *finale*, one of the genuinely weak pieces in Bruckner, and the movement that bars the Fourth from comparison with the Fifth. But it has a wonderful *coda*, which Rosbaud handled magnificently.

The broadcast of No. 5 left me roused and breathless, though scarcely half as breathless as the B.B.C. Orchestra must have been, for Sir Adrian (twice in two days) slammed in fifty minutes through a symphony that normally takes seventy-five. Yet the performance had its merits. Boult was the first conductor in my experience to follow precisely the score (this apart from his actual *tempi*, which were for the most part far too fast) : having chosen his speeds, he did not deviate unless

Bruckner gave him permission. He carried his devotion to the letter so far as to observe the *alla breve* time-signature in the *adagio*, which consequently went much faster than usual. The effect, though it commanded respect, was far from convincing, for though Boult must have made his two beats as slow as was humanly possible, he would have been wiser to assume that Bruckner has overestimated the length of the conductor's arm. The first theme sounded well enough at the quicker pace, but the second was ruined. But by keeping a firm hold on the architectural conception, Boult did demonstrate the tensile strength of the symphony. He could, however, have achieved this fully with a generally much broader treatment of the *tempi* : those he adopted suggested a desperate attempt to avoid dullness at all costs. The orchestra could hardly articulate the notes and was unable to be other than grossly insensitive. Some passages, such as the fugue in the last movement, were horribly scrambled, even ludicrous.

It is usual to accuse Bruckner of covering the same ground in each of his symphonies, and much harm is done when an Austrian like Dr. Mosco Carner writes (in an article supposed to commend Bruckner to the English public) that when one has heard one Bruckner symphony, one has heard all nine. A more devastating condemnation could not be devised ; and it is not true. If one has recognised the austere grandeur of No. 5, is one deemed also to have experienced the iridescence of No.6, the firm euphony and glowing tranquillity of No. 7, the immense dramatic force of No. 8, and the profound penetrations and quests of No. 9 ? At all events, there is a striking contrast between Nos. 5 and 6 : Bruckner thought the latter his most original work ; it is rarely played. Rosbaud again showed his fine insight and his performance went far towards eradicating the nasty taste of one previously heard from Holland, by the *Concertgebouw Orkest* under Flipse, who so slimed the music with soapy *portamenti*, *ritardandi*, and flabby *rubato* that it came to resemble Scriabinated Franck. The chief glory of the Sixth is its very beautiful slow movement, one of Bruckner's rare voyages into true sonata style : the *Scherzo*, too, is unique in its elusive mystery, and to some extent anticipates Mahler's *Nachtmusiken*. Van Beinum's recording of the Seventh Symphony is now fairly well known and since I have reviewed it elsewhere,* there is no point in discussing it here. It seems, however, a pity that (admirable as this recording is in some ways) no attempt was made to broadcast the original version of the work, which contains some very individual features, and which has not yet had an adequate performance in this country.

The recording of the Eighth Symphony was no better than the others, but the performance was almost fabulous in its precision and breadth. The first movement certainly shows the most concise design in all Bruckner's work (apart from his *scherzi*, which are in a *genre* of their own), and its colossal power was marvellously held in the playing : this piece seems to me the greatest of its kind since Beethoven's *Coriolan* Overture, with which it has some striking points in common, notably the way in which it rises to a titanic Promethean climax, ending with a grim and fearsome collapse. While No. 8 is in some ways the most

*Disc, No. 9, Winter 1949.

Beethovenian of Bruckner's symphonies, its very processes are alien to those of Beethoven, with whose spirit it shares only a certain terrific driving force. The *scherzo* is like some stupendous, celestial reciprocating engine, accumulating vast energies by continuous action. In the slow movement Bruckner evokes a new atmosphere of rem ote, one might almost say interplanetary, contemplation of strange worlds, while the *finale* is an embodiment of the exploring mind of man, now pressing forward, now waiting to consolidate new territory and muster strength for the next venture. It is in such a movement as this last that Bruckner's style is open to misunderstanding by the transitionists. A Bruckner *finale* is not fundamentally an *allegro*, nor is it a slow move-ment : it is a synthesis of both and its function is to expand in the world created by the first three movements rather than to continue and finish a strictly dramatic scheme. It is therefore active and static by turn, almost in the way of an architect who enters his own newly-built cathedral. In such a movement Wagner's " art of transition " would as a general method be hopelessly out of place, except where the music is definitely active : at such times Bruckner shows himself master of it. When the music is static it is so at cardinal moments : the one crushing argument against the transitionists is that such breaks in the movement could be made beautifully " transitional " by any blockheaded Bachelor of Music, that had he wished, Bruckner himself could have written some smooth Wagnerian bars to this end. Bruckner knew what he was about ; his mastery of mere technicalities staggered many of his eminent Viennese contemporaries, and he spent six years polishing the Eighth Symphony. It is simply silly and im-pertinent to suggest that in a lifetime of intense creative activity Bruckner never learned to do what any ordinary hack could do : the fact is that he had other aims in mind. It is necessary to grasp these aims in order not to be baffled by their reverse side.

There is one other criticism of the B.B.C's. manner of presenting Bruckner. Why were most of the broadcasts given at such a late hour ? Who dares to listen in comfort to the last climax of No. 8 in a flat at midnight ? This consideration apart, such works need the full application of a fresh mind. Very few minds are in this condition after nine o'clock at night. The series has not been a success : if such another takes place in the remote future, someone in the B.B.C. must take Bruckner a little more seriously. ROBERT SIMPSON.

On Rehearing Wagner

TO open an operatic tetralogy under water, to carry it through earth, cloud, fire and flood to universal downfall, with a large cast and orchestra no member of which can afford to be less than outstanding in his allotted role is to ask a triumph of spirit over matter any reasonable approximation to which deserves our gratitude. My tribute to the Covent Garden Wagner season is a sincere one ; but both performance and works raise fascinating problems.

To begin in more senses than one at the bottom : this orchestra, never good, and doubtless exhausted by its varied labours, imprecise, ill-blended and poor in tone, is simply incapable of providing the indispensable *continuous* Wagnerian glow of glowing sound. Inter-

31

mittently is not enough. True, Rankl too is sometimes at fault. Usually his tempi are excellent (Wagner's chief test of a conductor) ; even his slow *Liebestod* is no slower than Walter's—but perhaps it takes a Walter to draw the tension so dangerously fine. Often the tempo felt slower than it was because the pulse began to flag. Often the effort to extract too much spoils what cannot be bettered in its own natural pace. On the other hand, restraint can also be exaggerated. Isolde's long wait in Act II *before* Tristan's arrival should grow electrically and impetuously to a supreme climax as she waves to her approaching lover ; but Rankl held back up to the very meeting itself, which thus lost half its own intensity for want of preparation. (The distant—in this performance all too distant—hunting horns for the first time in my experience failed of their usual mingled threat and haunting, otherworldly beauty). And how can the end of Götterdämerung rise to its wonted climax if the crescendos and sudden pianos (each with their minute preceding silence like a catch of the breath, and their immediate surge to the next crescendo) are smoothed over and tamed, or if the swirling string and woodwind figures are kept below the (rightly) shattering brass modulations (an instance of the many cases where it is the accompaniment which needs prominence, the themes being safely left to take care of themselves) ? The greatness of Bruno Walter's Götterdämerung hung like an unappeased ghost over Rankl's lesser cataclysm. It would be wonderful to hear the Ring or Tristan or the Meistersinger again with a better orchestra and a guest conductor of Walter's or de Sabata's or Barbirolli's calibre.

Yet Rankl's virtues are very real. His restraint in prize passages like the *Ride of the Valkyries*, the *Journey to the Rhine*, or the *Funeral March*, where so many conductors break loose (" here comes my celebrated *Funeral March !* ") works enormously to the advantage both of these passages themselves and of the general proportions. Scenes in themselves quiet, like Tristan and Isolde's duet *after* they have mutually accepted union in death as the one triumphant outlet from their intolerable dilemma, gained a rapt quality from the same orchestral restraint combined with inspired singing. This miracle was not achieved in Siegfried's poignant recall (under the influence of the second magic potion) of Brunhilde's love and Brunhilde's music within moments of the tragic death prepared for him to our knowledge but not to his ; but here the failure was Svanholm's. A truly memorable Tristan, a fascinating Loge, a satisfactory Siegmund and a very good Siegfried, Svanholm lacks (though he more nearly approached it in the Tristan passage) that fey and ravishing tone which Melchior kept for this moving scene, so that Svanholm narrating and dying was much the same vocally as Svanholm bullying and loving. He is a magnificent actor and musician, free of Melchior's occasional vulgarity, but also considerable short of Melchior's supreme vocal splendour.

Flagstad falls short of nothing. To beauty of tone, presence, acting and countenance she adds the effortless power to cleave the orchestra (with nothing held back to spare the singer) like a bird in flight, thus achieving the full Wagnerian sonority and rapture. She has all Isolde's intensity and Brunhilde's spiritual significance, dwarfing the stage at her final entry as Brunhilde must. She always had the voice ; now her greatness, like Brunhilde's, has wonderfully matured.

Hotter's beautiful voice too often lacks a clean cutting edge ; but he is a good (if possibly miscast) Gunther, a splendid Wotan and a really great Kurwenal (how moving he makes that fine study in simple loyalty). Peter Klein, who sings instead of barking Mime, and acts superbly, is the best I have heard ; he and Grahame Clifford's Alberich made a terrific quarrel of it outside Fafner's cave. As to Fafner : Norman Walker (an admirable King Mark) sang him well enough ; but why not give him really heavyweight, electrical amplification, as the one character who can be encouraged and should be enabled to roar the theatre down ? (When Mime barks and roars, Act I of Siegfried fails at once, as does Act III at the least lapse from heroism into vulgarity). Fafner is, of course, tired of slavery to his own hoard, and nourishes an unconscious death wish ; but he is still formidable, and should sound it if he cannot look it. Though even a stage dragon could swing and *raise* himself more than our new friend, otherwise commendably alarming.

Mm. Bourman, Abercrombie and Shacklock were pretty Rhine-maidens, musical and accurate, in Götterdämerung ; more so than Mm. Rae, Raisbeck and Watson in Rhinegold, for whose first scene they were hampered by fishtails (absurd in drapery, however fascinating in the nude) and fins (absurd and unmermaidenly anyhow). For the last scene they were more gravely handicapped by being placed not merely offstage, as Wagner directs, but half-way to Bow Street Police Station, so that their moving interruption of the godly procession fell short of its customary effect.

Constance Shacklock also sang Brangäne, quite enchantingly, making the utmost of this important and sympathetic role. Edith Coates, a too scowling and too nagging Fricka (we must feel some sympathy and respect for Fricka, or the tragedy unbalances) sang Waltraute memorably. Here are two English voices of Wagnerian dimensions, allied with the brains to use them properly. Trevor Anthony is an intelligent but insufficiently evil Hunding (a matter of natural timbre) ; Ernster's Hagan was capable of anything and pleased me well. Doree's Sieglinde and Gutrune are vocally beautiful : perhaps a lighter timbre conveys better the pathos of Gutrune's almost innocent involvement in a tragedy stronger than herself (almost : but she does consent to the drugging of Siegfried, thereby taking that small first step which can change one's moral direction from South to North). A rather weightier Erda than Edith Furmedge (? Mary Jarred, ? Kathleen Ferrier) adds to her impressiveness, as would less fitful illumination, she being not a ghost, after all, but a goddess. Shirley Russell has the right lightness for the wood bird, but could be a little nearer and brighter. The Norns, with their superb music, were a disappointment : themselves swallowed in obscurity (why not silhouette them darkly against a pallid sky ?) they took their revenge by swallowing their words, and a good many of their notes as well.

A convincingly underwater Rhine ; a formidable conflagration round Brunhilde's rock ; a resounding Götterdämerung collapse ; fine costumes, and sets nicely balanced between unfeasible realism and incongruous modernity ; not too many fireworks (but too noisy and thus too distracting); not an all too real horse (one acute anxiety the less); returning giants who almost trip over the coveted hoard without noticing it ; moonlight outside as Siegmund breaks *into* Hunding's hut despite an orchestral thunderstorm sufficient to remind any producer of the prevailing weather ; Wotan appearing simultaneously with Hunding, Siegmund and Brunhilde for the combat instead of five crucial bars later as Wagner directs ; a turf uprooted with no visible effort ; splendidly active ravens, but the shape of ducks ; funeral logs lit at a touch without twigs or kindling . . . on balance a production of unusual merit.

And the Ring itself ? My advice is : study the libretto. Advantageous as it is to have learnt the musical themes well enough to recognise Wagner's orchestral references to such basic concepts as nature, intuition, hate, will, obligation or frustation, it is surprising how if you look after the libretto the themes will look after themselves. They are, in fact, designed for that very purpose. They establish the exact mood or rather moods (for it is of their essence to combine and melt one into the other, as it is of Wagner's genius to have invented themes fluid enough to do so yet distinctive enough to be memorably significant) whether you consciously detect them or not. But read the words carefully, immediately beforehand, and in both German and English if you have a little but only a little German, and you will find yourself following the stage situation and even the poetry in vastly enhanced detail. All those supposedly boring speeches and interminable interludes at once spring to life (how can a speech not bore you of which you do not follow a word ?) and you will make the curious discovery that it is in these very passages that the drama offers its profoundest interest. For despite its operatic trappings the Ring is a drama of ideas, and not merely of ideas, but of realities of which even these ideas are but the containing symbols.

Scratch the surface of the Ring, and you find, as Shaw found in his *Perfect Wagnerite*, a fascinating allegory of capitalism and socialism, greed and bravery, morality and love : powerful forces operative in our external world. But look still deeper, and you will uncover a symbolism so intimate that no two interpreters will read it alike, a symbolism not of the outer world but of the inner, and like all inner meanings dependent on what you yourself have to bring to it in the way of vision and experience. In short, a myth.

We all benefitted from Shaw on Wagner ; but what we now need is Jung on Wagner. As Wagner very well knew, a myth is not just a " fairy-tale " (though a true fairy-tale may be a myth). It is, unknown (at the conscious level) even to its creators, a statement about realities of the kind which we generally apprehend only through symbols. Because symbols speak directly to the unconscious, we respond to them whether we understand them intellectually or not. Hence their strange power ; hence both the durability and the mutability of the myth itself. A myth will mean, for you, precisely what your own inner wisdom can find in it ; but it is bound to mean something. It releases ; it expresses ; it is closed to you only in the measure in which you close your heart to intuition.

Sophistication of that superficial kind which disbelieves whatever it cannot intellectualise, and reduces a symbol to its mere outer semblance, is the real enemy of intuition. A Jungian analysis of the Ring could not but enlarge our understanding, whilst actually enhancing our intuitive response. Wagner was not consciously aware of the archetypal symbolism by which water serves to represent the unconscious itself with all its amoral innocence and immediacy ; but Jung would have something to say of the sureness with which he picked on the Rhine symbol, and wedded it to music heard not merely when the river but (far more significantly) the associated state of nature is called to mind. Erda's music is derived from it : so, by a stroke of genius which may or may not have been unconscious, is that inverted and literally descending version associated with the Gods' downfall and the completion of the cycle back to nature. When Wotan consults Erda, he consults his own intuition (and finds her clouded by his previous surrender to self-will) ; when he confides in Brunhilde, he confides in his true will (but is divorced from her by that same surrender and the commitments and compromises in which it has already entangled him). The truth outs in Act I of Siegfried, after Wotan has learnt his lesson and decided on renunciation as the one escape from accumulating evil. There he calls Alberich " black-Alberich " and himself " light-Alberich " ! Thus acknowledging in so many words that he and his old enemy are but the two faces of the same medal. Self-will for noble ends and self-will for ignoble ends are an inseparable pair of opposites, like light and darkness, pain and pleasure, good and evil. You cannot have the one without the other : they imply one another.

This is a truth typical of those better (because more directly) conveyed by symbols than by metaphysics. The Ring is full of them. We all have a Loge in us, our clever side, too clever by half if we do not watch it closely. We have all had dealings with Fricka, curtailing our own freedom for the benefits of law and order ; we have all at times turned to Erda, and perhaps plucked out intellectual conceit as Wotan plucked out an eye for the privilege of drinking at the well of inner wisdom. We have not always been on speaking terms with Brunhilde, and may easily have silenced our unconscious will by casting on her a magic sleep only to be broken by a Siegfried denied our conscious aid and undeterred (as our ego cannot be) by the seeming flames of our own private moral censor. Was not the Garden of Eden guarded by a flaming . . . ah yes ! dear editor, I quite agree. Enough is enough. Merely let me add that if you have not read the libretto, cannot read the libretto, and have no intention of ever trying to read the libretto, the power of the enacted symbols will still draw you on provided you have not left all your sensibilities at home, or armour-plated yourself in cynicism, or been born tone-deaf. Wagner's music will take good care of that.

ROBERT DONINGTON

Book Reviews

SERGEI RACHMANINOV *by John Culshaw :* Contemporary *Composers' Series. (Dennis Dobson) 8s. 6d.*
    Rachmaninov might not be pleased at being included in a series devoted to such composers as Satie, Ravel and Martinu, for he was completely out of sympathy with the music of his own later times.

However, this broadens the conception of contemporary music and makes the issue, already confused, more polemical.

Mr. Culshaw hovers between apology and admiration. This is a difficult composer to deal with and the impression given is that since the music has arrived and seems likely to stay, it had better be faced up to. Mr. Culshaw has studied every work that he could find. He has given detailed analyses of most of them, but has not found the dividing line between an extended programme note and an informative generalisation. Few authors have succeeded in maintaining this necessary balance. The trouble is that while one welcomes evidence such as Mr. Culshaw puts forward with an informed scholarship, one is left rather in the dark without the music to study.

On the Symphonies Mr. Culshaw finds himslf in a quandary. They are not as good as they ought to be, yet Rachmaninov was such a delightful personality that it seems a shame to have to say so. On the Concertos he is enlightening, particularly as regards the Third which I have always thought the best ; I am pleased to find that my opinion is confirmed. The excellent prêcis plan is adopted with this work, but it ought to be more detailed. Over the Second Concerto the author makes the astonishing statement that " those who persist in saying that the music is neurotic (how can music be neurotic ?) are wrong ; the neuroticism is not in Rachmaninov, nor in his music ; it is in themselves." This is begging the question a little too easily. Many find it erotic, aphrodisiacal in fact, and it is interesting to read that the composer was very far away from this state.

On the Piano Preludes Mr. Culshaw is excellent and finds himself on sure ground ; many will agree with him, for even if one does not like the idiom, one must admit that Rachmaninov knew how to write for the piano. A book of this nature should immediately arouse a desire for wider knowledge, and if there is no enthusiasm in the reader at the start, he should have risen to some by the end of the book. Mr. Culshaw writes too modestly and too apologetically and does not give the impression that he is really enthusiastic.

There is only one other composer I detest as much as Rachmaninov. This book is inclined to modify my detestation, but not to cure it. It has aroused in me a desire, but not a burning wish, to read " The Isle of the Dead " and to re-consider " The Bells." I am surprised that Mr. Culshaw thinks so little of the Cello Sonata.

This book may annoy the Rachmaninov " fans " but it will be salutory for them, as it will curb their inordinate admiration. The production is excellent and the musical examples printed in a size that will give joy to the most short-sighted reader. Generally speaking it is an excellent assessment, plainly written in rather a sober style. I do wish, however, that it were not necessary to use the word " discography " for what is simply a list of recorded music.

N.D.

THE CONCERTO by Abraham Veinus ; Pp. 330 (Cassel & Co., Ltd.) ; 16s. 0d.

" In the piano concertos from Mozart onward, the dominance of the solo instrument is a direct consequence of its frank opposition to the orchestra." Like pretty well every writer on the concerto, Mr.

Veinus makes too much of the rivalry between solo and *tutti*. Thus, while he proposes to take " a close view of the Mozart concertos," he overlooks what from the viewpoint of concerto technique is the most important feature of the last, B flat Concerto (K.595), i.e., the absence of any opposition, frank or frail, between piano and orchestra. This instrumental concord is one of the exoteric effects of the concerto's esoteric transcendence. The work was born out of the death of struggle.

" There are several good reasons for believing that the . . . 'cello concerto in D major, long attributed to Haydn, is not his work at all but was composed by Anton Kraft . . ." No. " [Mozart's] comments in his letters on matters of style and technique show a shrewd and critical intelligence." How delightful to know that Mozart's musical intelligence satisfies Mr. Veinus' requirements. " Torelli, however, did clarify the boundary line between solo and orchestra, and for the edification of future concerto composers he did establish, for better or for worse, the precedent of entrusting the leading musical ideas to the orchestra while the solo entertained with virtuoso display." What other precedent could he have established ? Logic is indeed the weakest point even in some of our best music-critical minds. Consider, for another instance, Mr. Veinus' attack on Schweitzer's view of Bach's clavier concerto arrangements. Schweitzer is confronted with two " more searching explanations " which contradict each other. However searching, one of these must be wrong, while Schweitzer needn't be, even if the other is right.

But I hesitate to complete the list of representative flaws, for merits predominate. Everybody can learn from Mr. Veinus' book, including even the eminent newspaper critic who thought the scheme of Bax's recent *Concertante* " original," not to speak of the distinguished author who thinks that Beethoven invented the instrumental recitative. So that this history of the concerto must be recommended to everyone who wants to know about what he knows, and to be made eager to acquaint himself with what he doesn't.

H.K.

CONCERNING HANDEL *by William C. Smith (Cassell, 21s. 0d.)*.

Now that Mr. Smith, who was for many years Assistant Keeper, Department of Printed Books, British Museum, has published his researches concerning Handel's life and works, the composer's future biographers will have no excuse for repeating accounts, long current, of Handel's poverty, bankruptcy and loneliness, which Mr. Smith shows largely to be imaginary. Nor should it be said again that the singer Gustavus Waltz was Handel's cook, or that Handel ever met Gastone dei Medici in Hamburg. On these and many other points Mr. Smith corrects most of Handel's previous biographers while acknowledging that "many of the less acceptable stories about the master can only be questioned and not emphatically contradicted."

It is a pity that the author did not devote one of his chapters wholly to the errors of Handel's biographers. As it is, though he mentions Chrysander, Rockstro and Streatfield, he ignores Leichtentritt's enormous, indispensable, but practically unreadable volume, first published in 1924, and also the handsome volume by Herbert Weinstock, published by Knopf in 1946.

It is hardly necessary to say that Mr. Smith's book will appeal chiefly to musicologists and bibliographers—two of his chapters are devoted to the earliest editions of the *Messiah* and of the *Water Music*— but even the general reader, if not so passionately addicted to Handel's music as Samuel Butler was, will find interesting details about the composer's life and works on many of these pages, and two of his letters never before published. The book, which is very well produced, contains fourteen illustrations, of which six are portraits of Handel.

A.R.

A SHORT HISTORY OF MUSIC *by Alfred Einstein. Pp. 397 ; 14s. 0d. (Cassell).*
MUSIC : *A Short History by W. J. Turner. Pp. 105 ; 6s. 0d. (A & C. Black).*

As Dr. Einstein knows so much more than oneself about mediæval music and illustrates his points so copiously with music examples, one must accept his publisher's statement that the student will find here " a sure guide to musical history." But some of Dr. Einstein's statements in his *Modern Times* section makes one doubt his " wisdom." Did Liszt indeed surpass Berlioz " in taste and intellectual power " ? Is it sufficient to write of the composer of *Les Noces* and the *Symphony of Psalms* that " Barbarism, triviality and mechanism are all conjoined in the work of Igor Stravinsky " ? Hindemith is dismissed in rather less than three lines and Schoenberg's late music described as "almost entirely unintelligible." All these statements can be checked against the evidence of one's own ears, but the rashness of them must inevitably make one doubt Dr. Einstein's enthusiasms and aversions in the earlier periods of music of which he writes.

The faults of W. J. Turner's even shorter history are so numerous that it would take pages of this journal to list them all. The chief one is, of course, that Mr. Turner was no musician : a fact that stares at one from almost every page. I fancy that Bartok (oddly joined to Webern by Mr. Turner) would have been surprised to learn that he had used the 12-tone system with more success than Schoenberg himself.

D.M.

MUSIC AND CRITICISM : A SYMPOSIUM EDITED BY RICHARD F. FRENCH. *pp. 181 (Oxford University Press for Harvard University Press)* 16s. 0d.

This volume consists of a collection of eight papers delivered by various experts in the course of a Symposium on Music Criticism held at Harvard University in May, 1947. Apparently the Music Department at Harvard had felt for some time that someone ought to do something about music criticism ; so it planned this Symposium, choosing the titles and selecting the experts to write the papers concerned.

One or two of the titles seem unfortunate. As might be expected, nothing much emerges in the course of the address on *The Critical Nature of a Work of Art*. And sometimes the real issues implicit in the titles are evaded—as is the case with *The Future of Musical Patronage in America*.

In the midst of this assembly—or, rather, at its head—appears E. M. Forster. His instructions were to discuss the *raison d'être* of criticism in the arts ; and this he proceeds to do, dipping into the well of his past experience as novelist, critic and amateur of music as he goes along. After careful investigation, he fails to find that criticism has given substantial help to artists ; and this conclusion is certainly not shaken by any of the arguments put forward by the rest of the contributors.

E.W.W.

MUSIC LOVER'S ANTHOLOGY. *Compiled by Arthur Jacobs ; pp. 227 (Illustrated). (Winchester Publications Ltd. 12s. 6d.)*

This pleasant and well-produced anthology ranges perhaps too wide, embracing even short stories, poetry, and a section of humorous writing (most of which, including two naively unfunny oddments by D. B. Wyndham Lewis, would have been better omitted). Those passages descriptive of composers and performers are the most attractive, for in them one seems to catch hints of a design for greatness. Christopher Hassall and Scott Goddard contribute original articles, and there is an interesting section, which might well have been expanded, on *The Musician and his Work*. Milein Cosman's drawings have considerable character.

C.H.S.

CECIL GRAY'S AUTOBIOGRAPHY : Musical Chairs or between Two Stools, being the Life and Memoirs of Cecil Gray. *Home and Van Thal. 16s. 0d.*

On p. 165, *Dolce* should be *Dulce* and *disipere, desipere*. May the second edition look to that ! This is not only a book for Scotsmen, though I know of none recently written that so signally exemplifies those three words of Buchanan : *praefervida ingenia Scotorum*. It is a book for any adventurous and ambitious soul, constructive and critical, albeit sensitive, who wishes to learn how to win through with least sacrifice of integrity and to safeguard his spiritual gains by presenting a façade of comparative failure to a catalytic world. It reads to me, in my simplicity, as honest an account as any creative artist can reasonably be expected to give of his progress, mental make-up and associates. In one way, though of so vastly different a scope, it resembles *Memoirs of a Fox-hunting Man*, in that it traces the development of a shy introvert childhood to a manhood as prudent and extrovert as that of any musician who comes to mind. In laying it down, I am not at all sure that the lack of interest shown till lately (say before Mr. Gorer's article in *The Music Review*) in *The Temptation of Saint Anthony*, *Deirdre* and *The Trojan Women* will not be found to have materially assisted those works, which may even be more Wagnerian than their composer cares to imagine. We are, apparently, treated to the spectacle of a divided mind ; the boy who writes histories at twelve desires at all costs to be a musician. Creation on both planes is a continuous agony, and the solitary's sole alleviations are travel and convivial frolics with boon companions. Some years back, when I read Mr. Gray's brilliant life of his friend ' Peter Warlock' (only manhandled by the rambling egocentric section contributed by the poet Robert Nichols) I noted mentally that a biographer who could so sympathetically analyse the causes of a suicide so complex as that of Philip Heseltine, whom I knew slightly, might be expected to produce a work of truthful analysis (a quality most rare in ' lives ') with himself as his subject. In this judgment I was not aided by knowledge of Mr. Gray's historical writings on music, for I had not read any of them. No, I simply detected in the ' Warlock ' book a real analyst of character and achievement who was not afraid of appearing to make a fool of himself, as so many of us are. I did *not* detect there what is abundantly clear from many a passage in the book before me, a true stylist with a sense of prose rhythm and harmony. Take for instance the prophecy at the start of Chapter 8, relating to the outbreak of the third world-war :

> I hope and anticipate that the atomic bomb will have become an obsolete weapon, and given place to bacterial warfare, whereby the human race, with a few chosen exceptions, as in the parallel instance of the Cities of the Plain, will be exterminated, while their redeeming creations, in the form of historical buildings and works of art, will be preserved, like ghostly Chirico cities, through which the few survivors will bat-like flit.

While suggesting that ' their ' should be ' its ' (as referring to ' the human race '), look, I ask you, at that highly original final cadence ! Only a person with an innate sense of style would close the paragraph with short words like those. *Ex pede Herculem.*

But the most refreshing features of this prose production, all things considered, are that it states and does not apologise and that there is little or no technical clap-trap on music or instruments. The works analysed appear at the close and it is noteworthy that they are not analysed thematically but objectively in the main, as *plots*. Nor, in the extremely diverting accounts of musicians, Sibelius, Van Dieren, Delius, Busoni (admirable !) Walton, or, the Sitwellian scene, does the writer's aloofness appear high-brow or otherwise objectionable. In his notes on his connections by birth I was, in one instance, able to follow him, since, as a schoolboy I vividly remember the pale strained face of Stewart Gray, leader of the hunger-marchers (on whom the headmaster had threatened to turn the hose if he addressed Harrovians in the ' Bill-yard '). It was my first real vision of a human being *outside society*, though I did not associate it with my spiritual loneliness then as Mr. Gray's word-picture of his cousin makes me do now. Be *that* as it may, in the long dialogue, not without humour, between the author and his *Doppelgänger* (pp. 161—167), with its allusion to the painter Haydon, not a word is thrown away and the reader is made to feel instinctively that no one can be permitted to write the life of Cecil Gray but Cecil Gray. Even if his own lack of interest in the performance of his compositions seems at first sight forced, or even a pose, the trend of his narrative as a whole impels the conviction that here, actually here, this descendant of an engineer is a wise smith of his fortunes. Nor can there have ever been a better story told against a Scotsman by a Scotsman than the episode of the photographs of the Sistine Chapel, which alone would keep these 324 pages alive in any but an addled memory.

I know that a *review* is expected to be a *précis* in these days, though I have not had the agonizing Fleet Street adventures that Mr. Gray details so trenchantly ; but if I do not leave the impression that this life-history up to 1939 is, some heady and splenetic flippancies expected, a mature and considered piece of writing, very subtly put together, as well as thoroughly readable, I shall have failed in my job. The writer's sensitivity exaggerates here and there, certainly. To illustrate the difference between Bach and Beethoven by saying that in the latter's work there is no element of divine inevitability (p. 31) is stressing a distinction by a captious paradox ; to insist that the lure of women with titles was a wish-fulfilment of a *leit-motiv* that D. H. Lawrence was unable to realize in life, is not allowing sufficient weight to the fact that Lawrence did, as I have always understood, marry a German aristocrat ; to insult the Cornish peasantry for their highly natural suspicion of a covey of interloping Chelsea fry, during a war with *Kultur*, is hardly to concede a Caledonian reason to Western Celts. But, in all these cases, there is a latent truth that has been forced into the service of paradox or epigram, so that one is never in a position to say that Mr. Gray is talking abject nonsense. I neither know him, nor, after reading his autobiography, do I desire to meet him ; but I should not desire to meet Augustus himself, were he alive, after reading the *Monumentum Ancyranum*. E.H.W.M.

FROM KEYBOARD TO MUSIC, *by George Woodhouse. Augener, Ltd., 4s.*

There is nothing which reads more enigmatically than any sort of attempt to put the technique of playing an instrument, and especially the piano, into words. In fact, the more one knows, the more inarticulate is one's explanation. The result usually reads like a Riemann edition of a Bach fugue—the simplest things become impossible to comprehend. For this reason, Mr. Woodhouse's well-intentioned book fails, as it inevitably must. He is sincere, and he knows much that is true, as well as much that is demonstrably untrue in practice—as, for instance, his triumphant quotation of Chopin's actual fingering for certain passages in his own works. The one given on page 42, Fx. 19 (e), which indicates the thumb for every note of a right-hand descending arpeggio, looks ridiculous, but was actually sound sense—in Chopin's time. Mr. Woodhouse has merely overlooked the fact which the editors he anathematizes have remembered, that Chopin's piano would have a loose action and generally softer tone, whereas any such attempt on a modern piano, with its stiff action made for voluminous tone, would be courting disaster. What we have gained on the roundabouts we must be prepared to lose on the swing, especially Chopin's.

What Mr. Woodhouse and any such instructor must remember is that a word or image accompanied by adequate demonstration will leave its mark on and have an accurate meaning henceforth for any attentive student, but the same word or image merely written can have any one of a dozen meanings, most of them quite inaccurate. Every such system suffers from these faults—no player can describe accurately what he does, not even Schnabel, whose description of his technique, quoted by Mr. Woodhouse, bears no relation to what he actually does. H.T.

41

New Music

PRELUDE AND FUGUE IN C MINOR. DOUBLE FUGUE IN
E FLAT. For Piano—*Havergal Brian*. *Augener, 3s. and 5s.*

That Havergal Brian is one of the major composers England has
so far produced, I have no doubt. When the public at large will have a
chance to find out for itself it is impossible to say. I do not agree with
the critic who, when reviewing Nettel's book " Ordeal by Music," said
that Brian had had his chance—in other words, it had come and gone
and it is now too late. For whatever reason, he has not had it. The
story of the constant string of misfortunes which has attended as
baulked a career as can be found in musical history can be read fully
in the book mentioned above. The same critic implied that, the day of
large orchestras having gone by (has it ?) along with the romantic era,
Brian was a back number. It would be interesting to know what works
and performances of Brian the reviewer had heard.

The passing of the large orchestra is an illusion. All that has passed
is a reason for using it. English scoring, as a general rule, is not a
strong point, and composers like Vaughan Williams, Britten, **Walton**,
Rawsthorne, etc., are now using large orchestras for the mere production of noise, and employing unnecessary doublings which make a
Schumann symphony, always the subject of much ado about nothing in
this respect, a model of good scoring by comparison. They have completely failed to understand the good sense of composers such as
Bruckner and Mahler—the latter especially understanding fully that, in
order to produce the chamber effect which is his aim in all the major
symphonies, it is necessary to use a very large orchestra, not to double
or even quadruple every part and so produce a noisy blur, but to have
as many strands clearly audible as possible. There is not a note in these
scores which cannot be clearly heard in even a bad performance ; I
defy anyone to say the same for the Vaughan Williams 4th, 5th or 6th,
or Britten's " Sinfonia da Requiem," or Walton's " Symphony," or
Rawsthorne's " Symphonic Studies " and " Violin Concerto."

This Brian clearly understands also, and, in the scores I know at all
well, the " Dr. Merryheart " Overture, "The Fantastic Variations on an
Old Rhyme " and the " Gothic " Symphony, he shows a mastery
which is rare in that every instrument is necessary and contributes its
quota to a texture clear in every detail.

As to the music, everyone must find that for himself. I know its
importance for me, but I shall not presume to dictate to others. What
is necessary, before Brian can be either accepted or dismissed with
fairness by the musical public in general, is an adequate number of
performances of his major works. That the music is romantic is true,
but it is true in a way that musicians to-day misunderstand. Part
of the reason for this misunderstanding lies in the problem
of large orchestras and in the size of the works concerned. Almost the
only thing which to-day governs the length of a work for a listener,
musician, critic or otherwise, is the clock. What makes such works as
the symphonies of Bruckner and Mahler, and, I will say, Brian,
independent of this mechanical device is their magnificent sense of
proportion—one of the prime reasons for the size of the orchestra used.

And, in Bruckner and Mahler's case, the origin of this proportion lies in a great achievement of Schubert which is obscure to-day, merely because proportion has disappeared from our scheme of things. Until this is seen, composers will continue to produce short works for large orchestras, which actually sound much longer and ten times more tedious than any Bruckner or Mahler symphony, because there is no proportion, and therefore no sense.

Brian has this sense of proportion, in fact, whether it is there consciously or unconsciously, there is evident to me, in such work of his as I know, a definite Schubertian ancestry (I speak of structure and of nothing else) which reduces his enormous creations to normal size—that is, the right size for our ears.

At the moment, his larger works must wait for their due appreciation, which will inevitably come, until some return to a sense of lasting values and proportion has been effected, although, in the process of delay, we may lacerate a man's soul. That is the old, the human way of thanks, and Brian, no doubt, has by now learned it to the full. In the meantime, we may well occupy our time in getting acquainted with such of his smaller works as are available, and be grateful to Messrs. Augener's for thus belatedly publishing these two works for piano. (They were composed in 1924 !) They are both fine examples of his mature way of thinking, in a texture which owes more than a little to Reger, although only in a few rare instances does the sound approximate to the German master. The Prelude and Fugue are fine to play and easy to read, with a mastery in distribution of effect which is content not to anticipate climaxes, and shows a view of the piano as essentially pianistic as his orchestral thinking is essentially orchestral.

The Double Fugue is a huge structure which might well take its place beside the great series by Reger. Its effect is as immediate on the hearer as in the Reger fugues, but its layout is marred by one fault. No doubt with the intention of making it easy to read, Brian has in many places laid out the four parts on four staves. In practice, this makes superhuman demands on the reader, and it is a pity that such a magnificent work should be placed at such a disadvantage, one which can be easily put right. It is to be hoped that in a future edition this will be done.   H.T.

PICTURES OF CHILDHOOD—for Piano Solo.   *A. Khachaturian.*
Anglo-Soviet Music Press Ltd., 4s. 6d.

Soviet composers as a whole continue to give no evidence that they have either anything of any value to say, or any great interest in saying it. This may or may not be due to the ideology which controls the workings of their minds. Personally, I think it has everything to do with it. But, so far, individuality being against the interest of the masses, they are reduced to a choice between being fatuously banal, or idiotically innocuous. These pieces of Khachaturian represent a slight upward step from those of his larger works which I have heard, in that they are completely innocuous, only very slightly idiotic and are without a trace of the fatuous.

H.T.

VARIATIONS ON A THEME OF ROSSINI, FOR VIOLONCELLO AND PIANO ; THREE MADRIGALS FOR VIOLIN AND VIOLA—*Bohuslav Martinu. Boosey and Hawkes, 5s. and 7s. 6d.*

Martinu gets better and better. I had begun to think that his attractiveness would wear thin, since he was in danger of becoming a slave to certain rhythmical tricks. These variations reassure one. They are still very much Martinu, but have a solidity of musical expression and an interest in formal construction which is rare in music to-day. Nor has he yet, apparently, reached the absurd stage of treating music as a science, and proclaiming " discoveries " of to-day, all of which were known to composers from Bach onwards, and used by them as and when they wanted to, as making a classical (or " romantic," if you wish) style out-of-date. A large part of practically every well-known modern composer, for example, Hindemith or Britten, is already far more out-of-date than the romantics will ever be. He who writes for the times must be content to perish with the times. Fortunately Martinu does not fall into this trap, and, although his variations are not a great masterpiece, they are of value in that they know their theme, and can afford to ignore it without forgetting it. A very fine work.

The choice of the name " Madrigal " for Martinu's three duets for violin and viola is a little obscure, since there is nothing of a vocal nature about the music, and, although the parts, insofar as these are real parts, are free enough, it is hardly the sort of freedom implied in the term " Madrigal." However, that aside, these are three quite pleasant pieces, spoilt by too little melody in either an old or a modern application and too much of Martinu's stylised rhythmical tricks. Nevertheless, in the singular dearth of music for this difficult combination these excellent studies are to be welcomed.   H.T.

PRELUDE, PASSACAGLIA AND FUGUE, for VIOLIN AND VIOLA—*Gordon Jacob. Joseph Williams—Score, 2s. 6d. ; Parts 3s.*

If the Martinu pieces are excellent studies, this is the solid work to which they could lead. Jacob is a much underrated composer, who has the, to-day, singular virtue of humility. Precisely because he does not claim to be a great composer, he invariably says more than he knows. Like most English composers, he has difficulty, in sonata-works, in the difficult art of transition, but with this difference, that he knows and admits it, as he did on one occasion to me. But, precisely because he knows it, it is far less apparent in his work than in that of most of his contemporaries. He is also rare among modern musicians in that he is fully aware of the great contrapuntal mastery which animates the whole of Schumann's work, from the smallest piece to the largest symphony.

These three pieces are a finely-drawn unity, and, although, or perhaps because, there is singularly little double-stopping, they are a test of real musicianship. There is a slight Mahlerian feeling in the high canonic writing in the Prelude.

The Passacaglia is based on a theme of the good old traditional type which Bach, for all practical purposes, instituted (will composers ever write a passacaglia on any other type of theme ?). It looks on paper extremely angular and uncomfortable, but proves to be extremely flexible and capable of sustained and impressive treatment, which it gets.

The Fugue is like a certain type of Regerian fugue, seen through Jacob's eyes, and makes an exhilarating finish to a sensitive and finely-wrought addition to a scanty repertoire.
H.T.

FULL SCORES

NOCTURNE FOR FOUR VOICES—*Phyllis Tate* (*Oxford University Press*). *8s. 6d.*

This is a setting of a poem of the same name by Sidney Keyes, who died in enemy hands in North Africa in 1943 at the age of twenty, and posthumously won the Hawthornden Prize for Literature in 1944. The music bears the date December 1946, and was first performed a year later under Dr. Mosco Carner, to whom it is dedicated.

The composition is for soprano, tenor, baritone and bass soloists, string quartet, double-bass, bass clarinet and celesta. In this striking combination, the celesta enters fully into thematic development and is not used merely for colour. It says much for the composer's skill that the concentration on male voices produces no lopsided effect in the music. There are five sections, in contrasted mood, but the work is continuous and has a single thematic structure. This structure is closely integrated and very interesting : basically, it contrasts subjects dominated by the " harsh " interval of a semitone (used both melodically and harmonically) and others dominated by the " gentler " interval of a falling third, variously major and minor.

The poem is a dialogue : the girl, lamenting her dead lover, is urged by other voices to drown herself. The music for the girl (soprano) is tender and moving ; the other voice-parts give some impression of strain—a strain, that is, in their musical language, not merely in their representation of something nightmarish. Particularly awkward is the point at which the composer, apparently to keep the bass voice occupied while the instruments are piling on the " atmosphere," drops (for the only time in the work) into word-repetition : " The fury, fury, the fury in your head, the fury, the fury in your head, in your head," and so forth.

Not, in my opinion, an entirely successful piece. But promising, significant, and courageous : for here, as all too rarely, is an attempt to meet a contemporary poet on his own ground. In this well-produced score, the would-be Italian terms " delicamente " and " pochetissimo " have slipped past the proof-reader.
A.J.

VOCAL SCORES

THE BEGGAR'S OPERA : A BALLAD-OPERA BY JOHN GAY in a new musical version, realised by Benjamin Britten. *Vocal score by Arthur Oldham* (*Boosey and Hawkes, 37s. 6d.*).

Originally *The Beggar's Opera* was at once a sophisticated treatment of popular material, and a popular treatment of the sophisticated. A middle-class product, the ballad-opera guyed the aristocratic pretensions of Italian opera, while at the same time it presented, for a fashionable audience, the roistering vigour of low life within a scheme of conventional courtesies. Its musical techniques depended on a rapprochement between popular folk material and the fashionable academic conventions of the time.

All through his career Benjamin Britten has been interested in the problem of effecting a rapprochement between what one might call the more provincial elements of English musical styles and the cosmopolitan techniques of Europe. *The Beggar's Opera*, no less than the music of Dowland and Purcell, has thus a particular relevance to Britten's own problems, and any regrets about his marring the ballad-opera's 'primitive force' with his pernickety sophistications seem to me to be sentimental and inapposite. Dr. Pepusch was sophisticated too ; his realisations ' civilized ' the barbarities of the Vulgar. Nowadays we are more self-conscious about it than the eighteenth century had need to be, because we're less sure what we mean by being civilized. None the less, I can see no justifiable objection on theoretical grounds to a twentieth-century realisation.

The validity of the principle accepted, we are prepared to find that Britten's version displays his customary expertise ; and we are not disappointed. The contemporaneity of Britten's realisation doesn't rest mainly in the application of extraneous harmonies to folk tunes or eighteenth-century melodies, but rather in his copious invention of instrumental counterpoints to the themes. Such incidental harmonic oddities as occur in the score are usually a consequence of this free growth of orchestral part-writing. The instrumental figuration is often suggested by a brief phrase of the melody—as in the use of the Scotch snap phrase in the setting of ' The miser thus a shilling sees.' The characteristic virtuosity in the use of the few instruments is of course inseparable from this seemingly inexhaustible creation of accompanying figures that don't merely accompany. In the scene in the Condemned Cell, especially in the Lament, the nature of the instrumental material and the virtuosity in the treatment of it imbue the music with a touchingly poetic evocativeness. This is a contemporary re-creation which one does not need to ' justify ' because it is supremely beautiful.

W.H.M.

JOHN BLOW : SALVATOR MUNDI, *anthem for chorus and organ, ed. H. Watkins Shaw. (Hinrichsen).*

This is perhaps the greatest example of the church music of a composer whose work is still insufficiently known. It is, with its chromaticisms and dissonant suspensions, a highly emotional piece which has much of the operatic intensity and theatrical glamour of the mid-seventeenth century. Yet it preserves the devotional and liturgical spirit of the previous century—or rather translates that spirit into slightly different terms ; nothing could be more remote from the perfunctory secularity into which much Restoration church music degenerated. This edition is to be energetically recommended.

W.H.M.

MINIATURE SCORES.

PROKOFIEV : CINDERELLA SUITE NO. 1 (*Boosey and Hawkes, 12s. 6d.*).

Hard on the heels of a sold-out season of Cinderella at Covent Garden comes a score of the first suite, almost coinciding with a recording of some of the music. The sequence of movements on the records does not agree with the score, and is probably not intended to do so. The music shows Prokofiev in two minds : he is not sure whether to be simple or subtle, and while the themes tend to favour the former virtue, the scoring sticks to the latter, but only a score could show this. The present production looks like a photographic reduction of a handwritten full-score : if this is the case, the writing is extraordinarily clear except for one or two cramped-up *tuttis*.

D.W.S.

BARTOK : FIRST AND SECOND RHAPSODY FOR VIOLIN AND ORCHESTRA (*Boosey and Hawkes, 5s. 0d. each*).

Dedicated respectively to Szigeti and Szekely, these two well-organized rhapsodies show Bartok in congenial frame of mind, with folk dances as the basis of his work, and violin technique stretched far beyond the wildest flights of the village fiddler's imagination. Harmonics, varying rapidly with natural notes, and guitar effects in plenty make these rhapsodies colourful and showy, but the cool, calculating head is behind it all, and the hard brilliance rarely absent. Both works have the same slow and quick sections (*Lassu* and *Friss*), with an alternative finale for Rhapsody No. 1.

D.W.S.

MUSSORGSKY: PRELUDE TO *Khovanchtchina* (*2s. 6d.*) ; *Boosey and Hawkes.* NIGHT ON THE BARE MOUNTAIN (*5s. 6d.*) ; *Boosey and Hawkes.*

Some day Mussorgsky will be considered worthy of an *Urtext Gesamtausgabe*, but until that happens, we must make do with the carefully contrived orchestrations of Rimsky-Korsakov. There is, however, the danger that the hand that alters the scoring may alter the harmony, and if Rimsky-Korsakov's wife was capable of the latter type of emendation when dealing with a Tchaikovsky score, there is every reason to believe that her more illustrious and versatile husband would do the same with Mussorgsky. Be that as it may, his versions are eminently playable, and they never go to the extreme (as Stokowski does) of making the violins in a body play whole tunes in consecutive artificial harmonics. This kind of effect is risky enough when entrusted to a single instrument only : in *tutti* it is so fantastic as to savour of musical bathos. The Prelude to the unfinished opera *Khovanchtchina* is attractive, and we are as sorry to know that this scheme petered out as we are with *Salammbo*, whose Carthaginian colour was apparently not strong enough to combat Mussorgsky's idleness and procrastination. Both of these scores (nos. 653 and 654 of the series) are up to the usual Boosey and Hawkes standard of printing.

D.W.S.

STRING QUARTET III : *Michael Tippett* (*Schott*) ; 5s.

This work outstrips the F sharp major quartet only in size, for though it could not have been written by any other composer, it has not the fluidity of the earlier work. Often this Quartet in C labours, though it does contain some very fine things. Tippett's sense of tonality is delicate and always imaginative, even where his melodic invention does not equal it : a case in point is the *andamento* subject of the first movement fugue, establishing C as a centre merely by the orientation of its answer rather than by any direct statement. But the *andamento* itself seems unworthy of its composer and fails to hit the ear smartly enough to make it ring for the rest of the piece. The preceding introduction arouses high expectations and deserves more than its rather heavily worked sequel, though it succeeds in enlivening and deepening the end of the fugue with two interjections of its characteristic muttering monotone. The slow movement is one of Tippett's best inspirations.* After a preludial viola solo accompanied by *arpeggiando pizzicato* chords on the 'cello, a long, well-sustained *cantabile* begins in A major, with a full counterstatement ending in a *codetta*-like reference to the prelude : then comes the reply ; the *cantabile* starts again in A minor, by no means a literal transcription, but full of subtle changes of melodic inflection. It achieves considerable pathos and finally subsides over the guitar-like chords, fading into an inconclusive E minor.

The contrapuntal *scherzo* that follows is, like the first movement, marred by overcrowding and not very distinguished subject matter, though there is plenty of ingenuity. The sound, however, is busy rather than energetic. The introductory fourth movement is highly dramatic, mysterious, declamatory, and excited by turns, leading after a silent pause to the fifth and last section, *Allegro comodo*, mainly in C minor, though approaching that key from an oblique angle. It is fundamentally the simplest of all the movements, and the comparative plainness of its melodic rhythms recalls the style of Hindemith. Its best elements are the swinging 3/4 tunes that sometimes spring to the surface, but its loud ending over a long pedal C, with a somewhat Regerian *allargando* does not altogether convince : its internal details are not vital enough to sustain it.

The quartet as a whole seems to me unequal : perhaps its real lack is melodic tension as opposed to contrapuntal and dynamic tension. Perhaps this accounts for the seeming absence of a unifying mood for the complete work. Undoubtedly Tippett has aimed higher in this than in the Second Quartet : if he has instead fallen short, it may be because he persevered at moments when it would have been better to wait for the lost freshness to return. Probably the work is transitional and will prepare the way for a genuine masterpiece : one can only hope that the Fourth Quartet will blend the lucidity of the Second with the intellectual grit of the Third. Add to these qualities the beauty of Tippett's natural melody and nothing less than a great work could result.   R.S.

*The nearest "classical" parallel to this form might be found in Brahms' song *An die Nachtigall*, Op. 46, No. 4. There it is, of course, dictated by the mood of the poem.

Opera

WOZZECK, *Alban Berg* ; *Albert Hall, 16 March, 1949 ; B.BC. Symphony Orchestra, c. Boult.*

THE IMMORTAL HOUR, *People's Palace, 4 April, 1949 ; London Philharmonic Orchestra, c. Rutland Boughton.*

AVON, *Inglis Gundry* ; *Exploratory Opera Society, Scala Theatre, 11 April, 1949 ; W.M.A. Opera Group, c. Geoffrey Corbett.*

TITUS, *Mozart, Guildhall School of Music, 28 April, 1949 ; City Opera Club* ; *Musical Director, Alec H. Dempster.*

A great performance of this very great opera was given—one which proved for once and for all that expressive, lyrical and dramatic music can be written within the strict confines of the twelve-tone system, given, of course, a composer of genius. In Berg we have a genius of a very rare order. Sir Adrian Boult rose magnificently to the occasion and Heinrich Nillius made an unforgettable *Wozzeck*. The remainder of the cast were, without exception, much more than adequate, but for Suzanne Danco, who seemed lost as *Marie* and was not as sensitive as she might have been in the famous *Lullaby*. Most composers take this episode too fast (witness the recent Ormandy recording of the *Three Fragments*) and Sir Adrian could have been a little more leisurely.

The *Immortal Hour* is more important historically than musically, but nevertheless deserves an occasional revival, if only to remind us how perverse Wagner's influence can be on a slender talent. Scene I of Act I is about as dull as the first half of Act I of *Siegfried* ; and Mr. Boughton is no Wagner. The real fault with the work is its inconsistency of style, an odd mixture of hot-house emotionalism and folk rhapsodizing ; and its very bogus mysticism is far removed from life, musical or otherwise. The opera was badly produced but well played and sung, particularly by Glenda Raymond and Arnold Matters as *Etain* and *Eochaidh* respectively.

Mr. Gundry's *Avon* was a disappointment and not as successful as his previous rather uneven *The Partisans*. The libretto (the composer's own) was stagey, to say the least, and the music quite undistinguished. No amount of costumes, historical accuracy and genuine Elizabethan street-cries can compensate for a score essentially so commonplace.

Mozart's *La Clemenza di Tito* may or may not be great music. It would be quite impossible to tell from this performance of it. However much one may praise the City Opera Club for their enterprise, one can only regret that the production must have surely fallen far short of their own ideals and ambitions.

D.M.

II TABARRO AND GIANNI SCHICCHI, *Puccini ; Sadler's Wells ; 5th April, 1949.*

To the Puccini-lover, *Il Tabarro* and *Gianni Schicci* must come as a surprise, even more than *Turandot*. Not that the musical vocabulary has changed in these two works, but the choice of words has suddenly become refined. Always when a poet or a composer begins to select carefully from his vocabulary and to condense judiciously, he loses his wider public, who miss his usual racy immediacy. This perhaps accounts for the neglect of these two works ; it is to be hoped that they will now stay together in the Wells repertoire. What makes them so palatable is, I think, the simplicity and shortness of their one-act stories. Puccini has to pack into the space of an hour not only so many arias and recitatives but also so much painting of atmosphere and dramatic build-up. This makes his style extremely concise, if not indeed epigrammatic. To be sure, the arias get their proper length and relief, especially in the serious *Tabarro* when there is a need for numbers in the grand style ; Puccini would not be the great dramatist he is if he insisted on musico-dramatic recitative throughout for the sake of conciseness. But he has other means to keep the " numbers " in their proper place within the framework of an one-act story. In *Il Tabarro* for instance, he has a genuine formal key-system. Now, this is something one would hardly credit him with, and which remains hidden to most of the audience, like Alban Berg's, Britten's and most of Wagner's key-systems. But as a means of composition it heightens the dramatic impact of the music even for the ordinary listener. In this story of an elderly and moody Parisian bargee who, after trying in vain to regain his wife's love, watches out on his barge for his suspected rival and kills him, the Parisian atmosphere prevailing at the beginning is depicted in C major. This is heightened to G major at the arrival of the balad-seller, who offers the story of Mimi for sale (a very curious, half-mocking self-quotation here). On the other hand, Giorgetta's music is in B♭, and the duets later on with her husband are in Bb, E♭ and D♭, the " emotional " keys of the work. In the centre stands a furtive and tormented love-duet between the heroine and Luigi in the wildly illicit key of C minor. At nightfall, the Parisian C major is dulled into A minor—a strange scene this, where the husband sits brooding over the identity of the lover to some vague polytonal strains off-stage. At the catastrophy, " Paris " and " Love " meet forcibly in the common C minor. (When the dying Luigi confesses his love there is a last-flickering of C♯ minor.) This ingenious lay-out is supported by a 3/8 (also 6/8 and 9/8) rhythm, at once suave and menacing, which is brilliantly used in all important scenes, and firmly ties the beginning of the work to its end. The performance was sensitive and effortless, all the roles well cast, Miss Sladen's strong dramatic sense dominating the scene.

Gianni Schicchi is a work of pure delight, a *Falstaffian* comedy, swift, malicious, improbable, and wholly convincing. As in all classical comedy, that is, the characters convince, while the plot is improbable— even if, according to Dante, it really should have happened. Such improbability is of course artistically highly desirable. In the music too, (as in Verdi's *Falstaff*) there is on the one hand the naturalistic, mercilessly true exegesis of the characters, and on the other hand, the flights of fancy into abstract comicality ; passages of an irresponsible iridescent humour which seem to epitomize not so much the situation in hand, but Comedy of Manners in general. Unfortunately, there are also the " atmospheric " and the " emotional " elements, which here, unlike in *Tabarro*, are expressed jointly in a few musical numbers, chiefly Rinuccio's sentimental salute to Florence, and the popular " Oh, my beloved daddy " of Lauretta. These are remnants of an earlier, cruder Puccini ; especially the latter, mitigated though it was by Elsie Morison's stylish performance, is a real blotch on the opera. Puccini may here have pandered to popular taste, in a work that otherwise, for all its fun, makes no concessions to his audiences ; which theory is borne out by the self-irony of the scene where Schicchi paces the room in search for a solution of the task put upon him, and the two lovers break into the most " Toscan " bits of duet-singing every time he says " it can't be done," only to be cut short by his next utterance. Altogether, I think, Pucinni in this opera knew very well what he was doing, and it makes one wonder, by comparison, how naïve, or else how calculating he was when writing *Tosca* and *Butterfly*. Perhaps he was both.

Like all good comic music, this score incites one to think about the inherent expressive contents of short motifs. Never before has it struck me that the downward slur of two notes, repeated in close sequence, which denotes grief and resignation, needs only a quickening of pace, a slight loosening of its sequential order, to acquire an air of supple, feline mockery. This is what happens with the false lamentations of the relatives. The score is full of such things, in close concentration, and I wish musicians would go to hear this opera five or six times.

What stands out about the Sadler's Wells production is its skilful direction by Alan Gordon, and the décor by Peter Hoffer. Individual singing lets one down sometimes, but the ensembles are spirited, and that is what here matters most. Edmund Donlevy is an excellent " all-round " Schicchi, stressing the versatility of this character.   P.H.

HENRY WOOD CONCERT SOCIETY : " PARSIFAL " CONCERT. *B.B.C. Symphony Orchestra, Goldsmith's Choral Union, one dozen soloists, c. Boult, Albert Hall, 13th April, 1949.*
If there is one thing more foolish than to say that Wagner did not believe in the religion of his last work, it is Dent's contention that it does not artistically matter whether he did. The musically self-evident belief behind *Parsifal* does not, however, reach so deep as the truth of *Tristan* or the message of *The Mastersingers*, for which insufficient reason Scott Goddard writes in his notice on the present performance of the " morbid ecstacy of the work." What is morbid is the anti-Wagner stench that once again pervades the air, for so insecure have we become in our own, neo-classical emotions that an unclassical panic seizes us lest we submit to those of a none too gentle genius.

The concert was enjoyed by all who did not mind, say, the rich variety of C majors at the end of Act I.   H.K.

COSI FAN TUTTE, *Mozart. Sadler's Wells Opera, 11th May, 1949, c. James Robertson.*
This was an interesting attempt to extract by action the maximum of the comic from the score. Occasionally this led to a distraction from the musical interest, particularly in the duets—in Act II—the wit lies in the music, and not necessarily in the wiping of noses archly to the accompaniment. But within the aims of the production the principals did well, even if the ensemble fell apart in the *Finale* to Act II.

Fiordiligi's Rondo-Aria *Per pietà, ben mio, perdona*, ought to be sung if the balance of so finely-balanced a piece of characterisation is to be maintained. After the Wagner-Verdi-Puccini debauch, however, it is a thing of some consideration that without too great a loss of integrity this alien and intelligent music could come over in the contemporary opera house.

P.J.C.

SCHWANDA THE BAGPIPER, *Weinberger. Sadler's Wells Opera, 6th May, 1949, c. James Robertson.*

Schwanda is perhaps the only genuine contemporary comic folk-opera. (*Albert Herring* with all its sophistication must be excepted.) *Schwanda* not only succeeds musically but is amusing as well—the scene in Hell *is* funny, but remains several stages removed from pantomime for all its devils' tails and thunder and lightning. A great deal of the music is finely conceived—obvious, perhaps—but always expert, skilfully contrived and wholly enjoyable. It has no distinct musical personality and is full of reminiscences of Dvorak and Strauss, contrapuntally spiced with Reger ; but its intentions are so admirable that its cosmopolitan character becomes a positive virtue. The opera was brilliantly produced by Dennis Arundell. Roderick Jones as *Schwanda* and Howell Glynne as the *Devil* stood out from a more than competent cast.

P.G.H.

Concerts

LONDON PHILHARMONIC ORCHESTRA. *Albert Hall, 17th March and 12th May, 1949, c. van Beinum.*

The orchestra may be congratulated on giving two of the best public performances of a Bruckner symphony and Mahler's *Das Lied* that I have heard. The Buckner *Third* was particularly notable but for an occasional ragged pause and some uncertain moments in the brass. Not one of his greatest works—the *chorales* in the *adagio* never seem to fulfil themselves—but it is a very delightful one and should, of course, be heard more often. Mr. van Beinum seemed to me to be happier with Bruckner than with Mahler : in *Das Lied* the orchestral detail (as always with this conductor) was carefully thought-out, but he had a tendency to drag the *tempi* of the quick movements which sapped the essential bitterness of the music ; and in *Der Abschied* the pulse was so slow that when Mr. van Beinum accelerated the pace he had to work up a great climax in a very few bars : as a result the climaxes were rarely achieved and the orchestra asked to perform impossible athletic feats. Mr. Richard Lewis sang the tenor part with commendable vigour and understanding, and Madame Zareska the contralto with real sensitivity, but too little fulness of tone. A voice of immense proportions is needed if *Das Lied* is to succeed in the Albert Hall.

D.M.

TWO BRAHMS REQUIEMS *at the Albert Hall, 25th March, 1949 :
New Era Concert Society, Philharmonia Orchestra, Alexandra
Choir, c. Austin, with Schwarzkopf and Hotter, 9th April, 1949:
Royal Choral Society, L.S.O., c. Sargent, with Baillie and Pizzey.*
One good performance is better than two bad ; these two were
worse than none at all. In better form and in a better performance,
Hotter and Schwarzkopf might have been excellent. Schwarzkopf
almost was. Unforunately, however, she sang, well-nigh throughout,
a vibration flat. Too critical ? I think that only when one is able to be
dead in tune may one, in fact should one be out of tune. Which is to
say that only if one's ear is sensitive and conscientious enough to detect
the finest differences in pitch, even though the notes are produced by
oneself, is one capable of what may be called creative intonation, i.e.
of such minute deviations from normal pitch as enhance the music's
meaning. Off-hand I know of only three interpreters whose intonation
is creative. One—Bronislav Huberman—is dead, the second hardly
ever performs publicly, the third is Peter Pears.
Apart from one lapse, Schwarzkopf's phrasing was impeccable,
though not very profound. Hotter attacked the music at a deeper level,
but while Schwarzkopf's voice was perfectly even, his vibrated lavishly
and most disturbingly. In the Chorus—" Behold, all flesh is as the
grass," the Alexandra Choir rendered the (from the point of view of
colour) difficult, soprano-less passages in unison and octave unison
surprisingly, if not very well, perhaps because the tenors were too weak
and un-tenorlike to obtrude.
Geoffrey Sharp writes in the May issue of the *Music Review* that
the New Era performance " was the worst . . . of the Requiem
we can remember." He missed his chance to hear the worst we can
foresee.   H.K.

BOYD NEEL ORCHESTRA under BRITTEN, with PETER PEARS and
DENNIS BRAIN. *Chelsea Town Hall, 28th March, 1949.* BRITTEN :
Frank Bridge Variations, Serenade, Prelude and Fugue ; PURCELL :
*G minor Chaconny ; first performance of Arthur Oldham's
' Summer's Lease ' (Seven Sonnets by Shakespeare, for Tenor and
Strings).*
For once, music and musical interpretation at once. Something
has happened to Pears. His refined technique, always servant to his
unique understanding, is now served by a new ease. Mr. Oldham is a
young pupil of Britten. It was a mistake to include his gifted Britten
imitations in a Britten programme, where they were bound to
embarrass the most benevolent ear.   H.K.

SONATA FOR PIANO *by Alan Rawsthorne (First Performance) :
James Gibb, Wigmore Hall, 8th April, 1949.*
A good, solid piece, full of interesting points. Four short movements run without a break, and thus the Sonata is like a new set of
" Bagatelles." Although the themes of the first three movements
seemed related, this did not help to create the impression of real
4-movement form since the material, though weighty enough, is not
worked out to all its " obligations " (to use a term of Schoenberg).

In short, I wished the piece had been longer. Apart from this formal criticism, Rawsthorne's idiom is assured and convincing, due, in no small part, to his keen sense for harmonic progressions and telling bass-lines which always prevents him from giving way to the merely sensational or coloristic. Nevertheless, the piano-writing is difficult and brilliant, and thanks are due to Mr. Gibb for his straightforward performance, and his feat of memorizing this complicated piece.

P.H.

ST. MATTHEW PASSION (BACH) : *London Philharmonic Orchestra and Choir, conducted by Eduard van Beinum. Albert Hall, Easter Saturday.*

Eduard van Beinum is certainly one of the most versatile of conductors. He is equally at home in modern music and in the music of the past : we may expect his interpretation of a Szymanowsky symphony to be as convincing as his interpretation of Beethoven's Fifth : we know that, with his famous Haarlem Roman Catholic Chorus, he can excel in Palestrina and Victoria, and that at Amsterdam he can give inspired performances of the Protestant " St. Matthew Passion," making it there as much a Holy Week institution as it has become here in England. Throughout the work he displays a profound knowledge and understanding of the score. It was a most impressive performance ; and the orchestra and choir, who have recently (under Ansermet) given us such a magnificent recording of Stravinsky's " Symphony of Psalms," proved themselves on this occasion as worthy as ever.

The soloists were, on the whole, good. Peter Pears, as the Evangelist, was quite outstanding : a more artistic and carefully-thought-out handling of this rôle it would be difficult to imagine. His phrasing and diction were excellent, and his wide range of expression—from calm detachment to dramatic intensity—always in perfect taste. Robert Irwin, Isobel Baillie, and René Soames all sang well. The great disappointment was Rosina Raisbeck, the contralto soloist, who has a very unattractive wobble in her voice. The wobbling disease of singers is at present more widespread than usual.

Some of the *tempi* in this performance seemed rather strange—especially that of the alto aria " See the Saviour's Outstretched Arm," which was surely too fast to feel at all comfortable. And to perform the chorales consistently loud throughout was also rather a strange practice—sometimes impressive, but not very appropriate when the words are reflective or penitent in character.

The performance was perhaps somewhat marred by applause (well-meant, no doubt, but quite out-of-place) breaking forth at the end from the large and enthusiastic audience.   D.C.

L.C.M.C. *B.B.C., 17th May, 1949. First performances of works by Wilfrid Mellers, Constant Lambert and Humphrey Searle. B.B.C. Chorus, c. Leslie Woodgate, Philharmonia Orchestra, c. Leighton Lucas.*

Stravinsky's two piano sonata (excellently played by Mary and Geraldine Peppin) is dry stuff, but the work of a musical mind that

54

cannot stop producing music even when the level of inventiveness is not particularly high. Even in this desert there was an oasis in the shape of the second movement's *Theme and Variations*. Mr. Lambert's *Trois Pièces Nègres sur les Touches Blanches*, for piano duet, proved to be a complete mirage and not as interesting as their title. Devoid of thought, or indeed any intrinsic musical merit, they merely irritated the ear. It is a pity that Mr. Lambert's talent for composition should be so heavily tarred with a 1920 brush. A surer judgment could be made of Mr. Meller's *Motets in Diem Pacis* (*The City of Desolation, The City not Forsaken*) at a second performance where the choir was larger and the brass less overwhelming. Nevertheless they were impressive, particularly the first which was a good deal more distinguished than its partner. Mr. Meller's choral writing is flexible in the extreme, and at times comes near the lyricism of Delius without the latter's chromatic flabbiness. About Mr. Searle's *Gold Coast Customs* for Two Speakers, Male Chorus, Chamber Orchestra and Percussion, it is difficult to write, simply because one would find oneself writing about Mr. Searle. The work was honest, uncompromising, most serious in its intent, expertly written and magnificently performed by a Section of the Philharmonia under Leighton Lucas, with Constant Lambert and Miss Edith Sitwell (whose text it was) as the readers. Whether or not it was music I am not prepared to say, but whatever it was it had a savage power and burning intensity that certainly cannot be ignored. It had something that must be faced up to. The gentleman who hissed at the end of it was merely running away from the problem.

D.M.

LONDON PHILHARMONIC ORCHESTRA, *Albert Hall, 19th May, 1949 ; c. Victor de Sabata.*

Sabata gave an extremely personal reading of the Brahms *First* which upset a good many critics who sat with their noses stuck in their scores and their ears shut. I have not heard the *Andante* played better or the finale better integrated. The whole symphony was infused with a kind of nervous suppleness and Sabata brought out a new clarity in the texture of the orchestration which I have not noticed previously. Ghedini's *Pezzo Concertante* was given in the second half of the programme, the obbligati violin and viola parts being very ably played by David Wise, Albert Chasey and Frederick Riddle respectively. An amiable piece of music, it was neat and concise in style and preserved a nice balance between the contemporary and old *concerto grosso* idiom.

D.M.

L.P.O. UNDER KLEIBER, *Albert Hall, 21st April, 1949. Handel, Overture to " Berenice " ; Mozart, G minor ; Beethoven, " Eroica."*

One advantage of Kleiber's programmes is that they are short. One flaw is that they are too short, in that his tempi tend to be too quick, at any rate for the L.P.O., whose indisputable improvement under Beinum has been exaggerated. There are two amateurish arch-sins in fast execution, i.e., haste and retardation. The Mozart's Andante, which Kleiber took rather rapidly, showed the first sin in its first, the second in its second part. In the last movement the first violins were even unable to play simultaneously. In fact this department had a particularly rotten night. Wrong notes abounded ; nor did the players bother to finger tolerably alike. Thus at one point some played a d″, or rather an inevitably rich variety of d″'s as natural harmonics, while others availed themselves of the A string for this single note, without the right hand's regard for the A string's different timbre. While the newspapers call the results of such combined operations " fine string playing," we would suggest desk-by-desk rehearsals.

As interpretation, the G minor was nothing against that of Ian Whyte (who would soon be known as a front rank conductor if he had an *orchestra* to conduct), despite the thrilling leading back to the first movement's recapitulation and the finely felt trio. The beginning of the symphony was dreadful—no restrained tragic passion, no prolonged, tensing up-beat phrasing, but a cheaply advertised *expressivo* that left nothing for later. The " Eroica," on the other hand, in spite of all the unintended vagaries of tempo, was colossal in the sensible sense of the word.

Though a man of calibre, Kleiber has his mannerisms. Not, to be sure, the choreographic variety. On the contrary, *ff* is for him the sign to stop conducting altogether and, as it were, to inspect the parade. This is alright, I suppose, as long as he enjoys it and the orchestra can take it. One famous orchestra, under another conductor, once couldn't. He reviewed rather than conducted the fifth of Brahms' Haydn-Variations, until they had to start afresh.

H.K.

LONDON PHILHARMONIC ORCHESTRA : *Beethoven. Missa Solemnis and Verdi ; Requiem, Albert Hall, May 26 and June 2*

Two supreme masterpieces, and a conductor to match. Of all de Sabata's triumphs, he will never surpass that of making a large English choir sing with accuracy, passion and articulation. The first, perhaps, the second conceivably : but all three combined ! We have smaller choirs of wonderful purity and musicianship ; but in the Vatican, for example, they add to these qualities such a sharpness of articulation, such a fire of declamation, as make our best (and I am not belittling it) seem merely so much raw material for genius to take in hand.

In the person of de Sabata, genius did take a hand. By simply persuading all concerned *to leave a silence* (longer or shorter) *between every note* that is not deliberately *legato*, he sharpened the serried Philharmonic ranks into an instrument of precision and emotion— incidently saving Beethoven's repeated high B's from the flagging due to the exhaustion of sustaining them in the usual glutinous fashion. The orchestra was similarly electrified : only the soloists retained traces of our traditional glutinosity, the legacy, I suppose, of past oratoriorical excesses. But I must not withold a word of special praise for Constance Shacklock.

R.D.

MORLEY COLLEGE CONCERT SOCIETY. *Central Hall, 27th May, 1949. Kalmar Orchestra, Morley College Choir, c. Walter Goehr. Richard Lewis (Tenor), Ralph Downes (Organ).*

Of the new music played at this concert, Schoenberg's *Variations on a Recitative for Organ* Op. 40 was indisputably great. This judgment is not based on the sight of the music for I have not seen the score, but solely on the evidence of my ears. I cannot claim to have understood the structure of the work, but the *Cadenza* struck me as being one of the most dramatic and the *Fugue* one of the most purely beautiful (in the strict meaning of those over-worked terms) I have ever heard. The whole was inexpressibly moving and a quite overwhelming musical experience.

Matyas Seiber's *Ulysses* Cantata was original and independent, continuously interesting and always musical. It was also extremely clever, but always clever in a musical manner, and one must always be grateful for intelligence. Nevertheless some of the music was more intelligible to the eye than the ear—the concluding 8-part fugue for instance. Mr. Seiber seemed to me to be more successful with the infinitesimal creatures of the earth than the vastness of the Universe ; and James Joyce's text had an obstinate habit of remaining greater than the music in which it was enveloped. **D.M.**

A HAYDN WEEK-END : *Glyndebourne, 28th and 29th May, 1949 ; Royal Philharmonic Orchestra, c. Sir Thomas Beecham.*

The series of concerts began badly with an untidy performance of the G Major Piano Trio (RP Trio—Betty Humby-Beecham, David McCallum and Anthony Pini). The sense of disppointment was not dispelled by a section of the orchestra playing under Beecham a very dull *adagio* from *Notturno No. 1* and an *Echo for Two String Orchestras.* We could have done not only without the echo but also the commonplace music which gave rise to it. The *Divertimento for Hurdy-Gurdy* was more substantial although its musical interest was somewhat clouded by the elaborate joking from the rostrum, which consisted of Sir Thomas versifying (badly) and Mr. Christie appearing with a dog. The Hurdy-Gurdy never appeared (one feels it was never meant to) and its part was filled in by individual members of the orchestra. The concert ended with a disastrous performance of the *Emperor* Quartet by Messrs. McCallum, Rosen, Verity and Pini which provided the worst quartet playing within my experience. I find it hard to believe in recollection that such insensitivity can have been perpetrated by such talented musicians.

But the evening concert set matters aright with incomparable performances of Symphonies 102 and 97 and a quite amazing version of the D major *Harpsichord Concerto* which is great Haydn, a great Concerto, and should be more frequently played. Lucille Wallace was a superb soloist, particularly in the *adagio* where the cascades of chromatic ornamentations were played with incredible artistry and virtuosity. Margaret Ritchie and Richard Lewis sang excerpts from " *The Seasons* " very excellently : but oratorio remains generally dull, even Haydn's. The final Sunday concert placed between two late symphonies the *Bb Sinfonia Concertante* for Oboe, Bassoon, Violin and Cello (principals from the orchestra playing the solo parts) and the E♭ *Trumpet Concerto* in which Richard Walton was the expert soloist. The *Sinfonia Concertante* is not the best Haydn apart from some moments of muscular development in the first movement and some interesting contrapuntal writing for the ensemble. The *Trumpet Concerto*, apart from its extrovert charm, is chiefly remarkable for its likeness to the Mozart Horn Concertos, both in style and technique. Symphonies 93 and 99 are masterpieces and were conducted with undeniable genius. The first movement of 93 has an astonishing fugal development—astonishing for its power and brevity. No. 99 (perhaps the finest of the Haydn symphonies) cannot be written about in a few words such is the richness of its invention and variety of expression. Another 36 hours of Haydn would have convinced me (no doubt wrongly) that not much has been done with the Symphony since.

P.G.H.

CHELSEA SYMPHONY ORCHESTRA, *c. Norman Del Mar.*
Chelsea Town Hall, 31st May, 1949.

The Chelsea Symphony Orchestra only succeeded in becoming an orchestra after the interval, fortunately in time to cope with the Mahler *Ninth*. The Strauss *Die Shweigsame Frau* Overture was hardly intelligible and although the ensemble playing had improved for the Horn Concerto (No. 2 in E♭—first performance) it was still far from perfect. But even the orchestra's deficiencies did not succeed in concealing Strauss's fine workmanship—the beautifully timed and placed entry of the solo horn in the *Andante* for instance. But the new Concerto is not important new Strauss. Dennis Brain was the expert soloist.

Mr. Del Mar should be entrusted with frequent performances of Mahler's music. He obviously understands it and the peculiar quality of the composer's mind. The orchestra responded nobly to his persuasion and gave a quite remarkable performance of the gigantic Ninth Symphony. In the first movement Mr. Del Mar's *tempi* went astray in one or two places. At bar 205 he increased the pace quite arbitrarily : *Leidenschaftlich* can be conveyed without any change in time. The wildness is in the notes, not the speed at which they are played. The same fault marred the climax at bar 385, although the immediately preceding section, with its curious resemblance to a chamber-orchestra style, was admirably and moreover accurately performed.

The *Laendler* went well except at [26] where the trumpet remained silent : although it has only three notes to play it is one of Mahler's characteristically brilliant touches of orchestration and its absence made itself felt. The middle section of the *Rondo Burleske* suffered from the erratic hit-or-miss methods of the first trumpet, and the end of the *Adagio* from woolly counting on the part of the strings, no doubt due to the extreme slowness of the music at this point. Nevertheless, the finest performance of a Mahler symphony I have heard given by English musicians.

D.M.

Two Italian Concerts

CHERUBINI'S C MINOR REQUIEM.

THOSE privileged to be in the hall of the Accademia at Florence on the evening of April 26 heard, conducted by Adriano Lualdi, the first performance in Italy of the work that Beethoven valued more highly than any other Requiem and that Berlioz regarded as Cherubini's masterpiece. Its history is odd. It belongs to France rather than to Italy. Written for the anniversary of the execution of Louis XVI, it was first sung at the Abbey Church of Saint-Denis in 1817 and not again till 1820, at the same church, for the funeral of the Duc de Berri. To see it, therefore, in its proper prospective, one must go back in thought to the worst excesses of the French Revolution ; it celebrates a tragedy, the inhuman murder of a king. Heard in Florence in 1949, it seemed to focus attention on the tragedy of Italy in the last war. The festival was in honour of the composer, his portrait on a large plaster medallion, on a background of pink brocade, was suspended from the gallery, where the chorus, in black, took their places ; a lecture preceded the performance, and the programme was embellished with three portraits of Cherubini, one of them from a sketch for Ingres' famous portrait, and reproductions of four of his own drawings. The strings were not particularly strong and an interval after the *Dies Irae* somewhat obscured the effect of the whole ; but the Accademia Nazionale " Cherubini " is to be congratulated on a notable achievement, for the singing was never forced and the pathos of certain sections, notably the Introit, the *Pie Jesu* (foreshadowing Rossini's *Quando corpus morietur*) and the solemn intoning of the C's over the poignant orchestral phrase to the words *lux perpetua luceat eis* at the close, went straight to the heart. Nor, in the *Tuba mirum*, was one unaware that Verdi had learnt from this work, which can be said to have Beethoven's intense intellectual gloom, without his forward drive, and indeed bears some affinity to the revolutionary canvases of J. L. David, in spite of their different political implications.

A PAGANINI RECITAL.

At Rome, on May 5, in the great hall of the University, Julius von Ujhelyi, accompanied by Libero Barni, not unsuccessfully invoked the ghost of the most famous of violin virtuosi. Unfortunately only the first movement of the Concerto in D, in Wilhelmj's arrangement, was given, the rest of the programme consisting of six of the twenty-four unaccompanied Caprices (Op. 1), the 'Campanella' Rondo, familiar through Liszt's piano transcription, the 'Streghe' variations on a theme by S. Mayer, the once acclaimed Fantasia for the fourth string on the 'Prayer' in *Moïse* (ludicrous) and a 'piccola sonata.' Only the Caprices seemed to have musical value, particularly the imitation of the bagpipe, though in all, when the pyrotechnics are excluded, there remains a sediment of romantic melancholy not far removed from Field's. One realized at once how much the garish emaciated figure of the composer must have contributed to the original effect of these pieces and regretted that the recital was not confined to the Caprices played in their entirety. A stricter tempo and less sentimentality on Ujhelyi's part would have served him and the composer in better stead.

E.H.W.M.

FROM THE NORTH.

ST. MATTHEW PASSION : *Liverpool Philharmonic Concert, April 10th, 1949.*

Sir Malcolm Sargent prepared the ground for his performance of the *St. Matthew Passion* in an interview with the *Liverpool Post*, which suggested that only pedants would object if all the extraneous Nineteenth Century paraphernalia of the *Messiah* were added to Bach's austere masterpiece. With the result that the critic arrived for the performance in the state of mind described by Berlioz when he expected the opera to be ruined by an irresponsible conductor's jiggery-pokery.

The performance, however, was correct if a little beefy. Granted that Bach's oboes tend to stand out of any body of tone subdued below a *mezzo-forte*, the tone of concerted numbers in the first part never sank below a stolid *forte*, and the early Chorales, in which delicate points of balance do not arise, were encouraged to heartiness. The Chorale tune in the first chorus barely emerged from the seething movement of the restless polyphony, over which it should ride with culminating grandeur ; details of orchestration—the malicious jibing of the flute in the first *Let Him be Crucified*, were practically inaudible. The point is, of course, that too large a choir can easily obscure polyphonic movement by its mere weight, but offers some special beauties in spite of that—the tremendous bass entry of the fugal chorus in *My Saviour Jesus Now is Taken* and the mighty unison on *I am the Son of God* at the end of *He Trusted in God*.

The soloists—Misses Edna Morrison and Miss Mary Jarred, Messrs. William Herbert, Gordon Clinton and Harold Williams, sang with remarkably intelligent phrasing, although the ladies hardly did justice to the overwhelming power of this music. It is just not enough however to sing prettily. Mr. Herbert apparently had no difficulty whatever with the appalling pitch of the Evangelist's music, although the recent German gramophone records, in which the part is sung by Karl Erb, demonstrate that this music repays an entirely calm approach, whilst in common with most tenors, Mr. Herbert was inclined to emphasise the tragedy.

H.B.R.

HALLÉ CONCERT : *Het Residentie Orkest, April 21st, 1949.*

The credit for the exchange of programmes and halls between the Hallé and the Residentie Orchestra from the Hague is all, apparently, John Barbirolli's, and it is a pity that such a fine orchestra should be heard for the first time in this country in Manchester's cramped, malacoustic Albert Hall. Nevertheless under its conductor Johannes Adrianus Out, the orchestra succeeded in overcoming these difficulties and gave Manchester the brighest, most enjoyable musical evening this season.

Two works by Dutch composers—Johan Wagenaar's overture, *The Taming of the Shrew* and Leon Orthel's *Third Symphony*—were brilliantly performed.

Cyril Smith gave a commendable performance of Rachmaninov's 3rd Concerto, and the concert ended with Ravel's *Fragments Symphoniques* from *Daphnis and Chloe.*   B.N.

BEECHAM : *Liverpool Philharmonic Concert, April 27th, 1949.*

James Agate once wrote that a good actor could offer a moving performance and he would be suitably impressed, whilst a great actor could reduce him to a state of gibbering terror by the recitation of the multiplication table. Sir Thomas Beecham came to Liverpool two days before his 70th birthday, and, as we expected, his concert exceeded expectation.

These notes have shown that the Liverpool Orchestra has, during this season, offered a reasonably catholic choice of music and played it rather well. On April 27th we heard it play with all its potentialities realised, not having realised before that some of them existed at all; playing with a rapt response to the demands of colour and phrasing, imbued with an excited enthusiasm, and as much at home with Haydn and Mozart, the neglected masters, as with Schumann. The performance of Haydn's Symphony No. 102 was the first Haydn symphony we have heard this season, and whilst all was graded, balanced and moulded—not the least of Beecham's gifts is that of shaping a movement which seems to happen by spontaneous combustion—it glowed, sparkled and shone by virtue of its own vitality. With Mozart's Sixteenth Concerto (K.451) we passed from Augustan happiness to Olympian majesty, a measured grandeur of emotion too rarely imagined. Almost every Mozart Piano Concerto is his greatest, and this, rarely performed as it is, offers no small delights. Lady Beecham sustained an elegant and sure melodic line, but suspicious things occasionally happened beneath it, while Sir Thomas at times pleaded for unimaginable orchestral subleties. There was no attempt to galvanise either tempi or dynamics ; the mystery of a lovely performance lay in a sense of phrasing and nuance, in the scrupulous attention given to the relative weight of each note.

The concert ended with a performance of Schumann's *First Symphony* so urgently impetuous and filled with youthful excitement that blemishes in orchestration and text-book doubts were forgotten. The degree of sympathy that Beecham shows for all the works he plays is astounding ; at the end of the concert we wonder which offers him the greatest delight.

In all respects this was a great occasion and it is pleasant for a time to drop the critic's robe and indulge in deserved hero-worship ; one's recollections of splendid performances by Sir Thomas go back to childhood, for one thing, and for another we realised that the orchestra, which has done good work for us in the last six months, largely due, it seems, to Mr. Rignold's careful and catholic methods, is potentially at least much better than good.   H.B.R.

HALLÉ CONCERT : 5th May, 1949.

It was with some enthusiasm that John Barbirolli was welcomed to the Albert Hall, Manchester after an absence of six weeks. Mr. Barbirolli is the able puppeteer (indeed many of his movements could be attributed to Delvaine) and he controls his " puppets " with skill—and a polished display of histrionic mime ! Under its conductor, the Hallé has made bold strides during the past season, but the brass section still requires attention.

This inconsistency of the brass was particularly noticeable—and at times embarrassing—in the overture from Borodin's " Prince Igor." Haydn's Symphony in B Flat was dexterously performed. It embodies two interesting curiosities. The theme of the second movement is based on our National Anthem and a violin solo (adroitly played by Laurance Turner) is employed in the last movement.

The eighty-five-year-old composer Richard Strauss has written a " Duett Concertino " for clarinet and bassoon with string orchestra and harp especially for the Hallé, and courtesy appears to be the only reason for its being performed in this context. Strauss strives for modernity and youth, but, in spite of the string orchestra's brilliant work and impeccable solo performances from Pat Ryan (clarinet) and Charles Cracknell (bassoon), the concertino remained little more than salon music.

Sibelius's powerful Second Symphony concluded the concert.
                                                                      B.N.

BRYANSTON SUMMER SCHOOL.

We recommend to the attention of our readers the Summer Music School to be held at Bryanston from 13th August to the 3rd September, 1949. The School has gathered together an extremely distinguished staff of lecturers and performers and the subjects for discussion range from Monteverdi to Stravinsky, by way of Beethoven and Bartok. A stimulating curriculum.

CHAMBER MUSIC COMPETITION.

A prize of £20 is offered by the ALFRED J. CLEMENTS MEMORIAL FUND (South Place Sunday Concerts) for the best Chamber Music Work composed and submitted by a British Subject. The work shall be for any combination from 3 to 6 instruments to last not less than 20 minutes or more than 30. The adjudicators for 1949 are : EDMUND RUBBRA, MATYAS SEIBER and BERNARD STEVENS. Full particulars may be obtained from the HON. SECRETARY, 9, ASMUNS HILL, GOLDERS GREEN, N.W. 11.

[A number of Reviews of Books and New Music, and our normal Gramophone Record Supplement, have had to be held over to our next issue, owing to lack of space.—Eds.]

MUSIC SURVEY

(KATHLEEN LIVINGSTON   WILLIAM W. LIVINGSTON   DONALD MITCHELL)

VOL. II, No. 2   CONTENTS   AUTUMN, 1949

Published for MUSIC-SURVEY by NEWMAN WOLSEY, Publishers, 244, HIGH
HOLBORN, LONDON, W.C.1.

EDITORIAL CORRRESPONDENCE should be addressed to the EDITORS,
MUSIC SURVEY, OAKFIELD SCHOOL, WEST DULWICH, LONDON, S.E.21.

All enquiries relating to advertising space in this journal should be made to :
THE ALDRIDGE PRESS, LTD., 15, CHARTERHOUSE STREET, HOLBORN
CIRCUS, LONDON, E.C.1.

Editorial : Short and Bitter

NOTHING is further from the truth of music than its partial understanding.

While the beautiful is always right, the ugly is not always wrong. Which makes many deem the ugly beautiful.

Every composer must start by imitating others. None should end up by imitating himself.

Genius remains genius. When a talent is born into the storm created by genius, it rarely remains a talent : The billows bear it either high or drown it.

The great have done more and been less than the small think.

Good music cannot prosper without the support of those who pretend to like it.

The God of Art is an angry god, for he makes the talentless industrious.

Intellectual music is emotional music we do not understand.

A conscience without originality is pitiable ; originality without a conscience is a pity.

The modern need for simplification, unlike the classical need for simplicity, is the result of the decrease of leisure among the intelligent and the increased literacy among idiots.

There isn't such a thing as a courageous artist. When you have something to say you need no courage to say it.

What seems morbid music frees the feelings our morbidity makes us fear.

The bad artist is created by his times. The mediocre creates for his time. The better artist creates for posterity. The great creates posterity.

A truism is a truth stated without having been re-discovered.

The need of the hour is mental birth-control.

The mature artist's ability to live up to his ideals is increased by his willingness to live down to his limitations.

" The appreciation of music " makes as much sense to me as " the appreciation of God."

H.K.

Wilfrid Mellers

By ARTHUR HUTCHINGS

ERNEST NEWMAN recently compared methods of publishers' journalists who " make an easy reputation as accoucheurs of masterpieces " with those of Mr. Perker and the electioneering agents who sent the Hon. Samuel Slumkey to the head of the poll at Eatanswill—" He has come out . . . He has patted the babies on the head . . . He has kissed one of them," the crescendo reaching climax at " He's kissing them all " ! The future of English music is not likely to lie in the hands of those thus advertised. The young composers who once made the biggest stir and were claimed by Parry and Stanford as their most gifted pupils, even where they have become excellent composers, administrators or teachers, do not stand beside Vaughan Williams of whom little fuss was made when young ; middle-aged Vaughan Williams was frequently bracketed second with Holst. So to-day Rubbra, who towers head and shoulders above his contemporaries, is hardly ever mentioned by the casual journalist who feels called upon to show his acquaintance with the names of modern British musicians.

There is always a suspicion, largely justified by history, that the greatest composers are not theorists and critics, but those who write in catharsis ; we are at a stage, however, when no composer can develop a purely inherited technique ; it is almost impossible to write significant music without system, and for the first time since the 17th century, when the polyphonic system had reached its decadence, it is more likely that things of permanent worth will come from the conscious, studious, and critical composer than from one brilliantly endowed, extravagant with score paper, as were so many of the classical giants, and hoping ultimately to garner a number of first-rate works from a prodigal harvest of mixed quality.

The output of Wilfrid Mellers is now large enough to cause discontent with the generalisation that he is " an intelligent and provocative critic and musicologist, and a composer of some achievement and yet more promise." Nobody can play Perker to Mellers ; he is no baby-kisser. While the direct stimulant, the passing instrumental effect, and the programmatic high-light are what please the musical public, he has chosen, like Rubbra, to show affection for tradition and system. Ansermet has illumined the truth of platitude in a recent article dealing with the theories of Schoenberg and Stravinsky. He writes:

> " All that can be expected from any *system* of composition is that it will provide the means of making an architectural construction. . . . No system can give a formula for making good music."

Ansermet does not show a corollary—namely that, in certain epochs, brilliant musicians fail to write first-rate music for lack of system and " means of making an architectural construction." We see this in the short-windedness of those Purcell works whose brilliant parts do not make a brilliant whole ; we see it when the conservative Gibbons tries his hand at verse-anthems and the new music of his day which ousted polyphony and heralded the baroque. The finest art is produced when the systems are used, not merely by experiment or after *a priori* selection, but naturally in contentment with a tradition not fully developed, or from fertilisation of a decadent tradition by admiration of an imported one. There are some who suppose that the second of these conditions serves Mellers ; he uses no conscious Englishry for, as he says in his book " Music and Society," Vaughan Williams and others before him made that unnecessary ; neither has he chosen the narrow æsthetic and the refined taste of a man like Finzi. The English tradition is fertilised by the theories and achievements of Schoenberg and Stravinsky, brought to this country directly and through the teaching of Wellesz, although I personally see more affinity between Mellers and Bartok than between Mellers and the recent Viennese School.

With Vaughan Williams and Rubbra alone as examples we should be careful nowadays not to make the assertion : " One who is genuinely creative should show the fact in his teens. We cannot expect significant music from one who begins writing in mid-twenties after a prolonged education. We already have enough respectable and donnish music of the type called scholarly." To such a remark malice could reply : " We also have far too much hit-and-miss music written by those who improvise at the piano and write down the fortuitous tone-combinations that please them, either because they cannot remember that they have been used before, or because they depict whatever mystical idea, or literary programme, or mood phase happens to suit them at the moment." The hit-and-miss composer depends on passing effects, and whether he writes sonatas, concertos or songs, they all sound like film music. He lacks the construction which can only go hand in hand with a system. Much of his work begins, continues and ends at high tension and, if not actually prolonged, enjoys a passing popularity with a nerve-ridden public. Such a composer uses passacaglia, fugue, and other time-honoured musical formalities, not with a Purcellian or Bachian freedom, but in an attempt to supply the form which a carpenter imposes on a chair or table. His music lacks the organic form of a plant or tree, which has its roots in the system or nature of the species, be it oak, plane or poplar.

Mellers would have been a composer whether or not he had refrained from publishing before pursuing his studies. He, too, has used the hit and miss method popularly called " trusting to inspiration " ; and he has had one or two very enjoyable hits, such as the Carols and some of the incidental music written for the Birmingham production of " Prometheus."A glance at these scores and those of two motets " In Diem Pacis " reminds us forcibly of

Holst whose tireless experimenting would have made him a first-rank composer had his time and place offered him the means to push forward a basic technique. Mellers himself has said : " I am conscious of some debt to Rubbra, but rather to that side of him manifest in " The Dark Night of the Soul," an aspect that most directly comes from Holst. My Englishness must be involved with a certain exoticism, including chromatic and pentatonic melismata, melodic augmented seconds, etc., which may derive via Wellesz from Mahler, who crops up in the most unlikely places—even in Britten and Berkeley."

When sufficient time has passed, we shall be able to see what continental and " exotic " elements, apart from the temporary and permanent influence of Ravel, are to be detected in Vaughan Williams's mature works, but we may be certain that his wide interest in all contemporary techniques, and not just in the English tradition which he himself helped to vitalise, prevented his being a composer only for residents in the more pleasant parts of southern England, in the shires and university cities. The Viennese element in Mellers crops up most obviously in " The Forgotten Garden " and in the ' mad ' parts of " Prometheus," less obviously in the little Shakespeare part-songs (which look difficult on paper but come off wonderfully in performance), but most successfully in his most recent and, I think, impressive work. This is a set of " Five Songs of Night " on poems from the Greek, scored for contralto, cor anglais and string quartet. These intense and passionate songs strike one as being among the finest English works for their medium since Warlock's " The Curlew." The String Trio, a work better known than most of Mellers's compositions, since it was by it that he first scored a notable success in London, is also in Mellers's more sophisticated and " Viennese " style.

Personally, that is to say because of my age and training, I am prejudiced to a greater affection for his more direct, diatonic, " English " works and, despite the emotional virtuosity of the Greek songs, think it likely that he will follow his natural bent towards a more simplified vocal type of writing. As the Rubbra symphonies show, it is almost impossible for one who has given time to a study of English music before it lost its vigour and was swamped by Italian baroque not to have acquired a style bastically vocal. For those who sympathise with this fact, and have themselves given time to the same study, Mellers's finest achievement will seem to be the dramatic oratorio " Ruth." Its four scenes bear much the same relationship to each other as do the movements of a classical symphony : " The Road to Bethlehem " is the dramatic first movement, built on the idea of tonal conflict, and its orchestral prelude and chorus of lamentation make a " first subject group " opposed by the atmosphere of the arias for Ruth and Naomi ; " The Harvest Field " is an engaging pastoral scherzo; in the slow movement, " Nightpiece," occurs what seems to be the emotional climax of the whole work; I refer to Ruth's aria of benediction in which the harmonic simplicity and general expansiveness are deliberate and highly effective; the finale must thus assume the nature of an epilogue and summing up, making extended use of material from the prelude. Despite the intense grandeur and vigour of the big chorus in " Prometheus," it is " Ruth " that we ought to hear broadcast if we are to appreciate Mellers's most sustained achievement. One naturally supposes that this and " Prometheus " should lead to an essay in opera, and it is good to learn that Mellers is already formulating his reactions to a libretto on the life and death of Bunyan.

His future? The future for any British composer? Mellers is more likely than most modern composers to know at least the next little move. In his excellent essay " Rubbra and the Dominant Seventh " (now reprinted in " Studies in Contemporary Music ") he deals with one task—to make dissonance, or something that will perform the function of dissonance. Among the many inadequate but suggestive definitions of counterpoint is " the art of dissonance." Dissonance cannot be established without the establishment of consonance, and these are both matters of tradition which vary with times and places. (See for instance Yasser's " Medieval Quartal Harmony " for a commentary on the fact that for centuries the fourth, not the third, was regarded as the more consonant interval.) When resources are so enormous, when tradition no longer gives a composer strict limits, he cannot call upon passing notes, suspensions, auxiliary notes and other dissonances to give music a momentum. The old polyphony had its electrons, its active particles, its dissonances thrusting forward to consonance. The life and activity (like the construction mentioned by Ansermet) came from the system itself; and not even the metrical ictus of baroque and rococo, or the rhetoric of Beethoven's technique, made vociferous by large instrumental forces, could give so strong and certain flow to texture. Remove Beethoven's genius and we see why the theorists of his day preached the virtues of an older discipline. Mellers is among those who have embraced that older discipline with affection, and not as something imposed by an academic course. There are good reasons to expect from him a series of fine works that will show the results of his labours, without archaism or pedantry. He himself is his most astute critic, and those of us who have smarted at his diagnosis of our chief weaknesses can testify that he is more merciful with us than with himself. May both music and letters flourish with him.

A LIST OF WORKS BY WILFRID MELLERS :

CANTATAS, ETC.

The Song of Ruth, Cantata for soprano, mezzo soprano, baritone, chorus and orchestra (Lengnick: in the press) ..	1948
Prometheus, Cantata for soprano, baritone, tenor, chorus and chamber orchestra	1947-8
News from Greece, Cantata for mezzo soprano, mixed chorus, three trumpets, two pianos and percussion	1949
Conversion in the Garden, Cantata for baritone and string orchestra	1947
The Forgotten Garden, Cantata for tenor and string quartet ..	1945

Chamber Works.

String Trio (Lengnick)	1946
Sonata for Viola and Piano (Lengnick)..	1946
Five Songs of Night, for contralto, cor anglais and string quartet	1949
Sonata for Solo Violin	1944

Choral Works.

4 Shakespeare Songs for women's voices (O.U.P.)	1944
4 Carols for boys' voices and celeste (Lengnick)..	1946
2 Motets *in Diem Pacis*, for mixed chorus and brass (O.U.P.) ..	1945

Orchestral.

Sinfonia Ricercata	1947

Songs.

3 Canticles for soprano and organ	1949
3 17th Century Poems for baritone and piano	1948
4 Latin Hymns for soprano and flute	1944
4 Catzonets for soprano, clarinet and piano	1945
4 Songs of Spring for soprano and violin	1949
3 16th Century Poems for countertenor, flute and guitar ..	1949

Piano Works.

Epithalamium..	1944
Prelude and Canzona	1945

MUSIC SURVEY, Vol. I, Nos. 5 and 6, contained an article by Dika Newlin on *Schoenberg in America.* In No. 5, Richard Gorer contributed *An Interim Report on Humphrey Searle's Music.* Wilfrid Mellers in No. 6 wrote on *Sibelius and " The Modern Mind."* The first part of Arnold Cooke's essay on *Paul Hindemith* appeared in Vol. II, No. 1. In the January issue, 1950, Vol. II, No. 3, René Leibowitz writes on *A New French Composer — André Casanova.*

Further to the Schoenberg-Mann Controversy
By ARNOLD SCHOENBERG

In his letter accompanying the following communication, which we here publish for the first time, Schoenberg writes that the matter " may perhaps be stale " by now. So it may, but the character document of a master never is. The authorized translation and the annotations are mine.

H.K.

IN my reply to Mann's letter to the Editor of the *Saturday Review of Literature*(1) I confined myself to making clear that I had nothing against the application of my Twelve-Note Technique, as I have indeed already shown it to my pupils twenty-five years ago and have delivered explanatory lectures about it at several American universities. It was, however, inadmissible to transfer its authorship on to someone else(2). I then pointed out that the sole purpose of Mann's letter was to hide his conduct behind a flood of words. Thus he does not quote his actual note(3), namely—" It does not seem supererogatory to inform the reader that the form of musical composition delineated in Chapter XXII, known as the twelve-tone or row system, is in truth the intellectual property of 'a' (4) contemporary composer and theoretician, Arnold Schoenberg. I have transferred this technique in a certain ideational context to the fictitious figure of a musician, the tragic hero of my novel. . . ," but gives an explanation(5) which would be acceptable despite its superfluous " poetry," particularly if one had translated it into sober German, usual for such a purpose.

(1) i.e., Schoenberg's reply to Mann's own reply to Schoenberg's first letter whose first paragraph ran : " Sir : In his novel ' Doctor Faustus,' Thomas Mann has taken advantage of my literary property. He has produced a fictitious composer as the hero of his book; and in order to lend him qualities a hero needs to arouse people's interest, he made him the creator of what one erroneously calls my ' system of twelve tones,' which I call 'method of composing with twelve tones.' " (By permission of Arnold Schoenberg and *The Saturday Review of Literature*, New York.) I find it, by the way, surprising that Mr. Peter Stadlen, who has the reputation of being a Schoenberg expert, entitled his radio talk on June 16, 1949, "Schoenberg and the Twelve-Tone System." Or was the title the B.B.C.'s ?

(2) Leverkühn, the hero of *Doctor Faustus*. Compare Paul Hamburger's article on the book in the last issue of this journal.

(3) The acknowledgment which Mann printed at the end of the book upon Schoenberg's private protest, and about which Schoenberg says in the first letter to the *Saturday Review* : " But Mr. Mann was not as generous as I, who had given him good chance to free himself from the ugly aspect of a pirate. He gave an explanation: a few lines which he hid at the end of the book, in a place and on a page where no one even would see it. Besides, he added a new crime to his first, in the attempt to belittle me: He calls me ' *a* [a !] *contemporary* composer and theoretician. Of course, in two or three decades, one will know which of the two was the other's contemporary."

(4) Schoenberg's inverted commas.

(5) In *Der Monat*, Berlin, March, 1949, I find the German original of Mann's explanation of his note : " ' Ihr müsst wissen', besagt sie [i.e., the note], ' unter uns lebt ein Komponist und musikalischer Philosoph namens Arnold Schoenberg; der hat in Wirklichkeit die Zwölf-Ton-Kompositionsmethode erdacht, nicht mein Romanheld.' "

The gratitude he shows Mr. Adorno(6) in the "Story of a Novel"(7) for services rendered goes far beyond the recompense afforded in the actual novel. There he confines himself to ascribing Adorno's analysis of the variations from Beethoven's last piano sonata Op. 111 to another author ! This is apparently a tactical manœuvre. Besides, however, he adds one of those small (very small) extra presents which preserve the big (very big) friendship : He lays Adorno's father-name, "Wiesengrund," under the opening of the variations' theme. And here, too, something awkward happens. It emerges that Leverkühn has no feeling for the rhythmic values in a phrase, that he does not know how to declaim. Adorno should have told him : " I'm not called

but

All the more astounding, this, since Leverkühn comes from an era when one took such things even more seriously than today. If he really died in 1941, he must have been at least 75 years old and must have been born about 1866. Or (which is more probable) he is a remainder from the 70's, when those Burgerts, Dräseckes and other Wagnerians sought to excel their model by extended dimensions. It is not, after all, surprising that Mann depicts so antiquated a composer as the hero of his novel, since he himself comes from that past period and has not, at any rate as far as music is concerned, grown into the present.

Hence, too, Leverkühn's amateurish idea of the true essence of composition with twelve notes that it suffices each time to play off the twelve notes or their inversions, and that this means composing. I am therefore convinced that Mann's " Lamentation of Dr. Faustus " ought to bear the sub-title " Leverkühn's Twelve-Note Goulash." What he there throws together into one pot may be tasty—wherefore I shall perhaps find the time to analyse it and to show a journalist how things have to be founded in order to live on after they have been " Book of the Month."

(6) Wiesengrund-Adorno, a pupil of Berg, and Mann's adviser in Twelve-Note technique.

(7) Thomas Mann's book, *Die Entstehung des ' Doctor Faustus.'*

I find it more and more repulsive to see the obstinacy of an, after all, respected writer lead to his seeking to uphold an untenable position by misrepresentations, though it would have been so easy to accede to my wishes. A tiny footnote—" These descriptions or deductions rest on Schoenberg's Method of Composition with Twelve Notes "—would have entirely sufficed. He could not bring himself publicly to own this. Those pretended stylistic reasons(8) are of course complete nonsense. For in that case he should not have done it at all(9), and why then this revenge ?(10). This punishment by degradation ?

But now one would think he would at last see his wrong and stop, since I have not continued any further. However, he now publishes this "Story of a Novel" and continues his unfair behaviour. To be sure, it seems to be downright impossible for him to speak out as plainly as is necessary ; otherwise he could have safely said that he asked me for my *Harmonielehre*, and that when I lent him one of the few extant copies of the work, I also sent him the *Jakobsleiter* with a nice dedication. But he can only continue to degrade me and although there is no reason why he should censure me without, moreover, the least substantiation, he cannot refrain from saying about the *Jakobsleiter* that its " religious poetry " is not fully brewed.

Here, justly, something happens to him that happens to others in similar situations. It is very peculiar that when someone hits at me in a particularly nasty way, fate seizes him by the collar and the following things happen : Prof. Dr. Richard Wallaschek of the Vienna University reproaches me with the fact that Hugo Wolf could not give a song recital with singers as good as mine, and adds : " But then, when one has a friend for an opera-director and a brother-in-law for a conductor, it's easy, naturally." What this idiot wanted to say was of course: ' When one has an opera-director(11) for a friend and a conductor(12) for a brother-in-law . . .' Still better was what happened to Elsa Bienenfeld when she congratulated me upon my 50th birthday by twitting me with, *inter alia*, the small number of my published works : " He hasn't published much, he can count the number of his works on the twelve fingers of his hand." And thus, too, Mr. Mann :

(8) Mann says in his " Story of a Novel " (7) that to mention Schoenberg name in the text would not only have been out of style, but also " almost something of an offence," because of the divergence between Schoenberg's thoughts and Mann's *ad hoc* version thereof. The idea of the Twelve-Note technique, Mann suggests, assumes a character in the sphere of his book— " this world of the devil's pact, and of black magic "—which it does not possess in reality, and which makes it in a sense his property, i.e., that of the book. It was for this reason, and also, to a lesser extent, because the printed acknowledgment somewhat disturbs " the spheric completeness " (spharische Geschlossenheit) of the novel, that Mann printed his note " a bit against his conviction."
(9) i.e., should not have printed any sort of acknowledgment anywhere in the book.
(10) The form of Mann's note.
(11) Mahler.
(12) Alexander von Zemlinsky, 1872-1942.

79

Not only is the *Jakobsleiter* no religious poetry. Indeed I say quite expressly that it is founded on Swedenborg's theosophy, as I know it from Balzac, for " I was never known to pocket papers not my own "(13), and I admit it quite openly. The *Jakobsleiter* is not, then, poetry, nor is it religious, but, as I said, theosophical philosophy. But whatever else it be, it is difficult to imagine that it could be fully brewed, for poetry does not brew. Doesn't start to brew and, consequently, doesn't cease to brew. A scientist like Thomas Mann ought to know that. If one wanted to speak in his style, one could describe his sentences from a page's top to bottom as fully stretched noodle-dough, or *Strudel*-dough, or perhaps as fully brewed tapeworms. Again his behaviour is most unfair. Again it is only his endeavour to disparage me. Again it is only revenge which, however, cannot put him in the right. It is precisely as if somebody who had stolen a car explained exactly how bad this car was—but steal it he did all the same. If this is Mannly, it is not, at any rate, fully brewed.

(13) *Meistersinger*, Act III, Scene III, Sachs to Beckmesser.

Paul Hindemith—II

By ARNOLD COOKE

[CONCLUSION]

THE symphony *Mathis der Maler* is probably Hindemith's best-known work. The opera from which it derives has only once been performed in England, in a concert version by the B.B.C. As one can thus get but a limited idea of an opera, it is not possible to form a clear opinion of it ; but it is obviously a work of great importance. It has an excellent libretto by the composer himself, based on incidents in the life of Matthias Grünewald, the great German painter, and on his period. The earlier opera *Cardillac* was the brilliant culmination of Hindemith's youth, the first great work of his early maturity ; *Mathis* is the climax of the succeeding period, which included the *Gebrauchsmusik*, a number of concertos and the oratorio *Das Unaufhörliche*. In it we see in the clearest form yet attained the simplification and clarification of style for which Hindemith had been working since *Cardillac*. The symphony is in three movements, and represents three of the paintings in the great Isenheim Altar piece of Grünewald—a Concert of Angels, the Entombment of Christ, and the Temptations of St. Anthony. The first movement is one of the finest of Hindemith's achievements. The opening with its wide-spaced chords of G major on the strings and the strand of melody rising in the woodwind creates immediately a feeling of spaciousness and grand design, while the fine melodic themes, fluent counterpoint, and precision of form throughout produce a sense of classical poise. The slow movement is equally fine ; short, concise and economical, it is of great depth and beauty of expression. The last movement depicting the Saint beset by devils is naturally the most dramatic and exciting, though perhaps not so satisfying from the formal point of view as the first movement. It is, however, a very effective and powerful finale, and one is surprised that this symphony has not yet established itself as a regular feature of our concert programmes ; for as modern works go it is quite easily approachable, nor difficult to perform.

Before winding up I should like to mention some of Hindemith's chamber music, the best of which belongs to his most personal work. Of the five string quartets, four are early works, and of these only the last is consistently Hindemithian in style. The others are eclectic, though No. 3 (1922, Op. 22) has some typical things in it, and is moreover a very effective and stimulating piece of music. The intimate third movement is particularly attractive. No. 4 (Op. 32), written in 1924, is bigger and more mature, and is full of that vigorous contrapuntal energy which became his chief characteristic in the next few years. Then there was a gap of twenty years before the fifth String Quartet in E flat (1943) appeared. This is surely one of the finest of modern string quartets, worthy to rank with some of those of Bartok, the greatest modern master of this form. It opens with a slow and expressive fugue leading into a lively allegro in which the use of a motoric triplet figure pervades the whole and binds it together. The slow movement is a set of variations on a lyrical theme. The last begins broadly for the first part, which is succeeded by a fugal peroration in which the themes of the first movement reappear and are combined with the first theme of the last movement. The final section is a delicate Allegretto, very quiet and mostly *pizzicato*, in which some of the other themes of the last movement are rhythmically transformed.

In the twenty years between the last two quartets, Hindemith wrote a mass of chamber music, including a large number of sonatas for various instruments with piano, and also for piano only. Some of the finest are amongst the piano works, the Third Piano Sonata, the Sonata for Piano Duet and the Two Piano Sonata. Hindemith is not a practised pianist, and his writing for that instrument is not always as successful or imaginative as for other instruments; but he has written some fine music for it, and these three works in particular are very effective. Both the solo Sonata and the Two Piano Sonata end with a massive fugue, in which form Hindemith showed an increasing interest at this time. Another chamber work of great interest is the Quartet for Clarinet, Violin, 'Cello and Piano, an elaborate and brilliant piece of writing, containing a remarkably beautiful slow movement. These later chamber works show an assurance and maturity of style, an inventiveness and expressive power beyond most contemporary work of their kind.

A glance at a catalogue of Hindemith's works shows that it covers practically every branch of music. By modern standards his output is prodigious, and it is not to be expected that everything should be of first rate quality. In fact with a composer so gifted with every technical resource and a natural facility, there is always a danger of the talent running to seed as it were, and ending up in mere fabrication of music ; and there were some who feared at one time that this would happen to Hindemith. Fortunately the growth of his personality kept pace with his technical expansion, and in the years after attaining maturity his art underwent a broadening and deepening process which gave it fresh life and impetus and enriched its content. Very few composers today can show such a consistent spiritual and stylistic development whilst maintaining such a high output.

Although there will certainly be differences of opinion as to Hindemith's place in music, there can be little doubt in the minds of those who know his work that he has achieved the position of a master. I would not suggest that he is among those who have reached the highest flights, but there are a number of composers to whom this has been denied, and whose indisputable greatness rests on their unique contribution to music, and their command of the whole field of their time. One thinks of Schumann and Brahms as typical examples, and perhaps they can be considered the most likely parallels in a previous age. Hindemith has something in common with these two predecessors in the German tradition, from which he is descended through Reger. He has youthful freshness and vigour, originality and spontaneous inventiveness similar to Schumann, and the constructive power and formal sense that is found in Brahms. Perhaps it may seem strange to some to compare Hindemith with a composer apparently at the opposite pole of feeling like Schumann the Romantic ; but it must be remembered that this is largely a matter of period, and it is only in relation to their respective periods that one can compare such artists. Besides, there is quite a streak of the German Romantic in Hindemith. It comes out occasionally in the operas, and in many of his slow movements, but it is a romanticism entirely free from exaggeration and sentimentality. His position in relation to his time is comparable with that of Brahms, whose task it was to re-establish absolute music, to re-assert the importance of form and construction in his time, as Hindemith has done for the present—with this great difference, of course, that whereas Brahms ends a period, Hindemith begins a new one. There is often the feeling in Brahms' music that he is looking back to a better past, but with Hindemith the whole feeling is of the present, and looking forward to the future. Whatever his ultimate position in music, his importance for the present and for the immediate future can scarcely be overestimated. Perhaps more than anyone else, he has succeeded in achieving an assured and balanced order of the musical possibilities of our time, by creating a style which is not in any way derivative and yet traditional : that is to say in line with past musical experience—a style which includes the diatonic in the chromatic, and the simple triad along with the most complex dissonance. There are some who say that this is a compromise and therefore a weakness, but actually every true style is a compromise, a balancing and ordering of the conflicting forces of the time, a synthesis between old and new. No art can be absolutely new and cut off from the past. The attempt to produce such art would lead to sterility, while to remain content with the old ways too long is the sign of exhaustion and decadence. One may say that it is the task for every creative artist to find the right synthesis for, as well as his own adjustments to, his time and place. The extent to which he can accomplish this is a measure of his importance.

Apart from this consideration, Hindemith is one of the most gifted all-round musicians of our time, as composer, theorist and teacher ; and in the executive domain as a great exponent of the viola, for which he has written three concertos. This practical contact with music as a whole permeates all his work. It ensures that his compositions are always playable and well conceived for the particular instruments involved, and though at times difficult, never outrageous. And if it is good from the players' point of view, from the listeners standpoint also it is a sane and balanced music, a music of order and restraint, not of excess, which should appeal to an age that has had more than enough of violence and sensationalism. This is not to say that it is half-hearted or what the French call ' discret.' On the contrary, it can be remarkably intense and passionate, but the emotion is expressed musically from within, not extraneously. It is in fact the music of an integrated personality. At its worst it may be dull, but never cheap. At its best it has strength and beauty.

Lessons from Salzburg
By GEOFFREY SHARP

WITHIN a week of my return from the Salzburg Festival I was fool enough, as it turned out, to attend a Berlioz/Strauss " Prom." at the Albert Hall. I know, of course, that it isn't fair to compare Promenade with Festival performances, . . . BUT it is more than time that English audiences realised that the kind of noise made for their supposed entertainment on this particular evening has nothing at all to do with music-making as Continentals understand it. The chauvinists who believe that English standards are quite high enough are advised to read no further.

I do not like to see alleged soloists playing in public with the music in front of them ; while it is surely beyond dispute that a conductor who finds it necessary to divide his attention between the score and the players, will compare unfavourably with any otherwise similar colleague who has taken the trouble to learn his score and can therefore keep his eyes on the orchestra.

If, on this particular occasion, the conductor had kept his eyes on the players, he would have seen (even if he could not have heard) that some of the strings were contributing less than they might, while others found it expedient to substitute less energetic variants for some of Berlioz' faster flights of fancy in *Harold in Italy*.

This sort of humbug must not be allowed to pass for professiona music-making, not even at Promenade concerts ; indeed, it would be deplorable in the efforts of the Dankpuddle Amateur Orchestral Society whose members, being unpaid, cannot be forced to attend rehearsals. Our professionals, on the other hand, are subject to rehearsal, but insufficient in quantity and often in intensity also. The Musicians' Union, concerned as it is (and rightly) with " the rate for the job " and its members' RIGHTS, would do well to encourage its members to do their job properly. Our orchestral players' ability to give just tolerable performances of all sorts of music almost at sight is not a credit to their virtuosity so much as a reflection of the conditions under which they are accustomed to work. There is a tradition of inadequate rehearsal about English music-making ; and sight-read approximations to the music of the masters have followed in its train.

All this is fact : not merely conjecture, nor biassed opinion. Yet I have no confidence in the prospect of any early or lasting reform ; for there will be no change of heart until our public, players, conductors and concert-promoters realise, or have the realisation forced on them that music cannot be made properly without sweat. To fiddle lackadaisically during working hours and to campaign for Union rights on a soapbox between performances may promote the mental unbalance of a whole hoard of little Hitlers, but it will contribute less than nothing to the health of the musical profession.

All this lies dormant at the back of one's mind year in and year out, occasionally to be stirred to the point of eruption by some manifestation of peculiar ineptitude, but liable to crystallization only as a result of steady experience of authentic performance, compared with which the counterfeit can only infuriate.

No English Festival would have presented Bruckner or Mozart as Salzburg did this year. Nor, to be fair, would I have expected comparable intensity or finesse from any native orchestra in Delius, Elgar, Holst or Vaughan Williams : for our orchestras do not match the Vienna Philharmonic in quality, a fact which none of our pretending has any power to alter.

This does not mean that remedies cannot be found for the future. But of these the most important is by far the most difficult to achieve : a complete change of heart within the profession. Only when our leading musicians " get " Music in the sense that the Old Testament prophets " got " Religion shall we see and hear any real signs of the revival of the musical health of the community.

The kind of earnestness that I am advocating is not popular in England to-day, whether in music or any other pursuit except perhaps some branches of sport, but it will have to be accepted and practised if our music-making is to develop full adult tendencies out of the childish shambles sold as " professional music " by impresarios part fool, part knave in proportions I would rather not asesss.

I have called this essay *Lessons from Salzburg*. The first and most important of these I hope I have now made abundantly clear.

It was best illustrated by Furtwängler's performance on August 7th of Bruckner's Eighth Symphony and by Bruno Walter's of the great Mozart G minor on August 21st. Both these were given in the Festspielhaus which has rather " forward " acoustic properties, by which I mean that it gives full value to orchestral climaxes, like the Manchester Albert Hall which, though it looks like a public lavatory, yet remains a wonderful showcase for the Hallé Orchestra. There the comparison ceases, for the Festspielhaus is bright, comfortable and attractive, needing only a centre-gangway to make it ideal. The Bruckner held the entire audience spellbound for eighty minutes, a fine tribute to the composer who has, however, been dead long enough to need no such exceptional advertisement even in England ; it also provided positive proof that Furtwängler's powers of concentration can still span vast paragraphs and even whole chapters of sound—that unique characteristic of the man which put his finest pre-war performances beyond the range of most of his colleagues and, be it said, of most of our critics.

Each of these symphonies has its own problems of " balance." If Bruckner's are more obvious than Mozart's they are also, as one would expect, less subtle. Walter played the G minor Symphony with clarinets and a small body of strings and refuted once and for all the claim, made by many musicians, that it looks better in score than it sounds in performance.

Orchestral " balance " emerged as the most important factor from these two concerts. But in England the majority of performances are prepared with only the scantiest regard for the resultant orchestral sound and when, as almost always, the concert fails to satisfy it is the hall that is blamed for its shocking acoustics. Better blame the conductors for their asses' ears and the players for their lack of application. But even Midas himself would, I think, have been dissatisfied with the Royal Albert.

The other musical reforms at which I have hinted would all follow upon the change of heart which I regard as essential. Readers may gather a crumb of comfort from one final lesson from Salzburg, as it were in reverse. The Salzburgers have at least one exasperating habit : at the end of any concert, and in the intervals too, they rise as one man (or woman), make for the various exits and then stand there in a solid phalanx, talking, shouting and applauding, . . . and most effectively preventing thirsty people like me from keeping appointments for liquid nourishment. The English do at least keep out of the way if they do not happen to want a drink.

Britten's "Let's Make An Opera," Op. 45*

By DONALD MITCHELL

ONE of the best of Walter de la Mare's poems tells of the fly to which Small things appear Large. It has struck me recently that quite the reverse often happens with our critics : Large things appear Small, and, alas, it must be added, Minutiæ appear Mountains. It would be a pity if Britten's " Entertainment for Young People " were to meet this thoroughly undeserved fate through the perversity of those who have cried aloud for so long for a work of this nature and now decline to recognise its arrival.

Elsewhere† has been given a brief but comprehensive account of Britten's interest in the young which makes a recapitulation unnecessary in this journal. Mr. Keller, at the close of his article, ventures the opinion, " not a Great Work but an intriguingly simple, finished little piece of great potential purport." With that verdict I wholeheartedly agree except that I should probably call *Let's Make an Opera* a great work nevertheless. Intriguingly simple ? Of course. Too simple to be understood by those with (literally) simple minds who are intrigued only by complexity. Nowadays, when there is a premium on the complicated, simplicity is more likely to be misunderstood than ever before. So it is that when true art stares us in the face we are unlikely to acknowledge it.

Childhood is a period of immense significance ; we find it inconvenient and embarrassing to be reminded of it, if only because we have replaced the involuntary honesty of the child by the voluntary dishonesty of the man, an uncomfortable adolescence serving as a bridge between the states of innocence and sin. Awareness of this curious transformation has by no means been confined to the professional psychologist: it has influenced most creative artists and either consciously or unconsciously played a fundamental part in their processes of composition‡. All too often a concern for childhood can lead to a neurosis of unalleviated nostalgia, but Britten is peculiarly fortunate in that he has been able to preserve intact his understanding of the child mind, a preservation free from regrets. He has written the perfect work both to be played and enjoyed by children : his cast acts and sings exactly as he likes, because he knows exactly

---

*Performed at the Cheltenham Festival, 1949. Cast and Production, both musical and dramatic, were admirable ; but a special word of praise must be reserved for Norman Del Mar who, as conductor-compère, made a particularly brilliant contribution.

†Hans Keller : "*Britten and the Young*," *The Listener*, 29th September, 1949.

‡See my earlier and rather inconclusive article on this subject, " *Music and the Literature of Childhood* " in *Music-Survey*, 1/4/48.

how they like to act and sing. And the adult is not excluded, provided he is sensitive enough to perceive at the back of the music the experience of a completely integrated artist. The work is written for children but is never childish. The young by their active involvement in the opera must miss a certain level that can only be appreciated through the passive observation of the adult. What is an entertainment for them has a moral for us, and we can ill afford not to be reminded of fundamentals most of which we were familiar with in childhood but have since cared to discard.

The first part of this Entertainment (text by Eric Crozier) consists of a short play (no music apart from the rehearsals with the audience) related to the miniature opera *The Little Sweep* which follows. We see the trials and tribulations of the producer, the tricks of the children, and some individual scenes are played over : we learn painlessly from the dialogue (no preaching) what an opera *is*. All this is charmingly done, although it could safely be cut in a performance for adults only.

As a title *Let's Make An Opera* must be taken at its face-value, for it applies not only to the performers, but the audience as well are expected to participate in four songs throughout the course of the opera. The libretto tells of the eight-year-old boy who has the misfortune to be in the brutal clutches of a sweep, Black Bob (all the adult parts are taken by adults) intent upon forcing the shivering Sammy to climb his first chimney in a country house, c. 1810. The children of the house, on discovering a tearful and blackened Sammy, show signs of social indignation and determine to effect his rescue ; but they are practical enough to remember to bath him, conceal him overnight in a toy cupboard and arrange for his exit the next day in a large trunk to another kindlier home—all this with the assistance of Rowan, a sympathetic nursery-maid, and in spite of the machinations of Miss Baggott, the apopleptic house-keeper. The tale is divided into the classic three acts (scenes) which are linked together by the audience, who provide a vocal overture, two interludes, and join in the finale. The songs are important, not only as evidence of Britten's amazingly spontaneous melodic invention, but also as the nearest approach to genuine folk-tunes that has been made by a contemporary composer. Although the first song is written in $5/4$, Britten overcomes the audience's mathematical confusion by a constant repetition of the initial rhythmic line that once sung, or rather sung once, is continuously and permanently memorized. The second, " Sammy's Bath ", is a gaily syncopated $3/4$ with cross-rhythms which are hard on the uninitiated eye but come easy to the ear. Britten ingeniously varies the treatment of the theme in the orchestra (string quartet, piano, duet and percussion) throughout the song's four stanzas. The third, " Night Song " is a serene $6/8$ piece for which the audience is divided into four, each geographical area making its own bird-noise when it has completed its stanza. In the final verse the audience-areas unite and combine in a motley, but not cacophonous *cadenza* of the four bird-noises, owls, turtle-doves, chaffinches and herons.

In the fourth and last, the " Coaching Song," which constitutes the opera's *finale*, the cast from the stage and the audience in the theatre alternate in bidding farewell to the good brown mare that carries Sammy off to freedom.

The remainder of the music is substantial and the action realised to such an extent that when in Scene I the reluctant and struggling Sammy is thrust up the chimney by the sweep and his assistant, the full horror of that brutal 19th century tradition is conveyed without reserve. No fairy-tale this, but undiluted social realism. After the child's emergence from the chimney, his pleading " *Please* don't send me up again ! *Please* don't send me up again !" on a simple chromatic phrase, is remarkable for its psychological insight into the character singing it ; and in such a situation, with such a text, no other music would have done other than that written in the score. Its inevitability is its strength. Rowan, the maid, anxious to secure Sammy's release sings a quite exquisite piece " Far along the frozen river " which in emotional range, beauty of conception and above all in its real passion, does not lag far behind some of *Albert Herring*. In the last scene there is a most skilfully managed children's *ensemble* in which Sammy's reponse to the greeting " 'Morning, Sammy, lovely weather " is " 'Morning ! Morning !" on an ascending and descending fourth ; the timing is perfect, the music makes its point. And soon Sammy, seated on nursery furniture that has been magically converted into a coach and horse, rides away, leaving some of the audience perhaps in a more sober than riotous mood, certainly those who can recall at short notice the dirge from *Albert Herring*, both music and text.

> In the midst of life is death
> Death awaits us one and all.
> Death attends our smallest step
> Silent, swift and merciful.

This *Entertainment for Young People* then is what for years our musical educationalists have been begging our native composers to produce. The instrumental forces required are modest; it could be staged in any village or school hall. Children like acting and they like singing, and here is ample opportunity for them to do both and to listen to music that is written *for* them if not altogether *of* them: here the whole problem of community-singing is solved through direct musical participation by the audience: and the plot has a social bias that should satisfy our musical sociologists. It is well to be reminded now and again that children should not be exploited physically, although our present tendency would seem to be ill-treatment of their minds rather than their bodies. If we ensure that *Let's Make An Opera* (and works like it, if and when they are written) reach the audiences for whom they are intended, perhaps we shall not in later years be accused of irresponsibly cheating our children of contact with the cultural renaissance of which, in one sense, they have heard so much but of which in reality they have heard so little.

In Memoriam : Richard Strauss, 1864-1949

ONE experiences an acute sense of loss on hearing of Strauss's death. Although, at his advanced age, the news was to be expected, one feels as if a mountain-range, long familiar on one's musical horizon, and seemingly " aere perennius," had suddenly disappeared ; and one has to reassure oneself that the fruits of Strauss's spirit will remain. The range of this mountain, that is, the extent of Strauss's musical thinking, is truly amazing : it reaches from beer and skittles to Greek tragedy and Oscar Wilde, from domestic joy and worry to a sunrise in the Alps, from the home-spun song to the intricacies of modern opera. He appears in guises, a Proteus-nature, in the Brahmsian style of his youth, in the Teutonic Wagnerism of " Death and Transfiguration," in the Viennese " Rosenkavalier," in the Italianate "Ariadne," in the blood-and-thunder febrility of " Salome" and " Elektra," in the classicism of his late style.

One could almost call him a universal genius, for he was a mighty sorcerer in the realm of music, wielding miracles of power and beauty with the magic wand of his technique and inventiveness. He was all-knowing ; was he also all-feeling ? His detractors have tried to blacken the white magic of his art. They were wrong, for he did have feeling, warmth, humanity ; in short, he had the " anima " worthy of his staggering " animus." But what could one do with a " soul " at the turn of the century when one might neither be blissfully unaware of its workings, nor wear it on one's sleeve ? The sages of the day, misunderstanding Nietzsche, said : " Objectivate your soul. Give it to a task, a community, the world, and you shall be redeemed this side of the grave." So, Mahler gave his soul to mankind, struggling and straining to reach it ; Elgar gave his to King and Empire, and to the Manes and Penates of the English hearth ; Scriabin to occult science ; Sibelius to himself. Strauss—it sounds paradoxical—gave his soul to Music. There it grows rank, it luxuriates—a great lonely soul, severed, à la mode, from both its maker and its bearer. There, it comes aglow in the pyrotechnics of his orchestration, like the mannikin in the alchemist's phial ; there it also stagnates, growing lush and fatty, whenever the coercion of Form and Technique abates, as in his songs. Oh yes, Strauss's music has soul-content ; but the proposition of Soul: Technique, Content : Form, Anima : Animus, presents itself with Strauss in a singular manner, different from all other composers of his stature. Whereas in your " normal " genius " form," " idiom," in short, everything masculine, surrounds and protects (consciously or unconsciously, that is not the point here) an instinctive and im-pulsive utterance of the soul, in Strauss (but not in Berlioz or Liszt !) " form," " technique," " esprit " strive to be repleted, to be anima-ted, by maternal creative power.

Now, if Strauss's soul were too poor to fill the vagaries of his technique, his case would not interest us. But since Strauss has a psyche as truly hermaphroditic as any great composer's, his problem was not, " Do I have enough soul for my technique ? " but rather, " Is my soul pliant enough to enter the ramifications of my ever-spreading, ever-greedy technique ? I can set to music the cold froth of Munich beer ; I can also, at a pinch, embrace Sophocles and Molière to oblige the choosy fancies of my technique—but how much more will my demon ask of me ? " Some such reasoning seems implied in Strauss's modest doubts in his own strength, expressed in his correspondence with Stefan Zweig. He fled from his demon into conducting, into money-making, into a comfortable bourgeois life, and, most significantly perhaps, into card-playing. Haggling over royalties or bluffing at " Skat " was so easy : one's actions produced ascertainable results; means and aims grouped themselves into the normal causal nexus instead of being bewitched by the demon to work conversely. For a time, it seemed that this demon of technique and effect, the only one Strauss, the magician, could not subjugate, had got the better of him : in " Arabella," " Schweigsame Frau," etc. But then came the late instrumental works where the problem, while not being solved, is sensibly evaded.

Where, then, lies Strauss's genius ? It lies in his lively imagination, resourcefulness, industry, in his visions of harmony and orchestral colour and their clear and strong statement ; it lies in the inborn greatness of his feeling, and in his versatility. His failings are that the relationship of feeling and form is strained, and that, in consequence, his versatility is enforced, and can not be called universality. Versatility becomes Universality only in some geniuses of very high order : Shakespeare, Bach, Goethe, Mozart. In others it could be called lack of singlemindedness. Only posterity will decide whether those composers, by comparison narrowminded, like Debussy, Sibelius, Schoenberg, or whether Strauss was the greater.   PAUL HAMBURGER.

[*Note.—Strauss's last opera " The Love of Danae " will receive its first performance at the 1951 Salzburg festival.—Eds.*]

Richard Strauss
(1864-1949)

When Germany had fallen, and her name
Was hated through the Nations for the blend
Of cruelty and system without end
That had eclipsed her years of glorious fame,
One leapt to purge her story of its shame
With the assurance of a faithful friend
Who had conserved pure Grace, and yet could bend
In admiration of Art's changing game.

His oboe sounded through the Tiergarten,
That retribution made of proud Berlin,
As the frail rapture of convolvulus
Nurses a ruined wall; the wild beasts' den
Was purged by an old Cavalier from sin,
Rose-bearer still, still Kammermusikus.

E. H. W. MEYERSTEIN.

RICHARD STRAUSS

Aspects of American Musical Life*

EVERY English visitor to the United States has to learn how to make " adjustments," a process almost as tedious as contending with the language of a country where English is not spoken. For the musician this necessity can be disconcerting—more so perhaps than for the scholar or literary man, who will have had opportunities to discover beforehand many particularities of the state of letters on the other side of the Atlantic.

Most English people have by now accustomed themselves to a situation in which the serious novelist or poet can assert himself economically and yet retain his integrity as an artist. But they still assume silently that a musician or painter ought to be exempt from the business of making money. The Americans don't feel like this at all. Their honourable pre-occupation with what Matthew Arnold called the " almighty dollar " implicates all classes of society except mystics, vagrants, and out-and-out duds. The fine arts are affected by it in many subtle ways. In music one result of things as they are is that the average professional musical career tends to take shape in a different pattern from that which is customary in England. The antagonism between " light " and " serious " music is not so sharp ; in fact one finds outstanding composers and performers active in both these fields with seeming impartiality. An inquiry into the lives of big-time performers will sometimes reveal that they began their professional life as dance-band musicians, Tin-Pan Alley accompanists or arrangers of jazz ; and young composers often go straight from graduate school to participate in the musical side of ephemeral theatrical productions current on Broadway. Musicians who have an eye to business know that there is money in the entertainment world, which they therefore enter in order to obtain financial security before aspiring to more ambitious openings. There are, of course, vocational training schools similar to the Royal College, the Royal Academy and the Guildhall School in London. But even there the students don't seem to regard highbrow music as their sole responsibility. No disgrace attaches to the acceptance of a contract in popular entertainment—if there's money in it, it may bring you one step nearer to becoming an accredited virtuoso.

But while the trade of light music takes on enormous proportions in the States, the concert- and recital-giving industries are also immense. The subscription-concert principle, used much more extensively than it is in Britain, is devoted to satisfying the demands of an intensely buoyant, keen, and not unduly discriminating public which loves and

---

*These notes are intended to serve as a follow-on to Mr. Andor Foldes' short essay on the New York musical scene, in MUSIC SURVEY, Vol. I, No. 5. I must apologise if they seem to apply too exclusively to affairs in the eastern part of the country. But there, after all, several important centres of culture are located within reasonable distance from one another, and communication between them is easy. In a continent as large as the United States the " roving reporter " is something of an anomaly !

gets its Beethoven, Brahms and Tchaikovsky. A multitude of sub-scribers enables the concert-promoters, once they have made certain of financial sufficiency, to secure the services of eminent leaders and to allow adequate rehearsals ; this makes possible the performance of many large-scale works, which could not be attempted if standards of austerity had to be observed. The Americans always admire visible superiority : the man who can control a hundred-and-twenty performers stands a better chance of laudation than a mere string quartet leader. Conductor-worship is rife : even comparatively young conductors (especially if they have recently come from Central Europe) soon become legendary figures whose personal fads and fancies are known to thousands. (An interesting phenomenon last autumn was the appearance in several cities of the 9 year-old Italian boy, Ferrucio Burco, as director of an " International Symphony Orchestra " !) Singers probably come next in popularity, and then pianists. The subscription-giving public, however, takes little account of the nerve-racking competition which every artist who struggles to bring off a " début " at Carnegie Hall has to face. And few of those who are thrilled so regularly by the playing of the permanent symphony orchestras and the productions of the big opera companies ever realise that most of these organisations are hotbeds of intrigue and egregious self-seeking.

That is inevitable, in such a bureaucratic community, and it doesn't happen in the United States alone. The standards of per-formance shown by American orchestras, however, is staggering. In fact the flawlessness with which an ensemble like the New York Philharmonic can render a work such as " Till Eulenspiegel " or a Mahler symphony leaves one wondering whether the whole thing isn't somehow unreal and too coldly perfect to be musical. And when finely disciplined orchestras from Cleveland, Minneapolis or Cincinatti play Mozart or Haydn without the slighest trace of effort or incon-sistency of phrasing, one questions oneself as to the possibility that in the attempt to achieve the ultimate, some of the essential spirit of the music may have been lost. But American musicians have a reply to one's questionings. They have organised a number of smaller orchestras equipped to perform less heavily scored classical items and modern works which call for unusual combinations of instruments. Such organisations include the ' Little Orchestra ' under Thomas Scherchen, the ' Saidenberg Little Symphony ' directed by Daniel Saidenberg, and the ' Chatham Sinfonietta ' conducted by Emmanuel Vardi. These groups are not to be confused with those employed by the purveyors of " symphonic jazz." They perform serious works which are seldom included in the standard orchestral repertoire—an interesting symphony by Boccherini or Gluck, and such things as the early suites of Stravinsky or Milhaud. These small orchestras have a counterpart in the various choral ensembles, of which the most famous is the ' Robert Shaw Chorale.'

It is significant that Robert Shaw (who, though only thirty-three, has held many important assignments in the past ten years or so) began his musical career as the conductor of a Glee Club when he was an undergraduate at Pomona College, California. Every American university has its Glee Club, and some of these groups achieve enviable standards of enthusiastic performance. In one or two cases they make substantial contributions to musical culture by undertaking the study of vocal works that would normally be labelled " For Connoisseurs Only." Robert Shaw's ' Chorale,' which consists of about thirty singers and assisting instrumentalists, has made great advances since the days when it was known as ' The Collegiate Chorale'. It has a big repertoire, including many madrigals and motets, early Bach cantatas, Poulenc's Mass in G, Hindemith's *Six Chansons*, etc., as well as specially commissioned works by American composers. It fulfills extensive broadcasting and recording engagements, and performs with great delicacy. The admirable balance which the ' Chorale ' achieves is largely due to Shaw's unusual methods of presentation : instead of having the several voices standing together in contending blocks, he disperses them in order to obtain unity and sonority.

And though the vast majority of music-lovers are content to go on listening to the well-worn classics, the more adventurous can get in touch, through gramophone records and magazines (the gramophone record supplement of the *Saturday Review of Literature* is especially good in this respect) with a considerable range of music which in England would only be heard at rare recitals and on the Third Programme. While I should not say that America is the connoisseur's paradise, the enquiring musical mind has a very good chance of satisfying itself in a way that is hardly possible in England ; it is indeed easier in America to justify an enthusiasm or follow up a particular interest without meeting the discouraging snobbery of *noli-me-tangere* specialists. America has, of course, " specialists " galore, but they don't seem to shut themselves up in musicological ivory towers. In several parts of the country, for instance, special " societies " undertake the cultivation of otherwise neglected music. At Boston there is the ' Society of Ancient Instruments,' a kind of American Dolmetsch family. In New York a ' Society for Forgotten Music' has recently been formed. This exists for the purpose of performing the work of former masters who have narrowly missed being remembered outside of textbooks and dictionaries—men like Dussek, Stamitz, Spohr, and others who do not deserve to be dropped entirely, whatever their shortcomings. The Committee of this Society (which gives concerts at the New York Public Library and arranges periodical " live " broadcasts) includes eminent musicologists. Through organisations of this kind musicologists are able to make contact with the world of " ordinary " listeners, much as in England they are introduced to the public *via* certain magazines and radio talks.

On the question of radio it is fairly easy for an English onlooker to be smug and satirical. It seems strange to anyone used to the B.B.C. services that with so many technicians and such a large body of advisers to call on, the majority of American radio programmes have to be so puerile, at any rate in setting. Some directors of American radio stations, however, are far from apathetic towards the state of affairs as it now exists. They admit that commerical sponsorship is an evil of questionable necessity, and are prepared to co-operate in any effort to alleviate its bad effects. There are two stations in the New York area, for example, which have managed to arrange for the transmission of practically nothing but serious music. The real objection to most musical programmes, however, is that they are restricted almost wholly to what is available in recorded form. Some time ago, for instance, I wondered why Glière's Symphony No. 3 was appearing so regularly in the schedules—until I learned that there is an acceptable recording of it available in the States, and that it plays for a convenient length of time. Most American listeners with whom I have spoken regard the B.B.C's Third Programme as an object for considerable covetousness : " Such a thing would be impossible over here," they say regretfully. At the same time New York has at least one first-rate musical commentator in the person of David Randolph, whose radio talks—mostly introductory notes—cover a wide range of musical interests. And one item which attracts many intelligent listeners is the broadcasting on Monday evenings of recordings made earlier in the day at a rehearsal by the Boston Symphony Orchestra under Koussevitsky. So far the B.B.C. has only given fragments of rehearsals ; the Boston recordings have shown how exciting twenty or thirty minutes of such an occasion can be.

As for American attitudes to English music of our time, almost universal respect is shown for the genius of Vaughan Williams. Last autumn the Mercury Record Company issued a version by Mitchell Miller and the Saidenberg Orchestra of that composer's Oboe Concerto—an admirable tribute and a really beautiful performance. The usual charge that American recordings are raucous and tasteless does not in fact apply to the Mercury, Vox and Concert Society discs I have so far heard. Elgar, by the way, has never really caught on in America : a friend of mine whose choir and orchestra recently performed Vaughan Williams' *Serenade to Music* with great success and enjoyment told me that he had never heard Elgar's Cello Concerto, and had never heard of the *Introduction and Allegro*. The modern British composers who *are* well-known are Britten, Walton and possibly Arthur Bliss. It is safe to say that Rubbra, Rawsthorne, Lambert, Ireland, Berkeley and Bax are unknown except to the people who keep up with the musical periodicals.

But then, what do English listeners know of contemporary American composers like Howard Hanson, Harl Macdonald, Deems Taylor, Charles Ives (a wickedly neglected artist) and David Diamond— to quote a few names at random ? Modern American composers are not all—as many people in England seem to think—committed to the business of reeling off dime-store music for quick consumption. Perhaps unfortunate experience of the " jazz " tradition still prejudices many English music-lovers against acquainting themselves with American composers. But the music of say, of Aaron Copland, or Gail Kubik, though occasionally jazz-like in externals is usually scornful of jazz's more commonplace manifestations. It may not be too much to hope that further acquaintance with American serious music and with the results of research into the nature of jazz idioms and the native American tradition will enable more and more Europeans to appreciate what is genuine and differentiated in the music of American writers.

ERIC MACKERNESS.

Notes on The Frankfurt Festival

THE Week of New Music was held in Frankfurt from the 18th to 25th June, and had many of the customary virtues and vices. The programme tended to be too long and a great deal of the music of an indefinite and nebulous quality, and the performances were not of an equal standard. Works with a difficult if fascinating texture, such as Schoenberg's Variations for orchestra, need a really first class performance. The Schoenberg concert, in fact, while offering some excellent playing in the Violin Concerto by the talented young Hungarian violinist, Tibor Varga, did no more than sketch the outlines of Variations for orchestra and the Pieces for orchestra. Since, however, the Frankfurt Orchestra was not in the same category as the Hamburg, or even the Baden-Baden orchestras, it is perhaps unfair to attribute these shortcomings to the extremely painstaking conductor, Winfried Zillig, who at least possesses a thorough understanding of Schoenberg's work and is himself a composer of considerable talent.

Of the orchestral concerts, the first, given by the Northwest German Radio Symphony Orchestra, conducted by Hans Schmidt-Isserstedt, was an example of how a modern music concert should be designed and conducted. The programme consisted of Tippett's *Concerto for Double String Orchestra*, Bartok's 3rd Piano Concerto played by Monique Haas, and Stravinsky's *Le Sacre du Printemps*. The playing was of great brilliance and accuracy. Rosbaud's concert with the Baden-Baden Orchestra erred on the side of length, but included a pleasantly vigorous performance of Stravinsky's *Orpheus*. The first performance in Germany of Hindemith's 1945 Piano Concerto was given with great intelligence, but perhaps insufficient technique by Karl Seemann. The programme also included Roussel's *Suite en Fa*, and a lamentable neo-Straussian *Symphonie mimee*, called *Horace Victorieux*, by Honegger. The playing was generally competent, but quite often, and in particular in the Roussel, indefensibly coarse. The Frankfurt Orchestra, in a concert conducted by Kurt Schroeder, performed a *Week-End Prelude* by Norman Lockwood (rather a bad joke), Krenek's 3rd Piano Concerto with Peter Stadlen as soloist, and Boris Blacher's *Great Inquisitor*. The quality of the performances obscured the works, though Stadlen gave a considered reading.

There were a mass of chamber music concerts, including the first German performance of Hindemith's very dynamic 1948 Cello Sonata, excellently played by Ludwig Hoelscher and the highly competent organisor of the Festival, Heinz Schroeter. Tippett's *Boyhood's End* received a musical performance and completed a successful double event for the visiting British composer. The first performance of Wolfgang Fortner's 3rd String Quartet gave an impression of a definite talent, though the first movement promised

95

a quality which was not maintained throughout the work. The young Hans Werner Henze, regarded in many quarters as the white hope of modern German music, showed in his *Apollo and Hyacinthus* that his new-found allegiance to the cause of 12-tone music does not yet suit his eloquent style as he would have it do. A first performance of a Chinese Song for Contralto, Tenor and Piano by Rolf Liebermann from Switzerland made curiously little effect. Perhaps a commentary on the rather pedestrian standard both of performance and of the works (with one or two honourable exceptions) was made by the triumphant success of Bartok's Sonata for 2 Pianos and Percussion, which ended the last chamber music concert in a blaze of glory.   HOWARD HARTOG.

The Cheltenham Festival, 1949

ELSEWHERE in this issue† I write of the new Britten Opera which was performed during the Festival, and elsewhere* have I written at greater length of Arnell's music, with special reference to the 4th Symphony, which received its first public performance by the Hallé and Barbirolli on the 29th June. Nevertheless I must add that my impressions, speculations and prophecies regarding this composer were all strengthened and confirmed: the first movement of the symphony seemed to increase in weight and importance on closer acquaintance ; in particular its epilogue has about it a quality that I can only describe as "inevitability" (a subject I hope to deal with in a not too distant article) and which promises much for the future. The symphony generally was acclaimed by the press, but, while not grudging Mr. Arnell his rightful praise, most of his critics liked him for the wrong reasons and were moved by what for me were the weakest moments in the music. Another new work to receive its first public performance in this country was Arthur Benjamin's *Concerto for Viola and Orchestra*, originally written for Viola and Piano. The arrangement for orchestra, to Mr. Benjamin's credit, does not sound as if it were arranged, but the viola part needs substantial editing. Mr. Riddle's tone was not as big as it might have been, although a mere increase in volume would not have been the real solution to the problem of a viola which was busy visibly but inaudibly. The final movement, a spirited *Toccata*, is possibly Jamaican and Carribean by turns, but that should prevent no one from under-estimating the rhapsodic (and perhaps unexpectedly serious) *Elegy* that opens the Concerto. An *English Suite for Strings* by Alec Rowley also received its first hearing. It was well played, but why it was chosen for a Festival of contemporary music it is hard to understand. It might be suitable for a school band of average ability although both Milhaud and Britten have shown how to write music for the young that is both original and contemporary: Mr. Rowley's

†See pp. 86 ff.
The Listener, 23rd June, 1949.

style is made up of the clichés of a previous generation. Barbirolli contributed an arrangement of some Handel pieces for viola and orchestra—a Concerto in name but little else. The programme notes informed us that " there is genius in selection as well as arrangement." Barbirolli's genius must have deserted him on both counts on this occasion. And if the pieces were arranged with " exquisite taste", they were certainly not exquisitely performed by either the Hallé strings or the soloist (Riddle).

Unable to hear the *Theme and Variations for String Quartet* of Bernard Stevens at the Festival, I attended a rehearsal in London. Mr. Stevens' slow variations were better than his quick. In attempting to impose on his variations normal four-movement form, he has strained after something hardly possible to achieve in a work of brief dimensions mainly concerned in perpetually varying its theme and texture. It was odd to find Reger's ghost (as distinct from Hindemith's) stalking through Mr. Stevens' final fugue, though Reger would have avoided the short-winded conclusion Mr. Stevens gave it. My review must end with a reference to the event that began the Festival badly : The Critics' Forum. This was a brainstrust (?) of some of our more distinguished musical fraternity, presided over by Mr. John Denison of the Arts Council. A large gathering of the public should have noticed that, with the honourable exception of Mr. Charles Stuart of the *Observer*:

(*a*) Most of the questions were more intelligent than the answers they received;

(*b*) The standard of articulation was extremely low: are critics deprived of their pens deprived of their literacy also ?

(*c*) Humility, an essential part of the genuine critical apparatus, was conspicuous by its absence.

All this, therefore, should have made the public ask itself: " Of what use are music critics—on this showing at least " ? But judging by the Prom-like applause at the end of the Forum I fear that such was not the case. I suggest that next year there be more questions from the floor : perhaps we shall discover more critics among the audience than on the platform. DONALD MITCHELL.

Barbirolli's 4th Dvořák was the best I have ever heard. Among his feeling solutions of phraseological details were the ravishingly precipitate second beats in the restatement of the scherzo theme: an exceptionally sensitive realisation of Dvořák's urging accents, and of the highly de-accented first beats they imply. Barbirolli's 4th Brahms, however, stated what should have been developed.

After a disappointing performance of Haydn's Op. 20, No. 2, wherein the fugue was too quick and the first movement too generous in its number of *tempi* (the *détaché* semiquaver triplets being accorded a pace of their own), the Blech Quartet gave the first performance of Richard Arnell's excellent 3rd String Quartet, Op. 41. The work does not perhaps seem very important in the composer's eyes, but then important creators always squint; at some time or other Goethe thought his *Farbenlehre* his most important work. Being facile and 20th-centurian, Arnell no doubt ethicizes effort, and since the present quartet cost him probably far less trouble than the 4th Symphony, he does not think as much of it. In its light-weight kind, and apart from two repairable blemishes, it is in point of fact a better piece. It also sounds better; indeed, its sound is a function of its form (a rarity nowadays): listen to the structural rôle of the, in a string quartet, brilliant key of D major.

For those who had heard, not long ago, the Buschs' largely exhaustive interpretation of Beethoven's C sharp minor, the Blechs' came as a shock; a fortunate one, for musical ignorance is unmusical bliss. It is not possible to give a general impression of a performance which did not itself give one. A few symptomatic details, then. Perhaps it would be unfair to say that the opening was too quick, but it certainly had too little of that beyondish, though nowise tensionless peace or breadth or timelessness which is of its essence. To write about the metaphysical content of music is, strictly speaking, impossible, but vaguely speaking I should say that what this movement needs above all is the subordination of its never-ceasing tension to the assurance that springs from the awareness of eternity. To return to earth in the form of the Eulenberg score, the 'cello's minim in bar 24 is d sharp, not d natural.

When the Blechs reached the B major, the movement received a jolt: an arbitrarily new tempo popped up. And No. 2 showed *the* rhythmic fallacy: Some of the second half-bars' trochaic feet were arbitrarily shortened, almost approaching duplets. The *più mosso* of No. 4 was too quick: again no logical transition of tempo. The successive *pizzicati* in the first Adagio variation were not the only notes which led a far too isolated existence. But the most deeply depressing desecration was that of No. 6. Here you have to show how near you are to Beethoven's God. In the Busch rendering, Adolf Busch's entry contradicted Hugo Gottesmann's blasphemic utterances and lifted the movement up to where it belongs. In the present performance, the first violin made no attempt at redemption: its none too refined emotion continued to take the place of the music's sublimest spirituality.

I have the greatest respect for many of the Blech Quartet's achievements, and even for some inspired moments in the present interpretation, but moments are not enough for this work. The early and middle Beethoven always manages to fight his way through even a bad performance, but even the greatest possible representation does not do justice to the late Beethoven, and anything worse is worse than nothing. This is not perfectionism, but a reminder that the performer's responsibility towards the public should depend on his reponsibility towards the composer: If you cannot give the composer his due, soil his linen in private. Of course each of us must play late Beethoven from the cradle to the grave, but most of us should only let the listener in when we can already see our grave, and maybe our way out of it.

Phyllis Tate's Saxophone Concerto shows gifts and shifts, but as a matter of purely personal taste I prefer music.

HANS KELLER.

Edinburgh, 1949

INDIGESTION of the ear and diarrhœa of the pen are the occupational diseases of a music critic reporting the Edinburgh Festival for a daily newspaper. For the holiday-maker, however (or should it be " the pilgrim " ?) the profusion of musical events—at least one every evening, nearly every morning, and some afternoons—allows a maximum quantity of good music for the minimum expenditure on the overheads of food, shelter, and souvenirs. Brevity here bars a complete or even representative review of performances.

Bloch's " Concerto symphonique " for piano and orchestra was played by Corinne Lacomblé and the B.B.C. Scottish Orchestra under the composer. In blown-out, rhetorical vein, it lacks almost entirely that sense of striving exaltation which hitherto seemed to be characteristic of Bloch. It is oddly uncontemporary in idiom, with Rachmaninovian piano heroics which may, paradoxically, increase the composer's popularity.

This was the only work billed as a Festival première. Printed programmes, however, were deficient in information as well as (generally) badly annotated; and in Hans Gál's " Concertino for Organ and Strings," Herrick Bunney and the Jacques Orchestra were in fact giving a first performance. This pleasant work makes refreshing use of the organ as an intimate chamber instrument ; in the middle one of the three movements, however, which is written for organ alone and is canonic in structure, the pleasure is perhaps unduly intellectual.

" The General Shepherd," by Allan Ramsay, is a play of 1725 interspersed with lyrics set to popular tunes of the day—a ballad opera in pastoral setting. With the most conventional of rich-man-loves-poor-girl plots, it succeeds through its poetry (in Lallans), Tyrone Guthrie's clever open-stage production, and Cedric Thorpe Davie's musical arrangement for eight solo singers (distinct from the actors), wind quartet (flute, oboe, clarinet, bassoon), and an antique square piano (played by himself). Not so impressive, perhaps, is Davie's overture, which is a pastoral to end pastorals, incorporating such things as a quotation from the Pastoral Symphony in " Messiah." But the setting of the songs is excellent, and adds to the already high service given to the Festival by Davie's music to another play, " The Three Estates," revived again this year.

In a sense, Davie's work is more important than the Festival appearances of Bruno Walter, Rudolf Serkin, the Glyndebourne Opera, the orchestras from Berlin and Paris and Geneva, and the rest. For the two plays are *of* Edinburgh as well as in it ; they are special to the Festival, and not something that could be put on just as appositely in Liverpool or Liége. Of similarly distinctive interest

99

was " William and Lucy," a later 18th-century Scottish ballad opera by an anonymous author, presented outside the Festival but at the same time by Moray House Training College. Tom McCourt's musical arrangement was uncomplicated (rightly, since the company was amateur) but charming.

Festival fare was an improvement on last year. There were some worthy American items, including Roy Harris's third symphony. Unfamiliar music included Jean Rivier's attractive and unpretentious piano concerto, Martinu's " Sonata da Camera " for cello and orchestra, and Frank Martin's concerto for piano, harp, harpsichord and double string orchestra, which I was almost alone in finding dull and monotonous. Vocal and instrumental music from Dufay to Dowland came in two concerts by the Pro Musica Antiqua group from Brussels, who handle their old instruments like modern professionals and not (as many such teams) like well-meaning scholar-dabblers.

The Glyndebourne Company put on a really impressive performance of " Un Ballo in Maschera ", with Ljuba Welitsch, Mirto Picchi, and Paolo Silveri as the first-night leads. But " Cosi fan tutte" was a disappointment after last year*, despite a Fiordiligi and Dorábella (Suzanne Danco, Sena Jurinac) as good as could be wished.

The Ballets des Champs-Elysées, with a mainly British orchestra which disgraced the Festival, bravely brought to Edinburgh " La Sylphide," tartan tights and all. The dramatic climax of Jean Cocteau's ballet " Le Jeune Homme et la Mort " is in the middle, when the walls collapse ; but the musical tension, in Bach's Organ Passacaglia in C minor (orchestrated by Reinecke), goes on mounting to the end. The success of this contrasting combination seems to be related to the aesthetic principles of both Pudovkin (see his remarks on film music) and Gluck.

Several Scottish items in the concerts failed to justify their inclusion ; and the contribution of British music as a whole, though not skimped, was unsystematic. No Walton, no Britten, no major Delius, no Holst except one folk-song arrangement—a poor offering, surely, for Britain's greatest gathering of music-hungry foreign visitors. Some central musical feature of British interest seems to be needed—perhaps, as I have suggested elsewhere, the professional production of a Purcell or Handel opera.

None the less, the Festival is, after its third year, a remarkable success. How, one wonders, did we ever do without it ?

ARTHUR JACOBS.

*A disaster both this year and last. See *The Music Review*, Nov., 1948, and Nov., 1949, for my lonely but verifiable verdict.—Ed. (H.K.)

Film Music

LOUISIANA STORY—I.

A FILM score from America at last. Not nearly so good, to be sure, as Frederick W. Sternfeld*—whom we had to reproach with over-estimation on a previous occasion—or indeed many musicians in this country would have it; yet a remarkable attempt to use the still more remarkable musical opportunities of a highly dramatic, but at the same time unhurried and largely speechless picture. It comes from Virgil Thomson, who combines musical competence with film-musical experience, having written the music for *Plough*, *River*, and the election film *Tuesday in November*, as well as, together with Marc Blitzstein, for *Spanish Earth*. And now, in *Louisiana Story*, Thomson has been fortunate enough to collaborate with director-producer Robert Flaherty, for whom, by the way, Richard Arnell wrote his so far only film score, *The Land*.

Louisiana Story's strictly thematic, ternary title-music in F major comprises the score's best and worst. Its middle section is a well-nigh sublime, four-line chorale, twelve-tonal in the outer and tonal in the inner parts: " ambitonal," one might say. This double pers-pective gives rise to various, captivatingly fleeting tonal im-plications in the " atonal " parts, for instance of C and D. The tonic of the harmonic middle parts, however, is E, though both at the beginning and before the end, the E upstairs poses as dominant of A minor. The chorale is one of the most natural and most logically orchestrated pieces that have ever legitimately found their way into the cinema. Linked as it is leitmotivically with one of the protagonists, the derrick, it fortunately reappears twice in its entirety in the course of the film.

So far, so fascinating. Alas, the outer sections of the title music offer nothing but an episode from the later passacaglia, obviously a Cajun song, and a rotten one. In the overture it appears in F major, in the passacaglia in E major. (For my two music examples in Parts I and II of this article I have of course to rely on acoustic memory.)

I find it difficult to imagine that this, for our ears, infantile affair can impress anybody but the most regressively sophisticated. What notes it struck in Mr. Thomson's mind (apart from some con-secutives) I am unable to say. Not his most brilliant treatment can make this tune a tune, and I am sure the critic Thomson would have felt the same, had not an uncritical feeling made him feel otherwise. Nor, indeed, am I at all certain that as a critic, Thomson would pass

*" Current Chronicle," *The Musical Quarterly*, New York, XXXV/1, January, 1949, pp. 115-121.

the so-called passacaglia*, of which this tune attempts in vain to form a part. Mr. Sternberg grows quite excited about this porridge, and has an explanation for all its lumps. It is, we learn, " loose in structure " (one of the most convenient euphemisms of modern musical journalese), and " since the movement lasts about 14 minutes, constant repetition of the bass would have been tedious both dramatically and musically." Of that bass, certainly. Upon its initial statement I immediately thought that as a passacaglia theme it did not seem a happy choice, but quickly admonished myself that it was not my thoughts which mattered, but the composer's. These, however, were not greatly in evidence. The counterpoints, that is, are rather uninspired and, where they are repeated, repetitive. The first one is downright enervating; its first phrase having ended on C-D♭-C (home-key: F minor), the second proceeds to D natural, for no other apparent reason than to avoid landing on D♭. There is hardly anything more paralysing in thematic structure than this sort of apologetic construction; Dvorák seeks a similar egress in the opening of the E♭ piano quartet's first movement.

Mr. Sternberg further observes on the passacaglia that " relief is offered in several passages. . . . [by] folk song episodes." My impression, however, was that upon the passacaglia's failing to develop, it was put aside as a bad job, all the more easily since the film offered the composer an excuse for amusing himself as a folklorist in an aggregate, or rather an arbitrary array, of so-meant episodes. After you heard the piece, you did not know what was more episodic, the episodes or the passacaglia. (When at a later point in the film the passacaglia was resumed in a shortened version, i.e. without episodes and without the previous four twelve-tone codettas, its form had a better effect.) In any—not only in Mr. Thomson's extreme—case, an episodically interrupted passacaglia is no joke. I know only of two recent examples of such an attempt, namely, Britten's concert version of the *Grimes* Passacaglia and his *Condemned Hold scena* in the *Beggar's Opera*. The *Grimes* interlude annexes the end of the scene that follows it in the opera, whereby the ground bass is cut from under our feet until it reappears at the very end in the dominant. At the same time this epilogue gives us an inversion of the Passacaglia's initial viola solo (the boy's theme), on which all subsequent variations are based, and which, moreover, derives from the passacaglia theme itself. Thus the link-up is successful, even though it may not be able to conceal its existence. In the *Beggar's Opera*, Britten takes the greatest pains not to let the listener lose the thread of the ostinato which he interrupts—or rather sustains, ties up— again and again at various points, in order to insert the songs of the *scena*. The theme is constructed in distinct view of the last song, *Greensleeves*, with which it coincides contrapuntally. Thus a build-up is achieved that is not only orderly, but organic and extra-ordinarily original. Mr. Thomson, however, far from solving the problem, does not even seem to be alive to its existence, or else he depends on the picture to solve it for him.   HANS KELLER.

(To be continued in the next issue.)

*The first part of the movement came over extremely indistinctly when I heard it, but I do not think I missed anything of great importance.

Reviews of Music

Single reviews are arranged in alphabetical order of composer's
names ; joint reviews appear at the end.

*BACH : A Little Prelude in E Minor. Arr. for Piano Solo by
Harold Darke. (O.U.P.) 2s. 6d.*

WHEN will arrangers of organ music recognize that in nine cases out
of ten *quality* is mutilated by spread chords in the bass ? The sole
portion of this arrangement that sounds authentic to my ear is the
greater part of the *sotto voce* on the third page, where this obvious
device is reduced to a minimum ; the effect of the rest is grandiose,
bark, not Bach.

E.H.W.M.

*BACH : ' I call upon thee, Lord.' Arr. for Two Pianos by John Lovell.
(O.U.P.) 3s. 0d.*

THE arrangement of this choral prelude, in the two piano series
edited by Ethel Bartlett and Rae Robertson, is, on the assumption
that such metamorphoses are musically necessary, blameless.

E.H.W.M.

*BARTOK : Second Piano Concerto (Two Pianos, 4 Hands). 22s.
Forty-four Violin Duets, Vols. 1 and 2. 4s. 6d. each.
Hungarian Peasant Songs (Miniature Score). 3s. 9d.
All published by Boosey & Hawkes.*

THE second concerto, so important a landmark in the evolution of
Bartok's style, was finished early in 1931, the year in which the violin
duets were also produced. Leading away from the first concerto, it
did not lead up to the third (now the most popular of the three) but
paved the way rather for the fine *Sonata for two pianos and percussion*.
The present reduced version of the orchestral part has been made by
the composer himself. The three years immediately following 1931
saw Bartok engaged more in matters of scoring and harmonization
than of actual composition. It was in a sense a period of renewal of
energy, the outcome being the *Fifth String Quartet* and the *Music for
strings, percussion and celesta*. While the 44 duets cannot be classed
as major works, they are significant in that they show the elements of
Bartok's craft, and provide an approach to his harmonic and
rhythmic ideals which is almost without parallel. The *Hungarian
Peasant Songs*, dating from 1933, are a brilliantly-conceived score
consisting of a ballad and ensuing dances: one feels that the composer enjoyed harmonizing his native folk-music almost as much
as he enjoyed composing. All these items are well-printed on stout
paper which will endure, like the music it bears.

D.W.S.

ARTHUR BENJAMIN: " *Carribean Dance* " and " *Two Jamaican Street Songs* " *for two Pianos* (*Boosey & Hawkes, 5s. 0d. each*). " *From San Domingo* " *and* " *Jamaican Rumba,*" *arr. for Violin and Piano.* (*Boosey & Hawkes, 2s. 6d. each.*)

Is there a recipe that mixes passion-fruit, cayenne pepper, pineapple, limes, and a dash of rum ? Ask Arthur Benjamin—he has one. And he mixes his ingredients so dexterously that we swallow his brew as smoothly as—well, if not mother's milk, at least brandy punch. True, Milhaud and Constant Lambert used the same cookery-book—but what matter ? In the hands of a " gentleman "-cook every recipe acquires his individual tang, and only the " players " may, to their own loss, confound, in the sampling, the various finesses of three distinguished chefs. To adhere to terms culinary : two grand pianos are the ideal vessels—hard, cool, big and clanky—in which this heady draught should be served. But if we get it bottled for export by Boosey & Hawkes, in small, shapely violin-flasks—we cannot complain.   P.H.

D. MOULE EVANS : ' *The Haunted Place,*' *for strings* (*Joseph Williams*). *Score : 5s. 0d. ; Parts : 1s. 0d. each.*

REPETITIONS of two undistinguished themes interspersed with some scrubby quasi bogey-bogey music, the whole covering exactly eight pages constitute this indifferent piece of film background music which has nothing to commend it for any other purpose. It is difficult to see why Reginald Jacques should have played it, why the composer should have written it or why it should ever have been published.
                                   N.D.

HOWARD FERGUSON : Sonata No. 2 for Violin and Piano (*Boosey & Hawkes*). *7s. 6d.*

WHILE the idiom of the entire sonata is Frenchy, there is a curious difference of language between the César Franckian first movement, and the other two which seem informed by much more recent preceptors. In the first (and weakest) movement, sentimental semitone-appogiaturas and enharmonic modulations abound (e.g. in the " clever " introduction which takes us from B♭ minor to the home-key F♯ minor) ; there is also a very naive German Sixth in the 2nd subject (A major) which comes up again in the Coda of the last movement. Mr. Ferguson's style is much freer in the slow movement, especially at the beginning and end (figures 0—5 and 7—10) as well as in the last movement, a sonata-rondo with a 6/8 *détaché* theme which, though not very original, certainly has vigour. Where Mr. Ferguson falls down is in his climaxes, where simplified statements of the themes are presented in modulating sequences *à la* Franck. Ferguson's themes, acceptable enough in their ordinary form, will not stand up to monumental simplification. (See 1st mov., figures 17—18; 2nd mov., 5—7; last mov., 25—27 and 31—32). But the saving quality of his style is its being academic in the French rather than in the German way, i.e., he does not use

104

his undoubted technical skill to obscure the relative insignificance of his ideas, but admits frankly what and how much he has to offer, leavening and sweetening the dish with traditional French *savoir-cuire*.   P.H.

BENJAMIN FRANKEL : String Quartet No. 3 (Augener), 4s.6d.
IT is the custom to speak of austerity and arid textures whenever one of Mr. Benjamin Frankel's cerebrations appears. This quartet, however, compels admiration not only by virtue of its cogency of thought, but also by the interesting variety of thematic material to be found in each of its five movements. Although the work may not always reach a high level of inspiration, it has moments of some intensity and an integrity that commands respect.   R.L.

JOHN IRELAND: Overture, 'Satyricon' (Joseph Williams), 25s. 0d.
THIS spirited little work is prefaced by a quotation from the Satyricon of Petronius, telling us "to be merry, and put life in our Discourse with pleasanter Tales." This laudable resolution is duly observed by John Ireland in this well-written and crisply scored piece. The brisk and highly rhythmic opening, which forms the basis of most later developments, leads through an animated sequence of some interest to the second group, both elements of which are equally undistinguished and share a certain facile lyricism which fails to convince. The work is, however, refreshing, has moments of considerable sparkle, and is devoid of pretence. It was completed in 1946 and first performed at a Promenade Concert the same year.   R.L.

DARIUS MILHAUD : 'Chansons de Ronsard.' Reduction for Voice and Piano ; English translations by Henry Pleasants. (Boosey and Hawkes.) 5s. 0d.
THESE four settings date from 1941 and were composed for voice and orchestra, for Lily Pons. They are outside the compass of any but the highest soprano who needs considerable sense of musicianship to negotiate the wide intervals, particularly in the second, " à Cupidon." The orchestral score has apparently proved easy of adaptation, for unlike so many transcriptions the piano parts look as if they had been originally conceived for the instrument.
The translation is fair, but in several places the accents get all wrong ;
¾ With | ev'ry thresh | ing floor ex—claim,
for example, is bad. Ronsard is one of those poets who are actually untranslatable in terms of English poesy ; it is better not to make the attempt. There are many singers of the required calibre capable of singing in French.
The B.B.C. might consider this group in its original form· Milhaud has caught the right spirit and his texture is sufficiently slender to give perfect balance.   N.D.

E. J. MOERAN : Overture for a Masque (Joseph Williams).
Score: 25s. 0d.

THIS is just the kind of work which one has been waiting for, as it is extremely suitable for opening a concert and is not too difficult in execution. No particular Masque seems indicated but it carries out the functions of a comedy overture. The quiet middle section gives it an English flavour which Moeran excels in and it is typical of the freshness of the composer's idiom.   N.D.

MONTEVERDI : Vespro della Beata Vergine, edited by H. F. Redlich. (Universal Edition, Vienna.)

GIULIO STROZZI, in giving an account of a performance of a mass by Monteverdi, stressed the instrumental part of the music, and the " tears and sighs " it drew from the listeners. Whether it was indeed the *stile concertato*, or simply the solemnity of the occasion, which exerted this powerful effect on the congregation, is a matter open to doubt. Monteverdi himself must often have felt guilty about this wholesale transfer of operatic style and method into certain of his works composed for the Church. He was (as Dr. Redlich points out in the Introduction to this edition) for many years concerned with the moral and artistic justification for " this tremendous stylistic antithesis." Moreover, he may (for reasons best known to himself) have preferred to stress the rigorous style of earlier contrapuntal models, more than the operatic, or rather monodic compositions which came from his pen. The title of the Amadino publication of 1610 bears four lines in heavy type referring to the Mass (*In illo tempore*)—the Vespers are relegated to the bottom of the page. Was this because the Mass was composed in the old style, and the Vespers in the new ? And is it only a coincidence to find in a letter from the singer, Bernardo Casola, a reference to " una messa a sei voci di studio et fatica grande," yet no mention of the Vespers ?

Dr. Redlich has given us an excellent practical edition of Monteverdi's setting of the Vespers. It is high time we had such an edition, for seventeen years have elapsed since the *editio princeps* of Malipiero, whose faithful transliteration of renaissance note-values has been criticised by Curt Sachs as " inflation-bill script." Not that all the notational problems have been solved. *Duo seraphim* starts off with the note-values halved: then at the words " alter ad alterum " there is a reversion to the original notation, thus avoiding an embarassing superfluity of hemidemisemiquavers, which would unnerve modern singers as much as the virtuosi—Adriana Basile, Caterinuccia Martinelli, and Settimia Caccini—who doubtless took part in the original performance. Problems of notation are invariably bound up with the problems of tempo: the composer realised this when he directed the singer of the alto part in *Et exultavit* to "go slowly because the tenors have to sing semiquavers." It is a pity that Dr. Redlich has not kept this and many other remarks by Monteverdi —always eminently practical remarks—instead of supplanting them by poor English translations of a German *Verhaltungsbefehl*.

It is more of a pity that the Foreword has not been carefully checked, especially as the words " Letchworth, England " have been appended to the signature. Several grammatical and spelling mistakes need correction, and the whole essay needs to be purged of Germanic compounds like " allembracing " and " timevalues." Many readers may wonder what is meant by a " sequel of items," and why the plural of *Antiphon* should appear time and time again as " Antiphona's." It is stated that two of the original fourteen items have been omitted " for practical reasons "—the German version has " aus klangästhetischen und aufführungspraktischen Gründen." What is wrong then, from the aesthetic point of view, with the sound of *Nisi Dominus* and *Lauda Jerusalem* ? Why not omit *Pulchra es*, which according to Bettina Lupo is " tedious and scholastic " ? In any case, three (not two) of the fourteen items have been omitted, for we have only the seven-part *Magnificat;* the six-part version, *non concertante*, is not included. It would surely have been advisable to mention the fact that Vespers, according to the Roman rite, is the only service where music other than plainsong is permitted— and the counterpart is Lauds, not Matins. Apart from these few reservations, the 1949 edition by Dr. Redlich should be indispensable to all who wish to perform the *Vespro*.

D.W.S.

First publication of MOZART, Oboe Concerto C major, K.314.
Pocket Score (Boosey & Hawkes), 5s. 0d.

THE same work as the Flute Concerto in D of the same Köchel number. In his new edition of Köchel (quoted as introduction to the present score) as well as in his *Mozart* book (p. 283), Einstein suggests that this is in fact the composition of which Mozart writes in his Mannheim letter of February 14th, 1778: " . . . then Herr Ramm (by way of a change) played for the fifth time my oboe concerto written for Ferlendis, which is making a great sensation here. It is now Ramm's *cheval de bataille.*" This concerto was composed in '77 for the Salzburg oboist Guiseppe Ferlandis, and Einstein explains that Mozart re-wrote it in Mannheim early in '78 as one of his two flute concertos for the Dutch amateur flautist H. De Jean, " out of sheer lack of time and money." Surely not " sheer " ? Mozart's just-quoted letter also suggests lack of creative power when writing for the flute: " It is not surprising that I have not been able to finish [the pieces for De Jean], for I never have a single quiet hour here. I can only compose at night, so that I can't get up early as well; besides, one is not always in the mood for working. I could, to be sure, scribble off things the whole day long, but a composition of this kind goes out into the world, and naturally I do not want to have cause to be ashamed of my name on the title-page. *Moreover, you know that I become quite powerless whenever I am obliged to write for an instrument which I cannot bear. Hence as a diversion I compose something else, such as duets for clavier and violin* [K.301-6], *or I work at my mass.*" (My italics.) One's last reason is often one's first.

Einstein (*Mozart, ibid.*) also points out that " it is significant that Mozart later returned to the Rondo theme [of the present concerto] in composing Blonde's aria ' *Welche Wonne, welche Lust*' in *Die Entführung aus dem Serail.*" Less obviously, but just as tangibly, the concerto looks into its past, too—cf. bars 19f. of the Adagio with the opening of the early, and in itself uninteresting E flat quartet K.160 (1772). The phrase may seem conventional, a thematic type; indeed, its skeleton is. But in this particular shape it does not, I suggest, appear anywhere else. The interest of such comparisons lies in the difference in Mozart's approach to, and treatment of the same thing, and in the light thus thrown on the none too early growing up of a mind that outgrew life.

H.K.

SCHUBERT SONGS

AUGENER LTD. have issued sixty solo songs of Schubert separately, with English versions by R. Capell and others. R. Capell is responsible for the four to hand, i.e. *Prometheus* (1s. 6d.), *Grenzen der Menscheit* (1s. 6d.), *Am Bach im Frühling* (1s. 0d.), *Bei dir allein* (1s. 0d.). These accredited translations are more singable than precise, so why complain ? The two from Goethe, being unrhymed, are less catastrophically clichéd than the other two; but to render ' *und Moos und Gras wird neu und grün* ' (Schober) by ' to all the land new life they bring ' and ' *empfind*' *ich, dass ich liebe* ' (Seidl) by ' dost comfort bring and blessing ' brings these admittedly minor lyrics into the region of the Victorian drawing-room ballad; they did not deserve quite that evasion of a translator's job.

E.H.W.M.

SMETANA : Sonata for Two Pianos, 8 hands (Hinrichsen), 10s. 6d.

A CURIOSITY which should prove good fun for amateur pianists. Pleasant and well-written, although not the best Smetana can give us. Georg Kuhlmann's very explicit, sometimes aggressively verbose footnotes seem out of place. Surely, string-quartets are never told by an editor how to come in together ? What is needed now are really good critical editions in the much more serious domain of duets for one piano. I wish Schnabel would give us the collected Schubert-duets, annotated in the manner of his Schubert Sonatas.

P.H.

ALEXANDRE TCHEREPNINE: Fantasie for Piano and Orchestra.
(Eastern Chamber Dream, Yan Fei's Love Sacrifice, The Road to Yunnan). (Henrichsen.) 10s. 6d.

THIS is a score after perusal of which I feel in need of a bath; a bath in the form of a Bach 2-part invention. The melée of styles, idioms, " naïve " and " spicy " harmonies, pentatonic meanderings, tumble-down brass-chords, tumble-up pianoforte-glissandi, rolls on the cymbals, bland oriental ditties on the flute—this " highly effective " piece is a *Chinoiserie* in the grand manner. One would have thought that Puccini's artificial pagodas, comparatively stable as they are, would have been the last edifices of their kind. But no, the Parisian " salon," after having originated the *Chinoiserie* in the visual arts of the 18th century, now inspires the kindred soul of the composer, as he says in his preface, to " dreams about the legends of Old China." There have been quite a number of artists, especially Chopin, who were strong enough to take the draughts of a town with a notably " artistic atmosphere," and to benefit from them. Which brings us to the crux of the matter, namely the question whether the contemporary artist is entitled to write descriptive music in an outlandish, seasoned-up style for the stimulation of a highly civilised and blasé public. In my opinion, he is, as long as it is good as music, and not merely as literary " romance." And it can only be good as music if there is heart in it. On this point, pieces like Ravel's *Asie*, or De Falla's *Nights in the Gardens of Spain*, score heavily. Compared with them, or even with some technically very similar pieces by Villa-Lobos, Tcherepnine's *Fantasie* seems heartless, contrived, disingenuous, in spite of all its verve and colouring.   P.H.

JOAN TRIMBLE : Two Irish Tunes for Two Pianos. Arranged from the Herbert Hughes collection of Irish Country Songs. (Boosey & Hawkes). 2s. 6d.

THE art of writing simply yet sonorously for two pianos is by no means an easy one, but Miss Trimble has had such experience in it that she creates—almost unwittingly, one would think—just the right lay-out. These are light, pleasant pieces, and when Miss Trimble deviates, for variation's sake, from the " natural " harmonic implications of the folk-tunes, sailing forth into a kind of " development," she does so tastefully and unpretentiously, especially in the second piece. (I hope that the G flat in the bass of the 3rd bar on page 12 should read G.)   P.H.

J. S. BACH : " Sheep may safely graze " (from " Birthday Cantata "); " I step before Thy throne, O Lord " (Chorale Prelude ; BUXTEHUDE : " Nun bitten wir den heil'gen Geist " (Chorale Prelude). Transcribed for piano by Egan Petri. (Boosey & Hawkes, 2s. 6d. each).

THESE transcriptions, easy though the notes are, are not for amateurs, as only the surest tone-gradation will make them intelligible. In the " Sheep," the voice and the two flutes of the original often meet in 3-part writing for the right hand which is a perfect study for sounding certain notes in close chords. (A pity Petri has not given us any fingerings, very professional ones being needed here.) The enchanting dissonances (read : consequential counterpoint) by which Bach banishes all traces of sugariness from this pastoral piece, become even more apparent in the one-coloured piano-transcription than in the original (see bars 3, 4, 9, 15, 16, 19, 29, 32, 34, 35, 39, 45, 51, 52, 55, 56.) Players who are wont to play all of Bach's slow

movements pastorally will go astray in " Before Thy throne . . .",
Bach's last work, dictated from his death-bed. Petri's excellent
metronome-mark ($\frac{1}{4}$* 46) indicates that this Adagio with its diminu-
tions, inversions, and strettos of the chorale has to be played with
the most fervent Protestant " Innigkeit." The Buxtehude, written
about fifty years earlier, is just as " Protestant," in the more common
milder, quietist manner. Formally, it is rather akin to the Bach,
both being in G, 4/4 time, having similar chorales and figuration.
Petri's frequent expression marks in these pieces show the spirit of
a great artist. The classics would be better performed to-day if
they had made use of Petri's " quasi forte." P.H.

*AARON COPLAND: Danzon Cubano. For Two Pianos (Boosey
and Hawkes). Hoe Down, arranged by the Composer from the
ballet Rodeo for Violin and Piano (Boosey and Hawkes).*
ALAN RAWSTHORNE: Sonatina for Piano (O.U.P.).
ROBIN ORR: Sonata for Viola and Piano (O.U.P.).

THE two Copland pieces are both in the composer's more popular
manner. The Cuban dance manages to be an experiment in an
exotic genre while remaining consistent with Copland's urban
temperament. It is, I think, better music than *El Salon Mexico;*
the diaphanous scoring for the two pianos gives the rhythmic complexities—characteristic both of Cuban popular music and of
Copland's American style—a lucent serenity. Though a ' light '
piece, this is a work of maturity. *Hoe Down* makes an effective
frolic to end a recital; divorced from its context it possibly seems to
be too much like the real thing and not enough like Copland.

Rawsthorne's Sonatina contains no movement built on the
dualistic sonata principle of the eighteenth and nineteenth centuries.
The first movement is monothematic and toccata-like, creating a
typically glinting and astringent sound from the keyboard. The
slow movement is lyrically sustained, reaching a most impressive
climax; and the humour of the last two movements has a rather
Waltonian acidity. It is testimony to the power and integrity of
Rawsthorne's mind that the consistent and continuous keyboard
figuration hardly ever ceases to fulfil a musical purpose.

The Orr Sonata seems to me the best work of the composer I
have come across. The always impeccable texture here carries an
unexpected emotional range and warmth, especially in the Elegy
and the trio of the Scherzo, which has an unmistakably celtic
flavour beneath its fastidious elegance. In this sonata, as in the
Rawsthorne, cosmopolitan sophistication gives maturity to, without
stifling, a native English vitality. We are far from the antiseptic
and clinical atmosphere that is typical of so many of the minor
disciples of Stravinsky and Hindemith. Of the two works the
Rawsthorne has the greater force and personality, while the Orr
has the greater concentration and the more careful organization.
W.H.M.

*$\frac{1}{4}$ = crochet.

FRANZ REIZENSTEIN : Sonata for 'Cello and Piano. (Alfred Legnick). 9s. 0d.

E. J. MOERAN : Sonata for 'Cello and Piano (Novello).

COMPARED with his Violin-Sonata, the new Reizenstein is more mellow, more spacious, perhaps more sonorous, if not so daring and intense. This comes from the nature of the instrument which demands more lyricism, and, with its wide range, dovetails easily with the piano, as treble, middle-part, or bass. The problem of letting the 'cello come through in all these positions is brilliantly solved—as it also is by Moeran, in exactly the same way—by clever part-crossings, wide piano-arpeggios with the 'cello winding its way in between, and all solid chord-writing being well above or below the 'cello-line. The two works are not only similar in texture, but also in the origin of their lyrical passages, which in Moeran's case is of course Gaelic, while the theme of Reizenstein's first movement, or the beginning of the slow introduction to the Finale, could be by Moeran. Also some transitional passages built on chords show a striking similarity, e.g. bars 7—10 on p. 26 of the Moeran and bars 1—4 on p. 15 of the Reizenstein.

It is in their contrapuntal passages that these works part company. With Moeran, these are the development, the setting in motion of the quasi-folkloristic melodies, out of which they grow very naturally. With Reizenstein, one feels that the themes are the preparation for the " real job," namely the remarkably skilful polyphonic passages and fugatos of the work. It is here that Reizenstein must make jump from simple melody-writing to the manner of composition germane to him: the counterpoint of the Hindemith-school. Sometimes this change is too sudden, as at the beginning of the last movement proper where an " Allegro amabile " theme in the vein of Dohnanyi, changes character in the 5th, and then again in the 14th bar. On the other hand, this " amiable " theme is harmonized much more boldly on page 51; but since this comes after the first rondo-episode in " Hindemith "-counterpoint, it sounds like the proper resolution of the preceding dissonances. My classificatory references to Hindemith do not imply plagiarism. Mr. Reizenstein has an original mind; and at the same time, this brand of modern counterpoint is too big a field to be treated by one man alone. There cannot be enough of it, and one is grateful for passages of strong and clear polyphony, like the 3rd subject group of the first movement (pp. 12-13) or the main part of the scherzo, which is shaded off by a masterly trio of the type where a dreamy solo-voice is followed by thematic meditations in the other parts. This is in a certain tradition of trio-writing, stemming perhaps from Schubert's string-quintet, and used sometimes by Bruckner and Dvořák. In the trio and elsewhere, e.g. in the development-section of the first movement, or in the introduction of the finale, one witnesses the rise of inspiration. Whenever this happens—and it happens often enough in Schubert and Brahms—one experiences sympathy. Inspiration is taken for granted in a work dispensed in its entirety by divine grace, but the spectacle of inspiration rearing its pretty head is disarming.

However, perhaps the best analysable feature of this sonata is its compact formal mould. The scheme of the last movement, a Sonata-Rondo, is :

$$a — b, \quad a — B, \quad C, \quad a — c, \quad D, \quad a + c, \quad a + b, \quad d;$$

where (a) is the first subject ; (b) a quaver-sequence growing out of it; (B) the enlarged quaver-sequence; (C) the first episode in form of triplet fugato; (c) a bridge-passage taken from (C); (D) the development, using (a) and (b); (a + c) and (a + b) a compressed, partly superimposed recapitulation; (d) the simplified (D) used as a coda.

All this is not merely clever on paper, but really comes off.

The form of the Morean is perhaps just as strict, but not so complicated. In the first movement, for instance, a restatement of the first subject, rhythmically simpler, harmonically richer than at the start, serves as development-section; and in the coda, both the 1st and the 2nd subjects are treated at length in changed settings. Vague ? Yes—but with a purpose. What really matters in this style is to efface all outer signs of construction while getting the balance of the sections exactly right. Moeran is a past-master at this. The Sonata breathes the fresh air of improvisation while keeping in perfect shape, and though the tempo changes frequently, there is a somnabulistic certainty about the length of every section. A real " peroration " like the marvellous passage before the final " presto " of the Finale could not be a bar longer or shorter (as at the end of the Dvorák 'Cello Concerto). It is hard not to wax poetical about this work, for the essence of Moeran's style is poetry ; the poetry of the cool, distant, western sky and of the Atlantic seascape, tempered by a retiring but very genuine human warmth and understanding. Without being in the least picturesque, this music seems nourished by the careful and loving observation of nature and its seasons, and the simple life. The mood it induces, and perhaps was written in, is one of wonderment ; a mood veering between reserve and admiration in face of man and the works of God. All the elements of this music, its apotheosized Irish tunes, its outbreaks of manly passion, its shivery, twilit dialogues, its processions of tritons and sea-urchins—all this is encompassed by the wondering love of a true poet.   P.H.

IGOR STRAVINSKY : *Oedipus Rex* (*Boosey and Hawkes*), *11s. 3d.*

Oedipus Rex is sub-titled ' opera-oratorio.' This should mean, not that it can be played as an opera *or* an oratorio, but that if it is given on the stage, the action should be immobilised, and if it is given on the concert platform, the performance should have some kind of setting and be in costume. In this country, it has never yet been produced in these conditions. There have been one or two concert performances. But that is all.

For this neglect, the composer himself is partly to blame. Cocteau's version of Sophocles's tragedy as set by Stravinsky plays just under an hour and does not fill an evening's bill. It is difficult to find a suitable work as companion to it ; and even if such a work is found, the public's aversion to a double or triple operatic bill is usually fatal. In addition, the dog Latin of the libretto acts as a deterrent. Nevertheless, *Oedipus Rex*, when properly produced, completely achieves the cathartic effect of great tragedy.

Twenty-two years after its first performance in Paris, it is good to be able to renew acquaintance with it through the score of the 1948 version. Here lie revealed such memorable passages as the noble sweep of the chords with which the work opens, the slow pulsing chant of the chorus of tenors and basses, the conceited and over-decorated utterance of the still illusioned Oedipus, the serpent-like venom of Jocasta impugning the authority of the oracle, the rusticity of the hesitant messenger, and the luminous revelation of Oedipus's final *Lux facta est.*

Although Stravinsky is supposed to have newly revised this score, it contains a number of unfortunate mistakes. The worst of these is the metronomic direction :$\frac{1}{4}$*=88, instead of :$\frac{1}{8}$*=88, at section 110. This, if followed literally by a subservient conductor, would wreck one of the most important passages of Act II.

One final complaint. The French stage directions are so badly and inaccurately translated ('*figure*' translated ' figure,' for instance) that it is essential to get a really good version of the Speaker's running commentary for English performances.   E.W.W.

---

*$\frac{1}{4}$=crochet ; $\frac{1}{8}$=quaver.

Book Reviews

Arranged in alphabetical order of titles, with a joint review at end.

THE BOOK OF MUSICAL DOCUMENTS, *by Paul Nettl.* $5. (*Philosophical Library, New York.*)

A NOT particularly useful anthology of musicians' letters, extracts from diaries, funeral orations, poems, archives, newspapers, etc. The headlines for each quotation (for which Mr. Nettl is presumably responsible) are particularly fatuous: " Beethoven Did Not Dislike Pretty Women." D.M.

" CÉSAR FRANCK," *by Norman Demuth. Pp. 310 ; 12s. 6d.* (*Dennis Dobson.*)

UNTIL Mr. Demuth has enjoyed Fowler's *English Usage* he should stop writing ; yet Messrs. Dobson's publishers, rather than Mr. Demuth, are to be rebuked for passing so many mis-spellings and offences against grammar and style. A few factual errors may be mere slips, pardonable in a first edition ; Liszt was not the first to express the sublime with diminished sevenths, for they served Bach wonderfully ; and Habaneck could not have played each new Beethoven symphony as soon as it arrived ; Beethoven was dead before the Conservatoire Society Concerts were founded. For none of these faults shall Mr. Demuth be reprimanded. His enthusiasm for Franck is genuine and timely; with a little more care and scrutiny, he could have held us with sheer verve and gusto— qualities that have redeemed many a poorer musician and writer.

His book has been hurriedly and carelessly botched, and he knows it; he states in his preface that repetitions and contradictions are forthcoming, and he scamps the chapters which do not deal with the music in which he is interested. Does he think he can disarm censure by forestalling it ? Could not Mr. Demuth have done a little reading and thinking about the æsthetics of opera, or was he hurried by his publishers ? These remarks are made with deep regret by one who has enjoyed much that Mr. Demuth enjoys, including some of his own music.

It is good that a modern composer champions Franck, even if enthusiasm leads Mr. Demuth to declare that a certain piece is worthy of Bach and another of Beethoven. Franck had qualities enough to bear witness to his greatness, whether or not single works bear comparison with the achievements of the greatest. He achieved a personal style more idiomatic than that of either Liszt or Berlioz, or of any nineteenth century composers except the giants, and Mr. Demuth does well to contradict those pitiful little coxcombs who never dare find fault with a single bar of Bach or Beethoven, but do not tire of pointing out the obvious weaknesses of Schumann, Mendelssohn, Tchaikovsky or Franck. He is aware of Franck's weaknesses, but shows that some of them exist in single works which had special tasks. The repeated jibe about orchestration that resembles organ registration is seen to apply only to the symphony, and Mr. Demuth shows where and how it applies. He makes several illuminating remarks on Franck's grappling with new problems of structure, including ' cyclic ' form, in the history of which the early *Ce qu'on entend sur la montagne* is shown to be important, though Schubert's *Wanderer* fantasy is not mentioned.

Mr. Demuth holds that Franck's best music is not to be condemned for containing passages that remind us of improvisation ; this treatment is inherent in the materials, and can be found even in the works for which Mr. Demuth reserves his highest eulogies—the quartet and quintet. (Suppose we knew only the violin sonatas, quartets and quintets of Brahms and Franck ? Should we not think almost as highly of Franck's chamber music as does Mr. Demuth ?). It is a great pity that so few people except organists know the " Six Pieces " and the " Three Chorals," and that few organists play the first two of the Chorals, such apotheoses of the improvisatory style, yet such masterpieces of Franckian structure; this corrective commentary is needed, as are Mr. Demuth's remarks on Franck's personal character. Franck was upright and generous at a time when envy, hatred, malice and all uncharitableness seemed to be the attributes of most of the leading musicians in France, and when morals, sexual or commercial, were lax. We are made to see that, though Franck was a sincere churchman, he was neither ascetic nor mystic, except in so far as all composers are potential mystics, and that his reputation has suffered by D'Indy's iconography (the only likeness of the composer known to English readers, in Mrs. Newmarch's translation) and by false quasi-mystical interpretations of the symphony and other works. French criticism soon cleared away D'Indy's portrait of Franck, and it is a pity that some of the French accounts of the composer have not been translated. Meanwhile some of their opinions and comments have been sifted by Mr. Demuth.   A.H.

DESIGN IN MUSIC, *by Gerald Abraham. Pp. 55 ; 3s. 6d.*
   (Geoffrey Cumberlege : Oxford University Press.)
An alarmingly absorbing attempt to explain the truth in wrong, i.e. " simple terms and colloquial language." If that were possible, not even a man of the author's calibre would ever do anything else. I should have loved to send this series of articles (which originally appeared in *Hallé*) for review to the writer who reminded us once in *The Sunday Times* that there was far too much easy writing about music, or something to that effect. None would have judged the booklet better, but alas, it is by him.   H.K.

A DICTIONARY OF MUSICAL THEMES, *by Harold Barlow and*
   Sam Morgenstern. Pp. xiii + 656 ; 30s. 0d. (Williams &
   Norgate.)
THIS awe-inspiring effort has justly become the talk of the town, to which one or two supplementary observations may here be added. While the absence of expression marks in the quoted themes does not matter much, the omission of slurs is irritating. There would seem to be quite a number of misprints in the themes listed ; two chance

glances disclosed three (Dvorák, 315, 316). The quotations from the Introduction (here, as often elsewhere, called " Prelude ") to Act I of Pfitzner's *Palestrina* do not include the opera's most important theme: When the authors did not know a work, they did not apparently always consult someone who did. The plan to include (hardly any other than) " practically all the themes which can be found in compositions that have been recorded " at the time of compilation, furnishes some grotesque results. Thus Franz Schreker is represented by nothing but *The Birthday of the Infanta* and the *Kleine Suite* for chamber orchestra, Schoenberg by Op. 4 and 19, Britten by the four Sea Interludes from *Grimes* (i.e., not the Passacaglia), the oboe quartet, the *Simple Symphony*, and the Bridge-Variations, while Berg or Franz Schmidt do not appear at all. " It is hardly likely that a music student will be haunted by a theme from a composition not yet considered worthy of recording." In point of fact the student is far more likely to be haunted, say, by *Grimes*' Passacaglia theme than by anything from Britten's Phantasy-Quartet. Nor indeed does the main purpose of the book appear to be to appease the haunted music student: " We feel that the book contains almost all the themes [of instrumental works or pieces] the average and even the more erudite listener might want to look up." While the answer to this is a definite NO, neither you nor I would have made a better job of it.   H.K.

GESPRAECHE UEBER MUSIK, *by Wilhelm Furtwangler. Pp. 139 (Atlantis-Verlag, Zuerich, 1948).*
SEVEN talks about music, that is seven monologues by Furtwängler, subtly egged on by the conductor Abendroth in best Boswellian fashion. A slender volume of such clear thinking and timely importance that we should like to write a 500-page comment on it. Instead, we can only give Furtwängler's essentials as we see them (the numbering refers to his chapters) :
(1) The public contributes to the valuation of music only by its involuntary (nowadays mostly repressed) reactions. These become, in the long run, conscious and positive if the effect of a work springs from an entirety of thought (as opposed to the " illegal " effect of details), thus rendering a mere mass of listeners into a community.
(2) The technique of composition is limited by the receptivity of the human ear. The classics, recognizing this, were complicated in *one* department only (e.g. Bach in counterpoint, Beethoven in rhythm). When the grand architecture (i.e. the identity of form and feeling) is lost, the composer's intellect becomes separated from his instincts, emotions, etc., and makes for " arrangements " of impulsive but short-winded effects.
(3) As in poetry, so in music the epic precedes the dramatic. The three aggregate states of all music : " being " (Bach), " happening " (Mozart), " becoming " (Beethoven). Unlike in poetry, the tragical has to be overcome by joy in order to induce musical catharsis.
(4) Thoughts on Beethoven. The determinedly simple articulation of his ideas lays him open to " literary " explanations.
(5) The composing of an age is always reflected in its reproductive

art. Thus, the great technique of modern performers and conductors is a thing of training, away from the living music. In rehearsing, details are decided on and " bottled up " for performance. Our fear of improvisation in a performance springs from the insecurity of our musical instincts, while, on the other hand, all the great musical forms have been developed empirically from improvisation.

(6) In the strife of musical factions (old *v.* new, European *v.* nationalistic) the material (or idiom) of a composition is mistaken for its content (Wagner's tragedy). But this idiom soon ages, and only then we can judge whether the composer was a mere individualist or obeyed the natural laws of music. Nowadays, this issue is confused by the historian trying to teach the composer.

(7) Diatonic music is " natural " since it conforms to " vital biological values," viz., key-centre : sense of locality ; cadence : tension and relaxation. Atonal music is instinctively refused by most as being hostile to life (all art being, in essence, anthropomorphic) ; but it keeps its place since it expresses the despondent intellectualism of our age. The geocentric Ptolemaic-Christian cosmology which up to now has unconsciously informed all music, is superseded in atonal music for the first time by the composer's acute awareness of a large, mechanical, inhuman cosmos " beyond good and evil."

It may seem from this précis that Furtwängler is utterly didactic— but, far from this, his writing is explicit, warm, urbane, with a welter of good reasoning supporting his contentions. " Man is the Measure of all Art" could be written over it—an admirable maxim, yet one that is hardly understood to-day, though a lot of unthinking lip-service is paid to it. My only quarrel with Furtwängler is that his concept of Artistic Man is too narrow : Man is certainly bound by the biological limits of his physis but only the smallest part of these limits have been explored yet. For instance, it is quite conceivable that when psychology has shed light on the interaction of intellect, impulse and emotion, the postulated antagonism between speculative practising and improvisation in a musical performance will simply fall away—as indeed it does to-day in some lucky individuals like Furtwängler himself. Also—in the case of atonal music—the step to the Copernican system has now been made in all the arts, for good or ill, and we shall have to wait and see how music will come to terms with what we have so far narrowly considered its one and only biological attachment. Furtwängler is clearly biassed here, for what he says elsewhere about the public's conscious reactions and about factions in music invalidates his own argument in talk No. 7. But these are defaults of courage, not of sense. For its eminent, and quite uncommon sense the book should be read by every thinking musician,   P.H.

HARPSICHORD MUSIC, *by Max Kenyon; pp. 256; 18s. 0d.* (*Cassell & Co.*)
THERE is something to be respected in the unguarded zest with which Mr. Kenyon has assembled his strange assortment of fact and fancy, of intuition and idiocy. I can understand how this book came to be written, though not how, in its present form, it came to

be published. There are, after all, good scholars in Mr. Kenyon's field. There is the Royal Musical Association; there is the Galpin Society with its team of diverse specialists, willing to help enquirers on any question of instruments or instrumental music likely to have entered Mr. Kenyon's head. They could have pruned out for him the mistakes now staring from every other page. Why offer the fruits of such keen laborious endeavour in so unripe a state, driving every knowledgeable reviewer to reluctant censure ? Even a bad book takes a great deal of writing ; it is no pleasure to condemn it. But as it stands, Mr. Kenyon's is certainly a bad book, despite his directness and his marked though undisciplined talent for writing. The following brief selection is unfortunately typical :

" The spinet is quite unimportant, in exactly the same way as the baby grand, which it vaguely resembles . . ." (Vaguely is the word.) " But the virginal is of great importance." " To my mind there is no real difference between the virginal instrument and the spinet instrument."

" The harpsichord was the great instrument of Europe : it dominated the opera, the oratorio, what passed for orchestral music " (why the sneer ?) " and it was essential for, though it did not dominate chamber music." (Overstatement amounting to distortion.)

" The English Virginal school is the one branch of instrumental music in which this country is pre-eminent." No; our viol music and virtuosi were acknowledged leaders in the 17th century.

" At the time when we began to import our Kings we also began to import our composers." Vivid, but pre-dated by over half a century, and only partially true even then. " Shakespeare " (in his 128th sonnet) " should not have said 'jacks,' 'keys' was the right word." Poor Shakespeare was not, however, the only Elizabethan to use ' jack ' in this unusual sense. (Premature rejoicing.)

" Gibbons is Jacobean and even Caroline." Gibbons and James I both died in 1625. " In English musical history, there was a diminution, almost a gap, during the reign of Charles I and the ensuing Commonwealth." A hoary chestnut this, though Charles I seems to be an addition of Mr. Kenyon's own. (Unfamiliarity with the commonplaces of recent research.) " A peculiarity of French clavecins is that they usually have two sets of strings, instead of only one set." Two (or more) sets of strings are not of course peculiar to French harpsichords ; but I think Mr. Kenyon is merely trying to say that French taste was particularly insistent on this feature. Incidentally, to call an English harpsichord a harpsichord, a French one a clavecin, an Italian one a cembalo and a German one (of all far-fetched names) a Flügel*, is a lapse into pointless and confusing pedantry surprising in our unpedantic author, who to cap it writes of the German music of J. S. Bach: " In modern times we have

---

*The French term is at least exact, but the German isn't. Nowadays, Flügel (lit. ' wing ') is almost exclusively applied to the grand pianoforte, while the ' German ' word for ' harpsichord ' is ' cembalo.' The *Grove* article on ' Flügel ' is therefore misleading.—Ed. (H.K.)

Flügel (or to be pedantically precise, clavecin) recitals giving this music on the instrument for which it was composed. But there are only a few harpsichordists . . ."

" At the French Court music had little place." As a description of one of the most brilliant musical centres of Mr. Kenyon's period, inadequate. Couperin cited : " on ne peut enfler, ny diminuer ses sons." Mr. Kenyon commenting : " Couperin is quite clear. The clavecin is a beautiful but inexpressive instrument." Couperin is certainly quite clear ; but that is not what he said. " Clavichords made in the twentieth century usually . . . have one string to a note." Two. Clavichord tone " may be increased, decreased or prolonged not so well, but in the same manner, as the human voice." The clavichord is a wonderfully expressive instrument, but this is an optimistic account of the *Bebung* technique. The harpsichord jack is " knocked downwards with sufficient escaping action as to avoid striking the string twice." It is not the jack which escapes, but the plectrum, and this does not avoid striking the string a second time, though almost noiselessly, on its return journey. " The Purcell Suite in G Minor seems almost to consist of delicious double wobbles, presumably executed before the beat." Why presume when contemporary authorities clearly prescribe ornaments not before but on the beat ? Why casually dismiss " the authoritian Dolmetsch " (who also happened to be a genius) as laying down " laws " (in fact he merely quoted them from numerous early authorities) " which if followed always and followed exactly, would dehydrate most music ?" As well practise psycho-analysis while dismissing Freud. " Personally," writes Mr. Kenyon, " I distrust these quotations from Quantz." Personally, I distrust these whimsies from Mr. Kenyon.

R.D.

HINRICHSEN'S MUSICAL YEAR BOOK. *Vol. VI. 1949/1950. Pp. 416 ; 15s. 0d. (Hinrichsen.)*

MR. HINRICHSEN continues his invaluable work. The mixture is much the same as before (as it necessarily must be where indices and bibliographies are concerned), but we have news of music in Iceland and Egypt, a fascinating list of all the known names of British bell-founders, and a discerning account of " The Year's Opera " by Desmond Shawe-Taylor. Mr. G. Handley-Taylor's perfumed and precious account of " Italian Ballet To-day " (" the names . . . still sparkled like scintillating dewdrops in the twilight webs," etc.) is the only weak piece in an otherwise informed and scholarly production.

D.M.

KATHERINE DUNHAM, HER DANCERS, SINGERS, MUSICIANS. *Edited, and with an Introduction by Richard Buckle ; pp. xvi+79; 20s. (Ballet Publications.)*

RICHARD Buckle's handsome tribute to Katherine Dunham shows the enormous advances made in recent years in the action photography of ballet. On most pages the text is confined to brief captions; the emphasis is on Roger Wood's photographs, skilfully adjusted as to size and position by the editor so as to make a varied and exciting impact on the eye. In fact Roger Wood's photographs are so good that they flatter Katherine Dunham's choreography, which is rarely as effective as it here appears. She makes use of a certain number of interesting traditional movements, but these are padded out with a mass of routine steps which are characteristic of the American free dance, and which have no precise expressive significance. Fortunately she has trained a splendid company; they work like demons to bring out every nuance in the choreography, and their vitality is apparent in every photograph.

F.H.

THE NEOHELLENIC FOLK-MUSIC, *by Solon Michaelides. Cyprus, 1948.*

I AM a little vague as to the purpose of a book which does nothing but (a) repeat for the thousandth time the history of those modes which have affected the tonality of Western music, and (b) quotes a number of Neohellenic Folk-tunes. H.T.

" OPÉRA COMIQUE," *by Martin Cooper ; pp. 71 ; 7s. 6d. (Max Parrish.)*

THE books in " The World of Music " series are the best value on the present-day market. The chief difficulty about them is that so much has to be compressed into so small a space that much of interest has to be left unsaid. Mr. Cooper succeeds better than one or two of the other contributors to this series, probably because he has had a good journalistic experience. The book is, of course, factual, and although now and again the reader gets an insight into Mr. Cooper's personal opinions, I should have liked to have seen more of them. Mr. Cooper writes easily, although I can find no real signs of that " Gallic lightness of touch " which the " blurb " tells us is there. At any rate he avoids that schoolboy enthusiasm which is the hall mark of the amateur.

Two details require comment. The name of Charles Simon Favart does *not* " grace to this day the small square " in which the present Opéra-Comique stands.   The square in question is the Place Boïeldieu ; one of the streets crossing it is the Rue Favart, the one the other side being the Rue Marivaux, A small point but one liable to lead Mr. Cooper's readers into difficulties. Secondly, he tries to shiver a lance in defence of Cherubini by ascribing his reputation of being a pedant largely to the malice of Berlioz. Surely he knows that there is more factual evidence than this, since he has studied the period. If he has not read Cherubini's book on counterpoint, I suggest that a week-end with it may give him the insight into Cherubini's attitude.

One other small criticism, which also applies to many other books : Quotations from foreign texts should always be translated, even if the translation has to be literal. Not all Mr. Cooper's readers have his familiarity with the French language, and these books are not for experts.

I have nothing but admiration for the adroit manner in which Mr. Cooper steers clear of Opéra when so often it would have been easy to have drifted along its tempting channels. I regret that there was no space for more details about the actual theatres. What information there is I find fascinating. The book, written with all the authority of careful research which I am perfectly willing to take for granted, is very readable—and enjoyable.   N.D.

THE PROMS, by *Thomas Russell ;   pp. 72 ;   7s. 6d.   (Max Parrish.)*

MR. Russell writes critically of the Proms that " more attention is given to the problem of attracting a steady audience of five thousand a night than leading the audience along new paths in music." But the whole essence of the Proms lies in their popularity. They provide a broad base on which more selective tastes can subsequently be raised. Mr. Russell should address his pen to the arrangers of week-end concerts in London.

For the rest, he has told the story of the Proms well, and the illustrations to the book are interesting. Particularly enjoyable is a sketch of Sir Henry Wood by Edmund Knapp. It captures quite exactly the stance of the conductor and the characteristic sweep of his baton.   P.He.

SIXTEEN SYMPHONIES, *by Bernard Shore, with a Foreword by Sir Adrian Boult; pp. 387; 17s. 6d. (Longmans, Green & Co.)*

THIS pleasantly unbuttoned book strikes me as better value than many far more pretentious volumes. It may bring the adult reader up short for a moment to be told that " horns now add their popples of approval "; yet after all, I know at once and exactly what it is Mr. Shore means. The stylist in me cannot quite repress a frown: so I turn to the O.E.D., there to find, to my own astonishment, that popple has even a statutory existence: " rolling, tossing, ripple." Popple be it then; and having swallowed popple, I shall certainly not strain at the rest of Mr. Shore's slightly unconventional vocabulary. He is eminently readable. The book alternates between general discussions of his sixteen selected composers and detailed descriptions of single symphonies by each of them. The general chapters conjure up, by a palatable mixture of biography, anecdote and comment, an atmosphere favourable to an enjoyment of each symphony. The detailed chapters are in the form of glorified programme notes, describing the musical material in the order of its appearance, and drawing attention to a dozen or two of especial felicities on the way. As befits this approach, there are excellent photographs to bring us closer to the composers, and musical quotations to illustrate their symphonies. What raises the whole far above the programme note level is a real gift for interesting writing. Like a good talker at ease, Mr. Shore lets fall the occasional inanity (" Schubert, seemingly fresh as when he began the symphony . . . ") which is the price of informality; but his touch is always light and generally sure. All writing about music that is not technical is metaphorical; Mr. Shore's choice of images is refreshingly free, inventive, and successful in conveying both information and excitement. It is imbued with that unmistakable ring of conviction which only a good craftsman writing about his own craft can evoke. Mr. Shore has left the orchestral desk from which he conceived his previous and perhaps more original book, *The Orchestra Speaks;* but he carries with him his inside knowledge of the symphonic experience. It would be a dull talker with whom we never disagreed. I really did jump to learn, for example, that " no such good music as the Pastoral Symphony has been written by anyone since "; even so I can sympathise with the mood in which this peculiarly reckless statement was penned.

The composers are Haydn (88th Symphony), Mozart (40th), Beethoven (Pastoral), Schubert (Ninth), Schumann (D Minor), Brahms (First), Dvořák (G), Berlioz (Fantastic), Franck (D), Tchaikovsky (Pathetic), Sibelius (Second), Elgar (Second), Vaughan Williams (London), Holst (Planets), Bax (Third), Walton (B Flat). In some respects a very personal choice, as a result of which, however, the author's heart is in his work.

R.D.

THE MAKING OF MUSIC (' *How to recognize and understand orchestral music*), by *Cedric Cliffe. Pp. 335 ; 12s. 6d. (Cassel.)* THE ORCHESTRA, *by Adam Carse. Pp. 71 ; 7s. 6d. (Max Parrish).*

MR. CLIFFE likes to admit to " purely personal " prejudices—about modern music, about old music, about Mahler, about Delius —but then, a book is not a chat in a pub, and why pay money for " personal prejudice " and the slang of the officers' mess if we can consult better opinion ? " A book by an amateur written for amateurs " simply will not do.* There are experts (whom Mr. Cliffe is pleased to call " pundits ") for that job. As might be expected, Mr. Cliffe lowers music to the man-in-the-street, instead of pulling him up to it. He pleads for the " normality," the " common sense " of music, and first of all, for the sporting fun of spotting the composer. This kind of shilly-shallying is absolutely harmful, in art as in religion. Mr. Cliffe's second general mistake is his quasi-evolutionary view of musical history : everything gets bigger and better, and Beethoven's orchestra is " better " than Bach's. *But:* some of the quieter passages are written with real educational clarity, and there are some brilliant ideas (for instance his comparing Bach's and Handel's styles via the " Air on the G-string " and the " Largo "). On the whole, if I for one be allowed to venture a " personal " opinion, Mr. Cliffe would make a good educator if he underwent two years of Pythagorean schooling.†

Mr. Carse's book is much smaller and less ambitious, but here is a man who really knows how to educate the music-lover by putting things clearly and non-technically while never lowering the station of music. With its prints and coloured reproductions the book is both charming and good value.

P.H.

*The blind leading the blind ?—ED. (D.M.).
†Mr. Cliffe might learn that Hugo Wolf has only one F in it—not two as in his book.—ED. (D.M.).

Concerts and Opera

Arranged in chronological order.

ELGAR FESTIVAL. *Albert Hall, May 30th—June 15th.*

A WELCOME opportunity of making up our minds. To speak my own: Elgar's greatness lies in his symphonic works. As Shaw characteristically insisted at the time, all oratorios (with barely exceptions enough to prove the rule) are boring; Elgar's, despite their sincerity, contrive to be churchy without being religious. Some splendid singing and some sanctimonious : but no material injustice was done to the composer.

Both symphonies are long and loose enough to collapse beneath their own weight in a bad performance. But not so in a good one. Striding; brooding; triumphing: if your temperament is congenial at all, they mould you to their mood from first note to last. Boult did even better with No. I than Barbirolli (who for once sacrificed momentum, slightly, to nuance) did with No. II. Barbirolli's *Enigma*s neared perfection; Boult and Fournier rose fully to the Violoncello Concerto, the subtlest and most concise, as it is the last of Elgar's masterpieces. *Falstaff*, his most mercurial, went well enough under Sargent. Heifetz is too steely for the Violin Concerto; but in any case this is a far less even work. Mary Jarred's contralto soli in the (for an Elgarian choral work) unusually spontaneous *Music Makers* were so magnificent that I must applaud them, though space forbids a detailed appraisal of the singers.

R.D.

LONDON PHILHARMONIC ORCHESTRA, *Royal Albert Hall, 9th June, 1949, c. George Szell.*

MR. SZELL has few mannerisms and makes little fuss. All is very precise and orderly ; he is strict but not a martinet. Beethoven's 8th Symphony appeared to its great advantage from Mr. Szell's scholarly but bright and energetic reading. Not so Strauss' " Don Juan." Here the bare bones were a little too noticeable, highly polished, but nevertheless lacking their decent covering of flesh. It is never wise to expose a Strauss skeleton at the expense of all else, and Mr. Szell pushed Don Juan through his multiple *amours* at such a vigorous pace that romance went by the board and only the mechanics of copulation remained. Mr. Clifford Curzon was the admirable soloist in Beethoven's E♭ Concerto.

D.M.

LONDON PHILHALMONIC ORCHESTRA, *Royal Albert Hall, 16th June, 1949; c. Jean Martinon.*

THE experimental reduction in prices at this concert was a decided success: four times the usual number of seats were sold, yet the takings still failed to balance expenses.

The orchestra played without unusual distinction ; in the "Paris" Symphony the sensitive, quiet reading was marred by some rather imperfect ensemble, expecially in the wood-wind. A thoughtful, carefully shaped performance of the Elgar Serenade for Strings lacked breadth and warmth of feeling, particularly in the slow movement.

The orchestra and conductor were at their best in the vital and brilliantly-scored Roussel suite, " Bacchus et Ariane." The principals of the orchestra were outstanding in the many difficult solo passages.

Berlioz' Symphonie Fantastique was given an unexciting performance lacking in bite and drive in the more frenzied passages. The Conductor's departures from the score in the use of *rubati* were misplaced and irritating and served only to weaken the power of the music.

R.T.

W.M.A. SINGERS, *King George's Hall, 16th June, 1949, c. Alan Bush.*

THIS programme included the first performance of Wilfrid Mellers' " News from Greece," for mezzo soprano (Esther Salaman), chorus (W.M.A. Singers), two pianos (Paul Hamburger and Helen Pyke), three trumpets and percussion. Owing to the smallness of the stage and the consequent overcrowding of choir and instrumentalists it was difficult to judge whether or not Mr. Mellers was justified in his scoring. Nevertheless it was apparent that much had been accomplished with little means, and the simple narrative made its point both musically and politically, without the politics obscuring the music or becoming a bore. Mr. Mellers' lament rang true enough, particularly in the cantata's third and last part, where much of the best music lies. The work is an interesting example of what M. René Leibowitz* has termed " committed " art, i.e. art which has extra-artistic characteristics. But it would be hard to say on this one hearing whether Mr. Mellers has succeeded in so realising his artistic preoccupations that they have become "a vivid expression of, and a real tribute to " the social realities that provided the initial impulse for his composition. D.M.

**Horizon, XX/116/1949.*

PELLEAS AND MELISANDE, *Covent Garden, June 16th.*

IN the long tradition of opera, *Pelléas* is one of the greatest and most remarkable achievements. It is at once the debtor and the antithesis of the Wagnerian music drama. Debussy's chromatic harmony stems like so much twentieth century music from Tristan ; the manner of its use does not. Where Wagner is passionate, Debussy is poignant ; where Wagner intensifies, Debussy understates. In the upshot, Debussy comes nearer than any composer, Wagner not excluded, to the avowed aim of the first Italian founders of opera : his characters appear to be quietly talking—but, as it happens, in music. Brief and disjointed as the scenes appear, reticent as the singers must remain, there is a naturalness and inevitability in all that is said and expressed, which by the climax of the opera, the scene of Pelléas' avowal and death, have mounted to an uncanny completeness. What carries them there is, of course, the quality of the music. There is no romantic passion, nor much architecture. But there is an unfailing glow, like a subterranean fire. The flow of melody, so unobstrusive but so lovely, never flags; the harmony, so economically proportioned to the situation, never falls below it. To achieve that apothesis of sensibility, Debussy must have been not merely inspired but possessed.

Desormière, by a miracle not less remarkable in its kind, brought our weary Covent Garden orchestra into a very creditable semblance of the soaring, melting tissue of sound demanded by this celestial score. But the Opéra Comique singing was more than a semblance; I had little fault to find. Etcheverry's Goland was the most powerful performance, not unnaturally since this is the only rôle which calls for, or admits of power. Mélisande is scarcely a woman, merely the undeveloped potentiality of one, and the passivity of Irène Joachim's acting struck me as well in character, while her pure, supple singing gave great pleasure. Pelléas is scarcely less fey, and still more innocent; Jansen both sang and acted him as he should be. From Jacqueline Cellier's Yniold to Froumenty's Arkel, the cast were admirable; the production was unfussy; the sets were colourful, sketchy, and all the better for leaving so much to the imagination.

R.D.

THE PROMS, 1949 : FIRST PERFORMANCES.

ALAN RAWSTHORNE : CONCERTO FOR STRING ORCHESTRA, *11th August.*

THE laconic style, as opposed to mere "bitty-ness," is much rarer in music than in literature, since only few composers, and still fewer listeners, are keen-eared enough to perceive, *and* leave unsaid, the associative links between several lapidary statements. Rawsthorne is one of these few, making us feel, rather as T. S. Eliot does, by his meaningful conciseness, that our musical, or general, education has been far from thorough. Nor can one say of his latest full-scale work, as one could of the Sonatina,* that its material is not worked out in all its possibilities : here it is just a case of very individual material asking for so much working-out, and no more. This is most apparent in the first movement, in strictest sonata form, with three well-defined subjects, the first contrapuntal, the second a lyrical passage for solo viola (the few solo passages occur in the 1st and 3rd movements, the slow movement being, as it were, a solo for the whole orchestra); a short development in double-counterpoint being followed by the emotional climax of the movement, a quiet solo-violin passage over a string-tremolo; followed in turn by a shortened recapitulation. The 2nd movement, a kind of chaconne, has the same 4-note motto as "La Folia," used by Corelli and others, and has some of the grave charm of those early Italian chaconnes. Whether the quotation is conscious or not, one thing is certain: Rawsthorne's musical roots strike very deep. Lastly comes a serious *Rondo*, thematically related to the first

*See my review in Music Survey, Vol. II, No. 1.

movement, with a quiet, almost stagnant first episode, and a fugue as second episode. The main section is progressively shortened until at last the few firm chords of the 2nd subject that are left put their foot down and call a halt. The work should speedily be published in miniature score.

WILLIAM ALWYN: CONCERTO FOR OBOE, STRINGS AND HARP, *12th August*.

GRATEFUL writing for the oboe, but otherwise a very sorry makeshift. The orchestral lay-out, with its long sequences of 6/5/3 and 7/5/3 floating gently around a key-note *à la* Delius, and its little tidal onrushes crowned with a bit of dripping harp-seaweed, is filmy in more senses than one. Add to this the " effective " beginning (orchestral motto—oboe cadenza—motto—cadenza—motto—real start) where Tristan's shepherd, obviously long after his master's demise, is treated to a holiday by the Irish sea. Add further the kittenish, it's-fun-to-be-coy nine-eight rhythm of the *Vivace*, the styleless interspersion, in the same movement, of modal harmony with whole sequences of leading-note transitions into secondary functions, and the academic bass and treble pedal-notes plus sliding chords above or below, of the last section. There is any amount of motivic work within and between the movements, but none of it is cogent. For instance, the motto of the beginning (keynote—semitone down—keynote—semitone up—keynote) is simplified later on, one of the semitonal steps being inverted into a major 7th—a good, normal device, it seems but in the context quite unconvincing. The very last 12 bars or so struck me as excellent.

GORDON JACOB: FANTASIA ON THE ALLELUIA HYMN, *16th August*.

A FRIENDLY and homely improvisation in the true and trusty key of G major. Unpretentious in its neat if obvious design, it includes several sections of charmingly scholastic polyphony, culminating in a big brassy statement of the hymn-tune. As Hubert Foss' programme-note says: a very good piece for the semi-amateur orchestra.

LEIGHTON LUCAS: CHACONNE IN C MINOR, *29th August*.

CONDUCTOR's music ?—Yes. The orchestration is brilliant. But how much more ? The form is certainly as it ought to be, with its pungent, if somewhat sudden, restatements of the theme, its quiet episodes for solo instruments, and its accumulative use of theme-plus-countersubjects. As to the substance of the music, I find myself at a loss. The work exhibits much of the uncompromising ebullience of, say, the later Bartok, and also the unexpected probing into unknown territory found with the better of modern composers. One is apt to regard these as the symptoms of a strictly logical mind at work; but whether Mr. Leighton Lucas gives us the genuine article, or just " une attitude de logique", I should only be able to decide upon seeing the score.

126

BLOCH: 'CONCERTO SYMPHONIQUE' FOR PIANO AND ORCHESTRA (*First London Perf.*, *Sept. 6th. Piano: Corinne Lacomblé; c. by the composer.*)

Two matters pictorial impress themselves on the listener in all of Bloch's bigger works: (a) we seem to travel up and down Jewish history, i.e. Bloch's music is not written in a definite tense but slides continuously between Present, both Perfects and Pluperfect, with occasional glimpses of Future.* (b) The unquestionable nobility of his music is not one of rank but one of deserts—in other words: this music is great not because it has been written but because it was possible to write it. By which I do not mean at all that Bloch is a mediocre talent made good by hard work, but rather that his original approach, the fact that he compels music to speak like this, makes us overlook much that is trite in the nature of his musical substance. Since both (a) and (b) are, strictly speaking, processes alien to the laws of music, Bloch is always in danger of being more interesting than beautiful. While a work like " Schelomo " deeply impresses us by Bloch's meritorious courage of stating the only just Beautiful, in the " Concerto Symphonique " the balance is tilted towards the interesting, and the trite. I am aware that this is a very severe pronouncement, and I hasten to add there are many arresting details: his beginning the recapitulation in the first movement with a solo cadenza on the first subject, followed by the second subject as orchestral-tutti ; the gradual brightening in the major trio of the scherzo, and the superb orchestration. But, on the whole, the alleged " Roman legions " of " Schelomo " never stop moving—they parade, quick-march, run and trample in the variegated 2/4 step of all the movements—the muted horns never cease calling to action, and the grief of the oppressed hangs like a dark cloud over their infrequent rejoicings. All this is symbolized by the treatment of the solo part: In " Schelomo," the truly " concertant " (contesting) 'cello stood for the individual, receiving support and suffering opposition from the orchestral masses; in the " Concerto Symphonique," the pianist is vanquished by the orchestra while being constitutionally unable to become a part of it: This is the individual crushed by the masses.

*His codas (for instance the one in the first mov. of this work) are the nearest ever approach to " Futurum exactum " in music—as though Bloch were saying: " Sometime, what I have told you will be clear to you."

LENNOX BERKELEY: " COLONUS' PRAISE " (*Yeats*) *for Mixed Choir and Orchestra*, *September 13th; c. Leslie Woodgate.*

AN excellent work, but given its wealth of musical ideas and its elaborate apparatus, much too short. One can quite see the problem this poem presents to the composer: on the one hand, the jolly, jerky allusiveness and the rhapsodic, though short-breathed lyricism of Yeat's poem suit Berkeley's style admirably; on the other hand, any poetry set to music has a natural tendency to bide its time; to blossom out into a welter of musical invention which, by its sheer compositional impact, must needs stretch the form. Now, Berkeley was quite right here not to give way to this " natural tendency" of music, for one cannot spin out the poet's exuberance, nor can one break his teasing allusiveness by long orchestral interludes. One can but find musical equivalents for these qualities, and this Berkeley does with unfailing instinct: the fanfare of the beginning returns in short gusts of brassy chords; the many *a cappella* sections are followed by immediate orchestral tutti or are punctuated by solo instruments gathering towards a tutti; all fugal parts are short and lively; and the few quiet passages have just the touch of maudlin sentiment that underlies Yeat's fervour. Yet all the time, musical substance clings and clusters round the poet's words crying out to be treated at length. The only solution I can think of would have been to combine " Colonus' Praise " with some similar poem in Yeat's graecizing vein, using the same musical material for building an overall musical structure.

P.H.

Gramophone Records

HAYDN : The Seven Last Words from the Cross. Op. 51. Griller String Quartet. Decca. AK 2139—2147. 42s. 9d.
A sensitive and even recording of major music.

MOZART : Divertimento in D. K.131, and Minuet and Trio from Divertimento in B Flat. K287. Royal Philharmonic Orchestra (Sir Thomas Beecham). H.M.V. DB 6649-51. 18s.
No one can question the excellence of this set. It is good Mozart, good Beecham, and very good engineering. Of the seven movements the opening *Allegro* and the final *Allegro Assai* seem the most diverting.

MOZART : Concerto for Piano and Orchestra in E Flat. K. 271. Lili Kraus and the Philharmonia Orchestra (Walter Susskind). Parlophone. R.20570-3. 24s.
A bad and ill-recorded performance. I prefer the earlier Gieseking recording.

HAYDN : Symphony No. 40 in F Major. Royal Philharmonic Orchestra. (Sir Thomas Beecham.) H.M.V. D.B.6823-4. 12s.
A mature work of Haydn's middle period, outstandingly played and well 'recorded. It compels a hope that more such will be resuscitated.

MOZART : Sonata for Piano in B Flat. K.570. Artur Schnabel. H.M.V. D.B.6839-40. 12s.
The contrapuntal texture of this late sonata is intelligently delineated without a loss of the sense of the total structure. The finale is an interesting example of Mozart's interests and achievements in the last years of his life.   P.J.C.

*Strongly recommended.

SCHUMANN : Symphony No. 1, Op. 38. National Symphony Orchestra (Coppola). Decca. A.K 2151-4. 19s.

Coppola should have concentrated more on the architecture of the symphony; over-emphasis of its lyricism makes it flabby and unconvincing. The best played movement is the unexpectedly severe *scherzo*. The orchestra is competent but rather lifeless.

*NIELSEN : Sinfonia Espansiva. Radio Symphony Orchestra, Copenhagen (Erik Tuxen) ; and Overture—Maskarade. Decca A.K. 2161-65. 23s. 9d.

Decca must be congratulated on their initiative. This is not music that strikes one immediately as original, but closer acquaintance reveals a genuine musical personality and a musical mind into the bargain. It seems a pity that solo voices had to be dragged into the slow movement ; they give the music a programmatic tendency, and a rather self-conscious pastoral flavour. The last movement finds it difficult to live up to the tune with which it starts. The work (is it a symphony ?) is magnificently performed and recorded.

*STRAUSS : Don Quixote, Op. 35. Royal Philharmonic Orchestra (Sir Thomas Beecham). Leonard Rubens (Viola) and Paul Tortelier ('Cello). H.M.V. D.B. 6796-6800. 30s.

As might be expected, Beecham gives an authoritative reading of this score ; one which must be very close to his heart. A brilliant set very satisfactorily recorded. The eloquent 'cello part might have been a little more rhapsodically played.

*STRAVINSKY : Symphony of Psalms (1930). London Philharmonic Orchestra, London Philharmonic Choir (Ernest Ansermet). Decca A.K. 1753-5. 14s. 3d.

A superb performance of this great work, perfectly recorded. Ansermet pays meticulous attention to the instructions of the score, save in the third movement where Stravinsky's *non crescendos* in the tenor line are ignored.

OFFENBACH : " O mon cher amant je te jure" : "Ah Quel diner" : " Mon Dieu, Que les hommes sont bêtes " : " Je t'adore " : " Belle Nuit, O Nuit d'Amour." Jennie Tourel with Orchestra (Maurice Abravanel). Columbia. L.B. 79-80. 8s.

These extracts from " La Périchole " and " The Tales of Hoffmann " are most expertly and stylishly sung. Interesting to observe that Ravel's declamatory vocal line is a direct descendent from the Paris music halls. The recording is good, although the orchestra, particularly the strings, might have been further amplified.

WAGNER : Overture, "Die Meistersinger von Nürnberg." Orchestre de la Suisse Romande (Hans Knappertsbusch). Decca K.1905. 4s. 9d.

A resonant recording, but the performance has neither the vitality nor rhythmic excitement of the Beecham Columbia, which is to be preferred.

*Strongly recommended.

*BERLIOZ : Roméo et Juliette, Op. 17. N.B.C. Symphony Orchestra (Toscanini). H.M.V. D.B. 6665-7. 18s.

Strange music, not truly romantic ; rather the product of a keen analytical mind, dissecting the human heart with as little real passion as a scientist. The recording is not as harsh as most from America and the performance less mechanical than might have been expected of Toscanini. An important set.

*BACH : Concerto in E major. Gioconda de Vito (violin), London Chamber Orchestra (Anthony Bernard). H.M.V. 6884-5. 18s.

A quite outstanding recording. The soloist is brilliant and the orchestra does more than provide a sympathetic accompaniment. This set supersedes the old Menuhin. A very fine issue indeed.

STRAUSS : Suite from " Der Rosenkavalier," Op. 59. Philadelphia Orchestra (Eugene Ormandy). Columbia L.X. 1183-5. 18s.

The recording is strident and the music disagreeably overplayed and romanticised beyond all measure. In addition the orchestra seems to have a faulty sense of rhythm; the beginning of the famous trio from Act III is suspended in a vague mist of tremulous hesitancy, which bears little resemblance to the score of the opera.

*MILHAUD : Scaramouche, Suite for two pianos and Benjamin : Jamaican Rumba and Mattie Rag. Phyllis Sellick and Cyril Smith. Columbia D.X. 1554-5. 8s.

A delightful suite, capitally played, and recorded at a range that includes the high and low registers of two pianos. More Milhaud must be recorded—particularly the orchestral Suites Provençal and Française.

DEBUSSY : La Mer. Orchestre de la Suisse Romande (Ernest Ansermet). Decca A.K. 1606-8. 14s. 3d.

A performance that stresses the sinister aspect of Debussy's miraculous score. The orchestra is good although the brass is rough in places. It would be a help if the labels stated the version of the score recorded.

BOCCHERINI : String Quartet in D Major, Op. 6, No. 1. New Italian Quartet. Decca. A.K. 2173-4. 9s. 6d.

Boccherini did write some extremely effective and interesting quartets of historical importance. It is a pity that Decca chose to record this early work which is quite undistinguished and has nothing to commend it but the excellent playing.

STRAVINSKY—trans. DUSHKIN: Pastorale for Violin and Wind Quartet. c. Igor Stravinsky, and Russian Maiden's Song. Szigeti (Violin) and Stravinsky (Piano). Columbia L.X. 1174. 6s.

The Pastorale is an amusing piece which none other than Stravinsky could have written. The reverse side is unbelievably dull and uncharacteristic. The recording has an edge like a saw to it.

*Strongly recommended.

PROKOFIEV : " Cinderella." Royal Opera House Orchestra, Covent Garden (*Warwick Braithwaite*). Columbia D.X. 1562-4. 12s.

When the music is alive and deftly descriptive as in the *Midnight Waltz*, the *Gavotte* and the *Sewing Scene*, it is successful and interesting to listen to; but in the *Pas de Deux* and the *Seasons* the ballet spectacle is needed and the music declines to stand on its own feet. The orchestra plays with more spirit than it does normally at Covent Garden and the suite is competently recorded.

D.M.

SIBELIUS : Symphony No. 2 in D major. Op. 43. Philadelphia Orchestra (*Eugene Ormandy*). Columbia L.X. 1175-9. 30s. London Philharmonic Orchestra (*Basil Cameron*). Decca A.K. 2127-32. 23s. 9d.

With monotonous persistence the American companies continue to issue inferior recordings ; possibly long subjection to such aural assaults has weakened their critical faculty.

The Philadelphia recording is a travesty of that orchestra's tonal quality, made in an unresponsive studio which imparts a harsh edginess to the strings. However, the recording cannot be blamed for the inartistry of the performance. The conductor takes unforgivable liberties with the score, particularly in the matter of tempi and dynamics. Mr. Ormandy adopts an excessive speed in the third movement and an unduly slow one in the Andante; in fact, the whole performance is explosive and unfeeling. Subtleties of phrasing and detail are all overlooked in the conductor's desire to emphasise the broad romantic outline of the work.

The Decca set avoids the excessive volume and bad balance of the American recording and is altogether more pleasing. Yet, despite its softer tone it has actually a wider dynamic and tonal range. This is most noticeable in the ff brass passages, which have a firm sonority. The strings of the L.P.O. lack the weight of the Philadelphia's but nearly everywhere their smaller numbers are an advantage and Mr. Cameron obtains greater purity of style, though not greater precision of attack. Added to this is more gracious wind playing and a rich bass. The interpretation has authenticity and restrains within proportion the strong emotional element in the symphony, which belongs to Sibelius' early and more extravagant period.

R.T.

BACH : Passacaglia and Fugue in C Minor. Fernando Germani (*Westminster Cathedral Organ*). H.M.V. C.3866. 4s. 0d.

While the sound of the 11th, 17th, 19th and 20th variations and of the fugue's greater part is a mess, and the interpretation, especially in the fugue, not the best, the music makes us recommend the rest.

HAYDN : Fantasia in C Major. Dennis Matthews. Columbia D.B. 2545. 3s. 0d.

A fair recording of a rushed performance, not up to this pianist's musical and technical standards.

*MOZART : " Madamina !" (Leporello's aria from ' Don Giovanni,
Act I). Erich Kunz with Vienna Philharmonic (Otto Ackermann).
Columbia L.B. 81. 4s. 0d.

Leporello's first phrase is of the last importance, Kunz' rendering
of it ravishing. He knows in fact everything, barring the formal
function of the crotchet in the Andante's bar 36. The recording
is good.

*BEETHOVEN : Sonata in C Major, Op. 2, No. 3. Solomon.
H.M.V. C.3847-9. 12s. 0d.

Excellent, of course, though Beethoven's ' con brio ' makes
Solomon's brilliant passages too brilliant. But what exceptionally
clear understanding of the various meanings of various *sforzati* !
The first movement's coda is a pure and rare joy. The second's
dominant seventh in bar 10/2 is too strong in view of the following
bare octave (not so, therefore, after the theme's return). The fourth
is almost perfect. As for the recording, the end of side 1 would
almost have prevented us from highly recommending the set.

BEETHOVEN : Sonata in C Minor, Op. 30, No. 2, and
SCHUMANN : Allegretto from A Minor Sonata, Op. 105.
Wolfgang Schneiderhahn and Frederick Wührer. Columbia
L.X. 1190-3. 24s. 0d.

The Beethoven is being given a performance of mixed (occasionally
superior) quality in which the violinist unduly dominates the pianist.
He cannot refrain, in syncopations held over the strong beat, to give
the latter a push; shows an exceptionally musical technique in his
changes of position; plays a bit sharp in the 1st movement's second
subject and, both times, at the end of the trio; manages the *cresc.*—
[*subito*] *p* in the slow movement's bars 40—41 well, and that in the
first movement's bars 98—99 ill; shares his partner's ignorance as to
the difference between crotchet and quaver at the end of the Adagio's
C major scale runs.

Schumann's accents on the off-beats do not deter Schneiderhahn
from accenting the beats, and the c' in the 17th bar before the end has
a big tummy. Towards the end of sides 1, 4, and 5, the recording
badly deteriorates.

*SCHUBERT : ' Heidenröslein ' (Op. 3, No. 3) and "Wiegenlied "
(Op. 98, No. 2). Irmgard Seefried with Hermann von Nordberg.
Columbia L.B. 78. 4s. 0d.

Miss Seefried's rarefied voice is excellently recorded ; not so the
piano. The ' Heidenröslein ' (which the label translates as ' Hedge-
roses,' omitting, moreover, its Opus number) is definitely as
' lieblich,' if not quite as lovable as Schubert wants it. There are
some slightly sharp notes before the 2nd strophe's first fermata, and
the differentiation between the end of the last and that of the other
strophes, though well-intentioned, is terribly exaggerated by both
performers. In the lullaby one hears too much breathing.

*Strongly recommended.

VERDI : ' Morrò, ma prima in grazia ' (' Un Ballo in Maschera,'
   Act III) and ' Pace, pace, mio dio ' (' La Forza del Destino,'
   Act IV). Joan Hammond with Philharmonia (Warwick Braith-
   waite). H.M.V. C. 3879. 4s. 0d.
All right rather than right.   H.K.

BRAHMS : Piano Concerto No. 1 in D Minor. Rudolf Serkin and
   Pittsburgh Symphony Orchestra (Fritz Reiner). Columbia
   L.X. 1162-7. 36s. 0d.
In spite of many fine moments, the recording is spoilt by the
blatancy and coarseness one has come to associate with American
recordings. In the performance, the worst fault spoils what is
perhaps the outstanding moment in the whole great first movement,
and is made worse by the negligence which failed to remedy it before
the recording was issued. This is the moment of return, when, over
the rolling pedal D, the piano bursts out, not with the original chord
of B flat, but with a chord of E. The right hand top E is not there,
and the remainder of the chord is a blur until the end of the bar, so
that one of the nineteenth century's greatest flights of structural
imagination goes for nothing. But where was Serkin's integrity, that
he could allow it to be issued in this state ? The finale is superb, and
I have no fault to find with it, except that in the triplet octaves which
swoop down the bass of the second return of the main rondo
subject, the right hand split octaves are not split, but played as
straight octaves. There is no warrant for this alteration, nor is there
for a tied G in the slow movement, at the end of the bar preceding the
transition.
   The interpretation has the real grip of this agonized reaction of
one sane mind to the tragic and inexplicable breakdown of another.
The Backhaus recording I have only heard once and therefore will
not compare with it. The Schnabel is still, in spite of certain wrong
notes, the deepest and most understanding performance of this work
I have heard, but Serkin's is below it only in an understandable
failure of stamina in parts of the first movement and something short
of the deepest perception in the slow movement.   H.T.

VERDI: Un Ballo in Maschera. Complete opera, with Tullio Serafin
   conducting soloists, chorus and orchestra of the Rome Opera
   House. H.M.V. DB9075-9091. £5 2s. 0d.
Narrow-minded Neapolitan censorship tried unsuccessfully to
transplant the seventeenth-century Swedish characters of Scribe's
libretto into mediæval Florentines: but the first performance saw a
Bostonian background, which made the plot even more ridiculous
than ever. Verdi had the strength of mind to triumph over literary
set-backs of this kind, as the present recording shows. The extracts
received give an impression of vivid tone-colour, often (from the
singing angle) a little hard, but well in keeping with the dramatic
feeling. Maria Caniglia, as Amelia, is well cast: she enjoys her two
big arias, 'Ma dall arido stello divulsa' and 'Morrò ma prima in grazia.'
Gigli, as the Governor of Boston, is less convincing, but shows
surprising gubernatorial agility in E scherzo od è follia. The cast also
includes Elda Ribetti, F. Barbieri, Gino Bechi, Tancredi Pasero and
U. Novelli.

PURCELL: If music be the food of love; Music for a while. Alfred Deller (counter-tenor) with Walter Bergmann (harpsichord). H.M.V. C.3890. 4s. 0d.

One of the criteria of musical excellence to-day seems to be bound up with an ability to arrange Purcell. Such arrangements are often far from being successful, and in fifty years' time many editions will have to be purged of their accompaniments, just as mediæval music has been shorn of its false feathers gained through chance excursions into the Victorian drawing-room. In this record, the realizations ring true, however, and the voice is a delight.

MOZART: Symphony No. 41 in C. Vienna Philharmonic Orchestra (Karl Böhm). H.M.V. C.3884-7. 16s. 0d.

Böhm's orchestra in Dresden understood him well, but the Viennese seem (in this recording) a little wary: there is even a suspicion of a clash of temperament which prevents the interpretation from bring either thorough-going on the one hand, or lyrical and translucent on the other. There is ample solidity apparent when Böhm is compared to Walter (with the same orchestra) and many may like their Mozart this way. Some movements gain, others lose—the minuet, for example, lacks the delicacy essential to so chromatic a subject. The recording is good, nevertheless, and space is left for the little overture to *Der Schauspieldirektor*.

BEETHOVEN: Symphony No. 1 in C. New York Philharmonic-Symphony Orchestra (Bruno Walter). Col. LX.1204-7. 24s. 0d.

Walter brings out all the lithe virility, the daring and the self-assurance of this early work. The *con brio* of the first movement is accentuated without distortion, and the strings have a fine crispness about them in the *fugato* passages of the slow movement, rich already in that typically Beethovenian scheme for motives in contrary motion. The third movement, as Walter plays it, makes us understand why this piece inspired Elgar to compose: it has a vigour and dash all of its own, almost without equal in Beethoven's other youthful works. The finale sounds brilliant, though the tempo is about normal. A recording to be recommended, though for some reason there is only $1\frac{1}{4}$ ins. of music on side 2. The available space could so easily have been used up by a Bagatelle, or a talk on Bonn.

GOOSSENS: Oboe Concerto (in one movement). Leon Goossens (oboe) and the Philharmonia Orchestra (Susskind). Col. DX.1578-9. 8s. 0d.

Goossens had at one time a pre-occupation with monothematic structures which often put a strain on his formal conception of a large work. This one-movement Oboe Concerto does not suffer in this way, and there is adequate colour in the accompaniment to fit, and yet stand out from, the flowery solo part, which is impeccably played by Leon Goossens.

IRELAND: The Forgotten Rite. Hallé Orchestra (Sir John Barbirolli). H.M.V. C.3894. 4s. 0d.

There is no programme for this brief, finely wrought tone poem: it evokes, rather than depicts, the darkness and light of pre-history. This atmosphere the Hallé Orchestra seems to understand, through the medium of their guide and conductor, and the playing, especially of the solo flute, is sensitive and imaginative.

D.W.S.

THE ENOCK INSTRUMENT DEMONSTRATED.

At his studio before a small number of critics, Mr. Joseph Enock showed " what could be done with a modern gramophone record." Despite the, for me, painful over-amplification of sound, there seemed to be no doubt that the ' Enock Music Reproducing Instrument ' is what it claims to be, namely, unequalled in fidelity. My only request is that Mr. Enock should not head his prospectus, " Music Re-created." A [machine never (re-)creates, though the majority of contemporary musicians, led by that truly imposing master machine, Toscanini, would persuade us otherwise.

H.K.

MUSIC SURVEY

(KATHLEEN LIVINGSTON   WILLIAM W. LIVINGSTON   DONALD MITCHELL)

VOL. II, No. 3   CONTENTS   WINTER, 1950

MUSIC SURVEY is published quarterly by NEWMAN WOLSEY, 244, HIGH
  HOLBORN, LONDON, W.C.1. Annual Subscription, including postage, 11s.
EDITORIAL CORRRESPONDENCE should be addressed to the EDITORS,
  MUSIC SURVEY, OAKFIELD SCHOOL, WEST DULWICH, LONDON, S.E.21.
All enquiries relating to advertising space in this journal should be made to :
  THE ALDRIDGE PRESS, LTD., 15, CHARTERHOUSE STREET, HOLBORN
  CIRCUS, LONDON, E.C.1.

REVIEWERS :

R.A.	RICHARD ARNELL
N.D.	NORMAN DEMUTH
R.D.	ROBERT DONINGTON
P.A.E.	P. A. EVANS
R.F.	RUDOLF FISCHER
P.H.	PAUL HAMBURGER
H.K.	EDITOR
E.D.M.	ERIC D. MACKERNESS
E.H.W.M.	E. H. W. MEYERSTEIN
D.M.	EDITOR
H.B.R.	H B. RAYNOR
R.S.	ROBERT SIMPSON
D.W.S.	DENIS W. STEVENS

Editorial

IN view of the fact that the widely-read Pelican *Symphony* book (Ed. Ralph Hill) is of extremely uneven quality and has been incompetently reviewed by responsible journals, we have decided to assemble a symposium on the work whose essays by different authors will be examined by H. F. Redlich, Norman Demuth, Robert Simpson, Charles Stuart, William Mann, E. H. W. Meyerstein, A. E. F. Dickinson, John Culshaw, etc., and members of the editorial staff.

This symposium will be published in the Summer issue. The Spring issue will be devoted to discussions from various representative viewpoints of Benjamin Britten's music. It will, incidentally, include a children's symposium on the children's opera.

Obituary

MUSICOLOGY and musical bibliography have suffered a grievous and untimely loss by the sudden death of *Dr. Alfred Loewenberg* on January 2, 1950. Born in Berlin in 1902, he emigrated to England after 1933, where he found a permanent haven of refuge. Later on he became one of this country's most outstanding bibliographers. The crowning achievement of his painstaking and persevering scholarship was the publication of the momentous volume " Annals of Opera " (Cambridge, 1943). As editor and executive officer of the " British Union Catalogue of Periodicals," as chief contributor to Grove's Dictionary (4th and 5th edition), as a widely acknowledged authority on opera librettos and plays with incidental music, Loewenberg held a unique and universally honoured position. He leaves many friends behind who will never forget the sterling qualities that distinguished alike the man and the scholar.

HANS F. REDLICH.

Stravinsky: The Dialectics of Dislike
BY CHARLES STUART

SOMEWHERE in his writings on music George Bernard Shaw tells us that he distrusts judgments based on dislike. If judgments based on dislike are bad, dialectics based on dislike are worse. The contemporary object lesson here is Igor Stravinsky, who has been the target of more sophistry, misconception and general nonsense than any composer since Wagner. In the eyes of the average English critic *Petrushka* is the masterwork. Stravinsky has sinned by not rewriting *Petrushka* once every eighteen months for the past forty years. The more a man's music changes the more it must say the same thing, preferably in the same way. Newness makes us stir on our pillows and mutter mutinously in our half-sleep. The mixture as before is soothing, restful, trouble-saving. Dislike of the post-*Petrushka* works, not because of any internal demerits but simply because they *are* post-*Petrushka*, has made many a good man incapable of seeing, thinking or hitting straight.

1

Let us look at Grove. In the 1928 edition the late H. C. Colles wrote in the article on Form :

> So far as may be judged by the later works of Stravinsky . . . the maintenance of a continuous rhythmic movement *takes the place of recurring features*, and tone colour . . . can become a prime factor in the preservation of unity. While this new technique remains in its present inchoate state, it is impossible to suggest what its outcome in Form may be. (Italics here and in later quotations my own.)

It will be noted that " later works " are undefined. Where in Stravinsky's output did the old formalism end and the new inchoateness begin ? Could not Colles have given us a dividing line ? Hardly. The division does not exist. There are recurring features, thematic and harmonic, all the way through from *Firebird*. The curious thing is that at the time Colles was writing and editing, the principle of recurrence in Stravinsky's music was more evident than ever. The coverage of the 1928 Grove is up to the end of 1925. How could Colles have failed to notice five variations on an air in the Wind Octet of 1923 ? Or the recapitulation of the largo introduction to the Piano Concerto of 1924 ? Or the constant restatements of thematic material in the 1924 Piano Sonata ? Structural characteristic of this kind (there are others more subtle) do not have to be looked for with pneumatic drill and microscope. They leap to any seasoned ear on a first hearing. It would be uncharitable to conclude that Colles was writing about music he had never heard. One is obliged to assume that initial dislike stopped his ears against characteristics that are as plain as a pikestaff.

I turn to the Grove article *en chef*, Eric Blom's Stravinsky essay. I am not greatly concerned in this context with Mr. Blom's violent aversions from particular works. Mr. Blom is entitled, I suppose, to let us know that he finds the Piano Concerto dreary and hollow, *Perséphone* bankrupt of inspiration. (Whether a musical dictionary is the proper place for such a parade of personal taste and its limitations is another matter.) What does concern me is Mr. Blom's efforts to be objective, especially the following passage from the 1928 edition, which I have been re-reading and puzzling over these twenty years :

> The dominating principle that governs the art of Stravinsky from *Petrushka* onwards is *his belief that music should make a purely physical appeal to the hearer*, and should be free from any literary and pictorial associations which address themselves to the intellect. . . In his mature ballets we may observe how his music is raised from the subsidiary form of a mere accompaniment to the dignity of an independent organism *by being made to appeal exclusively to the senses*, while the scenario occupies the mind. The composer's intention is that the two entities should make their impression simultaneously on two distinctly separate faculties.

When, and in what terms, did Stravinsky avow the extraordinary belief that is here imputed to him ? Mr. Blom gives us neither chapter nor verse. I am fairly well acquainted with the Stravinsky record. Never have I come across anything in book or newsprint which remotely resembles this " purely physical appeal " doctrine. E. W. White's recent book (*Stravinsky, A Critical Survey*), which is well documented, certainly makes no mention of it. In any case, the doctrine, as applied to Stravinsky or any other composer, is nonsense.

Stravinsky's music, like all other music, derives its nature from *relation*, the relation of note to note, of note-group to note-group. Relations are apprehended, they are analysed and synthesised, by the intellect, whether or not the intellect reflects while so doing on what it is about. To argue that music may be "addressed to " and therefore assimilated by one's body is so much gibberish. Mr. Blom endorses it. Having endorsed it he refuses to budge. Stravinsky's views on music were expounded in *Chroniques de Ma Vie*. Nowhere in this work does he advance the " purely physical appeal " hypothesis. On the contrary, he defines music as construction in Time which satisfies the human craving for order. As a definition of music this does not get us farther than most. What clearly emerges, however, is the metaphysical, as distinct from physical, character of Stravinsky's approach. The *Chroniques* came out in 1935; the coverage of Grove's 1940 Supplement takes us up to the end of 1938. Surely there was opportunity here for Grove to bring itself doctrinally up to date ? But no: what Stravinsky really thinks about music is ignored by the 1940 Supplement. To this day we are fobbed off by the mumbo-jumbo of 1928.

2

And now for the dread Mr. Newman. When, in *Poétique Musicale*, Stravinsky detrimentally compared Beethoven as a melodist with Vincenzo Bellini, a scandalised howl went up from many whose knowledge of Bellini is confined to the Druids' March in *Norma*. Mr. Newman had three angry articles in *The Sunday Times* (May 2, 9 and 16, 1948) which painstakingly pointed out to Stravinsky matters of which he was aware already. Thus :

> Only a man of simple mind could talk about the ' melody ' of say a Bellini and the ' melody ' of a Beethoven as if the terms meant the same thing in both cases. A melody of the Bellini type is self-generating and self-sufficient. A Beethoven melody, however, is neither self-sufficient nor the main exponent of the musical idea. It is not absolute but contingent, *just one of the many forms in which the complex of forces within the music finds expression.*

In what material sense does this differ from the following passage in Lesson 2 of the *Poétique* (" The Phenomenon of Music ") ?

> The art of music speaks to us with many voices at once. Let me again call your attention to Beethoven, whose grandeur derived from a stubborn battle with rebellious melody. Suppose for a moment that melody were the whole of music. *What would become in that case of other forces, all of greater importance than his melodic faculty, which go to make up Beethoven's musical greatness ?*

The original French text is awkward. I have done my best to clarify it in translation. But the general purport is clear. Stravinsky thinks that melody is only one weapon in the Beethoven armoury. Mr. Newman thinks the same. Why he should fly into a pet is hard to understand. In his heat he misses the point at issue. Stravinsky's main contention is that among the elements which constitute music melody should be supreme. Melody, he argues, is ruler of the musical hierarchy. It follows from this doctrine that Bellini's average practice, whatever the absolute merit of his music, is aesthetically sounder than Beethoven's.

Is this doctrine wrongheaded ? Stravinsky's adversaries are too busy shouting abuse to pay serious attention to what he says. Refutation is never to be expected from those who are most eager to refute. For my own part I think on the one hand of the opening movement of the Ninth Symphony, the " ethics," the muscle, the magnificent polemics of it. On the other hand I think of the B flat major trio, *O ! di qual sei tu vitima* in the first act of *Norma*, an unflawed, tranquil world whose orbit intersects those of *Cosi fan tutte* and the C sharp minor Waltz of Chopin. Between Beethoven's world and Bellini's the choice is harder than may appear to those who write off Bellini unheard.* If Stravinsky leans, on grounds of aesthetic principle, to Bellini we must not forget that few have paid more penetrating homage to the genius of Beethoven. The references in *Poétique Musical* are to be read in conjunction with the *Chroniques*, where Stravinsky writes warmly, movingly even, of *ce prodigieux musicien* and in particular of the rare sobriety which characterised his genius. Above all we must remember the Beethoven tincture in certain of Stravinsky's piano music. Of this Alfred Cortot has written with signal insight and admiration. The Adagietto of the Piano Sonata and the Notturno of the Two-Piano Concerto, not mere echo or aping, are a transubstantiation of Beethoven, a restatement of the Beethoven quiddity in the idiom of a later day. To assert (as has been asserted on the strength of the *Poétique* lecture) that Stravinsky's appreciation of Beethoven is shallow betrays a laughable ignorance of the data.

3

In *The New Statesman and Nation* of January 4, 1947, Edward Sackville West wrote apropos the Symphony in Three Movements:
> Stravinsky's new symphony was all too precisely what one would expect from a composer who has committed himself to the following categorical statement: " I hold music to be essentially powerless to express anything whatsoever, be it a feeling, an attitude, a state of mind or a natural phenomenon." What wonder that a spiritual condition of such evident bankruptcy should produce music of a determined vacuity ! Mastery of the orchestra only aggravates the offensiveness of these brittle, charmless, logarithmic movements.

*The choice is fortunately quite unnecessary.—EDS.

Restated syllogistically Mr. Sackville West's position is as follows: Composers whose aesthetic theories are unsound write bad music. Stravinsky's aesthetic theory is unsound. Therefore Stravinsky writes bad music. The major premise need not detain us long. Writing music and theorising about it depend on different faculties. It follows that the bad theorist may be a good composer, and vice-versa. The minor premise reflects one of the most deeply cherished superstitions of musical England: that every good symphony tells a story. Frank Howes never tires of informing us that Vaughan William's F minor Symphony expresses the violence of the Fascist decade, his E minor the horrid realities of war. Vaughan Williams lets it be known that this is news to him. But V.W. is only the composer. What does he know about it ? His protestations are jovially waved aside.

Stravinsky doctrine, running counter as it does to the prevailing academic and critical current in this country, is traditional and unparochial. Mr. Sackville West and other English commentators quote only its negative aspect. Music, says Stravinsky, cannot express, cannot depict anything external to itself. What we must look for, he adds, is its intrinsic value. This, once perceived, endues the hearer with delights of a higher order and more powerful character than any mere evocation or portrayal of normal emotional experience. In short, the actual (as distinct from garbled) text of the *Chroniques* presents us with the classical teaching that the emotions engendered by music are *sui generis*. Mr. Sackville West appears to regard the " spiritual bankruptcy " of this teaching as axiomatic. Or was he merely suffering from a rush of words to the pen ?

Having demolished the premises, we could afford to let the conclusion take care of itself. But Mr. Sackville West is not to be let off as lightly as that. He asserts that the Three Movements are brittle, charmless, offensive; which means merely that Mr. Sackville West, poor man, happens to find them so. Other hearers, whose musical qualifications compare not unfavourably with those of Mr. Sackville West, find them (a) sappy as distinct from brittle, (b) charming as distinct from charmless (c) attractive as distinct from offensive. It will not do to say that on this point Mr. Sackville West's opinion is as good as the next man's. The judgment of people who derive emotion *sui generis* from a piece of music is valuable; the judgment of those who derive none is of no value at all.

The fact is that Mr. Sackville West does not see the point of the Symphony in Three Movements. Instead of envying those who do he kicks the composer.

A concluding quarrel, this time with Mr. Edmund Rubbra, who, in an article on Stravinsky's Mass (*The Month*, April, 1949), says:

> In the new Mass he seems to have borrowed the mediaeval costumes of Jacopo da Bologna or Matheus de Perusio, fourteenth-century composers whose freedom of polyphonic speech plus the accompanimental use of odd wind instruments would make a special appeal to him. To go back thus far to forms and textures upon which he could model his musical speech was a very logical thing for Stravinsky to do, for in many ways the musical situation in the present century is akin to that of the thirteenth and fourteenth centuries: then, as now, experimental methods prevailed, and style was not consolidated enough for rules to be deduced from it.

This is very learned and frightening. I do not say the scent is false. What I do urge is its irrelevance. We are asked to travel to Birmingham by way of Beachy Head. Why go tunnelling back six hundred years for the idiomatic origins of the Mass when most of them, implicit or explicit, are to be found in *Les Noces*, the Symphonies for Wind Instruments dedicated to the memory of Debussy, and the *Symphony of Psalms*? Stravinsky has made occasional use of modal devices ever since his so-called " Russian " period. His rhythmic fluidity has been Gregorian these thirty years. The harmonic values of the Mass are not to be assessed at a gulp. With Stravinsky it was ever thus. The hasty hearer is tempted to agree incontinently with Mr. Blom, that Stravinsky's harmony is not subject to any " laws of progression or combination." One has to be patient and listen again, preferably with score on piano desk. Many of music's major pleasures have to be worked for: they are not carried in by the butler on a card tray.

But let us make no mistake about it. *Pleasure* is the operative word. The purpose of harmony is to please, to rejoice our musical sense. I borrow a score of the Mass to recapture beauties suspected rather than seized in performance. I transcribe for the piano the Hosanna section which is supposed to go by (I regret to say) at the speed of a non-stop Underground train. I play this page again and again, unable to keep my fingers off it, lost in a solid, glittering world of major thirds and sixths which march and clash and countermarch *self-justifyingly*. There is the test of harmony. Does it draw you again and again to your piano ? Does it get into you like a fever ? Does it give you no peace ? Does it make you feel bitter and intolerant against the deniers of beauty ?

Mr. Rubbra ends his article as follows: " Whether the Mass is a lasting contribution to the corpus of liturgical music it is impossible to say, but at any rate it is an original one. The listener must judge whether this originality is inspired . . . ' by a meaningless striving after extraordinary effects ' or by a true desire to give new form and meaning to ageless words."

What I had rather hoped for was Mr. Rubbra's own judgment. That he should pass the buck to " the listener " is symptomatic.

While we would not agree with each of Mr. Stuart's fiery observations, we enthusiastically endorse his main thesis—that Stravinsky is dangerously (because none too obviously) misunderstood and underestimated.—EDS.

A New French Composer: Andre Casanova
BY RENÉ LEIBOWITZ

A SHORT time ago the French Radio recorded the works of a young and little known French composer: André Casanova. These recordings will soon be heard over the air—a very good undertaking, I think, for there are few musicians nowadays who show such remarkable gifts as Casanova and who use these gifts with similar earnestness and lucidity.

André Casanova was born in Paris in 1919. As a young boy he showed genuine musical gifts and studied the piano. He was also studying law when the war broke out. In 1940 he was demobilized and decided to devote his whole time to music. At first he concentrated on his piano playing, but he also began—without any tuition—to learn harmony and to compose. After a few years of struggling in this field, he felt that he was not really finding his way; when I met him in 1944, he was almost desperate. He played me some of his music which showed definite signs of talent, but was completely void of control and skill. We decided that he should begin harmony and counterpoint all over again, in order to acquire a solid background. For a few months Casanova, taking a lesson every day, wrote only exercises, and obviously enough, made very rapid progress. Then, one day, at the end of July, he came to a lesson, bringing with him a few measures of a piano piece. He had composed them quite spontaneously, in a few minutes, and although he did not quite know what to do with them, he felt sure that he had managed to express something which he had vainly tried to say before. He wanted my advice as to whether he should go on with the piece. I insisted that he should; during the next few lessons we would always devote some time to this work. I was quite surprised by the idiom of this composition as well as by the profound changes undergone by my pupil, but I did not talk to him about it, and when correcting or advising, I would stick to very general principles of composition. About a week later the piece was finished; it was the first composition ever written by a Frenchman which was using quite consistently, though quite unconsciously, the idiom of Schoenberg and his school.

I must say now that Casanova had no idea of this and that, generally speaking, he had no knowledge of the music of Schoenberg nor of the principles therein involved. It is true that, many years before, he had heard *Pierrot Lunaire*, an event which made such an impression on him that it became the origin of his desire to compose, but it is also obvious that when he was writing the present piano piece, his memories of *Pierrot Lunaire* were far too vague actually to influence him.

The spontaneous adoption of some of the chief elements of the Schoenbergian principles of composition by a young French musician proves several interesting points. In the first place it shows that these principles have become part of the musical language of our time and that they are, therefore, accessible to any musical mind groping for certain radical means of expression. In the second place it contradicts a theory—which used to have many adepts—according to which the music of Schoenberg was supposed to be a purely local Viennese and expressionistic affair,* thus being completely incompatible with the aims and inclinations of a " Latin " mind.

Here now was a young Frenchman who had written twenty-five measures of music which showed a complete emancipation of dissonances, as well as certain very characteristic and subtle Schoenbergian features. The piece begins with the following figure, Ex. 1, in which all the twelve tones of the chromatic scale

are used. This figure does not actually play a functional role in the future development of the piece and never assumes

*It is interesting to note that Freud's revolutionary contribution to psychology, which in some respects parallels Schoenberg's revolutionary contribution to music, was belittled in a similar way. Thus William McDougall, describing Freudian " doctrine " in 1936 (*Psycho-analysis and Social Psychology*): " And again, since every male infant practises masturbation (at least in Vienna), and every parent threatens to castrate him as punishment for such conduct (again in Vienna) . . . "—ED. (H.K.).

the function of a *row* (Casanova was not yet aware of such a possibility), but certain of its motives are used and varied, so that the whole structure becomes articulate and coherent. A very significant feature is the final chord, Ex. 2, which reproduces

Ex. 2

the first four sounds of the initial figure. Not only does it create a logical ending, but, what is more, it shows that the famous Schoenbergian principle of the unity of the horizontal and the vertical has now become a universal principle which can be grasped by someone who has no theoretical knowledge of it.

I must repeat that I did not think it advisable then to draw my pupil's attention to all these facts, preferring him to find out for himself. He was very much stimulated and encouraged, merely because he had actually finished a piece, something which he had been incapable of doing before, and, a few weeks later, he had completed a second composition, this time a song for voice and piano. It is in very much the same style as the preceding piece and stresses some of the elements which we have discussed. The tendency towards a consistent use of the total resources of the chromatic scale is still stronger here. The beginning of the piece shows three clearly delimited sections wherein all the twelve tones are used each time before one of the tones is repeated.

This procedure is still, so to speak, unconscious in the song, but when, in September, Casanova undertook to write a second piano piece, he found that he had to make constant use of it. The exigencies of his compositional mind had now become such that he found the repetition of a tone (before the unfolding of the eleven other ones) disturbing, because such a repetition would create an " overweight," tending to give to the repeated tone a privileged function (something like a tonic), which, on the other hand, could only be contradicted by the context. Thus the whole second piano piece is made up of continuous twelve-tone sections.

After this I found it necessary to have my pupil acquainted with the laws of the twelve-tone technique; considering that he had reached such an advanced stage all by himself and in such a natural way, an awareness of the consequent handling of the chromatic material could only help him further and give him more freedom and solidity. I was right: Casanova still talks of the day when I explained to him the Schoenbergian method of composition as of one of the most significant days of his life; he then suddenly felt that all he had been striving for had immediately come within his reach. He undertook to compose a third piano piece, thus wishing to complete his opus 1. For both structural and sentimental reasons he chose the initial figure of this first piece (Ex. 1) for the basic twelve-tone row, and built the first phrase of his opening theme on it, as shown in Ex. 3.

Ex. 3

This third piano piece shows new improvements, above all in its dimensions. Whereas so far Casanova had only been able to express himself in short pieces of fifteen to twenty-five measures, his Op. 1, No. 3 totalizes seventy-two measures. This is not surprising: the rigorous handling of the twelve-tone technique enables the composer to discover many structural devices which make vast forms possible. In Casanova's previous pieces unity had been obtained through a highly economic treatment of a few basic motives. Contrasting elements had been introduced cautiously, had never been allowed to unfold up to the point where they could become *themes* themselves. Thus the dimensions had to be kept down to the limits prescribed by the possibilities of the given material. Any extension beyond these limits could only have led to useless repetitions and to tautology. In the present piece, Casanova manages quite naturally to overcome such obstacles. A contrasting idea is built up in a " closed " form and becomes a proper second subject. The unity of the whole is not endangered, because every feature of the piece is based on the fundamental twelve-tone series, the only thing which varies from one idea to the other being the specific handling of the series itself. Thus instead of unfolding the original basic set horizontally (as in the case of the first subject), the present passage is derived from a vertical treatment of a transposition of the row.

Needless to say, other results are achieved by similar procedures, and recapitulations are no longer mere repetitions because they too derive from different forms (such as inversions and retrograde motions) of the row. Thus in his very first twelve-tone composition[1] Casanova has been able to express himself in a relatively long form.

(1) It is important to note that this piece is the first twelve-tone composition ever written by a French composer. Its success was partly responsible for the interest in this technique aroused among many other young French musicians, who adopted the same method during the following months.

After this, Casanova decided to compose two more songs which, along with the one he had written in July,* were to form his Op. 2. They occupied him during the months of December, 1944 (the third piano piece having been completed in November) and January, 1945, and gave him ample opportunity to become familiar with the most important devices of the twelve-tone technique and to acquire increasing fluency in its application. They show, moreover, the general progress of the young composer. Formal structures, treatment of voice and piano, unity and variety of musical features, harmonic control, polyphonic aspects, all these fundamentals of musical thought are used here in a more and more mature way.

From the specific point of view of the setting of the *Lied*, there is also a definite step forward. Whereas the first song did not quite avoid a certain " recitative " allure, a very common defect in song-writing today which often degenerates into a completely "loose" expression, the new songs are much more closely knit and show some remarkable passages wherein voice and piano are magnificently interwoven. Ex. 4, chosen at random (from Op. 2, No. 2), may give a good idea of what I mean.

The next few months were devoted to all sorts of research work. Casanova was planning to undertake a large instrumental work in order to get acquainted both with chamber music style and symphonic forms, but he hesitated quite a while about the actual instrumental combination. Then, suddenly, in the late spring of 1945, he decided on a trio—a very unusual one—for flute, French horn and viola. His idea was to use a " representative " of the three main instrumental species: wood wind, brass and string, and to blend them into a proper contrapuntal unit. The work was to occupy him for over a year, its date of completion being September 16, 1946. It lasts just under 15 minutes.

*August ? See Leibowitz' preceding dates.—EDS.

It was a most interesting experience to watch the care, the pains-taking control, which Casanova brought to every one of the two hundred and thirteen bars of the piece, but it would be utterly false to believe that such an effort was due to lack of inspiration or to poverty of ideas. Quite on the the the contrary, the Trio op. 3 shows an impressive wealth of musical features; Casanova's foremost difficulty was to avoid chaos and disorder without his actually depriving himself of the profusion of thoughts which came to his mind. He was moreover, striving towards an extreme condensation of form, so that whatever length was to be achieved, it should only be due to the possibilities inherent in the given material, which in its turn was to be treated as economically as possible. Thus the Trio adopts a very concentrated and strict form (comparable to some of Mozart's Fantasies) :

I. A slow introduction ($\frac{1}{8}$* — 66) of 26 bars. Its character is free, its mood slightly " vague " and mysterious. Although it is based on the developing variation of a few basic motives, the structure remains loose and open, so as to prepare for the closed form of the following Allegro.

II. The main part, mostly fast, of 161 bars. It opens with an energetic theme, Ex. 5, whose antecedent is given by the viola alone, while all three instruments combine in the consequent codetta.

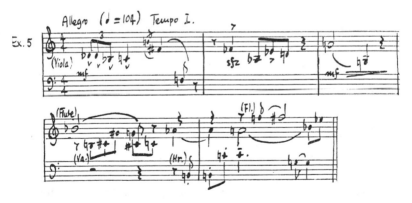

A very interesting moment is to be found in the last transitional bars before the contrasting section dominated by the second subject, Ex. 6. The idea is to create a composed *ritenuto* based on a motivic liquidation, a standstill equivalent to the dominant in the realm of tonal composition ; also, the impression of a modulation is created when the new tempo and the new subject are reached in bar 64.

*$\frac{1}{8}$=quaver.

153

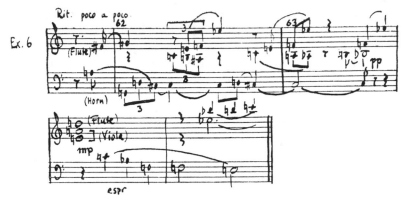

Ex. 6

The second subject gives birth to very intense contrapuntal treatment and leads to a third idea, in which the energetic character of the beginning is re-established. This conclusive section constitutes a coda group which is resolved by a transition (Tempo III, $\frac{1}{4}$*=72) to the central elaboration. After this follows a recapitulation of the first part in a highly varied form. The coda of the recapitulation dissolves quietly and leads to:—

III. A long slow conclusion of 26 measures ($\frac{1}{8}$*=66) which is a varied recapitulation of the introduction (I). It ends with a remote echo of the Allegro's first subject, Ex. 7 (viola part, cf. Ex. 5).

Ex. 7

Most of our young composers do not know what they want, and when they think they do, they go about it with great lack of responsibility. Some of them believe that today one is allowed to write anything, others, who have adopted some radical idiom—for example the twelve-tone technique—think that this is enough to become " modern " or " advanced ". Most of them forget that in order to compose valid music, one must not only have ideas but that it is equally necessary to know what to do with them. From our descriptions of Casanova's work and personality it may have become clear that his whole attitude shows a complete awareness of these problems.

*$\frac{1}{4}$=crochet, *$\frac{1}{8}$=quaver.

A few months after the completion of his Trio, Casanova began to work on a symphony which will be finished by the time this article appears. Again he was compelled to work very slowly and, again, this is not due to sterility, laziness, or to lack of imagination. The explanation is that with every work which he has so far undertaken, Casanova has tackled problems which were new to him. Not only has he—consciously and conscientiously—explored, one after the other, some of the main musical *genres*, piano, vocal, chamber music, and now orchestral music, but, what is yet more important, he has always endeavoured to question the very act of composing, to start so to speak from scratch, as if he had never composed before.

It is not our task to draw any conclusions as to the absolute value of the works thus produced (time will take care of this), but it is our duty to draw attention to a composer who in the midst of many false values, represents something which is serious and genuine.

Observations on the ' Jena ' Symphony

BY ROBERT SIMPSON

THESE notes are not the result of extensive research; I wish to thank Miss Marion Scott and Dr. Hans Redlich for their advice. The main purpose is to show what suggestions may be based on internal evidence; the music alone proves absorbing enough and it has itself stimulated what follows below. Perhaps these few hints may impel more patient mortals to greater industry in actual musicological detection.

This C major symphony, attributed to Beethoven, was published in 1911 by Breitkopf and Haertel after its discovery in Jena. No score was found—only a set of parts, in an unknown hand. On the second violin part was written " *Par Louis van Beethoven* " and on the 'cello part, " *Symphonie von Beethoven* " (sic !). The published score was edited and introduced by Fritz Stein. He indicates that there is no doubt that the MS. dates from the end of the XVIIIth Century and shrewdly remarks that at that time Beethoven was not famous enough to attract the attentions of forgers. Therefore, he says, it is not likely that the inscriptions (which seem to be in the copyist's hand) are deliberately misleading. Various theories about the work have been advanced and it is by no means widely accepted that the music is by Beethoven himself. Marion Scott, for instance, suggests that it might be by his grandfather (also Louis), and Tovey (I hope whimsically) hinted that it might be a symphony of Haydn, let drop by him on his way to or from London on either of his journeys in the 1790's. The first of these theories seems a little far-fetched, but it is the soberest scholarship compared with Tovey's, which on internal evidence is fantastic and, moreover, is almost unbelievable from one who elsewhere has shown a keen grasp of Haydn's later symphonic style.

Reference to Haydn brings about the main topic of this article. Let us begin by looking at the " Jena " symphony. First, it is clearly an immature work: the mature Haydn would never have written it. Moreover, it has not the lean refinement of the earlier Haydn (compare it with No. 26 in D minor, No. 31 in D, or No. 40 in F, to quote three widely differing examples), but its style suggests the strong influence of Haydn's last works, imperfectly digested. To be more precise, its first two movements are quite plainly modelled on the older master's 97th symphony in C major; it is incidentally interesting that Stein notes in passing that there are similiarities between the " Jena " symphony and Haydn's 93rd and 97th. These similarities are surprisingly systematic in the case of No. 97, especially in the first movement, not only in the actual themes but (far more important) in the inner structural details, as if the composer of this intriguing work had deliberately used the Haydn masterpiece as a ground-plan.

The two slow introductions suggest no parallels: that is not surprising, as an immature composer always has no trouble in writing an introduction; his real problem lies in preventing his composition from becoming totally introductory. Therefore it is reasonable to imagine this musician allowing himself a free hand at the beginning (the better to conceal his later reliance on a prop). It is the *Allegro* that sees him turning to Haydn for support. The main subject of the movement can now be compared with that of No. 97:

Such resemblances as this could be justifiably dismissed, were it not for a further chain of events. Haydn follows his main theme with some subsidiary material and then a powerful *tutti* that sweeps with great breadth (through a striking Neapolitan inflection) on to the dominant of G. The other man is wise enough not to try to match this superb fling and he contents himself with building a schoolmasterly and somewhat pedestrian transition, based chiefly on the quaver motion of (b). Notice that he has not Haydn's un-inhibited delight in throwing off one new idea after another. The next similarity is in the two second themes (or, more strictly, those which start the second groups). They both have in common a prominent anacrusis, turned to account for its own sake. The stylistic similarity between them is quite striking.

More striking, however, is the fact that the unknown symphonist also includes the cataract of triplets that interrupts Haydn's tune. Unlike Haydn, he separates it from the theme by a short and rather trite *tutti*. Like Haydn's triplets, his lead to a soft little cadence-theme that also employs the characteristic upbeat rhythm. Haydn's exposition ends with this *piano* idea: Mr. X conceals his debt with five bars of formal bluster.

At every point it will be found, of course, that Haydn is the bolder, if only because he has more experience: accordingly his develop-ment thrusts straight forth into E flat with the main *arpeggiando* subject. The comparative novice is content to stay in G with his. Haydn soon follows with a characteristic and highly expressive woodwind passage, punctuated by soft flashes of (a). This finds a mild echo at bars 130-4 of the " Jena " symphony (at this point Haydn is in D minor, " X " in F). Both passages are brushed aside by decisive *tutti* paragraphs which in both works lead directly to the restatement. Compare the two returns.

The free inventiveness of Haydn's exposition gives him, as usual, great scope in rearranging his recapitulation. This is a point his imitator has missed and the latter's restatement of the first group and transition is as featureless as its original: he is quite unable to indulge in the masterly shortening that Haydn makes here in order to leave room for later expansion. The old man also intensifies the rhetorical force of his triplet passage (after the restatement of Ex. 2) and it breaks off suddenly, to give way to unexpected deep modulations in the direction of A flat and D flat. Now look at bar 244 of the " Jena " symphony. Is it not convincing? This seems to me conclusive, the last link in the chain of evidence.

Mere coincidence could scarcely stretch so far as all this. The rest of Haydn's movement is gloriously expansive, the spacious modulations returning to a theme hitherto omitted from the restatement, and thence to a final rousing *fortissimo*. Mr. X dare not sustain his tonal inflections for long and ends with a lame repetition of his cadence group.

Equally remarkable similarities may be found in the slow movements of both symphonies. Compare, for instance, the outlines of the two themes (both used for variations of similar types). The young composer (for such he must be) even duplicates the essence of the second half of Haydn's tune.

The *minore* variations are also strikingly alike in character and construction, and it is amusing to see how the imitator (so unlike what one knows of Beethoven) forgets that, in contrast to Haydn, he has made his theme's first sentence end on the tonic: his minor variation has a cadence in A flat at the corresponding place (the usual key to fit in place of the dominant of the original major). Even the earliest Beethoven variations never forget their theme. This suggests even more strongly that this composer was concerned with an almost limpet-like adherence to Haydn's scheme, an adherence in which his powers of observation did not always sustain him. In such an article as this it is obviously not possible to pursue the matter in great detail, and it must suffice to say that there is no doubt at least in my own mind, that this " Jena " symphony could not have been composed before Haydn's first London symphonies. No. 97 was written about 1792 and I am grateful to Miss Scott for the suggestion that it can hardly have been published on the continent before 1795 or 1796. In 1795 Beethoven produced works of far greater scope and quality than this; the B flat piano concerto, the piano sonatas of Op. 2 (think of the F minor !), the three Trios of Op. 1, and *Adelaide*. On the other hand, Beethoven had lessons from Haydn in 1792-3 and although he asserted that he learned nothing from the master, it is not impossible that he had the chance to study some of Haydn's later symphonies, including No. 97. Perhaps he did not care to admit the extent of his debt: a case could, no doubt, be constructed for his having written the " Jena " symphony as an exercise during that period. Whatever is asserted must remain inconclusive: would the dates have allowed it, delightful speculation could have been raised on the idea that Haydn's 97th symphony (at least in its first two movements) was inspired by an exercise of Beethoven ! But even the most fanciful of musicologists must bow to the authority of dates; unfortunately No. 97 had been played in London before Beethoven went to Haydn for lessons.

It must be concluded at least that whoever wrote this symphony did so after 1792: Beethoven might possibly have done it at that stage in his development. But if (as seems more likely) it was composed after the actual publication and fairly accessible performance of the Haydn symphony in question (that is to say, probably about 1796), I, for one, refuse to believe that Beethoven was responsible for it. This brings up the question of the rest of the work. What of the minuet and finale ? Of the minuet, not much can be said: it is conventional in style, though it contains a pleasant turn to E flat in its second half. The trio consists of a very plain woodwind theme decorated by triplet figures on two solo violins (in this it reminds one slightly of the corresponding passage in Schumann's 4th symphony). The finale is a different matter: it is by far the best piece in the work and has a quite brilliant sparkle, both in its matter and its orchestration, the treatment of the woodwind in particular showing strong individuality: its form and style are more suggestive of early Beethoven than anything else in the symphony. There is here more than a trace of Beethoven's characteristic blend of Mozart's symmetry with Haydn's rough unpredictability. It is, indeed, a marked advance on the rest and leads me to a further suggestion. Is it impossible that the young Beethoven, to oblige someone else, added a finale to an unfinished symphony, much in the same way that Mozart aided Michael Haydn ? Such practices were very common in a period when composers had the attitude of artisans and thought nothing of helping each other out of a difficulty: Beethoven was generous enough and would certainly not at this time have developed the rugged intractible individualism of his later years. The more often I hear the work,* the more gripping does this thought become, though there is, of course, no possible way of proving it. The fact that the finale alone may have been by Beethoven need not be annulled by the copyist's inscription: he could easily have been under a misapprehension that the whole work was by that composer simply because he had heard the name associated with it. Copyists are not always sharply aware of matters beyond their mere professional accuracy: in this case he has scarcely troubled to see how the name is spelt. (Of course, spelling at that time was fluid, but this does not necessarily invalidate the point.)

No doubt all these matters are controversial; but a controversy is far more interesting than a sleeping mystery.

---

*There is a recording available (H.M.V. DB9047-9), but the performance by the Los Angeles orchestra under Werner Janssen is abominably pompous and romanticized.

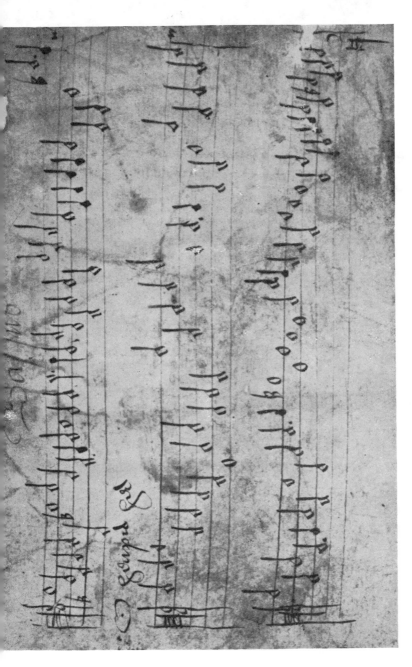

PUBLIC RECORD OFFICE. S.P. 1/246, f. 16.
Bassus of part-song "O heapid hed"

A Part-Book in the Public Record Office

By DENIS STEVENS

THE discovery of a *Bassus* part-book, in manuscript, dating from the latter part of Henry VIII's reign, would have made little impression in the year 1848—the year which saw the addition of the State Paper Office to the existing organization of repositories for Public Records in London. Comparative musicology was a science unknown at that time; and such remnants of the greatness of Tudor music as had come down to Victorian scholars, endured a spate of irresponsible misrepresentation which lasted nearly until the end of the century. True, Dr. Rimbault had gone so far as to publish, in 1841, the *Mass for Five Voices* of William Byrd, but he showed unforgivable neglect in his attitude towards other music of the period, even when it was actually in his possession. He owned, for example, the Mulliner Book, a manuscript " of the greatest importance for a knowledge of keyboard music in England during the first half of the sixteenth century."[1] The only piece he transcribed from it, and published, was a *Gloria tibi Trinitas* by Blitheman,[2] the least interesting by far of a set of six pieces based on the same plainsong, and by the same composer. Before coming into the hands of Rimbault, the manuscript had been the property of John Stafford Smith for nearly sixty years, and this worthy too had given evidence of his utter lack of discrimination by printing three unattractive skeletons of French dance-tunes from " this splendid proof of English musical skill."[3]

Now there is a connection between the Mulliner Book and the *Bassus* part-book from the Public Record Office. The latter document was discovered by the present writer in 1948 (exactly a century after the State Paper Office had become part of the P.R.O.). It is, indeed, listed among the State Papers (Domestic) of Henry VIII, but was not mentioned in the main series of calendars because it lay among a group of miscellaneous papers which had accumulated during the period of publication. An accumulation of this kind can be well understood when it is realized that the Deputy Keeper of the Records had in his "custody, charge and superintendence" more than fifty million documents, ranging from a certain " scrap of paper " to a fifteenth-century Plea Roll weighing half a hundredweight. The Miscellaneous papers were, however, eventually published in calendar form, in 1932, as *Addenda* to the *Letters and Papers, Foreign and Domestic, of the Reign of Henry VIII*.[5] Item No. 1880 describes " a book of the bass parts of songs, some of which are written out in full, others only indicated by the opening words," and the general heading to the section states that " the letters and papers following are almost all of the latter half of Henry VIII's reign or not much later: but it is difficult to assign dates to them and no arrangement has been attempted." The part-book is accordingly bound in with a number of documents relating to piracy, prophesies, and magic.

Of the twenty-five songs in the book, four (Nos. 13, 16, 24, 25) correspond to keyboard transcriptions in the Mulliner Book. The correspondences are, moreover, close enough to indicate that the two manuscripts have much in common with regard to date. According to the section-heading quoted above from the *Addenda,* the part-book dates perhaps from 1540 to 1550; the Mulliner Book, on the other hand, is usually placed between 1560 and 1565.[6] Musical historians tend, however, to forget that the Mulliner Book is a cumulative production and a composite one: it is an organist's private anthology, and was completed, doubtless, only after many years of patient work. The binding and paper have been certified as belonging to the latter part of Henry VIII's reign,[7] and the original beginning of the book (ff. 9-17) with its twelve-line staves,[8] could easily date from 1550.

Mulliner (if it was he who made the keyboard transcriptions) must have used part-books as the basis for his material. In certain of the arrangements, problems of alignment do not appear to have been successfully solved[9] and our sympathies go out to this pioneer score-maker, his anxious eyes flashing from one part-book to the other, as his pen compounds the harmonic essence of his linear guides. It is tempting to think that this *Bassus* part-book was one of that very set, for the numbers in question re-appear in the Mulliner Book in exactly the same order:

		Bassus		*Mulliner*
My friends	.. ..	f. 22v	..	f. 65v
Benedicam Domino	..	f. 24v	..	f. 81v
O Happy Dames	..	f. 28v	..	f. 107
The bitter sweet	..	f. 29	..	f. 109

In no instance has Mulliner transposed, nor has he changed the outline of the bass part except occasionally when he has written one semibreve in place of two repeated minims. Yet this part-book cannot have been his source, for the *Benedicam Domino* stops short just before the section in triple time, which is given in full by Mulliner.

It may be as well to examine the songs individually: let B = *Bassus* and M = *Mulliner*. *My friends* is thus titled (by incipit only) in both B and M. Neither manuscript gives any indication of the composer, and it is not only difficult, but risky, to assign the music to anybody in particular. Often the composer was none other than the writer of the lyric, for specialization was no part of the Tudor life. But in this instance the lyric can be traced. A sixteenth-century collection of poetry in manuscript, now in the British Museum, contains a paraphrase of one of Martial's *Epigrams* by the Earl of Surrey. The first of the four verses is as follows:[10]

> My friends, the things that do attain
> The happy life are these I find.
> The riches left, not got with pain,
> The fruitful ground, the quiet mind.

(The spelling has been modernized, as in all the succeeding examples). This stanza fits the bass part very suitably indeed, customary and effective repetitions of phrases helping the short verse to cover the existing music. Such repetitions can be seen throughout B whenever the text is given in full, and they are shown in the usual way- -://: Henry Howard, Earl of Surrey, was not, however, endowed with any special talent for musical composition, and in his case therefore poet and composer are not one and the same man. As will be seen later, his poem *O Happy Dames* came to be set by John Shepherd. The re-construction of *My friends* from B, M, and the textual source gives birth to a part-song of rare delicacy and feeling, which shows the Tudor school to have acquired a simpler, yet no less subtle technique (in this kind of music) than the far-famed Elizabethan madrigal composers. Of notational interest is the absence of the b-flat key-signature in B, where the only accidental to appear is a solitary e-flat in the second line.

Benedicam Domino[11] is presented in B as a grace with polyglot text, no composer being mentioned by name:

> Benedicam domino in omni tempore
> Semper laus ejus in ore meo.
> O Lord with all my heart and mind
> I will give laud and praise to thee,
> Thou art so loving and so kind
> Thy majesty preserved me.
> Therefore semper laus ejus in ore meo.

In M there is a careful keyboard arrangement, with voice-leading clearly shown by means of crossed-through stems, an idiosyncracy of Mulliner which must not be confused with the ornamentation which the same sign implies in the later virginalists. The version in M, however, has a second section in triple time (shown ꜗ), which is entirely lacking in B. The text for this second section, as well as that for the first, is found among a number of arrangements for lute and solo voice in a British Museum manuscript[12] almost contemporary with M. The *mode d'emploi* of this manuscript is evident from the lay-out of the music: on each *verso* page, facing outwards, are to be found the treble parts of the songs, while on the *recto* page, facing towards the reader, is the lute music. The treble part of Benedicam Domino (duly ascribed to Johnson, as in M) appears on f. 60v, and the complete text is underlaid. Here is the second section of the text, corresponding to the above-mentioned rhythmical change:

> Let us give laud to God most high,
> And for our Queen now let us pray,
> That she may reign to God's glory,
> Who may rejoice both night and day
> To praise his name where ever we go.
> Laus ejus in ore meo.

Who is the Queen mentioned in the second line of this stanza ? Anne Boleyn, perhaps, if the Johnson who composed this part-song is the Johnson who was appointed chaplain to her, as Nagel supposes.[13] There are, we are told, documents teeming with Robert Johnsons, " ranging in degree from the Archdeacon of Leicester to Queen Elizabeth's mole-catcher." But the great Johnson of Tudor times was undoubtedly the composer of this song, and of *Defiled is my name*,[14] and of the motet *Domine in virtute tua* to which the garrulous scribe of a certain Scottish psalter[15] has appended this information: " set in England by ane Scottish priest being diletit (=summoned before an ecclesiastical court) to have beine ane heretyke fled thair lang before reformation." Anne Boleyn was executed in 1536, so this setting of *Benedicam Domino* may have been composed a year or so previously, when both the queen and her chaplain were in a more optimistic frame of mind.

O Happy Dames is anonymous in M, besides being a poor transcription. J. S. Smith traced the poem from the incipit given by Mulliner, and accordingly wrote " Earl of Surry " above the stave, which misled Anderton into thinking that the music might be the work of the poet also.[16] The version in B is completely underlaid, and has the real composer's name written at the end: She*p*d. This song is a valuable addition to the known works of Shepherd, who has been hitherto represented by sacred vocal music in profusion and a *Poynte* (constantly reprinted from M f. 37 for no apparent reason) which van den Borren rightly " passes over in silence."[17] Shepherd gives the impression of being a prolific song-writer from the entry in the 1557 list of " New Year's Gifts given to the Queen's Majesty "[18]:

> By Sheparde, of the chapell, three rolls of songs,
> delivered into the chapell.

The poem *O Happy Dames* is found in Tottel's Miscellany, first published in 1557. Collation of B with M helps considerably to straighten out the tangles in the latter source, and a successful reconstruction has been made, and used.[19]

The bitter sweet is anonymous in both B and M, though the lyric is known to be the work of Jasper Heywood, under whose initials it appears in the *Gorgeous Gallery of Gallant Inventions* (1578). The date of the published miscellany gives little indication of the date when the lyric was written, for, as Bruce Pattison points out, " amateurs of high rank intended their poems primarily to circulate among their friends, and manuscript copies of them were usually well known long before any enterprising printer laid hands on them."[20] The reconstruction of this part-song—a composition of quite exceptional merit— brings into relief a suave and delicate vocal contour, coupled with a highly individual feeling for contrapuntal colour, "affecting not only the ears, but the very arteries, the vitall and animall spirits " as Robert Burton used to say.

One other song in B deserves special consideration; *Vain is the fleeting wealth*, the lyric of which is elsewhere described[21] as "The vanity of man's life." At the end of the song, only just visible (owing to the advanced state of decay of the margins) is the remark:

$$\text{finis quod } \overset{W}{\underset{\wedge}{}} \text{ } p\text{sons}$$

The sign *p* of course stands for " per " (as in the previously cited name, Shepherd). But the most interesting thing is the caret, and subsequent addition of the intitial W. The scribe obviously wrote the surname first, then, remembering that a younger man also called Parsons was steadily making a name for himself, added the W in order to avoid any ambiguity. Had numerous of his fellow-scribes been as conscientious, the confusion that has long reigned over the identity of the two Parsons would never have arisen. Biographical data concerning Parsons (William) is, and always has been scanty, but entries in the Communar's Paper Book at Biddisham (near Wells, Somerset) throw some light on his activities before he went up to London to contribute music to Day's *Psalter* (1563). The relevant entries are:[22]

1551	Feb. 11	Paid to William Parsons for divers songs and books by him made and to be made. 16s. 4d.
1552	Mar. 2	Paid to William Parsons for divers songs and books. 12s. 0d.
1552	Aug. 29	Paid to William Parsons for 15 books containing three masses and a primer, 5s. 0d.

1559   Paid to William Parsons for making and pricking of certain songs in English. 20s. 0d.

The " certain songs in English," not only pricked, but made (be it noted), might well have included compositions like *Vain is the fleeting wealth*, whose five four-line stanzas were treated by Parsons in *durchkomponiert* manner, the rhythm changing to a brisk *tripla* at the words

> Where is become that wight
> For whose sake Troye town
> Withstood the Greeks till ten years' fight
> Had razed the walls adown ?

But until more material is forthcoming, it will be impossible to reconstruct either this song or the twenty others remaining.

Of these twenty, numbers 2, 3, 6-8, 18-23 are the only ones with texts fully underlaid. The others have only an incipit, and texts are so far untraced save for that of No. 11, where the music fits fairly well to the poem by Richard Edwards, printed in the *Paradise of Dainty Devices:*

> When May is in his prime, then may each heart rejoice . . .

Additional evidence of this matching of text and music may be seen in the fifth line of the poem, which begins with the word *All*. This very word (looking rather solitary) is written near the beginning of the third and last line of music on f. 21v of B. Though only a small matter, it does help to rule out any suspicion of instrumental performance, which theory is often put forward as soon as a textless song appears. Sixteenth-century singers memorized many of the better known texts of the day, hence there was no need to copy them out in full: memories had to be good in times when there were no card-indexes. An odd word in a part-book, however, would serve as a useful guide in the extemporaneous underlaying of texts.

Most of the texts in B are English: the three exceptions include the polyglot text of *Benedicam Domino* already noted, and in addition one Latin text, *Benedicite Dominus* (no. 19), and the French incipit *J'ai content* (no.17). The notation too may be said to embody English features: it is straightforward, sometimes inconsistent, and often concerned with personal as opposed to standardized methods of conveying information to the reader. Its straightforward nature may be gathered from seemingly small matters like the almost total absence of ligatures: the only two in the whole manuscript occur in nos. 19 and 20. Change of rhythm appears only once, when the sign $\frac{C}{3}$ is found in no. 6. There are no complications regarding bar-lines. These are rarely met with, and serve merely to confirm (as in nos. 2, 4, 19, 23) what has already been suggested by a *corona*, or pause.

One inconsistent feature is the use of clefs. The usual form of a sixteenth century bass clef obtains, except in nos. 4 and 5, (where the latter part of the sign is missing) and in no. 9 (definitely a C-clef), and lastly in nos. 10 and 11 (where the more modern form is used). The originals may be seen in the thematic index which accompanies this article. Early song-form often called for a repeat of the refrain or final couplet: and here is the other inconsistent feature. In nine of the songs the music is written out in full (nos. 5, 6, 7, 8, 13, 16, 17, 19, 24), but two others (nos. 4, 11) have a condensed repeat which has apparently no relation whatever to shortage of paper.

The personal aspects of the notation may be seen in the improvised sub-division of a semibreve by means of a sign like this: // (no. 11). Or in the odd way in which accidentals are scattered upon staves which bear no key-signature. The only accidentals used are b-flat, b-natural, e-flat, f-sharp, and (in no. 25 only) a-flat. One gathers the impression that the scribe, whoever he was, had a practical turn of mind; and he was certainly no pedant, but more likely *paterfamilias*, as portrayed in Holyband's *The French Schoole-maister* (1573)—

Father: Roland, shall we have a song ?

Roland: Yea sir: where bee your bookes of musick ? for they bee the best corrected.

Father: They bee in my chest: Katherin take the key of my closet, you shall find them in a little til at the left hand . . . . behold, ther bee faire songes at fouer partes.

Roland: Who shall singe with me ?

Father: You shall have companie enough: David shall make the base: John the tenor: and James the treble. Begine: James take your tune: go to: for what do you tarie ?

James: I have but a rest.

Father: Roland, drink afore you begine, you will sing with a better corage.

Roland: It is wel said: geve me some white wine: that will cause me to sing clearer. I should not be a singing man except I could drink well . . .

Guest: There is a good song: I do marvell who hath made it.

Father: It is the maister of the children of the Queenes Chapel.

Guest: What is his name ?

Father: Maister Edwards.

Guest: I heard saie that he was dead.

Another: It is alreadi a good while ago: ther are at the least five yeers and a half.[23]

There must have been very many of these domestic collections of songs of which B is an example, though very few of them have come down to us. The real Tudor part-song is dwarfed by its sleek successor, the Elizabethan madrigal, and but for Wynkyn de Worde's fragmentary song-book of 1530 and the present example from the Public Record Office, evidence might be even scantier than it is. The songs of a nation, or of an age, are true historical testimonials of human interest, and it is by no means out of place to have them preserved among national archives, rare though these songs may be. The matter is perhaps best summed up by a paragraph in a recently published guide to the Public Records:

" Of the subjects pursued by so many persons with such an immense aggregate of patient research through so vast a quantity and variety of Documents it is impossible to speak in detail: but no one can be for long engaged officially in the work of the Department without realising that there is literally no subject of human interest studied in this Country which might not potentially find illustration in its Public Records."[24]

(1) C. van den Borren: *The Sources of Keyboard Music in England*, p. 17, n. 11. The Mulliner Book has been in the British Museum since 1877 (Add. MS. 30513).
(2) Rimbault: *History of the Pianoforte* (Appendix no. 1).
(3) Davey: *History of English Music*. p. 120.
(4) S.P.1. Vol. 246 ff. 16-29.
(5) Those responsible for the transcription were Mr. James Gairdner, C.B.; Mr. R. H. Brodie, I.S.O.; and Mr. A. C. Wood. The texts only of the songs were published—not, of course, the music.
(6) cf. Apel, Davey, Parry.
(7) Hughes-Hughes: *Catalogue of Manuscript Music in the British Museum*, vol. III, p. 77.
(8) See example in Wolf: *Handbuch der Notationskunde*, vol. II.
(9) E.g. the alto part of *O Happy Dames* (f. 107).
(10) British Museum: Cotton MS Titus A XXIV f. 80. The version in Add. MS 36529 f. 54v begins: *Marshall, the things that do attain.*
(11) The melody is based on the plainsong used in the earliest secular motet with English words: *Worldes blis/Domino* (Wolfenbüttel 677 f. 7v-8).
(12) British Museum. Add. MS 4900.
(13) Nagel: *Geschichte der Musik in England*, vol. II page 53.
(14) Another link with Anne Boleyn. She was said to have written the " complaint " while imprisoned in the Tower of London, awaiting her execution.
(15) British Musueum. Add. MS 33933, f. 68v.
(16) Anderton: *Early English Music*, p. 226.
(17) C. van den Borren: *op. cit.* p. 18, n. 14.
(18) " From an original roll, formerly belonging to Sir William Herrick of Beaumanor, and still in the possession of his immediate descendant, William Herrick, Esq." (*Illustrations of the Manners and Expenses of Ancient Times in England.* 1797).
(19) Together with the next song (*The bitter sweet*) it was included in a group of Tudor part-songs, broadcast on April 2nd, 1949 in the Third Programme of the British Broadcasting Corporation. The B.B.C. Singers were under the direction of Leslie Woodgate.
(20) B. Pattison: *Music and Poetry of the English Renaissance*, p. 34.
(21) British Museum. Sloane MS 1896, f. 42. (*Religious and Moral Poems*).
(22) Historical MSS Commission: *Wells Cathedral*, vol. II, p. 274, 287.
(23) From the extract in M.St. Clare Byrne: *The Elizabethan Home.*
(24) *Guide to the Public Records, Part I: Introductory* (London, His Majesty's Stationery Office, 1949).

THEMATIC INDEX

No.1 f.16
O heaped head

No.2 f.16v
With hea-vy heart I call and cry

No.3 f.17
Judge as ye list, say what ye can, tho' trouble try

No.4 f.17v
If writers words

No.5 f.18
Hey downe downe etc

No.6 f.18v   (W. psons)
Vain is the fleeting wealth wherein the world stays

No.7 f.19v
If ye love me keep my commaundements

No8. f.20
Shall I des-pair then sudden-ly

No.9 f.20v
Who list to hear this song

No.10 f.21
Who list to learn to thrive

No.11 f.21v
When may

No.12 f.22
The fierce and wanton colt

No. 13 f.22v
My friends

No. 14 f.23
Walk-ing a-lone

No. 15 f.24
Sudd-en-ly methought I heard a sound

No. 16 f.24v
Be-ne-di-cam Do-mi-no

No. 17 f.25v
Jay content

3 pts. No. 18 f.26
For-tune a-las is this thy chance

3 pts. No. 19 f.26
Benedicite Dominus

No. 20 f.26v
Mar-vel must I why death is ha-ted

No. 21 f.27
Is it not sure a dead-ly pain

No. 22 f.27v
Wavering and wandering are womens wits

No. 23 f.28
If I had space now for to write

No. 24 f.28v (shepd)
O happy dames that may embrace

4 pts.

No. 25 f.29
4 pts The bit-ter sweet that strains my yielded heart

Analysis versus Inspiration

A CRITICAL COMMENTARY TO JULIUS BAHLE'S
PAMPHLET " HANS PFITZNER UND DER GENIALE
MENSCH " (CURT WEILLER VERLAG, KONSTANZ,
1949)

By HANS F. REDLICH

THIS is an intriguing yet repulsive attempt to deduce the artistic
worthlessness of a great composer from his allegedly insufficient
humanity. It is an ill-tempered, ill-mannered booklet, written by a
distinguished psychologist who fell foul of Pfitzner, because the
composer would not accept his doctrine of the true nature of
musical inspiration and preferred to entertain his own views on the
mystery of musical creation right up to the bitter end.

" Musikpsychologie "—a new species of psychological research,
probing into the inner recesses of the creative mind—had only
recently come into the full limelight of publicity, after its scientific
foundations had been secured by Carl Stumpf, Ernst Kurth and a
number of German researchers,[1] among them Otto Selz, Julius
Bahle's mentor. Bahle himself embarked on his career as a psychologist of musical creation with his meritorious thesis " Zur
Psychologie des musikalischen Gestaltens " (Leipzig, 1930). His
later publications[2] are little more than repetitive extensions of this
central subject, on which he has focused his entire attention ever
since. Bahle's analysis of the processes of musical composition,
culminating in the establishment of creative phases — called
" Vorbild, Gegenbild und Leitbild "—championing the method of
working with particles of motifs (in the manner revealed in
Beethoven's sketchbooks) and pooh-poohing any idea of a " heaven-
sent inspiration " and of long stretches of genuine melody, was
based on the self-analytical explanations of some 30 distinguished
composers (among them Richard Strauss, G. F. Malipiero,
Alfredo Casella, Ernst Krenek and others) whom he had approached
in a circular letter. Among the composers who refused to
collaborate with him was Hans Pfitzner (whose " No " is fully
reproduced in facsimile on page 85 of Bahle's pamphlet). But
Pfitzner went even further. He dared contradict an article by Bahle,
published in the " liberal " newspaper *Frankfurter Zeitung* by
another article, published—*horribile dictu*—in Hitler's own

---

(1) Carl Stumpf, *Tonpsychologie* (1883/90); Ernst Kurth, *Musikpsychologie*
(1930).
(2) *Der musikalische Schaffensprozess*, 1936 (Konstanz, 1947); *Eingebung und
Tat im musikalischen Schaffen* (Leipzig, 1939).

Voelkischer Beobachter[3] and he finally crowned this audacity by publishing an essay on Bahle's " private subject " under the title of " Die musikalische Inspiration " (1940), in which he dealt rather unkindly with his adversary, as he had done so often in the past in his exasperating polemics with Paul Bekker, Ferrucio Busoni, Alban Berg and others. The book under review is Bahle's reply to Pfitzner's last lucubrations on the subject of musical inspiration; completed in December 1948, it was published just in time to cast a final shadow over the ebbing life of the octogenarian composer, who died on May 20, 1949, in Salzburg.

Bahle tries to prove the alleged low quality of Pfitzner's music by the admittedly controversial features of his personal character. He seriously believes that denigrating statements on his opponent's character may be used not only as *argumenta ad hominem* but also *ad rem*. He even goes so far as to assert (p. 38): " . . . Zum Masstab fuer Pfitzner's Bedeutung als Komponist dient uns aber das Wissen um das hohe Menschentum . . . der grossen unumstrittenen Genies der europaeischen Kulturgeschichte . . ."[4] Surely such arguments are invalid for the assessment of a composer's ultimate value. If Bahle thinks little of Pfitzner's music, he should have stated his case in terms of purely musical analysis. It is well known that the moral characters of some of our finest composers are not without blemish, which fact in no way reflects upon their artistic merits. On many pages of his pamphlet Bahle cites Pfitzner's admittedly nationalistic bias as an indisputable proof of his artistic inferiority. While completely agreeing with Bahle on the desirability of a super-national type of music (as envisaged by Chr. W. Gluck), I find it useless to overlook the fact that many great composers have entertained a vehemently nationalistic outlook. The five letters of Verdi's name became the symbol of Italian " Risorgimento," just as Weber's and Wagner's music fanned the blaze of modern *Furor Teutonicus*. And even the gentle Claude Debussy began to call himself rather stridently " *Musicien Francais* " on the title pages of his last publications after 1914 !

Among Bahle's special " bêtes noires " are certain German Romantics, like E. T. A. Hoffmann, who play an integral part in

(3) *Der " Einfall " im musikalischen Schaffen* by J. Bahle, publ. *Frankf. Zeitung*, Sept. 18, 1935.
Was ist musikalische Inspiration ? by Hans Pfitzner, publ. *Voelkischer Beobachter*, Jan. 10, 1936.
Both articles are reprinted in full in the Appendix of the book under review.
(4) " Our yard-stick for assessing Pfitzner's significance as a composer is our knowledge of the high humanity of great and undisputed geniuses in the history of European culture . "

Pfitzner's world and are therefore abhorrent to his detractor. He is also at pains to prove the comparative unimportance of free improvisation at the keyboard (p. 58ff.)—a creative process very dear to Pfitzner, which incidentally played a much underrated part in the virtuoso careers of Mozart and Beethoven.

Bahle's attempt to use the comparatively low number of Pfitzner's works as an argument against their creator seems particularly undignified. It is very easy to compare Pfitzner's 50 *opera* in a lifetime of 80 years unfavourably with Mozart's and Schubert's high opus numbers. By using this purely statistical argument without any sense of historical discrimination, Bahle reveals his fundamental lack of insight into matters of musical technique, thereby justifying Pfitzner's doubt as to his qualifications as arbiter of good and bad music. In discussing his opponent's low output, Bahle does not mention the fact that three out of Pfitzner's five operas are of truly Wagnerian dimensions [5]. Every student of music knows well enough that the mental and physical effort necessary for writing an operatic score like " Meistersinger " or " Palestrina " cannot be compared with the " scrittura " of an opera in the times of Mozart or even Schubert. Nobody would dare to call Wagner's musical output small, because he composed very little besides his 13 operatic scores. Yet Bahle is juggling with numbers in Pfitzner's case, in order to make him appear a composer of sluggish imagination. The innate dishonesty of Bahle's arguments becomes evident from the fact that he carefully excludes Beethoven's name (so frequently quoted on other pages of his pamphlet) from this argument, because he knows very well how poorly Beethoven would compare with his paltry 9 Symphonies as against Haydn's 104—if it really were a case of numbers. Pfitzner's own analysis of musical creation and his theory of " musical inspiration " are dismissed airily as the concoctions of a layman's mind, untrained in the technique of philosophical analysis (p. 49 *et passim*). Unfortunately for Bahle, the testimonial of a great composer like Hans Pfitzner will always carry greater weight with any student of this problem than the reasonings of a psychologist, who has obviously never experienced "the kiss of the Muse." And to make matters worse, Pfitzner's theory of musical inspiration has received succour from the most unexpected quarter. Arnold Schoenberg (incidentally one of the composers who assisted Bahle in his original experiment), published only quite recently[6] the following confession

[5] *Der arme Heinrich* (1894), *Die Rose vom Liebesgarten* (1901), *Palestrina* (1917).
[6] From the article *Rueckblick* by Arnold Schoenberg, publ. *Stimmen*, No. 16, Berlin, 1949.

which is certainly grist to Pfitzner's mill and must be gall and worm-wood to Bahle and his doctrine, which altogether discards the mystery of inspiration and the irrationalities of genius in favour of "iron work" ("stramme Arbeit" — to use an apocryphal dictum of Max Reger's). Schoenberg says:—

> ". . . Bei dieser Gelegenheit will ich auch von den wunderbaren Beitraegen sprechen, welche das Unter-bewusstsein leistet. Ich bin ueberzeugt, dass in den Werken der grossen Meister viele Wunder zu entdecken sind, deren unbegreifliche Tiefe und prophetische Vorraussicht ueber-menschlich genannt werden muss. In aller Bescheidenheit will ich hier zwei solche Faelle ans meiner Kammersymphonie erwaehnen. . . um die hinter unserem Bewusstsein wirkende Macht ins rechte Licht zu stellen, indem ich Wunder nenne, fuer was ich persoenlich keine Anerkennung bean-spruchen darf. . .
>
> Ich glaube aber ausserdem, wenn man seine geistige Pflicht mit ruecksichtsloser Aufopferung erfuellt und alles, soweit man kann, der Vollendung nahegebracht hat, dann beschenkt einen der Herrgott mit einer Gnadengabe, indem er Zuege von Schoenheit beisteuert, die man mit seinem eigenen Talent niemals haette hervorbringen koennen. . .[7]

Schoenberg, the founder of the method of composing with 12 tones, the most cerebral of all living composers[*], is talking unblushingly of a " miracle," of the " grace of God " and is praising the wonderful contributions made by the " subconscious." He is using here words from Pfitzner's musico-psychological vocabulary which are anathema to Bahle. Pfitzner is dead, leaving to posterity to decide finally whether " Palestrina " and the String Quartet in C sharp minor are strong enough to obliterate the nauseating spectacle of their creator's polemics with contemporary adversaries, but Schoenberg at 75 is still very much alive. Will Bahle have the courage to take him to task ? Bahle really believes that " genius is impossible without high humanity," that it is only to be found " where man considers

(7) " In this connection, I also want to say something about the subconscious mind's miraculous contributions. I am convinced that in the works of the great masters many miracles can be discovered whose unfathomable depth and prophetic vision can only be called super-human. In all modesty, I would here mention two such instances from my chamber symphony. . . in order to put the power behind our conscious mind in the right light . . . calling " miraculous " what I, personally, must not claim any acknow-ledgment for . . .
I believe, moreover, that when one does one's spiritual duty with unflinching devotion, bringing everything as nearly as possible to per-fection, then God graces one's work with beautiful features which one's own talent could never have produced . . ."
*The greatest mind springs from the deepest heart.—ED. (H.K.)

174

himself a citizen of the world and abandons himself to the eternal values of the True, the Good and the Beautiful . . ." (p. 115). But in the world of reality things do not turn out in such black-and-white fashion. The shattering greatness, the utter novelty and hypnotic quality of Wagner's " Tristan " continue to obliterate the repulsive aspects of Wagner's shady qualities, i.e. the cheap antisemitism of " Das Judentum in der Musik," or the anti-French jingoism of " Eine Kapitulation." The possibility of such tremendous contrasts in an overriding genius indicates history's condemnation of Julius Bahle's pet theory of artistic values.

Bach's Fugal Craftsmanship—I
By A. E. F. DICKINSON

THE aural interests of a musical society at any given time are bound to be drawn in certain directions at the expense of others. At the moment the speciality is probably the textures of contrasting instrumental groups and of personal harmonic sequences; so would, indeed, the texture of personal harmonic systems be, if criticism were sufficiently abreast with creative achievement to reveal these. Structure is less considered, except in so far as the classical symphony or concerto constitutes an established background of experience, a mental custom which retains its appeal and remains a standard for the integrity of contemporary expression. Nevertheless, every cultivated musician nowadays has been through a symphonic stage and, without necessarily having covered the initial, comparatively primitive period through which even the greatest composers of the later eighteenth century had to pass, he knows most of the recurrent and changing patterns through whose reverberation the Viennese masters and their predecessors achieved clear thought and a com-pelling richness of utterance. To detail the general features of sonata form here, for example, would be provocative.

To expound fugue in this enlightened age, expecially Bach's, seems equally superfluous on first consideration. Yet fugue (i.e. complete or characteristic sectional expression through the imitational treatment of at least one main subject or phrase) claims its firm place amongst other genres, not as the constant resort of most major composers in the development of absolute music since 1600, but as the steady vehicle, in one unforgettable case, for instrumental expression, aery light fancy, immortal longings. Fugue has also proved indispensable, not only to well-meaning writers like Frescobaldi and Pachelbel, but, at certain moments, to a few great composers from Beethoven onwards, and there is no telling who may not catch the infection even tomorrow. In spite of this signal pursuit of fugue, extending in Bach's case to a range and a final intensity parallelled only by Beethoven's development of sonata form, the general experience of whole fugues through keyboard and organ recitals remains for most listeners, I fancy, a big buzzing confusion. Or at best it is an impression of a tricky piece of juggling with subject and answer, followed by an equally hazardous and fortuitous balance of episode and entry, some examples of which make better musical sense than others, but why, is a mystery. Nor have the grammarians been much help to the common listener. Even the thorough Prout, one of the first writers to expound fugue in terms of compositions that command the wide assent of musicians, was the correspondence coach *par excellence*. He was concerned with what we may call the gymnastic or automatic side—canonic treatment and (in a separate manual) invertible counterpoint—and turned a less attentive ear to the quality of the material or of its articulate development. Nor, apart from quoting two fugues in full, did Prout sort out the various (and not numerous) plans of fugal expansion adopted by Bach, or attempt to evaluate the intrinsic qualities of each. Aesthetic relevance was not his concern here, but how to make bricks and models with straw.

It thus happens that the close of two centuries from the death of Bach finds a listening world in singular ignorance of his positive contributions to the art of fugue. It is not yet established whether he is a traditionalist, a revolutionary or a historical imperative. There has been a prodigious and indeed monstrous time-lag between his monumental achievement and an intelligent and comprehensive social response, such as no one would dream of denying Mozart or Beethoven if he claims more than a nodding acquaintance. A fresh survey, more definite than has so far been apparent, is needed to do justice to the range of basic material, its typical expositions, the alternatives of subject-development and episode, and some points of signal creative penetration.

Inevitably *The Art of Fugue* (to be called A.F. henceforward) contains the closest packed examples of what fugue as such meant most firmly to Bach: not only the " research " factors of close canon, inversion and virtuoso counter-subject, but the careless profusion of episode and the wider range of fugue on two or more subjects. Hence, Tovey's *Companion* to this work has revealed many details of Bach's final craftmanship. Yet A.F. is chiefly the concentration of an art which had been attending Bach's creative expression from the various mature organ works to the two successive, entirely distinct, and nowise complementary " books " of the

Forty-eight. Research qualities are rare in the breezy, rhapsodic atmosphere of the organ works. The first Book of the Forty-eight unfolds a fresh and miniature art, and thematic expansion is commonest in the second Book and in A.F. But in the organ fugues much use and wont crystallised, and in general the successive maturities of the later collections were the product of a sparer or more exhaustive invention, rather than of an entire change in method. The present account of Bach's fugue does not, then, hinge on the specialist treatment of A.F. except in a few virtuoso and consummate aspects. The analysis of any of the main collections applies to some extent to other groups. The only qualification advisable is that the organ fugues rely more confidently on bravura treatment and a general insouciance, structurally, than the keyboard fugues.

We may begin briefly with the expository elements, on which didactic comment has mainly fastened. Certain formalities stiffen the opening display of theme. Bach's subjects vary from a plain and even equivocal group of whole-beat notes to the accomplished bravura or balanced phrases of a long subject, but there is always a firm underlying melodic outline, however short or slight. With negligible exceptions the starting point is the tonic or dominant, and the main subject lies, more often than not, either between d and s, or in the rest of the octave (s-d'). If it ascends from d in melodic substance—harmonic adjuncts in the subject being disregarded—a certain vocal effort is implied, after which any descent will be easier and normally more rapid. The sequence $dr(s,)d$, however, is a common outline, and makes a firm enough curve, spread out by rhythmic detail. A subject beginning with s tends to fall towards d, either at once or after a preliminary sls or sd' stretch upwards; and similarly a subject may descend from d' to s. Subjects are found that move, or twist erratically, from one half of the scale to the other, or traverse the entire descending scale, but they are not common. Thus ds, sd' and the reverse of these remain the prevailing terminals of two opposed types of quasi-vocal melody, one stretching upward, the other gravitating less assertively to a lower pivot. We might call them the active and passive mood: summons and appeal. Each may be enlivened by ornamental figures suited to the instrument.

In so far as one pair or another of these pivotal degrees is an essential part of the initial melodic span, it will be answered at the next entry by the complementary pair, as in the working balance of authentic and plagal compass established by experience in modal music. That is, ds is answered by sd', sd' by ds, and similarly for these in reverse melodic direction. With this recurring qualification, a canon a fifth higher strikes a responsive pitch of intonation but avoids too sharp a turn from the initial pivot-line, such as *sr'* or *rs* might give. Further details are a matter of rhetoric, dependent on context—the composer's concern, not the listener's. The key-centre meanwhile usually changes to the dominant with the raising of the pitch a fifth (at some octave), but the first answer may avoid this step. If the key pivots from *d* to *s in* the subject, it is desirable that the answer should pivot back sooner or later. Bach's rhetoric is singularly consistent in these matters, and these " tonal " answers are more musical than an exact canon, for the fifth and answering fourth are the most natural and familiar intervals of sound, more natural at first than the arbitrary curve of a subject, which has to establish its validity.

The counter-subject, if any, is normally shaped in contrary motion against the curve of the subject and in cross-accent at the obvious points of plasticity. Occasionally it is more consonant. It will thus have some shape of its own; but its main function is to make durable harmony with the subject, if it is to survive the exposition. This happens in rather more than half the fugues. In the rest Bach extemporises counterpoint each time. Developing counterpoint, linearly free or already determined or both, enlivens the remaining entries of subject and answer, as settled by the number of " voices " assumed to be concerned. A short but suggestive episode, slight enough not to snap this chain of almost epigrammatical phrases, may divide one pair of these opening entries if they are reasonably positive in themselves. An extra entry may carry the rejoinder of tonic and dominant a turn further and thus close or open the outlet to fresh keys via the dominant. This orderly and often stylised exhibition of the subject, as the prevailing refrain or salient phrase in a richer polyphony, ranges from the grand scale of the organ works to the swift *exposé* of keyboard miniatures like the first C sharp major. In three-part fugues descending, in four-part ascending voices (or all ascending but the last) are the most prevalent and inevitably the firmest arrangements of texture. For four-part fugues (the full choir) accumulation of material over the natural base; for three-part, suspension from the lighter thought that first finds utterance.

In a significant minority—over one third of the main output at each stage—a counter-exposition by two or more voices amplifies the exposition, varied in voicing, in order of subject and answer, or occasionally by inversion of the subject and by impromptu extensions or developed episodes, yet maintaining the original orbit of key throughout or substantively. This again ranges from the brief process of the first E major fugue to the finality of the same book's F sharp minor, or to the spacious exordium of the late organ fugue in D minor (usefully miscalled the " Dorian "), which is concluded by a resonant pedal entry.

The subject thus set forth, succinctly or expansively, it may now recur in single entries (each in part a token of the exposition) separated by episodes or comparative digressions. These entries and attendant or dividing episodes occasionally group themselves by key into two sets, one pulling away from the tonic, the other returning to it, possibly from the nearest key on either side (dominant or subdominant). But usually the recovery of the tonic, midway or finally, is far too perfunctory to suggest a formal rejoinder to the exposition, for which there is no need whatever in fugue. This broad development, rounded in varying degrees by the final entries or a free coda, forms the main body of the fugue, of which the exposition has shewn the main material. It remains to consider the three or four lines on which such development proceeds, each making a different kind of appeal to the listener.

(To be concluded in the Summer issue).

A Note on Tonality
BY RICHARD ARNELL

It is now often very difficult to relate contemporary harmonic structures to the simpler terms used previously. A musical phrase or chordal structure predominantly in the key of C major might nowadays modulate so rapidly as to retain little theoretical relationship with this key centre. Nevertheless, however complex the modulation or chromaticism might be on paper, there is often left with the listener the firm sensation of a major tonality.

Similarly, and more frequently perhaps, a certain kind of protracted dissonance, combined usually with a melodic line containing many augmented and diminished intervals, provides an equally strong sense of the minor mode.

Since there seem to be no terms to describe this novel state of affairs it might be helpful to musical aesthetics to coin the concepts of " chromatic major " and " chromatic minor."

As an example, the first movement of Stravinsky's *Symphonie de Psaumes* might be described as being in the key (or orientation) of the " chromatic E minor "—a description which could encompass the many figures constructed on chords such as B♭ major, C minor, far removed from E minor in the strict sense, but easily acceptable to the modern ear.

After Schoenberg's 75th Birthday

TO BECOME RECOGNISED ONLY AFTER ONE'S DEATH . . . !
By ARNOLD SCHOENBERG

(Author's translation of facsimile letter sent to his friends and well-wishers, in reply to their birthday greetings.)

September, 1949.

I have been given during these days much personal appreciation, which I have enjoyed immensely, because this showed me that my friends and other well-meaning people respect my aims and endeavours.

On the other hand, I have for many years closed my account with the world, bowing to the fact that I may not hope for plain and loving understanding of my work, that is: of all I have to express in music, as long as I am alive. However, I know that many of my friends have familiarized themselves thoroughly with my manner of expression and have acquired an intimate understanding of my ideas. They then might be such who carry out, what I have predicted 37 years ago in an aphorism.

" The second half of this century will spoil by overestimation, all the good of me that the first half, by underestimation, has left intact."

I am somewhat embarrassed by so much eulogy. But in spite of this, I find in it also some encouragement. Is it readily understandable that one does not give up, though facing the opposition of a whole world ?

I do not know how the Great felt in similar situations. Mozart and Schubert were too young to be forced to occupy themselves with these problems. But Beethoven, when Grillparzer called the Ninth abstruse, or Wagner, when his Bayreuth plans seemed to fail, Mahler, when everybody named him trivial—how could these men continue to write ?

I know only one answer: they had to say things which had to be said.*

Once, when serving in the Austrian Army, I was asked whether I was really " that composer " A.S.

" One had to be it," I said, " nobody wanted to be, so I volunteered."

*We have taken the liberty of re-translating this sentence.—Eds.

Perhaps I also was commanded to express certain ideas, unpopular ones at that, it seems, but ideas which had to be presented.

And now, may I pray that you, all of you who procured for me real joy by honoring me and wishing me luck, accept this as an attempt at expression of my deeply felt gratitude.

Many cordial thanks.

RECENT SCHOENBERG PERFORMANCES

SCHOENBERG'S seventy-fifth birthday occasioned a number of performances of his works which, if small, spotlit their almost total neglect under which both the composer and the public likewise suffer. The disparity between Schoenberg's fame and people's knowledge of his music can only be compared with Wagner's situation in his day. The hostility of most critics could only, in fact, be maintained in the absence of performances, the method being to set up a scarecrow called " twelve-tone system " and then declare "it can't be music." Having thus frightened musicians and audiences, the whole of Schoenberg's output, whether twelve-tone or not, can then be written off.

Admittedly Schoenberg's music is " difficult " in the sense that it makes the utmost demands on both players and listeners, but so does Beethoven's. And the parallel continues because, once the summit is reached it is seen to include the deepest and most far-reaching outlook over the art and thought of his age.

Schoenberg is one of those artists who created, not followed, the norms of their time. At every stage he wrote the music by which the period will be historically designated; he profoundly influenced composers of a variety of schools and traditions; and at the present time the " technique " he invented is being used by many composers writing music completely different from his own.

The most suitable birthday present to one who for fifty years " bestrode the narrow world like a colossus " (and not such a narrow world either) would be performances of works from his earlier periods. This was done in a Schoenberg programme at the Frankfurt " Week of New Music " last June, when the " Song of the Wood Dove " from " Gurrelieder " (1900), the " Five Orchestral Pieces " (1908), the orchestral " Variations " (1928), and the violin Concerto (1936), directed by Winfried Zillig with Tibor Varga as soloist, produced an overwhelming experience. Earlier in the year the present writer broadcast a series on the B.B.C. Third Programme, " Turning Points in Contemporary Music ", which included the First String Quartet (1904/5), the Symphonic Poem " Pelléas and Mélisande " (1903) and the two transcriptions for String Orchestra of " Verklaerte Nacht " (1899) and Second String Quartet (1907/8) conducted by Hermann Scherchen.

That such performances serve the recognition of Schoenberg as one of the greatest living composers was further demonstrated at the London Contemporary Music Centre's concert in November when " Pierrot Lunaire " was given by Marya Freund and the wonderful Ensemble of the Accademia Filarmonica Romana under the direction of Pietro Scarpini, who also played the Piano Pieces Opp. 11 and 19. All these occasions were so many revelations to audiences who were hearing the works mostly for the first time and will doubtless lead to their inclusion in the repertoire of soloists, string quartets and orchestras.

The later works are obviously a harder nut to crack. Their content needs reflection to assimilate; but the music is there and familiarity and some hard work (why not ?) will bring their reward. First class performances are essential and in this connection I must congratulate the London String Trio on theirs at the introduction to this country of the String Trio, Op. 45 (1948) at the London School of Economics Music Club. No one present could doubt, even at a first hearing, that here was one of the masterpieces of contemporary chamber music.

EDWARD CLARK.

SCHOENBERG: *Pierrot Lunaire,* Marya Freund and the Ensemble of the Accademia Filharmonica Romana, London Contemporary Music Centre, 8th November; and *Verklaerte Nacht*, Boult and B.B.C. Orchestra, 9th November.

Pierrot Lunaire: 1912 ! Its idiom is just becoming natural to those well in touch with the newest developments, though not yet to the uninitiated; so it was with Beethoven's posthumous quartets. At all events, *Pierrot Lunaire*, like *Wozzeck*, overcame me with an overwhelming sense of genius revealed: revealed in its passion; its sureness; its compression; its texture woven from fragmentary melody, uncompromising harmony and sparse instrumentation into sounds as vital and in their economical fashion as rich as *Wozzeck's* huge explosive orchestra. You must go back to *Tristan* for another such challenge and new departure.

The genius-leap to *Pierrot Lunaire* could not have been more forcibly underlined than by Boult's admirable performance next day of *Verklaerte Nacht*. Mahler, not Schoenberg, was the last post-Wagnerian of genius. The mastery and the integrity alike of this early romantic tone-poem put most contemporary outpourings to shame; but outpouring was just what was in truth most foreign to Schoenberg: he had to start again.

ROBERT DONINGTON.

"ARNOLD SCHOENBERG'S ' SURVIVOR FROM WARSAW,' OR THE POSSIBILITY OF ' COMMITTED ' ART."

IN this remarkably level-headed article in "Horizon" (Vol. XX, 116), René Leibowitz discusses Schoenberg's latest work—a dramatic oratorio, concerning the Warsaw ghetto and the Nazi gas-chambers —in its aspect of art committed to topical social or political reality. His conclusion that " only a great work of art (that is, a work achieved through the masterful usage of purely artistic means) can, if inspired by social realities, become a valid expression of, and a real tribute to these realities " is neither understood in Moscow, nor by the reactionaries in the West. For the latter, M. Leibowitz has this to say: " . . . the deep sense of our great artistic tradition lies precisely in the boldness and in the subversion of those who have made it, so that one is justified in saying that this tradition finally amounts to an infinite chain of acts of freedom." He contends that Schoenberg's new work is both artistically free and topical; and by his more detailed description of it he makes one wish to hear the " Survivor " soon in this country.

PAUL HAMBURGER.

Musical Life in Australia
By CURT PRERAUER (SYDNEY)

SINCE our last report (January, 1949) things have proceeded smoothly—perhaps too smoothly—along their vaunted path. For some' time the New South Wales and Queensland orchestras have been supported by the respective States and their capitals. Now South Australia and Victoria have followed. The scope of the orchestras' activities has widened. Permanent conductors are now to be appointed also for the two new State-Municipal orchestras. The management of the orchestras lies still in the hands of the Australian Broadcasting Commission (" A.B.C."). And things could be a lot worse. With the A.B.C. acting as concert-management (besides some private firms who are Muse-importers, too), we are provided for every year with a large number of visiting artists, including conductors. Kubelik has terminated his second Australian tour which was even more successful than his first. Now we await Otto Klemperer. We had good luck with singers: Ninon Vallin and Todd Duncan. Australian Marjorie Lawrence is certainly spectacular, even if she includes " Danny Boy " and " Annie Laurie " in her programmes. But didn't Melba advise Clara Butt " Sing 'em muck ! " ?

Most prominent figure in Australia's musical life is still Eugène Goossens. When he arrived here, more than two years ago, all the hopes of Australia's musical life were focussed upon him. He has proved himself a competent conductor. Also, being simultaneous head of the Sydney Symphony Orchestra and the New South Wales State Conservatorium, he had to be very diplomatic in order to avoid clashes. The improvement of the Sydney Symphony Orchestra has been most noticeable. But Goossen's programmes, which at first elated us through the inclusion of " modern " or semi-modern literature, have meanwhile revealed a sort of one-sidedness, an inclination towards French rather than British works. The latest British schools of composers, Cooke, Searle, Berkeley and others, are hardly represented at all. True, the latest French names share this fate, but there's plenty of Ravel, Debussy, and also Prokofiev, Roy Harris, etc. Inevitably, we have our share of Tchaikowsky. Melbourne's Sir Bernard Heinze conducted Honegger's *King David* in the Southern capital, and Kubelik the same composer's more recent second Symphony for strings. Kubelik also included Martinu and Janacek in his programmes. We have not heard any of the later Hindemith works, nor have we heard any of the major works by Bela Bartok, or any of the Schoenberg works (except, of course, the *Verklaerte Nacht*). But we did hear Kodaly's *Galanta* Dances.

Chamber music, too, is calmly jogging along, with the Sydney " Musica Viva " unjustly dubbed " Musica Mortua." They are doing a Beethoven cycle this year, and their playing is respectable. The competition of the newly-founded quartet of the Australian Broadcasting Commission will probably be exceedingly salubrious.

Talking opera is one of Australia's favourite cultural occupations. An Italian company has been here for almost 12 months, going from capital to capital, from Australia to New Zealand and back again. The usual repertoire . . . however, *Turandot* was there, too

(no, not the other great Italian's, Busoni's work of the same name !).
Don Giovanni was promised—but not kept, maybe fortunately !
The public wallowed. Goossens, however, did Verdi's *Falstaff*
with the Conservatorium Opera School, probably the only time in
the history of music that any conductor ever dared to perform this
work with students.

There is, however, in Melbourne an attempt to build up opera.
So far there have been two seasons annually. Whether this attempt
will be successful or not will largely depend on whether the energetic
and ambitious founder of the " National Theatre Movement,"
Miss Gertrude Johnson, concedes influence to experts or to
amateurs. The best performance so far was a remarkable *Fidelio*,
with production and musical direction united in the hands of Hans
Zander, of best Berlin pre-Hitler tradition.

Tyrone Guthrie, reporting on the possibilities of an Australian
national theatre, declared that the talent available entitled Australia
to the greatest hopes for the future, if certain conditions were
fulfilled. He is being constantly attacked for not acknowledging the
incumbent state of affairs as something simply wonderful. He is
right, all the same.

New York in the Fall of 1949

THE musical season of New York City was officially and traditionally
opened by concerts of the New York Philharmonic-Symphony
Society and the visiting Philadelphia Orchestra.

The Philadelphians (whose concert marked their first appearance
in New York since their tour of Great Britain) opened their programme with Ormandy's instrumentation of Bach's well-known
organ Toccata and Fugue in D minor. This transcription compares
favourably with Stokowsky's, in that it reproduces the colours of the
organ rather faithfully. It was played for all it's worth by the
Philadelphia people, who for sheer beauty of tone are really hard to
beat. In commemoration of Schoenberg's 75th birthday, the
" Transfigured Night " was played in the string orchestra version
which the composer prepared from the original score of his Opus 4
about 5 years ago. This post-Wagnerian product still retains much
of its youthfulness and bears throughout the marks of a genuine
genius. Mr. Schoenberg, who a few weeks ago wrote a biting letter
to the Sunday New York Herald Tribune in which he took to task
the Big Three among United States conductors (Toscanini, Walter

and Koussevitzky) for not having given him adequate hearings, would probably have enjoyed the beautifully transparent performance of the Philadelphia Orchestra, though a later work would have been more representative of the great Viennese master's oeuvre.

Coming two days after the Philadelphia concert Mr. Stokowsky opened the series of the New York Philharmonic-Symphony concerts (in which he will share the leadership with Mitropoulos, while Bruno Walter, Leonard Bernstein and de Sabata will each have a few weeks of guest conductorship) with his well-liked interpretation of Brahms's Symphony I. As a novelty he gave us the first local performance of Aaron Copland's Concert suite from his movie score " The Red Pony " which proved to be an agreeable, if not overly exciting piece of work.

Among solo recitals the Greek soprano Elena Nikolaidi, who scored such a tremendous success with her début last season, repeated her triumph in a recital in which she achieved her best in Schubert and Hugo Wolf. Solomon gave a magnificent piano recital before a half empty hall; especially his interpretation of Schumann's *Carnival* made a great impression on an audience which was primarily made up of fellow-pianists, students and musicians in general. Yehudi Menuhin gave a recital in Carnegie Hall (his first in two years), playing Bach, Prokofiev, Bloch and Paganini, as well as short pieces by the young American composer Alexei Haieff.

The New York City Center Opera Company under the energetic leadership of Laszlo Halasz opened its pre-Metropolitan Opera season with a rousing performance of Strauss' "Ariadne auf Naxos" (in memory of the composer). The work chosen for the opening of the Metropolitan was " The Rosenkavalier ".

New York City's Municipal radio station, WNYC instituted an interesting weekly series of recorded concerts in which some live music is occasionally featured. Entitled " Hands across the sea", this one-hour programme introduces each week the music of another European country. Herman Neuman, the excellent conductor-director of the station who recently returned from a successful European concert tour, is the master of ceremonies; during the month of October the English show brought works by Vaughan Williams, Alan Rawsthorne and Richard Arnell.

ANDOR FOLDES.

Film Music

PROKOVIEV'S " NEVSKY " CANTATA*

WHEN asked to arrange for the concert hall his background music to a film, the composer usually finds that very little of it has any significance in itself. To take a recent example: the concert suite that Walton arranged from his music to " Henry V " is of very modest proportions when one remembers the large quantity of music of high quality which the film contained and its important dramatic function. How was it possible then that Prokofiev was able to include so much of his music to Eisenstein's film in a cantata for the concert hall ? The explanation is to be found in Eisenstein's treatment of the subject as a pageant opera with its opportunity for formal songs (even of a strophic nature), choruses and dances. In addition, the momentum of the music frequently controlled the momentum of the film itself, as in the Battle on the Ice. Prokofiev's task in arranging this cantata was therefore unusually simple. However, for one who, like myself, retains a vivid impression of the powerful impact of this great film and for whom this impression becomes even more vivid when he listens to the cantata, it is impossible to estimate the degree of success of this arrangement for the concert hall.

The most remarkable feature of Prokofiev's development as revealed in this cantata is the influence of Moussorgsky, particularly of " Boris Godunov." This re-assertion of Moussorgsky is extremely important at the present time when many Soviet composers are still influenced by the Belyaev circle which degenerated into the academicism of Glazounov. Under the influence of Moussorgsky, Prokofiev has developed considerable powers as a choral composer since his Paris days. They are shown at their best in the fourth movement, " Arise ye Russian people," with its contrast of declamation and *cantabile*. The second movement, " Song of Alexander Nevsky," however, lacks melodic distinction and is rhythmically rigid; Prokofiev has tried to create a melody of medieval strength and ruggedness, but it compares unfavourably with Walton's treatment of the Agincourt Song in " Henry V." Some of the most terrifying shots in the film were those of the Crusaders, but the third movement, " The Crusaders in Pskov," does not fully express the ruthlessness of the Teutonic Knights.

The really memorable moments, however, are to be found in the orchestral sections, particularly in the desolation and remoteness of the first movement, " Russia under the Mongolian Yoke," and in the exultant last section of the fifth movement, " The Battle on the Ice," before the Crusaders disappear beneath the ice. Incidentally, there is an extraordinary similarity between Prokofiev's use of the divided lower strings and Walton's use of the harpsichord to suggest medieval " mechanised " warfare.

The miniature score is printed with all the transposing instruments written at the sounding pitch, a practice which is of great assistance to conductors and score-readers and which, it is hoped, will be one day universally adopted. While the piano transcription by Atovmian cannot be expected to achieve more than a black and white likeness of Prokofiev's richly coloured orchestration, and though it is unavoidably difficult, it is effectively recast in terms of the piano: a very rare phenomenon in contemporary transcriptions.

Serge Prokofiev: Cantata, " Alexander Nevsky " Op. 78. Miniature Score, 12s. 0d.; Vocal Score, 15s. 0d. Anglo-Soviet Music Press Ltd.

The human quality that pervades Prokofiev's later works augurs well for his opera, " War and Peace " which, it is to be hoped, will soon become available in this country.

BERNARD STEVENS

LOUISIANA STORY—II

CORRIGENDUM
Some copies of our last issue had " C-D-C " instead of " C-Db-C "
in Part I of this article, page 102, line 14.

THE second best movement is the concentrated (and formally concentric) quadruple fugue in A minor, brilliantly prepared by the passacaglia's last variation with the theme up in the strings, *tremolo*. " Where are you ? " the anxious father has just been shouting; and when, upon the fugue's interpretation of the first stage in the boy's encounter with the alligator, the camera switches again to the father: " Where are you ? What' you doin' ?," the woodwind stretti of the fourth subject contribute a moving contrast to the fugue's and scene's dramatic action. The rest of the piece has been well described by Sternfeld* who does not, however, mention the finish, where we get a novel application and dramatisation of a practice $4\frac{1}{2}$ centuries old. To the boy's " He killed my coon ! " the father replies, " Never mind, we'll get him . . . we'll get him . . ."; and on the second " get," the fugue resolves into the Picardy third: a particularly liberating and hopeful sound which does not give the faintest feeling of a formula, owing to the tritone terror of the fugue and, I suppose, the dramatic situation and resolution. Mindful of Bernard Stevens' remarks above, I should like to know whether for one who has not seen the film, the cadence sounds brand new in the concert hall too.

For the following quotation of the score's most attractive Cajun folksong I have to rely on acoustic memory. After the fugue, the tune reappears in F, whence it is immediately and charmingly transposed to D.

Supposing, that is, that the quote may be said to be in C major. Its tickling tonality is really ambicentric (F and C), with the hexatonic scale which make up its notes " gapping " the distinguishing degree between F and C, i.e. the latter's leading note. Nor does F's leading note get an unfair advantage, for it only comes in where it isn't F's leading note. So the tune keeps a choice of two keys in the window, and two modes (Lydian F and Mixolydian C) under the counter. True, C prevails, but does not prevent a strong suspicion of its being the dominant.

The thematic end of the score, with the inverted pedal on G serving as dominant of the "chromatic C minor"† seems at first, not unlogically, to stay in this key, i.e. the dominant minor of the overture's and the passacaglia's

* Sternfeld, F. W., " Current Chronicle," *The Musical Quarterly*, New York, XXXV/1, January, 1949; pp. 117 ff.
† See Richard Arnell's " Note on Tonality " on p. 179 of this issue.

home keys. But suddenly we are torn to, and tucked away in D, on A. I was quite unable to find a valid musical or dramatic reason for Thomson's particular choice of progressive tonality which, whether you could define it or not, must have added to your impression of the score's lack of unity. In view of film music's temporal discontinuity, composers should approach the question of progressive tonality with far greater care than they very generally do. The commentators don't approach it at all.

HANS KELLER

A NEW FILM MUSIC CRITIC

HAVING pleaded the need for competent film music criticism for quite a time, I welcome the birth of a colleague: Mr. Antony Hopkins, film music critic for *Sight and Sound* (*Books on the Film*, British Film Institute, 2s. 6d.). I have had opportunity to attack Hopkins' film music as well as his ideas about music in general and applied music in particular, and judging from his first, none too substantial film music article I shall no doubt have the pleasure of attacking again. But the fact remains that here is a musician writing about music, which makes a nice change.

H.K.

Reviews of Music

Arranged in alphabetical order of composers' names

BENJAMIN BRITTEN : " *Saint Nicolas* " (*Op. 42*). *Cantata for tenor, mixed chorus, piano duet, strings, percussion and organ ; text by Eric Crozier. Pocket Score* (*Boosey & Hawkes*). *12s. 3d.*
THE year's top score. Vocal score reviewed in *this journal*, I/6 (1949), p. 206 ; underestimated elsewhere. While the composer is supposed to be a lucky star, this major work has so far only received one inauspicious London performance which could not disclose it. Composed 1948.

H.K.

ANDRE JOLIVET : " *Trois Chansons de Ménestrels* " (*Heugel-United Music Publishers*). *4s. 0d.*
DESPITE their title, these songs are medieval neither in the nature of the text nor of the music. The melodic line has an archaic flavour which, however, is not supported by the sophisticated harmony. The second song (Lamento de Jésus - Christ) is distasteful in its familiar approach to Christ's agony; the third, with its effective contrast of minor and major, is the most successful. While Jolivet has been associated with atonality, the songs are clearly tonal, in fact unusually easy to sing.

P.A.E.

MARCEL MIHALOVICI : 3rd String Quartet, Op. 52 (*Heugel-United Music Publishers*). *Score : 8s. 9d.*
Rumanian by birth, Mihalovici trained in France, notably under d'Indy. His style has progressed beyond the Wagnerisms of his master to their logical outcome—atonality. In this quartet, atonal technique is combined with a use of the basic classical structures: the first movement is in sonata form, the finale a fugue, and the scherzo and slow movement are in simple A-B-A form. As used by earlier composers, these forms were built up on contrast of material

and/or tonality. The atonal composer, however, is denied this latter means: he can reproduce a subject at a different pitch but as there is no tonal centre the device has not the powerful effect of the classical " subject in a related key." Thus, in the first movement, Mihalovici restates much of the original subject matter as a literal transposition, one semitone higher. It may be argued that this gives greater tension to the restatement, though I suspect that the listener who possesses neither the score nor absolute pitch will remain ignorant of the change. The second and third (slow) movements are better balanced, with contrasting middle sections and more distinctive material; the slow movement contains some of the most satisfying music in the quartet, spoilt only by the persistent use of a niggling demisemiquaver figure. The fugal finale abounds in stretti and other contrapuntal devices, which look impressive in the score, but would prove barren in performance.

P.A.E.

DARIUS MILHAUD : Ier Trio à Cordes (Heugel-United Music Publishers). Score : 4s. 6d.

MILHAUD long ago proved that chamber music is an excellent medium for his crystallized thought; and those who look for real string writing in three real parts will find it here. This is the music of a cool brain with a mastery of technical subtlety. I like the way the cello enters at bar 6 with a three-note figure and drops one in succeeding bars. The third movement, "Sérénade," is obvious in treatment rather than in result. The fourth movement, " Canons," is a good example of 20th century counterpoint; the composer is careful to indicate exactly what he is doing with his themes. The fifth movement, " Jeu Fugue", may not be sufficiently contrasted with the first, but the polyphony's easy flow makes attractive music, and as a fugato it is completely successful. A splendid little work, worthy to rank with Roussel's string trio. A quaver rest is missing in the first violin's bar 69, page 17.

N.D.

DARIUS MILHAUD : Quatrains Valaisens (Heugel-United Music Publishers). 1s. 3d.

FIVE settings for four mixed voices of short Rilke poems. There are probably a good many composers who could do as well as this. The vocal writing is not unduly square, but not once does the contralto part cross the soprano; hence the songs suffer from monotony of timbre. Quavers and semiquavers are joined together regardless of syllables. Mixed quartets will find this cycle very useful and simple to sing, though the brevity of the individual settings makes for scrappiness and precludes partial performance.

N.D.

HANS PFITZNER : Concerto for Violin and Orchestra in B minor, Op. 34 (Boosey & Hawkes). 12s. 6d.

PFITZNER is a genius lacking all talent, just as Strauss is a genius with too much talent*. By " talent " in a composer I do not mean technical ease (of which Pfitzner has plenty) but a capacity to give an intelligible, unequivocal surface to his own depth. Downright honest natures like Pfitzner who are unable to do this, and to grasp that extreme artfulness can be a sign of genius, will impute insincerity to the man who lures the public by the glitter of a polished surface ; they would rather give up their craft than join in such a swindle. Hence Pfitzner's deep mistrust of Strauss† who in many respects is his brother-in-arms in the lost battle of post-Wagnerian chromaticism. It is amazing how many individual positions were open to the defender of the late-romantic style. Pfitzner's is one of the most original: it is not the overloaded compound chord of the chromatic dissonance that interests him, but the interval of two notes, made absolute. In no composer is there such a difference of meaning between a third and a tenth, a fifth and a twelfth; the violin concerto is full of spacious difficult playing over the strings. With creditable pugnacity, Pfitzner tackles all the wayward, intractable intervals of the diatonic scale: the tritone, the minor 2nd, major 7th, minor 9th, augmented 2nd, and augmented 5th. His discords are neither spicy chromatic conglomerations nor telegraph-poles supporting a number of polyphonic strains, but the meeting-places of his favourite intervals. The result is a complicated, though strictly tonal style. As the angular beauty of an old woodcut is determined by the difficult material used, so Pfitzner's expressiveness is sustained by all that is problematic in the common major and minor scale.

The form, too, highly personal: the four joined movements are built on four " themes " (indicated by the composer himself in the score), whose first and second are main and second subject respectively of the short first movement, while the third follows closely as the subject of seven variations, and the fourth appears after a long time as the main subject of the final sonata-rondo. The third theme, which appears after the heroic first movement, is in itslf a motif from the first theme. The variations stand in place of a scherzo, working up to a furious dance, and receding again. After a solo cadenza comes the very profound slow movement for orchestra alone. Built on the second theme, it is strongly reminiscent of " Palestrina," with its sad falling sevenths. An unquiet partial repeat of the first movement leads to the rondo. The fourth theme appearing here, after so much obstinate profundity, is of a gaiety so naive, foursquare, and contact-seeking that one is tempted to put an arm round the old fighting-cock's shoulders and look him mildly into the eyes. But many things have still to happen before the movement is allowed to end in a triumphant B major. All four themes are now in full sway, with cross-references which seem completely musical, i.e. not promoted by a programme.

Now that this work is available in England, on with our leading violinists ! This concerto challenges any player with a big tone and a strong left hand who is also a musician.

P.H.

*Soon after we received the present review, Ernest Newman (*Sunday Times*, 18th September, 1949) observed likewise on Strauss.—EDS.

†See Hans Keller's " *Hans Pfitzner : An Unpublished Letter*," *Music Survey*, II/1.

PROKOFIEV : *Adagio for Cello and Piano, Op. 97. Gavotte from " Classical Symphony," arranged for piano by the composer. (Boosey & Hawkes.) 2s. 0d. each.*

APART from one of Prokofiev's charming little *carillons*, and his ubiquitous knack of falling on the tonic chord at the right moment, this is not one of his happiest pieces. Nothing can be gained by arranging the " Gavotte "for piano except some extra royalties.

P.H.

PROKOFIEV S " *Alexander Nevsky* " *Cantata is reviewed under FILM MUSIC on p. 187.*

*ALAN RAWSTHORNE : Street Corner Overture for Orchestra (O.U.P.)
6s. 0d.*

I HEARD this work twice in one day at the recent Cheltenham Festival (rehearsal and performance) and discovered that once was enough. But that doesn't mean that it is not an extremely effective overture and bright enough to begin many a festival of contemporary British music.

D.M.

GEOFFREY ROBBINS : " Bagatelle " for Flute, Oboe and Piano (United Music Publishers). 3s. 6d.

As little has been written for this combination, wind players may welcome the piece. As music, it is workaday stuff, relying on the overworked chords of the seventh. The joinery is not always convincing; the pompous ending out of keeping with the title.

P.A.E.

PETER WISHART : Four Pieces for violin and piano (O.U.P.). 7s. 6d.

THESE neatly formed and moderately difficult pieces should find a place in some recital programmes.

P.H.

JOHN WRAY : A Simple Suite for Viola Classes (O.U.P.). 3s. 6d.

EXCELLENT for its purpose, whatever that may be. If you don't play the violin, don't learn the viola; if you do, you don't need a simple viola suite. Have a look at the viola part of a Haydn quartet and play it next week; if you can't, you definitely can't.

H.K.

Book Reviews

Arranged in alphabetical order of titles, with a joint review at end.

CLAUDIO MONTEVERDI—LEBEN UND WERK, by *Hans Redlich. Pp. 232; Fr. 11.60 (Verlag Otto Walter, Switzerland).*

DR. REDLICH summarizes in this book some twenty years of unremitting research into Monteverdi's life and work. It is not, however, a purely popular book, as its gorgeous cover might suggest. The approach is at once scholarly, and efficient, and the author's argumental momentum is never once disturbed by such a thing as a footnote. They are all relegated to the end of the volume, where in addition may be found useful tabular information about Monteverdi's whole output, together with a *Lebenslauf* and a remarkably complete bibliography. Especially interesting is the chapter which shows how Monteverdi's work has fared since the time of his death: due homage is paid to the many editors who have (like Dr. Redlich himself) made available to the musical world practical editions of the operas and religious works. The problem of editing is dealt with very fully in the succeeding chapter, and light is thrown into corners where once there was only darkness and prejudice. An English version of this indispensable book is, we understand, in preparation. Also, it may not be out of place to mention that a list of misprints in Dr. Redlich's edition of *Vespro* (*) has now been issued.

D.W.S.

(*) Reviewed in *Music Survey*, Vol. II, No. 2.

ESSAY ON THE TRUE ART OF PLAYING KEYBOARD INSTRUMENTS, *by C. P. E. Bach, translated and edited by William J. Mitchell; pp. 449; 30s. 0d. (Cassell).*

THE musical reader who possesses Editha Knocker's translation (the first in English) of Leopold Mozart's *Versuch einer gründlichen Violinschule,* published last year by the Oxford University Press, should lose no time in setting this first complete englishing (with an admirable introduction) of C. P. E. Bach's *Versuch über die wahre Art das Clavier zu spielen* beside it. It has not the quaintness and individuality that make Leopold Mozart's work a joy to the curious bibliophile; it is a treatise, not a book, with no charms or idiosyncrasy of style. Here, most lamentably, it is presented in a truncated form, i.e., without the eighteen lessons (*Probe-Stücke*) in six sonatas, mentioned on the original title-page and continually referred to by the great composer who wrote it. True, in a note (p. 37) the translator lists editions of these, but the work should not be reprinted without them, either in a slip-pocket, or as an additional volume, since this one runs to 449 pages already. Proud C. P. E. Bach, who devotes seven sections to them in his introduction to part one, would certainly have gibbed at the description of this edition as " the first complete English translation," for these " lessons " are the apex of the achievement. With this exception and the observation that the facsimile title-page on p. 26 is not of the first edition, as stated, but of the second, as the words " zweyte Auflage " and the date, 1759, clearly show, nothing but praise can be accorded to the format and lay-out of this classical text to which subsequent composers, of the Viennese school especially, were so deeply indebted. The aid afforded by the succinct notes is particulalrly gratifying; they are full of learning and present controversial matters in simple terms.

E.H.W.M.

FROM BEETHOVEN TO SHOSTAKOVICH: THE PSYCHOLOGY OF THE COMPOSING PROCESS, *by Max Graf. Pp. 474; $4.75* (Philosophical Library, New York).

AN author who could have written a good book on this subject offers instead an uninformed, unscientific, uninformative, repetitive collection of, at their best, quarter-truths which are based (*inter alia*) on drawing room versions of, beautifying improvements upon, and reactionary phantasies around, the discoveries of Freud, indebtedness to whom is not acknowledged. It is the first book I am reviewing without having read it to the end, believing as I do that nobody who is capable of reading it to the end is competent to review it.

H.K.

KEYBOARD MUSIC FROM THE MIDDLE AGES TO THE BEGINNINGS OF THE BAROQUE, *by G. S. Bedbrook. Pp. xvi + 170; 21s. 0d. (Macmillan).*

THIS book is at first attractive, in fine disappointing. Amply illustrated, both pictorially and musically, it sets out to cover some four centuries of European keyboard music, a period which is almost completely covered (and well-covered during the Renaissance) by manuscripts of our own composers' work.

Let us examine the treatment accorded our own composers. In the 47 pages allotted to music before the Renaissance, three-quarters of a page suffices for English music, the only composers mentioned (repeat, mentioned) are Redford and Taverner, and the latter is credited with " organ pieces " which are in fact nothing more than transcriptions of vocal works. Ex. XXXIV is not called *Lucem tuam*, and I much doubt whether it is by Redford. It is bound upside-down into a manuscript in the Bodleian Library (Mus. Sch. C93) and is there described as "a very good verse called Redford's meane." Redford, who died in 1547 (not 1545) is, however, at least correctly placed at the end of a chapter which deals with the early sixteenth century. But, after 65 pages devoted to the Spanish, German and Venetian schools, he appears again, this time as a member of the " North European School." Previously described as being under the influence of the Flemish school, now as a member of the " St. Paul's" organ school, Redford may be visualised as the possessor of an enviable quantity of old school ties. In point of fact, as his music shows, he was a remarkably independent character. Nevertheless, it is not true that " Redford's works appear the most developed, interesting though some of Blytheman's pieces are." Reverse the position of the two names.

No writer with any conscience could dismiss Add. 29996 as " a very extensive book." No mention is made of the very important feature of composite binding, nor of the panorama it gives of keyboard music from 1530 to 1630, nor of the mystery pieces which Fellowes once ascribed to Byrd, of all people. English music is stated to exist in " various libraries of England, Europe and America," no attempt being made to list even the most important of the manuscripts, though Merulo, the Gabrielis, Sweelinck and Frescobaldi are given full and detailed treatment. For keyboard music in England we are referred to a list of " authorities " whose work is obsolete, and/or misleading.

English music is not alone in being accorded scant treatment: three pages suffice to describe the whole of Spain's output during the Renaissance. Tomas de Santa Maria, a most important theorist and executant, is all but ignored, though a library in Glasgow possesses one of the few extant copies of his treatise of 1565 dealing with keyboard technique. Diruta, the Italian, is nevertheless quoted extensively, but not comparatively. The chapter on the " Spanish School " ends: " Certain it is that Cabezon was, outside the Venetian school, amongst the greatest of the keyboard composers of the first half of the sixteenth century." Mr. Bedbrook is obsessed to an alarming degree by the questionable achievements of the Venetians, and the beneficial influence of the schools, to which he might profitably return for a short while before producing another book.

D.W.S.

MAX REGERS 75. GEBURTSTAG. MAX REGER *by Joseph Haas;* REGER UND UNSERE ZEIT *by Hans Mersmann. Pp. 24 (Max-Reger-Institut; Ferd. Dümmlers Verlag, Bonn).*
THE first publication of the newly founded Reger Institute, consisting of two lectures which duly exaggerate the importance of a near-great composer whose undue neglect over here would seem to make their translation advisable.

H.K.

MUSIC: A REPORT ON MUSICAL LIFE IN ENGLAND, *by the Arts Enquiry. Pp. 224; 15s. 0d. (Political and Economic Planning).*
ALL thoughtful musicians are agreed that the present state of the art in this country is far from healthy. This survey, sponsored by the Dartington Hall Trustees, supports this assertion. The shortage of concert halls (only 18 in the British Isles seat over 2,000), the difficulties of opera production, and the complete lack of " live " music in the rural areas are disadvantages to which we are accustomed; but we now find that no professional musical activity can

be run at all without large subsidies from public and other funds. Although standards of performance are almost uniformly mediocre, this does not account for constant running-at-a-loss. The main trouble lies in our widespread musical illiteracy, but the chapter on musical education gives little hope for any improvement, as music either has no place in the schools or is left to quite incompetent teachers. The report is presented with a minimum of comment (nor is it needed in such a dreary document) but a concluding section ends on a hopeful note. I wish I could echo it.

In such a compendium of facts inaccuracies are inevitable, but it is rather unfortunate that in the first paragraph of Chapter I we are told that Mozart was born in 1745.   P.A.E.

MUSIC TODAY, *edited by Rollo H. Myers. Journal of the International Society for Contemporary Music. 7s. 6d. (Dennis Dobson).*

This spasmodical (as Abraham calls it) has already widely and competently been commented upon. We give a review of one of its articles which has not.—EDS.

MUSIC OF THE NEW WORLD, *by Carleton Sprague Smith.*

THE article suffers only from its author's encyclopædic knowledge and treatment of his subject. It is hardly possible to compress into less than nine pages so much information about the vast continents of North and South America, encompassing as they do every possible musical style from the primitive to the most sophisticated.

Most of the *names* are mentioned and neatly pigeon-holed, including some of the younger ones—with the notable exception of John Cage, an exotic composer who writes for most unusual instruments—" prepared pianos," flower pots, etc. One may laugh at such preoccupations, but a culture is always the richer for its eccentricities.

Copland, Harris and Piston are given pride of place in the North; Villa Lobos, Guarnieri and Chavez in the South—probably a just enough appraisal, allowing for my lack of detailed knowledge of the more tropical continent.

There are few native 12-tone composers. This has an invigorating effect on the musical life: contemporary music there is not weakened by the split between " tonal and atonal " which causes so much devitalizing discussion in Europe.

Sufficient mention is made of the iconoclast, Charles Ives—son of the New Englander who was perhaps the first to notice the interestingly bi-tonal clash of the organ with a street-band, playing in a different key. Ives was quick to exploit his father's experiments and in the early 1900's was writing almost anarchistic dissonance. Being such a pioneer unfortunately isolated him, seemed to turn inward a talent that might have produced a work of the very first rank.   R.A.

NIGHTS AT THE OPERA, *by Barbara McFadyean and Spike Hughes. Pp. 410; 12s. 6d. (Pilot Press).*

THE authors have produced a book which excludes Monteverdi, Gluck, Handel, Beethoven, Weber, Wagner and Strauss, and concentrates instead on the " most popular and satisfying operas " from " Figaro " to Puccini (via Mascagni and Leoncavallo).

It turns out to be another collection of plots, told clearly, if not always elegantly (" The Count, with one thing and another, is in a bit of a spot ") and with adequate musical quotation. Professor Dent's Pelican remains excellent value.   P.A.E.

THE ORATORIOS OF HANDEL, by *Percy M. Young. Pp. 245; 18s. 0d.* (*Dennis Dobson*).

THIS book shows some signs of slackness in composition and Mr. Young is far too sparing with his references and footnotes. Bibliographies are sometimes an unnecessary evil: but not where eighteenth century music is concerned. Mr. Young quotes fascinating passages of prose and verse to illustrate his argument ; but he seldom tells us where they occur. The book's chief merit lies in the fact that its author has first experienced *Esther, Theodora, Joseph* and the rest as living music, and then tested his estimate of them against the standard acclamations of the past. Of the *Messiah*, for example, Mr. Young believes that its uniqueness lies in its homogeneity: and he shows how certain of the other oratorios (*Israel in Egypt*, for instance) are less successful because Handel's music fails to live up to the " conception " he has built up for himself around the literary framework. Mr. Young goes on to demonstrate how Handel's attitude towards the Biblical material he approached served to dictate a certain " interrelation of aria and recitative and the logical disposition of key centres " quite unlike that of his other oratorios, where different philosophies of life had suggested more " dramatic " or " introspective " musical treatment. With this and other considerations in mind we can see why contemporary critics thought the work inferior to Handel's other operas and oratorios (Sir John Hawkins), or that he "might have done better" (Charles Jennens). " Within limits," Mr. Young comments " Handel might have done better. He might have been more demonstrative, but Handel's judicious, though anachronistic conclusion was out of place. This sobriety spreads also to the orchestration, which is throughout restrained."

Mr. Young's sections on Handel's orchestral writing are full of perceptive comments. He notes that Handel, far from relying on a standard instrumental grouping for his various works brought in several fresh combinations for special purposes—from the solo cello, archlute, bass and continuo as an accompaniment for the melancholy " Gentle airs, melodious strains " in *Athalia*, to the large "noisy" orchestra of *Saul* which employs three trombones, carillon, kettle drums and a separate organ part. In this experimentation (as in other things) Mr. Young insists on Handel's being a near-romantic artist, a point he returns to several times. More important, to my mind, is what he tells us about the conditions which made the England of the early eighteenth century—with its tradition of bravura singing, its Vauxhall Gardens and its opportunities for manifest charity—the ideal place for the flowering of Handel's genius. The introductory chapters on the development of the oratorio as a musical genre will perhaps strike some readers as a trifle elementary. But the later ones, which deal with Handel's music in performance, contain criticism and advice which is of the utmost importance to anyone modest enough to accept it. Mr. Young implies that present-day performances of the oratorios ignore a great many of Handel's essential demands; they disfigure his outlines by making unwarranted abridgements, and detract from his desired total effect by allowing a performance to pass as an *omnium gatherum* instead of a musical interpretation.

In spite of its stylistic deficiencies Mr. Young's handsomely produced book can be regarded as a useful contribution to current musical knowledge.

E.D.M.

THE SCORE, *edited by William Glock; thrice yearly. Pp. 48; 5s. 0d. (I.T. Publications).*

THE most important article in this issue is (or rather, should be) Henry Boys' first instalment of " Stravinsky," sub-headed: " Critical Categories needed for a study of his music." This turns out to be a digest of an apparently excellent " Essay in Aesthetic " by the Russian writer Boris de Schloezer, with Stravinsky's views on music interspersed now and again, for comparison. While nobody would envy Mr. Boys his task of condensing a strictly philosophical book which, in itself, is a condensation, we think he should have devoted two articles exclusively to de Schloezer, bringing in Stravinsky only in a third essay. As it is, his treatment of de Schloezer on ten pages is too cursory, and needs several readings with annotations to make sense.

Douglas Newton, in " The Composer and the Music of Poetry," tries to prove that the composer always gets the better of the poet in their unequal struggle. The article strikes me as biased. " The Æsthetics of Ornamentation in French Classical Music," by Edmond Appia, and " Monteverdi and the Madrigal," by Prof. Westrup, are excellent contributions by specialists in those particular spheres. G. F. Kosuszek, writing on a new German composer, Boris Blacher, in the manner of a " close-up " in one of the popular weeklies, is altogether too naive and not worthy of the " Score." Of Blacher's symphony Op. 12, he says : " [its] contrapuntal sternness does not really suit the broad symphonic form." Indeed ?

I hope that the " Score " will not embark on reviewing, but will continue to devote what space it has to matters æsthetical and theoretical. This may limit its readership, but will cover it with glory in fifty years' time.

P.H.

EDWARD ELGAR, *by Mrs. Richard Powell. Pp. xii + 134; 12s. 6d.* WHEN SOFT VOICES DIE, *by Helen Henschel. Pp. 180 ; 12s. 6d. (Both Methuen re-editions.)*

Two records of the actual stuff of life as experienced by two geniuses for living as well as for music. The comparative artlessness of the telling is positively an advantage, leaving the personalities concerned, including the two charming authors, to stand out naturally and sincerely. It is of such personalities that civilization consists.

R.D.

Concerts and Radio

Arranged in chronological order.

I. London and Cambridge

VIENNA PHILHARMONIC *under Walter and Furtwangler, Albert Hall, September-October, 1949.*

WALTER'S concert would have been unblemished, had not the violas introduced the Andante of Mozart's G minor symphony all too openly, devoted to their beautiful tone rather than to the mood and shaping of the movement; and had they not allowed themselves the same narcissistic emphasis in the bridge to the second subject as well as in the recapitulation.

The Furtwangler concerts showed the musical that there was, after all, such a thing as music. They culminated in a uniquely unifying interpretation of Beethoven's Ninth, imbued with musical religion. We remember every bar.

Our colleagues of the daily press, on the other hand, remembered what they had always been used to; it is these—admittedly not unselective—memories which supply most critics with their standards of criticism, and which make most criticism popular and irrelevant. On September 29th we read: " A Furtwanglerised performance of Beethoven's Seventh . . ." (*Daily Telegraph*); " I prefer a baton less lingering and more lively . . ." (*Daily Express*); " Beethoven's Egmont Overture and 7th Symphony were marred by Furtwangler's eccentric tendency to exaggerate slow and soft passages . . ." (*Daily Herald*); ' . . . it may be propounded contrary to generally accepted opinion (*sic*) that his outstanding gifts do not find their best outlet in Beethoven . . ." (*Times*). No notices on the Ninth appeared in *Express* and *Times* of October 9th. The others wrote: " As soon as the music begins . . . his reverence vanishes, and instead of Beethoven's we have Furtwangler's Ninth Symphony " (*Daily Mail*); " Dr. Furtwangler . . . coloured the performance with his irrepressible temperament, and here was in some respects an example best disregarded " (*Daily Telegraph*); " Beethoven's Ninth . . . was a most un-Titanic affair, full of fine detail . . . but tame as an interpretation " (*Daily Herald*). This critic supplemented his view with a somewhat divergent one in the *Spectator* of October 14th: " The night before, Furtwangler had conducted the same orchestra in Beethoven's Ninth, an individual reading which, compared with the Walter concert, brought forcibly to my mind Goethe's perhaps too easy equation of the romantic with disease and the classical with health." It is time to remind Martin Cooper that he tends to find morbid music wherever he turns his ears. Maybe music is morbid altogether: Goethe didn't suffer from it. For the rest, the only point we are able to extract from all these verdicts is that whatever is more than nothing is Furtwanglerised, and the only advice we can give our colleagues is to attend a few Furtwangler rehearsals in order to find out what he aims at, since they have not found it in actual performance. When future musicologists will compare Vienna's or Zürich's or Basle's notices on Furtwangler with London's, they will arrive at the conclusion that there must have been two distinguished conductors of that name.

H.K.

MAHLER CONCERT. HENRY WOOD CONCERT SOCIETY: B.B.C. SYMPHONY ORCHESTRA *with B.B.C. Choral Society, Doorn, Ferrier; Albert Hall, 1st October, 1949; c. Walter.*

AFTER a painless and unspontaneous performance of the *Kindertotenlieder*, Walter gave us the 2nd Symphony (not one of Mahler's best). It was received with remarkable acclamation by the press; and that, perhaps, was the most remarkable thing about the concert. Nevertheless the first and finest movement had to be labelled claptrap by somebody (and was). Claptrap ? Exactly.

D.M.

B.B.C. SYMPHONY ORCHESTRA: BACKHAUS, *Albert Hall, 12th October, 1949; c. Boult.*

BACKHAUS is a very good concerto soloist, who brought about a distinguished if not memorable performance of Beethoven's 3rd Piano Concerto: if memorable at all it was for the length of its first movement's cadenza and the beauty of the unusually slow tempo of the last movement.

R.D.

LONDON PHILHARMONIC ORCHESTRA: CONCERT OF WORKS BY ERNEST BLOCH, *Albert Hall, 13th October, 1949; c. Bloch.*

BLOCH'S " Suite Symphonique " was tame and jovial, excepting the brilliant finale. Miss Nelsova's tone in " Schelomo " was not too small : the orchestra was too loud. The " Sacred Service " excelled in detail but lacked unity. The liturgical text, consisting of prayers and responses, makes for antiphonal effects, but one begins, after a time, to miss long sustained numbers, such as fugues. I do not know to what degree Bloch's melodic and harmonic invention is based on Jewish folk music, but he achieves with it profound and piquant effects when he moves in minor keys or minorish modes; when the words prompt him into a major key, not even he is able to avoid a certain Mendelssohnism which has been the bane of Jewish sacred music for a century. The 5th part of the service (" Epilogue ") is completely integrated, Bloch being a master in the writing of codas.* Here some new, visionary quality enters the music and lifts it into the realm of real greatness.

P.H.

See my review of the " Concerto Symphonique " in M.S. II/I/49.

LILA LALAUNI: *Wigmore Hall, 13th October, 1949.*

THIS recital revealed a sound musical approach to various styles, an often manly touch with an occasionally blurring *ff*, and a technique which is sincere if not flawless.

Two compositions of her own: *Fantasia* is obviously a study which Rachmaninov forgot to compose, and *Capriccio*, based on three themes from *Rosenkavalier*, is a kind of entertainment which thrills any musical salon in any age.

R.F.

B.B.C. SYMPHONY ORCHESTRA: *Albert Hall, 26th October, 1949; c. Kubelik.*

MARTINU'S *Bagarre:* technique piquant, content slight. Ida Haendel in Brahms' violin Concerto: we have a handful of great musicians who play the violin, but this is genius for the violin as such. Rafael Kubelik: a great conductor in the making, for whom the B.B.C. orchestra played very well indeed in Berlioz' magnificent *Symphonie Fantastique.*

R.D.

TCHAIKOWSKY FESTIVAL : LONDON PHILHARMONIC ORCHESTRA, *Albert Hall, November-December, 1949; c. Malko.*

TCHAIKOWSKY is not the most suitable of subjects for a six-concert festival. But how right the popular audiences are to love him as they do ! Splendid at his most vulgar (1812 overture), intensely moving at his most neurotic (Pathetic Symphony), he is only unbearable when he is being respectable.

Malko is a highly competent conductor who can give and hold the right tempi but is not quite flexible enough in varying them to draw the last intensity from each passing phrase. The L.P.O., neither the best nor the worst of the great London orchestras, is worth castigating for not going all the way. Strings : you are out of tune ; *that* is why you lack the " Viennese bloom "—in common with other English orchestras.

Of the soloists I can only find room to suggest that if Gioconda de Vito were as magnificent a musician as she is a violinist, she would be a genius indeed; and that Iris Loveridge is one of the most musicianly of pianists. If you chose to regard my silence on at least one of the other soloists as eloquent, I shall not go so far as to contradict.

R.D.

HANS PFITZNER'S SYMPHONY IN C: VIENNA PHILHARMONIC, c. Furtwangler. B.B.C. Third Programme, 2nd November, 1949 (recorded on August 7 from the Salzburg Festival).

FOR many this must have been their first Pfitzner; unless they are warned that it is nowise among his best it may remain their last. Most aspects of the symphonic problem are in fact ignored or evaded. The would-be continuous structure† is forced and uncompelling. The first and third (last) sections ("movements" would be franker, but then they aren't movements either) seek too early refuge in C major, wherein the first breaks down; maybe it should not have ended in the home key at all. Part of the slow section (in the relative minor) is beautiful. For the rest, invention runs into epigonous debt. The principal subject which, all too expectedly, turns up again at the end together with the third section's saltarello rhythm, is banal in the extreme.

Since the B.B.C. announcer only said that the work was written "towards the end of Pfitzner's life," some actual information may be welcome. It was finished and first performed in 1940, nine years before the composer's death. The first Viennese performance, in the same year, was given by the conductor and orchestra of the present one. Op. 46, the Symphony is the third and last work to which Pfitzner gave this title.

H.K.

†Pfitzner was preoccupied with "Einsaetzigkeit" (single movement structures) and joined movements. See Hans Rutz, HANS PFITZNER: MUSIK ZWISCHEN DEN ZEITEN, Vienna 1949, pp. 37, 135; and Paul Hamburger's review of the Violin Concerto on p. 190 of this issue.

CONCERT OF WORKS BY DMITRI KABALEVSKY: Anglo-Soviet Music Society, London School of Economics, 8th November, 1949 (Sonatina Op. 13, No. 4, and Sonata No. 3 for piano, 7 Nursery Songs and 8 Preludes for Piano).

KABALEVSKY'S quasi folktunes and marching rhythms enchant me for a while and I am impressed when things begin to move (as in the developments of the 1st and 3rd movements of the Sonatina and the Sonata). But when the same trifles return I am irritated. Is this because I enjoy Kabalevsky's simplicity with a smirk, and not with a smile? In that case, I and those like me could be said to "intuitively strive to approach new democratic standards while, rationally, continuing to delight in sophistication." This is what Kabalevsky himself said about Soviet composers in general at the Central Committee Conference of Musicians (January, 1948)*. I do not think that he meant to exclude himself. There is in his music a definite streak of irony directed against both popularity and formalism, the good and evil of the Soviet artistic conscience. An interesting working hypothesis, and Kabalevsky thrives on it, except when the form is too small to allow for its application.

*See Alexander Werth's "Musical Uproar in Moscow," p. 78 (Turnstile Press).

Since, at its best, Kabalevsky's mixture of popularity, formalism and irony is, chemically speaking, an " unstable emulsion," it would not do to precipitate the irony through the acid of an intellectualised performance. This was felt by the three excellent pianists of the evening (Miss Susan Slivko, Mr. Leonard Cassini and Prof. Kabalevsky himself) who gave a teasingly smooth, almost glossy polish of perfection to the music.

P.H.

HAYDN ORCHESTRA: *Conway Hall, 18th November, 1949; c. Harry Newstone.*

HAYDN's Symphony No. 19 in three movements (the openings of the first two based on the common chord, and strings alone in the *andante*), was followed by Mozart's *Sinfonia concertante* (K.364), but without the delicacy and nuance that this most temperamental work demands. Of the soloists, the viola, Miss Jamieson, seemed more suited to the feat (for such it is) than Robert Masters, though neither showed fear in attack. The concert concluded with Haydn's B flat symphony (No. 9 of the Salomon set). The design of this magnificent work was made abundantly clear by the conductor and the only comment I would make is that the imposing minuet was played too *pesante* for my taste. A word should be added about the programme, which seemed intended to contrast Haydn and Mozart to the latter's disadvantage. Nobody with an ounce of sense ever saw Haydn " as an inferior Mozart," nor is a remark on Mozart's " apparent inability to face moral problems, in his life or his music " (even if true) called for in such a place. One pays one's sixpence for a musical analysis, not a sermon to an ethical society.

E.H.W.M.

LONDON PHILHARMONIC ORCHESTRA AND CHOIR *with Fisher, Shacklock, Stephenson, Anthony; Albert Hall, 20th November, 1949; c. Malko.*

BEETHOVEN's Ninth was on the programme and nowhere else. We are gratified to learn that the L.P.O. has appreciated our detailed comments, even where they were unfavourable, but in the present case it must be said that the interpretation, as distinct from the execution, was beneath criticism. Not, to be sure, below notice: the misrepresentation of a great work is probably more harmful than the presentation of a bad one.

H.K.

PHILHARMONIA ORCHESTRA : BEETHOVEN'S NINTH, *with B.B.C. Chorus, Schwarzkopf, Watson, Schock and Christoff ; Albert Hall, 25th November, 1949 ; c. Karajan.*

KARAJAN's version commanded more than usual respect: his fine feeling for balance and fluidity of colour produced many lovely orchestral sounds; the playing was polished in the extreme, the phrasing graceful and " artistic." None of this, however, compensated for the lack of strength in the first three movements: the polish, in fact, caused a fibreless effect, and the first movement in particular suffered. The strings (as so often with British orchestras) must be held largely to blame, especially in the climaxes, for thin anaemic tone, but the conductor himself did much to damp the spirit of the performance. His sudden reduction of the *tempo* at the *basso ostinato* completely destroyed any point the music had already made. This habit of unexpectedly pulling back (without drastically altering) the speed also dimmed the fire of the *scherzo* at bar 77, and again at 296, while his handling of the *coda* of the *adagio* caused a lamentable flagging sensation. The finale went better than the rest, though it, too, was not entirely free from artistic blemish. Little could be sillier or more damaging to the total effect than the long-drawn *ritardando* from 525 to 543 (the magical passage that leads from the thrilling 6/8 fugato, which ends on the dominant of B, to the sweeping entry of the main theme in D major on the full chorus). The maintenance of the *Allegro assai vivace* is here absolutely vital to Beethoven's whole idea; it has something of the effect of a sudden appearance of the augmentation of the subject at the end of a fugue—at a slower tempo its connexion with what has just passed is seriously weakened. The singing of the chorus was very good, and a word of praise is due to the solo quartet, which was the best-balanced I remember. There were some curious noises from the trombones in the last movement.

R.S.

HOMERTON COLLEGE MUSICAL SOCIETY : *Cambridge, 26th November 1949; c. Rimmer.*

WILFRID MELLERS' *Ruth* is simple music free of banality, at moments deeply moving, and almost consistently imaginative and individual: that is to say, a work of rare talent.* Rimmer conducted his mainly amateur forces to good effect; the choir sang beautifully; the soloists (Pauline Lewis—a new soprano with a limpid voice and an expressive intensity that will take her far—Margaret Orr and Robert Powell) deserved well of us. The orchestra needed more rehearsal, but I suspect a certain poverty of texture in the orchestration, a certain monotony in the inner and lower parts. Mellers' strength is in his melody, sinewy, unobvious, with sevenths, ninths, tenths and other fashionably unvocal (!) leaps much to the fore, but also a curiously expressive play with the much less " modern " major sixth. We shall hear more of all this.

R.D.

Cf. Arthur Hutchings on *Wilfrid Mellers* in *Music Survey*, II/2.—EDS.

EXPLORATORY CONCERT SOCIETY : *Queen Mary Hall,30th November, 1949.*

As a composer only moderately and to me unsympathetically exploratory; as a pianist rather dexterous than romantic, Reizenstein shone in that uneven masterpiece, Hindemith's *Ludus Tonalis.*

R.D.

NEW ERA CONCERT SOCIETY: *Albert Hall, 6th December, 1949.*

A section of the Philharmonia Orchestra was conducted by George Weldon, the soloists being Elisabeth Schwarzkopf and Jacques Thibaud. The centre part of the arena was used for the performers, who were mounted on a square platform with ropes: it might have been a boxing ring. In the Albert Hall, it did not look unnatural, and it did not sound unnatural. Indeed, it seemed as though the elusive acoustical genie of the place had at last been forced to give way. Balance was good, in defiance of the many changes in size and content of the small orchestra. Haydn's *Divertimento*, Wagner's *Siegfried Idyll*, and Grainger's *Hill Song No. 1* were all played with a good sense of style, though the idiom of the third piece was unfamiliar but none the less attractive, with a pronounced open-air tang not entirely due to the presence of saxophones.

Schwarzkopf proved herself to be almost at home in the capricious, mock-serious mystery of Sauget's *La Voyante*. The chiaroscurist is given an ample, subtle melodic line, with that touch of the *insaisissable* which belongs to the best of French song. Weldon's accompaniment was more successful here than in the Mozart Concerto (G major) which Thibaud played. His beat proved somewhat inflexible for the demands made upon Mozart's rhythm by the veteran soloist, who nevertheless maintained a fine rich tone which is in direct contrast to the tiny strand of sound one hears from so many violinists of to-day.

D.W.S.

B.B.C. SYMPHONY ORCHESTRA AND CHORUS: *Albert Hall, 7th December, 1949; c. Cameron.*

HONEGGER's *Joan of Arc* is just the thing to set the critics by the ears. On two counts it sails very near the wind: sentimentality; and whatever the word is for using all the tricks. But it outsails them both. The performance was well conceived, well rehearsed, well produced, in many respects magnificent; the music is not less passionate than skilful; and I for one was greatly moved.

R.D.

BOYD NEEL ORCHESTRA: *Chelsea Town Hall, 12th December, 1949; c. Boyd Neel.*

THE Holzbauer Symphony in E♭ shows just how great was Mozart's achieve-ment. Almost any movement from the comparatively early (K.250) *Haffner Serenade* (played last in the programme) was more symphonic than Holzbauer's Symphony. Alan Rawsthorne conducted his own *Concerto* for String Orchestra which must be one of our civilization's few civilized pieces.

D.M.

II. Liverpool

LIVERPOOL PHILHARMONIC CONCERTS:
15th October, 1949.

THE strings of the Liverpool Philharmonic Orchestra, conducted by Rafael Kubelik and ably abetted by piano and tympani, played Martinu's *Double Concerto* with a conviction and ferocity that roused a startled admiration from the audience at a " Popular " Concert.

It is the hysterical violence of the *Double Concerto*, where the themes are racked and pounded into disintegration, that is its most notable feature. That there is richness of mind as well as passion behind the music is immediately obvious; throughout the first movement the piano is in support, underlining the surging motion of the strings by reducing it to chords that are no more than the basic facts of musical life. New and promising relationships are established here, and one realises that from this protean outburst has already sprung Honegger's less satisfactory *Symphony for Trumpet and Strings*. The two works were written in similar moods of extra-musical compulsion, though Honegger, we realize now, was equally outspoken with less to speak about. The structure of the second movement is easier to perceive: it grows to anger from an agonized solemnity of wide chords that round off both this and the last movement, which exists to hurl contradictory, dissonant phrases against a theme that has only the ghost of melodic interest but a satisfactorily distinct tonality.

25th October, 1949.

THE revised version of Lennox Berkeley's *Concerto for Two Pianos*, played brilliantly by Cyril Smith and Phyllis Sellick with Sir Adrian Boult conducting, seems to have gained in clarity and force over the original, making its points with acute judgment and shrewd economy of gesture. We may accept this Concerto as the justification in practice of its composer's eminently sensible discussion of atonalism in *Music Today**: it demonstrates that there is still musical capital to be made made from the clash of simultaneous tonalities or the creation of a sense of key from a tonally vague background.

The soloists played splendidly, but the orchestra fell at times a little short of the high standard they set: the brass lacked the necessary degree of civilization, and the theme of the *Allegro Moderato* in the first movement— a delightful tune—scampered out so raggedly on its first appearance that it made little impression. A clear case of under-rehearsal.

*Music Today. Dennis Dobson, Ltd., for the I.S.C.M.

12th November, 1949.

THOMAS PITFIELD'S *Piano Concerto*, given its first performance by Stephen Wearing and the Liverpool Philharmonic Orchestra, with Hugo Rignold conducting, has the Lancastrian virtues of honesty, craftsmanship and forth-right speech accompanied by a sturdy independence of diction and an inborn gravity that transcend locality.

Emotional and intellectual honesty are the key-notes of this music: if Pitfield had been a thought less honest and allowed the pianist a little more solitary splendour, we would feel more certain of the work's future. Few pianists really like to exist in the state of strict parity which Pitfield demands.

It seemed obvious that in the first movement, which is beheaded un-expectedly, the performance exceeded rehearsals in speed, so that it did not die quite the death its composer demanded.

15th November, 1949.

THE *Psalmus Hungaricus* is a noble work, beautifully written, fascinating in its treatment of voices, and extremely concise. This, and Kodály's more recent *Concerto for Orchestra*, were conducted at a Liverpool Philharmonic concert by their composer, forming an occasion to which the musical élite of Liverpool failed to rise. One would be hard put to it to think of another work of this decade so essentially gay as this Concerto: in spirit, it is of the old days; its polyphony ranges across the Schoenbergian hinterland, but for effects rather than structures. The concerto is fertile in excitement and surprise of development, and on this occasion it received a finer performance than we dared to expect, lacking only the ultimate excitements of virtuosity.

6th December, 1949.

A PERFORMANCE of *Das Lied von der Erde* which turned out, after a rather untidy opening, to be the best and most moving I have yet heard.

The classical masters benignly resolve the tragedies of life: they look at them with detachment and give them formal coherence: however bitter their anguish, they are above the battle, and to share their experience is to reach catharsis. But *Das Lied von der Erde* comes to no such conclusion; its sorrow is unresolved, as though the *"ewig"* of the closing bars is an eternity of dying. This music is unique, for it is a distillation of pure sorrow, not fired by anger or sharpened by bitterness, but existing in its own integrity, so that even the gaiety of the central movements is clouded by the awareness of an eternal loss.

Richard Lewis sang well ; Kathleen Ferrier greatly, with a sense of style for which one can be humbly grateful. Hugo Rignold conducted.

H.B.R.

Opera

Arranged in chronological order.

I. Covent Garden

THE OLYMPIANS : 1st October, 1949.

I believe Bliss may be one of those very near misses who are the Muses' real victims. Sincere to his finger-tips, enviably gifted and accomplished: has it been granted him to conceive one phrase which could be no one but Bliss ? I can only recall the sense of Puccini, Strauss, Wagner and Vaughan-Williams jostling uncomfortably in the wings. Yet I was touched more than once at the time. Wotan-Sachs-Jupiter quietly expounding the far from obvious truth that only the eternal fire is changeless, our role being to let it burn through us acceptingly and thereby find both peace and joy when least we expect them, was so admirably sung by Kenneth Schon, and brought the Priestley-Bliss partnership into such fruitful union, that it reached momentary greatness.

R.D.

BORIS GODUNOV, with Boris Christoff : 5th December, 1949.

CHRISTOFF received well-deserved ovations after each of his three big scenes. I am too young to have seen Chaliapine as Boris, but I should imagine that this is about his measure.

P.H.

THE LOHENGRIN REVIVAL: 15th December, 1949.

IT never pays with Wagner to take matters at their surface value. On the surface, Lohengrin, after an excellent beginning as the romantic lover and champion of a pure but misunderstood heroine, proves touchy at the first tiff and caps Elsa's petulant curiosity by a still more petulant withdrawal. And how bourgeois Elsa's doubts: "After all, we don't know who his parents are ! " But bring to this superficially arbitrary plot some responsiveness, no matter how unconscious, to the power of all genuine mythology to clothe in symbols the most elemental realities, and Elsa's curiosity will no longer seem idle nor Lohengrin's withdrawal pointless. For she is the type of all initiates summoned by opportunity before being inwardly ready for it, and thus vulnerable to the satanic forces represented (and in the person of Edith Coates how magnificently represented) by Ortrud, with her weak and corruptible tool von Telramund.

It is of the essence of initiation that the novice shall not demand to know what in any case cannot be imparted, but only learnt in the ripeness of time from inner experience and development: the heart of the mystery. Try to force that door before it is ready to open of its own accord, and you arrest your own further growth, by falling short of the confidence in your master on which growth depends. Lohengrin made no enquiries into Elsa's credentials. Elsa, in expecting her own cause to be taken on trust but failing to do as much for

205

her champion, made it literally impossible for their union to proceed, for the perfectly simple reason that trust cannot exist in one direction only. Relationship is mutual. Thus Elsa fell into a peculiarly subtle and insidious form of that most insidious of human illusions: trying to have your cake and eat it. She would trust him, of course; but with the slightest and surely most innocent of mental reservations—she could ask him to whisper his secret just into her private ear; it would go no further. Fatal, as mental reservations invariably are ! There are situations in every lifetime when the attempt to keep open the loophole of escape spells certain failure. Burn your boats; take your life in your hands; or the mystery will pass you by.*

Taken literally, then, Lohengrin is rather cruel melodrama; taken ritually, it is ripe wisdom for any human couple. That is why Wagner chose myths and legends for his subject matter; he sensed intuitively their hidden content, so pre-eminently suited in its simplicity and universality for music drama such as he slowly evolved. Lohengrin came before his style fully matured; it is inferior to Tristan and the rest; but it is also greater than a superficial view of it suggests, both in its libretto and in its music. Like all Wagner, however, it must be taken enthusiastically or not at all.

The Covent Garden revival marks a high point in that much berated management's patient nursing of a truly English operatic tradition. With an almost entirely English cast, a standard was reached higher than we have hitherto achieved here, and taken all round (i.e. ignoring for the moment phenomena of the Flagstad order) higher than the international Ring last summer. Even the orchestra shares vastly in the improvement. Space forbids a more detailed appraisal; but we have undoubted grounds for sober congratulation and encouragement.

ROBERT DONINGTON.

*In an article on Gustav Mahler (The Canon, III/2, Hunter's Hill, N.S. Australia), which our reviewer cannot have seen, Schoenberg recalls how he once observed to Mahler that he was " unable to decipher the deeper meaning of the text of Lohengrin . . . In spite of the great impression made by the summons to patriotism and by the consecration of the Grail, it was hard to blame Elsa for wanting to know Lohengrin's origin, even if Ortrud had not aroused her suspicion. ' It is the difference between man and woman,' explained Mahler. ' Elsa is the sceptical woman. She is incapable of having the same degree of confidence in the man that he showed when he fought for her without questioning her guilt or innocence. The capacity for trust is masculine, suspicion is feminine.' Certainly, suspicion originates in the fear of the one who needs protection, while trust results from the sense of power of her protector, the protector of Brabant. This interpretation reveals the deeply human background of the rather theatrical Nie sollst du mich befragen." —EDS.

COVENT GARDEN: GENERAL SURVEY.

THE autumn's best production was Grimes, the worst wasn't Salome. Not nearly so good as the original Wells production (1945) from which it has taken over the conductor and five principals, the Garden's Grimes could easily be bettered by greater adherence to stage directions and score, and by such profound interpretative measures as trying not to start a crescendo so loudly that you can't grow any louder. Martha Mödl proved a potential Carmen, Erna Berger an impossible Gilda and an improvable Sophie: since the Rosenkavalier offered her nothing better than a mere top C sharp, she made many of her top notes, by way of compensation, sharp and loud, including the piano b″ in the first " Ewigkeit " before the end. Act she does not. Shacklock's

Octavian was made to exaggerate the tête-à-tête : no trace of " sehr weich " in her " Die schöne Musi ! " She is, however, developing. Rankl's approach was good, the orchestra bad; and the production, scorning stage directions as usual, was depressing at its most unmusical and debatable at most of its best. Alan Pryce-Jones' English version of the most untranslatable libretto cries for emendation. The deadest performance was Stella Andreva's Violetta; poor unfortunate newcomer, you thought it was Verdi who bored you stiff ! Incidentally, Gerant Evans (Germont) seems convinced of his b flats in the 2nd act's duet's bars 11/2 and 13/2. We agree with most critics about Brook's *Salome*. Had most critics agreed with us about his far more serious devaluation of *Figaro* (*this journal*, I/6), we might have been spared the later débacle. And while the production of *Figaro* has meanwhile improved, it remains more unmusical than that of *Salome*. An unintelligent *Figaro* production, that is to say, is worse than a stupid *Salome:* the theatrical implications of Mozart's music are the most definite imaginable, so that unless you understand it you can't go right.

H.K.

II. Sadler's Wells

DON GIOVANNI: 25th October, 1949.
MUSICAL honours to the conductor, James Robertson, and his orchestra; to Minnia Bower's Zerlina; and to Stanley Clarkson's Commendatore. A constrained Ottavio (Gerald Davies); a good Donna Anna (Victoria Sladen) save when she swooped on her *coloratura*—a too fashionable vice.

Donna Elvira (Marjorie Shires) most moving, except when threatening to make her betrayer pay, pay-hay, pay-hay-hay-hay the cost; just as Ottavio told us all about his eart, har-har-har-heart. Good singing from Leporello (Edmund Donlevy) and Masetto (George James), and good restrained acting *to begin with;* a Don Giovanni (Frederick Sharp) who sang as well as he looked. In fact, generally excellent acting, against exceptional settings. But what is to be said of a producer who encourages such prodigies of stage business, and justifies the greater part of it triumphantly, only to debase the statue and supper scenes and Donna Elvira's last unhappy words by such a background of Leporellidiocy as I have never seen ? To sneak a laugh in the wrong places is to throw the *tragi*comedy away and the music with it. I ask the talented Geoffrey Dunn to listen to the music and think again.

R.D.

FALSTAFF: 13th December, 1949.
WHAT a virtue to be able to hear nearly every word of the rather well-translated (H. Proctor-Gregg) libretto, thus catching much of Shakespeare's own magic in this most touching of comedies; and to watch a vocally admirable Falstaff (Arnold Matters) who is never in the smallest doubt that his first duty is to bring out the pathos, and above all the dignity of his wonderful part, leaving the comedy to take care of itself with the music's aid. Good acting, fussy production (Tyrone Guthrie): that seems to be the present fashion at Sadler's Wells, and the second half of it goes far to destroy what this excellent cast builds up in the first. Add to this a determination to underline every least opportunity, legitimate and especially illegitimate, for comedy of the broad unsubtle sort with three times three, and the comparative failure of this far from unmeritorious performance is largely accounted for.

Rather notable singing by Elsie Morison as Nannetta and Rowland Jones as Fenton, and a not unsatisfactory standard, if on a smallish scale, all round. The orchestra conspicuously failed to glow; the conducting by Michael Mudie was average; the final choral fugue was a disappointment, and no wonder with that horde of Windsorians packing a small stage and the principals playing general post at every second bar. Yet I believe this performance could be pulled together.

R.D.

Gramophone Records

*DONIZETTI: "In questo semplice modesto asilo" (Betly). Margherita Carosio (Soprano), Philharmonia Orchestra (Leopoldo Gennai). H.M.V., D.A.1910. 4s.
Singing of pin-point brilliance and deliberate pre-1848 humour. Spacious recording.

PUCCINI: " Oh my beloved daddy (Schicchi) and " Love and Music, the have I lived for " (Tosca). Victoria Sladen (Soprano), Philharmonia Orchestra (Stanford Robinson). H.M.V., B.9755. 4s.
Good lyrical singing though hardly rich enough for Puccini.

*FAURÉ: "Les Berceaux" and "Le Soir." Pierre Bernac (Baritone), Francis Poulenc (Piano). H.M.V., D.A.1907. 4s.
Best vocal interpretations of these songs I have ever heard. I wish Poulenc's playing were less hurried and anti-sentimental. Recording nicely intimate but piano-tone tinny.

*MOUSSORGSKY: " Monologue of Boris " and " Dialogue of Boris with Prince Shouisky." Alexander Kipnis and Ilya Tamarin (Bass and Tenor). R.C.A. Victor Symph. Orch. (Nicolai Beresowsky). H.M.V., D.B.6482. 6s. MOUSSORGSKY: " The Death of Boris." Raphael Arie, L.S.O. (Joseph Krips). Decca, K.2229. 4s. 9d.
Both Kipnis and Arie have immense dramatic power; Arie's tone is perhaps a trifle purer. Both conductors accompany well, Krips getting much of the atmosphere on the Decca disc which is a better recording than the H.M.V.

*BEETHOVEN: Sonata in A, Op. 12, No. 2, for Violin and Piano. Max Rostal and Franz Osborn. Decca, A.K.1958-9. 9s. 6d.
Only the most intimate knowledge of the score will show how right this version is, always granting, as I do, that over-considered phrasing and strong accents suit early Beethoven. Recording excellent but first and second break impossible.

HANDEL: Sonata in A minor for Recorder and Harpsichord. Carl Dolmetsch and Joseph Saxby. Decca, K.2175. 4s. 9d.
Dolmetsch's exquisite tone is recorded faithfully but the harpsichord sounds a bit thin. Very nice Handelian style : we are glad to get away from the cresc.-decresc. of German editors.

*Strongly recommended.

SCHUMANN: Waldszenen, Op. 82. Clara Haskil *(Piano).* Decca, A.K.2110-11. *9s. 6d.*

Miss Haskil's always nimble and sensitive playing is shown at its very best in "Vogel als Prophet" and in passages like the last 12 bars of "Einsame Blumen." Otherwise, her rubato is apt to be just a bit too aimless for these parochial middle-German landscapes. The tone of the recording improves towards the end.

HANDEL: Overture and Pastoral Symphony (Messiah) R.P.O., Beecham. H.M.V., D.B.6879. *6s.*

The "Pastoral" becomes a new piece when Beecham tenderly brings out its siziliano rhythm with all the various shadings inherent in it. Is it too much to ask for better ensemble and cleaner string playing ? Recording fair.

*CHERUBINI: Overture, " The Water Carrier." Bournemouth Municipal Orchestra, cond. Rudolf Schwarz. H.M.V., C.3865. *4s.*

An extremely well-studied and lively performance, with all the players pulling their weight. Fine, spacious recording.

*WEBER: Preciosa Overture. Turin Symph. Orch., cond. Mario Rossi. Decca K.2184. *4s. 9d.*

A boisterous, exhilarating, clear-cut performance of the military-band-plus type. Top range of violins edgy in reproduction.

*GLINKA: Jota Aragonesa. Philharmonia Orch., cond. Nicolai Malco. H.M.V., C.3878. *4s.*

A turmoil of colour in which Glinka never loses his common sense nor his dry humour. Performance and recording are absolutely first-class.

DVORÁK: Symphonic Poem " The Golden Spinning Wheel," Op. 109. R.P.O., Beecham. H.M.V., D.B.6658/60. *18s.*

Very dull Dvorák. As always when he ruminates at length on his own style, I come away saturated with " Czech " chorales and endless rows of exposed fifths. Beecham very sensibly conducts with the leisurely bonhomie of an old Austrian band-master. Recording fair.

*SMETANA: " Dance of the Comedians " and " Polka " (The Bartered Bride). B.B.C. Theatre Orch., cond. Walter Goehr. Decca, K.1667. *4s. 9d.*

Conducted with the grip and gusto of an old theatre-routinié, played with real response to the conductor's demands. Recording clear.

*ELGAR: Serenade in E minor, Op. 20, for strings. Hallé Orch., Barbirolli. H.M.V., B.9779-80. *8s.*

This set is a great credit to Barbirolli. The string playing is remarkably rounded and well-recorded (except for a rattle on the first side of my set). Perfect intonation save for three fleeting moments.

P.H.

*Strongly recommended.

Correspondence

4, Elfin Grove, Bognor Regis.
19th December, 1949.

Sirs,—I strenuously maintain the right of any reviewer to express an unfavourable opinion provided that it is fair and unbiassed. As I can think of no reason why Prof. Hutchings should be biassed against me personally or against anything I may do, I must point out, in all fairness to the publishers of my book on César Franck, that Prof. Hutchings does not appear to have read it properly.

He is of the opinion that it was rushed—" botched, and he knows it." He justifies this opinion by stating that I admit to repetitions and contradictions. In the Foreword I said: " The book is intended for reference purposes as well as for general reading and there are several instances of statements appearing in the biographical section which must reappear in the consideration of the works. There are not so many that the general reader will experience any annoyance." There is no mention of the word " contradictions " and, indeed, there are none. Will Prof. Hutchings kindly explain why he refuses to believe me, assuming that he has read the Foreword ?

As for his remark that I have " scamped " the chapters which deal with the music in which I am not interested—how does he know ? Does he think that anybody will write a book on anything which does not interest him ? Certainly some music interests me less than others, but since I have devoted twenty pages to Franck's chamber music, I can hardly be accused of " scamping " it— for, Prof. Hutchings may be surprised to learn, it is the chamber music of any composer which interests me least. Does Prof. Hutchings know Franck's operas ? If not, why does he assume that I have done no thinking about the subject ?

Prof. Hutchings is generous enough to allow me the error of stating that Liszt was " the first to express the sublime in diminished sevenths," a piece of nonsense which could never enter my head and, therefore, I did not say it.

I regret having to reply to criticism in this way, but Prof. Hutchings's carelessness requires some kind of answer, since the words of a man in his professional position may well be taken literally and thus work to the detriment of the book.

Yours truly, NORMAN DEMUTH.

Department of Music,
University of Durham,
6, Owengate, Durham.
12th January, 1950.

Sirs,—I have re-read parts of Mr. Demuth's book and scrutinized my review of it. Your passing to me of his letter has done him little service, for it has confirmed my belief that my comments were generous, and also made me examine the opinions of reviewers in other monthly publications. At the time of reviewing I was strongly biassed in Mr. Demuth's favour, for I had appreciated certain remarks in his book on Ravel, am an ardent Franckian, and rejoice when a composer can be persuaded to write about a composer. I understand that Mr. Demuth is well known for his tenacity under criticism, but must assure him that he would be wiser to seek benefit from it than to re-expose his weaknesses by the extra advertisement of bickering letters.

Yours truly, ARTHUR HUTCHINGS.

MUSIC SURVEY

(KATHLEEN LIVINGSTON   WILLIAM W. LIVINGSTON   DONALD MITCHELL)

MUSIC SURVEY is published quarterly by NEWMAN WOLSEY LTD., 4, HOLBORN PLACE, HIGH HOLBORN, LONDON, W.C.1. Annual Subscription, including postage, 11s.   U.S.A. $2.50.

EDITORIAL CORRRESPONDENCE should be addressed to the EDITORS, MUSIC SURVEY, OAKFIELD SCHOOL, WEST DULWICH, LONDON, S.E.21.

All enquiries relating to advertising space in this journal should be made to : THE ALDRIDGE PRESS, LTD., 15, CHARTERHOUSE STREET, HOLBORN CIRCUS, LONDON, E.C.1.

Editorial

THIS Britten issue explains itself, both as to purpose and content. Suffice it to say that the traditional method of systematically exploring the explored has been replaced by an unsystematic welcoming of new ideas. Fortunately, two contributions—Arthur Hutchings' and Paul Hamburger's—were not completed in time ; otherwise the issue would have generously overflowed. The articles will be published in forthcoming numbers.

REVIEWERS:

J.A.	JOHN AMIS
P.J.C.	P. J. COVENEY
J.C.	JOHN CULSHAW
N.D.	NORMAN DEMUTH
R.D.	ROBERT DONINGTON
F.H.	FERNAU HALL
P.H.	PAUL HAMBURGER
R.A.H.	R. ALEC HARMAN
H.K.	EDITOR
W.S.M.	W. S. MANN
W.H.M.	WILFRID H. MELLERS
E.H.W.M.	E. H. W. MEYERSTEIN
D.M.	EDITOR
H.B.R.	H. B. RAYNOR
E.N.R.	E. N. ROSEBERRY
C.H.S.	C. H. STEPAN
D.W.S.	DENIS W. STEVENS
C.S.	CHARLES STUART
H.T.	HAROLD TRUSCOTT

A Note on St. Nicolas:
Some Points of Britten's Style

By DONALD MITCHELL

*" . . . Britten is now engaged on a further opera and indeed
there seems no end to his industry and resource. But the world
is still waiting for him to produce a genuine masterpiece, that
will appeal to the heart as much as to the brain."*
      Stephen Williams in " The Canon," Australian Journal of Music,
      Vol. 3, No. 2.

INDEED there seems no end to the misunderstanding of Britten's
music by Britain's critics. It is not the first time that doubt has been
cast on the partnership of heart and brain in Britten's works : it
has been said before and will be said again. Perhaps it would be
unfair to expect originality from Mr. Williams. Nevertheless, if he
hasn't discovered a " genuine masterpiece " amongst Britten's
output to date—and he lists *Grimes, Lucretia, Herring* and what he
cares to call " an audacious rescoring " of *The Beggar's Opera* (an
audacious inexactitude as rescoring has less than nothing to do with
Britten's realization)—then Mr. Williams I fear will wait for ever.
Possibly the *Spring Symphony* or even *Let's Make an Opera* will call
some of Mr. Williams' Australian chickens home to roost.

It may be that in these days when so often an Oversized Heart is
accompanied by an Undernourished Brain, or vice-versa, the
perfect fusion of the two evident in Britten's music must go unnoticed.
Music that shows either an extreme cerebral or extreme emotional
tendency is both easier to understand and write about. Perfection is
a horrid thing to face as there's little to accord it but respectful
recognition : and that, particularly where Britten is concerned, few
critics are prepared to do. It's not without significance that Mozart
remains a notoriously difficult composer to discuss intelligently :
much of what he did seems to lie completely outside the scope of
discussable " art."

Which was exactly what E. M. Forster wrote in a broadcast on the
1949 Aldeburgh Festival, and more especially of the entry of the
three small boys in Britten's Cantata *St. Nicolas* with their joyful
"Alleluia":

220

Milein Cosman.

" It was one of those triumphs outside the rules of art which only the great artist can achieve." Mr. Forster was indisputably right, except that it was really a stroke of musical genius anticipated pages back in *Nicolas* by the stepwise descending and ascending passage that closes each stanza of the brittle *esitando* waltz celebrating the Saint's birth. The rhythmic drag of these interpolated bars in $\frac{2}{4}$ (Ex. 2), serves to isolate the melodic phrase which is later to become so important.

What did Mr. Forster mean by " outside the rules of art " ? Perhaps the words don't convey much unless we understand what Mr. Forster felt on hearing *Nicolas* at Aldeburgh, which is something of altogether greater analytical interest.

A distinguished contemporary composer's comment : " Britten has an extraordinary sense of beauty", is relevant. I don't know that I fully understood what was meant at the time : but his opinion was confirmed for me by my first hearing of *Nicholas*, when I was so confused by its progressively overwhelmingly impact that all I could find to say was : " This is too beautiful." My apprehension was considerable and amounted almost to physical fear at being unable to bear the burden of further listening. I record this " subjective " opinion unashamedly : it may tell you as much about me as about Britten. But I have yet to be convinced that a strong musical response, in its context, is of no value.

This " sense of beauty "—which lies " somewhat outside the rules of art," and is not necessarily part of every composer's equipment— Britten has to a most penetrating degree. When coupled to his unfailing musical sensibility, it results in the kind of purely musical experience that both Mr. Forster and I seem to have shared at more or less the same point in the *Nicolas* cantata. Not that the experience seems to have been a general one : the wide-spread underestimation of *Nicolas*, and in much the same way of *Let's Make an Opera*, is a most depressing symptom of the prevailing low standard of response from ears all too eager to be seduced by the harmonic " subtleties " of a Ravel.

Even Britten's (I am sure) sincere admirers seem to be infected by this odd unwillingness to give the right reasons for liking the right things. Thus Imogen Holst on *St. Nicolas* (*Tempo*, No. 10, Winter 48/49) and more particularly on its eighth movement *His piety and marvellous works :* writes Miss Holst : " . . . the listener becomes increasingly grateful for the fact that Britten is a composer who is never afraid of sounding obvious " ; and she proceeds to quote in support of her claim a choral passage of 4-part harmony that is about as unobvious as anything to be found anywhere in the cantata. The only obvious thing about it is its absolute musical and dramatic rightness : and this is what Miss Holst meant but curiously couldn't bring herself to set down in print. This extraordinary tendency to treat common chords as suspect and dub them as simple, innocent or obvious, is one of the more interesting psychological reactions to Britten's music. Something must be wrong : the composer must be cheating. Miss Holst underrates her own perception. Why be afraid of designating genius as genius ? Soon we shall learn that what is obviously genius is obviously genius and then perhaps we shall stop obstinately misunderstanding what we really understand.

Unity of heart and brain : how else could Britten have achieved coherence in a work of such dissimilar moods and contrast of dramatic action—*Nicolas from Prison*, the ship-wreck, the communal hymns, the ceremonial crowning of the Bishop ? Over and over again in *Nicolas* we see Britten developing germinal ideas that cohere and integrate as the music unfolds, giving it complete consistency of style. In this connexion it's not unrewarding to recall the dismay of the press after the *Spring Symphony's* first performance† : " It's not a symphony " was the protest. Their search for something that wasn't prevented them from finding something that was : a structure with a strict internal logic of its own.

Perhaps one of Britten's greatest assets is that his structural effects make their point without conscious recognition on the part of the listener ; in other words we needn't play the tiresome game of recognising themes, their transformations and transubstantiations : yet the emergence of this wild theme (*Nicolas from Prison*) :

from the Introduction :

is of more than mere academic or even local significance. We have only to think of the Storm Interlude from *Grimes* to see the same mind melodically at work.

†See page 237.

St. Nicolas is a source-book for proof of Britten's astonishing ability to build a cohesive form from initial musical ideas, although he by no means presents all his ideas in his first movement : some eggs remain to be hatched in later baskets.

As we have seen, Ex. 2 from the second movement acts as a binding force in the seventh. Even the unadorned octave E's in the very opening bars of *Nicolas* are echoed in the persistently repeated " God be Glorified " that interrupts the waltz, which, for all its (unremarked) structural importance, has proved a stumbling-block : once again the music is too " obvious " ; and this in spite of the fact that Britten's predilection for using the waltz as a musical form has proved a fairly constant factor in his work : in the early *Frank Bridge* Variations for String Orchestra, the man-hunt scene in *Grimes*, *Sammy's Bath Song* in *Let's Make an Opera*, and the last movement of the *Spring* Symphony—to mention only a few instances. We should beware of making superficial observations which may mean that we haven't penetrated the surface. The tonic/dominant insistence in the *Nicolas* waltz makes the D major dip at the words " His glory spread a rainbow round the country-side " all the more exhilarating ; and that, in its turn, further intensifies the last state-ment of " God be Glorified " *ff* by the tenor. The waltz tune (which owes its special brightness to Britten's relentless use of the sharpened 4th of the scale) is in itself only part of a not-so-simple whole. We haven't heard this kind of thing before in spite of some people's endeavours to convince us (and themselves) otherwise. It is not even pastiche : it is characteristic Britten.

But the common-chord, simplicity bogey dies hard and Britten's unaffected use of triads still bemuses and disconcerts although some of his most deeply felt music had been conceived in such terms. He is often at his most profound when his harmonic texture is at its simplest : as when Grimes ponders on the " Great Bear and Pleiades " (Act I Sc. II) and Britten (with discreet canonic writing in the strings) ponders on an almost undisturbed E major : or in Herring's outburst " It seems as clear as clear can be . . . " (Act I Sc. II) : or Nicolas' " The mother's cry is sad and weak " in *Nicolas and the Pickled Boys*—incidentally a wonderful *agitato* recollection of Ex. 2. Strangely enough it is in one of the communal hymns in *Nicolas*, " All people that on earth do dwell," where through considerations of practical necessity Britten has had to restrict his imagination, that one of his most dramatic and imaginative harmonic strokes occurs :

Ex.5
(NICOLAS CHOSEN BISHOP)

firm - ly stood

The unexpected arrival at C minor does not disturb the untutored congregation who sing the tune in a safe unison. Britten's mind tends to be at its most ingenious when working under a self-imposed or external discipline. His skill at sacrificing exactly nothing musically, even when faced with the disposal of untrained forces is nowhere more evident than in *St. Nicolas* or in *Let's Make an Opera*. And of course, Ex. 5 has already been anticipated by a figure in the movement to which the hymn forms the conclusion (No. V. *Nicolas comes to Myra and is chosen Bishop* : see bar 1 and its even more striking development 3 bars before [29]). Too much stress cannot be laid upon the strict thematic consistency in Britten's music.

Whilst European influences have been noted in Britten's work, most of them have been wrongly attributed. The *Spring Symphony's* first peformance gave rise to any amount of not very perceptive comment on the work's " orchestration " : it's not much appreciated that only bad orchestration reaches the ear as orchestration *per se*. To write of Britten's " melodic invention " and his " orchestral manipulation " of it, is demonstrably meaningless : it is dividing the indivisible. Only recently have we come to realise the absurdity of viewing Mahler as an " orchestrator " : even the superb one that his detractors permit him to be. As Ernest Newman acutely observed on one occasion, if we are to quote Mahler we must quote him in full-score. To write about the orchestration of the *Spring Symphony* without inevitably writing about the *Spring Symphony* would be impossible ; although that fact won't deter many from making the attempt. Apart from the opening of the first movement of Mahler's Ninth Symphony, I know of no other contemporary music so plainly conceived in terms of pure sound than the *Spring Symphony's* introduction.

Mahler himself being distressingly misunderstood in this country it is not surprising that his influence on Britten should have been both over- and under-estimated. There is no doubt that Britten learned a great deal from Mahler : but while the *Sinfonia da Requiem* shows that learning only partially digested, it would be difficult to point to passages in Britten's mature works and make the accusation of plagiarism, although it is clear enough that often what is absolutely and unmistakably Britten's, has made use of certain of Mahler's characteristics for its own purpose and ends. This digestive assimilation of influence has always played its part in the growth of the creative process towards a personal idiom. Britten's case is especially interesting in that he is the only major British composer who has in any way reacted positively to the closing stages of the 19th century Viennese school, which would include Alban Berg but exclude Schoenberg, at least from *Pierrot lunaire* onwards. When the time comes, this aspect of Britten's music will make him of quite exceptional historical significance.

While Mahler remains undervalued over here, it is obvious that Purcell should be recognized as the important influence he is in Britten's vocal style : but even a cursory glance at some of Mahler's and Britten's scores will reveal stylistic resemblances. Britten must have gained much from a study of *Das Lied von der Erde*, particularly the contralto's protracted recitativic-melodic vocal line in *Der Abschied*, as these two quotations suggest ; but the semitonal descent in the *Nicolas* extract would have occurred to Britten only :

Ex. 6
MAHLER:
Das Lied
von der Erde.
Ich spüre ei-nes feinen Windes Wehn ...

Ex. 7
(PRAYER OF NICOLAS)
Pity our simplici-ty,

Britten's liking for a stepwise melodic line was a late preoccupation of Mahler :

Ex. 8
MAHLER:
Das Lied
von der Erde

Ex. 9
BRITTEN:
(Albert Herring) I.2.
It seems as clear as clear can be that Sid's i-deas ······ are very

The actual thematic cut and shape of Britten's orchestral writing frequently bears a relation to that of the Viennese master's, particularly in its subtle rhythmic suspensions. (Compare the orchestral interpolations in the Introduction of the *Spring Symphony*, or the orchestral *codetta* to Ellen Orford's " Glitter of waves and glitter of sunlight " *Grimes*, Act II Sc. I, to almost any orchestral passage in *Der Abschied* from Mahler's *Das Lied.*) A closer examination of Britten's style might well disclose hitherto unsuspected roots. Britten's is a rich mind that has been nourished and stimulated by sources not over-familiar to English ears.

The most expert of contrapuntists, Britten has an unerring architectural facility that enables him to sustain an involved *ensemble* structure and drive it through to its conclusion as few composers have done since Mozart : the finale of *Lucretia* shows just that instinctive feeling for a developing structure that characterises the finale of *Figaro's* Act II. It is as apparent in the masterly *ensembles* of *Let's Make an Opera :* the interaction of real counterpoint that generates not the mere manipulation of themes but an integrated, self-sufficing form. Britten is peculiarly fond of canonic imitation : a device prominent in much of the choral writing in *St. Nicolas*, and in the *Ceremony of Carols* (see No. 6 : *This Little Babe*). There is no better example of Britten's inspired contrapuntal craftsmanship than in the middle (*Allegro pesante*) section of the *Spring Symphony's* last movement at [14] : " now little fish on tender stone begin to cast their bellies." The theme is given to the soprano, alto and tenor soloists who work it out imitatively between them ; after a few bars they are joined by the choir who separately enter in their four parts with the theme in its inversion. The canon in " Fair and Fair " (*Spring Symphony*, third movement) is a self-evident master-piece.

There is no space to discuss either Britten's sociological importance, or his stature as a religious composer : his actual influence on the musical life of this country has been little explored. At the very least we have an artist with a social conscience and a sense of public responsibility, and, let it be said, an acute understanding of the human heart and mind which leads him to be sad when we might think him most gay :

Those who understand the disquieting function of the pedal in the above quotation (analogies may be found elsewhere : see *Spring Symphony*, first movement, " The Driving Boy,") are probably in a position to recognise the tragic inflection of Britten's many-sided genius.

Resistances to Britten's Music : Their Psychology

By HANS KELLER

Perhaps the true secret of Freud's immense influence all over the world is to be found in the fact that he was the first humanist in clinical psychology, which although it followed a humanitarian tradition had become rather static and indifferent toward the deeper psychology of man. The fact that Freud's system grew out of therapeutic effort and continued to remain wholly dependent on therapeutic work for its scientific research was another potent factor which in itself is a derivative of humanism.　　　　　GREGORY ZILBOORG

Because each individual science is dissatisfied with its own isolated knowledge, it seeks a closer association with all available knowledge.　　　KARL JASPERS

In clinical psychoanalysis the quest for ubiquity has long since been supplanted by that for specificity. In the attempt to apply psychoanalytic concepts to other fields, similar progress has not always been evidenced.　　　ERNST KRIS

I. PROBABLE MISUNDERSTANDINGS ELIMINATED

THIS article is unfair. It attempts to explain hostility towards Britten's music on the assumption that from an intra-musical standpoint his major works are largely unassailable. Thereby many a respected colleague's unfavourable opinion of Britten is countered below the musical belt. Since, however, for me there is no doubt about Britten's greatness which indeed I tried to imply in a previous study (Keller [1])*, I have no honest choice for my line of intellectual action. At the same time, the results of the present investigation will be found to retain at any rate some of their significance even for the man who dislikes Britten. For they claim implicit validity in the case of any other composer inasmuch as he shows the musical character traits discussed in section II and is placed in the sociological situation outlined in section III below. The anti-Britten reader may moreover find that while he sees no reason to alter his musical opinion, he recognizes the extra-musical, depth-psychological sources which may lavishly supply it with energy ; he might even admit that with such powerful agents behind one's aversions, one must have a critical eye on one's criticisms lest they become exaggerated. Such, as I see it, is the deeper realistic meaning of Bernard Shaw's distrust of judgments based on dislike.

The countering of one's opponents' musical opinion, not by argument, but by psychological analysis—and this is really what the present article amounts to—hits below other belts beside the musical. For instance, it is tactless. This alone would not greatly disturb us, for tact has not altogether been found to have a precipitating influence upon the discovery of psychological truth. More serious scientifically is the fact that while the discovery of motives behind reasons does not as such dispose of the reasons, one yet

* Bibliography on p. 236.

tends to give the continuous impression, by concentrating on the irrational aspect of rationality, that one's adversaries' beliefs are false. Needless to say, they are, but it is scientifically unfair to imply that psychologizing proves it. One careful claim psychology can nevertheless make : if we are able to discover sufficiently strong motive powers behind a certain piece of alleged rationality for this to exist, there is sufficient reason for the allegedly reasonable to be unreasonable. In a word, the allegedly reasonable *need* not be valid, though it still may be. For example, I know enough about the psychology of my resistances to Sibelius to be able to say that what I have every artistic reason to believe to be my artistic objections to his music need not be artistic. But then I never write about Sibelius.

II. INDIVIDUAL PSYCHOLOGY : THE POLYCRATES COMPLEX
Timeo Danaos et dona ferentes. Virgil, *Aeneis* II, 49.

THE term " individual psychology " is here used not in its factious sense, *i.e.* as denoting the theories of Alfred Adler in opposition to those of Freud (psychoanalysis) on the one hand and Jung (Analytical Psychology) on the other, but simply as distinct from " social " or " group " psychology. Under the present heading, then, we have to consider which mental forces, other than those determined by its sociological and historio-geographical context, are likely to oppose Britten's music. But our individual-psychological considerations must, at the same time, take the sociological fact of Britten's popularity into account, *not* because this appears to be ultimately a function of his character and would be much the same in a different society, but because in any case we have to concern ourselves with the individual psychology of reactions to what Cicero called *aura popularis*, the shifting breeze of popular favour. For as far as art is concerned, these reactions tend to show that nothing makes a man more unpopular than his popularity. There is of course a certain justification in the highbrow mistrust of lowbrow appeal. " All really modern music after Strauss has remained esoteric " (Eisler). " Since 1870 artists have become accustomed to despise the public. The stupidity of the public is an accepted fact " (Cocteau). Nor need we accept these narrow historical qualifications ; the most modern times have merely intensified a state of affairs which the searching observer is able to detect throughout our cultural history : " The real intentions of all great creators of the occident were only comprehensible to a small circle. Michelangelo said his style was predestined to breed fools . . ." (Spengler). The exoteric, however, need not exclude, but can on the contrary often enclose the esoteric : Britten and Mozart. " In great art the superficial gratification which a first approach affords to the public may only be a bait ; the artist, as it were, draws his public closer into his net " (Kris). A recent critic, confused as her reflections often are, does realize that " much of [Britten's] work, like [for instance Michelangelo's] is esoteric " (Manning), though for her esoterism is the outcome of neurosis ; but then she doesn't know what a neurosis is.

Now what are the reasons why even many otherwise understanding musicians refuse to be drawn into Britten's net, why they regard not only his lucky stardom, but even the most immediately striking of his musical endowments and attainments—his effortless ease and productiveness, his supreme craftsmanship, brilliance, virtuosity, his spontaneity, inventiveness, cleverness, agility, versatility, not to speak of his so-called " eclecticism" (always demonstrably individual) —with the gravest suspicion, as if these qualities were in themselves defects and went to prove an absence of the inner, the deep, the lasting ? A logical reply depends on methodical sub-questions.

(1) What have all these abhorrent characteristics in common ? (2) Britten having after all also an individual psyche to be reckoned with, what are his own reactions to them ? (3) Do we know of any highly intelligent musician's aversion to them being so strong that it results in a provably and absurdly distorted opinion whose psychology can thus be conveniently examined on the surface, involving as his attitude must a minimum of logical reasons and a maximum of powerful psychological motives ?

To (1) : Britten's most obvious qualities all imply an overmeasure of good and easy artistic fortune—partly really, partly seemingly. From the extra-musical (psychological as well as merely material) gains which he derives from his talent for popularity, to the intra-musical comfort (fearfully overestimated by the outsider) of his " taking the gifts of his epoch, intact, and as self-evident matter, utilizing them at his will," of "shuffling [them] like a pack of cards " (as Lang says of Mozart), of his " yielding to an influence quite ingenuously, quite in the feminine fashion " (as Einstein says of Mozart), Britten's gifts convey the exceptional impression of being gifts : of his not having to pay for them.

To (2) : Surprisingly perhaps, Britten's own reactions to his exalted position do not in psychological essence appear to differ greatly from those of his detractors : he does not seem altogether alive to his genius—he clearly has ideas below his station.* Bach could be unaware of the extent of his genius ; Mozart stood at the

* I hardly know him personally, but am relying on printed and indeed well-known documentary evidence.

border of genius's self-knowledge ; Beethoven, with his character behind him and 19th century history before him, ruthlessly invaded the realm of self-cognition. At the present, over-conscious stage of our culture it is not easily possible for talent or genius not to be fully conscious of itself and its significance, unless strong endopsychic resistances put a stop to self-recognition. That Britten's mind would seem to harbour these can be gathered not only from his extreme modesty, but also from the fact that just as his depreciators minimize the value of his various " lucky " qualities, so he minimizes the part they play in his art and doubtless overestimates the contribution of his hard and regular work. I have pointed out elsewhere [2] that " the very fact that work plays such an important role in art makes it easily possible to magnify its importance, for it is only the exaggeration of something unimportant that will readily show up." Since, as I have shown in the same place, the moralisation of hard labour in art belongs to the guilt-laden psychology of our age and plays into the hands of the reaction against the Romantic Artist, while modesty does not only likewise but also receives the ethical support of English tradition, Britten is able to levy mental forces *en masse* against his full self-evaluation. Whether these can in themselves be considered sufficient to have brought about his complete victory over self-importance is a further and decisive question to which the cautious investigator will be inclined to reply in the negative.

To (3) : Fortunately from our, the psychological standpoint, the most unintelligent comment on Britten printed comes from one of the most intelligent writers on music (Adorno) who speaks of Britten's " meagreness playing trumps "—so far, so unverifiable—and of his " lacking command of technique "—an easily disprovable proposition which we need not trouble to contradict, since most other critics of Britten reproach him with what they feel to be his dangerous technical facility. How then did Dr. Adorno arrive at so grotesquely distorted a judgment ? It offers its own psychological key : the " trumps."

While Britten himself reacts to his utter intra-musical self-assurance, his " easy " musical victories, with social modesty, Adorno likewise feels uneasy about the obtrusive ease with which Britten's music attains its aims : there must be something wrong with what seems to be too perfectly, too sweatlessly right. Naturally there needn't be, but man is not natural, and one of his most powerful complexes commands : Thou shalt not be too lucky. It is this complex which makes us worry about having nothing to worry about, unhappy about happiness.

The human "need for punishment" (*Strafbeduerfnis*) was discovered by Freud, who showed it to be the result of tensions between ego and superego. Once one knows of the need's existence one can with one's naked eye observe it in the guilt- (obsessional) neuroses which dominate our culture ; the guilt psychoses, *i.e.* the depressive states, wherein the mind is yet far more thoroughly swayed by unconscious conflicts between ego and superego than in the obsessions, offer moreover an enlarged picture of man as a punishment-seeking animal. To Prof. Flugel [1] we owe the delineation and delimitation of the whole complex* that roots in the need for punishment, and also a telling and colourful label—quite in the psychoanalytic tradition :—

> If we do not experience sufficient pain, if things go too well with us and we have too much luck, we begin to feel uneasy because our need for punishment has not been met. Hence at bottom the fear of Hubris, of arrogance or 'uppishness,' which the ancient Greeks, themselves a relatively guilt-free people, were yet able to discern as a fundamental human trait . . . It is not surprising then that throughout history those who have sought to increase human power and understanding should have aroused a degree of suspicion and distrust that has often led to martyrdom, for at bottom it is felt that such pioneers are guilty of Hubris, and that if they had their way they would involve all mankind in the penalties incurred by those who presume 'above their station' . . . In our own civilization all of us probably experience this need [for punishment] in some degree ; we all tend to be suspicious or 'superstitious' about good fortune and successful enterprise, but some far more than others. In this respect we would appear to be the victims of a complex comparable to certain other complexes of widespread (perhaps universal) incidence but varying intensity, such as the Oedipus complex, the castration complex, and some others with which psychoanalysis has made us familiar. I would suggest that it be called the Polycrates complex, after Polycrates the tyrant of Samos . . .

It was for instance, I believe, the Polycrates complex which was responsible for Oscar Wilde's fate : unable to tolerate his easy and complete success on the one hand and his amoralistic philosophy on the other, it drove him by every available means—*i.e.* both through his offences and his subsequent behaviour—into one of the most savage forms of self-punishment great talent has ever meted out to itself. It was, I think, the Polycrates complex too that made this section's motto ('I fear the Danai even when they bring gifts') into a universal saying, for the Polycrates complex tends to smell a rat in every gift, and the proverb serves as rationalisation. "Oh rats !" indeed the Polycrates complex exclaims when it encounters the all too good luck, both extra- and intra-musical, which Britten owes to his particular gifts, their assured artistic manifestations being duly taken for procacity, their sparkling

* In view of the general—popular as well as psychological—misuse of this term (which was introduced into psychoanalysis by the so-called " Zürich School " [Bleuler-Jung]), *e.g.* in the scientifically misleading phrase " inferiority complex," we may be allowed to restate its psychoanalytic definition : " A group of emotionally invested ideas partially or entirely *repressed*." (Jones[1]; our italics.)

exoterism for lack of esoterism. And it would seem to me that it is Britten's own Polycrates complex that is at the bottom of his resistances to self-recognition and makes possible his complete victory over what would be considered a presumptious attitude.

By making Britten the scapegoat for our own unconscious guilts (which are the source of the need for punishment), we are by no means freeing ourselves from *self*-punishment. Quite apart from the fact that the projection of guilt which is the basis of vicarious punishment might in itself be regarded as a special form of identification (Jones [2]), " the public puts itself," on any but the most primitive level of aesthetic experience, " at least for a moment, in the artist's place, identifies unconsciously with him to however a slight degree " (Kris). By depreciating Britten we punish ourselves for identifying ourselves with his presumptious music : a special manifestation of the general law according to which the critic criticizes himself. As soon, however, as something seems manifestly " wrong" with a particular Britten work, the Polycrates complex relaxes its hold over the critic's judgment, since in such a case Britten no longer presumes above his station. Thus, in the case of the " Spring Symphony," after it had been (wrongly) established that it was not a symphony (for the motives behind this finding, see section III below), enthusiastic praise came forth from the otherwise most punitive quarters. Yet more striking support for our hypothesis may be gathered from the reactions to the children's opera : " It looks as if this small scale opera would have the broadest appeal of [all Britten operas] " (Stein) ; it even appealed to Britten's sternest critics. From the point of view of the Polycrates complex the work has not only the general advantage of being admittedly slight and therefore appeasingly imperfect, but it descends from the level of Polycrates —the involuntary usurper of parental omnipotence—right down to the level of the child, thus assuaging all our childish fears. That Britten's adult music is often accused of childishness and immaturity strikes us now as a matter of psychological course.

III. SOCIAL PSYCHOLOGY : GROUP SELF-CONTEMPT

Paepstlicher als der Papst sein. (German saying)

Britten's work meets with far more understanding and far less resistances abroad than in his own country. The proverb " *Nemo propheta in patria* " springs to mind ; Latin proverbs, however, have a way of starting with " *Nemo*," which may be as it should be in the case of " *Nemo ante mortem beatus*," but argues an unwarrantable generalisation about prophets and their like. The proverb is true in regard to some of them ; unfortunately I cannot pretend

232

to know which. In the specific case of Britten, however, I have arrived at a piece of truth.

We take our cue, not from a specimen of British resistances to Britten, but again from Adorno's attitude. On the more musical plane this is determined by his understanding running along the lines of the Austrian and German rather than of the more Eastern and Western traditions. Now since " all through his career Benjamin Britten has been interested in the problem of effecting a rapprochement between . . . the more provincial elements of English musical styles and the cosmopolitan techniques of Europe " (Mellers [1]), it is impossible to get the feel for his style and indeed his forms for one who finds it emotionally difficult to move far beyond the Vienna school. The twentieth-century composer of opera in England " is committed, from the start, to self-consciousness ; he will be highly sophisticated, a virtuoso, a rhetorician, and—in no discreditable sense—an exhibitionist " (Mellers [2]). From Adorno's words (see section I above) it can be gathered that he does not altogether take kindly to Britten's exhibitionism—that the historio-geographical limitations of his understanding allow his Polycrates complex to storm freely, and, conversely, that the latter may even inhibit his intellectual appreciation of Britten's historical significance. " In his best work, Britten has succeeded in creating a fusion, not a confusion of stylizations ; and he has succeeded in making his ' baroque ' opera a part of the English tradition . . . undoubtedly the cleverest thing he has done is, almost single-handed, of his own thought and creative effort, to have succeeded where Purcell failed " (ibid). Britten's forms, his monothematicisms, variation- and ostinato-structures are bound to be thorns in Adorno's side, who is really disgusted at Stravinsky's " harmonic-rhythmic ostinato-cement " and can hardly perceive the wide arc which Britten describes from Purcell beyond Stravinsky. But what have Austro-German prejudices to do with the predominance of English resistances to Britten ?

In the investigations which Margaret Phillips and I have undertaken into the psychology of small social groups (and on which each of us has so far given only a preliminary report) I encountered, in the diary of an Auxiliary Fire Brigade's group life during the war, a social-psychological attitude to which I have given the somewhat unprecise name of " group self-contempt "*, and which seems

* A group has no self ; once metaphorical terms are introduced into science one never knows what may happen to them : the metaphor may in the end be taken for real. I do not wish, however, to saddle my musical colleagues with a new technical psychological term denoting an unfamiliar attitude ; for our present purposes the descriptive term " group self-contempt " will do.

to me to make its invariable appearance in any group as soon as certain clearly definable conditions are fulfilled. I shall here confine myself to the wider groups in which I have observed the attitude, *i.e.* women, Jews, prostitutes, and incidentally also populations under Nazi occupation during the war (in regard to which I have relied on second-hand information published in the *Lancet*). The reader may wonder how these groups, different as they seem from each other in every conceivable respect, can be thrown under one hat, where in fact the *tertium comparationis* lies. They all, however, display the necessary degree of exclusive identification which makes the application of the term " group " convenient and indeed psychologically justifiable—exactly how justifiable can be gathered from the very phenomenon of group self-contempt, whose aetiology is, I submit, this :—

A group is dominated by another group in superior position : women by men, Jews by Gentiles, prostitutes by society and so on. Since the dominated group inevitably feels the dominating group to be *in loco parentis*, the former's members project part of what might loosely be called their common superego† on to the dominating group, with the result that they turn part of the aggression which they would but can't release towards the dominating group back against their own group.   The introversion of frustrated aggression originally directed against a parent (figure) is a process that has been well channelled from infancy onwards, but the present course of psychic events is more complicated and, for the average individual, more satisfying. It is not a simple in-turning of aggression, but rather an aggressive flow whose objects lie both in the outside and the inside world : inasmuch, that is to say, as any member of the dominated group identifies himself with it, his group self-contempt is directed against himself, while insofar as he feels himself to have remained a separate individual, his group self-contempt consists of out-turned aggression : moralized (superego) sadism taking his group, as distinct from himself, as object.   One can only describe the process by dividing it, but I do not imagine it to be necessarily divided : the phenomena of female misogynism, Jewish anti-semitism, prostitutes' anti-prostitutionalism and so forth seem to show that one can after all sit at once on two stools. This capacity seems to vary from individual to individual : many must no doubt pay for group self-contempt with lively internal conflict.   And all must pay in terms of realism and logic ; but reason has always been found to be a small price for emotional gratification.

† In order to make group formation at all possible, they had in any case and in the first place to project their individual superegos on to a leader or leading idea(s).

British anti-Brittenism is, I submit, a prominent aspect of British musical group self-contempt, though in this case the dominating group which, together with the contempt it displays, (" Das Land ohne Musik "), serves as model for the group-self-contemptuous attitude, has its centre—the bulk of the Austro-German tradition's exponents and followers—in the past and only its periphery—the Adornos—in the present. But while this self-contempt can be heard at work in many English compositions themselves, it does not readily direct itself against the more exclusively English composers who have developed at a safe distance from Austro-German techniques, so that they are not so easily felt to offend against them.

The " specialist " reactions to the " Spring Symphony " go to support our interpretation. Since the work is vocal and lacks the " Viennese " sonata-developmental approach, while on the other hand presuming up to Mahler's symphonic station, group self-contempt denies it the Austrian honorary degree " Symphony," notwithstanding its extended intra-musical unity and its, at bottom, classical symphonic scheme which is *not* a mere matter of classical succession of tempi, as several writers seemed to believe, true to the critical tradition of keeping to the surface. The reactions to the " Spring Symphony " also offer some insight into the possible interaction of the individual and social psychology of resistances to Britten : group self-contempt having ascertained beyond doubt that not all is well with the work, the Polycrates complex is appeased.

But the question remains—why is (or was until a short time ago) British group self-contempt often more severe than Austro-German criticisms of British musical life, why indeed has highbrow Britain adopted a more Austro-German attitude towards Britten than Austria and Germany ? The reasons appear to be twofold. On the one hand, they lie in the particular structure of British musical self-contempt, which takes its orders from Vienna's past (and its emigrants abroad), while Vienna itself doesn't. In fact there seem to be subtle signs that British musical developments are about to exert a powerful influence on Vienna, so that in the not too distant future we may get the reverse spectacle : Austrian group self-contempt with the renascent English tradition as dominating group. Meanwhile we have to reckon with the bewildering picture of a state of flux produced by the historical overlapping between two opposite forms of group self-contempt. The weakening of Austrian dominance can already be felt in the slight weakening of British resistances against Britten, similarly as the weakening of male dominance has resulted in a decrease of female misogynism. On the other hand, the general nature of group self-contempt, wherein lies the second lot of reasons for the English group's over-Austrian attitude, is more conservative than one may hope. We must not forget that the primitive, unconscious superego is at the root of the trouble, that infantile moralizing agency whose " excessive severity does not follow a real prototype but corresponds to the strength which is used in fending off the Oedipus complex " (Freud [1]). That is to say, similarly as in childhood the superego did not just arise out of an incorporation of the parents' prohibitive and maybe aggressive attitudes, but rather out of a combination of these with the child's own savage, frustrated, and hence in-turned aggression, so in group self-contempt the dominated group's superegos, or at any rate the more relentless among them, may not rest satisfied with taking the dominating (parental) group's contempt or commands as prototype, but may be pleased to add plenty of backward-flowing sadism of their own. Thus they will tend to be over-obedient to the dominating group, " to out-pope the pope "(*papas*), as our present section's motto has it; it is well known that many a Jewish anti-semite is, like Weininger, more anti-semitic than his models. And the more you out-pope, the later will you be prepared to cease poping altogether. In fact, group self-contempt meets diverse needs of the Polycrates complex, and for me, the superficially, most respectable resistances to Britten boil down to primitive guilt.

BIBLIOGRAPHY

Adorno, Th.W.: *Philosophie der neuen Musik*, 1949. Brill, A. A.: *Freud's Contribution to Psychiatry*, 1945. Cocteau, J.: *Opium*, 1933. Einstein, A.: *Mozart*, 1946. Eisler, H.: *Komposition für den Film*, 1949. Flugel, J. C.: (1) *Man, Morals and Society*, 1945. (2) *The Psychoanalytic Study of the Family*, 1939. Freud, S.: (1) *An Outline of Psychoanalysis*, 1949. (2) *Das ökonomische Problem des Masochismus*, in *Internationale Zeitschrift für Psychoanalyse*, X, 1924. (3) *Massenpsychologie und Ich-Analyse*, 1921. (4) *Zur Geschichte der psychoanalytischen Bewegung*, in *Jahrbuch für psychoanalytische Forschungen*, VI, 1914. Glover, E.: *Psychoanalysis*, 1939. Jones, E.: (1) *Papers on Psychoanalysis*, 1918. (2) *Einige Faelle von Zwangsneurose* (II), in *Jahrbuch für psychoanalytische Forschungen*, V, 1913. Jung, C. G.: *Diagnostische Assoziationsstudien*, 1906-10. Keller, H.: (1) *Britten and Mozart*, in *Music and Letters*, XXIX/1, 1948. (2) *Kyla Greenbaum and the Psychology of the Modern Artist*, in *Music Review*, X/4, 1949. See also Phillips. Kris, E.: *Approaches to Art*, in Lorand, S. (ed.): *Psychoanalysis Today*, 1948. Lang, P. H.: *Music in Western Civilization*, 1942. Manning, R.: *From Holst to Britten*, 1949. Mellers, W. H.: (1) Review of Britten's *Beggar's Opera* in *Music Survey*, II/1, 1949. (2) *Stylization in Contemporary British Music*, in *Horizon*, XVII/101, 1948. Phillips, M. and Keller H.: *Some Sociological Concepts of the Group*, 2 papers to British Psychological Society, Social Psychology Section, 1947. Spengler, O.: *Der Untergang des Abendlandes* (I), 1923. Stein, E.: *Benjamin Britten's Operas*, in *Opera* I/1, 1950. Weininger, O.: *Das Judentum*, in *Geschlecht und Charakter*, 1908. Zilboorg, G.: *A History of Medical Psychology*, 1941.

A Note on the Spring Symphony
By BENJAMIN BRITTEN

I WROTE the Spring Symphony in the Autumn and Winter of 1948/9, and finished the score in the late Spring of 1949. For two years I had been planning such a work, a symphony not only dealing with the Spring itself, but with the progress of Winter to Spring and the re-awakening of the earth and life which that means. Originally I had wanted to use mediaeval Latin verse and had made a selection of fine poems ; but a re-reading of much English lyric verse and a particularly lovely Spring day in East Suffolk, the Suffolk of Constable and Gainsborough, made me change my mind.

The work is written for a large orchestra, mixed choirs and boys' choir, three soloists (soprano, contralto and tenor) and a cow-horn. It is in the traditional four movement shape of a symphony, but with the movements divided into shorter sections bound together by a similar mood or point of view. Thus after an introduction, which is a prayer, in Winter, for Spring to come, the first movements deal with the arrival of Spring, the cuckoo, the birds, the flowers, the sun and "May month's beauty"; the second movements paint the darker side of Spring—the fading violets, rain and night ; the third is a series of dances, the love of young people ; the fourth is a May-day Festival, a kind of bank holiday, which ends with the great 13th Century traditional song "Sumer is i-cumen in," sung or rather shouted by the boys.

A Children's Symposium
on Britten's Children's Opera

(1) Lyric Theatre, Hammersmith.

BEFORE I went to see Britten's children's opera, "The Little Sweep," I knew nothing at all about opera. Now I know that opera sets out to tell a story, supplementing the words with music which, as one of the actors said, brings to the surface and emphasizes all the exciting, romantic things lying beneath ordinary, every-day happenings. I think that this was illustrated very well in the opera where Miss Baggott is on the verge of opening the toy room cupboard and discovering the little chimney-sweep. The music screws you up to a point of quite nerve-racking tension which would be very difficult to achieve in an ordinary play.

The scenes before the actual opera gave this fundamental explanation, introduced us to the story and helped to make the opera a more personal affair, but I think that these scenes could have been used more profitably. The title was " Let's Make an Opera " but, although it was very interesting to hear the children's adventures in finding a hip-bath, and to watch the scenery put up and hear some of the songs beforehand, we did not learn very much about how the opera was actually *made*. For instance, we were told that one of the aims of an opera-writer was to try to vary as much as possible the different combinations of voices, but we never learnt how the different combinations were chosen for the various songs.

Most of the songs I liked, particularly the one which the children sang when they held a consultation in the nursery about what was to be done with the Little Sweep; I think the music to the little chimney sweeper's plea, " Please don't send me up again," is rather moving. That is an example where, however well the actor had spoken, words alone could never have expressed all that the music did. The only part of the opera I did not enjoy was the part where the children pulled the little boy down the chimney. The firm way in which they pull the rope and the way the song matches their actions—gently first, now a little harder, now a *tug*—is so effective that it is horrible. I shuddered to think how painful it must be to be stuck in a chimney and pulled down with such difficulty.

It was great fun singing the songs arranged for the audience. I thought at first I should hate this since I am generally very embarrassed at that kind of thing, but the songs were so irresistible and Mr. Norman Del Mar created such a friendly atmosphere among the audience that it was perhaps the pleasantest part of the afternoon.

By the end of the opera, when all the actors ran back on to the stage and sang the stage-coach song, I was really excited and this last song seemed to harmonize exactly with this excited feeling. It trotted first, then
> " Let me see you canter, canter, canter
> Good brown mare,"
then the song galloped, but everything must come to an end, as we realized when the song slowed down to a walk and finally stopped.

I am not musical, and I never thought music could excite me so much. I used to think opera was quite beyond my sphere and suspected that I should find it rather dull. Now I have changed my mind and want to hear more opera. " The Little Sweep " has at least removed my indifference.

ELIZABETH MULLEN (16).

(2)   Concert Hall, Broadcasting House.

I went to Britten's opera, " The Little Sweep," which was performed at the B.B.C. I had previously heard it on the wireless, and the idea of the audience singing was a novel one to me ; so I was looking forward to joining in myself. In the first song for the audience, " The Sweep's Song," the music for the words " Sweep, sweep," sounded most discordant, yet it did not grate on my ears. The conductor, Norman Del Mar inspired you to sing lustily, and the result was not unpleasant.

When Sammy the sweep-boy, was stuck in the chimney, one could not hear that he was frightened or suffocating. I liked the song " Please don't send me up again," the most in all the opera.

The Night Song sounds very sleepy and slow, and the cries of the different birds are most realistic.

The opera ends with the Coaching Song, in which both the stage and the audience join in, having different parts. The song gets faster, until the words " Let me see you gallop, good brown mare " are sung ; after which the music, words and horse "slacken pace, and the journey is ended."

As I came out of the B.B.C. I had a lovely feeling inside me ; a feeling of contentment at having seen something worth while.

NORA FRANEY (13).

(3)   Surveying both productions.

THE most important thing I have to say about this experimental opera is that I enjoyed it very much indeed. I have actually seen the whole of it twice ; the first time at the B.B.C. and the second, as it should be seen, at the Lyric Theatre. Seeing it at the B.B.C. was like listening to it over the wireless as there was no movement and no distracting, colourful costume ; therefore full attention could be paid to the very infectious music. I maintain I certainly got more out of the music on my first hearing than when I *saw* the opera.

I do not know whether making an audience sing and play a part in an opera is an original idea but I do know that in this opera it is a very successful one. I am sure that one of the main drawbacks of this is that the audience may not get to know the songs well enough to sing them successfully or it may not wish to sing. In the particular opera of which I am writing, both these difficulties are overcome admirably. The songs are so haunting, so catching, that they can be sung almost without learning them and are so pleasant that the audience overcomes its diffidence, saying, " Even if I'm not a brilliant singer I can still have a try," and roars out lustily in company with the comic gestures of a very enthusiastic and helpful conductor, Norman Del Mar. I think that it is through him that the atmosphere between stage and theatre is so pleasant.

A few details : in the first scene the sweep and his son sing a very effectively gruesome duet, which makes one realize why the children are so concerned about Sammy's fate. The audience's bath song, although a nice tune in itself, does not sound as " bath-like " as I think it could. The song which all sing together after Juliet's assumed faint is, to my mind, the best of the opera.

The various melodies are so haunting that I find it very difficult to keep them out of my head ; but, I think, humming through my favourite phrase, why should I ?

ENA FRANEY (15).

The Significance of Britten's Operatic Style
BY HANS F. REDLICH

THAT it must be difficult even for the well-informed and discerning critic to arrive at a balanced assessment of Britten's creative achievement at the present stage of his career was forcibly brought home to me by this remark of Desmond Shawe-Taylor after the recent Albert Hall performance of the " Spring Symphony": " . . . . We must, I think, firmly part company from those sincere, but misguided persons who find Britten merely imitative and eclectic. His signature appears all over the work . . . . In this work he has brought his personal idiom to full and splendid fruition . . . . "[1] This statement may contain the seeds of future misunderstandings and—despite its obvious sincerity and good-will—ultimately be responsible for an historically faulty approach to the phenomenon of Benjamin Britten.

Britten appears to me as a composer of unquestionable creative spontaneity and of remarkable originality in his mental processes. Yet it is undeniable that the actual substance of his music suggests a strongly eclectic bent of mind. A paradoxical situation ? Not so much, perhaps, as worried sympathisers like Shawe-Taylor try to make out. Britten is—in contradistinction to a considerable section of his British audiences—a shrewd and penetrating student of post-Wagnerian operatic developments who uses the achievements of his forerunners as models for the pattern of his own musical imagination: Wozzek, socially ostracised and disenfranchised, fighting against a community of sadistic philistines (a preconception of the dramatic situation in " Peter Grimes ") ; Stravinsky's statuesque Opera-Oratorio " Oedipus Rex " (a blueprint for the dramatic processes in the " Rape of Lucretia "); opera-parody as automatic reaction against Wagnerian " pathos " (Hindemith's " Das Nusch-Nuschi "

240

(1921) with its King Mark parody anticipating the satirical " Tristan" quotation in "Albert Herring "[2]), as well as Brecht-Weill's " Dreigroschenoper " (1927), especially its Finale, " Des Koenigs reitender Bote kommt," which coins the stylistic vocabulary for the rehearsal of the children's chorus in " Herring," the parodistical operatic patterns in " Let's Make an Opera " and the contrapuntally rigged-up ensembles in Britten's version of the " Beggar's Opera." The list might also include Pfitzner and Busoni, Richard Strauss and Verdi.

In his works for the musical stage Britten has epitomized the operatic achievements of the last half-century, presenting his audience frequently with an artistic synthesis, the elemental composition of which was often quite impenetrable for his listeners. We may choose to call that artistic eclecticism, but certainly Britten is here in the very best company. He is as much an eclectic as Monteverdi, Mozart and Wagner, who in turn epitomized in their mature works the stylistic innovations of their contemporary and preceding epoch. It is the " eclectic " Monteverdi's " Favola d'Orfeo," 1607 (fusing Florentine recitative, Marenzio's madrigal and Giovanni Gabrieli's orchestra), which we associate with the origin of Opera, not Jacopo Peri's original pioneer work " Euridice," 1602, which is now as dead as a doornail. For us today, Mozart's " eclectic " " Figaro " and " Don Giovanni " represent the acme of Italian buffa and dramma giocoso, not their original models, Piccini's " Buona Figliuola " (1760) and Gazzaniga's " Convitato di pietra " (1787). Finally, it is Wagner's unashamedly imitative and eclectic " Lohengrin " (1850), which has ruled the stage for exactly a century, and not Weber's earlier, musically richer and more original " Euryanthe " (1823). To round off one paradox by another : the fact that Britten is so firmly established as an eclectic composer, of Mozart's type, seems to me the best guarantee of his lasting importance as an operatic representative for his own epoch. Britten's " eclecticism " goes even further. He recovers the secret processes of classical composition, a technique all but forgotten during the progressive turmoil of the last decades with their often herostratic protagonists. Again, Britten's music is subject to a severity of formal purpose, at present only to be found in some works of members of the dodecaphonic school.[3]

I should like to prove this assertion by a significant example taken from Britten's opera " Albert Herring," a work which contains undoubtedly many scrappy and hastily improvised passages, particularly in its recitative sections and in those scenes where Britten's predilection for adolescent fun occasionally gets the upper hand over the innate catholicity of his method of composition. I am here referring to the melodic paragraph associated with Albert's gradual spiritual transformation from a repressed sucker into an emotionally normalised youth. This important Leitmotif of the Opera[4] may have been suggested to Britten by a passage in Verdi's "Falstaff"[5], the choice of which is in itself a pointer towards Britten's own artistic goal. The relationship between model and derivation and the transformation to which the musical elements of the model are subjected in the latter's digestive process, might determine Britten's own stylistic converging point. Verdi's passage, satirically paraphrasing romantic and "spookish" sensations by appropriately "guying" highly romanticised harmonies of Weber-Wagner flavour, describes the dreaded midnight appearance of Herne, the dark hunter [6]. It contains an element of counterpoint between voice and French horn, contrapuntally independent in Britten's duologue* for bass flute and bass clarinet, and propelling Britten's music irresistibly forward where Verdi has to round off his paragraph with a conventional cadence.

Britten subjects his characteristic motif to a number of transformations (variations), reflecting the different stages in Albert's gradual process of mental awakening. They cannot all be enumerated here, but I should like to mention one in particular, which occurs in the symphonic interlude, chiefly devoted to an initial "plugging" of this important motif.

*See footnote on p. 243

This beautiful (two-part) counterpoint, deftly canalised in a kind of Barcarolle rhythm—surely one of Britten's happiest inspirations—has in turn served as a model for one of his finest songs : "Canticle I," the beginning of which is quoted below.

A subtle, but organic link between Britten's operatic music and his lyrical style.

Examples of such convincing part writing* and logical consequence are significant pointers towards a future synthesis of style, which ought to become important even beyond the aquatic boundaries of Britten's homeland.

No doubt, there are chinks in his operatic armour. He might profitably outgrow his apparent obsession with the (rather transitory) fun of Opera-Parody.[7] Richard Strauss (with whom Britten shares some characteristic features) was equally addicted to it in the days of his youth, when planning (and ultimately suppressing) the opera " Till Eulenspiegel," of which the purely symphonic " merry pranks " have alone survived, and later, when revelling in the amiable shallowness of Wolzogen's " Ueberbrettl " atmosphere of " Feuersnot." Britten might also try to widen the ambit of his dramatic subjects. So far he has been almost exclusively occupied with one single operatic subject, the dramatic admissibility of which is not beyond doubt. " Grimes," " Herring," " Lucretia " (even " The Beggar's Opera " and the forthcoming " Billy Budd ") are essentially determined by the root problem " Ego versus community," a theme which has rarely been treated with lasting success on the operatic stage.[8] This problem becomes even more complicated through the psychological abnormality of the principal characters in Britten's operas.

Grimes—at once flagellant and sadist ; Tarquinius—obsessed with the sexual craving of a maniacal satyr ; Albert Herring—a model of pathological repression and mother-fixation : it is true that these heroes of a new operatic stage seem to reflect faithfully the psychological abysses into which our present " dark age " may

---

*Simplified music examples given here ; the scores themselves must be consulted for a full examination of Britten's counterpoint.—Eds.

be tumbling. But is that quality of tormenting topicality enough to make them " aere perennius " ? Is it Gesualdo's hysterical experiment or Monteverdi's creative sanity that has survived the holocaust of posterity ? And what remains of the proverbial " horrors " of the Opera of the French Revolution ? Only Beethoven's " Fidelio," which transforms sordid historical antecedents into an idealistic paean for freedom. The occasions are indeed extremely rare, when emotionally abnormal characters endure in Opera. Marschner's Vampire and Hans Heiling, Wagner's Klingsor and Kundry, Verdi's hunchback Rigoletto, Strauss' Salome and Elektra are cases in point. They are the distinguished members of an operatic " chamber of horrors," willingly avoided by everybody who has a chance to escape into the elysian spheres of Monteverdi's, Gluck's and Mozart's operatic world.

In order to fulfil his creative destiny Britten may have to return to the elemental foundations of operatic processes. In choosing a subject for operatic treatment he should not overlook the eternal validity of E. T. A. Hoffmann's dictum :

". . . Eine wahrhaftige Oper scheint mir nur die zu sein, in welcher die Musik unmittelbar aus der Dichtung als notwendiges Erzeugnis derselben entspringt . . . ."* (E. T. A. Hoffmann " Der Dichter und der Komponist," from " Die Serapionsbrueder," Vol. I. 1819),
to which could be added Richard Wagner's early confession :

" . . . Ich kann keinen dichterischen Stoff ergreifen, der sich nicht durch die Musik erst bedingt : mein " Saengerkrieg ", wenn das dichterische Element darin vorwaltet, war meiner hoeheren Absicht nach aber auch ohne Musik nicht moeglich . . ."† (in a letter to E. Hanslick, dated January 1st, 1847)
and which might be rounded off by Claudio Monteverdi's moving confession to his faithful librettist A. Striggio jun.:

Cl. Monteverdi (in a letter, dated Venice, December 9th, 1616, rejects a suggested libretto " Le nozze della Tetide," a " favola maritima," because of its apparent lack of fundamental human interest) :

" . . . Come caro Signore, potro io imitare il parlar di venti, se non parlano ! Et come potro io con il mezzo loro movere li afretti ! Mosse l'Arianna per esser donna, et mosse parimenti Orfeo per essere homo et non vento . . . . L'Arianna mi porta ad un giusto lamento, et l'orfeo ad una giusta preghiera . . . ."‡

Are Britten's opera librettos truly conditioned by music in the sense of these three axiomatic statements ? A negative interim reply to this question has been volunteered by one of his own librettists, tacitly confirming that Britten so far has not found the ideal poet companion of genius and musical understanding comparable to Mozart's Da Ponte and Richard Strauss' Hofmannsthal. With disarming modesty Eric Crozier confessed[9] to be " neither poet nor playwright " and to the belief " that a librettist is a craftsman working for an artist." Such an axiom may spell certain danger for the composer, depending on the practical results of such " craftsmanship," without always being able to recondition them as effectively and ruthlessly as Verdi did with the products of his librettists. In E. T. A. Hoffmann's dialogue between the poet and the composer, in Wagner's truly amazing creative symbiosis between these two incompatibilities and in the letters, exchanged between Strauss and Hofmannsthal, Britten's friend and adviser might find altogether different conceptions of the poet's function in his collaborative union with an opera composer. It must be the sincere wish of every music lover, that Britten may find in time this complementary personality, who alone will be able to help him to carry out his creative mission as the first English opera composer of universal importance.

(1) Cf. *New Statesman and Nation*, March 18th, 1950.
(2) Cf. Vocal Score, Act II/I, p. 184, 6 bars before cue No. 19.
(3) Their music—needless to say—is moving on a plane which is, technically and structurally, totally different from Britten's.
(4) Cf. " Albert Herring ", vocal score, p. 245. It turns up in various rhythmic and melodic variants whenever Albert refers to his spiritual change. Cf. also V.Score p. 250 *et passim*, 278 (cue No. 99) and p. 354 (cue No. 63).
(5) Cf. full score (Ricordi), p. 330 cue No. 14, Act III, part 1. This is a work whose general technique and special atmosphere must have exercised a formidable and beneficent influence on Britten for a long while. Verdi's melodic sentence is repeated at cue No. 15 of Act III in a characteristic variation (based on an ostinato motif in the third horn) in which the spiritual relationship to Britten's passage becomes even more self-evident.
(6) Cf. Shakespeare's " The Merry Wives of Windsor," Act IV, Scene 3.
(7) Cf. the parodistic " Threnody " in " Albert Herring," Act III, and its serious counterpart in the " Rape of Lucretia," Act II/2, Vocal Score, p. 197 *et passim* (" Alla marcia grave").
(8) Berg's " Wozzek," Moussorgsky's " Boris " and Pfitzner's " Palestrina " come most readily to mind in that context. The two latter are dramatically inconclusive because they lack fundamental dramatic polarities. They fail because neither Dimitri nor Cardinal Borromeo are more than sparring partners for Boris and Palestrina. Wozzek alone succeeds, because the central antithesis Wozzek-Marie all but obliterates the social tug of war between Wozzek and the surrounding world of " *larvae et lemures*."
(9) Cf. the libretto of " Albert Herring ", 1947, foreword p. 6 *et passim*.
* " It appears to me that in a real and true opera the music must immediately spring from the words as their necessary product . . . "
† " I cannot lay hold of any poetic material that does not make itself first dependent on the music : according to my ultimate intentions my ' Singers' Contest ' [The singers' contest on the Wartburg (" Tannhaeuser," Act II)] was not possible without music even where the poetic element predominated . . . ."
‡ " . . . How, my dear Sir, can I imitate the speech of the winds [i.e. the Four Winds, mythological characters in the suggested libretto] if they do not speak, and how can I, with only half of them, stir the emotions ? Arianne stirs the emotions through being a woman and in the same way Orfeo through being a man and not a wind . . . Arianne inspired me to write a lament and Orfeo to write a prayer . . . "

Britten's Sinfonietta in D minor, Op. 1

By HAROLD TRUSCOTT

ALMOST the one outstanding early instrumental work by Britten, the Sinfonietta is a real achievement as a courageous attempt to develop a coherent style and to get to grip with larger issues. Written in 1932, when he was 19, it shows, somewhat unequally but positively, a grasp of sonata-style which was only to come to fruition many years later.

A classically-rooted but personal instrumental style is notoriously more difficult to come by than a vocal style ; those who trace instrumental mastery to vocal origins are being misled by appearances. Nor should an easy instrumental technical mastery deceive. This has been a stumbling-block to Britten, but the Sinfonietta shows a clearer instrumental vision than he had for many years afterwards.

He has always been a tonal composer ; sometimes instinctively, as in the present instance, sometimes, it would appear, merely because he did not believe in atonality—a negative attitude now being replaced by a consciously positive one.

Each of the three movements has its clear tonal build, dramatic in the first movement (the gradual arrival in midflow at the second key, F major, is superb) ; lyrical in the second ; and lyrico-dramatic in the finale, in a straight drive through one key at an unlyrical pace, with various parts of the key as resting-places, buttress-fashion.

The highest point of form and eloquence in the work is the first movement's merging of development into recapitulation, with an impact of development on the main material that Schubert would have loved. In fact, the whole movement shows a kind of formal mastery which is rare in English music.

The shape and its coherence are abetted by the material. The main theme of the first movement grows from the first bars into a huge and curving paragraph. The slow movement is least successful ; its theme is too indeterminate for the variation-fantasy built upon it. The finale is the right energetic finish to a highly sensitive and finely organized work : the main theme of the first movement is not only the seed of the tarantella rhythm, but proves to be the finale's eventual aim and goal.

246

Britten " The Eclectic "

By CHARLES STUART

MOST people of middle age remember the reign of the Holy Ego. An artist's first duty was to *express himself*. Like all vague phrases, this had to be elucidated by metaphor. The artist's spirit was a quarry where his artworks were hewn and shaped. Everything came from deep within. Self-communing and umbilical contemplation were the order of the day. The artist's psyche was a delicate flame or flower : he had to shield it with cupped hands or hothouse glass. And so on. It was this centripal trend that produced the music of Delius and the mature Scriabin : " soulprint " music of great beauty and (for many of us) great tedium.

On these and related points I have had two or three talks with Britten at various times. Here is an agreed summary of his views on the relation between music and its composer :

> It is all largely a matter of when one was born. Had I been born in 1813 instead of 1913 I should have been a romantic, primarily concerned to express my personality in music. The rot (if that isn't too strong a word) began with Beethoven. Before Beethoven music served things greater than itself. For example, the glory of God, or the glory of the State, or the composer's social environment. It had a defined social function. That was the kind of setting in which Mozart and our own Purcell worked. After Beethoven the composer became the centre of his own universe. The romantics became so intensely personal that it looked as though we should reach a point where the composer would be the only man who understood his own music ! Then came Picasso and Stravinsky. They loosened up painting and music, freed them from the tyranny of the purely personal. They passed from manner to manner as a bee passes from flower to flower . . . I do not see why I should lock myself inside a narrow personal idiom. I write in the manner best suited to the words, theme or dramatic situation which I happen to be handling.

The Holy Egoite of thirty or forty years ago would have rolled up his eyes and thrust out a repudiating palm at all this. A composer, he held, must devise his own manner : it must be a different manner from that of everybody else, recognisable a mile off ; and, once devised, it must be stuck to mystically and excludingly for better or worse. The bee was scorned. Passing from flower to flower was written off as contrary to common sense and good taste. Against extraneous manners and styles the composer sat on watch and ward year in and year out, with anxious biting of nails.

Down went two pages of sonata first-movement or cantata to text by Walt Whitman at his hairiest. Then you went over what you'd written with a weedfork, uprooting reminiscences : here the ghost of a *Pelleas* phrase, here a stray bar from *Le Coq d'Or*, here a fleck of Franck, here, God help us, an echo of the Silver Rose music in *Rosenkavalier*. A man was mortally afraid to be anybody but himself. He defiantly flashed his identification card long before the thing had been invented. Scriabin, Delius and to some extent Debussy and Ravel became refined monomanias, music generally a set of stuffy personal compartments like sleepers to Edinburgh.

It was the so-called neo-classicists of the 'twenties who first broke the party walls down and let in new air, reasserting the classical principle that in the matter of music, as of the other arts, we are members of one another, producing our best under mutual stimulus and the auspices of tradition. Do not run away from the Masters. Let the Masters canalise your own genius if you're lucky enough to have any. That was the preachment. In effect Britten is saying the same thing a generation later. The doctrine is unpalatable in this country, whose musical spirit looks like being dominated by romantic individualism for another half century.

The listener's immediate and main concern, however, is not with the doctrine but with its fruits. A cursory glance at Britten's output is sufficient to show the aesthetic increment from his impersonal approach and stylistic range. Consider *Grimes*. The perky opening bars for woodwind (Lawyer Swallow's tune) might have been lifted from one of the Brandenburgs. Here we have a morsel of Bach woven into the general fabric with a deliberation and aptitude which automatically rule plagiarism out of court. Among neo-classicists, however, the use of Bachian formulae has long been common form. A more daring deviation is the act-three hornpipe, with burgesses singing " Goodnight ! " across it in sixths and the rector warbling amiably about his roses. This is sheer Schubert. It is safe to say that no pre-1930 English composer who cared for his reputation would have risked so patent an evocation. But the stresses of the scenario plainly prescribed some sort of light musical relief before the excitement of the man hunt. What better solution than a five-page interlude in Schubertian manner ?

An insert of this kind must never, of course, be a tinker's patch, with rivets round the edge. The secret of using other men's styles is to make them blend with the surrounding tissue ; they must become organic, part of the living body. That happens to be one of Britten's peculiar skills : he is a great blender, a great grafter in the surgical sense of the word.

Britten has never been afraid of " wrong " notes. I think of bitonal or polytonal pressures in, for example, the Dies Irae (*Sinfonia da Requiem*), the *Grimes* interludes, *Let us take the road* (*Beggar's Opera*) and the craggier bits of the *Spring Symphony*. These things are very much of to-day and yesterday. Britten is prepared to go harmonically all the way with Alban Berg. But " wrong " notes have never been his golden rule. Like Stravinsky, he has the courage to be pretty on occasion. When Albert is missing, Mrs. Herring hands the police his photograph (" took on the pier at Felixstowe ") to an adorable waltz accompaniment on the harp. The intention, I admit, is parodistic. A generation earlier, however, the parody would have been pointed by false relations, say an inner part one semitone out, as in the case of the *Tabarro* waltz interlude. It is significant that Britten prefers to let prettiness here speak for itself. He doesn't hide a snigger behind his cuff.

He has, indeed, the pluck to cultivate prettiness in contexts where the excuse of parody cannot arise. A case in point is the episode of the saint's birth in the *Saint Nicolas* cantata. Here again we have a tiny waltz, stale as to idiom, fresh as paint in effect. Hearers who take their modernism seriously were scandalised. Whether or not they believed in saints wasn't to the point. What they did believe in was the right application of decent musical conventions ; and celebrating a saint's birth with strains worthy of a street piano was hardly the thing. So much for the panic flight from prettiness, one of the most curious quirks of our age.

The most fruitful and readily definable of all Britten's " adopted " manners is the Purcellian. Listening not only to Britten's outright realisations of Purcell's vocal music but also to the chacony of the second string quartet, the passacaglia of the neglected violin concerto and certain *Beggar's Opera* numbers (*Virgins are like the fair flower** and the Condemned Hold scene), I sense an affinity so deep as to be almost filial. Britten uses the Purcell idiom, applying it to new purposes, with as much assurance, flexibility and affection as if it were a peculiarly personal inheritance. Yet the legacy remains essentially an impersonal thing. Purcell wrote to the requirement of royal and ecclesiastical masters. His main concern (like that of Bach, Mozart, Haydn) was to satisfy the ceremonial and cultural needs of the outer world, not to satisfy the whims and impulses of the sacred Ego. His music stands majestically apart,

*The air is Purcell's.—EDS.

detached from its maker, like a Wren palace or church. The formal richness and severity of it are the product of outreaching, not of any inward burrowing and quarrying. And these are precisely the values we often get in Britten. I think of the grandeur of the violin concerto's closing pages. Purcell could not have written this music. Nor could Britten himself have written it had his mind not been moved and fired by the Purcell tradition.

To summarise. I find it hard to lay my finger (I am happy to say) on any bar or stave and say, "This is quintessential Britten."* His technique and imagination are too widely ranging to permit of any such pin-pointing. His technical weapons come from the general musical armoury of the Western world, no school or period barred. Those who lament this are themselves to be lamented as upholding a shallow and outdated subjectivism.

*We don't—EDS.

Film Music

There are great possibilities in music for the films, but it must be taken seriously by the director and composer, and used as an integral part of the whole thing—not just as a sound effect, or to fill up gaps during the talking. The nearest approach to this I've seen has been in the Disney cartoons and a few French films.

BENJAMIN BRITTEN

BRITTEN

BRITTEN's film music includes (a) the G.P.O. Film Unit pieces *Coal Face*, *Night Mail* (both 1936), *Line to Tschierva Hut*, *The Calendar of the Year* (both 1937), *The Savings of Bill Blewitt* (year ?), *Sixpenny Telegram*, *The Tocher* (both 1938); (b) *The Way to the Sea*, *Around the Village Green* (both 1937), *Advance Democracy* (1939) ; *Village Harvest* (year ? ; its Irish Reel is available on record), *Instruments of the Orchestra* (1946 ; available in score and on records : " The Young Person's Guide to the Orchestra ") ; and (c) his only feature score *Love from a Stranger* (1937). For *Coalface* (which I don't know) and *Night Mail* he collaborated with Auden. Both documentaries have become classics and have as such been widely, if not altogether deeply, commented upon in film literature and film talk ; Grierson described *Night Mail* to Manvell as a kick in the belly. For me the kick was less localized, whence I may be allowed to add, as far as distant memory of a dreadful projection at the Hampstead Everyman's Cinema permits, a musician's additional observations to what has already repeatedly been said about the sound track.

I. FILM-MUSICAL FORM :
The economy of the total amount of music, and the consequent utilisation of natural sound and silence, are formally all the more impressive since (overture apart) music and poem are deferred to near the end of the film, where they are prepared by the sound of the wind and the leading (train) rhythm. Both an extreme contrast and an extremely strong link is achieved between the realistic first part and the artistic climax ; or to put it another way, the sound track's gravitation urges up, not down : the film lifts itself from phenomenal up to metaphenomenal stylization, giving the impression as if for once someone had succeeded in pulling himself by the hair into the air.

II. THEMATIC AND TONAL STRUCTURE :

The title music with its post-call in A and its train rhythm in C (a highly significant key for the composer straight up to the " Spring Symphony ") is strictly expositive, not only thematically but also tonally. Both the overture and the body of the score—and hence the entire music—proceed from A major to C major. The final C major, however, is only reached, via the initial fanfare, at the very end, with the E, after some hesitation whether to be dominant or mediant, deciding upon the latter function. Hence, while the total tonality is not just progressive, *but also doubly concentric* (a compelling means of varifying unification in a short, but extendedly discontinuous structure) the body of the film may be said to be in A. Yes, of the *film* : for the overture's A major and the actual film music's A major are linked, in the musicless, realistic part of the film, by the recurring train-whistle's portamento up to and down from a".

III. TOTAL TEXTURE :

The treatment of the melodramatic problem is already highly characteristic of the composer, *i.e.* careful and clean. The musical film-goer whom overwhelming experience has forced to the conclusion that " the acoustic incongruity of the spoken word and of music " (Apel) is inescapable, realizes here that it isn't.

IV. PROSPECT :

IF and when film music embarks on a musical history, *Night Mail* will be found— despite or indeed partly because of its elementary simplicity—among those legitimate points of departure from which so many of its successors have illegitimately departed.   HANS KELLER

BIBLIOGRAPHY :

Apel, W.: *Havard Dictionary of Music*, Boston 1944, article *Melodrama*. Eisler, H.: *Komposition fuer den Film*, Berlin 1949. Huntley, J.: *British Film Music*, London 1947. Keller, H.: *A Film Analysis of the Orchestra*, in *Sight and Sound* (British Film Institute), XVI/61, London 1947. Lindgren, E.: *The Art of the Film*, London 1948. London, K.: *Film Music*, London 1936. Manvell, R.: *Film*, London 1946.

Schoenberg

As long as any great music needs partisanship we shall be found to be partisans. From now on, every issue of this journal will reserve space for the special subject of Schoenberg until, with our help or without, he has ceased to be a special subject. If we are the first who, while not members of the Schoenberg school, decide upon such constant support, this is Schoenberg's merit as well as a reminder of history at which we are ourselves, as it were, surprised.—EDS.

JACQUES STRING ORCHESTRA : *Wigmore Hall, 11th January, 1950 ; c. Harvey Phillips*. LONDON STRING TRIO : *B.B.C. Third Programme, 14th January, 1950.*

THE main attraction at this concert was Schoenberg's *Verklaerte Nacht*, performed with partial, if sympathetic, understanding and rather less than adequate orchestral technique. It remains a work of singular beauty and outstanding historical interest. Compare the composer of *Verklaerte Nacht* (aged 25) with the composer of the recent String Trio (aged 72) : in these two pieces we have the young man writing with superb resourcefulness an old man's music, and the old man writing in a post-contemporaneous idiom of unparalleled vigour, intellectual energy and optimism.   D.M.

ARNOLD SCHOENBERG JUBILEE ISSUE OF "THE CANON"
AUSTRALIAN JOURNAL OF MUSIC. Vol. III No. 2 (*Distributor in the U.K. : Hinrichsen*).

THIS issue of *The Canon* is an interesting phenomenon in itself ; but the most interesting thing in it is Schoenberg's own contribution : a reprint of his essay on Mahler. René Leibowitz's " Arnold Schoenberg's Recent Tonal Works and the Synthesis of Tonality " is outstanding : Rudolf Kolisch, Otto Klemperer and Edward Steuermann write warm-hearted, if effusively fussy, birthday tributes. The " British Musicians' Congratulations " are rather sparse (but of course there aren't so many when one comes to think of it) : some of our critics might bear in mind a remark of Schoenberg's from his piece on Mahler : " . . . the great artist must somehow be punished for the honour which he will enjoy later. And the esteemed music critic must some-how be compensated for the contempt with which later times will treat him."

D.M.

THE 16th issue of the Berlin *Stimmen* (edited by H. H. Stuckenschmidt and Josef Rufer) is an excellent Schoenberg birthday number. Contributions by Roger Sessions, Margot Hinnenberg-Lefèbre, René Leibowitz, Fritz Stiedry (same note on " Schoenberg Rehearsals " as in the Schoenberg Jubilee Issue of the Australian *Canon*, reviewed above), Peter Gradenwitz, Dallapiccola, Boris Blacher, Paul Dessau, Werner Egk, Wolfgang Fortner, Karl Amadeus Hartmann, and the two editors, are framed on the one hand by two highly important articles of Schoenberg himself, and on the other, light hand by delightful " Schoenberg Anecdotes " reported by Alfred Keller, as of the composer's retort to a new pupil's introducing himself by stammering some-thing about his " diplomas " : " For heaven's sake, no diplomas ; if you want to study with me you have to know that you don't know a thing " ; or of his grieved reaction to the news of the sudden death of a famous and maliciously anti-Schoenbergian critic : " Well, and what about the others ? " Schoenberg's first article, a " Rückblick " (retrospect), gives a penetrating account of his stylistic development and replies to recent questions whether certain of his compositions are "pure" twelve-tone music or in fact dodeca-phonic at all : " Indeed, I do not know. I am, after all, still more a composer than a theoretician " ; while his second, shorter article " *On Revient Toujours*," replies to a pupil's enquiry what to answer when asked—in view of the Band Variations, the 2nd Chamber Symphony, the Suite for strings etc.—whether Schoenberg had given up composing with twelve notes, by drawing a parallel between his own deflections to tonality and the classical composers' deflections to strict counterpoint. " It was not given to me to continue in the way of the ' Verklaerte Nacht,' the ' Gurrelieder,' or even ' Pelleas und Melisande.' Fate forced me on to a harder road. But the wish has always been alive in me to return to the earlier style, and from time to time I yield to the desire. Thus it is that I sometimes write tonal music. For me, stylistic differences of this kind have no particular significance." Nor should they have for the music lover's or critic's evaluations, though alongside their classical parallels they certainly merit the musico-psychologist's closest attention.

In " Rückblick " Schoenberg points out that composing with twelve notes is only to a small degree a " prohibiting," exclusive method. " In the first place it is a method that should ensure logical order and organisation, and whose result ought to be easier intelligibleness " (awkward translation mine : I wish to keep exactly to Schoenberg's words). A logical paradox, for without

252

harmonic prejudices the method's clarifying function would be obvious. That Schoenberg's proposition ought to be a truism struck me forcibly before I read it, i.e. when on January 29th the B.B.C. gave us an opportunity of hearing Webern's Variations op. 27. Schoenberg's own Five Piano Pieces op. 23 which introduce his " classic " twelve-tone period, and which Peter Stadlen played in the same recital, I found more difficult, in spite of the simplicity of the twelve-tone waltz's (No. 5's) series. But then I am not convinced that Stadlen altogether understood the work ; indeed, without wishing to diminish the importance of his services to the Schoenberg cause, I would suggest that a virtual performing monopoly over advanced music is a bad thing. No single player is likely to understand such music completely : neither composer nor listener should be entirely at his mercy. Various performers, on the other hand, will be likely to clarify different parts and aspects of the same work. As for the help to understanding which current writings on atonal music proffer—

> " HOW TO JUDGE A WORK OF MUSIC " (" 10 Questions " in *World Music*, ed. Ralph Brewster, Vol. I, Vienna-Florence-London 1949 ; Question 2b running thus) : " *Does* this work *wander occasionally or entirely beyond the limits of tonality ?* " This is not a technical question, because tonality is a law of nature felt even by people who are not very musical. It is the anchor or pivot round which a passage or phrase turns. Virtually all European music from the XVIth up to the beginning of the XXth century is tonal. The most important feature of so-called *modern* music is the break with tonality, introducing that vague grey colour and that feeling of disorientation, of not knowing where you belong or what direction to follow.

By its pitiable nature, stupidity has the redeeming intelligence to criticize itself.

H.K.

When shall we hear the *Survivor from Warsaw* (1947) in this country ? France has no Third Programme, but the Paris radio broadcast the work in December, 1948.—EDS.

Opera in Italy

THE Scala season of 1949-50 has thought fit to revive Bellini's *I Puritani*—the last of the three operas of his short life—*La Sonnambula* and *Norma* completing the list. It was first performed at the Théâtre des Italiens on 25th January, 1835. Called a *melodramma seria* in 4 acts, it is a pleasantly lyrical work, but dramatically it is guilty of a fatal weakness : it contains insufficient villainy. The protagonists are creatures of rare nobility : imprisoned in a Puritan castle in Plymouth (uncompromisingly solid), they behave like true-born Englishmen to the extent of making ample restitution for their baser acts. The dramatic effect is excitement without conflict and without resolution. The hero, a Cavalier, gallantly smuggles out Queen Henrietta in place of his bride, Elvira, who is promptly deprived of reason. He is denounced by the " villain," a Puritan, who, being in love with Elvira, is so moved by her demented pleading that he resolves to restore her the hero. The end of the Civil War settles all problems, even those of insanity, and the gallant villain is forgotten in the general rejoicing.

Musically, the opera progresses by a series of melodies and *recitative accompagnato* on a simple harmonic basis. The orchestration is effective and there are some good *ritornellos* for clarinet or horn. Bellini is a Janus who looks backwards and forwards. He has the delicacy and formal clarity of the 18th century and the exploitation of sensation which belongs by right of adoption to the 19th. For the most part the arias (or ariosos) are beautifully shaped. Sometimes they degenerate into melodies built not for shape but for climax, and the rhythms become imaginably trite. There is a marked lack of homogeneity in the work ; I suspect a break of composition between the first and last 2 acts. The duets in the 4th act anticipate early and middle Verdi. In the first act the voices are treated almost instrumentally, and weave simultaneous patterns independently of each other. This is very effective in the scenes between the bass (Sir George—Cesare Siepi) and the coloratura soprano (Elvira—Margherita Carosio).

The level of orchestral performance was high, particularly among strings and high woodwind. Franco Capuana achieved admirable contrasts of dynamics and *tempi* without which the work would be nullified dramatically. The singing amongst the men was of a quality I have not yet heard in Italy : the American tenor, Eugenio Conley (Lord Arthur) and Paolo Silveri (Sir Richard Forth) had parts very grateful to their rich and even voices ; but Margherita Carosio (Elvira), was not well-cast vocally (her lyric soprano is not light enough for this (low) coloratura part), nor particularly convincing dramatically.

Nicola Benois' sets were conventionalised and heavy—incidentally very similar to those used for 19th century operas in the State Opera at Budapest. But they achieved a creditable semblance of Gothic *àl'inglese* ! The chorus, influenced perhaps by its surroundings, behaved with great sobriety in countless military processions and static ensembles.

The next night saw *Falstaff* under de Sabata—a broadcast performance. The sets followed Verdi's stipulations, and were similar to the Rome production which I had seen a month earlier under Gabriele Santini. Thus it was possible to assess the superiority of the Milanese soloists and orchestra without hindrance. It would be a hard task to improve on Mario Frigerio's production.

In spite of its jocularity, Stabile's masterly Falstaff has a split-second timing about it. He has a knowledge of the score which any conductor might envy. By comparison, Gino Bechi spread himself too much : the part lost precision.

The synchronisation of movement, voices and orchestra made the Scala performance quite exceptional. No unnecessary moments were lost, particularly in the scenes with the women ; and leads followed pat on the heels of their cues—some tribute to the ensemble rehearsals.

The Scala's Nanetta (Alda Noni) had the spirit of a Susanna, while Elena Rizieri gave her charm without character. In neither case did the exquisite " Sul fil d'un soffio etesio " achieve the floating *pianissimo* which is needed to balance the aeriness of the fairies. Francesco Albanese played Fenton in both productions : his tone is sometimes nasal and even rough, but he gives the part just the right amount of animal vitality.

For sheer production and scenic value, I much preferred the Scala's version of the 3rd act. The set was more palpable and more spacious. It gave a real sense of perspective from the enormous tree in the dark, shadowy centre to the lighter fields beyond. The Roman production ended up in a crowded riot of excitement : at the Scala the stage was left empty but for the echoes of the voices.

There was little to choose between the choruses, but throughout the opera the soloist ensemble was better at the Scala, and the comedy slicker and more exaggerated—without, however, degenerating into buffoonery. I was glad to have seen both performances and grateful that the Scala's came second.

CYNTHIA JOLLY.

Reviews of Music

Arranged in alphabetical order of composers' names.

BACH : The piano concertos after Vivaldi, Marcello, Telemann, etc., edited by Arnold Schering (Peters) ; 10s. 6d.

THIS fairly recent edition is based on the old Dehn edition, and on the Bach Gesellschaft, both of which " ascribe to Vivaldi all the original compositions upon which Bach's arrangements are based." In the meantime, some of the models have been identified as Marcello, Telemann, and the young Duke Johann Ernst, Bach's patron in Weimar. Only the academic scholarship of the 19th century could have made such a mistake ; it must be clear to every sensitive layman that while even the Marcello differs in style from all the Vivaldi's, the German models, although Italienate, are a world apart from them. Nor is Vivaldi such a shining paragon of concerto-writing. Next to a really inspired movement like the " Largo " of No. 2 we find the trite sequential symmetry of the last movement, No. 5, reminding us of the weak passages in Johann Ernst (No. 11 and 13) who is better in his themes than in his working-out sections. The most individual piece is No. 8 by an unknown master, in free fantasia form. Bach, though mostly cleverly adapting the strings of the " tutti " for the keyboard, sometimes contents himself with a faithful copy : see the " unplayable " passages in No. 2, 6 bars from the end, and No. 8, 5 bars from the end.

P.H.

JOHN BLOW : " Begin the Song " (ed. H. Watkins Shaw). (Hinrichsen) ; 0s. 9d.

" BEGIN the Song " is fine music, much of it worthy of Purcell, particularly the Overture and the " Duet and Ritornello on a Ground." Music was most refreshingly young in these days, full of ideas and experiments ; the middle-aged complacency which harmonic formulae and melodic clichés gave to so much early 18th century music is entirely absent. It is sincerely hoped that Mr. Shaw will edit, and Hinrichsen publish, many more works by this scandalously neglected composer.

R.A.H.

BENJAMIN BRITTEN : A Charm of Lullabies, for Mezzo-Soprano and Piano ; Op. 41 (Boosey & Hawkes) ; 6s. 0d.

APPARENTLY thrown off between bigger tasks, these five songs show by their very lack of effort how easy and instinctive Britten's style has become. Hidden in their fittingly simple design we find gems of declamation and harmonic daring. As always with Britten, it is not the richness of harmony that is extra-ordinary but its very personal, yet generally valid, cadential progressions (e.g., I, bars 22—29 ; III, bars 17—27). Blake's " Cradle Song " (I) with its steady 3-part counterpoint is the most substantial piece. Britten's empathy with the most diverse poets is uncanny : he boldly steps from the unsophisticated Scottish lilt of Robbie Burns' " Highland Balou " (II) to the exasperated blue-stocking latinity of Thomas Randolph's " Charm " (IV). " Sephestia's Lullaby," by the Elizabethan Robert Greene (III), with its alternating blank and doggerel verse, is full of a wistful awareness of the changing fortunes of life : its style approaches Wolf's " Rat einer Alten." Again, the well-meaning starchiness of John Philip's nurse (V) is expressed by what can only be called tenderly purposeful music. We are glad that Britten has found the time to show again his gift for the nocturne. As in the Nocturnes of " Lucretia " and " Herring," he gives us not Landscapes by Night but People by Night : five cradle-singers as different from each other as they can possibly be. Composed December, 1947.

P.H.

GEOFFREY BUSH : 4 Pieces for Piano, and Nocturne and Toccata (Augener); 2s. 0d. and 3s. 0d. respectively.

" IF this is modern music it's not too bad " as the county-ladies say in the remoter Music Clubs of Great Britain. It is there, I am afraid, that these platitudinous pieces will be performed, to the easy satisfaction and artistic detriment of all concerned.

P.H.

GEOFFREY BUSH : La Belle Dame sans Merci. Set for Unaccompanied Chorus and Tenor Solo (O.U.P.) ; 1s. 0d.

KEATS' poem is rendered with great precision of detail by Mr. Bush, who uses his eight-part chorus to good effect, vocalizing a harmonic background now with lips half-closed, now open. The word " thrall " ends with a four-part glissando, and bare octaves follow to depict the " starved lips in the gloam." Descending chromatic triads make their way down the " cold hill's side," and so on.

D.W.S.

MARIUS CONSTANT : Trio for oboe, clarinet and bassoon. Miniature Score (J. & W. Chester) ; 3s. 6d.

THIS composer's name is a new one ; I understand that he is a Rumanian who lives in Paris. It seems not inappropriate that he should be published in London.

If one does not seek for individuality, then this is an admirable little work in four movements, full of the deft touch of the early Milhaud. The medium is so sparsely provided for that this trio should find a niche ; but there are many British composers who could do, and have done, as well. Formal balance excellent and texture very clear. The one blemish is a long and unenterprising Cadenza for the Clarinet in the fourth movement. The score is beautifully printed, but why no parts ?

N.D.

GERALD FINZI : Before and after Summer (Boosey & Hawkes) ; 7s. 6d.

HARDY's poems of the West country take on a new and poignant meaning in Finzi's highly sensitive setting. There is in the music a feeling of slight under-statement, a quality which is not only pleasant in itself but helpful wherever there is a touch of bathos in the poetry : thus the blend is as it should be. These ten songs for baritone and piano may be considered a sequel to the earlier set based on Hardy's poems.

D.W.S.

BENJAMIN FRANKEL : *The Aftermath (Op. 17), Song Cycle for Tenor, String Orchestra, Trumpet and Timpani (Augener) ; 7s. 6d.*

ROBERT NICHOL's cycle of six poems of a *crise spirituelle* played against the sombre background of a northern seashore which provides the imagery for the poet's despair in life and God, rings subjectively true, but is, with its establishment of morose, loveless beauty as the ultimate reality, objectively questionable. However, in the last poem deliverance comes to the poet who is now able to say : " I look not on myself again, but if I do I see a man among men." This is one better than the desperate conclusion of Moussorgsky's neglected but influential song-cycle " Sunless," a parent, in fact, of " The Aftermath." To be sure, Nichol's poetry is better than Count Golenistchev-Koutousov's, and Frankel's music speaks its own, very personal, modern idiom. Yet the two composers have a number of qualities in common :—(a) They do not paint naturalistically but delineate realistically, their characters and scenes ; thus it is by the sheer rectitude of their sparse texture that they give an uncanny feeling of the astral. (b) The same rectitude, taken in its moral aspect, enables these composers to be father, confessor, and consoler to their poets ; to sympathise with, but not patronise their misery, and thus to ennoble it. When, in the last song " Deliverance," the poet comes to terms with life again (a problem with which Moussorgsky is not faced), Mr. Frankel proves himself a most tactful friend : he begins the song with the trumpet-theme of No. I in order to join the problem to its solution, but after that refrains from jubilation in the orchestra, while letting the singer voice his newly found strength in purely diatonic strains. (c) While Mr. Frankel's more outwardly descriptive passages come from Debussy's water-music to the song " De Grève," most of the intrinsic features of his style have their roots in Moussorgsky : his skill in finding dissonant fundamentals for a series of common chords, his revealing the tonic of a song only in the last cadence, his ostinato basses that often go in the interval of an augmented fourth, and his plangent counterpoint, most expressive when approaching or leaving obliquely a major or minor second.

Read F♭ for F, p. 19, last bar, and B♭ for B, p. 29, first bar, both in the piano-reduction.

P.H.

P. RACINE FRICKER : *String Quartet in one movement. Miniature Score (Schott); 5s. 0d.*

FRICKER was born in 1920 and wrote this piece (dedicated to Matyas Seiber) at twenty-eight. Talking about the symphonic problem in *Music Ho!* Lambert says " it is by the standard set by the greatest creations of Beethoven that any succeeding symphony must be judged." Similarly with the symphony's sibling, the string quartet, at any rate from a moral standpoint : it is a regal responsibility. Fricker, like many of the few equally gifted, does not altogether think so ; otherwise he would not have published the present work, though he would (and should) have written it. Not that he can be counted among those who, upon the string quartet's emergence into public life, have replaced considerations of conscience by concessions to consumption. It is by his potential maturity that this premature publication stands condemned. We shall follow his development with respectful and rising interest. Meanwhile and beside the point, we are intrigued by his accents on successive semiquavers in the tempo ¼=c. 112.

H.K.

NORMAN FULTON : Three Pieces for Two Pianos. (*Waltz, Polka, Air*). (*O.U.P.*) ; *5s. 0d., 4s. 6d., 4s. 6d. respectively.*

THIS is an example of what Hindemith* calls " a manner of writing which puts tones together according to no system except that dictated by pure whim, or that into which facile and misleading fingers draw the writer as they glide over the keys." Particularly the latter, I suspect : some composers believe they can let themselves go in the two-piano medium.

There is not a single phrase where the tune and the harmonic progressions are not trite while the filling parts and the actual chords are unreasonably complicated. To give a simple example : In the 8-bar phrase starting the Waltz proper (Meno mosso), bars 1 and 5 are a simple I_9, bar 4 a VI_7^d, and bars 7, 8 a very smug $II_{5\,(flat)}^7$. Therefore bars 2 and 6 cannot possibly be $V^{7\,(sharp)}$, nor bar 3 a tonic with a superimposed flattened leading-note triad. And so we find, throughout the pieces, harmony that is not merely bad, but wrong. The music is called " light," but this term is contradicted by its very lay-out (see the "Air," for instance). It is a complete mystery why the O.U.P. should have published these excerpts from an uncorrected exercise-book.

P.H.

HANDEL : " *Foundling Hospital Anthem.*" (*Hinrichsen*); *3s. 0d.*

ALL flows along so smoothly, so comfortably ; sequence follows sequence in orderly succession and we are soothed but rarely excited ; even the promise of the Hallelujah Chorus at the end fails to compensate.

R.A.H.

HOLST : " *Mars* " *from* " *The Planets*," *arr. for two pianos by the composer.* (*Curwen*); *6s. 0d.*

THE purpose of this arrangement of a movement from one of Holst's weaker works escapes me. It is akin to playing Rimsky-Korsakov's " Scheherazade " as a piano solo.

H.T.

ANTHONY HOPKINS: Partita in G Minor for Solo Violin (Chester); 3s. 6d.

THIS lively and well-contrasted suite of five movements, lasting eleven minutes, will certainly not elicit the polite boredom which certain of its illustrious forebears are wont to spread over a concert audience ; it is also good music. The composer being under the double obligation of writing brilliantly for Solo Violin, and making his form and tonality clear under self-imposed restrictions, succeeds better here than under relatively freer conditions, as often happens with modern composers. In the absence of filling-in parts which could carry the rhythm over its dead points, Mr. Hopkins' occasional contractions of 16 semiquavers into $(4 + 4) + (3 + 3)$ or $(3 + 3) + (3 + 3)$ are natural and good ; not so his occasional $(4 + 4) + (3 + 3 + 3)$, which, adding up to an odd number, audibly destroys the smallest common denominator (2) of these rhythms.

P.H.

*In his introduction to " The Craft of Musical Composition," fourth paragraph.

ANTHONY HOPKINS : *Sonata No. 3 for Piano in C minor (Chester);* 7s. 6d.

THIS work's well-sustained mood of austere aggressiveness results from the close observance of a scheme of motivic relationships : all themes are built on (a) a rising scale motif or (b) a fourth or a fifth combined with an adjoining semitone. This scheme works best in the slow movement whose sections, built on (a) or (b), alternate not without finesse. But looking at the form of the other two movements, one finds the motivic plan, albeit strict, extraneous. The development of the 1st movement actually is on a lower level of dissonance than the exposition, and matters are not improved by the 2nd subject appearing here in its original shape, nor by the " judicious " dismissal of this subject from the recapitulation and its obvious reinstatement in the coda. Of the four entries in the fugal introduction to the last movement, Nos. 2 and 3 are on the same degree, a tautology which further prevents the fugato from mixing, as it is meant to, with the ensuing Allegro's development ; and the diminution of the fugato-subject into scurrying unison-triplets which serves as a coda is simply childish. One hopes that Mr. Hopkins' extraneous orderliness, whether conscious or not, may soon develop into that unconscious sense of form which, ideally speaking, it presupposes.

P.H.

KHACHATURIAN : *Three Dances from " Gazaneh " Ballet. Miniature Score (Anglo-Soviet Music Press);* 3s. 0d.

ONE of the conditions of writing for the ballet, forgotten occasionally by the most famous of ballet composers, is that it must be music. This isn't. As Music for the People, it is hard on the Russian intelligence.

H.T.

ROBIN MILFORD : *Idyll, " Under the Greenwood Tree," for Violin and Piano (O.U.P.);* 3s. 0d.

A PLEASANT work in Milford's later manner—if his manner can be said to have changed except in so far as it has increased in opulence. It isn't merely the quotation from Hardy that suggests that its relation to early Vaughan Williams, Delius and " the English tradition " resembles that of the music of Finzi. It is genuine and moving music, which one feels one has heard too often before.

W.H.M.

ROBIN ORR : *Music for Sophocles " Oedipus at Colonus." Vocal score (O.U.P.);* 10s. 6d.

COMPOSED for the Cambridge 1950 production, this is the kind of incidental music which cannot be profitably commented on apart from the production for which it was intended. It doesn't come across very effectively in this pianistic form, but that may be because it is well conceived orchestrally. So far as one can tell it would seem to strike an appropriate balance between a highly civilized precision and an almost primitive starkness. It is, as the music for a Greek play should be, subservient to the text.

W.H.M.

THOMAS B. PITFIELD : *Bagatelle in E♭ (Augener);* 2s. 0d.

A PURELY diatonic piece of gentle playfulness, with a few chromatic changing-notes thrown in rather incongruously, but equally playfully.

P.H.

THOMAS B. PITFIELD : Sonatina for flute and piano (O.U.P.); 5s. 0d.

THIS might be described as a slightly uneasy alliance between Poulenc and the English academic tradition. The first movement is well written and eupeptic without being facetious. But four movements are a few too many. Poulenc could get away with the juicy chromatics of the *andante* only because he has the French theatrical tradition to help him.

W.H.M.

IGNAZ JOSEPH PLEYEL : Symphony in C, arranged and edited by Adam Carse (Augener); 4s. 6d.

PARTLY charming, partly boring. Form and orchestration are good throughout (*cf.* the 1st movement's development). On the other hand, the themes and the harmony are, in about equal parts, (a) charming, (b) too naively simple, (c) too naively complicated. For (a) look at the minor introduction to the first movement (perhaps the best part of the symphony) ; further, at the disguised beginning of that movement's recapitulation (letter I) and at the very individual 10-bar phrase starting the finale. Examples of (b) abound in the movements most closely modelled on Haydn, i.e. the first and the Minuet. The first movement's main theme and the theme of the Trio are symmetrical text-book phrases. (c) is most interesting to us. Here are experiments with fairly new modulations (as the beginning of the 1st movement's development), new chromaticisms (as the sudden colouring of bar 7 in the Mozartian Adagio) and new figurations (as the Czerny-like passages, letter B—C in the same movement). All these sound incredibly gauche to our ears attuned to the niceties of Haydn and Mozart. But I have no doubt that they were, to contemporary ears, fairly indistinguishable from their more illustrious counterparts.

P.H.

PROKOVIEV : Musique d'Enfants, Op. 65 (Boosey & Hawkes); 6s. 0d.

PROKOVIEV completely avoids the common fallacy of writing modern music for children as if they were untutored grown-ups steeped in the last generation's second-best, and whose authoritative " I-know-what-I-like " taste has to be pandered to. These twelve easy piano pieces (though full of changes of position wholesome for young hands) hide a good deal of uncompromising art. The D major section of the " Tarantelle," for instance, is the simplest, and yet truest, educational statement of " extended tonality " I have ever seen. An unspoilt child growing up with these pieces will have a good chance of becoming an intelligent lover of modern music.

P.H.

PROKOVIEV : Third Piano Concerto in C, Op. 26. Full Score (Boosey & Hawkes); 50s. 0d.

EXTENDED comment is hardly necessary on what is now an established concerto. The score is very clearly printed ; transposing instruments are written as they sound.

D.M.

RACHMANINOV: Etudes-tableaux, Op. 29. (Boosey & Hawkes); 3s. 0d. each (Nos. 1—9).

ANOTHER instalment of the Gutheil edition, beautifully produced except for the appalling lower-case typesetting on the covers. The pieces are technically more difficult and musically less interesting than the Preludes. The best : Numbers 1 (C minor), 7 (C minor) and 9 (D major).

J.C.

RACHMANINOV : Songs. Op. 4, No. 1, Oh stay, my love, forsake me not ; Op. 4, No. 3, In the Silent Night ; Op. 14, No. 8, O, do not grieve ; Op. 26, No. 10, Before my window. (Boosey & Hawkes); 2s. 6d.

FOUR representative songs, of which Op. 26, No. 10, is perhaps the best. The texts are printed in Russian, French, English and German. The English translations are sometimes clumsy, and generally Mr. Calvocoressi's French is preferable.

J.C.

ALAN RAWSTHORNE: Sonata for Cello and Piano (1949) (O.U.P.); 8s. 6d.

IT is symbolic of the inspired precision of one of our greatest masters of form that this Sonata starts with a 6-bar (not even an 8-bar) phrase, consisting of two motifs à 3-bars (a and b) in which every note of the whole sonata is contained like the chicken in the egg. Only a few examples : The first movement proper begins with (a) in diminution against (b) in inversion ; its (chordal) second subject is a particularly interesting form of (b) shared between the instruments ; the second movement begins with (a) in canon ; the last movement theme is compounded of (b) direct and inverted. Since all these derivations are not superimposed but inherent in the material, the result is " Variety in Identity "—a considerable achievement for a composer. A similar relationship, perhaps expressible as " Individuality within Tradition " applies to the contents of Mr. Rawsthorne's music. As I have indicated elsewhere* he does not copy, or paraphrase, the manner of the great masters. What he does constantly† is to utilise their victories over the acoustic material, and colonise the territories they discovered. Now these " victories " of the masters, as distinct from their styles, are partly ineffable, partly not examined yet. They cannot be *copied* by a modern composer—but they can be *assimilated* by a strong instinct for tradition, which Mr. Rawsthorne has. In the " Poco piu mosso " of the Adagio he " colonises " the contrapuntal variation-form of one or two masters I will not name. In the first movement, the same happens to another's organisation of florid, but thematic middle-parts. As in all good modern music, so it is here ; the traditional begins where the general public hears dissonances.

P.H.

ALAN RICHARDSON : French Suite for Oboe and Piano (O.U.P.); 7s. 6d.

BEAUTIFULLY written and a delight to play. But I always find something a bit forlorn about this kind of superior salon music without a salon to play it in. Entertainment music without someone to entertain—without a stable relation to a society—can only become academic exercise or pastiche. About this there's nothing particularly French except the titles—and the elegance of workmanship. The last two pieces suggest Koechlin in his lighter mood, though they don't achieve his subtle and personal poetry.

W.H.M.

Music Survey, II/2/50.   †As does Britten.

ALEC ROWLEY : Etudes in Tonality (Peters); 3s. 6d.

REALIZING that Mr. Rowley is a first-class educational composer, and that his eight essays on tonality (Modern Tonality, Modal, Pentatonic, Diatonic, Chromatic, Whole-Tone, Polytone, Atonal) are written *ad usum delphinum*, I still find these pieces tame and unimaginative, illustrating unessential and often purely pianistic aspects of the tonalities concerned. The " Modern Tonality " is old-fashioned even for 1937 (the year of publication), and as for " Modal " and " Pentatonic," I could show Mr. Rowley plenty of better examples from his own " Nautical Toccata."

P.H.

DOMENICO SCARLATTI : Sonata No. 6 in D minor for Violin and Clavier, arranged and edited by Lionel Salter. (Augener); 3s. 0d.

MR. Salter suggests that this Sonata and its seven brothers written in open score were intended as violin sonatas. Whether he is right or wrong, the result will please the Scarlatti fans among violinists (I know there are some). Invention : not quite so good as in Scarlatti's best piano works. Realisation : very good, except in 1st mov., bar 6, 2nd half.

P.H.

JOHN STANLEY : Concerto No. 3 in G. Edited and arranged by G. Finzi. (Boosey & Hawkes); 7s. 0d.

THIS score should serve several purposes—to enlarge the repertoires of string orchestras and keyboard players, to acquaint the public with the work of John Stanley (1713—86), and to disprove the idea " that English composers of the 18th century were mere imitators of Handel." These words are taken from Mr. Finzi's Introduction, which explains in detail the ambiguity of the original publications, in which the same music was used as a concerto grosso and as a keyboard concerto (organ or harpischord). Mr. Finzi has turned this piece of bibliographical small-talk into an eminently practical idea, resulting in a score which gives both versions, and a suitably padded part for those wishing to use the piano as solo instrument. This work (four movements, eight minutes) is well edited, though it is at the same time a " pure text."

D.W.S.

RICHARD STRAUSS: "Don Quixote," Op. 35. Miniature Score. (Novello); 7s. 6d.

THE print could be better, the misprints worse.

H.K.

PHYLLIS TATE : Sonata for Clarinet and Cello (O.U.P.); 6s. 0d.

THERE is something brave about the way in which Miss Tate tackles the thorny problems of modern, melodious, 2-part counterpoint. In the main, she never leaves any doubts as to the harmonic implications, and even the tonality (circumscribed as it is) of her two, or sometimes more parts. This is in spite of most brilliantly using all the instrumental possibilities of cello and clarinet, wide and narrow positions, flageolets, part-crossings, etc. There are, however, some passages, built on a chromatic 3-note motif, and increasing in length and importance, where our sense of tonality is purposefully obscured. The Finale is the most important movement. Interesting as the form of the whole is, it does seem punctilious. Is this because of the thin texture ?

P.H.

*IAN WHYTE : An Edinburgh Suite for piano (Asherberg, Hopwood & Crew) ;
5s. 0d.*

IN the verses of Don White which preface " Holyrood " (2nd movement), the
ruined wall and the palace lawn in the moonlight are inaptly called " a sweet
(sic !) historic stage." In the same spirit, Ian Whyte deems it " sweet " to make
his music a stage for the shapeless phantoms of Vaughan-Williams, Ireland,
Debussy, and even Reger. Yet the first two movements have a certain
peripathetic charm. But this very charm turns sour when in the last movement,
a " Waltz-Reel," the composer has to activate his historical conglomerations
of harmony. The last six bars of F♯ major chords, much too bright after all
this glum gambolling, prove convincingly that stylistic perambulation, forced
by super-imposed form into active utterance, results in parochialism.

P.H.

*DAVID ZEIKEL : " The New Yorker " and " Music for Julie," for un-
accompanied Violin (American Composers' Guild); $3.00.*

THE three movements of " The New Yorker " are : (1) " Broadway ; After
Midnite " ; (2) " Central Park ; Before Dawn " ; and (3) " Riverside
Drive " ; the " Music for Julie " consists of " Casa del Suena " and " Hollywood Snapshot " (" Fast as Possible "). No metre. Special effects : steamboat
whistle, auto (truck) klaxon, street-car bell, ambulance siren, and a train
growing gradually louder and faster. Technicolor by quarter-tones. Boy,
how modern.

H.K.

Book Reviews

Arranged in alphabetical order of titles.

ESSAYS AND LECTURES ON MUSIC, *by Donald Francis Tovey ; collected,
with an Introduction, by Hubert Foss. Pp. ix + 401 ; 18s. 0d. (O.U.P.).*
TOVEY is unreviewable. Considered against this fact, the more responsible
reviewers—quite especially Gerald Abraham in *The Spectator* of February 3rd
—have made a fine job of this book ; their efforts need not be doubled. Only
an over-length essay could do, as well as mete out justice to any single Tovey
piece. The harm he has done for which he is to blame is equal to the harm he
is doing for which he isn't, while both together are commensurate with his
greatness. Tovey, who wrote down to highbrows, will never risk underestimation. Listen to everything he has to say, and meet it all with deep,
paranoic suspicion. According to *The Listener* (March 9th), the study on
" Haydn's Chamber Music " belongs to the essays which " are Tovey at his
best—and at his best Tovey is the greatest critic of our age has produced."
Writing of Haydn op. 33 (pp. 50f.), Tovey explains how " Haydn has now
completely solved the problems of all kinds of form in a slow tempo . . .
The secret . . . lies in the composer's realizing that a bar of slow music is not
a bar of quick music played slowly, but an altogether bigger thing." I realized
this when I heard my first slow music ; Haydn knew it in the womb. Since
one cannot conceivably attribute to Tovey the amount of temporary idiocy
needed for innocently tearing a master's thoughts through muddled readability,
one finds oneself in the painful position of having to regard his essays not just
with humility on the one hand and distrust on the second, but sometimes also
with disgust on the third.

H.K.

INTRODUCTION TO THE MUSIC OF BRAHMS, *pp. 78 + 6 ;*
INTRODUCTION TO THE MUSIC OF ELGAR, *pp. 68 + 2 ; both by*
W. R. Anderson at 3s. 6d. (Dobson).

PROGRAMME-NOTE commendation, plus many happy touches which are more.
But when shall we get " introductions " which are critical ?

R.D.

INTRODUCTION TO THE MUSIC OF MENDELSSOHN, *by Percy M.*
Young. Pp. 85 + 7 ; 3s. 6d. (Dobson).

THIS is a shrewd and interesting little study, ably setting the composer in his
milieu and emphasizing, particularly in the section headed " Mendelssohn's
Philosophy," his high culture and intellectual polish. The query on p. 85 how a
further century of musical experience will affect the relative status of
Medelssohn and Brahms is acute. Mr. Young puts the six preludes and fugues
(op. 35) rather than the *Variations Sérieuses* at the head of the piano works,
omits the *Fantasia* (op. 28) and in spite of Sir Henry Wood, has little to say for
the second piano concerto. *Elijah* passes with honours and *St. Paul* is found
"worthy of its theme." There is a good word for *Lauda Sion*, for the songs
(with words) and the early piano quartets. The D major quartet is regarded as
a typical work, the Italian preferred to the Scotch Symphony, and the
composer's Mozartian use of the minor noted. In short, this is the kind of
preliminary study of his work that Mendelssohn, were he living in these
debunking days, might reasonably be expected to appreciate, since his father
is quoted (p. 55). But, even in so short a sketch, more should have been said
about Weber, not only from a cultural point of view, but as the originator (by
his *Concert-Stück*) of the continuity of movements in the Mendelssohn
concertos, and the tragic reserve of the 43rd *Song without Words* (composed
on the same day as the " Spring Song ") might have earned a footnote at
least. An old error is perpetuated by the translation " the musical papers "
apropos of the *Melusina* overture (p. 51), for the reference is to Schumann's
critique in the *Allgemeine musikalische Zeitung ;* it was Matthew Arnold, not
Johnson (p. 85) who said that Gray " never spoke out." Maybe an
" introduction " to Mendelssohn is not the place to mention *Camacho's*
Wedding, that early failure, but some Mendelssohnians would have driven it
home. The library of the B.B.C. has recently acquired a copy of the score
(engraved at the Mendelssohn family's expense in 1828), so a hearing of this
delicious work may soon burst on a public infrequently acquainted with the
overture only, so familiar to a past generation of Promenaders.

E.H.W.M.

LOHENGRIN, *by Hans Redlich. Pp. 38 ; 2s. 6d. (Boosey and Hawkes)*

AN invaluable introduction, to which I would only add that I see Elsa as the
initiate who, in a failure of that mutual trust which is of the essence of love,
tries to force a knowledge that can only grow slowly from within, thereby
wrecking her own initiation : a situation so typically human and set to music
so expressive of it as to move us far more profoundly than its romantic trappings
seem to warrant.

R.D.

SADLER'S WELLS BALLET BOOKS: 1. THE SLEEPING BEAUTY, *by Sacheverell Sitwell, Joy Newton, Tamara Karsavina and Dyneley Hussey; Pp. 56.* 2. JOB *and* THE RAKE'S PROGRESS, *by Joan Lawson, James Laver, Geoffrey Keynes and Frank Howes; Pp. 48.* 3. HAMLET *and* MIRACLE IN THE GORBALS, *by Michael Benthall, Clemence Dane, M. H. Middleton, Arnold L. Haskell and Eric Blom; Pp. 46.* 4. CARNAVAL, LE SPECTRE DE LA ROSE *and* LES SYLPHIDES, *by Lincoln Kirstein, Arnold L. Haskell and Stewart Deas; Pp. 40. The series edited by Arnold L. Haskell. 2s. 6d. each (Published for the Governors of Sadler's Wells Foundation by The Bodley Head).*

IT is only right and proper that the first (and longest) booklet should deal exclusively with *The Sleeping Beauty:* to a large extent the occupancy of Covent Garden by the Sadler's Wells company has been based on this ballet.

Unfortunately there is no attempt to set *The Sleeping Beauty* in its historical background. Instead, Sacheverell Sitwell makes a long-winded and lavishly question-marked attempt at " re-living " a performance of the ballet. (" Princess Aurora is about to come on: the Four Princes, her partners, are already waiting . . . Who will it be ? ") The best essays are Dyneley Hussey's detailed analysis of the music and Karsavina's reminiscences of the first production in 1895.

The second booklet contains an interesting account by Joan Lawson of Ninette de Valois' development as a choreographer. Miss Lawson's analysis of that fine ballet *The Rake's Progress* is short but excellent; her analysis of *Job* much less satisfying. Geoffrey Keynes contributes a first-rate account of the genesis of *Job*.

Helpmann's dance-dramas lend themselves admirably to literary exposition, and as one might expect the third booklet maintains the highest average standard of the four. The chief defect is that only Eric Blom (writing on the Bliss music for *Miracle in the Gorbals*) has sufficient space to come to grips with his subject. Michael Benthall throws out some stimulating epigrams and is almost alone among the contributors in suggesting that some of the performances are less than perfect; but no one could deal adequately with a subject like " The Dance-Drama " in five small pages.

The Sadler's Wells Ballet has never been happy in its attempts at the subtlety and lyricism of the romantic ballets of Fokine, and the booklet dealing with these ballets is inevitably the least satisfying of the four.   F.H.

THE CONCERTO, *by John Culshaw. Pp. 72 ; 7s. 6d. (Max Parrish).*
THAT rare bird, a popular explanation which is both popular and an explanation.   R.D.

THE ORGAN WORKS OF KARG-ELERT, *by Godfrey Sceats. Pp. 50 ; 6s. 0d. (Hinrichsen).*
THIS is the second edition (first, 1940) of a study by an organist who with two others concerted Karg-Elert's one visit to England in 1930, three years before his death (following an American tour), of a singularly humourless personality, who at Reger's advice proceeded from harmonium to organ composition and succeeded him as Professor of Composition at the Leipzig Conservatorium. I had all but written " Crematorium," because I read on p. 32 that " Elegiac Poem," the third of " Three Impressions " (op. 108), originally bore the title " Cremation," but that this was altered at the publisher's request. He seems

to have gone literally one better than Reger by composing sixty-six Choral Improvisations as against the other's sixty-five, so he said, but Germany (unlike the late deeply deplored Harvey Grace) did not rise to the colossal significance of this narrow majority, and disgruntledom, culminating in playing one day " on a fabulous cinema organ (costing 80,000 Marks)," set in with fatal results. Blom's *Dictionary* states that Grieg persuaded Karg-Elert to devote himself to composition, but you would not guess that from the two references to the Norwegian here. The author is generous in descriptive analysis and hints how to render the pieces listed. In no. 4 (" Idyll ") of op. 76, in which the whole fifty bars are played under an inverted pedal (the dominant E), " it will usually be found easy to keep this note down throughout by placing a short length of pencil on the key and pressing it forward, point first, so that it forms a wedge."

E.H.W.M.

THE RHINEGOLD, *by Berta Geissmar. Pp. 34 ; 2s. 6d. (Boosey and Hawkes).*
IN this welcome addition to the Covent Garden Opera Series Dr. Geissmar has woven, scene by scene and with as much detail as the limited space permits, story, symbolism and *Leitmotive* into a coherent and readable synopsis of the opera, and a valuable introduction to the understanding of the *Ring*. The illustrations are of considerable interest, the last (inadequately captioned) coming nearer to the imagination's scale than most stage materialisations of that elusive sublimity.

C.H.S.

THE STORIES BEHIND MUSIC, *by Robert Elkin. Pp. 152 ; 7s. 6d. (Rider).*
A VERY useful collection of the stories behind 138 symphonic poems, descriptive pieces, and overtures, always based on the composers' own explanation, or on the authentic statements of his circle. Two minor slips : the name of Gottfried Keller should have been mentioned in connection with Delius' " Walk to the Paradise Garden," and three out of the four condensations, by various authors, of Nietzsche's " Zarathustra " quoted à propos Strauss's work are lopsided, to say the least.

P.H.

WAGNER NIGHTS, *by Ernest Newman. Pp. 767 ; 35s. 0d. (Putnam).*
IF you read this most fascinating book through from cover to cover you'll know all you ought to know about the Wagner opera you're watching and probably more than the people performing or producing it. I've often wondered why Covent Garden hasn't made use of Mr. Newman's inexhaustible knowledge : he might have saved them the worst of their Wagnerian *extravaganzas*. In *Parsifal* an interesting entry from Wagner's Venice Diary is quoted: "Nothing touches me seriously save in so far it awakes in me fellow-feeling, that is, fellow-suffering. This compassion I recognise as the strongest feature of my moral being, and presumably it is also the fountain-head of my art." So far we haven't recognised fellow-feeling as the strongest feature of Wagner's moral being, but perhaps we ought to consider *Parsifal* afresh and think again. Mr. Newman's definition of an " amphora Heldentenor " is worth remembering, as amphora apparently = " a two-handled, big-bellied vessel, usually of clay, with a longish or shortish neck and a mouth proportioned to the size, sometimes resting firmly on a foot, but often ending in a blunt point . . . "

D.M.

Periodicals from Abroad

See also under *Schoenberg*, p. 252

CONTREPOINTS : Sixième Cahier. Pp. 188 (Richard-Masse, Paris).

THERE are some priceless, provocative articles in this excellent volume. Fred. Goldbeck (editor), whose style is inimitable and not to be imitated, acts as compère to the many famous contributors : Ansermet, Koechlin, Lefebure, Moreux, Pincherle, Virgil Thomson and others. Of outstanding interest is the re-printing of Alban Berg's thirty-year old essay in musical analysis. John Cage, who is known to have doctored pianos, contributes a number of musical maxims : e.g. " The more one considers music objectively, the more one realizes that it is not an object." René Chalupt examines the musical significance, and the many musical references in Verlaine's poetry, while Yvonne Lefebure discusses, from a pianist's point of view, a recent book on Chopin by André Gide, and a recent Sonatina by Alan Rawsthorne. Festivals are well-covered if they happened to take place south of Cheltenham, and two first performances are thoroughly reported on by Claude Rostand. They are the Oratorio, " Golgotha," by Frank Martin, and the Ballet " Abraxas " (on a Faust theme) by Werner Egk. Last, but not least important in this volume, is a fine appreciation by V. Federov of the late Mme. Yvonne Rokseth.

LA RASSEGNA MUSICALE : XX/1. Pp. 92 (Rome).

HEREIN are four first-rate articles : an appeal for a broad-minded approach to musicology and musical philology, by Lugi Ronga ; an introduction to a critical evaluation of Puccini, by Gianandrea Gavazzeni (of whose forthcoming book on Puccini this article form a chapter) ; an account of the deficiencies of the opera-house régime, and suggestions for improvement, by Fernando Previtali (conductor of the Rome Radio Orchestra) ; and a valuable discussion of a series of quintets for wind and strings composed by G. G. Cambini (1746-1825), by Alfredo Bonaccorsi. A. M. Bonisconti contributes a note on the later works of Strauss, and there is a list of compositions and writings by Dallapiccola, Roman Vlad, and Riccardo Malipiero. Book and music reviews are accorded ample space, and there is a useful section devoted to gossip from all parts of the musical world.

D.W.S.

Concerts and Opera

(Arranged in chronological order)

I. London and Birmingham

WILFRID MELLERS : Extavaganza for speaker, counter tenor, piano, harpsichord, celesta, guitar and percussion ; City Art Gallery, Birmingham. 18th January, 1950.

MUSIC both witty and touching, a further stage in the evolution of an important composer.

R.D.

ARTHUR OLDHAM : Divertimento for Strings. Derby String Orchestra, Wigmore Hall, 21st January, 1950 ; c. John Pritchard.

GOETHE on the physicist-humorist Lichtenberg : " Where he cracks a joke, a problem lies hidden." This describes the musical humour of Britten but not yet that of his pupil Oldham. While the jocularity of this extremely gifted young composer lacks the tragic undercurrent of Britten, or, for that matter,, Mozart, his quieter passages have real individuality, like the theme of the 2nd and 3rd movements, and all manner of bridge-passages where formal problems are solved with astonishing precision. As I am told that Mr. Oldham has in the meantime completely revised this work, final judgment must be suspended.

P.H.

BOYD NEEL ORCHESTRA : Bach Programme, Chelsea Town Hall, 23rd January, 1950 ; c. Boyd Neel.

HALF-WAY to a Bach-like performance—and that is a lot. Sewing-machine rhythm, insufficient articulation, some thick string tone, piano (but beautiful— Denise Lassimonne) for harpsichord, 'cellos for gambas, muffed ornaments account for the other half.

R.D.

RAYMOND RUSSELL with Boyd Neel Orchestra ; Chelsea Town Hall ; 31st January, 1950.

INTELLIGENT harpischordist with inflexible rhythm and shocking touch.

R.D.

STRAVINSKY : Sacre du Printemps, B.B.C. Symphony Orchestra, Albert Hall, 1st February, 1950 ; c. Sargent.

To be the object of uneasy derision from the uncomprehending is perhaps the sincerest of tributes, because the least intended. In music, Schoenberg, so driven, so moving, is the chief target ; but Stravinsky, whose fires have largely sunk, still draws his share. Sargent gave us a really splendid revival of the *Sacre du Printemps*. No wonder bold spirits still walk out in baffled protest ! If ever there was a masterpiece culled straight from that teeming, terrifying jungle we call the unconscious . . . (but supreme art has worked the chaos into a dream-world logic of its own, thereby completing a necessary stage which surrealists omit). Many worthy people are ill at ease with cats, instinctively sensing in their sleek prowl and independence all that is least tamed or tameable in ourselves : nature triumphant. Such persons the *Sacre* can only distress. But for those in fruitful contact with their own dark underside, the *Sacre* is a rite indeed, conducted through music of almost incredible technique and inspiration.

R.D.

TIPPETT : Symphony (1945). Central Hall, 1st February, 1950, Royal Philharmonic Orchestra ; c. Walter Goehr.

OF all the English performances of the Symphony, it was the best. But will this work ever come off ? Tippett's idiom is linear, rhythmically complex, non-padded, and occasionally suffers from being over-intellectual. A symphony in such an idiom is extremely difficult to orchestrate, and orchestration is by no means Tippett's greatest gift. Imperfect instrumentation makes the understanding of a difficult work more difficult, and makes the music hell to play ; unwilling playing doesn't help the conductor.

The composer's own hieroglyphs for each of the four movements are helpful : arrow, circle, star and question-mark. Tippett has solved his finale problem with a fine double fugue that sounds quite thick for all that it stays in three parts : the very end, where the music is brought to a stop by stammering on the first fugue subject's trill, punctuated by loud thumps on the dominant, is an imaginative master-stroke. At the same time he has failed to make a formal success of his opening allegro ; too many meaty groups of themes mill about in the most difficult of the four movements to listen to : a psychological error. The second movement is a large-scale adagio on a ground-bass that does not always retain its initial length or key. The scherzo has a flavour of hocquets and Perotin.

I passionately admire this Symphony and feel much of its matter to be important and moving ; but I fear that its presentation may obscure its greatness. J.A.

PHILHARMONIA ORCHESTRA *with Gioconda de Vito ; Albert Hall, 2nd February, 1950 ; c. Galliera.*

THE only thing as bad as trying to impress one's personality on a work is trying not to do so. Since both sins are due to unspontaneity, they are not seldom found together, as in Galliera's handling of Brahms' Haydn Variations and the Violin Concerto, notwithstanding his intermittent proofs of immediate insight, e.g. in the brilliantly rendered, but alas wilfully isolated 8th variation. As an obvious example of the first evil the senseless *ritardando* at the beginning of the 3rd variation's second part's modified repeat may be quoted, while the second evil manifested itself in what for the *Times* critic was a laudable lack of " over-romanticizing." In addition, the traditional features of second-rate conceptions were all there, such as the heavy scanning of the 4th and the siciliana variations, the ill-balance at the end of the *Vivace* (though in this variation the scanning approach proved of course beneficial), or the absurdly beautiful, i.e. open and undeveloping beginnings of the concerto's first and second movements ; instead of entering into the second movement, the violinist could thus have packed up and gone home. (Boult is here more far- and form-sighted than both Galliera and even Sabata.) De Vito herself was as energetic as enervating : over-masculine, her interpretation inhibited its own passion by aimless espressivos which fierily paralysed the melodic flow, creating the same feeling as the nightmare which chains you ever more strongly to the spot the more you feel you must run. Significantly enough, the largest good section and the best larger section was the cadenza, whose formal requirements are least definite, so that intense, but short-range intentions go a long way. Paul Hamburger tells me that a few days later de Vito gave an excellent account of the Beethoven Concerto. I almost feel as if the Brahms Concerto had died with Huberman.

The changing quality of performances and interpretations exhausted me so much that I could not stay for Beethoven's Seventh. H.K.

ROBERT WALLENBORN : *First English recital, Wigmore Hall, 4th February, 1950.*

WALLENBORN comes from America. He brings with him athletic hands, an assured and often brilliant technique and (I suspect) a tendency to be unduly on guard against languor and sentiment. In the Bach A minor Fantasia and Fugue, the fugue (like some of his Couperin) was cautioned for loitering, and the " Kreisleriana " made me wonder whether he really had his heart in Schumann. But at all times there was uncommon lucidity. It is rare to meet a pianist who, in a miscellaneous programme, so consistently keeps out the mud. I do not expect to hear the fugal finale of Hindemith's Third Sonata (1936) expounded with less clatter and greater clearness. Another Third Sonata in the programme was that of Dello Joio, an American pupil of Hindemith who doesn't sound in the least like his master, an unusual thing. A fluent and blameless work which has no more chance of reaching posterity than a snowflake.   c.s.

PHILHARMONIA ORCHESTRA with Schwarzkopf ; Albert Hall, 20th February, 1950 ; c. Kubelik.

Though short, the programme—Mozart's final symphonic trilogy and the early " Exsultate Jubilate " motet—was overburdened with musical weight. A born and inspired musician, Kubelik will yet mistake his mind's ear for the listener's, so that at times one is in doubt whether to believe one's ears or his hands. Not that all his intentions were right ; he would, for instance, arrive too soon with every *subito piano*, including even, in the " Jupiter's " first movement, the pianos after the exposition's and recapitulation's introductory ritornelli, or, in the development of the E flat's finale, the violins' G minor entry after the violent octave unison in G major and the ensuing bar's rest : some time is needed to restrain, and thereby to communicate, the world of emotion that lies behind this silence. Masterly on the other hand were all his *Rückführungen*, as well as his extended upbeat phrasings, a particularly welcome example being the ever further upbeating theme of the G minor's opening movement, where he succeeded surprisingly at what would in theory have seemed an impossibly exaggerated speed. Weakest movements : the E flat's and G minor's minuets, whose titles he took all too literally—one would rather have danced than listened to them. Especially the G minor minuet was downright grotesque in its pedestrian one-two-three. Best movements : the Andantes ; the opening of the G minor symphony's slow movement and the corresponding entries in the bridge to the second subject and in the reprise were more logical than under Walter (see last *Music Survey*, p. 197).

Doubtless perfunctorily rehearsed, Schwarzkopf's nervous interpretation was not as a whole up to her badly recorded version with the same orchestra under Susskind. In some particular instances, to be sure, there were new subtleties, for example in the exquisite softness with which she sang the echo and its continuation in the first movement's penultimate coloratura, or in the recitative which, in the face of an audience, she shaped more theatrically and freely than in the recorded performance. The " Hallelujah " fell to pieces.

                                                                H.K.

OPERA

LA TRAVIATA : Sadler's Wells, 21st February, 1950.

If Covent Garden won't become better, the connoisseur will soon overrate Sadler's Wells, particularly in view of Joan Cross' largely musical production of *Traviata*, as well as of Michael Mudie's musical intentions, as far as they do not remain latent. Marjorie Shire's remarkable Violetta will become memorable when she calms down to the job, so that she will be in tune at such harmonic junctures as ask for fair intonation for the sake of sheer recognisability, while the orchestra will show its appreciable improvement to greater advantage when the brass will have looked after itself. General praise to diction ; particular objection to Violetta's distinct oral movements which in Act I mark conversation against the rhythm of the chorus : a newcomer might for some precious seconds get lost here, believing her to be singing. The whole interpretation ranges from very good to pretty bad, with more important things than the words being translated into English.   H.K.

LONDON PHILHARMONIC ORCHESTRA : *Albert Hall, 23rd February, 1950 ; c. van Beinum.*
BEETHOVEN'S " Coriolanus " overture and the Tchaikovsky violin concerto (with Alan Loveday, otherwise worthy, playing several high notes out of tune in the cadenza) preceded the first English performance of Prokoviev's Symphony No. 6 in E flat minor (Op. III), with which the rest of this note is concerned.

Tunes are the stuff for an enlighten'd proletariat. They come off Prokoviev's assembly belt all shiny, not very new, anxiously showing their profiles and other charms. The opening of the middle movement (Largo) promised something more symphonic. Squeal of woodwind and belch of brass over a dark river of sound from drums and tremolo double-basses : all this was original and exciting. But overleaf the tunes were sprouting impenitently as before. One of them had a trite chromatic tail and was stated on loud fiddles with an edge of trumpet tone at the top of its curve. The first page or two of the concluding Vivace were, at first blush, capital, but they came back rondo-wise and quickly lost their bloom : in any case the facetious vamped rhythm of this movement is enough to squash any thematic material, however good.

Once or twice the essential Prokoviev put in an appearance. The first movement has a slowish interlude over a tick-tock rhythm for the bassoons among other things. Here were the old insouciance and clarity which first charmed Europe thirty years ago and have been popping up at odd intervals ever since.

The Sixth Symphony, likes its predecessor, makes one speculate as to the real, as distinct from surmised, effect of Party-line pressure on composers in the U.S.S.R. Has Prokoviev deflected or adulterated himself for ideological reasons ?* Or are his weaknesses preordained, something latent in his music from the start ? There's a thesis here for somebody.   C.S.

HURWITZ STRING QUARTET : *Conway Hall, 5th March, 1950.*
I CAME into the Andante of Haydn's op. 64, No. 6, in time to hear that the B flat minor middle section was exceptionally little out of tune. While the *dolce* character of the trio was largely neglected—the point about the short appogiatura is that it is long : a tender *portamento* with the ornamented note being none too strongly accented—and the viola's E flat semiquaver passage in the finale slowed things up as usual, the interpretation was on the whole very much alive. What appeared to be the first London performance of Bernard Stevens' string quartet convinced us again of the unity of the slow theme, its eleven variations and the final fugue on a new subject. Both this work and Britten's " Spring Symphony " are novel non-sonata organisms growing from and beside the classical four-movement scheme. Neither form is as simple as it sounds ; I shall return to either.   H.K.

If so, without success : Moscow condemned the Sixth.—EDS.

HINDEMITH and VERESS : *Dorian Singers, c. Seiber, Tibor Varga (violin), Ilona Kabos (piano) ; Wigmore Hall, 6th March, 1950.*

RILKE's French poems are, says E. M. Butler, all in a sense *juvenilia.* The examples which Hindemith set, as *Six Chansons*, in 1939 are notable for delicacy of imagery and for a tenderness that seems far from the burning force of poems even so fragile as, say, the Sonnets to Orpheus. It is almost as though in employing another language, Rilke had become another poet. Hindemith has undergone a similar metamorphosis. His harmony is fluid, translucent here, even winsome in its gracefulness. If the soothing chromaticism was not so reminiscent of Massenet's France, one might suspect the intrusive influence of Charles Wood. The performance suggested that these chansons are grateful to sing but, for the listener, Rilke's transformation is considerably more interesting than Hindemith's.

Sandor Veress's violin sonata was also heard for the first time at this concert. Its two-movement structure has patently come into being on purpose, not simply as a result of finale trouble, since its intention is to discuss the implications, melodic and rhythmic, of its material. Obverse and reverse fall well into contrast ; where the work fails is in the integration of accumulated musical experience ; particularly in the first movement, heterogeneous techniques and vocabularies can be felt warring with one another and this admixture of *meum* and *tuum* affects the eventual coherence of a composite picture that involves much of beauty and something of individual significance. Tibor Varga and Ilona Kabos were enthusiastic and assured protagonists.

W.S.M.

BRITTEN : *First English performance of the Spring Symphony, Op. 44 ; Albert Hall, 9th March, 1950. London Philharmonic Orchestra and Choir, Lambeth Schools' Music Association Boys' Choir, Joan Cross, Anne Wood, Peter Pears ; c. van Beinum.*

SO THEY SAID.

COMMENT was varied and instructive and revealing of the commentators. Martin Cooper in the *Spectator* decided the *Spring Symphony* " . . . scarcely adds anything to Britten's reputation." Likewise Mosco Carner in *Time and Tide :* " Does it add another cubit to Britten's stature ? It is doubtful." But Desmond Shawe-Taylor in the *New Statesman* took rather a different view : " In this work [Britten] has brought his personal idiom to full and splendid fruition." *The Times* devoted a thoughtful, if evasive, Friday column to a review of the score, " concerned not with the effect of the work or its artistic value but with the composer's methods." During this discussion appears the statement that the *Spring Symphony* follows " more closely " than Beethoven's Ninth or Mendelssohn's *Lobgesang* " Vaughan Williams's *A Sea Symphony*" : Dyneley Hussey in the *Listener* complained however that " There is nothing symphonic in [the *Spring Symphony's*] composition, save possibly the fourth part. The organization of a composition symphonically into a coherent whole, as Vaughan Williams did in the ' Sea Symphony,' is something different . . . " Mr. Carner thought " the text rather than the music is the unifying agent " : Mr. Capell in the *Telegraph* found Auden's poem out of place in an "anthology of spring poems, principally of the 18th and 17th centuries " but " the admirable music (the slow movement of the " symphony ") remains consistent enough." The *Spring Symphony* struck Mr. Carner " as by the same

272

Britten who wrote the wonderfully suggestive *Serenade* and the delightful carol music . . . " We were struck by the same thought too but didn't think the inevitable worthy of record. The fact that there was no " orchestration " whatsoever misled some critics into ingenuous judgments. Thus Felix Aprahamian in the *Sunday Times* with his " slenderest musical material manipulated with mastery, and what appears doubtful on paper is realised in actual sound with astonishing success." Mr. Carner has been skilful in defending Mahler against this old heresy but seems determined to perpetuate it in Britten's case : " . . . Melodic invention runs sometimes thin, concealed though this is by clever orchestral and textural manipulation . . . " *The Times* was warier and more accurate in its approach, with " sound-colour that can roughly be called orchestration." While Mr. Shawe-Taylor wrote that the *Spring Symphony* belonged to a category of works of art celebrating, among other things, " simplicity and innocence," and Mr. Cooper discovered the finale to be " a children's musical game on a big scale," Mr. Stanley Bayliss of the *Daily Mail* must have found the rules somewhat complicated, as he was throughout " longing for the warmth and simplicity of Haydn's ' Seasons'." Few critics were able to bring themselves to pronounce the *Spring Symphony* the masterpiece it undoubtedly is: only Mr. Shawe-Taylor stated this conviction without ambiguity ; and he can take the prize for being completely and undeniably right.

D.M.

LONDON CONTEMPORARY MUSIC CENTRE : *R.B.A. Galleries, 14th March, 1950. Aeolian String Quartet, John L. Davies (clarinet), Helen Perkin (pianoforte).*
First Performances : J. R. Lubbock, String Quartet in G ; Dorothy Gow, String Quartet ; Iain Hamilton, Clarinet Quintet.
Edwin Evans Memorial Prize, 1950 : Pianoforte Sonata by Mervyn Roberts.
The only music on the programme was Milhaud's captivating Suite for clarinet, violin and piano written in 1936.

D.M.

ARTHUR OLDHAM : *First Performance of the Violin Sonata, Wigmore Hall, 17th March, 1950 ; Suzanne Rozsa (violin) and Paul Hamburger (piano).*
The Sonata shows undeniable talent, individual and imitative, though little invention. The combined influences of Mozart, Prokoviev and Britten are well to the fore. What spoils the fun ? A certain ambiguity of intention. Sly parody can be very diverting, but becomes suspect if not instantly recognisable, and downright offensive when prolonged indefinitely. An unsubtle joke can soon turn into an insult particularly if it's repeated : which was the fundamentally uncivilized error of most of Mr. Oldham's sonata and of all its second movement. He was well served by his performers.

D.M.

GINA BACHAUER : *Wigmore Hall, 18th March, 1950.*
It should be an axiom in musical criticism that any performer who, without the composer's express desire, and certainly without mentioning the fact in the concert programme, subjects a work to truncation (other than the omission of repeats, and of those not invariably) forfeits thereby all right to be considered as an interpretative artist. The motive, whether fear of boring an audience or

273

honest belief that the work improves by mutilation, is unimportant. What should we think of a conductor who, in the last movement of Brahms' fourth symphony, should omit some of the variations ? The case of playing Reger's *Variations and Fugue on a Theme of Bach* minus variations 5, 7, 8, 9 is exactly comparable, for the fact that Reger, like Brahms, did not number his variations is a *proof* that he regarded the piece as an organic whole. People who do these atrocious things, by some curious law of nature, generally betray their insensitivity in other ways also. All nuances might have been struck out of the score from which this pianist did not play ; you could not hear the figuration of the treble because the web of harmony was wholly lost in the reinforced concrete of sonority. Her attack, in other words, was synonymous with pounding. Moussorgsky fared hardly better. There was stridency right enough in his rich Jew, but no *parlante* in his poor one, his market place at Limoges was a buzz of noise, not of sound ; nor would anyone from this rendering have detected an anticipation of Debussy's outlook in his children at play in the Tuileries Gardens. There are three classes that tend in practice to overlap: interpreter, executant, executioner. This performer, on this occasion, gravitated towards the last.

E.H.W.M.

BACH CONCERT : *Stuttgart Chamber Orchestra, Central Hall, 20th March, 1950 ; c. Karl Muenchinger.*
APART from the individual excellence of the soloists, the first half of this concert had that quality of meticulously embalmed flawlessness which the Germans call " stilvoll musizieren." In the second half, some unevenness in the string playing witnessed the triumphal entry of life and great interpretative art. But the tempo of the G minor organ fugue, played in a string transcription as an encore, would have tied in knots the feet of any organist.

P.H.

BACH CONCERT : *Stuttgart Chamber Orchestra, Central Hall, 21st March, 1950 ; c. Karl Muenchinger.*
WE all long instinctively for the new vision of Bach promised by the slightest approach to his own intentions, as opposed to the outweighted forces and fatty style which still afflict him. What Stuttgart offered, and gained unstinted applause for offering, was : the colossal advantage of chamber-size forces ; splendid technical accomplishment ; patent sincerity and devotion ; enough correct ornamentation to underline the absurdity of the remainder ; a harpsichordist (Lechner) with a touch like steel on steel ; a fiddler (Barchet) alone among his company in sensing some of the requisite transparency, sensitiveness and crisp articulateness ; a conductor with a metronome for a conscience. Size right ; style wrong, and nearly as far from the truth about Bach in terms of (a) flexibility, (b) incisiveness, (c) clarity, (d) phrasing and (e) nuance as our old mammoth tramplings, to which it merely applied an exquisite telescope for looking through the wrong end of.

R.D.

B.B.C. SYMPHONY ORCHESTRA AND CHORUS : *Albert Hall, 22nd March, 1950 ; c. Boult.*
NOT much went right in the Brahms Third Symphony : the complete Ravel "Daphnis and Chloe" was better performed because easier to conduct. But even Boult's understanding, lively and at times enjoyable reading of the score didn't lessen the infuriating tediousness of Ravel's restricted harmonic vocabulary which only succeeds in irritating the ear after all its potentialities have been exhausted

in the first five minutes. Potentialities then become crashing inevitabilities and all Ravel's " sophistication " and delicacies of nuance and timbre are seen as nothing but essentially primitive and unsubtle assaults on our aural response. The wind-machine was as embarrassing to listen to as it evidently was to the percussor who had to turn the handle. As for balance and performance, seeing a row of open mouths shouldn't be the only way an audience knows a choir is singing *pianissimo*.

D.M.

KRENEK : *Sonata for Organ, Op. 92. Organ Music Society, King's College Chapel, 23rd March,* 1950 ; *Denis Vaughan.*

MR. VAUGHAN's immediately preceding performance of Bach's Concerto No. 2 in A minor didn't convince me that the Krenek which followed was in very safe hands. However, certain musical facts were not obscured. The sonata is neither atonal nor in " free twelve-tone technique " as the programme note had it. A strong tonal basis was apparent throughout which was not disguised by an intense and rather angular chromaticism reminiscent of middle-period Reger. I should like to hear this impressive piece again when I shan't expect something that wasn't what the programme said it was.

D.M.

VAUGHAN WILLIAMS : *The House of Life, R.B.A. Galleries, 23rd March,* 1950 ; *Richard Wood, acc. Paul Hamburger.*

1903, the date this song-cycle was published, saw Vaughan Williams free of modal influences and conversant with Lieder of Schumann, Schubert and even Brahms. His annoying tendency to drive a cadence to death, a habit which has remained in differing contexts ever since, is noticeable throughout. Unimaginative ballad rhythms obtrude and intrude. The third song is structurally ingenious but would have been better without the weak accompanimental coda. A very capable performance by Mr. Wood whose diction is to be admired.

D.M.

NEW ERA CONCERT SOCIETY : *PHILHARMONIA ORCHESTRA, with Livia Rev ; Albert Hall, 28th March,* 1950 ; *c. Kubelik.*

MARTINU's Double Concerto for strings, piano (soloist : Sidney Crooke) and timpani, of cyclic build and—like his Concerto Grosso—progressive tonality, should be heard in a hall where its counterpoint can be listened to, and some of its dynamics checked. Chopin's E minor piano concerto, played with often deeply feeling finesse by Livia Rev who is in fact growing into a musician-virtuoso, is worth its sporadic, yet hypnotizing suggestions of original genius, despite its pitiable treatment of the orchestra. Kubelik's conception of the 2nd Brahms Symphony was sometimes based on profound and markedly individual insight, *e.g.* in the 1st movement's third theme's intense build-up, both hesitant and urgent, un-flowing without being scanned and, as it were, spoken as well as sung ; whereas at other moments the interpretation became simply stupid, for instance in the same movement's bars 315 ff., where the violas' *mp* and " hairpins " as against the flutes' and bassoons' *p* must on no account induce the conductor to give prominence to the semitonal clashes. Alas, Kubelik is leaving us for Chicago.

H.K.

II. Liverpool

LIVERPOOL PHILHARMONIC CONCERTS :

17th January, 1950.

FRANKEL'S *May Day* Overture, opened the concert and gave an impression of lively orchestration and vigorous cinematic romanticism, born out by a subsequent broadcast with the same orchestra and conductor (Rignold). Mainardi played Schumann's dreary *Cello Concerto* with an almost sacramental beauty of tone and phrasing, and the orchestra did full justice to Ravel's version of *Pictures from an Exhibition.*

31st January, 1950.

To a number of recent fine performances, Beecham added *Brigg Fair,* and the Sibelius *First Symphony,* reaching the zenith of the orchestra's achievement in Mozart's 34th Symphony, which was a revelation of what, under favourable conditions, we may hope for from an orchestra normally no more than pleasing in performance.

14th February, 1950.

D'INDY'S *Symphonie sur un chant montagnarde Français :* rarely has so little been made to go so far. It is acceptable because of its sincerity and technical skill. Under Rignold, who is a powerful force for musical education, Kathleen Long and the orchestra gave a performance which amply justified this resurrection.

18th February, 1950.

CONSTANT LAMBERT'S *The Rio Grande :* the idiom of the 1920's was beautifully realised, though no pianist glitters in the work as Harty did in early performances. Somebody might have remembered that the preface to the score demands " a more dramatic style of singing than is usually practised."

28th February, 1950.

BARBIROLLI and the Hallé based their programme on the Sixth Symphony of Vaughan Williams and the fourth of Brahms. Their treatment of the Vaughan Williams work pays more attention to tonality and phrasing than any other I have yet heard, with the result that the second movement dwindles a little in stature with its theatrical insistence on a small rhythmic formula. Certain obscurities in the *Scherzo* seem to arise from the shock tactics of juxtaposition on which the composer has depended for effect, but there is grandeur in the first movement, and an intensity of loneliness in the last. The Brahms symphony was infinitely moving, and I have never heard the first movement open with a more beautiful statement of its principal theme.

14th March, 1950.

BY playing the *Concerto for Strings* shortly before *The Firebird,* Malko, conducting with unfussy efficiency, demonstrated that Stravinsky had to go to school with the lesser masters of the 18th century in order to learn the fundamental architecture of composition before producing the works of his maturity ; and whatever we may think of the series of works consciously derived from classic models, its outcome, the works of Stravinsky the precision—*Oedipus,* the *Symphony of Psalms* and the recent *Mass,* for example, have assimilated imposed form as the basis of expression. The *Concerto,* with its mastery of concise statement is an entirely satisfactory work on these terms. More than any other living composer, Stravinsky has recovered the secret of expressive form, and failure to grasp the essentials of his later work indicates that the listener has not yet come to terms with music as an art of structure and balance. H.B.R.

III. Manchester

THE HALLE SEASON : *Winter/Spring* 1949/1950.

Iт's high time the level of critical sensibility were raised on the Hallé programme—or they stop having notes—or they stop charging sixpence for a musical judgment that in all seriousness can declare Haydn to lead his audiences up the garden path (*sic*) in his opening *adagios*. It's a good thing John F. Russell doesn't communicate his programme note interpretations to Sir John Barbirolli.

The Hallé Orchestra is an adequate playing mechanism but like most of the major English orchestras it lacks the stature and a conductor really worthy of its musicianship. Considering how well it can play, and has played—in its performances this season of the Strauss *Metamorphosen* or Reger's Variations and Fugue on a Theme of Mozart—it seems the more unfortunate that it should be frequently satisfied with the ragged or slick, the dry or melodramatic. I have never heard before a Mozart *ritornello* played without any accentuation (K 595 in Bb, soloist Eileen Joyce); and a *Tod und Verklaerung* followed which was as bad as it vulgarly could be. The orchestra has been most successful in music where blatancy in performance is not a vice but a virtue.

That the Hallé is developing two tones, the harsh and the sentimental, is a pity. The causes and effects of the present deficiencies were exposed in a performance of the Bartok *Concerto for Orchestra*. Too busily occupied in score-reading, Barbirolli never achieved a total effect from the work's subtle orchestration and texture. Sentimentality is not always enough where good music is concerned.

From a particularly jarring orchestration of the National Anthem to the clatter of Verdi's *Forza del Destino* overture to a Hadyn Symphony (that managed to sound like Brahms), there is always apparent the same *angst* over the first violins, with only an infrequent care for what happens to be going on elsewhere.

The season has been remarkable for outstanding performances of the Sibelius and Walton violin concertos by (the late) Ginette Neveu and Frederic Grinke respectively. The Walton was like reading early Auden, symbol as it was of genius undeveloped. In November, Kathleen Ferrier sang Lennox Berkeley's *Four Songs of St. Teresa of Avila*. Although continuous comparisons with Britten's *Serenade* were continuously encroaching, the quality of the work and the performance suggest that it should be more frequently heard. Later in the programme she sang Brahms' Alto Rhapsody. The religiose music, sung with a virtuosic religiosity, attuned well with the Victorian architecture of Manchester's Albert Hall.

It would be inadequate in a general review to deal with the Sibelius cycle in which all the symphonies are to be performed. Barbirolli's Sibelius is good. Significantly, of the six symphonies so far performed the retrogressive fifth emerged as the most effective.

Previtali has conducted three concerts but left no outstanding impression. Monique Haas under his direction didn't play the Bach D minor Concerto as if it was written after 1800 which was refreshing. Lyvia Rev played the Beethoven C minor as if it needn't have been written at all.

Suggesting to a Mancunian the possibility of a quantitative if not qualitative difference between music in the southern and northern metropolis, he replied that he only needed to hear the Hallé once a week and he was satisfied. If he is, I am not—quite.

P.J.C.

Third Programme

See also under *Schoenberg*, p. 251.

BRITTEN : St. Nicolas. 7th January, 1950 ; Ena Mitchell, Joan Alexander, Anne Wood, Richard Lewis, Henry Cummings, Huddersfield Glee and Madrigal Society, Blackpool Girls' Choir, B.B.C. Northern Orchestra, c. Leslie Woodgate.

AN inferior performance of a superior cantata discussed elsewhere in this issue : it's odd that no one has yet remarked on the real glorification of God apparent in Britten's music, though it would have been hard to tell so from the flat agony of the small boy who was required to sing at this crucial juncture in the score. Notable was the persistence of the choir in keeping out of tune: both reception and balance were bad.

D.M.

BRITTEN AND MAHLER :

THANKS are due to the B.B.C. for offering a second English performance (March 20th) of the *Spring Symphony* so soon after the first (*vid.* p. 272 ; same performers on the present occasion), and for remembering the existence of Mahler's First Symphony. The hoped-for improvement in the standard of performance of the Britten, however—and we are thinking even of such pre-musical requirements as roughly the right notes—did not ensue. The work is in fact difficult to perform, unusually so for Britten. Every unusual thing must be done to ensure the necessary facilities—both temporal and acoustic—for the future rehearsal of a masterpiece that needs all the more hearings for seeming clear at the first.

H.K.

Gramophone Records

FRANCK: Chorale No. 2 in B minor. Marcel Dupré (organ). Decca AK. 2188-9
Dupré coaxes a near-Parisian swell chorus from the organ at St. Mark's Church, North Audley Street, though this chorale is for the most part meditative, and among the best of Franck's later works.

MOZART : Duo in G major. Szymon Goldberg (violin) and Frederick Riddle (viola). Parlophone R.20576-7.
Intonation not always impeccable, especially in the faster, note-against-note passages, where the players seem to think it doesn't matter. Otherwise a musical performance.

BRIAN EASDALE : Ballet Music, "The Red Shoes." Philharmonia Orchestra (Muir Mathieson). Col. DX.1597-8.
In the colour sequence in the film " The Red Shoes," this music had little need to be evocative : now it is precisely this quality which strikes the ear. Brilliant ideas and orchestration ; performance much alive.

SCHUBERT : Symphony No. 8 in B minor. Philharmonia Orchestra (Kletzki). Col. LX.1222-4.
The reading is highly imaginative, the orchestral response more than adequate. Yet there are no uncommon departures from printed score or accepted phrasing.

BEETHOVEN : Piano Concerto No. 4. Rubinstein and the Royal Philharmonic Orchestra (Beecham). H.M.V., DB.6732-5.

Rather matter-of-fact in the first movement, but the Saint-Saens cadenza adds lustre in a lusty kind of way. The truer Beethoven is reached in the *Andante*, though deep sympathy with its tragic utterances comes naturally neither to pianist nor conductor. The finale, however, is played in excellent style, and with an unaccustomed but welcome gracefulness.

BRAHMS : Piano Quartet in G minor. Serkin, Busch, Gottesmann, Busch. Col., LX.1217-21.

A fine, full-blooded performance of a youthful and prolix score. A transfusion is called for in the second movement owing to exaggerated phrasing from the violin and viola in the main motive, which is made to sit down heavily where it was never meant to. There is only one other fault—one which is unfortunately apparent from the first side to the last—that is the sluggish position-change of the first violinist.

DVOŘÁK : Cello Concerto in B minor. Fournier, with the Philharmonia Orchestra (Kubelik). H.M.V., DB. 6887-91.

In spite of beautiful tonal qualities which seem peculiar to this cellist, in spite of a fluent, masterly technique, this performance has a strange lack of continuity about it.

CORELLI, distorted by PINELLI : Suite for string orchestra. Philadelphia Orchestra (Ormandy). Col., LX.1214.

The name of the café in which Mr. Pinelli earns his living is not revealed to us, but we respectfully suggest (a) that he leave the classics alone in future, (b) that the Columbia Gramophone Company refrain from thus encouraging and perpetuating such travesties.

RAVEL : Alborada del Gracioso. Orchestre de la Suisse Romande (Ansermet). Decca, K.1609. 4s. 9d.

The labelling suggests that there are two *Alboradas*, No. 1 and No. 2. There is, of course, only one ; and the transcription for orchestra is Ravel's own. Tempi must necessarily be slower than in the original, but such details matter little in a harlequinade of this kind. Both recording and performance are good.

WAGNER : " Wahn ! Wahn ! überall Wahn " (Sachs's aria from Die Meistersinger, III, 1). Paul Schoeffler, with the National Symphony Orchestra (Rankl). Decca K.1573. 4s. 9d.

The voice is a little too forward, the orchestra better at *forte* than *piano*. Schoeffler sings the monologue with noble restraint, and has an ample reserve of power. **D.W.S.**

*BRAHMS : Variations on a Theme by Haydn, Op. 56 (a). Vienna Philharmonic Orchestra (Furtwaengler). H.M.V., DB.6932-4.

Perfect. Compare with the previous H.M.V. Toscanini version to see why.

*WAGNER : Siegfried Idyll. Vienna Philharmonic Orchestra (Furtwaengler). H.M.V., DB.6916-7.

See review above : but on this occasion compare the H.M.V. Bruno Walter recording. Furtwaengler wins hands, feet, down.

*Strongly recommended.

279

DELIUS : *On Hearing the first Cuckoo in Spring.* Royal Philharmonic Orchestra *(Beecham). H.M.V., DB.6923.*

A very sensitive and evenly recorded performance of a slight piece played too frequently, but rarely as well as it is here.

LAMBERT : *The Rio Grande.* Philharmonia Orchestra and Chorus *(Lambert)* Kyla Greenbaum *(piano),* Gladys Ripley *(contralto). Columbia, DX.1591-2.*

A performance where it is evident (and perhaps not altogether surprising) that not one of the performers believe in what they are performing. Perfunctory playing simply doesn't suit Lambert's calculated flippancies.

PURCELL : *Thy Hand Belinda* : *When I am Laid in Earth (Dido and Aeneas, Act I) ed. Dent.*

GLUCK : *Che faro senza Euridice (Orfeo, Act III). Flagstad, Philharmonia (Braithwaite). H.M.V., DB.6913.*

Flagstad sings the Purcell with understanding of its passion even if she does scoop her top notes. The Gluck she doesn't understand, whence it is passionless and painless where it should be painful : the notes are there but not the music.

*BRAHMS : *Variations on a Theme by Paganini, Op. 35. Michelangeli. H.M.V., D.B. 6909-10.*

An extraordinarily brilliant performance which proves that the Paganini variations only become laborious technical exercises when played by those whose techniques are not equal to the task. No doubt everybody will squabble happily for months over Michelangeli's rearrangement of the order of the variations.

BEETHOVEN : *String Quartet in F minor, Op. 95. Griller String Quartet. Decca, AK.2185-7*

A brisk, business-like performance. In the slow movement's *fugato* the Grillers are musicians enough to realise that a fugue subject (particularly Beethoven's) can have a personality of its own on each separate entry.

D.M.

BACH : *Violin Concerto in A Minor.* Tibor Varga with the Philharmonia *String Orchestra (Anthony Bernard). Columbia, DX.1586-87.*

A clean performance, if a little mechanical in the swinging counterpoint of the first and last movements. Well recorded.

BEETHOVEN : *Sonata for Piano in A flat, Op. 26. Walter Gieseking. Columbia, L.1230-1232.*

A slight difference of opinion between Gieseking and Beethoven concerning the time value of a certain note in bar twelve of Variation I, some quaver passages in the scherzo badly rushed and the Funeral March is long enough without repetitions ; but generally speaking this is fine Beethoven playing. " Für Elise " occupies the last side. Recording somewhat uneven.

*Strongly recommended.

CHOPIN : Preludes. Op. 28. Moiseiwitsch. H.M.V., C.3905-06.
A tinny recording of probably well-played (but too often played) music.

CHOPIN : Nocturne in G minor, Op. 48, No. 1. Mazurka in E minor. Op. 41,
    No. 2. Columbia, LX.1228.
        Fantasia, Op. 49. Nocturne in C minor, Op. 27, No. 1. Columbia,
        LX.1211-12.
        Malcuzynski.
The quality of these two records is much superior to that of the Moiseiwitsch
set mentioned above. Malcuzynski's playing is both sensitive and brilliant.

DAQUIN : Noel No. 10.
MULET : Toccata " Tu es Petra " Fernando Germani (Westminster Cathedral
    Organ)—H.M.V., C.3928.
The Daquin is a pleasant and seasonable trifle, well played, if messy in parts ;
rubbish on the reverse.

LAMBERT : Suite from the Ballet " Horoscope." Philharmonia Orchestra
    (Constant Lambert). DX.1567-68.
Racy, nostalgic stuff. Both performance and recording are competent.

MENDELSSOHN : Violin Concerto in E Minor, Jascha Heifetz and the
    Royal Philharmonic Orchestra (Beecham). H.M.V., DB.6956-6958.
The concerto is brilliantly played and there are no vulgar sentimentalisations.
Beecham keeps the orchestra on its toes to provide a light accompaniment
throughout. Altogether a well polished performance competently recorded.

RACHMANINOFF : Rhapsody on a Theme of Paganini for Piano and
    Orchestra, Op. 43. Cyril Smith and the Philharmonia Orchestra (Sargent).
    Columbia, DX.1608-1610.
A brilliant pianistic display, faithfully reproduced.

TCHAIKOVSKY : Symphony No. 6 in B Minor, Op. 74. Vienna Philharmonic
    Orchestra (Karajan). Columbia, LX.1234-39.
A rather undistinguished, Teutonic affair, but the exciting performance of
the march, with its brassy bite, would stimulate the most jaded appetites. The
recording is uneven.

RAVEL : Daphnis and Chloe Suite: No. 2. Orchestra National de la Radio-
    diffusion Francaise (Kletzki). Columbia, LX.1215-16.
This set is to be recommended. It has clarity, fulness of tone, delicacy,
refinement and ample verve and vitality. A superb presentation of Ravel's
rich score.

SIBELIUS : Symphony No 7 in C, Op. 105. Hallé Orchestra (Barbirolli).
    H.M.V., C.3895-97.
An authoritative performance of a great symphony. The string playing is
magnificent throughout, and the brass really sonorous. The last four bars—
a terse summing up of the whole symphony—sound final and deliberate. The
performance is well recorded.   E.N.R.

BEETHOVEN : Symphony No. 5 in C Minor. Paris Conservatoire Orchestra
    (Carl Schuricht). Decca, AK.2253-2256.
Possibly the best records of the work.   H.B.R.

Correspondence

132, CROMWELL ROAD, S.W.7.

March 29th, 1950.

SIRS,—Your Autumn 1949 issue contained a generous appreciation by Donald Mitchell of Benjamin Britten's children's opera. May I correct one published statement about this work ?

It has been said that Britten wrote it in eight days. Perhaps it is true that the actual notes were set down on paper in that space of time, but the writing, in its full sense of conception, consideration and formal planning, began in August 1948, and took about eight months of intermittent work. During these months Britten was also busy planning, sketching and scoring the " Spring Symphony."

Britten's uncanny skill for swift writing has often deceived his critics into thinking him a superficial worker. They underestimate his gift for preparation. There are few composers who write more quickly than he, but his speed is due to the fact that he never begins to record a work on paper until he has mastered its formal problems and has decided exactly what its contents shall be. Then, as I have several times heard him say, the main task is to " find the right notes " for ideas and forms that have already taken shape in his imagination.

Yours sincerely,

ERIC CROZIER.

4, ELFIN GROVE,
BOGNOR REGIS,
SUSSEX.

23rd March, 1950.

SIRS,—With reference to Curt Prerauer's " Musical Life in Australia " (MS II/3/50), *Falstaff* was produced with an all student cast and orchestra at the Royal Academy of Music under Barbirolli in 1938 or 1939, so that the Australian claim is not quite accurate.

Yours truly,

NORMAN DEMUTH.

A POSTCARD FROM MR. CHAPMAN

24th March, 1950.

The next time that I read that a piece of music " totalizes seventy-two measures "* I shall come round to Oakfield School with a loaded revolver, and if I die as well as you it will be well worth while.

For pity's sake, what does it mean in PLAIN English ? And PLEASE let Editorial footnotes† to other people's contributions stop with the present issue. It's a temptation—but it MUST be curbed.

ERNEST CHAPMAN.

* For obvious reasons, René Leibowitz's English is American. We have only translated it where its meaning was not plain.
† Editorial footnotes are either right or wrong.—EDS.

MUSIC SURVEY

A Quarterly Review

Vol III   No 1.   1950

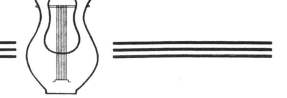

MUSIC SURVEY

(KATHLEEN LIVINGSTON   WILLIAM W. LIVINGSTON   DONALD MITCHELL)

VOL. III, No. 1   CONTENTS   SUMMER, 1950

EDITORIAL CORRESPONDENCE should be addressed to the EDITORS, MUSIC SURVEY, OAKFIELD SCHOOL, WEST DULWICH, LONDON, S.E.21. Annual Subscription, including postage, 11s. U.S.A. $2.50.

All enquiries relating to advertising space in this journal should be made to MUSIC SURVEY at the above address.

Obituary

THE shockingly sudden and premature death of Kurt Weill, who died of heart failure in New York on April 3rd, 1950, at the age of fifty, while planning a new opera on the subject of Mark Twain's " Huckleberry Finn," throws into high relief the topical tragedy of the emigrant artist. To date, the smug complacency and hypocritical shallowness of our present musical life have successfully prevented any serious discussion of this problem, although it is a well-known fact that most of the representative composers of this age (Schoenberg, Stravinsky, Bartok, Hindemith, Krenek and Kurt Weill amongst them) have been driven into exile by indiscriminate forces of political factions which brutally denied them vital contact with their respective national climates. This sorry fate overtook Kurt Weill while still in his early thirties and nothing can express more poignantly the sinister implications of this enforced exodus than the simple fact that Weill's mature music, composed by the homeless artist in France, England and ultimately in the United States, has remained a *terra incognita* even to his admirers.

Born on March 2nd, 1900, at Dessau, but educated in Berlin, Weill was a typical representative of the new democratic stratum slowly emerging in Germany after the defeat of 1918. A pupil of Busoni, his early operas on librettos by Georg Kaiser seemed to link him with the expressionist wing of young intellectuals. In his later association with Bert Brecht, one of the most daring and original German poets in those uneasy years between two world wars, Weill quickly discovered his artistic mission. He succeeded, where others failed, in creating a musical style expressive of the disruptive, subterraneous forces in pre-Hitler Germany, by cleverly mixing jazz, cabarets, " Ueberbrettl," and neo-classical experiments into the heady cocktail of his unforgettable satirical " songs," which form the musical backbone of his " Zeitopern " (Topical Operas). Brecht-Weill's " Dreigroschenoper," produced in 1928 and played all over Central Europe in a unique *succès de scandale*, is a flaming indictment of the social evils of its age and of Hogarthian sincerity of purpose. It is unfortunately unpalatable to English audiences because of its unabashed attempt to make the Gay-Pepusch *Beggar's Opera* of 18th century Soho relevant to 20th century Berlin N. Both authors achieved more in their aggressively political opera " Aufstieg und Fall der Stadt Mahagonny " (1927, revised 1930) and in their students' opera " Der Jasager " (1930). The latter work, with its primitive topicality and its easily communicable rhythms, blazed a trail for Hindemith's and Fortner's " Lehrstuecke," and for Britten's recent children's opera. Weill's cunningly simplified jazz rhythms and the threatening leer of his jaunty melodies had a peculiar quality of lingering on in the memory of his contemporaries. An effort to forge a new operatic type in " Die Buergschaft " (1932) was nipped in the bud by the advent of Hitler's forces, whose openly proclaimed dislike of his music must have been deeply flattering to the exiled composer. In the U.S.A. Weill succeeded once again in becoming one of Broadway's most acclaimed composers of music for the stage and screen. His operas " Knickerbocker Holiday " (1936), " Lady in the Dark," " Street Scene " (1947), the student's opera " Down in the valley," his last serious " musical drama ", " Lost in the stars " (1949), and his film music "A touch of Venus," have yet to be heard in the old world, which was prepared to exile and to forget him, but quite inclined to listen attentively to his American followers (Gershwin, Blitzstein, Menotti) and to glamorise his German imitators (Wagner-Regeny, Carl Orff, Fried Walter and others). There is no need to shed crocodile tears over the unkind treatment of Franz Schubert at the hands of his contemporaries. The case of Kurt Weill proves that our own age, when confronted with a composer of unmistakable originality and irrepressible genius, whose music vividly reflects its own vices, weaknesses and despair, is quite capable of similar callousness.

H. F. REDLICH.

Symposium on a Symposium

RALPH HILL (EDITOR): THE SYMPHONY. PENGUIN BOOKS, 2s. 6D.

" Only fearlessly honest and responsible reviewing can protect the book-buying public and force up the standard of accuracy."
(Editorial, *Monthly Musical Record*, November, 1949.)

" At the price these essays on twenty-one symphonists, written by authoritative critics, are remarkable value . . . the general level is high . . ."
(A.H.K.'s review of *The Symphony* in the same journal, same issue.)

NOTE : After this symposium had been set up in type, we gathered from Mr. Hill that " some (not all, unfortunately) of the misprints have been corrected in the 2nd edition of the Symphony, now on sale. This book was born with considerable labour pains caused by my illness, a *blind* copyist, and certain contributors who neither copied correctly nor checked proofs from sources." Had it been sent to us, we should have been glad to review the revised edition too.—EDS.

RALPH HILL: *Introduction. The Symphony and Its Development.*
A. K. HOLLAND: *Beethoven.* HUMPHREY SEARLE: *Liszt.*
WITH a kind of diffidence Hill speaks of Liszt's symphonies as " borderland cases," as if their inclusion in this book needed some special apology. I personally think that the acceptance of Humphrey Searle's brilliant essay on these much maligned compositions is one of the happiest features of the book. But I fail to understand, why—even if Bizet, Balakirev, Chausson, Rimsky, etc. had to be excluded because of their relative unpopularity with modern audiences—the editor neglected the symphonies of Richard Strauss, three of which—the early one in F minor, the " Domestica " and the later " Alpensinfonie "—belong decidedly to the post-classical pattern of the species and are certainly more symphonic in technique and substance than Berlioz' " Fantastique " and " Harold." A whole " Salon de refusées " could be added to the name of the grand old man of Garmisch. No mention is made of the 6 symphonies of the great Danish composer Carl Nielsen (d. 1931), whom many connoisseurs (outside the United Kingdom) consider at least as important as Sibelius. Nor is there a word on Scriabin's symphonic works, although their connection of style with Berlioz' and Mahler's " Mammoth " scores is apparent to any serious student of the symphony. It would have been a gracious gesture to mention Arnold Schoenberg, whose two " Kammer-sinfonien " are by far the greatest contribution to a derivative species, and old Mjaskowsky with his 25 Symphonies . . . It seems rather an arbitrary decision to rule out any living symphonist under 60 years. The point could have been easily stretched in the cases of Rubbra and Prokofieff—the one nearing 50, the other 60—with their important contributions in this field.

Ralph Hill's survey of the development of the symphony makes, as a whole, enjoyable reading. But there are signs of defective scholarship and editorial haste. As an early instance of the usage of the word "Symphony," Hill mentions the introductory " Sinfonias " in the experimental operas of the Florentine " Camerata " of 1600. He omits to explain, however, that in those days the word " Sinfonia " was synonymous with Overture and that orchestral compositions of a pre-symphonic character were called " Sonate." The " Sonate " and " Battaglie " of the great Venetians (A. and G. Gabrieli, Annibale Padovano and Cl. Monteverdi) originated in the second half of the 16th century, giving the symphony an even older pedigree than Hill indicates.

A strange example of editorial carelessness is the *repeated* mis-spelling of Donald Jay Grout as D. J. Grant (page 17). A worse blunder occurs just overleaf, when Hill calmly refers to Carl Theodor, the Elector Palatine, as " the Duke of Mannheim." A Dukedom of Mannheim is of course as fabulous as a Dukedom of Hampstead. In the 19th century Mannheim belonged to the Grand Duchy of Baden, created by Napoleon, but in the days of Mozart and the Mannheim Symphonists it was a part of the Palatinate (Bayrische Pfalz).

The further story of the symphony, from Mannheim and Vienna to the Romantic movement, is well told. It is only when Hill speaks disparagingly of Mahler's " tonal monsters," that the spirit of contradiction begins to reassert itself. It seems somewhat unfair to compare the orchestral tables of Beethoven's Vth and Mahler's VIth Symphony and to hint at the latter's inferiority, *because* of its colossal orchestral forces. Similar " tonal monsters " had been composed much earlier than Mahler, their perpetrators being Liszt, Berlioz, Beethoven himself (in his Battle Symphony), Lesueur and Orazio Benevoli. The fashion to write for an orchestra of 12 players, so popular in our present day, will one time be derided as an aesthetic " fad " much as we today jeer at the " tonal monsters " of the late Romantics. I quite agree with Hill's final dictum that size in itself is no criterion of aesthetic and intellectual values. But that axiom will cut both ways. Surely, Britten's " Rape of Lucretia " is not superior to " Peter Grimes " *because* it employs only an orchestra of 12, in contrast to the full band employed in the earlier work ? And if Ralph Hill thinks that the decline of the " colossal " symphony is one of the redeeming features of our age, why, oh why, has he omitted Arnold Schoenberg's two " Kammersinfonien " (of 1908 and 1945), the first of which certainly indicated the " turn of the tide " in the sense of his own argument ?

A. K. Holland's " Beethoven " essay gives a good, if necessarily all too terse, account of the salient features in the nine symphonies, though these have certainly been treated more sympathetically by such distinguished scholars as Donald Tovey and Marion Scott. But one misleading error should not pass undisputed, as it tends to befog the unsuspecting mind of the uninitiated. When discussing the " Eroica " Mr. Holland refers to its original programme and to a copy of the full score, " in which words (in German) ' composed on the subject of Bonaparte ' may still be read." There is practically no title-page of a composition by Beethoven, written in German, before opus 101 (Sonate fuer das Hammerklavier), when—in a letter to his publisher Steiner, dated January 23, 1817—Beethoven decrees, half humoristically, that henceforth all headings and title-pages of his compositions should be printed in German. (A passing phase, as late works of Beethoven show). But a mere glance at the original of the " Eroica " (or at the facsimile of its title-page, reproduced in many books on Beethoven) could have enlightened Mr. Holland to the fact that the original title of the score runs as follows: " Sinfonia Grande—intitolata Bonaparte " : in plain Italian, as is practically every title-page of Beethoven in those years.

After the somewhat pedestrian treatment of Beethoven in Mr. Holland's contribution it is pure joy to read the scholarly and exhaustive study of Liszt's " Faust " and " Dante " symphonies by Humphrey Searle, whose excellent Liszt bibliography (in the Suppl. Vol. of *Grove*, 1940) has already placed him in the forefront of scholars conversant with this sadly neglected musical pioneer. An analytical study by Searle of Liszt's music in general and of his 13-odd symphonic poems in particular would certainly fill one of the worst gaps in English musicography. It would be equally stimulating if Mr. Searle were to include in his discussion of Liszt's imaginative treatment of Goethe's and Dante's poems a paragraph on the approach of other notable composers to these favourite subjects of musical Romanticism. A comparison between the achievements of Spohr, Berlioz, Wagner, Schumann, Liszt, Tchaikowsky and Mahler in this direction would ensure a much deeper insight into the workshop of these composers.

I was particularly interested in Mr. Searle's contention that Wagner had made considerable use of the principal motif of Liszt's " Faust " Symphony in his " Goetterdaemmerung," and I only wish he had indicated the relevant bars in Wagner's score.

There are a couple of bars in Liszt's " Faust," which (to my mind) exercised a formative influence on the music of the 1st act of " Tristan ", composed about 3 years after the completion of Liszt's score. I hope Mr. Searle will investigate the extent of Wagner's indebtedness—especially in " Tristan "—to Liszt's " Faust " Symphony.

Searle's discussion of the " Dante " Symphony is equally valuable. But again the full story of the relationship of this rather unequal work to Wagner (to whom it is dedicated) remains to be told. Also, the fact that both works offer alternative endings (even in the printed full score—a feature they share with Bartok's Concerto for Orchestra) would warrant a more detailed psychological investigation, which no doubt Mr. Searle was unable to carry out because of lack of space.

H. F. REDLICH.

STANLEY BAYLISS: *César Franck.*

In his six pages of letterpress Mr. Bayliss leaves us with the impression that he is not interested in either Franck or his Symphony, and regards them as a couple of bores who have to be dealt with in a symposium devoted to the Symphony. He postulates some new angles upon the quality of Franck's music, and deplores the fact that " the emotional content of the second movment of the Symphony " is " something quite different to (sic), and of a lower order than, that in the Allegretto of Beethoven's Seventh or in the slow movement of the Ninth Symphony." Further, commenting on the fact that Franck's Symphony is in three instead of the usual four movements, he says that it " has affinity with the *Symphonie Fantastique*," and hastens to assure us that he knows the latter to be in five movements. He then proceeds at some length to show how wrong all Vincent d'Indy's theories and opinions are. He

7

is right to draw attention to the remarkable fact that Franck's representative works were written in the last twenty years of his life, but goes astray when he says that these are all the works by which he is known, thus forgetting the " Six Pièces " for organ (written in 1860) which have been in regular use by organists for years. I doubt that the Franco-Prussian War of 1870 really did " release a spring in his mind."

This introduction should have placed Franck and his work within the panorama of the Symphony. He is sufficiently important to warrant this. A writer genuinely interested in the matter could have been fully enlightening and informative on the point, to the advantage of the type of reader for whom the symposium is intended.

The programme note is adequate, but till now I have never heard or read that the principal subject of the third movement "quite definitely does afford a healthy contrast to the morbid or sick-room atmosphere of much of the other movements." It is to be feared that the uninformed reader will gain little from this pessimistic piece of musical assessment.

NORMAN DEMUTH.

RICHARD CAPELL: *Bruckner*.

MR. CAPELL'S familiar rhapsodic treatment of Bruckner has the undeniable advantage of catching the imagination. Whether it is really likely to help the cause of a composer who is all too often thoughtlessly condemned for excess of rhapsody is another matter. Of the twelve pages of this essay, eight are " introduction " and four are devoted to the Fourth and Seventh symphonies (plus two pages of music quotations). His descriptions, though eloquent, do little to dispel the common idea that Bruckner " rambles " and is weak in construction, largely because the writer himself does not appear to have grasped the real structural methods of this composer, methods that are well below the surface of the music. There are a number of statements that reveal a looseness of thought and terminology that may cause confusion to the ordinary listener. The opening theme of No. 4 for instance, is said to be " first in the major, then in the minor." What is one to make of that ? Does Mr. Capell regard the use of the flat sixth as a change to the " minor " ? Further, he clings in his analyses to the prop of sonata-form far more tightly than poor Bruckner was said to have done by Tovey: this makes his treatment of No. 7 very misleading indeed, for that work contains but one true sonata design—its *Scherzo*. Its first movement is planned on other lines (which I have described in another journal).* This critic's sense of tonality has not enabled him to hear this structure for himself: otherwise he would not have referred to the " second subject " as beginning *in* B; the theme he means (which is emphatically not a " second subject " in the bad old sense) begins not *in* B but *on* B— a fact on which great issues hang. No doubt Mr. Capell would defend his over-simplification of the form of the *Adagio* as a " Rondo " by pointing to lack of space; but his introduction could have been reduced by half. The *Scherzo* is said to have " a wealth of themes and power of motion commensurate with its great length " ; this piece is thematically derived entirely from its first twelve bars (really three large bars) and it lasts four minutes.

Music Review, VIII /3 /47.

These are the kind of loosenesses which should put the reader on his guard. However, one should be grateful that one of our most influential writers is willing to speak up in favour of Bruckner, and it is to be hoped that Mr. Capell's sincerely felt and finely expressed eloquence will encourage many more people to discover this music for themselves.   ROBERT SIMPSON.

WILLIAM McNAUGHT: *Schubert.   HERBERT WISEMAN: Brahms.*
MARTIN COOPER: *Tchaikovsky.*
HERBERT WISEMAN adulates, Martin Cooper deprecates; while only William McNaught has the right attitude of critical admiration towards his symphonist. Mr. McNaught's happy mixture of scholarship and shrewd comment single out his contribution from the rest of the book. Where have we come to when a serious author feels the need, apropos of a harmless little formal graph of the Unfinished's 2nd movement, to *apologise* for one of those " alphabetical schemes that incur the frequent reproach of being non-musical ? " It should be clear by now that metaphorical comment is welcome only on the basis of a strict formal analysis, including bar-numbers (as given by Mr. McNaught). If the reader cannot be expected either to use a score, or to have the music by heart, the writer ought to give him his, avowedly personal, impressions of the music, and those only. The same with key-schemes. Mr. McNaught never mentions a key-relationship without showing its formal purpose (see pp. 146, 154, 158), while Mr. Wiseman, for instance, splashes keys over the pages of his article as if Brahms were one of the lesser *al fresco* painters (see pp. 251, 257).

Among Mr. McNaught's many hits are an excellent introduction to Schubert the symphonist, including this definition of the quality commonly called " Schubertian ": " .   .   .   it is not a parallel to other adjectives of the kind, such as Chopinesque, or Brahmsian, for it is little concerned with a personal idiom. It stands among other things for the way in which small and curiously engaging effects keep on cropping up from nowhere; they have an element of surprise, but with it an air of naturalness." Of the great C major symphony he says: " It has spontaneity of both kinds; for Schubert, we know, was quick to arrive at his final thoughts; yet the music gives that sense of ready self-growth and natural connection that most composers achieve with great labour or not at all. *It has something more: a sense of the unpremeditated in the course which the music runs after it has given itself birth.*" (My italics.)

Now for some detailed criticism of Mr. Wiseman's Brahms.

Department of General Remarks. " The truth about [Brahms'] orchestration is that he wrote what he wanted to be heard and that, after all, is what matters." " No amount of verbal description will enable one to hear the key-changes and the modifications of the theme." " The movement [No. I, 2nd mov.] proceeds upon its lovely way .   .   ." " The movement [No. II, 2nd mov.] has moments of rare beauty .   .   ." " It all ends [No. III, 2nd mov.] in a mood of supreme ecstasy and wonderful beauty .   .   ." " The slow movement [No. IV, 2nd mov.] is sheer beauty."

Department of Non Sequitur. " It is as if Brahms, after a long development section [No. II, 1st mov.] had resolved to save a little time in the recapitulation .   .   ." " It is a complex movement [No. II, 2nd mov.] and perhaps a little difficult to follow completely, but (sic !) it has moments of rare beauty .   .   ." " It grows in intensity and in power [No. IV, 1st mov.] until the final bars where four drum-beats *only serve* to make the finish all the more impressive.'⁹

Department of Coinciding Metaphors. Mr. Wiseman: "The symphony [No. I] opens on a note of *gloom* and deep tragedy." Mr. Cooper: ". . . The introduction [to Tchaikovsky No. V] . . . a *gloomy* theme in the lowest register of the clarinet." Somebody must be using the wrong dictionary; I think it is Mr. Wiseman. Which brings us to Mr. Cooper's Tchaikovsky. I wonder why he has undertaken to write about him when he believes that the symphonies are no more than " artistically arranged bouquets of opera and ballet music." This is probably wrong in the case of the first movements of the 4th and 6th, and of the whole of the 5th Symphony in which every single theme springs from the introductory E minor phrase. Mr. Cooper also reads more " hectic anxiety " and " self-pity " into every symphony than is really there (I wonder how he feels about Dostoievsky ?)* " Introspective melancholy and self-pity is the unifying principle of the whole 5th Symphony, informing the middle and last movement as well as the first." If Mr. Cooper had said that only a man possessing, among others, the above traits, could have written the 5th—yes; but as to the " unifying principle "—no. Speaking of the second subject of No. V's 4th movement: " This too has a solemn march-like character." Being much faster than a march, this flute-solo over the ostinato has to me the significance of a pennant flying over a heavy ship. There is no quarrelling over images, but surely the 2nd movement of No. VI is not a macabre, but a wistful valse (is Chekov macabre ?); and the 3rd movement of that Symphony is no more " in the nature of a divertissement " than the 3rd movement of Brahms' Fourth, both of which fulfil exactly the same function in the life-work of their composers.

PAUL HAMBURGER.

*His quotation from Freud should read " frei flottierende Angst," not " flottende."

HUBERT FOSS: *Borodin.*

BORODIN (Mr. Foss tells us) " had an unrivalled capacity for crowding an immense quantity of truth and significance into the shortest possible musical phrase." Thus are virtues made out of vices, and we muse upon Molière's *Eliante*, who showed how a fat woman became majestic, and a thin one became graceful, in the eyes of a suitor. Mr. Foss, in courting Borodin, does tend to minimise the faults: the repetitive (or to be kinder) epigrammatic themes, and the too often static basses. It would have been worthwhile to point out that the " Five " had a penchant for Schumann, whose music is full of similar characteristics, and whose symphonies lacked a Rimsky-Korsakov-cum-Glazunov orchestration. The analyses given by Mr. Foss are straightforward and should prove useful in the concert hall. DENIS STEVENS.

ALEC ROBERTSON: *Dvořák.*

ALEC ROBERTSON writes amiably of Dvořák. The affinities with Schubert warm his heart, and he is sensitive on the other hand to the Brahmsian links. I could wish, however, that he had been more specific about home-bred elements in the symphonies. To say of a given tune, or even of a whole work, that it is obviously Slavonic, patently nationalist, or characteristically Bohemian, is hardly enough. The reader is, I think, entitled to some pedigree or provenance in support of such judgments. The tendency (and danger) is to take nationalism in music rather for granted. Ever since the days of Maestro Mica (1694-1744), whose Symphony in D makes such astonishing hearing,

Czechoslovakia has been reacting to as well as from European classical procedures, alternately bringing gifts and taking gifts away. In the case of Dvořák a thorough sorting out of these processes would have been worth while. One minor point of emphasis. Mr. Robertson quotes a loved march tune from the last movement of the Fourth and says there is something very Elgarian about it. But surely this is cart before horse. Dvořák takes precedence over Elgar both in time and in international eminence. All that we can safely say is that Elgar occasionally sounds Dvořákian.

CHARLES STUART.

CECIL GRAY: *Haydn*. GEOFFREY SHARP: *Mahler*. H. G. SEAR: *Bax*.
MR. GRAY is always a lively and stimulating writer and he worships Haydn's music. So far, so good: but the results are less satisfactory than the credentials.

For a start it is the manner of presentation. Instructive on the whole, Mr. Gray is led by his enthusiasm into emphatic but woolly generalizations. The symphonies which he describes in detail are: *La Reine*, the Oxford, the Surprise, the Military, the Clock, No. 102 in Bb and the Drumroll. The analyses are fairly readable without containing much of instructional importance or musicological individuality; Mr. Gray expends too much space in ramming home unessential points. Haydn's originality is more surprising than the *fortissimo subito* chord that gives No. 94 its nickname: a diverting point but hardly worth constant plugging. Again Mr. Gray admires Tovey (as who does not?). But to quote the *Essays in Musical Analysis* as often as he does shows a streak of laziness and is not really profitable, since most music-lovers have those classic volumes at their shoulder anyway. It is the detail rather than the chapter *in toto* that is disagreeable. Haydn, though widely, is not yet universally given his proper due of devotion and Mr. Gray's enthusiasm deserves to win more converts to the cause; in point of fact, however, I finished the chapter inclined to prize Mozart's symphonies the more, and Haydn's the less.

The first grace-note in Ex. 14 should be e″, not f″.

I always thought that Mr. Geoffrey Sharp liked Mahler but, from his chapter on that composer, an almost diametrically opposed opinion might be deduced. He is constantly at pains to depreciate Mahler's art as a symphonist; he plainly does not know the majority of the symphonies at all intimately for he commits the most elementary howlers in dealing with them ; and he states his case with an inconsequential and perfunctory bluntness that only underlines his ignorance.

There is no space here to tabulate all Mr. Sharp's errors of fact or conjecture, but a few may conveniently be listed for the benefit of those who may turn to this chapter seeking enlightenment.

The 5th movement of the 2nd Symphony begins " In Tempo des Scherzos " but broadens out after 17 bars. It is *not* a Scherzo; that designation is reserved for the 3rd movement, though Mr. Sharp does not tell us so. He fails to identify the Adagio of the 10th Symphony as the first movement; Krenek only completed the orchestration, most of which had already been satisfactorily done by Mahler before his death. He makes no mention of the connection between the first and second symphonies, that of life, death and judgment. The term " Wagnerian symphonism " does not refer to Wagner's early symphony but to the symphonic architecture of his later operas, e.g.

11

Tristan. In the analysis of the 4th Symphony, he happily adopts Tovey's for once erroneous " farmyard noises " explanation of the sleighbells, which are actually intended to depict the ride to *Kinderland*. This movement is not a free rondo; it is in sonata form with double exposition. Nor is the second movement a rondo either; it is a scherzo of the same type as is found in Beethoven's Seventh Symphony. " Not sufficiently contrasted " with its predecessor is ridiculous; apart from the formal differences, the idiom is considerably more acrid, and this combined with the contrasted orchestral setting and the use of a solo violin with strings retuned, produces a weird atmosphere far-removed from the delightful freshness of the first movement. The finale was intended for the 3rd Symphony as " What the child tells me "; Mr. Sharp forgot to tell us. He might well have given the descriptive titles of the 3rd Symphony's constituent movements, rather than the numerous offensive jibes that litter his pages. They are: *Introduction, Pan awakes— Summer marches in; What the wild flowers tell me; What the forest beasts tell me; What Man tells me; What the angels tell me; What Love* (originally God) *tells me.* Voices are not omitted from the 9th Symphony because Mahler had found them unsuitable for symphonic construction; the symphony's theme was too intimate for words and singing.

At a time when the growing appreciation of Mahler as a song-writer is leading people more and more to seek something of the same nobility, pathos and touching simplicity in his symphonies, a sympathetic and instructive introduction to this wonderful corpus of musical philosophy would have been of great value. Mr. Sharp's blindness to Mahler's merits and insensitivity to the workings of his creative genius are poor qualifications for the task; the chapter neither does Mahler justice nor Mr. Sharp credit.

The musical examples are full of errors. Ex. 2, 3rd crotchet of 1st full bar: lower voice should read G not A. Ex. 3: 4th quaver of bar 2 is A not B. Ex. 5, bar 1: 2nd violas play D not E. Ex. 10a, bar 2: second horn G♯ not G. Ex. 10b: the first two As are tied. Ex. 11b: first note correct; the rest is printed as for clarinets in B♭ with two sharps in key-signature (i.e. a tone too high). Ex. 14: grace note G between bars 2 and 3. Ex. 15: A in bar 2 makes more sense if correctly notated as B♭♭. Ex. 18 : grace-note B♭ between bars 1 and 2. Ex. 19 : grace-note E♭ between bars 1 and 2. Numerous accents and phrase marks are also missing.

Mr. H. G. Sear's chapter on Bax is admirable; enthusiastic and knowledgeable, he is by no means blind to Bax's weaknesses as a symphonist but, like all good enthusiasts, he suffers them gladly. He makes no criticism of that architectural loose-limbedness that seems to me Bax's weakest point in symphonic construction, the feeling that this music, beautiful as it is, would be better suited to such a medium as the tone-poem—to which in fact Bax has contributed some fine specimens.

Our knowledge of Bax's symphonies even in this, the country of his birth, is absurdly limited. We hear so little of them. The seventh has been performed several times in recent years and might have merited a closer analysis but Mr. Sear was doubtless limited by space; he has chosen the Third, which is recorded and therefore readily available for study, and the Sixth, presumably because of the special features that distinguish it. He writes fluently, with a pleasantly appropriate predilection for sonorous and unusual adjectives. They are vivid analyses too that excite immediate interest, and will doubtless win many converts to Bax's symphonies.   WILLIAM MANN.

J. H. ELLIOT: *Berlioz.*

Mr. J. H. ELLIOT, in finding it " fairly transparently evident that his wells of inspiration were not deep," confesses in effect that he is hardly the ideal writer on Berlioz for a series like this. A note of apology (" graceful if not very distinguished melody," for *Un Bal,* " not a very good tune I fear " for the march proper in the penultimate movement), as of one afraid of exposing himself to ridicule in a professional caucus, pervades his analyses of the *Symphonie Fantastique* and *Harold in Italy,* the only " symphonic " works of Berlioz he touches. Anyone with historical, if not musical, imagination would recognize that the *Marche au Supplice* is, in essence, a tonal expression of the Reign of Terror, a delayed-action bomb, as it were, from the France of the early 1790's. Something too he might learn from Berlioz in the matter of literary style. A bar stroke has fallen out of the second example (6) on p. 178.

DYNELEY HUSSEY: *Mendelssohn.*

Mr. HUSSEY's article on Mendelssohn's symphonies is hardly adequate, even when one sympathizes with him for dismissing the *Reformation* and the *Hymn of Praise* with a bare mention. The drawback of the absence of deep distress in his life and music was noticed as far back as Grove's long article in the *Dictionary* and this should have been stated. " The First Symphony in C minor " (actually No. XIII) was composed at fifteen, not twelve; its slow movement is not Mozartian but in the exquisite early manner of that in the Octet, and its trio in style looks forward to the second subject of the overture to *Athalie.* The fact that its composer did not turn away from this work in later life should have ensured it attention. Nor is it stated that Mendelssohn was dissatisfied with the Italian Symphony, which was not published in his lifetime.

E. H. W. MEYERSTEIN.

F. BONAVIA: *Elgar.*

THIS essay has the virtue of defending with eloquence two symphonies often derided as " unsymphonic " by listeners whose temperaments are unsympathetic, but never by those attuned to Elgar's poignant if rather ample inspiration. To the latter, the accusation is meaningless: there is such a thing as the unmistakable symphonic experience compounded by the organic development (not the mere statement) of musical material itself pregnant and moving. To the former, the light will not blaze forth from these gentlemanly pages. Excellent points are made; but they are not pressed home, doubtless from fear of that damned soul the general reader whose patience must not be tried too far. Why not drag him to the difficult, exciting facts for a change ? I cannot be convinced that it mattered either to the A flat symphony or to its present hearers that Edward VII died while it was half-completed; but that its coda (though absurdly misdescribed as " one of the finest things in *modern* music "—my italics) is " extremely moving and extremely stately " does matter and is worth saying, even in this general form. Such enthusiasm is contagious; what is lacking is the close, factual argument to carry it home. Out of place in such a book as this ? then so much the worse for such a book as this.

ROBERT DONINGTON.

SCOTT GODDARD: *Vaughan Williams.*

It is perhaps characteristic of the modern English symphonist that there is or has been a struggle for expression. Scott Goddard emphasises the rhapsodic element that even now tends to be the abiding popular impression of Vaughan Williams's art. Rhapsody, in his estimate, might have disintegrated both the third and the fifth symphonies if it had not been subject to a discipline which the composer has made peculiarly his own. For these and other reasons a musician may consider first the thematic material quoted. Here are nine good pages of first-hand, accurate and well selected information. We may regret the omission amongst other things of "Token of all brave sailors" (an inspiring setting and a passing reminder that V.W. could ascend to a sharpened seventh in its own right), but the frequent quotation of the harmony makes this cross-section of the musical texture a revealing history. Turn on to the top of page 44 (Rachmaninov No. 2, Adagio theme); the freshness of Vaughan Williams's approach once more hits the ear. Turn back to the later Vaughan Williams; chromatic disturbances and atonality appear, but the comparison of Nos. 4 and 56 (the last example) shews a consistent personality.

The elegant, persuasive and reasonably thorough analysis of the symphonies, which the citation of these first or typical occurrences supports, is objective rather than critical. At the same time, Mr. Goddard says much too little about the shaping of movements in the light of material. A broad hint of the composer's employment and abandonment of sonata-form—especially in regard to the presentation of second subjects, if any—and of the many " cyclic " uses, would have been a useful pointer for the school-child (of all ages) who has found meaning in dominantward second subjects and so forth. As regards background, *Job* does not account for the fourth and sixth Symphonies as readily as Mr. Goddard implies.

The structural generalisation, " No perorations at the end," is surprising. The epilogues of all the symphonies except the third are epitomes of what has been maintained before, and often vital strokes at that. Incidentally the reference to Parry of the " orator's gambit, the final, unquestionable peroration " is a clumsy " abusage."

In his account of the last movement of *A Sea Symphony* Mr. Goddard hardly does justice to the problem of absorbing " restless exploration " in a coherent structure. The subtle half-recapitulation in the Allegro of *A London Symphony* might have been mentioned, and also the salvaging of a second Trio (original version) in the coda of the Scherzo. The epilogue is rather taken for granted. The *Pastoral Symphony* suits Mr. Goddard's tranquil narrative; here natural trumpet and wordless soprano enter without question. The concentration of each movement of the fourth Symphony is well emphasised, but not the blend of minatory and pathetic elements. The analysis of the fifth Symphony is illuminating, that of the sixth is the most persuasive. The general impression is of a reserve of more exact thinking than is stated. This is reassuring but sometimes baffling.

A. E. F. DICKINSON.

JULIAN HERBAGE : *Sibelius.*

Julian Herbage thinks there is a close connection between Tchaikovsky and Sibelius as symphonists. I don't. He finds certain passages in the Sibelius symphonies " bell-like " or " dance-like " or " pastoral " or what-not. In practically every instance I don't. What's more, although he obviously knows these symphonies very familiarly indeed and gives ostensibly factual accounts of their structures, I—who also know them well—differ over and over again from him in his analyses, sometimes very radically. I don't feel that it would be logical of me to argue with him—even when he asserts that "the main Allegro energico" (No. 1., first movement) "starts in G major," or that the middle movement of No. 5 "has a guileless simplicity". Can it be that expounding the form and content of seven symphonies, even with Mr. Herbage's exemplary conscientiousness, is no suitable task for anyone's 9,000 (or, come to that, 90,000) assessing, descriptive, explanatory words ?   RALPH W. WOOD.

STEPHEN WILLIAMS : *Schumann.*
HERE is the mixture as before—assumption of omniscience and china-shop blundering. It is probably too much to expect the official music-journalists to learn that no criticism is justified which does not attempt to consider the oldest work as though it were new, or from its own view-point.

Mr. Williams shows gross misunderstanding of what is symphonic, of what purpose development has in the scheme of things, and of what is or is not admissible in orchestral doubling. His half-hearted initial defence is allowed to crumble in the face of specious and vituperative arguments ; he has nothing with which to combat them except the music itself, of which he shows little knowledge but a vague liking. (It has not struck him for instance, that in the introduction to the Second Symphony the trumpet plays an important theme ; or that the main theme grows to full stature from this introduction). His only defence is unconscious and meant as a condemnation—" his (Schumann's) themes are too terse for anything so spacious and continuous as a symphony." There is no rule in these matters, but the balance of symphonic history is in favour of terse themes. Schumann's expand by movement and tonality as and when he wishes. (Tonality is out of Mr. Williams' ken also, as witness his remark anent the sub-dominant leaning of the new coda-tune in the First Symphony's first movement).

There is no sign of helplessness anywhere in these four symphonies, and so far from the movements being independent, each work is obviously conceived as a whole from the start. Moods complement each other, apart from structure. Schumann's developments are not sections and know what Mr. Williams does not ; how to develop otherwise than by themes alone.

Two misfortunes are insufficient data upon which to base accusations of bad scoring.

Mr. Williams has supplied the perfect summing-up of his chapter : " . . . . the most sensible thing is to forget all I have written . . . . and plunge into the symphonies themselves."   HAROLD TRUSCOTT.

ROBIN HULL: *Rachmaninov.*
MR. HULL provides conventional programme notes for the Second and Third Symphonies, with plentiful allusions of the "restrained passion," "dramatic outburst" type; strangely, he does not examine the First Symphony, psychologically in many ways the most penetrating of the three. Since the analytical method used by Mr. Hull is the same as that used by the other contributors he is doubtless on the side of the gods, but whether any chapter in the book will "guide the intelligent listener towards a deeper understanding" (blurb) is, to say the least, dubious. Only McNaught, Herbage and

Goddard manage to convey something more than the bare mathematical bones of structure. Mr. Hull's phrase-by-phrase analysis is impeccably accurate—but how does it lead to deeper understanding? The concept is not to be achieved by a system that merely indicates the order of musical sequences. In his introduction, Mr. Hull shows that he really understands Rachmaninov, and it is from this section that the reader must draw his conclusions; the rest is like a guide book to a city: it tells you so much, but what really matters is that which it cannot describe.

JOHN CULSHAW.

ERIC BLOM: *Mozart.*

" There must, we tell ourselves as we listen spellbound to a Mozart symphony, be something else than the contrivance and manipulation of structure about the creation of music in this or any other form " (p. 62). Which, says Blom, is best called individuality. Quite possible, of course, that " the intelligent and serious listener " to whom this book is addressed will not stop to reflect that while all greatness has individuality, not all individuality plus faultless contrivance of form is great. " But if Mozart's individuality is easily enough apprehended . . . it becomes tantalizingly elusive directly one tries to describe it on paper. Who is to say why . . . the opening of the . . . G minor Symphony gives a peculiar impression of just that apprehensive agitation, just that foreboding of tragedy? *A technical explanation, that the movement is fast and the key is minor, does not help, for someone may remind us that the scherzo in Mendelssohn's "Midsummer Night's Dream" music is also fast and in a minor key (in fact the very same key, as it happens)* . . . " (p. 62f.; my italics.) Having thus informed the intelligent reader about the nature of technical explanations, Blom concludes that great inspiration remains a mystery; by which time he has spent more than 600 words on precisely and provably less than nothing. The present writer would be prepared to accept the above-italicized words as a challenge, i.e. to furnish an analysis of the G minor's opening—comprehensible to everyone who has music in his blood and Blom's musical dictionary at his elbow—of which Mr. Blom would say: " It does help."

The rest of the essay is more like what we have reason to expect from its author, though occasional omissions and confusions continue to constern. The symphonies discussed are K.201, 297, 338, 385, 425 and " the " four. As in Blom's *Mozart* book, the most important point about K.201's first subject, i.e. the bass, remains unmentioned and unquoted. We are advised not to call the Haffner's first movement " monothematic," and to label as " second subject " what is really the second countermelody at, harmonically, the second subject stage. In order to prove himself wrong Mr. Blom need only look up " subject " and " theme " in Blom's *Everyman's Dictionary of Music.* But he is in no mind to do so: "All that happens is that the first subject remains present as a counterpoint, for the simple reason that it chances to combine ideally . . . with the new theme" (p. 71). All that happens is that the heart continues beating because life chances to combine ideally with man's activities. The " theme " is moreover of pronouncedly transitional character: an " open," sequential melody, driving on the dominant's tonic pedal (omitted in the music example) from the *Wechseldominante* (the dominant's dominant) back to the dominant, which it thus confirms. Apropos of K.543's Andante, Blom points out that Mozart rarely writes in A flat. It would have

16

been worth while somewhat to enlarge upon this important observation. On the one hand, apart from the present movement, three of Mozart's greatest slow movements are in A flat: " the " E flat quartet's, the second E flat violin sonata's, and the Adagio from the string trio. The slow movement of the E flat quartet K.160 is also in A flat, and while that of the E flat quartet K.171 is in C minor, the trio is here in A flat, as is the first trio of the string trio's second minuet.   In the four E flat piano concertos, on the other hand, Mozart consistently avoids going into the subdominant for the slow movement, whereas he chooses this degree for the middle movements of twelve out of the other 17 piano concertos in major.   Nor of course does he go into the sub-mediant in the C minor concerto, whilst in the D minor he does.   As a matter of fact he never goes from C minor into A flat.   Blom touches upon another important question of tonality when he notes that the E flat symphony's trio " rather unusually remains in the tonic key " (p. 86).   Generally true, this assertion is somewhat misleading as it stands: of the six symphonies with minuets which Blom discusses, three have their trios in the tonic key.   The *Linz's* tonic trio goes unobserved, while the *Jupiter's* is only indicated by a reference to its " gentle calls in C major."   And the B flat symphony K.319, whose trio is also in the tonic key, is not discussed.   In point of fact the later works of Mozart show (as has not, I think, yet been noticed) an increase in tonic trios.   Among the six later symphonies with minuets, four have their trios in the tonic key.   We find two tonic trios among the " Ten " string quartets; none among the earlier ones.   (There is one in the A major flute quartet of 1778—one year before K.319.)   The last two string quintets have tonic trios.   (The tonic trio of the clarinet quartet, as also that of the string trio, is another matter, for these works have two minuet movements.)

It is untrue that " the only time Mozart showed that he was capable of being clumsy was when he wrote *A Musical Joke* . . ." (p. 74).   There are examples of unintentional and very considerable clumsiness particularly in the early quartets, e.g. K.160 in the very respects, too, in which the later master excelled.   It is untrue that the " false start " in the development of the *Prague* is " humorously made to hoodwink listeners who have not the gift of absolute pitch" (p. 79).   One need not have absolute pitch in order to hear (as one absolutely must) that the " start " is in the wrong key, and Mozart's structural intentions do not include the hoodwinking of his unmusical listeners. But then, Blom addresses himself more than once to the unmusical.   " The intelligent and serious listener " who has to be told that in the G minor's Andante " the fervently lyrical second subject " is " first in B flat, later in E flat " (p. 89) can go and bury himself, and he for whom the cross-rhythm of the same movement's bar 20 " appears to turn the time for a moment from 6-8 into 3-4 " (*ibid.*) must be fatally short of rhythmic breath.   Nor can Mr. Blom yet have met an intuitive and really musical listener if he thinks that " the incomparable flow and polish " of the Jupiter's finale is all that " the hearer who remains unaware of its polyphonic problems " enjoys (p. 63).

The references to Exx. 14, 15, 16, 17, 18, 19 are misprinted, as are, most lavishly, 44 of the 56 music examples themselves.   In fact the music appendix will make an excellent game for parties of intelligent listeners: Who can, without recourse to the scores, detect more misprints ? (No prize for anyone who finds less than 40.) Blom's chapter, then, combines unexpected demerits with expected merits.

HANS KELLER.

A Note on "Gold Coast Customs"

By HUMPHREY SEARLE

THE combination of speech and music is a perennial problem with which composers of all ages have tried to grapple. The essence of the problem is to decide whether the music should be purely incidental, without any particular shape of its own (in which case it often might just as well not be there at all), or whether it should be a more or less independent entity (in which case it may distract from or drown the words). On first reading Dr. Edith Sitwell's magnificent poem, I felt that it was a work to which music might possibly add something in the way of background atmosphere, but that a purely choral setting would not be appropriate. A good deal of the violent emotional impact of the poem is due to the use of a very subtle poetical technique (which Dr. Sitwell has analysed in the preface to her Collected Poems and elsewhere.) In attempting to write music for it I did not, of course, try to parallel this exactly (which would be impossible), but rather to write a work which, though entirely ancillary to the poem—the music would make very little sense if performed without the words—would yet have a structure of its own ; i.e. it is an attempt to make a rough equation of poetical and musical form.

The poem consists of three sections, of which the first is by far the longest ; I divided this in half, and cast the music in four continuous movements corresponding to those of the normal symphony ; Allegro, Adagio, Scherzo and Finale. Further, the whole work falls into twenty-six sections which build up the characteristic shapes of each movement—Allegro in sonata form, Adagio in ABABA form, Scherzo with two trios, and Rondo-Finale. The following analysis may make this clear :—

Section	First movement—ALLEGRO.	First line.
	Exposition.	
1	First subject (A)	One fantee wave Is grave and tall
2	Second subject (B)	One house like a ratskin Mask flaps fleet
	Third subject (C)	But at Lady Bamburgher's parties each head

18

19

Fourth Movement—RONDO.

22	Primary section	*When, creeping over* *The Sailor's Street*
23	1st alternative section	*Where (a black gap flapping,* *A white skin drum)*
24	Primary section	*The leaves of black hippopotamus* *hide*
25	2nd alternative section	*But yet when the cannibal Sun is* *high*
26	Primary section	*Gomorrah's fires have washed my* *blood*

These sections are, of course, of varying lengths, and some of them are subdivided—Section 18 (Sally's monologue) for instance consists of an introduction and a set of variations within itself ; but the table above shows the main design of the work.

The music uses the twelve-note technique of Schoenberg ; the fundamental series is shown at A. By taking every third and sixth note respectively, two subsidiary series, B and C, are arrived at.

(It will be seen that, as these are symmetrical series, the retrograde form is the same as the inversion). A is mainly associated with the " basic " ideas of the poem, and the greater part of the work is derived from it. It appears at the very opening in two-part chords on the pianos, but is most easily recognisable at the first entry of the brass, before the words " Striped black and white Is the squealing light " ; this upward-rushing phrase is associated with the idea of " the light " throughout the work.

A is also the basis of the trombone chords which are associated with the " stone coffin " ; these first appear in the fourth section.

> " I only know one half of my heart
> Lies in that terrible coffin of stone,
> My body that stalks through the slum alone."

The pizzicato double bass phrase which follows the chords represents the theme of " stalking through the slum " which frequently recurs, particularly in the monologue of Sally the prostitute in the third movement.

Series B, which first appears at the beginning of the second section, is mainly associated with the idea of the " rag houses " and the " Sailor's Street." The figure of two repeated quavers is important throughout the work.

B also appears as a counterpoint in some of the more lyrical passages, for instance at the words " O far horizons and bright blue wine " in the third movement (section 16).

The third series, which is first exposed in the second half of the second section, usually appears in the passages describing Lady Bamburgher's parties, normally in its inverted form.

Its original form, however, also provides a lyrical clarinet solo in the second movement (section 11).

21

"The negress Dorothy one sees
Beside the caverns and the trees".

The only other important themes, both derived from A, are, firstly, that associated with the Worm, and first appearing in section 3, "The shapeless worm-soft unshaping Sin" :—

and the main theme of the Scherzo :—

"Gold Coast Customs" is scored for what might be described as an enlarged jazz combination :—speaker, male chorus, 2 flutes (doubling piccolos), oboe, clarinet, tenor saxophone, bassoon, two trumpets, three trombones, four percussion players, two pianos and double basses. There is no actual imitation of African music, though certain effects are borrowed from it—for instance the use in section 3 ("So our wormskin and paper masks still keep") of groups of 4, 5, 6 and 7 quavers continuously repeated against each other ; and in the last movement at "Bahunda, Banbangala, Barumbe, Bonge" (section 24) whip, rattle, bass drum, two piccolos and a shouting chorus make an effect suggested by an African war chant, whistled and shouted to the accompaniment of tom-toms and clapped hands. In addition, in the first and last movements a tenor drum beats continuously in the background ; and though I have not tried to reproduce the intricate rhythms of African music in detail, there is some use of an irregular five-beat rhythm, which appears in the slow movement (section 12) on percussion alone, and recurs several times in slightly varied forms.

On its other appearances the last semiquaver of each group is tied to the first of the next, giving a more ambiguous effect (e.g. in sections 9 and 14). The jazz passages (accompanying Lady Bamburgher's parties) are, of course, frankly parodies, and do not try to imitate any particular school or period of jazz ; an eminent authority tells me that they are best described as " shimmy fox."

The chorus (which is silent throughout the first movement) sings little of the poem, apart from five lines on its first entry (" How far is our innocent paradise ") and occasional interjections later (" Sally go pick up a sailor ") ; it principally provides a background of colour by singing vowel-sounds, especially in the more lyrical passages. My reason for thus limiting its role was, of course, to try and ensure that the words should be heard as clearly as possible. I had originally hoped that the work could be scored in such a way that the speaker would be audible without amplification, but this proved to be far too optimistic an idea, and a public address system is necessary in the concert hall. At the first performances the speaker's part was shared by Dr. Sitwell and Mr. Constant Lambert (to whom my musical setting is dedicated), and the alternation of the two voices, was, I think, generally agreed to be effective. The words are notated in rhythm but not in pitch, and though the voice is not treated like an instrument (as in some passages of " Façade," for instance), more or less exact synchronisation with the music is desirable. (There is, by the way, a musical quotation from the *Popular Song* from " Façade " in section 7, " Beckoning negress, nun of the shade," and shortly afterwards one from " Tristan "—" Lady Bamburgher's romantic heart ").

There is no need for me to weary my readers with further elaboration ; I can merely say that I have enjoyed writing this work more than anything I have done before, and only hope that I have not done an injustice to Dr. Sitwell's tremendous poem ; Dr. Sitwell has indeed collaborated most kindly and enthusiastically throughout, and I would like to express my sincere gratitude both to her and to Mr. Lambert, as well as to all those who made it possible for the work to be brought to performance.

Dr. Sitwell's poem is published in " The Canticle of the Rose " by Messrs. Macmillan, Ltd., and Humphrey Searle's musical setting by Messrs. A. Lengnick & Co.; the quotations are reproduced by their kind permission. " An Interim Report on Humphrey Searle's Music " by Richard Gorer, appeared in *Music Survey*, 1/5/49.—EDS.

For The Edinburgh Festival:
(1) "Ariadne"—Phoenix of Opera
By H. F. REDLICH

STRAUSS' and Hofmannsthal's *Ariadne auf Naxos*, cropping up for the first time in their famous correspondence early in 1911 as " die kleine Molièresache " (the Molière trifle) and—even more modestly —as " Zwischenarbeit " (interim work) between operatic conceptions of exceptional magnitude (*Rosenkavalier* and *Frau ohne Schatten*), has nevertheless become one of the decisive turning points in the history of 20th century music. Its historical significance—as it appears today after almost forty years—seems in no way inferior to that of Monteverdi's and Rinuccini's earlier *Arianna*, whose famous Lamento elicited so many sympathetic tears from its Mantuan audience in 1608, ushering in the age of operatic emotionalism which seems so definitely terminated by the *Ariadne* of 1912. The latter work—the fragile and subtle realisation of a poet's dream, desiring a new Mozartean age to rise out of the dying embers of post-Wagnerian sensualism—is the first premonition of a novel artistic creed which, guided by the spirits of Lully and Gluck, revives forgotten loyalties of form and proportion. It was indeed a poet's operatic vision that descended upon the surprised composer of *Elektra* and *Rosenkavalier* in that famous letter of March 29th, 1911 :—

" 30-Minuten-Oper fuer ein kleines Kammerorchester, die in meinem Kopf so gut wie fertig ist, benannt " Ariadne auf Naxos " und gemischt aus heroisch-mythologischen Figuren im Kostuem des 18. Jahrhunderts, in Reifroecken und Straussenfedern und aus Figuren der commedia dell' arte, Harlekin und Scaramuccio, welche ein mit dem heroischen Element fortwaehrend verwebtes Buffo-Element tragen. . . "*

The " small chamber orchestra " of this letter became the igniting spark for Strauss' receptive mind. The fragrant tissue of his score (for a handful of winds, soloistic strings, pianoforte and percussion : 36 players in all) offered to a new generation a way out of the suffocating forest of modern mammoth orchestras. In 1911 we are definitely at the borderline of two artistic epochs. The gargantuan scores of Strauss' own *Elektra* (1909), of Mahler's VIIIth Symphony (" Symphonie der Tausend ") and Schoenberg's *Gurrelieder*—both

---

*" *Thirty minutes' opera for a small chamber orchestra virtually finished in my head, called* ' Ariadne auf Naxos ' *and mixing heroic-mythological figures in 18th century costume, crinolines and ostrich-feathers, with figures from the* commedia dell' *arte, Harlequin and Scaramouche, in whom the buffo element is continuously interwoven with an heroic element. . .* "

published in 1910—and Skrjabin's *Prometheus* (1911), represent the twilight of post-Wagnerian Baroque, while simultaneously the first experiments in the direction of a quite different sound ideal are being launched. In 1908 Franz Schreker uses a "chamber orchestra" for the first time in history to accompany a Ballet (*Birthday of the Infanta*); this had been preceded by Schoenberg's first *Kammersymphonie* Op. 9, composed as early as 1906. How deeply Strauss himself was affected by Hofmannsthal's novel conception and how keenly he felt the import of their artistic achievement in *Ariadne*, may be gathered from a letter of his, written in August 1916, at the end of the five long years in which *Ariadne* slowly (and painfully) matured into the masterpiece it eventually became.

"... Ihr Notschrei gegen das Wagner'sche ' Musizieren ' ist mir tief zu Herzen gegangen und hat die Tuer zu einer ganz neuen Landschaft aufgestossen, in der ich, von Ariadne und besonders dem neuen Vorspiel geleitet, mich ganz ins Gebiet der unwagner'schen Spiel-, Gemuets- und Menschenoper zu begeben hoffe. . . Ich verspreche ihnen, dass ich den Wagner'schen Musizierpanzer nun definitiv abgestreift habe. . . "†

Between these two letters the slow gestation of *Ariadne auf Naxos* took place. Originally it was planned to supplant the "Turkish ceremony" in Molière's *Bourgeois Gentilhomme* as a kind of operatic intermezzo in a play (to which Strauss had contributed ravishing incidental music). That first version of *Ariadne* was first performed at Stuttgart, on October 25th, 1912, with Max Reinhardt as producer. It achieved for the time being no more than a *succès d'estime*. A complete revision of libretto and music eventually resulted in the second (and now universally performed) version—first played in Vienna, on October 4th, 1916—which dispensed altogether with Molière's play, starting with a completely new dramatic Prelude (to which Strauss' letter alludes) and containing a wealth of beautiful new music. Molière's *Bourgeois* in a new adaptation by Hofmannsthal ultimately received much more incidental music from Strauss' pen and has existed since 1917 in its own right in two arrangements : as a play with music and as an orchestral suite, occasionally using dance tunes of Lully and transforming them into something intensely Straussian.

† " *Your cry of distress against Wagnerian ' music-making ' has gone deeply to my heart and has pushed the door open to an entirely new landscape where, led by Ariadne and particularly the new Prelude, I hope to proceed straight into the realm of the un-Wagnerian* Spieloper *of human sentiment. . . I promise you that I have now definitely divested myself of Wagnerian musical armour. . .*"

Every student of opera should read the letters exchanged between poet and composer in those years of arduous toil. They represent an ideal initiation into those problems of opera which have been with us since the far-off days when the fate of Arianna, abandoned by Theseus, for the first time moved an operatic audience so profoundly. The music of this later *Ariadne* (with its heroine forgetting her grief at last in the divine love of Dionysos himself), its limpid orchestral climate, its daring coloratura arias, its buffo ensembles, secco recitatives, and its unique amalgam of the heroic and the burlesque, is likely to remain Richard Strauss' most potent appeal to a new artistic age—to which his own librettist had "pushed the door open."

BIBLIOGRAPHY :

Richard Strauss : *Briefwechsel mit Hugo v. Hofmannsthal* (Berlin, 1926).

Hugo v. Hofmannsthal : *Ce que nous avons voulu en écrivant Ariane à Naxos et Le Bourgeois Gentilhomme* (*Mercure Musicale*, VIII, Nos. 9/10, Paris, 1912.)

(2) A Note on Bartok's Viola Concerto
By DENIS STEVENS

A COMPOSER'S unfinished sketches have always proved a temptation to his friends and pupils. Imitation of his style during his lifetime counts for little more than pastiche : after he has died that same imitation becomes a sacred duty, which it is possible to carry out more or less well, according to the taste and talents of the musical executor. A composer's last testament is not always his greatest, but it may often be of such interest as to compel eager expectation from the whole world of music. That world will turn, however slowly, from admiring to despising if either taste or talent is lacking in the completion of a symphonic or operatic torso.

Where Rimsky-Korsakov failed, and Alfano rounded off, Tibor Serly (who has prepared Bartok's Concerto from the composer's original manuscript) has succeeded, not only as a highly-skilled palaeographer*, but as contrapuntist and orchestrator. He has given to the world, and more especially to the violists, whose concerto literature is discouragingly sparse, a work which has the imprint of Bartok's hand, though it was made up by an almost unimaginable feat of synthesis from " odd loose sheets of music paper." Serly (in his preface to the concerto) goes on to say: " Bits of material

*See the facsimile in the Viola/Piano edition (Boosey & Hawkes).

that came to his mind were jotted down without regard for their sequence. The pages were not numbered nor the separation of movements indicated. The greatest difficulty encountered was deciphering his correction of notes, for Bartok, instead of erasing, grafted his improvements on to the original notes."

Serly admits that the orchestration proved the easiest part of the work, and he has used what might be called a sub-normal classical orchestra, the omissions being a fourth horn and a third trombone, to agree perhaps with Bartok's stipulation that " the orchestration will be rather transparent, more transparent than in the Violin Concerto."†

From the point of view of structure, the work has much to recommend it. There are no tortuous corridors, no beams to crack the unwary skull. The first movement has an air of classical logic about it, and is graced by several themes of outstanding character. Not least remarkable is the skill shown by Bartok in elaborating a theme, so that the result has an air of improvised re-creation, like that of a figured plainsong :

The return of this theme is contrived in a manner which has been made familiar by countless concertos : here, there is no sense of staleness as the melody enters quietly just before the end of the cadenza. Throughout the recapitulation, there are many subtle changes of line and colour which only Bartok, or one who understood to perfection his mental processes, could achieve. The slow movement is full of a tranquil angularity, with the melodic leap of a fifth in the foreground. Echoes of the Fifth Quartet are heard in the section marked *piangendo*, but the tranquil mood returns, and with it the main theme of the first movement. In the finale, an *ostinato* double pedal sets loose a scurry of semi-quavers which lends an anxious kind of brilliance to the whole movement, so typical of later Bartok. Needless to say, the resources of the viola are thoroughly displayed, for the virtuoso style which is so essential a part of every concerto is by no means overlooked by the composer. Indeed, Bartok was nothing if not a realist. It is to be hoped that his last work will find a permanent place in the repertory of viola soloists everywhere.

†Letter from the composer to William Primrose.

Bach's Fugal Craftsmanship—II.

By A. E. F. DICKINSON

ONCE the exposition is completed, a fugue may continue by more or less impromptu methods of changing the voicing, polyphonic content and key of the entries, or by exploiting the contrapuntal possibilities of subject, counter-subject or a freshly-announced subject. These entries are joined, varied or forced apart by anything from a slight extension to a growing episode of rival interest. Each way of development shows a different attention to the subject and so far a distinct type of appeal, like the varying relation between first and second subject in a sonata. The first method, spaciously carried out in most of the organ fugues and executed in miniature in many fugues in the first Book of the Forty-eight and in a few in the second, is thematically casual and relies mainly on a flow of fresh counterpoint. The second is a more consciously virtuoso manner, but it may range from an introspective and cumulative close canon or vigorous invertible counterpoint between subject and counter-subject to an overwhelming expansion of two or even three or four subjects in a rich integrity. Either method may, or may not, be amplified or qualified by parallel interludes—successive in time but parallel in effect. In the final version of A.F., Bach went to some pains to define the order in which his established methods of subject-development could best be placed, if the same subject was to be preserved substantially. He put close canon, which appears to be the modern obsession, into a group of manifestly " exhibition " fugues, employing the fugal craft lightly and brilliantly before the main subject moves into a wider and more absorbing world. Multiplicity of subjects may prove conclusive, but it is not necessarily an asset. Just before Bach died, he was grappling with this very problem. Each structural appeal must in short be *heard* on its own merits after its recognised kind. We may now distinguish these in their classes.

(1) In many fugues the combination of subject and counter-subject with a variable third or fourth part is conveniently disposed by means of a slight variety of key. In major-key fugues, the relative minor, and less often the supertonic or mediant minor and the sub-dominant, are the prevailing changes. In minor-key fugues, the relative and submediant and leading-note major, with the sub-dominant, are commonest. Further modulations are rare and notable. The contrast of major and minor is always effective. It lets in, or removes for a spell, the antinomies of polyphony in the minor.

The big G minor organ fugue is a vigorous exemplar on a large scale. The first C minor fugue of the Forty-eight is a slight and wiry specimen of the closer-bound structure of Bach's keyboard invention. It heralded very many others. The B minor at the end of the book attempts a more cumulative effect in a tortuous chromatic vein. Alternatively, the counterpoint may be " free " all the time, as in the second F minor fugue* and A.F. No. 4. This type may be regarded as the adaptation of vocal fugue to the keyboard, by the development of finger and foot movement to replace the interest of music fitted to words by piquant interludes.

(2) Occasionally the subject is treated in close canon, in two isolated pairs of entries (never less) or in a cumulative insistence. This, the vocal tradition in fugue, appears potently in the late D minor organ fugue, in each Book of the Forty-eight and in the witty trio, Nos. 5-7 of A.F. Canon can be passed off lightly, as in the first fugue in F, as well as being pressed in the service of a concentrated imagery, as in the C major preceding. Inversion (usually from the dominant, reversing a *d-s* curve) often attends these research fugues, establishing the inverted subject as a working alternative to the subject. This is a conspicuous variant in the first fugues in D, E flat and A minor, and in the second B flat minor. Occasionally inversion is used by itself, as in the first F sharp minor and B major fugues, both subtle examples. Both canon and inversion may be absorbed in a developing polyphonic movement.

Ex.1

Subject
(Inversion of main subject)   Canon

Augmentation is employed casually in the second fugue in C minor, and in a thorough-going manner in the first E flat minor fugue and A.F. No. 7. Close canon appears constantly in one of the most satisfying fugues, the second E major ; but it is all so smoothly worked that the craft is never uppermost. None of Bach's canonic fugues could be named Musical Jokes. *O si semper omnes !*

(3) Counter-subjects, old or new, may be developed at fresh intervals with the subject, or doubled in thirds and sixths. The

*References will be to the Forty-eight unless otherwise stated. A.F. = *Art of Fugue.*

second G minor fugue and A.F. No. 9 are *loci classici,* supported lightly by the second C sharp minor and B major fugues, the organ fugue in C (beginning *d : r/m : f*), and, without any exploitation of fresh intervals, the first C sharp minor fugue, one of the greatest. In nearly every case the surrounding polyphony perpetually changes its face at the same time. Alternatively, one or even two fresh subjects may be announced separately and combine later with the first. The organ fugue in F, the second G sharp minor fugue and A.F. No. 10 show two subjects ; the last with a scintillating variety of invertible counterpoint, duly absorbed in a wider polyphony. The organ fugue in E flat, the second F sharp minor and A.F. Nos. 8, 11 and 14 show three subjects. In the E flat the principal subject attends and integrates the other subjects in turn ; the F sharp minor and A.F. No. 8 lightly combine their three subjects at the end, the second subject functional rather than characteristic. A.F. No. 11 treats the inversions of the subjects of No. 8, and naturally exploits their combination at the end.

These methods merely ensure a certain automatic development of two or more figures of expression, and the results vary. The sturdy subject of the second G minor fugue lends itself to humorous contrapuntal gymnastics around it. The supporting fugues named above take invertibility in their stride and are maintained by a succession of polyphony and episode and key-interest. Only the sharpest ear would detect that the counter-subject changes its relation to the subject. The first C sharp minor fugue works its two counter-subjects with the subject in a rich tapestry of three to five threads, and effects a concluding section by means of close canon, abandoning the first counter-subject ; an unexpected and tense moment.

Of the double-fugues, the organ fugue in F has such a spacious exposition that the second fugue is a positive relief, and the Combination, breezy, unrestrained and yet concise, makes an easy climax. A.F. No. 10 is so compact of spontaneous polyphony

First subject, inverted at the tenth, in the alto.

Ex 2

Idée fixe, here the second subject, answered in the dominant (counter-exposition)

and episode that it only needs to switch and combine the variant

30

degrees of entry to keep up a sense of movement. The subject of the second G sharp minor fugue, on the other hand, is anything but capable of the record length which the fugue happens to hold in the Forty-eight ; nor does its studied chromatic auxiliary rescue it, or the equally forced episodes.

The second F sharp minor fugue combines a jaunty first subject, an almost episodic second phrase, and a garrulous, irrepressible third, all comfortably united in the final section, without strain or emphasis. A.F. No. 8 exposes and expands a pungent subject, descending irresistibly down the complete octave ; introduces a voluble and rather trenchant counter-subject to promote further counter-exposition ; announces a third element, the *idée fixe* of the series, inverted) ; and finally combines the three with a sharp screwing up of the harmony, which relaxes in later entries. The subversive *idée*, breaking in almost a century before cyclic events became a positive trend, is sufficiently controlled not to overwhelm the fugue, but rather to enhance the cumulative effect. In the equally long and symmetrical treatment of inversions of these three subjects (A.F. No. 11), the new subjects are virtually *idées fixes* from the start, and each is freer to enter anywhere without a sense of disturbance. The problems of syntax beguiled Bach. But the inversions (with the second subject dragging *up* an octave and the third subject's suspensions resolving upwards) prove fatal on such a scale and as a sequel to the parent fugue. A.F. No. 11 is a resourceful but pathetic fugal progeny, and its modern presentation as the pretentious climax of an orchestral setting is about as impressive to an alert intelligence as the World Economic Conference of twenty years ago. Such *folie de grandeur* is no compliment to the subtle wit and intimate tone of the fugue. Bach's own reaction was to work out two completely invertible fugues as a preliminary to the invertible quadruple fugue which (happily) he did not live to write, and to embark upon a normal quadruple fugue, whose execution up to the triple stage shows a queer lapse to the awkwardness of *fugato* sections, and to promise a foregone conclusion, no more. Even with Tovey's brilliantly conceived finish, this perplexing final fugue is best reserved for the lecture-room, not dragged into publicity.

(4) It has been convenient to detail the various expansions of subject first. These entries, so variously reinforced by free or organic counter-phrase, are usually joined or pushed apart by episodes of various dimensions and qualities. They range from an impromptu extension, whose relevance (e.g. in the common sequential treatment of the bass) is so spontaneous as to be unconscious, to

expansive passages of apt imitation and sequence, on the one hand, and independent developments, on the other. The latter may depend on a stray ascending or descending line or cardinal interval (fourth or fifth), or on a cheerful Alberti figure ; or there may be

more special *jeux d'esprit*, as in the late organ fugue in D minor, the second keyboard fugues in C sharp minor, F, F minor and B flat, and A.F. Nos. 1, 4, 8, 10. The salient impression is that Bach is rarely gravelled for lack of varied connective or contrasted matter—the first F minor and B minor fugues, and the second E minor, are definitely exceptions—and remains unexcelled in continuity of style. Where an episode develops a pronounced cross-rhythm of its own, the resultant tension against an expanding subject is of the same order as that of the two-subject fugue.

Broadly, then, Bach's methods of development are not numerous ; nor can it be said that he always chooses the only alternative possible, or even that he always exploits his subjects. But what method and length he chooses usually shows an uncanny observation of his themes and of their potential contexts. That is something which no one else has done in a hundred fugues that bear more than technical scrutiny. Not the bluff Handel, nor the versatile Mozart ; not even Cherubini or Klengel. Since Bach's time, fugue has suffered re-valuation. It has become at best the composer's reserve and improvised vehicle. If it took Beethoven to unforgettable receding horizons, it fell later into the exuberant but casual grasp of Mephistopheles-Liszt and Falstaff-Verdi. Modern revivals are either pungent and strained attempts to maintain fugue in a proud atonality, or somewhat mild, old-fashioned essays in the neo-classical. Fugue remains as a texture, but as a typical structure it is out-of-date, a conscious anachronism. Its use by composer students at the expense of more fruitful things is highly debatable. Yet this is no reason for ignoring the vast and intimate experience that has been unlocked by its sterling key at the touch of a master, or for regarding an inability to hear an inversion at the twelfth or a *stretto maestrale* as a claim to superior musical understanding.

The Libretto of " The Secret Marriage "

By WINTON DEAN

THE two-hundredth anniversary of the birth of Domenico Cimarosa*
has very properly provoked stage and radio performances of his
best-known work, the opera buffa *Il Matrimonio Segreto*. Musical
reference books assure us that the first performance, in Vienna on
7th February, 1792, so delighted the Emperor Leopold II that he
promptly invited the entire cast and orchestra to supper and then
ordered them to repeat the opera *in toto*, thus setting a symbolic
seal on the century that had enthroned the *da capo* aria. But they
do not mention the curious and enthralling fact that on that very day
the Emperor also concluded with the King of Prussia the treaty of
alliance against revolutionary France which was to plunge Europe
into almost continuous war for more than 23 years, sweep away the
last vestige of the spacious world of patronage and aristocratic ease,
and confer on Cimarosa the distinction, rare among operatic
composers, of being sentenced to death for his political opinions.
No wonder the Emperor felt like refreshing himself with a comic
opera ; and, since the new work was among the most sparkling
and witty of its kind, and free from the undercurrent of heart-break
and unease that had disfigured the similar works of the late Mozart,
barely two months in his grave, no wonder he wanted it all over
again. He had his desire ; but whether he laughed too much at the
opera, or partook too much of the supper, or worried too much over
disturbing the ant-hill of European politics, or for some quite trivial
and irrelevant reason, within three weeks he was dead. Perhaps the
monarch who ignored the greatest genius among his subjects and the
greatest composer of his age, only to confer the greatest *da capo*
of all time on a foreigner and an inferior, was required by an even-
handed destiny to pay a forfeit in proportion : within minutes of his
passing out of the world there passed into it, in a foreign land and a
humble family, Mozart's true heir in the empire of *opera buffa*—
Rossini.

One more fact we learn about *Il Matrimonio Segreto :* the libretto
is based on an English play, *The Clandestine Marriage*, by George
Colman the elder and David Garrick, produced at Drury Lane in
1766. It is always worth examining the source of a successful opera
libretto : not only does it throw up a fascinating profusion of curious
details, but by showing the librettist at work, accepting here, altering

*17th Dec., 1749.

and rejecting there, it illuminates as nothing else can the contemporary attitude to opera. Occasionally it even uncovers an original which ought never to have been buried. An inspection of *The Clandestine Marriage* does all these things. It turns out to be one of the funniest and best constructed comedies in the English language. After reading a few pages we are tempted to cry " Sheridan ! " or perhaps " Goldsmith ! "—until the laws of chronology point out that at the time of its production Sheridan was barely fifteen, and *The Rivals* was still nine years and *She Stoops to Conquer* seven years within the womb of time. We do not know the proportion in which the authors shared their labours. The editors of the British Theatre series, publishing the play in 1792, the year of the opera, considered from internal evidence that " the design, if not even the execution of Ogleby"—of whom more in a moment—came from Garrick, who incidentally does not seem to have acted in the play. Clearly Colman was the chief agent. He was a lawyer turned dramatist, who spent seven years trying to run Covent Garden Theatre, then as now a controversial establishment, quarrelled several times with Garrick, moved on to the Haymarket, begat a son of the same name and profession, and died in a Paddington lunatic asylum in 1794 when his grandchild the opera was already famous. But to the play.

Garrick's verse prologue connects it with yet another of the arts by informing us that it was deliberately modelled on Hogarth's *Marriage à la Mode*, the series of six pictorial satires now in the National Gallery. And a satire it certainly is, though like Beaumarchais's *Figaro* cycle it largely lost this element in the process of operatic transubstantiation. The best way to discuss it is to place the two versions side by side and then draw the necessary distinctions. Briefly the story of the opera is this. Geronimo, an old rich miser, lives with his two daughters, Elisetta and Carolina, and his widowed sister Fidalma, who acts as house-keeper. He has a clerk, Paolino, who having fallen in love with Carolina and in the hopelessness of persuading the old man to accept him as a son-in-law owing to his lowly social position, has married the girl in secret. In order to ingratiate the old man he negotiates a marriage pact between his patron Lord Robinson and the elder sister Elisetta, an arrangement that satisfies Geronimo's social pretensions at the expense of his purse. Unfortunately Lord Robinson refuses to have anything to do with Elisetta, who is a tartar, and presses his suit on Carolina, gaining Geronimo's assent by waiving half the proposed dowry. At the same time Fidalma precipitates her ageing charms on the bosom of Paolino, who creates a nice dramatic aposiopesis by faint-

34

ing in the middle of a duet and is discovered in this compromising situation by Carolina. We thus witness the delicious spectacle of Lord Robinson, Carolina and Paolino trying desperately to lower their own estimation in the eyes of Elisetta, Robinson and Fidalma respectively, to the confusion and mortification of old Geronimo. Finally the latter, pressed by Elisetta and Fidalma, decides to send Carolina to a convent ; she and Paolino prepare to elope ; the two rejected and resentful ladies, hearing voices in Carolina's bedroom in the middle of the night, gloat over the prospect of unmasking his lordship, only for him to emerge from his own door and take them in the rear ; the young couple entreat forgiveness ; and thanks to Robinson agreeing after all to marry Elisetta everything ends happily.

So far as the outward action goes, the librettist, Giovanni Bertati, followed the play with unusual exactitude. His only notable additions are Fidalma's love for Paolino, the scenes in which the various victims try to evade their unsought admirers, and Lord Robinson's final change of front. All these are stock ingredients of opera buffa, and all except the last are dramatically justified. That indeed is the one blot on an admirable libretto ; it goes clean against the character, and was obviously introduced merely to supply the *seconda donna* with a husband. Even the incontravertible fact that all foreigners believe a British peer capable of anything cannot excuse it.

But if Bertati has preserved the bones of Colman's play, he has altered the spirit out of all recognition. It is fascinating to see two things—and two good things—at the same time so similar and so utterly different. The target of the play's satire is the always contemporary vice of snobbery ; it is anatomised with an acute observation and a merciless pen. The miserly father, suitably named Sterling, is the successful *nouveau riche* business man whose only item of faith is the wealth by which he has risen and which has brought him a country estate replete with all the latest absurdities, from a " high octagon summer-house " raised on the mast of an East-Indiaman to a delectable pile of ruins " ready to tumble on your head," from a maze (" all taste—zig-zag—crinkum-crankum— in and out—right and left—to and again—twisting and turning like a worm, my lord ! ") to a bogus parish church " to terminate the prospect." His own object now is to penetrate the inner ramparts of high society by buying a title for his elder daughter Elizabeth, and he calculates the cost to a nicety. But he can be mighty self-righteous withal. When asked to forgive his erring daughter at the end, he replies : " I am a father, my lord ; but for the sake of other fathers, I think I ought not to forgive her, for fear of encouraging other silly girls like herself to throw themselves away without the consent of their parents." Surely an apt secretary for the Fathers' Union.

Elizabeth is a termagant with no standards and a dirty mind ; her ambition is bounded by the mental horizon of the London season. " Love and a cottage ! Ah, give me indifference and a coach and six ! " To which her sister Fanny replies " And why not the coach and six without the indifference ? " Mrs. Heidelberg, the aunt, is a far more formidable figure than Fidalma. The widow of a prosperous Dutchman (" a warm man—a very warm man ; and died worth a plumb at least ; a plumb ! ay, I warrant you, he died worth a plumb and a half"), she has all the vices of her brother and niece and others of her own, including an almost sadistic lust for family domination. She knows that Sterling covets her wealth, and trades on the fact by threatening to convey it to her husband's relatives in Holland whenever she requires to bring him to heel. She leers at everything of the male sex (above a certain income), and her speech is common and affected : she is for ever concerned with " people of qualaty " and the honour of " the fammaly." Other specimens of her vocabulary are " wulgar," " dish-abille," " purluminary " (preliminary) and " flustrated." She has something of both Vanbrugh's Lord Foppington (in a much debased form) and Sheridan's Mrs. Malaprop ; and it is not impossible that remarks like " as perfect a pictur of two distrest lovers, as if it had been drawn by Raphael Angelo " may have given Sheridan a hint. These three characters bring us plenty to laugh at, but we cannot laugh with them as we can with their counterparts in the opera. Indeed they are so unpleasantly true to life that the comparative gentleness of their final taking off leaves us faintly dissatisfied.

The two lovers are not much altered by Bertati, doubtless for the sensible reason that newly-weds are much the same everywhere. Robinson is a synthesis of two characters. His title he inherits from Lord Ogleby, his status in the plot from the latter's nephew Sir John Melvil, a hot but impecunious baronet. These two represent the genuine aristocracy and, of course, easily see through the entire Sterling family ; but, true to type, though they have titles and estates they have no money, and are therefore forced to bargain. Both lay siege to the younger, married and seemingly also pregnant sister ; Lord Ogleby even deludes himself (no difficult task) into believing that she loves him in return ; neither could possibly pair off with the termagant Elizabeth at the end. Ogleby, an amusing compound of vanity, shrewdness and hypochondria, is conceived almost in terms of farce. Among the minor characters, who all disappear in the opera, are Canton, Lord Ogleby's Swiss retainer, who combines " the language and the impertinence of the French, with the laziness of Dutchmen," a number of servants comic or faithful, and three lawyers, caricatured in a very funny scene for which no doubt Colman drew on his early legal experience (Mr. Serjeant Flower, after laying down the law to his junior colleagues, summarises in a sentence of titanic length the document he has drawn up for Sterling, whereby, inter alia, " the whole estate, after the death of the aforesaid earl, descends to the heirs male of Sir John Melvil, on the body of the aforesaid Elizabeth Sterling lawfully to be forgotten.") The addition of these extra characters to the uproar in the bedroom corridor makes the finale even more entertaining than in the opera. The play's construction is remarkably tight, and the characters are observed with a rich humour that connects the generation of Vanbrugh and Congreve with that of Sheridan and Goldsmith, and suggests that further treasures may await the enquirer into the annals of 18th Century English comedy.

Bertati, no doubt wisely, dropped the satire, which his audience would hardly have understood, and exchanged the humour of character for the farce of situation, thereby providing the perfect vehicle for light trippant music in a style long established by convention. He transferred the scene to Italy ; the only link with England is one which was not, and could not have been, in the original—the caricature of Lord Robinson as the absurd English milord so dear to continental comedy. (We meet him again in Auber's *Fra Diavolo*, though by that time the species had acquired a more romantic quality through the well-publicised activities of Byron.) This stroke of genius—it is surely nothing less—not only shifted the dramatic kaleidoscope and pointed the contrast between the members of Geronimo's household and the sole outsider ; it made the libretto more irretrievably Italian than ever. The six surviving characters have become the stock figures of opera buffa, the two pairs of lovers, buffo bass and comic house-keeper or servant whom we meet time and again in slightly varied forms. Mozart immortalized them (reducing the buffo to a minimum) in *Cosi fan tutte ;* we find them in Scarlatti, Rossini, Donizetti, Sullivan and even (much subtilised) in *Falstaff :* modern composers like Wolf-Ferrari in *I quattro rusteghi* (*The School for Fathers*) and Arthur Benjamin in *Prima Donna* still delight in putting them through their paces.

Colman's comedy and Bertati's libretto are both types (so, of course, is Cimarosa's music) ; but they are very different types. The remarkable thing is that an almost perfect specimen of English satirical comedy should have been transpirited into an almost perfect specimen of Italian opera buffa with such success that although the skeleton remains the same the flesh retains no disfiguring marks of manipulative surgery. Only those who have studied the muddle that usually results when a play—even a native play—is gutted for the operatic stage can appreciate the rarity of this phenomenon.

Schoenberg

THE VERY FIRST PERFORMANCE OF SCHOENBERG'S " GURRELIEDER "

By HANS NACHOD

" SING that to me," said Arnold, my elder cousin, showing me a piece of paper on which a song had been written down not very legibly in pencil. It was lunch time and I was visiting the Schoenberg family to meet my friend Heinrich Schoenberg, Arnold's younger brother. Heinrich and I were friends throughout our whole life until he was killed by Hitler's hechmen. We were of nearly the same age, but Arnold was nine years older, giving him an authority over his younger associates.

The Schoenberg family lived in those days in one of the poorer Jewish quarters of the Leopoldstadt in Vienna, just behind the Taborstrasse. It may have been in 1905, though I am not quite sure of the date ; Arnold was about to become known as a young composer of whom Hanslick, the famous critic of the main Austrian paper " Neue Freie Presse", had written on the occasion of the first performance of his forgotten string quartet, played by the Prill Quartet : " It seems to me that a new Mozart is growing up in Vienna." Pauline Schoenberg, Arnold's mother, and my father's sister, was a poor widow, living on her children's earnings. Just before entering the university, Arnold, the eldest, had to give up his studies because of his father's death. To earn money he became a bank clerk, but resigned after a short time in order to devote himself to music only. It was a hard life for him, and for the whole Schoenberg family. Arnold tried to earn money as a chorus master of some workers' choirs in one of the remotest suburbs of Vienna and I remember that he often had to walk there because he could not afford the fare. Later he earned money by orchestrating operettas and scoring compositions. I had to help him for some while by copying manuscripts and myself gained some pocket money in this way. It was a grim but gay life. Schoenberg never lost his humour ; but the family, all the uncles and the aunts, were gravely displeased and blamed him for his mother's worries, who badly missed his income as a clerk. I remember many family discussions about Arnold, resulting in an attempt to persuade him to go back to his job at the bank. Only my father defended his decision to devote himself to music, because his artistic instinct felt that in Arnold Schoenberg there was developing a genius. As for myself, I never had any doubt that Arnold was a genius, and I always felt a great admiration for him from my earliest days. His sparkling eyes, his way of talking, his wit, his whole personality deeply impressed both me and Heinrich. Perhaps this admiration, the fact that I refused to embark upon a bank career (I wanted to become a writer, actor or anything connected with art), and my father's attitude towards his musical ambitions, were the reasons for Arnold Schoenberg's liking of me. I assume that he took a liking to me. He never said so—on the contrary, he was always rather careless with me—but I knew it, because there was always something behind his rough mask which was so lovable, because he liked working with me, and because from the first he liked my singing. He introduced me to his friend and teacher and later brother-in-law, Alexander von Zemlinsky, who became my conductor and teacher for twelve long years.

"Sing that to me," Arnold said. "If you play it to me on the piano, I might be able to sing it," was my answer. Schoenberg smiled, sat down and played "So tanzen die Engel", "Waldemar's Song" from the first part of the "Gurrelieder." I sang it once, I sang it twice and I sang it again and again. I don't know how often I sang it, but I have known it by heart ever since then. Arnold beamed at me after we had finished and said : "You have the right voice for this song and I hope you will sing it one day, when it is performed." I did not know what it was I had just sung, but I was very excited and profoundly impressed by its beauty, and still more by Arnold Schoenberg's praise of my singing. I was very happy.

Years went by. Arnold Schoenberg's reputation rose like a star. By now it was already a great privilege to know him, and the Nachod family was proud to have such a son. It was the Nachod family which gave him his gift for music, because the whole family had been musical for generations, and there was hardly one of them who did not either sing or play an instrument ; but I think it was Schoenberg's father, a very remarkable man, from whom he inherited his genius. Now my father was able to say : "I told you so."

In the meantime I had taken up singing and was studying at the Academy of Music in Vienna and had gained some fame as a promising young tenor. Amongst many offers were engagements to both Vienna opera companies, the Court Opera and the Volksoper (People's Opera). I decided to begin my career at the Volksoper where a great ensemble under the management of Rainer Simons, who was also the main producer, and the musical direction of Alexander von Zemlinsky, was doing astonishingly well. The singers included Josef Schwarz, Marie Jeritza and others. I was now an established opera singer, and Arnold came to many of my performances and followed my professional progress, because he had something special in mind for me. One day he disclosed what this was—I was asked to sing "Waldemar" in his great work the "Gurrelieder." A full orchestral performance of the "Gurrelieder" requires several hundred musicians and costs a great deal of money. Because of the high finance of such an undertaking it was difficult to obtain backing, and Schoenberg's friends suggested that the first section of the "Gurrelieder," which consists of solo parts only, should be played with piano accompaniment in order to bring out the work's great beauty and to stimulate a full performance at a later date. I gladly agreed to sing and we began to rehearse immediately. For "Tove," Madame Winternitz-Dorda, the wife of the conductor Winternitz, was chosen, and the mezzo-soprano role of "Waldtaube" was given to my colleague from the opera, the English singer Drill-Oridge. Our coaches were all pupils of Schoenberg : Anton Webern,

Alban Berg and Heinrich Jalowitz. I studied mainly with Webern, because he was also in those days coach to the Volksoper. We were keen and ardent. The idiom seemed very new, although the " Gurrelieder " was by no means the Schoenberg of today and very much rooted in the style of its period, at least as far its first part was concerned. We were children of our time, the time of Wagner and Hugo Wolf. As soon as we were acquainted with what we had to sing and had studied it intensively, Schoenberg took over. Naturally, he could not play the piano score of his " Gurrelieder " ; either Alban Berg or Anton Webern played at rehearsals. To study with Schoenberg is an inspiring experience, which cannot be explained in words. His over-powering personality carries one away. The best explanation of Arnold Schoenberg's personality was given to me once by Prof. Egon Wellesz when he said : " Schoenberg's personality is dangerous, one cannot escape its influence." I had the privilege of working with Richard Strauss and many other great composers of my day, but the long, the " heavenly long " rehearsals with Arnold Schoenberg belong to the happiest memories of my life. Wherever it happened, in Vienna, in Berlin, in Leipzig, in Amsterdam, my greatest musical experience was never-ending work with Schoenberg. He was tireless and expected the same qualities of endurance from his collaborators. In Amsterdam we often worked from twelve to fourteen hours a day for more than four weeks, but not once did I feel the least fatigue. When one considers that we rehearsed this first performance of the " Gurrelieder " in addition to our daily routine work as opera singers it can can be imagined how strenuous those days were. During these rehearsals Schoenberg discovered again and again new versions and expressions of his music. He listened to his performers and sometimes adopted their versions. It was not rehearsing, it was creating ; and it was an adventure. Then came the day when I participated in one of the great events in the history of music : the very first performance of the " Gurrelieder." In the Ehrbaar-Saal in Vienna a large and important audience gathered to listen. The whole musical world had sent representatives : the piano part was performed on two pianos by Alban Berg, Anton Webern, Heinrich Jalowitz and another pianist (a woman) whose name I have forgotten.

I gladly remember the praise which I received on this occasion from Artur Nikisch and Felix Weingartner. There was no division of opinion, only general excitement.

This was, as is not widely known, the very first performance of the " Gurrelieder." The first *full* performance of the whole work followed much later, on the 23rd February, 1913, in Vienna, under the direction of Franz Schreker, and I again sang the tenor part and witnessed the enthusiasm of the Viennese public.

A Note on Carl Nielsen's Third Symphony

NIELSEN developed slowly and we may be sure that what he published is but a tithe of what he wrote. Beethoven's sketch-books are full of apparent waste, the off-scourings of a hypercritical mind. One would like to see what was thrown away to produce a Nielsen symphony. It is not, as a rule, the most spontaneous minds which produce the most spontaneous scounding music ; indeed, the first impression of any large scale work by the Danish composer is its spontaneity. It is a dangerous impression in these days when thought is at a premium.

One cannot speak of a work by Nielsen or any other large-scale composer as representative. Only the small produce representative work, i.e. " the mixture as before ". Nielsen does not do so ; those who think he does will not progress beyond a very slippery surface. Listen to recordings of the third symphony, produced in mid-career, and the clarinet concerto, which is almost his last work. Similar in texture, rhythm and melodic material, these works are as typical of each other as a tortoise is of a snail.

The happiness of the third symphony is full of meaning, similarly as Haydn's cheerfulness. " Sinfonia Espansiva " he called it, and while this may, as has been suggested to me, have a definite application to the slow movement, it could well stand as a description of his whole work : all his music expands from a fixed centre.

The first movement is a glorious symphonic waltz which ranges over all the known (and some unknown) sonata-country without fuss or self-consciousness, does what it wishes when it wishes, and presents a scheme as inevitable as a Bach Fugue. The most stately dance of seraphic joy in the " Sanctus " of Bach's B minor Mass could have no more energetic and quietly ecstatic rival than this wonderful movement.

The succeeding slow movement is of the same kind as the lovely Prelude to the second act of his opera " Maskerade " : it has—erroneously, I believe—been deemed pastoral ; for me it inhabits a far more rarefied atmosphere. It is crowned by one of the few existing completely natural uses of the voice as a purely orchestral instrument, raising the symphony to a high plane of sexless but virilely pure emotion. It closes with a curling chromatic flute figure which also ends the next movement, a curiously puzzling scherzo with some of the soft, half-light character of Sibelius's Sixth Symphony. Its colour is grey yet it is radiant.

The Finale is a buoyant hymn of praise, buttressed with a most audacious tune, the most subtle point of which is its bass. The duty of a tune is to be itself and turn up at the right moments ; its function here is its buttressing. It is therefore not surprising to find the action which it offsets confided to other material, in particular a passage which has all the admirably quiet and delicate suggestion of a fugue without, in this context, the painful duty of being one.

Nielsen, in the current but misleading jargon of the day, forged for himself a personal language out of the materials of an older age, which is merely to say that he is sane and an individual. Again and again he thrusts at us the " obvious," which we discover, with no little surprise in these sophisticated and tasteless days, to be so far from obvious that we have missed it all along the line. The prime difference between the great composer and the small is that the former continually reminds us of that which the latter makes us forget. Nielsen has shown that one language is capable of far more fine shades of meaning than a fussy working out of a new one, which never knows its starting point, for each successive work.

This third symphony, an admirable introduction to Nielsen's ways of thought, provided one is humble enough not to assume omniscience with one or two hearings, might well have been called " Four Aspects of Heavenly Joy," a fit subject for Aquinas. What St. Thomas did not write has been aptly supplied by Nielsen in an even more untranslatable language.

HAROLD TRUSCOTT

41

Film Music

REPLY TO PIZZETTI.

DOUBTLESS presented with a misleading translation of my speech on *Featured Music* : " *Classical* " *Quotations* at the first international film music Congress (the 7th *Congresso Internazionale di Musica*) at Florence, the president, Italy's veteran composer Ildebrando Pizzetti, gave in his turn a somewhat misleading critical account of what I said. I quote *verbatim et literatim* from the official translation of his closing speech on May 19th :—

> Hans Keller, a critic who is evidently most scholarly and thoughtful about the aesthetic problems regarding the art of the sound film, has said, in " *Quotation from classical music in the film*," many things worthy of meditation. For my own part I must confess that I remain very doubtful about the reasonableness and efficacy of quotation from classical music in the film. For example, when faced with that extract from " Symphonie Pastorale " which Keller showed us where the execution of a Bach prelude on the organ accompanies the meeting in church of two young people unconsciously attracted to each other by an awakening love, I cannot attribute to Bach's music any value which is psychological or dramatic, that is, linked to the sentimental development of the characters. In this episode the sound of the organ and the solemnity of the place, that is to say the church, are suggestive. But if, instead of playing a Bach prelude, the young organist had played another piece of music the effect would, I consider, have been the same. At that point, in my opinion, in order to express or suggest the feelings of the characters the composer of the music in the film should have contrasted the Bach prelude with other musical expressions which could be referred to the sentiments of the actors.

I didn't just talk about classical quotations, but about the integration of " featured " music in general and of classical music in particular. I didn't dream of defending, in principle, the use of classical music ; in fact I spent quite a time cursing typical examples of hair-raising quotations and moreover suggested that film makers suffered from a downright quotation compulsion which was due, *inter alia*, to our age's artistic insecurity and to the consequent need for what was, psychologically speaking, the classical quotations guilt-assuaging parental approbation. At the same time I would never have gone so far as to smell an *a priori* rat in every quotation ; indeed, as a matter of critical principle, I dislike *a priori* rats—nor does Pizzetti give any reason for his wholesale suspicion. The quotation of Bach's Weimar A minor organ Prelude I played as " *the most successful example I remembered of the integration of a partial quotation*." I went on to say :—

> The meaningful interruption of the Bach reinforces the sensitively delayed, music-less transition to the most strongly contrasting tango at the dance, after which follows that dramatically climactic waltz which hero and heroine dance, whence the two are brought back again, both discreetly and contrastingly, to the church organ, this time for organ practice. A more complete reversal of the preceding contrast would not have been tolerable, for the way from the sublime down to the primitive is shorter than the way from the primitive up to the sublime. Striking continuity is maintained in this scene under the most precarious circumstances. We remember Auric's [the film's composer's] own words :—" A tight-rope walker and a dancer are the two creatures combined in any artist who moves me. Every new work is a tight-rope stretched above an ever-lasting track. . . " In these contrariant, but unified sequences the tight-rope stretches over the whole compass of the relationship between the two people, indeed almost over the whole compass of the human mind. . .

The Bach assumes its full significance in the sound track's wider context ; but this Pizzetti has not considered at all. I submit that he does not in fact appreciate the creative intentions behind these scenes if he thinks that any old organ piece would have done equally well : only the Bach—the most popular of sublimest organ pieces—could produce that extreme horizontal contrast whose significance I have described. As for Pizzetti's concluding suggestion, it not only contradicts his own initial " doubtfulness about the efficacy of quotation," but its execution would have landed us in Hollywood *Kitsch par excellence*, because (1) instead of being followed by a music-less transition to the dance, the prelude would have been stabbed in the back by, inevitably, hostile music ; (2) instead of the extreme contrast between Bach and dance, whose unification is helped by the sound track's *Keeping to the realistic level*, the music would have jumped from the realistic to the interpretative (" background ") level without artistic purpose ; for (3) Pizzetti's purpose, i.e. the " expression of the feelings of the characters," is completely achieved by the visual, and the interpretative background music would have been tautological.

I hasten to add that the above excerpt is nowise typical of the Maestro's suggestive speech ; in fact its coda—

> I have thought it my duty to express, briefly, what I think about the various papers. Are mine the observations of a man who, by age, aesthetic education, and personal moral sense, cannot feel and argue with the sensibility and mentality of men who are younger and more closely bound to certain characteristics of the life of the last twenty years, which are precisely the years of the sound film ? Maybe ; however, they are observations—I do not claim that they have any value as judgments—which someone can bear in mind if only to contest or refute them. . . .

—is far too modest. As probably the youngest critic at the Congress, I may say that Pizzetti's artistic seniority, his " aesthetic education and personal moral sense," are exactly what is needed for an art still in its first childhood.

HANS KELLER.

Aldeburgh Festival, 1950

I WAS present for the final week-end only. Most memorable was Britten's appearance as combined conductor and pianist in Mozart's G major Concerto K. 453 (25th June). As I expected he showed such an in-, out-, and around-sight of the music that his own superb piano technique was quite transcended, and impressed itself long after the concert was over : I realised the art before I recognised the artifice. Two things excited me : first, his extraordinary handling of arpeggios and passage-work ; they were transformed into soaring melodic curves—perfect proof that Mozart's scales are more than scales if you have a pianist who can see beyond his one-note-at-a-time nose ; second, Britten's phrasing of the jaunty variation theme of the last movement. I have heard nobody achieve such perfect pace or convey such a sense of adventure, of revelations to come. I can only compare it in its spontaneity and newness of conception to Britten's accompaniment of the first *lied* in a recent broadcast of *Die Schoene Muellerin* with Peter Pears, which had just this quality of unfamiliarity. Pianists should note and take to heart : the simpler the texture became, the more cautious was Britten's dealing with it ; simplicity meant increase of tension rather than its relaxation. Britten's rehearsals with his gifted instrumentalists were of special interest : one of his comments, made while working at the Mozart A major Symphony K. 201, has stuck in my memory. Following instructions to the orchestra came the rejoinder : " These aren't the kind of things you can write in your parts, but this is the way I want you to *feel the notes*." (My italics). Under the spell of such musicality the orchestra acquitted themselves well, apart from understandably fatigued contributions from the horns.

A choral and orchestral concert in the Parish Church (24th June) included a first hearing of a Festival Overture for Strings and Trumpets by Antony Hopkins which began promisingly but petered out in its finale ; " the brilliant conclusion " (composer's programme note) was just what it lacked. After a deeply moving Purcell D major *Te Deum* (Deller-Pears-Parsons, two boy trebles, Festival choir and orchestra, Britten conducting), came the first public performance of Britten's " Wedding Anthem " (Cross, Pears, as soloists). The anthem, if a slight piece, displayed expected features of Britten's style. Exceptionally musical was the soprano and tenor duet " These two are not two, Love has made them one." In some ways, stylistically and in its highly imaginative imitative and canonic structure, it is prophetic (or reminiscent) of " Fair and fair " from the *Spring* Symphony. Astonishing is the uncanny mirroring of the poetic content in the musical conception. No less than a short article would do justice to its subtlety. There is space for no more than a mention of notable singing by Miss Cross and Mr. Pears in an operatic programme (accompanied by Britten, 23rd June), and an overcrowded production of Britten's realization of *The Beggar's Opera* (24th June) which was dullest when the music stopped : allowing for the acoustics of the Jubilee Hall, it was apparent to me that, in this form, survival of the original airs is certain. Mr. Erwin Stein's grudging note to the Mozart Symphony concert was rather surprisingly inadequate ; some of its judgments were debatable to say the least.   DONALD MITCHELL.

The Brussels I.S.C.M. Festival

THE 24th I.S.C.M. Festival, held in Brussels between 23rd-30th June, certainly seemed to be one of the best arranged that the Society has ever had. The I.N.R. (Belgian Radio) put their orchestras and choruses at the disposal of the Society, and all the concerts were held in the magnificent large studio in the I.N.R. building. In addition, adequate time was allowed for the rehearsal of difficult orchestral works, and as the concerts were broadcast on a strict schedule, there were none of the irritating delays experienced at some other Festivals.

In the first three days of the Festival two I.S.C.M. concerts were given, as well as a " side-show " concert of Belgian orchestral music provided by the I.N.R. This last is perhaps best passed over in silence as far as musical quality is concerned, though there were some imaginative orchestral effects in Fernand Quinet's *Trois Mouvements Symphoniques*. The first I.S.C.M. concert was for chamber orchestra, and included an outstanding event—the first performance of Webern's last work, his *Second Cantata*, Op. 31, for sorpano and bass soli, chorus and small orchestra. This not only shows his lyrical and dramatic powers at their finest, but is one of his more easily intelligible works, the continuous vocal line holding together the astonishing orchestral fabric of sound. Though it is his most extended work, its six movements last barely a quarter of an hour, and so it was possible to play it twice consecutively—an excellent idea. The performance, under Herbert Haefner, appeared to be admirable on the whole, though the final chorale was taken much too fast : the soprano, Ilona Steingruber, showed great capability in attacking an almost impossibly difficult vocal line. Altogether it was a very moving experience, and one which must certainly be repeated in England as soon as possible.

In the same concert Alan Rawsthorne secured an excellent performance of his *Concerto for Strings*, the expert craftsmanship of which entirely put in the shade a dullish piano concerto by Marius Flothuis (Holland) and also a curious *Sinfonietta* by Hans Eisler for a " chamber orchestra " which included a piano and an organ ! The latter certainly contained some interesting moments, but was far too long for its material.

England was also well represented in the second concert by P. Racine Fricker's *String Quartet* (admirably played by the Amadeus Quartet) which created a very favourable impression by its originality and intelligence. Nothing else in this long concert was outstanding, though a 'cello sonata by Wolfgang Fortner (Germany) was interesting in a dryish way, and the *Hommage à Schoenberg* of Eunice Catunda (Brazil) was a curious combination of South American rhythms with the twelve-tone technique. The quartet of the South African Arnold van Wyk suffered by coming at the end of an over-long programme.

The most notable of the remaining concerts was the second programme for chamber orchestra on June 27th. It began with a Japanese work—*Ten Haikai of Basho* for chamber orchestra by Syukiti Mitsukuri—short, sensitive musical paraphrases of Basho's poems which successfully translated Eastern ideas into Western terms. In this same programme were two Belgian compositions—five children's counting rhymes provided with an acidly effective accompaniment by Pierre Froidebise, and three pieces by Karel Goeyvaerts, a pupil of Messiaen , in spite of a number of unusual effects, including the use of the Ondes Martenot, these gave an impression of monotony and shapelessness. Much more valuable was René Leibowitz' " L'Explication des Métaphores," for speaker, 2 pianos, harp and percussion ; the solid basis of the twelve-tone technique gave this work a kind of abstract strength. Equally solid and more easily assimilable was Roman Palester's " Cantata of the Vistula," for speaker, chorus and instrumental ensemble ; it showed genuine musical and dramatic feeling, and apart from one passage for speaking chorus which was not quite successful, it was a very satisfying musical experience.

The two concerts for full orchestra provided quantity rather than quality. The first included an effective *Toccata and Fugue* for piano and orchestra by Arthur Malawski (Poland), though it did not reach the level of his *Symphonic Studies*, heard at the Amsterdam Festival of 1948. The *Sinfonia Giocosa* of Klaus Egge (Norway) was neither jocose nor of much interest, and André Jolivet's " Psyché " revived both the spirit and letter of the " Poème d'Extase " with great efficiency. After the interval came another pretentious work, the cantata " La Naissance du Verbe " by Giacinto Scelsi, which contained some original ideas, but lacked cohesion and was inflated almost to bursting-point.

In the second chamber concert no work was particularly outstanding the most vital being perhaps the second quartet of the young Czech Kare Husa, which at any rate showed promise. Milhaud's choreographic suite " Rêves de Jacob " was written with his customary expertise, as was also the second sonatina of Conrad Beck (Switzerland). But in general the level of inspiration was not high.

The final orchestral concert began with a longish symphony for strings by Karl Amadeus Hartmann of Munich—romantic, almost Mahlerian in parts, but showing a strongly original mind as well. The flute concerto of Hans Henkemans (Holland) was clearly meant to be no more than a pretty pastiche, and as such was effective. So also was the chamber concerto of Niels Viggo Bentzon (Denmark) for 3 pianos, wind, percussion and double bass ; here a pseudo 18th century concertante style was fairly successfully exploited. The fifth symphony of Harald Saeverud (Norway), written in the form of variations, showed some originality, but was far too extended and bombastic for its material.

Though most of the music performed at this Festival showed a high level of technical competence, very little of it was of any real musical value. Most of the composers seemed to be more occupied with writing within a given framework than with expressing new ideas of importance. There was little experimentation—in fact a good many of the works borrowed elements from earlier periods—but there was a general feeling that the majority of the composers were not quite sure of themselves and were producing works which would be at any rate effective, if no more. Whether this tendency will persist remains to be seen ; in any case one will look forward to next year's Festival in Frankfurt. HUMPHREY SEARLE.

Music in Cambridge

(1) *General.*

IT is among the smaller Cambridge College groups that one looks for genuine musical enterprise. The series of three recitals given earlier this term in Emmanuel College Chapel deserve mention because they were shared by different organists, and the Music Club's Bach commemoration concerts were somewhat exceptional in that they were open to all, which meant that the aspirations of mere clubbability did not crowd out the claims of the music itself. This year's madrigal singing on the river was favoured by almost perfect weather.

The rest of the May Week concerts offered little more than musical fun and games. Only two of them, in fact—apart from Lully's incidental music to *Le Bourgeois Gentilhomme* which was heard at the Jesus College presentation reported below—invited serious attention. One was the production of Monteverdi's *Orfeo* at Girton College (see (3) below) ; the other was a concert of music by Vivaldi given in the Music School by the Fitzwilliam House Musical Society.

Most of the Vivaldi works were being heard in England for the first time. An Oboe Sonata had been specially transcribed and the continuo part realised from a manuscript in the University Library ; the programme as a whole was the result of research begun earlier in the year at Turin University. The two overtures played (*L'Incoronazione di Dario*, 1716 and *Il Giustino*, 1724) turned out to be sprightly works ; but it was in the fine Violin Concerto in A that Vivaldi's true musical personality became manifest. The Bassoon Concerto (" The Night ") is less distinguished music ; but its programmatic scheme is not without interest.

The most revealing items in this concert, however, were the vocal pieces. Three operatic arias from *Tito Manlio, Arsilda* and *Farnace* are charming, if not profound ; but the *Stabat Mater* and *Fiume che torbido* for bass voice possess a majesty and dramatic range as moving as anything in Handel. The *Confitebor* for three voices, which concluded the evening, left me at least convinced that there is nothing trivial about the religious aspects of Vivaldi's art, however inconsequential some of his secular pieces may appear to be.

The standard of performance at this concert was very high. The orchestra numbered only fourteen players ; but the conductor, John Lanchbery, was able to secure adequate interpretations throughout. Apart from the music performed, the occasion was gratifying for several reasons. This, surely, is just the kind of activity a University music department ought to be engaging in as a matter of regular policy. It can only be done through disinterested co-operation between people who are fundamentally interested in music as a cultural force, and are brave enough to ignore its " social " amenability. It would be ungentlemanly to suggest that such people are not to be found among those who hold important positions at Cambridge University. Never-theless, one cannot help wondering whether it is not in rather unexpected places (Fitzwilliam House is not normally regarded as a " Musical " college) that the real function of a university is given the serious consideration it demands. E. D. MACKERNESS.

(2) Lully's *Le Bourgeois Gentilhomme* at Jesus College.

In this country Lully's music, if known at all, has usually to be read rather than heard. It was with considerable interest, therefore, that Cambridge musicians attended two recent performances (given in English) of *Le Bourgeois Gentil-homme*. These were held in the cloisters of Jesus College during May Week. Lully's incidental music for Molière's play, sung to the original polyglot words, came across—as it should do, of course—more like the contents of a modern " musical " than anything in the nature of " opera " *pur sang*. But the Jesus College performance brought out all its *galant* charm, and pointed up its dramatic effectiveness. As a work of literature Molière's drama may have a few slight structural faults ; but Lully's leaping rhythms compensate for any minor insufficiencies in this great masterpiece of European comedy.

The Jesus College instrumental ensemble of strings, woodwind and harpsichord was conducted by Raymond Slee. All the music came to life in a remarkable way ; and the whole performance (dances, costumes, lighting, etc.), had an air of authenticity which made one long to know what the original presentation before Louis XIV at Chambord in 1670 was actually like. Perhaps the most appreciative comment one can make on the Jesus College production is to say that this year's *Bourgeois Gentilhomme* will stand comparison in every respect with previous Cambridge triumphs, such as the *King Arthur* of 1928, and *Samson* in 1932. C. L. CUDWORTH.

(3) Monteverdi's " *Orfeo* " at Girton College.

GIRTON College Musical Society and Miss Jill Vlasto, its moving spirit, already have to their credit last year's performance of Cavalieri's opera-oratorio " Rappresentazione di anima e di corpo " (1600). Now they have put lovers of Renaissance music under considerable obligation by a magnificent effort devoted to Monteverdi-Striggio's " Favola d'Orfeo " of 1607. The open-air performance in the Woodland Court of Girton on the 8th June was quite in keeping with the peculiarities of courtly intermedium and festive masque from which early opera sprang. Monteverdi's expressive *recitativo* was handled with skill and understanding by Keith Miller (Orfeo), Jane Goddard (Euridice) and Ena Mitchell (Spirit of Music and Proserpina), while the madrigalian part of the work was rendered in a thoroughly enjoyable and expert manner by the society's choral group. In the pleasant arrangement of graceful dances, and in the suggestive handling of chorus and soloists, the experienced mind of Jill Vlasto could be felt. It seems a pity that she abstained from conducting, leaving the baton in the hands of an undergraduate conductor, inadequately equipped for this responsible job. Choice of this conductor (who was also badly placed on one side of the stage and not visible to all the performers) resulted in some lack of synchronisation between orchestra, chorus and dancers—especially unfortunate in an open-air performance with its unavoidable acoustic vagaries. Even so the beautiful tone of Robert Donington's viola da gamba and the impeccable harpsichord style of Thurston Dart could be greatly enjoyed. It was indeed a remarkable experience to observe how easily the implications of Monteverdi's musico-dramatic style were grasped by a new generation of enthusiasts, to whom the divine Claudio is evidently much more than the object of mild historical curiosity. The distinguished audience included Professor J. A. Westrup, whose excellent edition had been used for the performance, and Professor E. J. Dent, who had greatly contributed to the edification of the listeners by his programme note. Girton's bold and imaginative reading of modern opera's most venerable ancestor met with delighted appreciation.

H. F. REDLICH.

Reviews of Music

Arranged in alphabetical order of composers' names.

H. ALBICASTRO DEL BISWANG : " XII Sonate a tre " (Sonate X-XII) edited by Silvia Kind. (Universal Edition, Vienna) ; no U.K. price available.

THE well-known Swiss harpsichordist has scored and edited three Sonatas from Albicastro's Op. I, originally published in Amsterdam c. 1700 and linking this enigmatic Swiss (who, according to Miss Kind's scholarly preface, may after all turn out to be a Bavarian or Austrian) with Torelli, Corelli and Vitali, champions of the then new type of " Sonata da chiesa." These instrumental Trio-Sonatas are—oddly enough—meant to be played by at least *four* different instruments (2 violins, cello, harpsichord), but the solemn beauty of their *Grave* sections would certainly gain much by an orchestral interpretation. Miss Kind's very practical arrangement provides for both alternatives, besides adding sensible suggestions for the improvisation of cadential bridge passages and sound dynamics. Excellent bowing marks have been supplied by Professor Robert Reitz. This commendable edition appears as part of the UE collection " Continuo," the professed aim of which is to make forgotten chamber music again easily accessible. The excellent print, carefully distinguishing between " original " and " realisation," and registering throughout the figures of the original *basso continuo*, deserves special praise. An obvious misprint however in Miss Kind's preface should be corrected. Surely it must read " 12 Concerti a 4 " (referring to Albicastro's Op. 7, Amsterdam, 1703) and *not* " 2 Concerti a 4," as printed in the table of his preserved compositions ? H.F.R.

VICTOR BABIN : " *Ritual,*" *a song for Baritone and Piano.* (*Augener*) *;*
  2s. 0d.
RITUAL implies a profound harmony of agreement between God, priest and people. This Mr. Babin has not yet discovered, or words, voice and piano would not disagree. H.T.

J. S. BACH : " *In our hour of deepest need.*" *Transcribed by John Barbirolli.*
  Score. (*O.U.P.*) *;* *3s. 0d.*
THIS is a transcription of Bach's last chorale-prelude for viola I and II doubled by violoncello I and II, violoncello III supported by double-bass, and four horns in unison and trumpet. Should such an intimate deliverance be brought into the concert-room ? There is a strong case against transcriptions of old music, apart from the elimination of obsolete instruments ; and more than enough original orchestral music waits to see the light. The substitution of conscious and coloured polyphony for the smooth, modest harmony of the original pays the music, here as elsewhere, a doubtful compliment. Educationally it may fill a place in orchestras where there are more lower strings than violins. A.E.F.D.

J. S. BACH : *Musical Offering.* (*Peters-Hinrichsen*) *;* *8s. 6d.*
THIS is a reprint of the original Peters edition of the collection, with an appendix containing the pedal-piano (or organ) version of the 6-part fugue and the " solution " of the canon at the fifth which Bach calls *Fuga canonica*. (The latter is surely for flute, violin and bass, rather than piano and violin or organ as indicated here). The text is clean, besides being well printed. The Trio and Canon for flute, violin and bass are precisely phrased, but the realisation of the figured continuo part is left to the player. A programme-note in English would have been useful. It is to be hoped that *The Art of Fugue* will soon be available again in the same edition. A.E.F.D.

BRITTEN : *Spring Symphony, Op. 44.* " *The Little Sweep.*" (*Let's*
  Make An Opera), *Op. 45.* *Vocal Scores by Arthur Oldham.* *A Wedding*
  Anthem (*Amo Ergo Sum*), *Op. 46.* (*Boosey and Hawkes*) *;* *15s. 0d.,*
  12s. 6d., 4s. 0d., respectively.
No very satisfactory comment on the structure of Britten's *Spring* Symphony has yet been forthcoming : Erwin Stein's analysis in the current *Tempo* (Spring, 1950) tells us that " symphony " must be accepted " in the metaphorical sense." Of the twelve vocal movements he also writes that " No

thematic connection between them is apparent. . . . " On that point he is factually wrong as a quotation from " Waters above " appears in the succeeding " Out on the lawn I lie in bed." Nor am I so certain that the symphonic form of the work is as metaphorical as he supposes. Hearing the *Spring* Symphony convinced me that it had a structural unity quite apart from mere handling of moods or rough grouping of movements according to normal symphonic procedure. How Britten has achieved this unity I have not yet succeeded in proving to my own satisfaction, but I fancy there are certain thematic derivations and transformations which imply organic growth : for instance the opening phrase given to the wordless chorus in " Out on the lawn I lie in bed " seems to evolve from an orchestral interpolation in the Introduction at [5] *et seq*. Possibly more important still is the binding element of the interval of a fourth which haunts a great part of the vocal writing throughout. It is extremely prominent both in the Introduction (where it is uncompromisingly and suitably bare) and in the Finale, though in the latter its function is tonally and spiritually more positive (" Rejoice ! Rejoice ! ") and powerfully reinforced by the cow-horn's restricted contribution which was built as it were to a " fourth " specification and unable to sound outside that dimension. Indeed in the *Spring* Symphony we may have an outstanding example of a newish principle of symphonic structure—unity by interval. Of " The Little Sweep " something has already been written in this journal.* A closer inspection of the score not only confirms my previous impression of its extreme sensitivity and small-scale bigness of conception but also the absolute consistency of Britten's style, an impression which an examination of the " Wedding Anthem "† does nothing to shake. Protestations of his lack of personal style seem to be largely legendary and hallucinatory : a subject to which I shall return at greater length on a future occasion.   D.M.

**Music Survey, 11/2/50.*   †*See also p. 44.*

AARON COPLAND : Four Piano Blues. (Boosey and Hawkes) ; 3s. 6d.

ON first glance merely a study in what the catalogues call " truly pianistic sonorities" ; cf. the jazzy rhythms, the well-spaced middle-parts, the sonorous tenths in the left hand. This conscious slickness makes me doubt whether these Concert Blues have evolved as naturally from their local tradition as, for instance, Strauss' Concert Waltzes from Viennese folk music. Unless, of course, this very slickness is by now part of the American folk-idiom. In that case, these pieces would stem from a degenerate branch of folk music.

P.H.

IVOR R. FOSTER : Three Pieces for Piano. (Augener) ; 2s. 6d.

THESE pieces clarify the cause of the revolt against smug complacency which has itself now settled down to a complacent old-age. The original motive of the revolt was to enforce an exact examination of every word one utters. This Mr. Foster has not done. The sentiments he sententiously expresses were old when Mendelssohn penned his more sentimental " Songs without Words," still revolutionary in comparison.
H.T.

GIROLAMO FRESCOBALDI : Orgel und Klavierwerke, Gesamtausgabe nach dem Urtext von Pierre Pidoux. Four volumes (edition in progress). (Baerenreiter Verlag, Kassel-Wilhelmshoehe) ; no U.K. price available.

THIS is the first serious attempt to present us with a complete edition, promised by Frescobaldi's first editor F.X. Haberl as early as 1887. Once Vol. 5 has been issued, the complete corpus of Frescobaldi's *instrumental* music will be available in a reliable modern edition, in which the complicated original notation is reduced to two staves only (playable on harpsichord and organ alike) and presenting a very scholarly and convincing revision of the frequently faulty musical text of the rare first editions supervised by the composer. The editor has also embodied the titles and fascinating prefaces of Frescobaldi's original issues, to which useful comments are added for the benefit of the modern executant on either instrument. It is a pity that these prefaces and commentaries have been published only in German. It would have been useful for scholars and amateurs to be able to consult the original Italian alongside a modern translation. The print is impeccable, the quality of the paper very poor indeed. If after the issue of Vol. 5 editor and publisher could be persuaded, to re-publish Frescobaldi's *vocal* compositions also, one of the worst lacunae of modern musicology would at long last be abolished.

H.F.R.

P. RACINE FRICKER : Four Fughettas for Two Pianos, Op. 2. (Schott) ; 7s. 6d.

TECHNICALLY and musically brilliant examples of how to write modern Fugues. The great problem of using Tonic, Dominant and Subdominant as *degrees*, as in the classical fugue, while freely moving in the *functions* of chromatic tonality is solved by Fricker in these ways : (a) All his subjects can be followed by *real* answers, thus avoiding the adjustments of *tonal* answers which would weigh too heavily on his extended key-system. One justified exception to this is the subtle adjustment at the very end of the 4th fugue's answer (bars 10, 11) ; an unjustified one the A in the first answer of fugue 1 (bar 5) which never recurs. (b) There are very skilled modulations at the end of each development-section (see No. 2, bars 31-33, No. 3, bars 10-11), taking us rapidly back not only into the home key, but on to the Tonic and Dominant entries of a counter-exposition. In Fugue 4, which is more spacious than the others, there is even a false recapitulation, consisting of twice 3 bars of the subject, followed by the real counter-exposition of twice 6 bars of answer and subject (bars 52-57 and ff.). (c) Episodes are kept very short and near-thematic. It is only here and in the Codas that parts are divided to allow for some harmonic colour (No. 1, bars 14, 22 ff ; No. 2, bars 24-27). (d) Fricker's choice of keys for the development-sections stresses his modern tonality while the degrees on which the subjects enter conform to classical rule even in these sections. In fugue 2 (F minor), the development-section (bars 27-33, B minor) is a tritone apart from the home-key, thus stressing the most important interval in that particular fugue-subject. But the entries themselves of this section occur in multiple stretto at a bar's distance on V-I-V-I.

To end with, here is an analysis of the short fugue 3 (*Lento*, 4/4, in D) which perhaps best shows Fricker's organising powers.

51

Exposition, bars 1-7. Subject of 1 bar length in Treble, answer in Alto (2nd bar), Subject in Tenor (bar 4), Answer in Bass (bar 5). Bars 3 and 6 establish the two main counterpoints. Thus, the " lamentoso " subject with its narrow intervals appears in the form of two canonic duets.

Development, bars 7-11. Answer, inverted in the 6th below, in stretto at a half-bar's distance with subject (direct), against 1st counterpoint (soprano, bars 8-9), against a figure from 1st counterpoint (Alto, bars 8-9), and against 2nd counterpoint direct and inverted (bar 10).

Counter-exposition, bars 11-14. Answer-Subject-Answer-Subject (a re-arrangement) in S-A-T-B, in home key, now each at a bar's distance, the Subject simultaneously being inverted in the octave both times. Against this, an inversion of the first counterpoint (Treble, bars 12-13), the first counterpoint (Treble, bars 12-13), the first counterpoint direct and its first notes in augmentation (Bass, bars 11-13), and other near derivatives of both counterpoints.

Coda, bars 15-16. The last notes of Subject in imitation (Tenor and Bass, bar 15), against 1st counterpoint (Treble, bars 15-16). I must leave it to the reader to visualise the strong polyphonic equilibrium of this fugue from a careful reading of this analysis.   P.H.

C. ARMSTRONG GIBBS : Three Pieces for Cello and Piano, Op. 121.
" She loves me not," " Nocturne," " A laughing tune." (Augener) ;
at 2s. 6d.

I do not think that these un-modern pieces which smack a little of Ireland heather and Fauré violets, would really harm a young player's musicality. They can be recommended as Associated Board examination pieces.
                                                                          P.H.

ALEXIS HAIEFF : Five Pieces for Piano. (Boosey & Hawkes) ; 7s. 6d.

VERY gifted compositions, demonstrating likewise the blessings and the bane of the Nadia Boulanger school. On the one hand, Mr. Haieff certainly can compose. Every note is to the point, the form is logical, the rhythms supple and powerful. On the other hand, he is so exclusively bent on solving the problems posed by his own style that there is no trace of spontaneity left in the finished product which should always recapture the semblance of the improvisation from which it originally sprang, however inflexible the stylistic mould in which it has meantimes been cast. The scores of Palestrina, Schoenberg and Stravinsky, to name some " technical " composers, all bear witness to this second stage of spontaneity. If it does not show up in the scores of Mr. Haieff, one cannot, of course, blame him for not being greater than he is ; but perhaps one may suggest that, at least for a time, a looser method of composing may do more justice to his gifts than his ambitious aridity.
                                                                          P.H.

GORDON JACOB : Rhapsody for Cor Anglais and Strings. (Arranged for
cor anglais and piano). (Joseph Williams) ; 6s. 6d.

HAVING already written concertos for oboe and bassoon, Dr. Jacob now bridges the gap in the double-reed family. The cor anglais, however, an orchestral soloist most effective in small doses, becomes a bore when brought to the front of the platform. Frequent changes of mood in a short work prevent this to some extent, but are accompanied here by stylistic inconsistency. The solo part is aptly written, as we should expect, yet the work adds nothing to the composer's stature. Despite the " New World " atmosphere of the music, the alternative arrangement for alto saxophone admits only of a pecuniary explanation. P.A.E.

KARG-ELERT : Three " Modal" Interludes for Organ. (Hinrichsen) ; 1s. 6d.

A page of introductory remarks leads us to expect something better than the 26 bars of incredibly feeble music which follow. Any competent organist could improvise to better effect, and with more allegiance to the modal spirit and letter. P.A.E.

FRANK MARTIN : Ballade pour piano et orchestre ; and 8 Préludes pour le piano. (Universal Edition, Vienna) ; no U.K. price available.

THE peculiar technique of choral *parlando*—as employed in his impressionistic oratorios—has lately focussed much attention on the *doyen* of modern Swiss composers. His apparent predilection for tortuous chromatics especially noticeable in his piano music, coupled with a certain structural looseness, necessarily suggests associations with French music. In the diffuse dance rhythms of the " Ballade " the piano acts throughout as *primus inter pares* with a symphonically treated orchestra. *Tarantella* and *Waltz* motifs tinge the severe atmosphere with a hue of southern serenity. Much more convincing are the " Eight Preludes," composed in 1948, i.e. 9 years after the " Ballade." Although indebted to their distinguished predecessors Chopin and Debussy, they evolve a personal idiom out of patterns of a romantic past. No. 3 sounds like an atonalist's dream projection of Chopin's macabre Prelude No. 2. The strict canon in the lower fifth in No. 6, with the spidery skips of its principal motif, is a masterpiece of skilful and diaphanous contrapuntal piano writing. Perhaps the most original effort is No. 7 with its graceful pedal effects, combining the background sonorities of Liszt's and Debussy's colourism with a contrapuntal technique of austere nobility. No. 1 clearly indicates César Franck's organ music as a stylistic archetype for Frank Martin's pianistic experiments. The highly imaginative and superbly effective treatment of the instrument distinguishes this opus from much contemporary piano music, often designed with little consideration for the sonorous properties of the keyboard. H.F.R.

PROKOFIEFF : " Lieutenant Kijé," Suite Symphonique, Op. 60. Pocket Score. (Boosey & Hawkes) ; 8s. 0d.

THE preface (in English, French, Russian) tells us that this suite can be performed with or without a baritone, two entire versions of the second and fourth of its five numbers being provided. Tips on these alternatives are given to the conductor, the librarian, the orchestral manager ; and advice on the possible omission of some of the instruments that appear in the long list (in Italian but for the words " militaire " and " saxofono ") that, together with information in French and English that the work lasts 18 minutes, concludes the preface. Certain details are proffered about percussion, what it consists of and how it is to be played. The question of the transposing instruments, figuring here as non-transposing, is discussed. The one matter on which no hint is given, beyond the bare (French and Russian) titles of the movements, is what the piece is all about. In movements I, III and V Kijé is born, wedded and interred respectively. II is a romance and IV a troika, with texts (Russian, French, English, German) of a doggerel, folk-song type, casting no light on the situation. The English version of the text of II is illiterate and even at one point mis-spelt. Who was Kijé ? In what force was he a lieutenant ? And why ? How did he comfort himself ? In what adventures ? " Lieutenant Kijé " was a film for which Prokofieff wrote the music as one of his first jobs after returning to Russia in 1933. Anyone acquainted with the film (or with the short story by Yuri Tinyanev) will know the answers—how the valiant Lieutenant had, in fact, no existence at all, except on paper in the official records of the Imperial Army—will know into what dilemmas his " birth " was destined at various points to betray his fabricator, and what a relief his " interment " must have been. But will everyone who buys the score or hears the music have this knowledge ? I don't think the publishers have any justification for such an assumption. The suite—typical, though well below first-grade, Prokofieff—more or less holds its own as music pure and simple, and whether knowledge of its " programme " would really alter one's enjoyment, or otherwise, is a moot point. But people are bound to be curious and to think they ought to " know the story."   R.W.W.

PRIAULX RAINIER : *Suite for Clarinet and Piano.* (*Schott*) ; 5s. 0d.

A PERCUSSIVE piano part, largely dependent on 2nds and 9ths, linked to an ungrateful clarinet line, produces here a brittle texture which becomes tedious in a 5-movement work. Though the clarinet is exploited technically, it is confined too much to the incisive upper register, and forgoes the relief of the luxurious chalumeau. In the first movement, if the prescribed " vivace " is to be taken literally, then the clarinet's scales on p. 6 are unplayable ; if the tempo is to be governed instead by the fastest speed at which the clarinettist is physically able to play these scales, then the movement loses its vigorous impetus. This problem arises again in the last movement ; there are no metronome marks to suggest a solution.   P.A.E.

R. VAUGHAN WILLIAMS : *Pastoral Symphony. Pocket Score.* (*Boosey and Hawkes*) ; 10s. 0d.

THIS symphony needs to be heard in its period. Following on the pungent revision of *A London Symphony* which Boult, Wood and Godfrey had publicised as soon as it was made available by the Carnegie United Kingdom Trust in 1920, the Pastoral of 1922 seemed an unconventional but consistent embarkation on the wan or wayward waters of the Lento of the *London* and other things. Its fluid metre, medieval curves and unemphatic tone gave it a peculiar sanctity, in spite of the ruthless touches of nature as she is ; and the work soon found its way into the Three Choirs Festival. Its lack of rhythmic contrast rendered it a symphonic solecism, which it remains ; but it was not till *Flos Campi* and similar trends elsewhere threatened fixation that the Pastoral came to mark the beginning of a route which the composer must either master or fall into a rut. *Job* and the F minor thus appeared a break-away,

the D major a reversion, and the finale of the E minor a pronounced consumma-
tion of the linear counterpoint of the Pastoral. Yet this symphony claims
its own position in the chain, as by far the most consistent product of the
maturer Vaughan Williams to date. Its melodic bases are a document in the
new mode-ality ; its uncompromising counterpoint and melting cadences are
singularly well balanced ; and again and again when the manner threatens
to be overpowering, the symphony " turns over " and clinches a point :
(i) in the poignant Lydian touch of the inescapable *cor anglais* tune against
the final chord ; (ii) the direct, unusually natural melos of the trumpet
subject, and the chromatic yearning of the violins in the final solitude ;
(iii) the mixo-mixo-Lydian tune (piu mosso) and the equally effective escape
from the main theme at the end ; (iv) the gradual affirmation of rhythm and
harmony after the baffling, textless plainsong, and the poetic, simply contrived
reversal of this process at the very end. By a coincidence this symphony was
first performed after a piano concerto which "screamed Liszt," making clear
once and for all that precise in texture as it was, it abjured all the conventional
rhetoric of the springing rhythm, the buoyant curve and the brilliant climax.

A.E.F.D.

R. W. WOOD : Three Studies for Piano. (Joseph Williams) ; 3s. 0d.

LIKE true studies, these short pieces exploit particular points of both pianist's
and composer's technique. One appalling passage of overlapping double
octaves in No. 1, presenting the only extreme difficulty in performance,
yields to redistribution of the notes between the hands.

Dated 1939, this is Wood's first published composition (long overdue)
and shows his thorough and individual craftsmanship. Metronome indications
and more marks of expression would be welcome : in the rather arid No. 3, a
laconic " con ped." raises more questions than it answers. P. 2, bar 2—
for B-and-C, read presumably octave C's ; p. 3, bar 6—the right-hand
note-values add up incorrectly ; p. 3, bar 13—sharp signs wrongly enclosed
in parentheses.

A.J.

*THOMAS WOOD : " Over the Hills and Far Away " (" A Ring of Nursery
Rhymes New and Old ") ; and " Chanticleer " (after Chaucer's " The
Nun's Priest Tale"). (Stainer and Bell) ; no prices stated.*

TWENTY-FIVE and forty-three minutes respectively of *a cappella* music might
tax the powers of any choral composer, but Dr. Wood has such a strong
grip of all the possibilities, beauties, tricks and what-not of writing for choirs
that there should not be a dull moment in a performance of these works.
His ideas are those of a skilled technician : conventional, but never tasteless.
Similarly, his music shows more sense of humour than humour ; but what
fun there is, is companionable, clean and beloved of choral societies. It
can bear, in a way that a coy style could not, the quotations from " Judas
Maccabeus," " Meistersinger," and " Cherry Ripe," which Dr. Wood
makes in " Chanticleer."

P.H.

NOTE: We regret that in our last issue Robin Milford's " Idyll " (Under the
Greenwood Tree) was attributed to the Oxford University Press ; the publisher's are, of course, Augener Ltd.

Book Reviews

Arranged in alphabetical order of titles.

JOHANN SEBASTIAN BACH, *by Karl Franz Mueller. Pp. 48 ; S. 18. (Austria Music, Emerich Florian, Vienna).*

In his preface the author says that through many years' study of Bach's work he has arrived at " special and new results."   We offer a prize of 5 guineas to anyone who finds them.   H.K.

CHAMBER MUSIC: *The Growth and Practice of an Intimate Art, by Homer Ulrich. Pp. xvi + 430 ; 45s. 0d. (Columbia University Press. London : Geoffrey Cumberlege).*

The scope of Mr. Ulrich's useful book is sufficiently broad for us to gain a clear view of the chief trends in chamber music from its origin in the chanson and canzona up to the present day.   Nearly half the book is devoted to chamber music prior to Haydn.   Mr. Ulrich defines chamber music as being for not less than three players, excluding wind ensembles but not combinations of strings with wind.

He has drawn extensively on Riemann and an unpublished work by Miss Eunice C. Crocker, " An Introductory Study of the Italian Canzona for Instrumental Ensembles," in the earlier part of the book.   The short section in triple metre found in the canzona is shown to be the germ from which the second movement of the sonata and the symphony grew, and Mr. Ulrich studies the relation of the canzona to the *sonata da camera* and *sonata da chiesa,* and considers the *sonata a quattro* of Alessandro Scarlatti to be not the first " string Quartets " but " Baroque works which happen to be written for four string instruments. . . . "

The trio sonata is given the importance which it deserves, but there and elsewhere more attention is given to composers who made innovations than to those who didn't.   The fantasies of Purcell, for instance, are barely mentioned, but his trio sonatas are discussed fully.   Several composers, Loeillet among them, are only mentioned in the list of published music and recordings at the end of the book.   Space forbade discussion of the work of Spohr, Boccherini, Chausson and Glazounow.   Schoenberg, Bartok, Milhaud and Hindemith have a place in the final chapter, which ends with four pages on American composers ; an undue proportion since 20th century British, Italian and Spanish composers are dismissed in about the same number of lines.

A few mistakes have crept in.   K. P. E. Bach was not Sebastian's oldest son (p. 164).   In the chart on p. 199 Haydn's Op. 1, No. 4 is indicated as a three-movement symphony instead of No. 5, and Op. 3, No. 4 should have only two movements.   The footnote on p. 286 implies that Schubert wrote only 15 string quartets.   Brahms' second cello sonata is stated to be in F minor instead of major (p. 330).   Erik Satie is given a membership ticket of " Les Six" in place of Durey (p. 372), Honegger is given French nationality (p. 376), and Alessandro Scarlatti is confused with his son in the index.   It is incorrect to say that " Debussy made but one contribution to chamber-music literature "

(p. 357). Can Dvorák reveal " depth of feeling " (p. 352) and only touch a " surface emotion " (p. 353) ? And was he really " second to none in technical ability " and in " formal perception ? "

These, however, are minor blemishes in a lucid, readable, and generally accurate and well-informed book.   J.C.

THE COMPLETE OPERA BOOK, *by Gustave Kobbé* (*completed and supplemented by Katharine Wright and Ferruccio Bonavia respectively*). *Pp. xxiv + 990 ; 30s.* (*Putnam*).

THE fifth English edition, revised by Bonavia, of a necessarily incomplete book of well-told (but, of course, nevertheless unreadable) opera stories " together with Leading Airs and Motives in Musical Notation." In a further revision, some (to say the least) harmless excisions might make room for some highly desirable additions. The point is not perhaps quite untopical : the present edition may well sell rapidly.   H.K.

COUNTERPOINT, *by Walter Piston. Pp. 235 ; 12s. 6d.* (*Gollancz*).

IN the Foreword to the English Edition Professor Piston explains some of his technical terms to the English reader, including the self-explanatory " leading-tone," but excluding the term " voice-leading " which he later uses, and which only those who are acquainted with American or German terminology will understand (*Stimmfuehrung ;* English : part-writing). Like Dr. Andrews (see the review of *The Oxford Harmony* below), Prof. Piston does not prove himself a master logician; in fact, he gets himself into a similar mess over the subject of the rhythmic weight of long notes. Few musical theorists are willing to embark upon a piece of logical abstraction ; as Mendelsohn was the first to point out, musical thinking is extremely concrete.

> When tones of unequal time values are associated, the longer notes usually seem to possess more rhythmic weight than the shorter ones, whether or not they are given more stress by the performer. Thus in example 34 [meaning the 3rd variation, i.e. the actual theme, of the *Eroica's* finale] the dotted quarter notes make strong beats by comparison with the eighths [p. 31].

If Prof. Piston will replace the dotted crotchets by quavers and the quavers by dotted crotchets he will, we dare predict, make a weighty discovery.

On pp. 34f. the melodic rhythm of a passage from Mozart's Flute Concerto, K.313, is wrongly analyzed, and the section on " Metric Relationships" in the interesting chapter on *Harmonic Rhythm* contains again two severe illogicalities (p. 63). As this chapter arrives at " Static Harmony," the opening of Beethoven's Op. 59, No. 1, serves as an excellent example, but static harmony is not static everything, and to introduce the theme by saying that " the effect of this static harmony is of relaxation and immobility" is absurd, though many a bad interpretation would support the author. Quite apart from the *a priori* fact that an opening subject's function can't be relaxation because it hasn't got anything to relax, the present subject represents a typically Beethovenian thematic evolution based on a steady and far-reaching accumulation of tension. Nor is this only achieved by melodic, textural and dynamic means : by its very restraint, by the pressure which the harmonic immobility exerts upon the nowise immobile tune, the static harmony contributes essentially to the tensioning process. For the rest, we would earnestly ask Prof. Piston to re-feel himself into the terrific tension of the great " chaotic " (Furtwaengler) beginning of Beethoven's Ninth : the apotheosis of the Static in the service of the Dynamic.

> The author has not tried to establish or perfect an individual style, or to determine minutely the proper conduct of individual notes in counterpoint. He has intended to present the principles by which the contrapuntal element has operated in the works of composers in the belief that these principles will have lasting validity in any instrumental music based on harmony and rhythm [p. 231].

In fact the single reference to twelve-tone method (called of course " twelve-tone system ") is misleading, and the student may find Krenek's *Studies in Counterpoint* (1940 ; Schirmer, New York) a welcome complement. If he can think independently, Prof. Piston's often highly stimulating and unconventional textbook will prove enormously useful ; at times it will prove harmful if he can't.   H.K.

FROM HOLST TO BRITTEN : A STUDY OF MODERN CHORAL MUSIC, *by Rosemary Manning. Pp. vii + 80 ; 5s. 0d. (Workers' Music Association).*

INTERESTING chiefly in its unintentional sidelight on the psychology of undevoted discipleship : how, that is, one who has projected an essential part of his conscience on to a group ideal (Marxism in this case) satisfies his conscience's original and/or reactive urges for independence by disagreeing just as much with representatives of the idealized school as will not injure the projected part of his conscience—the central tenets of the ideology.   For the rest, there are a few islands of insight, but Marxism or no Marxism, the author lacks both the musical and the scientific knowledge—if not indeed, for the time being, the scientific conscience—necessary for the criticism and interpretation she has undertaken.   H.K.

A HANDBOOK ON THE TECHNIQUE OF CONDUCTING, *by Sir Adrian Boult. Pp. 47 ; (Hall the Publisher, Oxford). 5s. 0d.*

SIR ADRIAN, in a foreword, anticipates the most obvious charge that might be made against his tiny handbook. He apologises for its " telegraphic style, written as it was for students with whom I was in almost daily contact." It is, indeed, very much a book for students only.   Sensible, and in no way highfalutin', for outsiders, it is rather distressingly brief and terse ; and here and there it could be written more clearly.   Only when we probe to certain wide basic assumptions, relating to music as a whoie rather than conducting, is there ground for argument.   R.W.W.

HARMONY FOR LISTENERS, *by Douglas Turnell. Pp. 190 ; 15s. 0d. (Cassell).*

IN effect this a harmony book and must be judged as such.   Mr. Turnell's idea of harmony " for listeners " is ingenious, but in the end the listener's harmony is everybody's harmony and the only way to learn harmony is to learn it.   Mr. Turnell's short-cuts and over-simplifications can only baffle and boggle his readers. There is vast danger in our present-day tendency to play down a complicated subject in order to make it palatable to that mythical creature " the listener." For instance Mr. Turnell's few lines on the modes are worse than useless, particularly as far as his listener is concerned, since he fails to give any clear indication, and no concrete examples, of the features that distinguish for an attentive ear a mode from the major/minor scale. Mention of the slow movement of Beethoven's A minor quartet Op. 132 is precious little help. The listener meeting it for the first time on Mr. Turnell's introduction won't make much of its modality though he may well comprehend other and more important things. In chapter after chapter Mr. Turnell's intelligence is sacrificed to his under-estimation of the intelligence of his listener. As many times as the latter is enlightened he is left in the dark, or mis-led. We are interested to know that the tonic, sub-dominant, and dominant seventh chords " are all that are required to harmonise large sections of the works of Haydn, Mozart and Beethoven." The minor truth begets the major error.   D.M.

HAYDN, *by Rosemary Hughes. Pp. 244 ; 7s. 6d. (Dent).*

IT is not easy to discuss the life and work of a great composer in a book of under 250 pages. To attempt it with Haydn is a task indeed, and Miss Hughes must be congratulated for the measure of success she attains in her addition to the Master Musicians series.

The biography, which is most attractively written, takes up about half the volume, and the Appendices and Index just under 50 pages. Miss Hughes in the circumstances does very well with the 84 pages left in which to discuss the music. It is rather a pity, therefore, that she cannot resist the temptation of comparing the " crudity " of one of Haydn's earlier works with the " unattainable perfection " of one of Mozart's latest, especially as the Haydn Symphony No. 39 in G minor is one of those remarkable works written around 1770 with a bareness and power which could not have been expressed in any other way. It is one of the wonders of Haydn that, cut off at Esterhaz and composing at the rate he did, his technique was always equal to his creation. Considering his output it would be fairer to him (as also with Mozart) to perceive the occasional inequality of his inspiration. That Haydn's development is easier to plot than Mozart's is due, as Miss Hughes points out, to the great difference in their respective maturing rates. Finally it is a pleasure to come across a writer on Haydn who understands what she is writing about when dealing with the evolution of Sonata Form ; a surprisingly rare accomplishment.   H.N.

IN MEMORIAM RICHARD STRAUSS, *by Willi Schuh. Pp. 23 ; no price. (Atlantis Verlag, Zurich).*

IN twenty-three closely packed pages the composer's official biographer and faithful friend in the years of his Swiss exile, epitomises the life and achievement of " the last of the giants." Dr. Schuh especially stresses the Goethean quality of Strauss' genius. Strauss longed for Mediterranean sunshine in his Bavarian eyrie just as much as the old Olympian in chilly Weimar. These pages are more than the customary eulogy of a great artist, grown old and somewhat remote. They contain valuable and deeply moving insights into the innermost recesses of Strauss' complex soul. There is an authentic ring about the intimate confessions which are quoted, such as the composer's proud and yet modest statement that his relation to Wagner might be compared with Tintoretto's relation to Titian. High hopes are raised with regard to a future authoritative Strauss biography, a task for which Dr. Schuh received every encouragement from the composer himself.

H.F.R.

JAHRBUCH DER MUSIKWELT, *edited by Herbert Barth. Pp. 696 ; 38s. 6d. (U.K. distributors: Hinrichsen).*

Leo Kestenberg's " Jahrbuch der Deutschen Musikorganisationen " (1931), and Hinrichsen's six volumes of his " Musical Yearbook " have obviously inspired Herberth Barth and his editorial team to an even more ambitious undertaking, the first of its kind in post-Hitler Germany. It contains excellent contributions to musical Bibliography, listing all first performances of new compositions throughout Europe during 1945/48, and it attempts to survey Germany's recent contribution to music and musicology without overlooking the musical achievements in the Western hemisphere. It contains—very much like the recently published English volume " Who's Who in Music "—names and addresses of all Germans, in any way connected with the creation or execution of music. In a section of articles dedicated to musical research, the book tries hard to do justice to modern French, Danish and American music, its professed aim for future issues being international completeness. The editorial preface is already issued in trilingual fashion, a method of presentation which will be adopted for the textual part in later volumes. The emphasis is as yet perhaps too much on German music which—if compared with musical developments in other western countries—looks insignificant enough. The admitted lack of information about British music is simply deplorable but unfortunately typical of any such publication, compiled and produced in the American zone of Germany. It is high time American cultural centres stopped this successful imitation of British " insularity."

H.F.R.

KEYS TO THE KEYBOARD : *A book for pianists, by Andor Foldes. Pp. xii + 65 ; 5s. 0d. (O.U.P.).*

Very sound advice on many technical and some musical points, for beginners, advanced students and concert-pianists. If less chatty, would be weightier ; but possibly not so persuasive. Contains a number of excellent technical exercises. Two minor criticisms : Mr. Foldes fails to warn the young pianist that gramophone records, though they may help the student, should never be consulted while preparing a work for performance. Secondly : he does not qualify his repeated advice to practise passages (especially scales) *staccato.* Out of the four or five ways to produce *staccato* on the keyboard, only two would be of help in this connection, and one of them is a *portamento.* I have horrible visions of unpianistic goings-on prompted by a misunderstanding of Mr. Foldes.

P.H.

THE OXFORD HARMONY, Volume II, *by H. K. Andrews. Pp. vii + 241;
15s. 0d. (O.U.P.).*

IT becomes obvious that the length of a note has almost as much influence
on its accentuation as its position in the bar [p. 192]. A long note on a
weak beat, however, if it is immediately preceded by a short note on a strong
beat, need not necessarily carry any accent at all. The amount of accent
taken by a relatively long note is therefore dependent upon its position in the
bar and the phrase [p. 193].

Archbishop Cranmer's campaign for economy in the number of notes
placed over a syllable was a sound one. It is specially important in solo song.
The days of operatic coloratura are past. Runs, trills, and other vocal
gymnastics bring a cheap spectacular element in at once ; furthermore they
obscure the words, and hold up the action. It must be granted that Bach,
Handel, and Purcell (and some others) did remarkable things with florid
passages, but the present-day tendency is to get on with the job, and it is a
good one [p. 196].

The book " is intended to follow Dr. R. O. Morris's *The Oxford Harmony*,
Vol. I, and deals with Chromatic Harmony and Modulation, and practical
matters such as writing for string ensembles, pianoforte accompaniment,
setting words to music, etc." The unreserved praise it has received elsewhere
has necessitated the above pillory ; qualified praise remains due.

H.K.

THE ROAD TO MUSIC, *by Desmond MacMahon. Pp. 75 ; 5s. 0d. (Paxton).*

OF " The Road to Music " I can find not one good word to say. It seems to me
altogether too complicated, muddled, abbreviated, and full of assumptions of
knowledge in the reader, to be of any use to the absolute novices for whom a
series of grotesquely highfalutin' preliminary declarations informs us it is
written. On the other hand, anyone more advanced than an absolute novice
is bound to be infuriated by its inaccuracy, ill proportion and lack of compre-
hensiveness. The actual writing is not merely undistinguished but sometimes
verges on the illiterate. A book so fantastically bad that its being printed at
all not merely dismays but astonishes this reviewer. R.W.W.

ROBERT SCHUMANN, *by Karl H. Woerner. Pp. 371 ; no price. (Atlantis
Verlag, Zurich).*

THIS is the first Schumann biography to make full use of W. Boetticher's
two publications (1940/41) with their numerous reprints from Schumann's
hitherto unpublished diaries and notebooks. It succeeds in drawing a far
from Victorian picture of this often misrepresented Romantic, discussing
frankly the lurid aspects of his mental disease, and courageously linking the
style of Schumann's later, often disastrously misunderstood works (the
opera " Genofeva," the music to Goethe's " Faust " and to Byron's " Man-
fred ") with that of his great contemporary and Saxon compatriot Richard
Wagner. Expertly presented analyses of neglected works like the later
songs and a deep psychological insight into the schizophrenic organisation of
Schumann's earliest creative processes enhance the value of this brilliantly
written book. It deserves the honour of an English translation, in spite of
Miss Joan Chissel's recent meritorious volume on the same subject.

H.F.R.

A SHORT HISTORY OF WORLD MUSIC, *by Curt Sachs. Pp. 400 ;
18s. 0d. (Dennis Dobson).*

THIS book was wanted, not only by the "layman" for whom, says the dust-
jacket, it was " designed " ; it is the *only* short history of music, written in
English during the last few years, which one could commend whole-heartedly
both to the advanced student and the beginner. Why have so many summaries
of musical history been written, and why are those by reputable scholars even
poorer than those by insular writers with a gift for elegant generalisation ?
Obviously there is a sale for them, for the present reviewer, who claims
neither scholarship nor elegance, has been asked by two publishers to provide
a short history of music—not a history of technique, of styles, of instruments,
of the relations between music and other arts, or of what Mr. Mellers has called
" Music and Society." Smooth yet vigorous condensation, such as is found
in Trevelyan's shorter histories, comes at the summit of a scholar's powers,
after his slower pacing through the tracts of time. Dr. Sachs, having earned a
place of honour by his writings on the origins and early stages of music, on
oriental musical practice, on various musical epochs and on the aesthetics of
music, now gives us a bird's eye view of musical history with as little disproportion as is humanly possible at this stage of our knowledge.

The inequalities one might expect from a specialist are extremely difficult
to find ; an ungracious and jealous eye notes, at the end of chapters dealing
with composers since 1800, that one or two books which might have been
suggested for " Further Reading " are omitted in favour of inferior books or
studies now superseded. For the general student, this short history will be
used in stages, before and after some of the " Reading " and " Listening "
recommended. (By the way, " Anthologie Sonore " discs *can* be obtained
from English gramophone dealers, though they are costly ; " Two Thousand
Years " discs cannot.) Dr. Sachs is to be congratulated when so much of it
can be read at a session for its sheer intrinsic merits, for no short history of
music covers so much ground or keeps so clear of all but essential details of
composers' biographies ; the history is of musical expression, from the primi-
tives and the first oriental schools to modern times, and of the materials which
made that expression possible. " Short " the history may be, yet it contains
facts that are not found in longer works.

Thus, the chapter " The Age of Josquin " has sub-divisions on Protestant
chorale, Tablatures, Viols, Temperament, Treatises on Music, Printing ;
that on " The Age of Bach and Rameau " includes Bach's Instruments,
Beggar's Opera, *Style galant* and *Style bourgeois, Crescendo and diminuendo,*
Criticism and public concerts, Pitch ; yet in all this Dr. Sachs, who uses
music type only to illustrate mode or notation, intends that the reader shall
be sent to the music of the period, whenever printing or recording make it
available. The final chapter alone, covering 1886-1948, is inadequate and
teutonic in outlook : last year one found advanced music students in Germany
who knew Byrd only as a composer of some pieces for " clavecin," supposed
Holst's " Planets " to be the high-water mark of modern English music and
judged Fauré by " Après un rêve " ; one can be patient for another half
century while scholars of Dr. Sachs's calibre suppose that Mahler, Wolf,
Strauss, Schoenberg and Stravinsky are the only " names " between 1886

and 1948, while other composers can be classed under a list of twenty-ish-
" isms "—verism, bruitism, expressionism, barbarism, naturalism, archaism,
neo-classicism.   Malice itches to add another which would insult a fine mind
which has produced a fine book on a subject botched by other fine minds.

THE SONGS OF HENRI DUPARC, by *Sydney Northcote. Pp. 122 ;
8s. 6d. (Dennis Dobson).*

MOST of us know Duparc only as a Franck pupil beloved by other musicians
of his time, who was instrumental in founding the Societé Nationale, and
composed some dozen songs which, once fully known, form a treasury indispensable to a survey of French artistic growth during the second half of the
last century.   " Artistic " is deliberately written instead of " musical," and
this book splendidly illuminates the distinction.   Though one could not
wish the musical analyses and technical criticism to have been better done,
Dr. Northcote's study is of interest not only to singers and professional
musicians, nor is it merely the first book in English on a subject that is important while quality ranks above quantity.   It is really a series of essays which,
one hopes, will be expanded either in articles or in other books from the same
pen.   " Seldom has any creative artist laid so small an offering on the altar
of fame " as has Duparc, and Dr. Northcote's study could not have added up
to a book—which it certainly does—had some of its most interesting parts been
amplified, and the main subject been lost in fuller discussion of the man, his
poets, and the spirit of his age and race.

Duparc was born in 1848 and died in 1933, so that Fauré was three years
his senior.   " Duparc's longevity is misleading.   His practical interest in
music began only in adolescence, and the last fifty years of his life were overshadowed by a tragic nervous disease."   He was a lawyer by profession, and
although in old age his sight failed and he became paralysed, the nervous
affliction which prevented him from composing from his early thirties onwards
did not seem to affect his outward appearance of robustness and geniality.
Dr. Northcote tries to discover Duparc as husband, parent and mayor of his
city.   There was nothing about him to suggest the petulant and hyper-
sensitive artist, and the extracts from his letters, though quoted to show his
opinions on literary and artistic matters, also show his shrewdness, frankness
and kindness.   In only one activity does he seem to have been over-fastidious
—in the seeking of artistic integrity, to a standard abnormal even among the
great composers.   A letter to Chausson criticises that composer's treatment
of verse in terms that might have come from Wolf, and have brought a
coolness to a less intelligent friendship.

Duparc became a disciple in composition only after Franck ceased to
regard him as worth serious training as a pianist.   He had shown no marked
aptitude for music in boyhood, yet Franck thought him his most inventive
disciple ; all his music is " early," but his songs are those of a distinct musical
personality, a genius that could not fulfil its promise.   Though one of them,
" Lamento," is dedicated to Fauré, and though, as Dr. Northcote shows,
Duparc and Fauré of that period had common mannerisms, Duparc is no
second-rate imitator of his great contemporary ; after full acquaintance with
the marvel that is Fauré and the marvel that is Wolf, we still do not leave
dusty the few justly favoured songs of Duparc.   He tried to destroy every

trace of inferior composition, every incomplete sketch and arrangement ; " Le Galop," which escaped his suppression of his early songs, yet is, in Dr. Northcote's words, " somewhat reminiscent of the graphic pace and strength of *Erlkoenig*," shows the composer's degree of self-criticism.

His poets were Parnassians. Perhaps the best pages in Dr. Northcote's book compare the ideals of artists belonging to different epochs that have witnessed an outburst of poetic and musical lyricism ; particularly vivid is the explanation of common ideals and reactionary techniques in the succession romantic—Parnassian—symbolist. We are not allowed to dismiss Duparc merely as representing a middle stage of technique, a musical Parnassian mean, between Franck and Debussy or late Fauré. These 118 pages, like their subject, have a quality that makes them worth knowing.   A.H.

TWO CENTURIES OF BACH, *by Friedrich Blume. Translated by Stanley Godman. Pp. 85 ; 6s. 0d. (O.U.P.).*

THIS well translated brochure is a fresh survey of Bach-appreciation, from Scheibe to Dilthey and Schweitzer.   The thesis is that the church works are what matter, and that their insight into the *coincidentia oppositorum* of Christian consciousness must be the basis of every major book on Bach.

It is true and worth saying that Bach's church music cannot be considered a mere ornamentation of the ritual, as fit for the concert hall or studio as for St. Thomas's.   But theology cannot maintain art in a hundred cantatas, a monumental Mass, and another hundred instrumental works without an equally categorical imperative or " instress " (G. M. Hopkins) from the pursuit of sound-relationship.

A religious bias need not dismiss as trifling Bach's modest, unforced, undramatic pursuit of phrase and counterphrase for its own sake.   " It is all inside a Christian world-scheme," testifies a writer in a penetrating and pertinent analysis.*   For that connection between religion and universal human freedom Prof. Blume shows little concern.   Many readers may sympathise with his vision of a new and more comprehensive conception of Bach.   But when we read in this context " With the catastrophe of the Second World War the era of specialisation has come to an end," we cannot but recall that Bach's Lutheranism produced, not only *coincidentia oppositorum* but (significantly in the vernacular) " I am a good shepherd," " Prince of Peace ! ", " Wake up," " See that your righteousness is not pride," and " My Sin it was that bound Thee." There is nothing obscure or evasive about these works: their gospel message is clear and binding, whether war is being waged or not. They call for renewed attention to their serene but characteristic sureness, rather than for fresh light.   A.E.F.D.

*T. R. Milford : " What is Christian music ? " (*The Student Movement*, May/June, 1950).

THE WELL-TEMPERED STRING QUARTET, *by Bruno Aulich and Ernst Heimeran. Pp. 147 ; 7s. 6d. (Novello).*

" MORE than any other sport," says the translator D. Millar Craig, " chamber music does weld its devotees into a community of spirit. . . " Quartet playing is as much of a sport as praying, and the authors' jokes, even when good , are misplaced. As for the " practical hints " (by amateurs for amateurs), some of them are obviously wrong and harmless, others subtly wrong and dangerous. The unwitting humour of the authors' attempts at musical analysis could not be bettered. The book should sell very well.   H.K.

WITH STRINGS ATTACHED : REMINISCENCES AND REFLEC-
    TIONS, *by Joseph Szigeti* (*with 15 half-tone illustrations*). *Pp. 323 ;
    17s. 6d.* (*Cassell*).

A MASTER speaks, so it behoves us to find the truth in every wrong thing he says, and says surprisingly well. The right things are, of course, pure gold—

> The unsuspecting millions are . . . none the wiser as to what is being done to their listening habits, how they are being conditioned by the mass—and mess—of sound that is aimed at them. They hear the cinema organ's wobble and probably they like it because it reminds them of the human voice or of the vibrato of a stringed instrument. But they don't realize something that came to me with a shock the other day when I was listening to a popular music broadcast : that the process is being reversed nowadays, that we seem to have reached the point where *the string orchestra is imitating the cinema organ.* Thus the vicious circle seems to be completed.

—though by no means sporadic. " ' Message,' " shudders Szigeti, " there shall be none, if I can help it." You can't help it : no artistic mind can, even though it may be the reader who has himself to act as messenger. Only one little factual correction has to be made :—

> The absence of this insular attitude and the degree of the artist's *Einfuehlungsvermogen* (inadequately translated as " capacity for indentification ") always seemed to me the hallmark of an artist's worth, the yardstick of his stature.

The adequate (if colourless) translation of " *Einfuehlungsvermogen* " is " capacity for empathy."   H.K.

Periodicals from Abroad

CHORD AND DISCORD : II/6. Pp. 190 (New York).

THE *Bruckner* (read : Bruckner-Mahler) *Society of America's* bulky yearly (1950), edited by Gabriel Engel : an important and prospectively good magazine. Best : Robert Simpson's analysis —" the first reasonably complete one in English to be made from the original score "—of Bruckner's Eighth as well as his note on Bruckner's Ninth. Worst : Ernest J. M. Lert's leading article, most promisingly entitled " Instinct and Reason in Music," and arriving after 10 pages of ignorant psychology and muddled philosophy at two world-shattering conclusions : " 1. That music, originally, was not an art for art's sake. It was, and still is, a vital part and function of human life.—2. That vital music is not an arbitrary product fashioned by cerebral workmanship without involving any extra-musical emotion. Music is primarily the expression of extra-musical instincts." Desmond Shawe-Taylor's " objective " discourse on " The Length of Mahler " would seem to lend strength to Oscar Wilde's reminder that all unbiassed opinions are absolutely valueless, as well as to Schoenberg's biassed opinion that the middle way is the only one which doesn't lead to Rome.   H.K.

Concerts

I. London.

PHILHARMONIA CONCERT SOCIETY : Philharmonia Orchestra, Albert Hall, 13th April, 1950 ; c. Boult.

BALAKIREV'S first symphony was the plum of this concert and should be heard oftener, as it is consistently interesting and *entraînant*. Though dated 1898, much, according to Rimsky-Korsakov, was sketched in 1866, and it is impossible to believe that the scherzo, that starts in a Mendelssohnian vein and continues on native Russian lines, was not conceived long before the vanishing of Mendelssohn's afflatus on European music. The introduction and first movement are the most astringent and seemed, on a first hearing, to have least contrast. The *andante* sounds like a naive forerunner of the third movement of *Scheherazade* (1888), exotic but not dazzling ; but the finale (coda in particular) conveys beneath its undoubted brilliance a peasant mysticism, a lonely jubilation which, if harking back to Glinka in manner, is as intense as Mussorgsky. This is a work that, repeatedly heard, will become greatly endeared, not least because of the trio and the original harp cadenza linking the last two movements. Whatever Karajan's rendering may be, Sir Adrian Boult's is nervous, earnest, and adequate.

E.H.W.M.

FESTIVAL OF ISRAELI MUSIC : London Philharmonic Orchestra, Frank Pelleg (piano), Martin Lawrence (baritone), Albert Hall, 17th April, 1950 ; c. van Beinum.

A PECULIARLY interesting concert. The backsighted and unhistorically minded would have heard nothing but rather crude reflections of a long familiar and outdated colouristic romanticism. In fact, these Israeli composers, and in particular the piano concerto of Paul Ben-Haim, displayed a vitality and experimentation normally found in those composers who were in at the beginning (and in some sense were the founders) of the romantic/nationalist movement. For Israeli musicians this use of a romantic idiom is historically right, and, genuinely felt by artist and audience, can provide a valid musical experience. Not all the works were as " crude," in the sense I have qualified above, as the concerto : Joseph Gruenthal's " Exodus," a choreographic poem for orchestra with baritone solo, showed a mature assimilation of strong European influences—notably, and not surprisingly, Mahler's. We must view Israeli music in rather the same way as the Israeli State : as a considerable achievement, something of an historical oddity as well as an historical necessity. If we can, as it were, adjust our ears to a new historical situation there is not a little to admire and much to be looked for from the future.

D.M.

MAHLER'S SONG OF THE EARTH : London Symphony Orchestra, Albert Hall, 23rd April, 1950 ; c. Krips.

KRIPS is more than a good, he is a great conductor ; he made the L.S.O. sound beyond belief. But what counted most was his understanding of that infinitely volatile and daemonic spirit that is Mahler. Nuance, tempi, balance—everything to a hairbreadth. Englishmen *have* temperament ;

they *can* play as beings possessed : but since that is not our national tradition, we must be conducted into it. We were ; and Mahler triumphed. Kathleen Ferrier is now a great singer, and Richard Lewis a very good one ; both were magnificent. I don't think many left the Albert Hall in any doubt that the *Song of the Earth* is one of the two or three greatest compositions of our century. R.D.

PHILHARMONIA ORCHESTRA UNDER KLETZKI, WITH MENUHIN. FIRST EUROPEAN PERFORMANCE OF SCHNABEL'S RHAPSODY: *Albert Hall, 27th April, 1950.*

ALL that earnestness can do towards creating music, Schnabel has done before and here does again. There is something more than pathetic, almost tragic, about the results ; for of the life-force itself there is not a breath. Tovey's music (though in a worse because uncontemporary idiom) was just the same. There is no substitute for musical invention, and this cannot be commanded by sincerity, not even Scotch or Teutonic sincerity.

Menuhin rejoiced me by returning in Beethoven's violin concerto to that pure, inspired and carefree talent, his hold on which has of late seemed so precarious.

Kletzki conducted Ravel's inspired orchestration of the Mussorgsky *Pictures at an Exhibition* with prodigious verve, to every ounce of which the Philharmonia responded. R.D.

THE LONDON GUILD OF ARTS : *Capriol Orchestra, Margaret Ritchie (soprano), Alan Loveday (violin), Iris Loveridge (piano), David Mason (trumpet), Central Hall, 5th May, 1950 ; c. Roy Budden.*

THE Capriol Orchestra needs strict sectional training before interpretations are attempted. The Bach Cantata No. 51 was unrehearsed and too fast for both our own and Miss Ritchie's liking, who, however, sang well in the long sections with continuo and was excellently accompanied by Walter Bergmann. Alan Loveday's playing of Mozart's A major concerto had a certain meaningless technical fluency combined with a disregard for Mozart's most basic and recurrent phraseological traits. Miss Loveridge's clean playing and boisterous humour made the most of Shostakovitch's concerto for piano and trumpet. P.H.

AIMÉE VAN DE WIELE : *Harpsichord recital, Wigmore Hall, 6th May, 1950.*

I CANNOT agree with some critics that Miss van de Wiele's rubato in fast pieces was excessive. I found it daringly original and very satisfying, suiting, as it did, the capacities of her instrument. But I can well see that her kind of partly halting, partly gushing phrasing in, for instance, the last movement of the *Italian Concerto*, may have offended ears expecting the necessarily milder forms of rhythmic movement familiar from performances on the pianoforte. Miss van de Wiele is a great artist, and the *Goldberg* variations, their great arch rising out of the very minutiae of composition, were shaped by her much as Schnabel shapes the *Diabelli* variations. P.H.

SONATA RECITAL : Eleanor Warren (cello) and Walter Susskind (piano),
Wigmore Hall, 7th May, 1950.

WHILE Miss Warren's technique is almost equal to her fiery imagination,
Mr. Susskind's playing, though brilliantly effortless, was musically too timid.
In Beethoven's Op. 102, No. 1, the players' disregard of the score's *crescendi*
at the crucial moment, i.e. a quaver before a sudden *piano,* was symptomatic
of a performance that did not quite achieve its intentions. The same goes
for the Debussy and the Rawsthorne* sonatas although Miss Warren's treatment of the latter was very imaginative. The players were completely at their
ease in Rachmaninoff's Sonata which is technically grateful and offers no
musical problems. But the piece has not aged well, and now that it is no longer
in vogue, it is as improbable as a fossilized jellyfish.   P.H.
*For my review of the work, see *Music Survey* II/4/50.

MORLEY COLLEGE CONCERTS SOCIETY : Central Hall, 12th May,
1950 ; c. Michael Tippett and Walter Goehr.

Clear performance of Gibbons by Morley College Choir who are getting
better and better. Stravinsky's " Ode " in memory of Natalie Koussevitsky
(1943) : more than a self-copy but less than a new work. Haydn's " Maria
Theresia " Mass : good singing by Elsie Morison and good *tempi* by Walter
Goehr. Why is this work not done by our Choral Societies instead of the
more hackneyed classics ?   P.H.

SONATA RECITAL : Helen Kwalwasser (violin) and Alan Richardson
(piano). First performance of Alan Richardson's First Violin Sonata ;
Wigmore Hall, 15th May, 1950.

THE undeserved immediate success with the crowd of Mr. Richardson's
sonata makes one almost believe that a good work of art must be unpopular.
Of course, this is not so—but a bad piece of music need only " fall pleasantly
on the ear " to be acclaimed. Only the slow movement had some musical
substance which relieved the moist shadiness of the first, and the " Here we go
round the mulberry bush " jollity of the last. Mr. Richardson proved himself
an ideal partner in a very concerted performance of the Franck sonata.
" Concerted " (in its various modern senses and in its Latin sense of " con-
certare ") is the word for Miss Kwalwasser's musical personality. With
perfect control of the violin, in neat and concise phrases, and even with a tinge
of inspiration (*sit venia verbo*), she gives a concert with the concerted support
of all her powers, contending earnestly for the approval of the great masters
and the public. Her matter-of-fact seriousness goes a long way, but both
charm and greatness elude her. To put it very rudely : the one thing that is
worse than a complete amateur is a complete professional.   P.H.

AMADEUS QUARTET with Dennis Brain (horn), John Alexandra (bassoon),
Frederick Thurston (clarinet), Edward Merrett (double bass) ; Mozart :
Quartet in G, K.387 ; Schubert : Octet ; Wigmore Hall, 26th May, 1950.

THERE can be no doubt that the " Amadeus " have become, in a relatively
short time, one of the leading quartets of Europe. They possess the two
qualities which are necessary for a chamber-music ensemble of international
standard : perfect unity of intention and spaciousness of conception. Unity

of intention is, of course, much more than good ensemble-playing : it is the utter musical self-assurance of players who know that however much they may thrash things out at rehearsals, at the performance they will be safely oblivious of details and feel and play as one person. No amount of conscious rehearsing, or rather, only an enormous amount of conscious rehearsing of this and other works, followed by an instinctive suppression of settled details, can have produced, among other things, the rhythmic and tonal unity between the semibreve- and the quaver-passages in Mozart's last movement. As for spaciousness of conception, this is an elusive quality mostly found, or at least most obvious, in great conductors, and has much to do with the role of objective and subjective time in music.* It means really that the formally most significant passages of a movement or an entire work (its architectural mainstays, as it were) are allotted so much time and significance, that the details crowding round them in the form of bridge-passages, modulations, embellishments, etc., are also sufficiently distinct although never pressing, or weighing upon, these main stresses. Thus, in a spacious performance, the third dimension of a score, its depth, will be so enhanced as to make the listener feel that he travels not only on one, but on several lines of time, at various subjective speeds, but in the same instant of consciousness—a feat of magic expressed in Thomas Mann's saying " Music is ennobled Time." In consequence, a spacious performance of a well-known work seems much longer than usual while it lasts, but, in retrospect, appears to have gone like a whiff. When, in the Schubert, there came the tragic introduction to the last movement, the very beginning of the work, to which it formally points back, might have been centuries ago—so much " ennobled Time " had flown, meanwhile, under the bridges of the strings and through the apertures of the wind. But after the performance, I wondered whether six movements were enough to express fully the Octet's musical world.   P.H.

*About which a thesis by an aesthetician would seem to be overdue.

LONDON PHILHARMONIC ORCHESTRA: Albert Hall, 1st June, 1950; c. Koussevitzky.

KOUSSEVITZKY has his detractors ; but for me the sheer electric force of the man is worth oceans of musicianly correctness. I heard only his first programme, with Prokofieff's Symphonie Classique (one hears here the genuine basis of Prokofieff's by now inflated reputation), Mussorgsky's Prelude to Khovantschina (the supremely un-conscious genius, as Brahms is the over-conscious), Debussy's La Mer (how Debussy's greatness grows) and Tchaikovsky's 5th Symphony (how Tchaikovsky repays full-blooded performance) ; each of these fitted Koussevitzky's best qualities (while the earlier classics might collide with them). The L.P.O. evidently agreed, and played as I cannot remember hearing them before.   R.D.

TIBOR DE MACHULA : Cello recital with Gerald Moore ; Wigmore Hall, 1st June, 1950.

FIRST London appearance of this Hungarian Cellist, recommended by Furtwaengler. Tone : big but inexact since place of contact changes too much. Left hand better. Musicality : sweeping and sturdy but diffuse, spoiling Bach's solo sonata in C by seemingly free and easy, but actually careless, cross-phrasings. The same happened in Beethoven's Op. 102, No. 2. Gerald Moore was much more consequent in his part.   P.H.

CHELSEA SYMPHONY ORCHESTRA : Peter Pears *(tenor),* Denis East *(violin),* Chelsea Town Hall, 6th June, 1950 ; *c.* Norman Del Mar.
THIS is my relation to Britten's *Our Hunting Fathers* which was performed for the first time since 1936 and sung to perfection by Peter Pears. (1) A study of the score : it looks scrappy, incoherent, both horizontally and vertically, *risqué, outré.* (2) The performance : I am shocked and bewildered by something so wildly sad, or sadly wild, that I might as well laugh about it. (3) The score studied after the performance : things fall into their places, the ruling hand of the composer appears as it must have limned the savage panorama, hatching in certain areas, leaving others free. (4) I hope for more performances, for my own and those critics' benefit who were jolted into opposition by a single hearing.

By way of contrast, my reactions to Hindemith's Violin Concerto (1939) would never undergo radical changes, although they may be intensified by repeated hearings. No doubt a number of unobtrusive felicities would be revealed, but in inspiration this concerto compares unfavourably with even so slight a work as the piano-duet sonata of 1938. The noise of a full orchestra in Chelsea Town Hall is so shattering that I dare not chip in critically ; only in quieter passages I would like to have said : " A little more roundness of tone, strings ! " P.H.

BACH, HANDEL, PURCELL : Anne Alderson *(soprano),* Maurice Bevan *(baritone),* Integer String Quartet, Cowdray Hall, 7th June, 1950.
MR. BEVAN : good, ringing middle-register ; extremes of voice weak. Very musical in Bach's cantata No. 82 ; German could be better. Miss Alderson : musically not so mature. Pleasing voice, but does not raise soft palate on vowels e, i, resulting in inferior tone. Instrumental playing amateurish, programme good. P.H.

NEW ERA CONCERT SOCIETY : MARCEL DUPRÉ, *Bach recital ;* Albert Hall, 12th June, 1950.
TECHNICALLY, it could not often have been better ; musically, it often could not have been worse. The Bach year's deepest possible disappointment.
H.K.

RUTH HUGGENBERG : Wigmore Hall, 16th June, 1950.
MISS HUGGENBERG's exclusive preoccupation with good tone made Schumann's *Phantasiestuecke* more agreeable than they sometimes are, but, while dulling the Haydn F minor variations, made her *Sonata Pathétique* one of the most unintelligent readings of Beethoven I have ever heard. Good tone is the means, good phrasing the end—not the other way round. P.H.

ST. JOHN'S WOOD ORCHESTRA : Erich Gruenberg *(violin),* Gervase de Peyer *(clarinet),* Everyman's Theatre, Hampstead, 18th June, 1950 ; *c.* Francis Oakes.
ORCHESTRA : courageous, enthusiastic, musical, almost too sensitive for present technical standard. Conductor : gifted, knows his scores. After setting rhythm of a piece, should detail his movements more. Trio of Mozart Symphony in A (K.201) should have same speed as Minuet. Both this and the

Minuet of Haydn's " Farewell " symphony were too fast. Excellent playing by Mr. Peyer and Mr. Gruenberg, especially the latter's slow movement of Mozart's Violin Concerto in G, at once intimate and intense. First performance of Concertino for Clarinet and Strings by young composer Josef Horowitz : well worked, if not original, in strident passages (first movt. devel., last movt. first subject), banal in lyricisms (first movt. second subject, last movt. first episode). Form does not grow out of material, particularly noticeable in second movt. which was not deep enough to bear continuous ostinato of chords, and in faulty A-B-A-B structure of Rondo. Brilliant treatment of clarinet part. All in all : too much conscientiousness about details, too little about the whole. But promising talent.   P.H.

VICTORIA DE LOS ANGELES *with Gerald Moore : Covent Garden, 18th June, 1950.*

MANY years ago Ernest Newman wrote in the Birmingham *Daily Post :* " Melba's singing was uninterestingly perfect and perfectly uninteresting." A triple accent on ' perfect ' and the quip applies to Los Angeles' recital : her voice is perfect, her natural technique unequalled perfection ; and her indefatigably tasteful approach to matters phraseological, her inexhaustible tenderness make you marvel and marvel until you are sick of it all, which I personally was after 10 minutes. For the real musical result was strictly nil. Underneath the unique civilization of her execution (marred only by a tendency to go slightly off pitch) there lay a yawning lack of culture which one would have been glad to call barbarian if only there had been more life, more imagination to it. Let those who disagree compare her " Wer hat dies Liedlein erdacht ? " (Mahler, No. 4 from *Des Knaben Wunderhorn,* as the programme would not know) with Peter Pears' or Beryl Hatt's, her Mozart Alleluia with Schwarzkopf's or Maria Stader's. I hold no brief for comparisons between interpretations which stand, as they should, on their own feet. But to compare different and independent interpretations with a hidden lack of interpretation is musico-logical.

Are we witnessing the attempt of a culture to commit suicide with the very weapons with which it has achieved its victories ? So far it would be no more than an attempt.   H.K.

––––––––

In our last issue (p. 268) we wrongly attributed a performance of Stravinsky's *Sacre du Printemps* to Sargent ; the conductor was in fact Sir Adrian Boult.—EDS.

II. Liverpool.

OFFICIALLY, the season ended on March 28th, when Archie Camden played the Bassoon Concertos of Gordon Jacob and Eric Fogg with expected virtuosity. Although two Bassoon Concertos in one evening is one too many, Fogg's work impressed with the genuine poetry of its slow movement, whilst Jacob's is a job of little importance neatly accomplished by a skilled craftsman. No sooner had the regular season finished than Sargent, with the Philharmonic Choir and Orchestra, performed the *Mass in D* to very creditable effect (April 18th).

Given a chorus to deal with, Sargent becomes a good conductor, and, whilst on his last visit he had vulgarised the vulgar Respighi orchestration of Bach's C Minor *Passacaglia*, he led the Chorus through the Mass with a discreet awareness of its appalling difficulties and an exultant delight in its dramatic power.

These activities gave way to a series of four " Spring Concerts," three of " popular classics " under Rignold, and one of French Music under Albert Wolff, in which Roussel's *Fourth Symphony* was given its first Liverpool performance (May 30th). The orchestra's account of the first movement was tentative, but their sympathy awoke during the *Lento*, and the joy of Roussel's remarkably humane music, so temperate and " proportioned," in E. M. Forster's sense of the word, appeared as it should. Wolff added *Nuages* and *Fêtes* to this : the performance of the latter as good as can be heard anywhere. The rest of the programme was an orgy of Ravel, including the unspeakable *Bolero*.

These notes have been devoted to the rarer works which have been performed, but Rignold has given us more Mozart and Haydn than we have heard before in a single season. Schubert's *Unfinished* Symphony and Mendelssohn's *Italian* have been given performances of rare spontaneity and freshness, and Beethoven's *Pastoral* one of a deep meditative beauty that the local press found altogether too meditative. The critic in Liverpool is in the happy position of realising that, though there are weaknesses he might attack, the orchestra's policy leads to a lively and intelligent musical life, and that a continually increasing repertory is developing its expressive power. H.B.R.

Opera

I. Sadler's Wells.

HUGH THE DROVER : Sadler's Wells Revival, 12th May, 1950.

DESPITE superficial appearances, this is an opera of high emotional tension ; passion smoulders beneath the surface in the English way, and is not burnt to atoms beneath our noses—both methods may achieve genius. *Hugh the Drover* is quietly and profoundly moving, and producer (Mr. Powell Lloyd), conductor and cast combined to handle it with an interpretation to match these qualities. I missed, perhaps, a certain sensual generosity in the vocal tone which would have lent still more splendour, but I have no intention of apportioning this criticism beyond hinting that it lay more with the female than with the male element. What mattered was the rightness and beauty of the whole performance. R.D.

II. Covent Garden.

WAGNER'S " RING " : First complete cycle, 8th, 10th, 14th, 17th June, 1950.

THE new Covent Garden presentation of Wagner's Tetralogy (as far as I was able to attend it*) is a very creditable achievement and worthy of its laudable purpose to win over a new generation of listeners to a just appreciation of Wagner's magical art. If it fell short of generally accepted continental standards, that was not the fault of the singers, the majority of whom rose magnificently to the occasion. Flagstad's Bruennhilde is an unforgettable experience in the perfectly homogeneous authenticity of its interpretation, combining as it does flawless singing with superbly restrained (yet never merely statuesque) acting. Her " Todesverkuendigung " (" Walkuere," Act II) in its monumental poise and the extra-mundane ring of a unique soprano, conjured up treasured memories of great Bruennhilde's of the past. It was certainly not easy to live up to her standard. Yet Svanholm's Siegfried managed to avoid eclipse by his partner, impressing deeply with his mimetic gifts and the psychological penetration of his part in both " Siegfried " and " Goetterdaemmerung " ; he had sung with gusto the easier part of Siegmund, to which Sylvia Fisher had added her beautiful and convincing Sieglinde. Andreas Boehm's Wotan is obviously the result of careful study. As the Wanderer he agreeably surprised us with the sudden emergence of hitherto suppressed *bel canto*, doubly welcome after the somewhat dessicated " Sprechgesang " of his part in " Walkuere." Boehm seemed as little at home on the rocky cliffs of the *Bruennhildenstein* as his predecessor Hotter, slipping twice and prematurely breaking his spear in a misguided effort to impress Erda, the inveterate dreamer. (Could nothing be done to improve the topographic knowledge of visiting Wotans at Covent Garden ?) Ludwig Weber contributed a very impressive Hunding, even surpassing this effort in best Wagnerian style with his sinister, yet flexible, vocally powerful and psychologically very arresting Hagen. Paul Schoeffler's mature style enlivened the decadent figure of Gunther with welcome heroic elements. Erich Zimmermann's experienced Mime wearied through overacting and a misapplied dose of " Sprechgesang," which deprived listeners quite unnecessarily of the thematic delineations of his part. Graham Clifford's Alberich suffered from singularly poor pronunciation of the German text. Other English singers however—Edith Coates as Fricka and Waltraute, Jean Watson as Erda, Doris Doree as mellifluous Gutrune, Norman Walker as very humanised dragon—tackled the thorny problems of Wagnerian alliteration with ease, assurance and a remarkable degree of audibility. A special word of praise is due to the perfect vocal ensembles of Valkyries, Rhinemaidens and Norns and to the thunderous male chorus in the second act of " Goetterdaemmerung." Production, costumes, settings and lighting tried hard and on the whole—not unsuccessfully—to strike a sensible balance between the old fashioned naturalism of days of yore and the deplorable tendency of our own age to oversimplify and to fight shy of any realistic stage property. In this respect the beautiful and convincing vistas of "Feuerzauber" and the end of "Goetterdaemmerung" surely constituted the high-water mark of stage craft in present-day Covent Garden. The lowest ebb was reached in the timid scrapping of Wagner's poetical stage transformation between Scenes 2 and 3 in Act III of " Siegfried," when the beautiful transitional music (in this instance preceded by a most ugly cut) had to be played against a lowered curtain. Reece Pemberton's settings for " Walkuere," Act I, were singularly impressive, as were many décors and choral movements in " Goetterdaemmerung," which as a whole showed signs of more careful preparation than previous works of the cycle.

The orchestra undeniably had its great moments ; large parts of " Goetterdaemmerung," but unfortunately not Siegfried's *Funeral March*, totally lacking as it was in nobility, and mistaking indiscriminate noisiness for Wagnerian monumentality ; the " Waldweben " in " Siegfried " with its immaculate woodwind and horn solos ; the whole Act I of " Walkuere " with its careful phrasing and sensitive tonal balance, but not the pedestrian " Feuerzauber " with its gate-crashing glockenspiel. Frequently brass and woodwind did not blend properly, the former—especially at the lower borders of its tessitura— playing occasionally out of tune. The percussion section—although rhyth- mically precise—seemed to suffer from the cheap quality of some of its instruments. Throughout, Karl Rankl conducted with the utmost conscien- tiousness and care and with a sincerity of purpose that should have borne better fruit. Unfortunately his beat tends to be fussy, and his left hand is all too often high up in the air when it could be employed more profitably as a damper for overzealous trombones. Wagner's " Ring " undoubtedly benefits more from a less emotional and better balanced style of conducting, such as Weingartner adopted, whose " Ring " interpretation invariably achieved (what seemed denied to Rankl) a satisfactory blending of all orches- tral groups into one homogeneous whole.

H.F.R.

*I had to miss " Rheingold " on June 10th for a performance of Monte- verdi's " Orfeo " at Girton College, Cambridge on the same day. See p. 48.

TRISTAN : 29th June, 1950.

NEVER in my life which, however short, has been rich in *Tristan*s have I heard a Kurwenal that approximated to Paul Schoeffler's musical, vocal and histrionic realization, though the latter had to fight the producer's heavy opposition. To enlarge upon Flagstad's ever-developing virtues is unnecessary at this time of the day. It is in deep deference to them that I still think what I felt when I first heard her as a boy : that her phrasing, however naturally it emerges from her body, however magnificently sure it is of itself, is not always naturally —let's have it out : musically—conceived. A melodic curve, that is to say, will sometimes forget to descend ; the opposite of an upbeat (phrase)—the Germans use the telling word " abfallen "—will not be allowed to serve its dis-tensioning function : in fact, a feminine ending will suffer from a strong masculinity complex. Shacklock's promising Brangaene could greatly im- prove if someone told her that she tends to beat the bar with her body, com- plete with hands, head and, alas, throat. Svanholm's Tristan has not greatly changed since last year, though his acting has yet further improved : I thought his entry in the 1st act's fifth scene exceptionally impressive. But then the producer, Friedrich Schramm, spoilt it all by one of his incredibly stupid improvements upon Wagner : upon Isolde's near-rhetorical question " . . . warum ich dich da nicht schlug ? " Tristan was made to jump forward towards Isolde and to give a three bars' dumb show of an intense question mark (" Quite so, my dear Isolde, why for heaven's sake didn't you ? ? "), in flat contradiction of music and words. And while Schramm has now abolished Isolde's Blind Man's Buff game at the end of the 2nd Act to which I objected last year (*Music Review* X/3), Marke (Norman Walker) still enquired of the audience why they had betrayed him. It was, however, the last scene that was completely mismanaged : what, for Wagner's sake, is wrong with Wagner's stage directions ? The very end of the 2nd act, on the other hand, was produced with exceptional clarity. The orchestra, under Rankl's periodic- ally well-intentioned stick, was for the greater part a sorry sound, even where it was not technically deficient ; Mr. Joseph Shadwick, for example, contributed a café-inspired violin solo. The males of the Covent Garden Opera Chorus hardly emitted anything that could by any stretch of the term be described as a note, and an eminently intellectual section of the audience hardly said anything that betrayed recognition of a masterpiece : we suggest that next year there should be No Admission for Idiots.

The least one may ask of a daily newspaper is a report that is journalistically adequate, but *The Times* of June 30th commented upon the production without mentioning the producer.   H.K.

Gramophone Records

FIVE FACETS OF THE L.P.O.

No man may serve two masters, but many orchestras must serve many conductors, the more so in these modern times. Lucky the bands who manage to keep both their temperament and their temper amidst so many perplexing changes of direction. The L.P.O., playing music by Franck, Elgar, Mozart, Ravel and Verdi, have in nearly every instance found the right interpreter. Nobody could be more sympathetic than Franz André in doing justice not only to Franck but to Bürger, who supplied the literary framework for " Le Chasseur Maudit." (Decca AK 1485-6). Eduard van Beinum appears as a champion of Elgar, in a brilliant performance of " Cockaigne," the brass to be as much praised here as the woodwind were in the previous item. (Decca AX 296-7). Celibidache's version of the earlier G minor Symphony of Mozart shows the orchestra in classical trim, with spick-and-span phrasing and careful, well-timed rhythms. (Decca AK 2197-9). Jean Martinon takes over, quite rightly, for Ravel's suite " Le Tombeau de Couperin " : but if the Forlane is a Venetian Dance, should it race so ? Or are gondolas now propelled by engines ? (Decca AK 1838-9). The last of the five is Georg Solti, who brings off all the stage tricks in Verdi's Overture, " La Forza del Destino " : an operatic, as opposed to a concert performance. (Decca X 298).

Other Decca orchestral issues include contributions from Amsterdam, Paris and London. Brahms' First Symphony, under van Beinum, shows up the strong features of the Dutch orchestra, the performance being precise yet warm and flexible. Tempi are good throughout, and problems of interior balance in the last movement are nicely solved. (AK 1895-9). The two extracts from " Romeo and Juliet " by Berlioz are played complete (except for one small cut) by Münch and the Orchestra de la Société dCdCdP. The solo oboe could have been better in the " Reverie," but the strings are good, with a fine, keen tone. (AX 293-5). Nor is the oboe over-inspiring in Jorda's records of " El Amor Brujo," the orchestra being the National Symphony. The cellist, too, sounds unhappy in his 7/8 tune. The strong point here lies in the orchestral dynamics, which I suspect Jorda achieved by the sweat of his brow. This suite by de Falla is backed by an excerpt from " Iberia " by Albeniz—" El Puerto ". (AK 1332-4).   D.W.S.

SIBELIUS' SIXTH SYMPHONY

IF Sibelius ever wrote a romantic symphony, it is this work which most properly deserves the title. Appropriately has mellowed his characteristic austere orchestral texture with a harp and Beecham has done well to emphasise the part. Although divided into four movements the symphony has a continuity of thought which clearly foreshadows the organic whole of the seventh and much of its technical content was due to reappear in the seventh with added significance. There are two notable weaknesses. First, sequential padding which brings the music to a standstill. Second, trite harmonic clichés which banally obtrude. Sequence is the principal thematic device of the whole symphony.

The glory of the sixth symphony is its finely divided string writing, to which the strings of the Royal Philharmonic Orchestra do full justice—especially in the polyphonic opening, the grave antiphonal dialogue between upper and lower strings of the last movement, and the latter's final passionate flights. Beecham understands Sibelius' idiom profoundly and his performance is full of imaginative nuances. The recording is resonant and the performance well reproduced. (HMV DB.6640-6642).   E.N.R.

A dryish performance of Mozart's *Jupiter* by Boehm and the Vienna Philharmonic (H.M.V. C.3884/6) is no improvement on the existing Walter version from the same company. Only in the Minuet does Boehm get a rhythmic pulse that Walter doesn't. The tympani's quavers make themselves felt. Haydn's *London* Symphony by the London Philharmonic (Krips) (Decca AX.287/9) is the best set to date. Coarse orchestral playing of the Liverpool Philharmonic (Rignold) in the *Military* does not completely disfigure the startlingly original instrumentation of Haydn's second movement which should prove to the attentive ear that some idiosyncracies of the late 19th century Viennese school have very deep roots. (Col. DX.1623/5).

Janacek's *Sinfonietta* is very understandingly played by the Czech Philharmonic under Kubelik ; it needs some understanding, particularly the rather eccentric inflation of the brass section and consequent problems of instrumental balance. (HMV Special List C.7671/3). Mozart's C major oboe version (K.314) of the D major Flute Concerto is said to be arranged by Paumgartner. Edited would be more accurate a description. The miniature score (Boosey & Hawkes) could usefully be consulted on this point. Competent recording of an unremarkable performance from Rothwell and the Hallé conducted by Barbirolli ; the former's phrasing is not always all it might be. (HMV C.3954/5).

Altogether satisfactory performance and recording of Britten's *Variations on a Theme of Frank Bridge*, Op. 10, by Boyd Neel and the Boyd Neel String Orchestra. Now we are all convinced of its " brilliance," perhaps we can start considering the music. (Decca AK.2307/9).

Haydn's C Major Quartet, Op. 33 No. 3 (Bird), finely and intelligently played by the Koppel Quartet. They realise what most other Quartets don't—that the terseness of Haydn's style is almost in inverse proportion to the importance of his ideas. (Col. LX.1254/5).

Richard Strauss : Excerpts from *Elektra*, Op. 58, expertly sung by Welitsch, Schluter, Schoeffler and supporting cast, with the Royal Philharmonic conducted by Beecham. Virtually *Elektra's* closing scene. Since the opera is an organic growth and relies a good deal for its drama and effectiveness on a sense of first-to-last-note gathering of momentum and cumulative climax, this fragment is disappointingly fragmentary. The recording could be better. (HMV Special List DB.9393/6). More acceptable are the scenes from *Rosenkavalier* " The Presentation of the Silver Rose," (Schwarzkopf and Seefried) and the finale to Act II (Weber and Herrmann), both with the Vienna Philharmonic conducted anonymously but efficiently. Scoreless and unfamiliar listeners will have some difficulty in distinguishing Octavian from Sophie. (Col. LX.1225/7). Outstanding musically is the lamented Mario Cebotari's superb recording of "Es gibt ein Reich " from *Ariadne auf Naxos*, a great aria which shows Strauss still had something new to offer in voice-orchestra relationship after the *Salome/Elektra/Rosenkavalier* trinity. Vienna Philharmonic, nameless conductor. (HMV Special List DB.6914).

Frederick Fuller's Wolf *lieder—Epiphanias*, *Auf dem Gruenen Balkon* and *Ach, des Knaben Augen*—recommended for musicality, good diction, and good German. Daniel Kelly accompanies. (HMV C.3851).   D.M.

FAURÉ'S " LA BONNE CHANSON," Op. 61.

This recording atones for the English neglect of Fauré, the " ordered fantasy " of this song-cycle being ideally realised in a beautifully controlled performance by Sophie Wyss and Kathleen Long. Comparison with the Debussy and Ravel songs on the last side of this issue leaves Fauré's mastery undisputed. Recording is very good. (Decca AF.9414/18).   P.A.E.

Clues for the reviews below: DB—II.M.V.; DX, LX, and TX—Columbia ; F, K, X, and AX=Decca. Single asterisk : Recommended. Single asterisk in brackets : Recommended despite defects in performance and/or recording. Double asterisk in brackets : Strongly recommended despite such defects.

BEETHOVEN : Schnabel's and Fournier's Op. 102, No. 2 : The grudging recognition given to the 1st subject's *diminuendo*, the emphasis on the upbeat *a* in this theme's recapitulation, and the slow movement's premature first *crescendo*, are typical shortcomings in an often masterly interpretation. The defects of the discs are multiform (DB.6829-31) (**). Through a mostly rotten —harsh, shrill, and indistinct—recording, through Clifford Curzon's periodical nervousness (surest sign : notes which should be given more than their value are given less), through Szell's (LPO) neglect of the slow movement's " *un poco mosso*," the E♭ Concerto fights its way to the listener. What a towering masterpiece, whose every new hearing reveals how superficially one has hitherto understood it ! Where Curzon is good he is, of course, excellent (AX.282-6) (*). G major Concerto, Casadesus with Philadelphia under Ormandy : a ghastly set (LX.1198-1201). G major Romance, Tibor Varga with Philharmonia (c. Bernard) : The pitch of the factory sample I have received for review oscillates so strongly that I refuse to listen. What I heard, i.e. the opening double stoppings, are awkwardly phrased and in fact completely spoilt by an impossible *vibrato*. But then Beethoven is not in this place entirely free from blame, and the F major Romance would have been a better choice. (DX.1615). Gerard Souzay's baritone (L'Orchestre de la Société des Concèrts du Conservatoire de Paris, c. Edouard Lindenberg) wobbles through *In questa tomba oscura;* the *Air de Demetrio* from HANDEL'S *Berenice* with its well-sung quavers is more enjoyable, though the recording is ill-balanced (K.2290). SCARLATTI'S sonatas in D (Longo 461) and G minor (Longo 499) are better played (Jacqueline Blancard) than recorded (K.2247), while an excellent recording of the MENDELSSOHN Violin Concerto is marred by phraseological mistakes of van Beinum (LPO) and particularly Campoli, whose at times impressive execution includes, moreover, three attempts at re-composition, two of them stupid and outrageous (AX.290-2) (*). There are some ill-defined phrases, too, in Münch's largely commendable rendering (L'Orchestre de la Société des Concerts du Conservatoire de Paris) of the *Queen Mab* scherzo from BERLIOZ' *Romeo and Juliet* (X.281)*. WAGNER : *Todesverkuendung* from *Walkuere* with Flagstad, Svanholm, and Philharmonia under Boehm : Flagstad's accentuation is not immaculate (cf. " . . . *der scheidet vom Lebenslicht* "), nor her intonation as assured as usual (hear, for instance, the terribly sharp D♭ in "*Wotans Tochter reicht dir traulich den Trank !* "). Incidentally, she makes an unfortunate mistake on " *Dir Waelsung. . .* " (d″-d″ instead of d″♯-e″). While the difficult recording problems have not been solved, the set offers enough to produce a state of ecstasy in the receptive, not to speak of the understanding listener (DB.6962-3) (**). Love Duet from *Tristan* with Helen Traubel, Torsten Ralf, Herta Glaz, and the Metropolitan Opera Orchestra under Fritz Busch : Everything that was possible under the circumstances has gone wrong with the interpretation, execution and recording ; whereas for the concluding B major chord Fritz Busch shall for one year roast in hell (LX.1243-4). MOZART : Backhaus disappoints in K.331. The theme shows no trace of its *grazioso* character ; in point of fact it has 4 beats to the 6/8-bar. The first variation is snobbish, the third a piano teacher's, the fifth desultory. As a matter of principle, Backhaus rushes those continuations which introduce small ternary structures' middle sections. In the 8th bar of the minuet's second part he destroys a harmonic juncture by playing, both times, c″♯ ; I haven't seen the ms. but if Mozart did not put a natural he forgot it (DB. 6810-11). If you want to hear nine seconds of a top F♯ and some topmost A flats (a‴♭) and things, as emitted by the "German nightingale" (I believe that's what they call her) Erna Sack, buy JOSEF STRAUSS' badly recorded *Dorfschwalben in Oesterreich* and JOHANN STRAUSS' *G'schichten aus dem Wienerwald* on K.2270. And if you want to hear a flat top F, buy LX.1233 with Lily Pons " and orchestra " doing Rosina's Cavatina from the *Barber*. Not that it is fair to concentrate on this single note, for the rest isn't in tune either. OSCAR STRAUS is a commercial man with invention, but there is a longer way *From Strauss to Straus* (New Symphony Orchestra, c. Straus) than he appears to believe (K.2269). Cantor Salomon Stern is heard in (more or less) his own interesting religious improvisations : they require stylistic analysis and defy evaluation, except that they are perhaps too much beside good and bad and too little beyond. The labels have not been checked by someone who knows Hebrew (F.9266-9). H.K.

A considerable number of record reviews had to be held over.

Competition

MUCH ingenuity is devoted all the year round to solving the literary competitions of our more select weeklies. In introducing a kind of competition that calls upon musical knowledge as well as literary skill, we cannot claim to be " responding to a wide-felt demand "—but we should like to create such a demand for self-expression among our subscribers, and we shall welcome any suggestions for the development of this feature. We realise that a gap of three months between the setting of the problem and publication of the results may strain expectations to breaking-point, and even deter some from competing ; but we hope nevertheless that the competitors' ambition, curiosity—and healthy acquisitiveness—will prevail.

COMPETITION No. 1. Set by P.H.

Imaginary conversations, not exceeding 400 words, are invited between any one of the following pairs of composers :

(a) Bach and Handel in 1750.
(b) Beethoven and Schubert in December 1826.
(c) Wagner and Verdi in 1880.

A first prize of 3 guineas, two second prizes of 1 guinea each. Results and winning entry to be published in the autumn issue. Entries by September 25th, marked " Competition."

Correspondence

JOSEPH'S,
THE STREET,
TAKELEY.

June 23rd, 1950.

SIRS,—There is one sentence in the Spring issue of your journal which you ought not have passed for publication, i.e. on p. 277, paragraph 2 :

"The Hallé Orchestra . . . lacks . . . a conductor really worthy of its musicianship . . . ."

This is bunk, and mischievous bunk at that. I am not usually dogmatic to this extent ; but I saw a good deal of Barbirolli's work in the early stages of building a band of fair quality out of some of the rawest possible material. I have, literally, spent many hours at his rehearsals of Bruckner's Seventh and Strauss' *Don Quixote*. I can assure you and your Manchester correspondent that Barbirolli, so far from being unworthy of the orchestra, has in fact made it what it is. I know that both he and the band have their limitations, but let us have the thing in the proper perspective.

Yours sincerely,

GEOFFREY SHARP,
(Editor, *The Music Review*).

I agree, except that I take a yet more serious view of this quite incompetent notice. Owing to my function at the Florence Music Congress I did not see it prior to its publication, and it is my duty to act as a bad colleague and dissociate myself from it.—H.K.

HULME HALL,
VICTORIA PARK,
MANCHESTER 14.

July 23rd, 1950.

SIRS,—I think with orchestral performances you either judge them from absolute standards, involving taste and interpretation, as I did in the Hallé review Mr. Sharp refers to, or you judge them from relative standards involving questions of what is possible with the material in hand and how much conscientiousness has gone into rehearsing, as Mr. Sharp is doing. I would be last in casting any doubt on Sir John Barbirolli's great achievement in making the orchestra what it is. Expressions such as worth and unworthiness sometimes suggest pejorative meanings beyond the momentary intention. I would apologise for any bruised feelings that these words may have caused, reserving the judgment that in performance there are frequent signs of careless phrasing, tendencies toward sentimentality, and a lack of an integrating perspective of a work's organic development, symmetry and meaning. The playing now seems beyond the musical mind that informs and directs it. Give the Hallé a Beecham, Furtwaengler or a Koussevitsky and all would be more than well.

Yours sincerely,

P. J. COVENEY.

MUSIC SURVEY

(KATHLEEN LIVINGSTON   WILLIAM W. LIVINGSTON   DONALD MITCHELL)

VOL. III, No. 2   CONTENTS   DECEMBER, 1950

EDITORS :

DONALD MITCHELL
HANS KELLER

EDITORIAL BOARD :

ROBERT DONINGTON   PAUL HAMBURGER   E. D. MACKERNESS
H. B. RAYNOR   DENIS W. STEVENS   RALPH W. WOOD
CHARLES STUART   DENNIS DOBSON

EDITORIAL CORRESPONDENCE should be addressed to the EDITORS, MUSIC SURVEY, OAKFIELD SCHOOL, WEST DULWICH, LONDON, S.E.21. Annual Subscription, including postage, 11s. U.S.A. $2.50.

All enquiries relating to advertising space in this journal should be made to MUSIC SURVEY at the above address.

Editorial

EXCISIONS AND INCLUSIONS :

IN this issue we have been forced to hold over our normal Music and Book Reviews, certain Gramophone Record Reviews, and the *Film Music* feature. These excisions are due to the fact that we have received an unprecedented number of surveys of musical events both at home and abroad which, if their topicality is not to lose its point, must appear without delay. With regard to Record reviews we shall, in future, review fewer records at greater length. Very competent shorter notices of all new recordings are available in *The Gramophone* and *The Music Review* for instance, and *Music Survey* sees no sense in duplicating the good work done by its contemporaries in this field. Our record reviews will contain a separate technical report on recording standards beside detailed comments on performances and interpretations as well as, in the case of new music, on the scores themselves. The change over to the new style review may not be accomplished in one issue, but our next number will certainly make a start in that direction.

The March issue will include an article on Anton Webern by Humphrey Searle and a centenary piece on Vincent D'Indy by Norman Demuth : the postponed *Film Music* feature will deal with the " Harry Lime Theme."

TYPOGRAPHICAL :

No doubt it will have been noticed that in recent issues of the paper the percentage of small type used has substantially increased. Normally we reserve the smaller type for features and reviews and print our leading articles in (we hope) a clear 10pt. Times Roman. Nevertheless we have on occasions, for space considerations, been obliged to set a main article in the smaller type : an example is Paul Hamburger's dialogue in this issue. Had we printed this article in 10 pt. we should have had to divide the article into two parts : rather than inconvenience our readers in this manner and destroy the physical continuity of Mr. Hamburger's argument, we felt it preferable to subject them to the lesser evil of reading the whole dialogue in 8pt. This course is liable to result in issues which are typographically somewhat below the standard we and our printers set ourselves, but we trust our subscribers will appreciate the motive behind our seemingly erratic typography. Where an article may be harmlessly dissected, surgery shall intervene in the interests of readability of type.

COMPETITION :

The small number of entries received for the competition commenced in our last issue suggested that the period during which entries might be submitted was by no means long enough. We have, therefore, decided to reopen the competition and fix the new final date for receipt of entries at the 1st of February 1951. For the convenience of readers who may not have seen the original announcement we reprint the competition on p. 142 of this number. Past competitors need not, of course, re-submit their present entries, or devise new ones.

PUBLICATION DATES :

In order to avoid the Summer doldrums *Music Survey* will in future be published in March, June, September and December. This decision explains the (for once) deliberate time-lag in the publication of this number.

ERRATUM :

Music Survey III/1/50 p. 17 line 25: For "quartet" read "quintet."

Obituary :
George Bernard Shaw (1856—1950)

ACCLAMATIONS of Shaw usually embrace such clichés as " despiser of convention," " fearless denouncer," and so on. But his distinction as a music critic lay in the fact that before approaching the subject of music in a professional capacity he had given himself time to arrive at serious deliberations about Art and Life. In the process he evolved a critical vocabulary that was all his own. Consequently he never had any need to shelter himself behind the " technical " double-talk of professorial bumbledom. Shaw could recognise instinctively the living from the dead in the musical works that came under his notice : and he was equally skilful in detecting the difference between sound performances and shallow exhibitionism. How essentially *right* some of his enthusiasms turned out to be ! His book *The Perfect Wagnerite* (1898) is notable for being one of the least confusing dissertations on the question of Wagner's dramatic intentions. And the *Music in London* volumes (originally published in *The World* between 1890 and 1894 after Shaw had already done similar writings for *The Star*) have that inevitable honesty and economy of statement which usually characterises durable literature. There was no trickery about Shaw's prose style : he was above adopting that nauseating tone of knowing *politesse* which forms the staple currency of a mutual admiration society. His death therefore serves to bring home to us the extent to which criticism—of the Shavian standard—is in abeyance among the fraternity now deputed to undertake the kind of work he once did with such challenging mastery.   E.D.M.

A Marginal Critic of the 18th Century
By E. D. MACKERNESS

ACCORDING to Sir John Hawkins, the English translation of Francois Raguenet's *Parallele des Italiens et des Francais, en ce qui regarde la Musique et les Operas* (1702) was made by John Ernest Galliard. Hawkins also claimed that Galliard was the author of a *Critical Discourse upon Operas in England* which was appended to the English edition of that work, published in 1709. The Cambridge University Library(*) possesses a copy of the *Comparison* which contains some curious marginalia written in an eighteenth century hand by an individual to whom the names of both the French author and the English translator were unknown. The notes would appear to have been made at the request of a friend who wanted a candid opinion on the views expressed in the original text. They are obviously the work of a person whose general level of musical cultivation was high. And though expressions of impatience and disgust are frequent among them (e.g.: " This is all stuff," " Impertinent," " Mighty Witty," etc.), the general drift of the comments given is not without interest.

Many of these marginal jottings are taken up with an attempt to show how far the author of the *Comparison* (and also the writer of the footnotes which accompany the English version of it) is guilty of muddled thinking and deficient in musical knowledge. Thus when Raguenet tries to get away with the proposition that the French *operas* are better than the Italian ones because there are more bass voices to be found in France than in Italy, the annotator remarks : " Bass voices have certainly a very good effect in some compositions and I suppose the Italians are not wholly without them (and he does not say they are) . But supposing they had none the dispute in this place is of the Advantages of french musick wch does not turn upon theyr having more of one sort of voices than the other."

(*) References and quotations in this article are given by kind permission of the University Librarian, H. R. Creswick, Esq., M.A.

He censures other diverting irrelevances in the same way. And he writes off Raguenet's description of the Italians use of " cadential reconciliations " in dramatic situations with the words " All this is French tattle ! " Of the two styles of music mainly discussed, it is the Italian which most pleases him. He appears to have a considerable knowledge of many of the Italian composers : he knows Stradella, Merula, and can vouch for having seen works by Scarlatti " where he has varied his stile from very good wch is his usuall stile to very Bad." And to the footnote on page 31 dealing with Italian church music he adds this comment (after confessing that he does not know what the annotator means by Unison Ariettos) : " I don't doubt but Lelio Colista deserved to bee namd as a Composer & Gratiani : & Frescobaldi perhaps was as great a musitian as any of em."

Perhaps the most interesting parts of these marginalia are those which commend Purcell, by comparison with the Italian composers. The author of the *Critical Discourse* refers rather piously to the several " beautiful Strokes, composed by the late Famous Mr. *Henry Purcell*." Here the notes in the margin are " I will only·àdd to this that I have seen much Italian musick. And of all that wch ever came or could come to Mr. Purcells sight I never saw any thing but what I could have matchd with something of his as good att least." Earlier, speaking of choruses which Raguenet's English editor had characterised as " Interruptions," the author of the marginalia had observed : " Chorus's are out of fashion it may bee but any man that understands musick must certainly not think a Chorus of 5 or 6 parts finely managed such as one might name 20 of Mr. Harry Purcels, an Interruption. . . . " And then, criticising the laudation of two songs by Scarlatti given in a footnote to page 16, he writes : " I wonder how the annotator came to forgett mr. Purcels Cold scene when he was thinking of veder parmi wch is very good but not better than, what Power art thou." This reverence for Purcell provides fair confirmation (if such were needed) of a statement made in Allotson Burgh's *Anecdotes of Music*, Vol. III, page 381 (1813). Burgh is speaking of Daniel Purcell and the music prize for which he competed in 1702. " He appears, indeed, to have had little other merit than that of being brother to Henry Purcell, whose Music of all kinds was at that time in the highest favour throughout the kingdom."

The marginalia which relate to musical custom and the reputations of performers are amusing and occasionally outspoken. The footnote to page 42 represents the habit of beating time at the opera as having ceased only when Italian performers came into northern Europe. The marginal author writes : " The Reason of the Beating time att the opera att Paris and att those of Mr. Purcells was because the Instrumental musick is of more parts than that of the Italian operas generally is and the Chorus consisting of as many beeing performed by numbers it woud bee Impossible that they should come in Just to the time without such an help The Italians beat time to theyr church musick for the same reason." Of Corelli his opinion—at variance with the usual accounts—is that he is " a Conceited fellow half madd ffor all he is so great a master." And of the captivating singer Nicolino of Naples : " Nicolino is undoubtedly a wonderful master but surely the Annotator does not commend him like one that understood his value A ladys footman that reads Romances or Plays would commend him just soe in the 12 penny Gallery "(†). Of the soprano La Rochoix, whose praises are sung so highly by Raguenet, the annotator says : " La Rochoir was a little woman (as I remember) with a good voice sung the disagreeable French manner but was certainly one of the best actresses that ever came upon the Stage not inferior to Mrs. Barry her self."

The footnotes to the English version of the *Parallele* were obviously the work of someone other than Raguenet. But certain dates and facts set forth in them indicate that they can hardly have been by Galliard either : for reference is made to the author's having been present at performances in Italy which took place when Galliard was still a child. As for the authorship of the *Critical Discourse* which follows the *Comparison*, the writer of the marginalia in the Cambridge University copy (commenting on the remarks passed on Thomas Clayton's opera *Rosamond*) will have it that " This seems to bee writt by a frenchman ! " The mention of Clayton's operatic pieces gives us a fair idea of the annotator's critical position. The author of the *Critical Discourse* comes down heavily on *Rosamond*, and the way it disappointed the town. In the margin we find this note : " This very town whose judgement the Author has complimented several times did not stick to commend Arsinoe(‡) above poor mr. Henry Purcells Performances, Tho it damned Rosamond, wch (not with standing this author) I think better much than Arsinoe tho far from good." The author had censured Clayton for beginning his overture with an Allegro and ending it with an Adagio, " without Sense, Reason, or Harmony."

(†) The upper or twelve-penny galleries of theatres at this time were the cheapest part of the house. " In contemporary Prologues and Epilogues," notes Montague Summers in his edition of Dryden's *All for Love,* " there are disdainful references to the denizens of this lofty tire."

(‡) *Arsinoe* (1705) was also by Thomas Clayton.

The marginal comment on this runs : " There may be .... occasions where it may bee as sensible reasonable & harmonious to begin an overture with an allegro as an Adagio." The writer of the *Critical Discourse* is particularly severe on what he calls the Swiss operas, which he thinks are the most unlikely to please the town. This, presumably, is a reference to the works of Martin Heidegger, whose *Thomyris* and *Clotilde* are singled out as particularly unsuitable. It should be observed here, perhaps, that the tone of the *Critical Discourse* is petulant in the extreme, and often directly abusive. It is not surprising, therefore, that in the final marginal jotting our anonymous annotator should take a last fling at the author for not fulfilling the intentions advertised on his title-page. " Woud not any one have thought," he says, " that this promissor magno Hiatu would have proposed something for the Improvement of musick in England Instead of that hee has been labouring all along pro viribus to prove that we must have an Italian Opera (wch wee knew before) and that wee cant have an English one (wch I dont know yet) and by his spleen to Swiss musick that wee must naturalize all forreign musick but Protestant. I was never so tird in my life."

These marginalia contain one or two fragments of technical discussion which perhaps have a pedantic interest(§). But it would be absurd to claim that they are of much importance in comparison with the main substance of Raguenet's famous *Parallele* itself. The age in which they were written, however, was (as the text books always tell us) one of incessant wrangling among musical partisans. And so the practical logic which this annotator brings to bear on the reading of his text repays examination. Later in the eighteenth century we find William Jackson of Exeter (**) warning us that an exclusive preoccupation with Handel's idiom is making it hard for English composers to speak out in their own native musical language. Purcell was explicit about his imitation of the most famed Italian masters. The author of these marginal embellishments to the *Comparison between the French and Italian Music* (probably a non-professional musician) shows a certain spirit of resistance in the face of musical *imposition* by foreign practitioners which contrasts favourably with the attitude displayed by those members of the " town " audience in his time who accepted indiscriminately all that the Continental virtuosi had to offer.

(§) On page 35, for instance, he refers to " admirable passages closes, etc., wch in English are called Takings (sic) by those that profess musick. . . . " The art of *taking* or resolving discords is discussed in Playford's *Introduction to the Skill of Musick* : see page 120 of the 1700 edition.

(**) In his *Observations on the Present State of Music in London* (1791).

Notes on the Statue Scene in Don Giovanni
BY LUIGI DALLAPICCOLA

" OVER and above the absolute and individual greatness of artists, there exists a greatness of a somewhat special kind : that of those who, endowed with particularly keen sight, not only created works of aesthetic perfection, but were able to catch a glimpse of the future and throw over bridges towards it . . . " I wrote these lines in an issue of the Florentine paper *Mondo* dated 21st April, 1945.

At that time I came across an article by Heinrich Jalowetz in the *Musical Quarterly* of October, 1944, entitled " On the Spontaneity of Schoenberg's Music " ; in it, he pointed out how Mozart, in the development section of the finale of the Symphony in G minor, had made use of a series of ten different notes :

Ex.1

Of course, it did not need Heinrich Jalowetz's acute observation to convince me of the unparalleled audacity of Mozart's genius ; while still an adolescent, I had been amazed by the asymmetric effect of the opening bars of the Overture to *Il Seraglio*, created by a succession of phrases of 8 plus 6 plus 8 plus 10 bars. Later, studying Arnold Schoenberg's *Harmonielehre*, I found certain surprising passages in the Symphony in G minor underlined with particular emphasis :

Ex.2

Nor had I, for my part, failed to observe with what scrupulous care Mozart had applied himself to the setting of the syllables of certain verses ; one case amongst many is to be found in the aria " Madamina. Il catologo è questo."

When Leporello enumerates for the second time his master's mistresses,

>   In Italia seicento e quaranta,
>   In Almagna duecento e trent'una,

it would have seemed to Mozart too obvious, perhaps too easy, to follow in his music the regular, mechanical stresses of the verse. (How many interminable and identical strings of octosyllables are there in the operas of his predecessors and contemporaries, and how many do we find in those of his successors !) And so, suddenly, in a flash, he begins the third line

>   Cento in Francia, in Turchia novant'una,

on the strong beat of the bar. Thus, by means of a trifle light as a ir, the whole page is flooded with a new light.

However, Heinrich Jalowetz's observation made such an impression on me that I decided, although I was no specialist in the study of Mozart, to write a few notes on a passage sung by the Commendatore in the finale of *Don Giovanni ;* a passage, which, both on the written page and in its realization in the theatre, can only be regarded as an anticipation of what in our day is called " expressionism " :

Ex.3 IL COMMENDATORE :   Ri - sol - vi ?   Ver - ra - !

It would be superfluous to relate how many contributions to the development of writing, language and expression, have had their far-off origins in the necessities of technical organisation, and to insist on the fact that, in art, every stroke of the pen is subordinated to the most diverse conditions[1].

Thus, if Domenico Scarlatti has written, in one of his sonatas, the following passage :   Ex.4

it does not in the least mean that he has consciously (and for the first time in history, as far as I know) made use of the whole-tone scale. It is the fundamental rhythm, clearly established beforehand at the beginning of the piece, which forced the composer to write these notes and no others, in order to fill the existing space between the D flat and the C. Of course it is obvious that, having pointed out the supreme interest of such an extraordinary passage, and indicated its aesthetic consequences, I am unable to state definitely whether Scarlatti realized the implications of his boldness. Personally, however, I am inclined to believe that he was at least vaguely conscious of them.

Let us take another look at the passage in the *Harmonielehre*, where Schoenberg, with his inimitable perspicacity, comments on the much-discussed beginning of the fifth movement of the *Pastoral* Symphony :   Ex.5

" That Beethoven was clearly conscious of this anomaly is shown by the fact that his sense of form has led him to oppose to it a further anomaly, as if to *resolve it*, and with perfect congruence :

namely, the entrance of the tonic harmony on the weak beat of the bar, which rhythmically, is so extraordinarily efficacious."

If we now apply the same method to the passage of Domenico Scarlatti quoted above (Ex. 4), we shall find that the first irregularity (that is, the use of the whole-tone scale) is immediately opposed by another : the three notes which follow the afore-mentioned scale are independent of it ; thus we encounter another series of diverse notes. The second irregularity is intended to counter-balance the first. In passing, I will also mention the fact that the second part of the sonata does not begin in the dominant.

Now the passage in *Don Giovanni* (Ex. 3) is also fully justified in its aesthetic consequences ; but this is a subject which has never even been touched on. However, before proceeding further, I must first clear up a point on which I have reflected for a long time. *The Commendatore*, to my way of thinking, *is the protagonist of the opera.*

As is well known, Soren Kierkegaard has not the slightest doubt that the protagonist is Don Giovanni himself: " Except for the Commendatore, all the characters stand in a certain erotic relation-ship to Don Giovanni. He has no power over the Commendatore, because the latter represents conscience ; all the others, however, are in his power. Elvira loves him, which puts her in his power ; Anna hates him, which puts her in his power ; Zerlina fears him, which puts her in his power ; Ottavio and Masetto are linked to him by bonds of kinship, and the ties of blood are strong." (Kierkegaard, *Don Giovanni.*)

In any case, it is worthy of note that the Commendatore is recognized as having a place apart. But even more significant is the following passage : " The music suddenly makes of him something much more than a mere individual : his voice is amplified to the point where it becomes the powerful voice of a spirit." (*op. cit.*)

But the Commendatore is not the protagonist merely because he represents spirit, conscience. From the *musical* point of view he is the protagonist because, appearing in the introduction and in the final scene, he fixes the two points on which is erected that great arch which is the construction of *Don Giovanni*. (The apex of the arch is the scene of the masks.) His two utterances and his " Yes ! " in the Graveyard Scene are only an introduction to the final scene, similarly as the *Andante* which follows the fall of the fatally wounded Commendatore is only a pendant to the introduction.

He is the protagonist, then, and above all because he constitutes the law which dictates the musical construction of the opera. One cannot fail to notice that the Commendatore falls *to the same chord of the diminished seventh* which we hear again at the moment in which the Statue makes its entrance (*see diagram*).

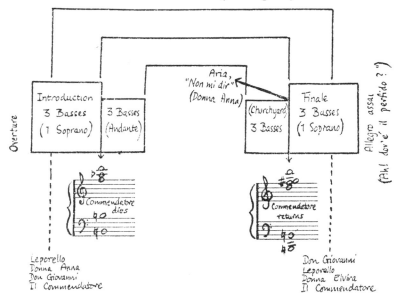

" But Donna Anna's aria," it will be justly objected, " the aria ' Non mi dir, bell' idol mio,' comes between the graveyard scene and the finale." It is precisely this aria which caused Berlioz to pen words of fire. "Je veux parler de l'allegro de l'air de soprano (No.22) au second acte, air d'une tristesse profonde, ou toute la poésie de l'amour se montre éplorée et en deuil, mais ou l'on trouve, néanmoins, vers la fin du morceau, des notes ridicules et d'une inconvenance tellement choquante, qu'on a peine de croire qu'elles aient pu échapper à la plume d'un pareil homme. Donna Anna semble là essuyer ses larmes et se livrer tout d'un coup à d'indécentes bouffoneries . . . Il m'était difficile de pardonner à Mozart une telle énormité. Aujourd'hui, je sens que je donnerais une partie de mon sang pour effacer cette honteuse page . . . " [2].

And in a note at the foot of the page : " Je trouve même l'épithete de *honteuse* insuffisante pour flétrir ce passage. Mozart a commis là contre la passion, contre le sentiment, contre le bon goût et le bon sens, un des crimes les plus odieux et les plus insensés que l'on puisse citer dans l'histoire de l'art."[3]

It is my firm conviction, however, that Berlioz attached excessive blame to the *vocalises* of Donna Anna (let us admit that they stand in the greatest contrast to the state of mind of the woman who loves and yet hates Don Giovanni). I think I can guess, on the other hand, what it was that he found so unbearable (although he did not realize it) : it was the point at which the aria No. 22 is inserted in the opera. Berlioz was not aware that Mozart's error was one of *construction* (that the aria may well have been written at the last moment for some prima donna or other ?) and that the same piece, at another point in the opera, would not have had such a sinister effect. But, ir˙ ˌrtcd between the Graveyard Scene and the finale, it interrupts the action which is driving towards its inevitable conclusion, and seriously unbalances the total architecture of the work (*see diagram*).

I personally maintain that, when this aria is omitted from performances of *Don Giovanni*, the greatest service will have been rendered to the public which comes to the theatre to rejoice in a masterpiece.

It will be seen, then, that the Commendatore falls and rises to the same chord of the diminished seventh. All the rest, the whole opera, is a parenthesis ; the most beautiful and delightful parenthesis in the history of opera, but still a parenthesis. Ferruccio Busoni, I remember reading, once observed that the character of Don Giovanni is already, in the libretto, a little cold. It is true that Don Giovanni is not the character in the opera on whom most emphasis is laid ; this arises from the fact that he is really the evil genius of the Commendatore. We are witnessing, in fact, a parenthesis in life : Don Giovanni is damned from the very moment in which he kills the Commendatore. From that moment not one of his amorous enterprises reaches a happy ending. And we see him as the prey, around which a circle of pursuers draws ever closer and closer.

No surprise should be felt that the Commendatore, the mysterious protagonist, is led to express himself in a manner so exceptional for his time (Ex. 3), at the culmination of the great drama, in the scene which has never been surpassed or equalled by any of the great masters of music in the theatre : the Commendatore is a being from beyond the grave, and his mode of expression cannot be that of other men.

But perhaps it was not only considerations of an aesthetic and transcendental nature which led Mozart to his extraordinary innovation : perhaps it will be necessary to appeal to *technical and practical considerations*.

Mozart has arrived at the culmination of the drama, where it is rushing headlong to its conclusion. The characters must now, more than ever, be drawn with the utmost precision. The least imperfection, at this point, would bring about the failure not only of the scene in question but of the whole opera. Mozart, we know, considered that the delineation of character must be based above all on the human voice. But in the Statue Scene, the three characters are *three basses*, and that means that the composer lacked that fundamental and principal means of psychological characterization: diversity of vocal timbre.

Everyone knows what this diversity signified for the great masters of music in the theatre. If we examine the original sketches of *Rigoletto*, we see how Verdi, in the duet " Si, vendetta, tremenda vendetta," having noted in full the baritone melody and reached the point where Gilda joins in, contented himself with writing :—

Verdi did not even write the resolution I have added in brackets. He left the phrase incomplete, with the simple note : *repeat the motive.* His phenomenal instinct as man-of-the-theatre told him that the change of tonality (Rigoletto, A flat major ; Gilda, D flat major) and, above all, the change of vocal timbre, would suffice to infuse the page with the sense of a sharp blade thrust deeply into the flesh— an effect more than sufficient for the complete musical and dramatic realization of the scene.

But for Mozart it was a question of differentiating three characters, moreover in the most delicate and crucial moment of his opera, without being able to count on the perspective which different vocal timbres establish naturally. A desperate problem, if there ever was one in the theatre.

Let us see how he came to grips with the problem, and solved it.

Of the three characters, the one which causes least anxiety is that of Leporello. And Mozart relies on the ' parola intonata ' which had already rendered inestimable service to the composers of *opere buffe* and *drammi giocosi.*

By this means, the differentiation of Leporello from the other two basses is established ; he now stands out with absolute clarity.

Don Giovanni, unlike his servant, needs the orchestra for his characterization. In the whole opera, there is only a single moment in which the Don, usually imperturbable and dominating, seems to waver : the moment in which the Statue appears on the scene. What has happened to Don Giovanni, confronted with the apparition of the SPIRIT ? What has he become, this man who has laid siege to, and overcome, two thousand and sixty-five women, if Leporello's catalogue is correct ? :

Don Giovanni hardly manages to stammer out " Non l'avrai giammai creduto " ('Tis an honour unexpected), and it is the orchestra, with its syncopated movement, which gives us the idea of fear, the fear which freezes, not that which finds relief, melodramatically, in a cry..

Don Giovanni is aware of his momentary weakness, and is ashamed of it. This becomes quite clear if we observe how the passage quoted, heavy with anguish (Ex. 8), returns at the end of the dialogue with the Commendatore, and more particularly at the words ' A torto di viltate tacciato mai saro ! ' (Shall it be said of me, then, a coward's part I played ?).

Don Giovanni needs to reassert himself, to wipe out his shame. And he is not slow to do so. ' Ho fermo il core in petto. Non ho timor verro ! ' (I know what I am doing. I fear you not, I'll come) :

If just now I pointed out the sudden weakness of the man, confronted with the apparition of the spirit, it must be recognized that his fresh metamorphosis is equally surprising, if not more so. The " young and extremely licentious nobleman," according to Da Ponte's description, suddenly turns into a hero. Don Giovanni has never been so great as at this moment. A man moulded of clay, he has never understood anything that was not of this earth. Perhaps he has succeeded in dominating the earthly scene so completely, only because all that concerns the spirit has remained for him, as it were by his very nature, outside his ken.

The musicians play at his table. The third and last operatic excerpt intended to enliven his meal, is the " Non piu andrai, farfallone amoroso " from *Figaro* (but no longer in the original tempo—*allegro* ; no longer in the bright tonality of C major !).

Leporello, who is competent in matters of music (or would Don Giovanni have turned and asked him ' Che ti par del bel concerto ? ' —' What do you think of this fine music ? ') asserts that he knows this strain only too well.   This coincidence, a most strange and certainly not a casual one, escapes Don Giovanni.   " Non piu andrai, farfallone amoroso " (Now your days of philandering are over) is the musicians' burden.   Don Giovanni does not realize that it is the first of the three warnings which come to him from beyond.

The musicians, then, write on the wall, as it were, the three words which appeared to Belshazzar.   But if they express themselves somewhat cryptically, Donna Elvira adds a further warning, when she enters and implores the man she loves so much to change his way of life.   Don Giovanni once more remains insensible. And even the appearance of the Statue does not succeed in convincing him that it is something more than human.   With his terrible " No !", he stains himself with the sin for which there is no pardon.   Don Giovanni has persevered deliberately in final impenitence. But his gesture is such that, in damnation, he will not be alone. A great brother awaits him : Capaneus[4].

The Commendatore is differentiated from both Don Giovanni and Leporello by his vocal line, which has the character of an arioso: his declamation abounds in leaps of an octave and unusual intervals,

which, as the action proceeds in a continual crescendo, become more and more difficult and extraordinary :

until we arrive at the passage (Ex. 3) in which I claim to have discovered the first example of expressionism in the theatre.

As is well-known, expressionistic music has habitual recourse to the widest intervals, and it is to this that we owe the discovery of the peculiar *tension* which exists between the most widely separated sounds.   That the interval of the *tenth* is now felt to be something very different from (I would say *independent of*) the interval of the *third*, should no longer require a lengthy demonstration.   However, those who still speak today (even though they base their views on ancient and famous treatises) of the interval of the *third or tenth* should try replacing the two *tenths* of the Commendatore (Ex. 3) by *thirds*.   The tension contained in the wider interval will be immediately destroyed.

96

There is, finally, one further particular which it seems to me indispensable to set in its true light.

During the whole scene, right up to the *Piu stretto*, the declamation of the Commendatore is underlined, with a precision I cannot believe to be purely fortuitous, by the inexorable rhythm which resounds in the orchestra :

If certain typically expressionistic composers have conceived the idea of a *ritmo principale* (Alban Berg's ' Hauptrhythmus ' in *Lulu* and the Violin Concerto) as an essential *musical* element throughout an entire composition, this ' Hauptrhythmus ' has found already, in the scene in *Don Giovanni* to which I have drawn attention, a most complete and convincing aesthetic and technical application.

From this, I believe it to be not entirely due to chance that in this very scene we find the first example of expressionism in opera. Expressionism, the culmination and ultimate experience of romanticism, is already contained, in a nutshell, in that utterly romantic scene, the finale of *Don Giovanni*.

(Translated by Deryck Cooke)

(1) " Ainsi j'étais déja arrivé à cette conclusion que ne sommes nullement libres devant l'oeuvre d'art, que nous ne la faisons pas à notre gré, mais que, préexistant à nous, nous devons, à la fois parce qu'elle est nécessaire et cachée et comme nous ferions pour une loi de nature, la découvir." (Proust, *A la recherche du temps perdu* : *XV, Le temps retrouvé*.)

(" Thus I had already reached the conclusion that we are in no way free in the matter of art ; that we do not create it according to our own will ; it is pre-existent, and we, because it is necessary and yet hidden, must, as we would do in the case of a law of nature, discover it.")

(2) " I refer to the allegro section of the soprano aria (No. 22) in the second act, an aria of intense sadness, in which all the poetry of love is poured out in tears and lamentations, but in which, nevertheless, towards the end of the piece, such ridiculous and shockingly inappropriate sounds occur that one can scarcely believe they could have escaped from the pen of such a man. Donna Anna seems suddenly, at that point, to dry her tears and indulge in coarse buffoonery . . . I found it difficult to forgive Mozart such an enormity. To-day, I feel I would give some of my blood to expunge that shameful page . . . "

(3) " Even the adjective ' shameful ' seems to me insufficient to blast that passage. In it Mozart has committed, against passion, against feeling, against good taste and common sense, one of the most hateful and senseless crimes that can be quoted in the history of art."

(4) Capaneus is one of the figures in Dante's Inferno. He was one of the " Seven against Thebes " ; climbing the wall of the city, he boasted that no one could stop him, not even Jove himself, and was struck by a thunderbolt. Dante placed him in the seventh circle of the Inferno (that of those who defied God) and put into his mouth words of contemptuous defiance and impenitence. [Translator's note.]

[We are indebted to the Editor of *La Rassegna Musicale*, Rome, for permitting us to reprint this article from his journal (April, 1950) ; we must also thank Signor Dallapiccola for his co-operation, and last, but not least, Mr. Deryck Cooke for his skilful translation.—EDS.]

Mainly about Britten

By PAUL HAMBURGER

A : . . . . so you find that there are passages in Britten which one cannot explain to oneself, or even analyse to any advantage ?

B : Yes. I have often listened to certain pieces which very clearly come from Purcell, and somehow I felt that this is more than a past. . . .

A. : Pastiche ? Oh, surely . . . .

B : No, no . . . , what I meant to say is : This is not just how a composer of Purcell's turn of mind would compose in the twentieth century, there is a personal note to . . . .

A : Come, come, you would surely allow Britten a personality of his own ? Like Brahms relating to Schumann, or Wolf to Wagner, you know ?

B : Of course ! What I mean is, there is in Britten's music a personal note of a *special kind.* Something, how shall I say . . . , unprecedented, something which convinces one immediately ; and although you may rack your brain to find the musical tradition to which it tags on, yet you cannot find it.

A : But you were just speaking of Purcell. And what about all the others ? What about Mozart, Mahler, Berg, the modern English School ? It should be easy to see how an eclectic composer fits—quite legitimately I will admit—into the history of music.

B : That's just the puzzling thing about it. Somehow it isn't a question of style. When you hear a passage in Brahms which comes from Schumann, you know at once that Schumann could not have written this, but also that it could not have been written before Schumann. But with Britten and Purcell, or Britten and Mahler, you may find passages that could have been written by either, save for one tiny birthmark, an interval, a rhythm, an odd note, which stamps them indelibly as the property of one or the other. Or again, it may only be the place of that passage in the entire work. The position here is rather the one of Mozart to Haydn, or Bruckner to Wagner.

A : So the meaning of music is altered by traits that either defy analysis, or else whose impact is greater than can be proved analytically ?

B : Yes. And this in spite of the score openly brandishing its family tree, for everyone to see.

A : Well, perhaps I can help out here. There seems to be in Britten a marked difference between style, and meaning or content.

B : But isn't the one the sensual realisation of the other ?

A : Not quite. That is, strictly philosophically, yes. But not psychologically. You see, you can connote styles rationally, if you are a scholar of music. If you are a good listener you can, to the same end, connote, or understand, styles by your unconscious, or semi-conscious memories of music. But the content of music, that is, the meaning of each single, concrete work in its entirety, is ineffable, and immanent in its complete form, and that is all one can say about it.

B : If I get you, you hold that our understanding of a composer's idiom, of what is, as it were, his temporal language, works by unconscious or semi-conscious comparisons, or even by comparisons on the notional level. But if the contents of music themselves cannot be compared, how can we understand them ?

A : Oh, yes, they can be compared, though not rationally, but instinctively, by the full use of our entire aesthetic personality : what they called in the eighteenth century our " sensibility." Only, they tried hard in those days to overlook its transcendental aspect.

B : How does this comparison, or understanding, work ?

A : It works in two ways : by similarity, or by contrast. All things that need sorting out are sorted out by this method. If you sort out the contents of a sewing-box you can line up all the buttons according to similarity and size : these would be the conservative composers, recognised and ordered according to class of musical content. On the other hand, the hooks and eyes would be recognised by their contrasting shape and would complement each other when put together. These would be the revolutionary composers and those against whom they revolt (though the latter might be conservative : here our sewing-box lets us down). The understanding of *revolutionary* contents will take the form of association by apodictic contrast to something known. But just as this way of sorting leaves out of consideration the weight of the buttons and hooks, so our musical classification says nothing about either rank or style of these composers. The later Stravinsky, for instance, while his style is still sufficiently revolutionary, creates contents that cotton on—excuse sewing-box language !—to the classics. Or take Haydn : in his match v. P. E. Bach & Co., he cribbed the style of his antagonists, but his musical meanings rise up against rococo-music. But then again, style and content may coincide : in Schoenberg v. the Rest, both the letter and the spirit fight on the barricades.

B : And where does Britten fit in here ? Is he a button or a hook ?

A : Britten, and a number of others, do not fit in here. To be sure, they are also in the sewing-box—it's all one world. They are the odd objects in the box : the thimble, the pin-cushion, the scissors—the things which, though no better than any single button or hook, occur only once and are unlike those others and unlike each other. Musically speaking : their styles may be conservative, or revolutionary, just as the material of the thimble may be the same as that of a hook, but their contents cannot be connoted even instinctively for lack of other comparable contents. A savage coming across our sewing-box could form the notion " buttons " from seeing a number of them, but he could never form the notion " thimble " from seeing only one.

B : Well then, we all live in this musical box of yours. There is no outside for us. So how can we understand these—er—unhistorical composers ?

A : Unhistorical is just the word. We must understand their musical contents as we understand everything that is outside our space-time perception : by direct insight, or divination. But I hasten to add that the contents *per se* of conservative and revolutionary music are just as much outside space-time, that is, they are also non-verbal and immanent in themselves. Only their understanding by us takes the form of a comparison or dialectical progression, while dialectical understanding is not possible in the case of the latter class of music for lack of a *tertium comparationis*.

B : What would you call this third class of musical contents ?

A : I would call it hermetic music.

B : What, just like a sealed bottle of fruit ?

A : If you like. Or again, like the hermetic rites of the Freemasons, intelligible only to the initiated. Note, by the way, that not only Britten, but also the hermetic composer Mozart—whom I name in the same breath just for this quality, not in order to assess Britten's rank prematurely—was in his own time accused of logistic practices although his music does, in fact, more than that of other composers, demand an understanding of an extra-logical kind.

B : Has this classification of musical contents, as distinct from styles, been attempted before ?

A : Not to my knowledge. But it has always been in the air and has given cause for some misunderstandings.

B : Such as ?

A : Some people believe, though not in so many words, that revolutionary music should be a *priori* superior (or inferior) to conservative music, or, more subtly, that both conservative and revolutionary music should be superior to hermetic music since they are founded in the dialectic process of Life—with a capital " L ". This is Moscow's musical dilemma. The answer is, of course, that the musical contents of Bach, Haydn and Mozart—the conservative, the revolutionary, and the hermetic—are equally immanent, and that only the form of understanding differs as between the first two and the last.

B : Any other misconceptions ?

A : Well, one concerns us here in connection with Britten. Some hermetic composers are invariably called eclectics. The confusion of style and contents again. Even when speaking of style I should say that the hermetic composer is no more an eclectic than the conservative in his affirmative, or the revolutionary in his negative assimilation of models. But in the absence of these contentual associations which would carry the understanding by way of similarity or apodictic contrast, an unconscious feeling of fear is bound to develop in the listener ; a fear which will be pleasurably relieved at the recognition of a model, while taking its unconscious revenge by denigrating the provider of this relief. Any obvious eclecticism will always be picked out by the frightened listener with a broad grin.

B : Sounds very Freudian to me.

A : So it is. Here is an example from real life. The other day, I played and sang some of the *John Donne* Sonnets to a tenor who had so far found all Britten's vocal music " unnatural, concocted and written

100

against the voice." My own croaky singing gave him an amused re-assurance of superiority which Pears naturally cannot provide, so that, his unconscious fear of these songs assuaged, he found them " much better than he thought they were, in fact, quite extraordinary."

B : I hope his enthusiasm will last. . . . But now that we have mentioned Britten's songs—he's called a vocal composer, isn't he ? In fact, operas and songs are his main line. How does that agree with the hermetic quality of his music ? Why is he inspired by the word, the vehicle of dialectic history, when what you call the hermetic quality of his meanings even prevents their being compared to the meanings of other composers?

A : If you'll listen to me, I'm going to show you some strong musical and psychological reasons for Britten's love of the word.

B : Well ?

A : But first I must tell you that the musical meanings of Bach, Schubert and Wagner are not any less immanent, nor do they any the less signify themselves and nothing else, through being wedded to a text.

B : Not even if it is a bad text ?

A : No. Some people even say that this is the ideal case. I do not agree with those musical voluptuaries, but I do hold that if a piece of vocal music has the immanent meaning which every healthy musical organism has, then bad poetry can do it no harm.

B : Good poetry must have an immanent meaning too, then ? And is this linked up with its form ?

A : Yes. A poem has two meanings : a communicative and an artistic one. The communicative sense cannot be excluded from poetry, and it is, according to Paul Valéry, the main business of the poet to establish a real relationship between it and the artistic meaning. But this latter is as immanent as the meaning of music, and, as in music, it is sensually incarnated in the poem's entire form, together with its members.

B : And you think that only good poetry should be set to music ?

A : Yes and no. I am quite satisfied with the Bach cantatas for what they are, that is: superb music; but Wolf's Goethe songs are in a different category of art which has its own musico-poetic laws. Wolf, in contra-distinction to Bach, considers a poem neither a mere communication, to be set to music pictorially, nor the vague instigation for writing an intra-musically satisfying form. Far from " setting a poem to music " he chooses an immanent musical meaning from the store accessible to him to be mirrored in an immanent poetical meaning from the vastly larger store of world literature.

B : But this surely never happens in opera ?

A : In opera and oratorio, the word-music problem is, in view of the more extended form, different from that in song. Let us confine ourselves to songs. Schubert in his touching modesty, did not always write " songs " in our strict sense of " an immanent poetic meaning mirroring itself in an immanent musical meaning." But often he did.

B : How does the composer take his choice in this mirroring process ?

A : We do not know yet. Much too little is as yet known about the common ground of all arts but one thing we do know because it happens on the rational level, and it is this : in the same way as the immanent sense (or entire form) of a poem is mirrored in the immanent sense (or entire form) of the music, so its communicative sense will be mirrored in, or rather translated into, the actual style of the music, with its symbols for action in space and time.

B : Very interesting. And now, shall we have a cup of tea ?

A : By all means, but we still have to see how the conservative, revolutionary and hermetic composer each deal with the word-music problem ; and after that we have to find our way back to Britten.

B : All right, but make it snappy. I want to get back to Britten.

A : Very good, Sir.—The conservative and revolutionary composer will, by affinity of spirit, turn to the poetry in the main stream of literature, including, of course, those revolutionary poets who, by having successors, became part of that main stream. Schubert's Heine settings, for instance, are the mutual mirroring of two revolutionary *contents* while the style of poetry and music is conservative. For the listener, the added poetical content (always meaning the form as a whole) will further strengthen those instinctive connotations which, as we said, are the basis for the understanding of conservative and revolutionary music. Now, as to the hermetic composer. . . .

B : Do tell me which composers fall into that class ?

A : I consider that the following have, either always or on occasion, produced what I call hermetic musical meanings: Purcell, Mozart, Beethoven (last period only), Chopin (sometimes), Bruckner (throughout), Mussorgsky, Berg (but not Schoenberg) and Britten.

B : But how can you place Chopin and Bruckner. . . .

A : I am sorry we can't go into that now. We shall have to stick to our point and disregard for the present the instrumental writers as well as the operas of Mozart, Berg and Britten. Strictly according to our definition of " song," we shall also have to disregard Purcell and Mussorgsky because, owing to the inferior quality of most of the poetry they set, it is not their word-music meaning, but only the meaning of their music that is hermetic. It turns out that Britten's songs afford, if not indeed the first, at least the clearest example of a hermetic composer's relationship to poetry. This again is not in itself a measure of Britten's rank as a composer ; it only means that Britten, almost in spite of his musical gift, is cultured enough to fall for first-rate poetry only. In consequence there is in his songs no superiority of either words or music, no dialectical pull from the one to the other, no slavish adherence of the music to the single turn of phrase, nor complete disregard of poetry ; but the immanent meaning (or form) of the great poem tallies completely with the immanent meaning of the composition.

B : But, speaking of Britten's poets, I don't think one can call the poetry of Michelangelo or Tennyson hermetic ?

102

A : Certainly not. But as long as a poem *has*, in fact, an immanent meaning, though it be of the conservative or revolutionary class, its union with hermetic music can be effected. On the other hand, Britten has certainly shown a predilection for hermetic poetry, such as Donne's, Blake's, Rimbaud's and Auden's. Be it here said again that the style and communicable thinking of, for instance, Donne, while making him one of the so-called metaphysical poets, does not necessarily make his poetry hermetic ; it is the absence of other poetic immanent meanings comparable to his that makes it so.

B : So Britten does, after all, show a liking for hermetic poetry ?

A : Yes, but this is not as self-evident as it may seem at first glance. If we remember that our definition of hermetic art is, and must be, a purely negative one, we must admit that it is statistically improbable that two hermetic contents should ever complement each other. If they do, after all, meet, as in the case of Britten and Donne, or Britten and Rimbaud—meet, that is, across the boundaries of distinct artistic media —we are logically forced to the conclusion that two negatively defined categories have a property other than negation in common, and we can expect that by virtue of this positive property some immanent meanings of sculpture and architecture will also mirror the immanent meanings of Britten or Donne.

B : What is this positive property ?

A : This cannot be stated by language. Its subjective impact, called synaesthesia, may one day be defined psychologically.

B : But how then, if even the single hermetic meaning has to be divined, can a word-music meaning of the hermetic class be understood ?

A : As the immanent content of any work of art is by virtue of its singularity concrete, and the comparison of conservative and revolutionary meanings the step to abstraction, it follows that, since the single concrete hermetic meaning has to be divined, the understanding of two mirroring hermetic meanings takes the form of an abstracted divination. This is indeed the *non plus ultra* of dialectic : the super-rational and super-instinctive connotation of immanent concretes, resulting in the ultimate and therefore Platonic, abstraction.

B : Lucky we aren't having tea yet, or I would have bitten a large piece out of my cup just now.

A : Poor you. But do you gnash your teeth when you hear the *Dirge* from the *Horn Serenade* ?

B : Oh, no. I rather like that.

A : But you like it, I hope, because you understand it. And your understanding must take the form of what I said.

B : It may. I know nothing about it. I enjoy it because it reminds me of Mahler, a favourite composer of mine.

A : Is that all ?

B : No, it isn't. That's only a detail. The piece as a whole, including the words, has a very peculiar savour, I admit. To speak in your language, it reminds me of something I may have known in another life.

A : In *my* language, my foot ! But it's good enough.

B : Don't mention it—rather tell me, is Britten aware of all this ?

A : I should hope not. These are merely aesthetic speculations. A good composer knows nothing about aesthetics.

B : But, according to you, it's curious that he should be inspired by the word, didn't you say so ?

A : You said so, but I will formulate the question again : why does a creator of immanent musical meanings, that is, a complete master of form, whose meanings, besides, are hermetic like Britten's, take up the word ?

B : What would Britten answer ?

A : In the first place, one oughtn't to ask him. It would be bad form. But if asked, he would perhaps say what he has said on other occasions, namely, that he'd like to find the right music for everything. This is, of course, superficially correct : he has a most uncanny capacity for finding convincing musical symbols for every action, emotion or situation presented by the text, and I daresay it gives him great pleasure to exercise this gift. But this does not explain why he should not be content, at any rate more frequently, to build his new world of immanent musical meanings in the isolation of absolute sound.

B : What is your explanation, then ?

A : Any explanation must be tentative because we are dealing with a living composer. Also, even if we had the self-confessions of a composer's whole lifetime, many of these would be self-delusions or superficialities since the unconscious processes of creation are benevolently withheld from the creator's reason. This understood, I would submit that the isolation imposed by so-called absolute music creates in the hermetic composer—who, we remember, is doubly isolated from extraneous meanings and from the immanent meanings of his colleagues—a suffering pride, an ironical disbelief of, and a deadly serious belief in isolation, in short, " the pathos of loneliness." This ambivalent reaction towards the feeling of loneliness will be seen to be the counterpart of the afore-mentioned fear of the listener in the face of Britten's music. The difference is, of course, that the listener, being on the outside of this complex, can take his revenge, while Britten, being sufferer, battlefield and hero of this compositional trauma, can only take revenge against himself. Now, if Britten had by an unfortunate coincidence strong masochistic tendencies, he would by now be dawdling down the path of Mussorgsky. Luckily, his psyche is integrated enough to find the way out of this conflict. This way out is not a decisive victory over the self-destructive tendencies evoked by loneliness—such a victory is only given to simple natures like Bruckner. The way out is, characteristic of our time and perhaps also of Mozart's, a continuous mercurial suspense between a liking for and a dislike of isolation. This results, amongst other things, in the ironical popularity of some of his music and, important for us here, in his curious relationship to poetry. Setting the composer aside for the moment and speaking of his music anthropomorphically, we can say that the attitude of Britten's hermetic musical contents towards the immanent meanings of their poems is one of admiration, reluctant charity, ironical self-assertion, pity and self-pity. Introducing the composer again, or rather his subconscious mind, we should say that he takes the cross of the word upon himself in order to be saved from hermetic isolation or, when setting hermetic poetry, in order that music and poetry may find their salvation in each other.

B :   Can you give me some tangible evidence for this from Britten's style ?

A :   Not directly. You remember, this was a discussion of the word-music problem on the philosophical plane, and our findings apply to Form, or Meaning, in its entirety, which always transcends actual style. But we can come down now to the cognitive level on which a composer's style can be recognised, and see how the poet's communication is translated into music. Perhaps the stylistic manifestation which goes nearest to our problem is the musico-poetic symbol.

B :   What is this ?

A :   It is a formula which translates a poetic image into music.

B :   How would you define a poetic image ?

A :   For our purpose it will suffice to define it as the communication of a single and definite thought, action, state or sensation.

B :   Is there an accepted way of creating a musical symbol ?

A :   There are roughly four kinds of symbols that have been used throughout the ages. First, there is *Direct Depiction*, applicable, of course, mainly to the aural and visual image, as in baroque music and in naturalistic programme music. Secondly, there is *Indirect Depiction* of sensual perceptions with a stress on their subjective meaning, as in impressionist music. Thirdly, there is the *casual attachment* of a musical formula to a poetic image, producing, through repetition, a conditioned reflex in the listener, as with Wagner's leitmotifs. Lastly, there is the *instinctive attachment* of words and music, operating, in the absence of a direct cognitive link through subconscious intra-literary and intra-musical associations.

B :   Which of these does Britten use ?

A :   He uses, in this respect like Purcell and Schubert, the first and last constantly, while almost completely excluding the second and third. As to *Indirect Depiction*, the impressionistic symbol, he once tells us by way of musical charade what he thinks of it. The music of a certain two bars in the sixth *John Donne* Sonnet declares the impressionist to be the man who, although he has found immediate artistic perception and " had his thirst fed by it," is still " melted by a holy, thirsty dropsy."

B :   Hardly fair on Debussy, but it fits Britten's case, I suppose—What about *leitmotif* technique ?

A :   This hardly enters into songs, of course. But within the framework of a song cycle, Britten uses, as in his operas, not indeed the *leitmotif*, but certain *leit*-modulations and *leit*-forms à la Mozart. For instance, the swift, exciting modulations by third-relationship in *Villes* of *Les Illuminations* turn up again, significantly, in the last song, *Départ*, in wide, calm spacing for the words " Assez vu .... assez eu .... assez connu."

B : To come now to the symbols Britten uses frequently, don't you find his *Direct Depiction* sometimes as naive as Purcell's ?

A : Yes, there are very naive examples in the spirit, if not in the style, of Purcell's ornaments. They abound in the early *Our Hunting Fathers* and *On this Island,* and also in the folksong-arrangements. Later, when Britten chose poetry less pictorial, this symbol became rarer but it still turns up, with great felicity, in as late a song as *Canticle I,* Op. 40. There, the confluence of two brooks is described by the meeting of two scales in a manner that would have delighted not only Purcell but also the Kuhnau of the *Biblical Sonatas.*

B : Why does Britten use this crude symbol ?

A : I would call it crude only in Kuhnau, not in Britten, where it does not obtrude on the form and makes musical sense even without reference to the words. But here again Britten seems, out of his isolation, to want to make a contribution to history : for, apart from a few ventures of Schubert and Wolf, nobody since baroque times has dared to use this symbol and it wants restating in modern idiom.

B : And what about that other symbol Britten uses ? Your label " *instinctive attachment* of words and music " sounded a bit vague.

A : I'll give you an example in a minute. First let me say this. When a poetic image is attached to an apparently fortuitous musical image in a way that immediately convinces the intelligent listener, one is tempted to see in this a recurrence on a smaller scale of the " mirroring of two immanent contents." In so far as this " mirroring of two complete forms " has to happen in the dimension of time, I would agree. Understanding of music means taking in one detail after another and afterwards reconstituting the whole, thus arriving at a perception of beauty which is more than the sum of all beautiful details, and which we called the immanent content of the work. But the very fact that we are able to single out beautiful moments, that we can speak of harmony, counterpoint, or musical symbols, means that even an elusive feature of style must, to a certain degree, be definable and analysable.

B : You hold that it is only the meaning of the complete work that defies analysis, whereas every detail must pertain of the qualities of style ?

A : Yes.

B : But what if one just cannot find a stylistic reason for the pertinence of a detail ? You said yourself that these instinctive musico-poetic symbols work in the absence of a direct cognitive link.

A : Yes, but the word " instinctive " is the clue. To find the operating association, one must cast one's net wide enough to catch instinctive, and as such, subconscious connotations. This is not always practical, nor indeed desirable. But sometimes these connotations emerge into consciousness by chance, and then you get an insight into the workings of this symbol.

B : You promised me an example of this.

A : Here it is. In Sonnet LV of Britten's *Michelangelo* Sonnets, the very simple chordal setting of the words " That which in thy lovely face I yearn for and seek to grasp, is but ill understood by human kind," has always struck me as extraordinarily suited to the words, for no apparent intra-, or extra-musical reason. Until one day I happened to look at the score and found that the chord sequence was a Britten-ish version of those modulating sequences of secondary sevenths that appear from Buxtehude in Bach, in the Viennese classics, in Verdi and Puccini, and again in Vaughan Williams, and other contemporary composers. As every harmony teacher knows, these sequences can be extremely dull, but in the hands of a master they are poignantly expressive. Now Britten's sequence, while starting completely symmetrically, gains sudden depth by the dissonant C in the bass of its third bar, to the words " ill understood by human kind." It now dawned on me that both words and music were a profound comment on symmetry in art, and the dangers of, and misconceptions about, this high artistic principle.

B : You mean that Britten broke the symmetry of his sequence because it was just becoming dull ?

A : There is more to it. What kind of faces do you like, pretty ones, interesting ones, or beautiful ones ?

B : Oh, I couldn't say. . . . I like them all.

A : I guess I do too. The C in the bass is there to chide us. Michelangelo obviously preferred a beautiful face, in its complete symmetry, to both a pretty one, whose symmetry is merely dull, and an interesting one whose irregularity may fascinate.

B : I see . . . . you mean, the same goes for musical sequences ?

A : It goes for all form in music. Britten is quite capable of writing a sequence that would be beautiful yet not pretty, in spite of its perfect symmetry ; but when Michelangelo says that we don't understand this kind of symmetry, Britten falls in with him and breaks his sequence.

B : I see . . . . but how complicated for the listener.

A : Not at all, neither Britten nor the listener can gain anything from being aware of this. I was merely trying to explain why this passage may stir the listener, and to show how the " indirect attachment " of words and music works.

B : So you believe that the hermetic composer has a special liking for this class of musical symbol because it comes nearest to the hermetic meanings of his music ?

A : Not really. The conservative and revolutionary composer will also, when writing " songs " in our strict sense, make more use of this last word-music symbol than of any others.

B : Why is that ?

A : I am afraid that would be the subject for a new discussion. Anyway, we are only groping our way to a general theory of musical hermeneutics.

B : What's hermeneutics ?

A : Come on, let's have our tea now.

Einstein's " The Italian Madrigal "[1]

By R. ALEC HARMAN

THERE is a tendency amongst contemporary writers on music to link up their subject, be it a general history or a specialized study, with other branches of human activity ; Dr. Einstein's " The Italian Madrigal " is an outstanding work of this kind, for not only does it give us the most complete survey yet produced of Italian secular music in this fascinating age, but also, as the author states in his preface " . . . seeks to define the function of secular music in the Italian life of the sixteenth century . . . " This aim is brilliantly accomplished, for the author's detailed knowledge of the history, literature and customs of the period is immense, and only excelled by his knowledge of the music, of which he has transcribed from original sources over 8,000 examples during the 40 years in which he has been assembling his material. The fruits of these labours appear in two volumes of text containing 24 illustrations (chiefly portraits) and a third volume of musical examples ; all three volumes are handsomely printed and bound.

To an admirer of Burckhardt's classic, this book not only more than supplements the pathetic three pages on music (and mainly instrumental at that !) which is all the older author gives us, but also much of it is indispensable to the general student of sixteenth century Italy, especially the student of literature, for Dr. Einstein includes a liberal selection of the very varied types of verse (some of it sheer doggerel) which was set to music. By far the greater part of this literature is identifiable, the names of Petrarch, Tasso, Ariosto, Sanazzaro, Bembo, Cassola and Guarini occurring again and again, and it is interesting to note in this connection how very few of the texts of the English Madrigal School have been identified—less than one-tenth. Admittedly 16th century England did not possess Italy's wealth of lyric talent, but whereas in both countries a certain amount of verse appeared first in music prints, proving the close relationship between poet and composer, in Italy, unlike England, much of it was subsequently published either by the author or in anthologies, a fact which clearly shows that lyric poetry was much more widely appreciated in Italy than in this country, as does the following passage from Michel de Montaigne's " Journal de Voyage " (July 2nd, 1581) quoted by Dr. Einstein, where Montaigne is surprised " to see these peasants with lutes in their hands and even the shepherdesses with Ariosto on their lips. *But one sees this everywhere in Italy.*"

On the purely musical side the book is richly furnished with examples both in the text and in the third volume which contains 97 pieces ranging from c. 1470-1613. Most of these cannot be found in any of the standard publications such as Torchi, Kiesewetter, etc., and in fact Dr. Einstein's selection has been largely governed by what has not been reprinted by other scholars ; even so it is a great pity that he does not include at least one of Gesualdo's madrigals (an omission which also occurs in the author's " The Golden Age of the Madrigal "), and one of Monteverdi's, despite the

(1) Princeton University Press (London: Geoffrey Cumberlege). 3 vols. 10 guineas.

publication of the latter's complete work. The omission of examples by, and detailed discussion of, Giovanni Gabrieli, Croce, Giovanelli and other Venetian and Roman composers is explained in the preface as follows : " In order to keep within reasonable limits, I have confined myself to a characterization of the most important masters whose works lie along the direct line of development . . . " I hope that Dr. Einstein will in the near future produce a further book dealing with these composers.

The first two volumes are divided into ten chapters, the first of which deals with the " barren " 15th century, the development of a national feeling and of musical forms such as the frottola, capitolo, strambotto, etc., and the rise of music printing. Dr. Einstein is not convincing (to me at any rate) in his explanation of the total lack of outstanding native musical genius in the 15th century, for he argues that " The northerners satisfied every want in sacred and secular artistic music. There was no reason to compete with them, and since there was no native school, in those times the indispensable condition for a transmission of knowledge and technique from master to disciples, there naturally arose no native genius." But he also maintains (and rightly) that " the spirit of the Italian music of the Trecento must have remained alive," and that the music of the Quattrocento involved " the spontaneous invention of a melody with a simple " harmonic " accompaniment ; an art of improvisation, an ability to recite effectively a sonnet, a ballata, a capitolo, or a strambotto. As yet no one had thought it worth the trouble to put such music on paper, but it was certainly being practised." Now surely if Burgundian music was so satisfying, a specifically native art which contrasted so sharply with the other would have found no support ? This was the case in 18th century England but with the difference that there were no native undercurrents which blossomed forth in the 19th century, whereas 16th century Italy clearly shows that there must have been a 15th century musical practice with aims quite different from the Burgundian polyphonic style. The statement that there was no native school (in the accepted sense) is true so far as we know, but Dr. Einstein makes no attempt to explain why this was so ; the Burgundian influence is no explanation : after all Tromboncino (for example) composed his frottole etc. when the Burgundian influence was still very powerful. Why there are no examples of this Quattrocento music extant is surely not due to no one bothering to write it down, but rather to it having been lost or destroyed ; new sources are still being unearthed (for example, the Aosta Codex of recent years) and it is still possible that we may discover some of the secular music of this enigmatic period, a period which must have remembered and treasured the exquisite bloom of the Trecento Florentine school, and one which also boasted the greatest theorist of the century.

In the all too short sections on " Printing " Dr. Einstein clearly demonstrates that many of the early frottola prints of Petrucci and others were not meant to be sung from, but served only for codification ; indeed he queries whether this " part " music was intended for four singers and leans towards the idea that it was sung by a solo voice with lute or viol players condensing the other three parts. This seems very probable if one remembers the improvisatory character of 15th century Italian music, and the wheel thus comes full circle, for the book makes it quite clear that the *a cappella* madrigal and motet were essentially " bogus " forms in that there never was and never can be complete equality of voices—" an upper voice cannot help but dominate, a bass must support and thus assume a subordinate function, inner parts must " fill in " and thus surrender a part of their independence " ; hence we find accompanied song at the very beginning and at the very end of the century. Unfortunately the author does not give us any account of the format of the madrigal prints.

The second chapter is the best in the book for it presents the " Origins of the Madrigal " in a manner which is both erudite and lucid. It begins with a comparison between the madrigal of the Trecento and Cinquecento, and continues with the effect of the motet style on the frottola, the first madrigalists, the relation between the poets, their poetry and music, the various Academies, and finally 16th century musical aesthetics, including a fascinating and amusing section on " Eye Music " and an excellent section on the much discussed " Musica Reservata." In the section on " Eye Music " Dr. Einstein has not, I feel, attached sufficient importance to the use of Proportions, for while dealing fully with colouration (e.g. black notes for " night "), figuration (e.g. quaver figures for "rushing ") and inclination (e.g. a rising scale passage for "ascending heavenwards "), he only mentions Proportions *en passant* in a piece by Anerio. Yet Proportions, though less purely " Eye Music " than colouration, for they could and did introduce a metrical complexity which could be heard, were frequently used as a means of " imitating nature."

The next chapter deals with " The Early Madrigal," its chief contributors— Verdelot, Festa and Arcadelt, their successors Alfonso della Viola, Domenico Ferrabosco, Palestrina, and finally Willaert. The oft debated question as to whether Festa or Verdelot should be regarded as the first madrigalist is fairly stated by Dr. Einstein who gives both sides of the argument. If " the presence of more traditional features could be used as criteria, Verdelot would have to be considered the earlier master " ; moreover Willaert clearly regarded Verdelot as the father of the genre. On the other hand it seems clear that Festa's three-part madrigals (admittedly composed in motet style) were written before Verdelot's four-part, but that the latter influenced Festa's later work. This should be the last word on the subject.

Another topic on which many have differed is Palestrina's attitude to secular music, for twice (in 1569 and 1584) he rejects such music and regrets his former essays in this field, and yet he continued to contribute to collections, and in 1586 published his second book of madrigals for four voices. Dr. Einstein calls this " pure hypocrisy," using the same epithet later in the book. This I feel is a trifle harsh, for on both the occasions mentioned above Palestrina was dedicating a book of motets to a high ecclesiastical dignitary with whom he was naturally anxious to keep on good terms. In an age when composers were servants (albeit respected ones) and fulsome flattery was commonplace, Palestrina's remarks hardly deserve so severe an interpretation. (Lasso incidentally gets off much more lightly, despite the fact that he published a collection of secular songs (many of them obscene) in 1581, which though written earlier he must have revised in 1580 ; this at a time when he was an avowed penitent and a complete convert of the Counter Reformation). In his judgment of much of the music, however, Dr. Einstein bestows great praise, and scouts the idea that Palestrina's greatness rests solely on his church music, a point of view which anyone who has studied this composers's madrigals will endorse.

Chapter four is concerned with " The Lighter Forms "—the villotto, mascherata etc., which are superbly classified and differentiated from the madrigal. What incredible stuff some of this is—the range of subject matter, the characterization, the wealth of expression ; the English School did not produce anything to compare with it, though a few isolated examples almost certainly stemmed from their Italian counterparts ; Gibbons' " The Cries of London," for instance, being undoubtedly related to the mascherata, despite its polyphonic instrumental accompaniment and ' monodic ' vocal line. The first great master of these forms is da Nola, a comparatively obscure figure until one has read Dr. Einstein. In fact one of the most notable features of this book is the way in which certain composers receive an altogether new importance and others less than one would expect, for instance Lasso, whose " historical importance is relatively insignificant . . . Unlike Verdelot, Willaert, Rore, he invents nothing ; he never seizes control of the development; he uses an already existing store of formulas." Alternatively, Rore is the outstanding example of a composer who, though admittedly mentioned in all the lexicons, has never occupied such an exalted place as he does in the present work, and chapter five, " The Post-Classic Madrigal," is largely concerned with him. Rore was the first composer to use in most of his work the new and revolutionary black notation or *note nere* indicated by the half-circle and corresponding to our $\frac{4}{4}$ time, in which the crotchet is the harmonic unit ; the standard signature until his time had been a barred half-circle ($\frac{4}{2}$) with the minim as the harmonic unit. Now, however, " a new freedom of incalculable consequence has been won. The madrigal may now change its tempo in two ways, according to its expressive need. With the [barred half-circle] sign it may accelerate the tempo, while with the [half-circle] sign it may retard it " (page 404). Dr. Einstein then points out that here is a method by which one can estimate Italian influence on any ultramontane composer, a suggestion that should be followed up. The English School for instance, seem largely to have failed to grasp the significance of these two signs, for one often comes across pieces with the barred half-circle but in *note nere*, and vice versa (some of the barring in the English Madrigal School is misleading because of this). Even Morley, the teacher and admirer of Italian clarity and logic, though he correctly differentiates between the two signs in the text of his " Plain and Easy Introduction," consistently uses the half-circle wrongly in the examples which he gives, the only exceptions being the 6th Duo at the end of Part I and the two Italian Canzonets after the Peroratio. Unfortunately Dr. Einstein does not make it clear whether the new sign does in fact mean a retarding of tempo, for on page 374 he says " From 1530 to 1540 the madrigal is in principle always written in $\frac{4}{2}$ time. The introduction of $\frac{4}{4}$ is not necessarily connected, from the point of view of the mensural technique, with a more rapid tempo. But it is a fact that the livelier note-picture in *note nere*, in black quarter and eighth notes, did affect the tempo and manner of performance also." Again, on page 407, in speaking of Rore's first book of four-part madrigals (1550) he says that the only piece in the whole book which is in $\frac{4}{4}$ time contains the line " *Piu vivace* che mai nell' alma sento," and that the choice of *note nere* here is perhaps a reflection of the text—" If this interpretation is correct, it should indicate that $\frac{4}{4}$ time was associated with the idea of a faster tempo after all." The solution of this problem is an important matter vitally affecting performance. On the one hand there seems to be some justification for supposing that in the late 15th and early 16th centuries when the barred half-circle was used Proportionally, this sign did in fact imply a slightly quicker pulse or tactus. If it did not, its use would frequently have little significance, an interpretation which bears out the statement on page 404. On the other hand if the actual look of a page had something of the same affect on 16th century performers that it had on those of the late 17th and early 18th centuries, then the use of *note nere* would involve a faster tempo. With Rore also the five-part madrigal became the norm, resulting in a complete change in the internal structure of the madrigal, terminating the pairing of the voices and bringing us a step nearer the " stile concertante". In fact Dr. Einstein maintains that Rore could no more be ignored in the 16th century than Wagner could in the 19th for " he had introduced much that was new—the revolution on the rhythmic side, the use of daring harmony for daring expression, the sublimation and spiritualisation of music through the choice and treatment of its texts . . . In his work the high point in the development of the madrigal was not only reached but even over-stepped," a claim which the examples in this book go far to substantiate.

" The Three Great Oltremontani", Lasso, Monte, and Wert, occupy the whole of chapter six, and here again the importance of the last named is completely at variance with the position accorded him in the standard works of reference. But Dr. Einstein claims that " as a musical personality Wert can hold his own in comparison not only with Monte, but also (or very nearly) with Lasso ; aside from this his later influence was far greater than theirs, for he was one of the real intermediaries between Rore and Monteverdi and his role was by no means limited to that of the mere intermediary " ; in fact " the later Wert is no longer Rore's successor ; he is the contemporary of Marenzio, Gesualdo and the young Monteverdi, and one of the forerunners and founders of the music of the 17th century". Needless to say the author supports his contention in a completely convincing manner, and we are left to marvel that it has taken 350 years to establish the historical and aesthetic importance of this composer.

As regards Lasso, Dr. Einstein makes an interesting comparison with Mozart, for while Palestrina and Boccherini were fully understood by their contemporaries, Mozart and Lasso were not, yet both proved the more " actual " to posterity. This kind of illuminating remark which links up with personalities and principles outside the century can be found all through the book ; I quote a few examples, some of which are perhaps a little sweeping. " The spirit of music cannot be lost in any nation, considering the unified development of European music." " The greatest genius in art . . . can only affect the pace of the development, not the development itself." " The virtuoso will always show a tendency to level the expression of a work of art instead of raising it."

The next three chapters deal with the rise of pathos and drama in the madrigal, the " New Canzonetta " and " The Great Virtuosi "—Marenzio, Gesualdo, Monteverdi and Gagliano. Here, as we approach the 17th century, we come across numerous foreshadowings of the future, and in fact this book contains much that is of great value to the student of early opera—from Rore to Monteverdi there is a direct line containing the seeds which later blossomed into opera and cantata. Of the composers mentioned above Marenzio receives the greatest attention, which is as it should be, for the refinement of his personal expression, his ability to unite the two opposing trends, sensuality and austerity, the catholicity of his literary taste and his influence on contemporary poets make him the culminating figure of the Italian madrigal. The last word has been said, and the sections on Gesualdo, Monteverdi and Gagliano, and the succeeding chapters (which include first-rate dissertations on Striggio, Vecchi and Banchieri) simply show the increasing disintegration of the madrigal, a disintegration which had begun with Rore. They are nevertheless (or perhaps because of this) among the most fascinating and instructive in the whole book, particularly the last two chapters on " Pseudo-Monody and Monody " and " Monteverdi and the Madrigal Concertato " which, by linking up directly with the next century, provide a fitting conclusion.

It is impossible to give any idea in a single article of the immense wealth of information and the painstaking scholarship which have gone to the making of this great work ; it is a tremendous achievement, and my admiration for its author is in no way diminished by the following criticisms.

Dr. Einstein has set out with the intention of defining " the function of secular music in the Italian life of the sixteenth century." In order to do this adequately he quite rightly insists that " the history of an art-form in which poetry and music are one is possible only on the basis of a knowledge of music and poetry, of poetry and music " ; hence the liberal quotations of the verse on which the madrigal and other musical forms were based. Dr. Einstein's knowledge of Italian is more than merely native : it is philological. But to the vast majority of people to whom this book will be a constant source of delight and information, a great deal of the verse will mean little or nothing. The quotations from theorists, historians, etc., are excellently translated, but these are in the main the very passages which anyone with a good smattering of Italian, can struggle through. Verse is a very much more difficult problem, for the poetic vocabulary and idiom in any language is less straightforward than in prose, especially when it comes to dialect. The fact that only two out of the numerous examples of verse are translated considerably mars the purpose and value (both entertainment and academic) of this book. I do not necessarily suggest that the translations should be in exactly the same form as the originals (though in the same author's " The Golden Age of the Madrigal " all the texts are most beautifully and poetically translated by Gustave Reese), but some kind of free translation (as in the " Historical Anthology of Music " by Davison and Apel) would enable the reader to appreciate much more fully the extraordinary range of this literature.

My next main criticism concerns the music and more especially the retention of the Soprano, Alto and Tenor clefs. This procedure is defended by the author on the following grounds : 1) The use of the treble and modern tenor clefs in place of the above mentioned clefs results in a great number of ledger lines, or, in the case of the latter, in the reading of a perpetual transposition. 2) The book is addressed to musicians and " the musician who is unable to read the three older clefs . . . will also be unable to read a modern score or even the score of a string quartet" (sic). As regards the Alto and Tenor clefs there is something to be said in favour of their being kept, but the Soprano clef is completely defunct as far as modern scores are concerned, and its use here is an unwarrantable hindrance ; furthermore the replacement of the Baritone by the Bass clef is exactly the same alteration as the replacement of the Soprano by the Treble would be, except the former results in more ledger-lines above the stave, and the latter below. The Alto and Tenor clefs also should both be replaced by the modern tenor clef for it is high time Alto singers became accustomed to singing from this clef ; as to the criticism that this would involve reading a perpetual transposition I can only reply that this particular form of aural adjustment is far more common today than the reading of the two clefs in question, not only because of modern vocal practice but also because (to use the author's own argument) the modern score contains more instruments which transpose than those which use C clefs. In any case it renders volume III useless for performance by the ordinary singer ; whereas it should have been possible for four or even five people to sing from this collection, the temptation now will be to copy the music out in the customary clefs. Moreover Dr. Einstein is not consistent in his replacement of the Mezzo-soprano clef, for he sometimes uses the Soprano clef, sometimes the Treble, even when the latter involves two ledger-lines. A similar inconsistency is shown when using short score : on some occasions he condenses the Soprano and Alto clefs to the Soprano, and on others he uses the Treble, again resulting in two ledger-lines ; and when he combines the Treble and Soprano on one stave he chooses the latter clef ! There are other equally abitrary instances.

With regard to dotted notes intersected by a bar-line, the author adopts the principle of placing the dot at the beginning of the next bar, a procedure which has little to commend it. Dr. Fellowes' contention in " The English Madrigal School " that it makes it easier to detect the point of imitation is true (but he only uses the dotted crotchet thus !). Unfortunately the dot often gets overlooked by the singer or omitted by the printer (as in this book where by no means all the omissions are noted in the Addenda and Corrigenda) ; if the note is tied over the bar-line both these disadvantages are overcome and a few words can explain that there must be no accent on the first note of the bar so tied. Oddly enough this latter procedure is the one adopted by Dr. Einstein in " The Golden Age of the Madrigal " although in the present work he forgets occasionally. (Morley, incidentally, defined the dot as a kind of ligature ; as ligatures are indicated by slurs in modern editions why not dotted notes ?).

All this boils down to the general complaint that volume III is clearly not ntended for practical use but only for the delectation of scholars. In addition to the above criticisms there are no speed indications and (which is more serious) no statement as to the principles which have guided the author in his application of Musica Ficta (some of his superscript accidentals appear to be both dubious and arbitrary). This is a great pity, for it is perfectly possible in a work of this kind to cater both for the specialist and for the more discriminating music lover. Besides which the book is inadequately indexed ; although composers and places are given, there is no means by which one can refer to poetic or musical types unless they form a chapter or sectional heading, and even this is clearly insufficient. Neither is there a bibliography which the number of books, monographs and articles referred to by the author in the text makes absolutely essential.

It is inevitable in a work of this size and complexity that there should be errors both in the text and music. The astonishing thing is that there are not a great many more. Most of them are merely misplaced single notes or omitted dots which I shall not enumerate ; but the following should be mentioned :—

Vols. I and II.

p. 43 Beatrice d'Este died in 1497 not 1597. Why did not Isabella (d. 1519) live to see Beatrice's sad end ?

p. 80 " De no de si de no " is correctly described as an Oda in the text but as a Frottola in Vol. III.

p. 80 The key sequence in the Frottola " L'Amor Donna . . . " is F—A minor—B♭ not E♭.

p. 598 Vol. III does not contain Conversi's " Zefiro torna."

p. 839 Some of the stated missing leaves are given in the index ; moreover some of the pieces are presumably so short that another piece is at least begun on the same page (10, 12, 13, 14, 40, 45), while others are presumably long enough to cover three pages, or is the indexing at fault ? The following pages are not included in the index : 1, 3, 4, 6, 19, 21, 24, 25, 32, 34, 36, 41, 42, 44, 47 ; 19, 32, 34, 47 are explained but the others are not.

Vol. III.

p. 16 The Bass part at the end does not fit in with the note values of the other parts. The Longs (here and in all three vols.) have their tails down on the *left* side.

p. 25 Line 2, bar 6, surely a superscript natural not ♯ over the Bass F.

p. 28 Line 4, bar 1, the last four notes in the Tenor should be A, G, A, B.

Finally, let me reaffirm my opinion that this book is an outstanding contribution to our knowledge and enjoyment of 16th century Italy in general and its music in particular ; my only hope is that Dr. Einstein will now do three things :

1) Make the second edition (and there must surely be one) more easily appreciated by the non-specialist student, by translations of the verse and the use of modern clefs.

2) Give us (as previously suggested) a detailed account of the Roman and Venetian secular schools.

3) Write a stylistic analysis of Italian secular music in the 16th century, considering such matters as the rise of tonality (or the breakdown of modality), Musica Ficta, key signatures, the use of dissonance and chromaticism (including chromatic chords and false relations), the clash between the native ' harmonic ' style and the Burgundian polyphonic, the influence of the Spanish ' Villancicos ' and the French ' Chansons,' the development of the melodic formulae which accompanied the " Imitazione della Natura," underlaying, form, imitation, and archaisms (e.g. the use of the so-called ' Landini sixth ') ; for no one is better equipped to tackle these subjects than the author of this book.

Schoenberg

"A SURVIVOR FROM WARSAW", Op. 46.

It is the evening of September 13th, 1950—Schoenberg's 76th birthday. The setting is the annual International Festival of Contemporary Music in Venice. The elegant audience in the beautiful 18th century theatre, La Fenice, is restive and Scherchen, who is conducting the Rome Radio Symphony Orchestra, has been having a rough passage. Milhaud's 300th opus, a Suite for two pianos and orchestra, has been politely received, but without undue enthusiasm. A study for "Il processo" of Kafka by Bruno Maderna, a young Venetian who has recently discovered dodecaphony, had almost been stopped by mock applause and hissing, and only Scherchen's strength of character had averted a catastrophe. "Seven Aspects of a Dodecaphonic Series" by Vogel seemed too long in spite of the fact that two Aspects had been cut.

This was the atmosphere in which Schoenberg's "A Survivor from Warsaw" began, and this was the bored and restive audience which, when it was finished, called insistently for a repeat, any opposition silenced by the very nature of the work. Scherchen, smiling happily at this unexpected close to an exceptionally trying evening, announced that he wished to play the repeat performance in honour of the master's birthday which fell that day.

Thus a circle was completed ; for Schoenberg, commissioned by the Koussevitzky Foundation, began work on the score of "A Survivor from Warsaw" on his 73rd birthday. Having heard of a young man who had survived the German massacre of Jews in the Warsaw ghetto, he had asked him to visit him. From his account, Schoenberg wrote the text, which is in English except for the Nazis' orders, which are rapped out in German. The words, magnificently spoken in Venice by Anton Kubinsky, are moving in their simplicity and truth. The Jew recites his confused memory of the massacre and of his semi-conscious survival . . . "And they were all dead . . . then miraculously they all began to sing 'Shema Yisroel' ! " (I quote at random.) Whereupon the work closes with a unison male chorus in Hebrew and a final triumphant cadence on the trumpet.

The music, which was written in ten days and finished on the 23rd September, 1947, is built up of unifying elements in Schoenberg's habitual technique, the raw material of the series being treated with constant variation. The four opening notes—semiquaver triplet f′♯—g′—c″ and crotchet a″♭—immediately serve to establish three other inverted forms, and from the very start the division of the series into several fragments serves as an exact basis for the different sections of the work. Likewise the theme of the "Shema Yisroel" chorus, which is introduced a few bars after the opening, is used at the centre of the work as a *cantus firmus* on which are embroidered counter-melodies (chorale prelude), whereas the presentation of a characteristic and recurring chord is reminiscent of Wagner's use of the *Leitmotive*, a practice well illustrated in Schoenberg's "Five Pieces for Orchestra," Op. 16. These various devices which ensure constant but unified variation have been exploited by Schoenberg for 40 years, and the summit of dodecaphonic writing with speaker which he has attained in the eight minutes of "A

Survivor from Warsaw " can be placed in a direct line of development from the finale of the "Gurrelieder" (1900) through "Pierrot Lunaire" (1912), "Die Glueckliche Hand" (1913), " Kol Nidre " (1939) and the " Ode to Napoleon " (1942).

But none of the above observations can truly convey the dignity and unerring sense of proportion of " A Survivor from Warsaw," nor the magnificent sense of inflexion, timing and pauses in the text, which are expressively accompanied but never interfered with by the orchestra and which culminate in the final climax and completion of the choir. These concentrated eight minutes appear to contain an infinity of time and experience; and Schoenberg's humanity, which is that of a master and not a theoretician, carries the work far beyond the sphere of coteries. There were many in the audience in Venice who understood neither English nor dodecaphony. The origins of " A Survivor from Warsaw " and its historic reception at La Fenice should give food for thought to those who persist in contending that Schoenberg's work is cerebral and dry paper-music.

In the present state of the world, where distortion continues to undermine our judgment and sense of values, we would do well to accept this work, not only as an exceptional and revolutionary technical achievement, but as an artist's expression of humanity and faith—" Lest we forget."

CHRISTINA THORESBY

Cheltenham and After

SOME FIRST PERFORMANCES

ARNOLD BAX : Concertante for Orchestra with Piano Solo (left hand). Soloist : HARRIET COHEN.
P. RACINE FRICKER : Symphony, Op. 9.
RICHARD ARNELL : String Quintet, Op. 60. (Blech Quartet, Kenneth Essex, 2nd viola).
WILLIAM ALWYN : Symphony No. 1 in D.
ANTHONY COLLINS : Symphony No. 2 for Strings.
FRANCIS BAINES : Concerto for Trumpet and String Orchestra. Soloist : ERIC BRAVINGTON.
[Except for the Baines, which was performed by the Boyd Neel String Orchestra conducted by the composer, the orchestra resident throughout the Festival was the Hallé under Barbirolli.]

BAX must be quite our most static composer (and that's putting it moderately). This last work of his sounds not a note different to the music he was writing as a young man ; he is now 76. The kindest thing that can be said in the piece's favour : it was a gallant gesture made to a temporarily disabled musician. If the Bax need never have been written at all it was obvious that Fricker's Symphony had to be—at least from Fricker's point of view : and that is the first, if not the last, of the necessities for the successful creation of a work of art: the not-to-be-denied will to create of its creator. I have reviewed the Symphony (as far as I understood it) elsewhere.† In view of the recent publication of the miniature score (Schott's—to be noticed in this journal in the near future) it would seem wise to postpone further discussion ; another performance meantime—which the symphony more than deserves—would

†*Music Review*, 11/III/50.

help. Arnell's recent Quintet, for two violins, two violas and 'cello, displayed the now to be expected features of his style. His strong contrapuntal tendency, an almost whimsical delight in flouting any preconceived formal notions we may possess, his droll humour, his gift for amiable parody of his elders, and his liking for assembling beneath one roof the widest possible range of musical materials : so to speak, a deliberate, responsible eclecticism. Arnell, in spite of the variety and contradictory nature of his ideas, achieved a remarkable consistency of idiom, eccentric as it often is. His use of the medium was an object lesson in imagination ; and his finale, with its sectional treatment of the instrumental resources, was proof of his independent and antiphonal approach to the textural problems a string quintet sets. The Alwyn Symphony both disappointed and dismayed : if the Arnell Quintet was deliberately eclectic the Alwyn was distressingly, indiscriminately and probably unintentionally so. Strauss flirted with Sibelius—quite un-formally in the most impolite meaning of the word. No one was surprised to find the symphony un-symphonic : indeed only the reverse would have caused a stir. But that such commonplace stuff should have issued forth from a by no means commonplace musical mind was astonishing. To say stick to film music will be considered abominable bad taste : but that's my advice to Mr. Alwyn. Why stop doing what you do better than most others, in order to try your hand at something where you fail as badly as the worst of the rest ? Anthony Collins' Suite (we can safely ignore its more pretentious title) was loose and episodic in structure and continuously rhapsodic in manner. For all this it was curiously un-English, although the composer shares with other English lyricists an inability to write a refrain for solo violin over a subdued harmonic accompaniment which is not alarmingly sentimental. Mr. Collins' first movement, the most interesting of his four, eschewed the modality of the English renaissance and favoured instead the richer texture offered by a very free neo-romanticism. Thus the movement was often reminiscent of Schoenberg's *Verklaerte Nacht*. The fact that the latter work belongs to the 1890s (if only chronologically) makes its own comment. What Schoenberg was doing then is not historically possible now : nor is Mr. Collins a Schoenberg. The Baines was an insult to everybody's intelligence, the composer's included. I should like to know on what musical grounds the concerto was chosen for performance. According to the programme note it was written in 1937. Someone should have let this sleeping dog die.

D. M.

CHELTENHAM FESTIVAL (SECOND WEEK : JULY 10TH-15TH) : BRITTEN'S " BEGGAR'S OPERA " (AT CHELTENHAM AND AT THE " LYRIC," HAMMERSMITH, JULY 17TH-AUGUST 5TH).

THE second week of the festival brought the English Opera Group to Cheltenham for three performances of " Albert Herring," two of the " Beggar's Opera," and two of " Let's Make an Opera." Let there be no doubt : in spite of the general success of these operas, their music is still far from being understood. The general public takes to them because their plots are ingenious, their action lively, singing good, dresses lovely ; and because the music, or how much people hear of it, seems to them authoritative, even if unintelligible. Some of the critics, on the other hand, are still professionally unable to discern the voice of authority in a composer who intentionally

118

spurns its grandiose trappings. Reading statements like " the false aesthetical premises " of "Albert Herring " (" Times "), or hearing the " Star," the " Evening Standard " and the " Evening News " all bemoan the good old days of the Austin-Playfair production of the " Beggar's Opera " (18th July), one becomes doubly grateful for the meticulous care that is lavished by the English Opera Group on the production, direction, playing and singing of these operas : for one hopes that performances of such polish, admitted even by adverse critics, will tie these operas over to a not too distant time when the real significance of Britten's music will be grasped by both the public and the press.

Now for some detailed remarks about the performances. *Albert Herring*. Britten's tempi (July 10th) generally faster than Del Mar's (July 12th, 14th). Music better served by Britten, capacity of audience and singers better served by Del Mar. Britten's abrupt conducting deprecates the underlying seriousness of the music ; it may offend listeners by cheating them out of their fun and their awe alike. Even on purely musical grounds, Del Mar's speed of the threnody is preferable to Britten's, which is about 8 metronome beats faster. Production smoother, wittier, more kaleidoscopic than ever. Whoever thinks this is too much for his eyes and ears must just come again. People *will* chatter in second act interlude. Old Sadler's Wells drop-curtain of nocturnal Loxford used to help them concentrate. Marvellous singing and impersonation by Peter Pears as Albert Herring. Twice, his natural gentleness curbs him : both his outburst in the 2nd act, 2nd scene, and his turning against his mother at the very end could be more explosive. At Sadler's Wells he used to point at his mother with outstretched arm, singing : " You ! ! ! . . . " Now, he is almost consoling. But otherwise, what musicality, what intuition ! What balance between country bumkin and Parsifal at first, between rake and Prodigal Son at last ! Nancy Evans (Nancy) and Frederick Sharp (Sid) are a well-matched pair—just one in a million of ordinary, decent, level-headed young couples, one feels. The pathos of courting—" our love is a private world-event. Yet it happens to millions : is that a bond or a barrier ? Are we gods or may-flies in love ? "—this pathos is written all over Britten's music for Sid and Nancy. Evans and Sharp brought it out to perfection (especially on July 14th) in their snugly frightened, uncomfortably pleased singing of the two love duets. Joan Cross (Lady Billows) and Gladys Parr (Florence) successfully tackle the comic duplicity of their parts. The former *sings* like one who most certainly is in " Debrett," but *acts* as if she would not mind getting into " Punch " ; the latter *sings* like one who most certainly would like to be in " Debrett," but *acts* as if she would loathe getting into " Punch." Otakar Kraus (Vicar), Roy Ashton (Mayor) and Norman Lumsden (Budd) would neither look for themselves in " Debrett," nor would they recognize their own likenesses in " Punch." This means that their acting and singing can combine to produce those comedy characterisations whose humour is supposed to reside solely in the onlooker's mind—a task which they solved brilliantly, deflecting from pure singing just as much as necessary and no more. Margaret Ritchie found the right warbles for the repressed emotions of Miss Wordsworth ; Anne Sharp (Cis) was excellent as always. I know this opera is devilishly hard to sing, but, all the same, the ensembles could be improved. The quartet in the last act (Mrs. Herring, Nancy, Miss Wordsworth, Vicar) and also the threnody, sound as if the singers daren't listen to each other, with the result that slight inflections in pitch (which are unavoidable) are not followed up by the other singers, at least not until the next simple passage is reached.

The Beggar's Opera. Still finding unsuspected beauties after twelve hearings of this opera, I can hardly follow any more the arguments advanced against Britten's setting, compounded as they are of mental laziness and a wrong conception of musical history. That it is not only intellectual snobs like me who are taken in by Britten, is shown by the example of the public who continue to flock to the show, and by at least one stage-hand at the " Lyric " who, having served in the Austin-Playfair production, began by violently disliking " this ' ere 'oifalutin' music," but came round after a few performances and now admits to enjoying it. At the time of writing, the production has become very smooth (in places almost slick), and the dialogue safely accelerated, now that the enunciation of the singers is very assured. But I am certain the dialogue could be cut even more than it already is, to make room for Mrs. Peachum's " A maid is like the golden ore " and her exquisitely rude canon with her husband, at present left out. Basil Coleman's direction very aptly oscillates, as does the music, between the characters' depravity, avarice and bawdiness, and their pretensions at social status, sound business-sense and good manners. Of the two conductors, Mr. Del Mar is more experienced and safer, if sometimes inflexible, while Mr. Renton lets the singers have their way, sometimes justly so, sometimes at the expense of good ensemble. Speaking of the singers, Bruce Boyce looks, acts and sings like a perfect Macheath. He has been blamed for a lack of " swagger," but I believe a character who has to be credible in the passacaglia and terzetto of the Prison Scene (credible to Britten's climactic music, that is !) could not put on another inch of swagger in the preceding acts without becoming farcical. Which goes to show, by the way, that a composer of Britten's rank was needed to transport the whole atmosphere of the opera, away from *operetta-glamour*, into the realm of *opera semiseria* where it belongs. David Franklin (Peachum) and Otakar Kraus (Lockit) give a brilliant portrayal of their roguish friendship and distrust. Their voices are well-matched too : Franklin's rambling, nicely gritty bass against Kraus' energetic heroic baritone. Lucy, one feels, is the rôle of a lifetime for Rose Hill—but then one remembers that one felt the same about her Despina. Her unfailing musical instinct always combines with the exact movements and facial expression needed at a particular moment. Nancy Evans' Polly, while always well sung, was a little stiff at first ; but lately she has found a way of stressing Polly's purity and sincerity while not making her fatuous or prudish. Gladys Parr, very well cast as the Beggar and Mrs. Trapes, nightly combines her long stage experience with untiring devotion to her rôles, and Max Worthley's neat tenor is an asset to Filch, and to Macheath's gang.† To proceed: In a concert at the Town Hall (July 11th) Peter Pears and Benjamin Britten performed Schumann's *Dichterliebe*, Arthur Oldham's *Five Chinese Lyrics* (1948) to Arthur Waley's translations, and some American folk songs set for them by Aaron Copland. In the performance of the *Dichterliebe* which was truer to the spirit of Schumann, and phrased more

---

† Our reviewer is the husband of Esther Salaman—a fact which explains why there is no mention in his notice of her dramatically accomplished and musically excellent performance in the rôle of Mrs. Peachum both at Cheltenham and Hammersmith.—Eds.

according to the form of each song than any I have heard, some of the best moments were : the aptly inconclusive end of the first song, Pears' patter in " Die Rose, die Lilie," Britten's rubato in " Wenn ich in deine Augen seh," the tenuous mezza-voce touch of both in " Am leuchtenden Sommermorgen," and the sensitive change in the dotted rhythm of " Am Rhein " from upbeat quavers to portamento quavers. Three criticisms : " Allnaechtlich im Traume " should have more lilt and a freer ending, more pedal would fetch out the fantastic quality of " Aus alten Maerchen," and Die boesen alten Lieder " should be slower and more processional. The *Chinese Lyrics*, a very good example of Oldham's style, translate the flowing rhythms and concrete images of their poems into uncrowded music of superior behaviour, with a florid vocal line. Similarly well-spaced are Copland's arrangements, most of them daringly, and effectively, old-fashioned.

One of the weaker works of Moeran, the String Trio (1936), was performed by the Carter Trio on July 12th. The modal and pentatonic academicism, and the partly gushing, partly meandering texture of its outer movements do not well agree with the older, more continental harmony of the slow movement. The Carters were joined by Leon Goossens in a first performance of William Wordsworth's Quartet for oboe and strings (op. 44). Although there are many beautiful moments (the second movement's second theme, and its first development section are Wordsworth at his best) one is disturbed by a certain negative quality of this idiom which tries to avoid modern English academicism without putting a more personal language in its place. The first movement's form, A - a - B - b - C - B - b - a - A, where A and a are related slow groups, B and b related fast groups, and C the development, will be seen to change round the order of a sonata-recapitulation. Though it does not come off in this work, the scheme remains an interesting possibility for the modern composer under special conditions of tonality. A similar case is the cyclic finish of the second of the two movements : the quotation of the first movement's A *and* B (in this order) makes the ending bizarre. The treatment of the oboe is not ideal : long cantilena passages are absent, and A is really a clarinet-figure.

The next day (July 13th), the Rubbra-Gruenberg-Pleeth Trio gave a first performance of Rubbra's Piano Trio op. 68. The, to my mind, genuine mysticism of this music makes me overlook many of its stylistic anachronisms (which in a mystical composer we should always forgive), its austere string writing, its ascetic invention, and the formal defects of its first section where a slow theme is treated rather aimlessly in the manner of a chorale prelude. The Cello Sonata (1946) which was also performed at this concert—" mystical " music too, but more inventive than the trio—succeeds in its very similar first movement through having a theme that is capable of acceleration and retardation, thus producing two climaxes within the movement. The *scherzi* of both works exhibit Rubbra's curious sequences which seem compounded of Italian baroque, Schumann, and modern English sequential trends, and are remarkably telling. But it is not until the last section that the Trio reaches the spiritual heights of the Cello Sonata. In the " Tema " and the two " Meditazione " a deeply serious, self-effacing and God-fearing musicianship is revealed.

P.H.

The Edinburgh Festival

Usher Hall, 2nd September : Hallé Orchestra, c. Barbirolli.

IN this, the first European performance of Bartok's posthumous Viola Concerto, William Primrose, partnered by Sir John Barbirolli, succeeded in transmitting the quintessence of Bartok the musician.* Barbirolli's feeling for the elusive and subtle colours of this dark-hued orchestration was matched by the sleek, tense tone of the solo viola—a large tone, often enough, for an instrument of such reasonable proportions. Primrose's technique is not without the indelible imprint of the U.S.A., which is to say the imprint of Europe at its best : the effortless cohesion of bow-arm and left-hand-work bore testimony to the broadest, yet keenest of minds, a mind non-insular and nonplussed, ever the servant of the music. It would be pleasant to see more of this attitude, but there is little hope of such an improvement until British viola players cease trying to imitate British violinists.

> * For another impression of the Concerto, see the review of its first London performance on p. 136.

King's Theatre, 4th September : " Ariadne auf Naxos."

A FANTASTIC and highly-varied synthesis of opera, ballet and theatre must inevitably appeal to a wider range of tastes than any of these *media* taken singly. So it was that *Ariadne auf Naxos*, brilliantly cast and produced by Carl Ebert, provided an entertainment of rare delight and ample proportions, for like every synthesis of the arts (not excluding Bayreuth) this one was not afraid of outstaying its welcome. For all the experimentation of Strauss and von Hoffmansthal, the opera has an unwieldy tail, which wags contentedly from one interrupted cadence to another in blissful unawareness of its marked tendency towards the prolix. But the two halves, play and opera, balance one another uncommonly well : both Molière and Strauss are Janus-headed. Whereas Molière looks back to Cervantes and forward to Beaumarchais, Strauss pays due homage to classical tonality yet contrives at the same time to be as modern as we like to imagine him. And in like manner, Miles Malleson's re-creative adaptation of Molière's play, and his sympathetic portrayal of Monsieur Jourdain fully matched the inspired conducting of Sir Thomas Beecham, who showed himself as partial to the gentle art of repartee as the best of the *Commedia dell'arte*.

Freemasons' Hall, 5th September : Hugo Wolf recital.

A RECITAL given by Elisabeth Schwarzkopf and Gerald Moore proved to be wise in its complete devotion to Wolf, whose settings of poems by Moerike, Goethe, Geibel and Heyse made up the entire programme. Here the singer's art was nicely blended with pianistic sensitivity of a high order, and the performances, thus scaled down to that intimate radius where lieder flourish best, lacked nothing in depth both of sympathy and interpretation.

Usher Hall, 8th September : Magnificat (Monteverdi). Orchestra, chorus and soloists of La Scala, Milan, c. Guido Cantelli.

THIS travesty of a masterpiece of the Baroque was brought about mainly by four things : too many instruments, too many voices, too much vibrato, and too much fuss. Under such fourfold disadvantage, no performance could hope to be good, and this one was bad. The mammoth effect which had apparently been sought after by Ghedini in his transcription put to shame the monstrous Handelian festivals which London knew a century or so ago. On such a scale as this, tempi and ensemble suffered badly, and the balance between the imitation cornetts (clarinets + oboes) and the rest of the band left much to be desired. Again, it was the scale which had to do with the distortion, time after time, of a simple little cadential tag of the Renaissance—a mere written-out-trill—yet another proof of the excessive fussiness of an overblown edition. It is to be hoped most sincerely that the Italians will one day learn to interpret their musical heritage in the right way.

D.W.S.

An After-note on Strauss' "Ariadne auf Naxos"

ONE aspect impressed me immediately after hearing the broadcast performance : *Ariadne* was not half as classical or neo-classical as either Strauss had wanted or I had imagined it to be from study with score and piano version. It seems that in the act of orchestration Strauss often defeated his own best intentions : the texture became Straussian against the composer's will. The small-scale Prelude to the opera itself is really something of an illusion : its very ingenious 18th century pastiche doesn't last long, and the effects of it are entirely dispersed by Ariadne's (admittedly great) aria " Es gibt ein Reich " which is as full-blooded and as full-blown as anything in *Rosenkavalier* or *Salome*. I notice in this issue* that one of our Salzburg reviewers writing about *Capriccio* (yet another of Strauss' intimate operatic explorations) feels obliged to make back-reference to *Rosenkavalier*. In this connection therefore it is not without value to re-examine once more the Strauss-Hofmannsthal correspondence and see how Strauss' verbal ambitions to revive the spirit of antiquity measure up to his musical achievements. He wrote quite plainly on a famous occasion :

> " Your impassioned protest against the Wagnerian method of music-making has sunk deep into my heart and opened a door on an entirely new landscape, in which, with ' Ariadne ' and more particularly the Prelude to guide me, I hope to find my way into the realm of un-Wagnerian opera where all is action, feeling, and human nature."

But how how far did Strauss realise his ideals in " Ariadne " and after ? Hans Redlich in his recent *Ariadne* article† reacts positively when he speaks of " the fragile and subtle realization of a poet's dream, desiring a new Mozartean age to rise out of the dying embers of post-Wagnerian sensualism."

Now I don't doubt for one moment that this was the objective at which both Strauss and Hofmannsthal aimed : nor do I doubt *Ariadne*'s indisputable historical significance. But its significance seems to me to be historical merely, and not musical : that it was rather Strauss' and Hofmannsthal's forward-looking ideas that have influenced operatic history, not Strauss' music.

I have suggested in an article elsewhere‡ that Strauss succeeds with " humane " characterisation and fails with the superhuman and mythological. This is an over-simplification ; but consider the gulf that divides *Till*, for instance, from *Zarathustra* : consider the intense psychological perception

*See p. 132.
†*Music Survey* III/1/50.
‡*Disc*, Spring, 1950.

and penetration which infuse *Rosenkavalier* and the inflated emptiness of the anti-social *Ein Heldenleben*. I wasn't in the least astonished to find that in *Ariadne* it was the music given to the comedians, the *commedia dell' arte* figures, which was the most convincing. Indeed I suspected well in advance that the advent of the God Bacchus was going to be a dreadful bore and my suspicion was proved horribly right : a fact on which Denis Stevens has made witty comment above. Even Ariadne's fine aria I have quoted is to an extent devalued by the earthbound Zerbinetta's staggering coloratura piece which is a musical *tour de force*. But as far as I was concerned Bacchus put an end not only to Ariadne's charms but to Strauss' never very musically concrete 18th century ideals besides. There is no point in complaining of this curious schizophrenia in Strauss ; this odd distinction between the humane and heroic which, in *Ariadne*, we have nakedly, if unintentionally, exposed for us by the composer in two separate compartments: a play within a play, as it were. Perhaps Strauss' humanism was the most 18th century thing about him, if we choose to regard it as contrary motion to the 19th century's prevailing tendency towards heroism. Whatever it was it didn't result in a fundamental stylistic transformation. Ultimately *Ariadne* disappointed me because it proved that Strauss couldn't be anything but Strauss.

D.M.

The Leeds Festival

LEEDS' Festival reminds its visitors that festival or no festival the city's business continues very much as usual. In the Town Hall's vestibule, more thronged with dinner-jackets than any similar gathering at Covent Garden, a large placard bleakly directed Tax Defaulters to the appropriate Court of Justice ; and during a performance of Holst's semi-exotic *Hymn of Jesus* the front stalls were assailed by an odour of distinctly boiled fish. It seems that the Civic Restaurant was in operation beneath the platform on which the Yorkshire Symphony Orchestra and Mr. Miles were doing their valiant best. The acoustics of the Town Hall were less alarming than its architecture ; fortunately so in view of the predominantly and traditionally choral nature of the festival. The Y.S.O., making its début as a festival orchestra, pleased us by its enterprising programmes, but disappointed by its poor *ensemble* standard, weak tonal resources and slovenly rhythmic sense. Its conductor, Mr. Maurice Miles, must learn to impress his personality on his band by more effective means than extravagant gestures and a partiality for unmusical *ritardandi* which strain phrasing and structure to breaking point—a tendency all too evident in his reading of Vaughan Williams's over-played Sixth Symphony. But we must be grateful to the Y.S.O. for a rehearing of Honegger's *King David* oratorio which is undeservedly neglected by our choral societies. Vigorous stuff, it makes its elementary points with bold strokes of vocal and instrumental colour, in the manner of a very good poster : often blatant, never vulgar, and always sincere. The one unsatisfactory soloist was Margaretta Scott, the Narrator, who roared the Biblical text rather in the style of an Ibsen heroine at bay. The Hallé succeeded the Y.S.O. as a more accomplished resident orchestra and was responsible in its final programme for the Northern première of Britten's *Spring* Symphony. The composer was to have conducted but illness intervened and at the last moment his place was

124

taken by the festival's chorus master, Mr. Herbert Bardgett. In the emergency circumstances created by Britten's absence Mr. Bardgett did extremely well : " I'm having a bash—why don't you ? " he cried out during the rehearsal when his chorus made tentative hits at the un-Handelian intervals of Britten's wintry introduction. Those who feared for the subtleties of Britten's music in the hands of this genial Yorkshireman could have been less anxious : the performance was both a musical and public success. The hundred-odd Leeds schoolboys who added their uninhibited gusto to the already large orchestral and choral forces, proved, at the very least, that English kids can whistle as straight as their opposite numbers in Amsterdam.

D.M.

Chester Arts Week

DONIZETTI AND MILHAUD

THE first English performances of Donizetti's *The Night Bell*, and *Le Pauvre Matelot* by Milhaud, were given by the London Opera Society in the Gaumont Theatre, Chester, as the most enticing event of Chester Arts Week. A plush super-cinema is not the place for small-scale opera, and the Milhaud would show to better advantage on a smaller stage ; but both operas were well set and produced, and the Boyd Neel Orchestra, under Edward Renton's taut conducting, played finely throughout the evening.

The singers had some difficulty at first in making contact with the audience across the no-man's-land of an improvised orchestra pit, but Jennifer Vyvyan, as the Matelot's wife, sang impressively, while the music of the other characters gave them little opportunity to make any impression. The heavier demands of Donizetti were met with considerable success by Ian Wallace as the tormented apothecary—his every word was magnificently audible—and Gwyneth Owen managed the bride's coloratura neatly, though neither showed the richness of voice the music demands. As the gay and wicked hero, Bruce Boyce was disappointing—he has been known to sing with far more spirit—but he looked the part and romped through it with engaging *panache*.

Little need be said about *The Night Bell*. It has the gaiety, the sheer physical joy and the inventiveness of *Don Pasquale* or *L'Elisir d'Amore*, but its small scale prevents Donizetti from exercising his gift for lengthy, flowing melody. The translation, by Christopher Hassall, is in the Dent tradition, but ruder.

Le Pauvre Matelot is not good opera. The situation could have been made theatrically strong if it had been built up more firmly in the libretto :—A sailor returns to his obstinately faithful wife after fifteen years' absence. Unrecognized, he pretends he is a friend, and tells his wife that her husband is in hiding because of his debts. As he sleeps, she murders him for a pearl necklace he carries ; with this she will save her husband. The sailor's deception has no motive ;* until the last scene the *dramatis personae* discuss banalities in curt dialogue. Milhaud has no material with which he can make his people convincing.

Verdi, Mozart, Richard Strauss, would have bullied the librettist—Cocteau, in this instance—until fidelity, deception and the determination to murder, which the heroine must mime and not sing, were matters for strong arias ; the crux of opera is its creation of character by music sung, and to say that

* The motiveless and innocent deception finds its dramatic fulfilment and justification in the irony of the final premeditated murder.—EDS.

Cocteau and Milhaud did not wish to write as Verdi would have written is to say that they turned their backs on theatrical effectiveness.† The music throughout is disturbing, imaginative and beautiful ; Milhaud employs a chamber orchestra with mastery, but only in the last scene is there any attempt to marry the events of the stage to the activity in the orchestra. Then, to a fascinating perversion of *Blow the Man Down*, the wife seizes and holds the stage with the only truly vocal phrases in the work.   H.B.R.

> † But quite consciously and deliberately so. Both Cocteau and Milhaud knew what they were about when they substituted a naturalistic speech-song for the extended arias our reviewer misses. The validity of their method is, of course, another matter.—EDS.

La Scala, Milan

THE best musically : Verdi's *Otello, Requiem* (Sabata) and Beethoven's Seventh (Cantelli)—the latter a rapid substitution for Monteverdi's *Magnificat* which was a power-cut casualty ; in any case we don't seem to have missed much. (See this issue p. 122 for a review of the Edinburgh performance.) The best production : Donizetti's *L'Elisir D'Amore* (Capuana). The worst all-round : Verdi's *Falstaff* (Sabata). The Italian company's welcome visit was much publicised in the national dailies, weeklies and elsewhere, and a long report here would seem to be superfluous. Eric Blom said all the right things in *The Observer* on two consecutive Sundays. If Covent Garden could have learned much from La Scala's example, Sadler's Wells could have taught the Milanese something about *Falstaff*.   D.M.

The Darmstadt International Summer School

THIS year's international summer school, organised by the Kranichsteiner Musikinstitut of Darmstadt, provided a very valuable survey of the position of modern music in many countries today. About 150 students, teachers and guests from 14 different countries were able to meet and study together a variety of contemporary problems. There were composition classes, given by Wolfgang Fortner, Edgar Varèse and Ernst Krenek ; piano and violin lessons by Peter Stadlen and Tibor Varga, and an ensemble class under the direction of Maurits Frank of the Amsterdam Quartet. In addition, Hermann Scherchen gave some valuable informal lectures on the problems of conducting modern music, and Theodor Wiesengrund-Adorno discussed various aspects of contemporary musical criticism. Apart from these there was a comprehensive survey of the music of Bartok, including performances of all six string quartets by the Végh Quartet, a recital of his piano and violin works, and several lectures illustrated by recordings or live performances of most of his other major compositions. Finally, the curriculum included a number of separate items of interest ; three illustrated lectures on electronic instruments, a symposium on the work of the younger French, German and English composers, a talk on Schoenberg's methods by Josef Rufer of Berlin, and another by Hans Mayer of Leipzig on " Epic Theatre and Modern Music," with particular reference to Bert Brecht's theories.

Side by side with all these activities came a series of public concerts in the Stadthalle. Ernst Krenek, who celebrated his 50th birthday during the festival, was represented by a number of recent works, including his 4th Symphony and 7th String Quartet (heard at the London I.S.C.M. Festival in 1946). In the same concert as the symphony, given by the Darmstadt Landestheater Orchestra under Scherchen, came a notable event—the first German performance of Schoenberg's " A Survivor of Warsaw "—the moving and terrifying story told by one who escaped from the battle of the Warsaw ghetto. It is one of Schoenberg's finest and most mature works, and is long overdue for performance here.* It was followed by another remarkable piece—Edgar Varèse's " Ionisation" for 41 percussion instruments, written as long ago as 1932, but never before (it seems) performed in Europe. It is a most interesting combination of complex sonorities, though the use of a couple of sirens brought unfortunate associations which perhaps were not so noticeable in 1932. A suite from Fortner's ballet, " Die Weisse Rose " (based on Oscar Wilde's " The Birthday of the Infanta ") completed the programme ; it makes an individual use of the twelve-tone technique and is sensitively scored ; clearly it is music for the stage rather than the concert hall.

A chamber orchestral concert under Scherchen included, apart from two works by Krenek, the first two movements of Berg's Chamber Concerto with Varga and Stadlen as soloists, and a movement from Josef Matthias Hauer's " Zwoelftonmusik," Op. 73—a pleasant but curiously ineffective little piece. The festival ended with four concerts of music by composers born between 1915 and 1930 ; as might be expected, a certain number of immature works were performed, but there were also some interesting contributions. Two young Italian twelve-tone composers, Bruno Maderna and Luigi Nono, showed a good deal of originality in handling a somewhat fragmentary and Webernian technique in two works for small orchestra ; Hans Werner Henze proved himself the most accomplished of the younger Germans in his dramatically scored 2nd Symphony, though there were also effective, if less striking contributions by Bernd Aloys Zimmerman, Matthias Siedel, and Hans Ulrich Engelmann. The outstanding works in the chamber concerts were the 2nd String Quartet of the Belgian Victor Legley, which showed a mature mastery of its material as well as a definite individual personality, and Peter Racine Fricker's String Quartet, which met with an extremely warm reception. The reactions of the audience were in fact extremely violent, and the weaker works were heartily whistled at. The whole atmosphere of the school was invigorating ; the students were out to absorb as much knowledge as they could, and the general tendency was radical. Hindemith and Nadia Boulanger seem to have been replaced by Bartok and Schoenberg, at any rate for the moment, as the chief influences on the younger generation, but there was no particularly doctrinaire attitude prevalent, and most of the students seemed willing to try out any idea provided it was interesting and progressive.

HUMPHREY SEARLE

* As pointed out in *Music Survey* II/4/50. So far no one has caught up with our seven months' old plea.—Eds.

[Next year's school will take place from 23rd June to 15th July, and composers born between 1916 and 1931 are invited to submit orchestral, chamber orchestral, or chamber works, by 15th January to : Kranichsteiner Musikinstitut, Darmstadt, Lagerhausstr.,9.—Eds.]

Bach in Lueneburg : 1700—1950

REPORT ON THE CONGRESS OF MUSICOLOGISTS AND ON THE SECOND
WORLD CONGRESS OF MUSIC LIBRARIES, JULY 15TH-22ND, 1950.

EXACTLY 250 years ago, that is in March, 1700, J. S. Bach was accepted at
the school of St. Michael's church in Lueneburg, where for three consecutive
years he was to learn the rudiments of musical craft, occasionally acting as
singer and player and eagerly imbibing the elements of Boehm's and Reinken's
organistic skill. The present state of political cleavage, dividing Germany into
Eastern and Western zones, has lately focused attention on this picturesque
Hanseatic city of ancient guildhouses and Gothic church spires. With the
existing zonal boundaries it happens to be the one and only township in the
Western zones which may claim to have been a place of Bach's one-time
activities. To hold a Congress of Musicologists in the year celebrating the
200th anniversary of Bach's death in a town boasting of a genuine Bach-
tradition (be it only the tradition of the " alumnus," i.e. " Mettenschueler ")
would give a firm enough backbone to any gathering of musical scholars,
always in danger of becoming dilatory and obtuse. It was therefore an
excellent idea on the part of Germany's newly-founded society of musicologists—*Gesellschaft fuer Musikforschung*—and its admirably active president
Professor Friedrich Blume (Kiel) to have invited scholars from all over Europe
to attend a Congress which was devoted simultaneously to the furtherance
of their science in general and to the worship of J. S. Bach in particular. By
combining this first International Congress of Musicologists in Western
Germany since the cessation of hostilities with the Second World Congress of
Music Libraries (a successor to the previous Congress in Florence), Professor
Blume was able to include an even greater number of interested scholars,
students and librarians and so enhance the truly international character of
his enterprise. Both congresses were held in close succession within one week
and their participants met during a delightful excursion across the famous
solitude of Lueneburg Heath. Beside the actual proceedings of the congresses with their numerous sectional meetings, lectures, public addresses and
discussions, there was also a series of concerts, chiefly devoted to Bach's
inexhaustible art. These Bach concerts were undoubtedly highlights of the
Lueneburg days, culminating in a very competent, if slightly too hurried,
performance of the *St. Matthew Passion* under Richard Liesche (Bremen).
Amongst many other notable events came a beautiful reading of the rarely
heard Cantata No. 169 " Gott soll allein mein Herze haben," performed as
part of a Lutheran church service at St. Michael's, on the very organ loft
where Bach himself used to sing as a young chorister ; a performance of three
a cappella motets, interrupted by a selection of Schuebler Chorales and
Organ Fugues ; a choice programme of his secular works—including the
curiously Italianate Cantata No. 209 " Non sa che sia dolore," which, if
authentic, is certainly a clever imitation of style—and finally, a masterly
performance of the Goldberg variations, played by Fritz Neumayer in the
nave of the ancient Klosterkirche on a harpsichord with 2 keyboards. These
concerts found their legitimate counterpart in the papers specially devoted
to a deeper understanding of Bach's personality and art. Of remarkable
interest in that respect was the paper read by Professor Arnold Schmitz
(Mainz) on the rhetorical qualities of Bach's music and on its organic

association with the rhetorical figures of traditional poetic ornamentation (a subject which he has treated at greater length in his recent study *Die Bildlichkeit der wortgebundenen Musik J. S. Bach's*, Schott, Mainz, 1950). Professor H. Besseler (Jena) lectured on " Bach als Wegbereiter," while Fred Hamel (Hanover) discussed Bach's work as reflected in the short but lively history of the gramophone record. Prof. R. Haas (Austria) spoke on " Bach und Wien " and H. Engel (Marburg) on the sociological aspects of Bach's personality. The present writer read a paper on " Anfaenge der Bachpflege in England, 1750-1850," in which he was able to show that the lion's share in the achievements of early English Bach enthusiasts should go to A.F.C. Kollmann, who was first in the field to start a faithful reprint of the " Wohltemperirte Clavier " (1799), after having recognized the peculiarities of Bach's instrumental style in earlier publications from 1788 to 1796. He also corrected the recent error of H. T. David and A. Mendel (in their *Bach Reader*, 1945) who attribute the English translation of Forkel's Bach biography (published 1820) to R. Stephenson, whereas a letter from S. Wesley (dated September 23rd, 1820) to the organist Emmett proves beyond doubt that Kollmann himself was the author of this translation. Among the numerous papers read on other topics, two seemed of special value : W. Boetticher's new chronology of Orlandus Lassus' work, culled from the huge Catalogue of works he is preparing on that vast subject, and H. Chr. Wolff's thoughtful paper on " The Value of History." Among notable German scholars reading papers on a bewildering variety of subjects ranging from " Cantus Gregorianus " to Metastasio's librettos, were K. G. Fellerer (Cologne), H. J. Moser (Berlin), Anna Amalia Abert (Kiel) and R. Gerber (Göttingen). Especially attractive were lectures on problems of Italian musicology contributed by the distinguished Italian team of Fausto Torrefranca, Federigo Ghisi and Ottavio Tiby. A great number of papers were devoted to problems of musical folklore. Among these should be mentioned at least A. Bake's scholarly account of " Die altindischen Tongeschlechter in Bharatas Natyasastra " and Eta Harich-Schneider's most vivid account of Japanese music. In the subsequent Congress of Music Libraries, most ably presided over by Mr. Valentin Denis (Louvain, Belgium) and attended by a galaxy of leading music librarians from all over Europe, some papers were of special interest to the English student : J. H. Davies' interesting lecture on " Music Librarianship for Broadcasting," as well as Irmgard Becker-Glauch's paper on " The English Music Libraries in Germany." Perhaps the most valuable work of this Congress was done in committee, where the way was prepared for a future issue of a General Catalogue of Music (as envisaged already in 1943 by O. E. Deutsch in his important article " Music Bibliography and Catalogues," London, The Bibliographical Society) which would at long last replace the *Quellenlexikon* of Eitner ; and where practical means were found for a closer collaboration and intercommunication between music libraries in Europe. Both congresses did their best to fortify cultural contacts with the Eastern Zone of Germany, represented by few if prominent personalities like Professor W. Vetter, Berlin, and they both received official blessing and even a promise of financial support from UNESCO, ably represented on this occasion by Dr. Robin Laufer (Paris).

H. F. REDLICH

129

The Salzburg Festival

Beethoven : " *Fidelio*."

Furtwaengler's *Fidelio* was the greatest operatic event of the Salzburg Festival and one of the greatest in my life. Unfortunately I could not be sure that any of the critics I talked to in Salzburg understood Furtwaengler's achievement sufficiently to be entrusted with noticing it for this journal ; whereas I myself was " covering " the Festival for *The Music Review*. Happily, however, a musician was passing through the town on the day of a *Fidelio* performance ; I persuaded her to submit her impression.—ED. (H.K.).

A GLORIOUS performance. Not being stylized, *Fidelio*'s formalities easily become stilted. By the sureness of Furtwaengler's touch, however, which was caught by all the singers, the danger was entirely avoided ; nor was there for an instant any pushing and pulling between stage and orchestra. A vigorous feeling pervaded the interpretation from the eminently rhythmical (though by no means hasty) first notes, a feeling too, of complete inevitability of design.

The casting—Florestan, Patzak ; Leonore, Flagstad ; Fernando, Braun ; Pizarro, Schœffler ; Rocco, Greindl ; Marzelline, Schwarzkopf ; Jacquino, Dermota—was entirely right. Flagstad noticeably restrained herself in the ensembles in order to subdue the quantity of her voice, which effort strangely roughened its quality. But where great strength and exuberance were needed she gave with all her generosity. Her acting had real dignity ; only her hands did not collaborate. Schwarzkopf's arm and body movements, on the other hand, were often platitudinous as against the true refinement and beauty of her singing. Patzak is blessed with the perfect timbre for Florestan : a voice both manly and sorrowful, with flawless purity of musical line.

The performance roused us all to such excitement that somehow the interval seemed an effort. The climax was the 3rd *Leonora* which flashed through one's imagination as if Beethoven had been there moulding it. Upon the over-powering coda, whose intensity derived from the growth of the whole movement, the entire audience—in mid-act and in the darkened theatre—stood and literally roared.

Guenther Rennert's production and Emil Pretorius' designs were straightforward and spacious ; brilliant white mantillas and light clear colours emphasized the feeling of sunlight in the crowd scene, wherefrom a presentiment emerged of the finale of the Ninth Symphony.

E.S.

Boris Blacher : " *Romeo and Juliet*."

As an opera *Romeo and Juliet* (15th August) amounts to almost nothing. For the most part it hovers uncomfortably between mime and oratorio, and it had much better been left in its original state*. Little appararent attempt has been made to achieve continuity between scenes, with the result that there is no interest in development of character and no possibility of dramatic climax. Scene follows scene with monotonous haste and the whole effect (since the piece lasts only an hour) is fragmentary and unsatisfying. Blacher's resources

*(Written during the war as a concert work, it was subsequently adapted for the stage.)

130

are eleven singing characters—of whom only Romeo and Juliet are of importance—full four-part chorus, ballet, and orchestra of flute, bassoon, trumpet, piano and strings. If the ballet was a charming inessential the treatment of the chorus was positively inept. Whereas, in *The Rape of Lucretia*, Britten's chorus remains almost wholly detached from the action, palely spot-lit and made-up ashen-grey, Blacher's choir, seated in pews, was in no such way set apart—so that one continually expected them at least to take notice of the action. But no. Immobile they remained, comically commenting upon what they were (clearly) not allowed to look at !

Musically, Blacher shows no very strong influences. In solo work he is less free, melodically, than Britten ; though less wayward and less intricate also. In choral passages he shows close affinities to Kodaly. He has also a briskly rhythmic manner which, though it lacks the fevered aimlessness, recalls one side of Walton. In general, the music is remarkable for an assured harmonic sense which reconciles without strain romantic and modern idioms.   There is certainly no suggestion of the consistent use of a " modern " system of tonality.

The performance was very good. Holm is extremely musical, but at times he is inclined to over-phrase—with a resulting dislocation of line.   Gueden reminds me of Rita Hayworth, but as a singer she is now very nearly in the Seefried class, with a voice that is bright without hardness, and exceptional breath-control. The orchestra under Krips was impeccable.

R.N.P.

Britten : " Der Raub Der Lukrezia."

SALZBURG'S was the first Austrian production of Britten's *Rape of Lucretia*, and it sounded like it. Or, to be exact, a small part was surprisingly better, another disappointingly worse than, and the overriding rest precisely as bad as was to be expected from an interpretation which had to do without the help of composer or tradition. Vocally, to be sure, one even heard some better efforts than in the English Opera Group's production.

If, however, the composer had no time to advise Prof. Krips in detail, the publisher of the work ought to have sent an expert to Salzburg, preferably Erwin Stein, to watch the rehearsals from the beginning. As it was, the severest defects consisted in wrong tempi (that Prof. Krips misread the metronome indication of the lullaby was not much of an excuse, since the structure of the music made his express speed an impossibility anyhow) as well as wrong phrasings.   Rhetorical declamation often took the place of musical accentuation : if you don't understand the music you cling to the words. But while one could not yet expect the virginal performers to read between the lines, they could have heeded the lines themselves more conscientiously, singing at least the right notes and note values, not to speak of a logical textural balance in the ensembles. As the work was thrown together with Blacher's *Romeo und Julia*, it had to be played without a break : an anti-formal informality.

The chamber orchestra was taken from the Vienna Philharmonic ; the singers were Julius Patzak as Male Chorus (who despite his elsewhere, e.g. in *Fidelio*, unsurpassable musicality, did not understand this music at all),

Annelies Kupper (Female Chorus), Kurt Böhme (Collatinus), Alfred Poell (Junius), Hermann Uhde (Tarquinius), Elisabeth Höngen (Lucretia), Dagmar Hermann (Bianca), and, last and best in every respect, Hilde Güden as Lucia.

Josef Gielen's production was better than the musical performance in proportion as it is easier. Caspar Neher's designs were impressive, though in my—here a layman's—opinion not up to John Piper's.

I did not, *literally*, meet an Austrian listener who didn't take exception, in the strongest terms, to the German translation. All the objections I heard were based on literary grounds, though musically the translation is not adequate either. It needs thorough revision.

Otherwise, the work was enthusiastically received, obviously for the wrong reasons, since the venture (for which we remain sincerely grateful) could not offer more than a glimmer of the right ones.

H.K.

Strauss : " *Capriccio.*"

CAPRICCIO, though given in Germany in 1942, had what was in effect its world première on August 12th at Salzburg. It was intended as the third of a trilogy of operas of which the first and second were *Friedenstag* and *Daphne*. It is, however, self-contained and requires no reference to the other two. Strauss describes it as a " Konversationstueck", and any criticism which does not take this into account is off the point. Dramatically, it represents a discussion, in the Shavian manner, of the relative importance, in opera, of words and music.

The scene is Paris ; the date " about 1775," at the time of the publication of Gluck's Preface to *Alceste*. The Countess Madeleine, who is at the centre of the discussion and who perhaps represents the opera-listener, has as her suitors the composer Flamand, and the poet Olivier. The remaining protagonists are the Count her brother, the dilettante ; La Roche, the impresario ; and Clairon, the actress. Madeleine is wooed by Flamand and Olivier both as lovers and, for the sake of the argument, as musician and poet respectively. La Roche, besides cherishing fantastic ambitions in the theatre, has a shrewd understanding of the issues involved. The dilettante is obsessed with the actress, and neither is interested in much more than the glamour of the stage. It remains with Madeleine to state her preference. Since both words and music must play their part she must accept both. But in real life she rejects Flamand and Olivier.

Musically, *Capriccio* looks back to *Rosenkavalier*. Strauss treads no new ground, but the opera has the repose which one has come to expect from his later work. The temperature is lower, the atmosphere no longer suffocating. The mood of the piece is set in a tranquil introduction for string sextet, reminiscent of the *Metamorphosen*. Individual touches recall *Rosenkavalier*, but the prevailing mood is more well-mannered, for passion never runs high. What linger in the memory after one hearing are the introduction, Flamand's aria, the trio for Madeleine and her lovers, the " argument octet "—a brilliantly witty piece of contrapuntal writing—, La Roche's great outburst, which has all the virtuosity of the best of the Ochs passages (and more musical substance), and Madeleine's final monologue, which, as it strongly recalls the Marschallin's, can as easily bear comparison with it. Strauss's invention remains amazing—the tinsel has gone, but there remains, here and there, a sugar-plum or two. He uses a small orchestra with restraint, economy and taste : his consummate mastery of orchestral colour is employed, as it should be in what is, after all, a kind of operatic last will and testament, to underline the characterization of the protagonists in the argument.

The presentation was entirely worthy of the occasion. Lisa della Casa—a singer new to me —gave a peformance of the highest artistry. Her voice, if it perhaps at present lacks the range of expression, is reminiscent of Lehmann's —very pure and even throughout, with a characteristically German production. Schoeffler (undisguisable as ever) was in every way a highly accomplished La Roche and his conception of the rôle was, for a first night, remarkably mature. Dermota, as Flamand, gave some lovely singing and was only very occasionally uncertain in intonation. Braun, as Olivier, was curiously ineffective. Neither of the lovers acted as well as he sang. To the evening's additional delights Klein contributed a remarkable character-study, Wilma Lipp and Karl Friedrich an altogether delicious parody of contemporary Italian opera. The playing of the Vienna Philharmonic, under Böhm, was beyond praise.

It is an unhappy thought that *Capriccio*, largely because it is essentially a " musicians' opera " and partly because of the severe demands it makes upon the listener— it lasts for 2 hours without a break—is unlikely to have a very wide appeal outside Germany.

R.N.P.

Viennese Preview
[Manuscript received at the end of September.]

FRITZ Busch has just come to Vienna to conduct at the State Opera for a month—for the first time since 15 years. Previously, at the beginning of this month, we had Georges Sebastian, [musical] director of the French Opera ; he will be returning at the end of October.

The concert season starts in the middle of October. Both the *Konzerthausgesellschaft* and the *Gesellschaft der Musikfreunde* have issued comprehensive and promising programmes. The *Konzerthausgesellschaft* is planning a big orchestral cycle with international conductors and soloists, each concert presenting a standard work from our musical literature, a modern work, and a famous soloist. A second soloist with a chamber orchestra under Franz Litschauer is above all intended to offer such masterpieces as have rarely or never before been heard in Vienna. In this cycle, too, great soloists will be heard. A third cycle of seven evenings gives a selection of Schubert's best songs, chamber music, symphonies and masses, while a fourth, of six evenings, will be devoted to chamber music alone : one Haydn quartet, one contemporary and one standard work in each recital. At the present time there is an amazing amount of remarkable talent in Austria ; but while members of the younger generation have already proved their accomplishments at various competitions, they are not yet sufficiently known to the wider public. The *Konzerthausgesellschaft*'s fifth series of concerts will therefore consist of eight solo recitals by young Austrian artists. Finally, there will be eight concerts of great chamber music played by Austrian as well as foreign ensembles, and nine appearances of celebrated international soloists,

But the climax of the *Wiener Konzerthausgesellschaft*'s programme will be the IVth International Music Festival which is to take place from March 31st to April 15th, 1951, in the Konzerthaus. The chief works whose performances are planned are the oratorio *The Grand Inquisitor* by Boris Blacher, Stravinsky's *Persephone*, Monteverdi's *Vespers*, Hindemith's *Das Unaufhörliche*, Britten's *Spring Symphony*, and a concert performance of an opera by Ernst Krenek. The first concert under Karl Böhm will offer three first performances, i.e. of Richard Strauss' waltz *An München* [*To Munich*], a song of praise [*Hymnus*] for contralto, choir and orchestra by Gottfried von Einem, and a Concertino for violin and 21 wind instruments by Alfred Uhl. A further first performance will be Elisabeth Schwarzkopf's of Hindemith's new Motets. These concerts, two of which will include works of living Austrian composers, will be conducted by Ernest Ansermet, Karl Böhm, Igor Markevitch, Hans Rosband, Paul Sacher, Karl Schuricht, and Eugen Szenkar. Besides, the Festival will proffer recitals of chamber music and *Lieder*.

The *Gesellschaft der Musikfreunde*'s plans are similar to the *Konzerthaus-gesellschaft*'s : eight orchestral programmes, two successive performances of each, under the title " The Great Symphony," each time under a great conductor* with an internationally known soloist. Then there will be a special " Karajan Cycle," i.e. six double concerts under Karajan comprising the B minor Mass, the Verdi Requiem, a concert performance of *Aida* with Italian artists and three orchestral programmes. Eight recitals of *Lieder*, six of chamber music (Schneiderhahn Quartet), four choral concerts and sixteen evenings with great soloists—this, in short, is the programme of the *Gesellschaft der Musikfreunde*.

The Vienna Philharmonic has already started its season with a concert under Furtwaengler, the conductor of four out of its nine concerts ; Clemens Krauss will conduct two, while for the remaining three Fritz Busch, Hans Knappertsbusch and Rafael Kubelik will be responsible.

The Austrian section (founded 2 years ago) of the international society *Jeunesses Musicales* has also a bigger programme this year than last. The society's principal aim is to unite the world's youth culturally, providing it with opportunities to attend the best concerts at reduced prices. The programme includes, above all, a cycle of eight choral and orchestral concerts, almost all of them repeat performances of the *Konzerthausgesellschaft*'s concerts. Membership of the *Jeunesses Musicales* also makes it possible for young people to listen to the rehearsals of the Vienna Philharmonic, as well as to attend other concerts and operas at reduced prices. In a word, the society's intentions could not be worthier, and it has already contributed a great deal towards mutual understanding among the young.

Among smaller-scale activities, those of the International Society for Contemporary Music, the Austrian Society for Contemporary Music, and of several private organisers should be mentioned : altogether a tremendous bill of fare, sometimes really too much at a time for the Viennese public which is unfortunately neither big nor solvent enough to digest all these programmes which are of very high cultural rank, but often very difficult.

DARIA COUNTESS RAZUMOVSKY† (VIENNA)
[Trans. H.K.].

*We may be provincial, but we do not know of eight great living conductors. —EDS.

†A descendant of ' the ' Count Razumovsky.

Concerts

I. Ken Wood and London

KENWOOD HOUSE : Members of the Boyd Neel Orchestra, 23rd July, 1950.

No sooner was the architecturally beautiful Kenwood house re-opened to the public than small chamber concerts, easy, informal, restful, gay and intensely enjoyable, were presented in surroundings as idyllic as you will find within a day's march of London. I had no fault to find with Maurice Clare's little group giving Beethoven's early Septet, a divertimento in all but name, and Schubert's great Octet, a living proof that the peculiar graciousness which goes to make a serenade (again not in name : but this is what I mean by Serenade) can blend with the most finely wrought emotions music can convey—there is no more moving compound.

R.D.

FIRST PERFORMANCES AT THE PROMS

August 4th : Prelude, Fugue and Postlude by Honegger. London Symphony Orchestra, conducted by Basil Cameron. (First performance in England.)

So far as I can make out, the only really successful recipe for writing a good fugue since and including Beethoven is not to write a fugue. No matter how you handle the fugal texture, the real spirit of fugue implies a ruthless symmetry very near the heart of Baroque music, and a thousand miles distant from the twentieth century. That subtly, infinitely varied but inescapable pattern ; that powerful classic reassurance as the final entries come surging into place—what has all this to do with our fluid fantastical era ?

Whatever the text-book view, I don't think Honegger has written a fugue. I enjoyed the piece, and the fugal alchemy seemed successful and of our own age. However, this is not a major work. It was well performed.

R.D.

August 23rd : Organ Concerto in C by Leo Sowerby. E. Power Biggs and B.B.C. Symphony Orchestra, conducted by Sir Malcolm Sargent. (First performance in England.)

As a concerto it misfires. Mr. Sowerby appears deliberately to avoid the many opportunities offered by the unique tonal character of his instrument, and strives to make the organ simply an extension of the orchestral texture. How far this impression was due to Mr. E. Power Biggs' screamy registration, it is difficult to say upon first hearing.

Musically the material itself is disappointing ; too many of the quieter sections were reminiscent of parish church improvising, and the more brilliant movements, for all their apparent complexity, seemed to be weak both thematically and in development. The incessant pedal-points revealed a basic poverty, in spite of the elaborate superstructure.

Much of the material would be acceptable as a rhapsodic improvisation. The essential problems of the concerto form were not faced.

R.J.

135

August 25th : " May Day ": A Panorama, Op 22, and Prelude for Orchestra
by Benjamin Frankel. London Philharmonic Orchestra, conducted by Basil
Cameron. (First performance in London.)

THIS received a vivid performance which contrasted oddly with the sleepily inefficient *Pastoral* which preceded it.

Much that is attractive, but no integration ; it is a suite of short impressions rather than one complete work. Form is a much-abused word but it has a meaning, which is the coherence that gives speech a connected significance. There is none here : a pity, for the work is worth it.

H.T.

September 5th : Viola Concerto by Bela Bartok. William Primrose and London
Philharmonic Orchestra, conducted by Basil Cameron. (First performance
in London.)

EVERY genuine musician must respect and admire Tibor Serly's earnest and sincere attempt to put on record, as nearly as possible, Bartok's very much incomplete last work.* It is an understandable service to the memory of a revered master and friend, but whether it was a wise one is dubious in the extreme. If the work was complete except for the orchestration, Bartok's method of sketching made its completeness very difficult to perceive. Since we shall never know whether Serly's result is as Bartok would have left it, we can only express regret that this tinkering should have been done and examine the work as we find it.

It is certain that, as it stands, it does nothing to prove that the viola is an ideal solo instrument. The first movement is, as William Mann stated in his programme notes, a sonata movement, but only as Bartok understood it. There are violent changes of tempo. True, these can be absorbed, but usually they spell danger. Here they are not absorbed and the movement sags wearily, patently wondering what to do next, and never finding out. Nevertheless, it is the best of the three.

The slow movement appears to be little more than a sketch, or it is an ineffectual attempt at a profound understatement. A middle section makes laborious play with a figure of clashing false relations which is as old as modernity and is certainly no younger than Wilbye.

There is no credit in discovering that the finale of Grieg's Piano Concerto hovers over the Magyar merry-making of Bartok's finale.

The " fierce preoccupation with problems of musical structure " of which William Mann writes was always a matter of attention to details whose relevance should not arise until the structure is determined, and, with Bartok's notion of a " virtuoso " style, is on a par with Spohr's " classical " style, i.e. " with shakes at the end of the passages." He has got no nearer to it in this last work.

The performance on this occasion left much to be desired. Particularly was the soloist's tone extremely rough, but as this was partly a result of the placing of the work ; it is as much a criticism of the writing, or a further proof that the viola is no concerto instrument. But the air of boredom which pervaded the last movement was entirely William Primrose's fault. I understand he asked for the work. Now he has got it, it is unfair, to say the least, to show complaint.

H.T.

* For another impression of the Concerto, see the review of its first European performance on p. 122.

September 8th : Viola Concerto by Elisabeth Lutyens. Frederick Riddle (Viola)
and B.B.C. Symphony Orchestra, conducted by John Hollingsworth. (First
Performance.)

COMPARED to this, the Bartok is a model of concerto-writing. If Primrose had difficulty in extracting a musical tone from his instrument in many places, we did at least hear all but a few phrase-ends. But the sight of a soloist playing vigorously and apparently producing no sound is a sight hitherto only experienced during a cinema sound-breakdown. It should be kept there. Mr. Riddle is no weak player, but the fiendish battery employed in this work to defeat him won all too easily.

At the risk of being pedantic I think it is time Miss Lutyens and others of her ilk ceased to hide behind the cover of " twelve-note " or any other technique and came out into the open with some music or " forever hold their peace "—and ours, too. The programme note informed us that " the viola unaccompanied expounds the first movement's theme. Gradually the orchestra takes it up, refashioning and analysing it, often dovetailing fragments together, in the way we associate with Sibelius." The reverse impression was mine.

Of the second movement : " The *Adagio Elegiaco* is like a song in three stanzas with a *ritornello* separating the verses." A song without a melody is not a new experience, unfortunately, but it is an illiteracy which should be fiercely repressed.

The " jovial " mood of the third movement escaped me. But I have noticed that these simple human emotions have undergone enormous changes as the human race becomes more enlightened. Perhaps the real solution is merely to switch the old familiar labels.

I will take the composer's word for it that the last movement is a Passacaglia, and merely recommend her to do a little research on the exact connotation of " concerto."

H.T.

[We print these impressions of a largely meritorious work for those who liked it : it is, we suggest, important to realize how wrong even an otherwise highly competent and imaginative musician—himself an interesting composer —can go when he does not understand a work and is indeed opposed to the technique it employs (and, incidentally, when he hears it from an unfavourable acoustic angle). An appraisal of Miss Lutyens' Concerto will be found in the article on *First Performances* in the November issue of the *Music Review*. —EDS.]

September 15th : Fantasia (Quasi Variazione) on the old 104th Psalm tune, by
Vaughan Williams for Piano Solo, accompanied by Orchestra, Organ and
Chorus. Michael Mullinar (piano), Royal Choral Society, B.B.C.
Symphony Orchestra, conducted by Sir Malcom Sargent. (First performance
in London.)

VAUGHAN Williams is a composer who rarely appeals to me ; as I liked parts of this work very much at first hearing, I am naturally suspicious.

Seldom does a Vaughan Williams texture convey clearly what it means, and this is no exception. There are few composers who can do the right thing in the wrong way so brilliantly. But the textural mistake in this case is something of a landslide. *Fantasia* was the right name—*quasi variazione* a bad afterthought.

Nevertheless, there would have been a tautness in the structure had not the piano insisted upon interfering with a quite pointless and clumsy display of glitter. A feeling of purpose in the music was continually frustrated by these silly interludes.

The performance had great gusto, marred by instability on the part of the pianist, and was received with the usual homely air of rapturous acclaim which sits so delightfully on a Prom audience. The moron who gave a maniacal whoop while the last chord was still sounding has now achieved his life-long ambition to broadcast. Let us hear no more of him.

H.T.

FERRIER, PEARS, BRITTEN : United Nations Association, Song Recital. Central Hall ; 25th September, 1950.

" MR. BRITTEN is an incomparable accompanist," wrote *The Times* after the event ; and in so doing pointed out the most singular aspect of an altogether memorable concert : which is not, by any means, to underrate the combined contributions made by Kathleen Ferrier and Peter Pears, but merely to take note of the obvious. Just good, factual reporting.

D.M.

JACQUES ORCHESTRA : Wigmore Hall, 26th September, 1950 ; c. John Pritchard.

I ASSUME this to be Mr. Pritchard's first concert with the orchestra since he replaced the retiring Dr. Jacques. Perhaps allowance should be made for stresses and strains inevitably present on such an occasion, but the instrumental balance in Strauss' *Metamorphosen* was worse than it need have been (particularly in its middle section), and the Mozart *Adagio and Fugue* (K. 456) suffered from a ruinous lack of rhythmic precision. The orchestra could do with a month's rigorous rehearsal : for instance, the violas were uncomfortably toneless and tuneless in the Strauss. Generally, Mr. Pritchard should pay attention to graduation of tone. From that point of view the Strauss was a special mess.

D.M.

II. Liverpool

INTEREST centres at present on the Philharmonic Orchestra's prospectus for the coming season. The various other musical organisations, notably the Rodewald Society, which provides programmes of chamber music, continue to flourish, but their plans are not so progressive as to create immediate excitement.

The Philharmonic is providing its customary series of subscription concerts and offering several novelties, probably the most exciting amongst them being the first English performance of Martinu's Violin Concerto on January 30th (Soloist : Henry Holst). The number of Sunday Concerts and Saturday evening " Pops " has been reduced, and four of the eight Sunday fixtures feature visiting orchestras. The worthy " Industrial Concerts," supported by various Merseyside business houses, offer eight good but conventional programmes, each played on four successive nights, and the scope of the " Junior Phil " concerts has been increased. One wonders how the players will survive.

Last season, a disquieting tendency was the failure of Liverpolitans to fill the hall for the big Tuesday events ; but as the Saturday and Sunday Concerts were each of a very high standard, the rearrangement this season should remedy the problem.

The summer has pursued a blankly unmusical course, broken only by two concerts given by the London Philharmonic Orchestra under Martinon, on July 7th and 8th. The first of these included a luscious performance of Beethoven's *Pastoral* beside the inevitable Debussy and Ravel, and Sibelius' *En Saga*. The Debussy was *Nuages* and *Fêtes*, which it seems every visiting conductor must play. Martinon did well with them, but no better than has been done by the Liverpool players. The Ravel was *La Valse*, and Martinon, realizing that the music was over, set out to enjoy himself. One doubts whether his enjoyment was worth the headache he gave us.

The only other event was the visit of the New York City Ballet. It was suggested that to see George Blanchine's version of Mozart's *Sinfonia Concertante* would lead one to a liking for ballet. It made one realize how limited against Mozart's vocabulary, is that of the choreographer : the physical action could by no means be said to " express " Mozart's score.* The Covent Garden Orchestra's contribution was coarse, crude and unmusical. Stravinsky's *Orpheus*, with its classically lovely lament, faired rather better.

H.B.R.

*In fact, it could not have abused it more stupidly.—ED. (H.K.).

Gramophone Records

AN ANTHOLOGY OF ENGLISH CHURCH MUSIC
(Recorded on Columbia LB 91-95 and LX 1283-1289)

" ENGLISH Church Music is a subject " says Doctor Fellowes in the tract which accompanies this collection of records, " the importance and value of which deserves far wider recognition than has usually been accorded to it." Lost causes, including musical ones, invariably deserve recognition. That they do not more frequently gain it is a fact more lamentable than inexplicable, for in the cause presently to be reviewed—that of English Church Music—the root of the matter lies no deeper than that suspect sub-stratum of our intellectual soil which has long been assumed the one and only nourisher of taste. It is perhaps unfortunate that musical taste in matters liturgical is even more all-embracing than the Established Church itself, and if there is one truth which emerges from the present anthology, it is that which sets a limit to taste, and denies the sincere Christian music-lover a simultaneous acceptance of Robert Fayrfax and Alan Gray, of Thomas Tallis and Samuel Wesley. The proof is now on record (LX 1283, LB 95, LX 1284, LX 1287) and may profitably be rehearsed in that order.

No sooner has Doctor Fellowes pleaded for wider recognition of this music, than he proceeds to circumscribe its very function, and to proscribe (by inference) all those who are not members of the Church of England : " [the music] can have no place in a concert programme . . . it can be heard with proper effect nowhere but in a church in association with a religious service." Liturgically speaking, however, an anthem is not an essential part of a religious service. For the past twenty years I have attended Church of England services which rarely contained an anthem, and I am quite sure that my experience is not unique. On the other hand, I have heard some fine performances of English anthems presented in a church, but in an extra-liturgical way, that is, in a concert programme. And if for full appreciation the music " must be heard in some great cathedral with its special acoustic properties " why record the music at all, since it is fore-doomed to regurgitate itself from a small box, with its special acoustic deficiencies ?

But it is when we are told that " [English Church Music] cannot have any place in the religious worship of continental cathedrals and churches " that we realize what Doctor Fellowes means by English Church Music. He means that music which is printed, as opposed to that remaining in manuscript ; and that known to him, as opposed to that " known only to specialists." In other words, those parts of our repertory which were considered good enough for export to Munich, Bologna, Turin, Modena and Trent, in performing editions during the fifteenth century, are to be brushed aside as being not only unfit for English churches (where they saw the light) but for continental churches whose liturgy was necessarily at one with ours. So we bid farewell, before we even see them, to the

> Hympnes, proses, messe, motez,
> Comme Dompstaple et du Fay,
> Qui tant doulcement en leur temps,
> Par bel et devost passe-temps
> Ont composay . . . (1)

We bid farewell, before we even hear them, to the fifty-odd compositions of Dunstable which have been listed by Bukofzer (*Acta Musicologica* VIII, 102) and partially transcribed by Rudolf von Ficker (*Denkmaeler der Tonkunst in Oesterreich* XL) ; for us the rich manuscript collections of Plantagenet and Tudor music in Oxford, Cambridge, Eton, Ware and Edinburgh might just as well not exist. Or perhaps they do not exist for Doctor Fellowes.

For he is plainly so little interested in what happened in the sphere of English Music before 1550 that the one and only pre-Reformation composer whose work is represented in this anthology has been re-christened as Thomas Fayrfax. The " T. Fayrfax " at the top of the page is no printer's error : for the mistake has been confirmed by Doctor Fellowes in the second paragraph of his essay. Worse than this, the version of the *Agnus Dei* from the " Missa Albanus " was not taken from the early sixteenth century sources in Bodley, Peterhouse, Lambeth, or Caius, but from a transcript made by H. B. Collins for practical use in the Oratory, Birmingham. Since the leisurely course of pre-Reformation ceremony encouraged equally spacious musical settings of the Mass, Collins's practical edition involved a certain amount of judicious cutting, for which there was every excuse. But there is absolutely no excuse or pardon for an "amateur"* who seizes upon a mutilated masterpiece, alters it still further by the substitution of utterly ridiculous text repetitions, and allows the result to be committed to wax, pressed, and circulated throughout the wide world as a specimen of the music of Fayrfax. It is not as though there is nobody in England who has studied Fayrfax, nobody to whom Doctor Fellowes could have had recourse in his quest for a suitable excerpt. Several scholars would

(1) Eloy d'Amerval : *Livre de la Deablerie* (Paris, 1508).
*cf. Fellowes : *Memories of an Amateur Musician* (Methuen, 1946).

have been able to point out the wisdom of selecting a verse from a motet. The first verse of *Ave Dei Patris filia*, of *Salve regina*, or of *Aeterne laudis lilium* would have fitted comfortably on to one side of a twelve-inch record, and so avoided the awkward break which occurs in this raw, bleeding hunk of Renaissance polyphony which has been served up to us on LX 1283. Little wonder that the performance on this record by the choir of St. Paul's Cathedral sounds uncomfortable and unconvincing. With such a text, it could not have been otherwise.

One cannot leave an exposure of editorial mis-management such as this without quoting a curious sentence found immediately beneath the list of items, on page two of the tract. After eleven credits to Doctor Fellowes on the records themselves, and ten credits in the tract[2] we find this platitudinous peroration of puffed-up pride :

" The works arranged by Dr. Fellowes are also scored by him."

If this kind of statement is to be tolerated, we may look forward with bated breath to the concert programmes of the future, which, in a misguided attempt to follow in the paths of righteousness, may choose to print the following :

" The works scored by Mozart are also harmonized by him." Or :

" The works arranged by Ravel are also scored by him." Indeed, there is no limit to the gullibility of the musical public. They are not to know that sixteenth and seventeenth century practice caused music to be copied or printed in part books, one book for each voice, or at the most, one book for two voices. This was a departure from the earlier tradition of the choir-book, which had all the voice parts, even if there were as many as nineteen[3], writ large on adjacent pages, so that they could be seen even at a distance by every member of the choir. In both cases, a modern performing edition could be produced merely by copying and duplicating the parts, on the analogy of orchestral parts. But singers have been spoilt for the past two centuries by a profusion of mass-produced scores, so that any editor who wishes to publish choral music nowadays must of necessity score what he edits. The palaeographer scores music for a different reason : so that he can check up scribal errors by paying attention to the harmony resulting from linear counterpoint. In neither instance is the process of scoring anything more than pure routine work, and as such need not be brazened abroad as if it were a secret technique or a gift so rare as to be bestowed only upon those who think they have invented it.

A word or two about the performances themselves.

They are given by a gamut of choirs, seven in all, referenced from A to G. First on the list is Canterbury Cathedral Choir which sings with tolerable fervour a dull anthem by Wesley and a slightly less dull one by Crotch. *In jejunio et fletu*, which has been chosen in preference to the infinitely more typical *cantus firmus* motets of Tallis, is sung by this same choir with a lack of phrasing, expression, and understanding which has to be heard to be

(2)   These are correctly spelt, of course ; but not so the names of some of the choir-trainers. Dr. Dykes Bower appears four times as Dr. Bykes Bower, Dr. H. K. Andrews three times as Dr. H. R. Andrews, and Dr. W. N. McKie three times as Dr. W. W. McKie.

(3)   Cf. *O bone Jesu* by Robert Carver (National Library of Scotland, Adv. MS., 5/1/15, ff. 6v-13).

believed. Next on the list is the choir of King's College, Cambridge, whose interpretation of sections from Byrd's four-part Mass is marred by their decision to sing the music fast enough to be crammed on to two sides of a ten-inch record. The Gibbons anthems fare better, but the singing can scarcely be called Elizabethan. Nevertheless, a certain Bishop of Worcester and Salisbury could hardly fail to have approved it, since he deemed the common singing men " . . . a bad society, and yet a company of good Fellowes, that roare deepe in the Quire, deeper in the Taverne. They are the eight parts of speech which goe to the *Syntaxis* of Service, and are distinguish't by their noyses much like bells, for they make not a Consort, but a Peale."[4]

The choir of New College, Oxford, contributes a mediocre motet by Stanford, and anthems by Morley and Purcell, which though nicely sung are spoilt by the omission of the organ part in the full sections. From St. George's Chapel, Windsor, comes a modern group : the *Te Deum* in G by Vaughan Williams, a *Sanctus* by Alcock, and an anthem by Harris which is full of very clever D.Mus. modulations. The tone of the choir is disappointing. The performance of Fayrfax by the choir of St. Paul's Cathedral has already been mentioned. They have also recorded *O nata lux de lumine* by Tallis, with a wrong c sharp by Fellowes. This typically Tudor clash (appropriately enough at the words " pro perditis ") is not only missed : it is lamented. The Boyce verse-anthem *I have surely built Thee an house* is beautifully sung, and is without doubt the one redeeming feature of this anthology. Westminster Abbey choir sing two anthems by Purcell : the eight-part *Hear my prayer* and the well-known *Rejoice in the Lord*, which is given with accompaniment of organ and strings, the latter from the Jacques Orchestra. The style of singing leaves something to be desired ; the style of orchestral playing leaves nothing undone in the matter of slovenly bowing, audible changes of position, and complete ignorance of seventeenth century string technique. York Minster is last on the list, with Charles Wood's *Hail gladdening light* and Gray's *What are these*, the latter noticeable for a blaring and vulgar tuba solo on several inches of wind.

What *are* these ? A set of records which, with a little planning, fore-thought, and care, could have been a credit to their compiler and to the nation. As they stand, they have only one good point, and that is the all-round technical excellence of the recording, which must often have been carried out under difficulties. But of what use is good recording without superlative performances ? Sackcloth and ashes for the British Council, for all their auspices ; and may Heaven help the British taxpayer.

D.W.S.

(4) Dr. John Earle : *Microcosmographie* (1639).

COMPETITION No. 1. Set by P.H.

Imaginary conversations, not exceeding 400 words, are invited between any one of the following pairs of composers :

(a) Bach and Handel in 1750.
(b) Beethoven and Schubert in December, 1826.
(c) Wagner and Verdi in 1880.

A first prize of 3 guineas, two second prizes of 1 guinea each. Results and winning entry to be published in the March issue. Entries by 1st February, 1951, marked " Competition."

Correspondence

KELLER ON TOVEY ON HAYDN

I have not Mr. Keller's inside knowledge of Haydn's experience in the womb, so I cannot tell if he is right in saying that Haydn realised in that place that " a bar of slow music is an altogether bigger thing than a bar of quick music played slowly." But from Tovey's description on p. 21 of the book under review * it seems clear that by the time he came to write the finale of his quartet op. 3. No. 1, he had forgotten the converse of this pre-natal knowledge. So if even the great can forget, and rediscover later what they once knew, it is even within the bounds of possibility that Mr. Keller himself will sometime discover—and surely he must have heard enough music in which the composer has evidently no knowledge of whether his music is moving fast or slowly—that the distrustful disgust with which he read Tovey's profound remarks on this so little understood problem of movement, is simply due to some psychological resistance of his own.

WILLIAM WORDSWORTH

*Music Survey, II/4/50, p. 263—Eds.

" He speaks with angels," said one of the Master's disciples. " How know you that ? " I asked. " He himself admits it," he replied solemnly. " But suppose he lies ? " I persisted. " What ! " he exclaimed, " a man who speaks with angels capable of telling a lie ? "

I am quoting this duologue from the *Encyclopaedia Britannica*'s article on the *Circulus in probando* because judging from Mr. Wordsworth's argument he may find it an attractive line of thought. He uses, that is to say, the very fact he wishes to demonstrate—the profundity of Tovey's opinion on Haydn's sense of tempo—as a premise. What Tovey says in the place to which Mr. Wordsworth refers is this :—" As for any sense of pace, Haydn might just as well have used bars of double length with quavers and semiquavers and called it andante." The interested reader may now like to look up the *Presto* of op. 3, No. 1, and form his own opinion.

I agree with Mr. Wordsworth that this problem of movement is little understood. He is right, too, in assuming that I must have heard plenty of music wherein the composer didn't know whether he was moving fast or slowly. But, believe it or not, Haydn's was not among it.

H.K.

24, St. Aubyn's Road,
Upper Norwood,
S.E.19.
4th September, 1950.

Sirs,—Mr. Sharp's outburst in the last issue of *Music Survey* (III/1) seems to be a little disproportionate. I fancy the Hallé Orchestra has got exactly the conductor it deserves.

No doubt the lengthy preparation given to Bruckner's *Seventh* and Strauss' *Don Quixote* is laudable enough ; but did Sir John and his band prepare with equal care their flagrant misrepresentation of Reger's *Mozart* Variations—

a preparation which "included" the complete omission of the fifth (technically most difficult) variation, and a perfunctory scramble through the concluding fugue ?

If so the question of conductor's and orchestra's capacity is not so much beyond doubt as either Mr. Sharp (or Mr. Keller for that matter) would seem to suggest.

HAROLD TRUSCOTT

22, MELBURY ROAD,
KENSINGTON, W.14.

8th September, 1950.

GENTLEMEN,—I wonder what you had in mind when you selected my humble person as the target of your aggression. I am not a critic. If I write articles occasionally it is mainly to let youngsters benefit by someone's lifelong musical experience. My wonder was mingled with a slightly malicious amusement when I read in your Summer Issue the assault on my article about Benjamin Britten's Spring Symphony, and on my Aldeburgh Festival programme note. Whatever reputation your magazine has gained during the past few months was largely due to your blunt exposure of irresponsibility and incompetence ; now you yourselves have committed the very blunders you are uncovering.

Mr. Donald Mitchell says, in what is supposed to be a review of the vocal score of Britten's Spring Symphony :—

> Erwin Stein's analysis in the current Tempo (Spring, 1950) tells us that the " symphony " *must* (my italics) be accepted " in the metaphorical sense."

What I wrote was :—

> . . . if someone has too hard and fast a notion of what a symphony should be, let him accept the word here in the metaphorical sense. But if a symphony means integrating the manifold aspects of one idea, here is a true example of the type.

Surely it needs not much intelligence to see that in the first sentence I intended ironically to anticipate objections to the title, and that the " if " in the second sentence is not really conditional. Of course it is a symphony, and I myself strongly advocated the title when a discussion about it arose before the first performance. Mr. Mitchell goes blundering on when he says:—

> Nor am I so certain that the symphonic form of the work is as metaphorical as he supposes.

Of course I supposed no such thing.

Further, my article is no analysis, but a description. An analysis would have been useless without the complete music there to illustrate it.

And here is another of Mr. Mitchell's distortions of my article :—

> Of the twelve (*clearly I was referring to the five movements of part one*) vocal movements he writes, " No thematic connection between them is apparent." On this point he is factually wrong, as a quotation from " Waters Above " appears in the succeeding " Out On the Lawn I Lie in Bed."

Does Mr. Mitchell believe that a quotation is a thematic connection ? Surely there is some confusion in his mind about the meaning of such terms as thematic, structure and unity. He seems to have no idea what the function

144

of musical form is. Few people have, maybe this is a comfort to him. But I am well prepared to give him a few private lessons if he should care to learn, in order to avoid in the future such nonsense as the following :—

> Indeed, in the Spring Symphony we may have an outstanding example of a newish principle of symphonic structure—unity by interval.

Intervals are by necessity a basic element of any musical structure. Nor is it a " newish principle " to give a certain interval prominence in a piece of music, symphonic or otherwise. However, it is hopelessly underrating Britten's creative imagination to suspect that the unity of his symphony has to do with the recurring interval of a fourth. There are hundreds of other means at his disposal of which I mentioned only a few in my article—if Mr. Mitchell would care to read it. Britten gives overall unity to the musical form more often through co-ordination of the sections (not what Mr. Mitchell calls " rough grouping of movements ") than through integration of the thematic material. This is one of the features of his style, and seems to my mind more important than the recurrence of an odd interval. By all means analyse every detail and discover all links and relations, but please, Music Survey, keep a sense of proportion.

This admonition may also suffice as a rejoinder (I suppose this is the correct use of the word ; see page 44, 2nd line of your Summer Issue) to the sweeping censure of my note on the Aldeburgh Mozart concert. Some of Mozart's minor and more conventional compositions had purposely been selected to show that the spell of his music is not restricted to his major works. In particular if they are as superbly played as in Aldeburgh.

ERWIN STEIN

On one point Mr. Stein is undoubtedly right and I am wrong. My " must " was far too strong. Apologies. Perhaps I was misled by the very opening sentence of Mr. Stein's article. He wrote : " *Spring Symphony*—the accent is on the *first* word." (The latter italics mine). But perhaps Mr. Stein was being ironical again.

As for my other " distortion " of his article, Mr. Stein has only himself to blame. The distinction he makes between the twelve vocal " pieces " and the four " parts " into which they are grouped was not at all clear in the text.* His terminology doesn't seem to be very exact. We have " parts," pieces," and " movements " to cope with : what were " pieces " in his article have become " the five *movements* of part one " (my italics) in his letter. I am well prepared to offer Mr. Stein a few private lessons in the regular use of accurate terminology if he should care to learn.

Mr. Stein asks me if I " believe that a quotation is a thematic connection." If one piece-part-movement quotes thematic material from another, there is just that amount of " thematic connection " between the two, that and no more. A " thematic connection " may or may not have structural significance. Mr. Stein may remember that my review not only suggested provisional explorations of the *Spring* Symphony's structure but also of its accessory integrating factors. If I remember correctly the " thematic connection " I specified is the only one of its kind in the work : I think it a feature worth pointing out : Mr. Stein evidently didn't and doesn't.

Mr. Stein in quoting my " Indeed, in the Spring Symphony we *may* have an outstanding example etc." carefully avoids resurrecting any of the earlier statements in my review which substantially qualify the sentence he has chosen to stigmatise as "nonsense." I wrote quite frankly : "How Britten has achieved this unity *I have not yet succeeded in proving to my own satisfaction.*" I suggested " certain thematic derivations and transformations " and continued : " *Possibly* more important still is the binding element of the interval of a fourth which haunts a great part of the vocal writing throughout " (my italics). Mr. Stein has treated my tentative propositions as papal infallibilities. If I had written " The *Spring* Symphony *is* an outstanding example etc." Mr. Stein would have had more reason to complain. I meant what I said : in the *Spring* Symphony we have the consistent use of an interval which acts as a " binding element " (one, surely, of many ?), which helps to give the music both coherence and integration, and is, moreover, one often overlooked by those " youngsters " for whom it seems Mr. Stein writes his occasional articles.

Mr. Stein accuses me of " sweeping censure " on his Aldeburgh programme note. I don't understand why naming a musical opinion " debatable " should be considered extravagantly censorious. Mr. Stein wrote originally : " The pieces selected are perhaps not the greatest Mozart ever wrote, yet, perhaps, they represent an important aspect of the composer and show him from what may be called the conventional side." The repetitive " perhaps " suggests that Mr. Stein may be less sure of his opinions than I am of mine : that the G major Concerto (K.453) is neither a conventional nor a minor composition.

D.M.

* See also review of the *Spring* Symphony in *Music Review* 11/4/50.

THE ELMS SCHOOL,
COLWALL, Nr. MALVERN,
WORCS.

7th November, 1950.

SIRS,—Some music critics, when challenged, seek refuge behind the superficial armour of :—

(a)   Their journalese and blurb—(i.e. " integrating perspective of a work's symmetry").

(b)   Not being required to qualify their irresponsible remarks by quoting from the score.

With regard to (b), I defy Mr. Coveney to be capable of quoting the exact portions (in the Hallé Concert to which he refers) which were, he alleges, performed with " signs of careless phrasing " and " tendencies towards sentimentality."

Who would dare refute Barbirolli's " worthiness " of the Hallé had they heard his interpretations of works so widely ranging in diversity as Ravel's " Daphnis and Chloe " Suites, Berlioz' " Symphonie Fantastique " and Elgar's 2nd Symphony, in all of which he excels ?

These examples are cited at random and were just a few of the memorable performances that have taken place over the last twelve years.

Mr. Coveney apologises for any " bruised feelings " his words may have caused, but I would suggest that the only thing thus affected by his words would be the mind which conceived them.

GUY HARLAND

MUSIC SURVEY

(KATHLEEN LIVINGSTON   WILLIAM W. LIVINGSTON   DONALD MITCHELL)

VOL. III, No. 3   CONTENTS   MARCH, 1951

EDITORIAL CORRESPONDENCE should be addressed to the EDITORS, MUSIC SURVEY, OAKFIELD SCHOOL, WEST DULWICH, LONDON, S.E.21. Annual Subscription, including postage, 11s.   U.S.A. $2.50.

All enquiries relating to advertising space in this journal should be made to MUSIC SURVEY at the above address.

Editorial

IN his article on *Don Giovanni* in our last issue, Dallapiccola suggests that, for musico-architectural as well as dramatic reasons, Donna Anna's aria " Non mi dir, bell' idol mio," Mozart's " error of construction," should be omitted in order that the Finale may immediately follow the graveyard scene. Dent has already observed in his *Mozart's Operas* that Anna's number "has no reason whatever for its existence," and eight years ago Geoffrey Sharp (*Don Giovanni : Some Observations, Music Review*, IV/1) proposed, for similar reasons and indeed in almost the same words as Dallapiccola, to play the Finale at once after the cemetery scene, though not to omit the aria altogether : "By following [' In quali eccessi '] with the big scene for Donna Anna and Don Ottavio (' Crudele ? ') we are able to increase the sense of resentment against Don Giovanni, and to prepare for the ultimate catastrophe which may then sweep from ' O statua gentilissima ' right through to its dramatic conclusion." It may be remembered that Dallapiccola leaves a door half open for the transplantation of the aria when he assumes " that the same piece, at another point in the opera, would not have had such a sinister effect [upon Berlioz]." On the other hand, Sharp's article strongly recommended the removal of the Finale's last section, a cut whose possibility Dallapiccola does not mention, though it would give yet greater prominence to what he considers the pillars of the opera's structural arch : the initial death and the final return of the Commendatore to the same diminished seventh chord ; nor would Sharp's recommendation be without weighty precedent (as he did not himself seem to realise), e.g. the Mahler tradition's at the Vienna State Opera. Nevertheless, once one recognizes that the last scene's final *subito piano* is of all his operatic endings the only one wherein Mozart's original genius is fully, sublimely apparent, the objections to the inclusion of the Finale's finale lose their interest. Since Mozart research has so far by-passed this unprecedented and unequalled passage, fascinating alike in structure, texture and spiritual text, we intend to analyse it in our projected Mozart Issue, in which we desire to say nothing that has already been said and some things which ought to have been.

Meanwhile, we have thought it our musical duty, in view of the forthcoming publication in this country of Schoenberg's *Style and Idea*, to counter certain pseudo-authoritative and savage attacks upon its American edition without delay ; whence we have no space left for the article and music example of our promised Film Music feature on the *Harry Lime* tune : this will be published in the next issue, while in the present number a topical Film Music survey takes its place—and our reform of record reviews its first decided steps.

D.M. *and* H.K.

Obituaries

BEFORE the old year ended, music lost two precious apostles. E. J. MOERAN was prized almost exclusively in Great Britain and, one supposes, Ireland, for his music is too special in style to appeal to other than those who feel for our ways of thinking and who love our diverse countrysides. Something of a mystic, touched to the core with romantic ideals, it was in Ireland that Moeran found his strongest inspiration, though the Norfolk landscape, where he had so valuably pursued the quest for folkmusic, was a stimulus too ; indeed we can learn from his music that there is not such a great gulf fixed between the bogs of Ireland and the fens of Norfolk after all.

Moeran matured at a time when English Folksong was an exciting and novel subject for research, and he enthusiastically joined his contemporaries in unearthing fresh bequests in our national heritage of song. Its idioms flowed naturally in the veins of his melodic inspiration so that echoes of far off things swim to the surface of his tunes—" The Last Rose of Summer " in the symphony, " The Keel Row " in the cello sonata, " Tom Tom the Piper's Son " in the violin concerto. From friendship with Delius and Peter Warlock he acquired something of the first's spaciousness and of the second's tenderness and passion for Tudor Music ; but Moeran's work could on occasion draw on sources more dynamic and robust, as in the Rondo of the violin concerto. The songs of the people were, for him who had met them at first hand, not the pretty charmers that tyros imagine but vivid protests of a tough proletariat. Patrick Hadley recalls an authentic imitation of proper folk-singing by Moeran that brought worried policemen to the door.

His first symphony (I say first in optimistic hope that the MS of his second, commissioned for this year's Cheltenham Festival, may yet be discovered) makes probably the broadest appeal to a musical world in which nationalism is mostly unwelcome when it is not one's own. For me his most haunting music is in the slow movement of the cello concerto and the first and last of the violin concerto. Both concertos are rather rhapsodic cantabile works than vehicles of virtuosity, but Moeran had formal neatness sufficiently in his bones to control his musical dreaming. There is an innate sympathy with the English Choral Tradition, as well as a melodic freshness in his songs (characteristically he set A. E. Housman and James Joyce, the

153

latter with real sympathy) and the *a cappella* cycles " Songs of Springtime " and " Phyllida and Corydon." I, for one, can claim that his setting of " Weep you no more sad fountains " even manages temporarily to obliterate Dowland's glorious version from my mind.

He said, not long ago, that he would not go back to Kenmarg. He did, and never returned.

DINU LIPATTI had been ill for a long time but his death came as a sad shock. I first heard him play at the 1947 Lucerne Festival in a performance of Mozart's D minor Concerto with Hindemith conducting, and was amazed at his extraordinary sensitivity to Mozart's piano writing, the welling virtuosity, firmly yet how imperceptibly controlled by the demands of eighteenth century style. And yet in Schumann or Chopin he could command a staggering fullness of tone. He talked with prodigious and integrally digested knowledge of every style and branch of music, and of the other arts too; this highly developed cultural appreciation proclaimed itself in the musical rightness of every phrase he played, every movement he set his fingers to unfold. I never heard another pianist—no, not another interpreter—who so superbly made the inspired decision at every turn, who projected the composer's mind so surely, faithfully, vividly before the listener's astonished ears.

W.S.M.

Vincent d'Indy
1851 - 1931 - 1951
BY NORMAN DEMUTH

I FIRST came across the name of Vincent d'Indy in 1916 at a time when I was in hospital. I had received a present of books, among which was a translation of Romain Rolland's " Musiciens d'Aujourd 'hui." The name d'Indy meant absolutely nothing to me, but as I read I became more and more certain that this man, was, for me at least, everything that I had always imagined a composer should be. My friends and relations were sent in search of miniature scores but could discover only the " *Istar* " *Variations*, the *Symphony in B flat*, and the *Piano Sonata*. I then and there decided to explore the possibilities of becoming a student, as soon as the war was over, at the Schola Cantorum* which, I understood, had been founded by d'Indy himself. Circumstances however, forbade this.

It was not till later that I was able to collect a fully representative number of his works, although the three masterpieces I had found were sufficient to give a very clear all-round view of his ideals. When
*Now the *Ecole César Franck*.

154

I discovered, in Holland, Vol. II of the " Cours de Composition musicale," I knew that I had found my musical bible at last. I determined that one day I would meet d'Indy personally, although as time went on I grew in increasing awe of him. I even plucked up enough courage to write to him on some pretext or other, but the letter was unanswered.

In 1930 I attended a performance by the Schola Cantorum students of *La Légende de Saint Christophe* at the Salle Pleyel, in Paris. Arriving early, I saw the venerable figure of d'Indy in the foyer, receiving and enjoying the homage of his friends. A French acquaintance offered to present me, but I asked him to find out first of all if d'Indy himself would be interested. d'Indy turned away with a shake of his head, and everybody proceeded into the hall.

Undaunted, I called at the Schola Cantorum just at the moment when d'Indy, by a lucky chance, was going out. The Cerberus at the door explained that I wished to see him. I looked rather a youngish thirty-two, and when invited to sit down in d'Indy's very austere " bureau," I soon gathered that he thought I wanted to enrol as a student. He immediately launched out into a long explanation of the Schola and its aims, his eyes brimming with kindness and enthusiasm. In due time I managed to impart the information that I was a professor at the Royal Academy. With wonderful self-control and self-possession, he did not flicker an eyelid. I quickly told him that I had studied many of his works and that I admired them and his ideals intensely, all of which was perfectly true. I spent a very pleasant and impressive thirty minutes with him. Although his manner was friendly, it seemed disinterested ; I did not know then that this superficial frigidity was natural to him, and that in all probability he was full of sympathy for the rather young enthusiasm with which he was faced, an enthusiasm expressed in a brand of French which was original, to say the least. It is possible, if not probable, that I talked too much, but he never once mentioned English music, the R.A.M., England, or my own work. Unfortunately, I made a mistake which I have ever since regretted. I left without asking him for a photo. When next I was able to go to Paris, I had no opportunity of approaching him, and he died shortly afterwards. I remember now that towards the end of this interview he seemed to be waiting with an air of expectation ; but I have always been diffident at asking great men for their photographs unless I have needed them for some specific purpose.

Vincent d'Indy was an aristocrat by birth, and a man of the highest spiritual and artistic integrity, with which went a strong sense of morality. Instead of following the easy path of the dilettante he preferred to go through the mill like everyone else. A performance of any work was almost a religious rite with d'Indy, and he approached a Dalcroze demonstration with the same high-mindedness of purpose as the B minor Mass. In his musical judgment he kept a broad objectivity. Although the aesthetic of *Pelléas et Mélisande* was at the opposite pole to his own, he wrote sympathetically about it on its appearance, realising that it stood for a genuine musical expression. Privately, he confided his opinion that the work would not live " because it had no form." He was an active propagandist of Monteverdi and Rameau, while his efforts, and those of Charles Bordes and Alexandre Guilmant at the Schola, completely reformed the performance of Gregorian music in the Roman Catholic Church in France.

His regret at the absence of form in *Pelléas*, together with the word " tonality," represents almost the entire creative creed of Vincent d'Indy. He stressed the former more than any other teacher. His sense and feeling for tonality made him decline, with chapter and verse, to transpose an accompaniment to one of Chabrier's songs, while Vol. III of the " Cours " discusses opera almost primarily from the tonal point of view.

He became a master of variation and symphonic development, taking his line of departure from Bach and Beethoven. He referred everything to the Great Masters of every period—not for d'Indy the authority of a mere text-book. An advocate of the ' cyclique ' style, he became firmly convinced that symphonic continuity was possible only in this style. It must be remembered that at the time of the opening of the Schola as a general school of music, symphonic music in France was almost non-existent. The only symphonies of note were those by Lalo, Franck, Saint-Saens and Chausson— Dukas' solitary example appeared just about that time. Students at the Conservatoire were bound up in opera and the Prix de Rome. Franck had been the first to " teach symphony," as it was said, and his pupils d'Indy, Chausson and Guy Ropartz followed in his footsteps. Although a perfervid Wagnerite, d'Indy maintained that this musical style was not one which French composers could or should copy. He and others have been too loosely charged with trying to permeate French music with this insidious German element ; but in actual fact, all they did was to treat opera as a continuous entity, with guiding cellules used symphonically, thus eradicating the established sectional nature of the genre. d'Indy based his symphonic conception upon Beethoven's. He maintained that Symphony was a purely musical expression enclosed within the classical (or accepted) framework, although he was careful to point out to his pupils that " it is the music which decides the form, not the form which decides the music." Symphony, therefore, he saw as a monumental edifice built upon a series of cyclical or germinal processes, and upon tonality and key relationships.

d'Indy's music has often been regarded as being too severe. This is but one of the misconceptions which have arisen through his insistence upon classic design. He was never an opponent of programme music provided that it was expressed in the classic manner. His fondness for the cellule has led to his being accused of a deficiency in lyrical spontaneity. However, a cellule is not a theme ; it is but the germ from which themes grow. In his Variations the themes have a perfect flow and ease of style, particularly in the *Piano Sonata*. In his deliberately symphonic works everything is derived from some germ, and the result is always satisfying and musical. His most popular work is by no means the best. The *Symphonie sur un chant montagnard français* for orchestra and piano (note this) was a sensation when first performed in 1886. It immediately showed kinship with the Concerto Grosso principle, in that the piano is treated as one of the ensemble. It brought the two conceptions of Symphony and Concerto into close relationship and indicated the latent symphonic powers which the (at the time) young Frenchman had within him. Thematically, it says remarkably little and the mountain song is never really disguised. The scoring is remarkable, especially in the last movement where the harp picks out the theme from the pianism. Of the works of that period, *Le Chant de la Cloche* (1879-1893) is the finest. This dramatic legend for soli, double choir and orchestra should be revived by the B.B.C. as soon as possible.

From the large-scale orchestral works one picks out the magnificent *Symphony in B flat* (1902-1903), " *Istar* " *Variations* (1896), *Souvenirs* (1906), *Jour d'Eté* (1905), the *Diptyque Méditerranéen* and the *Concerto* for flute, piano, cello and strings (1926), in that order of importance. The *Symphony in B flat* takes a place beside the greatest for sheer resource, invention, and musical feeling. Its germinal qualities bind it together convincingly and its general scope is immense. Unlike so much of the music of its period, it does not " date," because d'Indy had no mannerisms and his technique is universal. A performance some while ago by Charles Groves and the B.B.C. Northern Orchestra makes us await a repeat with some impatience. The inverted " *Istar* " *Variations*, so treated in order to conform with the underlying programme, have probably been played more than anything else. It is interesting to hear the theme revealed through a process of gradual stripping of decoration and ornamentation. *Souvenirs* and *Jour d'été* touch romanticism, particularly the latter ; the former is a personal document over whose publication d'Indy hesitated. The last big work, the *Diptyque Méditerranéen* shows the brain of an ageing man constantly alive and alert to a picturesque subject as expressed by classical means.

In the realm of chamber music, the three *String Quartets* (1890, 1897 and 1928-1929), particularly the second, the *Piano Sonata* (1907), the *Cello Sonata* (1924-1925) and the *Suite* (1927) for flute violin, viola, cello and harp are all worthy of attention, the last two showing a final approach to the dance styles of Rameau. The *Second String Quartet* is built entirely upon a Gregorian fragment and, while strictly formal and classical in outlook, is of a striking serenity. d'Indy's fundamental polyphony and his love of clarity made him very sympathetic to this medium. The *Piano Sonata*, a set of continuous variations in three movements, is, as far as I am concerned, seraphically beautiful. Technically, it is a model of resource and germinal expansion. It is not *piano music* for a great-part in the accepted sense of the term. The player unfolds an ever-increasing texture and builds an edifice in sound of great beauty ; but in spite of the difficulties of the technique, there are not many pages fully concerned with what is called " pianism." As an example of the Amplified Variation, the Sonata is a landmark.

The *Violin Sonata* (1903-1904) is long : d'Indy works his material to the last inch, and the work is so much a complete entity and so well-balanced that no cuts can be made. The *Cello Sonata* pursues its course in an uninterrupted flow of sheer musical dance thought.

His finest and most practical opera, in my opinion, is *L'Etranger* (1898-1901), although many prefer *Fervaal* (1881-1895). The latter has been called the " French Parsifal," a description which nearly succeeded in damning it. *La Légende de Saint Christophe* (1908-1915) is a work brim full of subtle propaganda, but at the time of its production (June 6th, 1920) Paris was in no mood for sermons and while the work was received with more than the respect due to the Grand Maître who had written it, audiences turned to more palatable subjects. *L'Etranger* is based upon redemption through sacrifice, sufficient in itself to bring a howl of execration upon its head from those who saw the Wagnerian virus of *The Flying Dutchman* in its pages. Actually, this is its only contact with Wagner. The power of the sea music, the absolute sincerity of the whole thought makes *L'Etranger* a landmark in the history of opera. Like so many other French works, it received its world première at the Monnaie, in Brussels.

d'Indy began and ended his life with an Opéra-Comique. Neither *Attendez-moi sous l'orme* (1876-1882) nor *Le Rêve de Cinyras* (1922-1923) received performance easily. In the latter case, nobody felt that it could possibly succeed owing to d'Indy's reputation as a neo-classicist. Eventually it was received with some surprise and enthusiasm, and showed an adaptability quite unsuspected in such a serious-minded composer. At the time of his death d'Indy was sketching a fourth *String Quartet.*

d'Indy's opus numbers run to 105, and they are mostly considerable works ; he was not happy in small pieces. This may not seem a very high aggregate in a life which lasted so long, but d'Indy not only controlled the adminstrative and composition sides of the Schola Cantorum, but was a Professor at the Conservatoire, wrote books and articles, and gave lectures all over France. Branches of the Schola were founded in many towns and cities, and all these demanded his attention. His life was a full one ; he worked hard, and liked it. The late Pierre de Bréville told me that when Franck suggested that de Bréville studied orchestration with d'Indy (" he knows much more about it than I do "), d'Indy gave him an appointment for his first lesson at five a.m. His composition lessons always laid emphasis on the necessity for the creative artist to have vision and ideals. At the same time, they were practical and covered a wide range. He was a hard task-master and the discipline at the Schola was such that only the strongest could survive. Taking names of Schola Cantorum students at random, one finds Roussel, de Séverac, Samazeuilh, Erik Satie, Marcel Mihalovici, Edgar Varèse, Roland Manuel, and a host of North and South American composers. As a teacher, d'Indy may be said to have been the Nadia Boulanger of his time. Of the younger generation, he admired Honegger particularly, since he saw in him a continuance of his symphonic ideals. Of his contemporaries, he detested Schoenberg.

His aesthetic may be summed up from certain general statements, among which we single out " All processes are good provided that they are the means to an end (i.e. making music) and not the end in themselves," and " Music will proceed along the path indicated by the next composer of genius."

d'Indy was a great man and one beloved by all his friends and by those who took the trouble to understand him. He formulated the French Symphonic School upon the foundations laid by Franck and his work was immediately furthered in this respect by his pupil Albert Roussel (1869-1937) and, after Roussel, by Milhaud, Honegger and the younger composers, whether Schola Cantorum (Ecole César Franck) students or otherwise. He was one of the first to give French music world significance and, while basing his principles upon the finest examples of the great classical tradition, he maintained his Gallicism through clarity and imagination.

Not inappropriately d'Indy died working. He was engaged upon his book on Wagner when a sudden heart attack struck him down.

Schoenberg and the Men of the Press

By HANS KELLER

The decisive happens despite.

NIETZSCHE.

The critic stumbles along behind the artist.

J. ISAACS.

WE gather that Schoenberg's new book *Style and Idea* will very shortly be published in this country (Williams & Norgate). This seems the moment, then, for dispelling some of the prejudices which may have been aroused against the work by certain reviews of its American edition (1950), immoral at their worst and ignorant at their best. With Richard Capell's *Daily Telegraph* review, entitled *Schoenberg's Ideas*, I have dealt in an article (under my present title) in the February issue of *Colophon*, where I have also examined John Amis's (*Tribune*) and Frank Howes's (*The Times*) latest verdicts on Schoenberg's music. Richard Capell himself bequeathed this subtly ironical title to Winton Dean, inviting him to produce what turned out to be an extended tirade on the book in *Music & Letters*, and it is against this article-review as well as against Richard S. Hill's review in *Notes* (Washington) and Professor Gerald Abraham's emissions *ex cathedra* Monthly Musical *opinionis* that I here propose to defend the composer.

Nothing is easier, and nothing more convincing to the ignorant, than to sweep over the deep. Nothing is more relieving than to talk about what one doesn't know, for it's the easiest thing to be done about it ; besides, it promotes solidarity among the light-minded, promotes that jolly good highbrow fellowship which keeps the music critic's conscience ever supple and easy. Artistic stupidity hides behind anti-artistic intelligence which takes everything into humorous account except genius. Genius tends to be a disturbing phenomenon for the critic, for its recognition depends upon the creation of new standards of evaluation. Music criticism justifies itself where an inspired vision of the future supersedes all acquired illusions of the past. Otherwise, it merely judges itself : perhaps it is because the critic criticizes himself that he doesn't want to be criticized by anybody else. Or perhaps it is because he feels more certain than secure. In any case, one has to grant him that his certainty is based upon his professional knowledge ; but, alas, most professionals who construct this body of knowledge are amateurs without the imagination of amateurs. They know enough to judge the past by its future, but when it comes to the present they judge it by its past. As for the future—that, they say, can look after itself. " Can " and " must," however, have no future tense, and what can and must be known and said, can and must be said now.

It may seem unfair to reproach Gerald Abraham with insufficient knowledge, not only because he stands far above the common music(ologic)al pressman both as a scholar and as a musician, but more particularly because he has written on Schoenberg for *Grove's* Supplementary Volume (4th Edition). A *Grove* article, however, depends on exoteric knowledge, whereas the appraisal of genius, and of the man in whom genius burns, depends on esoteric knowledge. In simpler words, in matters out of the emotional or spiritual ordinary, it all depends on whether you know things outside in or inside out.

In the case of Winton Dean, however—a valued contributor to this journal upon other subjects—there does not even seem to be any exoteric knowledge capable of utilization. In fact, all that emerges from his piece is his staggering ignorance of every aspect of Schoenberg's work, mind, and background. A real knowledge of the twelve-tone technique, to be sure, can only be derived from the actual compositions ; just as a real understanding of Schoenberg's work, including his writings, can only be arrived at by way of one's insight into the development of his genius, or rather *into strongly developing genius in general* (Beethoven, for instance, or Freud, or Picasso). Mr. Dean, however, far from realizing as much as his factual ignorance, and quite unconscious of the dangers of spiritual ignorance, writes about Schoenberg's essays as a teacher would write about the efforts of a none too gifted, if far too self-satisfied pupil. He is careful to grant Schoenberg no more than a "reputation" and a " position," whereas he uses the words " genius " and

" master " for the purpose of ironisation. I am indeed in a difficult position, for humility in the face of genius is not half as readable as humour in the face of the unfaceable. Before we plunge into the morass, moreover, we have the ungrateful task of teaching the editor of a leading musicological journal *mores :* that he should have entrusted an article on Schoenberg's book to someone whose knowledge of Schoenberg equals mine of Sibelius is inexcusable.

There is good humour, there is bad humour, and there is the worst kind of humour, which is good humour misapplied : " Schoenberg's latest work is written in the twenty-six letter system." Thus Mr. Dean sets the mood of his article, and the *Musical Times* was quick to quote the sentence with relish. Upon the following excerpt from Schoenberg's essay *On Revient Toujours—*

> . . . a longing to return to the older style was always vigorous in me ; and from time to time I had to yield to that urge. This is . . . why I sometimes write tonal music. To me stylistic differences of this nature are not of special importance. I do not know which of my compositions are better ; I like them all, because I liked them when I wrote them.

—Dean comments :—" The [penultimate sentence], which belies a great deal elsewhere in the book, will perhaps disconcert both friends and adversaries ; the [last sentence] reveals a parental tenderness and fidelity almost unique in creative artists." Mr. Dean here proves himself unable to distinguish between the evolutional, historical point of view, wherefrom the stylistic differences are of special importance, and the extra-historical evaluational standpoint, from which they aren't. And sure enough, Mr. Dean's complete mis-interpretation of the excerpt's last sentence, which he has not understood at all, brings us to the crux of most criticisms of the book: the critics' inability to view Schoenberg *in terms of his development.* What Schoenberg means is what, in the simplest possible words, he says : he likes all his compositions because *each is true to the stage of creative development at which it was written.* Now, Schoenberg's more recent tonal compositions correspond to the stage where, having fully mastered his most advanced style, he is able to progress by regressing : to let the older methods gain by the new. The mastery he has achieved in his new technique makes it possible for him to revert to the old techniques without slackening his ever further urging development, without impeding his extra-diatonic thinking : he can now symbiotically combine contradicting methods without contradicting himself. Of course, if you cannot grasp his development, he seems to contradict himself, in his music and in his writings. He contradicts himself as much and as little as Beethoven's late B♭ quartet contradicts his early one. If Schoenberg did not thus " contradict himself "—that would be a ground for criticism ! Genius's first debt to art is dynamic evolution, while the critic's original sin is static evaluation. Thus Mr. Hill : " . . . there are constant indications in the lecture on *Composing with Twelve Tones* of how his method has changed and evolved. Obviously, he could not have been ' right ' both before and afterwards, and Schoenberg would be the first to admit it." Being the author of a study on *Schoenberg's Tone-Rows and the Tonal System of the Future (Musical Quarterly*, New York, January, 1936), Mr. Hill is most unfortunately regarded as an authority on Schoenberg, and his pseudo-favourable review of the present book is doubly dangerous : a trap for the virginal reader, all the more effective because the trapper doesn't know that he is trapping. Exactly what right has he to give categorical information on what " Schoenberg would be the first to admit " ? If he understood what lies behind Schoenberg's " changing method," if he had a musical approach to the development of Schoenberg's music, if he knew it from the inside, he would not be able to pronounce such overbearing nonsense. Those who experience Schoenberg's musical contents, know that he wouldn't admit anything of the sort. On the extreme contrary, he would say that he was right both before and afterwards, that in creative growth what was right yesterday won't be right tomorrow ; and that what is wrong for the pupil is right for the master. A truism ? Not many apply its truth to the case of a genius who, once his own pupil, became his inner master's master.

Discussing this essay on twelve-tone composition, Dean lets Schoenberg appear " convinced that the old tonality had been outmoded." Nowhere does Schoenberg—himself still (better : again) in creative touch with " the old tonality "—express or imply such a conviction. If Mr. Dean knew something about Schoenberg apart from the present book, he would perhaps realize the naiveté of his ideas of " Schoenberg's Ideas " ; he would know, for instance, Schoenberg's often-expressed aphorism that " there is still plenty of good music to be written in C major." In today's labile state of musical history, one and the same *time* comprises a bewildering variety of historical, developmental stages : history does not altogether parallel chronology. What is already valid for one creator (and listener) is not yet valid for another, and manybody's today is somebody's yesterday ; while different stages of development may, moreover, co-exist and collaborate in the same musical mentality. That the complete emancipation of the dissonance represents an extreme advance in the inevitable evolution of music does not mean that all preceding stages are past ; on the contrary, it means that Schoenberg's new style is the future's emissary in the present. The consequent sense of a mission which goes through Schoenberg's writings, however, is stigmatized as arrogance. " Intellectual arrogance abounds " says Prof. Abraham. " One is tempted to call him egocentric and almost unbelievably conceited " says Mr. Hill. " Is it not the height of arrogance," asks Mr. Dean, " to assert that ' the time will come when the ability to draw thematic material from a basic set of twelve tones will be an unconditional requisite for obtaining admission into the composition class of a conservatory ' ? " I should say, that depends on whether the time will come. But Mr. Dean does not even comply with primitive logic : he does not admit the mere possibility that Schoenberg's is a realistic prognosis, in which case the term " arrogance " does not apply, for to arrogate means to claim unduly. In other words, Mr. Dean, who never tires of reproaching Schoenberg with begging questions, begs (among others) the most fundamental question of all, though he professes to leave it unanswered at the end of his article. Likewise Mr. Hill : " The world has not caught much warmth from his fire yet, and no one can possibly say whether eventually it will turn towards or away from that fire." I beg Mr. Hill not to prescribe to us what we can or cannot possibly say. Predictability is a function of knowledge. If, on the one hand, one recognizes the scientific validity of the twelve-note method, while on the other hand partaking of Schoenberg's (as of all good music's) secret science,* i.e. if one isn't what Schoenberg calls " one of these non-musicians who look in my music only for the twelve notes—not realizing in the least its musical content, expression, and merit " ; if, in short, one is a musical scientist (accent on either word) who understands Schoenberg's music, one is in no doubt about its future. If on the other hand, one thinks, with Prof. Abraham, that " the lecture on ' Composing with Twelve Tones ' tells us, what most of us already know, how to ' understand ' twelve-tone music—that is, how to read the cipher— but contributes nothing toward its aesthetic justification," one should not perhaps write about twelve-tone technique. For this sentence contains three radical fallacies. Firstly, inverted commas or no, the essay definitely doesn't tell us how to understand twelve-tone music (no musician's essay ever tells us how to understand music), nor does it encourage us to go twelve-tone hunting for the pleasure

---

* Schoenberg says in his essay on *The Blessing of the Dressing* : " Secret science is not what an alchemist would have refused to teach you ; it is a science which cannot be taught at all. It is inborn or it is not there."

of the hunt. It describes the development and application of a method and is addressed to the musician who likes to know about what, emotionally and spiritually, he already understands, as well as to the potential pupil. Secondly, there is no ' cipher ' in twelve-tone music ; in fact, with the greatest precision, Prof. Abraham uses the wrongest possible term : a cipher conceals, whereas the tone row clarifies. Thirdly, the evolutional theory, the genesis of the twelve-tone technique *is* the aesthetic justification of its application, and Prof. Abraham appears to ask for an aesthetic justification of an aesthetic justification. The theory of twelve-tone music cannot, of course, be more complete than its history : what absurdity to expect the first twelve-tone musician to complete it ! But in spite of his howlers, in spite even of his unwarranted and unpleasant slight at Schoenberg's " mental character "—" terribly like the portrait drawn by his enemies "—he does not quite descend to the schoolboy level of Mr. Dean, who does not shrink from giving Schoenberg a lesson in the Rudiments of Tonality ; one need not be an admirer of Schoenberg in order to marvel at Richard Capell's temerity in printing this among many instances of equal insight : " [In tonal music] the basic motive is not [as Schoenberg says] a derivative of the tonality, it is expressed in terms of the tonality, just as a Latin poem is expressed in terms of the Latin language—a very different thing . . . " I do not propose to prove to Mr. Dean that 2×2 is not 5 before someone supports him ; but meanwhile he might try to translate a tonal motive of his own choosing into other terms, "just as " one translates a Latin poem. He is indeed enamoured by comparisons ; they work like miracles to prove the rightest wrong : "Why should a reference to tonal harmony [in twelve-note composition] be ' disturbing ' in a pejorative sense ? The modes did not cease to fertilize music the moment composers began to use the classical tonic and dominant system," the absurd implication being that diatonicism is to modality as dodecaphonism should or could be to diatonicism. But the classical major and minor *are* modes, representing the survival of the fittest by artistic selection, whereas all atonal technique grows out of the disintegration of tonal unity and the emancipation (increasing intelligibility) of the dissonance. Thus, Mr. Dean's didactic comparison does not apply if we do not outright condemn an atonal approach ; and if we do, we are asked to improve the unimprovable. " ' False expectations of [tonal] consequences and continuations ' which, by the very fact of their existence, could have been of the greatest artistic service are condemned outright. Not the least subtle device at a composer's command is his ability to open up one vista and lead his listeners down another." Mr. Dean has not the faintest inkling of the radical change in compositional technique that manifests itself in twelve-tone music, whose evolutional aspect he is therefore once again unable to grasp. So-called deceptive devices in music—say an interrupted cadence (*Trugschluss*), or a " deceptive " (discontinued) imitation—are not intended to deceive anyone (good music never is), but, on the contrary, to show the listener that and how he has been deceived by his platitudinous prejudices, by his automatic expectations. For this purpose, the disillusionment must be stronger than the illusion. Now Mr. Dean proposes that a radically new method of unification should, while it is still in the making, " open up one vista " of an age-old and deeply ingrained method of unification, " and lead his listeners down " the new way. But how can they thus be led, if the illusion is stronger than the disillusionment ? Optimistically supposing that the composer did not himself fall a victim to the fata morgana he had conjured up, that, dead certain of the journey's end, he unhesitatingly continued on the new way—he would find, upon turning round, that his listeners had gone and perished the other way which promised to lead home but led to nowhere. This would be a real deception. Of course, the seasoned master of the twelve-tone technique can, as Schoenberg has shown in his music, lead the master-listener to new destinations by routes at once new and familiar, by routes whose unfamiliarity reveals itself all the more to the traveller when he becomes familiar with them ; but then Mr. Dean does not perhaps realize that the twelve-tone lecture is not addressed to masters. If, on the other hand, he does, he might re-consider one of its reminders : " ' Everything ' has always been allowed to two kinds of artists : to masters on the one hand, and to ignoramuses on the other." But what can one do with ignoramuses who proceed to teach the masters how to teach ?

When Mr. Winton Dean, who by the evidence of his article has not gone through a single twelve-tone composition, declares the teachable part of Schoenberg's method to be a " ' preconceived formula '* with a vengeance, hedged about with all manner of rules and prohibitions " ; when he criticises this method as if he had ever tried to apply it, one realizes that the time has come when the ability to draw thematic material from a basic set of twelve tones ought to be an unconditional prerequisite for obtaining permission to criticize the twelve-tone method *qua* technique (as distinct from any particular result of its application). Any criticism of the technique's alleged

* Apropos of Schoenberg's definition of a " method " as " a *modus* of applying regularly a preconceived formula."

166

rigidity is quite irrelevant if the limitations imposed upon horizontal construction are not considered against the freedom gained in vertical combinations. But so far is Mr. Dean's mind removed from the actual compositional processes involved in the application of the technique that such an elementary independent thought would never occur to him ; he closely sticks to his misreading of Schoenberg's essay, for that is all he knows. In my opinion, once the twelve-tone technique has securely established itself, has become second nature, the genuinely musical world will realize that no change at all has taken place in the degrees of freedom and of discipline : the limitations of tonal harmony will be seen to have given way to a harmonic freedom which corresponds to the relative melodic freedom in tonal structures, and to have changed their residence from the harmonic to the melodic and contrapuntal field. Meanwhile, it is absurd to suggest, as Mr. Dean does, that Schoenberg " has sought to elevate his own procedure to a universal rule." The essay on twelve-tone technique stresses very thoroughly how the development of his technique has been bound up with the development of his own creativity, and in the essay on *The Blessing of the Dressing* he points out that all his pupils

> differ from one another extremely and though perhaps the majority compose twelve-tone music, one could not speak of a school. They all had to find their way alone, for themselves. And that is exactly what they did ; everyone has his own manner of obeying rules derived from the treatment of twelve tones.

It is only the twelve-tonal, i.e. essentially extra-tonal principle on which his technique is based that claims universal validity (as distinct from universal applicability), and a creator whose technique is not based on a principle so universal that it is in harmony with the psychic universe may as well pack up and steal away before someone discovers the swindle which unwittingly pronounces its own death-sentence by calling itself " contemporary." Art is never contemporary, journalism always is ; which is why the musical journalists mistake journalistic music for art. Nobody minds the critics' going about their " quiet little jobs as cemetery watchmen " (Sartre), but when they start to employ themselves and one another as new life's grave-diggers . . . But stop, says Mr. Dean. He is not, he would tell us, passing final judgment on Schoenberg as a composer. Sartre : " Our critics never bet on uncertain issues." "But," says Mr. Dean," Schoenberg has ventured into the field of criticism." He hasn't. He speaks as a teacher whom you mistake for a critic when he talks about the work of others, and for a " doctrinaire " when he talks about his own. From what you and your colleagues-in-arms have written, readers who do not know much about Schoenberg must conclude that his prime concern is to push his compositional method down other people's throats, and that for the rest you can't learn anything from him, except " things that were commonplace to Prout " (Abraham). A mere musician, however, and not a twelve-toner either—Otto Klemperer—recounts :—

> Originally a pupil of Hans Pfitzner, I had the opportunity of studying with Arnold Schoenberg in Los Angeles during the years 1935-37. I showed him a number of my compositions, which he criticised ; he also analysed for my benefit many works of the masters, such as, for instance, the motets of Bach. I consider him the greatest living teacher of composition, although, strangely enough, during our long conversations he never mentioned the twelve-tone system.

Whereas Prof. Abraham's musicological conclusion is—" For the sake of their own reputations, let composers keep to lined paper ! " In fact, the critics of the book have not even derived any benefit from its masterly analyses of the masters ; but then, the best teacher is the bad pupil's worst. As for more than one reviewer's criticisms of Schoenberg's sense of humour, it is a particular pity that the humour of the following paragraph from the essay on *The Blessing of the Dressing* should have gone unobserved :—

> I once had a pupil who had started harmony with me. About two months later he stopped taking lessons. He had been offered a position as second music critic on a great newspaper and was afraid too much knowledge might have an unfavourable influence upon the spontaneity of his judgment. He made a career as a critic and even as a pedagogue.

[Schoenberg's book (*Style and Idea*) itself will be reviewed in these pages after its English publication—Eds.]

Schooldays in Brisbane
A FRAGMENT OF AUTOBIOGRAPHY
By ARTHUR BENJAMIN

I suppose that if I had been born in Europe, I should have become a prodigy-pianist. But out there in a small Australian city, the thought, fortunately for me, never entered my parents' heads, though from the age of 6 I was in constant demand at concerts. I once sang for instance, sitting on a swing surrounded by Brisbane's most glamorous little girls, all of us dressed in Watteau style, the " Swing " song from " A Child's Garland "—the poems by Robert Louis Stevenson, the music by Liza Lehmann. Of necessity my stage and platform activities had to take second place when I started to go to Bowen House School. I was a day boy and used to rush home every afternoon to spend an hour or so at the piano, mostly engaged in improvisations which went on and on and on. No doubt this cultivated a technical facility which came in handy later, though it was not until I began to take lessons that I *learnt* the scales and arpeggios. Naturally at this period I had become quite well-known as the " boy-pianist," and one day as I walked home from school along Albert Street, a pretty woman standing in her doorway asked me if I would come in and play something for her. When I started on her very ancient upright piano I broke down after a couple of bars. I was bitterly humiliated, tried again, broke down again and finally ran out of the house in tears. I understood the explanation much later. The old piano's pitch had fallen perhaps as much as two tones, and with my absolute pitch, I could not my persuade my fingers to go on playing the notes heard in my mind when the notes which actually sounded demanded completely different fingering. Nearly every house in Albert Street framed a pretty lady in its doorways, so I found out years afterwards. Brisbane was the terminal port for big ships, and sailors will be sailors.

Bowen House School, which I entered at the age of 7, was allegedly run on the lines of an English prep school. Certainly all the teachers were English. Of them I can only remember Buller (the head), Newman (second in command), Carson (Latin and French), Butcher (History and Geography) and Miss Palmer (beginners). The last was sweet to me and lent me her banjo. Buller was a heavy-jowled, terrifying person, who had a pretty touch with the cane. It was he who caned any boy who had been caned twice previously in a term by other teachers. Newman just toadied to him and imitated him. He took maths, for which I had no talent. Carson was young, enthusiastic and dapper. He became headmaster later on. The only thing I can remember about him is a sort of rhythmic refrain he invented which went thus :—

(Non troppo allegro, molto giusto e staccetissimo).

Put the | tip of the tongue on the | base of the teeth and say
(piano e leggiero)

"Tu" | not | "Chew"!
(dolce) (subito ff)

The T's and the B sounded like " pizzicato." Butcher (nicknamed " Lardy," not with affection) taught us History, Geography and General Knowledge. Perhaps I will not be believed, but this is the way we learnt History and Geography out of Longman's Primers —I think that is what the books were called. For homework, on the nights before the lessons, we had to memorize two or three pages. At the lesson Lardy would suddenly point to a boy who would be expected to recite the first line—the *line*, whether it left off in the middle of a sentence or not. Lardy would then point suddenly at another boy, who would be expected to continue from where the last boy had left off. This was to make sure that we were all wide awake. The result was this sort of thing :—

    1st Boy : Brazil is the largest country in South America. Its
                  principal exports are
    2nd Boy : nuts, diamonds, teak (and so on).

History went exactly the same. So did " Poetry." Our English class consisted mostly of parsing and analysis. (I cannot remember who " took " us in English : but there is really no reason why I should). To return to Lardy. If an unfortunate boy could not continue the recitation of Brazil's excellences, he would shout, fortissimo, " GET," and, pianissimo and sinister, " the cane ! " It sounded like this :—

whereupon the unfortunate child had to go and ask the Head for the loan of a cane, return to the class room, receive two or three " cuts " on the palm of the hand from Lardy (all this while the rest of the class waited in gloomy silence) and return the cane to the Head. Some of the more hardened criminals advocated rubbing resin on the palms, and it was believed that a human hair laid on the palm would split the cane. The only History I heard seems, at this distance in time, to have been about the Tudor Dynasty, though I distinctly remember the whole class chanting, in unison :

but that might have been in Miss Palmer's class, where we all learnt to write " copperplate "—a rather pleasing accomplishment I retain to this day. How it happens that I now am a lover of History I find it very difficult to explain.* " General Knowledge " consisted in hearing about the dimensions of the Pyramids and other useless facts. But on the one day in the month, when the post from England

*Today one would be surprised to find a school in Australia where not a word was taught of Australian History, with its adventurous story of discovery. But in those days Australia was very much a colony.

brought the old " Wide World Magazine " with its curious con-
glomeration of fact and fiction, the General Knowledge lesson became
thrilling. We heard of curious experiments with mysterious rays by
a German called Hertz, and of radium, and of something beyond
the atmosphere called " The Ether."

We all used slates, ruled on one side, plain on the other. We were
each supposed to have a little round tin containing a little wet
sponge with which to clean the slates ; but these erasers were either
stolen or lost or insufficiently wet. So we spat prolifically on our
palms. I still have a vivid memory of the acrid taste and smell.
Germs ? Well, I suppose most of us grew up strong and healthy
men ; a lot of us quite healthy enough to be killed or wounded in
two wars.

We sat on long benches behind long desks, each holding about 8
boys. So it was possible to pass objects along surreptitiously. The
inevitably more precocious boy would pass along a slate on which
dirty drawings of anatomical significance were chalked. Thus began
my sex education. I use the word " dirty " not out of prudishness
but simply because (as I learnt later) the drawings were quite
inaccurate. And so life continued from the age of 7 to 13. My
schooldays were not unhappy, merely boring in the extreme. Except
for AN EVENT. Music at Bowen House School consisted of a small
proportion of volunteers, appearing for one hour a week, to sing
under the direction of a Mr. Allen (Miss Palmer at the piano) such
songs as " John Peel " etc. in unison. These were preceded by sight
reading. Mr. Allen would write large semibreves, in the treble stave,
on a blackboard ; and with a pointer he dodged about from one
semibreve to another, upon which the class would yell, anything but
unanimously, the note which came into their heads. Naturally I
found this exercise easy. The day came when Thomas Dunhill
examined our school music for the Associated Board of the Royal
Academy and the Royal College of Music, London. The class
(having been given instructions to listen to me and to sing the note
as immediately after me as possible and, moreover, *fortissimo*) passed
its sight reading test with honours. Not that Dunhill was deceived.
He asked to be allowed to talk to me and put me through some ear
tests and asked what I did musically. This happened when I was
about 10 or 11. Before he left Brisbane, Dunhill was brought to our
house by a doctor friend (representative of the Associated Board in
Brisbane) and he asked me to play and to improvise ; and I showed
him my first composition. Dunhill told my parents he hoped I
should soon be able to go to study harmony and counterpoint with

him. From that moment it was my burning ambition by hook or by crook to reach London.

I discarded my collection of postcards except those dealing with London, music and the stage. Indeed when I did finally come to London I knew at once every one of the more frequented thoroughfares, and, thanks to my study of London maps, how to find them—an accomplishment of which few Londoners bred and born could boast.

A Note on William Wordsworth
By PAUL HAMBURGER

Four Sacred Sonnets (John Donne), (4s. 0d.); String Quartet No. 1 (7s. 0d.); String Quartet No. 2 (7s. 0d.); Four Lyrics (voice and string quartet), (8s. 0d.); Cheesecombe Suite (piano), 2s. 6d.), String Trio (6s. 0d.), Hymn of Dedication Chorus and Orchestra), (3s. 0d.); Piano Concerto (6s. 0d.); The Image (song) (2s. 0d.); (All Lengnick).

WHEN I first read through a selection representative of Wordsworth's work between 1941 and 1947 (given in chronological order at the head of this article), I did not look at the dates printed at the end of each score, but made my guess, hoping to be proved right in the end. But when, eventually, I did look at the dates, I found I had often been mistaken. To be sure, if there is no steady progress, neither is there a steady decline in Wordsworth's powers: I had been right in believing the two string quartets to be early works. But from 1943 on, which was roughly the time when Wordsworth found a more personal language, the order of his compositions is most bewildering. One finds the *Four Lyrics* of 1941, the fourth of which is genuinely modern, followed by the more assured but stylistically regressive *John Donne* Sonnets of 1944, and by the dull *Cheesecombe* Suite ; the String Trio, perhaps his best work to date, resting cheek by jowl with the academic *Hymn of Dedication*, which in its turn is a forerunner of the horrible Piano Concerto of 1947—a complete lapse from grace. Such unevenness of production, coupled with a considerably assured technique, makes one mistrust a composer, makes one suspect that a senseless sense of duty is injuring his intellectual honesty. Let me say at once that I have not found a single bar in these pages that could be called a deliberate fraud : even the cadenza of the piano concerto, which has all the emptiness of early Rachmaninoff without his bland showmanship, is not written by one consciously scheming to befuddle an audience with faded heroics in modern trimmings ; it is written, as indeed is the whole concerto, with an intense sense of obligation towards the rhapsodic manner ; it is an attempt to do justice to romantic improvisation ;

and indeed Wordsworth would probably have considered it a sign of failure if his intra-musical concerns had not produced, so to say on their own, a work of popular appeal. But here, of course, lies the whole " swindle "—if that be not too strong a word for fruits of the mind that turn sour in the making : one cannot rhapsodize dutifully, nor be popular under obligation. Luckily, it is only in this concerto that Wordsworth deems it his duty to be popular ; in his songs and chamber-music his sense of obligation is directed towards other objects, namely (a) the cyclic form (b) the English school, (c) modern dissonance. Here, Wordsworth's compositional disingenuousness occurs entirely on the intra-musical plane. He is, metaphorically speaking, the best pupil of his teachers, and therefore their despair. If I had heard the 1st movements of the 1st and 2nd string quartets not knowing the composer, I would have guessed at an English folklorist of 1900 who had a liking for Russian music and had studied with Reger and Busoni in order to stiffen his out-pourings with a sufficient dose of counterpoint. It is perhaps significant that these quartets get better as they progress : in the central section of No. 1's slow movement (from fig. 2), and in parts of No. 2's Scherzo, Wordsworth's compulsory behaviour relaxes. It stiffens again, unfortunately, with the taking up of the cyclic construction : the earlier material reappearing in later movements, mostly in the Finale, though by no means introduced in the form of blatant or nostalgic reminiscences, is yet not significant enough to be cyclic.

Even in the otherwise progressive String Trio, the motivic connection between the first and third movements which are separated by a brilliant Scherzo) witnesses merely the rebirth of the academic self-compulsion of the quartets. There are two reasons for Wordsworth's failure in handling cyclic forms. First, he is, in spite of his copious counterpoint, a musical miniaturist with the miniaturist's sense of obligation towards large forms ; secondly, his melodic invention hovers uneasily between the full-blown melody dictated by both romanticism and English folklore, and the motivic snippet desirable for symphonic, and especially cyclic, development. As a result, most of his themes (cf. the Piano Concerto, the last movement of the first quartet ; not, however, the last movement of the String Trio which offers a genuine theme) are hybrids that satisfy neither the romantically attuned ear nor the formally inclined mind. Similarly balancing between two stools is Wordsworth' harmony ; our suspicion of unconscious disingenuousness is substantiated in the technical realm. Caught between his conflicting loyalties to folklorism and modern dissonance, Wordsworth has neither the genius nor the audacity of a Vaughan Williams to alloy these elements into an original idiom. Instead, he works out an optimistically premature compromise of two sorts : (a) romantic academicism, (b) a personal idiom of proud limitations. The former consists of all the stock-in-trade of the English neo-romantic school : the parallel second inversions (Piano Concerto), the parallel major thirds (*Four Sacred Sonnets*) the pseudo-modality (*Hymn of Dedication*), the obliquely resolved bass-appogiaturas under a string of root-positions. Though academicism is more suspect nowadays than at any other time, and though " romantic academicism " is moreover a contradiction in terms which, alas, is rarely apprehended by its perpetrators, a less ambitious composer might get away with it. But with Wordsworth it is unpardonable, because it stands in stark contrast to his more ambitious approach. Manner (b), called into action when dramatic conflict, disquiet, or soul-searchings are to be depicted (see the " dividing swords of scorn " in the *Hymn*, p. 4 : oh, that the devils should be so much easier to draw than the angels !), is nothing but a repetition of (a) on a more esoteric plane. The " proud limitations " of this more properly personal idiom—limitations which try to further its intelligibility—are based on the misconception that you must not court evil or suffering even when depicting it. Since " evil " in this context would mean the oppressiveness of modern civilisation, creating suffering in the artist through its impact on his sensibility, this would be tantamount to saying " however much you suffer your art must not be radical," or " they'll only understand what they can take, you'll hurt them if you give more ; and what's more, you'll hurt yourself in the long run if you don't learn to understate your suffering." In Wordsworth's harmony, this implied, though, I am sure, not conscious maxim makes for the most curious twists a composer suspended between folkloristic romanticism and modern dissonance can be capable of. Many of Wordsworth's better-class dissonances are based on the six single and four double appogiatura resolutions of the augmented triad (see the fugue of the second quartet). This is typical : the most extreme dissonance of tonal harmony, a chord on the brink of being non-functional, and, in consequence, capable of diverse modulatory resolution, is used by the dilemma-ridden composer to slur over the sufferings of life and the ardours of composition ; is made to behave rationally, in a number of faintly surprising, yet strictly intelligible ways, when the psychological impasse is such that no outmoded rationality can any longer be of avail. Consequently, this harmony of avoidances becomes listless and drab (most so perhaps in the simple piano setting of the *Cheesecombe* Suite) and the philistine is not far wrong when he complains of these dreadful modern dissonances. But while this kind of harmony is not truly modern, neither is Wordsworth's allegiance to the English school quite stable. In " Weep you no more, sad fountains " of the *Four Lyrics* a tune in the manner of Dr. Arne is supported by harmony in 20th century English style. Very well, one says, a (quasi-) folktune in modern setting. But then (after fig. 1) the tune approaches more and more the style of the harmony, taking licences which Dr. Arne would never have taken, thus forfeiting the chance of a correct compositional solution of the set problem. This song is symbolic of Wordsworth's music : with all his knowledge, skill, endeavour and sense of obligation, he is not aware that—like this particular lyric—he "wants to have it both ways." But the adamant economy of art, its inner truthfulness as it were, won't have it.

And, when all this hectoring is done, what remains of Wordsworth's music ? There remain quite a few passages, and some promise. It is those passages where, the storm of conflicting duties having abated, he allows himself to be simple or fragmentary. Then he can even safely become complicated. The good, unsolicited simplicity of the fourth lyric's " Full many a glorious morning have I seen flatter the mountain-tops . . . " gives rise to the complications of " Anon permit the basest clouds to ride. . . . " as naturally as the changes in our atmosphere happen. The recapitulation and coda of the String Trio's first movement, in their fragmentary precision, give the refreshing impression of a composer whose improvisation sounds workmanlike and whose workmanship sounds improvisatory. It is on these lines that one hopes Wordsworth will go on—he has already given a token of it in some passages of the oboe quartet. I think he needs luck for it, more than anything else, for he has tried too hard trying hard.

ENGLISH KEYBOARD MUSIC OF THE SEVENTEENTH CENTURY, IN THE LIBRARY OF THE PARIS CONSERVATOIRE

SEVERAL important musical manuscripts were sold during the nineteenth century to foreign buyers, and many fine collections were irretrievably dispersed. Such was the fate of the music belonging to Dr. Thomas Bever, an Oxford lawyer and musical dilettante, whose books are now to be found scattered among the libraries of London, Tenbury and Paris. Mr. Denis Stevens recently presented to the Bodleian Library, Oxford, microfilms of four of these Paris manuscripts, which are briefly described below.

RÉSERVE 1122 (ACCESSION NUMBER: 18547).
THE bookplate is that of Thomas Bever, LL.D., Fellow of All Souls College, Oxford. The initial H on the outside and inside of the cover refers to an alphabetical table of music books in the possession of the Tomkins family. A full description of those from A to G (with dates) may be seen on the page following the index, but their whereabouts are not known at the present time. It is possible that some leaves from these books were bound up with Bodley MS. Mus. Sch. C 93, and British Museum Add. MS. 29996, both of which contain music in the hand of Thomas Tomkins.

The size of the manuscript is $7\frac{1}{2}'' \times 11\frac{1}{4}''$ and it is paginated (i-viii) + 1-189. The music is mostly by Thomas Tomkins himself, and is liberally annotated. There are also a number of pieces by Byrd and Bull. No printed description of this manuscript has yet been made, but Professor Stephen D. Tuttle of the University of Virginia, Charlottesville, Va., has made a transcription into modern notation which is due to appear in the forthcoming series " Musica Britannica."

RÉSERVE 1186 (ACCESSION NUMBER: 18546).
SIZE slightly larger than the previous MS.: $8'' \times 11\frac{1}{4}''$. Although it is ostensibly keyboard music the greater part of the repertoire is made up of transcriptions of vocal music. The composers mentioned in the index are as follows: Bateson, Wilkinson, Morley, Dowland, Creighton, Wm. Daman, Byrd, Henry Loosemore, Mr. Silver, Mr. Lever, Tallis, Gibbons, Mudd, Churchyard, Clarke, Bull, Lugge, Tomkins, Williams.

Printed descriptions may be found in " Revue de Musicologie " 1927 (p. 205); 1928 (p. 235); 1929 (p. 32).

RÉSERVE 1185 (ACCESSION NUMBER: 18548).
THIS is a manuscript similar in size to Rés. 1122. The initials M.W. (? Michael Wise, Gentleman of the Chapel Royal) are embossed in gold on the cover. The volume is a composite one, for the first part consists of *Parthenia*, the first printed collection of virginal music in England. (This is separately numbered as Réserve 1184, but included in the same accession number as the manuscript portion of the book).

The index to the manuscript is written on two blank pages at the end of *Parthenia*, and the date split up by the heading is 1652. The music is paginated 1-348, and represents a number of composers, including Bull, Gibbons, Lawes, Cosyn, and Formiloe.

Printed descriptions of the MS. occur in " Revue de Musicologie " 1931 (p. 22); 1932 (p. 86).

RÉSERVE 1186 BIS (ACCESSION NUMBER: 18570).
A COMPOSITE binding of two MSS. of different sizes, the first being $12'' \times 7\frac{1}{2}''$ and the second $11'' \times 7\frac{1}{2}''$. The binding seems to be the work of the Bibliothèque du Conservatoire, whose initials appear on the spine.

The first part is paginated to 30, then foliated. The composers mentioned are Gibbons, Blow, Price and Ffaranella.

The second part contains pieces by Tallis, Gibbons and Bull.

Printed descriptions may be found in " Revue de Musicologie " 1926 (p. 204); 1927 (p. 36). These articles, and the ones on the foregoing manuscripts, are by Mlle. Pereira.

Schoenberg

CHAMBER SYMPHONY, OP. 9

When I had finished my first *Kammersymphonie*, Op. 9, I told my friends:
" Now I have established my style. I know now how I have to compose."
But my next work showed a great deviation from this style; it was a first
step toward my present style. My destiny had forced me in this direction—
I was not destined to continue in the manner of *Transfigured Night* or
Gurrelieder or even *Pelléas and Mélisande*. The Supreme Commander
had ordered me on a harder road.

I. General Introduction

A section of the Philharmonia Orchestra c. Scherchen,
Third Programme, 22nd November, 1950.

I WAS deeply moved.

With most composers, a critic who contented himself with that confession
might be suspected of not wholly earning his keep. With the Schoenberg it
may well be the crucial point: I doubt if any composer has ever been more
bitterly accused of writing from the head instead of from the heart. Augen-
musik: eye-music; that is the burden of the opposition. The complaint is
perfectly sincere. I remember, no more than five years ago, being confirmedly
of the same opinion. If growing familiarity can open my ears (which are in no
way particularly notable ears, and are professionally, moreover, attuned to
Lawes and Purcell and Couperin and Bach rather than to Berg and Schoenberg)
and fire my heart, then there is that in the music to open ears and fire hearts.

It was an enormous advantage to have this music twice over in the same
programme, splendidly played into the bargain. The whole affair reflected
great credit on performers, organisers and the B.B.C. alike. No music could
be more condensed. At the first hearing, my impression was one of a compact
wealth of content, constructed with an extremity of craftsmanship, sureness and
economy, strangely poignant and heartfelt, magical but elusive. At the second
hearing, this subtle and fascinating texture of *sound* became profoundly imbued
(where I had previously only obscurely sensed it) with *feeling* not less closely
knit than the structure which conveys it. That was the stage at which I became
deeply moved.

Now over to my colleagues.   R.D.

II. Style

THE more Schoenberg I hear, the more difficult I find it to write intelligently
about him. The routine musical vocabulary ceases to obtain. " Styles,"
" periods," " influences," " characteristics " and so forth—the words don't fit
Schoenberg and Schoenberg doesn't fit them. My colleague calls Schoenberg
" a widely-developing composer " which is, of course, very true but apt to mislead
unless we remember that the term applied to Schoenberg takes on a new meaning.
" Widely developing " in relation to Schoenberg is something quite apart from
" widely developing " in relation to almost any other composer we care to
choose: for the very good reason that Schoenberg's development as a composer
is unique. It may best be expressed as follows: *Each work of Schoenberg is
simultaneously not only a development but a stylization and consummate fruition
of that development.* Whereas development normally implies a further step

177

forward in technique yet to come, in Schoenberg the step forward and the objective itself are both achieved in and at the same moment—a most remarkable phenomenon, and even more remarkable musical achievement. It is therefore inadequate to talk of Schoenberg's development as if it were a series of progressive steps forward each of which logically and inevitably leads to the next: such an attitude is likely to hinder rather than further understanding of Schoenberg—especially where the stylistic discrepancies between one work and its successor are so vast. In looking for a " development " we only succeed in muddling ourselves and others too. As it happens, the *Kammersymphonie*, Op. 9, could be discussed in more or less familiar terms, because throughout we can detect the " influence " of the late Viennese school, particularly Mahler. Mahler crops up in the wonderful clarity of Schoenberg's instrumentation (cf. the 1st movt. of Mahler's Ninth symphony—the chamber orchestral interlude just prior to the coda); and Mahler has obviously tailored the cut of many of Schoenberg's themes (cf. the 1st subject of Schoenberg's 1st movt.). Indeed, there is little " new " in the *Kammersymphonie* to make strenuous demands on our aural response. (I don't mean " new " in the historical sense; the revolutionary aspect of the work for its own time is obvious.)   Yet when all has been said and done, and we have comforted ourselves with recognising in the Schoenberg piece all that we have previously known in Mahler, we find we are left exactly where we were before. In other words, where Schoenberg is concerned historical familiarities and/or relationships don't help. Schoenberg's " developments " not only contain within themselves their seeds of origin, but also their own development (the " development of the development " so to speak) together with that development's stylistic fulfilment. To understand Schoenberg we need understand neither what came first (Mahler in this instance) nor what came afterwards—although it is doubtful if an understanding of Schoenberg's late music can exist where there is a misunderstanding of his early style. Schoenberg has to be musically approached, as it were, from the inside, and in strict relation to himself. History, largely a record of imperfection, fails us when faced with perfection—and of its kind I suggest the *Kammersymphonie* is perfect, though Schoenberg has written greater things since. If I say this is music you either do or don't understand, I'm not demanding or claiming any kind of exclusive musical perception: from an external stylistic point of view there's no reason why everybody shouldn't.   D.M.

III.   Texture and Form

THE performance was excellent where excellence was difficult to achieve, but not so excellent where it wasn't, for instance in the interpretation of accents which primarily have a negative significance, i.e. a de-accentuation of another (preceding) note—Schoenberg had not at that stage introduced his new sign for unaccented notes—or, more unforgivably, of the dotted figures in the subordinate theme, whose " smart " execution contradicted unwritten sense and written slur alike. But such things remained isolated blemishes on a powerful and meticulously thought-out rendering of this unequalled achievement in extended single-movement structure and chamber-symphonic texture whose revolutionary innovations are hidden from the superficial listener by what he mishears to be a conservative style. The daring scoring, at once chamber-musical and orchestral, is completely heard through, original yet assured in the smallest detail. It is not, however, the texture only which should throughout be studied under a double aspect, but also the form, whose every element functions as part of a one-movement structure on the one hand and, at the same time, of a five-movement structure on the other. One instance which struck me forcibly: from the standpoint of five-movement form, *the resumption of the first subject at the end of the exposition* goes to form the *quasi*-first-movement's ternary build, while in the actual, total one-movement form it corresponds to the repeat in classical sonata form (as well as to the first return of the theme in the classical sonata-rondo); or, on a more recent historical level and hence more directly and closely, to the opening of the development in the repeat-less first movement of Beethoven's op. 59, No. 1, where the first subject is resumed in the tonic after the exposition, forming not merely a transition between the latter and the development proper, but also what I would call a mental bridge between the (imaginary) repeat and the (real) development.

The first subject's tonic repetition after the exposition, as introduction to the development, celebrates a severely belated and seriously lifeless revival in the calcified sonata form that is the first movement of Prokofieff's 5th Symphony; whereas in the present work a new organism has grown from these historical roots, in that the repetition of the principal subject runs into the transition to the *quasi*-second-movement with scherzo function. It is interesting that Prokofieff, who under his superficial symphonic innovations (e.g. his short-term dislocations of tonality) adheres slavishly to classical formulas for harmonic-thematic building, considers Schoenberg a " formalist." H.K.

OP. II

PRAISE, thanks and respect to Robert Collet who, in his Wigmore Hall recital on January 29, included the never-heard Three Piano Pieces (composed in February and March, 1909; the Second first, on February 22) which show the composer well on the new way and are still news to many a newer muse, though not to Martin Cooper, who pronounced in the *Daily Telegraph* that " after 40 years, they have lost their novelty and with it all their historical interest." He must show us how things can lose historical interest if they ever had it, and tell us whether he is aware that these Pieces are the first without key-signature and with Schoenberg's innovation of " harmonics " on the piano (a device which recently recurs in the *Ode to Napoleon*). He cannot tell us anything about their form, style, and meaning, for if he could he would not judge them, as evidently he does, by a series of isolated impressions whose vertical aspect isn't so bad after all. We on our part were fully occupied in following the clear but complex logic of these ever-evolving and closely interrelated structures whose every note counts, and which in the outlines of their argument let you always divine what's coming, whereas in its particular development they always surprise you by what you ought to have thought of, but haven't in the least. The Second Piece's recurring pedal on D-F in compound-quadruple time quavers, which is linked with two different thematic constellations, seems to look back to the similar, and similarly recurring pedal in the *Song of the Earth*'s *Abschied*, while the whole opus's basic motif, to which everything possible happens in the course of the movements, would appear to look forward as far as the *Ode to Napoleon*, where one hears it reappear in a more defined and developed shape.

Mr. Collet gave intelligent and conscientious, if not very inspired attention to formal whole and detail, though our understanding of the Third Piece was marred by its and his technical difficulties. H.K.

" TRANSFIGURED NIGHT "

Hilversum Radio, Radio Chamber Orchestra, c. Maurits van der Berg, 10th February.

Less brilliant a performance, and less assured in intonation, than the St. Louis Symphony Orchestra's under Vladimir Golschmann (HMV, DB 9280/3; strongly recommended despite the recording's deficiencies), but far, far more inspired: in fact, the most understanding interpretation of the orchestral version we have heard.

It is as more than a curiosity that one should remember a certain Viennese society's refusal to undertake the first performance of the original sextet: the single dissonance B♭ - a♭ - e'♭ - g'♭ - c" - e"♭ was considered anarchic. Indeed, when the work was first performed in 1903, critics and public rejected it furiously because of its radicalism. However, times, as distinct from masterpieces, change. Today, the above-mentioned records bring Edward Sackville West to the conclusion that the *Verklaerte Nacht* is " an epitome of all that is most repulsive in German art," while John Amis finds it " the ripest sort of romantic music " which " may arouse in some people the conviction that Schoenberg was not a very good composer up to the time of the beginning of his atonal music." What was disgustingly revolutionary has become disgustingly conservative; it follows that all a masterpiece has to do is to wait until its criticisms have ruled each other out: until another phase of the eternal conflict between those who make the times and those who are, more or less successfully, made by the times, has subsided. H.K.

The Third Programme broadcast (9th January), mysteriously unrepeated, of the Italian radio recording of the *Survivor from Warsaw* will be reviewed in the next issue, i.e. well before, and as an introduction to, the first English performance of the work in June. A detailed review of the *Ode to Napoleon* records (Esquire, TW 4002-3), on the lines exemplified on pp. 215 ff., but also, of course, including analytical observations on the score itself, will be printed either in the same issue, or else, preferably, in the Schoenberg Issue we are contemplating.—Eds.

BERG'S " LYRIC SUITE "

Vegh String Quartet, Third Programme, 31st January.

From tone and attack, in fact, from the bowing generally, one could safely infer that the stultifying misbalance which at times actually drowned the principal line in the subordinate parts or even in the accompaniment, was not so much the scrupulous players' as the microphones' fault; the suspicion cannot easily be set aside that the balance test (if any) was not supervised by someone who knew the score. With this difficult and unfamiliar work, the grasping of whose form depends on a completely faithful presentation of the carefully differentiated strata of its texture, such neglect would appear to be a serious matter.

An amendment to Erwin Stein's instructive general description of the music in the Philharmonia pocket score:—I cannot readily agree that the first (twelve-tonal) movement is in binary form. It is in what the text-books call " modified " or " abridged " sonata form, which does not follow the binary scheme A - B, but A - A, and since in these circumstances the codetta of the exposition inevitably assumes the function of an inter*medium* between exposition and recapitulation, the ternary scheme A - (B) - A would seem to me to be relevant, denoting as the bracket does not only the middle which is left out (i.e. the development), but also an actual little middle. I am couching my criticism in personal terms because " binary " and " ternary " are highly controversial concepts. Unlike Paul H. Lang, for instance, Willi Apel is not prepared to consider the sonata form proper a ternary form (neglecting, in my view, the harmonico-structural standpoint), whereas one of the musicians who contributed to the symposium *Arnold Schoenberg: Zum 60. Geburtstag* (Universal Edition, Vienna) remarked to me some time ago that " everything is in ternary form, because everything has a beginning, a middle and an end," an observation which may seem a trifle optimistic, but which points to what I consider the fundamental defect in the application of this nomenclature: the lack of a clearly defined *tertium comparationis.*   **H.K.**

Film Music

VLAD AND MILHAUD

ROMAN VLAD'S score for the Italian *Sunday in August* was a disappointment. As we know him to be more than a talented composer, and a discriminating critic besides, it seems likely that he was subjected to dictatorial directorial pressure—a pity that Luciano Emmer didn't realise that to be both popular and popular is musically quite fatal. The problem with which we are faced in *Sunday in August* (assuming for a moment that we are all potential film music composers) is how to be popular yet not popular, nor, needless to say, unpopular either. If this sounds as if it were merely a matter of verbal paradox, take as concrete examples two composers who work successfully in and out of films: Arthur Benjamin and Darius Milhaud. Both have written music, popular in the best sense of the word, and much to the public taste. But " *to* the public taste " and " *of* the public taste " are quite distinct propositions separated by a wide gulf. A work " *to* the public taste " can still be tasteful (stylish also, and genuinely characteristic of its composer); a work " *of* the public taste " is bound to be tasteless, simply because the public hasn't got any. Not that my comment is intended as criticism: taste after all implies selection, and I don't see the possibility of selectivity being practised in unison on a multiple scale. As it happens, *Sunday in August* deals with the multitude—sectionally and individually at times to be sure—and more particularly with the citizens of Rome who take themselves off to the sea-beach at Ostia on a Sunday afternoon and pursue their various pleasures amidst surroundings akin to our Margate or Blackpool. The plot is episodic—the main virtue of the film is its sometimes acute observation of character and crowd,· and its re-creation of the atmosphere of a public holiday resort, an atmosphere not without its share of social symbolism and poignant sentiment.

As far as Vlad was concerned, the problem was hardly one of structure (one not posed in view of the film's discursive technique) but predominantly a problem of style. How to achieve popularity, yet at such a distance that some sort of detachment is ensured ? Moreover, a kind of literal distance in which the composer has room enough to move about and consider stylistic popularity in relation to his personal, necessarily non-popular self. What Vlad did,

181

voluntarily or involuntarily, was as wrong as possible. He associated himself so closely with popularity (in this case the kind of music we can hear any Sunday be it Blackpool, Ostia, or Nice) that his score was quite indistinguishable from the routine commercial tripe which intervened now and again on the sound track, and which, ironically enough, was contributed by other musical hands, not Vlad's. Realism of this kind, an increasingly dangerous snare for the film composer, here defeated its own ends. Popularity can have no knowledge of popularity, and Vlad, by adopting the all-too-common idiom precisely prevented himself from making any kind of musical comment on the idiom itself—which should and could have been the proper function of his score. Indeed, in the final analysis Vlad's score was more realistic (and therefore less successful) than the film, in that the latter was not content merely to reproduce public scenes, but selected private issues, made moral judgements, drew certain conclusions and generally endeavoured to take some responsibility for the consequences of the popularity it set out to portray. That is, it considered itself as a social phenomenon from an isolated, if social, point of view. Vlad's score, which had not an element of parody in it (a valuable stylistic device where "popularity" is concerned), and not a hint of an in-turned self-criticism, was a lamentable failure—it may well be for reasons not only directorial but temperamental besides.

Milhaud, faced with a rather similar problem in *La Vie Commence Demain*, fares better, and partly brilliantly. The film itself is a kind of popular exposition of the glories of life which (chiefly) science has to offer us tomorrow, atom-bomb permitting. The hero of the piece, an enquiring young Frenchman, has displayed to him visually the tenets of Existentialism, some rather bloody biology, the architectural ideals of M. Corbusier, the inanity of André Gide, the saltwater excursions of M. Piccasso and so forth; all liberally sprinkled with examples of mankind's present idiocies—concentration camps, famine, brutality and war. A document in fact of what is and what (God help us) might be. Again the question of structure hardly arises since the film is but a series of episodes, many of them of a quasi-demonstrational laboratory nature. Between episodes, more often than not, the young man is obliged to take a stroll and a much-needed breath of fresh and still indisciplined air—a sequence which acts as a bridge passage between more extended and arduous undertakings. Milhaud was quick to seize on the musical possibilities of this recurring sequence and devized for it music, often in his most endearing 6/8 *promenade au printemps* manner, which reappears in various guises and lends some semblance of continuity to his score. But for most of the time Milhaud has to reflect as accurately as possible the emotions of his young hero who acts as a pair of universal eyes; and taking into account the bewildering change of scenes and the scientific character of many of them, Milhaud guesses right on nearly every occasion and manages to identify himself with a gaping and gasping audience, without becoming any the less Milhaud for all that. Now and again realism raises its ugly head, but where it does Milhaud disposes of the problem with superb accomplishment: as in the sequence in the existentialist café where the music for the jazz band not only performs a realistic function as a string of superior jazz sonorities but also, because of its fractional parodistic element, makes the profoundest of comments on itself and its environment. I very strongly recommend *La Vie Commence Demain* to film-music lovers with tough nerves: but beware of the biology.

D.M.

Reviews of Music

Arranged in alphabetical order of composers' names.

VICTOR BABIN: "*Beloved Stranger,*" *Song-cycle for Low Voice and Piano.* (*Augener*); *7s. 6d.*

THIS set of songs has fewer banalities than the same composer's " Ritual," reviewed earlier, but that is almost the only gain. It does not matter that the poems are not first-rate. It matters a lot that they are not first-rate for singing or setting. Mr. Babin gets over this difficulty by virtually ignoring it. Even this would not grievously affect me, but they are certainly the most aggressive love-songs I have encountered in a most aggressive age.   H.T.

VICTOR BABIN: String Quartet. Pocket Score. (*Augener*); *7s. 6d.*

THIS of Mr. Babin's is an apparently very earnest lucubration that possesses no kind of character and makes no kind of impact. Distant reflections of Hindemith, Scriabin, Rachmaninoff, Prokofieff, and even ye olde modal folk-song, chase each other over the 70 (no fewer !) deadly dull bright pages of its surface. And surface is all there is. This production may be a bit thick, in some ways and places, but depth it has not ... Between superficially string-like and quartet-like passages the work lapses often into procedures that would be orchestral if the keyboard view of the orchestra *were* orchestral. So one must fear that it would be even as boring to play as to listen to.   R.W.W.

BORIS BLACHER: " *Romeo und Julia,*" *Chamber Opera in 3 parts after Shakespeare for Soli, Choir and an Orchestra consisting of Flute, Bassoon, Trumpet, Timpani, Piano and String Quintet. Vocal Score.* (*Universal-Edition, Vienna*); *no price stated.*

ON the whole, the score well realizes the composer's intentions: not a very difficult task, since at their root these seem to be almost exclusively negative, reacting as they violently do against the post- and sub-romantic hypertrophies cultivated by the Nazis. But castrating the sterile does not mean fertility, and nothing is more dangerous to art than much taste about nothing; nothing more foolish than economy without wealth. The real ideas contained in this score are extremely few; instead, there is plenty of sophisticated aesthetic ideology which breathes a late-Strawinskyian, sado-masochistic spirit, with (amongst others) the most important difference that Strawinsky is a master who has plenty of ideas big enough to produce form. The music's relationship to the drama seriously tries to shine by its absence. The work is also intended for concert performance, but though it is no opera, neither is it a cantata. In fact, its sole significance would seem to be that of a neurotic symptom which is so plainly anti-emotional, and expresses so widely accepted an attitude, that it has no difficulty in posing as healthy normality.   H.K.

ARTHUR BLISS & J. B. PRIESTLEY: " *The Olympians.*" *Vocal Score.* (*Novello*) ; *31s. 6d.*

YET another autopsy does not seem called for, though attention might be drawn to the weak harmonic structure. The inclusion of a German translation (by Werner Gallusser) strikes us as pathetic, since the work is unexportable.

H.K.

ALAN BUSH: English Suite for String Orchestra, Op. 28. Score. (Joseph Williams) ; 15s. 0d.

THIS is one of the works in which the composer is consciously trying to evolve a style that is, compared with his earlier eclectic sophistication, national and traditional. The attempt is successful. Bush has here created a music which can absorb English folksong without sounding in the least like the homespun folksy composers; it is indeed consistent with, and a development from, the style of *Dialectic.* In the first piece the fantasia style of English string composers of the seventeenth century lends itself admirably to metamorphosis in terms of Bush's " thematic " technique; while the Passacaglia on The Cutty Wren is a splendid example of the seventeenth century technique of divisions on a ground, imaginatively reborn. Both the craftsmanship and the scoring are masterly, though the piece is extremely difficult to play.   W.H.M.

DIETRICH BUXTEHUDE: Cantata, Jesu meine Freude; for two Sopranos and Bass, with two Violins, Cello, and Continuo. (Bärenreiter-Ausgabe); no price stated.

A SELF-CONTAINED, nicely-balanced work of this kind should attract singers and players who welcome a change from four-square chamber music or madrigal parties. The cello (or bassoon) part is distinct from the continuo, and makes an excellent instrumental trio to set off the three vocal parts. In a more extended performance, the *tutti* sections may be sung by a small choir. Editing is scholarly and yet practical, with full collation of sources (Lübeck and Uppsala).
                                                                          D.W.S.

' CAPELLA ': Musical Masterworks of the Middle Ages. Ed. by Heinrich Besseler. (Bärenreiter-Ausgabe); no price stated.

THIS slim, well-documented volume contains unaccompanied choral music by Dunstable, Touront, Obrecht, Dufay, Finck, and Josquin. Professor Besseler has taken pains to ease rhythmic problems, which are so often a deterrent to amateur choirs and their trainers. Thus the Dunstable motet "Quam pulchra es" has normal bar-lines; the motets by Obrecht (" Parce, Domine ") and Josquin (" In pace ") have *mensurstrich*, i.e. lines drawn between the staves leaving rhythmic patterns unbroken; while the other compositions use a combination of both methods, involving some tied notes.   D.W.S.

GERALD FINZI: " Intimations of Immortality," Ode for Tenor Solo, Mixed Chorus and Orchestra. Vocal Score. (Boosey & Hawkes); 10s. 0d.

THIS is Finzi's most ambitious work, but I do not think it adds much to his stature. The tenor solo sections are lovely, though rather self-consciously so, in his familiar " Lizbie Browne " manner. When he deserts this vein of nostalgia Finzi's musical personality deserts him too. The " noble " bits are quite good Parry, but not more. Though excessively long, one could describe this piece as a well-written representative of the Three Choirs genre. What Finzi has to say he seems to have said once and for all in the Hardy songs.   W.H.M.

BENJAMIN FRANKEL: " May Day," a Panorama, Prelude for Orchestra, Op. 22, Quartet No. 1, Op. 14, and Quartet No. 4, Op. 21. All Pocket Scores. (Augener); 5s. 6d., 3s. 0d., 4s. 6d., respectively.

THE obvious fault to find with " May Day " is that it is " bitty " (15 changes of tempo in some 230 bars); that, in fact, it bears all too much resemblance to Tovey's " bête noire," a series of introductions to introductions. The composer's obvious retort is that it is a " panorama " and that to base a judgment on standards irrelevant to his intentions is futile. The programmatic quality of the work is emphasized by the descriptive expression-marks, always prolific in Frankel's music but here fairly running riot. Everyone who heard this work at the Proms, or at its première in Liverpool, seems to have agreed on the brilliance of its orchestration. It should be mentioned, however, that the brilliance is of a rather special kind, extraordinarily economical, extraordinarily sure and clear, and quite Berliozian in its persistent thrusting towards each instrument's technical idiosyncracies and favourite sonorities. The bare counterpoint through which these finesses tend to be projected, and the vigorous melos informing that counterpoint, are almost as peculiarly Frankel's own as are certain other characteristics more prominently featured in, say, his string quartets.

To which now we come. Frankel has travelled a long way in the well-under-ten years that separate his Op. 14 from his Op. 21, but perhaps not so far as he travelled, or seemed to travel, when reaching his Op. 14 from his Op. 13 (the solo violin sonata). Yet it is possible to feel at the same time that he has hardly travelled at all, ever. Frankel's musical traits—the rather narrow range of moods that severally he recreates again and again, the always expressive but not often very distinctive motifs (mostly either winding or fanfare-ish) to which most of them impel him, certain very pronounced " finger-prints " in the way of rhythmic and melodic turns—all these have consorted with remarkable consistency from pretty well the outset of his career. Between the first and fourth string quartets lie the greater complexities of the second and third. It is true enough that in No. 4 we find longish stretches of regular rhythm, of ostinati, of comparatively stereotyped pattern-work, to which very few parallels can be found in the already elusive, shifting textures and tonalities, the already rather pell-mell fluctuations of emotion in No. 1. But, for example, the tender freshness of No. 1's opening movement (" echt " Frankel), always so touching to return to, *is* in fact returned to, under completely different externals, in the finale of No. 4. All the same it is true that some aspects of No. 4 mark a distinct change in Frankel's method. Broadly—only broadly, of course—one could say that in it he appears to have decided to sacrifice subtlety to clarity, questing to definition, something like the remote, perhaps, to the immediate. Between such alternatives it is difficult for a listener to choose. Up to a point—and for the same reason—it is unnecessary for him to choose; he has both, and each set of values, when Frankel's music is the medium, is equally persuasive. Nevertheless, the choice is possibly a crucial one for the composer himself. As a choice one feels it has presented itself to him. It would seem to be the conscientious critic's duty to point out, then, that the change in principle embodied in Quartet No. 4 (though not necessarily anything but a commendable move to think of making, for Frankel or for anyone else) does, in fact, seem to have produced here certain shadows of comparative failure. For example, invention has, in places, given way to mechanicalness. The quartet writing, as such, is less admirable in No. 4 than in its predecessors. Those predecessors I have described elsewhere as most superb, most quintessential, thinking in terms of the medium. The same could not be said of No. 4. It is effective, it " comes off," but only in the teeth, so to speak, of difficulties the composer has created for himself by using material and procedures that are by nature non-quartet-like and even non-chambermusic-like. . . Both these quartets, it remains to be said, are suspiciously like master-pieces. Neither inclines me to waver in the view I have now for some time held — that Frankel is one of the most considerable composers of the last fifty years, in this or any country. R.W.W.

BENJAMIN FRANKEL: Sonatina Leggiera, Op. 19, for Piano. (Augener); 5s. 0d.

THIS work adds nothing to Mr. Frankel's reputation.   H.T.

HANS GAL: Lilliburlero, Op. 48. Improvisations on a Martial Melody. Score. (Novello); 17s. 6d.

A WORK one would like to recommend for its clever craftsmanship, earnestness, sincerity, and the desire to please. Its great mistake is choice of theme. If ever a single theme could be found which lacks every quality necessary to variation procedure, it is " Lilliburlero." Calling variations " improvisations " is a mere confession of failure.

The theme does not, and never can, act as a bass; yet its first appearance is in that capacity, which makes for much of the mechanically-contrived, so beautifully fitting, and so lifeless counterpoint in which the work abounds.

H.T.

HANS LEO HASSLER: Vater Unser. (Bärenreiter-Ausgabe); no price stated.

THIS extended setting of the Lord's Prayer first appeared in a publication called " Psalms and Christian Songs, composed fugally for four voices " (1607). Actually one of the verses is for five voices (SATTB) which makes for variation in texture without putting too much of a strain on resources. The only slight disadvantage of this edition (German text only) is the range of the bass part, which is expected in several places to manage a bottom D. The work could be transposed up a tone with good effect.   D.W.S.

JEAN-LOUIS MARTINET: Prelude and Fugue for Two Pianos. (United Music Publishers); no price stated.

THIS work shows signs of a modest talent which could develop if it rid itself of superimposed " modernisms." Otherwise it will join the coeval army of mediocre composers, all striving to be what they are not, instead of bad, good and great, which is what they should be.   H.T.

WILLEM PIJPER: String Quartet No. 3. Pocket Score. (Lengnick); 5s. 0d.

PIJPER has been scandalously neglected here. He was an important figure in his own country, but as there is nothing sensational about Dutch music, it has not made any impact upon our moribund Concert Committees. The music of this three-movement work is gracious and deft. It subscribes to no " -ism " or " -ality " and is not concerned with thematic working-out or constructional permutation. Pijper had a fine rhythmic sense which is allowed full play within the limited scope of the work. Technically, there are only one or two places which may cause hesitancy. The composer is fond of the reiterated note effect, but this does not mar the structure, polyphony (such as it is) or thematic continuity of the work.

It is neither monumental nor significant. It is simply an attractive lyrical String Quartet.   N.D.

EDMUND RUBBRA: *Lyric Movement, for String Quartet and Piano, Op. 24;
8s. 0d.* *4 Medieval Latin Lyrics, for Baritone and Strings, Op. 32; 8s. 0d.*
String Quartet in F minor, Op. 35; 3s. 0d. *5 Spenser Sonnets, for Tenor and
Strings, Op. 42; 6s. 0d.* *Symphony No. 3, Op. 49; 8s. 6d.* *Symphony No. 4,
Op. 53; 7s. 6d.* *The Morning Watch, for Chorus and Orchestra, Op. 55;
2s. 6d.* *Soliloquy, for Cello and Small Orchestra, Op. 57; 10s. 0d.* *Missa
Cantuariensis, Op. 59; 3s. 6d.* *Sonata for Cello and Piano, Op. 60; 6s. 0d.*
3 Psalms, for Low Voice and Piano, Op. 61; 3s. 0d. *Festival Overture, for
Orchestra; 24s. 0d.* *Symphony No. 5, Op. 63; 7s. 6d.* *Magnificat and Nunc
Dimittis, Op. 65; 1s. 0d.* *Meditazioni sopra Coeurs Désolés, for Recorder
and Harpsichord, Op. 67; 2s. 6d.* *Piano Trio in one movement, Op. 68;
8s. 0d.* (*Lengnick*).

Rubbra's music is an assertion of civilization; unlike much twentieth century
music it implies positive assent—what used to be called belief. There is not
space for a " review " of these works; they do, however, prompt a few reflections
on Rubbra's development.

The first phase of his work lasted a long time, and was experimental; experimental not in the sense that it was amateurish, for Rubbra has always had an
assured technique, but in the sense that he was slow to discover just what he
wanted to say. The Piano Quartet movement, the Latin Lyrics and the Spenser
Sonnets show him moulding a personal style out of elements suggested by Holst
and by Tudor music. In the next phase—the period covered by the third,
fourth and fifth symphonies—Rubbra has reached mature expression. The
continuous lyrical germination, the contrapuntal discipline, the re-created
diatonicism—these form a style that is traditional and at the same time unique.
His music has always been technically efficient; but if one compares the lucid
flow of the piano parts of the Psalms or the noble cello sonata with that of the
piano quartet, one sees how technical assurance has become synonymous with
ripeness of experience. Still more, compare the part-writing and the scoring
of the fifth symphony with that of the first. The fifth symphony may be said
to sum up Rubbra's music up to this point; it is a work of transcendent power,
which will survive the vagaries of fashion.

The Piano Trio, however, represents a further stage of development—especially
the concluding " meditazioni." A treatise should be written on the manner
in which Rubbra has here created a completely new sound out of a harmonic
vocabulary of the most " reactionary " simplicity. I believe this is great music;
the work of a profoundly religious mind and in that sense not altogether typical
of our time; yet " modern " too in the sense that it is " news that *stays* news "
as Ezra Pound once put it. Its effect has nothing to do with its relative complexity or simplicity; or " modernity " or non-modernity. It depends on the
positive conviction which has given it a consistent style in the midst of much that
is chaotic. One may call that conviction religious, I think; for it is precisely
such a religious sense which is today difficult to achieve without affectation
or self-deception. w.h.m.

GODFREY SAMPSON: Suite for String Orchestra. Score. (Novello); 8s. 6d.

THIS is an enterprising little work. It is probably as much the fault of systematic training as of inhibited imagination that it is wrong even where it is right.

The string-writing is vigorous, with no more than a trace or two of Elgar. The outstanding flaw is the work's acute misunderstanding of tonality. So afraid is Mr. Sampson of modulating where he shouldn't, that all three movements (each logical in structure, though not in feeling) cling to the tonic for dear life.   H.T.

DOMENICO SCARLATTI: Four Sonatas for Violin and Clavier, ed. by Lionel Salter. (Augener); No. 1, 2s. 0d., Nos. 2 & 3 @ 3s. 0d., No. 5, 3s. 0d.

MR. SALTER has done good work in presenting these four sonatas as nearly as possible in their true guise.   H.T.

HEINRICH SCHÜTZ: Anima mea liquefacta est; Adjuro vos, filiae Jerusalem; Fili mi, Absalon. (Bärenreiter-Ausgabe); no price stated.

THESE extracts from the first part of Schütz's *Symphoniae sacrae* demonstrate the ample measure of expressive polyphony which the smallest of means can achieve: there is none of the polychorality here that we look for in so staunch a follower of Gabrieli and Monteverdi. Grandeur such as this was to come later. Dr. Rudolf Gerber has gone out of his way to make practical editions, transposing where necessary and adding alternative parts for cor anglais, as in the first two motets, where the composer has indicated " Fiffaro o Cornettino." The printing is clear and well laid out, with both Latin and German texts.   D.W.S.

SCHUETZ: Motet " Ponder my words, O Lord," ed. by W. K. Stanton. (Hinrichsen); 1s. 0d.

THIS is an admirable training-piece for choirs not skilled in sight-singing and the music does not move uncomfortably far from the prevailing key of F minor. Nevertheless, Schuetz's apparent hankering after the acknowledged " vocal " progressions is sometimes deceptive when the separate voices generate their full musical strength. This seldom heard work of Schuetz is worth an hour's rehearsal, especially with this useful edition to hand (a piano reduction is provided below the vocal score). Its full beauty can hardly be appreciated at a casual run-through.   E.D.M.

T. W. SOUTHAM: Two Songs for Voice and Piano. " Nemea " and " A Holy Sonnet." (Augener); @ 2s. 0d.

HERE are two fine little works, a welcome break in a long succession of " modern vocal " efforts whose main purpose seems to be the mutual annihilation of voice and piano. Mr. Southam's original idea seems to be to illumine the poem as much as possible, allowing the vocal line and instrumental part to aid each other, and actually to provide some singable music in the process. He has even contrived that speech rhythm and musical rhythm shall quite often coincide.

The finer is the " Holy Sonnet," the better poetry (not, however, of the front rank) producing a proportionately finer response from the composer, who has wisely avoided great poetry in either case since the songs would then tend to be superfluous.   H.T.

BERNARD STEVENS: *Theme and Variations for String Quartet, Op. 11. Score.* (*Lengnick*); *6s. 0d.*

MR. STEVENS considers this his best work to date, and I agree. A very well chosen Adagio theme is treated in twelve variations which are intelligently grouped into three coherent sections, i.e. Nos. 1-4, progressively accelerating and dissolving the theme, until it appears atomized in the pizzicati of No. 4; Nos. 5-11, working up from the profound Adagio of No. 5 to the Presto of No. 8, making the Adagio of No. 9 with its ragged rhythms the esoteric climax of the work, returning to the inversion of the theme in No. 10, and founding a temporary coda on the pedal notes of No. 11; and, finally, No. 12, marked " Finale," in which three fugue-subjects, derived from the theme, are treated in a fugue of three sections. Though extremely well written for their medium, these variations are not of the playful type where performer and listener alike are invited to feast on a seemingly unlimited wealth of invention; they are, on the contrary, written with an austere will to extract only the essential variations, and I doubt whether Mr. Stevens would have been able to find even one more variation of equal quality. Only once does he let us down: the first fugue-theme is angular and too sequential in itself to allow for good sequential treatment later on. But the second part of the fugue returns to the standard of the variations. The later Brahms apart, nobody until Schoenberg has followed up the later Beethoven's habits of thought, and I am glad to see some young composers of today, who are not dodecaphonists, base their style on an analysis of late Beethoven.

P.H.

RICHARD STRAUSS: *Tod und Verklaerung, Op. 24. Miniature Score.* (*Novello*); *no price stated.*

A WELL-PRINTED edition of one of Strauss' worst pieces. The poem which Strauss later found to satisfactorily interpret his music is reprinted in full after the title-page. The name of the author is, for some, or no reason, omitted. In case somebody needs reminding, the poet was Alexander Ritter. D.M.

TCHAIKOWSKY: *Theme and Variations for Piano, Op. 19, No. 6. (Hinrichsen);* *3s. 6d.*

ONE of Tchaikowsky's most attractive lesser works, and well worth reprinting, although it is not well conceived for the instrument. There is a superb lesson to be learned here in the harsh ineptitude of Tchaikowsky's earnest attempts to use Schumann's most brilliantly pianistic devices. These variations, like all Tchaikowsky's sets, are variations in so far as he ever understood them—which was not far enough. H.T.

ALEXANDRE TCHEREPNINE: *Trio for Three Flutes and Quartet for Four Flutes. (Boosey & Hawkes); no price stated.*

THIS composer, son of the below, after the normal rush of blood to the head resultant on sojourning in Paris, has now apparently experienced a reaction of pure simplicity, disarming at arm's length but suspicious at closer quarters. One can but give him the benefit of the doubt. The Trio appears to be the pithier work of the two; it has, in spasms, some expressive flute writing. The Quartet is perhaps shorter but more disjointed. The intentions seem to be good, although four flutes unsupported are a little more than most of us can take.

H.T.

N. TCHEREPNINE: Four Pieces in C for Piano. (Boosey & Hawkes); no price stated.

PLEASANT pieces, neither good nor bad, by a composer who once showed signs of bigness. The finale, a study in rhythm, comes nearest to possessing a personality.   H.T.

N. TCHEREPNINE: Andante and Finale for Violin and Piano. (Boosey & Hawkes); no price stated.

BETTER than the piano pieces, but blown out by attempted sonata-length developments of no more than epigrammatic ideas which, in the finale's insistence on mere rhythm, become almost epigruntic.   H.T.

ANTONIO VIVALDI: Sonate da Camera a Tre, Op. 1. (Book I, Sonatas 1-6; Book II, Sonatas 6-12). (Barenreiter-Ausgabe); no price stated.

HERE again we have a text which closely follows the Amsterdam edition, giving some excellent samples of early eighteenth-century chamber music. The editor, Dr. Upmeyer, suggests that the first eleven sonatas at least may be played with doubled string parts, plus contrabass: the twelfth is a work apart, far more virtuosic than the others, and destined only for soloists. It is based on the *Folia* theme, one of the most popular of baroque basses. Dr. Upmeyer has provided competent realizations of the continuo " for those players who do not prefer to improvise according to the old custom." His footnote explains that Vivaldi too knew of continuo players who needed either a figured or a written-out part, but the reference to Pincherle's book is a subtlety worth pursuing. Before sending Pisendel a certain Concerto in A major, the composer scribbled in some figuring at one point in the finale, with the following phrase: " Per li Coglioni "; which might mean one of two things, and probably meant both.   D.W.S.

ANTONIO VIVALDI: La Stravaganza, Op. 4. Concertos 1-3 for Solo Violin, Strings and Continuo. (Bærenreiter-Ausgabe); no price stated.

A REVIVAL of interest in the music of the " Red Priest " (hair, not politics) has prompted a generous flow of new editions, some more welcome than others, but all conducive to a fresh and enlightened assessment of Vivaldi's powers as a composer. What is remarkable as much in the present editions as in those published recently in Italy is the unevenness in musical quality within a set of, say, six or twelve works of similar type. The eighteenth century, to whose early years *La Stravaganza* belongs, was a period which saw the average good composer turning out good average music: even the best composers were on occasions thus employed. It is therefore something to Vivaldi's credit that his interest-factor chart shows an encouraging number of ups and downs.

Of these three concertos, the first, in B flat, is by no means outstanding. The second, in E minor, is by contrast a masterpiece of individuality and inventiveness. Here is the finest of Vivaldi, with all the brilliance and suavity of the true Italian brought together within three short movements. Repetitive figuration, elsewhere dull, is here thrilling: the harmony, actual and implied, is on a level which touches the best of Bach. And so we do not wonder when we learn that Bach himself arranged for clavier certain movements from two concertos in this set of twelve. Bach had not the advantage of consulting the printed edition of Etienne Roger (Amsterdam) which forms the basis of Dr. Walter Upmeyer's text. The editing is accurate, continuo adequate, printing excellent; and Dr. Upmeyer adds a useful and informative introduction. Those who wish to perform the works may add their own bowing marks and ornamentation, both indispensable for a lively interpretation.   D.W.S.

*JOHN WEINZWEIG: Divertimento I (for Flute and Orchestra) and Diverti-
mento II (for Oboe and Orchestra). Piano reduction by Harold Perry.
(Boosey & Hawkes); @ 5s. 0d.*

NOTWITHSTANDING Mr. Weinzweig's wise precaution in not calling these two
works concertos, they stem from the modern idea of short, bright, breezy works
for wind instruments which pass today as concertos among the more " enlightened." Shortness is the one quality which recommends these two efforts,
were it not that it extends to breath also. H.T.

*VAUGHAN WILLIAMS: Fantasia (quasi variazione) on the Old 104th. (O.U.P.);
7s. 6d.*

THIS Fantasia really is what it says—a work for solo piano, accompanied by
chorus and orchestra; and the unlikely medium comes off superbly. The piano
writing itself looks, on paper, equally unpropitious; and again it comes off—if
the player can negotiate its devilish intractabilities. The form of the piece is a
series of variations on the noble tune, interspersed with three extended piano
cadenzas all in different yet mutually consistent styles. The first is a kind of
elephantine toccata, remorselessly exploiting the piano's percussive bass. The
second is linear and often polytonal, reminiscent in its texture and rhythmic
complications of one of the more elaborate fantasias of Bull. The third is
crystalline in sonority, hollow in its part-writing, with interjections of bitonal
washes of chordal arpeggios, pianissimo. In the choral and orchestral sections
the choir indulges in exultant vocalises more related to V.W.'s " traditional "
manner. Though this is a "modern" and even an enigmatic work, it makes
one feel glad to be alive, however atom-dominated. It reasserts the dignity of
man; and his obstinate vitality. W.H.M.

Book Reviews
Arranged in alphabetical order of titles.

BERLIOZ IN LONDON, by *A. W. Ganz. Pp. 222; 15s. 0d. (Quality Press).*
IN theory, a book of this nature writes itself, especially if its hero possesses a
prose style as striking and fluent as that of Berlioz. But Mr. Ganz has wisely
intervened with a nicely-judged frequency, not only to give the reader a connected
narrative whose high points are taken from the composer's correspondence, but
to take the reins and tighten them whenever Berlioz steps across the border of
straightforward letter-writing and embarks upon a journey in the never-never
land of Memoirs. Apart from his skilfully-contrived commentary, Mr. Ganz
provides a mine of information in his footnotes, which elucidate many a strange
happening in musical London in the middle of the last century. This book is
enough to make one long for a complete edition in English of Berlioz's literary
works. D.W.S.

COLLECTOR'S GUIDE TO AMERICAN RECORDINGS (1895-1925), *by
Julian Morton Moses. Pp. 200; $3.75. (American Record Collectors'
Exchange, New York).*
A GIGANTIC labour of compilation, which combines the functions of catalogue
raisonné and check-list. The result is a publication full of historical interest
for the connoisseur, who, even if he happens to be English, need not be discouraged by the title. Many of the recordings listed were issued here as well
as in America, and something of their history and origin may consequently be
traced in this very useful guide. D.W.S.

CYMBALES ET CROTALES DANS L'EGYPTE ANCIENNE and MIS-
CELLANEA MUSICOLOGICA, *by Hans Hickman. Pp. 95 and 27;
no price.* (*Le Caire, 1949*).

THE proper person to review these papers with their graphs, charts and alluring
illustrations would certainly be an archaeologist interested in questions of
Egyptology. But even the completely uninitiated and guileless practical musician
will not read Dr. Hickmann's account of ancient Egyptian instruments and of the
quaint habits of Egypt's singers, players and dancers without profoundly
enriching his mind.   H.F.R.

A DICTIONARY OF MUSIC, *by R. Illing. Pp. 318; 2s. 6d.* (*Penguin*).

HOW NOT TO COMPILE A MUSICAL
DICTIONARY

BY common consent the compilation of a Dictionary of Music has always been
the prerogative of mature scholarship. Grove and Riemann were both elderly
men when they prepared their memorable first editions. In recent years musical
lexicography has also more and more tended to become team-work rather than
the encyclopædic effort of one single mind. Eric Blom's new " Grove " as
well as Friedrich Blume's " Musik in Geschichte und Gegenwart " draw on a
host of highly specialised scholars from both hemispheres. To ask a musician
in his early thirties, with evidently but little experience as a musicographer, to
undertake the task of compiling a reference book single-handed, is therefore in
the nature of an experiment.

Despite the censorious implication of this review's sub-title, I should like to
state at the outset that in my opinion Mr. Illing has responded to this formidable
challenge of his powers with great gallantry. Many of the dictionary's more
than 1,500 entries have been written with evident zest, competence and a happy
knack for the succinct formula. Among these should be counted the articles
on general matters of musical form and on instruments (the latter greatly
assisted by excellent illustrations, well arranged tables and graphs). It is in the
section dealing with composers themselves that I seem to detect Mr. Illing's
Achilles heel. Here he committed the fundamental mistake of completely
excluding all composers, born after December 31st, 1899, and by limiting himself
to the monotonously reiterated reference " still living " in the numerous cases
of contemporary composers born before that date. The results of this ill-
advised decision, which incidentally may have been tempting enough for the
harassed compiler, despairing of dealing satisfactorily with all aspects of his
vast subject on less than 320 pages, are as disastrous as they are quixotic. The
dictionary's lacunæ will be a special disappointment for the prospective readers
of a Penguin Reference book, who expect to find first and foremost references
to persons and subjects uppermost in the mind of the ordinary " man in the
street."

As a direct consequence of Mr. Illing's severe self-limitation his dictionary
has become least explicit on matters and persons of special importance for the
contemporary musical scene. Here are a few examples. Because still living,
no information on either Stravinsky or Vaughan Williams is tendered beyond the
date of their birth. Such treatment seems specially unsatisfactory in the case
of Schoenberg, the principal architect of Twelve-note composition, now in his
77th year, who is excluded from reference while both his deceased pupils Webern
and Berg receive enlightening comment, and Twelve-note music itself figures as
one of the most relevant entries in the whole book. Even worse is the example

of the 85-year-old Sibelius who, because " still living," is not dealt with at all, whereas his exact contemporary, Richard Strauss (+1949) gets a one-page article. The situation seems mildly grotesque since the " dead " master with his spate of posthumously published works still appearing is so much more alive and kicking than the " still living " Sibelius, who has remained persistently silent for the past 25 years. Even worse seems the complete black-out imposed on all composers under fifty. It is bad enough that this country's most successful living composer —Benjamin Britten—is totally excluded. But that Rubbra, its leading symphonist, and Walton, its representative composer between the two great wars— both very near fifty—should remain unnoticed, makes nonsense of the idea of an encyclopædia. The compiler, in an effort to offset these deplorable editorial restrictions, has tried to compensate the reader in the field of national musical history. He has faithfully included every possible—albeit obscure—English musician from William Cornysshe to Henry Youll, some of whom have received but scant recognition in Grove. In this respect I find Mr. Illing's compilation very helpful for the specially interested scholar, but certainly not sympathetic to the requirements of the " man in the street," who surely would prefer information on Walton, Britten and Stravinsky to articles on Michael East and Solomon Eccles.

That Mr. Illing is at home in the world of old English music, is implied in the foregoing. That he is habitually ill at ease with the music of Central Europe is evident from the host of printing errors dealing with German composers. Eyesores such as " Liepzig " and " Wursburg " could easily have been removed.

In addition, Mr. Illing might have let E. T. A. Hoffmann die in his poky little flat in Berlin instead of " in Silesia," and allowed Richard Wagner to face death in the Venetian Palazzo Vendramin rather than " in Vienna " (which Wagner never visited again after 1875). The choice of German musicians is certainly not catholic. It is surprising to find an enthusiastic entry for the mediocre Sigfrid Karg-Elert, but none at all on two composers of great significance: Heinrich Marschner and Hans Pfitzner.* In dealing quite inadequately both with Bruckner and Mahler, Mr. Illing is only falling into step with the majority of English musicographers. A special bee in the compiler's bonnet seems to be the urge to debunk the Teutonic origin of notable composers. So we find the hoary yarn of Haydn's Croatian origin exhumed once more; August Wilhelm Ambros is " born a Czech " (although that nation did not exist politically at the time of his birth; although he wrote all his books in impeccable German; and despite the fact that he was the nephew of the great musical scholar Kiesewetter, whose name certainly does not suggest Slavonic origin); and—of course— Gluck's name appears to Mr. Illing to be " Czech rather than German." It is quite in keeping with these strange principles of race-allocation, that Eugene D'Albert (whose Scottish-German origin is universally accepted) figures here as the " son of French parents." Even in the department of non-German Continentals Mr. Illing is apt to go astray. Giovanni Gabrieli did not die " ca. 1612 " but on August 12th, 1612. The Englishman Hugh Aston is today chiefly remembered for his " Hornpipe," much less for his sacred music. Alfredo Casella's (+1947) *oeuvre* includes several operas, of which no mention is made. The Castrati participated in Italian opera right from the start (Monteverdi's " Orfeo," 1607), not " in the 18th century " as the compiler suggests. It is also a pity to find in an English dictionary on music a reiteration of the old and universally discarded etymological derivation of " Virginal," while the compiler fails to register at all the explanation generally accepted today (virga=jack).

That no entry whatsoever on " Byzantine Music " may be found, is a serious omission. All these blemishes should be dealt with in a further revised edition of this handy little dictionary, the usefulness of which would have been much enhanced, had Mr. Illing not so implicitly trusted his own powers. H.F.R.

* Also omitted: Roussel, Chausson, Duparc, Lekeu, Schmidt, Ives etc., although all were born well before 1900. But Mr. Illing includes Harry Farjeon, Quilter, Sinding, Raff and Grovlez.—EDS.

ESSAYS IN OPERA, *by Egon Wellesz. Pp. 158; 10s. 6d. (Dennis Dobson).*

HERE is a book by a scholar who is also creative—a humane and civilised being. The first part consists of several essays dealing with one of Wellesz's " specialist " subjects, Italian baroque opera. Yet the scholarship is *used*; on its basis Wellesz has something to tell us which is of profound human significance. The most remarkable example of this is the essay on the *Balletto a Cavallo*, which reaches conclusions which bear on our understanding of baroque art as a whole:

> " the Baroque theatre possessed in the highest degree the power of binding society together . . . the theatrical performances of the court were a ceremonial in which the ruling class acted its own life . . . and its conception of authority and service."

There is also a fascinating analysis of Cesti's festival opera, *Il Pomo d'Oro*, which Wellesz edited, and an introductory chapter on the change from renaissance to baroque which provides a most lucid definition of these terms.

The second half of the book consists of the three lectures on the nature of opera which Wellesz originally gave at Oxford; and various brief papers on his own operas. These demonstrate how Wellesz's practice as an opera composer is related to his view of the form as a ritualistic microcosm of social life. Thus he thinks that the modern opera composer can learn much from the methods of baroque opera composers, and most of all from Gluck, who combined some baroque techniques with a re-created ethical and religious sense. The brief " history of opera " which Dr. Wellesz includes in these chapters is not just another Baedeker; it illuminates his theme.

It will be observed that although these essays were written over a considerable number of years they are not a miscellaneous gallimaufry. They make a book which is closely organised and richly satisfying; the more so since Dr. Wellesz writes English with lucidity and economy. Miss Patricia Kean's translation of those essays that were originally written in German is first-rate.

In conclusion, it is pleasant to be able to report that one of the most distinguished theatrical composers of our time is again devoting himself creatively to opera. The chances of our seeing *Alkestis* or *Opferung des Gefangenen* produced in this country are, alas, remote; but surely we may hope that now Wellesz is a British Subject and is writing an opera on an English text (after Sheridan), our experience of Wellesz's dramatic work may advance beyond hear-say. W.H.M.

GOING TO A CONCERT, *by Lionel Salter. Pp. 160; 7s. 6d. (Phoenix).*

A BOOK FOR YOUNG PEOPLE ?

WITH reservations, it is. Now and again Mr. Salter's literary style smacks of the Children's Hour. For instance: " Like a real grandfather, the bass cannot be too agile or skittish, but it is willing, and will not be left out of a romp if everyone else is having fun." Throughout there's much too much " I bet ! " and " Bless me ! " and Chapter 4 is far too complicated. I think it would have been better to have covered less ground more simply. Not every young person has access to musical scores, or to a music teacher, and I think Mr. Salter over-estimates the score-reading abilities of most music teachers anyway. From time to time Mr. Salter uses terms which he insufficiently explains in the text, i.e. " fa-la." Until somebody told me its meaning, I was considerably mystified by this Elizabethan phrase. It seems to me that children's knowledge and under-standing differ greatly, and the " Young Person" is a very vaguely defined section of the reading public. I have no means of knowing if I'm too old or young* for Mr. Salter's book except in so far as I understand or misunderstand it. But generally I learned a thing or two or three† from the first two chapters, the last, and in between, Nos. 5 and 8. With its comprehensive appendices and glossary of musical terms, it's a book which I imagine every young concert-goer ought to have. P.J.R.

*Our reviewer is actually 14.—Eds.
†cf. Groucho Marx: *Animal Crackers*.

JOSEPH HAYDN: HIS ART, TIMES AND GLORY, *by H. E. Jacob. Pp. xiv +368; 18s. Od. (Gollancz).*

The author aims in this book to depict Haydn and his associates as living people. Many of the details given about Haydn's friends are valuable, but in attempting to make the scenes vivid Mr. Jacob draws too much on his imagination. The sections on Napoleon show the invention of the author at its height. The short chapter on Haydn and Herschel the astronomer is attractive, though one would have thought the author's love of colour would have compelled him to mention that when George III walked inside Herschel's telescope the king took particular pleasure in showing the Archbishop of Canterbury the way to Heaven.

Mr. Jacob does well to stress that Haydn was born into a family of craftsmen and that he remained throughout his life an artisan. Occasionally the author is able to throw helpful illumination on some aspect of the composer's work. No explanation is given why Haydn is stated to have recommended Beethoven to withhold publication of the third movement of the latter's first piano sonata, rather than the third of the Op. 1 piano trios, which is generally regarded as the work Haydn frowned upon. Beethoven's age is given wrongly on p. 213, and on p. 96 the following peculiar statement is found: " He (Beethoven) lived to be only half the age of Haydn." Some keys are wrongly quoted, the second horn is said to depart twice in the " Farewell " symphony, and Haydn is credited with a salary four times too large.

It is Haydn's " Art " which receives the rawest deal in this book. Mr. Jacob appears to know " The Creation," " The Seasons," and some of the masses and symphonies well, but he mentions only three of the piano trios, in a couple of lines and without identifying them, and says little about the string quartets. It is strange that he does not mention which are the first quartets to adopt the four movement plan, and in pointing out that Haydn altered the character of the minuet, he omits any mention at all of Haydn's scherzi, even though he devotes a page to the " Russian " quartets. Except for the " Emperor " quartet there is practically no mention at all of any of the last twenty-seven quartets. The description of Op. 1, No. 1 is unbelievable. J.C.

INTRODUCTION TO THE MUSIC OF BIZET, by *Winton Dean*. *Pp. 61;*
3s. 6d. (Dennis Dobson).

AN admirable book, giving in its short space not Bizet's biography, but the
development of Bizet's style. Mr. Dean begins: " The best introduction to
Bizet's music is not one more essay in praise of Carmen " and goes on to say
that Bizet " was no mere one-big-hit composer like Mascagni or Leoncavallo
or Humperdinck " and that, had he lived longer, the ultimate success of
" Carmen " would have given tremendous encouragement to his self-esteem.
While justly damning much of Bizet's lesser-known music, Mr. Dean makes a
strong plea for some neglected masterpieces, specially the opera " Djamileh,"
some of the songs, and the suite " Jeux d'enfants " for piano duet. I do hope
that Sadler's Wells will give us " Djamileh " one of these days. Mr. Dean
makes perfectly clear the historical position of Bizet between the old *opéra-
comique*, Gounod, Verdi, and the later Italian *verismo*. He aptly remarks
(p. 45) that " . . . Bizet's *verismo*, unlike that of his successors, never trans-
gresses the bounds imposed by art. It is always a refinement, never an imitation
of life," and a little later (p. 47) " . . . he never takes sides; he allows the
characters to make their appeal to the audience, unlike Puccini who seems to
leave his place in the background and go straight for our emotions. He is thus
true to Merimée . . . " Everyone who has read Merimée's passionately objective prose will agree with this.   P.H.

MILITARY MUSIC, by *H. G. Farmer*. *Pp. 71; 7s. 6d. (Max Parrish).*

THROUGHOUT the 70 odd pages of this booklet Dr. Farmer cannot make up
his mind whether to write on music for military bands, whether to concentrate
on music for wind instruments in general or on music for military purposes in
particular. Hovering uneasily between these three alternatives he seems unable
to proffer relevant information on any one of them.

It is a little surprising to read twice about Lassus' alleged predilection for
cornets and trombones, but not once about the novel use of wind instruments in
the sacred compositions of the two Gabrieli's (" Concerti " of 1587), and to
find no mention of the important fact that Annibale Padovano and A. Gabrieli
wrote "Dialoghi musicali . . . ed due Battaglie a 8 voci per sonar de' instrumenti
da fiato. . . ." The special type of " Battaglia " music which took on such
proportions in the early Baroque under the impact of the Thirty Years War is
pointed out nowhere. The reader will also search in vain for a word on Monteverdi's " Madrigali Guerrieri " in which the vocabulary of the military music
of the future, with its typified tattoos, signals and " off stage " battle noises, is
authoritatively coined. That all operas of the early Baroque include battle
music, commonly labelled " Guerra," is not even alluded to. It is also odd to
see Gastoldi's " Balletti " of 1591 singled out as the beginning of a wider
application of instrumentally inspired music, when Willaert, the Gabrieli's, and
others, had written and published authentic instrumental music thirty to sixty
years earlier. Dr. Farmer asserts that " some of the works of Josquin de Pres
. . . were doubtless for wind instruments. . . ." Again this is a case of " non-
proven." But it can be proved that solemn masses—already before Josquin's
time—carried the inscription " Trumpetum," thereby indicating that they were
to be accompanied by brass instruments. The " Toccata " in Monteverdi's
" Orfeo " is mentioned (but given the wrong title " Intrada "), yet no comment
is made on the fact that Monteverdi used exactly the same " Toccata " three

years later as the instrumental background to the introductory number of his " Vespro " of 1610, thus transposing this theatrical trumpet piece into the ecclesiastical sphere. Instead Dr. Farmer dishes out Hubert Parry's remark " that Monteverdi's experiments sometimes look childish."

There are many more puzzling omissions in Dr. Farmer's account of military music and of the developing use of military instruments through the ages. Very appropriately a chapter is called " Mozart the Meteor," but in it the reader will look in vain for a word on the " Masonic Dirge " (K. 477) with its revolutionary treatment of the windband. It is incorrect to state that cymbals and drums had first been used for the " colourisation of rhythm " by Mozart (1781) and Haydn (1794). Gluck in his " Iphigenie en Tauride " (1779) had used them exactly in that sense several years earlier. To find Mozart's pupil and friend Suessmayer characterised as " the friend of Beethoven " is a minor grievance compared with the omission of Beethoven's most important works for military band. Not a word is said about either the (transposed) arrangement of the famous Funeral March for military band from op. 26, or the " Battle Symphony." As much overlooked is the type of " Concerto Militaire " for pianoforte and orchestra, so much in vogue during the period of the school of brilliant pianists from Kalkbrenner and Dussek to Field and Weber. Not a single reference (except for an illustration) is made to the specific type of Russian military horn music with its peculiar mosaic technique. A sentence, dealing with Strawinsky's treatment of wind instruments in general, and with his principle of orchestration as applied to " Le Sacre du printemps " in particular, is really unworthy of a scholar of distinction.   H.F.R.

MODERN ENGLISH BALLET, *by Fernau Hall. Pp. 340; 20s. 0d. (Melrose).*
FACED with the current, sudden splendour of British ballet, Fernau Hall is rather like the little boy in the story who said that the Emperor had no clothes on. His book is likely to cause as much annoyance as that little boy; for it disquietingly calls in question much that we have come unreasoningly to accept during the short but intense period of growth of our ballet.

But by taking us back to first principles this book should help towards the formulation of generally accepted standards.

It has its faults (among which I would place a weakness of pattern and an over-emphasis on certain aspects of our ballet history at the expense of others), but can be safely recommended as an excellent and timely attempt to explain why our ballet is getting rapidly into the doldrums, and how disaster can be avoided.   F.J.

MUSIC MAKING IN THE OLDEN DAYS, *by Henry George Farmer. Pp. 122; 15s. 0d. (Hinrichsen).*
THE title of this book is misleading. It is not another account of " ye olde Englishe musicke," but a history of the Aberdeen Music Society from its beginnings in 1748 until 1801, when it ceased to exist. Dr. Farmer has gone into great detail on the subject of the Society's organisation, and brings to light a good many interesting facets of concert promotion in the middle of the eighteenth century. Chapter 9 (" The Music ") is especially relevant in this respect; the programme for December 20th, 1758, reproduced on page 61, with its characteristic division into " acts," is particularly notable. But the " programme note " style which the author has adopted for the greater part of this study makes rather tedious reading. Dr. Farmer's concern with inventories,

balance sheets and lists of office bearers marks him out as a competent musical archivist; but it occasionally serves to deflect the reader's attention from the main outlines of an otherwise illuminating treatise.

This criticism, however, does not apply to the thirteenth chapter, called " The Geniuses of the Society." Here Dr. Farmer provides us with a succinct anthology from the writings of certain Scottish philosophers who were active members of the Aberdeen Society. The extracts from works by John Gregory, author of *A Comparative View of the State and Faculties of Man* (1765), James Beattie, and Alexander Gerard (whose *Essay on Taste* is an enjoyable book on æsthetics) are presented with explanatory comments. And enough is said to convince us that although the Aberdeen Musical Society confined itself to the works of accepted masters in building up its library (in the early days it was laid down in the Rules that " some of Corelli's Musick " should be performed each time the Society met) its activities did at least prompt several intelligent thinkers to investigate for themselves the nature of musical experience. This fact alone justifies Dr. Farmer's painstaking researches. He has not " discovered " any startling genius among neglected Scottish composers. But he has shown, incidentally, the high level of Scottish musical culture at a fertile period of its history.   E.D.M.

SACRED MUSIC, *by Alec Robertson. Pp. 72; 7s. 6d. (Max Parrish).*
AN unpretentious little book which contains much scholarship beneath its unassuming exterior. If one can quarrel with some personal judgments— " small masterpiece " applied to Bruckner's E minor Mass seems to me quite inadequate—there can be no quarrelling with the magnificently accurate and compressed history of strictly liturgical music, combined with an imaginative understanding of what Western music in general owes to this cradle of its art.

H.T.

THE ST. MATTHEW PASSION; *its preparation and performance, by Adrian Boult and Walter Emery. Pp. 75; 4s. 6d. (Novello).*
ALL the books in the British Museum, all the concerts in a score of seasons, all the gramophone records in the catalogue, will not teach us as much as the regular singing or playing of Bach; whence this thoroughly practical book deserves a warm welcome. It is addressed mainly to the small, unwealthy choirs who plough through *The Crucifixion* and *Olivet to Calvary*, but shrink from assailing such a musical fortress as Bach's *St. Matthew Passion*. Never fear, say Boult and Emery; think hard and rehearse hard, and you may well achieve a more satisfying performance than many a rich choral society with huge choir and expensive soloists. And they are right.

Tolerance is a commendable virtue; and these authors have their share, but not to interfere with their historical sense. After all, " it is better to perform the Passion with no accompaniment but that of a piano than not to perform it at all." And so they advise allotting solos to a few of the choir when necessary, rather than omitting the glorious and revealing arias; they offer other cuts, but add that the ultimate aim should be complete performance; and they are informative about scores and parts, sound and firm about continuo, and offer sensible notes on interpretation. I wish they had pointed out somewhere that a piano continuo (if such must be used) should sound as unlike a piano as possible, and that the player should play with detached touch and use sustaining pedal only for bass notes, not for changing chords. They advocate

Seiffert's realization, too, with which I can't agree; it is dull to a point of un-Bachishness. One of Bach's own realizations is printed as an example which, however, was written for a mediocre player; Bach himself was fond of rich and elaborate contrapuntal realizations (Kittel and Daube both affirm this in passages cited in The Bach Reader).

All in all there is little to quarrel with; the choir that follows these authors' advice will avoid mediocrity, enjoy an experience of the supremest musical worth, and be able, possibly for the first time, to see Stainer and Maunder in proper perspective.　　　　　　　　　　　　　　　　　　**W.S.M.**

THE STORY OF AN ORCHESTRA, *by Boyd Neel. Pp. 133; 10s. 6d. (Vox Mundi).*

In easy and agreeable style the author tells the story of the Boyd Neel String Orchestra from its foundation in 1933 up to last year, devoting more than half the book to their Australasian jaunt of 1947. As both he and the Orchestra are prominent features of the British musical scene, his book commands respect. Dr. Neel's account of his rehearsal methods (p. 25 *et seq.*) throws light on the chambermusic excellence of his performances, but also explains why he is so rarely seen in front of a larger orchestra. Friendly discussions on how the music goes may achieve results with sixteen players, but not with a hundred and six. The piquancy of the book resides in Dr. Neel's occasional airing of his (and our) present musical discontents.

Today, musicology and musical criticism go their way unruffled by such mundane considerations as audiences and the economic problems of public music-making. Few writers of the day are supplying the future historian of these matters with data on the " papered " Wigmore Hall audiences, the unaccountable voids at Chelsea for fine programmes and the tribal rites of the Promenaders. Nor does Dr. Neel, but his outspoken comments reveal more about the present public attitude to music in London than may be gleaned from whole files of our daily national press in which concerts are reported.　　　　　　　　　　**F.A.**

Concerts

Arranged in chronological order; joint reviews, where they exist, at the end of each numerical Section.

I. London

HAYDN ORCHESTRA: Conway Hall, 26th October, 1950; c. Harry Newstone.
The enthusiasm and musicianship of this orchestra does much to atone for the sometimes noticeable blemishes in its intonation and ensemble. The trenchant beauty of Haydn's earlier symphonic writing was well demonstrated in the spirited performances of No. 64 in A and " La Chasse " (No. 73 in D). The well-conceived solo part in the Stamitz Viola Concerto could have been more feelingly handled by the soloist, Frederick Riddle; the graciousness of the andante completely eluded him. In the Dittersdorf *Symphonie Concertante* for double-bass and viola, the difficult bass solo was ably played by Roy Watson. But the composer's preoccupation with the technical problem of utilizing the double-bass as a solo instrument does not permit of anything musically significant, while the viola is virtually left without a part worth playing. The repetition of the finale as an encore served to emphasise the paucity of the work's ideas.　　　　　　　　　　　　　　　　　　　　**R.T.**

SAMUEL BARBER: First English performance of Piano Sonata (1950); Wigmore Hall, 17th November, 1950; Robert Wallenborn (piano).

THIS piece, as often with Barber, sounds facile and superficial although a very definite, and to all purposes excellent plan of construction is in evidence from beginning to end. I believe that Barber's compositional conscience—a strong conscience, I should say—is satisfied the moment he has found a workable plan for the distribution of his material. But this is too soon: a sonata is not built for efficiency, even if this be the efficiency of form at its most abstract. The second step, namely the mutual penetration of form and material, a process both unique and defiant of established rules in every new movement ever written —this step is not taken by Barber. This becomes specially clear at those places where Barber thinks he knows where he is and what he is about, i.e. when his formalistic conscience has been satisfied. He *knows* " I am now writing a proper coda on a pedal-note for the first movement," and: " Here, a lively scherzo would be in place, based on material from the first movement," and again: " This had better be a fugue "—and every time he is perfectly right. Over his self-righteousness he goes comfortably to sleep—although that doesn't stop him writing brilliant piano passages. P.H.

FRANK MARTIN: First English performance of the Ballade for Cello and Piano; London School of Economics, 29th November, 1950; Rolf Looser (cello), Marguerite Kitchin (piano).

YOUNG Swiss composers still think in terms of post-impressionism even when they consciously try to break fresh ground. The result is a certain repressed respectability in the works of Messrs. Willy Burckhardt, Pierre Wissmer, Robert Oboussier, who all have original ideas but are too civilized to give them free rein, let alone impress form on them after their liberation. Frank Martin, the doyen of Swiss music, is, luckily, free from this tendency to nip one's own flowers in the bud. His Ballade is not only good music well-written for the cello, but has the superior freedom and self-assurance of the experienced artist when in balladesque mood. But it is not quite as good as his rhetoric would have us to believe. P.H.

ROYAL COLLEGE OF MUSIC: Concert by the First Orchestra, 7th December, 1950; c. Richard Austin.

THE programme included a concert overture by Kenneth Jones (student 1947-50) which was awarded a Royal Philharmonic Society Prize for 1950. It still remains a matter of wonderment to me that our academies haven't got beyond the stage of teaching their inmates how to turn out beefy Elgar pastiche. They might at least have caught up with Bartok. D.M.

SIGI WEISSENBERG: Piano recital; Covent Garden, 10th December, 1950.

THIS twenty-year-old player is not only in the possession of a technique that could be the envy of many older and better-known pianists, but he is also much more musical than most possessors of a virtuoso technique are apt to be. Out of the usual spate of Liszt sonatas we have had this season, his interpretation was by far the best in that he treated the ramshackle structure of this work as if it were a genuine sonata-form, thus making it sound a better piece than it really is. The same seriousness of approach, mixed with that child-like, almost awkward humour which Schumann retained throughout his life, distinguished Weissenberg's performance of the latter's " Kinderscenen." P.H.

HAYDN ORCHESTRA: Conway Hall, 14th December, 1950; c. Harry Newstone.

THE programme included Mozart's " Titus " overture and " Linz " symphony, Haydn's " La Reine " symphony, and a flute concerto, notable only for the superb playing of the soloist, Johann Feltkamp. As a doubtful work of Haydn, or by some unknown, it is best forgotten. Mr. Newstone is doing fine and unique work but a still higher standard of orchestral performance is a vital and overdue necessity. H.T.

RACINE FRICKER: First performance of Violin Concerto. Morley College Concerts Society, Central Hall, 10th January, 1951; London National Orchestra, Maria Lidka (violin); c. Walter Goehr.

THIS work, like an 18th century concerto, is very near to chamber music. The orchestra is small but used with colour and imagination. The solo part is real fiddle music and solo music at that—yet it successfully consorts with the orchestra on terms of intimacy. The musical content has evident integrity. The idiom is strenuous in general, and in places self-consciously so. The themes are not markedly memorable but they fit cleanly and exhilaratingly together, throwing up a texture with something of the fascination of Alban Berg. There is glitter and reflection and echo, a three-dimensional sound. The outer two movements are more obviously ambitious than the poetical *Andante*, the last particularly—an interesting fact in view of the notorious difficulty of composing an adequate finale to a modern concerto. There is one near-impertinent tune which might well irritate on greater familiarity; but the movement creates a mood both relevant and substantial, and serves its function with some brilliance. The fiddling was admirable and the orchestral performance effective. R.D.

SONATA RECITAL: Peter Mountain (violin) and Angela Dale (piano); Wigmore Hall, 18th January, 1951.

WELL-STUDIED and sensitive performances of Hindemith's serious 2nd sonata and the charming sonatina by Jean Français. Beethoven's Op. 30, No. 3 was jolly instead of witty; no wonder at this speed. Perhaps to spite their names, Miss Dale often stands out where Mr. Mountain falls flat: cf. their respective treatment of the second movement's main theme in the Beethoven. She is more developed musically and technically whereas he sometimes presses in the lower register and is apt to be scratchy when going over the strings. P.H.

LONDON CONTEMPORARY MUSIC CENTRE: R.B.A. Galleries, 23rd January, 1951; Vegh String Quartet. First performance of Quartet No. 3 by Elizabeth Lutyens.

THE quartet by Kadosa (a young Hungarian) showed, besides a considerable technique of composition and good handling of the instruments, a very independent mind; independent, that is, mainly of Bartok. Yet he shares one characteristic with the middle period of this master: he presents folk-material, in a state of advanced decomposition, not as though listening to the people but as though harkening back to a primitive state of his own mind. With great intellectual honesty, Kadosa demonstrates by the insertion of these passages into an otherwise utterly modern score, not only the growth of his own mind, but also the secret but powerful link between modern dissonance and primitivity. But if the critic of the *Daily Telegraph*, speaking of Berg's " Lyric Suite " where much the same happens, believes this to be " decadent," he forgets that the only valid definition of decadence is " to be blind (or, in our case, to be deaf) to changing reality," and *not* " to doubt what one has formerly believed to be reality." From this angle, it is precisely the composer who thinks " all is well with us " who is decadent, and not Berg or Kadosa who feel the pulse of the century. Miss Lutyens in her latest essay neither believes " all to be well " nor is she unduly perturbed by her contrary findings. This quartet is an impartial interim-report on her and our condition. Her great clarity, objectivity and technical skill, together with a certain lack of true inventiveness, make her select a number of modern methods of composition, including the 12-tone row. It is to her credit that not only her changes of method but also her unorthodox handling of the 12-tone row (as the rapid reduction of the slow movement's series into partial series) do not disrupt her style but are felt to be consistent. The playing was of high distinction throughout the evening.   P.H.

FIONA GREIG: Piano recital; R.B.A. Galleries, 25th January, 1951.

A FIRST recital of some promise. Though her playing of Schumann's " Kreisleriana " and Beethoven's Sonata Op. 22 was not quite mature, it showed that unbroken seriousness of youth which is a token that nothing has yet been spoiled.   P.H.

PHILHARMONIA CONCERT SERIES: Kingsway Hall, 5th February, 1951; Wiener Konzerthaus Quartet and Jorg Demus (piano).

HERE was a classic example of the travesty produced by good executants when they insist on their own " interpretation " of a work in defiance of the composer's explicit instructions. These artists are, individually, excellent string players, and, as an ensemble, practically impeccable. Yet their performance of Schubert's Quartet in G, Op. 161, bore little relation to the original, which was set down once and for all in 1826 by Schubert himself. For example, the first subject is not marked " Introduction : Andante " nor the second subject " Meno mosso," but each time these elements in the design appeared, the performers insisted that such was the case. In consequence it was impossible to appreciate the true nature of the movement, which achieves unity (of fundamental rhythm) in diversity (of character); diversity being over-exaggerated, unity vanished. The *Andante un poco moto* began as a pure *andante*, and seemed to be dragging a ball and chain; it tugged hard at it each time it reached the melancholy little cadence (incidentally nullifying the pathos of the *ritardando* marked by Schubert just before its last appearance) but only became *un poco moto* in the middle section. The scherzo, taken at Schubert's speed of *Allegro vivace*, came off best; but the Trio, a lilting *allegretto*, was turned into a sentimental *andante*, only picking up its true speed after the double bar. The treatment of the finale had to be heard to be believed. The first bar created a momentary apprehension that the whole movement would be taken *andante* (once more !)—and this might have been preferable to what actually happened: the racing chariot was refitted with square wheels, constructed on the principle " minor-major = slow-fast," and in the resulting boneshaker a miserable journey was had by all.

After this, it was a great relief to hear Beethoven's Piano Sonata in E, Op. 109, played with complete integrity by Mr. Jorg Demus. I wondered how he and the Konzerthaus Quartet would ever manage to compromise in a performance of Brahms's Piano Quintet, but, being fond of the work, did not take the risk of staying to find out.   D.C.

PEARS, BRITTEN: " *Die schoene Muellerin* "; *Friends' House, 13th February, 1951.*

SOBERLY speaking the best, spontaneously speaking the only recital of the season. Details sound silly unless there are enough of them; generalities may sound clever but tend to be meaningless. A way out of one's limited space is to concentrate on certain generalizable particulars,* to indicate these inter-preters' art of strophic variation and the subtle total build-up they thus achieved, for example, in *Das Wandern, Ungeduld, Morgengruss, Des Muellers Blumen, Die liebe Farbe* and *Des Baches Wiegenlied,* a new revelation usually emerging with the penultimate and/or last " variation "; or to point to Britten's art of *variational imitation,* e.g. after " so muss ich wieder gehen " in *Morgengruss,* where the imitation in the piano constituted a real variation of Pears's phrasing, i.e. a strong, developing modification retaining a strong underlying identity; or to contrast the strictly musical *rubati,* as in the recitativic part of *Der Neugierige* (" ' Ja ' heisst das eine Woertchen, das andere heisset ' nein ' "), with those passages which in their very rhythmical (as distinct from merely metrical) strictness bore *rubato-*character, in that they had the feel of phrasic freedom by rhythmic necessity, such as the stressedly strict " und soll es ewig bleiben " (particularly the last one) in *Ungeduld,* with its " ritardando " of nothing but expression; or to try to find a metaphor for the perfectly shaped unnotability of the piano's notes in background motion, as in the sextuplets of *Wohin?* or in the semiquavers of *Eifersucht und Stolz;* or to comprehend Britten's unique dynamics under some generalization, that synthesis of rigidity and flexibility, of sternness and tenderness, of commanding and obeying—hear the *forte-decrescendo-* (yet *subito-*) *piano* in the opening of *Am Feierabend,* not to speak of the virile resumption of the semiquavers before " Haett' ich tausend Arme "—a synthesis for whose description one is inclined to fall back on the vaguest and best of abstractions, i.e. passivity and activity, masculinity and femininity; or to delineate, perhaps by means of geometrical drawings, the arches of the arch that is a vocal line of Pears, though geometry can hardly give an idea of his infinite range and shades of expression, and of the expressive-ness of his restraint.

The programme gave only the English texts and titles. When there is only room for one version, we should always get the original: if we want to see anything, we want to see the sounds. The poetic meaning, or what we need of it, is clear from the music.   H.K.

*Not possessing the music I am relying for these on my memory and notes.

B.B.C. SYMPHONY CONCERTS: Albert Hall, 1st November and 6th December, 1950; c. Vittorio Gui and Albert Wolff respectively.

THE memorable mess Gui made of Brahms' 4th symphony was a strange introduction to his incomparable performance of Debussy's *Iberia* (*Images* No. 2) which could not be too highly praised. Busoni's fiddle concerto inter-vened with Szigeti as accomplished soloist; but, as so often with Busoni's uneven talents, it proved to be disappointing. Ultra-eclectic for no compelling aesthetic reason, the game of recognising old faces at even Busoni's Masked Ball becomes tedious after one movement. The Brahms went as wrong as it could in the finale where Gui's hit or miss tempi missed most of the time. Example: He started the movement at such a rate that half-way through it some sort of holding back was inevitable. Ironically enough he chose to slacken speed at the restatement of the ground—marked Tempo I. Gui's Tempo II proved to be what his Tempo I ought to have been, and the latter part of the movement was more in accord with the demands of the score. Even so, half a movement played approximately right is small compensation for three and a half movements played unrelievedly wrong.

M. Albert Wolff directed a resurrection of Debussy's " Le Martyre de Saint Sebastien " which was mostly obscured by the expert chanting of d'Annunzio's exotic text by Messrs. Judd and Redgrave. Very capable chanting, but distracting nevertheless. The music that penetrated these histrionic impediments was occasionally impressive in a muscular and masculine manner somewhat at odds with the preciosity of its literary origin: that the music now and again was swamped by the words didn't seem to matter much, musically speaking. M. Wolff seemed very much at home in the midst of these incidental fragments and I should imagine gave them an authentic performance. He was assisted by a section of the London Philharmonic Choir and a team of soloists: Maude Baker, Margaret Rolfe, Joan Alexander, Marjorie Avis and Suzanne Danco.

D.M.

LONDON PHILHARMONIC ORCHESTRA: Albert Hall, 2nd and 23rd November, 1950; c. Boult.

THE first programme was notable for a shamefully empty hall and a vigorous performance of Vaughan Williams' *London* symphony. Vaughan Williams is a composer I don't well understand, but this symphony, for all its crudities and inhibited and inhibiting nationalism, can be a refreshing musical experience. I should imagine its " local " historical significance can hardly be over-estimated.

The crudities we heard in Bach's B minor Mass were of quite another and less healthy species. Apart from Boult's tempi that were most of them misfits, the London Philharmonic Choir were more often than not toneless and tuneless and the number of ragged entries and untidy exits were beyond mathematical calculation. A slovenly exhibition. Of the soloists, Peter Pears sang best in spite of a cold: in the duet " Domine Deus, rex coelestis " his superior phrasing was at unhappy odds with the unfeeling vocal line of his soprano partner.

D.M.

NEW ERA CONCERT SOCIETY: London Symphony Orchestra, 5th December, 1950, and 30th January, 1951; c. Richard Austin and Josef Krips respectively.

THE first concert included the first performance of Martinu's indifferent violin concerto very capably played by Henry Holst. The work itself was dull throughout and its occasional and quite arbitrary dissonances (cf. 1st movt. introductory brass flourish) were even more tedious than its respectable Dvorákian lyrical consonances (cf. the andante and finale). Some composers won't learn that the odd wrong note can't make a fruity texture salty. In the second concert Ilse Hollweg sang Zerbinetta's aria from Strauss' *Ariadne auf Naxos* with a high proportion of accuracy and sometimes great purity of tone. Reger's Mozart Variations and Fugue, Op. 132, fared badly under Krips whose ecstatic grimaces would be more bearable if they produced correspondingly ecstatic musical results from the orchestra. As it was we had very poor phrasing and tempi almost always too fast—especially in Variation 8 where *molto sostenuto* was converted into a rollocking *andante*. Reger's extraordinarily long drawn out cadences and melodic extensions are admittedly difficult to handle, but Krips' high-speed policy was the worst and most unmusical of all impossible solutions.

D.M.

FURTWAENGLER

Mysore Concerts (November 13, December 11)—" The Ring " from
La Scala, Milan (Third Programme, December; recording)

As was to be expected, the most overpowering interpretations in the Philharmonia Orchestra's first two concerts under the greatest developer and deepest
experiencer among living conductors were those of the symphonic and evolving
works: above all the 5th Beethoven, but also the 5th Tchaikowsky, Brahms'
Haydn-Variations, and " The Hebrides," with whose development Mendelssohn
seemed, for objectively incomprehensible reasons, dissatisfied. The Tchaikowsky became not only a great, but even an immaculate work: does then its
weakness simply consist in its occasionally hiding its strength, which it needs a
Furtwaengler to uncover ? *Don Juan*, too, was a master-interpretation, but
while he was surprisingly at home in Walton's *Scapino* Overture, Furtwaengler
disproved himself a Bartókian in the Concerto for Orchestra, wherein one of
his most singular assets became his most serious liability: the handling of
transitions. Though there were isolated stretches which showed that a penetrating and music-loving conductor was at work, duty seemed to conduct more
often than inclination; whereas unification—let alone intensely inspired Furt-
waenglerian unity—there was virtually none. On the basis of this performance
I should venture the surmise that Furtwaengler does not altogether approve
of the work, that in fact he does not think much of its inner unity, thus trying to
give compensation by more superficial devices. He would seem to me to harbour
a misplaced sense of obligation to perform works which he deems modern-but-
significant. It will be recalled that he undertook the first performance, in stormy
weather, of Schoenberg's orchestral Variations (Berlin, 1928), though it could
not be clearer from his recent book *Gespraeche ueber Musik* that he does not
understand Schoenberg at all. And even Hindemith, for whom he stood up so
manfully under the Nazis, is by no means his kind of music.

Wagner is, and the Third Programme's decision to let us hear as much as
possible of this side of his interpretative genius cannot be praised enough.
It was a new and newly united *Ring* we listened to; it was even a new Flagstad,
for we have not previously heard her give so *musical* a performance. Things
like the intensification towards Wagner's heroic E flat major in the transition
to *Goetterdaemmerung's* Prologue's 2nd part, the latter's rising orchestral triplets
punctuating Siegfried's fiery exclamations of love, the subsequent *Steigerung*
together with the interlude before the main act, the functionally accented quavers
in the *Rheinreise* itself, the simultaneous *marcato* and discretion of the *Walküren-*
motif to Hagen's " Ein Weib weiss ich, das herrlichste der Welt " *et seq.*,
the hesitation, both strictly structural and immeasurably tender, in Siegfried's
" . . . von einer Lehre *lass ich doch nie*, den ersten Trunk zu treuer Minne,
Bruennhilde, bring ich dir ! " or the build-up, characteristically both restraining
and urging, to the *ff* before Siegfried's " Bluehenden Lebens labendes Blut "
in the blood-brotherhood episode—countless memories like these become
actually stronger the further they reach back, the more one thinks and feels
about them.   H.K.

205

SOME FIRST PERFORMANCES

Franz Schmidt—Rawsthorne—Cooke—Fricker—Gerhard—Timothy Moore

WITHOUT a Third Programme, Holland has yet already been given an opportunity to hear Franz Schmidt's (1874-1939) last work, the oratorium *The Book with Seven Seals* (Hilversum Radio, November 28: Brabant Orchestra and Bois-le-Duc Choir under Rob Gevers; first Dutch performance) which the composer of four important symphonies (in a tradition that did not die with Mahler) regarded as his most significant work. His one-time pupil in composition, Julius Patzak, sang the Evangelist—the most exacting and important of the five solo parts—with the same mastery with which he interpreted Florestan at Salzburg (see our last issue), and which is unlikely ever to be attained by anyone else. As for the work itself, first but least, it suffers from a few formal weaknesses, such as all too forehearable cyclicisms which are more leitmotivic than functional, more organisational than organic. Not so the big cyclic frame, i.e. the Evangelist's opening number which returns in a new, overwhelming light before the final *Amen*. The style of the C major score roots chiefly in Bach, Brahms, Wagner and Bruckner, darting across the classical period on the one hand, and ennobling and purifying post-romanticism on the other. It is, for the greater part, a masterly composition of both extraordinary depth and immediate appeal, offering a wealth of spontaneous imagination whose most daring and grandiose flight is the D major *Hallelujah* in Gipsy style before the final return to C major; a unique piece which succeeds in incorporating the zingaro's several freedoms, including even his characteristic kind of agogics, in the rhythmic-harmonic-thematic structure. In a future issue, a member of our editorial staff will examine the score in considerable detail: at times we find ourselves compelled to make our own Third Programme.

Back in London, Alan Rawsthorne's Symphony (Albert Hall, 15th November: B.B.C. Orchestra under Boult) has met with the lukewarm reception which its nowise lukewarm lifeblood made probable: it does not happen often that the public in general and the critics in particular forgive a composer for developing: for not copying himself. Amongst a considerable number of other things, the work is the first symphony since Britten's 2nd string quartet which at once faces and solves the modern sonata problem. (The difference between a string quartet and a symphony is that the string quartet is more symphonic.) I shall give my detailed first impressions of this form in my article on recent novelties in the May issue of *The Music Review*, where I shall also try to assemble the evidence for my first evaluations of the new works played at this season's first concert of the L.C.M.C. (December 12): Arnold Cooke's not very original, but clean, clear and enjoyable oboe Quartet (Carter Trio with Goossens) whose texture is particularly praiseworthy; Roberto Gerhard's pseudo-twelve-tonal and B major-ending pseudo-viola pseudo-sonata (Anatole Mines and Norman Greenwood); and Fricker's problematic violin Sonata (Maria Lidka and Margaret Kitchen), whose serious wrongs are more easily describable than its unquestionable rights ("You've got something there," said V.W. to one of our younger composers, "but I don't know what it is"). If I get the space, I should, moreover, like to go into Timothy Moore's (b. 1922) trumpet Concerto (Queen Mary Hall, November 30: Philip Jones with Capriol Orchestra under Roy Budden), an untalented work hiding a talent, and symptomatic of our elderly age in that it is not so much a composition as a translation.   H.K.

206

Vaughan Williams—Stevens—Lambert—Arnell

The 21st Birthday Festival Concert of the Rural Music Schools Association (Albert Hall, 18th November, c. Boult) included the first performance of Vaughan Williams' Concerto Grosso for string players of all and no standards. Not intended as a masterpiece it was nevertheless musical throughout and genuinely characteristic of its composer whose interest in amateur musicians is known well enough. That " only good can come of it " is not always to be said of similar educative musical experiments: here the phrase strictly applies.

At the R.B.A. Galleries (26th October) Helen Pyke and Paul Hamburger gave a recital of original compositions for piano duet. It included several first performances of works some of which were more original than others. A " Fantasy on an Irish Ho'hoane " by Bernard Stevens; Richard Arnell's Sonatina Op. 61; and the first public performance of Constant Lambert's " Three Negro Pieces for the White Keys." The Lambert was previously reviewed in *Music Survey* II/1/49, and a further hearing only confirms that adverse opinion of their irritant and irritating character—about as negroid as a Kentucky Minstrel on Brighton Pier. The Stevens Fantasy, for all its integrity and taste, didn't seem to escape monotony of texture and rhythm; perhaps because Mr. Stevens cared too assiduously for his Ho'hoane. It struck me that the piece was inhibited throughout. The Arnell was mostly and successfully gay, apart from the prologues and epilogues which made their customary (for Arnell) and substantial comment on their context. Arnell is never half as gay as he seems at first sight or sound, although his well-nigh impeccable texture led *The Times* critic astray. " Uncritical acceptance of the first ideas that come into the mind " was his verdict, thus showing unprecedented critical insight into the workings of a composer's creative faculty. How, we are obliged to ask, can *The Times* be quite sure Mr. Arnell accepted his " first " ideas for his sonatina ? And what's the matter with first ideas anyway ? Ideas may be either right or wrong, but certainly not for being first, last or even in-between. *The Times* should take its own advice and think not once but twice; perhaps a critic's " first ideas " are even more suspect than a composer's. Arnell's First symphony Op. 31 (Chelsea Town Hall, 23rd January, first performance, London Classical Orchestra, c. Trevor Harvey) proved to have more in common with the 2nd Divertimento for chamber orchestra (Conway Hall, 15th February, first European performance, Haydn Orchestra, c. Harry Newstone) than with the 4th symphony heard at Cheltenham's 1949 Festival. Both the First symphony and the Divertimento display some of the same faults: manufactured and unconvincing *fugato*, a far from lucid texture, or a texture so lacking sonorous depth that it pains the ears (especially in the over-resonant Chelsea hall); and often thematic ambitions that over-weight the structure: Arnell's energetic tunes outrun the potentialities of his forms. Which is not to say that there is no fine music in these earlier pieces, but that Arnell has done better things since. Whereas the First symphony received at the least an efficient performance, the Divertimento hardly received a performance at all. But Mr. Arnell should have been grateful that he was spared the treatment Mr. Newstone reserved for Mozart's E♭ piano concerto (K.449)—soloist: Kyla Greenbaum. So far 1951's worst act of musical aggression. **D.M.**

II. Manchester

AUTUMN AND WINTER, 1950

THE Hallé Orchestra's first concert this season included the Suite, *Escales* by Jacques Ibert—a not unhappy re-working of the exotic fields of orchestral colour. Harriet Cohen was the soloist in Bax's *Concertante for Piano Left Hand*. A disappointing composition, containing material in no way distinguished enough to invite serious development. In the *Adagio and Fugue* for strings (K.546) of Mozart the pleasing quality of the Hallé viola tone came through well. Parts of the concluding *Enigma Variations* had finesse and bite : but I was sorry to note that Barbirolli took the " Dorabella " section more hurriedly than is surely consistent with the dignified gentleness that really belongs to it.

A fortnight later, on October 26th, Joseph Schuster appeared as soloist in the Schumann Cello Concerto. He has an extremely fine technique; but his tendency to adhere to a " strict tempo " approach on this occasion caused him to lose sight of the " poetic " aspects of Schumann's genius. The Hallé played Sibelius' *King Christian* music as though it was their favourite selection. In the Roussel Third Symphony I found myself too often listening to the orchestra rather than to the music—a thing one never needs to do in the case of the more richly musical Fourth Symphony. My only criticism of this performance concerned the occasional rawness of the brass section.

In the absence of the Hallé players during their visit to Portugal in November, we heard concerts by the Boyd Neel, London Philharmonic and Birmingham Symphony Orchestras. The programmes offered by the two latter were too conventional (or shall I say *commercial*?) to need comment. On their return, the Hallé presented a Vaughan Williams evening, the one work not by that composer being (oddly enough) Beethoven's Violin Concerto. Barbirolli's reading of the Fourth Symphony in F minor gave a good impression of its gravity. Philip Newman's interpretation of the Beethoven Concerto contained some material not invented by the composer; it also made use of a fair amount of unintentional *col legno* playing, a sentimentally exaggerated *rubato*, and an adventitious piece of tuning-up just prior to the first cadenza.

On December 7th the *Abu Hassan* Overture served to warm up the wind instruments for Mozart's *Serenade* K.388. It was followed by Paul Dukas' dance-poem *La Péri*. Not so obviously successful as the better-known *Sorcerer's Apprentice*, this work has moments of great beauty. In Beethoven's Seventh Barbirolli gave the orchestra the reins. The first and last movements were occasionally choppy; but the slow movement was graceful and subdued to such an extent that *sempre pp* on the cellos and basses brought an effect that was " magical "—since it is seldom sustained so well.

Of the many concerts other than orchestral, I should like to make special mention of that given at the City Art Gallery on October 23rd by the Laurence Turner String Quartet. The members of this group are all Hallé players, and on this occasion they were joined by colleagues who assisted them in the performance of Mozart's *Adagio and Rondo* (K.617) with glass harmonica (or celesta), and the D major String Quintet, K.593. The Schubert Quartet Movement and Bartok's Fifth Quartet were also included in the programme. The pertinacity which enables this ensemble to keep all Bartok's quartets in their repertory is worthy of note at a time when practically most other English chamber players seem to be giving Bartok the go-by.   E.D.M.

III. Liverpool

THE season opened badly, with playing at the Philharmonic scrappy and dispirited, an inauspicious start due in part, perhaps, to internal disorders in the governing body. Martinon's *Sinfoniette* for Piano, Harp, Strings and Timpani (October 10th) is merely designed to explore the potentialities of its heterogeneous instrumental medium; all that results is a competent musicianship which suggests that Martinon's later works might be worth a hearing.

Krips brought about a considerable improvement on October 24th, when his programme included the *Allegro moderato* of Mahler's Second Symphony, played with real authenticity of style. With it went a reading of the Mozart E flat Symphony unusually weighty in the opening *Adagio*, but moving and profoundly felt. Vaughan Williams' *Benedicite* (Boult, November 7th) hardly deserved its resurrection.

By November 21st, when Rignold produced a witty and sparkling account of the Britten-Berkeley *Mont Juic* Suite, the orchestra had found its feet. A fortnight later, Sargent was able to restore our faith in Vaughan Williams' *London Symphony*, and, to end the half-season on December 19th, Rostal and Rignold were both masterly in Elgar's Violin Concerto, where excitement replaced boredom until the end of the *cadenza accompagnata*. Debussy's *Printemps*, closing the concert, received a sounder performance than one imagined possible.

The Welsh Choral Union's performance (Sargent with the Philharmonic Orchestra) of Berlioz's *The Childhood of Christ* gave us some fine playing and choral work, but none of the soloists—Elsie Morrison, René Soames, George Pizzey or Robert Easton, was within reach of the satisfactory. The work is a mixed blessing, and the cavernous solemnity of the soloists made the most of its drawbacks.

Pleasures: Krips' deliberate tempo for the *Allegretto* of Beethoven's Seventh Symphony. The splendid clarity of the Boyd Neel Orchestra (November 5th) in Handel's B flat *Concerto Grosso* and an early Mozart *Divertimento*.

Displeasures: Arrau, doing everything that can be done to Brahms' Second Concerto with two hands and a sustaining pedal, yet not showing a particular awareness of Brahms' intentions (October 10th).

Boult, performing the whole of Brahms' *Requiem* at an almost unvaried *andante moltissimo moderato*.

Fournier, marring an exquisite performance of the " Haydn " Cello Concerto by clusters of wrong notes at the top of his finger-board.

Lilli Krauss and Sargent roaring with Lisztian abandon through Mozart's D Minor Concerto.   H.B.R.

Opera

I. Covent Garden

BEFORE going to the *Queen of Spades* I ran through Tchaikovsky's letters to Nadjedja von Meck. There are three keys to this score. The first is Russian folk melody. The second is the *Pathétique* Symphony. The third is Mozart.

" I not only like Mozart, I idolise him," wrote Tchaikovsky. " I am so much in love with the music of *Don Juan* that even as I write to you I could shed tears of agitation and emotion. . . . When the Adagio of the D minor string quartet was played I had to hide in the furthest corner of the room, so that others might not see how deeply this affected me. . . . To my mind Mozart is the culminating point of all beauty in the sphere of music. He alone can make me weep and tremble with delight at the consciousness of the approach of that which we call the ideal."

On my way in the taxi from Hampstead I hugged to myself the thought that presently, act two scene one, I should be in one of my more select seventh heavens, listening to the neo-Mozartian masque with which Tchaikovsky adorns the ball at Catharine II's court. The heavenly sarabande which harmonically swings wide of Mozart, then swings back again; the Daphnis and Chloe duet with its tender overtones from *The Magic Flute*; the complex and ravishing finale, where Pluto's baritone counterweights the soprano and contralto voices.

" How silly," I told myself and everybody else within earshot in the Covent Garden foyer, " how silly to call the act-two masque Mozartian pastiche. Technically and æsthetically considered, pastiche is as ignoble as what the hairdressers call postiche. It implies that Tchaikovsky went through Mozart with a mouthful of hairpins, snipping bits here and sticking them there. Of course, Tchaikovsky did nothing of the sort. The masque music comes from an inner chamber of the man's being. Call it Homage to Mozart, if you like. No lesser phrase will do. An offering at Mozart's tomb: that's what we are going to hear tonight." In the event we heard not a note. A clean, brutal cut left *Queen of Spades* with no Mozartian residue except the cerulean G major duet with two-flute ritornello for Lisa and Pauline in the boudoir scene. Now, I am not to be taken as arguing that *Queen of Spades* is ruined beyond bearing. What's left at the Garden, even with the masque gone, is value for anybody's money. Tchaikovsky's symphonic apparatus, slimmed and adapted for the lyric stage, presents the English opera-goer with a new and exciting adventure, especially under Erich Kleiber's conductorship, which has made new lights shine in the C.G. orchestra. Messel's sets and Benthall's production are without freakishness, combining elegance with a sharp sense of place and period. The main singers (Hilda Zadek, Edgar Evans, Monica Sinclair, Marko Rothmuller and Jess Walters) didn't give us anything like true Tchaikovskian ensemble on the first night, but all were reasonably well cast and looked like being an impressive team when they had sung themselves in. Technically, Edith Coates' tottery and terrifying hag of a Countess is the most astonishing feat of make-up the London stage has seen in years.

In all these things I take relish, and on their account distribute flowers all round. But let nobody pretend that, with the masque out, Tchaikovsky's basic musical conception is available at the Garden. Some say than an uncut *Queen of Spades* would be too long, others that for technical reasons it would be too costly. Such objections do not apply in post-war Berlin at the State Opera, where I have seen the masque handled with lavish and loving care. If Berlin can give it—and take it—why not London ?

Kleiber, here for three months as guest conductor, made his bow on December 6th, and had a demonstrative round of goodwill applause as soon as he showed his head in the orchestral pit. The occasion was *Der Rosenkavalier*. From the chorus of praise which followed in the dailies and weeklies I do not materially dissent. While Kleiber is obviously incapable of turning all the C.G. orchestral leaders overnight into star soloists of pre-war L.P.O. standard, the fact remains that he woos real eloquence of phrasing from the string choir and rather more certitude and smoothness than we are accustomed to from the rest. But the glory of this *Rosenkavalier* was his tempi which, for the first time in my experience, took the glue out of Straussian sentiment and scoring, substituting therefor something aerial, tingling, double-distilled and triple-Viennese. The Marschallin of Sylvia Fisher gratified musicianly ears and minds: histrionically considered it was, like the same artiste's Elsa and Leonora, just Sylvia Fisher from top to toe. Howell Glynne achieved the rare feat of singing every note but one of the Ochs music absolutely on the dot as to pitch and rhythm. The exception was the prolonged and inhumane high G at the end of the lechery monologue. Glynne can't do much with this. Small blame to him, say I. Welcome to Uta Graf, the new Sophie. At first I judged her voice, though agreeably silvery, to be perhaps on the small side; but she gratified me by holding her own with ease and assurance in the third act trio. Schacklock looks Oktavian every inch; her voice, however, strikes me as a bit cumbersome for the part.

La Tosca (producer Christopher West) was sung against early-Edwardian sets of fruity vintage, including a first-act basilica that rippled from dome to pavement every time anybody opened a door. If Walter Midgley's agreeable tenor was sometimes obliterated, Warwick Braithwaite, who conducted, is not to be reproached in any degree. Puccini's orchestra must here be given its head. Cavaradossi's voice ought to be big enough to go through everything like a nicely oiled bandsaw. Zadek, in the name part, quickly recovered from her initial wobble and flooded the house with lustrous tone. Her second act with Rothmuller, a Scarpia out of the top drawer (despite a dauby make-up which would have killed any less powerful Scarpia at birth), was one of those authentic and unforgettable operatic occasions. A current went through the house that agreeably chilled all spines. The third-act shepherd was sung by a boy, Kenneth Nash. No improvement, I think, on the shrill, rather trembly young woman's voice which we usually hear in this part.

The Dutchman (cond. Rankl, producer Heinz Tietjen) aroused much wonderment and naive exclaimings during the intervals among youngsters whose experimental knowledge of Wagner, all of it post-war, has been confined to the mature works. Never did they suspect that Wagner was capable even momentarily of echoing what they took to be Donizetti. Yet the story and much of the music have a dark power and savour that are miles ahead of the " grown-up " *Tannhæuser* and *Lohengrin*. Fisher (Senta), Norman Walker (Daland) and Evans (Steersman) sang after their individual manners and talents rather than from the inner core of Wagner's conception. Josef Metternich's Vanderdecken was on a higher level. His baritone is rich and solid. More importantly, his Vanderdecken is truly a haunted, stricken being, with an anguish inside him beyond the telling. Dramatic tension sometimes contorts his rhythm. When I heard him he seemed to be turning every dotted note into a double-dotted note, thus imparting a jerkiness to the vocal line which Wagner didn't have in mind. This, however, was a fault of passion, so rare a thing on the current operatic stage that we had better be indulgent about it.   C.S.

II. Sadler's Wells

NORMAN TUCKER is that arch-rarity, an opera house chairman and day-to-day administrator, who knows his way not merely about opera but about operas. Not only has he adapted and lucidly translated *Simon Boccanegra* and *Don Carlos* for his own stage but in the course of unavoidable retailoring he wrote bits into or performed grafting operations on both scores. This latter is a dangerous proceeding, warranted only by hard necessity. We must not pretend that Mr. Tucker's interpolations are all of them miraculously on the Verdian beam. What we may assert is that they are workmanlike and serve their turn. I am supposed here to be writing a notice, not a profile; but a notice of current Verdian enterprise at the Wells without primary reference to the practical nature of Mr. Tucker's directorship would be unjust.

Influenza prevented me from analysing, as I had intended, Mr. Tucker's *Carlos* cuts, which reduce a five-hour piece to the commercial compass of three hours and a half. It is no bad thing, however, to judge what remains on its own merits, which are certainly greater than some critics have allowed them to be. Elizabeth de Valois is in love with Don Carlos one minute and accepting the marriage offer of Carlos's father, Philip II, next minute but one. Abrupt, yes; but, unless you have left your imagination along with your dufflecoat in the cloakroom, there's no difficulty here. Elizabeth's change of front is patently determined by *raisons d'état*, which are as powerful an element in the *Don Carlos* plot (still more in the *Don Carlos* psychology) as or than, the dramatis personæ themselves.

What's left of the score, though utterly independent of *Boccanegra*, ranges like that work from the warblings of Verdi's middle period to anticipations of *Otello*, with occasional hints of that very Wagnerism which Verdi at various times so hotly repudiated. All true Verdians will go to hear and rehear it, for the Wells production is worthy of both rehearing and re-seeing. Favoured by the iron-hard vocal acoustics of a smallish theatre, the voices, most of them pretty strong anyhow, achieve a truly Verdian amplitude which could hardly be hoped for at the Garden. With these qualifications borne in mind, it is certain that we shall never hear *Carlos* better sung in English than it was by Joan Hammond, James Johnston, Amy Shuard, Frederick Sharp, Stanley Clarkson and Hervey Alan, under Michael Mudie's conductorship. Roger Furse's sets and some at least of the dresses are capital. The first act forest was like something out of a Pollock toy theatre which (I say it in all earnestness) strikes exactly the right note of naturalistic improbability. Sharp, as Don Rodrigo in the palace at Madrid, was a Velasquez full-length against an El Greco background: improbable again, but profoundly right. For George Devine, the producer, a nosegay.

I am not of those who, before going into the theatre for *The Barber of Seville*, take off their sandals and lave their souls in purifying waters. Rossini is not as important as all that. Even so, I am bound to side with the critical majority in lamenting Tyrone Guthrie's production. Mr. Guthrie ludicrously fusses and overcrowds a stage which, at the best of times, is so small that you can't swing a cat or a contralto on it. The first act introduced an Almaviva who, got up in pants, topper, swallowtail coat, stock and high collar, looked all set for *Lilac Time*. Late-Regency costume is early Romantic: it makes us cock an ear for the magic of Weber's declining and Mendelssohn's blossoming years. But what Romanticism is there in Beaumarchais or in the *Barber* music, pray ? The night's ineptitudes were mitigated by one good and promising thing—the stageworthy Figaro of Denis Dowling, who has a satisfying voice and uses it with assurance.   c.s,

III. Elsewhere

PADDINGTON, B.C.

PADDINGTON MUSIC SOCIETY: Brian Easdale—" The Corn King," a ritual opera. Paddington Hall, 22nd November, 1950.

THIS story of fertility rites, harvest charms, and even ritual murder, takes place on the shores of the Black Sea, about 300 B.C. The music is in the manner of the early Stravinsky, but not so good. Apart from the orchestration which is brilliant throughout, only a few scenes show musical individuality. This being so, one asks why this opera, composed in 1935 when the savages were still interesting, should be performed in 1950 when ritual murder, Mr. Orwell assures us, is again just round the corner.   P.H.

LES TROYENS A OXFORD

OXFORD UNIVERSITY OPERA CLUB: Berlioz—" Les Troyens." Town Hall, Oxford, 2nd December, 1950; c. Westrup.

THIS performance, half-amateur, half-professional, was quite understandably only half acceptable. While it is permissible to sympathise with a producer who wishes to reduce two operas in seven sections to one opera in three, it is not fair to blame the composer if the resulting concoction takes its own time in coming to the boil. Strong as was the impression made upon me by the Oxford Town Hall chair, which I endured for over three hours, the impression of an all-too leisurely dramatic crescendo was even stronger. Time after time I leaned forward, expecting something to happen to this doctored masterpiece: and as frequently I relaxed again, silently cursing the omission of some of Berlioz's finest pages. Nevertheless, both production and singing were spirited, the one triumphing over problems posed by an unchanging scenic background, the other bidding fair to conquer the niceties of French diction.

The real point of this production, however, is not how well or how badly it was put on, but *why* it was put on. Horace, in the third satire of his first book, tells us of the singers who, unasked, yet persist in singing. What of conductors, who (though conducting be not their métier) persist in conducting? *Injussi nunquam desistant.* If Professor Westrup is to continue as conductor of the Opera Club, thus depriving undergraduates of much-needed experience in the noble art, I look forward to the day when Sir Thomas Beecham (sometime of Wadham College) is appointed conductor-in-chief of choral, orchestral, and operatic functions within the bounds of the University. The appointment being made, Sir Thomas would doubtless spend the greater part of his time giving lectures to the music students on various neglected aspects of musical history. Or should I say " giving lectures to various neglected music students on aspects of musical history " ? Indeed, I still have memories of paying ten guineas a term for " supervision of research " which amounted to less than ten minutes in the whole term, and since the operas in those days were no more complicated than " Idomeneo " and " The Beggar's Opera " I begin to wonder whether music students now receive any supervision at all. Rumours that " The Ring " is to be performed during the coming year suggests that the Faculty of Music will close down altogether.   D.W.S.

213

Third Programme*

MAHLER: SIXTH SYMPHONY (First broadcast performance in England). 28th December, 1950; B.B.C. Symphony Orchestra; c. Walter Goehr.

THIS highly interesting and problematic work is not, as Mr. Dyneley Hussey in "The Listener" (4th Jan. 1951) will have it—" . . . turgid, breaking down, like the poor old dinosaur, under the excess of its own load "—but constitutes an attempt at complete symphonic integration: its relative failure must be set against the high stakes at which it aims. As with all major works of Mahler, the gargantuan size of this symphony springs not from boorishness, megalomania, or even an implied philosophical programme, but from Mahler's conscientious compliance with the formal demands of late-romantic harmony. Thus, once Mahler had found the harmonic idiom and the main themes of this symphony, its size was, ideally, determined. At this point, he could still have reduced both its structure and its significance to the non-committal level of the symphonic poem by leaving out much that can be gradually developed from the themes, and also much secondary matter that gives symphonic depth to the main action; thus introducing a false artistic economy which might please a public of limited powers of concentration. It is a credit to Mahler's artistic integrity that he never took this easy way, but set out time and again to find a structure strong enough to carry the burden of his subject-matter. And here the tragedy begins. There can be no doubt that this symphony does span the gulf of its hundred minutes as superbly as a bridge spans a wide river. Of the many devices that make this feat possible, two of the most important are perhaps the expressionistic, i.e. not in the least histrionic, use of fragments of earlier material in the introduction to the last, and biggest, movement: a search for a new approach to an old thesis quite as convincing as the respective passages in Beethoven's Ninth and Brahms' First; and, even more important, the use of a major-minor motto throughout the work which, developing from the A major—A minor appogiatura of a fanfare between the first and second subject of the first movement, culminates in the major-minor bitonality of the complete sonata-recapitulation of the last movement. Now, it would be wrong to say that these devices together with the rich contrapuntal texture weaving allusions between the movements, are mere feats of skilful engineering. On the other hand, the structure of this symphony cannot truthfully be called a living form. The tragedy is that the vastness of Mahler's design, albeit caused exactly by his thematic material, makes, *in retrospect*, demands on this material which Mahler is not genius enough to fulfil. No use calling his invention trite: it is not a whit triter than that of many serviceable symphonic motives of other composers. But his material, by complying with the harmonic idiom of his late hour, sets in motion a form of such size that Mahler's invention cannot keep step with it. Mahler seems aware of this dilemma, for in every lead-back—the critical moment for his form— he gives the very best he has (cf. the last part of the first movement's development !); he disguises, enriches, re-orchestrates every recapitulation (cf. all the re-entries in the compound-ternary middle movements). He achieves a great deal here, much more than " engineering," but still fails formally : for Form in its highest meaning, though it knows of antagonism between its components, knows of no antagonism between its components and itself. An illustration: the chorale in which the first part of the last movement's development culminates

* See also pp 177ff and 205.

s broken up to make room for the second part's new beginning. This is inevitable on the *level of structure* since the symphony's by now accumulated material demands treatment in a sectional development. On the *formal level*, however, the chorale is too important an event to run to seed in the middle of a development: it ought to crown the development (à la Bruckner) and end it. The fact that it *does*, in vastly augmented shape, crown the last part of the development does not alter the inappropriateness, formally speaking, of its former appearance. On the other hand, this appearance was *structurally* necessary, since a link with the first movement, from which this chorale stems, was needed in exactly that place. Mahler being one of the first artists to put truth above beauty (like the expressionists after him), his choice in this dilemma was obvious.   P.H.

Record Reviews Reformed

BEETHOVEN: SYMPHONY NO. 4 IN B FLAT. OP. 60. His Master's Voice DB 21099-21103.

WAGNER: MEISTERSINGER, OVERTURE and DANCE OF THE APPRENTICES. His Master's Voice DB 6942-6943.

Vienna Philharmonic Orchestra, c. Furtwaengler.

I. The Recordings

WHEN I accepted your editor's invitation to discuss these two sets of records from the technical (i.e. engineering) standpoint I had no original intention of prefacing my review with any kind of introductory *apologia*. But in these days when record " reviews " are written by all and sundry, regardless of qualification or the reverse, it has seemed to me necessary to define my attitude.

First, what do I want from a gramophone record? If the reader is to have any chance of interpreting my remarks aright he must know, for example, whether I play my records on a commercial " radiogram " *sotto voce* with the " top " turned down, or perhaps on a twenty-year-old acoustic monster with periodic pauses for repointing fibre needles. In fact, what I want is the nearest possible approximation to what I should hope to hear in the concert hall; which disposes at once of both alternatives.

It may be useful to describe briefly the kind of apparatus which, in my opinion, can give the best account of modern standard " 78 " records.

The basic requirements for a good motor sound simple; it must maintain constant speed, despite fluctuations of the mains voltage and (in these days) frequency: and it must not be affected by any reasonable variation of running temperature: a third essential is that the unit shall contribute no electrical or mechanical noise to the output of the whole equipment. You will realise how simply all this can be achieved from the fact (as I believe it to be) that only one motor on the English market fills the bill, and that at a cost of nearly £20!

In the best modern practice pick-up and needle (or stylus) are inseparable. In order to save space, and because I am confident that in this I shall not be contradicted, I pronounce the following dogma: that the only adequate means of transferring a signal from a modern disc record to a fine amplifier is by means of a diamond stylus permanently mounted in a light-weight, carefully balanced, moving-coil pick-up. The old " changeable " needles of steel, thorn or fibre

215

belong to a past era; while the so-called " permanent " sapphire stylus is a snare and a delusion—have none of it. Whereas one can hear a thorn needle wearing out from the very first revolution of the disc, equally one can hear a distinct deterioration of quality in the performance of any sapphire after playing 10 to 20 sides. If you use a gramophone at all frequently a good diamond will prove cheaper in the long run and can be shown to cause less record wear.

This is not the place to delve into detail regarding the specification of an " ideal " amplifier. But a few basic essentials may be mentioned; first, and this is most important, its maximum output power should be about double what it is likely to be called upon to supply, even on " peaks ": for example, in a medium-sized room, where you might momentarily need some 8 watts for an orchestral *fortissimo*, you ought to employ an amplifier capable of giving about 15 watts without objectionable distortion. Other points to specify are adequate provision for independent treble and bass control, the employment of the modern negative-feedback technique (which is now almost universal though by no means always fully efficient) and very low " hum-level " *with the volume control turned right up and the bass control at maximum*: these last two being largely interdependent.

The speaker system should be of wide acoustic range and capable of handling considerably more power than it will in fact be required to do. There are several good ones on the market, but none of these are cheap and my final word on this subject must be one of caution: it is a great mistake to cheese-pare over the cost of any link in the record-reproducing chain if you are seriously bent on achieving the finest results. One inferior item will ruin the performance of the entire equipment.

The apparatus used for reviewing the records now to be discussed fulfils all the conditions just specified and incorporates a further refinement in that the treble and bass controls can be set to provide an exact match with the recording characteristics usually employed by Decca and EMI (which are not identical). The range of (audio-)frequencies covered is from about 35 cycles to something above 20,000.

Now to our records. First a few grouses about generalities: the most serious of these are surface-noise and deterioration of recorded quality towards the disc centres, with the periodic over-recording of climaxes a good third. Apart from general human fallibility, which in the long run can be made responsible for any misdemeanour, I recognise no excuse for any of these faults. Material has been developed from which " noiseless " records could be pressed: the deterioration towards the centre of the disc could be largely overcome by employing Deutsche Grammophon's *variable micrograde* technique and leaving a larger diameter " blank " at the centre, while the remedy for over-recording is quite simply not to do it. There are other ills, such as cutter-resonance, cross-modulation distortion, and excessive distortion in the recording amplifier, but our first three *desiderata* add up to a considerable first objective for our recording friends to strive after and I can think of few greater pleasures than to be able to congratulate them, in the not too distant future, on having achieved all three, which would be a major triumph.

Commercial practice, however, invariably lags far behind the ideals of the enthusiast and the fact must be admitted that these seven records exhibit most, if not all of the above defects, to a greater or lesser degree. But by far the most serious is the very marked deterioration of quality as the linear velocity of the groove decreases (i.e. as the stylus approaches the turntable spindle). So long as the volume of the sound recorded towards minimum radius remains below (approximately) *mezzoforte* the reproduction of that sound will probably seem satisfactory, particularly if no very high frequency components are involved; but anything approaching *fortissimo* always sounds harsh towards the latter part of the disc and, if the violins' E strings are involved, doubly so.

Nevertheless, once we are resigned to accepting something substantially short of perfection, these records will be found to store much valuable musical enlightenment and a great deal of pleasure of a kind the scarcity of which makes it all the more welcome.

The Beethoven occupies ten sides which will probably prompt some peevish grizzling about Furtwaengler's choice of *tempi*, a matter which I am happy to leave to the expert attention of Mr. Keller; from the practical angle, though, I must point out that had the Symphony been " squeezed " on to nine, or even eight sides, the recording stylus would have had to cut even closer to the spindle with proportionately more disastrous results.

To save space I propose to set out in note form the remarks I jotted down while listening:

BEETHOVEN, side 1: Background audible but not obtrusive, improving towards mid-side. Recording a little better (i.e. clearer and more spacious) than of the Wagner. Trace of the well-known Vienna " echo " in loud passages. Strings very hard and distorted at end of side.

2: Notice great improvement of quality compared with end of side 1. Strg. *pizz.* very good. Timps. also v.g. 2/3 through side and later. Last climax distorted.

3: *Sfz* at 2/3 side v.g. Coarse at end.

2nd movt.   4: Vlns. not natural at top of range when above *mf.* Otherwise g.

5: Woodwind at 2/3 side v.g. Violin tone inclined to be fuzzy.

6: Vlns. v.g. at perimeter. Instrumental definition exceptional at low intensity level.

3rd movt.   7: Climaxes coarse at end of side. Noisy run-out groove. Otherwise g.

8: Final climax very rough.

Finale.   9: V.g. *sfz* at perimeter, bad " break " to

10: A good side, apart from characteristic rasp of violins at end.

General: No extreme " top " in evidence, but for the most part satisfactory tonal balance is preserved. Lower registers particularly firm and well-defined. Surface noise rather high.

WAGNER, *Meistersinger Overture.* 1: Upper strings well defined, but rather hard in quality. Serious deterioration in last 1½ inches. Background low, only just audible.

2: Too much background noise causing lack of clarity in recording of inner parts. Last ½ inch coarse.

3: Background again too high (note outer groove before music starts). Trumpets coarse at mid-side. Last 2 inches over-recorded.

Dance of the Apprentices.   Some recorded hum throughout, surging at each revolution. Excellent string tone at beginning, but hardens at mid-side. Last climax coarse.

General: Despite the above faults, this set has " life," " atmosphere," " room-tone " or what you will. With judicious top-cut and some bass-cut a very acceptable result can be achieved.

These essentially bald notes constitute a new experiment in taking gramophone records to pieces. Despite a possible appearance to the contrary, all the sides here reviewed attain a general standard which is high when measured by the commercial yardstick. Ordinary reproducing equipment may not disclose all the faults enumerated and there is no doubt that much musical enjoyment can be derived without listening for electrical and mechanical troubles. On the other hand, if the record-buying public were to become more critical the manufacturers would obviously have to accelerate the improvement of their products.

GEOFFREY SHARP

II. The Interpretations

THE Beethoven's introduction immediately explains Furtwaengler's approach, who makes it the extra-duction it is: the evolution of the form out of subdued but pregnant tension. No statement here; only development. Observe the completely different meanings he finds in the *fp*'s of bars 13 and 29-30 respectively: the former no more than a flash, an intense start which is checked sooner than might have been thought physically possible, thus ensuring the ensuing *diminuendo*. The volcanic opening, not *of*, but *into* the body of the movement, over the emotionally and dynamically extensive three-note *crescendo* which leads up to the first *ff* (as also, later, the corresponding *Rueckfuehrung* into the recapitulation), shows that with Beethoven a transition is not a bridge, but rather a stream that could flood any bridge away—even when it seems no more dangerous than a brook, as for instance the first subject's only *pianissimo*, whose urging power Furtwaengler realizes by a wide breadth of suspended and postponed accents. The first subject's—i.e. the basic—tempo he wisely chooses in full view of the second's first theme, which demands a more restrained speed, and which he is thus able to hold back no more than is necessary for the dramatic, i.e. essentially complementary, contrast between the two. If, on the other hand, the imitations entered (as they so often do) with metrical regularity, there would be no unity, because nothing would be left to be united. In fact, Furtwaengler's interpretations, like Beethoven's compositions, always centre on the organisation of complements, of which process there could be no more immediately overwhelming example than the D major—G minor—E flat major imitations of the development. Lastly, the extensive *crescendo* that starts in the coda's 23rd bar sounds, in the assurance of its aim, like an increase of speed transmuted into a dynamic intensification.

With regard to the slow movement, Geoffrey Sharp's prognosis proved true no sooner than it was made. Before Furtwaengler next conducts this movement, he must first enquire what the readers of the *Musical Times* have found out about its tempo when " trying to play the Adagio on the piano "; for this is what we are asked to accept as musical evidence against Furtwaengler's " unmusical," " capricious spell." " You will soon fail," Mr. McNaught foretells his readers who are to have a shot at Furtwaengler's tempo. No doubt they will, firstly because dilettantes always run off in a slow movement and slow down in a quick one, and secondly because the musician will actually have to adopt a quicker speed if he wants to express these most unpianistic themes in terms of the piano. But thus far, and thus concretely, Mr. McNaught does not seem to have thought; he contents himself with unspecified references to " the natural pulse and breath of the music," " the character and feel of the melody," general phrases which you can use for attacking and defending any tempo.

While the *onus probandi* thus still lies on the prosecution, I am obliging enough to mention just one of the many musical particulars which could be brought forth in evidence for the defence, i.e. the principal rhythm quoted by the prosecution: the further you depart from Furtwaengler's slow tempo, the less will you be able to define what Beethoven meant and wrote, and the more closely will you approach what he was at pains not to write, i.e. dotted semi-quavers.

The scherzo offers what in these happy circumstances is an entertaining curiosity, i.e. the only wrong note. In the first reprise's 36th bar, a single player among the violins, who can be heard to have small hands, tries to stretch back to the c"♭ from the lowered third position: a valiant if eminently unsuccessful feat of over-compensation, for he never really gets down and has to glide up again to the g"♭ on top of it all, like an avalanche in reverse. I mention this accident because if he had taken the fifth on two strings, nobody would have heard anything amiss; but no self-respecting fiddler would nowadays do such a thing: for the sake of an unrealized evenness of colour or *legato*, we sometimes hear the most awful noises.

Among the widely functional details of the finale, the richly felt shape of the first subject's lyrical violin phrase merits particular attention, while the exceptional logic of the contrast between the *legato* of the second subject's antecedent and what we might call the Diabelli-slurs of the consequent in the *Wechseldominante* is so obvious that one would not have to mention it at all, were it not for the fact that in the recapitulation a new subtlety is added: now that the consequent is in the dominant and therefore on a higher level in the violins, it is, to begin with, bowed more lavishly; only the cadential motif, that is to say, is phrased in marked pairs of slurs—a dimly hoped-for surprise which satisfies the inter-related requirements of sound and meaning, in that it takes into account the timbre of the E-string, the more obtrusive force of the higher level of pitch, and, most important, the need for variational recapitulation, as well as for some emotional broadening-out in view of the closing up of the entire structure, whose continuing tension is yet ensured by the restraint of the last quavers. Typical of Furtwaengler, too, and unlike anything one hears elsewhere, is the *crescendo* of the exposition's closing section, or, on the other hand, the incredibly soft cello continuation at the beginning of the recapitulation, or again, in the coda's first part, where first and second violins alternate in the basic motif's descent to the tonic, the continuity of the phrasing across the parts, particularly of the *diminuendo*, or, finally, the stressedly indistinct, muffled basses after the first *fermata*.

Of the *Mastersingers'* Prelude, the present rendering is the greatest I have ever heard, even from Furtwaengler himself: an unassailable majesty and dignity and, at the same time, an ardent passion, expound the problem of the opera in musical form. Furtwaengler is the only conductor who really heeds Wagner's tempo indication (" Sehr maessig bewegt "—which, in " English," means literally *molto moderato mosso*, or, in a more familiar term, *moderato molto*), thus disclosing the self-respecting, assured heroism in the theme of the masters. At the end of the recapitulation this appears in a yet broader, but also yet more intense form, sustained as it were by elemental feeling which, instead of exploding, has turned round upon itself in order to help mastering itself, achieving a triumphant union of original genius and traditional knowledge, of inspiration and communication, of becoming and being, not without an inevitable note of resignation. In the matter of tempo it will further be observed that stricter and freer sections alternate according to the development of structure, texture, and concomitant poetic significance; perhaps most obviously so at the dominant juncture when upon the opening masters' theme the love motif enters and eases the texture, claiming first a slight increase and later a decrease in speed, while with the motif of the entry of the mastersingers (whose dactylic upbeat is, for once, rendered as an upbeat, losing thereby none of its firmness) we return to stricter time, though the weighty intensification of its continuation is enhanced by a tense broadening of the pace. The prize song in E major is again treated as freer section; and in its interplay with the ensuing motif of the A major part, short-term alternations of (in themselves nowise static) tempi serve to build up the climax that is interrupted by the development section. This, as far as the master's motifs (now humorously treated) are concerned, is once more in a stricter and, incidentally, unusually swift speed: a point unnoticed by the critics who think that the present interpretation is " too slow." The tempo of the interjections, on the other hand, is of course freer and urgent.

That of the *Dance of the Apprentices* (*Maessiges Walzer-Zeitmass*, i.e. moderate waltz tempo) takes very minute account of the later counter-melody in the celli, whose interpretation and execution will delight friend and critic alike. Less obvious, the unprecedented understanding of the two *forte* triplets which, standing at the end of *crescendi*, are followed by sudden *piani*. Least obvious, but perhaps of the most inspired mastery, the less than imperceptible hesitation in the a" which introduces—makes the *staccato* dance tune submit, surrender to—the cello cantilena.   H.K.

PERIODICALS RECEIVED:

    Etude (July, August, September, 1950).
    Musica y Artes Visuales (nos. 4, 5, 6).
    Musique et Radio (September, 1950).
    Opera (Vol. I, nos. 3, 4, 5).
    Union Compositores Escritores (nos. 45, 48).

MUSIC RECEIVED:

Stainer & Bell Ltd.
    Taverner: Dum transisset Sabbatum.
    Morley: My bonny lass she smileth.
    Wilbye: Adieu sweet Amaryllis.
    Thomson: The Old Fisherman.
    de Lara: Suite " In the Forest."
    Handel (arr. Foster): Mirth and Melancholy.

Paterson's Publications Ltd.
    Murrill: Humpty Dumpty (A Handelian Fragment).

Bærenreiter-Verlag.
    Sweelinck: Psalms 55 and 122.
    Telemann: Concerto for four violins.

Boosey & Hawkes Ltd.
    J. S. Bach: Gavotte (arr. for Woodwind Quartet by Noel Cox).

W. Paxton & Co. Ltd.
    S. Karg-Elert: Deux Ritornelles transcr. from J. P. Rameau.
    Handel: Royal Fireworks Musick arr. for organ by J. Stuart Archer.

Shorter Record Notices

CHAMBER MUSIC BY BACH AND OTHERS

Two contributors to *Music Survey* were unhappy about the Stuttgart Chamber Orchestra's Bach concerts in London last year, but to me its playing showed a musical face much liker Bach's than any of our customary simulacra here and Decca will, I hope, have been thanked by many more than me and my household for snapping up this band to record Bach's music. The *3rd French Ouverture* in D (AX 314-6) offers the orchestra's faults and talents in almost equal proportions. The string execution often seems mechanically cold (e.g. opening Largo or Aria) and the ornaments are realized with a flawless accuracy that excludes expressive meaning, a fault even more evident in this set's fill-up, an arrangement of the prelude " Ich ruf zu Dir " which enshrines Bach's art exquisitely but to a point of loveless impersonality. That is true, too, of the poker-faced reading of the famous Aria, from which continuo is obstinately and painfully omitted. But when we survey what is left—the clean tone, splendid trumpet playing and indeed general ensemble, excellent tempi, overall feeling of chamber texture and interpretative ideals—the set can still give enormous joy, even if the dots in the overture should be shorter and the ritardandi at the closing bars less emphatic. The *4th Brandenburg Concerto* has fewer faults of this kind, and it offers fine-toned, sensitive, happily conceived solo playing, though poorly supported by the band as far as balance in reproduction goes; but the tone is far more vivid than in the Ouverture (where the strings sounded boxed up). The finale only just gets away with a frenziedly precipitate tempo (AX 319-20).

Further to these Bach bicentenary recordings by Decca, one of the solo violin sonata in C (AK 2378-80) has been made by Ossy Renardy who has already proved himself (in a record of Paganini's *Le Streghe*) a wizard technician. His playing here is not altogether clean nor his intonation unimpeachable, and he scrapes rather; the double stoppings in the fugue especially are made to sound too much like hard work, so that it seems to be composed of lumpy chords, not melodic lines, while the Largo's subordinate harmonies mean next to nothing. The bad workman blames his tools and this set seems to suggest that the violin writing is incompetent which Campoli, Neveu and others before them have superbly denied.

Walton's violin sonata was indifferently, even unconcernedly played at its first performance, but the same artists, Menuhin and Kentner have now recorded it (DB 9514-6) with reassuring efficiency and enthusiasm. The ravishing passages more than make up, on repeated hearing, for the pot-boiling sequential transitions (which, when you are performing them yourself, seem actually worthwhile). *Pace* H.K., the greater part of this sonata had to be written by somebody and the rough is musico-logically necessary to the smooth of the beginning, recapitulation, coda and at least three of the variations. Esquire's exotic and often rewarding issues offer a minor delight, and a bewilderment, in Honegger's unaccompanied *La Chèvre* and Roussel's *Andante and Scherzo*, Op. 51, in which the flute is joined by piano (TW 3-005). Jean Pierre Rampal's tone wobbles foully—this is well-nigh stagnant vibrato, the equivalent in puff of quadruple tonguing)—but as the piano tone resembles cascades of broken glass the recording may be suspect. Honegger's lovely piece is quite well-known but the

Roussel deserves attention. The New Italian Quartet cannot work up much enthusiasm for Schubert's glorious *Quartettsatz*. Ensemble and attack leave little to be desired, but the leader's tone grows tenuous in high places and all the time there is this grey atmosphere of exhaustion about the reading.

Friedrich Gulda's début is made (AK 2168-9) with Mozart's piano sonata in D (K. 576). His rhythm is firm, pedalling possibly exaggerated by the recording (in the Andante almost more hammer than note is heard), approach certainly errant on the inflexible side. The phrasing of the Rondo's theme is aggressively curt and the Alberti accompaniments exude a sternness fit to rap the tunes over the head for their melodiousness. Not this pianist's piece nor, I suspect, his composer. Backhaus quits HMV for Decca (AX 361-2) with an authoritarian reading of Beethoven's Op. 109 sonata. His point would seem to be that, since the variations are the work's core, attention must not be distracted by the beauties of the preceding movements, which he accordingly rattles through like a traveller driving through, say, the Lake District with no concern in his head but to get from Doncaster to Edinburgh. Sonorous chord balancing in the variations and, by its lights, an impressive interpretation— but not a thrill to be had. The horrid reproduction vividly recalls those pianos fitted with running water that Dali is so fascinated by.

Lastly a batch of Lieder by Strauss. Ellabelle Davis, with a voice curiously like Marian Anderson's turned soprano—glorious timbre, shaky breath-control, and over-accentuation of imperfectly enunciated German words (" wie einst *ww-yim* Mai ")—nevertheless brings much beauty to " Allerseelen " and the less well-known " Befreit " (which opens magically with a characteristic modulation from E minor to D flat); the pianist sounds as if he is sight-reading (K 2381). Lotte Lehmann's voice comes off badly, and her pianist too, in " Wozu noch, maedchen," " Die Zeitlose " and " Du meines Herzens Kroenelein " (DA 1943). The old seduction of her inimitable singing pops up now and again but really it's a depressing issue. Chloe Elmo is unaccountably featured in the same composer's " Staendchen " and Brahms's " Feldeinsamkeit " (Cetra reprint R 30025)—voice, choice; style, vile.

RAVEL'S " RAPSODIE ESPAGNOLE "

BEINUM and the Concertgebouw of Amsterdam bring this celestial work back into the catalogue (AK 2093-4). Virtuoso execution and interpretation, magnificently recorded; note particularly the mellifluous cor anglais tone in the last movement. Beinum's dynamics in I and his tempi in III are surprising but as a display of orchestral control the set is a winner.   w.s.m.

BACH: CHROMATIC FANTASIA AND FUGUE
Schnabel. HMV DB 9511-12.

OF all Bach's harpsichord works, this and its great neglected sister-work, the A minor Fantasia and Fugue, most nearly lend themselves to the piano, even the modern instrument. A superb harpsichord performance such as has not yet come my way might tempt my aesthetic appreciation but it would not shake my conviction that such works give of their best on a piano.

For such a realization a pianist is needed who will not force the tone, who will treat the piano as nearly as possible as a harpsichord, allowing it to speak for itself, and is content to let the work shape itself by its own superb composition. Such performers are so rare as to account fully for the general dissatisfaction with the use of the piano for Bach's keyboard music at all. Schnabel's performance, however, fulfils all these conditions: there is no higher praise. He rarely plays Bach; when he does, it is noticeable that he chooses such works as the Chromatic Fantasia or the C minor Toccata, another of Bach's " piano " works. Maybe his rare abstinence in this matter of Bach's keyboard works indicates that he, too, feels that the works which lend themselves to the piano are few.

On the odd side he gives the D major Prelude and Fugue from Book I of the " 48," superbly played and as surely lacking in conviction. It needs a harpsichord.　　　　　　　　　　　　　　　　　　　　　　　　　　　　H.T.

SCHUBERT: SONATA, Op. 42
Lili Kraus.　Parlophone R 20585-8.

SINCE Schubert is one of the greatest visionaries and experimenters in music, whose visions are always applied direct to practical ends, his piano-writing is of supreme interest. Although it is orchestral in its origin, to use this fact as a derogatory criticism is thoughtless and absurd. Scarcely any other composer except Beethoven has revealed *in such variety* the capabilities of the instrument; and there is scarcely any vital nineteenth or twentieth century development that does not owe its inception to Schubert.

Miss Kraus's egotistic performance is not quite so bad as her previous annihilation of Op. 143, mainly because the latter's debatable issues are far more numerous and acute; but even so the interpretation practically obliterates the music. She cannot maintain one tempo for four bars at a stretch; after a slight ritardando she cannot remember the original tempo; she quickens where the texture lightens, thus facilitating the technique, and slows up where her fingers find difficulty; she presumably plays from a very faulty memory, for where Schubert writes the first strain of a variation twice to vary details, she plays the second version each time (the same thing happens many times in the finale, seriously affecting the balance of the movement); there are innumerable wrong notes; and her pedalling is that of a beginner who cannot control hands and feet simultaneously. Performances of this kind do incalculable harm.　　　　H.T.

ELGAR: SYMPHONY No. 1 in A♭, Op. 55
L.P.O., c. Boult.　HMV DB 21024-9.

REVALUATION set in very soon after Elgar's death in 1934, and, as is usual with such a big figure, went to extremes. Neither the partisans who see in him the embodiment of all that is English nor those for whom he is disgustingly and emotionally out-of-date have a true picture of this fine and spasmodically great composer.

His first symphony was long in maturing, as was Brahms's. It was the first really important work of the kind by an Englishman, or so his contemporaries believed, and the weight of responsibility while writing it must have been heavy.

He was always prodigal of material and sometimes rode horses he could not control. He could not batter into shape as did Beethoven, nor had he the cruel self-criticism of his beloved Brahms. Both his symphonies are attempts to do again what Brahms did wonderfully in his third symphony, a work which Elgar probably admired more than any other of its kind.

The first movement of this symphony presents a tonal idea worthy of Beethoven or Schubert—the clash of the tritone—but it is never worked out: only echoed, and, in addition, Elgar made two vital mistakes. First, by making the introduction cover merely the double statement of a tune, which is subsequently used only as a distracting motto: second, by inserting a second group in a fully established F major. From that point on one cannot see the wood for the trees, either tonally or thematically. F major should never have been established in its own right but used merely as an aspect of D minor, and the second group material should have been sufficiently dependent to be absorbed into the structure instead of obscuring it.

The Finale fails because it is an attempt to take up and resolve a problem the statement of which has been repeatedly foiled, but the two middle movements are most successful considered as one unit, and the slow movement is one of Elgar's most perfect utterances. Indeed, in spite of everything, including incidentally the blatant over-scoring of much of the symphony, Elgar comes here almost within reach of visions which will never trouble the bulk of our composers, who may rest easy in their beds.

This performance does homage to the letter of Elgar's spirit but is marred by: (a) too heavy-handed a treatment in all but the slow movement, which is superb; and (b) Boult's characteristic slow grasp of the music. In spite of its age and the vast subsequent improvement in recording matters, the original Elgar version is far finer and has a typical quivering nervous energy which this set lacks.   H.T.

GLAZUNOV: VIOLIN CONCERTO in A Minor, Op. 82

Milstein and R.C.A. Victor Symphony Orchestra, c. Steinberg.

HMV DB 21085-7.

IN spite of the organised reaction against " romantic " music much of it still remains popular. Glazounov was one of its most consistent, if lesser, practitioners. His violin concerto falls into two parts: the first a compressed Lisztian design of exposition, a very episodic slow movement development, and recapitulation, all extremely terse and proving to be but a prelude to a high-spirited Finale of great breadth. Glazounov's music has momentum from the very first bars and he knows how to make episodic development really develop, while Liszt never finishes beginning or begins to develop.

As a performance this is one of the finest concerto recordings in my experience. Milstein's playing is not only great violin-playing, but an object lesson in teamwork with the orchestra which is all too rare. The recording in every way matches the performance.   H.T.

PARLOPHONE'S " CETRA " SERIES

GEMINIANI: Concerto Grosso in D Minor, Op. 3, No. 2 (R 30011-2).

This is in the very worst tradition of 19th century performances of 18th century music. If proper tempi had been adopted the work would have gone on 10-inchers. The playing is dull and the continuo (on a piano) completely unimaginative. The performers shall be nameless.

CATALANI: " Ebben ? ne andro lontana " (*La Wally*) and
BOITO: " L'altra notte " (*Mefistofele*) (R 30005).

These two are sung with complete lack of subtlety by Onelia Fineschi, whose coloratura is not quite up to the rather tricky little cadenzas in the Boito. The dramatic values are enhanced considerably.

BOITO: " Son lo spirito che nega " (*Mefistofele*) and
VERDI: " O tu, Palermo " (*I Vespri Siciliani*) (R 30007).

Poor Boito, twice butchered to make a Roman holiday ! I suppose Signor Cesare Siepi would have been booed off the stage if he had dared not to insert the laughs and general bugabooery into Mefistofele's aria. I'm quite certain Boito would have loathed it. The enormous fermate on the top E flats are quite gratuitous. In contrast the Verdi aria sounds so noble as to verge on dullness, which is a great pity as it is a fine aria and Signor Siepi has just the right richness of voice for it.

(Both the above records are accompanied by the Orchestra Sinfonica della Radio Italiana, conducted by Arturo Basile. The recording sounds fairly spacious, but the voices are too near the microphone.)

VERDI: " Va pensiero, sull' ali dorate " (*Nabucco*) and
VERDI: " O Signore, dal tetto natio " (*I Lombardi*) (R 30008).

These two choruses are sung with obvious enjoyment by the EIAR Chorus, accompanied by their orchestra and conducted by Gino Marinuzzi; I'm glad to say that some of the enjoyment is communicated to the listener.

VERDI: " Sull fil d'un soffio etesio " (*Falstaff*) and
ROSSINI: " Selva opaca " (*William Tell*) (R 30004).

There's a lot to be said for saving the best till last, and these two arias sung by Lina Pagliughi are far and away the most satisfying of the bunch. In Nanetta's Fairy Song she is perhaps just a little too placid, but her tone is consistently beautiful. The Rossini makes one realise how superbly he wrote for the voice, and is well worth getting in spite of the fact that Pagliughi takes four breaths where two should have been enough, at the beginning of the second verse. She also alters the last few bars so as to finish on the top A flat. Nevertheless. the general impression is one of great beauty. Although the recording is a little boxy, the balance between voice and orchestra is quite good.   J.J.N.

Correspondence

31, ASHLAR ROAD,
WATERLOO,
LIVERPOOL 22.

15th January, 1951.

SIRS,—It was no concern of mine to suggest that Milhaud did not know his business; in the conditions of modern journalism, one can do no more than attend to the point at issue, which is surely that *Le Pauvre Matelot* is an ineffective opera. The music has passages of great beauty, is written with unfailing style and is never less than masterly in its deployment. But as it is music for a stage drama, its business is to comment upon, elucidate and point the significance of whatever is happening upon the stage, which, under operatic conditions, must be a matter of vocal expression, for the operatic composer can only create character in terms of vocal expression. Without the creation of character, there is no drama. The fact that Cocteau and Milhaud were aiming at " naturalistic " opera is irrelevant; the work must stand or fall on its dramatic appeal.

Naturalistic opera is so nearly a contradiction in terms that the critic feels it unnecessary to analyse in detail the failure of a distinguished work—for the Milhaud opera is certainly that—which deals in *sprechstimme* with banal dialogue. The work is bad drama, so it follows that it is ineffective opera. Every opera, from Gluck to *Albert Herring* and *The Little Sweep*, which has been an artistic or popular success, has depended on characteristic vocal statement.

H. B. RAYNOR

192A, PAMPISFORD ROAD,
SOUTH CROYDON.

17th February, 1951.

SIRS,—Signor Dallapiccola's quotation, via Schoenberg, from the 1st movement of Mozart's G minor Symphony reminds me of the following " revised " version of the passage I have seen in an old Breitkopf and Haertel score as well as in one by an English firm of the early 19th century (Stanley and Jackson, if I remember rightly):—

[*Stanley and Jackson*]　　　　　　　[*Dallapiccola*]

Ex. 1　　　　　　　　　　　　Ex. 2

HAROLD TRUSCOTT

226

MUSIC SURVEY

(KATHLEEN LIVINGSTON   WILLIAM W. LIVINGSTON   DONALD MITCHELL)

CONTENTS

VOL. III, No. 4

JUNE, 1951

Editorial

PROFESSOR J. A. WESTRUP—AN APOLOGY

IN our issue of March, 1951, under the heading " Les Troyens à Oxford" (Page 213), we published a review over the initials of Mr. Denis W. Stevens by the second paragraph of which it was implied that Professor Westrup, Professor of Music in the University of Oxford, was devoting so much of his time to conducting undergraduate operatic performances that he was unable to carry out his proper function of lecturing to music students and supervising musical research and that he was taking money from music students in respect of duties which he was not performing.

Both we and Mr. Stevens are satisfied that there is no truth whatsoever in the allegations made by the Article and both we and Mr. Stevens desire unreservedly to withdraw the same and to offer to Professor Westrup our sincere apologies for any injury to his reputation or otherwise caused by the Article.   D.M. ; H.K.

Thomas Roseingrave

PREFACE TO AN UNPUBLISHED EDITION
BY DENIS STEVENS

THE several fascicules of *Analecta Hibernica* are silent regarding the early history of the Roseingrave family in Ireland, although the Chapter Acts of Christ Church Cathedral, Dublin, mention the name in 1661. Daniel Roseingrave, the first prominent musical member of the family, was organist of Winchester Cathedral at the time when his son Thomas was born, in the year 1690. The family returned to Dublin in 1698, and Thomas entered Trinity College less than a decade afterwards, only to cut short his academic career in 1710 when he set out for Italy, aided by a travelling grant from the Canonry of St. Patrick's.

Two things influenced him in Italy : the harpsichord playing of Domenico Scarlatti, and the music of Palestrina. He became a firm friend of Scarlatti, whose Sonatas ("worthy the Attention of the Curious") he edited in London, and whose visit to Dublin in 1740 he may well have suggested, if not actually arranged. Yet alongside this high regard for the brilliance of Italian keyboard music there was a deep reverence and admiration for Palestrina's style, examples of which, on "scraps of paper" were said to adorn Roseingrave's bedroom.[1]

(1) Hawkins, ii.824.

The result of this enthusiasm for fine contrapuntal textures was a technique of fugal improvisation which excited the envy of Arne, Pepusch, Festing, Greene, and many other musicians of the day— even Burney and Hawkins, who nevertheless censured his " crude harmony and extravagant modulation "[2] and his lack of "elegance and variety."[3]

In 1725 a panel of judges (which was to have included Handel) appointed Roseingrave the first organist of St. George's, Hanover Square, a post which left him sufficient leisure for composition, "a Science too greatly my delight not to be continually my study,"[4] as he later affirmed.

A career full of promise was brought to a premature end by a broken heart, a " crepation," to give it the quaint Italianate term which Roseingrave himself, thereafter intermittently mad, was accustomed to use. Archdeacon Coxe[5] blamed the girl's father; Burney[6] blamed the girl. Roseingrave retained his post at St. George's until 1737, although for some years previously it had been clear that he was in no fit state to carry on his duties. He removed to Hampstead, then to Dublin, where his father had died in 1724 after bequeathing to him the useful sum of five shillings. Perhaps there had been a family quarrel, caused by Roseingrave's appointment at the Haymarket Theatre on his return from Italy, instead of his being " useful and serviceable to the . . . Cathedrall."[7] There were, however, other relations with whom he was on good terms, chief among them William, his nephew, who mentioned in a letter dated 1764 that he had with him his uncle " Mr. Thomas Roseingrave, whose name stands highly respected in the musical world."[8] It was in William's house, on or near the site of Salthill Hotel, near Dunleary, that the composer died in his seventy-eighth year.

(2) Burney, iv.265.
(3) Hawkins, *loc. cit.*
(4) Dedication of *XII Solos for a German Flute.*
(5) *Anecdotes of G. F. Handel and J. C. Smith.*
(6) Burney, *loc. cit.*
(7) Chapter Act of St. Patrick's Cathedral (December 14th, 1709).
(8) Historical MSS Commission, Var. Coll. iv. 138.

The Isolation of Elgar
By A. E. F. DICKINSON

ELGAR, born to bestride the narrow English world and some of the Continent as well, yet born almost out of time, is something of a problem figure. He holds an uncertain place in the heritage which comes to the first notice of cultivated musicians to-day as something which they should try to make their own. In the formative period 1880-1910 such music-making as may be termed English sprang from a provincial and often dilettante society, perpetually devoted to interminable oratorio of all sorts, especially the far from hardy perennials of Mendelssohn and Gounod. In 1873 Macfarren's *St. John the Baptist* was given an enthusiastic reception. Parry's shorter and more critical and concentrated choral settings (*Prometheus* and *Job*) were refreshing but not overwhelming contacts with the passions and accents of literature. *King Olaf* and *Caractacus* shewed a new and combative evangelism in an epic style, dramatically muddled and verbally often grotesque but musically much more impactive. In *Gerontius* Elgar strained amateur choralism (and Protestant tolerance) to an at first shaky point, but the oratorio was not long in placing him on the centre platform, thanks to Richter. The *Pomp and Circumstance* Marches exploited his invention on a broad and firm basis, and the adaptation of a perky Trio-tune from the second for the Coronation Ode, however unfortunate a treatment, made that basis nation-wide and immovable. Englishmen now knew that right or wrong, the composer was with them to the end, not worrying, like Parry, about war-making or class bitterness. *Cockaigne* confirmed this love of English things, and *Falstaff* won later an appreciation of its suggestive fantasia.

In oratorio *The Apostles* and *The Kingdom* maintained the new combination of fervent choralism and unparalleled orchestral virtuosity, and the two symphonies settled that Elgar was a considerable composer for the classical concert-hall as well as for aspiring choruses. The second symphony appeared to conserve a sense of national achievement, along with some terrifying hints of nemesis. Meanwhile Parry and Stanford had uttered no serious challenge, unless it was Stanford's operas, and as musical leaders they gave generous support to the spread of Elgar's major works, although Parry in particular cannot have wholly approved of so much pursuit of sensuous sound without the bracing sternness of the German classics.

After such going from strength to strength, to doubt Elgar's integrity or greatness seemed to question the nation's progress itself, and to this day Elgar's music is a subject on which liberal comment may arouse unexpected demonstrations of opinion at the highest level, like Wagner's disrespect for English divinities in the past. Nor must a recognition of Elgar's finer qualities be impaired by an impatience with some of his mannerisms of word or tone (cf. descent of a fourth and a second, or multiple sequences). They are so frequent that almost any page of his mature music is unmistakable. Yet plain questions have been* and must be raised about the quality and coherence of his music, and about the dramatic background or foreground which he has selected for musical treatment. We need not bother now about the mixed impressions of *Olaf* and *Caractacus*, and there is no space here for the consideration of the concertos or chamber music. But how far do *Gerontius* and the later oratorios add up to a masterly whole ? Do the symphonies justify their late pursuit of classical forms and idioms ? Clearly they must stand or fall as the last word in musical romanticism. Above all, what about the startling sequences of texture ? For every stratum of musical society there is, perhaps, an ideal style, from the lowly thatched cottage to the ivory tower. But just as rhapsodies on national airs often fail to relate two strata of thought, so a modern appeal to the common man (e.g. by an obsession with colour) may jar upon the more differentiated expression that springs from classical experience.

We may as well grasp the nettle and consider texture first. In Elgar's music there is a very considerable reliance on chromatic harmony and modulation for colour, ranging from palpable diminished sevenths, founded on the minor ninths of the dominant or subdominant (or related chords) to many ingenious touches of accented passing-note and almost audacious sequences. The influence of Smart has been suggested by some critics. These habits pass muster in themselves, but they can easily be overdone. Of the following, *a* is tiresome, *b* stretches a sequence to the utter limit for a climax, and *c* is trite and awkward. Parry's rejection (Oxford

---

* Mention may be made of Ernest Newman's cool treatment of certain works in his early monograph on Elgar, and of Ernest Walker's highly qualified tribute in his *History of Music in England*. See also the contributor's " The drama behind Elgar's music " (*Music and Letters*, April, 1942), not to mention the entirely unexpected counter-blast which it produced from an eminent but in every sense conservative critic. (Ibid, October 1942).

Lectures) of the " reckless profusion " of modern music may seem out-of-date. Yet profusion can be disturbing. With all his chromatics, Wagner's normal harmonic range is much more diatonic.

There is a very pronounced diatonic strain in Elgar too ; reflections of national song of many moods. There are (a) bouncing tunes of cogent rhythm, (b) aspiring phrases of marked curve, (c) dreamy, ethereal utterances, (d) revealing recollections of antique wisdom, (e) wayward phrases. It may be inferred that the *a* class

represents unruly elements which may easily burst their moulds. A very broad appeal carries its own associations ; so does a relish for the *minutiae* of experience. The first may be a relief from the second. Initially it may preclude symphonic development. Classes *b*, *c* and *d* may similarly halt a movement by an irrelevant obsession. Class *e* may be either acceptable and arbitrary musical incidents or inadequate responses to an important dramatic occasion. A simple melodic line or sequence may be a sign of tremendous concentration, like the climactic theme of Beethoven's Ninth Symphony and many Sibelius epilogues ; but it may be merely the plain insipidity of the completely parochial. In discreet measure the second type may pass unnoticed, but it may break down under the strain of would-be symphonic repetition. The prayer-theme in *Gerontius*, the conversion-motive of *The Apostles*, and the Pentecost theme, are examples of such phrases. It almost takes a German to write an *idée fixe* which will stand the wear and tear of the modern orchestra.

The contrast of orchestral textures, simultaneous or successive, is obviously the factor of which Elgar has gained the most confident control, and on which it is hardest to dispute values, since freedom to be exceedingly resonant or subdued, and unison or variegated, is one of a musician's rights of assertion. On the strength of this mastery, principally, certain themes are wonderfully transformed. Which of the friends pictured within the Variations is not flattered by the eloquent intensification or rarification of some characteristic trait or chance association ? *Falstaff* is equally resourceful. Both works have naturally their commanding moments. But moving in a near-Shakesperian kaleidoscope of infinite variety, they can relax easily, touched with a humour for which Gerontius and the apostles can find no room. It has to be replaced by the interplay of shattering and serene experiences, with external utterances (Gerontius's priest, Peter, Judas, Jesus Christ) as a sort of neutral objective ground. The proliferation of clue-themes also calls for special emphasis as they reverberate. Thus *Gerontius* and the later oratorios each achieve a tremendous climax by primarily dynamic means†. All too audibly the pitch has then to be lowered to that of a conventional semi-tutti. We may contrast, perhaps, the peak of *A Sea Symphony*, where a moment of vision illuminates a voyage which the soul is impatient to make. The flashing mystic moment is dangerously like the fire in which the Lord was not. The listener is scorched (if he is at all inflammable) but waits for more, something that could not be Walhalla aflame or any rake's progress—and is apt to pass on, disappointed.

A good deal of other evidence could be easily collected to shew a passion for over-emphasis, or perhaps for indiscriminate emphasis. Also, of a weakness for " light and shade." We may concede a certain pride and pomp of initial or final assertion in the symphonics and elsewhere (even *The Kingdom init.*). But the scherzo of the first symphony is constantly overscored ; in the first movement of the second symphony the final swelling out of the motto-theme is egregious ; in the next movement the transition is more exciting than the second subject ; and the first subject of the finale is vulgarised by insatiable splashes of colour. On the other hand, the rescoring of the first subject of the Larghetto is masterly.

The string *Introduction and Allegro* shewed once and for all that Elgar was not dependent on brass, and in fact his handling of wind and wind-string textures is almost a monument in itself. Yet

†*Gerontius* as the soul encounters the divine glance ; *The Apostles* at the commissioning of the disciples ; *The Kingdom* at the Pentocost revelation.

the consciousness of power is at times obtrusive, and Elgar is more prodigal of both tutti and semi-tutti than Wagner. A constant *glissando* of dynamic values (and melodic lines, cf. second Symphony, first movement, *fin.*) gives his orchestration a nervous and often spasmodic impression. The ear is never at rest. There is a certain dread of the obvious.

It remains to decide how far these pronounced and not obviously homogeneous impulses can make up a total that is more than the sum of its distracting parts. The popular Variations for orchestra are much more than a set of variants of a pre-determined pattern. Their happy colouring and portraiture have been stressed, and the resourceful expansion of theme, with freer fancy in three variations, is a thoroughly original and virtually symphonic accomplishment, well able to absorb the proud rhetoric of " Troyte " and " Nimrod " and (on the whole) "E.D.U."§ Yet *Gerontius* aims at much more. It challenges Parry (*Job*) on his own ground of a universal spiritual drama, with the orchestra at last on equal terms with the voices. In clear but informal stages a steady stream of vocal declamation (solo or choral) combines with a revealing orchestral development. The structural method of interlocking clue-themes is Wagnerian. The drama is not Wagnerian, nor is it external, but the ritual stages of the great transition gripped Elgar and carried him over the more loquacious lines of the long selection from Newman's poem. Choral interludes of considerable range and cumulative power culminate in an ecstatic outburst (Praise to the holiest). The final rapture of this passage (one of the most urgent moments in musical experience) is well and truly prepared by a process of gradually simplifying sequences, and it is intellectually convincing because it has already been shown how in perfect man the life of God has broken upon the world completely, and may continue to break now and again. The judgment scene is impressive, and the entry of the Angel of the Agony, but the aftermath and epilogue are surely too conventional. Yet here is a compelling work, in which a vital English oratorio tradition and Wagnerian music-drama find a true fusion. The moments at which the motives are noticeably worked in are rare enough not to disturb.

The later oratorios nominally apply the same methods to what was planned as a trilogy. In fact much of the text is neither dramatic nor epic but quotation, not necessarily calling for music at all. The

§The original finale was expressly extended to make it " more symphonic " (letter from Elgar to Richter, quoted in the appendix of Basil Maine's Life of the composer).

238

motives are correspondingly artificial and uneven in quality, and too often used in random, meaningless succession to keep up the rhythm. The Judas and Magdalene Scenes are not convincing, nor the disciples' improving speeches. Nevertheless, there are uplifting moments. It was thus difficult even for the composer, most convincing of conductors yet, to avoid a spasmodic effect in delivery. The last part of *The Kingdom* is a finely constructed fantasia, no more.

It is a clear case of trying to build up a work from a missionary plan, instead of by taking (or making) a text which needs music on the scale chosen. *Mastersingers* sets out to exploit the Guild teaching and message, but as singing manners, and so far musical ; where a mastersinger is didactic, he is humorously original or surrounded by counterpoint. Not so the canonised ! Again, in *Messiah*, neither epic nor dramatic in form, a rich imagery carries Handel readily from number to number, making an epic of the long-familiar symbolic phrases. Christian apologia lacks both drama and imagery.

The symphonies followed at leisure these oratorios and the two mature overtures, *Cockaigne* and *In the South*, both fine patterns round one main *Affekt*. It is not surprising that the first symphony, lacking words to explain each fresh turn, seems to aim at *embarras de richesse* in every dimension. A motto-theme encloses the sonata forms of first and last *Allegro ;* the Scherzo has at least three themes besides the Trio ; the finale-introduction has three themes. The crux is the first development, which labours the themes inconsequently and overloads some of them with orchestration.‡ Thus after the inevitable return-procession, the motto is just one more figure, though a brilliant one. The Scherzo, too, is laboured Till Owlglass humour or rhodomontade (which?), and the Trio is weak. The effective *context* and relevance of the shapely slow movement makes the loving sequences acceptable. (Compare, unfavourably, Borodin No. 2). The finale is the finest movement. The sublimation of the powerful second-subject theme in the centre of the movement is just what is needed to justify the triumphant restatement of " motto " as well as present material. Let us admit slips of style in this symphony, but not miss the final Schubertian abandon, in which the many strands of the work converge ; something of which the German, Czech, Russian and cosmopolitan schools were incapable.

‡Observe especially figures 15, 17, 27, 28.

The second Symphony is more deliberate in construction. Letting the first two movements pass, with a query for the 12/8 and incessant trochaic feet of the Allegro, we encounter a superb and revealing Scherzo-Rondo. The release from the devastating central episode by way of the bounding trochaic tune, like King Macbeth's porter the only one capable of carrying on in the face of doom, (see Example 2 a (ii)) shews Elgar's fine sense of occasion at a crucial point. The finale is blithe and loosely put together, and the cadences of the second subject (Example 1a) are rather repellent, as has been said earlier. The epilogue is satisfying in its wistfully chromatic style. There is no romantic symphony I should like to have conducted more.

No. 1 in A flat is an obvious choice for a commemoration of English music. It preserves a firm image of a resplendent, confident era. Even if its continental idiom and reckless pride are utterly superseded, there will always be an orchestra and an audience for its imperious *élan*, and not only in one nation.

The second Symphony has altogether a more thoughtful cast, and more haunting moods. Between them they constitute a dignified revival of thinking (without concepts) in more or less predictable classic stages, in a striking series of relationships between one tutti and another. It is odd that the third Symphony never came to fruition in the next twenty years. But how much more gauche to have produced it before it was truly composed. It joins Beethoven's tenth (and Sibelius's eighth ?) as a document in that glowing intimation which carries its own standard of expression and rejection. It would have taken English music much longer to gain confidence if, there had not first been the gorgeous and intimate flashes of self-assertion known as the mature works of Edward Elgar.

[We are grateful to Messrs. Novello & Co., Ltd., for permission to reproduce the music examples quoted in this article.—Eds.]

Richard Arnell

By PAUL HAMBURGER

RICHARD ARNELL was born in London in 1917. He studied composition at the Royal College of Music with John Ireland, and wrote, between 1936 and 1938, a number of works of which some have been performed in public. His " real start " dates from 1939, when he settled in New York to remain there until 1947. Opp. 1 to 47 were written during this time. (His opus numbers are almost chronological, the main exception being the second Symphony, written in 1942, but numbered among the *opera* of 1944.) His music was quickly acclaimed and the majority of his works publicly performed in America: a remarkable achievement for a composer of his age. Leon Barzin, to whom the fourth Symphony is dedicated, conducted Arnell's " New Age " Overture in 1941 and his violin Concerto at Carnegie Hall in 1946. His Cantata on Stephen Spender's " The War God " for soprano, chorus and orchestra was broadcast at the time of the first United Nations Conference at San Francisco in 1945. In 1947 he returned to this country, and Opp. 48 to 63 comprise the completed works written in England to date. His talent was recognized upon the performances of his fourth Symphony and third string Quartet at Cheltenham, and, more recently, of his *Sinfonia quasi Variazioni* under Norman Del Mar. The first London performance of his ballet Suite " Punch and the Child " under Beecham will be given at a Festival concert. His new ballet, " Harlequin in April," commissioned by the Arts Council, is at present in the repertoire of the Sadler's Wells Theatre Company.

Arnell is one of the most original of young composers. Since he has defined his style to a degree—and that not only in his recent works—which makes one exclaim, at characteristic places, " This is real Arnell ! " he should be entitled to be searched no longer, in the critic's customs house, for " influences." But seeing that, historically speaking, nothing comes from nothing, and that the evaluation of style is, as distinct from its appreciation, at best a matter of comparisons, I will say that he is a pupil of Prokoffief, fortunate enough never to have met the master; a pupil of Stravinsky, lucky enough to keep out of the Boulangerie, and a student of Hindemith's music who never set foot in the Musikhochschule. The sympathetic figure of Ireland, his one and only actual teacher, may have furthered the liberal humanism of his outlook, but has left no musical trace. It would indeed be difficult to find an English composer so much outside, yet not opposed to, the English musical renaissance. He understands, with the possible exception of twelve-tone music, every current musical style, and, moreover, every modern psychological attitude to the problem of composition : in his composition class at the Trinity School of Music he lets his students pose the subjects (which have included such unorthodox ones as " Climate and Musical Style ") and then just introduces the students' discussion with his own remarks. Yet, in his own writings, one can hardly call him an eclectic, not even in the good sense of this much-maligned word. He is too sure of the individual meaning of his music, even if his style should, especially in earlier works, point to Hindemith. The only label which could, conceivably, apply to some of the recent works, such as the piano Concerto and the piano duet Sonatina, is " neo-classical." But Arnell's neo-classicism has not the tendency of Hindemith's or Shostakovitch's to foster a musico-cultural tradition by pious exegesis or by mocking complaisance. It is not, in fact, tendentious at all, but merely consists in his mastery of presenting the most complex, at times even unnecessarily involved ideas in the simplest matter-of-fact manner.

He stands for no nonsense in the business of composing and has no pre-conceived ideas about it. Transitions are left out where conventionally they ought to be, while they turn up where Arnell wants to have them ; the counterpoint is harmonic rather than linear, denying itself the loquacious adroitness of Hindemith ; the form, with all its precision, wears, quite becomingly, the air of a genius' untrammeled arbitrariness. He approaches the problem of modern sonata form (and he has written a great many sonata movements) in a manner that fits his own style and nobody else's : at least three distinct groups of material are introduced in an exposition (mono-thematic structures are, on the whole, alien to him) ; the development is often inserted episodically in the re-capitulation ; the key-schemes are powerful but not at all *recherché*. Vertical and horizontal compression, as distinct from (or even adverse to) precision of speech, mean little to him : they are only occasionally used ; otherwise they would obscure the teeming inventiveness that lurks at the back of the printed notes. His cadences are simple but far from plain. They don't try to say what the last man hasn't yet said, but pursue a very personal image of expressive harmony, sometimes adhering to the same progression in a number of consecutive works. His own brand of chromatic major-minor harmony is hardest to grasp where it looks disap-pointing on paper; the stretches with the fewest accidentals are often harmonically the most extreme ones. He has a most uncanny knack of modulating, not by presenting the credentials of the new key, but by cashiering those of the old. Out of the ensuing inter-regnum, the strongest potential tonality pulls ahead. He is most rhythmical when he is most metrical : a very rare thing. Using the 7/4 or 5/4 extension of common time (openly, or implied) no more than occasionally in the course of a slow movement, he freely ranges up and down the multiples of the basic 2/4 unit without ever changing his time-signature. With him, a sudden change in an Allegro, from quavers to semibreves, acquires a new—at times angular, at times monumental—beauty. As is to be expected, augmentation and diminution come very naturally to him : he often arrives, as in the piano Concerto, at quadruple augmentation of a theme at the end of a work. Strangely, this never happens with the triumphant " I told you so " mien of Reger, perhaps because other forms of the same theme are hardly ever combined with these occurrences ; or if they are, they start in unison and hobble along for a while in what in lesser hands would be dangerously parallel octaves. Here again, Arnell does not set " point counter point," but lets the skeletons of two or more concurrent harmonic progressions find a mutual *modus vivendi*. The more one looks into his music, the more one sees that, with all his technical skill, he lets things happen rather than that he promotes them : a lucky circumstance (for him as well as for us), since his musical instinct equals the enormous driving power of his ideas. This has nothing to do with an " uncritical facility " for which he has sometimes— and at the demonstrably wrongest times—been blamed. Rather is his occasional romanticism a case in question : it is neither shamefaced nor sugary, but always happens at the right moment, and easily suffers the close proximity of very advanced compositional techniques and very differentiated musical meanings.

As is the case with every composer, Arnell's musical personality is more concentrated in some works than in others. While it is always strong enough to arouse interest, there is in Arnell a marked difference between the works that are more, and those that are less amenable to the general listener. It is, of course, in the works less readily understood wherein Arnell's musical character is at its strongest. One of these is his second violin Sonata whose texture alone, among other things, opens up entirely new vistas. I do not pretend to understand this work fully, but I have a strong inkling that the esoteric Arnell will one day be a great revelation to us.

RICHARD ARNELL
LIST OF WORKS
Op. 1.—Classical Variations, 1939. Associated Music Publishers.
Op. 2.—Overture. " New Age."
Op. 3.—Three Songs for Children. Boston Music Publishers.
Op. 4.—String Quartet No. 1.
Op. 5.—Divertimento No. 1 (Chamber Orchestra and Solo Piano).
Op. 6.—Overture, 1940.
Op. 7.—Divertimento No. 2 (Chamber Orchestra).
Op. 8.—Siciliano and Furiante (Piano). Music Press.
Op. 9.—Violin Concerto. Schott.
Op. 10.—Flute Quartet.
Op. 11.—First Sonata for Violin and Piano.

Op. 12.—" The Land," Suite No. 1.*
Op. 13.—Sinfonia quasi Variazioni. Associated Music Publishers.
Op. 14.—String Quartet No. 2.
Op. 15.—Secular Cantata for Chorus and Orchestra (Swinburne).
Op. 16.—Four Serious Pieces (Cello).
Op. 17.—Fantasia for Orchestra.
Op. 18.—Sonata for Chamber Orchestra. Music Press.
Op. 19.—First Organ Sonata.
Op. 20.—Prelude and Presto for Piano.
Op. 21.—Second Organ Sonata.
Op. 22.—Song for Soprano (Dylan Thomas).
Op. 23.—Passacaglia for Solo Violin.
Op. 24.—22 Variations for Piano. Mills.
Op. 25.—Piano Quartet.
Op. 26.—Chamber Cantata for Tenor, Flute and String Trio (Plato).
Op. 27.—Symphonic Suite (1939). Re-written 1943.
Op. 28.—Piano Fantasia G$\sharp$. Study in Thirds. Fugue.
　　　　 " The Land " Suite No. 2.*
Op. 29.—No. 1. Song, " Reach with your White Hand: to me " (Herrick).
　　　　 No. 2. " Never seeke to tell Thy Love " (Blake).
Op. 30.—Partita for Solo Viola.
Op. 31.—First Symphony.
Op. 32.—First Piano Sonata.
Op. 33.—Second Symphony.
Op. 34.—Baroque Prelude and Fugue for Organ. H. W. Gray.
Op. 35.—First Sonata for Solo Cello.
Op. 36.—Cantata : " The War God " (Stephen Spender) for Soprano, Chorus
　　　　 and Orchestra.
Op. 37.—Canzona and Capriccio for Violin and Strings. Music Press.
Op. 38.—Oboe Quartet.
Op. 39.—Song, " Red is the Womb " for Tenor and Piano.
Op. 40.—Symphony No. 3.
Op. 41.—String Quartet No. 3.
Op. 42.—Fugal Flourish for Organ.
Op. 43.—Ceremonial Flourish for Brass. Associated Music Publishers.
Op. 44.—Piano Concerto. Schotts.
Op. 45.—Cassation for Wind Quintet.
Op. 46.—Prelude : " Black Mountain," for Orchestra.
Op. 47.—Trio for Violin, Cello and Piano.
Op. 48.—Second Sonata for Unaccompanied Cello.
Op. 49.—Ballet : " Punch and the Child." (Op. 49A : Piano Arrangement).
　　　　 Recorded by Columbia (c. Beecham).
Op. 50.—Abstract Forms (Strings).
Op. 51.—Concerto for Harpsichord and Chamber Orchestra.
Op. 52.—Symphony No. 4.
Op. 53.—" Recitative and Aria " for Piano. Schott.
Op. 54.—Sonata da Camera for Violin, Villa da Gamba and Harpsichord.
Op. 55.—Second Sonata for Violin and Piano.
Op. 56.—" Caligula " : Ballet and Incidental Music to Play by A. Camus.
Op. 57.—" Blech " Serenade for Ten Wind Instruments and Double Bass.

Op. 58.—No. 1.   Andante and Allegro for Flute and Piano.   Schott.
Op. 58.—No. 2.   Allegro for Trumpet and Piano.   Schott.
Op. 59.—" Ode to the West Wind " (Shelley) for Soprano and Orchestra,
         Op. 59A, Piano Arrangement.
Op. 60.—String Quintet.
Op. 61.—Sonatina for Piano, Four Hands.   Schott.
Op. 62.—Concertino for Violin and Chamber Orchestra (in preparation).
Op. 63A.—" Harlequin in April " : Piano Score.   Op. 63 : Orchestral Score
         (Ballet).
   *From the film music for Robert Flaherty's documentary of the same title.
   Though the film was never released, a discussion of the music can be
   found in *Music Review*, XI/1, Feb., '50, pp. 52f.—EDS.

Lennox Berkeley
By H. F. REDLICH

AMONG contemporary British composers William Walton and Lennox
Berkeley—both in their late fourties—seem historically connected
by a similar approach to the interlinked problems of post-classical
sonata form and post-romantic extended tonality.   Among the under-
fifties they are the last composers to grow up in the comparative
security of the Brahms-Elgar tradition, and both have so far managed
to keep afloat in the vortex of modern cross-currents of style,
successfully integrating elements of atonality in their musical orbit
without jeopardising their artistic heritage.   What the Hindemith
of the early twenties meant to the Walton of " Façade " and the
viola Concerto, Nadja Boulanger and the artistic credo of *La
jeune France* of that period meant to Berkeley.   But here the parallel
ends, and the divergencies of different creative temperaments begin.
Walton established his style with several bold strokes, emerging
as the representative composer of his generation with the technical
masterpiece of his Symphony and the vocal *tour de force* of " Belshazzar's Feast "—an isolated undertaking ; he stopped short at
opera and came to a temporary dead end at the outbreak of the last
war.   Berkeley, whose formative years are similarly delimited,
i.e., by Armistice Day 1918 and the renewed outbreak of war in
1939, and who kept aloof from opera as well as from the more
ambitious vocal forms (with the one exception of the early oratorio
" Jonah," 1937), went through a much more prolonged period of
gestation than Walton.   He became a clear-cut artistic individuality
in the late thirties, i.e. at the exact time when Walton's creative
momentum began to slacken.   From 1940 onwards Berkeley
produced a wealth of instrumental music, starting with the Symphony
(1940) and with chamber music for various combinations (including
the excellent string Trio of 1944).   This music has gone a long way

to establish him as one of the prominent and most promising British composers. The decade between 1940 and 1950—so singularly barren for Walton's genius, except for the belated appearance of the string Quartet and the violin Sonata—yielded to Berkeley a full harvest of symphonic and concerto music, quite apart from a crop of delightful miniatures, such as the " Nocturne " for orchestra (1946), the de la Mare Songs (1948), the piano Preludes (1944) and the Three Mazurkas for piano (1951). In recent years Berkeley has repeatedly tried his hand at compositions for orchestra and pianoforte, emphasizing the exigencies of sonata style and quite deliberately breaking away from the Parisian post-impressionism and musical Pleinair-ism of his earlier years, of which the " Nocturne " is a late but welcome example. In his recent orchestral compositions—the Concerto for pianoforte and orchestra (1948), the Concerto for two pianofortes and orchestra (1948), and the " Sinfonietta " (1950)—Berkeley courageously endeavours to reconcile the rigid demands of traditional cyclic sonata form with the vagaries of his own weakened tonal feeling. A closer study of these works reveals the composer's predicament to find valid substitutes for the customary modulations and inter-relations of basic harmonies. These traditional processes of sonata development are being increasingly replaced by thematic subject-matter intended for variational treatment or canonic imitation, and by melodic growths assuming the air of deliberate stylistic masks :

[The Concerto]

Example 1 indicates how the theme (a) of the piano Concerto's 3rd and last movement reappears, at its recapitulation (cue number 20), in a truly pianistic variant (b), the orchestra supplying the theme in its original form (c). Berkeley's obvious virtuosity leads him occasionally to invent a type of *Tema con variazioni* in which formal pliability eschews to a certain extent thematic relevance, as in the following theme from the Concerto for 2 pianos and orchestra (Movement 2) :

—where the incipit x involuntarily leads to a thematic association with Wagner's early C major symphony (1832) and the incipit of its Allegro subject (xi), of which Wagner with mordant self-irony wrote in 1882 that it belonged to those principal subjects " mit denen sich gut kontrapunktieren aber wenig sagen laesst." In its smooth transformation in the horns (Variation I (Ex. 2(c)) it becomes a musical backdrop to the elaborate passages of the two pianos. Thematic growths of this kind present only the hollow shell of the classical sonata idiom. They live parasitically on the niceties of the texture, surrounding and gradually overgrowing it as ivy overgrows a tree stump. Passages from Chopin, Field, Cramer and other composers of the " brilliant " school of pianists of 120 years ago, act frequently as archaic blueprints for those contrasted subjects in which Berkeley likes to revert to the " premiers amours " of classical tonal feeling under the pretext of a witty stylistic disguise. The introduction to Var. VII (*Tempo di Valse*) of the Concerto for two pianos owes as much to Chopin's " Minute " Waltz as do the three brilliantly conceived Mazurkas (1951), which were quite openly composed in homage to the Polish genius. The wistful brittleness of a Berlioz *cantilena* (cf. *Roméo et Juliette*) is conjured up in the "cantabile" melody of the piano Concerto's second movement with its curious quasi-vocal stresses, the dissonant backcloth of the murmuring strings and the obstinacy of their rhythmic

247

pattern. Such extended melodic formulae lend themselves easily to contrapuntal treatment, particularly if they tend to split up into complementary motivic parts as is the case in Ex. 3. This *ostinato* motif in the accompanying orchestra dissolves in the movement's

coda into the neat and persuasive epilogue of a flute duo, one of the composer's happiest ideas. Example 4 is not an isolated case, but a standard formula used in Berkeley's contrapuntal analysis of melodies. A very similar passage is to be found in Section II of the " Stabat Mater " (1947)—a dialogue of implementing counterpoints in the clarinet and bassoon, echoing the duo of two solo sopranos (consult the vocal score). Berkeley's " Stabat Mater " excels in the sensitive sonority of a chamber orchestra which has successfully assimilated the harmonic austerity of Britten's *al fresco* style. The composer is obviously much more at home in the instrumental sections of this choral composition, as may be seen from the beautiful flexibility and rarified harmonic atmosphere of its orchestral introduction and postludium. These orchestral episodes contrast strongly with the angularity and four-squareness of the vocal partwriting. That the " Stabat Mater " indicates a critical stage in the composer's struggle for a stylistic synthesis is shown by its stylistic dualism ; a struggle most conveniently represented by two violently opposed passages, rubbing shoulders as it were in this work, yet each exactly negating the other :

248

A brilliant example of far-flung tripartite canonic imitation, harmonically buttressed by hardly more than an occasional pedal-point.

A beautiful *a cappella* entry, worthy to be compared to Hugo Wolf's choral settings of 1881, presents Berkeley's nearest approach to traditional romantic harmony. That such contrasts of style are possible within the boundaries of a short vocal work of limited proportions, is a measure of Berkeley's artistic dexterity, but also an indication of the constant danger inherent in any musical style in which the main issue of compositional processes remains as yet unresolved. Neither the sensitive and poetically conceived " Four poems by St. Teresa " for contralto and strings (1947) with the folk-tune lilt of the second song, nor Berkeley's most recent work, the "Sinfonietta" (1950), proffer a conclusive solution. In a way the latter work—charming in its gallic grace but also haunting in the brittleness of its melodic texture—reverts to the models of Poulenc and the Prokofieff of the " Symphonie Classique." That the tonal symbol of musical Romanticism—the chord of the Ninth—plays a determining part in the make-up of its principal subjects may or may not be a portent that a kind of neo-Romanticism is knocking at the back-door. It is a feature well known to the admirers of Britten's latest compositions, with which Berkeley is obviously in increasing sympathy. If these works are really fore-shadowing a new Romantic age in music, the problems of tonality and of integral harmony will have to be boldly faced. Perhaps Berkeley's first opera may prove conclusive where his instrumental pieces have proved evasive. He has certainly earned the right to expect universal sympathy and attention when embarking on the period of his full maturity.*

*The author wishes to express his gratitude to Messrs. J. & W. Chester, Ltd., for furnishing him so liberally with full scores of the works mentioned in this article.

Arnold Cooke:
The Achievement of Twenty Years

By JOHN CLAPHAM

COOKE was born on November 4th, 1906, at Gomersal, near Bradford. His father, Reginald Cooke, had lived there many years and worked in the family carpet manufacturing business. Music-making in the home was frequent, and two of Arnold's uncles, Cecil Stanley Cooke and Perceval Cooke, became professional musicians. Arnold began composing at about the age of eight and wrote a piano sonata when he was fourteen. Reginald Cooke and his family moved to Ben Rhydding near Ilkley in 1920. A year later Arnold was sent to Repton, where he remained for four years and showed a particular interest in the Classics. From 1925 to 1929 he was at Caius College, Cambridge, reading history and music, and on receiving his Mus.B. in 1929 he set off to Berlin to study composition with Paul Hindemith for three years at the Hochschule fuer Musik.

On returning to England in 1932 Cooke became Director of Music at the Festival Theatre, Cambridge. In the summer of 1933 he was appointed Professor of Harmony and Counterpoint at the Royal Manchester College of Music, a post which he held until 1938 when he moved to Hampstead.

The years under Hindemith have left a very strong mark on the music Cooke wrote up to 1936, the year in which the flute Quartet appeared. To Cooke contrapuntal thinking comes naturally. Canons and fugatos are frequent in his music, and when writing figuration for the piano he is often guided by contrapuntal considerations. He also almost invariably choses to write 'vocal' melodic intervals. This may be seen in all the musical examples which follow.

In large-scale works he is keenly aware of the need to apply architectural principles. In the Cantata " Holderneth " (1933-34), for instance, he adopts a symmetrical scheme. The work is in six sections, with the climax in the third and fourth. These are flanked by sections for baritone solo, and the work begins and ends with quiet choral numbers. The third and fourth sections are effectively contrasted. The third is a fugue, which is thrown into relief by the sombre introduction to the words " Midnight blackness " and a brief epilogue using the same words. The section that follows is in ternary form with the outer parts rejoicing to the words " O redolent light," while the middle section for women's chorus is more quiet.

In the instrumental works preceding the flute Quartet, Cooke freely adapts classical forms. Their tonalities, while often somewhat obscure, are concentric both in their entireties and in each particular movement. An exception is the first string Quartet, where the first movement, a fugue, seems to start in the key of G and ends with a bare fifth, A sharp-E sharp, after final entries of the subject in F sharp and D ; whereas the finale ignores any implications of key in the fugue and begins and ends in C. The harmony of the music of this period is astringent and dissonant, with few points of harmonic repose. Concentration on a particular rhythmic theme or figure contributes greatly to the compelling forward motion of the quicker movements. This may be seen in his Concert Overture No. 1, which gained third prize in the *Daily Telegraph* Overture Competition in 1934 and was performed at a Promenade Concert at the Queen's Hall in the same year. There is a noticeable preference for the milder dissonances in this work, a foretaste of his later style, but the Three Pieces for piano written in 1935 and the flute Quartet of 1936 are similar in style to the works which precede the Overture. The Duo for violin and viola of 1935 has been lost, but, judging from brief sketches of it that I have seen, it resembles other works of that period. Its finale combines fugue with sonata form.

The viola Sonata and the Sonata for two pianos, the two works which follow the flute Quartet, are of very great significance in Cooke's development. A casual glance at these two sonatas shows the style to be completely different from that of the flute Quartet and the other earlier works, and the change seems to have come about spontaneously. Cooke had been dissatisfied for some time with the music he had been writing, but had made no conscious effort to effect a change, and was himself surprised to find that he was writing the first movement of the viola Sonata in a new style and with more assurance. In writing the Sonata for two pianos he experienced a greater excitement in the work of creation than ever before, but he had considerable difficulty at first in composing its *Larghetto*.

Cooke had written little for the piano before these two sonatas. He had preferred to write contrapuntal music for several instruments, each playing a single melodic line, and when he wrote an Ostinato,

Intermezzo and Capriccio for piano in 1935 he composed in a rather similar contrapuntal manner. By contrast the piano writing of the sonatas is more harmonic and more typically pianistic. The striking breadth of the soaring viola theme at the beginning of the viola Sonata shows Cooke's newly-found freedom of expression :—

The feeling for tonality is stronger than before but it will be noticed that the composer writes in F rather than in F major or F minor. Sometimes one mode may predominate, but often in his second period works major and minor modes of the same key are judiciously mixed, and at times effective use is made of strings of false relations between major and minor thirds of the tonic chord.

In these sonatas the themes are more distinctive and purposeful than hitherto, and Cooke's sense of humour becomes more apparent : see the pawky theme in the last movement of the Sonata for two pianos :—

In both these works the dissonances are on the whole less harsh than in most of his earlier compositions, and the contrapuntal writing appears to be more logical and to have a clearer aim. The contrapuntal strands or harmonic progressions proceed through dissonances towards their destined goal, a concord. The influence of Brahms can at times be detected. But above all, Cooke here discovers himself and emerges with a significant personal style.

The two sonatas led during the next four years to four other works in which the piano has an important place. These are a piano Sonata, a violin and piano Sonata, a cello and piano Sonata, as well as a piano Concerto completed in 1940 : his biggest instrumental work at that time. This work shows how readily Cooke adapts himself to a new medium. He writes in a genuine virtúoso style for the piano, makes excellent use of the orchestral material he has at hand, and at the same time retains his own vigorous and objective personality. The concerto is an important contribution to modern piano literature.

When Cooke was at work on the first violin Sonata he felt the need to return to scherzo writing ; in this work he combines slow movement and scherzo. Two years later (1941), in the cello Sonata, he wrote his first outstanding scherzo, and, as in the first string Quartet as well as the Passacaglia, Scherzo and Finale, he wrote the movement as a continuous piece of music without a trio, a method he later again adopted in his Symphony. The cello Sonata's scherzo opens with one of Cooke's characteristic exact melodic sequences of diatonic and chromatic notes, a feature found in several places in the immature cello Sonata which he wrote while still at school, and which crops up in all his works. The scherzo begins as follows :—

The cello Sonata of 1941 is in four movements and is the biggest of the sonatas. It is a mystery to me why this work still remains in manuscript.

The Four Shakespeare Sonnets with orchestral accompaniment written for Sophie Wyss were composed in the same year as the cello Sonata. They show Cooke's sensitive treatment of poetry, and deserve to be better known.

Between 1941 and 1945 Cooke served with the Royal Navy and became a Lieutenant. With little time available for composition few fresh works appeared. His piano Trio, which might perhaps be described as a study in canon, was finished in 1944 and partly written while his ship was anchored off the Normandy coast during the period of the Allied invasion. Cooke settled in London again in 1946 and in the following year was appointed to his present post of Professor of Harmony and Composition at Trinity College of Music, London. After submitting his viola Sonata, the Sonata for two pianos and a newly completed Symphony to Cambridge University he had the degree of Mus.D. conferred upon him in 1948.

The Symphony, which has been discussed in greater detail elsewhere,* was written at the age of forty and given its first performance by Sir Adrian Boult and the B.B.C. Symphony Orchestra early in 1949. The inscription on the score, " Symphony No. 1 in B flat " is not without significance. Sonata form has very great attractions for Cooke, and here, as in Beethoven's Quartet Op. 59, No. 1, all four movements are in this form, which is kept alive by frequent unexpected alterations of detail and compressions. The main theme of the first movement has distinction and reaches an impressive climax; the slow movement is one of the most moving Cooke has written; and there is plenty of fun in the last two movements. The Symphony is one of Cooke's most deeply exciting as well as one of his most enjoyable works.

The cheerful " Processional " Overture, written just before the Symphony, shows the ease with which the composer confronts contrapuntal problems ; it reminds one in fact of the finale of the " Jupiter " symphony. The uninitiated is in neither case aware of the ingenuity of the composer. In the Overture two of the main themes are combined in a canon 3 in 1 at the unison and a canon 2 in 1 at the twelfth heard simultaneously. First performed at the Cambridge Festival in 1948, it was repeated in the same year at a London Promenade Concert. In the Concerto in D for string orchestra, commissioned by the B.B.C. and to be heard again at the Malvern Festival this year, Cooke goes back in spirit to the concerti grossi of Bach and Handel.

The post-war chamber works, a second string Quartet, an oboe Quartet, a piano Quartet and a string Trio, are all good examples of Cooke's fertility of invention and assured technique, and together they show a wide range of mood and expression. The string Quartet and piano Quartet both have fine scherzi, and the string Trio has for a middle movement an *Allegretto un poco scherzando* full of humour. In the oboe Quartet there is a notable *adagio* beginning with the expressive melody for the oboe shown here :—

* See Bibliography.

254

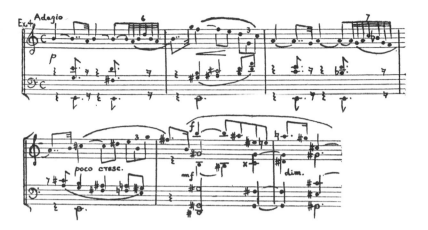

It is interesting to find Cooke turning to opera composition. He has been lucky to secure a well-constructed libretto based on Mrs. Gaskell's novel, "Mary Barton." As he had been brought up in industrial surroundings and also lived for a while in Manchester, " Mary Barton " has had for him a special appeal, and he has readily seized upon the chances the subject offers for delineation of character and emotional and dramatic expression. The choral writing in the Prologue is vivid and realistic. The opera is half finished.

Cooke's music is never complex. His writing is well ordered and he is economical in his use of themes. Vital rhythm is found alike in quick and slow movements. He has virility, humour and a healthy sanity.

LIST OF COMPOSITIONS

Chamber Music

Sonata for cello and piano in D minor (1925-26).
String Quartet in C sharp minor (1927-28).
Passacaglia, Scherzo and Finale : Octet for wind and strings (1931).
Suite : Sextet for brass (1931).
Quintet for harp, flute, clarinet, violin and cello (1932).
String Quartet No. 1 (1933), O.U.P.
Duo for violin and viola (1935) [Lost].
Flute Quartet (1936).
Sonata for viola and piano (1936-37), O.U.P.
Sonata for two pianos (1936-37), O.U.P.
Sonata for piano (1938).
Sonata No. 1, in G for violin and piano (1939), O.U.P.
Sonata for cello and piano in B flat (1941).
Piano Trio in C (1944).
Variations on an original theme for string quartet (1945).
String Quartet No. 2, in F (1947).

255

Oboe Quartet (1948).
Piano Quartet in A (1949).
String Trio in B flat (1950).
Sonata No. 2, in A for violin and piano (1951).

Orchestral Music
Concert Overture No. 1 (1934).
Passacaglia, Scherzo and Finale for string orchestra (1937) [Arr. from Octet for wind and strings].
Piano Concerto (1939-40).
Concert Overture No. 2, " The Processional " (1946).
Symphony No. 1, in B flat (1946-47).
Concerto in D for string orchestra (1948).

Miscellaneous Instrumental Music
Three Pices for piano : Capriccio, Intermezzo and Scherzo (1930).
Three Pieces for piano : Ostinato, Intermezzo and Capriccio (1935).
Suite in C for piano (1943).
Alla Marcia for clarinet and piano (1946), O.U.P.
Rondo in B flat for horn and piano (1951), Schott.

Cantata, Opera, Stage Music, and Songs
" Peer Gynt " : Incidental Music.
" The Merchant of Venice " : Incidental Music. } (1932-33).
Percussion accompaniment to a Greek Play.
" Holderneth " : Cantata for chorus, baritone and orchestra (Edward B. Sweeney), (1933-34).
" Bedtime Songs " : 12 children's songs (A. Rathkey), (1939), Augener.
" Labrador " : Song with pfte. acc. (Hart Crane), (1939).
Four Shakespeare Sonnets for voice and string orchestra (1941).
Song for tenor and small orchestra (Hoelderlin), (1945).
Four Songs for high voice (A. E. Housman, W. de la Mare, Thomas Nash, J. Milton), (1946-47).
Two Songs for baritone (W. H. Auden, Walt Whitman), (1946-47).
" The Death of Gunnar and Burnt Njall " : Incidental Music to Radio Drama (1947).
Music for *Colorado Beetle* Film (1948).
" Mary Barton " : Opera in a Prologue and 3 Acts (A Rathkey) ; adapted from Mrs. Gaskell's novel (1949-?).
" Rain " : Song with pfte. acc. (W. R. Morrison), (1949).

––––––

A piano Sonata (1921), an incomplete piano Trio (1923-25), a violin Sonata (1926-27), a horn Concerto (1928-29), a string Trio (1929) and smaller works have been destroyed by the composer.

NOTE.—Only the works with a publisher's name against them have been published.

[We are grateful to Oxford University Press for permission to quote the music examples from Mr. Cooke's *Viola Sonata* and *Sonata for Two Pianos*.]

Bibliography

Cooke, Arnold, " Paul Hindemith ": *Music Survey* Vol. II, Nos. 1 and 2, 1949.
" Personalia : Arnold Cooke " : *Musical Opinion* Vol. 59, No. 706, 1936.
Clapham, J., " Arnold Cooke's Symphony " : *Music Review* Vol. XI, No. 2, 1950.

Benjamin Frankel

By RALPH W. WOOD

AN article about a composer can be either a diatribe, a panegyric or an introduction—nothing else, to be worth writing at all. There is no ground in Frankel's output itself, and none in his interactions either with other composers or with the public, for a diatribe. Like that of practically any other living composer this side of 60, his work certainly needs, assuming that it merits, introducing to the public ; and since the natural and proper method of introduction—by sufficient performances—is not, as things stand, to be expected, one has to fall back on the other, however inadequate, method : instead of acquaintanceship creating appreciation and—so—demand, scribes and town-criers are necessary to prod into existence a demand that may lead to acquaintanceship being made possible, with appreciation to bring up the rear. As to panegyric, it is usually a fruitless, perhaps even self-defeating, indulgence, which we are well advised to reserve for discourse with people whom we already know to be fellow-enthusiasts. To claim that Frankel is a composer of such stature that his work does indeed merit being introduced to all who have ears, minds and hearts for music is anyway a piece of panegyric of some extremeness. Such composers do not grow on every tree or in every season. The claim is hereby made.

Intently, and quite unobtrusively, this still little publicized composer has assembled during the past twenty years a cluster of chamber-works that it would be reasonably easy under proper conditions for music-lovers to gather into their conspectus, to stack alongside the works of their dozen or so classics and handful of moderns, the accepted quite-familiar but ever-fresh objects of their continued affection and interest. " Under proper conditions " really means, of course, under some utopian dispensation when concert-givers and publishers alike operated with a divine insight into artistic values, and with an equally divine indifference to all but artistic considerations, when all first-rate music (after all, there's not so very much) was in print, and performed regularly, and available in recordings. As things are, the best that can be reported is that a substantial part of Frankel's chamber-music is in print, at any rate. To wit—a string trio ; an " Elégie Juive " for cello and piano and a "Novelette" for violin and piano ; a Trio for clarinet, 'cello and piano; a Sonata for solo violin; and four string Quartets. There are half-as-many-again chamber-works still in manuscript.

As a matter merely of statistics, this seems a rather remarkable output. One cannot think of many contemporary parallels. With a quiet, concentrated pressure this composer of, as it happens, more than usual technical many-sidedness (a flair for choral writing and a generous portion of the philosophical-cum-emotional interests implicit in such work, and again an extreme expertness and brilliance in handling orchestras of very various shapes and sizes, may be instanced) has turned out this series of moderate-length pieces for two, three or four instruments, not to speak of the Sonatas for solo viola and solo violin, that are as consistent in flavour as they are diverse in material detail ; and that, whilst employing a vocabulary markedly restrained and unesoteric, say to us things that are not the same as those we hear from any other music.

This combination of individual utterance, fairly conservative technique and remoteness from any kind of fashion is one of the most striking things about Frankel's music. And it certainly is one of the most important ; for, always uncommon, it is of course the combination that a glance round shows us to have been present in the music of very many of those whom time has proved to be the greatest masters of all.

Perhaps Frankel's most readily approachable work is the Sonata for solo violin. It has been performed a fair, if not a sufficient, number of times, and it is recorded. It necessarily lacks complication of texture. It happens to be exceptionally straightforward in harmonic procedures. " Happens " is perhaps the wrong word. Rather did its straightforwardness proceed from its very fine feeling for its medium. Not that it is child's play. There is plenty of scope in it, both structurally and harmonically, for academic minds to make mountains out of molehills, as is their wont. But no reasonably cultured listener is likely to be baffled by any of it. It is a work that, actually under beautiful control, has an effect of improvising, of moving along spontaneously alike when it is a matter of sombre brooding (first movement), robust joviality (middle one) or a gently intense searching (finale). This, too, this improvisatory manner, is peculiarly happy in a piece for solo violin. But what is important is that it is the manner of, in fact, nearly all Frankel's work.

Consideration of the Sonata is also an easy way of savouring something else that actually is present almost everywhere in Frankel's output. That is its exceedingly expert use of the medium, which reaches a profundity far beyond mere technical showmanship. (This violin solo Sonata is probably the most entirely satisfactory one, raising no qualms and needing no allowances to be made; as positive and natural a piece of music-making, as has ever been written.) Few composers are Frankel's peers in this respect, and he shares with them the quality of absolute untranscribability. Even in a negative way, one that is essential and far too rarely found, he preserves his sense of instrumental fitness, namely in the parts he gives to the piano when it is in harness with strings. Although he is himself a good pianist (as likewise a very capable violinist) such piano parts are markedly restrained. He refuses to ignore the fact that when violins and their kin are in use the less noise a piano makes the better. Accordingly, in such circumstances he confines it largely to held chords, basses, and thin single lines of figuration or counterpoint. (This attitude led him to write one work, the " Sonata Ebraica," Op. 8, for 'cello and *harp*—though practical considerations led him to mark the— extremely good—harp part " or piano.") His music for piano alone is quite another matter, though still notably spare.

The string quartets contain some of the most basically appropriate writing for this alluring but tricky medium that can be found anywhere ; in fact Frankel's thinking in terms of the quartet may be compared to that of Sibelius in terms of the orchestra. This is more than a mere matter of writing suitably for the instruments and of devising textures of the most effective kind for their combination. Quite properly, the medium seems to have affected the music's manner of progression, its rhythmic and harmonic details, its design —in other words the entire composing technique. The prevalent half-contrapuntal character, the tonal fluidity, the apparently artless, improvisatory, build-up of movements (an appearance contradicted, of course, by the power and placing of the climaxes and above all by the characteristic direct finishes, reached without warning, achieved without delay or prolongation, and always —or almost always—absolutely " right ") all appear to come by nature out of the medium. Frankel's methods do apply consistently to most of his work, but it is here that they reach their freeest and most integral use, and one finds oneself automatically regarding the quartets as the summit of his achievement, the truest and pro- foundest realization of his creativeness—though so to assume, thus early still in his career, is no doubt more bold than wise. Whatever their mood, the various quartet movements, entirely without padding, almost entirely without non-thematic material of any kind, have a meditative, " inward " quality that makes them in the best way of all difficult to parallel.

All of his music has an earnestness, remote alike from frivolity on the one hand and grandiloquence on the other, that gives it a peculiarly intimate, searching atmosphere. If you go with one of these pieces at all you go with it not through some delicious impression-bath, nor through some excellently satisfying equations of significant form, but—idea by idea, inflection by inflection of feeling—through an inquiry, a thought-sequence, an adventure of the mind (also, of course, of the heart), not so much talked to by the composer, not even so much listening while he thinks aloud, as sharing with him so to speak the unravelling, from initial entanglement to final orderedness and distinctness, of some emotional-cum-intellectual knot. Which actually sounds rather high-falutin' and difficult, when the truth is that this is music that, whilst not from any point of view facile, mirrors in its creator's reactions those of all men and asks for nothing more from any listener than concentration and sincerity. It is no easier to describe than any other good music is. And above all, of course, we must beware of going across the border into that cuckoo-land (inhabitated by the solemn non-musical philosophers, mathematicians, psychologists, mystics, and what not, of all periods) of actual interpretations, messages, visions, messiahships . . . First-rate music never owes its existence to, or depends for appreciation on the grasping of, ideas that can be either conceived or apprehended in terms other than those of music itself.

But meanwhile we do come to " The Aftermath."

In two compositions for string orchestra that, whilst full of character and altogether better than most " pièces d'occasion," are not quite in the same class as the chamber-works, Frankel, with peculiar purposefulness, wrote music charged with the implications enforced by extra-musical titles. His Mahlerian wealth of expression-consciousness, curbed in the chamber-works to an un-Mahlerian resolution to let the music speak for itself that has everything to commend it from viewpoints of composer and listener alike, was complicated there by a certainly un-Mahlerian desire to address himself to special non-connoisseur audiences. And then in one work he has chosen to seek entire explicitness. What is certainly to be considered as among his most significant products, and one by which he himself is inclined to set most store of all, is a song-cycle.

" The Aftermath " is a setting of six poems by Robert Nichols (for tenor, string orchestra, timpani and off-stage trumpet), but—this is the important fact—so far from starting from the poems and letting them dictate the character of the music, Frankel knew from the outset just what that character, that series of moods, was to be ; and he spent much time and care finding the sequence of poems that would match. So far as psychology, emotion, programmatic content, were concerned, it was a case rather of discovering words for music than vice versa. But that glimpse of the composer's approach (an approach, after all, less unusual than the layman might suppose) must not be allowed to obscure the fact that this was a juncture when all said and done, Frankel wished for once to touch into linguistic explicitness the communicatory gist that always in the chamber-music, though possibly no less precise, stands untranslatable.

In his copious supplying of film music, for both documentaries and features, Frankel tends himself to the view that much has emerged of a more-or-less perfunctory, director-dictated nature and only a small proportion (e.g. "Mine Own Executioner," "Daybreak") seriously representative of him as a composer. This is a refreshing candour, but not perhaps wholly reliable. For here we have a composer so natural, so innate and individual and, so to speak, possessed, that it is probably a lot less easy for him to write quite worthless and quite uncharacteristic music than he himself realizes.

Finally, a word is perhaps expected about Frankel's technical method. One approaches it gingerly. After all, if music has messages that cannot be put into words still less can they be decoded in terms of technical procedures. Belonging to no fashionable " school," marked by the clearest signs of spontaneous feeling and energy, his work is not grateful material for those who like to dig for " systems." He is consistently, and moderately, contrapuntal. He is diatonic, and chromatic, each in moderation ; and he often hints at a bitonality arrived at by the most natural of evolutions and on the spot itself (not by some previous, detached, theoretical decision-taking). Naturally his music is singing music, and full of phrases of real melody (nearly always short ones). It is from the polyphonic incidence of those phrases that the music derives its movement. He gives us frequent cadences, very often as beautiful as they are unexpected, but has to perfection the knack of avoiding their producing any feeling of bittiness. Both melodically and harmonically he has pronounced habits, " finger-prints "—quite futile to list or analyse. Ultimately of course, technique is not a separable factor at all. The "what" and the "how" can never be demarcated.

It is a fact, whether or not a technical one, that Frankel's music very often seems " difficult " at first hearing. Not because it is cacophonous or complex, but rather because its drift, its connections, are elusive. It seems almost too simple, too laconic, too austere, certainly too chary of the expected ; even the familiar has a way of arriving as a surprise. This is a matter much more of the idiom as such, the bar-to-bar build-up of texture and motion, than of the all-over design. The latter, to tell the truth, is rarely complex or subtle, on the one hand, or strongly gripping, on the other. In his almost always short movements (his few longer ones are invariably series of sections) he conveys balance and finality with exceptional sureness. He has yet* to show what he can do in the way of " development " and " growth," what he could make of a really extended movement.

* These words are written before the première (fixed for June 19th, 1951), and indeed before the completion, of the violin Concerto.

LIST OF WORKS

Op. 1   Three Miniature Studies, for piano.
Op. 2   Three Sketches, for string quartet (Version for string orchestra also exists).
Op. 3   String Trio (Augener).
Op. 4   Passacaglia, for two pianos.
Op. 5   " The Compact," Ballet.
Op. 6   Sonata for violin and piano.
—   " Elégie Juive," for 'cello and piano (Augener).
Op. 7   Sonata for viola solo.
—   Two Songs (Words from the Chinese).
Op. 8   " Sonata Ebraica," for 'cello and harp.
Op. 9   " Pezzo Sinfonico," for orchestra.
Op. 10   Trio for clarinet, 'cello and piano (Augener).
Op. 11   " Solemn Speech and Discussion," for string orchestra.
Op. 12   " Music for Young Comrades," for string orchestra.
—   " Pieces for Geraldine," Suite for piano (Augener).
Op. 13   Sonata for violin solo (Augener).
Op. 14   String Quartet No. 1 (Augener).
Op. 15   String Quartet No. 2 (Augener).
—   " Lament " (Wilfred Gibson), for tenor voice and unaccompanied women's choir.
Op. 16   " Novelette," for violin and piano (Augener).
Op. 17   " The Aftermath," for voice, string orchestra, trumpet and percussion (Augener).
Op. 18   String Quartet No. 3 (Augener).
Op. 19   " Sonatina Leggiera," for piano (Augener)
Op. 20   " Early Morning Music," for oboe, clarinet and bassoon (Augener).
Op. 21   String Quartet No. 4 (Augener).
Op. 22   " May Day," A Panorama—Prelude for orchestra (Augener).
Op. 23   Three Poems for 'cello and piano.
Op. 24   Violin Concerto.

Op. 25 " Ani Habatseleth Hasharôn," for soprano voice and orchestra.
—   Music for many films, e.g. " Julius Caesar " ⎫ British Council
                                  " Macbeth " ⎬ shorts.
                                  " The Seventh Veil "
                                  " Dear Murderer "
                                  " Mine Own Executioner."
                                  " Daybreak "
                                  " London Belongs to Me "

ARTICLES ON BENJAMIN FRANKEL

Robert Gill, " The Music of Benjamin Frankel," *Monthly Musical Record*, December, 1948.

Robert Gill, " The Music of Benjamin Frankel," *The Listener*, March 3, 1949.

John Huntley, ' Benjamin Frankel,' *Music Parade*, I/10 (A popular, but factually useful, article on Frankel as film composer by the author of *British Film Music*, London, 1947.)

A note on Frankel's music for the film " London Belongs to Me " will be found in the *Film Music* section in *The Music Review*, November, 1948.

EDS.

A Note on " Ulysses "
By MATYAS SEIBER

WHEN I began reading Joyce's " Ulysses " in 1946 I had no idea that I ever should set part of it to music. I started reading it casually and, I must confess, found it rather hard going at first. But the longer I read the book the more I became aware of its tremendous implications, of its symbolism, of its masterly capture and expression of the totality of human experience. The formal aspect of construction, the verbal virtuosity, the relevance of certain recurring motives which reminded me of musical composition, fascinated me ; and by the time I arrived at the penultimate chapter I was thoroughly in love with the work. This penultimate chapter, particularly, became my favourite and I was gratified to learn later that it was Joyce's favourite, too.

Written in a question-and-answer form, the chapter symbolizes Ulysses' return to his home. In the novel the hero, Mr. Bloom, returns home in the middle of the night with young Stephen Dedalus (Telemachos of the "Odyssey"), unnoticed by his wife who, as in the original, is asleep in the house. After some conversation Stephen leaves and Bloom sees him out. They emerge from the dark house into the starlit summer night. This is how Joyce describes the atmosphere of that June night :

> " What spectacle confronted them when they, first the host, then the guest, emerged silently, doubly dark, from obscurity by a passage from the rear of the house into the penumbra of the garden ?
> The heaventree of stars hung with humid nightblue fruit."

Seeing the starlit sky the hero's thoughts turn to the contemplation of the universe, to the vastness of the stars and galaxies, to the inconceivable distances of space and time. Then, at the other end of the scale, he remembers the minuteness of some living organisms, the divisibility of material into minute molecules and atoms which in the last analysis are only void space. Later his thoughts turn on the phenomena of eclipses and the sudden stillness which accompanies them. Finally he reaches the conclusion that all this is but a Utopia and that the " heaventree " might exist only in his imagination.

I can never forget the terrific impact these passages had on me. I felt as if somebody had expressed in the most perfect form my own feelings—that indescribable " cosmic awe " which overcomes me (and probably most people) when confronted with the starlit sky, and which, had I the power of words, I probably would have described in a similar way. At the same time I knew that I had stumbled on a passage which I simply *had* to set to music—I have not felt such strong compulsion ever before or after. To my mind these passages cried out for musical setting and they appeared to me the most perfect text any composer could wish for.

The text falls naturally into five sections and this suggested the plan of a Cantata in five movements. The first movement sets the scene ; it concentrates on the one evocative sentence :

" The heaventree of stars hung with humid nightblue fruit."

The music begins in a dark, brooding manner. The germinal idea is a three-note motif which becomes the central idea

of the whole work. It is, in fact, an interplay of the major third (or diminished fourth) and the minor third, which, in many different aspects, penetrates the whole fabric of the music. The basic motif and its inversion are developed in an austere two-part setting, the 3-note motif becoming gradually more extended into 4 and 5-note motifs :

This variant is, in fact, a modern version of the Palestrinian "Cambiata," i.e., the approach to a note, the leap over it and the return to it by an inward curve :

After the Solo Tenor has put the question in the first long sentence ("What spectacle confronted them . . . ." etc.), the chorus begins to sing the answer : "The heaventree of stars . . . ." The main motif displays again the basic major-minor relationship :

An extended vocalise on "ah" in close imitation, accompanied

by a fugal development in the brass, works up to a great climax at which appears the word "stars." At "hung with humid nightblue fruit" the music quietens down again and an extended orchestral postlude follows in which the motifs of the vocalise, of the "Heaventree" and the basic three-note motif are combined.

This movement could be described as "atmospheric" music ; it suggests the magic of the night, the opening-up of the summer sky. From the dark colour of the beginning it moves towards the light, ending on a single violin's high E.

The second movement's text deals with Bloom's meditations of "evolution increasingly vaster." Here the imagination soars into the vastness of the universe, to the moon, the milky way, to Sirius, Arcturus, to Orion "with belt and sextuple sun theta and nebula in which 100 of our solar systems could be contained," to the inconceivable distances, lightyears, to the immeasurable eons of time, compared with which human life is but a " parenthesis of infinitesimal brevity."

To express the accumulative weight of this passage, a ground bass movement suggested itself to my mind as the best-suited musical form. The Passacaglia theme is a modern version of the many traditional, chromatically descending ground-basses :

The theme appears not only in the bass but also on top and in the middle, sometimes interspersed with free developments of particles derived from it. The climax is reached in a fugue set against the ground bass, on the words " of our system plunging towards the constellation of Hercules."

This section works up to a cataclismic climax when the ground bass appears in a four-fold canon, piled up throughout the whole orchestra in fortissimo. Then the movement quietens down and the solo tenor takes over to conclude with the reflection on the brevity of human life. An eloquent two-part variation on the strings, in a way, sums up the argument, and the chorus repeats once more, quietly, the first sentence : " Meditations of Evolution increasingly vaster."

In the third movement the hero's thoughts swing to the other extreme : from Makrokosmos to Mikrokosmos, from the vastness of the Universe to the minuteness of the miriads of small organic existences on Earth ; to microbes, germs, bacilli, to the " incalculable trillions of billions of millions of imperceptible molecules " which make up even the smallest object. As a contrast, therefore,

I conceived this movement as a kind of " Scherzo " ; it is the only fast movement in the whole work. Its main section is a fugue with a quick, staccato subject :

This subject again derives from the basic 3-note motif of the beginning, but the relation of the major and minor thirds is reversed :

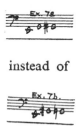

instead of

In this theme the basic three-note group is extended into a twelve-note series of regular structure, with alternating minor thirds and minor seconds. The second half of the series is an inversion of the first :

This theme the basic three-note group is extended into a twelve-note series of regular structure, with alternating minor thirds and minor seconds. The second half of the series is an inversion of the first :

The whole melodic and harmonic structure of the fugal section derives from this series, so that the whole fabric is dominated by the intervals of the minor third and minor second. There are 3 expositions of 3 parts each, the parts entering in 3 different rhythmic relations to the beat. In the second exposition the parts enter in reversed order and the third is in inversion. Between them there are two episodes.

A contrasting lyrical middle section (or Trio) for Solo Tenor reflects on the " Universe of human serum " with its red and white bodies which are themselves universes of atoms and molecules, consisting mainly of void space. Then the main section of the movement returns, the fugue theme appearing as " cancrizans," running backwards. The chorus takes up the words " dividends and divisors ever diminishing without actual division " and the music works up to a percussive climax based on an ostinato. The solo Tenor suddenly cuts into it with a long high A flat on the word " till . . . . " and the orchestral ostinato gradually fizzles out underneath. The Tenor then continues with the conclusion : " if the progress was carried far enough, nought nowhere was never reached." The orchestra recapitulates, for the last time, the fugal entries. This last appearance is the cancrizans of the first exposition, so that it runs back to the initial note E, punctuated by the choir repeating the triple negation " nought," " nowhere " and " never " with diminishing strength until it fades away in a whisper.

The fourth movement is based on a passage some 2 pages further on in the book. It is a beautiful, brief paragraph describing the sudden hush which descends on earth at an eclipse, " abatement of wind, transit of shadow, taciturnity of winged creatures, emergence of nocturnal and crepuscular animals, persistence of infernal light, obscurity of terrestrial waters, pallor of human beings."

I conceived this movement as a " Nocturne," shadowy and dim, hardly ever rising above a *piano*. It bears the subtitle " Hommage à Schoenberg " and its material is based on the two first chords of Schoenberg's piano piece Op. 19 No. 6, which somehow struck me as the embodiment of that quietness and remoteness I wanted to express. Here, again, I used the twelve-note technique. The 2 original chords :

I supplemented with two others, drawn from the remaining notes :

The whole movement is built on these four chords and on lines drawn from them. The quietest point is reached at the words " taciturnity of winged creatures," under which a 12-note chord, a combination of chords 1, 2, 3, and 4 gradually fades away, leaving the chorus alone. The orchestra now begins to come to life, depicting the strange sounds of the night at the words " emergence of nocturnal and crepuscular animals." Finally the movement quietens down again to the pale colours of the beginning and ends by the 2 original chords fading away, note by note.

The fifth and last movement, entitled " Epilogue," sums up the hero's meditations on the universe. He comes back to the original idea of the " Heaventree " and concludes that " it was not a heaventree, not a heavengrot, not a heavenbeast, not a heavenman. That it was a Utopia, . . . a past which possibly had ceased to exist as a present before its future spectators had entered actual present existence."

Just as the text refers back to the original idea, I based this movement partly on the material of the first. The movement begins where the first ended, with the inversion of the basic motif, played high up on a Solo Violin :

Now, however, the motif is extended into a 12-note theme

which develops into an 8-part fugato on solo strings, gradually descending in pitch. The counterpoint is formed from the inversion of the theme. In the subsequent development the movement recapitulates much of the material of the first movement : the " Heaventree " motif (in inversion) re-appears, and so does the long vocalise which, however, leads to a different climax. The whole development of this movement follows the reverse course of that of the first movement. Whilst the first developed from darkness to light, this one starts with the light colours of high strings and gradually descends to the dark, brooding mood of the beginning, slowly fading into nothingness and ending on the low E from which the whole work started.

Although I made ample use of the twelve-note technique in this work, I consider it essentially as tonally conceived. The central key is E and the five movements show a simple key-scheme based on the relationship of Tonic, Subdominant and Dominant :

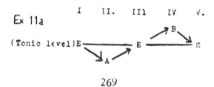

To conclude, just one more word about my relation to the text. I find there are two categories of people : those who see the beauty of this passage as I do, and those who seem to be entirely blind to it. In fact some keep on asking me : "How on earth could you choose just *those* words as a text for your Cantata ?" I must say that I fail to understand these people. To me this is one of the most beautiful passages which has ever been written and no matter how often I read the text —and I must have read it hundreds of times—it always gives me the same thrill as when I saw it for the first time. I do not feel, either, that I " chose " or " found " Joyce's words ; on the contrary, I rather feel that *they* captured *me*. Never was I more sure that I *had* to set a passage to music.

Some critics complimented me that I was able to do something with this " intractable," " indigestible " and " uninspiring " text. Whilst I am flattered by their compliments, I must, most respectfully, refute them. Quite the reverse, I feel that in composing the music I hardly had to do more than follow the words' lead and inspiration. Whatever the merits of my music may be, I feel, very humbly, that it can never measure up to the greatness, to the perfection of Joyce's masterpiece.

[The vocal score of " Ulysses " is published by Schott & Co., Ltd.]

Bernard Van Dieren (1887-1936)
BY DENIS APIVOR

WHEN the young and brilliantly talented Dutch pianist Frida Kindler came to this country in the decade before the first World War, there followed her a young composer who had made her acquaintance in Rotterdam,* through her brother Hans Kindler— later to become the founder and conductor of the National Symphony Orchestra of Washington. Van Dieren, who had an unorthodox education which included the study of science at Leyden, was already an excellent practical musician, and had a remarkable technical facility as a violinist. His official status in his early years in London, however, was that of a critic : he " covered " musical events for the Dutch papers.

The marriage of Van Dieren and Frida Kindler took place in 1910. For a while it was doubtful whether they would settle in England. She had been a pupil of Busoni, a member of the cele-

*Van Dieren's father was Dutch, his mother French. There is no substance in Mr. Lockspeiser's assertion in Edgar Thompson's "International Cyclopedia of Music and Musicians" that he was partly Irish. The date of his birth is often quoted incorrectly as 1884. He was born in 1887.

brated *Meisterklasse* in Weimar, and had worked and studied in Berlin—then the centre of the musical world. Van Dieren did in fact try living in Berlin for a while, but did not find the artistic climate congenial. There was talk of his settling in Paris. In this atmosphere of uncertainty the composer was suddenly struck down with a severe illness which, it later became apparent, was a form of kidney trouble. This malady, often painful and necessitating operations and long periods in bed, Van Dieren fought heroically for twenty-five years until his death at the age of forty eight in 1936.

That Van Dieren should have written so much music is remarkable. Composing is an exhausting form of activity even when one is in good health. But more remarkable still is the fact that his music is so frequently distinguished by a beauty of sound and a serenity which is quite rare in the works of contemporary composers.

The explanation of this special quality of Van Dieren's music is to be found where one might expect it—in the personality of the composer. It is clear from the testimony of those who knew him that his personality was an unusual one, combining as it did intellectual gifts of a high order with a spiritual integrity which was never forgotten by those who had experienced his company. This side of Van Dieren's nature which showed itself in a peculiar lack of self-advertisement as well as in a beneficial influence on other musicians might be called *religious* in the best sense of the term. His fine personal qualities were apparent in his very appearance and he became, at one time in his life, the model for Epstein's *Christ*, a figure in which suffering and nobility of mien are combined. Readers of Van Dieren's book of essays *Down among the Dead Men* might imagine that the composer was a Catholic. He was in fact considerably attracted by Catholicism but never became a member of the Church of Rome. Nor was he an ascetic : his spare time pursuits ranged from revolver shooting to an expert's application to food and wine.

Those who are interested in Van Dieren as a personality will find accounts of him in various publications dating from the early numbers of the *Sackbut* (1920), a magazine edited by Philip Heseltine and Cecil Gray, to the recent volume of Osbert Sitwell's autobiography *Noble Essences* which also contains an interesting photographic study of the composer. Mr. Gray himself writes of him in *Survey of Contemporary Music* and is, moreover, the author of a study of the composer called *The Modern Leonardo* which appeared in the *Radio Times* shortly after Van Dieren's death. The impact of Van Dieren on other famous personalities has been preserved in

271

the writings of Arnold Bennett, Jacob Epstein, and Busoni. Those whose memories do not reach so far back as the B.B.C. Memorial Concert in 1936, when a moving tribute to Van Dieren was made over the air by Sir Arthur Bliss, have recently had the opportunity of hearing Constant Lambert's account of the composer as a prelude to a broadcast performance of the *Spenser Sonnet* and the *Serenade*. Van Dieren was more than a personality who impressed his contemporaries ; he was a creative artist of unusual interest, whose music demands a hearing—and will continue to demand one so long as there is any sort of musical public for the more subtle manifestations of the creative spirit. Unfortunately, however, his work still has to contend with extraneous difficulties : a number of his most important works such as the *Chinese Symphony*, the *Serenade*, the *Diaphony*, and the opera *The Tailor* are still in manuscript, and the tendency of the concert-promoter and performing artist to avoid modern music which is unfamiliar, and requires a good deal of rehearsal, operates against Van Dieren's work. In addition, Van Dieren was a pioneer in the use of what one might call the *selective palette*. He chose the instruments for a number of his works in small groups as a painter chooses his colours—a course of action which is gradually becoming characteristic of much contemporary music, but which has not been parallelled by a change in the mechanism of concert-giving. Works which do not fit the standard orchestra, or require for example a group of wind instruments in addition to a string quartet, may fail to get a performance. Such works are easier to broadcast ; yet the time given to them even by the B.B.C. is not great.

Van Dieren was, however, not content to break new ground in the direction of subtlety of timbres alone. He was early in the field as a protagonist of the sort of contrapuntal approach which in the works of Schoenberg has influenced a whole generation. Look at any score of Van Dieren and you will observe a tapestry-weave of interlacing parts. Where the parts are all taken by smoothly toned dissimilar instruments, as in the *Spenser Sonnet*, the effect is the aural equivalent of a stained glass window, multicoloured and glowing. Where this contrapuntal obsession is carried into the accompaniments of songs the result is less happy, though once the difficulties are overcome the effect is one of homogeneity, and often very beautiful.

In many of his works, some of them written as long as thirty or more years ago, Van Dieren's constructive approach is similar to that which today is employed by such a composer as Dallapiccola.

There are the same wide leaps, the same pointillistic tendencies in the scoring. But Van Dieren's pointillism was never carried to the limits which have been explored by Webern, though there are frequent moments which are suggestive of such extreme lines of thought :—

Analysis of bars 63 and 64 of the *Spenser Sonnet* (O.U.P.).
The string parts have been omitted.

But while there are works of Van Dieren which might be described as tending towards " atonality " (so far as that term has any meaning) —see, for instance, the published song *Rapsodia from Levana and our Ladies of Sorrow*—his music tends more and more to limit itself to a complex chromaticism which, as I believe Mr. Rubbra once put it, fully explores the tonal territory of the seventh but does not go beyond it. The practical result of this limitation is an uncommon degree of euphony, an unmodern gentleness on the ear. This must no doubt have been perplexing to the critics who, expecting the composer to be a " revolutionary," did not find in his music the dissonance usually associated with the works of modern challengers for that title.

As Mr. Cecil Gray has pointed out elsewhere, Van Dieren's harmonic originality consists in the unusual way in which he employs familiar chords so that they come to have unexpected relationships to each other (though purely harmonic writing is uncommon in his work). The process may be seen to advantage in the following excerpts from the song *Weep you no more sad fountains* (Ex. 2) and from the first movement of the 5th string Quartet (Ex. 3) :

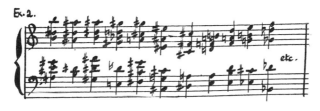

[From " Weep you no more sad fountains." (O.U.P.).]

Ex.3.

[From fifth string Quartet.]

The harmonic and contrapuntal aspects of music are relatively easy to describe and analyse, but the quality that characterizes a particular composer's melodic style is much more difficult to capture in words. The contrapuntalist is essentially a melodist, since for him all the parts must be saying something interesting. Now, Van Dieren's scores teem with melodies which seem quite out of focus with any particular tonality until one hears all the parts together. On the other hand there are frequent moments when he has recourse to a graceful and limpid *bel canto*—plainly the result of his assimilation of the melodic style of such composers as Donizetti and Bellini whom he so much admired and to whose music he drew attention in his essays ; see Examples 4 and 5 :

Ex.4. Adagio Cantando. Fifth Str. Quartet.

[This movement is metre-less.]

Ex.5.

[Published by O.U.P.]

Van Dieren was in fact a master of the string quartet. Of his six quartets, the fifth, dedicated to the Brosa Quartet, is possibly the most rewarding. A few copies of it were published by the *Cecilian Press* before the war, but this concern has now lapsed and the work remains in manuscript.

A similar fate has befallen the Sonata for solo violin which has been played in public and broadcast by Antonio Brosa since the war. This is a work of astonishing mastery and vigour and should be in

274

the repertoire of other violinists capable of doing justice to its technical difficulties.

A number of Van Dieren's songs (amongst other works) are published by the Oxford University Press, including the beautiful and moving *Der Asra* of Heine, as well as settings of Verlaine, Victor Hugo, Beddoes, and Walter Savage Landor. But it is perhaps not generally realized that there are many, and even better songs in manuscript. Of these the most outstanding is a superb group to words of Heine which includes *Seraphine* (an earlier song) *Mit deinen blauen Augen, Ach ich sehne mich nach Thränen, Mir träumte von einem Königskind* and *Was will die einsame Thräne*, all of which were written about 1930. English singers who might be disposed to include Van Dieren's songs in their programmes should know about two late songs : *Fly hence shadows* (Ford), written as a parting gift to a friend, and *A kiss I beg* (Edward Sherbourne), dedicated to the composer's wife, as well as about the existence of numerous unpublished settings of Keats, Shelley, and Byron.

At the time of Van Dieren's death he was engaged on a symphony which remained uncompleted. It is, however, to be hoped that an opportunity will be given to us of hearing some of the other larger works. The writer's impression of the *Chinese Symphony* (a work for five solo voices, chorus, and orchestra, based on translations of Chinese poems by Hans Bethge), from the performance given under Constant Lambert in 1936, was that it fully justifies the enthusiastic advocacy of Cecil Gray and Philip Heseltine during the composer's lifetime.

The opera buffa *The Tailor* contains many witty pages and much fine music in a relatively simple style. It should at least be given a studio performance by the B.B.C.— a method of presentation which has in the past enabled us to become acquainted with the sound of the operas of Berg and Busoni and which has recently been extended to such works as the *La Duenna* of Roberto Gerhard.

Of particular interest too, are the Overture *Anjou* (his last completed work) and an earlier piece—*Marginalia in Musica*, a setting of an amusing passage from De Quincey's *Murder Considered as One of the Fine Arts*. The latter should be ideal for broadcasting ; it requires men's voices only and is accompanied by a bravura piano part. It is almost a miniature operatic *scena* and solves with extraordinary wit and expertise the problem of recitative in the English Language.

[We are grateful to the Oxford University Press for their kind permission to quote the relevant music examples from Van Dieren's works published by them.—EDS.]

A Note on the 'Flower Aria' and 'Passacaglia' in "Lucretia"

BY DONALD MITCHELL

BRITTEN'S complete musical integration is as evident in the operas as elsewhere. Thus no surprise is occasioned by the development of the great *ostinato* finale to *Lucretia's* Act 2—fittingly the opera's deepest piece—from the Male and Female Chorus' unison chorale which virtually opens and closes on both the opera's dramatic action and its music :—

The relationship between Exs. 1 and 2—proof indeed of Britten's personal achievement of Schoenberg's dictum " Let there be unity " —has been well commented on. But in the particular instance I have in mind unity extends farther than has been verbally recognised,* and the promise of Ex. 1 is weightily affirmed in a phrase from Lucretia's Flower Aria (Act II, Sc. 2). Or to put it more accurately a glimpse of the *ostinato* is vouchsafed us long before the *ostinato* itself is revealed. More than a glimpse even, since the aria's eighth and ninth bars contain the *ostinato* figure itself :—

An arbitary quotation ? A leit-motif ? The context of Ex. 3 denies the former since the bars quoted are only meaningful when related to the whole expansive phrasual curve which is Lucretia's

---

* NOTE : Having written this piece I read for the first time Mr. Henry Boys' " Musico-Dramatic Analysis " of *Lucretia* (in *The Rape of Lucretia*, a Symposium, London, 1948), and found that he mentions the *Flower Aria-Passacaglia* relationship as follows : "In the aria which follows, ' Flowers bring to every year the same perfection,' she contemplates flowers as the only chaste existences on earth, 'For their beauty is so brief'—*this an image of her own funeral oration* " (my italics). Since Mr. Boys takes the matter no further I have decided to let my note stand in its original form. Perhaps it may usefully serve as an elaboration of Mr. Boys' comment. D.M.

first (stanzaic) expression of her grief. Nor is it a leit-motif, unless we care to consider it so in retrospect : its significance is not fully realized until the *ostinato* itself has been reached. No, it is more sensible to treat it as another example of Britten's astounding psychological-musical-literary penetration. " For their beauty is so brief " is Lucretia's lament in Ex. 3, and the *brevity of beauty* (the poetic *idea*) is, in itself, as much a dramatic-musical leit-motif in *Lucretia* as the *time*-motif is a dramatic-musical inner-principle in *Herring*. After Ex. 3 from the Flower Aria, what more natural than Ex. 4 from the *ostinato*—moreover to the words "So brief is beauty," the dominating motif of the whole structure, not only musically but also psychologically :—

The same idea, or poetic image, conditions and results in the same musical phrase : Lucretia, so to speak, musically foreshadows her own funeral *ensemble*. Unity could hardly go further. Given Britten's special gifts such unity may be inevitable, but it remains remarkable.

[*The Rape of Lucretia* is published by Messrs. Boosey & Hawkes Ltd.]

Schoenberg

A SURVIVOR FROM WARSAW

Recorded from Italy.

Third Programme, 9th January, 1951, Schoenberg-Time (6 p.m.).
IT is inexplicable why the Third gave only a single presentation of this short and extremely difficult work which, in New York as well as in Venice last year, had to be immediately repeated upon the audiences' request.

Severely enervated by the interference of a motor which completely extinguished one third of the broadcast and reduced the rest often to the almost indistinguishable, I was yet so overcome by what I could hear that I am driven to set down my impressions which, unaided as they were by score or a previous hearing, may not be altogether reliable.

Much is being said for and against the drastic newness of Schoenberg's technique which is here applied in strict fashion, but I think we do not sufficiently realise how new to music, indeed to our conscious minds, are the psychic regions from which this way of composing has emerged and which it explores.

Every honest and musical writer on music knows the paralysing state of " having something to say," for whenever we really have something to say about a musical content, we find that we can't say it : unfortunately one cannot express music criticism in terms of music.* Hence we escape, with full justification, into technical language, for though technical descriptions are far from expressing the whole truth, they have the advantage over metaphorical descriptions of denoting nothing but the truth. Their representational value, however, stands in direct relation to the reader's knowledge of the compositional processes from which they have been abstracted ; for instance, when I suggest that the first movements of Beethoven's op. 59, No. 1, and of Prokofieff's 5th Symphony form a bridge between the potential repeats of their expositions and their actual developments by starting off the latter with the first subjects in the tonic, you know what I mean because many classical sonata arches are part of your experience.

In the case of the *Survivor*, however, a technical description would be of the most limited avail, partly because the compositional processes from which twelve-tone-technical descriptions are abstracted are so widely unknown, and partly also because with this new music the process of analytical abstraction itself has not, to date, progressed very far : the completest technical description of the *Survivor*, from specialist to specialist, would be more incomplete than a popular description of Mozart's G minor Symphony from music critic to Promenader. Thus, while the *Survivor* reveals a new world of possible expressibles, I feel more paralysed than ever. One overriding impression however, I can formulate : Schoenberg has succeeded where psychology (despite Jung) has so far failed, i.e., in establishing the link between two kinds of depth—psychological depth, which is the primitive, the elemental, the instinctual, and artistic depth, which is the sublime, the supernatural. The Romans seem to have known after all what they were talking about when they said *altus* and meant either " high " or " deep " : the *Survivor* shows hell and heaven to be contiguous.

Some time ago I saw a play by Sartre, called *Men Without Shadows*, and dealing with the problems facing some members of the *Résistance* who are being tortured by the Nazis. The piece, complete with torture scenes on the stage, left me completely unmoved. The central point, if I understood and remember it correctly, is that these men who had everything to live and fight for, suddenly find themselves in a situation in which they have nothing left to die for. A very interesting point, in all conscience ; but it never occurred to any of those who, under torture, had given up all hope of survival ; I have seen hundreds of them and was one of them. They were either in religious ecstasy like Schoenberg's chorus, or fear-stricken, or, like myself, in a state beyond fear and courage, a state resembling tired and empty boredom. Sartre's dramatic situation, then, is emotionally unreal and impossible. Schoenberg's musico-dramatic content, on the other hand, is what Schopenhauer and Nietzsche call a "miracle," that is, in the former's description, something which is " impossible and yet real." In exacter words, Sartre shows us " survivors " how we couldn't have felt, while Schoenberg shows us how we really should have felt. Sartre is impossible because he isn't strong enough to imagine our emotional situation ; Schoenberg seems impossible because we would not have been strong enough to experience his message.

* Except for certain forms of unfavourable (including also corrective) criticism. Mozart's *Musikalischer Spass* is a piece of music criticism expressed in music.

278

His is a supreme case of applied music becoming absolute : feeling himself fully, with uncanny depth-knowledge, into the dramatic, still topical situation, he offers an immanent solution which only music can offer and which, to the musical mind, is all the more inevitable for that. Yet Sartre was in the midst of it all, while Schoenberg was on another continent. For the rest, what higher praise can the *Survivor* receive than a musician-survivor's confession that never since his escape from the Nazis did he feel, at the same time, so terrifyingly near and so redeemingly far from the memory of his experiences ?

Schoenberg's own libretto shows a stroke of genius which, *a posteriori*, appears to be self-evident simplicity itself, so that hitherto nobody has commented upon it : the trilingual structure. I write " structure " advertently, for the three aspects thus given, with the contrasts between them, are of basic formal import : the sergeant's German words, imitated by the narrator, pertain to naturalistic—and hence, in the music, psychic—realism ; the English of the narration itself means recollection, retrospection, re-experience, a dream-like catharsis and ab-reaction, and hence, in the music, a psychic " working-out," " development " and interpretation of the traumatic material ; and the final opening sentences of the principal Jewish (Hebrew) prayer correspond to the summit of the musical interpretation : the spiritualisation of the catastrophe. At the same time, from the standpoint and in the sequence of the " story," the alternation of the three languages is so realistic that it heightens the dramatic tension to a point which Sartre's stage tortures never approach. In order to make the narrator appear a refugee, his English should, I think, always be marked by a foreign accent, while the sergeant's German will best be a piercing Prussian. Both these requirements were splendidly fulfilled by Antonio Kurbinsky, whose musical interpretation, too, seemed beyond praise.

The music itself (8 minutes) is so condensed and compressed that it would be liable to burst if the pressure of the form upon the content were not just as strong as the content's pressure upon the form. It is not alone the ecstatic energy, but yet more the extremity of the contrasts which produces the score's powerful build-up of high tensions, a most obvious example being the lyrical and threnodic, yet virile cantabile for the cellos as opposed to the savage percussive cadences or to the shouting of the sergeant. But the most intense single tension, is, of course, the orchestral *accelerando* and *crescendo* which, in a terrific *Steigerung*, accompany the speaker's last words—". . . . they began again counting the corpses, as the sergeant had ordered them, first slowly : one, two, three, four, became faster and faster, so fast that it finally sounded like a stampede of wild horses and, quite of a sudden, in the middle of it, they began singing the . . . . "—and urge up to the massive coda, the figured *cantus firmus* " Shema Yisroel " (male chorus in unison with solo trombone) which a horn has foreshadowed early in the work over broken chords in the strings and a harp bass. The narrator's last word was his first *note* : a clear C sharp. I say " was " because I do not know whether it is Schoenberg's own intention to let the narrator storm into the prayer by way of sudden definite pitch, but in any case the effect was both logical and vehement ; so even if it was only the conductor's (Scherchen's) idea, I would suggest that it be permanently adopted. Neither the drive towards this culmination, however, nor the " Shema " itself, came out very well ; the recording microphones seemed to drown the chorus in the orchestra.

I am the last to minimize the danger of hearing tonal implications into atonal music and thereby injuring connections for the sake of clinging to old harmonic concepts, but despite the *Survivor*'s strict twelve-tone technique certain tonal tinges force themselves upon one's attention at first hearing— not because they seem to be there, but because they seem to be inter-related both harmonically and in regard to their respective positions in the musico-dramatic structure, so that they make a functional impression : hear the D major inkling after the narrator's " I must have been unconscious " and the G minor one after his unaccompanied " . . . whereupon the sergeant ordered to do away with us." This question awaits further hearing or an inspection of the score.

Finally, I can only hope I have said enough to stimulate the reader to hear for himself on June 19, when the work will be first performed in this country— hear for himself that the *Survivor* is destined to be one of the very few survivors from our war-worn musical age. By that time, *Radio Times* and Third Pro-gramme Noter will perhaps have become alive to the fact that the *Survivor* is not the first work in which the *Sprechgesang* " is written on and around a single line " ; the Third Programme listener, at least, should have been referred to the reciter's part in the *Ode to Napoleon* whose score and records he can obtain.   H.K.

Since this review was written, *A Survivor from Warsaw* received its first Austrian performance, again under Hermann Scherchen, at the Fourth International Music Festival in Vienna (April 10th).—EDS.

PELLEAS AND MELISANDE

B.B.C. Symphony Orchestra, Albert Hall, 14th March, 1951 ; c. Boult.

A highly laudable undertaking, a praiseworthy interpretation, a passable performance, an unsurpassable experience and, last but rarest, an excellent programme note (by Humphrey Searle). The younger generation gets to know its young Schoenberg in the light of the old—a fortunate reversal of History who, when she appoints Future's ambassador to the Present, makes the end the cause of the beginning.   H.K.

FIRST LONDON PERFORMANCE
OF VIOLIN FANTASIA OP. 47

L.C.M.C.—R.B.A. Galleries, 24th April, 1951.

MARTIN COOPER'S reaction in the *Spectator* of April 27 :—

It may be that, on paper and in theory, Schoenberg's *Fantasia* has . . . coherence, for he is certainly no joker, practical or otherwise ; but is paper enough, and has history any parallel instance to offer of music eventually recognised by all which was at first totally unintelligible— not merely unpleasing—to well-disposed and musically-trained listeners ?

The question of paper music does not in Schoenberg's case arise, whereas the answer to Mr. Cooper's second question is yes. Nor am I merely thinking of the obvious example of the late Beethoven quartets. Spohr, who himself did not understand Beethoven's 5th Symphony(!), writes in his *Autobiography* (anonymous and bad translation, London, 1864) :

> . . . I was invited to some music parties [in Berlin in 1805]. I first played at Prince Radziwill's, himself well known as a distinguished violoncellist and talented composer. I there met Bernhard Romberg, Moeser, Seidler, Semmler, and other distinguished artists. Romberg, then in the zenith of his fame as a virtuoso, played one of his Quartets with violoncello obbligato. I had never yet heard him, and I was charmed by his playing. Being now solicited to play something myself, I thought that to such artists and connoiseurs I could offer nothing more worthy than my favourite Quartets of Beethoven [op. 18 ! !]. But again I soon realized that, as at Leipzig, I had committed an error ; for the musicians of Berlin knew as little of those Quartets as the Leipzigers, and therefore could neither play nor appreciate them. When I had finished, they praised my playing, it is true, but spoke very disparagingly of what I had performed. Romberg, even, said very bluntly : " But my dear Spohr, how can you play such stuff as that ? " I was now quite doubtful of my own taste, when I heard one of the most famous artists of the day express such an opinion of my favourites.

Can we escape the conclusion that to Romberg op. 18, of all Beethoven quartets, was " totally unintelligible ? "

To me, however, this whole historical argument is somewhat boring, primarily because when a composer's music is part of one's life one does not care very much whether he acts according to precedent, but also because my own experience of musical history tells me that in any case things happen which haven't happened before : has history any parallel instance to offer of a great composer whose music had the fate of Bach's ?

At the same time it must be admitted that the *Fantasia*—Schoenberg's latest work (1949)—is difficult music, at any rate when played as on the present occasion : though Tibor Varga and Kyla Greenbaum were technically excellent and clearly tried their emotional best, the pianist had quite obviously no idea what she was playing, while the violinist's ideas were of a somewhat childish order, the chief one being apparently that the apex of every phrase is its expressive climax. While I am thus the last to claim to have already understood the work, and yet the first to emphasize its immensely powerful effect, I cannot refrain from recording two of my concrete impressions. First, the *Fantasia* seems to me renewed and strongest proof of what I feel to be Schoenberg's fourth period, which has already manifested itself in the string Trio and the *Survivor* (and perhaps, yet earlier on, in the Prelude to *Genesis* which we have not yet had an opportunity to hear). Beethoven, to whose musical character Schoenberg's bears affinities, is generally regarded as pre-eminent example of the three-period genius. I would suggest, however, that he did not live to develop his fourth, which op. 135 unmistakably announces. What exactly Schoenberg's—as well, and similarly, as Beethoven's—fourth period means I shall try to describe on a future occasion ; the return of his latest works to more or less " pure " twelve-tone method is not, of course, the most important aspect of the matter : it is a technical effect rather than a spiritual cause. Second, attention has not perhaps yet been drawn to Schoenberg's condensations of *rhythmic* structure : in this work it strikes one particularly how he leaves out self-evident rhythmic continuations and consequents, the actual consequence continuing or developing the implied and omitted one (or more than one). Perhaps this observation may help one or the other listener in following the thread which, unprepared for the omission, he would have lost. As for the general wailing about " sound," I submit that Martin

Cooper's above-mentioned article does not know what it is talking about. " No sounds," he writes in connection with the *Fantasia*, " are now in themselves unacceptable," implying that Schoenberg's dissonances would be unacceptables *par excellence* if there still were such a thing. He does not seem to have noticed that Bartok's first violin Sonata, which was played before the Schoenberg and which he appears to like, contains particularly " ill-sounding " and stressedly obtrusive consecutive clashes such as Schoenberg has never written and would never write. (I'll play them to him if he doesn't believe me.) I am not at the moment criticizing Bartok ; the fact is simply that Bartok's genius has a barbaric streak which the hyper-sensitie genius of Schoenberg hasn't. I cannot easily forgive an ear which mistakes its anxiety about the loss of tonal unity for a perception of dissonances and of the highest possible tension, and which yet makes its pen write about Schoenberg. The historical disintegration of tonal unity is interrelated, but, of course, by no means identical, with the equally historical emancipation of the dissonance. It would appear that paper music is what Martin Cooper does not listen to.

H.K.

HUMPHREY SEARLE ON
" STYLE AND IDEA "
B.B.C. " Music Magazine," Home Service, 29th April, 1951.

IN our last issue we have tried to show how unwisely certain editors in this country as well as in America have chosen their reviewers for Schoenberg's new book, *Style and Idea*. Meanwhile, the English edition of the work has appeared (Williams & Norgate), and whereas ignorant reactions are still forthcoming both in the general and in the musical press, the editors of the B.B.C's sundaily *Music Magazine* have earned the double honours of including, on this special occasion, a book review in a Review that does not normally concern itself with books, and of being the first to entrust this task to an authoritative reviewer—Mr. Humphrey Searle, who made an exceptionally brilliant job of the few minutes at his disposal, leaving the listener in no doubt about the value of the book. Apropos of Schoenberg's essay on *Gustav Mahler*, the reviewer pointed to the author's humility in the face of great art (a welcome *antiphonia* to the misreviewer's chorus on Schoenberg's " intellectual arrogance ") ; and upon playing an excerpt from the recorded Second Mahler in connection with Schoenberg's remembering " the first time I heard Mahler's Second Symphony[:] I was seized, especially in certain passages, with an excitement which expressed itself even physically, in the violent throbbing of my heart," Mr. Searle proceeded to illustrate certain of the book's analytical observations—on the relationship between the passacaglia theme and the first movement's first subject in Brahms' Fourth ; on the irregularities of the rhythmic structure of " Immer leiser wird mein Schlummer " ; and on the inversion and re-inverted retrograde form of the " Muss es sein ? " motif from Beethoven's op. 135 (the latter inversion resulting in the first subject's consequent)—with music examples on the piano as well as on records : an extremely happy idea which, with the amateur musician with whom I was listening to the talk, was particularly successful in the case of Brahms' IV, where Mr. Searle established the connection between the successive thirds towards the end of the finale and the opening theme of the work by playing the thirds on the piano in between the recorded excerpts as well as during the transmission of the opening. Altogether the review must have made it possible even for a small mind to gather some of the greatness of a great ; one hopes, moreover, that it dispelled some of the sinister air that surrounds a genius who is frank enough to admit his gifts. H.K.

After these lines had been set up in type, another noteworthy review of the book by Humphrey Searle appeared in the Spring issue of *Tempo*.
Style and Idea will be reviewed at length in our Mozart-Schoenberg issue (planned for Winter, 1951/52).—Eds.

TOO GOOD TO BE WRONG

" At the moment, however, we, in common with most of the writers whom Mr. ******† despises for their ignorance, are ignorant about Schoenberg ; so ignorant that we actively dislike his music."

[*Musical Opinion*, May,1951]

† Modesty forbids mention of this critic's name.—Eds.

Film Music
THE HARRY LIME THEME

For well over two years, the Harry Lime tune (from Carol Reed's production *The Third Man*) has pestered the diatonic world ; a recent visit to the Continent has shown that it is in fact becoming a classic : other tunes already quote it, and people who love it are even learning to whistle it.

Almost all popular hits seem vulgar, but since not all vulgarity is popular, the success of the tune asks for an explanation, all the more because one does not remember a previous instance of a hit-song which the light-music lover cannot sing, of a tune that is no tune at all. So far, two kinds of explanations have come my way, the circumstantial and the economical. The circumstantial, which is found among highbrows who pride themselves on their lowbrow practicality, has first been given by Antony Hopkins at last year's International Film Music Congress in Florence, and later also in the pages of *Sight & Sound*. It says that these notes have caught on because in the film they were played on the unusual instrument of the zither. The economical explanation, which I think I got from Benjamin Frankel, points to the commercial propaganda behind and in front of the tune. Both pointers are right ; neither is an explanation.

Not only are there plenty of sufficiently banal tunes which have flopped despite heavy commercial backing, but I have seen many people being struck by the Harry Lime Theme without having been subjected to any kind of conditioning, without even having seen the film and heard its zither. I am one of them. I never saw the film because I hate the zither. When I first heard the music, I at once detested it—as if it were important enough to be detested. As soon as I detest something I ask myself why I like it.

Particularly when I am shocked to find myself whistling it. It is, in fact, time that one turned one's curiosity to the music itself and tried to find an intrinsic explanation for its appeal. The striking, indeed the only feature about this " tune " is its submediant obsession which, avoiding any Aeolian insinuation, creates an extended *appoggiatura*, a suspense by a prolonged suspension, enhanced by the tonic-dominant bass as well as by the alternation of tonic chord and dominant seventh. The sixth is the inhibitory degree *par excellence*, because its opposition to the tonic is based on the strongest possible measure of agreement or *tertium comparationis*, including as only the submediant triad does the tonic third : hence the arch-inhibition, the interrupted cadence V—VI. Hence, too, the added sixth—a familiar jazz device—is the rightest " wrong " note, a harmonic non-harmonic note producing (*ceteris paribus*) the most primitive kind of dissonant chordal tension.

When I drew a colleague's attention to the fact that the Harry Lime Theme was not much more than a figured added sixth, using this degree instead of everything, including the tonic, he very sensitively remarked that the piece had the feel of a *coitus interruptus*—more precisely, of a prolonged *coitus*. In fact, just as the latter may be regarded as both the most elementary and the most elemental application, in adult life, of what Prof. J. C. Flugel (*Men and their Motives*) has called the " principle of increase of satisfaction through inhibition," partially regressing as it does to the unorgastic, fore-pleasurable sexual activities of childhood, so the prolonged submediant inhibition, the insistent suspension of the jazzy sixth, represents the most primitive application of this principle in the sphere of dissonant chordal formations. (In chordal progressions, the consequences of the interrupted cadence V—VI are, of course, the prototypical example of such an increase of satisfaction).

It is imagineable that the musical primitivity of this harmonic maneouvre corresponds to a relatively unsublimated amount of, perhaps, infantile sexual energy behind it ; this state of affairs would account for the " sexy " character of the tune to which a well-known singer has directed my attention, and which my own feeling confirms ; it would also account for one's disgust at (i.e., unconscious, infantile love of) the tune's banality.

I immediately asked this singer whether he could think of another such sexy tune, and his associations anon supplied the one-time hit *Sous les toits de Paris* (from the film of, I believe, the same title) where, sure enough, the submediant (likewise arrived at chromatically from the dominant) also plays a strong and inhibitory role.

The primitive itself is not bad, aesthetically or morally. Rather is it beyond —better: before—good and evil. Prolonged *coitus* may revert to infantile pleasures, but as soon as it is practised with a view to affording the woman gratification, it assumes a highly altruistic and thus adult significance.

Mr. Anton Karas's tune is in the main too primitive to be bad (except for the so far unmentioned and indeed unmentionable tonic resolution) : a bare harmonic structure with an ornamental pattern instead of a melody. That the same harmonic device (in the same " primitive " key of C !) can serve as basis for something good is shown by Kurt Weill's *Moritat* (from the Tobis-Warner production of the *Dreigroschenoper*) :—

Weill indicates " Blues-Tempo " ; to me the blues' influence seems even to extend to the melodic-harmonic structure, in that the tune apotheosizes that submediant which we hear in certain blues in place of the leading note and with a VI⁷ implication : by an extreme inhibition of the tonic, the submediant here downright usurps it. Owing to the quality of the melodic line, we are no longer disgusted at the primitive inhibition, though in order fully to appease our unconscious conscience we may have to murmur something about the decadent German twenties. Decadent the tune certainly wishes to be, an aim which it achieves by the submediant's *unbroken* dominance over the tonic : if we adhere to our psychogenesis, we may here be confronted with a musical phantasy of the so-called method of *Karezza*, i.e., prolonged *coitus* without *ejaculatio*. We in our civilization tend to regard this practice as decadent, but there are sects which have ritualized it, the purpose being a supreme and sublime test of will-power as well as concentration on the spiritual aspects of the beloved. From the purely medical point of view, it would seem that we are right, in that the practice is both physiologically and psychologically idiotic, but then, with Weill's tune, the medical point of view does not arise. Possibly, if unconsciously, Weill exhibits decadence as it were in inverted commas in order to show us that decadent art is never where we look for it : he seems to offer a parody, not so much of decadence, as of our conception of decadence. In any case, the art of love can tell us something about the love of art. Not much perhaps, yet much we do not readily think of.　　　　H.K.

Reviews of Music

Arranged in alphabetical order of composers' names ; joint review at end of section.

DENIS APIVOR : The Hollow Men. (T. S. Eliot), set for baritone solo, male voice chorus and orchestra. Vocal score. (O.U.P.) ; 10s. 6d.

IRONY is, I should have said, too definite a subject for music. When it is applied to such a forceful poem as this, it misses fire, because music can make no fresh points of its own (I except the tune of " Here we go round the mulberry bush " which is used organically, but even that is implied by Eliot's last verse and is not necessary). Nevertheless Apivor's setting is ingeniously conceived, and skilfully executed in a thoroughly consistent brittle manner. Manner is what saves this work, on the piano ; I judge that, properly performed, its colours would be striking. But it is a peculiar piece, for all that ; one cannot be sure how much is sincere, how much is ironic—there is a telling *cantilena* for the soloist in the second section, and some impressive choral writing in the fourth, but it is significant that when Apivor is setting words that are not satire, he falls back on styleless rumblings and crashings.

Scherchen says " Music is by nature positive." That is a questionable dictum, but this is certainly negative music to the last, beautifully written, semiquaver, and so, to my thinking, pointless ; which is one up to Scherchen.

　　　　　　　　　　　　　　　　　　　W.S.M.

WILLIAM BYRD : The Collected Works, ed. by E. H. Fellowes. Vols. XVIII, XIX, XX (Keyboard Music). (Stainer & Bell) ; 30s. 0d.

No praise can be high enough for Dr. Fellowes' pioneer work connected with Tudor Music in general and William Byrd in particular, but certain of Dr. Fellowes' avowed editorial principles must arouse grave doubts in the minds of any scholar. In his introduction (Vol. XVIII, page III ff.) Dr. Fellowes candidly reveals that he has deliberately sinned against the unwritten code of any modern editor of Complete Editions : the preservation of the original musical text at all costs. He has confessedly tampered with Byrd's musical text in order to adapt his edition to the requirements of the modern pianoforte. This argument has a somewhat quixotic ring at a time when the harpsichord is enjoying a tremendous vogue over all Europe and when readings of ancient keyboard music on a modern piano are openly discouraged by performers and audiences alike. There is no valid reason why any pianist should not adjust the musical setting to his requirements, following certain suggestions put forward by the editor in a prefatory note dealing with the problem, in Byrd's case, of *Auffuehrungspraxis*. The " thinning of some heavy chords in the left hand," to which the editor pleads guilty, certainly robs his edition of its supreme value. His excuse, that every existing keyboard piece of Byrd may today be found in modern critical editions presenting the *original* text, is not quite fair. He refers in that context to the volume " 45 Keyboard Works of Byrd hitherto unpublished," issued by the Lyre-Bird Press, Paris (ca. 1940) and edited by Dr. Stephen D. Tuttle of U.S.A. But this volume (not even to be found on the shelves of the British Museum) is certainly much less within reach of the average music student than his own new edition, which will disappoint the scholar even if it occasionally pleases the pianist.

In the vexed case of Byrd's ornaments Dr. Fellowes' course of action seems a trifle arbitrary. He has almost invariably interpreted those admittedly ambiguous signs as simple Mordants of a type more common in the later 17th and 18th centuries than in Byrd's own period, although it seems quite obvious that they are capable of different rhythmic interpretations. Once again an editorial note addressed to the modern performer, could have regulated the shape and number of these ornaments without spoiling the original text by a monotonous grace note, belonging typographically to a later century Neither print, nor general layout of these three volumes really conform to the standard adopted by other publishers in the case of the Complete Edition of a composer of William Byrd's stature.   H.F.R.

FRANCIS CHAGRIN : " Suite Romaine " for Piano. (Augener) ; 3s. 0d. Prelude and Fugue for two Violins. (Augener) ; 5s. 0d.

THE first consists of three energetic little movements, based on snippets from Roumanian folk music in modern settings. The near-Bartokian harmonization cleverly stresses the particular brightness which the Lydian and Mixolydian modes attain in many Roumanian folk tunes. The piano writing is sometimes unnecessarily awkward.

The second is a serious modern work in a very well managed, highly chromatic idiom which now and again reveals a glimpse of the basic tonic G. After a very imaginative prelude, a fugue theme of considerable length (thus obviating a third or fourth entry of the theme) is subjected to a great number of contrapuntal procedures (which are yet all in keeping with the medium) and serves, in close imitation, to build up a brilliant coda. In view of the technical difficulties of this piece, foremost the intonation which must be dead right to convey the composer's meaning, I should have liked the publication to be thoroughly edited, preferably by Rostal.   P.H.

GERALD FINZI : *Nocturne (New Year Music). Full Score. (Boosey & Hawkes) ; 15s. 0d.*

WE wonder at first what on earth Finzi is doing with Wagner's orchestra, although it has served others well on occasion. The mood of the piece, according to the programme note, hovers between Charles Lamb and Robert Bridges. The scoring, however, is effective, and the scheme of the piece, being roughly ternary, allows an identical bare fifth at start and finish. But undoubtedly the great moment is the 6/4 English tune, with marching bass.

D.W.S.

JOHN IRELAND : *Overture, " Satyricon." Miniature score. (Joseph Williams) ; 6s. 0d.*

THIS bright, tautly-constructed overture, which was first performed at a Promenade Concert in 1946, is here presented as the first of a series of miniature scores issued by Joseph Williams, Ltd. The music, on 6 x 9 inch format, is very legible indeed for a photographic reduction of a full score. A title on the spine would help in the matter of identification.

D.W.S.

JOHN JENKINS : *Fancies and Ayres. Edited by Helen Joy Sleeper. (Wellesley College, Massachusetts) : $3.*

IT seems that this charming volume was not only written but also printed entirely within the precincts of Wellesley College, which has a flourishing music department but no graduate course in musicology. All the more reason then, to welcome this as the first volume of the projected Wellesley Edition, for it gives proof of strong scholastic enthusiasm, and a genuine regard for the music of the seventeenth century.

Jenkins is a composer whose style is often more interesting than his music ; the form bids fair to outdo the content. To judge by the amount of music Jenkins has left us, and the state it was left in, one may do far worse than approve the epithet " voluminous " which the Hon. Roger North (*not* Sir Roger, please !) used in his " Memories of Musick." Had Jenkins been less voluminous and more self-critical, his music would not now be as little known as it is, and if English universities had one tenth of the gumption of American colleges, a complete edition of Jenkins would have been on the market years ago.

Miss Sleeper is to be congratulated on her interesting edition. On the credit side, there is a spacious introduction and ample critical notes, a facsimile of one of the composer's musical autographs, and a handsome spiral binding. The transcriptions are reliable, but not always practical. I do not know how many consorts of viols exist in the United States, but it would be safe to assume that they are outnumbered by chamber groups using modern instruments, and it is only right that these latter should be able to enjoy the " Fancies and Ayres." It is possible to play the five-part Fancies on a quintet of violins, violas, and cello, if viola 2 will beware the low note on p. 33. Similarly, the four-part Ayres would go well on a string quartet. The three-part Fancies, which were probably intended for violins (usurpers of the treble viol's place in the second half of the seventeenth century) present no problems in performance ; but the texture would benefit from a discreet keyboard part, such as Anthony à Wood tells us about in his description of the music meetings in Oxford. The sets of " Fancy and Ayres," true precursors of the trio-sonata, gain much from the intelligent realisations of Hubert Lamb, and it is a pity that he was not called upon to do as much for the " Fancy-Almaine-Ayre " sets for strings and organ. The organ parts must be filled out if the music is to make sense ; but the organ accompaniments to the five-part fancies can be used just as they are, since the harmony is quite complete without them.

If a cellist plays the gamba part, he will have to read the alto clef fluently, for this is used to notate the higher passages. Some players may be put off at first by the rather baroque sign used for a quarter-note rest : this is due to the fact that the music has been handwritten, not engraved. The copyist has a neat hand, but his smaller note-values are made indistinct in many places through over-inking, and ledger-line notes are often uncomfortably cramped. Miss Sleeper's *sigla*, including BoF, ChZ, and RoP, vie with the latest Californian creations—LoF, LoM, and TuB. One day musicologists will learn to call manuscripts by number, when they forget that musicology was invented by the Germans in general and Friedrich Ludwig in particular.

There is still no complete catalogue of Jenkins' music. That given by Miss Sleeper does not claim to be complete, but it is a useful supplement to the one in Meyer's " Die Mehrstimmige Spielmusik . . . , " where there are numerous mistakes and omissions. The selection of pieces gives a good cross-section of the various forms and styles used by Jenkins, though it is a sad thing to have no example of his six-part writing, either in the twelve Fantasias or the two In nomines. Jenkins must have been one of the last composers, barring Purcell, to write an In nomine. But Miss Sleeper has put us on the right road, and her edition is sure to prove highly popular with both scholars and players.   D.W.S.

E. J. MOERAN : Violin Concerto. Miniature Score. (Novello) ; 9s. 0d.

To my mind, Moeran's most personal and consistently absorbing work. Having written about his music, and this work in particular, for the last number of *Music Survey* I will confine myself to the information that the con-certo is scored for double wind, and brass (four horns and three trombones), harp, timpani and strings, lasts about 32 minutes, and is in three movements clearly and lyrically organised. The score is handsomely engraved on goodish quality paper ; my only complaint is that the reproduction might have been a shade larger, and thus more legible, as the score's size is already bigger than standard. It will be useless at concerts anyhow, I fear, since lights-out is steadily becoming the odious rule—though the new Festival Hall provides handsomely for both score-readers and sore eyes.   W.S.M.

BRUCE MONTGOMERY : Concertino for string orchestra. Score. (Novello) ; 8s. 6d.

Ecce iterum Crispinus, but by no means on top form, when compared with the *Requiem* reviewed below. Sluggish basses are again noticeable, and the the-matic invention is hardly striking ; too many consecutive triads (with or with-out clashes underneath) for my liking, and too much note-against-note texture. Finally I suspect that the persistent rhythmic patterns in the last two move-ments would prove tiresome.   W.S.M.

PARRY : Chorale Fantasia on an old English Tune, arranged for strings by Gerald Finzi. Score. (Novello) ; 3s. 0d.

A WORKMANLIKE arrangement of a lovely organ piece, obviously inspired by Brahms' Op. 122 preludes. The cellos are divided throughout, but only have real parts on the first pages—later they replace basses, or are doubled by them at the octave below. W.S.M.

PRIAULX RAINIER : Barbaric Dance Suite for Piano. (Schott) ; 3s. 6d.

THE percussive use of the piano (with a predilection for the percussive 2nd and 9th intervals*) noted in Miss Rainier's Suite for Clarinet and Piano is explained in this work, though not necessarily justified, by the title. I do not know whether Miss Rainier derives her remarkable rhythms from African music, or from her own fertile invention, but in the first and last movements of this piano suite their use, to the virtual exclusion of melodic and harmonic elements, leaves too little of the European conception of music for the listener to be more than intrigued (or irritated) by the subtly-accented noise. Though this " barbarism " may have its roots in native musical practice, yet the piano is a sophisticated instrument, and its use during the past two centuries cannot be wholly ignored. The second movement is bi-tonal, but does not attempt a harmonic fusion of the two keys : the left hand's succession of $\frac{6}{4}$'s, roughly in A minor, provides merely a rhythmic counterpoint to the primitive line of the right hand, in G flat.

Arithmetically deficient pianists will not quickly master the rhythmic complexities of this work, but otherwise the difficulties are, by contemporary standards, not excessive. P.A.E.

* The entire structure of Miss Rainier's string quartet has struck me as deriving its energy from the tension between the regions of C and C♯.—ED. (H.K.).

STEPHEN RHYS : Six Inventions for Two Oboes. (O.U.P.) ; 3s. 6d.

EMPHASISING intervallic relations rather than implied harmony, the clean two-part counterpoint of these inventions solves, unpretentiously, the problem of writing for two equal instruments of limited range. Nor are the oboe's other limitations forgotten : there is some appropriately perky writing in the fast movements but, wisely, no attempt at a true slow movement ; while sufficient rests in both parts prevent embarrassment. P.A.E.

ALAN RICHARDSON : Five Short Pieces for Piano ; " Jack in the Green " ; Sonatina. (Augener) ; 3s. 0d., 3s. 0d., and 4s. 6d., respectively.

THE " educational " Five Short Pieces educate, not only the young player's fingers but in places also his ear : hear the neat 7-bar phrase with which the first of them begins, as well as the " Walking Tune " where Mr. Richardson manages to walk quite briskly in 3/4 time with the aid of copious cross accents. In other places, however, their modernism *ad usum delphinum* is a bit sugary, especially in the rather insipid " Swing Song." " Jack in the Green," on the other hand, is semi-educational, i.e., a show-piece for the young talent going in for the higher Associated Board Grades. It misses its mark in that it has exactly that sham sophistication which will, unfortunately, endear it to many a " progressive " music master in the provinces.

The Sonatina is an entirely different proposition. Addressing himself to the finished player (though the piece is technically not unreasonably difficult) Mr.Richardson is here at liberty to display, in surprisingly graded assortment, the vernal pastel colours of his harmony . . . If we are too florid, so is this particular brand of harmony : it pays its tribute too readily to Flora, the goddess. Still, we like to follow the poet's enamoured eye as it wanders over the daffodils of movements One and Two ; especially since some very shrewd formal devices provide the gentle brushwork of these landscapes with a welcome perspective. But when Mr. Richardson, in the third movement, begins to gambol with the Easter lambkins, I, for one, look round for the nearest pub.   p.h

FREDA SWAIN : Two South African Impressions for Piano. (Joseph Williams) ; 3s. 0d.

PLEASANT drawing-room music, well written for the instrument, but musically undistinguished. In her footnote to " The Lonely Dove " (No. 2), Miss Swain assures us that her recurring 3-note phrase " . . . . approximates to the call of the doves whose plaintive and monotonous notes are heard incessantly in Cape Town." For once, I am in the happy position to be able to verify the genuineness of exotic musical noises. But I assure you that the continuous cooing, at times enchanting, at others tormenting, that floated down from the trees into my open window during a fortnight's illness at Cape Town, was much more chromatic than Miss Swain's prosy little C-B-A figure in A minor. Upon consideration, it would appear that the Cape Town doves could provide a quarter-tone composer with a heart-rending ostinato for a string quartet. P.H.

WALTON : Scapino, a comedy overture. Miniature Score. (O.U.P.) ; 7s. 6d.

The Columbia record, made by Stock and the Chicago Symphony Orchestra, followed the original version of this scintillating, neo-Rossinian piece. Last year Walton revised the score. He has, if memory and the gramophone record may be trusted, aimed generally at crisper, less grandiose texture— so much appeared from a performance by Boult and the L.P.O. at a tuning concert at the Festival Hall, though the acoustics on that occasion were giving prominence to brittle tone-colours—and at a compacter structure ; cuts have been made in four places.

The " miniature " (10 x 7) score is engraved at a size convenient for comfortable reading (even in the dim religious light referred to above) ; reproduced on the cover is not the familiar green and black design by Graham Sutherland, but Callot's engraving of Scapino—a break with Waltonian tradition that perhaps merits mention.   w.s.m.

WALTON : Two Pieces for violin and piano. (O.U.P.) ; 5s. 0d.

A Canzonetta and a Scherzetto, dedicated to " Vivien and Larry." The first, based on a troubadour melody, is simply set and sparely, but highly charac- teristically, accompanied. The second, nervous piece makes a disjointed effect, with its jumble of rhythmic tricks and flat harmonic scheme. Neat and unpretentious, not really difficult and not really distinguished.   w.s.m.

GRACE WILLIAMS : Sea Sketches for string orchestra. Score. (O.U.P.) ;
  10s. 6d.

THERE is something of the *tour-de-force* about these five pieces, " High Wind,"
" Sailing Song," " Channel Sirens," " Breakers," " Calm Sea in Summer."
The scoring is brilliant ; on each page the eye encounters an interesting
effect. The texture is organised and controlled with remarkable skill. But
the ideas, their clothing and their development are of the most commonplace,
and a performance of the work, would, I fancy, prove tedious in the extreme.
It is printed from a beautiful manuscript as are several of this Press's issues—a
more than adequate substitute for engraving in these days.   w.s.m.

TWO REQUIEMS

HERBERT HOWELLS : Hymnus Paradisi. Vocal Score. (Novello) ;
  6s. 6d.
BRUCE MONTGOMERY : An Oxford Requiem. Vocal Score. (Novello) ;
  5s. 0d.

   " *The great tradition of English church Music is a sacred trust* "
                                    COSMO GORDON LANG

THIS, I believe, is the only period in history when Sacred Music has acknow-
ledgedly clung to an outdated aesthetic—when a contempprary idiom has
been thought unsuitable, if not almost blasphemous, as the medium of man's
musical approach to the Almighty.

  In England, this timid creed has been fostered by the English Cathedral
Tradition, viz. approved musical conservatism. The sacred music of this
century would have stuck in Parryan bogs, if Vaughan Williams had not thrown
his own modernisms into the melting pot, suitably disguised by elements of
folk melody and the Gregorian Modes. As it is, his most uncompromising
religious work, *Dona Nobis Pacem*, is not often done, while the forces of Tradition, flying under the twin banners of the Three Choirs Festival and the
House of Novello, have sternly encouraged composers to imagine themselves
living forty or fifty years ago. *Belshazzar's Feast* was of its time when it
appeared (even though the I.S.C.M. saw retrogression in it) and it has flourished ; but since most audiences approach it as secular music, it is hardly
an exception.

  Yet, just as households that frown on refrigerators and television have almost
been forced to adopt electricity and the telephone, so even Three Choirs
composers have found themselves acknowledging Delius, Walton and the
more dissonant Vaughan Williams as accomplished facts. So the familiar
brown and ochre covers, which used to spell Victoriana, enclose music now
that could not have been written more than say twenty years ago in England.
Indeed, when one takes the thumbscrew of Tradition into account, then
Howells's *Hymnus Paradisi* and Montgomery's *An Oxford Requiem* are both
startlingly modern.

  Hymnus Paradisi would seem to be Howells's bid for a confirmation of the
greatness prophesied of him in his earlier days. It is brilliant, as he himself is
brilliant, though in a special sense presently to be outlined ; it is also very
moving in parts, even to one who reacts strongly against neo-Parry and bogus
modality. Its view of tonality is a good deal more fluid than its oratorial
predecessors'; when it accepts the past, it does so because Howells cannot help

it. He is aware of the present, and of the experience that has led up to the present ; his idiom, and his choice of what (rather rudely) may be called his musical sources, show that.

The *Hymnus* begins with an orchestral prelude ; slow in tempo, with flowing melodic lines in, at first, two-part counterpoint of a hazy nature. Dorian E minor, you might call it, for E is obviously the key note and the signature shows two sharps. But the tonality, or modality, shifts and the part-writing, as it expands, grows more chromatic. The dissonance norm is low, thus stressing the dissonant power of C minor $^6_4$ with added 6 natural, 7 natural, and F major $^6_4$ $+$ 7 flat, 9 natural, 11 natural, 13 natural (i.e., F7 flat and G superimposed) subsiding on to a G sharp minor triad, the harmonic climax of the section. The choral writing in the *Requiem* section, involving double choir, establishes this quasi-Dorian E minor, and sometimes resembles (aurally) that of Verdi's *Quattro Pezzi Sacri*. The third movement, a setting of Psalm 23, vividly recalls Vaughan Williams' *Dona Nobis* or parts of his *Pastoral* Symphony. The fourth, a highly successful blend of *Sanctus* and Psalm 121, raises the dissonant norm to what, for want of other terms of reference, I must call the *Belshazzar* level. This is an impulsive scherzo, with much use of soloists (soprano and tenor) floating rapturously over choral polyphony. The fifth section " I heard a Voice from Heaven " is short, contemplative and, for me, duller than the rest. The last movement builds up its luminous texture over a 60 bar pedal point on B♭ ; it begins pentatonically, in one pitch or another, but adopts the missing degrees of the scale of E♭ minor before enervation has time to set in. The part-movement* is indubitably Parry-sired, the harmonics ultra-modern Three-Choirs. The structure is wholly successful, dramatically, even to the (contextually) unexpected use of well worn old cyclicism at the end.

Howells's assimilation of other men's personal idioms is brilliant, for the result gives no impression of plagiarism, nor is there a suspicion of Elstree about the music. And yet, beautiful as I have admitted the work to be, I cannot see that it either leads English Church Music any forrader, nor that it sets a clearly definable creative personality before the listener (the music doesn't present a face, as a friend of mine is apt to say on such occasions).

Though a good deal less pretentious, and in some places positively undistinguished, Bruce Montgomery's score does move tradition along, and it does offer a " face." As the University title suggests, Parry, Allen and Warlock are the stylistic foundation stones of this work, which marks a notable advance in the composer's development. I have not heard a performance of *An Oxford Requiem* (as I have of the *Hymnus*) so I base my judgments on the vocal score only.

Like Howells, Montgomery is keenly sensitive to the colour of words— both are English scholars as well as musicians—and as in the *Hymnus*, so here the text, taken from the Psalms and the Burial Service, finds apt and picturesque (in the best sense) musical clothes. Chromatic harmony is Montgomery's *forte*, but the thematic germs that bind each movement together are in themselves striking. The weaknesses of the pieces are a tendency to drop on to a pedal point when things aren't going well, a general sluggishness in the bass, some very ordinary part-writing and a definite decline in character whenever the music turns toward diatonicism ; the principal idea of the last movement,

*Please note, *Haydn Society*, the English word for *Stimmfuehrung*.

deriving noticably from the *In paradisum* of Fauré's *Requiem*, seems out of style with the rest. All the same there is great beauty and a personality in the work.

Notwithstanding, it is necessary to adopt out-of-date standards—to pretend that Bartok, Hindemith, Schoenberg have never matured, perhaps never been born—if one is to appraise the qualities of both these works. The situation you will agree, is artificial—but then, sincerity apart, so is British Sacred Music today. The English Church is trying to bring its teaching up-to-date and music must march in step with this laudable effort (St. Matthew's, Northampton, has done valuable work here). I look forward to Searle in the 12-note technique, Fricker's *Crucifixion*, and Britten's *Christmas Oratorio* ; if you think that is a blasphemous hope, you are just being un-realistic.

W.S.M.

Book Reviews

Arranged in alphabetical order of titles.

INTERNATIONAL GALLERY OF CONDUCTORS, *by Donald Brook* * *Pp. 232 ; 16s. 0d. (Rockliff).*

DONALD BROOK's new book offers a considerable amount of information not included in his earlier *Conductors' Gallery*, and much which he claims is not available elsewhere. Many of his subjects are best known here from their gramophone recordings, but British conductors are represented very thoroughly. I can think of only one serious omission—Josef Krips, who seems to be one of the most important conductors at present working in this country. A work of this sort has an obvious value for purposes of reference, and Mr. Brook is not only readable, but adds sympathetic and informed comment on such matters as Furtwaengler's dealings with the Nazis, which are discussed with a common sense both admirable and salutary. The illustrations vary from startling action photographs to one of a relaxed, cigar smoking, dressing-gowned Beecham, and the volume is so produced as to be a credit to the most fastidious bookshelf.

H.B.R.

LITERARY STYLE AND MUSIC, *by Herbert Spencer. Pp. x + 119 ; 2s. 6d. (Watts).*

THE Thinker's Library's welcome, if idiotically mistitled, republication of four early Spencer essays, with an Introduction by Charles T. Smith. Only one of these claims the musician's attention : *The Origin and Function of Music.* That it still does so is due not only to its historical importance, nor to the mere fact that most musicians' scientific knowledge is of so far a past that they may well believe Spencer's theory to be after all true as it stands. No, Spencer's principal theme—that " all music is an idealization of the natural language of passion "—will probably return as a subsidiary subject in the scientifically comprehensive theory of music's origin. The main data therefor are already available ; that it has not yet been written is a deplorable consequence of the fact that Freud was completely unmusical, as well as of the circumstance that *most thinking musicians are at once too musical to escape into psychology, and unmusical enough to escape from it.* When the complete theory of music comes to be written, the history of Spencer's speech theory will show that not his most recent critic (Ernest Newman in

293

A Study of Wagner and later in *Musical Studies*) but, on the contrary, its first opponent had looked furthest ahead : Darwin, who held that music's origin lay in the expression of amatory feeling.

Since Freud, the Darwin of psychology (as, upon the testimony of the last half century, we may safely and in fact with considerable analogical precision call him), has discovered infantile sexuality, the perplexingly different activities of whose successive stages are yet linked with each other as well as with the adult's sexual act by the common characteristic of affective and conative *rhythm*, we are, factually and theoretically, in a position to re-value Darwin's musico-psychological foresight in a similar way as we have already revalued his biological vision. Not so, however, practically : whenever one of the one or two of us who are at last musically and psychologically qualified for musico-psychoanalytic investigations pushes ahead into the uncharted, well-chartable territory, he is met with, and hampered by infantile derision. For instance, while André Michel's *Psychoanalysis of Music* in last November's *Music Review* is by no means without musical and psychological blemishes (which I am trying to sift in the current [May] issue of that journal), it contains some conclusions which are courageous, new and true ; yet all the *Musical Times* has to say about this " really remarkable production," " this weightily-sponsored thesis," is that it " is the furthest point yet attained by the school which we prefer to call the psycho-anatomical. It would cause a sensation, if, say, it were read out to an orchestra." As a school magazine might ween, Freud isn't good enough to be obscene. H.K.

SIR ARTHUR SULLIVAN : *his Life, Letters and Diaries*, by Herbert Sullivan and Newman Flower. Pp. 306 ; 12s. 6d. (*Cassell*).

THE stiff wing collar, the profuse side-whiskers, the serious yet not unkindly gaze—Sullivan's portrait, no less than his music, allocates him directly to the Victorian age. His photographed profile dominates the dust-jacket of this book ; and the book is an essential document of that age, of which the music has been so little studied and so much abused. The late Herbert Sullivan was Arthur Sullivan's nephew, lived with him as a son for the last seventeen years of the composer's life, and duly became his heir. This book, which first appeared in 1927, has thus the status of an ' official ' biography. Sir Newman Flower, as the survivor of the collaborating authors, must assume responsibility for what is somewhat strangely described as a ' new and revised edition.' Strangely —for the alterations, where not trivial, are for the worse ; inaccuracies in the original edition have not been eradicated ; and statements remain which were once accurate but are now no longer so.

It was perhaps legitimate to omit from the new version the Introduction by Arnold Bennett, who claimed the credit for bringing the authors together. But it is disappointing that the original thirty-one illustrations, two of them in colour, have been reduced to seven, all in half-tone. It is worse than disappointing that the Bibliography, compiled by William C. Smith, instead of being brought up to date has been dropped. Mr. Smith's separate list of Sullivan's works is, however, retained. This list correctly gives the key of Sullivan's only symphony (1866) as E ; the text still persists in making it E flat. As in the original edition, Sullivan's pre-Gilbert operetta *The Contrabandista* is once referred to as *La Contrabandista*. And the absurd ' tragisit ' still stands as a mistake for the German ' tragisch ' in a reference to Schubert's fourth symphony.

Such uncorrected slips (and there are others) may well arouse dissatisfaction. But how far should a revised edition involve the revision of actual opinions— particularly if one of the authors is dead ? What of the almost indiscriminate praise heaped on Sullivan in this book ? *The Martyr of Antioch,* the reader is informed, showed that ' Sullivan as a composer of religious work was greater than ever.' *Onward, Christian Soldiers* is ' the world's greatest marching hymn.' *The Chorister* is a ' superb song ' ; and so on. It needs no great critical faculty to differ from these judgments ; nor to spot the beautifully unconscious German bias in the statement that ' Sullivan, at this stage, was entirely cosmopolitan in his musical beliefs. Apart from Schubert and Schumann, for both of whom he stood as the true apostle, he adored Beethoven, Handel, Mozart, Mendelssohn, and Weber.' Yet such expressions seem somehow appropriate to this book. Later authors can treat (and have treated) Sullivan more critically ; Herbert Sullivan could hardly be expected to assist in doing so, and would perhaps have failed had he made the attempt. Here he has not failed : the portrait, though partial, gives the impression of honesty as well as sympathy. The book itself, like its subject, is—as such spellings as ' clarionette ' remind the reader—a piece of history. The story of Sullivan's rise from humble origins to something like world fame is here told in the way that Sullivan himself would surely have told it.

Sir Newman Flower was therefore wise in not attempting a basic remodelling. But one would have welcomed elucidation on some points which are puzzling in the old edition and are still so. Sullivan's diary, when he was working in New York on the last stages of *The Pirates of Penzance,* gives the following entry for December 30, 1879 : ' Full dress rehearsal at 8. Press and some friends there. Excellent rehearsal ; everyone enthusiastic. Over at 1. Came home with Cellier, Clay and Gilbert ; all set to work at the Overture. Gilbert and Clay knocked off at 3 a.m. Cellier and I wrote till 5 and finished it.' Cellier and Clay were musicians, and so presumably helped copy the parts. But Gilbert—how did he ' work at the overture ' ? (This, by the way, was Alfred Cellier, later the composer of the enormously successful *Dorothy.* His brother François, who had by then become the regular conductor of the Sullivan operettas in London, was generally known as ' Frank ' Cellier. The present book confusedly indexes ' Frank ' and ' François ' Cellier as two different people.)

Also unhelpful is the bald statement that ' the impression he (Sullivan) received from the singing of the Russian choir '—on a visit to Kronstadt with the Duke of Edinburgh—' coloured his composing at a later stage. Many of the unaccompanied quartets, etc. in his Savoy operas are the outcome of that impression.' Did Sullivan himself ever admit that influence ? and if not, is there the slightest musical evidence for the statement ?

The reference to Mrs. Ronalds, the woman who mattered most to Sullivan after his mother, could also well have been expanded, if only by a footnote. Since this book originally appeared, Isaac Goldberg's lively American study of Gilbert and Sullivan has revealed much about this American ' society ' beauty, of whom the Prince of Wales (the future King Edward VII) remarked that he would travel the length of Britain to hear her sing *The Lost Chord.* Sullivan never married ; and both Goldberg and Hesketh Pearson (whose *Gilbert and Sullivan* has recently been issued as a Penguin) suggest that Mrs. Pierre Lorillard Ronalds, née Mary Frances Carter of Boston, was his mistress. It is hardly satisfactory to read now that ' the influence of Mrs. Ronalds '—the present book never mentions her christian names—' upon Arthur Sullivan has often been discussed and usually misunderstood.' The book reports that Sullivan had two earlier love affairs, but gives the name of neither woman. It is to be hoped that Leslie Baily's forthcoming biographical work on Gilbert and Sullivan, for which he has been granted access to family sources, will provide the illumination that has so far not been thrown on Sullivan's relationship with women and with his family. (' How do you think I could be otherwise than happy,' he remarked on his deathbed, ' when I am going to see my dear mother ? ' She had then been dead eighteen years.)

The style of this book is Flowery. Some of it would raise purrs of delight from such transatlantic parodists as Stephen Leacock or S. J. Perelman : ' So, in 1854, Mr. Plees of Bayswater might have been seen going up Great Portland Street with a boy of twelve trudging at his side—a boy in whom every nerve responded to excitement.' ' *In Memoriam* is the cry of a man in sorrow translated into Art and beauty as the best votive offering.' ' He appeared in Society, jocund, talkative, always interesting. And ere tomorrow's sun broke over the chimney pots of Mayfair he had rushed in the first train towards the North to conduct a concert.' One's relish is checked slightly when the facts do not live up to the flourishes. The score of Sullivan's *The Light of the World* is stated to be ' now the property of H.R.H. the Princess Louise ' ; but she died in 1931. And that description of Sullivan's birthplace in Lambeth—does it still hold good ? On a recent visit I found that it is now no longer true that ' all changing life has left little marked impression upon Bolwell Terrace.' For one thing, the address is now Bolwell Street, though the commemorative plaque on No. 8 still stands. For another, the iron gates and serried railings which formerly gave the street its prim, decorous quality were removed during the war for scrap. I confirmed this with a 73-year-old Lambethian in a neighbouring pub, and with a street-corner bookie not far off. Then I departed ; and, ere tomorrow's sun broke over the chimney-pots of Cassell's publishing house, I had decided that this book needs a *really* revised edition. A.J.

Concerts

Arranged in chronological order ; joint reviews, where they exist, at the end of each numerical Section.

I. LONDON

PHILHARMONIA ORCHESTRA : Albert Hall, 22nd February, 1951 ; c. Furtwaengler.

WE know and love our 7th Bruckner well. When we went to this concert, we proposed to ourselves to check once more certain formal inadequacies, chiefly in developmental and transitional technique, which had always struck us about this noble and profound master-score. When we left the concert, we realized that far from checking anything, our mind had not been anywhere near noting anything amiss. It would be rash to conclude that those formal flaws do not in fact exist. What we had not known before we heard Furtwaengler's interpretation was that they *need* not exist : *a failure of our own imagination* Public print this self-criticism deserved because it reminds us what a per formance can sometimes do and what a critic sometimes can't. H.K.

FIDELIO QUARTET : R.B.A. Galleries, 14th March, 1951.
QUARTET-PLAYING is a skill of maturity, which makes it hard to judge immature quartets ; but all quartets were immature once. I had the strongest impression that beneath the obvious defects of intonation (bad in the opening Haydn until nerves steadied) and rhythm (slight) which everybody could hear, this team has the rare essential qualities to grow with the years into a good quartet. There was a certain inwardness in the exacting Op. 59 No. 3 : a quartet well led took the place of four players of assorted personalities, imperfectly but authentically. The second fiddle being ill, Sheila Osmond took her part—more credit to all concerned. Peter Graeme was the excellent soloist in Gordon Jacob's oboe Quartet. R.D.

MALCOLM ARNOLD : First performance of Sonata for Clarinet and Piano ; R.B.A. Galleries, 20th March, 1951 ; Colin Davies and Geoffrey Corbett.
A VERY neat piece with a humour all of its own, especially in the last movement's " Furioso." The clarinet part, though grateful, could exploit more of the instrument's possibilities. P.H.

DUTCH HARPSICHORD TRIO : Wigmore Hall, 29th March, 1951.
MUSICIANSHIP : The leader, Feltkamp the flautist, is one of those rare spirits of creative interpretation whose least nuance is inspired and whose grasp of phrase, line and form is alike unfailing ; van Wering, a harpsichordist of fine touch, is not far short of the same exalted class, as her moving Chromatic Fantasy and Fugue made evident; Lentz, the viola da gambist, is a less profound and sensitive but still excellent musician. A real chamber group.

Authenticity : a standard blessedly higher than is in the least usual, though not without error (especially in ornamentation, which has more effect than is thought). There is one grave departure : Lentz plays the gamba with the technique of the 'cello, using a 'cello bow, strings of nearly 'cello thickness and tension, and a fingerboard deprived of the gut frets which give the gamba part of its individuality. Result : tone beautiful but rather 'cello-like ; articulation very 'cello-like. I know that the temptation for 'cellists to take this short cut is a strong one ; it has happened in this country too. It is a road of course, but not to the gamba, though seeming so. R.D.

UNDER THIRTY THEATRE GROUP : Whitehall Theatre, 1st April, 1951 ; c. Ionel Patin.
STRAVINSKY'S *The Soldier's Tale* complete with narration and play. Décor and acting were weak but enterprising ; the music was efficiently played and directed. What one first suspected to be Stravinsky in teasing, trivial mood unexpectedly developed into music of high tension and dramatic aptness ; particularly in the Chorale and the final dance of the Princess, Devil and Soldier where the music suddenly took imaginative possession of the narrative and the stage action. A complaint voiced by a leading composer present at the performance that " the music bears no relation to the story " just doesn't hold good. The music makes it. Few composers can do so much with so little and it's my bet that anyone and everyone could learn something from Stravinsky's brilliant instrumentation (violin, clarinet, bassoon, cornet, trombone, double bass, percussion) and his ceaseless rhythmic, innovatory and really inventive inventions. D.M.

B.B.C. SYMPHONY CONCERTS : B.B.C. Symphony Orchestra, Albert Hall, 4th April, 1951 ; c. Beecham.

PERFORMANCES of the C minor Mass (K.427) and the *Jupiter* both far above the average ; if that sounds patronising it isn't meant to. While very often I feel that Beecham aims at the superficially elegant and momentarily surprising, he frequently strikes as deep as the deepest—as in the *Jupiter*'s finale which I have not heard played better. Even the wilfully unbeautiful things—for instance the positively ruinous phrasing in the *Jupiter*'s slow movement— Beecham does beautifully on their own wrong level. His weak point as a conductor always seems to me to flaunt itself at, on, or over, all bridge passages : a weakness more apparent, of course, in the symphony than the Mass. Whereas with a Furtwaengler something organic happens : or to put this not so very simple musical matter in simple terms, we are in fact ' led back ' (or on, or over), with Beecham we jump our bridges before we come to them. For Beecham this is probably characteristic, but musically, and for Mozart, and for me, it is highly disconcerting. D.M.

NEW ERA CONCERT SOCIETY : First performance of Hindemith's Sinfonietta. London Symphony Orchestra, Albert Hall, 6th April, 1951 ; c. Hans Schmidt-Isserstedt.

HINDEMITH's new *Sinfonietta* isn't in fact very new. Indeed it suffers from a lot of Hindemith's old faults, notably his rhythmic monotony. On the other hand two considerations must weigh against a generally unfavourable impression : (a) in spite of Dr. Schmidt-Isserstedt, it was a very poor orchestral performance with really dreadful brass playing: (b) it was not until I had heard the new Horn Concerto for the second time that I was able to more accurately assess its merits (which I now think considerable). Nevertheless I think I can safely prophecy that the *Sinfonietta* won't prove to be a major piece—even at its most familiar. D.M.

NEW ERA CONCERT SOCIETY : Kirsten Flagstad, acc. by Edwin McArthur; Albert Hall, 17th April, 1951.

MME. FLAGSTAD's unfortunate lack of artistic identification with the rôle she portrays prejudices the songs of Hugo Wolf even more than it does her Isolde : there is much less time in Lieder to establish the character of the speaker, and the demands on the interpreter's empathy are consequently higher—highest of all in Wolf. The more conventional Grieg fared better, and the songs by Brahms were cleverly chosen for broad outline rather than literary and musical finesse. But even here, Mme. Flagstad's unconcern for both poem and music in a song like " O wuesst ich doch den Weg zurueck," which has come from Brahms' heart of hearts, only just avoided being offensive because it was, obviously, such a good-natured unconcern : a blank spot in the mind of an otherwise sympathetic person. Faced with Flagstad's unique voice and her insufficient, though quite unaffected musicality, one asks oneself where all the accumulated experience of life and art has gone which intensifies and diversifies the musical emotion of even the good amateur when he approaches his fifties. She has sung under the best conductors, met interesting people, travelled all over the world, and yet remained unspoilt : a remarkable achievement of character, but, alas, artistically only the negative prerequisite for something positive which did not happen to her. As a rule, it is invidious for the reviewer to bring up another artist for the purpose of comparison : but in view of the many listeners in the Albert Hall crowd for whom this concert must have been their first, and perhaps slightly disappointing, contact with Lieder, I am going to state here that any Lieder recital by Flora Nielsen is a much more important event than was this concert on April 17th. Of all the good English female Lieder singers, she lends herself best to comparison since she appears to be roughly of the same age and of the same pleasant disposition, and since her voice, though not on Flagstad's scale, is produced easily and well. But what a difference in musicianship !   P.H.

CARL TILLIUS : Piano recital ; Wigmore Hall, 28th April, 1951.

THE Swedish group, played with conviction by this Swedish pianist, showed up nothing very good or very new in the works of Messrs. Rangstroem, Stenhammer and Nystroem. But the " Kjempeviseslatter " of Saeverud is a very effective concert study in the form of a continuous crescendo.   P.H.

LONDON CONTEMPORARY MUSIC CENTRE : Twenty-Ninth Season, 1951.

THIS Season's third concert (20th February) was devoted to music from Scandinavia, a praiseworthy venture unhappily resulting in an evening of extreme musical boredom. The least cemetorial of the pieces presented was Ingvar Lidholm's Sonatina for piano (Frank Merrick), an immature work very heavily influenced by early Schoenberg. But apart from the unconvincing diatonic close to the second movement, the Sonatina had style, was consistent, and suggested that there might be some sort of future for its composer—unlike the remainder of the works in the programme which merely witnessed to their respective composers' unpromising pasts. On 27th March (Concert Hall, Broadcasting House) Paul Sacher conducted the Philharmonia in Priaulx Rainier's Sinfonia da Camera for strings, Matyas Seiber's Fantasia Concertante for solo violin (Rostal) and string orchestra, and Frank Martin's orchestral song-cycle Die Weise von Liebe und Tod des Cornets Christoph Rilke (Elsa Cavelti). I have examined these works in more detail in the May issue of the Music Review, but in view of the twelve-tonal Seiber's expectedly hostile reception by the majority of the press, it must be repeated here that the Fantasia was an exceptionally accomplished piece of great beauty. 24th April brought with it Bartok's first violin Sonata (Varga and Greenbaum), Iain Hamilton's Three (prize-winning) Nocturnes for Clarinet and Piano (Thurston and Hamilton), regressive in themselves and regressive when compared with Hamilton's own clarinet Quintet, Schoenberg's Fantasia for violin and piano, Op. 47 (see p. 280), Humphrey Searle's Quartet for violin, viola, clarinet and bassoon (Varga, Riddle, Thurston, Alexandra), which just failed to solve successfully all the textural problems it set itself, and finally Denis ApIvor's Concertante for clarinet, piano and percussion (Thurston, Greenbaum, James and Thomas Blades, c. ApIvor). ApIvor's texture was clarity itself, an essential for a work which is almost a satire on a satire though its irony be never very savage. But I doubt whether this kind of very civilized and valuable playfulness is sufficient to sustain a piece of such dimensions. Its very excellence demands something more—not more of itself, but something beyond it, or perhaps below it and thereby deeper. From this point of view, and in this Concertante, Mr. ApIvor made a vice of his own considerable virtues.   D.M.

II. THE PROVINCES

STRAVINSKY IN MANCHESTER
HALLÉ ORCHESTRA, 15th March, 1951 ; c. Weldon.

STRAVINSKY'S *1945* Symphony is not the work of towering genius which I took it to be when it first came out. It needs revision, and re-scoring in order to curtail the obtrusive piano part. And some of the motifs are so trite that one marvels the composer was not ashamed to recapitulate them. The slow movement (for a smaller orchestra) shows a better idea of the relationship between ends and means. But in the final section Stravinsky returns to the old job of musical pattern making, leaving us to contemplate yet again those harmonic barbarities that so shocked the '20s. Mr. Weldon made the best of a difficult task.   E.D.M.

STRAVINSKY IN LIVERPOOL
HALLÉ ORCHESTRA, 20th March, 1951 ; c. Weldon.

AT the Hallé's second visit, with George Weldon deputising for the indisposed Barbirolli, the *pièce-de-résistance* was Stravinsky's *1945* Symphony, which received a cogent and lucid performance. Like A. K. Holland, who, although he contributed an omniscient programme note to the work, confessed himself utterly baffled by it in his concert notice in the following day's *Liverpool Post*, we feel that our grandchildren will understand this work, enigmatically composed of grace, ferocity, *grotesquerie* and inspired logic ; we recognise its greatness because we are convinced of its logical and emotional coherence and appreciate the sense of inevitability that underlies its deliberate mastery of rhythmic and instrumental effect.   H.B.R.

Opera

I. Covent Garden.

VAUGHAN WILLIAMS' " THE PILGRIM'S PROGRESS." 26th April, 1951 ; c. Leonard Hancock, produced by Nevill Coghill.

" THE PILGRIM'S PROGRESS," advertised as the artistic curtain-raiser to the Festival of Britain, turned out to be much more ; namely, the epitome of a great composer's life-work. Vaughan Williams struggled with John Bunyan's visionary epic for decades, very much like Wagner with the mystery of the Holy Grail ; and he was equally careful to segregate his transformation of Bunyan's dream-allegory from the species of ordinary opera by calling it " a Morality." Unfortunately the libretto—despite its poetic depth—lacks essential dramatic contrasts, and lapses too often into solemn pageantry where we have a right to expect spiritual conflict. It is a " Magic Flute " without a Queen of the Night, a " Parsifal " without a Klingsor. Christian's pilgrimage proceeds a trifle too easily, and the sombre fight with Apollyon and the garishness of " Vanity Fair " suffer from a lack of musical devilry. Apart from these episodes the music flows on majestically and with all the mellow splendour of a unique—if carefully circumscribed—symphonic style. The choral pageants in the " House Beautiful," the stirring trumpet call at the threshold to the " King's Highway " speak the select language of the symphonist as unmistakably and eloquently as does the Woodcutter Boy's simple ditty.

" The Pilgrim's Progress " may not be a good opera, but it is a triumph of

English vocal music, and Covent Garden made an obvious effort to produce the work in a manner worthy of a festive occasion. The stage settings and costumes of Hal Burton were not unimpressive and conjured up a kind of Baroque Milieu, inspired by Burnacini and Claude Lorrain. Nevill Coghill's production was more conventional, particularly in the handling of the chorus. But the uncanny, serpent-like ballet in the " Vale of Humiliation " added to the atmosphere of sinister mystery, so well expressed by the looming figure of Apollyon. The Pilgrim was sung and acted by Arnold Matters with fervent devotion ; and the visionary poet Bunyan was effectively portrayed by the Maori singer Te Wiata. The work was conducted by Leonard Hancock, the youthful repetiteur of Covent Garden, who discharged his duties fairly enough. But a constitutional lack of dramatic temperament prevented him from intensifying the dramatic import of many passages, thereby emphasizing more than necessary the imperious monotony in the general flow of the music. The orchestra—as always at Covent Garden in the case of operas favouring a large brass section—sounded more often noisy than monumental, and failed to achieve that golden transparency of a Byzantine mosaic, so forcibly suggested by Vaughan Williams' masterly score.　　　　　　　　　　　　　　　H.F.R.

II.　Sadler's Wells.

JANACEK'S " KATYA KABANOVA."　10th April, 1951 ; c. Charles Mackerras, produced by Dennis Arundell.

THOSE who call this score a scrap heap or complain because it lacks full-fig arias and ensembles simply confess that they miss the point. I have nothing against the traditional *da capo* apparatus in the opera house. Let us by all means have suites of concerted pieces, from duet to septet with choruses and bands behind the scenes, in the grand architectural manner. But let us remember that other ways of opera-building may be quite as valid. Adding arias to *Katya* would be like painting the rose with red lead.

There is no occasion or room for set-pieces in Katya for the good reason that Janacek's procedures are sufficient without them. What he gives us in effect from scene to scene is a set of symphonic poems, musical incident cleaving to the physical and psychological happenings on the stage with singular fidelity and beauty. The vocal line never flowers into melody, remains in bud rather : but it is a singable line and intellectually satisfying once you relate it to Janacek's predominantly orchestral purpose.

That the music is so closely moulded to Ostrovsky's tale does not imply inchoateness. I would, in fact, go so far as to say that Janacek comes within hailing distance of formal grandeur. In act one, scene two, Katya has a lengthy monologue which expounds the childlike innocence of her nature, the stifling frustrations of her home life, the amorous temptation that is beginning to intoxicate her. Four scenes later she has a second monologue. Innocence has gone. Its place is taken by blank, stupefying despair. These two monologues, so widely spaced, are the psychological and musical pillars of the entire fabric. Listening to the first in anticipation of the second and to the second in recollection of the first, gives me precisely that feeling of broadly planned and sustained purpose which is the essential mark of great formalist art. Let us hear no more of the untenable judgment that Janacek here exposes himself as a shortwinded amateur who composes from hand to mouth.

301

There is framework, then : and, inside the frame, some of the loveliest musical detail I have heard in the opera house. Janacek's dates are 1854-1928 —roughly what one would expect from his harmonic sentiment, which ranges from Tchaikovsky, for Ostrovsky's more romantic moments, to Debussy and post-Debussian idioms when sorrow and its deliriums are in question. Listen to the extraordinary, stuttering brass writing against long-held choral harmonies in the catastrophic closing pages. This and other episodes have a craggy abstract power which surprised all who went to the first night expecting nothing but stale nationalism with overtones from Dvorak. Power has its pendant in tenderness. After two hearings I am haunted constantly by the gentle pulsing of major seconds deep in the orchestra which occurs during Katya's first monologue. It is detail of this kind which gives vitality and truth to the stage picture, turning a mere skeleton of story, which might have come from *Peg's Paper*, into a well of rare experience.

What we see on the stage is for the most part exquisitely right. The 1860 living room devised by Mr. Arundell and John Glass, his designer, so frugal, so snug, so bourgeois, is something more than an agreeable period piece : it is a backloth against which the personality of Katya (as played by Amy Shuard) shines out with a double radiance. Miss Shuard's Katya is credible, well-sustained and very moving for all its vocal faults. Miss Shuard has a way of singing her head off at the slightest provocation. Her Katya would be much improved by a bit of true *mezza-voce* and smooth, confident production on the lower dynamic levels. But the imperfections are not ruinous or anything like it. We make allowances for them as we go along. They do not get seriously in Janacek's way.

One extenuating factor is that, especially with Janacek's orchestra in it, Sadler's Wells is a rowdy little theatre. You might say that Mr. Mackerras ought to have given Miss Shuard a better chance by using the snaffle and the curb in the orchestra pit ; but that would have taken the nature out of Janacek's scoring. Acoustically we are in a vicious circle.

Katya is so much a one-part affair that for the rest I need only say that the production sports three tenors (Robert Thomas, Rowland Jones and John Kentish) without a bleat among them ; a tolerably convincing matriarch (Kate Jackson) ; a pert soubrette-ish type (Marion Studholme) ; and a stentorian Volga merchant (Stanley Clarkson), now tearful, now tyrannical, who consistently wears a top hat, ornate watchchain and his shirt outside his trousers. His name is Dikoy. We have often met Dikoy before—in Tolstoy, Turgenev, Schedrin, Tchekov and others. He is one of the grand stock types of Russian fiction. All the more credit to Janacek for giving him such unconventional music for his drunk act at the end of act two, scene one. c.s.

" KATYA " AGAIN

Mr. Desmond Shawe-Taylor has done a great service to music (and handsomely justified the courage of Sadler's Wells) by defending this unique score against the indolent listening-habits of most critics. In his two *New Statesman* articles he said most of the things that needed saying : that Janacek, far from being incoherent, is meticulously exact in his use of motivic material ; that an unobtrusive but potent Leitmotiv-technique faithfully mirrors the drama ; that the main interest is not in the orchestra but in the inseparable union of orchestral and vocal part-writing (as in every good opera since Wagner).

I should like to add that the appearance of fussiness, even fidgetiness, which the score presents to the all-too-casual listener, is founded not only in the typically " Russian " neuroticism of the story, but also in some kindred disposition of the composer's mind. After all, he had to find a plot that suited him. But this most emphatically does not absolve the critic from penetrating through the neurotic symptoms to the core of a very strange, very profound musical mind. The time will come when familiarity with Janacek's music will be *de rigeur* for the music critic, just as a knowledge of Dostojevsky is already indispensable for his literary colleague. The opera is certainly not an unbroken masterpiece : many of the lyrical passages, although not written with an eye for effect, sound trite by now ; and Janacek's invention is slow getting into its stride in the conventional first scene. But this is forgotten the moment Janacek's quite terrifying regard for artistic truth makes itself felt. I don't mean his exact verbal cadences—they would not sound in an English translation. I mean his sense of drama, so utterly more simple and compassionate than Wagner's or Puccini's, comparable only to the late Verdi's. Take the scene in the second act when the two pairs of lovers meet in the moonlit grove (compliments to Miss Shuard and Miss Studholme) and the music whispers : " This is not fairyland, not Elysium, nor yet the obscure trysting-place of a couple spurned by Society. This place is of this earth, by the banks of the Volga ; but, kind ladies and gentlemen, let it be sacred to these lovers, for they want it so." Or the scene of the last act when Katya publicly confesses her love affair during a thunderstorm. Lightning conductors have been discussed, and the crowd mills around in a disused summer-house. (They could have churned even more about on the stage). Or the long last scene of the heroine's suicide. Here the tragic event reflects no glory back on the composer, illuminating the laurel wreath on his illustrious brow. All this, one feels, is long past ; even the sordid has lost its attraction. The music merely registers the catastrophe ; it has stopped associating. For comment, as well as compassion, now rest with God alone.   P.H.

III. THE LYRIC, HAMMERSMITH
BRITTEN SEASON

" ONE pair of hands " laments Florence in *Herring's* Act I " are all too few for Lady B." And one pair of ears, lament I, are all too few for *Albert Herring*. Nevertheless I pride myself on being not as ear-less as a *Times* criticism of 3rd May which found "the first two scenes in the shop . . far too slender in substance to sustain interest throughout the time appointed to them." How depressing to read a review which says nothing more of the rest of the opera but that " the music . . . is slick in its wit "—as if slickness and wit were the whole *Herring* story. Here I'm afraid *The Times* notice proves itself wit-less too. It was this first performance of *Herring* at the Lyric's current Britten season which made me realise just how substantial the opera's first two acts are. Not that the last is not incomparable, nor that the interludal nocturne is not as musically and dramatically pivotal as it ever was. But where would the substance of the last act be without the substance of its predecessors ? Can something as substantial and as inevitable as the last act develop from the insubstantial and inconsequential ? For instance, how utterly pointless would be Albert's *grazioso* and *amabile* last act song ("And I'm more than grateful to you all ")— with all its expansive self-assurance—if it had not been for his previous Act I

Sc. 2 curtailed, interrupted and harmonically tense " It seems as clear as clear can be " and its subsequent even more passionate and therefore (for Britten) even briefer " Oh maybe soon I'll have the chance "—in any case a sequence of recitative and aria which repays examination from the strictly formal point of view. Albert hardly achieves melodic freedom until after the orgy—he is, as it were, liberated both dramatically and musically—a relaxation which would be musically meaningless without its very subtle preparation in Act I. I have not heard Mr. Pears sing a better Albert. His " And Golly ! it's about time, it's about time " was an astonishing feat—an unanalysable compound of irony, pathos, exasperation—room even for a hint of a wry smile. At this moment in *Herring* we find ourselves suddenly suspended over the deeps. The audience laughed, as sure a sign of insecurity as it is of partial understanding ; for laughter is not only near tears but nearer the truth than an impassive silence.

About *Herring* one could write not a small book but a large one. From its expert English Opera Group production the more musical of the musical might learn something more musical still. For instance how to phrase a single note. Mr. Pears' literally breath-taking entry in Act II Sc. 2 on " Why did she stare " is an example. His " Why " was in itself an infinity of phrases and feeling.

Newcomers to *Herring*'s cast included Victoria Sladen as a to-be very musically considerable Lady Billows, Bruce Boyce as a twice-worthy Mr. Gedge (pulpit and stage, so to speak), Tatiana Preston as a Miss Wordsworth who was demonstrably a Miss Wordsworth, not just a good Miss Ritchie, and a quite uninhibited Harry (Richard Tovell). As for *Dido*, Britten's very distinguished realization *cum* restoration was further distinguished by his own *continuo* playing, by a most accomplished production, and, on the night I saw it, by the respective musicalities of Joan Cross (Dido) and Peter Pears (Aeneas). Pears in this performance showed himself to be vocally extremely versatile ; the part itself was low, and yet there was no sense of strain nor an absence of his customary flawless phrasing. Regrettably, this notice has to go to press before we have had an opportunity of seeing the current production of *Lucretia*. Meanwhile *The Times* notice of *Herring* rather stupidly haunts my mind. How long, I wonder, before a contemporary masterpiece comes to be understood by its contemporaries ? Golly, it's about time, it's about time.

D.M.

Correspondence

21, KENSINGTON COURT GARDENS,
W.8.

18th February, 1951.

SIRS,—I should like to refer to the passage in Luigi Dallapiccola's article on " Don Giovanni," published in your issue of last December, in which he argues that the insertion by Mozart of the scene containing the aria " Non mi dir " between the Graveyard Scene and the Finale interrupts the action and un-balances the architecture of the work. This theory has its obvious attractions. It is certainly arguable that Mozart, possibly during rehearsals of the opera for its first performance, felt obliged to write a second aria for the prima donna concerned, and that this aria did not find a place in his original conception of the opera. On the other hand, its insertion elsewhere involves other problems:

(a) The aria clearly must follow the sextet; yet there the action is already delayed by individual arias given to Leporello, Don Ottavio and Donna Elvira; and to place " Non mi dir " as a fourth aria among this group would not seem to improve the constructional aspect of the opera at that point. (Clearly the aria could not succeed the finale.)

(b) The finale (in D major) would follow directly upon the duet at the end of the graveyard scene (in E major). This juxtaposition of two scenes without any intervening recitative, written in keys one whole tone apart, is, on the evidence of " Don Giovanni " and other operas by Mozart, very unlikely to have been planned or tolerated by him. The peculiarly strong opposition between keys placed in this relationship evidently caused Mozart to avoid the sequence. As the opera stands, the finale in D major follows (after a few negligible bars of recitative) directly on the F major of " Forse, forse "; this key-relationship is an extremely common one in Mozart's operas. If, therefore, Mozart had decided not to write " Non mi dir " and had preferred to lead straight from the graveyard scene to the finale, he would almost certainly not have written the graveyard duet in E major, but probably in F major; this would have involved a manipulation of the preceding recitative to make it end in F major.

(c) A minor point; but it might be thought mildly absurd for Don Giovanni to leave the graveyard with the intention of having the dinner prepared (" a prepararla andiamo ") and immediately thereafter to exclaim " Già la mensa è preparata." Donna Anna's aria, placed between these two scenes, at least has the merit of allowing time for the meal (and the scenery) to be organised.

J. N. A. ARMITAGE-SMITH

THE reader may find it convenient to examine this letter against both Dallapiccola's article in our last Winter Issue and our own Editorial in this year's Spring Issue.

Dallapiccola does not want to insert Anna's aria elsewhere ; he advises its omission. The possibility of its transplantation he only mentions when, and because, he tries to show that it was not so much the aria itself which " caused Berlioz to pen words of fire " as its present position in the structure.

Ad (*a*) :—In his paper on *Don Giovanni : Some Observations* (*The Music Review*, IV/1, 1943), Geoffrey Sharp proposes the following layout for Act II :—Eh via buffone "—" Ah taci, ingiusto core ! "—" Deh vieni alla finestra "—" Meta di voi quà vadano "—" Vedrai, carino "—" Sola, sola, in buio loco "—" Ah pietà, Signori miei ! "—OMIT " Il mio tesoro intanto "; INSERT Scena XIII beginning, Zerlina : " Andiam, andiam Signora " [from the material discovered by Einstein, see *Music and Letters*, October, 1938, p. 419]—"In quali eccessi, o numi"—" Crudele ? "—"O statua gentilissima"— Finale, without " Ah, dov'e il perfido." We are grateful to our correspondent for reminding us that the aria could not succeed the finale.

Ad (*b*) :— E major is the *Wechseldominante* of D major, i.e. its dominant's dominant ; Mozart is not in our opinion unlikely to have planned the " juxtaposition." The 6th scene of the *Entführung*, for instance, is in C major, the 7th in B♭, with just over 100 words of dialogue (*spoken*, of course) in between. Or, to turn to the very keys in question, the D major *Maestoso* following the E major *Allegro* within *Cosi*'s 2nd finale may amend our correspondent's apparent view on the function of the major supertonic in general and on its role in Mozart's dramatico-musical tonalities in particular, especially if he will have a close aural look at the *Allegro*'s central and eventual cadential A majors. One really should only talk about key relations when one definitely *feels* what one is talking about: no offence to Mr. Armitage-Smith, but rather a reminder to many. That Mozart " would almost certainly not have written the graveyard duet in E major " is, in our modest but decided view, nonsense : E major, which, of course, Mozart uses rarely, is by no means among his more multifarious keys (pre-eminently C major, D major, and E♭), so that any of his E major pieces is inseparable from its tonality ; Einstein has already drawn attention to the fact that the key of the graveyard scene is " the very embodiment " of its mood.

Ad (*c*) :—Geoffrey Sharp writes (*loc. cit.*) : " There seems but one cogent justification for playing *Crudele* ? between the cemetery scene and the finale, namely that it may be sung in front of a drop curtain and thus facilitates the task of changing scenery. A revolving stage would obviate this difficulty, otherwise the audience must bear the slight delay "—which would give our correspondent more than a hundred words' time to prepare himself for the shock of the tonic.   ED. (H.K.)

4. NORTON WAY N.,
LETCHWORTH,
HERTS.

29th April, 1951.

DEAR MITCHELL AND KELLER,

I was grieved to read Mr. Denis Stevens' report on " Les Troyens à Oxford," published in Vol.III/3, March, 1951, of *Music Survey*. It so happens that this was the first issue in which my name was added to the list of members of the Editorial Board. Although in such a capacity I was only asked to act as an adviser, bearing no editorial responsibility and barred from either devising or influencing editorial policy, I think it incumbent on me to dissociate myself *a posteriori* from that review, especially in view of the fact that friendly relations exist between myself and the Oxford Faculty of Music.

Regretfully I have come to the conclusion that only my resignation from the Editorial Board of *Music Survey* could clarify my position with regard to this review. I therefore beg you to accept this resignation together with my assurance of my continued sympathy with and interest in your artistic aims.

Yours sincerely,

H. F. REDLICH.

MUSIC SURVEY

A Quarterly Review

Vol IV   No 1.   1951

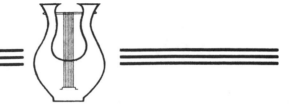

MUSIC SURVEY

(KATHLEEN LIVINGSTON   WILLIAM W. LIVINGSTON   DONALD MITCHELL)

VOL. IV, No. 1   OCTOBER, 1951

CONTENTS

EDITORS :
DONALD MITCHELL
HANS KELLER

EDITORIAL BOARD :
ROBERT DONINGTON   PAUL HAMBURGER   E. D. MACKERNESS
H. B. RAYNOR   RALPH W. WOOD   CHARLES STUART
                       DENNIS DOBSON

EDITORIAL CORRESPONDENCE should be addressed to the EDITORS,
MUSIC SURVEY, OAKFIELD SCHOOL, WEST DULWICH, LONDON, S.E.21.
Annual Subscription, including postage, 11s. U.S.A. $2.50.
All enquiries relating to advertising space in this journal should be made to
MUSIC SURVEY at the above address.

Obituary

Arnold Schoenberg
1874 — 1951

IN these times of revaluations, there is urgent need for those
for whom art is the loftiest expression of the human spirit to
hold fast, guard, and transmit to later generations one thing :
knowledge of and about mastery.

Egon Wellesz on Schoenberg's 60th birthday

[OSKAR ADLER, leading Viennese musician and philosopher who, as
Schoenberg wrote on repeated recent occasions, was his first musical teacher
and led the youthful quartet in which Schoenberg played the cello, may be
known to readers as the leader of the late Oskar Adler Quartet, whose cellist
was Franz Schmidt.* Schoenberg loved and admired his friend up to his
death. In a future issue we shall publish excerpts from Dr. Adler's as yet
sadly unprinted " Critique of Pure Music " (*Die Kritik der reinen Musik*),
an extended treatise of which Schoenberg thought very highly and which he
would have liked to see in print. Oskar Adler is 76 and lives as a naturalized
Briton in Hampstead.—EDS.]

INVITED to say a few words in remembrance of Schoenberg, as his
oldest and earliest surviving friend, I have to confess that I am unable
to give verbal expression to all I feel. To speak alone of what
bound us two together in the early days of Schoenberg's development would seem to me wellnigh sacrilegious. What I can compress
into a few words is no obituary [*Nachruf*], no epilogue, no necro-
logue, since for me Schoenberg has not died ; he strides on, true
to the opening words of his *Jakobsleiter* :—

> Whether right or left, whether forward or backward—
> one must always go on without asking what lies before or
> behind one.

Thus, always driven forward, uncompromising, following solely his
mission to which he had become alive at an early age, he grew to be
the initiator of a new musical epoch, far, far in advance of his
time—a lonely emissary from the land of the future which he had to
till for his contemporaries. Like a true prophet, he had to see and
lead the way where others could perceive nothing but wilderness,
those many others who faced his work devoid of understanding,
because " understanding " meant to them bringing everything new
and strange down to their own level. But then, as Goethe says :—

> We do not write to please you
> *You ought to learn. . . .*

Schoenberg has long since joined the chain of mankind's leading

*Cf. also *The Viennese School ?* in *The Music Review*, *XII*/2, May 1951
p. 154.

geniuses.   As I was able to write on the occasion of his 60th birthday, he brought mankind a twig from the Tree of Life.†   Already has it begun to strike root.   It will continue to grow until it has become a tree wherein the birds of heaven build their nests.

And if these lines are yet to be a *Nachruf*, I would call after [*nachrufen*] Schoenberg, from the bottom of my heart, words which at the present time are perhaps really felt by only a few, but which in days to come will swell into a mighty chorus :—

> Wherever you may be,
> Schoenberg ! we *thank* you.

OSKAR ADLER
(Trans. Ed. [H.K.])

Dr. Adler's German words are in *gehobener Sprache*, for which there is no English concept, and which one cannot in fact reproduce in English without sounding quaint.   I have therefore taken the liberty of slightly toning them down.
The translation of the *Jakobsleiter's* opening sentence I have taken from Dika Newlin.—Trans.]

Greatness can be measured from the distance only, lack of perspective destroys the proportions.   Therefore, it is not for us to be the arbiters of the great composer who has died.   His was a new conception of sound, gladly received by a few, violently rejected by many ; yet, directly or indirectly, every composer was influenced by it.   The phenomenon is that relatively few performances of the comparatively small number of Schoenberg's works should have had an impact which changed the language of music.   His works are still largely a secret.   He had to deliver a message which we can only decipher slowly.   ERWIN STEIN

I suppose it will take quite a few years and another generation to grow up, not impeded by the prejudice of modern contemporary slogans, to realize the real significance of Arnold Schoenberg, the greatest musician of our time !   KARL RANKL

The death of Arnold Schoenberg marks not so much the end as the beginning of an epoch.   His influence on the music of the last fifty years has been greater than any other man's, and the seeds he has sown will grow and blossom in ever greater profusion in the years to come.   Characteristically, he foresaw this in a sardonic aphorism, written as early as 1912, which he quoted in reply to congratulations

†Dr. Adler is referring to the closing sentence of his *Von der ewigen Jugend des Genies* in *Arnold Schönberg zum 60. Geburtstag*, Universal Edition, Vienna, 1934.—EDS.

sent to him on his seventy-fifth birthday : " The second half of this century will spoil by over-estimation all the good of me that the first half, by underestimation, has left intact." I feel there is no need to take a pessimistic view ; the genius that is in Schoenberg will not fail to find expression elsewhere. As an example I should like to quote from a letter recently sent to me by a young musician of 16 living in an English provincial town, a musician whom I do not know personally, and who, so far as I understand, is entirely self-educated musically. He writes " It seems very peculiar to me that after so many years of atonal and twelve tone music, there is still such a controversy over Schoenberg and his pupils. . . . Frankly I cannot see what the fuss is about. Surely if a mere newcomer to the world like myself can listen to his music with real enjoyment so can musicians of long standing. Admittedly some of his works are more difficult to appreciate, but two or three hearings should make them clear."

There speaks the voice of youth—and the same will be found in almost every country in the world. It is important to remember that Schoenberg's ultimate value lies in his *actual compositions* in themselves, more than in any technical procedures that may be deduced from them. A German critic recently wrote that Schoenberg " combines the expressive with the abstract in a convincing synthesis," and added "therein lies the secret and the greatness of his work." That is the point : many composers can achieve the expressive, and very many more the abstract, but Schoenberg, almost alone in our day, has the secret of both—a secret which all the great composers knew.

Among these great masters Schoenberg will find his rightful place when the dust of present-day controversies has long been blown away.

HUMPHREY SEARLE

I mourn the death of Schoenberg. Every serious composer today has felt the effect of his courage, single-mindedness, and determination, and has profited by the clarity of his teaching. The world is a poorer place now this giant is no more.

BENJAMIN BRITTEN

SCHOENBERG

Style and Idea : You had both ;
Beethoven shone through every mood.
With him and Plato you kept troth :
You stand with THE IDEA OF GOOD.

E. H. W. MEYERSTEIN

It is folly to approach a great mind with preconceived ideas. Great minds must inevitably alter our standards of judgment—that is if we are open to appreciate their greatness. Appreciation, indeed, is all that is possible to most of us, for real understanding involves a lengthy process of experience and adjustment. I have heard most of the major works of Schoenberg, but I cannot say I really know and understand them. Yet already I can realize the single-minded debt that music will owe to him for his completely individual and intellectual approach to his art. One does not need to be a dodecaphonist to appreciate what he has achieved. Schoenberg devoted his life to the creation and expansion of an innovatory musical technique, but the theories he evolved need not be confined to the practices he derived from them. Whether or not the twelve-tone system is to become the future language of music, Schoenberg's was a great mind, and it has opened up new paths which future composers must of necessity examine and explore.

JULIAN HERBAGE

PERSPECTIVE

Everyone dies too soon for someone, but not even every genius dies too soon for art, early though he may die for his years. Musically speaking, for example, Mendelssohn died almost too late, whereas not only Schubert, but also Beethoven died earlier than Mozart. It is not alone a question of development attained, but also of development attainable. Beethoven travelled unfathomably far, but as we begin to understand his latest works we fathom that he could have travelled far further. With Schoenberg it seems exactly the same. But in addition, he was born too early. It was really his premature birth which the newspaper obituaries, unintentionally, mourned.

Psychologically speaking, mourning is unconscious guilt. Morally speaking, mourning is conscious duty. We have not done enough for him ; we who feel and think, bear the responsibility for the many who don't. In the end, however, when all is said about, and little done for, the real, the real does itself. Meanwhile, we shall continue to say that a dying culture can, if it will, see the light beyond its grave. Will it ? There is nothing so painfully morbid as health to the moribund. Otherwise it would by now be common knowledge that Einstein, Freud and Schoenberg are the discoverers of the future.

HANS KELLER

Dear Hans,

I find I am quite unable to make a contribution to our own Schoenberg obituary in the manner which we had devised for our distinguished colleagues and ourselves. The formal approach defeats me. Writing a note to someone who understands Schoenberg may help me in my task.

When a great genius dies—particularly a genius who has mattered to me personally as much as Schoenberg has—I think not so much of the present loss, but of what the loss might have been had that genius never happened. In Schoenberg's case I don't find myself saying " What a grave blow to contemporary music " but, rather more optimistically and creatively, " Where would contemporary music have been without him ? "

I wonder what it is that keeps genius alive—alive at least as far as the world is concerned, since I imagine genius must be alive wherever genius exists, even if unrecognized. Thinking back over my association with Schoenberg's music—and that means a return of nine years to when I was eighteen—it strikes me that genius must always make itself known through flashes of revelation to a receptive heart—it's both as simple and as complicated as that. As I think we may safely assume that there will always be a few receptive hearts, we need have no fear that Schoenberg may fail to survive— survive as a creator, not as a " system," an author, not even as a thinker. I shan't (can't) forget the day when I first played " So tanzen die Engel " from the *Gurrelieder*—I knew after the first few bars—especially at " So lieblich klingt ihrer Harfen Ton nicht "— that here was a musical mind of quite exceptional beauty, a judgment I have never faltered in, although it was not consciously or analytically arrived at. All my later acquaintance with Schoenberg's music of any period has never for a moment given me any cause to alter that opinion. It was a revelation, remains a revelation, and it's hardly an exaggeration to say that all Schoenberg's work has been revealed to me through my memory of those four *Gurrelieder* bars and their initial, overwhelming impact. In relation to my own not-so-very-long life, my love of Schoenberg has been of quite long standing, and it has not been revelation alone, but *assimilation* also. As so often with the greatest art, it possesses one and becomes part of one.

I must admit that the thought that Schoenberg himself lived —that the mind which had created so much that was beautiful for me, was still actively creating, was always one of my sources of comfort and consolation. Somehow one could have more confidence in a world in which Schoenberg was alive. As Meyerstein remarks, Schoenberg stood " with THE IDEA OF GOOD " and as it's an idea which only receives minority support, I cannot accept the death of the creative power for Good that Schoenberg was with no more than a well-tailored phrase of grief. Of course we have Schoenberg's music with us still and for that we must be grateful indeed. But now Schoenberg is dead ; and a fraction of the best of all those of us who responded to the concept of Schoenberg alive lies buried with him.

We all died a little when Schoenberg died.

DONALD MITCHELL

Our regular *Schoenberg* section will be found on pp. 343, ff.

Editorial

THIS issue includes a note on Benjamin Britten and " The English Contribution to the Growth of Chamber Music "—two promised articles for which there was no room in our Festival number. Pressure on space obliges us to hold over our normal Film Music feature until December, and to further postpone publication of the projected dialogue on *The Consul*.

Regarding our review of the Glyndebourne Festival on pp. 372f., it must be pointed out that the lamentable news of Fritz Busch's death reached us when these pages were already in print. An appreciation of his achievement will appear in our next issue.

We have to thank one of our Directors, Kathleen Livingston, for her assistance in the preparation of the manuscripts of this issue for the printers, and three members of the Editorial Board, Dennis Dobson, Paul Hamburger, and Denis Stevens, for taking over the editing of it from the galley-proof stage. All are, of course, as exempt as usual from any responsibility for the paper's contents. At the same time we regretfully accept Denis Stevens's resignation from the Editorial Board : his considerable musical duties in another place make it impossible for him to fulfil this function in future. Denis Stevens has been associated with *Music Survey* almost since its inception ; his services have been so apparent that we need not enlarge on our gratitude.   D.M.; H.K.

CORRIGENDUM :—In the criticism of Martin Cooper's Schoenberg review on our last issue's p. 282, lines 11-13, ".... an ear which mistakes its anxiety about the loss of tonal unity for a perception of dissonances and of the highest possible tension ....," cut the " and " which slipped in by sub-editorial mistake.

On the Twelve-Note Road
By LUIGI DALLAPICCOLA

FIRST, I. must state my premises : what follows is not, nor does it set out to be, a study of the twelve-note system.

This will be sufficient justification, I hope, for the strongly and inevitably autobiographical character of my remarks ; inevitably, since my experience of twelve-note music began a long, long time before the publication of René Leibowitz's most useful books. I call them most useful, even if their usefulness has its unfortunate side : that of providing the most outstanding incompetents with the opportunity of passing themselves off as experts on a subject which is far from being strictly codified. It should be remembered that Arnold Schoenberg never gave lessons in the " twelve-note technique," and that as late as 1936 Ernst Krenek wrote : " Whoever speaks of, or deals with, questions arising out of the twelve-note technique, can even to this day only proceed on a basis of personal experience." (*Musica Viva*, Brussels-Zürich, No. 2).

As is well known, a single encounter can decide the orientation of a whole life. My orientation was decided on the night of April 1st, 1924, when I saw Arnold Schoenberg conduct a performance of his *Pierrot Lunaire*, in the Sala Bianca of the Palazzo Pitti. That night the students, with typical Latin gaiety, were indulging in the usual whistling before the performance began : the public for their part, caused an uproar, stamping their feet and laughing. But Giacomo Puccini did not laugh on that occasion. He listened to the performance with the utmost attention, following it with the score, and at the end of the concert asked to be introduced to Schoenberg.

Twenty-five years later, in a letter Schoenberg wrote to me on September 16th, 1949, the creator of the twelve-note system still remembered this gesture of our great popular composer, in these words : " Auf Puccini's Besuch der Pierrot-Aufführung war ich immer stolz. Es war sicherlich ein Zeichen menschlicher Grosse, dass er zu mir gekommen ist—und eine grosse Freundlichkeit."*

*" I have always been proud that Puccini came to see me after the performance of *Pierrot Lunaire*. His visit was truly a sign of human greatness—and showed great friendliness."

That he reproached me, in the same letter, for not having gone to shake his hand on that occasion, is another story. What qualifications had I, what fame of name or works, that I should dare present myself to the master ? Six years later, in Berlin, I still refrained from taking such a step. For at that time Fascism had not yet schooled people to presumption by means of that propaganda which one might define as *the artificial facilitation of life*, and which led to the consequences we all know.

In those days, to get one of our works performed, we had to wait in a long queue ; youths without works or fame did not hold positions in theatrical managements and concert societies ; to teach the most elementary matters of technique in a conservatoire, one had first to undergo examinations (stupid ones, it is true, but they demanded much hard work) ; and it was not the twenty-year-olds who dispensed judgment in daily press criticisms.

I, to be sure, like many others, wrote down my impressions of the outstanding musical events—but in my diary. In this way one could listen to music simply, *con amore* : free from the preoccupation of having to provide a considered judgment the following morning, as food for the public ; free from having to find at all costs a central idea on which to base a *piece* which would *read well ;* free from the fear of having to contradict tomorrow what one said yesterday ; free, finally, from the fear of offending with one's opinions some *employer* who might think differently from oneself. The " Littoriali della Cultura e dell' Arte "† had not yet been created; and everyone was convinced that the way of the artist was a very difficult one.

The night on which I saw Arnold Schoenberg, I felt I had to make a decision. It goes without saying that I did not consider whether I should become *atonal ;* for the time being, I decided to learn the trade.

In general, when people mention my name, they speak of me as a musician who has adopted the twelve-note technique ; and one authority has not hesitated to point out the singularity of my position. The singularity, that is, of having adopted the twelve-note technique at a time when I had no contact with the masters of the Viennese school (Schoenberg, Berg, Webern), nor with their disciples. Perhaps I am not the only composer of my generation to find myself in this position ; but I am ready to admit that it is a somewhat strange one.

†The " Littoriali della Cultura e dell' Arte " were a kind of cultural " games " held in Italy during the Fascist *régime ;* the best way to win a prize was to be a member of the Fascist Party. [Trans.]

319

" Etrange destin que celui de la musique atonale : voici qu'elle vient de devenir actuelle, elle, qui ne le fut pas, à l'époque de sa naissance. . . . "‡ Thus Gisèle Brelet begins her study *Chances de la musique atonale* (Alexandria, 1947). And she continues : " L'atonalisme est maintenant bien actuel : trop tôt venu, il lui fallait attendre que surgisse chez les musiciens la conscience des problèmes auxquelles il prétendait apporter une réponse."§

Now whether or not one agrees with Gisèle Brelet (it is obvious that Schoenberg, Berg and Webern were aware of the problems with which they were faced), it has to be admitted that the phrase " trop tôt venu " has an element of truth in it.

Truth, at least, in relation to other composers, to whom Schoenberg's boldness must have seemed frightening ; and also in relation to the public, even the most cultured and knowledgeable public.

The reason for this is that when the phenomenon of atonality gave its first signs of existence, the art of Debussy was still in full flower ; and Stravinsky, notwithstanding the noisy fiasco of *Le Sacre*, swiftly won over at least the ballet public which, listening to the music with its eyes, found justification for it that way.

The reasons for Ravel's favourable attitude towards the Viennese school must be sought elsewhere. Ravel had a natural distrust of giving too free a rein to fancy (a thing which can easily happen in the course of improvisation), and he loved to have problems to solve. (The Sonata for violin and cello is a typical example.) I shall never forget how warmly D. E. Ingelbrecht, who knew Ravel extremely well, agreed with me when I said that Ravel would have come to write a piano concerto for the left hand even if Paul Wittgenstein had not provided the occasion ; and precisely in order to limit to the utmost the danger of improvisation.

Years ago, a composer of tonal music who is a friend of mine declared, in the course of an interview, that when composing he followed his instinct ; that he was opposed on principle to any kind of system ; and that the word " *system* " itself appeared to him to be synonymous with " *trick*."

Now, although I am grateful to this musician for the friendship he has often shown me, and have frequent cause to admire his music, I must say that I have not the same admiration for his sense of logic.

‡" A strange fate, that of atonal music : it has only just become a living reality, which it certainly was not at the time of its birth. . . . "

§" Atonality is now a living reality : having arrived too early, it had to wait for musicians to become aware of the problems to which it claimed to provide an answer."

The word "*system*" is, according to him, synonymous with
"*trick.*" So far, so good ! By the very fact, however, that he
writes tonal music, he himself makes use of a system codified from
three centuries of experience, that is to say of a codified trick ; but
this is used unconsciously because it has been learnt at school and
because it forms part of us from the day of our birth. (It has been
wittily said that God, who gave us the moral law, also took care,
in His infinite bounty, to provide us with the tonal system). It
seems likely, moreover, that when music passed from the modal
system to the tonal system there was a critical period of uncertainty
perhaps not very different from that which, according to many
critics and listeners, is one of the most characteristic features of our
time : a time of considerable confusion, but one which only superficial minds can reproach with lack of faith.

Atonality, " trop tôt venu," was for a time abandoned : at least
in the sense that it was forgotten (hence the amazement of so many
critics at seeing it reappear again after the war). In the ten years
immediately preceding the last war in Europe, the only topic
of conversation was *neo-classicism.* Around 1930, Italian and
foreign magazines stated, without a flicker of the eyelid, that
" Germany had only one great musician : Paul Hindemith."
And performances of atonal or twelve-note music were made more
and more difficult by political events. The advent of Adolf Hitler
(a great connoisseur of art, like all self-respecting dictators) marked
the end of public performances of such music in Germany. In
Italy, performances were not forbidden, in the true sense of the word :
but every day some *aesthetician* (a critic-composer, of course)
publicly arraigned one or other of the composers belonging to the
so-called vanguard of *internationalism,* which in the language of
those days meant *anti-fascism* or, more precisely, *communism.*
Exactly how much attitudes of this kind have to do with strict
problems of aesthetics is not for me to say. It is enough to say
for the moment that even criticism has its *systems.* So-called
atonal music had very seldom been performed before the arrival
of Fascism, and was very seldom performed during the reign of
Fascism : so that no difference was to be perceived.

Just at the time when everyone had ceased to mention atonality or
twelve-note music, I began to be passionately interested in such
problems. (I am grateful to Guido M. Gatti for pointing out my
unrealistic position in a criticism on the Venice Festival of 1937.)
And already, in the first period of my activities as a composer (from

1934 to 1939, that is from the *Divertimento in quattro esercizi* to *Volo di notte*), series of twelve notes begin to make their, undeniably timid, appearance in my works ; in some cases they were used for purely colouristic purposes, in others with exclusively melodic intent.

At that time I had need of a helpful guide, or at least a confidant or a not too fanatical opponent ; but I could not find one.

Every first performance of a work by Stravinsky was the event of the musical year ; Hindemith was the fashion ; Bartok was to wait ten years, that is till after his death, to be tardily *discovered*. (They always come at the right moment, the discoverers !) Whenever I turned to anyone for light on the twelve-note technique, I always received the reply " It's finished." Someone advised me in a kindly way not to waste my time on such *unrealistic* matters. In Italy, at that time, baroque music was considered *realistic*, and an attempt was being made to write music equivalent to the architecture of Bernini. (Alas ! in too many cases it turned out to be merely an equivalent of the architecture of Piacentini . . .).

So I found myself practically alone. With the invasion of Austria by Hitler's troops, it became more and more difficult to obtain the works of the masters of the Viennese school : the few articles which had appeared around 1925 were no longer to be found, and those I did manage to track down were so schematic that they gave me no help at all.

From time to time, I tried my hand at analysing atonal works. I went wrong with many of them : with others I was more successful. I noticed that a system of analysis which held good for one work did not hold good for another. Far from being discouraged by the comparatively few results I obtained, I remembered a phrase of Ferruccio Busoni : " Avoid making art a routine. Let each work constitute a principle."

With the outbreak of war, the possibility of getting information became even more limited than in the years immediately preceding, and the solitude I mentioned above gradually became a necessity.

I am fully aware that what follows, an account of the way in which I arrived at an understanding of the twelve-note technique, will seem in these days very ingenuous ; in these days, I say, because everyone can now obtain the scores of the Viennese school, and René Leibowitz's books explain down to the smallest detail the system which attracted me, giving accurately prepared analyses with the notes numbered according to the development of the series. But in 1940 all this did not exist. Whoever wished to take the road

322

towards twelve-note music had to rely entirely on his own capabilities. At a distance of several years I can count myself lucky in having achieved so much on my own, notwithstanding many mistakes.

I have already pointed out, some time ago, that the difficulty of understanding twelve-note music is not due to the large number of *dissonances* it contains. I had realized this as early as 1935, when I heard in Prague, at the thirteenth Festival of the International Society for Contemporary Music, Anton Webern's Concerto, Op. 24, a work I admired because it seemed to me to express the composer's highest *ideal*, not because I had understood it as *music*. It was already clear to me then that the difficulty of understanding such music was due to other factors, especially to the fact that it made use of a new dialectic.

At the same Festival, when I heard Schoenberg's Variations, Op. 31, for the first time, I noticed something I had never been taught at the Conservatoire : that one of the most marked differences between classical music (I speak of sonata form, which is perhaps the highest achievement of classical music) and music based on a note-series could be formulated as follows. In classical music, the theme is nearly always subjected to *melodic* transformation, while its rhythm remains unaltered ; in music based on a note-series, the task of transformation is concerned with the *arrangement* of the notes, independent of rhythmic considerations. My first acquaintance with two great writers, James Joyce and Marcel Proust, date from this time.

Lacking treatises on twelve-note music and being unable to obtain the scores I needed, I found in the works of these writers confirmation of what I had dimly felt after hearing the works of Schoenberg and Webern.

In the works of James Joyce, above all in *Ulysses*, I was immediately struck by certain *assonances*.

Once already, years ago, I have had occasion to speak of certain *musical allusions* in the works of Webern, and to compare them with certain passages in *Ulysses* (*Il Mondo*, Florence, No. 15, 3rd November, 1945). The way in which Joyce exploits the name of Lynch, the young friend of Stephen Daedalus, is far from being a mere play on words.

In the brothel scene (corresponding to the Circe episode in the *Odyssey*) I found the following passage :
STEPHEN : Hm. (*He strikes a match and proceeds to light the cigarette with enigmatic melancholy*).

LYNCH : (*Watching him*). You would have a better chance of lighting it if you held the match nearer.

STEPHEN : (*Brings the match nearer his eye*). Lynx eye.

Again, in the same scene, another example :

STEPHEN : . . . . Married.

ZOE : It was a commercial traveller married her and took her away with him.

FLORRY : (*Nods*). Mr. Lambe from London.

STEPHEN : Lamb of London, who takest away the sins of our world.

LYNCH : (*Embracing Kitty on the sofa, chants deeply*). *Dona nobis pacem.*

The love of the word in Joyce, so near to the love of the note (regained in the music of our time), could even be carried over, in this case, into the famous French translation, maintaining fidelity to the original text.

STEPHEN : . . . . Mariée.

ZOE : C'est un voyageur de commerce qui l'a épousée et qui l'a emmenée avec lui.

FLORA : (*Appuie*). C'est M. Lagneau, de Londres.

STEPHEN : Agneau de Londres, qui enlevez les pechés du pauvre monde.

LYNCH : (*Qui enlace Kitty sur le* sopha, *psalmodie*). *Dona nobis pacem.*

Elsewhere, however, owing to the impossibility of transferring an assonance faithfully, the translators (helped, as is known, by the author) were obliged to re-create a passage entirely, so as to keep intact the love of the word. And so we find ourselves faced with a case like this, taken from the music-room scene, which corresponds to the episode of the Sirens in the *Odyssey*.

He heard Joe Maas sing that one night. Ah, what M'Guckin ! Yes. In his way. Choirboy style. Maas was the boy Massboy.

Which, in the French translation, is re-created thus :

Il avait entendu Joe Coeur chanter ça un soir. Ah, oui, M'Guckin ! Oui. Dans sa manière. Style d'enfant de choeur. Mais Coeur c'était l'as. L'as de coeur.

From this, I believed I understood up to what point in music an identical succession of notes could take on a different meaning by being *arranged* in a different way.

And I was also struck by Joyce's occasional use of an identical word first in its usual form and afterwards in its reverse form, beginning with the last letter and ending with the first (*cancrizans*, in music). At that time I did not know (Vladimir Vogel told me of it later) that, in some ancient languages, the roots of certain words of opposite meaning (*Dio—il Demonio ! la luce—l'oscurità*) are the same, and that certain words still have a meaning even if they are read *cancrizans*.

My observations on Joyce's prose encouraged me and showed me that, at bottom, the problems of all the arts are *a single problem*. The assonances I had noticed in Joyce had led me to realize that, in the use of a twelve-note series, the most careful and conscientious effort must be devoted to its *arrangement ;* contact with Marcel Proust gave me the opportunity of getting a definitive outlook on the new dialectic and new constructive method of the twelve-note system.

But, before proceeding, a parenthesis is necessary.

I had read somewhere (I do not know whether the writer was a competent person or a nonentity) that, in the twelve-note system, the twelve notes *have equal importance.*

It is obvious that, at the time when such a proposition could be formulated, many problems were far from being solved. It appeared evident to me that even if, from a *quantitative* point of view, the notes were equal in number, one factor of capital importance could not be overlooked : the moment, or the actual point of the bar, at which a given note makes itself heard. Hence we see *time* intervening, representing, as it were, the *fourth dimension* of music. It goes without saying that a note which falls on the weak beat of the bar will never have the same importance as the same note when it falls on the strong beat. The same may be said of notes which form part of a quick passage, compared with the same notes when they form part of a slow passage.

I know well that differences of this kind can also be found in classical music ; but how much more subtle and delicate are such relationships in twelve-note music !

Thus I came to the conclusion that if, in the twelve-note system, the tonic had disappeared, taking with it the tonic-dominant relationship, and if, in consequence, sonata form had completely disintegrated, there still existed, nevertheless, a power of attraction, which I will call *polarity* (I do not know whether such a definition has been used before, or whether there is another) : I mean by this term the extremely subtle relationships which exist between certain notes. These relationships are not always easily perceptible today, being much less obvious than that of tonic to dominant, but they are there, all the same.

The interesting point about this polarity is the fact that it can change (or be changed) from one work to another. One series can reveal to us the *polarity* that exists between the first and twelfth sounds ; another that which exists between the second and the ninth ; and so on. Here the *time* factor, which I mentioned just now, steps in, revealing its true importance : by this means we can establish the characteristic interval by impressing it on the memory more deeply than the others, and thus we have a chance of making our musical argument understood. (I do not speak of those who will not or cannot understand, nor of the innumerable heirs of Luigi Cherubini, who refused to go and hear the Fantastic Symphony of Berlioz, giving as his reason that " There is no need to go and hear how *not* to write music.")

And now I must give a brief account of my meditations on Proust.

Among the various characters in *La Recherche du temps perdu*, my choice fell on Albertine, but it will be readily understood that I could have taken as an example the Baron de Charlus or any other character.

Let us examine for the moment a passage taken from the first book of *A l'ombre des jeunes filles en fleur*, the particular passage in which this character's name is mentioned for the first time.

" C'est l'oncle d'une petite qui venait à mon cours, dans une classe bien au-dessous de moi, la fameuse *Albertine*. Elle sera sûrement très *fast* mais en attendant elle a une drôle de touche."

" Elle est étonnante ma fille, elle connaît tout le monde."

" Je ne la connais pas. Je la voyais seulement passer, on criait Albertine par-ci, Albertine par-là."*

It is true that, in the case of Swann or, shall we say, in the case of Odette, it was considered very *chic* to interlard the conversation from time to time with some English word or other. But here, the use of the English adjective *fast* must be interpreted in quite a different way. Gilberte does not use the English adjective because she considers it the thing to do ; it is Proust who, at the moment of introducing such an important character's name for the first time (it does not appear for the second time until about a hundred and five pages later) compels us, by using the English adjective, to pay particular attention to the name. It is by virtue of the English adjective that the name Albertine suddenly attracts our attention ;

* " He's the uncle of a little girl who used to come to my lessons, in a much lower class than mine, the famous *Albertine*. She'll certainly be very *fast* when she grows up, but just at the moment she's a bit of a sight."
" She's amazing, my daughter. She knows everybody."
" I don't know her. I only used to see her going about, and hear them calling ' Albertine ' here, and ' Albertine ' there."

and thus it remains inseparably linked with the adjective *fast*, an adjective which already seems to contain within itself a whole tragic fatality. *Albertine par-ci, Albertine par-là.* This repetition of the name is a subtle technical device, an invitation to the memory. When Albertine is mentioned for the second time, it is Mme Bontemps who introduces her name. " Et ma nièce Albertine est comme moi. Vous ne savez pas ce qu'elle est effrontée, cette petite."†

Here we are informed of another trait of this character, which is fixed in our memory by the adjective *fast*, and which, though it still remains off-stage, has an undeniable existence for us.

In the second book of *A l'ombre des jeunes filles en fleur*, we find only one mention of Albertine's name. But this time it is attached to considerations of such importance to the protagonist that we are obliged to pay particular attention to it, even if the action still takes place out of sight, off-stage.

Here is the passage in question :—

" Il y eut une scène à la maison parce que je n'accompagnais mon père à un dîner officiel où il devait y avoir les Bontemps, avec leur nièce Albertine, petite jeune fille, presque encore enfant. Les différentes périodes de notre vie se chevauchent ainsi l'une l'autre. On refuse dédaigneusement, à cause de ce qu'on aime et qui vous sera un jour si égal, de voir ce qui vous est égal aujourd'hui, qu'on aimera demain."§

Lastly, in the third book of *A l'ombre des jeunes filles en fleur*, we find Albertine's name four times, before seeing her *as a real person* on the stage. First of all, together with the *petite bande*, on the beach at Balbec. Proust gives us there, as it were, a portrait of the heroine, still unknown to the protagonist. He, shortly afterwards, hearing the name " Simonet " (" C'est une amie de la petite Simonet ") has the feeling that the name belongs to one of the girls of the *petite bande* : he enquires at the hotel and finds, sure enough, the name *Simonet et famille* amongst the latest arrivals. He meets a young girl on a bicycle, but he is not certain that it is definitely Albertine.

†" And my niece Albertine is like me. You've no conception how impudent that girl is."

§" There was a scene in the house because I did not go with my father to an official dinner at which the Bontemps were to be present, with their niece Albertine, a young girl, almost still a child. Thus the different periods of our life jostle one against the other. We refuse disdainfully, on account of something we love but shall one day no longer care for, to see the thing which today we do not care for but shall one day come to love."

327

And so, at last, we come to the *lyrical* passage, the *rhythmic and melodic* definition : " Tout à coup y apparut, le suivant à pas rapides, la jeune cycliste de la petite bande avec sur ses cheveux noirs son polo abaissé vers ses grosses joues, ses yeux gaies et un peu insistants ; et dans ce sentier miraculeusement rempli de douces promesses, je la vis sous les arbres adresser à Elstir un salut souriant d'amie, arc-en-ciel qui unit pour moi notre monde terraquée à des régions que j'avais jugées jusque-là inaccessibles."‡

Notice how, not until the eighth time of meeting Albertine's name, may we say that we begin to know her.

Shall we now try a comparison between this particular technique of presenting a character and that of the classical novel ?

Let us consider, for a moment, Padre Cristoforo, letting this great example serve for all. We see how Manzoni, on the first appearance of the character, is immediately careful to inform the reader of all his traits. Even that is not considered sufficient, however ; and so he informs us even as to particulars regarding the character's family, particulars which have played a fundamental part in forming his religion.

In music, this procedure is used in sonata form.

Sonata form demands that already in its first section (called the *exposition*) the two principal themes shall be exposed, and shall contrast with one another. The characters must be clearly defined from the beginning. Who does not know the theme of the Eroica Symphony ? Is it Napoleon, or someone else ? A hero, in any case. A character defined with a clarity of outline, a precision of design, which will not change throughout the whole first movement. Or let us consider the first thume of Mozart's Symphony in G minor. The rhythmic organisation of this miraculous theme undergoes no change, notwithstanding its many sensational adventures of colouring and modulation.

It is sonata form which demands this : a form once supremely alive but now, for some time, completely worn out. A strange thought that, from those very quarters where there is such opposition to *formalism*, there should come so many compositions written in the most played-out of all musical forms. But I will add nothing further on this subject : I am not writing a polemic. It was at

‡" Suddenly there appeared (on the road), following it at a rapid pace, the young cyclist of the little band, with her polo cap pulled down over her black hair towards her fat cheeks, her eyes merry and almost importunate ; and on that auspicious path, miraculously filled with promises of delight, I saw her beneath the trees wave to Elstir a friendly greeting, a rainbow which, for me, linked our terraqueous world to regions I had hitherto considered inaccessible."

Weimar in 1923 that Busoni, in his crystal-clear way, spoke, on the subject of form, words that seemed to me definitive :

" Man kann auch heute Fugen schreiben mit den überlieferten oder mit den modernen und atonalen Mitteln . . . . doch wird einer solchen Fugen immer ein antiquirter Charakter anhaften. . . . Denn die Fuge ist eine ' Form.' Als solche ist sie zeitgebunden, ' vergänglich.' Dagegen ist die Polyphonie keine Form, sondern ein Prinzip und als solches zeitlos und, so lange Musik geschaffen wird, ' unvergänglich.' "**

Is it necessary to emphasize that *canon*, which occupies such an important place in the twelve-note dialectic, is not a *form*, but part of the *principle* of polyphony ? (Perhaps Busoni, when he made the above definition, had in mind the dictum of Paul Bekker, " the crisis of modern music is a crisis of form " ?)

All this occurred to me after I had realized the difference between classical music and music based on a series : a difference of dialectic.

In music based on a series, instead of finding ourselves faced with a character rhythmically and melodically defined at the outset, we have to wait a long time : exactly as we had to wait a long time for the rhythmic and melodic definition of Albertine, " a rainbow which, for me, linked our terraqueous world to regions I had hitherto considered inaccessible."

Before reaching this rhythmic and melodic definition of the series, we may find it compressed into a single chord of twelve notes, two chords of six notes, three of four notes, four of three notes, or even six two-note chords . . . . to speak only of the most elementary possibilities. It will be understood that, in every such combination, the sense of *polarity* must be alive and present, so as to enable the listener to follow the musical argument.

And here I must mention once more the name of Proust. I have said that I could have devoted my analysis to the Baron de Charlus instead of to Albertine : what I wish to point out now is that both these characters find their *rhythmic and melodic* definition at Balbec.

Balbec, then, is not merely a geographical entity : it is something far more important. In relation to the constructional method of the novel, it is something analagous to what I called *polarity* in music based on a series.

** " Even today it is still possible to write fugues, using traditional or even modern and atonal methods . . . . yet to every such fugue there will always cling an antiquated character. . . . For fugue is a ' form,' and as such, time-bound, ' mortal.' On the other hand, polyphony is not a form, but a principle; as such it is timeless and, as long as music continues to be created, ' immortal.' "

To turn to a question one hears very frequently : is the twelve-note system a language or a technique ? To my way of thinking, it is even a state of mind. In any case, it seems to me a natural development of music, and Schoenberg's recent definition *nuova logica* will perhaps one day be thought as satisfactory as the definition *seconda practica*, adopted by Monteverdi three centuries ago.

For a long time the tonal system showed signs of being inadequate to convey all that musicians felt an urgent need to express : we can go back as far as Wagner and Debussy to find great composers who sought a code of rules by which to realize their poetic world. This movement towards the disintegration of the tonal world moved more and more swiftly : there arose, in quick succession, poly-tonality, atonality, the most unusual scales, quarter- and sixth-tones, until the arrival of twelve-note music, which is the most complete answer to the problem of the *method of composition*, in that it offers a basis on which to build. Personally, I have adopted this method because it allows me to express what I feel I must express.

The note-series technique is only a means of helping a composer to achieve coherence of musical argument. If anyone says that a work based on a series is automatically guaranteed such coherence, he is making a great mistake, since no artificial technique has ever guaranteed anything, and the unity of such a work will be, together with its melody, rhythm and harmony, an inferior product. It is not irrelevant to recall that the Wagnerian *leitmotiv* technique was merely a means of facilitating the musical argument and that, whereas in *Tannhäuser* and *Lohengrin*, this technique appears only sporadically, it reaches its fullest development in *Tristan*, the work in which the dominant-tonic relationship (once itself intended as a means of unifying musical argument) was weakened to the greatest extent.

Tonality still exists and will probably exist for a long time yet.

I am amazed when I am asked whether a given work is, or is not, strictly in the twelve-note system—as I was amazed when I heard that, during the Venice Festival of 1949, Schoenberg was accused of treachery for having presented a tonal work, his second Chamber Symphony. (Did not Dante continue to write in Latin, during the years he was engaged on the *Divina Commedia* ?)

We are once more at the *beginning of a period*. We see that each twelve-note work raises new problems and, if it is successful, finds new solutions. If it is successful, I say, because in art success is a very rare thing. (I dare say it will be admitted that, even in three centuries of tonal music, a few stupid works may have been written and that some may even have come from the pens of living tonal composers, at least one apiece.)

We see, again, that in the last ten years practice has somewhat abated the rigour of certain theoretical rules laid down previously. And we also see how works which, up to a few years ago, were generally regarded as unperformable and incomprehensible no longer seem so problematic.

Whatever one may say, no system (or so-called system) produced in this century has had more power than the twelve-note system to set things moving. No other system has been so persistently and acrimoniously opposed ; other systems, having once fallen into disuse, have never reappeared, whereas this one *did* reappear, and during the war years at that, in isolation and in all countries independently. Today, several twelve-note works have been acclaimed by the public ; the success of *The Survivor from Warsaw* at the Venice Festival of 1950 was particularly significant, notwithstanding the somewhat grotesque attempts of certain sections of the press to minimize its importance.

(It is a strange thing : if the public boos a twelve-note work, it has good reason, and whoever boos does so calmly and in good faith : if he applauds, on the other hand, it is because he knows, for example, that the day of performance is the composer's birthday, and he is consequently influenced by sentimental reasons !)

And even if, today, we are too near to events to write a history of dodecaphony, it is certain that, within a decade or so, the twelve-note movement will find complete justification, even in the eyes of those who today oppose it.

It will find historical justification, because *total chromaticism* has tried many times in musical history to confine itself within a narrow space : Heinrich Jalowetz found in the finale of Mozart's Symphony in G minor a series of ten different notes (cf. *The Musical Quarterly*, October 1944, *Music Survey*, December, 1950) ; Hermann Scherchen found a passage of twelve different notes in the finale of Beethoven's Ninth (cf. *Vom Wesen der Musik*, Winterthur ; English edition, trans. William Mann, Dobson, 1950) ; and I myself found a series of nine different notes in a sonata of Domenico Scarlatti, and—what is more strange—in these notes we find the whole-tone scale (cf. *Polyphonie*, No. 4, Brussels ; *La Rassegna Musicale*, April 1950 ; *Music Survey*, December, 1950). It will find aesthetic justification, based on artistic success, the only basis which counts, and the only one by which such works can be judged in the future, when polemics and personal rancour are things of the past.

For when we come face to face with an artistic success, we find that it automatically falls into its place in music as a whole, which knows neither present nor future, nor what is fashionable, nor what is out of date. An artistic success takes its place in history by virtue of its own merits.

(Translated by DERYCK COOKE.)

Britten: Thematic Relations and The 'Mad' Interlude's 5th Motif

BY HANS KELLER

I certainly think it necessary that the motivic web be clear to every hearer . . . One must get to know and understand a work by *thorough* study ; the deeper the music is, the more difficult one's study, and the longer does it take.
Mahler to an unknown addressee (15.5.94).

One thing I miss in your analysis of my 4th Symphony : did you overlook the thematic connections which are so extremely important for the idea of the work ? Or did you think you ought not to trouble the public with technical explanations ? In any case, please make a special search for these connections.
Mahler to Georg Göhler (8.2.11).

THEMATIC relationships are (1) cyclic or/and (2) derivative or/and (3) leitmotivic ; only one kind altogether excludes one other : (4) the repetitional and consecutive relations whose function is immediately connective rather than recapitulatory and thus not sufficiently extended to become cyclic. The " Spring " Symphony's thematic links and derivations are a good example of (4) (and (2)). The finale's " Sumer is i-cumen in," on the other hand, occurring at the point where nowadays a cyclic recapitulation usually appears, may be regarded as an extra-operic, intertemporal, historical cyclicism : an extremely subtle build-up once one admits the unifying function of a quotation of something that has not previously been stated. In any case, every form of cyclicism applies one or the other modification of the psychologically indestructible principle that the end is the beginning and the middle isn't, or that where the middle is, there are other middles in between. Being a basic formal device, a cyclic connection is, other things being similar, the most conscious thematic relationship to composer and listener : say, the opening and closing chorus in " Grimes," or the title-figure's reminiscences at the end of " Grimes," " Lucretia," and " Herring." Somewhat surprisingly, more purely leitmotivic and derivative relations are not always as conscious to the composer as they should be to the listener : someone told me that the relation I had pointed out between Lady Billows's arias in "Herring's" Scene I (Ex. 1) had not

Ex.1: 'ALBERT HERRING' SCENE I, Lady B's arias before and after the recitativic rondo.

Ex.2: 'PETER GRIMES'.

Act II, Scene I, bar 16 of ADAGIO.

Last Interlude, bars 15 ff.

been conscious to Britten, or had been vaguely conscious at the time of writing and then forgotten, despite its well-defined musico-dramatic significance. But the composer's unconsciousness is no excuse for the listener's, for after all the composer gets the thing out of his system and the listener into his ; in better words, the listener's unconscious is not so potent passively as the composer's is actively. Purely intellective theme-hunting does not, however, seem to me to be of the faintest use ; I take Mahler's reminders to mean that basically one's thorough study of a work should be emotional. I myself, at any rate, always let my emotional understanding drive the " motivic web " into the intellect; at the second performance of the " Spring " Symphony, the accompanimental relations between the middle section of " Out on the Lawn I Lie in Bed " and " Waters

Above," which I had not realized at the first performance, became suddenly clear to me when I got complete emotional hold of the structure. Thus only those analyses interest and help me today which I would have written myself tomorrow. But that may be I and my kind of music. Anyhow, while intellectual realization is no proof of understanding, lack of intellectual realization indicates incomplete understanding. Which is to say that Sackville-West's analysis of "Grimes" is, remarkable flashes of insight apart, superficial and insufficient ; nor does Stuart amend it. To take one of the most depressing instances of Sackville-West's heedlessness, i.e. the fifth motif in the ' Mad ' Interlude, a phantasy which is throughout thematic in that all its constituents are cyclic, derivative and leitmotivic. He shows the derivations of the first four motifs, but when he arrives at the passage here quoted, he just talks of " a grunting figure for two clarinets." Its origin is given in the quotation, which incidentally reminds us that whatever has become of Peter's stubborn outburst by the time of the Mad Scene, it is not the utterance of a pig. Peter's "Wrong to plan ! ", it may be added, inverts the minor ninth of his preceding " Out of the hurly-burly " and of his " Take away your hand ! " ; while these phrases in their turn do not readily betray their kinship with " We strained into the wind " (Act 1, Scene I ; reappearing conspicuously in Ex. 2's quotation from the ' Mad ' Interlude) though they also go on to the octave.

REFERENCES : Mahler, A.M. (ed.) : *Gustav Mahler Briefe*, Berlin 1925. Keller, H. : *The Rape of Lucretia, Albert Herring*, London 1947. Stein, E.: *Form in Opera : ' Albert Herring ' Examined*, in *Tempo*, Autumn 1947. Sackville West, E. : *Peter Grimes : The Musical and Dramatic Structure*, in Sadler's Wells Opera Book No. 3, London 1945. Stuart, C. : *Peter Grimes*, London 1947.

The English Contribution to the Growth of Chamber Music

By ROBERT DONINGTON

AMONG the rare advantages of a disillusioned age is a healthy disrespect for that religion of perpetual progress by which the genius of our ancestors is belittled, and therefore deprived of its fructifying virtue. The climate of our times at least encourages us to search the past not patronizingly but humbly. In music our gain is twofold : our composers, because the ancestral spirit can touch them and work through them (nothing to do with pastiche), stand once more in the chain of the generations and can produce creatively;

our listeners and performers, because they are content to recreate the original performing conditions (instead of replacing them with all the blessings of modern civilization) are learning how to give our ancestral music itself new life and the power to move and enrich our modern souls.

Still, everything must have a start. We can perhaps afford to laugh at the Victorians who called Haydn the father of the symphony, and Corelli the first instrumental composer : instrumental music is of the same primeval antiquity as instruments and has worn as many forms, from the temple bands of Egypt to the astounding harmony for two hands on the Celtic harp of which immemorial fragments survived to be written down by a belated Elizabethan bard.* It is not true, indeed it is a ridiculous assertion, that the 16th century witnessed the birth of instrumental music out of vocal music through the dance ; but it is true that a certain tradition of instrumental music supremely important to ourselves was so parented. It was the tradition which was to produce the late piano sonatas and quartets of Beethoven and which is still creative.

In this Festival year we may be proud that England made two major contributions towards launching our present chamber music tradition, one of which was unique. The story, which is still not familiar in all its details, may be briefly told as follows.

Concerning the Middle Ages, we can only be certain that instruments were numerous and freely used ; that they often doubled and alternated with voice parts in vocal performances ; that they accompanied solo singers such as the troubadours ; and that they played dance music.

Concerning the Renaissance, it can clearly be established, what was probably no novelty, that instrumentalists provided themselves with a large part of their repertory by borrowing vocal music. Now it was at this period an almost universal habit to embellish a written or traditional text with ornamental improvisation often so elaborate as to amount to new figuration, and in extreme cases virtually to a new composition. Both singers and instrumentalists employed this highly imaginative art, half creation and half interpretation ; but the instrumentalists exploited it in particular as a method of adapting music of vocal origin for the purposes of instrumental virtuosity. Their improvised figuration inclined more and more to idioms characteristic of the instrument employed : a sort of sketchy but richly suggestive counterpoint for the lute ; skips and leaps for

*British Museum M.S. Add. 14905.

335

the viol ; runs and arpeggiation for the keyboard, and so forth. What began as improvisation, besides continuing in that form, at least till the end of the Baroque period, also passed into composition. The result was a technique and a style, or rather a number of techniques and styles, intimately adapted to the main instrumental families of the late Renaissance because developed for and upon them. This development reached significant proportions in the course of the 16th century.

To avoid misunderstanding it is important to bear two corollaries in mind : (1) This was not the first instance of a specifically instrumental technique and style but merely the first of which we have much clear knowledge in our central European tradition: (2) In that tradition, it must be seen against a background of relatively pure polyphony, by which I mean a habit of treating the abstract lines of a polyphonic network as more important than the vocal or instrumental colourings in which these lines appear. Scoring in the late Renaissance was normally quite unstandardized. This does not mean that it was indifferent or casual ; but given a number of polyphonic lines to execute, the players used their own judgment in allotting voices or instruments to them, and any choice which was musically convincing (the operative factor), was equally legitimate. It was thus as an exception to established custom, though no novelty on the long historic view, that the instrumentalists of the late 15th and 16th centuries developed idioms and figures and formulae organically derived from the character of each individual instrument.

Here, then, was a stream of development stemming from vocal (and in the main polyphonically vocal) music, but intensely modified by the actual characteristics of various instruments, of which the chief were for the time being the lute, the organ, the harpsichord (not yet evolved at its most elaborate, and the viols, together with a number of melodic wind instruments (cornettos, shawms, flutes transverse and vertical, trombones, etc.) less individualized. With this stream there mingled another by no means devoid of vocal associations, but really in its essence opposed to the natural inclinations of vocal music : namely dance accompaniments, with their periodic symmetry and their strong pulsating rhythms. From such rhythms, some of the most characteristically instrumental figures took their origin, while the periodic symmetry contributed invaluably to the growth of abstract instrumental forms, as convincing and organic in their structure as those quite different forms whose framework is a complex verbal text.

336

Vocal polyphony and melody ornamentally embellished in ever more characteristically instrumental idioms ; dance symmetry and rhythms carried ever further from their primary purpose into the realms of abstract form : these are the twin streams from whose mingling in the 16th century flowed our present tradition of instrumental chamber music.

Now for the peculiarly English contribution. I have described it as a double one : I have in mind first that curious and uniquely English fashion for writing innumerable *In Nomines* for viols : second the astounding school of keyboard music, not uniquely English but superior to any continental parallel or precursor, which worked up from the mid-16th century to a brief but glorious climax in the last years of Elizabeth and the reign of James I. I shall not in this article have space to describe both, and concerning the keyboard music, which though still grossly neglected is the more familiar of the two, I shall merely say :

(1) It is technically, formally and emotionally as mature in its best examples as any school of music has ever been, and of an astonishing beauty.

(2) It is so well written for its own instruments that it sounds dry, bald and unconvincing if transferred to the piano—whence its previous neglect.

(3) Even more important than the right instruments is the right style, which is a closed book to most modern performers, and absolutely essential to the music.

(4) What with the association of Philips and Bull with Sweelinck (who taught Scheidemann who taught Reinken who profoundly influenced J. S. Bach) in Amsterdam and the adoption whether consciously or unconsciously of the English fingerings by Couperin, and through him by J. S. Bach again, we can be certain that the influence of our great keyboard school entered the main continental tradition with incalculable consequences for good

To understand the *In Nomine* we must return to the young manhood of Henry VIII, early in the 16th century. That versatile monarch, so cultured and so likable before hidden illness slowly warped his character, himself composed melodiously for viols in the instrumental idiom of his time : beautiful, quiet part-writing of a not specially instrumental character, entirely similar to the great secular collections in Italy and elsewhere, by which with his taste for Italian art and music he was certainly influenced.† Cornish and other contemporaries produced work of the same kind ; and there

†British Museum M.S. Add. 31922.

337

was dance music and some keyboard music moderately individual in character.

Not very late in Henry's reign, came an incident with consequences out of all proportion to its apparent significance. Some unknown group of viol players, possibly the Italians actually in Henry's employ, in the usual search for new material, found a passage particularly suitable for their purposes in a celebrated six-part vocal Mass by John Taverner (c. 1495-1545). The Mass is in the contrapuntal form then fashionable on the continent, and is, in fact, an early instance (before 1528) of the Flemish influence in England. It is of the type constructed on a plainchant melody, in this case the *Gloria tibi Trinitas* from which it takes its name. The passage in question is in straightforward duple time, unencumbered by complexities of notation frequent in contemporary church music but unfamiliar to most secular performers ; it is only in four parts ; its plainchant skeleton is set out complete in prolonged notes all of the same length, around which the remaining three parts weave a contrapuntal web of not very alarming complexity. It was, in short, a gift for the viol players. And the words of the text at this point begin " In nomine . . . "

The shape, the position of the climaxes, the whole character of the *Gloria tibi Trinitas* plainchant fit it extraordinarily well to serve as the framework of a motet-like composition of this character. Taverner's *In Nomine* acquired popularity as an instrumental piece. Other English composers wrote other pieces in the same form and on the same plainchant framework, specifically for viols ; the Elizabethan manuscripts contain an extraordinary number of *In Nomines* by almost every late Tudor composer of note. Their general nature remained motet-like and essentially vocal until near the end of the century ; thereafter the form was still the form of a motet, but the idiom became increasingly that of a truly instrumental chamber style. The two last of them were written by Purcell in 1680 ; and still they puzzled both contemporary and modern commentators by bearing the name *In Nomine* while standing on the plainchant *Gloria tibi Trinitas*. Each guess proved wilder than the last. Then in the oddest way four or five of us happened on the solution within a few months of one another. We shall never know which won the race ; shortly after I had stumbled on the passage in Taverner's Mass which gave us each independently the clue, I learned in casual conversation with Robert Thurston Dart that he had found it too, and we joined in an article in *Music & Letters* of April 1949—only to find Dom Anselm Hughes hot on our heels, not to mention dark hints that Gustave Reese in America knew all about it already. Who shall say that musicology lacks human incident ?

The English *In Nomines* of the later 16th century proved to be the link between the taut, concise construction of the vocal motet and the highly instrumental idioms which had been developing throughout the 16th century under the joint influence of extemporaneously embellished transcription and the rhythm and symmetry of dance music. The Renaissance court dances spread throughout cultured Europe ; the improvised embellishments seem to have been more continental than English (specimen workings of especial beauty remain from mid-16th century Spain, such as those in Ortiz's *Tratado* of 1553) ; the *In Nomine*, though its general pattern was familiar enough elsewhere, remained an English contribution in the specific form whose influence on the future course of instrumental chamber music was to prove so fruitful.

At the turn of the 16th and 17th centuries these several tributaries converged. One of our recurrent enthusiasms for Italian music was at its height ; the new Italian madrigals had been fashionable in English musical society for almost a quarter of a century, and the leaders of the still newer English madrigals had already begun to absorb the borrowed idiom into one of those splendid acclimatizations for which the English genius seems so apt. The result, as all the world now knows, was the most felicitous combination of a somewhat conservative structure (by 1600 Caccini and Peri and Monteverdi had already launched their revolution *away* from polyphony) with a passionately advanced harmony and spirit : the whole as English as the Cotswold hills in spite of its Italianate first inspiration.

Under a variety of names (fantasia, ricercare etc.) the 16th century Italians had also been composing instrumental works bearing considerable structural affinities to their madrigals, and influenced both by the improvised embellishments and by the dances. I do not know of any actual evidence that their fantasies for viols were brought to England ; but some of their equivalent keyboard compositions were. Roger North, looking back as a very old man in his *Memories of Musick* in 1728 on the days when, by general admission, " in vocall, the Italians, and in the instrumentall musick, the English excelled," after making a bad guess but no worse than usual at the *In Nomine*, attributed (and I think correctly) the early Stuart viol consorts to the converging of the Italian fantasies (together with all that lay behind them by the end of the 16th century) upon the English

In Nomines. That is not quite the whole explanation : there was some real English string music other than *In Nomines* or dance forms throughout the 16th century ; but there was not much.

If the Italian fantasies for viols did not travel to England, an English composer of fantasies for viols certainly travelled to Italy. He left this country at the end of the century as plain John Cooper ; he returned as Giovanni Coperario (c. 1570-1627), thus delicately hinting at his predilection for Italianry. His output of fantasies for 2, 3, 4, 5 or 6 viols was phenomenal ; his contemporary prestige and influence could hardly have been greater. His music, impeccably constructed, but only as a rare and notable exception achieving profound emotion, is classical to a fault. Nevertheless it is at its best truly instrumental, truly felt and truly chamber music, the first large body of English viol music of which all three could be said.

There is in the Fitzwilliam Museum at Cambridge a set of fifty 5-part fantasies attributed to John Bull (c. 1562-1628) though devoid of that romantic's usual fire, and close in style to Coperario. Byrd (c. 1542-1623) wrote a substantial total of fairly interesting viol music, difficult to date accurately over his long life ; Morley (1557-1603) a very little, and that little not truly instrumental.

At this stage, at the turn of the 16th and 17th centuries, the *In Nomine* dropped from its Tudor lead in favour of the more universal form of fantasy, no different in its motet-like construction, but resembling a motet built without, not a motet built upon, a plain-chant framework or *canto fermo*. In either case, a short theme is treated fugally though not necessarily strictly ; another follows, or a homophonic interlude ; and from a small series of such passages the entire work is constructed, to an average length of perhaps four minutes. Quite exceptionally, a single theme may persist throughout ; and the later the date of the fantasy, the greater the tendency to contrast each section dramatically rather than to dovetail it imperceptibly. Fantasy (or fancy, fantasia, etc.) is the general English term : an *In Nomine* is one species of fantasy.

By the same date, one particular dance form had risen to especial prominence as a vehicle of abstract music in the way such forms not uncommonly do (witness Bach's Sarabands, etc.) This is the Pavan, with or without an accompanying Galliard. The Pavan had been the accepted opening dance of every ball with the least pretensions to ceremony through the 16th century ; it is rather slow and dignified, and served to bring in the notables, young and old, impressively. The Galliard followed, fitting rapid and extremely virtuoso ballet steps into a slow musical pulse, and permitting the young gallants to display the utmost of their skill and virility. These dances were declining at the end of the 16th century, but their musical form subsequently rose to concentrated beauties often quite unsuitable and unintended for dancing. The Galliard may or may not be a transformation of the thematic material of the Pavan ; in either case, a suite-like effect results. But many of the greatest Pavans to be composed as abstract music stand alone.

The first stage merged into the second under James I. One of his court musicians, Thomas Lupo (exact dates unknown) developed an almost Schubertian vein of gloriously happy, warm and carefree counterpoint, as unlike the steely Coperario as could well be the case ; a leading figure among viol consorteers. Orlando Gibbons (1583-1625) wrote a limited number of viol works whose importance has been greatly exaggerated by historians dazzled by his vocal genius ; they are only occasionally of high inspiration. By far the greatest viol composer of the reign is Alfonso Ferrabosco the younger (c. 1575-1628), the English-born son of an Italian of the same name who came to England under Elizabeth and achieved fame for his vocal counterpoint. There are pavans for five viols by the younger Ferrabosco in a contemplative vein to be compared with Beethoven's Op. 132 slow movement ; *In Nomines* and fantasies in a contrasted vein of brilliance with a hint of Op. 59 about them. Ferrabosco is one of the great three of the English chamber music for viols.

The two others are John Jenkins (1592-1678) and William Lawes (?1602-1645). Both came into prominence under Charles I ; but Jenkins lived and worked prolifically to a very advanced age while Lawes got himself killed in an unnecessary foolhardy and typical manner at the siege of Chester, at the probable age of 43. Jenkins was a serene, Lawes a tempestuous figure. Jenkins was an assured and inventive composer with splendid lyrical gifts who throughout his extended life adapted himself successfully and promptly, but not too promptly, to changing musical fashions ; Lawes was a rebel of diabolical power and passionate nobility who impressed his contemporaries profoundly and influenced his successors more than is generally known, though less than if he had lived out his proper span. The two were a complementary pair, a little like the lyrical and the rebellious Beethoven separated. William Lawes was an altogether bigger composer than his brother Henry, and his loss was a grievous one to English music.

The chamber music of the viols continued to flourish so far as any civilized activity could flourish through the Civil Wars ; it suffered no marked reverse under the Protectorate (none fonder of music in general and the viols in particular than Cromwell himself) ; at the Restoration it collapsed. The impoverishment and disintegration of so many of the great country families where viol playing had long been indigenous was a leading cause ; the extreme dislike of the French-bred Charles II for any music to which he could not wag his head in time was a final blow to the passionate counterpoint of the viols at a time when half the gentry flocked to London to repair if possible their ruined fortunes, and when court fashion was thus exceptionally decisive.

Roger North (*op. cit*) called Matthew Locke (c. 1630-1677) the *ultimus heroum* of the viols (he should have written *penultimus*). This touchy but inspired composer wrote much chamber music on the border-line between viols and violins, and especially a set of six four-part suites for viols which rise at times (especially in their slow movements, called Ayres) to most exalted heights.

Purcell (1658-1695) made a careful study of his predecessors including those of the Elizabethan and post-Elizabethan age. He was certainly familiar with Locke and Jenkins, and from internal evidence I am convinced that he learnt deliberately from the burning dissonance and tempestuous counterpoint of William Lawes. There are many resemblances to suggest this in Purcell's fantasies (truly the ultimate ones till modern times) for viols, all written youthfully in 1680. They are a little uneven and at times technically unassured by comparison with the great age of viol music then rapidly being forgotten ; but some of those in 3 and 4 parts and each of the single examples in 5, 6 and 7 parts give it a triumphant ending. By an irony of history, it is above all through these belated and not entirely typical contributions to the viols' chamber repertory that its influence has reached the present generation of English composers. The knowledge which they may shortly gain of the main stream itself, played as it needs to be authentically, and upon the viols for which it is so masterfully scored, should have the force of revelation.

The rest of the story belongs not to the viols but to the violins. In 1683, at the age of twenty-four, three years after his viol fantasies (and in the self-same year as Corelli's first published opus, in the same form, at the age of thirty) Purcell published his first complete printed work, the first set of twelve trio sonatas for two violins, gamba and continuo. Once more an Englishman of genius had absorbed with ability and integrity an Italianate style which he immediately transformed into an English style and in this case, unmistakably a Purcellian style. The best of his work in this form (which is not, good though that is, the Golden Sonata) rivals the Italian for grace and mastery while excelling it for boldness and warmth and intensity of emotion.

English music took a blow from William Lawes's death at 43 in 1645 ; but a mortal wound from Purcell's at the age of 37 in 1695. Not for two centuries did Elgar shatter the intervening spell of subservience and relative unproductivity ; not until Vaughan Williams, a generation later, did any modern English composer of genius reopen his whole soul to the spirit of our ancestors.

Schoenberg*

THE PROBLEM OF INTERPRETATION

SCHOENBERG's death, the loss of his advice which, when he had the opportunity, he was not slow to give in decided terms, makes the problem of Schoenberg performances doubly acute. His works are not easily comprehended, whence their performance easily defies not only the listener's control, but also the performer's self-control. With music both unknown and intrinsically new, insufficient interpretations do not give the listener a chance, and the vicious circle of bad performances—rejection or misunderstanding of work—fewer performances—worse performances, has brought us to the point where every inadequate Schoenberg interpretation is disastrous, i.e., worse than none, because it does everything against and nothing for the so far uncomprehended work. There are too many Schoenberg performances because there are too few.

I. THE CHAMBER SYMPONIES

The first Chamber Symphony in E major (not E♭, as some of the Philharmonia miniature scores say), on which we enlarged in our March issue, was again performed on June 17, at the Aldeburgh Festival §§under Norman Del Mar. The second Chamber Symphony, in E flat minor (as the programme noter wouldn't notice), was performed by the RPO under Stokowski at the Albert Hall on June 4.

Del Mar's interpretation made largely sense and was not badly executed at the last rehearsal ; but the performance itself collapsed. The Stokowski rendering was technically proficient, but not noticeably musical. It is improbable that either performance should have taken place, though a receptive and imaginative listener could reconstruct some of the 2nd Chamber Symphony from the many accurate notes and the tolerable balance given by Stokowski ; while chaos reigned in the well-meant performance of the First, totally misleading the virginal as well as the seasoned listener about the music. There was laughter in the audience ; there was serious and protracted headshaking among the know-alls, who diagnosed a thick texture, whereas, in actual fact, as we have pointed out in March, the transparency of a texture that is by no means sparse is one of the Symphony's major miracles. About that aspect

*See also our obituary on pp. 312-317.
§§See pp. 368ff.

343

the Scherchen performance then noticed left the listener in no doubt, whilst in the present performance, principal parts were repeatedly and totally submerged : needless to say, the know-alls did not know that they did not hear them. The result which this both praise- and blameworthy undertaking achieved was best epitomized by the reaction of one of our leading pianists, who liked the music so much that he thought it should be heard after a good and generous dinner. The only satisfactory facet of the event was Erwin Stein's (the Symphony's first analyst's) programme note, which drew hitherto unawakened attention to the change in formal significance, " according to the Finale character of the section," of the exposition's and the Adagio's themes in the recapitulation.

It was the finale problem, too, which left the 2nd Chamber Symphony†—begun in the same year as the first (1906)—unfinished until 1940, when the composer, then in his period of occasional tonal reversions, added a second, scherzo- and rondo-like movement to the unfinal slow first ; the slow, extended, cyclically thematic coda, which assumes the significance of a finale movement, returns to the initial key of E♭ minor. The second movement proper thus functions as upper middle portion of the symphonic arch, the necessary increase in tension being partly due to an intenser " emancipation of the dissonance " than the outer sections evince, for though the Allegro remains clearly orientated from the region of the relative major's Neapolitan sixth (G major), it is (to use popular parlance) far more " atonal " than the Adagio and the coda. Schoenberg once wrote to Leibowitz : " The harmony of the Organ Variations fills out the gap between my Chamber Symphonies and the ' dissonant ' music. There are many unused possibilities to be found therein."‡) I would suggest that the Allegro of the 2nd Chamber Symphony itself contributes to the filling of this gap, and that the work is perhaps the only one in musical history *whose structure avails itself of widely different stages in the creator's development*, proceeding as it does from his earlier to his later style, and thence back to the earlier idiom, or rather to a synthesis of earlier and later harmony. It is as if, in 1906, the Adagio had left itself open for things to come. In general, when a composer completes or revises an early work, we may fairly safely assume that he will find the task difficult if he has undergone a far-reaching development, and easy if he hasn't. Thus Spohr writes to Hauptmann on May 21, 1852§ : " You have no doubt already heard that at the express wish of the Queen of England and of Prince Albert I have remodelled my opera *Faust* for the grand opera. This work has afforded me great pleasure, and agreeably engaged me for a period of three months, in which I have been as it were transported completely back to the happy days of my youth in Vienna. . . . I had . . . to place myself into the same mood and style in which I wrote *Faust* and I hope that I have succeeded in this . . . and that no one will observe a difference of style between the old and the new . . . " ; whereas Schoenberg himself writes to Alban Berg about his revision (1911) of the *Gurreleider* (1900-01)** : " When I completed the scoring I revised

†For the following observations I have unfortunately to rely on acoustic memory, no score of the work being yet available.

‡Leibowitz, R., " Arnold Schoenberg's Recent Tonal Works and the Synthesis of Tonality," *The Canon*, Hunter's Hill, Australia, September, 1949.

§Spohr, L., *Autobiography*, London, 1865, trans. anonymous and highly defective.

**Berg, A., *Arnold Schoenberg : Gurreleider*, Vienna, 1914, my trans.

only a few passages. It was merely a matter of groups of 8-20 bars ; particularly, for instance, in the piece ' Klaus-Narr,' and in the final chorus. All the rest—even some things which I should have liked to be different—has remained as it originally stood. I would no longer have found the style, and a fairly practised expert ought to find the four or five corrected passages without ado. These corrections have cost me more trouble than the entire original composition." The history of the 2nd Chamber Symphony, on the other hand, shows the reverse picture : originally its completion cost the composer so much trouble that he did not in fact achieve it, but in 1940 he extended and completed the work without difficulty. For once, a widely developing composer has made a structural virtue out of stylistic discrepancy, has resumed an early work with the delight of an undeveloping Spohr.

II. THE PIANO PIECES

On June 15 at the Institute of Contemporary Arts, Miss Else C. Kraus a Schoenberg interpreter of long and wide repute, presented the composer's complete piano works under the auspices of the London Contemporary Music Centre, having given the selfsame programme on May 27 at the exhibition of the Neue Rheinische Sezession in Düsseldorf. Her awe-inspiring feat of playing every note, wrong ones included, from memory may have intensified her crude dynamics and exaggerated, erratic agogics ; but while it would be rash to pronounce that she does not understand Schoenberg, a dangerous number of her conceptions of the music were so nebulous as to offer the listener's potential understanding no help whatsoever: if he was not receptive as well as bent on extremely active co-operation, he could not merely be forgiven for, but should indeed have been encouraged to, go to sleep. Particularly where Schoenberg's prose rhythms were concerned, she was in a helpless, though superficially purposive muddle. It is quite wrong to suppose that free rhythms ask for freer interpretation than symmetrical metres. The opposite is nearer the truth, for many a regular period implies what a freely pulsating sentence expresses. Often, moreover, when Miss Kraus's rhythms were not undermined by temporal distortions, her misplaced and supernumerary accents played havoc among them. The programme was really charmingly and quite wrongly introduced by E. J. Dent.

III. " THE SURVIVOR "

The severely belated first English performance of the *Survivor from Warsaw* for reciter, male chorus and orchestra (1947), given on June 19 by the B.B.C. in co-operation with the London Contemporary Music Centre at Studio I, Maida Vale, before an invited audience, was an unrecognized *débacle*. The L.P.O. and the musically inadequate section of the L.P. Choir were conducted by Clarence Raybould who, forgivably, did not understand the work at all ; while the speaker, George Baker, beside not being anywhere near the spirit of his part, was not even a musician. Consequently, the work, which had to be immediately repeated upon the audiences' request at its first performances in New York and Venice, left little impression, and the little was wrong ; thus Martin Cooper delivered himself of the clownish observation (*Daily Telegraph*, June 20) that the composition " provided suitably horrific background-music to an account . . . of an escape from a German pogrom," which the reader may like to compare with the effect of this music on ourselves (last issue) ; whereas *The Times* left the event unreported.   H.K.

345

Reviews of Music

WILLIAM ALWYN : Sonata Alla Toccata, for piano. (Lengnick) ; 3s. 6d.
THIS work is neither a sonata nor a toccata. It is all that can be expected
from the stylized conventions of the modern English school. I am afraid
its heart is as synthetic as its title. H.T.

*ARNE : Libera me, for chorus and organ. Edited by Anthony Lewis.
(Hinrichsen) ; 2s. 6d.*
A TRANSCRIPTION of a manuscript in the British Museum which shows Dr.
Arne in a very pure, almost purist, Italian manner. The style of this dirge is
agreeably straightforward (as are also Prof. Lewis's realizations) but its invention is hardly on a par with Arne's secular music. Mr. Hubert Langley's
claim that this " . . . being the only known example of Arne's writing for the
church . . . is therefore a very important addition to English Sacred Music " is
valid only from the antiquarian's point of view. P.H.

*BASSANO, LUPO, MORLEY : Fantasias for Three Viols. (Bärenreiter) ;
no price stated.*
BASSANO was a Venetian, and stayed in Italy ; the Lupo family came from
Italy to England, where at least three of them were active in the early years of
the seventeenth century. Thomas Lupo, four of whose Fantasias are here
printed, seems to have had the strongest musical personality of the family.
The last two pieces in the book are his, and they would tax the powers of modern
string players, leave alone viols. The solitary piece by Morley is taken
from his " Plaine and Easie Introduction . . . , " superfluous sharps and all.
D.W.S.

*ERNEST BLOCH : Concerto Symphonique for Piano and Orchestra. (Boosey
and Hawkes) ; full score, 20s. 0d.; reduction for two pianos by the composer, 17s. 6d.*
FOR a review of the first English performance see *Music Survey* II/2/49,
p. 127. The full score confirms one's impression that for long stretches
two orchestras are, in underlying fact, competing : the one is present in full
ruddy strength, the other one has sent a deputy—poor chap—to play a piano
reduction. But there are many beauties in the orchestration. P.H.

*BENJAMIN BRITTEN : Five Flower Songs for mixed chorus. (Boosey &
Hawkes) ; 7d., 7d., 10d., 7d., 1s.*
BRITTEN's first *a cappella* opus (47, No. 1—5, composed 1950, published 1951)
since the *Hymn to St. Cecilia*, Op. 27, 1942, though not of equal importance
either in itself or as showing a step in his development. Yet the simplicity
of the five songs—" To Daffodils " (Herrick), " The Succession of the Four
Sweet Months " (Herrick), " Marsh Flowers " (Crabbe), " The Evening
Primrose " (Clare), and " Ballad of Green Broom " (anonymous)—is adventurous : indeed, to the sensitive critic the composer's stature should, I
think, be evident from an inspection of this little formal masterpiece alone—
though my pronouncement may be coloured by my knowledge and love of
Britten. The progressive tonal structure takes the not unusual course to the
semitone below (E♭—D) ; as it were a journey home from the Neapolitan II,

with the central song's F major evincing the appropriate D minor pull. The texture is cautious, yet not without practical risks, *a cappella* choruses being what they are. As quite usual with Britten and Mozart, the superficially most effective stroke is perhaps at the same time the most profoundly original : the fun of the last song. H.K.

GEOFFREY BUSH : *Twelfth Night. An Entertainment for tenor solo, chorus and chamber orchestra. Vocal Score. (Elkin) ; 4s. 0d.*

A widely prevailing fashion of the contemporary English parlour-game of composition is achieving the " right " modern accent for synthetic Elizabethanism ; but sham never, in the long run, makes either customers or friends. Not the happiest of works to have been commissioned for this Festival year. H.T.

BUXTEHUDE : *Two Cantatas. Edited by Bruno Grusnick. (Bärenreiter) , no price stated.*

" LOBET, Christen, euren Heiland " is an adaptation of the editor, the original text being " Lauda Sion Salvatorem." It is a pity that both texts could not have been given. " Das neugeborne Kindelein " (four-part chorus, four strings and continuo) is more accurately set forth, and contains some fine and impressive music of the middle baroque. Three violins and cello are needed here. D.W.S.

ELGAR : *" The Wand of Youth," Suites 1 and 2. Pocket Scores. (Novello) ; 9s. 0d. each.*

VERY well printed, on excellent paper. One would like the print to be even larger, seeing how much marginal space there is. P.H.

HEINRICH ISAAK : *Choralis Constantinus, Book III. Transcribed by Louise Cuyler. (University of Michigan Press) ; $6.00. Office for the Epiphany and Nativity (from Choralis Constantinus Book II). Edited by Walther Lipphardt. (Bärenreiter) ; no price stated.*

AFTER an interval of forty years, the publication of a complete modern edition of Isaak's " Choralis Constantinus " (CC) has been rounded off by this handsome volume from the University of Michigan. In it, Dr. Cuyler presents not only that part of Isaak's *magnum opus* which was not printed in the 1898 and 1909 volumes of the Austrian Denkmäler ; she gives also an admirable account of the general background of the Flemish School (to which Isaak is usually assigned), and a detailed commentary on the music of Book III. The Mass settings only are omitted, and these Dr. Cuyler hopes to re-publish at a later date.

Isaak's remarkable series of Mass propers for the entire liturgical year has rarely been surpassed in the matter of sheer staying power, and if we exclude the Parisian organa for purely practical reasons, only William Byrd's " Gradualia " are available for comparison. Perhaps some scholar will attempt such a comparison, now that texts are fully available, and we may find more than one point of contact between the bold angularity which seems to be shared by these two musical giants. Isaak, who died in 1519, gives the listener a fleeting, but none the less immediate impression of sparseness and economy in texture : indeed, the four-part writing in CC is almost as much of a norm as the four-part texture of " The Art of Fugue." There are, very occasionally, five- and

347

six-part settings in CC, and at the other end of the scale there are a few for two and three voices. Whether or not the name of the publication, due in the first place to Formschneider of Nürnberg (1555) came from a Constance Gradual (none has survived to the present day)—or whether it was the result of a commission given to the composer when he visited the diocese, is not known. This and many other questions are fully discussed by Dr. Cuyler, whose article on the Sequences may also be consulted with profit.*

The greater part of this fine, noble music can be sung by a quartet of singers from one or two copies of the book, which should be in the library of every faculty of music worthy of the name. The independence of the parts, notwithstanding the ever-present plainsong as cantus firmus, is rewarding to solo singers, making for sonority, clarity, and (in many instances) sheer beauty of line. There are traps for the unwary, and opportunities to emend for those who amuse themselves in this way. Dr. Cuyler has not been too liberal with editorial accidentals ; and this very restraint, which is so often a great virtue, is here apt to falsify cadences, as on p. 83, where the editor's horror of the note g sharp has made nonsense of a perfectly straightforward cadence :

Small faults like these are easily rectified ; not so the rhythmical muddles on pp. 226 and 239, where *tripla* sections have given trouble. A consistent, and by no means minor blemish is the inconsistent underlay (" word-placement " to Dr. Cuyler) which often causes a point to appear in one voice with a different piece of text from its predecessor or successor of similar musical contour. The art of assigning correctly a given text to a musical setting of that text was an important part of the training of composers in the fifteenth century, and it should not be lightly treated by modern editors. Apart from these blemishes, Dr. Cuyler's edition is a fine and worth-while accomplishment, and it should do much to make Isaak's name a musical reality instead of a history-book symbol. Modern clefs, key- and time-signatures are used, and ligatures in the original are shown by the usual square brackets, thus demonstrating that the practical and the scholarly approach can most effectively go hand in hand.

The two versions by Walther Lipphardt derive from the DTÖ volume edited in 1909 by Anton von Webern. Clefs have been modernized, and some musica ficta added : more would be welcome. D.W.S.

*Journal of the American Musicological Society, III, p. 3.

*HERBERT MURRILL : Dance on Portuguese Folk Tunes for Two Pianos.
(Joseph Williams) ; 4s. 0d.*
THIS *Dance* might be described as being "good fun to play," which is probably all it was intended to be. It is a pity that the reprise places the material in the same position as at the opening ; a little thought would have suggested giving the second piano the tune at this juncture instead of repeating it on the first.

More antiphonal writing would have been welcome. Murrill's *Dance* does not add anything of any particular value to the two-piano repertory, but it certainly provides a jolly few minutes—even if they are of no great originality and smack too largely of the 1920's.   N.D.

TIMOTHY MOORE : Andante for Cor Anglais and Piano. (Schott) ; 2s. 0d.

UNPRETENTIOUS, well-composed, and laid out in a way that must ensure a good blending of this unwonted instrumental combination. The dissonances of the middle-part rise somewhat too steeply out of the first section.   P.H.

ALEC ROWLEY, ed.; From Ancient to Modern. (Boosey & Hawkes) ; 2s. 6d.

A VERY well selected album of piano pieces for the young, ranging from Purcell to Shostakovitch and Mr. Rowley himself. For once, the fingerings are not only ample but manageable by small hands, as distinct from most German collections where they merely look good on paper.   P.H.

ANTONIO SOLER : Six Sonatas for Pianoforte. Revised and edited by Leonard Duck. (Francis, Day and Hunter); Nos. 1-3: 2s. 0d.; Nos. 4-6: 2s. 0d.

THESE attractive little pieces are not mere Scarlatti-and-water, although their style is certainly less continuously inventive than that of the older master. They have occasional dramatic moments, and are easy enough to make a welcome addition to the amateur's repertory. Mr. Duck's editing consists mainly in the excision of a few rather unnecessary repeats, and in the clear presentation of the ornaments.   J.J.N.

RICHARD STRAUSS : Second Horn Concerto. Full score. (Boosey and Hawkes) ; 20s. 0d.

THIS child of Strauss's Indian Summer was written in 1942. It has not been much performed, at any rate in this country, chiefly on account of its fiendishly exacting solo part. While four English players have publicly essayed the sufficiently testing oboe concerto, the cornist who would tackle this concerto in a concert-room would be audacious indeed. Dennis Brain played it at Chelsea under Norman Del Mar in May 1949, and before that I believe under Sargent at Liverpool.

Strauss had a horn-player for a father, but even so he learned a lot about the instrument's potentialities between the appearance of his first horn concerto (also in E flat, Op. 11, 1884) and his second. The first is virtuoso enough but the agile solo writing that abounds in the later work cannot but recall Mozart's reference to his first Fiordiligi's " geläufige Gurgel."

Admittedly the solo part is notated in E flat which means, since the convention is outmoded, that written top C is only B flat with an F crook, or F with the B flat crook that Dennis Brain uses. Admittedly much of the thematic material derives from the harmonic series—the first two sentences of the Rondo's theme are made up from the (written) C major arpeggio. But these are dubious consolations. For the *tessitura* lies high and Strauss never could stay for long on the same diatonic plane ; the *Allegro* first movement makes much use in its first pages of a descending sequence of arpeggios : E♭, D♭, G, B♭, ending on a tonic E♭—and then what comfort is your harmonic series to the player ?

349

Those are rather dull technical particulars. More interesting is the chamber-musical atmosphere of the piece. Although Strauss divides his strings from time to time, and requires double woodwind, two horns, two trumpets and timpani, the concerto has the same wide-enhancing effect as we find in the scores of Wagner's mature music-dramas or in Strauss's own orchestral works after he turned round to Mozartian ideals of texture and sonority—the noise is so modest, for long stretches, compared with the number of players in the pit. There are three movements : *Allegro* leading without break into *Andante con moto* (as in the oboe concerto), and the concluding separate *Rondo*. I. The sequence of falling arpeggios has already been noted; it is thoroughly exploited in the first six pages and then Strauss drops it completely until the coda. The masculine side of the movement, which compels vigorous tuttis in Strauss's heyday manner, suggests *Don Juan ;* the feminine, which occupies a large part of the development, seems to have strayed out of *Daphne's* farewell to the day. II. Does the ghost of Berlioz stir itself in the first phrase of the main melody ? It vanishes anyway, for the rest of the tune is *echt* late-Strauss, viewing a *Rosenkavalier Klang-Ideal* through neo-Mozartian spectacles, and ending, before the soloist's entry, with a magically ingenuous modulating cadence—A major into F minor back to A♭. He eases the door from A♭ to D, for the middle section, with equally naive firmness ; the reprise incorporates material from that centre piece. I believe Strauss came nearer to a 20th century Mozartian aspect in this movement than anywhere in his late years, save possibly in *Capriccio's* mirror monologue (I haven't yet been able to see or hear the late wind serenades). III. The *Rondo* has something of *Till's* ebullient impetus ; the theme indeed has relations to the earlier score, and like them it can never keep out of earshot for long. But modulating side-slips or no, the music is more fundamentally diatonic, as is the case in the *Allegro's* kinship with *Don Juan*.

Is it slightly strange, in an English publication of a German score, to find the instruments named in Italian ? Perhaps not, for the directions inside are bilingual too. The list of instruments happily includes " Corono solo in Mib " ; this instrument I can only assume to be a masculine cigar.   w.s.m.

M. VAN SOMEREN-GODFERY : *Two songs.* " *Death, Thy Servant," and " The Day is no more." (Rabindranath Tagore). (Augener) ; 2s. 0d. each.*

THE voice line as such is well handled ; not so the metre and diction. I suppose the songs have what is called an atmosphere, but the harmony is crude, sometimes quite amateurishly so.   P.H.

STRAWINSKY : " *Madrid," for Two Pianos. (Boosey and Hawkes) ; 4s. 6d.*

AN arrangement from Strawinsky's " Four Studies for Orchestra " made by Soulima Strawinsky, with due regard to pianism which is, of course, what an arrangement or transcription should be. Doubtful, however, whether the listener could place the title from this version ; the music, brittle and un-compromising, is not far removed from the composer's neo-classicism. It is probable that the theme on pages 2 and 3 might give a geographical clue in its orchestral form. Although this arrangement requires neatness of technique and considerable stretch of hand, its percussive qualities are all in context and it is enjoyable to play. The two pianos are treated as one large instrument, but the technique is so slender that there is no obscurity of intention. It is a *tour de force* which just avoids virtuosity and in an otherwise serious programme should prove a useful and stimulating piece. N.D.

VIERDANCK : Two Cantatas. Edited by Hans Erdmann. (Bärenreiter) ; no price stated.

JOHANN VIERDANCK, of Dresden and Stralsund, achieved fame by his " Geistliche Concerten " of 1641. These are psalm-settings for two, three, or four voices with continuo, and occasionally have violins as well after the manner of Vierdanck's master, Heinrich Schütz. " Mein Herz ist bereit" is for two equal voices (either tenors or sopranos) with strings and organ : the texture is clear, lively, and not too contrapuntal. " Lobe den Herrn " is for three sopranos (or tenors) and continuo. There are adequate contrasts of time and intriguing alternations of fugato and homophony ; the vocal parts are not difficult at all. D.W.S.

PART SONGS

STRAWINSKY : Pater noster and Ave Maria. (Boosey and Hawkes) ; 6d., 5d.

PETER WISHART : Three carols for Christmas. (O.U.P.) ; 5d.

ARTHUR OLDHAM : My truest treasure. (Boosey and Hawkes) ; 10d.

ALL of these are pastiches of the devotional music of previous ages. Since they are also imitations of a past musical devotion itself, they should be suspect to a modern believer of C. S. Lewis's stamp. Most so the Strawinsky, whose block-harmony, interspersed with a few " free " passing-notes, lets you know, on the sly, that the composer is really a denizen of this blessed century. Much more responsible is Mr. Oldham's effort: he tries hard, and not unsuccessfully, to bridge the gap between his 13th century words and his setting, not only musically but spiritually. Let amateur choirs not despair of the, admittedly, difficult intonation. P.H.

CANTATAS

CHRISTMAS MUSIC : Cantatas by Buchner, Bernhard and Buxtehude. (Bärenreiter) ; no price stated.

FOR those who enjoy Christmas with a dash of music, these short cantatas, lightly scored for the most part, should prove very welcome. The first, by Buchner (1590-1669) has a Latin text " O quanta in coelis laetitia exuberat," and needs soloists and a six-part chorus. The accompaniment is for organ only, with optional doubling by a bass instrument, and (according to editor Adam Gottron) trumpets and trombones. The music is straightforward and effective. In " Fürchtet euch nicht " by Bernhard (a pupil of Schütz) two violins are needed besides the continuo instruments. This is a solo cantata for soprano, yet there is adequate contrast because of the frequent ritornelli which separate one verse from another. The musical text has been based on three manuscripts in the University Library of Uppsala. Buxtehude's setting of the macaronic " In dulci jubilo " stresses the Lydian nature of the melody, which is perhaps more familiar to us in other forms. A small three-part choir is needed, the instrumentation being for two violins and continuo. Parts for instruments and chorus are provided, and the realization by Dr. Grusnick is not to be despised. D.W.S.

Book Reviews

THE ART AND SCIENCE OF VOICE TRAINING, *by F. C. Field-Hyde.*
Pp. 223 ; 18s. 0d. (O.U.P.).

THIS book is completely comprehensive and eminently sane—one constantly
feels the life-long experience and sympathy of its author both as teacher and
singer and friend to all would-be singers. He covers a vast field of teaching
possibilities and explains almost every kind of pupil's dilemma, also giving
detailed treatment of specific defects of a physical, and sometimes psychological, kind. There is an excellent chapter on expression (diction and
interpretation) and a section on anatomical questions of vocalization, breathing-
resonance and registers. Here, there is a surprise for many readers in the
detailed view given that it is not the vocal chords themselves that give birth
to the pitch of the sung notes but, instead, the thyro-aretenoid complex of
muscular strands. The function of the vocal chords is to govern directly the
breath by their degree of closure effected during phonation.

Apart from anatomical considerations, I particularly enjoyed the author's
expression of wonderment at the working of the voice by the mind, e.g. " Can
there be a more marvellous phenomenon in all the relationships of mind and
body (or, indeed, in all nature) than that a simple thought can so activate
nerve-centres and currents as to issue in simultaneous adjustments of such
minute degree and selectivity in so varied a collection of muscles and other
organs which are situated in widely different parts of the body ? " (p. 127).

Many teachers will delight in this book, even though, as Mr. Field-Hyde
himself points out, every one of them will debate hotly both the aims at which
the singer should strive and every effort at obtaining them. The singing
process is invisible to the eye and often mysteriously unrecognizable to the
pupil himself, for which reason Mr. Field-Hyde wisely stresses the need for
developing a self-critical ear. In my view, teaching has to be a system of symbols
very personal to both teacher and pupil. A would-be singer may read a book
such as this one with the greatest admiration and yet unfortunately be not a
jot nearer the mastery of his own instrument. This means that however well
written is a book on singing, it still cannot for a moment replace lessons, as
an equally good book on piano-technique could, but remains, as this one does,
a most interesting and satisfying book of reference.   E.S.

JOHANN SEBASTIAN BACH, *by Hans Engel. Pp. xi + 252 ; DM 14.*
(Walter de Gruyter, Berlin).

WILLIAM MANN'S competent and, otherwise, fair review of this useful and
often interesting work in *Music and Letters* (January, 1951) is a trifle hard on
Prof. Engel's style, much of which is not only, by German standards,
refreshingly unpoetical, but also, some grammatical liberties aside, seductive :
Bach is alive in the author. Not that the " professorial manner " to which
Mann alludes is altogether absent ; readers will be fascinated to learn that
Bach wrote, in a certain well-known instance which shall remain anonymous,
" unusual intervals of . . . almost pathological character " ; and that in
addition to being—hats off, Gentlemen—" an extremely interesting harmonist,"
he " proves himself, in painting the word ' bekehren ' [convert] by a
' kehrend ' [turning] turn " of the musical phrase, " a trained philologist who
reduces the *compositum* to the denotation of the *verbum simplex*." Yet who is
even Bach when we compare him to " Nature herself," in whom the author

repeatedly recognizes " a powerful musician " ? It is grossly misleading to imply that the " picture of nature " of Beethoven's Sixth exists more " for its own sake " than " Bach's describing a storm " ; it is dead wrong to say that the words of Bach's vocal works tell us about the music's " spiritual background," its " depth and significance " : the contrary is the truth. That the syncopating ties which symbolize " tying " and " chains " " are not audible but only visible " is absurd ; in fact, it isn't so much the visible " tie " that counts, as the " binding " effect, rhythmic cum harmonic, of the syncopation.

You have to read very carefully if you do not want to overlook the fact that Mendelssohn had anything to do with the Bach revival, and indeed, when you read of Buxtehude's " truly Germanically-inexhaustible artist's soul " you may begin to wonder whether the author has, after all, remained quite unaffected by the Myth of the Twentieth Century.*

A substantial part of the book might, nevertheless, upon revision, profitably be translated, and a subject index added.   H.K.

*The title of Alfred Rosenberg's pseudo-philosophy.

A BIRD'S-EYE HISTORY OF MUSIC, by Eduard Reeser. Pp. 87 ; 7s. 6d. (Sidgwick and Jackson).

HERE is another history of music, written and printed abroad ; well-written and finely printed indeed, though the translation limps from time to time. Consider this sentence : " About 1880 a young generation of composers was at work which brought the stylistic development that had begun in the time of Bach to an end that was at the same time a preparation for a new transformation of music." The translation is that of Professor W. A. G. Doyle-Davidson, Professor of English in the University of Nijmegen. Proper names seem to suffer from under- or over-conversion, for the Tournai Mass appears as the Doornik Mass, and Gilles Binchois is anglicized into homely Giles.

The scheme of the book is a good one : it can be read quickly and with profit by those who need the " bird's-eye " view, and more slowly by those who wish to pause and digest the concise information which Dr. Reeser has skilfully put together. It does not, at any point, read like a catalogue be-it-never-so-slightly raisonné ; there is enough discussion of style and background to make the narrative continuously engaging, and a well-chosen array of pictures and title-pages to enable the eye to help the mind. Excepting only the bird-minds, this bird's-eye history will be welcomed by sage and tyro alike.   D.W.S.

FRANCOIS COUPERIN AND THE FRENCH CLASSICAL TRADITION, by Wilfrid Mellers. Pp. 412 ; 30s. 0d. (Dobson).

A VALUABLE book, well documented, conscientious and permeated with the enthusiasm of the writer, who has evidently chosen his subject because it appeals to him rather than for the less creditable motives which presumably inspire the slipshod, barely literate productions of those vulgarizers who exploit the growing popular interest in music.

With a breadth of view uncommon among musicians, Mr. Mellers has embedded his detailed account of all Couperin's works in a thoughtful and by no means conventional account of the social, political (this rather inadequately) and religious conditions of the grand siècle. While the advantage of this method is that the composer is solidly placed in his period, a danger lies in the tendency to attribute to the music itself elements of which knowledge is derived from other sources ; for all Mr. Mellers's skill in exegesis the reader sometimes exclaims "The Devil ! did he mean all that." For instance, that Mr. Mellers reads into Couperin's fourth book of Ordres " his habitual preoccupation with social values and states of mind " is more revealing of the writer than of the composer he is discussing.

A critic of a different school could with as much, or as little justification attribute Couperin's perfection of style and formal lucidity to mere " indifference to the appalling misery of the masses under Louis' dictatorship." The only information relevant to a piece of music, a picture or a poem is surely that contained in the work itself and the production that needs external annotation is, to that degree, incompletely realized by its creator. This weakness, however, if such it be, is implicit in the writer's approach, which is admirable in other ways, though one reader must confess to a recurrent irritation at the frequent use of the epithet " civilized." Some of his examples of this quality, like the story of the Chevalier de Lorraine and the " little dog," would admit of a different commentary less creditable to those concerned. In many respects the elaborate civilization of the French Court was a device to hold in check the unruly passions of men in whom privilege and idleness had combined to produce a dangerous violence of feeling. Though Mr. Mellers does not evade this aspect of his subject he does not dwell on it. One looks in vain among his well-drawn characters for a figure with the more truly " civilized " commonsense and dry scepticism of Montaigne. Such things are matters of personal preference ; to turn from the background study to the account of the music itself is to find a comprehensive, reasonable and sensitive account of everything Couperin wrote from the early organ masses to the whole corpus of his voluminous harpsichord music. The quality of comment is such as to inspire confidence in Mr. Mellers's taste and judgment, so that this part of his book should be invaluable to performers seeking to enlarge the absurdly limited repertoire of Couperin's keyboard music ; we may indeed be allowed some change from the eternal *Soeur Monique*, *Le tic-toc-choc*, *Les Moissoneurs* and so on.

There is a valuable account of Couperin's predecessors, though few would agree with the high estimate of the French lute composers. The numerous musical quotations are excellently chosen although in cases involving a continuo it would surely be better to give the figured bass than to print the " realization " which in the absence of the figures leaves room for doubt. This, which would incidentally save a line of music type, might be considered in the next edition.

In sum, Mr. Mellers has written not merely the first comprehensive study of Couperin, but a work of scholarship, industry and critical insight. My reservations apply only to the externals of his work ; as a whole it must be welcomed as a credit to English musical criticism. It is admirably produced and the high price is no doubt the result of an unusual generosity in music-type examples. B.R.L.

THE FOUNDATIONS OF SINGING, *by Franklyn Kelsey*. *Pp. 117 ; 7s. 6d.* (*Williams and Norgate*).

As a result of delving deeply into the probable background of the great period of Italian and international singing, Mr. Kelsey has come to some striking conclusions. He writes with the sureness and brevity of complete conviction, and lays the greatest emphasis on the importance of the use of " a continuous vocal gesture of the glottis." This he explains so well that this delicate and possibly dangerous subject can become of great value to the singer and teacher.

E.S.

ORLANDO GIBBONS and his family, *by E. H. Fellowes. Pp. 109 ; 10s. 6d. (O.U.P.).*

THIS little book, now in its second edition, is beautifully produced, and the cover is a delight to the eye. Although its purpose is mainly biographical, the music is briefly surveyed and in the main accurately catalogued. Definite evidence is now presented that the composer's birthplace was Oxford, and not Cambridge, as stated on the memorial tablet in Canterbury Cathedral. The accounts of William, Edward, and Ellis Gibbons are accurately set forth, and there is a useful supplement of wills and a genealogical chart of the Gibbons family. In the List of Works for strings there are said to be fifteen three-part fantasies in Dublin MSS.Z.2 Tab. 1, 13. Meyer contested this as long ago as 1934, and showed that nos. 1-8 were by Coperario (' Dessen Autorschaft ergibt sich aus dem Vergleich der unter Coperario genannten Quellen '). It is a pity that this one small fault was not put right : otherwise the book is admirable.

D.W.S.

THE HERITAGE OF MUSIC, Vol. III, *edited by Hubert J. Foss. Pp. 191 ; 10s. 6d. (O.U.P.).*

MR. Foss bequeathes a further volume to us, the heirs, and we sigh once more over the death duties. For in many of the essays there is very little substance left when we have stripped away all the phrases we have read somewhere before, the quotations which are somehow familiar, and the ideas which are sometimes trite. Oddly enough, those writers whose incursions into print are comparatively rare have come off better than those whose incursions are not rare enough. Dr. Thomas Armstrong contributes a magnificent essay on the much-misunderstood Orlando Gibbons, and Alan Frank writes an authoritative and carefully-illustrated study of the music of Bartok. But Philip Radcliffe's geminous offering on Corelli and Vivaldi should have been printed on stiff cards, which would then have served as a useful index. Mellers, in dealing with Lully, shows lacunae in his knowledge of the music, doubtless due to the unfinished edition of Prunières. He should go back to the Ballard scores, and so temper his enthusiasm for the Stokowski version of ' Le Triomphe de l'Amour.' Two essays which may be cordially recommended are those by Professor Dent (on Rossini) and Frank Howes (on Elgar).

D.W.S.

MODERN BRITISH COMPOSERS, *by Marius Flothuis. Pp. 60 ; 7s. 6d. (Continental Book Company A.B., Stockholm ; Sidgwick & Jackson, London).*

WE learn from Mr. Flothuis that the English composer's predilection for variation form, i.e. " the *sportive element* in English music," is due to the fact that the English are exceptionally fond of games ; that Britten's " Simple Symphony " is better than his " Young Person's Guide " ; that the embrace of Nancy and Sid in *Albert Herring* " is nothing less than obscene " ; that in the " epilogue " of *Grimes* " there is a quotation from Act I " ; and so on. Part of this volume is what one might call a new realization of the Pelican Book *British Music of our Time*, exclusions included ; thus, Arthur Benjamin is not even mentioned, but Joan Trimble gets 60 words to her composing self. The narrative is in fact as informed and almost as penetrating as a book of mine on Dutch music would be, with the difference that I should never get it published in Holland, whereas " Symphonia Books—A Series of Contributions to the History of Music " have had this effort well translated from the Dutch by Olive Renièr, lavishly illustrated, wonderfully produced on art paper, and thrown on the British market for the misguidance of Festival visitors. H.K.

THE NATURE OF MUSIC, *by Hermann Scherchen (trans. William Mann) ;* Pp. 193 ; 18s. 0d. (Dobson).

A THREE-PART rhapsody—" The Foundations of Modern Music (Joseph Sauveur) "—" The Secret of Creative Art (J. S. Bach) "—" The Imaginative Portrayal of Musical Material (Beethoven) "—on many things except the title's subject (" Vom Wesen der Musik "), with many wrong facts and as many right fancies, particularly when you can decipher the music examples ; strongly recommended as a stimulus. The translator has not often failed in his difficult task ; but some of his successes would seem to be improvable. H.K.

WAGNER—PARSIFAL, *by Hans Redlich. Pp. 55 ; 3s. 0d. (Covent Garden Operas, ed. Anthony Gishford ; Boosey & Hawkes).*

HIS indefatigable German interpunctions aside, Dr. Redlich has here produced an unconventionally constructed and, for this series, happily outsized analysis from which even the musician will derive benefit. If, according to a previous reviewer (MS, II/4), Dr. Redlich's *Lohengrin* booklet was " an invaluable introduction," his present piece ought to serve a yet more important purpose— as an ear-opener for those whose eyes, glued to the events misproduced on the stage, will not otherwise give their ears a chance. H.K.

POLITIKENS MUSIKLEKSIKON " MUSIKENS HVEM HVAD HVOR," *3 vols. Pp.416 + 400 + 416 ; no price stated. (Politikens Forlag, Copenhagen).*

MODERN Scandinavia decidedly has a penchant for Music Dictionaries. The enlarged second editions of T. Nordlind's Swedish *Allmänt Musiklexikon* (1928) and of H. Panum's Danish *Illustreret Musikleksikon* (1940) are now being followed by a Danish pocket Dictionary of Music (1950), highly original in form, layout and contents, and issued by the publishers of a great Danish daily paper. The Dictionary's original title could perhaps best be translated by " Music Who's Who and What's What." The enormous subject matter is dealt with in three pocket size volumes of 400 odd pages each, all richly illustrated. Volume I, called "Musikhistorie," sets out to collect the main facts of musical history from the days of ancient Egypt and Greece to the threshhold of the 20th century. Facts are arranged in strictly chronological order and from approx. 1500 onwards almost every single year is presented as a human all-round effort and condensed into a useful cross-section reaching from Scandinavia to Sicily. Every page is headed by a brief note describing the general political set-up and printing the year in question in bold letters. Excellent portraits of prominent composers as well as contemporary paintings of opera and concert performances interstice the text, which itself contains scholarly little articles on matters of more general interest (Monody, Madrigal, Opera etc.) besides biographical and bibliographical entries of the more usual lexicographical type. Volume I must come as godsend to Scandinavian lecturers on music, in that it will enable them to take in the general musical character of a period at a glance, and brief them succinctly on all musical events of importance in a few concentrated pages. Nobody will cavil at the tendency of the two chief editors Miss Nelly Backhausen and Mr. Alex Kjerulf to emphasize the musical achievement of Scandinavia, which anyhow is much too little known and appreciated in the western hemisphere.

Volumes II and III consist mainly of a biographical Dictionary, listing chiefly living (or recently deceased) musicians whose main activities fall into the period after 1900. This scheme could not be carried out without a certain amount of arbitrariness. Practically, it means that a still living composer like Jean Sibelius can only be looked up in Vol. I under the years 1899 and 1900 respectively, where he is treated as a historic figure. The same happens to Richard Strauss, Mahler, Pfitzner, Reger and Debussy, who, with the bulk of their work, belong of course to the first decades of the 20th century. The contemporary Dictionary of Vols. II and III, which lists composers as well as prominent performers and scholars and offers excellent catalogues of works besides new and often well produced portraits, includes a prodigious number of names. Quite understandably Danish composers and performers take pride of place. But England, the U.S.A., and Germany are well covered too, and the number of musicologists included from all European and American countries is surprisingly great. Very rarely a wrong or questionable date (as in the case of the date of Max Reger's death or Leopold Stokowski's birth) reminds the reader that even the indefatigable editors of this lexicon are occasionally prone to human fallibility. The third and last section of the Dictionary lists alphabetically 15,000 titles of famous compositions, selected according to their position in the programmes of modern performances. The selection will strike the non-Scandinavian reader as slightly quaint, including as it does a great number of popular songs, " hits " and drawing-room compositions which have not become universally popular outside the confines of the Scandinavian world.

It seems a great pity that this Danish Music Dictionary—so handy in size, so comprehensive in its contents, despite its local colour—should have to rely on the narrow circulation within the limits of Danish speaking humanity. It would certainly deserve to be translated into English. Thereby it could easily fill a noticeable gap in the phalanx of bulky Anglo-American music dictionaries. It would undoubtedly cast into lasting oblivion puerile attempts such as the recent Penguin " Dictionary of Music."   H.F.R.

INTRODUCTION TO THE MUSIC OF BACH, *by William Mann. Pp. 76 ;*
    3s. 6d.
INTRODUCTION TO THE MUSIC OF GOUNOD, *by Norman Demuth.*
    Pp. 62 ; 3s. 6d. (Dobson).

MR. MANN adopts an eminently practical plan. He begins with short chapters on " The Status of Music in Bach's Time " and " Bach's Heritage," which sketch in the historical background of the music. Bach's formative years are briefly dealt with and chapters on his style and " purpose " make illuminating comments on his music as a whole. So far our attention has been steadily drawn from general to particular, and Mr. Mann now embarks on a necessarily brief but surprisingly full study of the various types of music that Bach composed. At the end a few editions, critical works, and recordings are suggested. The style is lucid without any traces of condescension from the expert.

Mr. Demuth's first sentence—" For a great many years Gounod (1818-93) has been under a cloud in this country "—raised a hope that he would prove an ardent enthusiast, able to introduce the reader to hitherto unsuspected delights. What a hope ! In the first place Mr. Demuth seems singularly unsuited to introduce the music of Gounod at all ; he likes one or two of the operas, but has no sympathy at all for the sentiment of the religious works. And Gounod " had one besetting sin ; he was a snob " ; Mr. Demuth considers that the dedications of *The Redemption* and *Mors et Vita* spoil something or other (he does not tell us what). The form of the book suggests that Mr. Demuth's pen ran ahead of his thoughts : the General Summary to the chapter on the operas seems to be an undigested bolus of facts, many of which are repeated later, while the Summary at the end is a useless appendage. It is charitable to assume that the prose style is due to an attempt to write down to the ignorant reader ; the composer, at any rate, is patronized consistently. " Let us be fair," says Mr. Demuth on p. 48, " We are viewing this work in 1950. In 1867-82 this was how they did things." Well, let us be fair. We are, after all, reviewing this work in 1951.

It seems a little odd to me that the publishers should have considered that there was a need for a work on Gounod in their series, but it seems much odder that they felt that this work fulfilled it.   J.J.N.

INTRODUCTION TO THE MUSIC OF STRAWINSKY, by *Rollo H.Myers*. Pp. 64 ; 3s. 6d. (*Dobson*).
STRAWINSKY, by *Frank Onnen*. Pp. 58; 7s. 6d. (*Sidgwick & Jackson*).

THOSE who in the earlier years of the century witnessed with astonishment the often wilful prejudice and hostility with which Strawinsky's music was greeted can now enjoy the strange satisfaction of finding that while still in the plenitude of his powers he is becoming recognized as a classic. Although he is sole master of any composition that happens (like *The Rake's Progress*) to be actually under construction, his earlier music has now passed beyond his control and gained that strange independence that characterizes works of art when they have been accepted as part of the world's heritage.

Strawinsky is the first contemporary composer to appear in Dobson's series of introductions to the music of some of the great composers. In about 13,000 words, Mr. Myers gives all the needful information about his music to date. The author makes a virtue of concision by going straight to essentials and refusing to be side-tracked. His monograph is lucid in style and persuasive in exposition ; and his judgments command respect.

While Mr. Myers is accurate and dependable, Mr. Frank Onnen's study is marred by a number of outright mistakes. Some are directly attributable to inadequate translation (from the Dutch)—e.g. the statement that the *Dumbarton Oaks* Concerto ' has borrowed its name from the castle in the vicinity of Boston, which at that time belonged to the American maecena, Mrs. Bliss.' But this excuse can hardly be offered to justify such a critical ineptitude as the following judgment on the Sonata for two pianos :—' this piece . . . possesses only one pretension—that it has nothing to pretend.' Even the complete list of works ' chronologically arranged according to material supplied by the composer ' turns out to be inaccurate and incomplete in various respects. There are some interesting illustrations ; but as a whole the book is not to be recommended.   E.W.W.

Concerts

THE LONDON SEASON OF THE ARTS

MORLEY COLLEGE CONCERT SOCIETY : Festival Hall, Philharmonia Orchestra, 30th May, 1951 ; c. Goehr.

STRAWINSKY's " Babel " (first European performance) is better, if only in the sense of " more problematic," than his " Ode in memory of Natalie Koussevitsky," first performed at a Morley College concert about a year ago, and repeated on May 30th. A speaker recites some of the verses of Genesis dealing with the tower of Babel, against an orchestral accompaniment which obstinately refuses to be impressed by the story. God, although musically represented by male chorus, fares only a little better with his pronouncements. Rightly called, in the programme-note, a parergon, or by-work to the " Symphony of Psalms," " Babel " is yet more artificial, in that Strawinsky's impassive detachment (his unrealistic objectivity, as it were) which in the former very well expresses the Byzantine devotion of an amorphous mass, finds in the latter nothing to express. In the last, and paradoxical resort, it is nothingness which Strawinsky seeks to express here. Only sheer cussedness— and wicked cussedness at that—could have made Strawinsky accept a commission to set a story which, of all Bible stories, is most Greek, both in its Promethean aspirations and in God's jealous reaction to human hubris. This story cannot be made, as I readily admit psalms can, an occasion for a cool-headed, " objective," display of the processes of composition—a winsome play-thing under whose mask of sobriety lurks the grin of mockery. To do so, against all psychological, not to mention topical reality, is to deny basically the drama of man. Admittedly, we have suffered a surfeit of artistic representations of this drama; but then, the way to remedy this is not to take the sting of tragedy out of those myths where it patently stares us in the face. Courting the dichotomy between himself and all the others, and between all the others and God, Stravinsky ends up by composing it. It is as if one of the archangels for whose touchy snobbery the catastrophe of Babel seems to have been enacted, had written this musical account of his disguised, and not so disguised, *Schadenfreude*. Stravinsky is indeed an archangel amongst composers, but not even he can convey in music the hiatus of feeling which the faithful call obduracy before God. However lucid Strawinsky may be as a craftsman, it is one of the philosophical qualities of the void that it cannot be elucidated.

Michael Tippett, treating of a recent unfortunate consequence of the tragedy of Babel, is better equipped to understand God's dealings with man. " A Child of our Time," on repeated hearings, reveals again the composer's inspired sincerity and technical skill, and the treatment of the Negro Spirituals in the context remains one of the wonders of the modern English school.

P.H.

BERNARD FLAVIGNY (piano) : Wigmore Hall, 3rd June, 1951.

An unassuming young man with a brilliant technique and an almost mature grasp of impressionist music. The mannered phrasing of many Frenchmen (and especially women) was refreshingly absent. Groups of Debussy and Ravel played on end always impress me with the superiority of the former as a mind and an individual, of the superiority of the latter as an intellect and a composer.

P.H.

ZARA NELSOVA (cello) with ERNEST LUSH (piano) ; Wigmore Hall, 29th June, 1951.

Miss Nelsova's virtuoso technique shone in her small pieces, her musicality only in Benjamin Frankel's " Three Poems," an instrumentally extremely effective lyrical effusion that does not quite come up to Frankel's usual standard —but, then, Frankel's compositions are so good of late that one's expectations are correspondingly great. In Schubert's " Arpeggione," on the other hand, Miss Nelsova's no doubt strong innate musicality was overshadowed by an even greater vanity, prompting her into producing a fortuitous potpourri of interpretative ideas, with the sole purpose of making her instrument sound, and with complete disregard of Schubert's form and spirit. The most grotesque instance was the theme of the last movement where veritable sledgehammer accents were placed on every first beat. Since she hurried all semiquaver passages, Ernest Lush, sensitive as always, was in the unenviable position of being wrong through being right : he could not quite convince himself that she really meant all this fuss and pother. In her unbridled state, it would indeed be a difficult task to make Miss Nelsova see that stricter regard to the markings and spirit of the classics need not mean a loss of temperament and individuality but, on the contrary, could mean an increase of them on a higher level. Perhaps time will teach her.　　　P.H.

FIRKUSNY (piano) : Covent Garden, 3rd June, 1951.

By talent and achievement a player of international class, Firkusny is a cultured rather than a spontaneous musician. This refers not to his working habits about which I know nothing, but rather to their public result : what flows from his fingers is not milk and honey but vintage-wine. Its sparkle admirably suited the great Schumann Fantasy op. 17, whose formal capriciousness is, as with all of Schumann's larger works, cultivated rather than inevitable. It did not so well suit Mozart's C minor Sonata where deeper formal designs demand a deeper response. Mr. Firkusny is the happy owner of two very flexible wrists. The resulting ease of tone-production no doubt helped him to express himself in the romantics, but sometimes obscured, by sheer good tone, the phrasings of Mozart. After the Schumann we were looking forward to the Smetana pieces, but were put to flight by the prospect of having to sit through yet another performance of the Samuel Barber Sonata.　　　P.H.

BALLET AT BATTERSEA

Amphitheatre, Festival Gardens

ARTHUR BENJAMIN'S " ORLANDO'S SILVER WEDDING," with choreography by Andrée Howard, and lyrics, scenery and costumes by Kathleen Hale, presented by the Group Theatre ; c. Joseph Horovitz, produced by Vera Lindsay.

BENJAMIN at his most brilliant and wittiest ; a pity that the imaginative and lucid texture, including voices, was spoilt by the loudspeaker which the open-air performances seemed to necessitate. (The only scorings that sound well in the open air are those of wind serenades when they are out of tune). The music, which only some Frenchmen could have produced with equally economical wealth, maintains a subtle, but unmistakable personal idiom despite its expected eclecticism. The influence of the twenties makes itself strongly and fittingly felt, particularly that of *Façade*. The inexhaustible possibilities of parodying Wagner, first explored by Johann Nestroy, most musically utilized in *Albert Herring*, and most recently reverted to in Benjamin Frankel's highly humorous application of the *Walkürenritt* to Ken Annakin's film *Hotel Sahara*, are inventively remembered by Arthur Benjamin in a context where no one would have thought of them : at the first appearance of the Katnapper, we get a charming version of the *Götterdämmerung's* (not the *Rhinegold's*) Rhinemaiden's " Wei-a-la-la " (to a different text, of course), which returns at his return and is treated to and against a counter-melody, " . . . delicious fish." The element of harmonic, melodic or instrumental parody is indeed rarely absent ; when, at the reunion of Grace and Orlando, it is, the danger of anti-climax at a climatic juncture looms large. The tango at the silver wedding party itself, however, resumes that threefold burlesque with renewed finesse ; whence a first-rate polka brings the little masterpiece to (needless to say) a C major conclusion.   H.K.

A NOTE ON SUNDRY REVIVALS

To bring early music to modern audiences as a complete experience means :
(1) choosing only masterpieces, and not the first discoveries made by novices inexperienced in this difficult kind of treasure hunt.
(2) humbly yet imaginatively and informedly recreating the original conditions of performance, and not arrogantly assuming that we can do it all much better than our ancestors.

I have sampled a fair cross-section of the extensive early music making this spring and summer, with mixed results. I began with the Boult-Herbage-B.B.C. revival of Purcell's *King Arthur* music on February 21st. Here a bad start was made by using forces of a size into which Purcell's choir and orchestra would have gone five times over, thereby destroying at a blow that near-chamber music quality so essential to this as to most Baroque music. It is true that Purcell's largest theatre would likewise have gone five times into the Albert Hall : but that is no answer. We do not think it an improvement to quintuple Menuhin with Rostal, Heifetz, Giocondo de Vito and Ida Haendel under similar conditions.

In Baroque music, ornaments are not frills but part of the structure : playing them wrongly is like playing wrong notes—it *is* playing wrong notes. They are, for us, a new and very difficult study ; but though I am well hardened to our prevailing ignorance I was rather overwhelmed by the shoals of inverted mordents, an ornament passable round and about 1600, unfashionable to the point of social extinction well before Purcell's day, grudgingly readmitted by say 1740, but genuinely popular only as an erroneous modern substitute for the true or lower mordent in music of those periods most averse to it. As to the still weirder outbreak of lower-note (i.e. un-Baroque) shakes that spread grins (to my ruthless satisfaction) across the entire Albert Hall at a point where Purcell asks for a tremolando but apparently no one was prepared to believe that he meant it, here is Simpson writing (" Division-Violist," London, eds. 1659 to 1712) as if on purpose to provide the necessary evidence :

" Some also affect a shake or tremble with the Bow, like the Shaking-Stop of an Organ, but the frequent use thereof is not (in my opinion) much commendable."

The whole affair was typical of the immense musicianship, intelligence and expenditure which can be lavished on an early work and yet be marred by insufficient knowledge of crucial points of style, among which the ornaments were unfortunately but the least.

Compare with this the Sadler's Wells *Dido and Aeneas**, where the ornaments were not much better, but almost everything else was. Here was a chamber-music conception which at once set the music in an atmosphere it could breathe. The orchestra was small, and conducted by James Robertson with a genuine sense of Purcellian style in general, though much the usual ignorance of it (for which he is not to be blamed) in detail. Geoffrey Dunn, unfussy (as he is not always) and in rare sympathy with the music handled the production to match. Somebody had made (another rarity) a proper harpsichord part, well played. I thought the singing very good. Critical as I am where early music is concerned, I am not really hard to please : I could see many urgent points of style in need of rectification, but great inspiration and a sufficient fundamental soundness ; and I was deeply moved.

As to the two Wigmore Hall series (English composers 1300-1750 ; English Songs) I am restricted as a critic by having been also a minor participant, but can safely say : (a) the programmes were not altogether well designed, being by no means confined to masterpieces, and at times very scrappily constructed (both serious obstacles to the audience's enjoyment of early music) ; but (b) they included many items of the greatest importance and value. I must certainly draw attention to Henry Washington's *Schola Polyphonica*. First, the wonderful ring of authenticity on which everything else depends ; next, the controlled passion, the smouldering romanticism, the dramatic articulation combined with smoothness, the flexibility, the rhythmic clarity and justness, the dynamics growing from the music, the superbly moulded ritardandos—an art so difficult and so long forgotten that its revival needs a touch of genius. Michael Howard's *Renaissance Singers* fall short of this, but are still excellent ; Mátyás Seiber's *Dorian Singers* are not quite satisfactory, being less romantic than sentimental, and not particularly authentic.

The partnership of the countertenor Alfred Deller and the lutenist Desmond Dupré is another rare instance of exceptional musicianship combining with an acute sense of style to recapture the complete experience of works long forgotten, in this case the songs of Dowland and his contemporaries. Dupré originally used the guitar, a near but inferior relation to the lute ; and the contrast is very revealing, because Dupré has the talent to master the difficult lute technique and to draw out the sustained and incredibly colourful tone proper to that much abused instrument. We were also given lute accompaniments on the piano, skilfully played, but confirming with painful finality how much more of the magic is destroyed by this particular substitution than by any other to which laziness or wrong-headedness inclines us nowadays. Which is saying a lot.

John Tobin's *Messiah* has been cleaned like the pictures in the National Gallery and with equally startling results. Shorn of subsequent accretions, and still better of the overgrown choir and orchestra which usually stifles it, given a certain amount of free ornamental embellishment in the 18th century tradition, it glows in fresh colours and moves us anew. Tobin is not a substantial enough conductor in either technique or inspiration to achieve impressive results ; moreover the free ornamentation sounded rather artificial

*See also p. 366 for another review.

plastered on to a general style of playing not in the least Handelian but nondescript modern, while the smaller but more important bread and butter ornaments remained largely incorrect. But which of the greater conductors has even attempted so salutary a reform ?

The conditions in which music earlier than Haydn can move us as it moved its own contemporaries are very infrequently achieved. But then they are very difficult to achieve, and even our knowledge of how to achieve them is very recent and not yet complete.   R.D.

NOTE : In our next issue will appear further reviews of the London Season of the Arts including a comparative survey of the two performances of Britten's *Spring* Symphony.—EDS.

Opera*

I. Covent Garden

TRISTAN UND ISOLDE : 29th May, 1951 ; c. Krauss.

CAN music still convince one of the perpetual interest of the passionate exchange of one " laughing death " for another ? That is roughly the problem of a *Tristan* set in a world where passion can be contemplated rather closer than in 1865, and where laughing death is almost *vieux jeu* for the common man whose memory can pierce below the glittering surface of the new South Bank and other imposing edifices on the field of the monumental defiance of fantastic destruction.

Kirsten Flagstad, Set Svanholm and Constance Shacklock brought the laughing death of the first Act to a fine pitch of suspense and spontaneous, fatal release, somewhat spoilt by the faulty intonation of the final brass chord. In the second Act Svanholm's heroic voice, though dynamically subdued, seemed unsuited to Tristan's confidence in the world well lost. The third Act was a noble piece of ensemble work in both music and gesture ; the minor protagonists being Sigurd Bjorling (Kurwenal), Norman Walker (an unusually impressive and tragic King), and Geraint Evans (Melot), as well as tenor oboe, sorrowful strings and all. Clemens Krauss imposed shape and no little beauty on the various stages of passion, with Flagstad to ensure the coda. The first Act was rather too much broken up to hang together.

A.E.F.D.

PARSIFAL : 18th and 22nd June, 1951 ; c. Rankl, produced by Heinz Tietjen.

THE proof of the text lies in the music : an operatic rule without exception. All current disproofs and undercurrent reproofs of the Parsifal poem are thus so many shots which not only miss the point, but never aimed at it. Time may have invalidated the text as such ; the timeless and prophetic music revalidates it, recovers the poem's own timeless substance, makes one ashamed

*See also reports on Florentine, Aldeburgh, Glyndebourne and Cheltenham Festivals on pp. 368-375.

of one's precipitance, one's impatience, or rather the *Zeit-Ungeist's*. Of course there are boring stretches, unavoidably—no, necessarily so : the essence and end of this music is a new, simple, *quasi-opus-posthumum* sublimity which cannot be sustained for hours, and which yet needs hours to unfold, hours which, for the first time in Wagner, sublimize (not sublimate) the contrasting primitive itself. The central second act, moreover, sweeps even those necessary obstacles from its path : while its style is less elemental, its form is as compact and overpowering as that of the first acts of *Walküre* or *Tristan ;* yet the technique is more economical, and the ideas, above their deep passion, wise, though not worldly-wise in the poetic manner of the *Meistersinger*. Wagner foretold *Parsifal* to be his last work (conversation with the Bülows in July, 1862), and we could tell if we didn't know. Its religion, nowise unopposed but completely un-uncomplicated, is perhaps the most stunning surprise in the history of surprise *par excellence*, i.e., of genius's " third period." The drastic artlessness of the new style, especially of the diatonic interpretation of the Holy Grail, poses an intriguing problem with renewed urgency—the problem of Wagner's supreme solution of the problem of repeatability. How is it that Wagner can go on repeating, for example, the completely diatonic and unmodulatory A♭ Grail motif without losing any of the spiritual tension with which it invests the liturgical Saxon *Amen*, but, on the contrary, making every repetition into a tense expectation of the next ? Or why, on the other, chromatic hand, don't the combined sword- and woe-motifs in the same key become what repeated, undeveloping pain so often becomes in art, i.e., an enjoyable bore ; why, on the contrary, do they tear one's heart as if this task had not been achieved every other previous minute ? This question of repeatability is, of course, fundamental to the study of musical structures in general, but it is in view of Wagner's simplest leitmotivic builds that it takes its extremest form ; and our extremest answer—whose formula would have to be : you can repeat even x even n times if . . . —should solve the problem in general.

There will, to be sure, be those who say that we are begging our self-important question : that *Parsifal* is, in point of fact, a bore and worse. Indeed, the vast majority of the present audiences' sophisticated minority (critics, as usual, first) seemed to be of that opinion, which made me ask Wagner's pardon for having always disliked his letter to Angelo Neumann of September 29, 1882, wherein he confines *Parsifal* to Bayreuth. On these nights at Covent Garden I wished that the audiences had consisted of worshippers among whom I was the least, not, as it seemed the case, the most devout of my musical like. There even appeared to be quite a few who found the opera a sacrilege ; I found their presence such. Wagner's letter, of course, thinks of performances rather than listeners. But while Rankl and his forces (including Weber, Flagstad, Bjorling, Lechleitner, Otakar Kraus) would only seldom have satisfied him, there were not many stretches bad enough to remain incomprehensible or misunderstandable to the receptive novice.   H.K.

DIE MEISTERSINGER : *29th June, 1951 ; c. Beecham.*

AN aspect of this revival which seems to have been overlooked is that Beecham gave us every bar of the Wagner text. We went in at six on a sunny evening. At a quarter to midnight, the curtain calls having ended and the shouting died

364

down, we were able to scatter for our late trains. Traditional or occasional cuts which Beecham restored included :—

Act one, scene two. David's enumeration of the Modes (beginning *Der kurze, lang' und überlang'*) while Walther listens in dismay. There is much pretty music here which it was good to meet again, although Murray Dickie has some way to go before he can sing David's music as easefully as Heddle Nash did. Less well-known than Kothner's baroque trolling of the Masters' rules, this David monologue serves a similar purpose in affectionately reviving those roulades, turns and graces which Wagner the reformer was thought to have abjured for ever. Gay things go on at the same time in the orchestra. At mention of the Frog Mode, the strings give a squelchy hop. The Linnet Mode evokes staccato pipings, the Skylark Mode a frivol of triplets, the Lonely Gormandiser Mode a rolling chromatic unison, big-bellied and droll. At one point David sings of Hans Sachs's disciplinary strap. This occasions the first enunciation of the genial " cobbling " motif.

Act two, scene five. Sachs's hilarious *Jerum, jerum !* was done in its entirety. Hitherto the second stanza, with Beckmesser, Eva and Walther sticking in an unintelligible oar occasionally, has usually been shelved at the Garden. The tune is hearty and wholesome enough to bear the plugging which Wagner gives it. The same is to be said of Beckmesser's serenade tune later in the same scene, of which the second full statement is customarily cut. Wagner's intention, carried out by Beecham, was that we should hear the tune four times, with variants in the orchestra and ever-increasing discomfiture on Beckmesser's part. This provides an excellent musical run-in to the big riot ensemble which closes the act. Thanks to Beecham we now have some idea of the finale's true form and proportions.

Act three, scene two. The scene in Sachs's parlour between Sachs and Walther has long been a favoured quarry. You can blast out several chunks without making hay of the story. Beecham put everything back in its place. The most important restoration was the preliminary version of the Prize Song. Usually we hear the thing in bits (two stanzas and their " aftersong,") the bits being separated by Sachs's comments as he writes them down. What Wagner intended was that after dictating this first sketch, Walther should sing his creation through from start to finish without interruption. Beecham's restoration proved that in a formal sense Wagner knew what he was about. Scissors inevitably spoil him. Unfortunately, to my taste as to that of many others, the Prize Song does not lend itself to plugging as resiliently as Beckmesser's serenade. We have to hear it all over again a scene later in the Contest meadow ; and that is much too much.

Now about the performance. Yes, there was the odd orchestral blemish ; chorus, organ and Beecham were out of step rather and the rest of us on tenterhooks in the opening chorale ; and, as between singing and playing, the ensemble was rarely a glove-fit the whole night through. Yet most of us were in a state of high excitement, and with good reason. The orchestra was so welded and Wagnerian, so laden with golds and purples, that the odd instrumental blemish had no more significance than a fly settling on one's nose. The following night I heard *Tristan* under different hands. The difference in orchestral quality was startling. Lined up against a stucco wall at the prompt end of the pit (where Beecham had, with greater wisdom, chosen to put his *contrabassi*), the heavy brass barked away in detachment from the rest of the tonal mass. The cohering magic of the night before had given place to a box of spare parts, with the violins sounding at times like a palm court orchestra. Another joy of this *Meistersinger* was Benno Kusche's Beckmesser. Admittedly he overacts. He fiddled so much with his wig that I felt like handing him a comb over the footlights. But he is the perfect pedant, full of self-consequence, meddling and gall ; has never a gesture without style ; is capable of the evil grimace while producing good singing tone of a sort which, though the part is supposedly bass, sounds like high baritone, as is usually the case with good Beckmessers. Elisabeth Grummer's Eva was negligible until the quintet, which she launched with majesty : this is a superb voice but evidently needs its own line of country. Karl Kamman's Sachs had too hard an efficiency, not to mention a beard and wig that clung to his head like a loosely knitted balaclava helmet. The Walther of Peter Anders, knightly enough to look at, was rather less so on the ear, which yearned for richer tone. Nor was the mighty Ludwig Weber in his best vein for Pogner's Address. Miss Shacklock's Magdalene is, as you might expect, watchfully roguish. The programme said the producer was Heinz Tietjen : but I didn't notice any production at all. It was just *Meistersinger*, the same *Meistersinger*, rather musty and neo-naturalistic, that I have been seeing at the Garden since my nonage. In spite of everything a great night.　　　　c.s.

II.　Sadlers' Wells

DIDO AND AENEAS ; 8th June, 1951 ; c. Guy Warrack.

Prof. Dent's realization of *Dido* is, as was to be expected, scholarly. What it lacks in richness of detail, it often, but not always, makes up by sheer good spacing of chords. The Sadler's Wells scenery is gorgeous to the point of profusion, the ballet, often running, in the literal sense, counter to the singing, elaborated to the point of ostentation. Yet this show of imagination on the part of the producer (Geoffrey Dunn) is vastly preferable to any dry historical treatment ; especially so since Dido's " Lament " is an operatic climax that, distinct from the musical intensifications of other operas, needs to be prepared by contrast rather than by homogeneity. Those who criticized the mannered production of the closing dirge (magnificent catafalque behind gauze curtain, scattering of rose petals before, etc.), missed the point that after an expression of grief as regal as it is direct, the luxuriance of this opera, toned down by mourning, but by no means dwarfed by it, wants to be restated. Eleanor Houston, an excellent Dido, took cognizance, in her phrasing of the " Lament," of the five-bar ostinato underlying the vocal line ; an understanding which pleasantly announced itself in the recitative " Thy hand, Belinda " which is almost harder to phrase than the " Lament " itself. To these words, she did not, as I always feel Dido ought to, and as Joan Cross in the Britten version of *Dido* does, stretch a limp arm in Belinda's direction, eyes fixed on the horizon where, in operatically foreshortened time, (the intervening chorus would, in reality, just give him time to weigh anchor) Aeneas is already disappearing. But Miss Houston's curiously unearthly tone at this juncture in itself conveyed the impression of one who is receding to the horizon of her death. The other outstanding member of the cast was Anna Pollak as the sorceress. Her diction had bite and her phrases were properly clipped while the clippings remained mentally joined.　　　　P.H.

366

Radio

I. THIRD PROGRAMME

MAHLER'S EIGHTH SYMPHONY: 27th June, 1951; Vienna Symphony Orchestra, c. Scherchen.

THE orchestral playing, especially in the beginning of the second part, was excellent, the choir commendable, the soloists middling, the vocal ensembles messy, the conducting a mixture of all these. Patzak, although this tenor-part puts him under strain, delivered himself of it with great understanding. It was amusing to hear the contralto, Mme Anday, scoop as fruitily as ever she did when I last heard her in Vienna, fourteen years ago. To my mind, a great part of the second movement (to be exact, from the " pater exstaticus " to the final chorale, excluding either) was dated and cannot compare with the first part (*Veni, creator spiritus*) which I consider the crowning achievement of Mahler's life. But since many English listeners prefer the second to the first part, it may be my preoccupation with the Goethe text that makes me despair of anyone finding a proper setting for it. What is certain is that nobody would nowadays attempt the end of *Faust*, Part II, whereas many would succeed with a medieval Latin hymn. But in another fifty years, granted we are all still alive, my friends' and my own judgment may have turned full circle

P.H.

BENJAMIN FRANKEL : First performance of Violin Concerto ; 19th June, 1951 ; London Philharmonic Orchestra, c. Frankel. Violin : Max Rostal.

THIS inspired work is in logical succession to the 4th String Quartet. Frankel's qualities of lucidity, individuality, inventiveness, and absolute certainty of his own idiom, together with a command of instrumental writing that is not so much brilliant as unquestionable, are here displayed (or should one say " intensely understated " ?) in a medium which, although larger than the string quartet, is yet not so far removed from it. This chamber-musical quality, manifesting itself especially in the quite un-concerto-like last movement, will unhappily be a stumbling block to wider acclaim. After the resigned lyricism and the dark forebodings of the first three movements, the finale comes as a lesson from a wide-awake artist on how to find a modicum of happiness in this modern world ; a happiness on the brink of an abyss, as it were. Our composers cannot, in all consciousness, maintain in their finales the devil-may-care jollity of the 19th century concerto, except in the form of skits. There are two other alternatives : the heroic finale to the dramatic work, and a finale of quivering serenity to the lyrical. Frankel concludes this concerto in the right way, and finishes suddenly, though not abruptly, giving not a rap for " how a concerto ought to end." Rostal takes to Frankel's music as a duck to water ; there could not have been a better interpreter for it.

P.H.

II. PARIS.

STRAWINSKY MASS (1948) : *relayed by Radio Paris and Dijon from the Sainte-Chapelle, 28th May, 1951 ; c. Marcel Couraud.*

BY far the most musical and spiritual and vital of the five performances—including the Italian world *première** and the first three English performances†—I have heard. In fact, the intonation was good, even in the middle parts, and the basses were audible. Not so, however, the bassoons' double-dotted quavers in the *Benedictus* which, despite Strawinsky's carefully differentiated dynamics, have not to my knowledge yet been heard. Children's voices were at last employed and made a better job of their parts than the adults on previous occasions, which goes to show that Strawinsky may after all have known what he wanted.§ But the optional *soli* of the *Gloria* (as distinct from the obligatory ones in the *Sanctus*) were, perhaps wisely, sung by several. One trombone was somewhat rough, but only because it was so very well-meaning. For the rest, the zest, intensity and certainty of the phrasing made the *tempi* seem quicker than required by the metronome markings ; yet they weren't : the performance lasted exactly 17 minutes. For the first time, one was invited to understand the work.

One's previous impression of a sado-masochistic masterpiece† were vehemently and, as it seemed, finally confirmed, the aspect of mastery gaining a fuller meaning. Since this essentially pandiatonic —i.e., undeveloping—music achieves its static state by overpowering itself, it will always overwhelm those who understand it and seem powerless to those who don't.

Bar 6 of the *Gloria's* contralto part is misprinted in the Boosey & Hawkes Pocket Score : for g′—a′ read e′—f♯′.　　　　　　　　　　　　　　H.K.

*October 27, 1948 ; see *First Performances, Music Review*, February, 1949.

†February 19 and 20, 1949 ; see *First Performances, Music Review*, May, 1949.

§Mr. Denis Stevens informs me that in the Third Programme's own performance of the work on 9th April, 1951, children's voices were used.

Festivals

ALDEBURGH FESTIVAL

ALL reports I have seen and heard about the wonderful Aldeburgh atmosphere are wrong. All good festivals have a bad atmosphere ; otherwise they don't pay their way. Unmusicality cuts through all classes, but only the upper ones pay substantially for deceiving themselves into musicality ; the lower ones must needs employ other means towards the same end. The Aldeburgh atmosphere is concentrated. If you want to escape from the two ladies who, upon having to depart on the penultimate day, relieve themselves of the following reflections—

"It's a pity to miss the end, isn't it ? "
"Weeell, it's chiefly Schoenberg, you know."
"Yes, but it's the end all the same, isn't it ? "

—you run into the intellectuals with less money to spend than they spend, and with more knowledge than their constitutional snobbery entitles them to, who enlarge upon texture and orchestration and quality of execution and never get on to form, their minds being as short as they are narrow and as narrow as that of the too typical orchestral player who, however, can at times play an instrument. You finally seek oblivion with the young lady of economical judgment, bosom, and glasses, who has made the long journey from a cartoon of Saul Steinberg to Aldeburgh for the purpose of informing you that everything is very cute. Distinctly cute, indeed, every second thing is : after all, here is the only festival in the world under the direct or indirect leadership of two geniuses, one interpretative, the other creative and interpretative. At the same time there is no question of the latter's dominating the Festival, for Britten is the most moderate of all Britten fans, his active tolerance even wider than his creative eclecticism : while dodecaphonism is about the only contemporary trend that does not show in his music (though he has been influenced by a son of the father of the twelve-tone method, namely, by Alban Berg), the first performance of Roberto Gerhard's twelve-tonal piano Concerto was included in the choral and orchestral concert in the Parish Church on June 16, with Mewton-Wood as apparently excellent soloist and Norman Del Mar conducting. (For the first Schoenberg performance at Aldeburgh, i.e., of the first, pre-twelve-tonal Chamber Symphony, see our *Schoenberg* section on pp. 343ff.) The Concerto* immediately compels, but what seems its strongest movement, the central free variations under the title *Diferencias* (which the composer's programme note explained to be the Spanish equivalent for the English *Division*), is at the same time the avoidably weakest : it ends before it stops, and a cut at a definable point seems indicated. At the same concert, Britten conducted his far too rarely performed, and so far shamefully unrecorded *Saint Nicolas* Cantata, about whose under-recognized mastery this journal has not left its readers in any doubt. Peter Pears was the tired, yet supreme soloist in a performance whose choral aspect (Festival Choir) may have misled the newcomer about the work. The operas in the Jubilee Hall on the same night, *Il Combattimento di Tancredi e Clorinda* and *Dido and Aeneas*, with Pears in both, exhibited virtues and faults opposite and preferable to those of a first night : physical and mental exhaustion was paired with spiritual and musical freedom and relaxation. The final concert, under Del Mar next night at the Jubilee Hall, was too long, and the beginning was better chosen than the end : William Boyce's 3rd Symphony in C major formed an unusual and suitable introduction, but Saint-Saëns *Le Carneval des Animaux—Grande Fantaisie Zoologique* should not have succeeded Schoenberg's E major Chamber Symphony, but appeared elsewhere. The second item was, and shall remain, unwell known : Ernest Chausson's so-called Concerto for Piano, Violin and String Quartet in D major, for which Del Mar, Mewton-Wood, Manoug Parikian and the string quartet from the English Opera Group Chamber Orchestra did their best, is a structural, stylistic, and textural impossibility. It will always be interesting, on the other hand, to hear the *Siegfried Idyll* in its original chamber-musical texture, but it is difficult to agree with Del Mar's programme note that " the intimate nature of the Idyll is best preserved, and the supreme beauty and mastery of its counterpoint maintained when it is given in [this] setting." True, the Idyll's ideas are chamber-musical ; yet they are basically conceived, though not originally expressed, in orchestral terms. When performed as on the present occasion—and, mind you, the conducting was excellent—the texture is distorted, in that you hear, with the

*See also my *First Performances : Schoenberg—Schoenbergian—via Schoenberg* in the August 1951 issue of *The Music Review*.

most crystalline clarity, subordinate parts and figures which are not intended to obtrude, while on the other hand some of the most important shapes are pushed into the background, if at all definitely heard, owing partly to the fact that the strings are outbalanced. One hopes that the English Opera Group will give the Saint-Saëns, in which Britten brilliantly joined Mewton-Wood on the second piano, some time in London. H.K.

ALDEBURGH AND CHELTENHAM

First performances:—ALDEBURGH: Imogen Holst, " Welcome joy and welcome sorrow," 6 part-songs for Female Voices and Harp, words by Keats. *CHELTENHAM : William Alwyn*, Festival March, and Concerto Grosso No. 2 for String Orchestra. First Symphonies by *Arnold van Wyk, John Gardner and Malcolm Arnold. Maurice Jacobson*, Symphonic Suite for Strings. *Humphrey Searle*, Poem for Twenty-Two Strings. *Philip Sainton*, Serenade Fantastique for Oboe and Strings. *Alan Rawsthorne*, Second Concerto for Piano and Orchestra (2nd perf.), *Brian Easdale*, Opera " The Sleeping Children." Other performances of contemporary music included : *Benjamin Frankel*, String Trio, op. 3. *William Wordsworth*, Piano Quartet, op. 36. *Bernard Stevens*, Sinfonietta for String Orchestra. *Gustav Holst*, "The Wandering Scholar " (1-act Opera). *Arthur Bliss*, String Quartet No. 2.

It goes without saying that the following selection is very personal. Best of the pick : Rawsthorne, Arnold, Frankel. Upper Middle : Stevens, Jacobson, Easdale, Gustav Holst. Lower Middle : Van Wyk, Alwyn (Concerto), Sainton, Wordsworth, Imogen Holst, Bliss. Worst : Alwyn (March), Gardner. Open Verdict : Searle, which I did not understand (having missed its rehearsal, of all things), but have strong inkling that it belongs to the top class. Given benefit of doubt, and discussed therein. Series stated in six combinations of 12-part chords, then developed horizontally. From point of greatest contrapuntal concentration (too great, perhaps?) series devolved back to starting chords. In effect, a kind of *motus cancrizans* between harmony-counterpoint-harmony. Rawsthorne so sure of his style that he doesn't sound radical any longer. People think he's polite, and like him. Long tunes vary with close canons and augmentations (typical R.). 1st mov., between short expos. and recap., has one of the most varied devel's. of modern music. Scherzo in rondo form, last mov. rondo+Variation form, slow mov. scherzoid middle-part : all these stress *concertante* element. Self-confessed vulgarity of last mov. theme a bread-and-butter basis for most complicated harmonic experiments, brilliantly solved, specially the horse-play between the F♯ and G tonalities of this movement. 4-mov. form and treatment of piano come from 2nd Brahms Concerto.—Arnold the nicest musical exhibitionist ever : he exhibits not because he is unsure of himself, but because he is so convinced of his qualities that he disdains all frills of modesty. Luckily, this self-assurance is objectively justified. Not a single bar that doesn't say " Arnold." All conventional bridge-passages left out. Moods change musically, and not epically. This infantile realism of reactions found unforgivable by epically-minded " adolescents." Therefore some reviews bad. Makes one doubt whether people really understand Berlioz's technique of elision, or, come to that, the technique of Beethoven op. 135. Broad Italian ditty, marvellously mis-harmonized, that evolves from lacerated counterpoint of last mov. fugue, punctures the inflated belly of many a " grand " finale (for instance, Gardner's). Frankel's miniature punctures nothing, least of all unmusical ears. Its realism (for it is unepical, too) merely suggests to those who can still hear that they might, with advantage, have their ears overhauled if they don't understand this. A new kind of affect arises (in the deep slow mov. particularly) from renouncing all affected heroism. " That's that ; where do we go from here ? " is the only mature form of resignation. Some such " that's that " must have occurred before Frankel found the resigned language for this early work.

Of Stevens, only 1st mov. in the same top class as his recent string Quartet. 2nd mov. nicely lyrical but with touches of " good boy " writing, last mov. not inventive enough, in spite of formal niceties (complete inversion of reprise). String-writing bit awkward at times through being nearer quartet than orchestra lay-out. But piece, on the whole, concentrated and to the point. Jacobson not quite so concentrated, except in his cogently shortened reprises and brilliant codas ; but fairly wide emotional range. Part-writing in places knotty, obscuring the work's emotionality. Interesting ternary+(in middle) variation form of last mov.—Holst a charming, frivolous, medieval one-acter about a young wife, a lecherous monk, and a young scholar. Extraordinary how in late Holst the (ample) use of folk-material (" Whistle, daughter, whistle ! " is used as a programmatic *Leitmotiv*) has lost all national self-consciousness which, with all respect, it sometimes has in Peter Warlock. Holst should have been given *after* Easdale, not before, as satyric endpiece to the serious " Sleeping Children."* Story of boarding-school headmaster whose wife has been unfaithful with assistant master during the war. Head attempts to murder rival in a most scholarly way, but breaks down and lets the couple (and their expected child) go abroad. He has learnt forgiveness now and stays on to devote himself to his school. Sleeping Children (personification of Life with capital L) accompany action as a mystical chorus. Excellent libretto, realistically symbolic (Guthrie), and surrealist scenery (Koltay). Music fittingly nervous, to the point of short-windedness, well constructed with telling use of several *Leitmotiv* developing intra-musically in agreement with drama's extra-musical demands. Has been found boring by many, including those whose opinion I value highly, but I cannot agree, even after 4 hearings. I admit, however, that instead of the music's serious "clinical" observation of psychic processes, the unconscious dramatic self-identification of a genius's music would have been greater. Still, it's a very respectable score.

The besetting fault of the six works in the next section is academicism. Relatively freest from it the Van Wyk (although plenty of Sibelius in it ; but Sibelius himself just doesn't belong to any academy). Its main weakness, however, is structural : too homogenous material spread over too many movements (4, without break), and treated ambitiously with a polyphony that isn't quite borne out by the themes. Most academical the Alwyn Concerto, and that in both its frank Handel imitations and in its less frank " modern " developments. But well written for string orchestra. Sainton comes somewhere in the middle : its unconventionality of ten years ago is just becoming conventional now. Most hackneyed are its plain lyricisms and its sequences of jolly snippets in the Scherzo and other gay passages ; best its workable subjects (1st mov.) and the real developments. Also the form is, albeit extrinsically, satisfying. Very meaty oboe part.—The Wordsworth is, though apparently conceived with great earnestness, flat in both its structure and its effect. The Andante movements are muddy and listless rather than

*For details, see my review in *Opera*, September 1951.

sad, owing to Wordsworth's semi-modern harmony that doesn't quite put its cards on the table. The whole work (even the Allegro of the Scherzo) lacks rhythmic variety and instrumental distinction. On the other hand, Wordsworth's skill in horizontal manipulation for its own sake must be acknowledged. The Imogen Holst songs are precious and pretty-pretty through their extraneous allegiance to Britten's style. But even that gives them a certain polish, and the vocal writing is apt.

Lastly, if we pass over Alwyn's Festival March in silence, the Gardner. An uncivilized piece, lacking barbarian strength. Nothing half-hearted about Gardner's attempt to squeeze his, no doubt unconscious, cribbings from the English school, Sibelius, etc., into a good symphonic scheme, but result is just a laboriously contrived hotch-potch of sham-romantic film-music, which, fortified by the austere label of " symphony," outlasts and out-bores six film-scores.

Of performers and performances there is no space to mention the bad ones. Not that they would crowd out the good ones, but they'd ask for a lot of detailed statements. The best performances at Cheltenham were the 4th Vaughan-Williams by the Hallé (Barbirolli), Raymond Cohen's Elgar Violin Concerto, Brahms op. 25 by the Robert Masters Piano Quartet, Clifford Curzon in the Rawsthorne Concerto, Raymond Nilsson as Easdale's Headmaster, Pears as narrator in Monteverdi's *Combattimento* and as Aeneas in *Dido*, and the Grillers in Bliss's F minor Quartet. Back at Aldeburgh, Britten's playing and conducting of Mozart K.459 in F was a rare example of a performer's inspiration matching the one of his composer. One wonders whether Britten's own composing contributes to his insight into another one's music : usually, thing's don't work out that way. However that may be, here are a very few of the excellencies : the drily martial rendering of the orchestra's and piano's first tonic-dominant subject, with just a softening of its cadential ends that points out how much that isn't dry at all is going to happen to this theme in the course of the movement. The implacable wood-wind interruptions in the second movement's middle-part that were mollified, but not disavowed, by the piano's answers. The breeziness of the Rondo theme (complete with tiny *crescendo* and *accelerando* towards the quaver-bar) and the more abiding sparkle of the Rondo-interludes. Technically, Britten's limpid touch and capacity for minute tone-graduations are in a class by themselves (Gieseking in Mozart's C major K.467 comes nearest). His scales have just that little push, noticed only by the metronomic ear, that makes them actually more melodious ; under Britten's hands, that is. In short, Britten's yearly Mozart Concerto, as well as his more frequent accompanying, makes one regret that the composer Britten has no identical twin who could devote himself to a full-time pianistic career. P.H.

GLYNDEBOURNE FESTIVAL
IDOMENEO AND FIGARO [*see our Editorial on p. 317.*—EDS.]

" I HAVE it from Busch ! " a conductor retorted some time ago when he read my criticism of one of his Mozart *tempi*. Another man's *tempi*, however, are always wrong. Wherefrom it does not follow that a man's own are always right. Busch's own, for instance, seldom are. I have never understood the glorification of Busch's Mozart operas, nor, for that matter, of Ebert's ; and I understand it less than ever. If this is Mozart, I resign from Mozartianship.

Neither *Idomeneo* nor *Figaro*, while offering some unprecedentedly beautiful minute details, such as the perfectly characterized bass interjections in the 4 bars before Figaro's last act aria's triplets, ever showed a really well-shaped number, let alone a well-formed whole. There was as much inspiration in the conducting as in a piece of wood. When the emotionally heavy, pedantic, correct baton decided upon Mozartian lightness, the result was a lightness applied from without, lightness in heavy type. Far from being the moving power of the music, Busch's *tempi* were its exterior decoration. Since naturalness and spontaneity were lacking, every quick tempo, e.g. the *Idomeneo* Overture's, tended to be too quick, and every slow one too slow, e.g. *Idomeneo's* third act *marcia*, which provided a study in the opposite of *alla breve*, whereas in point of thematic fact it must be more animated than the corresponding priest's march in the *Magic Flute*, likewise an *alla breve* Andante in F major. Some of the singers and almost the whole of the orchestra were much better than the conductor, which made the whole affair all the more depressing : half-empty perfection, with the full half tepid. I had the sad opportunity to observe the effect thereof immediately after the *Idomeneo* performance I attended, when a sensitive musician who had just heard the opera for the first time " didn't think much of it." The better the singing and playing, the more difficult it is to realize that there is everything important wrong with them, unless you know and understand the music ; and since culture in general and music in particular have become so unfortunately respectable, the number not merely of amateurs, but also of expert professionals steadily increases who think they understand the music because they know it by what they have instead of a musical heart.

Ebert's production of *Idomeneo* was dominated by a flight of 3+4 steps on which was displayed, wellnigh continuously, the sort of " one-foot-up, one-foot-down acting " and singing which Alec Guiness* finds "particularly dispiriting." As for *Figaro*, it must remain a mystery to every musical opera lover in the country why an American had to be engaged for the rôle of Susanna who had not done it before and could not in fact do it, when the best Susanna (and Despina) alive and singing, Rose Hill, is trying her best to go to the dogs in London variety because, one has to suppose, she does not get enough, or sufficiently well-paid, serious work.

Glyndebourne's Assistant Conductor and Chorus Master, John Pritchard, has shown, in a recent concert performance of *Zaide*, that he understands Mozart ; until he takes over we shall do well to avail ourselves of cheap and unaccomplished Sadler's Wells, except when they have it from Busch. H.K.

*" My Idea of Hamlet," *Spectator*, July 6, 1951.

THE 14TH MAGGIO MUSICALE AT FLORENCE
WEBER'S "OBERON" IN THE BOBOLI GARDENS

BY all accounts, the Maggio Musicale, of which I saw only the grand finale, was only moderately good this year. " Haydn* and I are the only novelties " said Roman Vlad, whose one-act ballet *La Strada sul café* was unfortunately cancelled at the last moment through Russian performer-trouble. But the open-air performances of Weber's *Oberon* in the Boboli Gardens reached a very high standard, and rivalled in spectacular splendour many contemporary descriptions of Gonzaga or Medici festivities at the time of *Arianna* or *Orfeo*.

*Haydn's opera *Orfeo* was performed for the first time.

373

Grandstands were built by the side of a lake and the action took place not only on the island in the centre but even in the lake itself. The sheer visual effect of the mermaid ballet in Act 2 beggars description : Teresa Stich Randall as principal mermaid glided effortlessly on to a rock and proceeded to sing in a clear, perfectly controlled voice (with evident sangfroid) *O come grata sull'onde galleggiar* (" O 'tis pleasant to float on the sea " in the English original) with the mermaids circling round her in the water. The end of Act 3 saw the triumphal arrival of Titania in a fairy-barge propelled invisibly (*pace* a large swan) by some submerged mermaids whose breathing capacities deserve mention.

Even the Florentines found the scenic beauties far beyond their expectations. Herbert Graf shared the responsibility with the Boboli Gardens, which lent a formidable chorus of frogs, bats and crickets, not to speak of the unrehearsed cloud effect and a large yellow moon which slipped from behind the trees for the last scene.

But even if such effects are only suggested, as they were at Covent Garden in 1826, *Oberon* still succeeds, combining as it does some excellent qualities of exuberant German romanticism with the ballad-opera traditions so dear to English opera. Its value as a serious stage work lies less in its undeniable musical virtues as such than in the extraordinary skill with which Weber has merged all its incompatible elements into a powerful dramatic whole : witness the quality of the ensembles when all the weird assortment of characters finds a common denominator of proportion and discipline.

Inevitably this open-air production concentrated on the fairyland aspect and left the oriental colour to spring from the score and the behaviour of the characters in the harem scenes. The medieval chivalric side had more difficulty in making itself felt. The Charlemagne episodes were not used in order to focus attention on the mainspring of the plot, which is Oberon's quarrel with Titania. It came through with Sir Huon's heroic attitudes (Tyge Tygesen) and his attempts to reconcile love and honour.

Oberon presents such formidable problems that I am still astonished how successfully it was managed. The orchestra and chorus were placed immediately below island level above some illuminated fern grottoes which also served as landing stages, and as a lower level for the processions. The chorus was welded into the orchestral texture, being placed between the double-basses and the rest of the orchestra. When as in Acts 2 and 3 it was on the stage, it was kept as close as possible to the orchestra. Stage diffusion was harder to combat because nothing can add cubits to men's stature, or width to their gestures. The original spoken dialogue was retained and microphones used, with the stretch of water between singers and public as a powerful voice-carrier. Spot-lighting of different parts of the island effected the necessary changes of scene between Europe, Asia and Fairyland.

Strangely enough, working on such a large scale did not prevent the light-hearted courtship of Scerasmino (Melchiore Luise) and Fatima (Rina Corsi) from being the most effective scene. The baritone Luise gave a masterly characterization of this Papagenoish part, and Rina Corsi, while sometimes ungainly in her movements, was vocally extremely finished.

But however the work is staged, it is in Weber's vocal writing that the greatest dangers lie. His love of covering the whole range of the singer in two bars or less demands fantastic sureness of placing. The *vocalizzi* which form a large part of the arias are generally repeated *ad nauseam* as if the voices were instruments, and his singers require a stamina which in its healthy crudity militates against subtle interpretation. In fact, insufficient characterization is a very pronounced defect of the work, development being brought about almost entirely by sudden transitions in the score. In addition there are two protagonists (Oberon and Sir Huon) who are both tenors and the confusion is increased by their arias often being interchanged. Thus Oberon's aria at the end of Act 2 was sung by Huon in Act 1.

In this testing framework the singers made a remarkably good job. Gino Penno as Oberon had a magnificent bearing and a rich voice of immense volume but a tendency to take top notes too roughly and jab at them. Tyge Tygesen as Sir Huon was less impressive, but his voice is beautifully controlled and has a fine *legato*. Vocally speaking, Doris Doree as Rezia gave an excellent performance. Her voice was fluid and vibrant and she was the only one who really broke free of the fierce rhythmical punctuation of Weber's vocal lines which tends to occur whenever he is not being prayerful. Puck was played in traditional fashion by Gianna Pederzini. This extraordinarily gifted dramatic actress was gracefully mobile and her speaking voice is as seductive and well-modulated as her singing voice is powerful and even forbidding.

The Maggio Orchestra under Fritz Stiedry produced some very fine playing especially in the woodwind passages—e.g., the clarinets' and flutes' enchanting running figure in Oberon's aria at the end of Act 3. The various ballets were carried out in bare-footed fairy fashion (choreography by Carlo Faraboni) and, apart from the fairy lights, were as unremarkable as the costumes.

But except for inadequacies in certain of the component parts, the whole can be said to have succeeded as a magnificent *tour de force* and to have vindicated the frenzied reception accorded to Weber when he first conducted *Oberon* at Covent Garden shortly before his death.

Cynthia Jolly

Our next issue will include a report on the Salzburg Festival, with particular reference to the performance of Berg's *Wozzeck*.—Eds.

Gramophone Records

WALTON : *Violin Concerto.* Heifetz, with the Philharmonia Orchestra, c. Walton. HMV. DB.9611-3.

This is a new recording of a newly-orchestrated work : and let it be said at once that a great improvement is noticeable in the balance of soloist and orchestra. With the composer in charge, this version is as authentic as one could wish for, and it will doubtless be so regarded for many years to come. Heifetz brings his inimitable tone to bear on a virile and vigorous score which needs the steely touch : and there is brilliance and glitter in the orchestra too, as if they were galvanized by the presence of both composer and virtuoso.

DELIUS : *A Song of Summer.* Hallé Orchestra, c. Barbirolli. HMV. DB.9609-10.

The artists have seized the spirit of Delius's passion for the lush, bright richness of a continental summer, and they have given a sensitive reading of his romantic and colourful score. There is not too much definition in the recording, but this may be a deliberate attempt to stimulate a heavy, almost drowsy atmosphere. Unfortunately this drowsiness is communicated to the fill-up, a Mozart *Andante* taken from the Cassation in G major, K.63.

BERLIOZ: *Overture, King Lear.* Royal Philharmonic Orchestra, c. Beecham. HMV. DB.9614-5.

Beecham's strong sense of drama tells him to go slow in the introduction, and the greater contrast achieved fully justifies this attitude. Berlioz never told us where to find Lear and Cordelia in his music, but if we have guessed aright, Beecham confirms our reflections upon the tragedy, and effects a true catharsis in his fine interpretation. The playing of the woodwind is especially commendable.

WAGNER : *Forest Murmurs (Siegfried).* Hollywood Bowl Symphony Orchestra, c. Stokowski. HMV. DB.21238.

There is an astounding clarity in this recording, forever reminding us of the distance between Bayreuth and Hollywood. Every vein of every leaf, and every leaf of every tree is in its proper place. The plumage of the birds is brilliant to a degree hitherto unknown, and the forest no longer murmurs.

D.W.S.

HAYDN : *Divertimento in G, Op. 31, No. 1* (arr. Haas). London Baroque Ensemble, c. Karl Haas. Parlophone SW. 8118/8119.

The ensemble here consists of a string quintet, flute and two horns. Balance is generally good, though in the first movement the leading violin is inclined to be meek and wispy. The slow movement is of rather unusual design, and its elegance is enhanced by delightfully relevant phrasing. Except for one slight lapse of intonation, however, the final section is perhaps the most " fetching " of all. As fill-ups we have the Fourth London Trio for two flutes and bass (in which the cello tone is not quite authentic), and a Grenadier March for wind sextet and side-drum—very neat and perky.

MOZART : *Adagio in B flat, K. 440a.* London Baroque Ensemble, c. Karl Haas. Parlophone, R. 20592.

Originally scored for two clarinets and three basset horns. In this recording the lower registers of the clarinets are occasionally a little grotesque in *tenuto* passages ; but the music is ably interpreted.

PURCELL, arr. Bergmann and Tibbett (sic) : *Sweeter than Roses* and " *Epithalamium.*" Alfred Deller (counter-tenor) and Walter Bergmann (harpsichord). HMV. C.4044.

Deller's purity of tone and effective crescendo are well demonstrated here. The harpsichord accompaniment is nicely distanced, and not tinkly. One hopes for more of such recordings from these two artists.

BACH : *Brandenberg Concerto No. 4 in G.* Danish State Broadcasting Orchestra, c. Woldike. HMV. C.4073-4075 (five sides).

A clearly defined performance, with the three solo instruments playing much more like a *trio* than in any previous recording known to me. In the first movement the accompanying orchestra has a tendency to over-emphasize the obvious marks of punctuation, the basses especially. The harpsichord strikes me as a little too reticent (or maybe the realization of this part is not substantial enough). According to my reading of this work, the Andante is taken too fast ; it should avoid any feeling of languor : but here the *strict tempo* seems to have been too closely observed. The last movement, however, comes off very well, except for some inadequacies in the recording—which is a pity, for the solo passages are finely done. On the sixth side there is the Sarabande from the Sixth French Suite, played by Liselotte Selbiger, again (to my mind) a trifle hurried. E.D.M.

BARBER : *Adagio for String Orchestra.* Boyd Neel String Orchestra, c. Boyd Neel. Decca X.305.

An interesting study in the crescendo and sustained climax and a very lovely piece of music, worth many of its composer's later and more pretentious efforts. Its beginning and ending on the dominant is a stroke of genius in the handling of this simple framework. I have a feeling that its rightness would be more adequately demonstrated in its original string quartet medium.

HANDEL : *Overture (Suite) in C Major.* London Baroque Ensemble, c. Karl Haas. Parlophone, R.20581.

Mr. Haas and his players continually earn our gratitude for the many unusual pieces they recover for our benefit, and here is fresh cause. A trio for two clarinets and horn, it stands in brilliant contrast to the arid desert represented by so much of Handel's instrumental music, and in its freedom and easy working within narrow limits irresistibly reminds one of Mozart's little divertimenti for wind trio. The playing is magnificent.

WEBER : *Concerto for Bassoon and Orchestra, Op. 75.* Gwydion Brooke (Bassoon) with Liverpool Philharmonic Orchestra, c. Sargent. Col. DX.1656-7.

A little masterpiece of character-drawing, revealing little-suspected facets of the bassoon's nature and, incidentally, a finer work than the better-known Mozart. The performance is of a high order.

BACH : *Brandenburg Concerto No. 3, in G.* Chamber Orchestra of Palace Chapel, Copenhagen, c. Woldike. HMV. C.3947-8.

This performance is a delight ; an exactly right tempo which never degenerates into the unintelligent stomp we are so used to in this country, although it fails to achieve quite the consistent fluidity proper to the last movement. H.T

BALAKIREV: *Symphony in C Major.* Philharmonia Orchestra, c. Karajan. Col. LX.1323—1328.

A work of considerable vitality and charm, extrovert, brilliantly colourful, and evoking a sense of spaciousness in its moments of restraint.   It is not, however, a work to be heard too frequently ; with all its qualities, it is rhythmically and melodically restricted in the quick movements to the stamping vigour of Folksy Russian tunes which do not gather significance in development.   The slow movement is the height of the work, moving and sensuously beautiful, with no temperamental Slavonic tears.   The recording is true and finely balanced : Karajan's performance is in most respects all that could be desired.   In the slow movement it seems that the music demands some relaxation of strict tempo ; here Karajan's beat has more determination than the work he is conducting.

BEETHOVEN : *Piano Concerto No. 1 in C Major.* Gieseking with Philharmonia Orchestra. Col. LX.1312-1315.

Recording : the tone of the piano is dead for a few moments early on side two ; at the side's end the *tutti* is blown up out of focus, as is the drum roll at the conclusion of side seven.   For the rest, a most satisfactory set. Gieseking and the orchestra play with unfailing style and wit.   On the whole, a delightful. recording of an enchanting work.

MOZART : *Symphony No. 41 in C Major.* Royal Philharmonic Orchestra, c. Beecham. Col. LX.1337-1340.

The playing and recording are of a very high standard, but the interpretation has moments of irritating fussiness.   The performance is brilliant in tone and *élan ;* its displeasing points are matters of falsified detail which diminish the total value of what could have been a masterly set of records.

First Movement : tempo on the slow side.   The unison at the end of the first subject carries an exaggerated *ritardando* (a Beecham hallmark).   At one or two points the timpani are noticeably behind the beat ; rests are skimped of their full time values.   For instance, the five beat silence before the plunge into C minor, both in the exposition and in the recapitulation, is barely four beats long.   The sequential passage in bars 219-224 completely loses its sense of direction.

Second Movement : all the pathos is wrung out of the descending syncopated quaver figure ; each return of the principal subject is signalled by a perceptible slackening of pace.   More seriously, the various semi-quaver and demi-semi-quaver arabesques are caressed, hugged and patted out of recognizable shape : to find two, and at times three, sets of time values in a single sextuplet semi-quaver group is not uncommon. (Bars 41, 42, 43, and elsewhere).

Minuet and Trio : A pace so lugubriously slow that the semi-tonal descent that haunts the movement becomes an outrageously pathetic and self-pitying sigh.   The questionable tempo may have been adopted to give added momentum to the last movement.

Finale : very nearly a glorious performance apart from a mis-accentuated muddle between bars 172 and 185.   The brass suspensions in the recapitulation are exceptionally audible, and the tremendous *stretto* combination of themes is dazzling in its clarity.

BANTOCK : *Fifine at the Fair*.* Royal Philharmonic Orchestra, c. Beecham. HMV. DB.21145-21148.

This recording has been so widely praised for a variety of reasons that I offer the minority view with some diffidence.

A lengthy symphonic poem in loose " first movement " form, *Fifine* was inspired by a Browning text in which Don Juan meditates on carnal love, symbolized by the capricious flight of a butterfly which leads him both to Fifine, the fair-ground beauty, and the " sacred " devotion of Donna Elvira. The treatment and musical symbolism are inspired by Richard Strauss, but the material employed is less chromatic and more traditional than Straussian melody : moments parented by Wagner and Tchaikovsky are frequent. The work demands a vast orchestra, which is handled with considerable virtuosity.

Side One deals with Donna Elvira, whose suave but hardly memorable theme is disturbed by the distracting butterfly and finally silenced by the din of the Fair half way through Side Two. A showman thunders on a bass drum, a violinist tunes up and plays a duet with a piper, and half way through Side Three the orchestra breaks into a Waltz, the recognized Straussian symbol for carnality : this waltz, however, has more in common with Baynes's *Destiny* than with Baron Ochs or Salome. The Waltz completes the exposition and development continues until, on Side Six, a further waltz, slower and attempting languor, appears. The fair ground music provides a dynamic climax, and the finale, after chorale-like brass chords, allows the Elvira theme, with a suitable Lisztian " apotheosis," to triumph over the agitating influence of the butterfly.

Not only the method, but also the material is remarkably derivative : apart from its plummy richness, the work is without distinguishing features and offers nothing to which the mind leaps with any delight. There is real skill in orchestration, but whether or not there is any real music is something of an enigma.

Why was the work recorded, and why was the recording sponsored by the British Council ? As we know Beecham's taste for Occasional Edwardian, his share in the proceedings is understandable. We assume that, in conjunction with his proposed resurrection of *The Bohemian Girl*, this recording demonstrates the maestro's objection to the works of English composers. Having said so much on this subject, Sir Thomas has apparently decided that actions speak louder than words. We await his recording of *Maritana* with baited breath.   H.B.R.

*A further review of this recording will appear in our next issue.—EDS.

Correspondence

4, NORTON WAY N.,
LETCHWORTH,
HERTS.
2nd July, 1951.

SIRS,—In MS's Vol. II/4 (Spring 1950) your contributor E.H.W.M. published a report on a recital of Gina Bachauer (Wigmore Hall, March 18, 1950), in which he took that admirable and conscientious artist severely to task for having performed Reger's *Variations and Fugue on a Theme of Bach* minus Variations 5, 7, 8, 9. Since I share your contributor's (very forcibly expressed) opinion that " any performer who without the composer's express desire, and certainly without mentioning the fact in the concert programme, subjects a work to truncation . . . forfeits thereby all right to be considered as an interpretative artist . . . , " and since I was present at that recital (in which Miss Bachauer's playing moved me as profoundly as it disgusted E.H.W.M.), I tried to find out the reasons for Miss Bachauer's decision. I publish the results of my investigation with the artist's consent for the benefit of Reger students, and also as a vindication of Miss Bachauer's course of action which would undoubtedly have proved less controversial had she mentioned the incriminated cut in a programme note. Miss Bachauer had selected Reger's Op. 81 for her participation in the "Internationale Wettbewerb für Gesang und Klavier," Vienna, May 28—June 15, 1933, a musical competition under the presidency of Clemens Krauss. At the " semi-final," Miss Bachauer played Reger's work in its entirety, as published by Messrs. Böte & Bock, Berlin, 1904. After she had finished Moriz Rosenthal, who had listened as a member of the International Jury, congratulated her on her choice of work as well as on her interpretation. While expressing his great admiration for Reger's work, he deplored its excessive length and related to Miss Bachauer that he had discussed this question with the composer himself. He had pointed out to Reger that although one could easily play a sonata of about forty minutes duration, it was difficult to maintain the listener's interest for the same length of time in a more agglomerative type of work such as a set of variations. According to Rosenthal, Max Reger completely agreed with him and subsequently consented to the elimination of *three* variations (not four, as your contributor asserts). These authorized cuts run in the above-mentioned edition, from page 11, *Vivace*, to page 14 top, and from page 16, *Adagio*, to the top of page 20, *Grave*. Approved by the composer and practised by Rosenthal, they were accepted by Miss Bachauer. She subsequently played Reger's work in this shortened version at the " final," and received the " Ehrenpreis " of the city of Vienna, the highest award of the competition. The original diploma of June 1933 is at present in my hands. It bears the signatures of many prominent musicians, among them such pianists as Rosenthal, Backhaus, Lubka Kolessa, Paul Weingarten, Victor Ebenstein, Willy Rehberg, and Pantscho Wladigeroff. It is obvious that the International Jury knew of the cuts. Contrary to E.H.W.M., I myself, too, find them excellent and do not hesitate to recommend them to Reger students. They should indeed smooth the way for this superb but also superlatively difficult work towards popularity and immortality, and may prove as beneficial as the big cut in the second Act of *Tristan*, which was authorized by Wagner and is today universally accepted, although it is not mentioned in any reprint of the full score.

If Miss Bachauer has been too reticent about the reasons for her action, she has received more than due punishment at the hands of your contributor. The facts as disclosed in this letter should help to place her action as well as her artistic integrity into proper perspective.

Yours sincerely,
H. F. REDLICH.

As a Reger student I was particularly interested in Dr. Redlich's letter. It may well be that what Rosenthal told Miss Bachauer was perfectly correct— although to the best of my belief there is no mention of the matter in all Reger's voluminous correspondence. But it should be remembered that composers often have to agree to undesirable compromises in order to achieve a performance. We should not turn their own excusable willingness to negotiate deletions into an excuse for lazy listeners and lazy executants. Mr. Frank Merrick was able to play the work in its entirety, and with considerable success, at the Bechstein Hall on April 18th, 1910—during the composer's life-time. I am unable to understand why we should lag behind forty years after. I too was present at Miss Bachauer's recital—with music—and whether intentionally or no, the pianist exceeded even the " authorized " excisions detailed in Dr. Redlich's letter. I see no reason for changing my opinion that our reviewer's report was accurate and more essentially musical than Miss Bachauer's performance of Reger's masterpiece. ED.(D.M.)

66, ABINGDON VILLAS,
W.8.

2nd July, 1951.

THE UMMLAUT [*sic.-Eds.*]

SIRS,—I write to you, as a writer in and reader of your periodical, about a point of typography. This is the *ummlaut* [*sic.-Eds.*] which you are so assiduously trying to eliminate.

The *ummlaut* [*sic.-Eds.*] is an honoured member of the German vocabularic family. Its ancestry, like that of the French circumflex accent, is irreproachable and its use invaluable. Sirs, you are now making away with it. Schönberg may well become Schoenberg—he himself, I believe, has now adopted this Americanized spelling. But another musician whose name frequently appears in your columns, Dr. Furtwängler, is to be spelt, by your decision, Furtwaengler. And the passage that leads from the development to the recapitulation of a movement in sonata form is spelt by your magazine, not *Rückführung*, but *Rueckfuehrung*.

This ugly typographical periphrasis cannot be caused by the want, in your typesetter's armoury, of a's and o's with ummlauts [*sic.-Eds.*] on top. In your last issue but two, Schütz was spelt as I write him here, in one notice, and, in another, according to your own quaint prejudice—Schuetz.

Sirs, the two spellings are not symphonious ; the symbol ü is acceptably, if not exactly, pronounced like a stopped *ee*, but *ue* must be pronounced *oo-e* in so explicit an alphabet as German.

What is more important is that such spellings as *Muehlenraeder* and *Luenebuerger* [there is no such word—EDS.] look *unsightly*. Your magazine is designed to be *read* ; let it not be an offence to the eye.

I am, Sirs,
Yours faithfully,
WILLIAM S. MANN.

P.S.—What do you do about *Haüser* ?

Our respected contributor's attempt to write more than 250 words about nothing is completely successful ; less so his touching endeavour to teach me my mother-tongue. His observations on the *Umlaut* are in fact almost as well-founded as his spelling of the word itself. This was originally formed by Klopstock, and confined to its present meaning by J. Grimm in 1819. In any case, it means (as it says itself) sounds, not dots. There are three ways of spelling the *Umlaut* : (I) 2 dots, (II) a tiny " e " over, (III) an " e " after, the *umgelautet* vowel.   Nowadays, No. III is admittedly *Ersatz* (used, for example, in telegrams) whose general recognition derives, however, from its more honourable history : it actually antedates No. I in nouns with initial *Umlaut*, and most persistently in such foreign (Latin and Greek) words as *Aedification, Aegide, Aera, Oeconomie, Oedem, Oenomanie, Oesophag*, etc.   To suggest that " the two spellings are not symphonious " would therefore be inaccurate, even if Mr. Mann had chosen the right English word for what he wrongly means, namely, " homophonous."   The German latinist spontaneously speaks " *Caelius mons*," " *Asa foetida*," " *aegri deliria somni* " (never, of course, printed with ligatures) with *Umlauten*.   The tendency to pronounce " ae," " oe " and even " ue " as *Umlaute* is wellnigh all-pervading, affecting as it does two-syllabled vowel sounds.   Thus, although in 1915 *Duden* declares all No. III's to have been replaced by No. I's, and therefore spells the quadri-syllabic "*Aeronaut*" without the diaeresis (*Trennpunkte*) which Kiesewetter, in 1888, had applied, as a matter of course, to this word as well as to " *Lues*," both Schlessing-Wehrle and Brockhaus revert ruefully to " *Aëronaut* " in 1927 and 1935 respectively.   Brockhaus adds " *Aëroplan*," but while the diaeresis distrusts Mr. Mann, the spoken language mistrusts both him and the dictionaries at variance with him : today, true to Duden, nobody writes or prints " *Aëroplan*," but, in defiance of Duden, everybody says "*Ároplan*;" the only person from whose throat I ever heard an *Aëroplan* emerge was a Hungarian.

The discrepancies in our typography are due to the recent enrichment of our printer's armoury : our remaining No. III's had previously been set up in type. I feel the only words wherein No. III could conceivably offend are proper names.   ED.(H.K.)

P.S.—Previously we should have printed *Haeuser* ; nowadays we put your two dots in the right place.

REFERENCES :—Brockhaus, F. A. (publ. & ed.), *Der Sprach-Brockhaus,* Leipzig, 1935. *Duden, Rechtschreibung der deutschen Sprache und der Fremdwörter*, 9th ed. (Wülfling, E., & Schmidt, A. C.), Bibliographisches Institut, Leipzig and Vienna, 1915. Kiesewetter, K. (ed.), *Fremdwörterbuch*, 7th ed. (Scholtz, A.), Glogau, 1888. Schlessing-Wehrle, *Deutscher Wortschatz*, 6th ed., Stuttgart, 1927.

MUSIC SURVEY

(KATHLEEN LIVINGSTON   WILLIAM W. LIVINGSTON   DONALD MITCHELL)

VOL. IV, No. 2   FEBRUARY, 1952

CONTENTS

EDITORS :
DONALD MITCHELL
HANS KELLER

EDITORIAL BOARD :
**ROBERT DONINGTON   PAUL HAMBURGER   CHARLES STUART
DENNIS DOBSON**

EDITORIAL CORRESPONDENCE should be addressed to the EDITORS, MUSIC SURVEY, OAKFIELD SCHOOL, WEST DULWICH, LONDON, S.E.21. Annual Subscription, including postage, 11s. U.S.A. $2.50.

All enquiries relating to advertising space in this journal should be made to MUSIC SURVEY at the above address.

Editorial

HAROLD HOLT, LTD., is the only concert-giving agency in Europe which does not provide this journal with press tickets. We were not even honoured with a reply when we applied for admission to the Horowitz recitals. The suspicion cannot be avoided that Harold Holt, Ltd., is more interested in good publicity, however bad the criticism, than in bad publicity, however good (as possibly distinct from favourable) the review. Unless Harold Holt, Ltd., reacts to this suggestion, we are forced to assume that the firm measures the value of music criticism in terms of box office receipts. It would be what many regard as a normal attitude ; we should consider it disgusting.

The Third Programme's extended Schoenberg series will receive the fullest attention in our next issue which will in fact be devoted to the composer, and include the present issue's *Schoenberg* section for obvious reasons of context. The present issue's *Film Music* and *Review* sections have to be held over for less intrinsic, i.e. space reasons.

Constant Lambert
(1905 - 1951)
By HUMPHREY SEARLE*

I FIRST met Constant Lambert in 1936, so I cannot speak of the brilliant period when he burst upon the musical world as a very young man ; but the circumstances of our meeting are worth recalling, as they show a typical side of his generous character. I was a student at the time, and, through reading Mr. Sacheverell Sitwell's admirable biography, had recently become very interested in the late and unknown works of Liszt. I resolved to try to celebrate the 50th anniversary of Liszt's death, which fell in that year, by giving a concert of some of these works in Oxford, and wrote to Constant Lambert, to whom I was completely unknown, asking for his advice and help. In reply I received a most kind letter, in which he not only gave some valuable suggestions for the programme, but also promised to come down himself and conduct the *Malediction* for piano and strings. At that time he had recently completed *Summer's Last Will and Testament*, and was extremely occupied both with critical work and with conducting at Sadler's

*Mr. Searle's note is intended as no more than a personal appreciation ; it does not attempt to give a general account of Lambert's career.—EDS.

Wells and elsewhere ; yet for a cause which he had at heart he was prepared to come, at the request of somebody of whom he had never heard, to conduct an amateur orchestra in an extremely difficult work, without any thought of return.

Such actions were characteristic of him throughout his life ; he was always prepared to fight for the things he believed in, whether musical, artistic or social. Like Liszt, whom he so greatly admired, he threw out his influence in all directions ; his compositions, his conducting, his criticisms, his knowledge of painting and writing, his witty and brilliant conversation—they have all left their mark on our time. Some people have reproached him for not concentrating exclusively on composition. It is true that at times, circumstances made it difficult for him to do so, but there were so many things he could do well, and he enjoyed doing all of them. He flourished in a period when the old order of musical thought was being violently broken down by new ideas, and it is largely to him that we owe our present widespread appreciation of the Elizabethans, Purcell, Berlioz, Liszt, the Russian nationalists (especially Glinka, Balakireff and Mussorgsky), Sibelius (of whom he was one of the earliest admirers in this country) and the modern French school— not to mention such remarkable but less universally recognised figures as Satie and van Dieren. He was not particularly interested in academic tradition—though of course he had a thorough knowledge and appreciation of the classics, particularly of Haydn ; he preferred to break fresh ground, not just for the sake of being different, but because he was able to discover so many genuinely interesting things.

I do not think he ever saw himself as a " Great Composer "—he hated that particular kind of Teutonic aggrandisement ; but each of his works has a definite purpose and expresses a mood or feeling of its own. In spite of the enormous brilliance at his command, I feel that he was primarily a lyricist, and that he was at his best in such movements as the finale of the piano Concerto (which he wrote in memory of his friend Peter Warlock), the final slow section of *Summer's Last Will and Testament*, and the very moving " *Dirge* " *from Cymbeline*. The resounding success of *The Rio Grande*— certainly an admirable piece of its kind—tended to make the public think of him chiefly as a composer of brisk music with a jazzy flavour, and to overlook his real achievements in the fields of both ballet and symphonic music. In spite of his objective brilliance and his power of critical detachment, he was an essentially subjective person, who often felt things far more deeply than he cared to show.

This was evident in his conducting. Orchestral players liked working with him, because they felt that he was a real musician who was there to bring out the best in the music, and not someone who simply wanted to inflate his own reputation at the expense of the composer. As a result, they invariably gave of their best under him : one of the most remarkable experiences I have ever had was to hear him conduct a complete and uncut version of Liszt's *Faust* Symphony— a work which he had long awaited an opportunity to perform. Similarly, without his knowledge, personality and hard work, the Sadler's Wells Ballet could never have reached the pre-eminent position which it holds today ; and how many of the younger generation have profited by his brilliant and penetrating analysis of contemporary trends in *Music Ho!* Many young composers, too, benefited by his practical help, for he was always willing to perform new works, even of a kind which did not particularly appeal to him.

Constant Lambert will, I think, be remembered, not so much for any one facet of his achievement as for the sum total of them all, a potent and vital force in the music of our country and our time. All of us have many things for which we must be grateful to him, and his death is a most tragic loss for the world of music.

More Off than On " Billy Budd "
BY DONALD MITCHELL

[At this stage we consider it more important to deal with current critical misconceptions than with the music itself. To the latter we shall return—in detail—in a future issue.—EDS.]

1.

PRELIMINARIES

ONE of the opening pre- first performance shots was fired by Mr. Charles Reid in the London *Evening Standard* of November 29th, in a piece entitled " Britten Makes It Seven . . . " (Mr. Reid's mathematics are clear enough when one realizes that he starts counting the operas from the unpublished *Paul Bunyan* (1941) and includes the realization of *The Beggar's Opera*).

There are three legitimate possibilities open to the critic who writes about a new work prior to its première. (a) He can study the score and make provisional comments which the performance will either prove or disprove (a procedure adopted by Mr. Desmond Shawe-Taylor in the *New Statesman and Nation* of December 1st) ; (b) He can study old works afresh and prophesy likely stylistic characteristics of the new (a method not without its element of danger—witness the unfortunate article by Scott Goddard (" Britten as an Instrumental Composer," *Listener*, July 7th, 1949) which, as a preview of the *Spring Symphony*'s first broadcast performance, foresaw everything beside the *Spring Symphony*'s point) ; (c) He can write about the composer as a figure of popular interest, subjecting him to much the same sort of journalistic analysis as is meted out to politicians, actors, criminals or generals (to take a not-so-mixed bag of notorieties). A fourth possibility is to keep silent altogether until the first performance is over ; but that course is rarely an economic possibility.

Mr. Reid's article falls into category (c) and far be it from me to suggest that he be blamed for writing a gossip column piece for an evening paper. After all a genius is a genius, and even an inevitably superficial survey of his character can be of value. Faced with the unenviable task of writing an article which must be read and enjoyed by thousands of non-musicians the only question of conscience which arises is how to be as *harmlessly* entertaining as possible. Not, I should have thought, a very difficult task for Mr. Reid who is not only the most expert of journalists but also a music critic of uncommon perception (a judgment recently confirmed by his notice of *Wozzeck's* first English performance (*Evening Standard*, January 23rd)). For a Britten profile I could have imagined no happier combination than the journalist Mr. Reid working hand in glove with his music critical self. Here, in fact, was the chance to prove that the presence of good journalism need not entail the absence of musicality.

But what sort of a profile did Mr. Reid's *Evening Standard* article turn out to be ? I should be hard put to discover a parallel example of such tasteless fact and factless fancy. Much of Mr. Reid's information gives the impression that he was once Mr. Britten's bank manager : he specifies the amount left to the composer under his father's will ; the composer's initial fees for his joint recitals with Peter Pears (not a mention of the many occasions when both artists have given their services in a good cause) ; we are even told the price Mr. Britten paid for his motor-car. Such an extraordinary exposure of any man's private affairs is quite unwarrantable, and, in my experience of musical journalism, the article is without precedent.

Throughout this strange piece crop up emotive phrases such as " he felt very much at home with the *Bloomsbury Leftists*," or " now he has a solid, *bourgeois-looking* house facing the sea at Aldeburgh " [my italics], neither of which is very meaningful on close verbal inspection. There is no necessity for good journalists to borrow their vocabulary from bad politicians ; nor should Mr. Reid continue to use the time-dishonoured device of false juxtaposition. For instance :

> " . . . The man who in 1939 contributed anti-war music (including a satirical Dance of Death) to a Festival of Music for the People at the old Queen's Hall stood eleven years later as god-parent with Queen Mary and Princess Elizabeth at the christening of the Earl and Countess of Harewood's baby."

The first half of the paragraph is seemingly invalidated by the second, although a minute's shallow thought exposes the *non sequitur*. Meanwhile the inuendo has cast its shadow. As Mr. Reid has it : " . . . Britten's social life was beginning to glitter."

Mr. Reid winds up his piece with an off the mark comment or two on Britten's music, and introduces a group of fanatics (whom I have never remotely met) in order to demolish a ludicrous statement (which I could never imagine being made outside the confines of an asylum) :

> " . . . [Britten] has, I think, too much good sense to credit the extremist clique who say in all seriousness that *he is the most important thing that has hit music since Mozart* " [My italics].

If Mr. Reid can point to any such comment in print, we should be delighted to crown its author as the biggest musical idiot to hit this century.

As for Mr. Britten's views on other men's music we are told that " he has a rather childlike contempt for Puccini "—a remark which is more revealing of Mr. Reid's inexact terminology than of Mr. Britten's musical judgments. What does " childlike " mean in this context ? According to the Oxford English Dictionary the word is defined thus :

> " Belonging to or becoming a child ; filial. Like a child ; (of qualities, etc.) like those of a child. (*Usu. in a good sense, as opp. to childish*). [My italics].

As far as I am aware a contempt for Puccini is not a characteristic of childhood. It seems that what Mr. Reid really meant to write was " childlike " 's opposite—i.e. " childish " (O.E.D. : " Not befitting mature age ; puerile, silly.") But then Mr. Reid wouldn't have liked to stigmatize one of Mr. Britten's opinions as " puerile " or " silly " so he optimistically compromised with " childlike " which, strictly speaking, makes no sense at all. But, of course, the majority of Mr. Reid's readers on this occasion would substitute

" childish " for " childlike " anyway, so why should Mr. Reid have bothered ? Could there be any greater satisfaction than writing for an audience that will unconsciously attribute the opposite meaning to the printed word and thus arrive at what was presumably the author's original intention ?

So much for Mr. Charles Reid's curtain-raiser to *Billy Budd*. In one mouth at least it left a nasty taste.

2

INTERLUDE :
WHICH WAY TO THE SEA ?

" In the first act the shrill wind, the salt tang and the eternal swell and surge of restless water envelop the listener so that whatever happens aboard the Indomitable he can never forget this relentless conditioning of sailors' lives."

The Times, December 3rd.

" But where in the opening act was the tang of salt air and the sound of the sea that we expected of the composer of 'Peter Grimes ' ? "

Dyneley Hussey, *Listener*, December 6th.

3

RESISTANCES CONTINUED

IN our most optimistic moments we should never have imagined that one of our leading articles, printed well over a year ago, could have remained so topical. All those who doubted the validity of my colleague's analysis of resistances to Britten's music (this journal, May, 1950) should re-read it in the light of immediate criticisms of *Billy Budd*. If further evidence were needed, *Budd's* first performance has amply supplied it. Indeed with no little frankness it formed the first paragraph of Mr. Stephen Williams' review of the opera in the *Evening News* of December 3rd :

" One always resents having it dinned into one's ears that a new work is a masterpiece before it has been performed ; and Benjamin Britten's ' Billy Budd ' was trumpeted into the arena by such a deafening roar of advance publicity that many of us entered Covent Garden on Saturday (when the composer conducted the first performance) with a mean, sneaking hope that we might be able to flesh our fangs in it."

In the face of so astonishing a revelation of how some of our critics go about their occupation I find it difficult to make any comment— unnecessary, perhaps, since Mr. Williams makes his own. But let me point out without delay that Mr. Williams, in spite of this un-promising approach, acknowledged " with a full heart " before his review was over that " ' Billy Budd ' is, in its own right, a master-piece."

Mr. Williams, however, is not only critic for the *Evening News* but also (it appears) London music critic for the *New York Times ;* and to that distinguished overseas newspaper he contributed a notice of *Billy Budd* which included a short résumé of other English critics' opinions. (The date I am unable to identify since it is missing from my cutting).

While Mr. Williams had informed his London readers that the opera was " a masterpiece " it was not upon this theme that he enlarged for the benefit of the Americans. On the contrary, the greater part of his piece is taken up with a discussion of the " hysteri-cal ballyhoo " which accompanied *Budd's* first performance. In fact the *New York Times* review is an expansive elucidation of the motives which prompted Mr. Williams' first *Evening News* paragraph quoted above. The " publicity " seems to have got Mr. Williams' back up in no uncertain style :

> " Mr. Britten is in a class by himself. He is the golden boy of British music ; ' Hear Britten first ' might be the slogan of any English musical tourist agency. He is phenomenally clever and phenomenally lucky . . . "*
>
> " He has an astute and enterprising publisher who blazes his trail with blinding and deafening advance publicity. He had also fanatical disciples such as those who before the production of ' Billy Budd ' solemnly assured us that the libretto was to be compared only with Boito's ' Otello ' and the score only with the last works of Verdi."

At this point Mr. Williams must be referring to the very coolly factual preview of *Billy Budd* by Eric Walter White which appeared in the *Listener* of November 22nd. The two statements to which Mr. Williams seems to take a quite inflated exception run as follows :

> (a) " These collaborators [i.e. E. M. Forster and Eric Crozier] have succeeded in offering Benjamin Britten the best opera libretto *adapted from a literary masterpiece* since Boito's version of ' Othello ' " [My italics : Mr. Williams conveniently ignores this highly selective qualification].

*Mr. Williams was going strong on this subject in 1947 and in very much the same words. " . . . Then there is Britten. Britten is also a cult. He is indisputably the Golden Boy of contemporary music, immensely successful and immensely fashionable. His success is due to two causes : exceptional gifts and exceptional opportunities for putting them over." *Penguin Music Magazine,* No. II, 1947, pp. 70-72.

(b) " . . . in 'Billy Budd' Britten has written his maturest opera to date, one that in skill of construction,* psychological subtlety, and theatrical effectiveness can *without exaggeration* be compared with the later works of Verdi " [My italics].

The second of Mr. White's measured opinions is obviously the more important, and no doubt the attentive reader will mark Mr. Williams' substitution of " only " for Mr. White's " without exaggeration "— a slight but vital alteration which affects the whole construction and meaning of Mr. White's sentence.   In any case I have yet to hear that the comparative method of criticism is a crime, and Mr. White's suggestion that *Billy Budd* may be compared to the later works of Verdi is not only legitimate, but helpful to those finding their operatic feet in the history of music.

Oddest of all, as we have seen from the *Evening News* review quoted above, Mr. Williams himself considered *Billy Budd* to be a " masterpiece " ; and, ironical as it may be, he was, to the best of my knowledge, the only critic who used the term after the work's first performance.   Does then Mr. Williams object to one masterpiece being compared to another ?   And how do we account for the fact that what was a " masterpiece " in London has been modified for New York into no more than a " challenging, stimulating work of art " ?   Is it that Mr. Williams' resistances gained the upper hand of his opinions during their transatlantic crossing ?

Referring back to his own pronouncements on " hysterical ballyhoo," " advance publicity " and so forth, Mr. Williams concludes, " now all this kind of thing is very damaging "—while it doesn't seem to occur to him that his own efforts (especially in a foreign newspaper) are susceptible of like criticism.   If Mr. Williams doesn't think *Billy Budd* a masterpiece he shouldn't have written that it was ; if he does, then he should be glad of all the publicity the work gets, since great pieces these days are few and far between ; and he should certainly cease attacking those amongst his colleagues who voted it a great piece (with rather more musical explicitness) a few days earlier than he did himself.

One final word.   My own ears were unembarrassed by the deafening advance publicity to which Mr. Williams refers.   Surely he can't have been thinking of Mr. Reid's *Evening Standard* article ?

---

*Mr. Capell's contention (*Daily Telegraph*, December 3rd) that " Britten's score cannot be called much of a structure " is especially misleading. The highly organic nature of the opera's structure is a topic we shall return to in our future and more musical discussion of *Billy Budd's* music.

Now if Mr. Williams took exception to *that* kind of advance publicity, he would have my active support and sympathy. But, alas, he makes no mention of it. Can the awful din which so distressed Mr. Williams have been caused by that elusive " extremist clique " up to their old tricks again ?

4

INTERLUDE :

A CRITICAL TUNE WHICH SEEMS TO BE CATCHING

" [Britten] has . . . been daring enough to compose a score without one whistleable tune . . . "
Stephen Williams, *New York Times.*

" You will find no lovely tunes, but Britten's music is more melodious [sic] and warmer than in previous operas "
Sunday Express, December 2nd.

" One will go again not only to get a closer grip on the tale but to hear the music, which has hardly one memorable melody yet is nevertheless insidiously haunting "
Scott Goddard, *News Chronicle,* December 3rd.

" There were no arias [sic], no pretty tunes, but stern, stormy music, with the tang of the sea, with woodwind, brass and percussion dominating "
Reynold's News, December 2nd.

5

ROUND AND ABOUT THE LIBRETTO

(A)

As was to be expected, very large tracts of the after-criticisms of *Billy Budd* were taken up with discussions of the libretto and/or short synopses of Melville's tale. The opera's music received less attention and less space. In the present circumstances of newsprint shortage this can hardly be otherwise ; every reader wants to know what the opera is about.

On December 3rd, the morning after the first performance, the *Observer*, one of the two major Sunday newspapers, carried an article on *Billy Budd* by Mr. Eric Blom, while the *Sunday Times* made do with a short news item and a promise : " Mr. Ernest Newman will comment on the opera in *The Sunday Times* next week."

Was it worth waiting a week for Mr. Newman's piece ? In an article of some 700 words, as fairly as I can judge, not more than 51 words either relate directly to, or make direct statements about, the music ; possibly there are another 50 which imply musical judgments (though this is by no means clear from the text). This quite extraordinary disproportion could have mattered less had it not been for the very weighty *musical* conclusion Mr. Newman reached at the end of his first paragraph. Having explained that the " great emotional impact " Billy's tragic death made on the first-night audience was " merely a well-deserved tribute to Melville,"* Mr. Newman continues :

> " As far as I was concerned the new work was a painful disappointment. This seems to me the least notable of Mr. Britten's four operas ; I can see no such musical advance in it as I had hoped for."

Now this is very severe criticism (the severest of all the published criticisms of which I have knowledge), and in view of the authority attached to Mr. Newman's name and the reputation of the paper for which he writes, the very least the reader might have reasonably looked for was a factual substantiation of so forcefully committed an opinion. But not a bit of it. Mr. Newman's next paragraph initiates a lengthy examination of the libretto and he makes no decisive return to the music until the very end of his article.

Is it not a truism that as far as opera is concerned we can only evaluate the worth of a libretto in purely musical terms ? That a libretto's virtues and vices are speculative until they are minutely analysed in their musical context ? And at that stage may we not find that many of our preconceived literary judgments are reversed ? Mr. Newman considers that Britten " has been ill-served by his librettists." He writes that " The prime trouble with the opera, as I see it, is that hardly anywhere do the three principal characters come to real musical life." Mr. Newman is, of course, quite entitled to his wrong opinion. But it is symptomatic of the confusion in his mind that he lays the blame for this failure not on the composer, but on the librettists. What Mr. Newman considers to be Britten's inability to " back up " Claggart's ' Credo ' in the manner of Beethoven (Pizarro) or Verdi (Iago) seems to be of secondary importance :

*This well-deserved tribute to Melville certainly took the wrong turning if a *Daily Mail* report (December 3rd) is to be believed. It appears that at the opera's conclusion " The musical purists in the gallery pounded the plush-covered rails and shouted ' Bravo, Benjy ! ' " We must be grateful to Mr. Newman for exposing the gallery's misplaced enthusiasm.

" Melville's task was easy ; availing himself of the novelist's privilege to speak in his own person, he gives us a searching analysis of each of the three [principal characters]. But to translate these psychological subtleties into operatic terms is a difficult problem, and it is hardly to be wondered at that the librettists have failed to solve it. Claggart's brief soliloquising shows him only as an ineffectual cross between the Iago of the ' Credo ' and Pizarro, without a Verdi or a Beethoven to back him up musically in his confession of a natural bent towards evil."

Unlike Mr. Newman I don't expect the impossible of librettists ; achievement of the impossible belongs strictly to the realms of creative genius. Of course it is difficult to translate psychological subtleties into a libretto ; but it is exactly at this juncture that music comes into its own. Indeed, as a means of conveying psychological subtleties of character perhaps there exists no more perfect means of communication than music—to which *Billy Budd* testifies again and again. Mr. Newman's virtual obsession with the opera's text prevented him from realizing that the characterization and psychological subtleties he sought were only to be found in one place—in the opera's score.

I, neither, can achieve the impossible, and am unable to refute the charge that in this instance Britten is no Verdi or no Beethoven. Nevertheless certain features of Mr. Newman's remarks suggest to me that he has either so misheard or misunderstood the aria that one would be rash in the extreme to show much confidence in his judgment as expressed in its present form. For example his curiously misleading term " brief soliloquising." Why so " brief " ? To follow up one of Mr. Newman's own comparisons, Claggart's aria is actually as long as Pizarro's " Ha ! welch'ein Augenblick ! " from *Fidelio* (including the chorus even), and there is no doubt to my mind that the Forster-Crozier text is the Beethoven's literary superior.† Moreover I am surprised that the Mr. Newman who is so

† Nor is there much difference in length between Claggart's aria and Iago's " Credo." It occurs to me now, however, that Mr. Newman's " brief " may apply to the text *only*. But if we pursue the Pizarro-Claggart comparison, Claggart passes even this test with flying colours. Deleting all repetitions in both cases, while Pizarro has to make do with some 90 words, Claggart is liberally supplied with over 200. Textually briefer than Pizarro's, Claggart's aria certainly is not. Why Mr. Newman should imagine that Claggart's piece is less effectual and revealing than Pizarro's I am quite unable to understand—unless it is that he considers the following lines from the latter to be the very height of psychological penetration :
" And as I stand before him,
With deadly steel to gore him,
I'll shout into his ear :
' Tis I ! 'tis I ! 'tis I !
'Tis I who triumph here." [Trans. E. J. Dent].
[For German original, see p. 439].

conversant with the Melville tale seems to have missed the crucial significance of the aria's line " But alas, alas ! the light shines in the darkness, and the darkness comprehends it and suffers "‡ which is, as it were, a transformation of one of Melville's key observations on Claggart's character : a nature capable of " apprehending the good, but powerless to be it." In the libretto the external observation is translated into an internal observation actively made by the character about whom it was originally written. It is with these few bars that we feel for a fleeting moment (possibly for the first and last time) the impact of Claggart's own private tragedy ; and the music in fact runs as deep as one of the deepest of Melville's comments : " . . . Claggart could even have loved Billy but for fate and ban."

In short the characterization and the subtle psychology is there for those with ears ; and the libretto does exactly what is required of it : it provides the verbal clue to the dramatic situation (and very cunningly too). But the solution, the solution, Mr. Newman, lies in and with the music. A recognition of the fact that on their own account librettos and librettists can ultimately solve nothing is long overdue.

Mr. Newman's nagging insistence on the libretto merely supports my view that his musical understanding of *Billy Budd* was sadly limited ; an impression which is strengthened by his own final paragraph, the musical summing-up, so to speak :

> " Inexpert as the dramatic handling often is, for it keeps falling between the two stools of conventional ' opera ' and modern psychological music-drama§, the music, to me, is a greater disappointment still. It has several fine and some great moments, particularly in the third act ; but for the most part it indulges too much for my liking in a dry speech-song in the voices and disjointed ' pointings ' in the orchestra, and Mr. Britten has done all this much better elsewhere."

Mr. Newman's downshot is so vague and imprecise that it might apply to any opera composed during the last fifty years. In so far as it makes any ascertainable comment at all, his "dry speech-song"

‡A line which, I assume, borrows its imagery from *St. John* I, v. 5 : " And the light shineth in darkness ; and the darkness comprehended it not." The alteration in *sense* between the Biblical verse and its version in the libretto is, of course, plain ; as is, the correspondence between the aria's line and Melville's original comment. The librettists, so to speak, have poetized the moral proposition expounded in Melville's prose and added " suffering " as a logical consequence of " apprehension." For more on *Budd's* Christian symbolism see sub-section (c), pp. 398-400.

§That the whole opera takes place on two distinct " levels " Mr. Newman has evidently appreciated ; but the real significance of the dual action seems to have escaped him. See pp. 401-403.

would seem to be but an intellectual echo of what some of the lower-deck newsmen had written the Sunday previous, quite as wrongly but rather more concisely, i.e. : " This opera has no tunes." We had to wait a week for a repeat of that misinformative gem.

(b)

MR. CAPELL'S QUESTIONS

AFTER Mr. Newman's critical vagaries it is almost invigorating to find Mr. Capell making a straight-to-the-point inquiry in his column " *Billy Budd* " Questions (*Daily Telegraph*, December 7th). Writing of Act II's Scene 1 (" Act I, Scene II " in his text, but this must be a misprint) where the officers " are discussing the possibility of mutiny on board the frigate " he asks :

> " Is there not, by the way, a slip by the librettists here ? The Sailing Master makes much of Billy's shout, " Farewell, ' Rights o'Man' ! ", smelling in it disaffection; but only an hour before he had been informed that ' Rights o' Man ' was the name of Billy's merchantman, from which he had been pressed, and which must still have been in sight."

Mr. Capell may be partially answered by a reference to Melville. In the book, Billy, as he is leaving by boat for the *Indomitable*, suddenly jumps up and cries to his old ship and shipmates " And good-bye to you too, old *Rights-of-Man* ! ". To continue in Melville's own words :

> " ' Down, sir,' roared the Lieutenant, instantly assuming all the rigour of his rank, though with difficulty repressing a smile. To be sure, Billy's action was a terrible breach of Naval decorum. But in that decorum he had never been instructed ; in consideration of which the Lieutenant would hardly have been so energetic in reproof but for the concluding farewell to the ship. This he rather took as meant to convey a covert sally on the new recruit's part, a sly slur at impressment in general, and that of himself in especial. And yet, more likely, if satire it was in effect, it was hardly so by intention, for Billy, though happily endowed with the gaiety of high health, youth, and a free heart, was yet by no means of a satirical turn. The will to do it and the sinister dexterity were alike wanting. To deal in double meaning... of any sort was quite foreign to his nature."

As in the tale, so in the opera. Billy's farewell from the *Indomitable*'s deck is simply no more than a farewell, and " The Rights o' Man " is no more than the title of a ship with which he has been lately associated. It is the Sailing Master's and his colleagues' misunderstanding of Billy's adieu which results in the topic being raised once more in the Captain's cabin, not, to be sure, because the Sailing Master has *forgotten* the name of Billy's ship but because he has misconceived the whole incident as an example of potential duplicity on Billy's part (an impression which is all the stronger in the opera when some of the crew, in wordless chorus, pick up the theme of Billy's farewell phrase, previously heard as the working shanty " O heave ! O heave away, heave ! " It is at this moment that the shanty, as Mr. E. W. White correctly observes, " becomes identified . . . with the idea of mutiny " (*Listener*, November 22nd) *but on the crew's and officers' level of misunderstanding:* Billy is unaware of the tragic coincidence which is the very start of his misfortune). But how is it that this situation is operatically clear to those with no prior (and detailed) knowledge of Melville's story ? As I have indicated elsewhere the solution to the problems of librettos must always be heard with the ears, or looked for in the score. When we examine Billy's E major song " Billy Budd, king of the birds ! " we realize (hear) at once that its exultant innocence excludes the possibility of satire emerging as an element in its " farewell " conclusion. Mr. Capell in fact has fallen into exactly the same error as the Sailing Master for exactly the same reason : neither " understood " Billy's aria. But while it is dramatically essential in many an operatic circumstance that the characters show no signs of comprehending what the music is secretly revealing to the audience, there is really no need for the critics to follow suit.

In Mr. Capell's first review of the opera (*Daily Telegraph*, December 3rd) he had already complained of one inconsistency—
> " . . . the authors' inclination to represent George III's Navy as a hell on earth is not squared with their young hero's perfect satisfaction with all its rough old ways "

—and cast doubt on the authenticity of the Novice's flogging in Act I—
> " It would be interesting to know whether, in fact, a mere coxswain had authority in those days to inflict, on the spur of the moment, a flogging on a recruit who was guilty of nothing more than stumbling on the deck "

I can do no better than draw Mr. Capell's attention to Eric Crozier's authoritatively documented account of *The British Navy in 1797* (*Tempo*, Autumn, 1951) which proves that Covent Garden's *Indomitable* is a floating paradise when compared with accounts of contemporary naval conditions. Mr. Crozier points out that :

> " Men were flogged (and severe flogging crippled or killed) for the most trivial offences, for ' silent contempt,' for being last to obey an order. ' Starting ' a man—trouncing him with a stick—was common form for officers and petty officers."

It seems likely then that " a mere coxswain " (Bosun in the libretto) could have had the Novice flogged : that he did so to a recruit " guilty of nothing more than stumbling on the deck " is factually not quite correct, since the librettists have admirably paved the way for the Bosun's vengeance in a preceding scene where the Novice not only accidentally collides with the officer but omits to call him " sir "—for the Bosun an obvious case of " silent impertinence." It is the accumulated memories of these immediately previous " insults " which, on the Novice's stumbling, provide the rational (and dramatic) basis for the Bosun's action. In all conscience his action is peremptory enough, but certainly not as peremptory as Mr. Capell would have it.

As for Billy, Mr. Capell's objection to his singular acceptance of his environment was foreseen by Melville, not merely in relation to his tale but in relation to life itself :

> " . . . it is observable that where certain virtues pristine and unadulterate peculiarly characterise anybody in the external uniform of civilisation, they will upon scrutiny seem not to be derived from custom or convention *but rather to be out of keeping with these* . . . " [My italics].

The whole dramatic impetus of the opera lies in the " moral phenomenon " of Billy's character and should any hint of disaffection disturb his otherwise " uncomplaining acquiescence," the logic of Melville's story and Britten's opera would be seriously impaired, if not utterly destroyed.

(c)

BILLY BUDD'S SYMBOLISM

Very many critical evaluations of *Billy Budd* congratulate the librettists on their faithfulness to Melville's original. So far, so good. It is true enough that Messrs. Forster and Crozier invent mainly next to nothing but telescope and expand incident and dialogue with great brilliance. Nevertheless, in the one instance where they do radically depart from Melville's text—a departure which introduces an element of the utmost importance to the aesthetic understanding of the opera—none of the critics noticed it.

Briefly, *Budd's* Christian symbolism has gone unrecognized. I apologise in advance for the superficial nature of this contribution to the subject, but neither time nor space allow for anything deeper or more detailed.

I am, of course, aware that there exists already a body of *literary* opinion which views Melville's story in specifically Christian terms. For example Mr. Ronald Mason, in an article *Herman Melville and "Billy Budd"* (*Tempo*, Autumn, 1951) writes that "the story of Billy, owing so much to Christian symbolism, dramatises over again the victory of Innocence over the deadly Experience that had appeared to destroy it." Mr. Raymond Weaver, quoted in Mr. Rex Warner's introduction to a selection of Melville's short stories,* regards *Budd* as the author's "last word upon the strange mystery of himself and human destiny" and, according to Mr. Warner, "considered that now finally the author was attempting to justify the ways of God to man." On the other hand Mr. Warner goes on to quote Mr. William Plomer's comment on Mr. Weaver : " I do not myself perceive any such attempt at justification; I see the story rather as Melville's final protest against the nature of things " ; and Mr. Warner himself suggests " The ways of God are in no obvious sense justified, but . . . the dignity of man is upheld." These wide differences of opinion confirm my impression that nowhere in *Budd* does Melville commit himself on the Christian issue : his own attitude remains something of an enigma. In fact, the Christian content of Melville's *Budd* is potential rather than actual : for the opera, the librettists, so to speak, have *realized* it.

This Christian realization is plainly ascertainable from the librettists' additions to, and their one striking contradiction of, Melville's text. The revealing contradiction first : In the tale, when Billy is chained beneath deck awaiting execution, he is visited by the ship's chaplain— " . . . the good man sought to bring Billy Budd to some godly understanding that he must die, and at dawn." A paragraph later the Melville continues :

> " If in vain the good chaplain sought to impress the young barbarian with ideas of death akin to those conveyed in the skull, dial, and cross-bones on old tombstones ; *equally futile to all appearance were his efforts to bring home to him the thought of salvation and a Saviour.* Billy listened, but less out of awe or reverence, perhaps, than from a certain natural politeness . . . " [My italics].

Billy Budd and other stories, by Herman Melville ; *Lehmann*, 1951.

This unequivocal statement may now be compared with the libretto, Act IV, Scene 1, Billy to Dansker :

> " Chaplain's been here before you. Kind. And good, his story of the good boy hung and gone to glory, hung for the likes of me, the likes of me ... "

This awareness (however primitively expressed) is, as we have seen, denied him in Melville's original tale, and it finds its ecstatic fulfilment in the libretto in his subsequent and final (B♭) farewell to the world (which, unlike the major part of the libretto, has no germinal verbal equivalent in the story whatsoever) :

> " But I've sighted a sail in the storm, the far-shining sail that's not Fate, and I'm contented. I've seen where she's bound for. She has a land of her own where she'll anchor for ever. . . Don't matter now being hanged, or being forgotten and caught in the weeds. . . I'm strong, and I know it, and I'll stay strong, and that's all, and that's enough."

The imagery may be nautical but its meaning is apparent enough ; indeed it is vitally confirmed when Vere, in the opera's Epilogue, takes up both Billy's words and his music just before the opera's unambiguous B♭ conclusion wherein *Billy Budd*'s protagonists and conflicting tonalities (derived from the Prologue) are at last reconciled.

In the story, when Vere eventually dies of battle-wounds murmuring " Billy Budd, Billy Budd," Melville permits himself of a remarkno more enlightening than that " these were not the accents of remorse." But in the opera Vere is explicitness itself, and makes what seems to be a direct Biblical reference :

> " But he has saved me, and blessed me, and the love which passes understanding† has come to me."

Billy dies " strong " and the sorely tried Vere is saved by Billy's forgiveness. The opera's resolution on a Christian level should make us view *Billy Budd* more as a Christ parable than as a succession of ironical accidents‡ determined by an implacable and inscrutable Fate. " But I've seen a sail in the storm, the far-shining sail that's not Fate " sings Billy ; and is it not significant that we are informed in John Piper's and Basil Coleman's " *Billy Budd* " *on the Stage* (*Tempo*, Autumn, 1951) that the composer himself saw the Novice's scene in Act I " in terms of Stations of the Cross ? "

†Actually a compound of *Philippians* IV, v. 7, and *Ephesians* III, v. 19.

‡" Billy, that happy soul, comes to grief by what is, after all, only a chapter of accidents." ' R.C.', in the *Monthly Musical Record*, January, 1952.

PROLOGUE AND EPILOGUE

The vaguest recognition of *Budd's* Christian symbolism would have provided a vital clue to the work's relation to Britten's other operas. For the symbolism plus Vere's Prologue and Epilogue would have inevitably guided the listener back to *Lucretia :* and it is *Lucretia* with which *Budd* may be the most fruitfully compared both spiritually and stylistically (not forgetting the all-important and intervening *Spring Symphony*). But it was enough for most critical ears and eyes that *Billy Budd* was a sea-story with sea-shanties. *Peter Grimes* was taken as *Budd's* point of departure, and *Lucretia* went altogether unmentioned apart from a by-passing reference of Mr. Shawe-Taylor's. (*Herring*, of course, was even more emphatically excluded, except by Mr. Stanley Bayliss in the *Daily Mail* of December 3rd who wrote that " ' Billy Budd ' may reassure those who thought Britten's great talent had been diverted from its true path by trifles [sic] like ' Albert Herring ' . . .")

Had our critics been aware of *Budd's* link with *Lucretia*, they might have thought a little more deeply about the Prologue's and Epilogue's true purpose and spent less time misunderstanding their dramatic function. Dr. Mosco Carner in *Time and Tide*, December 8th :

> " In their endeavour to make the significance of the story as clear as possible the librettists had recourse to a prologue and epilogue, *a rather tame and undramatic solution of the problem* . . ." [My italics].

Or Mr. Philip Hope-Wallace in *Picture Post*, December 22nd :

> " . . . pages of prologue and epilogue (beautifully written *but not dramatically effective*) . . . " [My italics].

And certainly Mr. Eric Blom (in the *Observer* of December 3rd) would have been spared the trouble of unearthing the most minor and incidental of reasons to justify the reversal of his initial impression that the Prologue and Epilogue, as a device, was " rather cheap " :

> " But on studying the music I came to the conclusion that it must have been asked for by the composer, not only because the prologue and epilogue admirably round off his scheme thematically, but also because it enabled him to make a particularly subtle musical point. For when in the prologue Vere says " The good has never been perfect. There is always some flaw in it . . . some imperfection in the divine image," we first hear the music associated with Billy's stammer, that fatal defect which precipitates the tragedy."

Of course, the primary function of the Prologue and Epilogue (far from introducing Billy's stammer) is to " frame "—give perspective to—the opera's action, much as the Male and Female Chorus provide a timeless surround to the action in *Lucretia*. This element of timelessness is as important in *Budd* as it is in *Lucretia*. At some point in the opera's structure allowance had to be made for a removal of the action not only from the " historical present " (i.e. H.M.S. *Indomitable* in 1797) but also from the " contemporary present " (i.e. Covent Garden in 1951) in order that the action might be freely interpreted in terms which owe nothing to time or place. Relieved of all limitations of either past or present this is, indeed, the Epilogue's special duty. In it both Billy's and Vere's tragedies are transcended and the parable, translated from the sphere of dramatic action, becomes of universal import. The personal Prologue generates the Epilogue as a timeless platform on which this trans-figuration can occur. In fact I hear and feel Vere's Epilogue in much the same spirit as *Lucretia's* final Male Chorus. As for Mr. Blom's thematic anticipations (there are more than the one he describes) and " round off," no opera composer worth his salt would require a prologue and epilogue for such cyclic devices. (That *Budd's* Prologue and Epilogue bear the titles they do is, in a sense, misleading : " Epilogue," especially, severely underrates the piece's climatic importance).

But the Prologue's and Epilogue's timeless aspect by no means exhausts their significance. The following fragment of conversa-tion between Basil Coleman and John Piper (from their article quoted above) is strictly relevant :

" *Producer :* The main problem seems to me to decide how far we are going to be realistic and how far not. For me the most realistic scene is the Battle, Act III, i., where the crew have very definite things to do. . . Then the mist descends again and they are cut off from the enemy. But the mist is as much a mist of doubt and fear in the mind of Vere when he is about to close with Claggart at the beginning and finally at the end of the scene. And these dual planes of action seem to me to run throughout the opera, as they do in Melville.

Designer : Yes, and we must never lose sight of the fact that the whole thing is taking place in Vere's mind, and is being recalled by him."

In spite of the producer's efforts to stress these " dual planes " with all the theatrical means at his disposal (" . . . I can use the lighting in an unrealistic way . . . with scenes fading in and out to help the illusion of their having been called up by Vere ") they don't seem to have been very apparent to the critics. Witness Mr. Newman's comment,* or Mr. Blom's, who liked Mr. Piper's stage design but was evidently a little puzzled by its " detailed realism sitting rather oddly in an unreal frame of outer darkness which suggests the sea no more than anything else." Most muddles about an opera's libretto or its production proceed from muddles about its music—a dictum which applies above all to opera producers themselves, but not, on this occasion, to Mr. Coleman. Had Mr. Blom fully understood the Prologue, had he realized the contrast as well as the relations between the thematico-tonal structures of both Prologue and Epilogue on the one hand and of the body of the opera on the other, he would have become alive to the fact that the opera's frame, unlike a picture's, is of central significance : it introduces and solves the tragedy from the spiritualizing level which is the action's artistic *raison d'être* ; for without the perspective thus created, Britten's music would never have been interested in the subject.

6

AN INTERLUDE ON CAPTAIN VERE

" The outstanding performance of the evening came from Theodor Uppman as Billy Budd "—so ran a line in almost every post- first performance review. While I have no desire to lessen Mr. Uppman's achievement—as *Budd's* first Billy he will be long and gratefully remembered—I should have thought it obvious to every ear and eye that it was Peter Pears' Vere which was the supreme musical characterization of the first and subsequent performances ; I deliberately include the eye since I am sure that in Mr. Pears the singer the stage has lost a great actor. Yet who could have guessed the stature of Mr. Pears' performance from the reactions of the press ?

> " The tenor of the cast was Captain Vere, a stuffed uniform, but . . . Britten and Peter Pears gave him style."
> W.McN., *Musical Times*, January, 1952.

> " Theodor Uppman in voice (light baritone) and in person is ideally cast as Budd ; Peter Pears and Frederick Dalberg as the Captain and Master-at-Arms rather less so."
> Philip Hope-Wallace, *Manchester Guardian*, December 3rd.

*See footnote § p. 395.

" The part of the victimised Billy is very happily entrusted to a personable young American baritone, Theodor Uppman. If Vere (Peter Pears) and Claggart (. . . Frederick Dalberg), are both rather stiff, there are many lively, well-characterised and well-sung minor performances . . . "

Richard Capell, *Daily Telegraph*, December 3rd.

Wrong about much else Mr. Stephen Williams, to his credit, and in spite of curious agreement with *The Times* on a related matter (see below), was almost alone among critics in his accurate appraisal of Pears' performance :

" . . . Peter Pears played the Captain with such aristocratic poise and musicianship (with what delicate art he passed from the spoken word to the sung word) that the character seemed to belong exclusively to him."

New York Times.

Dr. Mosco Carner, in *Time and Tide*, thought " Peter Pears as Vere was every inch the noble Captain but seemed a little wooden and not quite at ease in the more intimate scenes in his cabin " ; but not satisfied with merely criticizing the performance, he declares elsewhere in the same article that " the scene in the Captain's cabin which opens the Second Act seems to me wholly superfluous." Since Dr. Carner has just previously complained that one of the opera's "serious weaknesses" is that " the richness of psychological detail so striking in Melville's portrayal of his principal protagonists is gone " and since, if anywhere in *Budd*, Vere's character is richly established in the very scene Dr. Carner unaccountably wants to be rid of, I may be excused for doubting his logic.

Why is it, I wonder, that moments of extreme culture go uncherished ? For it was during this scene that I was struck anew by Pears' marvellous singing and incomparable acting ; his every note and gesture added something to Vere's character and contributed to our total understanding of it. The result was superbly beautiful both to listen to and to watch ; a rare spectacle and a rare musical experience. Mine, I am aware, is a personal, probably a minority opinion, and does nothing to contradict the opinions of my colleagues ; but it certainly needed saying. Some of us are deeply grateful for the little real culture which infrequently comes our way. Most of us seem to have forgotten what culture is and no longer recognize it when either seen or heard.

According to *The Times* critic, however, Captain Vere shouldn't have been a tenor at all :

" . . . the composer has cast his voices upside down : the commander should have been the bass, the recruit the tenor "

—an observation approved of by Mr. Stephen Williams in the *New York Times ;* mysteriously, because Mr. Williams admits himself that " at the première I was not conscious of any disturbing anomaly." Of course he wasn't. There wasn't—and isn't— any anomaly to be disturbed by. Mr. Williams shouldn't allow himself to be bullied by *The Times* into thinking himself wrong when he couldn't have been righter. But for all that he felt himself obliged to bless *The Times'* heresy :

> " Psychologically [sic] quite sound. From a slender fair-haired stripling one expects a tenor voice, just as one expects a baritone or bass from a dignified middle-aged commander "

—an observation echoed by Mr. Philip Hope-Wallace in *Picture Post:*

> " The reflective part [of Vere] would more naturally suit a baritone with the tenor rôle reserved to the young sailor, Budd. Upside down casting ! "

Upside down thinking, gentlemen ! But having re-cast Britten's opera you might at least have re-composed the music as well. Has it not occurred to you that Captain Vere's music is " characteristic " to and of the tenor voice for which it is written ? Or do you suggest that a simple matter of transposition would enable a " dignified middle-aged " bass or baritone to take over ? What, in any case and in this context, does *The Times'* " should have been " mean ? What standards of comparison are we expected to use when we don't know what kind of music would have been forthcoming had Britten chosen such an improbable course ? All we *can* know is that a bass Captain Vere would be utterly unlike the Captain Vere of whom we have present, factual and musical knowledge. Meanwhile, acting on *The Times'* supposition, what happens to Britten's delicately poised balance between his male voices ? What happens when, for page after page in Act III, bass meets bass ? And in the same act and elsewhere what happens to Vere's conciliatory, characteristic and *characterizing* obbligatos ? I don't care if *The Times* thinks that Captain Vere's musical characterization is all wrong—even if the dramatic demands of the role have tenor writ large upon them. What I do care about is the expression of dogmatic judgments, seemingly based on ascertainable evidence, which, on examination, prove to derive from the purest realms of speculation. Speculators should stick to speculating. " Should have been " merely sticks in my throat.

I have always been suspicious of Gilbert and Sullivan's influence on English musical taste ; a suspicion confirmed by Mr. Newman's introduction of *H.M.S. Pinafore* into his notice of *Billy Budd** and by Mr. Williams' mention of a " dignified middle-aged commander." Is it necessary that operatic naval officers of the future, from admirals downwards, shall be Gilbertian parodies in reverse ? The last thing I should have expected of the commander who seems to have taken hold of Mr. Williams' fancy would be quotations from Plutarch. In fact the presence of the classics would have astonished me even more than their delivery by a tenor voice. Perhaps the librettists and composer should have been less faithful to Melville in this respect. After all it was Melville who wrote that " ashore in the garb of a civilian, scarce anyone would have taken [Vere] for a sailor " ; that " he had a marked leaning toward everything intellectual. He loved books, never going to sea without a newly replenished library, compact but of the best . . . " ; that " . . . he would cite some historical character or incident of antiquity with the same easy air that he would cite from the moderns . . . " How closely does Melville's Vere correspond to Mr. Williams' ? From such a remarkable, unconventional figure one could only have the right to expect the unexpected ; and it is the exception, not the rule, that we have in Britten's opera—tenor voice and all.

Music apart, I should have thought that this was one matter on which there could be no dispute. That for better or for worse the librettists' and the composer's Vere was strictly Melville's. But I was mistaken. Wrote H.S.R., in *Musical Opinion*, January, 1952 :

> " . . . this character, of all the characters in the opera, was the one which was *essentially alien* to that depicted with so masterly an economy of words by Herman Melville " [My italics].

The enquiring reader may refer to the book itself, or re-read the descriptive passages from Melville reproduced above. I myself must attempt to imitate Melville's verbal economy. No comment.

*He has since been joined by Mr. Winton Dean in *Opera*, January, 1952, p. 11.

7

A NOTE ON THE " INTERVIEW " CHORDS

Of all passages in *Billy Budd* none was debated with more fire and less fact than the end of Act III's Scene 2 ; the thirty-four chords which, according to the *Synopsis* of the opera in *Tempo*,

" tell of the fatal, invisible interview of the two men." Mr. Blom in the *Observer*, quite apart from giving a bewilderingly wrong reason for the chords' dramatic justification,

> ...." I can see that they foreshadow Billy's last resolve to die without weakening "*

states unambiguously that the triads are " harmonically disconnected " ; while Mr. Shawe-Taylor in the *New Statesman* votes for their being " distantly related but converging towards F major." Mr. Stephen Williams, in the *New York Times* not only declares the chords once more to be " harmonically disconnected " (if he's quoting Mr. Blom he doesn't make any acknowledgment), but that they are " certainly monotonous " besides ; and he adds a suggestion for their improvement : " [They] could be halved with advantage." (How would Mr. Williams set about this task ? By deleting each alternate chord ?) While *The Times* holds aloof by classifying the chords as no more than " antiphonal," Dr. Mosco Carner, in *Time and Tide*, approaches somewhere nearer the truth with :

> " Britten here writes a long series of chorale-like chords, all different harmonizations of the notes F-A-C (which define Budd's key) and scored in different ways."

It is a pity that Dr. Carner's imagination fails to keep pace with his perception ; for a failure of imagination it is when he writes that the chords are

> " effective and suggestive, it is true, but insufficient to serve as a *real* interpretation of that crucial scene [where Vere informs Billy of the court's verdict]."

While Dr. Carner is quite correct in pointing to the chords' centripetal relation to the F major triad†, his definition of the latter as " Budd's key " is superficial. Throughout the opera keys are not so much attached to persons as to aspects of the drama. More than just Budd, F major represents liberating resignation to the tragic inevitability of F minor. Aside from its descriptive role, the section stands as a highly compressed and formally concentrated survey of the opera's tonal area ; and, as so often in Britten, the feeling is intensified by the extreme terseness of expression.

*Mr. Blom must have been thinking of the chords' second appearance in Act IV, Scene 1, where their dramatic implication is more akin to moral resolution ; e.g. Billy's " I'm strong, and I know it, and I'll stay strong," etc. Two other references are made to the chords : in the orchestral " execution " interlude between Scenes 1 and 2 of Act IV, and in Vere's Epilogue.

†The whole section is basically in F major, or to use a term coined by Richard Arnell in his *Note on Tonality, Music Survey*, III/3/50, " F chromatic major."

In a reference to the chords' " wonderful realization . . . of what passed between the two victims of fate's malignancy, from which Melville hedges away," *The Times* does much less than justice to Melville's artistic integrity. Far from hedging, Melville had the honesty to desist from faking ; he was aware that any attempt to communicate literally the conversation between Vere and Billy was bound to be inadequate. Such matters run too deep for reported dialogue, and Melville's own moving conjectures on the subject leave the door wide open for music to enter and make explicit what is implicit in the prose :

> " Captain Vere in the end may have developed the passion sometimes latent under an exterior stoical or indifferent. He was old enough to have been Billy's father. The austere devotee of military duty, letting himself melt back into what remains primeval in our formalised humanity, may in the end have caught Billy to his heart, even as Abraham may have caught young Isaac on the brink of resolutely offering him up in obedience to the exacting behest."

So far, while everyone has either agreed or disagreed on the chords' theatrical effectiveness or their degrees of relatedness or unrelatedness, no one has yet offered an opinion as to why the passage takes the shape it does. Why, in fact, *common chords?*

It seems to me that Melville provides a clue—Vere let himself melt back into " what remains primeval " : so to speak a verbal rationalization of what most of us felt on hearing the chords for the first time. Melville, of course, is using primeval in the sense of fundamental, of the world's first age ; primitive, yes, but not elementary ; *elemental*, rather. And it is exactly a disclosure of the elemental that we experience in Britten's succession of slow triads— symbols, in a manner of speaking, of music's first age ; bearing in mind our own musical culture, they are perhaps the nearest we can approach to the emotionally-musical primeval without becoming self-consciously primitive (in its derogatory application). Our musical primitivity is limited by the history of our culture ; and the triad, relative to our culture, represents one of those limits. Britten himself, because of the peripheries imposed by his own culture, could go no further without peril of stylistic anachronism. The triad itself may be a highly cultured concept, the result of long historical development ; but in the context of *Budd* it expresses the fundamental, the cosmic even, in the most condensed (if contextually complex) terms. The chords, for me, are the true musical realization of the ultimate passions involved, when, in Melville's words, " two of great Nature's nobler order embrace."

Artur Schnabel

By KONRAD WOLFF (New York)

[We have not anglicized this article because we do not think that American is just bad English.—Eds.]

THERE are many thousands of us who have always regarded Artur Schnabel as one of the greatest musicians of our time, who owe him our happiest and most intense hours of listening, who see the impact of his genius in all of the best musicianship of today; and to whom, therefore, the short and almost indifferent newspaper obituaries which appeared in England and the United States came as a sad surprise. We remember the times in the twenties and early thirties— when each of Schnabel's concerts made news, when the era of recordings of masterpieces opened with his complete collection of the works of Beethoven, and when from America a great many of the most gifted young pianists went to Europe in order to study with him. Although he had partly retired in recent years as a pianist in order to concentrate on his composing, we felt sure that the public recognition of his *oeuvre* would have remained the same. The notices, however, simply describe him as a great scholar who, in his playing as well as in his lectures and editions, tried to demonstrate how music ought to be played and who, in his severity, became something of a Savonarola of modern concertizing. They have to add, however, that incongruously he composed some cacophonic and hypermodernistic music—symphonies, sonatas for solo strings, cycles of piano pieces, cadenzas to Mozart concertos, etc.—in which he appears a veritable Mr. Hyde as opposed to the Dr. Jekyll of the Beethoven Society.

What caused this change of attitude on the part of the musical press ? There is no doubt that in recent years mutual recriminations became increasingly frequent between Schnabel and the manufacturers of public musical opinion. Whenever one saw Schnabel he would complain about the general commercialism in music, about deterioration of taste, inferior teaching, and about competitiveness of young talent at the expense of devotion to art. Whenever the subject of Schnabel came up in a conversation with leaders of the so-called musical circles there would be somebody to blame him for his adamant attitude in the matter of programming and publicity, call him selfish and uncommunicative, not concerned with the public and its desires, and accuse him of playing for some abstract purpose rather than to living human beings.

On this level of discussion nothing can be gained for the truth. It can only be ascertained through contemplation of Schnabel's ideals and his musical personality.

In his youth Schnabel had been profoundly impressed by the philosophy of Nietzsche, and much of this influence went into his own philosophical concept. He shared Nietzsche's feeling for the importance of " Werden " (Becoming) as opposed to " Sein " (Being) in the manifestations of the universe.* Like Nietzsche he dreaded being tied down to a particular system, method or school. Even the rendering of music was possible for him only as long as it appeared new to him : as long as he could anticipate that new ideas might occur to him in the performance. As much as he despised the principle of " inspiration by the fingers," and emphasized, on the contrary, that conception must always precede execution, as much did he depend on inspiration during performance. It is true that his discipline and exterior poise were so great that his playing seemed completely planned and pre-arranged. The conception of the whole, the musical articulation, etc.—in other words, the reading of the score—were, indeed, entirely worked out and, what is more, re-worked for each performance. To the very last he never re-played any work (even if, like the Beethoven concertos, he had played it hundreds of times) without spending weeks of intense concentration on possible new angles that he might have neglected previously, and on revisions of his previous conception. But he also left room for spontaneity in order to be able to recreate the work each time through the active love and devotion to the music as it became audible. It did not matter whether the performance was a public one. He was quite sincere in his conviction that the presence of a public should not and could not influence the interpreter who was wrapped in the so much more formidable presence of the music he played. His most concentrated and inspired performances often occurred when he was playing at home for friends and pupils alone, and the public playing became a special experience only inasmuch as it created special acoustic problems and possibilities. Schnabel certainly was aware of the communication to be established between player and hearer, and the reproach that he despised audiences is most unjust. He always emphasized that the best music in the best possible interpretation was just good enough for any ordinary audience. But he did not believe that an artist should or even could

*An idea which has meanwhile become scientific fact : " . . . the present is the first period in which we have been able to grasp that the universe is a process in time . . . " (Julian Huxley).—Eds.

concentrate on the act of communicating ; communication should rather be the natural consequence of full devotion to the music.

To achieve, through intense study, a free, spontaneous delivery where he could sometimes surprise himself, remained Schnabel's principal preoccupation. The greatest compliment he could pay to a fellow-artist was to call his performance " alive " or " spontaneous " or " *con amore.*" Also, in judging compositions he greatly preferred warm, spontaneous music—even when on a comparatively low level—to intellectual or ambitious music without these qualities.

His Nietzscheism did not, however, go so far as to make him an anti-intellectual advocating *Leben* at the expense of *Geist.* He gladly used his intellect. " It does no harm to know," he would say in lessons when pointing out some musical detail. Only in performance was reasoning left behind in the direct experience of the music.

The healthy and concrete quality of his intellect made that very easy for him. Abstract reasoning was out of his sphere, and he was to a high degree unsystematic. Form as such, and compositional structure—as in a complex sonata form or in a fugue—had little interest for him, and he would never speculate on these subjects. He also was sharply critical of any attempt to introduce extra-musical concepts into musical reflections, to classify Mozart, for example, as " rococo " music, or to point out the " baroque " element in Bach. Such preconceived stylistic notions seemed unhealthy to him and therefore dangerous : they could easily create, in his opinion, an undue limitation of the music-making mind.

He also refused to indulge in philological quibbles. Although his conscientiousness and sense of order were meticulous in his work as in his private life, he was no pedant. He took accuracy for granted and saw as little cause for praise in it " as in not stealing silver spoons when invited." But at the same time he emphasized that true accuracy had to stem from a complete understanding of the music itself, not from musicological research. In his experience, a musician who grasped the spirit of the whole could achieve an accuracy of detail beyond the reach of anyone who, without a true understanding of the essentials, would go around comparing first editions, manuscripts, etc. Schnabel's editions of Beethoven's and some of Mozart's piano sonatas, as well as of Brahms' violin sonatas, are based on this conscientious, yet anti-pedantic approach to the problem of accuracy.

Schnabel's need of spontaneity in performance explains fully why he did not play a more varied repertoire. All those who have heard him in lessons know that he was one of the most accomplished and enchanting Chopin players, and that nobody could bring out better the inherent noblesse of Liszt's Sonata and Mephisto Waltz, or of Tchaikowsky's first Concerto. Some of these works he had played publicly in his youth, but they were not sufficiently close to his own nature to enable him to recreate them afresh every time. " I do not learn anything new by playing this music," he frequently said. For the same reason, during the last two decades, his performances of Weber, Brahms and even Schumann became less frequent. To Beethoven and Schubert he increasingly added Bach and Mozart ; only now did he feel equal to the task of performing these masters in public on a large scale.

It will be clear from all this that the act of performance always remained a hazard for him, and there were times when, to his and to the listeners' disappointment, the inspiration of the moment failed him. But this was the price he wanted to pay. As he phrased it, " security is for schoolmasters".

After forty years of public playing there were only a few masters left whose works could still be problematic to Schnabel and thus challenge his tremendous power of spontaneous inspiration every time he played them. He never played or taught the same piece in the same way (although the basic approach remained unchanged), and he frequently drove his students and assistants to despair when in every lesson he would make new and oftentimes contradictory demands as new means to realize his goal occurred to him.

It is with this in mind that we have to listen to Schnabel's recordings, now the principal documentary evidence of his playing. The mere idea of recording a performance was abhorrent to him, because of the suggestion of finality inherent in a record performance. For many years he absolutely refused to record, and he only gave in when he could hope to project his spontaneity on the disc. But even so, he frequently was tense and nervous when faced with the necessity of a " final " performance, and his records, therefore, on the whole, are not a complete projection of his normal playing. Those who have never heard Schnabel play, should bear this in mind.

Schnabel's personality, as unfolded in his playing, was *universal* in the sense in which this term is used for the *Weltanschauung* of Goethe—he created a microcosm. What he himself said of the compositions of Mozart and Beethoven, that they are " all-inclusive," was certainly true of his piano playing. I have often observed that different pianists, having nothing in common in their own playing, could agree in the mutual admiration and love of his. There are classicists and romanticists, sensuous players and crystal-clear analysts of the score, elegant and austere pianists, active and contemplative, proud and humble ones who all have received their principal inspiration from Schnabel's re-creations of music at the piano.

In this universalism Schnabel was by nature essentially different from most contemporary musicians—composers and executants alike. The majority of them have added one particular new manner to the existing music. Schnabel, while his personal note was as unmistakable as any composer's (and as inviting to slavish imitations), created a complete world. No greater injustice therefore could be done to him than to call him a " specialist," simply because he confined his public repertoire to a few composers.

Artur Schnabel was the most musical person I have ever known. There was perfect co-ordination of what his eyes read, his inner ear heard, his hands did, and his ears controlled ; co-ordination, too, of his intense emotional participation in the music and his intellectual grasp of every detail. Each faculty helped the other, but the central gift—a gift from nature, but consciously trained when he was young—was his musical hearing which included not only all simultaneous melodic lines and harmonic progressions, but, by vividness of the imagination, also the emotional and spiritual rays emanating from the music. This is why he was so overpowering in the face of any unexpected challenge, as when a pupil would come to him with a contemporary composition he had never seen. As soon as he began to read a score with a view toward playing or teaching it, the whole music became his—even when he was in disagreement with it. What he called his " loyalty " to music as such would compel him to put as much as possible into the interpretation and understanding of a work, to " give it the benefit of the doubt".

These qualities of Schnabel's natural musicianship came out most clearly when he played chamber music or accompanied Lieder, because in these moments he immediately and instinctively blended with his partners, inspiring them but also being inspired by them, and he then gave proof of such amazing swiftness of reaction and adaptation as I have rarely noticed with even the most experienced accompanists.

His amazing facility on the piano—when not under the strain of public playing there was absolutely nothing technical he could not effortlessly do at a moment's notice—grew entirely out of his musicality. His ear governed his movements at all times. He described the process of playing in all its complexity by pointing out that he always heard every bit in advance mentally, and then in retrospect physically. Bad acoustics in a hall could therefore easily throw him off, while the quality of the action of the piano did not make too much difference to him. He could immediately adjust to any piano and make any old upright (such as the one on which he used to teach) sound like the most perfect concert grand. As soon as he heard clearly what he was doing he adjusted his sonorities completely to the acoustic conditions, whether in a room or in a hall.

His much-admired sonorities on the piano were not the outcome of any particular physical gift—after all, he was not the only pianist to have a good hand for the instrument—but of his subtle and differentiating ear, for instance in chord playing where he heard and controlled every single tone in the chord. Basically, they were governed—as his whole playing was—by his feeling for the fluidity of all music. In accordance with his personality, he brought out the concept of " becoming " in music, that is, the fact that the essential of a composition is to be found in its live sequence of tones and chords, its *line*.

Schnabel's playing was therefore at all times eminently eloquent, and he devoted his main attention in practising and teaching to the connection and separation, emphasis and lightness which, in their alternation, constitute the musical speech. His approach to musical articulation was entirely new and creative and is not yet generally understood†. He saw the greatest danger to music at the piano in a certain type of percussive martellato in which successive tones would be hammered out with an almost machine-made equality. His tones could be even, too, but they came out like those " of a hummingbird," alike as much as the different leaves from the same tree are alike.

His practising therefore consisted mainly, not of training, but of experimenting : with an unparalleled imagination he constantly found new ways—fingerings or physical motions—to bring out the subtle and beautiful nuances of articulation which he heard inwardly, never shying away from untraditional ways of playing, if a particular effect could thus be secured.

†The author of this article, in collaboration with Schnabel, has prepared a textbook and treatise on these questions, summing up the principles underlying Schnabel's playing and teaching.

In his inspired moments, the complexity of what he heard in the music then dissolved itself into an overwhelming simplicity of the very kind which he admired so much in the late works of Beethoven. In these moments one could feel how close he was to nature and understood that (as he once phrased it) " air, not fire " was his principal element. It was, indeed, a predominant trait of his personality to be attracted to anything in the world which was as free as the air. This accounts for his manner of playing as well as for his preferences in music and his own composing. The more elastic and diversified the music, the more he could identify himself with it. Characteristically, the first pieces of Bach which he picked up after a long pause, were two of the most rhapsodic Toccatas. From there he moved on to the *Chromatic Phantasy and Fugue*, the last major piece which he added to his repertoire. In the same line of preferences one has to list Berlioz, the only French musician close to his heart, whose spontaneity and uncalculated irregularity he adored. His music was used as Schnabel's prime example to point out that in composition, as in everything, the true musical inspiration creates its own form of exteriorization, and he could become really furious when reading that Berlioz wrote " wrong " basses—just as he would not tolerate utterances about Schumann's alleged inadequacy in instrumentation.

This attitude perhaps gives the clue to Schnabel's own composi- tions. Although they are carefully written and frequently contain developments and inversions of themes and even, occasionally, clever intellectual games recalling those word puns and spoonerisms of which he was so fond, his music is essentially free of any system and does not want to prove anything. Speaking of his composing, he once said " I have always been more interested in the nature of things than in the means of their expression." Schnabel admired Arnold Schoenberg more than any other contemporary composer, but his music was essentially different. Unlike Schoenberg, Schnabel had some admiration, but no love for Wagner, and very little spontaneous sympathy for Mahler ; the vitality of Strauss's early scores attracted him more. Schnabel's atonality is entirely without preoccupation : free, bird-like melodies sing against a " neutral " yet meaningful background of veiled atonal sounds. The essence of these compositions is lucid only to those who have an ear for the rhapsodic cadence of the principal parts. The melodic line is in no instance tied down to any kind of rule approximating to the method of composing with twelve tones.

The harmonic system underlying Schnabel's scores remains, as yet, unanalysed. It is quite likely that some organic principles can be found here. The ultimate value of the compositions can only be judged if and when a generation of music lovers will arise whose ears are naturally attuned to music free of tonality. But there is no doubt that Schnabel, in his compositions, strives for the same ideals as he did in his playing : freedom and natural order.

It goes almost without saying that a man of such activity and universality did not confine his interests to his art alone. Schnabel was passionately absorbed with the world of today. He was an avid reader of newspapers and magazines and most outspoken in the stand which he took in any political question of the day. Also, although he seemed to withdraw from public musical life in the last years, he always kept in touch with musical events and reacted very bluntly when his dislike was aroused. If he was, in fact, often very bitter, the reason was that basically he was an optimist and believed in the possibility of a decent and constructive order of the world : hence his disappointment when the news of the day— whether political or musical—was sad and discouraging.

Never swayed by reversals, he thus became a pioneer in the field of music and has influenced our music-making perhaps more than anyone else since the times of Liszt and Bülow. Not only did he found musical schools and concert organizations and introduce concert habits which were generally accepted ; not only have his principles of teaching been followed by hundreds of pupils in many countries and will probably continue to live until the end of our era ; but he has also enriched our concert repertoire by adding to it a number of Mozart concertos and Schubert sonatas hitherto neglected. His intuitive understanding of this music finally transcended the traditional barriers erected against it by succeeding generations of teachers trained too exclusively on Beethoven and his pianistic school (Czerny, Cramer, etc.). There is no doubt that, for instance, if today we can hear Schubert's last two Sonatas frequently and adequately performed we owe it to Schnabel who, consciously acting as pioneer, has opened our ears to their beauty which he was the first to feel and communicate.

In recent years Schnabel became increasingly aware of his general mission which he could not completely fulfill by just playing and teaching the piano. It is for this reason that he began to lecture and write. But, although he disposed of an unusual word power, writing and public speech were, as media, essentially alien to him,

416

and therefore he was, on the whole, not understood. In the end, therefore, he concentrated on composing as the most suitable means for expressing his creative thought ; he could hope now that the day would come when people might be able to receive the essence of what he had to give.

The 1951 Bayreuth Festival

By JACK BORNOFF

GUSTAV MAHLER once said : " Tradition ist Schlamperei," roughly : " Tradition is an excuse for sloppiness." He was referring not so much to the outward aspect of a tradition, as to the tradition of performance : Mahler felt that the so-called traditional interpretation of music of an earlier age was often merely a way of avoiding coming to grips with it afresh, and re-interpreting it from a contemporary point of view.

From what we saw and heard at the 1951 Bayreuth Festival, Mahler's aphorism might have served as a watchword for its present guiding spirit, Wieland Wagner, one of the composer's two grand-sons. This young man of thirty-four affirms that Bayreuth had fallen into a rut : performances were given there in the name of tradition which, far from realizing the essential Wagner, merely submerged the music in clap-trap quite out of keeping with Wagner's original intentions.

There must be no compromise, says Wieland Wagner. Either we return to the original style of production, to the *Parsifal* of 1882 with its garlanded flower-maidens (which Heinz Tietjen—who reigned at Bayreuth from 1933 to 1944—did not shirk from resuscitating at Covent Garden in 1951) and gas-lighting ; or we must break completely with tradition and seek a new solution to the visual interpretation which will be in keeping with the concepts of our age. Wagner's music-dramas are not operas ; each one presents a separate problem, each requires a different approach. To treat in the same pseudo-realistic manner two works as far removed from each other as *Die Meistersinger* and *Parsifal*, as has been done in the past, seems to us today to be quite a misconception.

Wagner himself used to rail at the kind of decorations which had been designed " as if they were intended to stand there, all on their own, to be viewed at will, like a panorama, whereas I want them to be nothing but a silent background or environment, fitting a characteristic dramatic situation." How little satisfied he was with the practical realization of what were, and still are, unrealizable " visions", is apparent from the proceedings at the rehearsals for the first productions of *The Ring* and *Parsifal*. Wagner was continually changing his mind about the way his written stage instructions were to be interpreted, and, even after the first production of *Parsifal*, he made the comment that the moving backcloth in the second Transformation scene disturbed the music and should be cut out.

It would be a mistake, says Wieland Wagner, to use the technical improvements which have been achieved in the seventy-five years of Bayreuth's existence to attempt to carry out to the letter Wagner's stage instructions ; instructions which arose from the taste of his epoch, as indeed have all subsequent efforts at interpreting them. The spirit, as opposed to the written indication, of these " inner visions " is better served by allowing the music to speak for itself and by making the stage picture the " silent background " the composer desired. " . . . . now that I have succeeded in creating the invisible orchestra, I would like to invent the invisible theatre," said Wagner in 1878. A quip, of course. But his grandson has almost done so.

Never can *The Ring* have been pitched in such a low scale of lighting ; and there we have the keynote to Wieland's whole realization of *The Ring* and *Parsifal : lighting*. No longer is scenery the basis for the production of these works—not even a stage set used as a means of reflecting light. The basis is light itself—shafts of light of varying intensity thrown on to impressively simple planes of darkness. The purpose of this revolution in Wagnerian production is deliberately to blur the outline of the picture, and to suggest rather than to underline the action. As a consquence there may be some loss of detail, and many gestures we have always regarded as of vital importance to our understanding of the action may go unseen. But the result is to give to these legendary, as opposed to the historically and geographically fixed works of Wagner, a marvellous remoteness, a larger-than-life effect—either mystically as in *Parsifal* or symbolically as in *The Ring*.

Parsifal being the more abstract of the two works, it accordingly received the more radical treatment : the whole of the action was concentrated within—and on certain important occasions on the

fringe of—a slightly raised but flat-surfaced disc. In the first scene, the only properties were two mounds backstage, which enabled Gurnemanz, at the beginning, to make a group with the sleeping esquires ; then, in the second scene, this same disc formed the base from which the immensely tall, stylized columns of the Grail's temple rose up ; and in the first scene of Act 3, Kundry was discovered, significantly, in the same spot, *outside* the perimeter of the circle, on to which she had collapsed at the end of the preceding act ; the only stage property in this scene was a rocky mound from which flowed the holy water—but no hut, no woods, no " laughing meadow." All the rest was but light and shade : the vast yet strangely oppressive dome which represented the interior of Klingsor's tower ; the flower-maidens, sinuous bodies more felt than seen, in a garden of coruscating colours ; and the pale desolation at the end of Act 2.

Stripped to such bare essentials, the stage picture forced one to concentrate on the action. And the eye was continually rewarded by a revealing grouping and a telling use of the spotlight on features —the latter device all the more telling for being sparingly used. For example, in the first scene of Act 2 : Klingsor—a bald, severe head outlined in a blue light, motionless, high up and seemingly unsupported in space—a power of evil and not, as so often, just another cloak-and-dagger operatic villain ; and then, from the depths of the huge Bayreuth stage, a looming Kundry.

The Ring presents a different problem altogether : constructed like a Greek tragedy, its message is to be conveyed not, as in *Parsifal*, in terms of spiritual symbolism but through the course of human action—even when the protagonists are gods. But Wieland Wagner's theatrical principles are the same : sets of utter simplicity which contrast light and shade. In Act 2 of *Die Walküre*, the rocky gorge was formed by two cliff-faces rising sheer ; all the necessary cloud effects were seen in the narrow strip of sky showing between the cliff-faces ; and Brünnhilde appeared to Siegmund not from the top of one of the infinitely aspiring cliffs, but from within the rock face. In Act 1 of *Die Götterdämmerung*, the interior of the Gibichungs' palace had the one narrow, but immensely tall, opening to the light in the left background, with steps leading down from it into the body of the hall. Apart from this one shaft of light, black curtains took up the whole of the stage. After Siegfried's arrival, Hagen pulled a curtain across even that : the trap had closed.

Such a sweeping change in the stage picture demanded and received a corresponding revision in the handling of the action. By disposing the three protagonists of the Gibichungs' scene in an extended triangle which made full use of the size of the stage, Hagen at the back, Gutrune right and Gunther left front, Wieland Wagner was able to give Gibichung brother and sister each an individuality and still make it crystal-clear that they were only puppets, to be actuated as their Nibelung half-brother decreed. This Hagen was sinister enough, low-pitched, almost reticent, but doggedly weaving his plot like a true Nibelung until he had accomplished the penultimate deed in his mission, struck down Siegfried and avenged the perjury of his own machination.

This producer's whole conception of the part of Hagen, like that of every part in *The Ring*, derived strictly from his grandfather's writings : " Where we have in the past expressed operatic passion by means of wide outstretched arms, as if calling for help, we have now found that a half-raised arm, or even a characteristic movement of a hand, of the head are quite sufficient to convey any slight heightening of emotion ; and the effect of the true emotional climax will be all the greater for appearing to break out after having been long pent-up."

Still more startling was his treatment of Loge. As Wieland Wagner explained in an essay which appeared in the *Rheingold* programme notes, he saw Loge as an impersonal force of nature, neither good nor bad, equally warming or consuming, creating or destroying, as ready to help in forging the fatal ring as in purging it from the curse it bears. Possessed of a wisdom as great as that of Erda and her daughters, the Norns and Brünnhilde, Loge instinctively and disinterestedly speaks the truth. How is one to represent this vital element which, though present throughout *The Ring*, is personified only in *Das Rheingold* ? Not, surely, as the combination of " Mephistopheles and snake, liar and deceiver, intriguer and jester, demon and dancer " to which we are accustomed. Although these attributes are applied to him by other characters, that is merely how *they* see him. Since, within the conventions of Wagner's music drama, Loge must assume human shape, Wieland made him completely human, more human than gods, dwarfs or giants—intelligent and a thinker.

Another of Wieland Wagner's departures in *The Ring* was his treatment of the apparitions of Erda. Herself no longer seen, Wotan came down stage into a blue light projected upwards ; and it seemed as if the earth had opened up before him.

The Bayreuth costume designs were ruthlessly simplified ; much of the clatter and clash of steel was shed and though Parsifal still appeared in Act 3 " in shining black armour," there were no winged helmets for Wotan, Hunding or Hagen. This toning down of the picture was accompanied by a corresponding reticence of movement : gone were the posturing and exaggerated gestures that seemed so ludicrous to our mid-twentieth century minds. All the necessary underlining was done by the orchestra.

But even a Wieland Wagner must feel his way ; and whereas the characters of *Parsifal* were relieved of all unnecessary ornaments, Fafner, in *Siegfried*, remained the unwieldy dragon of the bad old days. Having gone so far,Wieland might have gone farther in his self-appointed mission and, even in *Parsifal*, spared us the sight of the falling swan of Act 1 and the hovering dove of Act 3. But I know what his answer would be : in *Parsifal*, there are four essential symbols—chalice and spear, swan and dove ; and whatever else disappears, they must remain. Perhaps he felt, like Pogner in *Die Meistersinger*, " Zu viel auf einmal brächte Reu " ; the old guard of Bayreuthians had been shocked enough. Nor must we forget that the new staging is, to a certain extent, a virtue made of necessity. Not all the simplification of the action was intentional or successful—certainly not the completely misdirected action in the final scene of *Die Götterdämmerung*.

As for the problem of casting *The Ring*, the 1951 Bayreuth was as far from a solution as was the first production there in 1876. The directors of the 1951 Bayreuth Festival wanted new blood. Their theories involved far too violent a break with the past for them to attempt to change habits—bad habits, they considered—acquired in the old school ; and, in many cases, they seemed to go out of their way to find singers with no previous experience of their roles. The results were sometimes disquieting : that the 24-year old Sieglinde had the right calibre of voice for the part was unquestionable, but, for all the natural beauty of her timbre and the warmth and sympathy of her interpretation, hers was not a performance of the finish one expects from the Bayreuth Festival. Nor, indeed, could one have supposed that a singer would have taken the stage at Bayreuth so obviously unrehearsed as the Hans Sachs I saw ; that he was not the interpreter of the role of the first cast is neither here nor there : this *was* a Festival performance. And the performances in several of the lesser roles could only be described as provincial. On the other hand in *Parsifal*, Ludwig Weber as Gurnemanz, Martha Mödl as Kundry, George London as Amfortas and

Hermann Uhde as Klingsor were as near to the ideal in their respective roles as we are ever likely to experience ; and Wolfgang Windgassen as Parsifal, though light in voice, certainly showed real promise. In *The Ring* there were quite a number of singers whom one would not wish to hear again. I expected the notorious " Bayreuth bark " to have become a thing of the past, yet both Nibelungen dwarfs were adepts at it ; and, moreover, their interpretations seemed to be considerably at variance with the new teaching. Only a very few of the singers—again Ludwig Weber, this time as Fasolt and Hagen, Martha Mödl as Gutrune, Herrmann Uhde as Gunther, and Elisabeth Schwarzkopf as Woglinde—could not have been bettered.

Forcing was one vocal defect mercifully not in evidence at Bayreuth. The covered-in orchestra, quite apart from its properties of integrating the sound of the various groups of the orchestra, allowed the conductor to unleash the full force of Wagner's climaxes without overpowering the singers. Sunken and disposed on tiers which prolong the rake of the auditorium to well under the stage, the Bayreuth orchestra is covered in from the front, i.e., from the auditorium side, by a roof curving over it to the extent of a third of the width of the pit, and from the proscenium side by another roof extending for the same distance in the direction of the auditorium.

I found it strange that the conductor of the *Ring* cycle I heard, Herbert von Karajan, should have seen fit to alter the disposition of the orchestra as laid down by Wagner himself for the only *Ring* performances he heard at Bayreuth. By bringing the violins from under the near cover of the orchestral pit into the open space between the two roofs, he gave added power and brilliance to the string tone ; but this hardly compensated for the loss in balance on the many occasions when the violins' subsidiary task should have kept them in the background.

Von Karajan is a conductor for whom I have a great admiration. In his Bayreuth *Meistersinger* he showed what he could do with a Wagnerian work of which he has the full measure. But in *The Ring* there were—next to some lyrical passages of extraordinary refinement and serenity—too many rough edges, too many occasions which disappointed through lack of a cumulative climax. The conductor treated each scene as a separate entity, whereas *The Ring*'s full majesty can only be revealed if we are conscious of the work's architecture as a whole.

For *The Ring* Wagner created his covered orchestra ; and *Parsifal* was the work Wagner wrote with the sound of the " mystische Abgrund " (as he called it) in his mind. *Parsifal* was given this year under Hans Knappertsbusch ; and here the sound that came from the " mystische Abgrund " had a most haunting quality—which was surely responsible for Debussy's reference to the " unique, incalculable beauty " of the work's orchestral writing.

[For another view of the Bayreuth productions, see pp. 426-430.—Eds.]

First Performances at the Proms (1951)

As was right and proper during the Festival year, contemporary British music played an important part throughout the 1951 " Prom " season with its uncommonly well-designed—save in one respect alone—programmes. While having ample opportunity to admire the splendid achievement of our established composers, such as Vaughan Williams, Walton, Rawsthorne, Constant Lambert, Ireland, Bax, Bliss, and others, the foreign visitor might have gone home with much less confidence in our less-known or younger composers on the strength of the summer's first London performances. Let it be said at once that Fricker's Symphony on September 14 was an honourable exception ; thanks to the Koussevitzky award, the Cheltenham Festival, and the Third Programme, its distinction is by now common knowledge. No other member of the younger generation was represented at all. Instead there was a Symphonic Suite for strings by Maurice Jacobson on August 3, a Cumbrian Rhapsody *Tarn Hows* by Maurice Johnstone on August 6, a *Serenade Fantastique* for oboe and strings by Philip Sainton on August 22, a *Galop Joyeux* by Gordon Jacob on August 25, Five Pieces for orchestra by Daniel Jones on August 31, and a Symphonic Suite *Piers Plowman's Day* by Alan Bush on September 7 (unavoidably missed by this reviewer).

Jacobson's Suite, previously only played at this year's Cheltenham festival, was at once the most ambitious and the least satisfying ; in its three extended movements the composer's naïve admission in the programme-note proved uncomfortably near the truth : " I now find myself uncertain of my own musical language . . . so I write and write, letting matter dictate manner, in the hope that in due course I shall find my own idiomatic feet." As a contrapuntal exercise it showed considerable ingenuity, but as music it lacked flavour and only the more introspective slow movement gave any evidence of creative compulsion. Scratchy string playing from the L.P.O. and a lethargic reading from Basil Cameron helped matters still less.

In *Tarn Hows*, Johnstone concentrates his " love of the lake district as a whole into a tone-picture of a favourite haunt at early morning, high noon and evening " ; the work is sufficiently delicately orchestrated and sensitively conceived (apart from one blatant, late afternoon interlude like the arrival of a charabanc of trippers) for the listener to enjoy it in spite of its out-dated, romantic idiom. Sainton's *Serenade* (another 1951 Cheltenham discovery) was a little, but not a great deal, more attuned to the times in its harmonic language, so that the composer's own pictorial guide to its scherzo-cum-trio form (escape from reality in wine and company at an inn—sleep and the ideal world of dreams—return to opening mood) to help the Promenader to come to terms with " contemporary music " proved hardly necessary. It was sympathetically scored for solo oboe, and the slow, dream-like middle section ravished the ear scarcely less than late Strauss.

Apt as was Jacob's *Galop Joyeux* to wind up proceedings on a Saturday night, it was a little hard on this composer to be represented only by this four and a half minute's worth of brilliantly orchestrated gusto, thrown off some thirteen years ago while he was orchestrating one of Liszt's galops for the ballet *Apparitions*. Nor did Daniel Jones's twelve years old Five Pieces for orchestra allow the Promenader any clue that here was a composer of symphonic stature, though his serious disposition was evident from his admission in the programme note that he regarded this very straight-faced work as entertainment only. Though grouped together, there was no thematic, programmatic or any other kind of relationship between the pieces, and the first three amounted to little more than note-book jottings ; but the more extended fourth piece gave the surest evidence of the composer's powers, both in the quality of the material and in its beautifully pellucid orchestration.

Of the four " imported " first performances, Goffredo Petrassi's *Partita* for Orchestra scheduled for August 6 was cancelled owing to Sir Malcolm Sargent's illness, and Castelnuovo-Tedesco's *Concerto da Camera* for oboe and strings (July 31) came on an impossible night for this reviewer. Bloch's *Scherzo Fantasque* for piano and orchestra on September 10 proved as uncharacteristic of the subtle, sensitive, visionary Bloch as his recent piano Concerto, from which the scherzo might possibly have been a discarded movement ; the surging energy and the vivid orchestration of the composer in his prime are here unfortunately lavished on thematic material of little distinction. Apart from Fricker's Symphony, in fact, the only new work of the season, British or otherwise, likely to establish itself in the repertory was Hindemith's four years old clarinet Concerto in four movements, which Frederick Thurston and the L.S.O. introduced on August 17. Not even the eloquently lyrical slow movement attempts to touch any extremes of feeling, but the music shows a concision of argument, a piquant lightness of texture, and an overall urbanity which make it very good company. As it was written for Benny Goodman, there is outlet in plenty for virtuosity—though it is every time a musician's rather than a showman's piece.   JOAN CHISSELL

Edinburgh Festival, 1951

THIS year's visiting orchestra was the Philharmonic-Symphony of New York under Bruno Walter and Dimitri Mitropoulos. Gloomy forebodings based on memories of the cold-blooded mechanical efficiency of the Philadelphia Orchestra were set at rest by the daily press the morning after the first concert (I had been at the Freemason's Hall hearing an enchanting programme of French Operetta performed by Fanély Revoil and Willy Clément, with Stanford Robinson such a brilliant accompanist that one was almost tempted to think he had missed his rightful vocation) so that the wilful manhandling of the Beethoven Fourth Symphony the next night came as the greater shock. As one graceless phrasing followed another and the whole misinterpretation culminated in the last movement's illogical and (for the woodwind) impracticable tempo, I thought back wistfully to my Beecham recording.

After the interval, a present to all the enemies of contemporary music, came Prokofiev's noisy, uncouth Fifth Symphony. Surely, few composers can show such falling off in maturity as the composer of *Chout* and the Third piano Concerto ? That this work is well thought of and much played in both America and the Soviet Union speaks sociological and cultural volumes.

The rest of the series of concerts was to provide the explanation of the dashing of my hopes. The conductor the first night had been Bruno Walter, and hearing his programme the following Sunday I felt I was listening to a completely different orchestra. Walter's performance of Haydn's Symphony No. 88 proved that he is our finest Haydn interpreter today ; solid and down to earth, he doesn't seek for subtle nuances where none is to be found. The main item was a fine performance of the Bruckner Fourth, played, very surprisingly, in the " revised " version (i.e. that published in the Universal score) and not the " original " version published just before the war by the Bruckner Gesellschaft. Bruckner, oddly enough, knew what he was about, and it is of small service to him to perform the rescored and in places structurally mangled versions made by his well-meaning friends.

Thursday night's Brahms concert—a repeat of the previous Friday's programme—was of the same high standard, and included a performance of the *Song of Destiny* by the Edinburgh Royal Choral Union. Either they are a quite exceptional choir, in which case we ought to be hearing more of them, or else Dr. Walter is an exceptional choral conductor. In either event, except for a few rather rough top notes, the singing had the same beautiful rounded quality as the New York Philharmonic-Symphony's strings ; and, a tribute to any choir, they sang at their best in the *pianissimo* passages.

Enough has been written already about Mitropoulos and suffice it to say here that I started with a strong predisposition in his favour. Here was someone active in the cause of contemporary music—though his Edinburgh programmes hardly showed it—and whose whole background seemed entirely on the side of what one might perhaps call *Music Survey*'s angels. But gradually the impression was built up, for me at least, of a personality almost devoid of musicality. Much has been said of his extraordinary showmanship and eccentric beat, or lack of it. This was put into high relief when, in the *Short Symphony* of Swanson (a work, incidentally, of no very great interest by a negro pupil of Nadia Boulanger) he behaved like any other conductor who prefers not to bother with a stick. Here, I felt, was a work comparatively new to the orchestra, in which Mitropoulos had decided that they needed immediate guidance and not a recollection of what happened at the rehearsal ; and I wondered what some other works would have sounded like if they had been thus honoured—whether, for instance Bax's *Overture to a Picaresque Comedy* would have tripped along somewhat more lightly than the parody of Richard Strauss which was what we heard.

But, all in all, £50,000 (in dollars too !) is a great deal of money to spend to reassure ourselves that our own Royal Philharmonic is a very fine orchestra, and the Philharmonia not bad either.

Of the large scale orchestral concerts, perhaps the most enjoyable was that given on a Sunday afternoon by the National Youth Orchestra of Great Britain under Walter Süsskind. The most intelligent programme included a new work specially written for the orchestra by Malcolm Arnold and Kabalevsky's Second Symphony. All the players were under 18.

The morning programmes followed what has now become a traditional pattern of chamber music and chamber orchestras. The Boyd Neel were responsible for half a dozen and were right on top of their form. They included an excellent performance of Stravinsky's *Apollon Musagète* and the next day, Richard Lewis sang Britten's *Les Illuminations* very beautifully.

The London Mozart Players were responsible for another four concerts. This is a first rate body of players, but I found myself wishing that Harry Blech had a little more of the finesse Anthony Bernard displays in his Mozart readings.

Two of the most interesting events of the Festival were, alas, two which lacked full houses. They were Suzanne Danco's programme of old Italian and modern French songs, which included superb performances of Milhaud's *Poèmes Juifs* and Ravel's *Histoires Naturelles*, and another, two days later, by Poulenc and Bernac, who were their usual supremely civilized selves.

It was virtually impossible to see more than a few of the festival films, but particularly noteworthy musically were the Soviet film on the life of Mussorgsky ; Alan Rawsthorne's ballet film *The Dancing Fleece*, made for the National Wool Textile Corporation ; and Racine Fricker's fine score to the Antarctic Exploration film *White Continent*.

Of the Glyndebourne Opera and Sadlers Wells Ballet I can say nothing, as *Music Survey's* Rover Pass was not deemed worthy of admission by the respective managements. The Yugoslav Ballet proved rather a disappointment. Here was neither good theatrical dancing nor good folk dancing but a rather unsatisfactory mixture of both.   DENNIS DOBSON

Salzburg and Bayreuth
BY GEOFFREY SHARP
with editorial inserts (H.K.) in square brackets and indented type.

A COLLEAGUE, more distinguished for his powers of persiflage than for his critical acumen, once thought it funny to upbraid your contributor for going to listen to music on his holiday. It would be unseemly to draw obvious inferences in so august a journal as *Music Survey*, so the worthy gentleman will, no doubt, continue to flounder in the profundity of his own wit.

Salzburg has unfortunately allowed the high standard of its 1948 Festival to be compromised by commercial considerations. High-pressure American colonization has made itself felt during the intervening years, and the principal emphasis can be seen shifting from the once so musical festival to the now prospering tourist resort. Even so, there were some good things.

By far the most important event, up to 8th August when I had to leave for Bayreuth, was Herbert Graf's production of *Otello*. Sickened as I am by the current messy-minded attitude towards opera as a *genre*—an attitude prevalent in, but by no means confined to England, as Salzburg took pains to prove with its pastiche of *Idomeneo*—this imaginative and resplendent fusion of the various arts, always lavish without ever lapsing into doubtful taste, recalled better days and has goaded me once again into campaigning for a more intelligent and enlightened approach to the whole problem of putting opera on the stage. There was, however, an important weakness : Ramon Vinay's voice was no more adequate to the part of Otello than his conception of it was Shakespearian. This may have meant that Paul Schöffler, as Iago, had a correspondingly easier task in establishing himself as the dominant character ; one can hardly imagine the part better played or sung. Certainly he proved, for those who did not already know it, that a strong Iago is as essential to Verdi's opera as to Shakespeare's play. All the other parts were adequately filled and in particular Dragica Martinis, once she had overcome her initial unsteadiness, gave a genuinely musical account of Desdemona and resisted every temptation to bawl her top notes. The Vienna Philharmonic played magnificently for Furtwängler, completely confounding those who had doubted whether this was his kind of music, and Herbert Graf provided an object lesson for the all too numerous class of critic which, having no understanding of theatrical procedure, proceeds to belittle its importance.

Next best was a piano recital by Friedrich Gulda. The juxtaposition of Bach's C minor Toccata and Beethoven's last Sonata emphasizes by contrast the problems of each. Gulda's solutions invariably seemed unbelievably mature for a young man of barely 21 ; apart from an occasional trace of youthful impetuosity in the Beethoven—and controlled impetuosity irks only the crabbed and ancient critic already bored with his pursuit—one could have imagined that here was Petri at his most magisterial and compulsive. The promise of Prokofiev and Debussy to follow had to be evaded ; the Brahms-Handel Variations would have completed the programme so much better.

Almost equally rewarding, and unexpectedly so, was a fine performance by Irmgard Seefried and the Schneiderhan Quartet of Respighi's little-known *Il Tramonto.*
[H.K. :—
Particularly unexpectedly in that Schoenberg's F sharp minor Quartet had been on the Festival programme and was dropped in favour of the Respighi without explanation or apology—barely 3 weeks after Schoenberg's death.]
The time, skill and care that had been devoted to its preparation will be understood from the fact that, in retrospect, it is difficult to believe that the music is really as good as it sounded.

If the technical ability of Joseph Messner and his collaborators came anywhere near matching the enterprise he shows in his choice of music, his Sunday evening concerts would long have been established among the highlights of the Festival. It was a pity that on this occasion his zeal for the unfamiliar was partially offset by the audience's aversion to fresh air, for the evening was very hot and Beethoven's *Mount of Olives*, indifferently performed, takes some sitting out in a stuffy atmosphere. It is a work we should all hear once ; whereas Bruckner's compact, brilliant and invigorating setting of the *150th Psalm*, which was over almost before it had begun, left us hungry for a repeat.

Of this year's *Zauberflöte* in the *Felsenreitschule* under Furtwängler's direction there is not much to say save that it was respectable but by no means epoch-making.
[H.K. :—
Another ear might hold that while many of his phrasings and formings were epoch-making, some *tempi* were by no means respectable.]
Seefried (Pamina) and Schöffler (Sprecher) both gave exemplary performances, Dermota was stiff and unconvincing as Tamino and Klein failed to exude anything approaching the full malice of Monostatos—but has any tenor

427

since Heinrich Tessmer ? The opera was largely spoilt by being strait-jacketed into the rigid and restricted arena of the vastly overrated riding school with its dead acoustics, minimal protection from the elements and intolerably hard seats ; there is no possible merit in one's posterior having to do penance for one's musical delights. The *Festspielhaus* would have been the proper setting for *Zauberflöte*, and for *Idomeneo* which was really disastrously man-handled.

Imagine this grand tragic opera unmercifully cut : then imagine the residue, spared from Dr. Paumgartner's garbage-can, lumped together to form a continuous one-act pageant. Imagine also this resultant *précis*, or *Moron's Digest*, cribbed, cabined and confined in the jaws of the all-consuming riding school, and you have a full quota of ingredients for a first-class musical *débacle*. After the simple dignity of Ebert's Glyndebourne production, which could also be criticized for its excessive " cuts," this bowdlerized, pseudo-Mozartian jamboree offended almost all one's canons of judgment. Of the cast Rudolf Schock (Idomeneo) alone appeared to have any idea of the *style* of performance required, while the Vienna Philharmonic under Georg Solti barely skirted the fundamentals of the score and never even hinted at the sombre luminosity of its finest pages. A fiasco : but let us be thankful for small mercies—at least the " cuts " were not compensated by unauthorized interpolations, Mozartian or otherwise.

[H.K. :—

Hilde Güden's Ilia, however unsatisfactory on the histrionic or stylistic side (whatever that may be), and however alive she may have been to her virtues of face, figure and throat, was a musical experience of the rarest order : a high-grade combination of interpretational sense and tonal sensuousness. The author of the present article suggested to me that she was singing for the gallery, in which case I seem to have been the gallery, which is all the more probable since I did not consider her marked prettiness a serious artistic drawback. She has the rare gift of feeling the logic of an extended melodic arch from its first note : her tense " *Padre !* " at the unconventional beginning of her G minor aria was in itself worth one's having travelled to Salzburg.

With Solti, one had to distinguish between execution and inter-pretation : the former as bad as our contributor suggests ; the latter, while not outstanding, better than many a more famed conductor's, in fact not unmusical.

After our contributor had left for Bayreuth, Furtwängler gave exhaustive interpretations of the Fifth Bruckner (original version except for the absolutely necessary doubling of the wind chorus in the final climaxes of the finale's chorale apotheosis), a master structure which lets you down only once, i.e. in the bridge to the resumption of the first violins' sustained melody over the first movement's second subject (bars 131 ff.) ; and of the Ninth Beethoven where, again, various mishaps in the performance deceived one or two critics about the quality of the conductor's conception (accent on " con- "). Irmgard Seefried, with a voice which in this work proved as tough as a horse's if it had one, got through the soprano part with flying tone-colours, though she is no longer able to reach the b'''s (" . . . Flügel weilt"): her voice is growing lower and beautifully darker.

We retract our previous intention to give a detailed review of Salz-burg's *Wozzeck* in view of the facts that (a) interpretation, performance and production were largely sub-mediocre ; (b) The Earl of Harewood has given an excellent report in his own journal ; and (c) the Covent Garden production, forthcoming at the time of writing, promises to be better and will naturally receive full attention in our next (Schoenberg) issue.]

To visit Bayreuth for the first time is a unique experience, but the unique does not necessarily encompass everything desirable nor exclude all that is inferior. This dirty old theatre with its flickering house lights and hellishly uncomfortable seats (worse than those in the *Felsenreitschule*), a fully appropriate appurtenance of Nibelheim, creates an immediate sense of depression which a sequence of five performances (*Parsifal* and the *Ring*) in barely relieved twilight did little to mitigate. Ignoring the precedents of Maskelyne and Cook, Wieland Wagner chose his own method of dealing with grandfather's stage magic : he ordained that his (stage) people should walk in darkness and we were left to imagine the toad, Brünnhilde's horse, all the rest of the difficult " props " and a good deal of the action as well. Ernest Newman has hailed this as a new technique which frees the listener's imagination. But isn't it simply cheating ? Of course, if the stage lighting is as dilapidated and inadequate as that in the auditorium—and your reviewer was offered no opportunity to find out—Wieland Wagner's peculiar kind of ingenuity may have been forced upon him : but some of the elementary lighting techniques were so badly carried out—inaccurate following, unwanted shadows, temporal contradictions, *etc.*—that one came to the conclusion that the Bayreuth electricians follow home rule rather than a lighting plot.

Any musician who has read thus far and wants to hear about the *Ring* is probably by now incredulous that a so-called music critic should waste so much space on mere stage fripperies. It is odd, isn't it ? But opera, and more especially Wagnerian music drama is not simply music with incidental diversions for singer-actors (of whom there are very few), scene-painters, electricians, stage-hands and a theatrical producer ; though the belief dies hard and Bayreuth this year made no attempt to be in at the kill. As theatrical productions, *Parsifal*, the *Ring* and *Meistersinger* were a multiple flop of a collective ineptitude that was hardly credible : but fortunately this was not all.

The acoustics of the building are fairly well balanced, that is to say no undue prominence is given to any part of the musical spectrum ; but the orchestra pit, which lies well below stage level, is covered—an interesting practice, if by no means wholly advantageous. There are three obvious merits in a covered pit : the musicians may wear comfortable clothes, the blanket of orchestral sound that the singers have to penetrate is less formidable, and the audience are spared the distraction of the musician's lights and the conductor's gestures. But in return much is sacrificed in the form of orchestral tone—far too much.

The orchestra, carefully selected from all over Germany, comprised something over forty violins and other instruments in proportion—that is to say it was about forty per cent larger than the largest British symphony orchestra ; even so, and despite the proven quality of the players, there were moments when the volume of sound was insufficient and one longed to hear the full brilliance of so many instruments in combination. The " lid " acted as a kind of communal mute and deprived the full climaxes of their rightful power and verve.

However, the human ear can be very accommodating and, this initial strangeness once overcome, the full, satisfying quality of the playing and singing emerged as the true glory of Bayreuth. Only in *Parsifal*, conducted by Knappertsbusch, was there any serious divergence from the set standard— one which, in England, would be regarded as literally incredibly high—

and here, for some unaccountable reason, unless it were fatigue, the last scene was allowed to fall to pieces from sheer inertia, ran approximately ten minutes overtime and completely failed to create its proper impression (10th August).

Herbert von Karajan's penetrating elucidation of the musical texture of the *Ring* tetralogy provided irrefutable evidence of his great musical ability and exceptional powers of concentration. The music was presented faithfully, imaginatively, yet entirely shorn of individual quirks or any of the forms of dross by which we nail the charlatan. The singing reached a high general level, above which a few achieved real eminence (notably those who could act!): Walter Fritz, whose Loge may prove to be the starting point for a new tradition, Paul Kuen (Mime), Ludwig Weber (Fasolt and Hagen), Arnold van Mill (Hunding), Leonie Rysanek (Sieglinde), Bernd Aldenhoff (Siegfried), Martha Mödl (Gutrune) and Hermann Uhde (Gunther). No member of the cast lapsed below a fair standard of professional competence, though the last minute substitutes for Elisabeth Höngen, who was indisposed, were not always happy in their work.

Die Meistersinger, produced by Rudolf Otto Hartmann, had two principal merits : it was played without " cuts " and we were permitted to see what was happening on the stage. Musically also it was thoroughly satisfying, though it seems worth suggesting that the opera be presented in two parts on consecutive nights. Act III could easily stand by itself—
    [H.K. :—
      And by what could Acts I-II stand, except by the bye ?]
—and we should thus escape being surfeited by a score which, despite its magnificence, needs a great effort for full assimilation at one session. Kunz played Beckmesser less broadly than does Benno Kusche, and Hermann Rohrbach, who was admirable in every other respect, could have done with a little more voice as Sachs. The other parts, especially the Masters, were very well filled—the majority in both senses, and the orchestra worked wonders for Karajan, including a Prelude to Act III which bordered on the miraculous.

[For another view of the Bayreuth productions, see pp. 417-.423—Eds.]

Periodicals

I. FOREIGN JOURNALS : NEW AND OLD

THE amazing resilience of the German people manifests itself not alone in their all-out effort to reconstruct their battered cities—with opera houses and concert halls as high priority issues—but no less in the fact that German musicography is once again flourishing. A host of music periodicals has grown up mushroomlike throughout the past six years, registering faithfully the almost feverish activities within the shrunken boundaries of the former Reich. Among the magazines representative of the western zones, *Melos* and *Das Musikleben* should be mentioned, both published by B. Schott's Söhne, Mainz. The latter was founded by Hermann Scherchen in 1918 and is again devoted especially to the propagation of progressive music. In this tendency it makes a point of championing the causes of Stravinsky, Bartok, Hindemith and younger German composers such as Werner Egk and Carl Orff, both hard at work to exorcise any lingering Romantic spirit from German opera. *Das Musikleben*, of more recent growth, often discusses topical problems of musical organization, education and sociology, but is not altogether averse to including, at times, subjects of historic or antiquarian interest. The chief editor of *Melos* is Dr. Heinrich Strobel, a well-known writer on musical matters and so far the only biographer of Paul Hindemith. *Das Musikleben* is edited by Professor Ernst Laaff, a notable younger scholar and professor of musicology at the university of Mainz, which was resurrected in 1946 by the French occupation authorities after a slumber of exactly 150 years.

More scholarly needs are satisfied by two periodicals published by Bärenreiter Verlag Cassel-Basel, a publishing firm famous for its admirable reprints of M. Praetorius and H. Schütz, as also for its formidable musical encyclopedia *Musik in Geschichte und Gegenwart*. Its Quarterly *Die Musikforschung* (now in the fourth year of its existence, and edited by Professor Hans Albrecht, Kiel) has become the official journal of German musicology, once more organized by the " *Gesellschaft für Musikforschung* " under the presidency of Professor Friedrich Blume of Kiel. This magazine at last fills the gap caused by the expiration of the once famous *Zeitschrift für Musikwissenschaft*. Among its regular contributors are the very best names of musical scholarship in Germany, including Heinrich Besseler, Rudolf Gerber, Walter Wiora, Walther Lipphardt, Hans Klotz and Hans Engel. Secondly, discussion of topical events as well as of problems of research are happily blended in the attractively illustrated monthly *Musica*, edited by Fred Hamel, the German gramophone expert. While it is comparatively easy to obtain regular copies of these periodicals of the Western zones, it seems strangely difficult to get hold of any music magazine produced in the Eastern zone. This is all the more regrettable as the above-mentioned journals deal only with musical activities west of the Iron Curtain. By a stroke of luck I recently received the first issue of a new periodical edited and produced in East Berlin and representative of the prevalent cultural trend in that part of the world. Its chief editors are Ernst Hermann Meyer, a distinguished scholar whose admirable *British Chambermusic* (London, 1946) is unforgotten and who has recently been appointed to the chair of sociology of music at the Humboldt-University of East Berlin ; and Dr. Karl Laux, a well-known musicographer, and the author of *Musik und Musiker der Gegenwart* (Berlin, 1949). The first issue of this new monthly which bears the programmatic title *Musik und Gesellschaft* (Music and Society), contains—apart from some articles clearly designed as cultural propaganda for " home consumption "—two valuable contributions on problems of musical research which should be brought to the early notice of western scholars. The aura of a little sensation surrounds the first publication of the facsimile of J. S. Bach's famous letter to Georg Erdmann (dated Leipzig, October 28, 1730), the most explicit autobiographical document from the composers own hand in which he asks his old friend of the far-off Lüneburg days to relieve him from his burdensome Leipzig appointment. Erdmann was Russian *chargé d'affairs* in Danzig, so that together with his other papers, this letter came into the possession of the Russian State Archives in Moscow. There it was discovered by Oscar v. Riesemann during his search for biographical data of Erdmann on behalf of Philipp Spitta, the Bach biographer. Spitta published first an abridged version of it and finally reproduced the whole text in Vol. 2 of his work, basing his reprint on a photostat which has been lost. Apparently Spitta never set eyes on the original, which is now admirably reproduced on 4 separate plates with a valuable commentary by Professor N. Notowicz. The facsimile bears on its four sheets the stamp of the Russian State Archives. It gives a wonderful example of Bach's penmanship and is of great value for modern Bach research. The other contribution of special interest to the western scholar is an article by Joachim Krüger-Riebow on Albert Lortzing, the " Mozart of German Biedermeier," who starved to death exactly a hundred years ago, and whose cause is but poorly served by R. W. Wood's short biography in Vol. II of " The Music Masters " (ed. A. L. Bacharach, publ. by Cassel, 1950). Krüger-Riebow's article surveys Lortzing's comprehensive posthumous manuscripts and notes which include, *inter alia*, several unpublished operas, among them *Caramo* (1839)—not " Caramor," as printed in Mr. Wood's article—and *Regina* (1848), a political opera reflecting the social upheaval of the German revolution of that year. The author's assertion is that *Caramo* as well as *Hans Sachs* (1840) have inspired some of the most famous motives in Wagner's Dresden operas. Both Wagner and Lortzing were in deep sympathy with the aims of the " Liberal Revolution." It is well known that Wagner had a sneaking admiration for Lortzing whose little opera *Casanova* (1842) is mentioned in his letters, and whose well-constructed librettos have earned him an approving footnote in Wagner's *Collected Writings*. How near Lortzing actually came to crossing Wagner's path in 1848 is revealed by the facsimile publication (*ibid.*, page 13) of a hitherto unpublished letter of Lortzing dated Vienna, July 31, 1848, and addressed to his Leipzig colleague Schmidt. It was written at the end of Lortzing's ill-fated conductorship in Vienna (1846/48) which was terminated by the closing of the opera on September 1, 1848, due in its turn to the general political situation. Lortzing, already desperately looking for a new job, and apparently " without salary," writes :—

> Dear Schmidt, Your Richard Wagner was or is still here with the intention, according to the local press, of reforming operatic activities in Vienna. A shrewd purpose ; I have my doubts, however, whether Herr Richard will succeed—I heard yesterday that Wagner had to leave Dresden because of his meddling in political affairs. Is there some truth in this or not ? Please explain. Perhaps there could be a chance for another one, that is to say, for me, but I fear the whole thing will turn out to be just gossip. In any case I beg you to reply . . .

This letter throws an interesting sidelight on Wagner's precarious situation during the last year of his conductorship in Dresden, and completely tallies with Wagner's own description of his professional vicissitudes which had been aggravated by his temporary political recklessness (see *Mein Leben*, 1911, Vol. II, pp. 200 ff.). When Lortzing aspired to succeed Wagner at Dresden he hardly had a premonition that Wagner would arrive at his Swiss exile less than eleven months later, and that he himself would have to die in the abject poverty of his ultimate Berlin job on January 20, 1851.

Among the small countries surrounding Germany, Switzerland has always been notable for its sturdy independence in matters cultural. Its chief musical journal (published in German and French), the *Schweizerische Musikzeitung*, now in its 90th year and edited since the early days of the last war by Dr. Willi Schuh, contains in its April issue two articles of unusual

*Trans. H.F.R.

importance. In an article on *Die Burrell Collection*, Julius Kapp, the Wagner expert and editor of Wagner's *Gesammelte Schriften*, 1914, draws attention to the fact that a part of the legendary collection of unpublished notes and letters of Wagner has at last been published by Macmillan & Co., New York (1950), under the title *Letters of Richard Wagner*, edited by John N. Burk.† This volume follows after an interval of half a century on the famous documentary publication of the *Burrell Papers* (London, 1898), which was issued privately in very few copies—rarities on today's market. The new book contains many hitherto unpublished letters of Wagner to his first wife Minna, neé Planer, which elucidate the tragedy of Wagner's first marriage, as well as the tragi-comedy of his love affair with Jessie Laussot-Taylor. The same number contains also a short article by Anthony van Hoboken, *Zum ersten thematischen Haydn-Katalog*, which announces the forthcoming publication of the first complete catalogue of J. Haydn's works ; thus a colossal work of compilation and research is being completed which started in the last years of Haydn's life. The catalogue—following closely on the heels of Wolfgang Schmieder's monumental *Thematisch-Systematisches Verzeichnis der Werke J. S. Bachs* (Leipzig, 1950), and of O. E. Deutsch's *Schubert : Thematic Catalogue of all his Works in Chronological Order* (London, 1951)—will be published by B. Schott's Söhne (Mainz and London) in three volumes. The first, with the complete instrumental music, will appear before the end of the year. The hope may be entertained that this important bibliographical undertaking is carried out in conjunction with the *Complete Edition* of Haydn's works recently started by the Austro-American Haydn Society Inc., Vienna-Boston ; it would be a misfortune if these closely related efforts were not co-ordinated.   HANS F. REDLICH.

†*Das Musikleben* deals in Nos. 3 and 4, 51, with this collection, reproducing long quotations from several letters in the German original, as well as a newly-found portrait of Minna Wagner.

II. *THE MUSIC REVIEW'S* FESTIVAL ISSUE

MR's MAY 1951 issue is the most substantial we can remember. Its contents ask for both appreciative and critical comment.

HANS TISCHLER'S analysis of MAHLER'S IMPACT ON THE CRISIS OF TONALITY forms one of the extremely few adult contributions to our undeveloped literature on tonality. But when the author replaces the newish term " progresive tonality "[1] by that of " dramatic key symbolism," " since this trait is not the product of purely musical considerations," one has to voice a decided musicological protest. First of all, no musical procedure is " the product of purely musical considerations," because purely musical considerations aren't. On the other hand, however, every symphonic procedure must satisfy purely musical requirements, must be valid in terms of purely musical considerations, and hence be abstracted into a term of purely musical reference; the extra-musical aspect of musical processes must be examined separately, like the physiological aspect of psychological processes. The history of pure music owes as much to Mahler's progressive tonalities as Mahler's symphonic dramatism owes to the history of tonality. There is, moreover, plenty of dramatic key symbolism (say, in Mozart) that has nothing whatever to do with progressive tonality, and there are plenty of progressive tonalities that have nothing to do with dramatic considerations. In fact, the development of progressive tonality does not by any means start with Mahler ; I have not yet seen recognized the revolutionary role which Schumann—one of Mahler's demonstrable parents—plays in this field: the body of the so-called A minor Quartet's (op. 41's) first movement is in F major ; and Mr. Tischler will agree that if the key scheme of this work owes something to considerations of dramatic symbolism, every sonata tonality does.[2] The evolution of progressive tonality can, of course, be traced far further back ; on the one hand over such movements as the finales of Beethoven's G major Concerto and E minor Quartet, or, on the other hand, over such operatic numbers as *Die Entführung*'s " Romanze," *Figaro*'s " Duettino " and " Marcia," or *Cosi*'s third trio (in which cases Mr. Tischler may indeed justly speak of " dramatic key symbolism "), to the first master of the sonata arch's tonal concentricity himself—Haydn, whose two B minor Quartets (op. 33, No. 1, and op. 64, No. 2) start in D major. It is not, however, this relative major at the beginning that is the ultimate source of progressive tonality, but the tonic major at the end—the 4½ centuries-old Picardy third.[3] In sum, " dramatic key symbolism " is a special aspect of (among other things) a special case of progressive tonality, and our terminology must decide whether it is dealing with music or the motivation of music. That the dramatic aspect of Mahler's symphonism is (i) unusually strong and (ii) unprecedentedly conscious does not mean that its musical aspect is the less " pure," i.e. less self-consistent and, as far as the undefinable but none the less definite laws of musical causality go, less self-determining and self-explanatory.

To MOSCO CARNER'S article, MATYAS SEIBER AND HIS *ULYSSES* —as well as to Seiber's own commentary on his outstanding piece (MS, III/4)— I should like to add that apart from its intentional quotation from Schoenberg's op. 19, the work harbours a hitherto unnoticed, extremely close relation to, amounting to virtual identity with, Schoenberg's thematic thought in the *Ode to Napoleon* (op. 41, composed 1942, first published 1944).[4] I mean the symmetrical tone-row of the (*quasi-*) *scherzo's* (No. 3's) main, fugal section, whose second half—f′′-d′′-db′′-bb′-a′-f♯′—is an inversion of its first half. The relation becomes audible to the twelve-tone-deaf in the upper part of the *Ode*'s bar 47 : g′′-e′′-eb′′-c′′-b′-g♯′-g′-e′ ; if you continue the *arpeggio*-like descending motion of Seiber's row for another 2 notes, i.e., by running again into the 2nd half's first two notes at the octave below (f′-d′), the two thematic units are, transposedly speaking, identical. Such a relationship cannot be chance. Either the *Ode* actually inspired Seiber (who wrote his Cantata in 1946-47), or else, more probably perhaps, he arrived at his row independently of, though *correlatedly to*, the Schoenberg, developing his invention from the same atonal premises. Significantly enough, while Seiber is unaware of the relation in his own description of the Cantata, Carner tells us that the series " came to [Seiber] as an afterthought." The " fore-thought " was, of course, the basic 3-note motif with its interplay of major and minor third ; and, to my ears at any rate, Schoenberg's configuration is an after-thought in much the same way—very much " after " indeed, in that I hear it stretching back, ultimately, as far as the basic motif of the *Drei Klavierstucke* op. 11 : b′-g♯′-g′ etc.! It is quite possible, of course, that it was in fact this motif, which to the receptive is very haunting, that set Seiber's mind unconsciously going on a work whose *Nocturne* was to bear the subtitle *Hommage a Schoenberg.*

To SCHOENBERG himself.

(a) H. F. REDLICH is dancing upon my nerves by his insistence—see May MR's Correspondence—on calling Schoenberg " the veteran champion of the boldest cerebral experimentalism in music." The only two accurate words are " veteran " and " boldest." Schoenberg did not champion his technique ; he had more important things to do, namely, to apply it. It is true that he foresaw the time when, in one form or another, it would be applied by many, but he never persuaded anyone, pupil or advice-seeker, to dodecaphonize. Again and again one hears it said or sees it written that he was intent upon propagating his method of composition and placarding his theories upon it, but in actual fact, as his pupil Dika Newlin, the editor of his recent book *Style and Idea*, has pointed out, " the important thing to keep in mind is that *Schoenberg* [did] *not teach his system.* [Her italics]. When young people, unaware of this fact, hopefully brought him their budding twelve-tone efforts . . . he used to be more irritated than otherwise. While he was . . . completely secure in his own use of the new technique, it seemed to be a matter so personal to him that he found it very difficult to impart advice on the proper use of the method to someone else." (*Schoenberg in America—I*, MS, Vol. I, No. 5, 1949). Nor is it generally realized that the essay on *Composition with Twelve Tones* in *Style and Idea* is Schoenberg's *first on the subject.* If Dr. Redlich is looking for a champion of dodecaphonism, Krenek is his man. Again, there is nothing experimental about Schoenberg's method, at any rate when he himself uses it. It is not a *modus operandi* evolved by trial and error, for there never was any error. The essential characteristic of an experiment is the possibility of an alternative ; none of the developmental stages in his creativity by which Schoenberg arrived at his *discovery* of the twelve-tone method admitted of an alternative : he did not know where it all led him, but his "it" knew, as we now realize, all along. Every single composition of his is, for its developmental stage, the only possible one. He does not try out his ideas ; his ideas tried him out. He passed the trial with honours, the honours—the reward—being the intellectual grasp of his method of composition. With profound understanding, William Hymanson (*Schoenberg's String Trio (1946)*, MR, August, 1950) calls Schoenberg the *prophet* of the twelve-tone technique. I leave it to Dr. Redlich to imagine the prophet at the experimenting table. As for Schoenberg's "cerebrality," it cannot be too strongly stressed that the undoubted power of his intellect did not involve its supremacy. Here MR's reviewer—

(b)—E. H. W. MEYERSTEIN says the rightest thing in the simplest words when, in his notice on *Style and Idea*, sensitively entitled A MASTER'S TESTAMENT, he explains that " the book, in a sense, is a justification of cerebrality, showing at every point that, granted the inspiration, no amount of logical thinking is unnecessary." Granted the inspiration. Dr. Redlich's phrase does not grant it and therefore misleads. Meyerstein's own review, however, is a masterpiece : one of the most exhaustively understanding and most beautiful pieces of appreciation that have ever been written. When I heard that MR's editor had given *Style and Idea* to a reviewer who was not, in my opinion, qualified for this particular task, I was furious. Now I repent.

I should have thought of Schoenberg's own observations on the layman—on certain laymen [my trans.] :—

And what, then, about the layman, who knows nothing of the tabla ture ? Schopenhauer explains mediocrity's respect for the work of art as belief in authority. This is doubtless true of the broad masses. But among laymen I have found individuals whose organs of perception are far sharper than those of most experts, specialists and professionals [als die der meisten Fachleute]. And I know for certain that there are musicians who are more receptive to painting than many painters ; and painters who are more receptive to music than most musicians.

[Harmonielehre.]

And poets. But it remains the exceptional merit of Meyerstein the poet that he fully recognizes Schoenberg the musical genius in Schoenberg the writer. It has to be admitted, of course, that unprofessional judgment, however deeply perceptive, can never be sufficiently technical, i.e., factual. But then, consider the curious facts with which our professionals provide us ! Consider what the chief music critic of Europe's leading newspaper makes Schoenberg say. In an article on *Intuition in Creation : Schoenberg and Sartre* (*The Times*, May 18, 1951), we read :—" [In the lecture on ' Composition with 12 Tones,' reprinted in *Style and Idea*, Schoenberg] first explains why the principle of tonality is exhausted[:] in this his aural psychology may be at fault ..." Far from giving any such explanation, Schoenberg never and nowhere stated or implied that the principle of tonality was in fact exhausted. On the extreme contrary, as Dr. Newlin recalled 2 years ago (in Part II of the above-quoted article, MS, 1/6) " a favourite aphorism of his " was that " there is still plenty of good music to be written in C major." And indeed, when we turn to the music Schoenberg himself composed after taking up residence in Los Angeles, we find that even in his own creative mind the principle of tonality had remained very much alive : the Suite for strings (1934) is in an undodecaphonic G major, the 2nd Chamber Symphony (1940) in E flat minor ; and the Theme and Variations for band (1943) even employ the key signature of G minor. In the Variations on a Recitative for organ (1943) the principle of tonality is immeasurably stronger than that of the twelve-tone method : though the theme contains the twelve notes, they do not function as a tone-row, and the work is quite obviously in D minor, including even the traditional Picardy third at the end of the fugue. In the twelve-tonal *Ode to Napoleon* (1942), too, the principle of tonality (E flat) clearly emerges by the end of the 16th stanza (" He in his fall preserved his pride, And, if a mortal, had as proudly died ! ") and leads the work to an E flat major conclusion. What Schoenberg does in fact explain at the beginning of the essay on *Composition with Twelve Tones* is (i) the disintegration of tonal unity in Wagner and Debussy, and (ii) the " emanicipation " (increasing intelligibility) of the dissonance in Wagner, Strauss, Moussorgsky, Debussy, Mahler, Puccini and Reger. The question of Schoenberg's " aural psychology " does not arise at all : he merely draws attention to hard—i.e., analytically provable—musical facts. So much, then, for a distinguished professional's factuality ; whereas Meyerstein's review does not show the shade of even a factual error.

HANS KELLER.

1Introduced, as he does not say, by Dr. Dika Newlin.

2Outside the fields of sonata on the one hand and drama on the other, Liszt's twelve *Etudes d'exécution transcendante* (1852) transcend the principle of concentric tonal organization, proceeding (or receding) as they do from C major down the circle of fifths (relative minors always included) to B flat minor : a genuine case of progressive tonality.

³After Walther von Stolzing has sung the second stanza of his dream, Hans Sachs gives a beautiful picture of one of the *psychic* sources of progressive tonality and of the deepest and most general of all " dramatic key symbolisms ":

> Ihr schlosset nicht im gleichen Ton :
> Das macht den Meistern Pein ;
> Doch nimmt Hans Sachs die Lehr davon
> Im Lenz wohl müss' es so sein.
> [You close not in the starting key :
> The Masters hate this thing ;
> Hans Sachs though can with you agree,
> It must be so in the Spring.]

" Ton " is an obsolete term for " Tonart," i.e. key : poor old Walther has ventured a dominant cadence. Incidentally, the passage reminds us of Wagner's own contribution to the bursting-open of tonal concentricity.

⁴As does, by the way, Malcolm Arnold's first string Quartet, whose first performance I heard since these lines were set up in type.

Correspondence

KÖLN.

October 6th, 1951.

SIRS,—You will have seen Our Music Critic's article in yesterday's *Times*,* in which he finally buries both Schönberg and Stravinsky (prematurely in the latter case, as I, writing from lively rehearsals of *Oedipus Rex* with the composer, can happily testify). This is the second major interment conducted recently by the *Times*'s Music Critic ; he can now have no serious rivals for the title of the Grand Undertaker of Music.

In this connection, might it not be suitable and rewarding for *Music Survey* to devote an early number to an " Inquest on Inquests," or might this seem premature ?

Yours etc.,

PETER PEARS.

[*Mr. Pears refers to " Two Revolutionaries: Schönberg and Stravinsky," *The Times*, 5th October, 1951.]

16, BELSIZE SQUARE,

N.W.3.

November 19th, 1951.

SIRS,—In your last number some of my earlier recordings are reviewed. Your reviewer, Mr. E. D. Mackerness, seems to misjudge the sound of the basset horns in Mozart's B♭ Adagio for 2 clarinets and 3 basset horns, K.440a. Since we have taken great trouble over this record, obtaining one basset horn especially from Edinburgh, I should be most grateful if you could amend Mr. Mackerness' misconstruction. He writes, " *originally* scored for two clarinets and three basset horns " (my italics), thus implying that we used a different combination, an arrangement. In point of fact, what Mr. Mackerness regards, and criticizes, as the sound of " the lower registers of the clarinets" is actually the sound of the basset horns which have *not* been replaced by any other, perhaps more familiar instruments !

Yours very sincerely,

KARL HAAS.

[It is sad that we find ourselves having published the very kind of review which we strive to banish from the musical earth.—EDS.]

SCHOENBERG

A HUMBLE PETITION AND ADVICE TO ENGLISH CRITICS

SIRS,—The last article by Mr. Eric Blom on Schoenberg, published in *The Observer*, raises no new problems, other than that of its own *raison d'être*—for despite the efforts of Schoenberg's supporters to rid the opposition of certain elementary misapprehensions, the latter have obstinately clung to opinions which differ little from the bewildered and hysterical views expressed in word and deed when the *Five Orchestral Pieces* were performed at the Queen's Hall in 1912. As the generations pass, these and other opinions have become hereditary in academic circles, and it would appear that they are to be accepted, along with Tovey's analyses, as a permanent fixture in the repertoire of the English Critic. It has, perhaps, been found that, like the Dictionary of Quotations, they save time and thought in the writing of obituaries. None the less, things have come to a pretty pass in this country when there is no better way for an aspiring critic to prove his intellectual, moral and political stability to certain musical giants left over from previous generations, than proudly to avow in print his complete inability to understand the works of Arnold Schoenberg.

Mr. Blom's article, although it had the virtue of courtesy denied to some of his colleagues when writing about Schoenberg, reveals a fundamental misconception which should not be allowed unchallenged enshrinement in the British Museum. The basis of his argument is that twelve-note music began as a system and developed into music, instead of beginning as a new musical venture and then being organised *a posteriori* into a system. Such a proposition reveals a lack of acquaintance with the history of twelve-note music in general and Schoenberg in particular, which for my part would make me more than dubious of essaying a full length article on the subject. The criticism of twelve-note music that it arises from a preconceived theory, should have more than a doubt cast upon it after a few moments spent reading Schoenberg's own account of how, having discarded tonality without having consciously put anything in its place, he discovered that he had been employing a primitive form of serial technique. To anyone who still doubts the legitimate birth of twelve-note music, I recommend a study of Schoenberg's later tonal works (notably the 1st Chamber Symphony and the second string Quartet), and their relation, first to the atonal works written before the formulation of the twelve-note system, and then to the subsequent works. It should then be clear that when Schoenberg laid down his principles of composition with twelve notes, he did so on the basis of what had already been achieved in purely musical terms. If this is not " a natural course of evolution " I do not know what is, and the line of continuity becomes more, rather than less, clear if it is followed back through German romanticism to the beginning of chromaticism.

As for Mr. Blom's isolated musical quotation, and his accompanying question as to " whether it is good in itself and likely to be fertile," I would like in turn to ask Mr. Blom whether he could honestly consider the following not unfamiliar theme " good in itself and likely to be fertile." did he not know its origins :

Surely it is unfair to extract a theme (not, it will be noted, a melody), and to ask for judgments thereon ? To criticize a theme *per se* is like judging a future bloom from a handful of seeds piled on a scrap of newspaper. And it is yet more dangerous to discuss, in isolation, the nature of an individual note row, which is the theme of the theme(s) rather than the theme itself. So much then, for Mr. Blom's article. I have selected it as being typical of a school of criticism which, while not committing itself too far, is content to amble along in an aura of genial inaccuracy and second-hand fatuities that are no more a credit to their authors now than they were thirty years ago. Dare I ask that whatever they may feel emotionally about Schoenberg's music, English critics in future attempt to practise a little of the gentle art of IN-VESTIGATION before writing articles for the edification of a public which eagerly imbibes their every word ? Had Mr. Blom cared to discuss the problems of extreme chromaticism as a whole, and criticized Schoenberg's organization of it in terms of acoustics, rather than measured it by the more fallible yard-stick of human comprehension, his article might have done the memory of a great man the honour it deserves. As it is, I have felt bound to cut the article out and place it in an envelope, now almost full, on which is written " Hobby Horses ridden by Eminent English Critics."

Yours sincerely,
DAVID DREW.

Nun, nun ist es mir geworden,
den Mörder selbst zu morden,
in seiner letzten Stunde,
den Stahl in seiner Wunde,
ihm nochs ins Ohr zu schrein :
Triumph ! Triumph ! Triumph !
der Sieg, der Sieg ist mein !

(See footnote † p. 394).

MUSIC SURVEY

(KATHLEEN LIVINGSTON   WILLIAM W. LIVINGSTON   DONALD MITCHELL)

VOL. IV, No. 3   JUNE, 1952

CONTENTS

EDITORS :

DONALD MITCHELL
HANS KELLER

EDITORIAL CORRESPONDENCE should be addressed to the EDITORS, MUSIC SURVEY, OAKFIELD SCHOOL, WEST DULWICH, LONDON, S.E.21. Annual Subscription, including postage, 11s. U.S.A. $2.50.

All enquiries relating to advertising space in this journal should be made to MUSIC SURVEY at the above address.

A Bedside Editorial for the B.B.C.

THE unexpected number of Schoenberg letters has necessitated the exclusion from this Schoenberg issue of all the reviews of Schoenberg concerts, books and records which we originally planned, as well as of our report on the Third Programme's Schoenberg series which, however, we have dealt with elsewhere.* The one review which we had commissioned before it became clear that space was getting short appears on p. 491, while the one talk in the B.B.C.'s series itself which will turn out to be of lasting value appears on pp. 472-489. For the rest, it remains for us to express once more our unreserved disgust at the utter mismanagement of this series which, by and large, was a protracted amateur performance in the worst sense, packed with factual ignorance, musical idiocy and incomprehensible interpretations of the most alarming order, and presided over by a General Editor (Michael Tippett) less than whose knowledge about Schoenberg even the B.B.C. would find it difficult to procure. At the same time—and this makes matters all the more distasteful—the series could be perfectly sure of safely sailing ahead, since there are only very few people who really know something about Schoenberg anyway, and the ignorant always prefer to listen to the ignorant. We shall no doubt be accused of the ' sour grapes ' line of argument, but the basic question is whether the grapes were in fact sour. Besides, one of us (Keller) had to spend many a working hour on gratis advice and information he had to give in reply to backstage enquiries from actual and potential contributors to the series ; no doubt Erwin Stein, the great Schoenberg expert who was not asked to contribute at all, had similar, if not worse experiences. That was when the grapes turned bitter.

Since we do not know what happens behind the scenes of the B.B.C.'s musical efforts, we, like the people in an autocratic state, have to depend on rumours. We don't know the names of the so-called listeners-in who report on the competence of performances. We don't know the names of that secret society, the Reading Panel, and therefore have no means of judging its score-reading abilities. But we hear insistent rumours that both Seiber's *Ulysses* and Searle's ' Poem ' for 22 strings were originally rejected by the Reading Panel because they weren't good enough.

It is for the B.B.C. to tell us what actually happened. If it doesn't, we shall know that those rumours are not altogether wrong. But

*The B.B.C.'s Victory over Schoenberg, by Hans Keller, with a footnote by Donald Mitchell, *The Music Review*, May, 1952.

We are grateful to Messrs. Rockliff for lending this portrait of Schoenberg which appeared for the first time in Norman Demuth's *Musical Trends in the 20th Century*.

sooner or later the B.B.C. will speak. Two or three years ago it may still have been possible for the slow-witted to regard us as the bad boys of music criticism and not to bother. Today, this journal's high prestige among composers, among musicians and musicologists all over the world, and our increasingly bad reputation among the common music critics, makes ours more than one voice in the wilderness.

Unpublished Schoenberg Letters:
Early, Middle and Late

Annotated, and the German letters translated,

BY HANS KELLER

The letters are arranged in chronological order. They are the property of their respective addressees, with whose kind permission they are here published for the first time. The original texts are faithfully reproduced, without any changes in orthography or punctuation. In the translations of the German letters, editing has been confined to a minimum.

We hope to publish a further batch of Schoenberg letters to Oskar Adler, Erwin Stein, Humphrey Searle, myself and others in a future issue.

Mrs. Marietta Werndorff, *née* Jonasz, widow of a Viennese orthopaedic surgeon, is a pianist who emigrated with her husband to America after World War I. She was a friend of Schoenberg. Items (1)-(7) are addressed to her ; the first antedates her marriage.

(1)   [Postcard]

[Rubber stamp :] Arnold Schönberg
                         Wien IX, Lichtensteinstrasse 68/70.
[Undated.—1907?]
[Gothic handwriting in ink.]

Verehrtes Fräulein, Ich muss Ihnen nochmals herzlichst danken für Ihre Mitwirkung bei meinem Schüler-Konzert. Es war wirklich ausserordentlich, was Sie in so kurzer Zeit geleistet haben und Sie können mit sich sehr zufrieden sein.
    Nochmals herzlichen Dank und beste Empfehlung

Ihr ergebener
Arnold Schönberg.

Translation :

> My dear Fräulein, I have to thank you again most cordially for your participation in my pupils' concert. It was really extraordinary how much you achieved in so short a time and you can be very pleased with yourself.
>
> Once more, cordial thanks and my best regards.
>
> > Yours sincerely,
> > Arnold Schönberg.

Item (2) is an undated postcard (stamp and postmark detached, apparently by Schoenberg himself) which Mrs. Werndorff had written to Schoenberg at Vienna, XIII., Hietzinger-Hauptstrasse 113, a house then owned by my mother, where he occupied a flat from 1910 to the summer of 1911, when he moved to Berlin-Zehlendorf. Schoenberg returned the card after striking out certain words and letters (below in double brackets) and inserting others instead (below in italics), thus transforming the text into a communication *from him to Mrs. Werndorff*. His red-pencilled alterations also include underlinings :

(2)   [Schoenberg's words, as Mrs. Werndorff's text, in Roman handwriting.]

Sehr verehrte Frau Werndorf
((Geehrter Herr Schönberg)) !

Ich weiss   *Sie*
((Sie wissen)) doch wohl, dass ((ich)) Mittwoch wie
            ?   *mir*   *en*
verabredet statt um 4 Uhr um ½5 bei ((Ihnen))   war .
Ich   *ich*
((Sie)) habe((n)) daran vergessen, ((Sie)) habe((n)) aber
                          Ihnen
auch daran vergessen ((mir)) ein paar Worte darüber zu
sagen. —

> > Mit Grüssen
> > *Arnold Schönberg*
> > ((Etta Werndorff))

((Ich spiele heute Abend Dr. Hertzka die Sonate vor.))

Translation :

My dear Mrs. Werndorf
((Dear Mr. Schönberg)),

$\qquad\qquad\qquad\quad$ *you* $\qquad\qquad$ *me*
((You)) doubtless know that ((I)) called on ((you)) on
$\qquad\qquad\qquad\qquad\qquad\quad$?
Wednesday, as arranged, at <u>half past four</u> instead of four

$\qquad$ *I* $\qquad\qquad\qquad\qquad\qquad\qquad$ *I*
o'clock. ((You)) forgot all about it, and ((you)) forgot,
too, to apologize with a few words.

$\qquad\qquad\qquad\qquad\qquad$ With regards,
$\qquad\qquad\qquad\qquad\qquad$ *Arnold Schönberg*
$\qquad\qquad\qquad\qquad\qquad$ ((Etta Werndorff))
((I'm going to play the sonata to Dr. Hertzka tonight.))

Item (3), an undated letter in Gothic handwriting (ink) with certain
words in Roman handwriting for the apparent purpose of emphasis
(below in italics or, according to Schoenberg's lettering, in heavier
type), enlarges further upon the same subject. The first (right) and
fourth (left) pages of the 4-page letter are reproduced in facsimile.

(3) $\quad$ Liebe, liebe, liebe Frau Doktor !
$\qquad$ Wess klagen Sie sich so hart an ?
$\qquad$ Dass Sie statt um 4 Uhr (wie verabredet ?)
$\qquad\quad$ um ½5 bei uns waren ?
$\qquad$ Das hätte ich Ihnen ja weiter gar nicht übel genommen,
da ich schon damit rechne.
$\qquad\quad$ Und nun :
$\quad$ auf eine offene,
$\qquad\qquad$ offene Karte ! ! ! ! ! ! ! ! ! ! ! ! !
$\quad$ schreiben Sie so
$\qquad\qquad$ Schreckliches ! ? ! ?
$\qquad\qquad\qquad$ Ach !

Wie hart strafen Sie mich für Ihre Un-
pünktlichkeit ! Oh ! . . . oh, Jammer !
Oh . . . .
$\qquad$ Ach ! . . . . .
Oder sollte es vielleicht sein :

$\qquad\qquad\qquad\qquad$ **Die Strafe**
für meine Vergesslichkeit . . . . ?
Ach . . . .
$\qquad$ Oh . . . . .

451

Ich schwerer Sünder,
   alle Qualen der Hölle
sind zu gering als Busse für mein
                  Ver-Bre-chen !*
A c h ! . . . .
                  O h . . . . !

Und denken Sie :
   Ich hatte vergessen, dass Sie um
4 Uhr kommen wollten.
   Und denken Sie warum :
      Weil Berg und ich verabredet hatten
dass er mich noch verständigt, ob Sie kommen
   Und denken Sie :
      Ich wurde nicht verständigt ! !
   Und nun denken Sie :
Ich hatte aber auch ausserdem vergessen !

         A c h . . . . . !
                  O h . . . . !

Und nun denken Sie :
   Wie wäre das also gewesen, wenn
Sie wirklich pünktlich um
      ¼4 Uhr bei uns gewesen wären,
wie Sie zuerst geschrieben haben ?
   Wir sind nämlich erst nach
      ¼4 Ur weggegangen
Weil ich vergessen hatte :
   Ach . . . .
            Oh . . *!*
Und denken Sie :
   Eine grause Mär berichtet :
   Einmal hätte ich,
                  der W Ü T E R I C H†

*This syllabication does not only serve slow motion emphasis, but also, with the help of the capital " B," an isolation of " brechen." " Verbrechen " means crime, " brechen " break, and the prefix " ver-" has a similar connotation as the prefix " for-."

†Schoenberg writes this word, in itself obsolete (meaning a bloodthirsty villain), in stressedly antiquated, Gothic sham calligraphy.

14 (vierzehn) leibliche, leib-
haftige Personen, menschlichen
Geschlechtes zu mir bestellt
und hätte sie aufsitzen lassen.
    So bin ich—dies mein
Porträt ! ! !
Ohhhhhhhhhh . . . ! Achchchchchchchch . . . !
Wie schlecht wird sich das in meiner Biographie
ausnehmen, wenn die Nachwelt dadurch mein wahres
Karakterbild erfährt !
    Ich bin
    zerknirscht

        ge-brrrochen

    zermuerrrrbt

        rrruiniert

    lebensueberdruessig

    tiefungluecklich

    verloren
                            weiter geht das Papier nicht !‡
        unrettbar Ach ! Oh !

Translation :
    Dear, dear, dear Frau Doktor !
    Whereof do you accuse yourself so severely ?
    That, instead of four o'clock (as arranged ?),
    You called on us at half past four ?
    This I would have taken in good part, since I have
    come to expect it.
            And now—
    Upon an open,
            open card ! ! ! ! ! ! ! ! ! ! ! !
    You write something so
            Awful ! ? ! ?
            Alas !
    ‡For the purpose of parodistic Romantic Irony, Schoenberg writes the
last line (see facsimile) so close to the bottom end of the notepaper that only
the upper parts of the words appear on it, and adds his marginal comment on
the right hand side.

How severely you punish me for your
unpunctuality !   Oh ! ... O misery, !
　　Oh . . . .
　　　　　Alas ! . . . . .
Or should it perchance be
　　　　　　　　The punishment
For my forgetfulness . . . . ?
　　Alas . . . .
　　　　　Oh . . . . .
Wicked sinner, I,
　　All the torments of hell
Are too slight an atonement for my

　　　　　　　　　　Mis-Deed !

A l a s ! . . . .

　　　　　　　　　O h . . . . . !

　　And just think—
　　　　I had forgotten that you wanted to come at
Four o'clock.
　　　　And just think why :
　　　　　Because Berg and I had arranged
That he would advise me whether you were still coming.
　　　　And just think—
　　　　　I was not advised ! !
　　　　And now just think—
I had forgotten anyway !

　　　　A l a s . . . . . !

　　　　　　　　O h . . . . !

　　And now just think
　　　　What then would have happened if
You had really arrived punctually at
　　　　Half past three,
as you wrote in the first place ?
　　　　For you must know we left only after
　　　　Half past three,
Because I had forgotten :
　　　　Alas . . . .
　　　　　　Oh . . /

454

And now just think—
Horrible tidings has it
That I,
   the BLOOD-THIRSTY VILLAIN,
Once appointed to see 14 (fourteen) incarnate,
bodily persons of human sex*, and that
I left them in the lurch.
  Thus am I—this is my portrait ! ! !
Ohhhhhhhhhh . . . ! Alassssssss . . . !
How ill will this show up in my biography, when
posterity thus discovers the true picture
of my character !
     I am

  contrite

   brrroken

 crrrrushed

   rrruined

 sick of life

 deeply wretched

 lost

   past saving Alas ! Oh !
       The notepaper doesn't
        go any further !

  How Schoenberg came to use, in a letter of 1916 (item (4)), the
old rubber stamp of his address prior to 1910 (a house in which
Zemlinsky had also occupied a flat), is a mystery which remains to
be solved by those who have nothing better to do. From December
1915 till September 1916, and again from July 1917 to October 1917,

*This intentionally wrong translation tries to retain some of the point of
Schoenberg's subtle and complex pun which in itself is untranslatable.
" Geschlecht " does not only mean sex and gender, but also species, race, stock
and generation. But in this context, the phrase " menschlichen Geschlechtes "
immediately conjures up the usual " männlichen Geschlechtes " (i.e. of male
sex), so that inevitably the picture arises in the reader's mind of mankind being
divided into two sexes, the human(e) and the inhuman.

Schoenberg was in the army ; at that time he lived in Hietzing (though not at the address of items (2) and (3)). Did he also use his old flat, or perhaps Zemlinsky's ? Mrs. Werndorff's explanation, if any, will not arrive soon enough for inclusion in this article.

(4)   [Card (covered on both sides) in envelope.]
        [Rubber stamp as *sub* (1).]
        [Gothic handwriting in ink.]

16/1. 1916.

Liebe Frau Werndorf, Ich freue mich sehr Ihnen was Angenehmes sagen zu können. Sie sehen also ich bin wirklich nicht boshaft, sondern nur sachlich. Sie haben wirklich ausgezeichnet gespielt und (was ein *sehr hohes* Lob ist) vielleicht *noch besser* begleitet. Klavierspielen kann ja ein Frauenzimmer bald. Eigentlich, wenns eine nicht kann, ists ja meistens nur so eine Art Versehen, oder Vergesslichkeit. Begleiten aber können die meisten Männer nicht, dazu muss man Musiker sein. Sie sind also : *Musiker.* Sind Sie jetzt zufrieden mit mir ? Ja ? herzl. Gruss und auf Wiedersehen Ihr Arnold Schönberg.

Translation :

Dear Mrs. Werndorf, I am very glad to be able to tell you something which will please you. You can see, then, that I really am not mischievous, but merely factual. You really played excellently and—*very great* praise, this—accompanied perhaps *even better*. Piano playing, after all, is something which a female can easily do. In point of fact, when there is one who can't, it's really in most cases a kind of oversight, or forgetfulness. But accompanying is something which most men are incapable of ; for that purpose one has to be a musician. You, then, are a *musician.* Are you satisfied with me now ? Yes ? Kind regards and *au revoir*, Yours, Arnold Schönberg.

Item (5) is a full face photo of Schoenberg which he dates and inscribes in Gothic handwriting (ink) :

(5) 5/6. 1917
    Arnold Schönberg
        wie er geleibt und gelebt hat, denn Leben
        kann man das jetzt nicht nennen.

ARNOLD SCHOENBERG   116 N. ROCKINGHAM AVENUE   LOS ANGELES 4Y CALIFORNIA

Dear Mr Keller, you have my book and
I assume you know, what it its
value — or not?

Enclosed you find a very
unpleasant review, written by
one of these non-musicians,
who look in my music only
for the twelve notes — not realizing
in the least its musical contents
expression and merits. He is very
stupid and insolent and would
deserve a treatment like that
you can give him.

I hope you are interested!
Now sharpen your pen.

Cordially yours
Arnold Schoenberg

See Item 11

Sie sollen mich so wie in meiner Biographie
ausnehmen, wenn die Nachwelt dadurch
mein wahres Karakterbild erfasst!

Ich bin

zerknirscht

ge - brrrochen

zermürrrrbt

rrruiniert

lebensüberdrüssig

tiefunglücklich

verloren

unrettbar

See Item 3

liebe, liebe, liebe Frau Doktor!

Wie klagen Sie sich so hart an?

Daß Sie statt um 4 Uhr (wäre verabredet?)

um ½ 5 bei uns waren?

Das hätte ich Ihnen ja weiter gar nicht übel ge-

nommen, da ich schon damit rechne.

Nur um:

auch eine offene,

offene Karte !!!!!!!!!!!

schreiben Sie — so

Schreckliches !?!?

Ach!

Zu solch starker Rücksicht für Ihre Un-

pünktlichkeit! Ach! ... Oh, Jammer!

Oh ....

ach! .....

Oder sollte es vielleicht sein:

Die Strafe

für meine ....?

Ach ...

Ach .....

Translation :

    June 5, 1917,
    Arnold Schönberg,
        exactly as he looked and lived, for you can't
        call it a life now.

This joke is not completely translatable ; " X wie er leibt und lebt "
means (to vulgarize and hence remain equally idiomatic) " the spit
of X " and has no perfect tense, though Schoenberg forms one for
his purpose.

Item (6) is a letter written on the notepaper of the William Taylor
Hotel, San Francisco. By now Schoenberg writes his German in
Roman handwriting, and he has changed the spelling of his name.
For the first time, incidentally, he spells Mrs. Werndorff's name
correctly, the previous mis-spellings (see items (2) and (4)) having
no doubt been due to the fact that " Dorf " means something
(village), whereas " Dorff " doesn't.

(6) [Block letters
    in ink :]

    ARNOLD SCHOENBERG   5/III. 1935
    5860 CANYON COVE
    HOLYWOOD CALIF.

    Liebe Frau Dr. Werndorff, wegen eines Konzertes hier,
erhielt ich heute Ihren Brief. Wir sind schon seit März
vorigen Jahres von Boston weg (nach New York) und
seit October in Hollywood. Auf der Reise dachte ich
daran, Sie in Council Bluffs zu sehen, hatte aber Ihre
Adresse nicht mit. Von Boston aus habe ich Ihnen
seinerzeit geschrieben. Und auch einem Musiker, der
sich, wahrscheinlich durch Sie veranlasst, wegen Stunden
an mich gewendet hat (wahrscheinlich war ich ihm zu
teuer).

    In Lincoln (Nebraska) ein Konzert zu dirigieren, bin
ich gerne bereit. Doch könnte ich es nur (Reisekosten-
frage ! !) tun, wenn ich in der Nähe noch wenigstens 3-4
andere Konzerte hätte (etwa höchstens in 12 Stunden
Entfernung). Das Mindesthonorar wäre $500-600.

Für Ihr Konzert kommt auf diese Weise mein Brief viel zu spät. Doch werden Sie gewiss noch so viel von mir gewusst haben, als das Publikum von mir zu wissen wünscht.

Wir sind sehr zufrieden in Hollywood. Vor Allem wegen des Klimas, denn ich musste Boston, dessen Klima mich beinahe umgebracht hat, verlassen, um mein Leben zu retten. Aber ich finde auch sonst dort viel Interesse und sehr viele Schüler und werde im Sommer an der Southern Cal. University einen Sommerchair besetzen und einen 6-wöchigen Kurs halten.—Im Herbst soll ich an die Juilliard-School nach New York, zögere aber noch wegen des Klimas !

So: nun schreiben auch Sie uns einmal Ausführliches von Ihnen und Ihrem Mann.

Viele herzliche Grüsse Ihnen beiden, auch von meiner Frau

Ihr

Arnold Schoenberg

Wissen Sie, dass wir eine kleine Tochter, die im Mai drei Jahre alt wird, haben ?

Translation :

March 5, 1935.

Dear Mrs. Werndorff, Today I received your letter regarding a concert here. We left Boston (for New York) as early as March last year, and since October we have been in Hollywood. On the journey I thought of seeing you in Council Bluffs, but I did not have your address on me. From Boston I wrote you at the time ; also to a musician who, probably at your instigation, approached me for lessons (probably I was too expensive for him).

I should be glad to conduct a concert in Lincoln (Nebraska). But I could only do it (a question of travel expenses!!) if I had at least 3-4 other concerts close by (say, 12 hours' distance at the outside). My minimal fee would be $500-600.

For your concert* my letter comes much too late now . However, I am sure you will still have known as much about me as the public wants to know about me.

We are very happy in Hollywood, above all because of the climate, for I had to leave Boston whose climate almost killed me, in order to save my life. But apart from that I find a great deal of interest there and very many pupils ; and in summer I shall occupy a summer-chair at the Southern Cal. University and give a six-weeks' course. In autumn I am supposed to teach at the Julliard School in New York, but as yet I hesitate because of the climate !†

Well then, now you, too, write us some time all about yourself and your husband.

Many cordial greetings to both of you, from my wife too,

Yours,

Arnold Schoenberg

Do you know that we have a little daughter who will be three in May ?

Item (7) is a printed notice Schoenberg sent out to his friends, ready, it seems, for whichever astrologer it may concern.

(7)   January 27, 1941, at 10:02 p.m.

a Son

has been born to the

very happy

ARNOLD SCHOENBERG FAMILY

We will call him

LAWRENCE ADAM

116 N. ROCKINGHAM AVENUE
BRENTWOOD PARK
LOS ANGELES, CALIFORNIA
PHONE : ARIZONA 35077

*Apparently a lecture-recital.

†Schoenberg, who was suffering from asthma, eventually declined this position, but he retained the Alchin chair of composition at the University of Southern California for one year. Thereafter, in autumn, 1936, he was appointed Professor of Music at the University of California, Los Angeles, from which post he retired in 1944 (see item (8)) as Professor Emeritus.

459

Erwin Stein, once the Benjamin of the old Schoenberg *garde,* is now the earliest and most thorough Schoenberg pupil alive, as well as a heavily authorized exponent of Schoenbergian thought.

(8) [Rubber stamp :] Arnold Schoenberg
116 N. Rockingham Avenue

[Deletion :] ▆▆ Los Angeles, Calif.
Phone ARizona 35077

[Typed addition:] Zone 24
[Red-pencilled circle around this address. Underneath, in the margin, Schoenberg writes in red pencil :]
note the little change in my adress. Los Angeles is now divided in zones and the post offices requires this form of the adress
[Typescript :]

November 22, 1943

Mr. Erwin Stein, 100 Cornwall Gardens, London S.W.7
or : c.o. Boosey and Hawkes
295 Regent Street
London W.

Dear Erwin : first let me thank you and Rankl for your cable congratulating me to my 69th birthday. I was very pleased to hear from you, because, as I had no reply to my letter from October 1942 (forty two ! ! !—quite a time) I was affraid you did not receive it. Have you got it ? If not I will send you a copy.

I was always thinking if you would have received my letter, you would have answered, because I asked you to try whether you could not record your performance of my Pierrot Lunaire or of others of my compositions.

I teach at present my last semester at the University of California. One must retire with seventy. But I have half a year of leave of absence to my credit, thus at the end of February I will teach the last time.

I think I have taught enough. It will be more than 45 years. But I intend to write now a few textbooks and finish —if possible my opera " Moses and Aroon " and the " Jakobsleiter." I have begun a textbook on counterpoint. It should be in thre volumes. First: Preliminary excercises;

second : Multiple counterpoint and contrapuntal compositions ; third : Counterpoint in the homophonic compositions of the ninetienth century (about 1770 to the present time). This last volume, for which I have made a good outline several years ago, will be something entirely new. At least I know of no book about that.

I have finished my piano concerto the last day of 1942. Since then I have written a piece : Theme and Variations for wind band and a version for symphony orchestra of the same. Besides I have worked on the counterpoint.

About my family : We are at present all well. Of course there are often flu's, as it is with children. I could be better if I would not smoke. My wife has much work to do, because we have no servant—there are practically none. I help dishwashing and preparing the breakfast.

Let me soon hear from you and your family.

Tell Rankl to write once. Do you know his adress ? Do you see Dr. Dent ?* Give him my best greetings.

Many cordial greetings from all of us to you and your family, and I hope to hear from you now soon again.

Most cordially, yours
Arnold Schoenberg

Upon the occasions of his 70th and 75th birthdays, Schoenberg sent printed letters of thanks to his congratulators. The letter of 1949 we have published in our Winter issue of that season (Vol. II, No. 3). Item (9) is the 1944 one, addressed, in this instance, to Dr. Oskar Adler, himself a musician and thinker of genius, and Schoenberg's first teacher and quartet leader† as well as his oldest and perhaps (as, *inter alia*, items (10),(12)and (13) tend to indicate) his best friend. The italicized passages show Schoenberg's penned additions and his pencilled address :

*i.e. E. J. Dent.

†See Schoenberg, A., *Rückblick*, in *Stimmen* No. 16, Berlin, 1949.— Incidentally, Prof. W. H. Rubsamen's reference to Dr. Adler in his article on *Schoenberg in America* (*The Musical Quarterly*, New York, October, 1951, p. 488, is without any factual foundation whatsoever, though Michael Tippett used this misinformation in his last broadcast on Schoenberg. The matter will be rectified in a forthcoming issue of *The Musical Quarterly*, where Prof. P. H. Lang (its Editor) has also promised me to take care of my correction of the date of Schoenberg's conversion, on which Rubsamen is wrong too. Meanwhile I have discovered one or two further factual mistakes in that article (which otherwise is highly interesting and informative). I propose to correct these, together with H. H. Stuckenschmidt's recent factual errors (*Arnold Schönberg*, Zürich, 1951, again an often valuable effort), in a separate note.

(9) *Dr. Oscar Adler*   *116, N. Rockingham Aven.*
                                    Los-Angeles
                                    California U.S.A.

Dear old Friend :   Los Angeles, California
[Schoenberg here changes his   October 3, 1944
lower case " f " into a capital
one.]

For more than a week I tried composing a letter of thanks to those who congratulated me on the occasion of my seventieth birthday. Still I did not succeed : it is terribly difficult to produce something if one is conceited enough to believe that everybody expects something extraordinary from you at an occasion like this.

But in fact the contrary might be true : at this age, if one is still capable of giving once in a while a sign of life, everybody might consider this already as a satisfactory accomplishment. I acknowledged this when my piano concerto was premiered and to my great astonishment so many were astonished that I still have something to tell. Or perhaps, that I do not yet stop telling it—or that I am still not wise enough to suppress it—or to learn finally to be silent at all ?

Many recommend : " Many happy returns ! "
Thank you, but will this help ?
Will I really become wiser this way ?
I cannot promise it, but let us hope.

Most sincerely with many thanks, yours

Arnold Schoenberg
Arnold Schoenberg

It is a pity I do not know your address. I know you must also celebrate your 70th birthday. I tried to reach you through Hans Nachod.† I hope he knows where you live. I think you are a few weeks older than I. Anyway : my most hearty congratulations and as a wish : that we meet soon again I‡ Your old friend Arnold.

†Schoenberg's cousin. See MS, Summer, 1950.
‡They never did.

462

Item (10) is an air letter in dictated typrescript, as the initials
" R.H. " (Richard Hoffmann, Schoenberg's secretary) in the left
bottom corner show. The double-bracketed words are struck out by
Schoenberg's pen and replaced, in his Roman handwriting, by the
italicized words.

(10) Arnold Schoenberg
116 N. Rockingham Ave.
Los Angles 24, California.

Herrn Dr. Oskar Adler   2. Juli, 1949.
88 Abbey Road
London N.W.8.

Lieber guter, alter Freund,

von Dir

So lange habe ich keine Adresse ((für Dich)) gehabt und
nun ist endlich die Gelegenheit gekommen, dass ich Dir
schreiben kann. Wie geht es Dir ? Ich habe gehört, dass Du
noch immer viel Quartett spielst, was ich leider seit langem
nicht mehr tue und ich bewundere Deine Aktivität. Wir
sind ja gleichaltrig und Du wirst auch heuer 75, oder bist
Du es schon ?

Leider ist meine Gesundheit, wenigstens augenblicklich,
oder seit den letzten fünf Jahren, nicht so, dass ich mich
sehr viel freuen kann. Viel Tage wo ich eigentlich nicht
arbeitsfähig bin und lieber ausruhen sollte. Immerhin
arbeite ich doch noch einiges und habe einiges zustande
gebracht :—ich habe ein Buch fertig, ein neues,
theoretisches, das den Titel " Structural Functions of the
Harmony " hat ; und ich habe ein Kontrapunktbuch zu
einem so grossen Teil fertig, dass ich es in einem viertel oder
halben Jahr fertig machen könnte. Aber ich habe keinen
Verleger für alle diese Sachen. Wir sind also nicht mehr
Oesterreich oder Deutschland, wo man aus dem Verlag
eines solchen Werkes nicht so viel Wesens gemacht hat.

Hörst Du manchmal Konzerte ? Hast Du also einige
meiner letzteren Werke gehört ? Lass mich einmal hören
wie Du dazu stehst. Ueberhaupt, schreibe Du mir doch
auch einmal.

Also, ich will lieber heute kurz sein und erwarte, dass Du mir doch noch einmal schreibst.

Mit vielen, vielen herzlichen Grüssen,
Dein alter Freund,
Arnold Schoenberg.

R.H.

Translation :   July 2, 1949.

Dear, good, old friend,

For such a long time I have been without your address, and now, at last, the opportunity has arrived for me to write to you. How are you ? I hear you are still playing quartets frequently; I haven't been playing for a long time past and I admire your activity. Indeed, we are coeval and you, too, will be 75 this year, or are you already ?

Unfortunately my state of health does not afford me very much joy, at least for the moment, or rather since 5 years. There are many days when I am not really able to work and had better rest. Nevertheless, I still work on a few things and have achieved one or two results :—I have a book ready, a new and theoretical one entitled " Structural Functions of the Harmony " ; and I have completed so much of a book on counterpoint that I could finish the whole in a quarter or half a year. But I have no publisher for all these things : we are no longer in Austria or Germany, where they didn't make so much of a fuss about publishing such a work.

Do you sometimes listen to concerts? In other words, have you heard some of my later works ? Let me know your attitude to them some time. Altogether, please do write me too.

Well, I'd rather be short today and I look forward to your writing me some day after all.

With many, many cordial greetings,
Your old friend,

R.H.   Arnold Schoenberg

Items (11), (12), (13) and (14) are from the last six months (and three days, to be exact) of Schoenberg's life. Items (11), (12), and the latter part of (13) are probably among the very few letters of this period in his own handwriting. The history of item (11), an undated air mail letter posted on January 10, 1951 and given in facsimile, began with Schoenberg's sending me a copy of his *Style and Idea* (1950), with a dedication, upon its publication—the first sign that he had taken note of my writings. I was just leaving for the Continent and remember writing him a note of thanks from the boat, adding that I would give him a detailed impression of the book when I had read it. Under the material pressure of a freelance existence, this remained an empty promise. Why the dedication as well as item (11) are in (Schoenberg's) English I do not know ; perhaps he assumed from my English writings that this was my mother-tongue. But then, item (8) is in English too.

(11) [Print :]
ARNOLD   SCHOENBERG   116   N.   ROCKINGHAM   AVENUE
LOS ANGELES 24 CALIFORNIA

> [" 24 " is struck out by Schoenberg
> and replaced by " 49."]

[Handwriting in ink :]
Dear Mr. Keller, you have my book and I assume you know, what it* its value—or not ?

Enclosed you find a very unpleasant review, written by one of these non-musicians, who look in my music only for the twelve notes—not realizing in the least its musical contents, expression and merits. He is very stupid and insolent and would deserve a treatment like that you can give him.

I hope you are interested !

Now sharpen your pen.

> Cordially yours
> Arnold Schoenberg

It is a sad thought that Schoenberg had to send this letter to Europe, and to a man personally unknown to him. Curiously enough, it arrived at the time of the completion of my article on *Schoenberg and the Men of the Press* (MS, March 1951). The reviewer in question is not only a musicologist of international repute but also one of those whom their colleagues regard as twelve-tone experts. I wired back to Schoenberg, "PEN SHARPENED," and immediately proceeded to apply the radical treatment required. I was in time for Schoenberg to see the published result before he died.

*Obviously " is." Apparently (see facsimile) Schoenberg was about to write " what its value is " (which would have corresponded to German syntax) and then decided on a transposition for the sake of what he thought was better English.

Item (12), a letter to Dr. Adler, was started on the day on which item (11) was posted (and probably written). Editorial scissors have been applied to passages of a private, personal and intimate nature, and also to the names of two contemporary executants because it would be unfair to let them be criticized by observations which Schoenberg never intended to be published ; Dr. Adler and I have moreover agreed that Schoenberg's choice of these two examples of what he had in mind was not the happiest. The cuts are indicated by 4 dots in the case of one or more sentences, and 3 dots in the case of words and phrases.

(12) [Print :]

ARNOLD   SCHOENBERG   116   N.   ROCKINGHAM   AVENUE
LOS ANGELES 24 CALIFORNIA

[" 24 " is struck out by Schoenberg and replaced by " 49."]

[Roman handwriting in ink :]

10. Jänner, 1951

Lieber guter alter Freund, es freut mich ausserordentlich, dass deine Astrologie nun endlich gedruckt wird. Du hast so viel Wertvolles geschrieben und das sollte alles bekannt werden. Kann dein junger Freund Keller nicht einen englischen Verleger dafür interessieren. Du hast ja auch über Harmonie geschrieben. ....

20/II. .... —*dieser Brief liegt nun so lange hier und ich bin aus 1000 Gründen nicht dazu gekommen ihn zu vollenden. Hauptsächlich Gesundheitsstörungen, aber auch ... und zudem jede Woche wenigstens ein Verlangen nach einem Artikel oder nach einem Interview—etc.

.... Es ist vor allem die grosse Konfusion der Tempovorschriften (Allegro, Andante, Presto etc), die äusserst unbestimmt sind. Im Allgemeinen scheint es mir, dass Beethoven wirklich Schnelligkeitsgrade damit meint. Wenn man aber bedenkt, dass er Allegro energico oder Andante cantabile anwendet, so werden das doch Charakteranweisungen. Und nun gar, wenn man seine Metronomzahlen vergleicht und sieht, dass er Menuette von (ich glaube) [einer Viertel pro Sekunde]† bis [zu einer Dreiviertel pro Sekunde]† vorschreibt, so zerstört das

*Schoenberg's dash, indicating the lapse of a month and 10 days (see his date in the margin).

†Schoenberg gives, of course, his metronome indications in the usual way, i.e. in musical notation. For the printer's sake, I have changed them into (the shortest possible) words.

jeden Versuch einer einheitlichen Erklärung. Das ist sowohl hinsichtlich Schnelligkeit als auch Charakter zu sehr verschieden.

Sich nach den kleintsten Notenwerten zu richten, ist vollkommener Unsinn, heute, wo die " grossen " Künstler, wie ... (und sogar ...) unbedingt wie irrsinnig zu laufen beginnen, wenn schnelle Passagen kommen. [To this sentence Schoenberg adds a footnote :] Die kleinen Noten im Grundtempo sind ihnen nicht schnell genug, um ihre brillante Technik zu zeigen[.]

Ich habe daran gedacht, aus dem motivischen Inhalt Schlüsse zu ziehen. Doch auch das ist sehr schwer. Ich habe den Ausdruck " Inhaltsschwere " angewendet, glaube aber nicht, dass dieser Begriff einen Masstab liefern kann. Wenigstens nicht ohne weitgehende Modificationen.

Es scheint mir eine der Hauptschwierigkeiten verursacht zu sein, durch die überstarke Betonung der guten Taktteile (1 und 3 in 4/4). Das steht jeder guten Phrasierung im Wege, die ja ihre eigenen Betonungsansprüche macht. In einer Phrase sollte nur *eine* Betonung zu finden sein. Ausgenommen, wenn es sich um eine besondere Charakteristik handelt.

Ich würde gerne wissen wollen, was du darüber denkst. Nochmals : Ich glaube, das der Motiv-Inhalt mit dem Gewicht zu tun hat und damit mit dem Tempo.

Viele herzlichste Grüsse
Dein

26.II.1951.   Arnold Schoenberg.

Translation :

January 10, 1951.

Dear good old friend, I am overjoyed that your Astrology† is at last being printed. You have written so many valuable things and these should all become known. Can't your young friend Keller interest a British publisher in them?‡ You have of course written on Harmony too ! ....

Feb. 20: .... This letter has now been lying about for such a long time and for a thousand reasons I have not found time

† See item (13) and its translation.
‡ Ourselves. As previously and somewhat prematurely announced, a forthcoming issue will contain excerpts from Adler's *Critique of Pure Music.*

to finish it. Mainly on account of my health, but also because of ... ; besides, every week I get at least one request for an article or an interview, etc.

.... [At the end of these omitted sentences, Schoenberg turns to matters interpretational which apparently had been broached by Dr. Adler :] Above all it is the great confusion of the tempo indications ; they are extremely uncertain. Generally it seems to me that by them Beethoven really means degrees of speed. When one considers, however, that he employs Allegro energico or Andante cantabile, these become, after all, indications of character. What is more, when one compares his metronome figures and sees that he demands minuets from (I believe) a crotchet per second to a dotted minim per second, every attempt at a uniform explanation is destroyed; the differences in respect of both pace and character are too great.

To let the speed be determined by the quickest notes is utter nonsense nowadays, when " great " artists like ... (and even ...) inevitably start to rush like mad when they get on to quick passages. [To this sentence Schoenberg adds a footnote :] The quick notes in the basic tempo are not quick enough for them to show their brilliant technique.

I have thought of drawing conclusions from the motivic content ; but that, too, is very difficult. I have used the expression " weight of content," but I don't think that this term can furnish a yard-stick. At least not without far-reaching modifications.

One of the chief difficulties seems to me to be caused by over-accentuating the strong beats of the bar (1 and 3 in 4/4). This is in the way of every possible good phrasing which, of course, claims its own accentuations. There should only be *one* accent in a phrase, except where some special characterization is involved.

I should be very glad to know what you think about all this. Once more—I think that the motivic content is to do with weight and hence with tempo.

With many most cordial greetings,

Yours Arnold Schoenberg.

February 26, 1951.

Item (13) is an air mail letter obviously written under physical difficulties. The first part (below in Roman type) is in Schoenberg's own (as distinct from his secretary's) typescript, the second (below in italics) in his Roman handwriting and in ink. His footnote is scribbled in pencil and shows his failing eye-sight most strongly. His two typed deletions are double-bracketed below.

(13) [Print :]

ARNOLD   SCHOENBERG   116   N.   ROCKINGHAM   AVENUE
LOS ANGELES 49 CALIFORNIA
                       [" 49 " typed over the printed " 24."]
Dr. Oskar Adler,   3 März. 1951
88, Abbey Road,
London, N.W.8
England.

Liebster Freund :
Eben erhielt ich Dein Buch, Das Testament der Astrologie. Ich habe mir einiges daraus schon vorlesen lassen, und finde alles was ich bisher kenne bewundernswürdig ; sowohl was Stil anbelangt, als was Gedanken anbelangt. Ich kann leider nicht selbst lesen—ich habe ein nervöses Augenleiden. Sehe, ich kann Schreibmaschine und kann sogar Zeitung eine ganz kurze Zeit lang ((lesen)) ohne Glas lesen. Glas kann ich überhaupt nicht ((lesen)) benützen, denn nach einiger Zeit verschwimmt mir alles vor den Augen. Deswegen muss ich es mir vorlesen lassen. Es tut mir besonders leid wegen deines Buches. Aber nach und nach [Here sentence and typescript break off.]

heute ist der 23. April und ich gebe die Hoffnung auf diesen Brief je zu vollenden. So werde ich dir vielleicht bald eine Sammlung*, die ich nenne :
" Psalmen, Gebete und andere Gespräche mit und über Gott "
senden und ich bin sicher du wirst mich verstehen. Also: viele innigste Grüsse,
                              Dein Arnold Schoenberg

[Schoenberg's footnote :] ich will noch vieles daran verbessern. Bis jetzt sind es 12—aber ich habe Material für 50 oder mehr : die religiösen Probleme unserer Zeitgenossen : [It is doubtful whether this is supposed to be a colon after which Schoenberg intended to add something, or whether he did not get his first full stop in the right place and therefore had to make a second one.]

Translation :

March 3, 1951
[to April 23, 1951.]

Dearest Friend :

I have just received your book, *The Testament of
Astrology.** I have already had some of it read to me and I
find everything I so far know admirable, in regard to both
style and ideas. Unfortunately I cannot read myself—I
suffer from nevous eye-trouble. I can see, I can type and
even read the paper for a very short time without glasses.
I cannot use glasses at all because after a time everything
fades before my eyes, which is why I have to have it read
to me. This grieves me particularly on account of your
book. But little by little [Here sentence and typescript
break off.]

*Today is the 23rd of April and I give up all hope of ever
completing this letter. So I may soon send you a collection†
which I call*

"*Psalms, Prayers and other Colloquies With and About
God*"
*and I am certain you will understand me. Well then, many
most affectionate greetings from the bottom of my heart,
Your Arnold Schoenberg.*

Item (14) is an air letter in typescript. Julian Herbage had asked
Humphrey Searle to suggest to Schoenberg a talk or series of talks
in the B.B.C.'s Sunday ' Music Magazine.' Herbage had not
attempted to suggest a subject because he felt sure that Schoenberg
would wish to talk about composing with twelve notes. The review
on which Schoenberg comments in his P.S. is Ernest Newman's of
Style and Idea in the *Sunday Times.*

(14)   Arnold Schoenberg
            116 N. Rockingham Ave.
            Los Angeles 49, California

May 25, 1951

*[Vienna-Mainfranken-Zürich, 1950.]
†[Schoenberg's footnote:] *I still want to touch up a great deal of it.
So far there are twelve, but I have material for fifty or more : the
religious problems of our contemporaries :* [see original above.]

Mr. Humphrey Searle,
44A Ordnance Hill
London N.W.8.
England

Dear Mr. Searle :

Your letter is at present in New York. If I should miss an answer to one of your questions, please repeat it.

—Your message that the B.B.C. will ask me for a lecture, to be spoken on a tape has suggested to me at once a subject : " Advice for Beginners in Composition with Twelve Tones." Unfortunately, when I conceived this idea, I had forgotten that television is not so general in use in England than in America. Thus I don't know whether this lecture which will use many musical examples, coming into effect only if one reads them, is acceptable for the B.B.C. There would still be a possibility to print in a cheap manner sheets containing the examples, if the B.B.C. can distribute them in time. Namely the examples will bring so many changes the improvement of which is perhaps less easily to realize by the ear than by the eye.

I must admit that this lecture will be very technical and direct itself to the higher educated musician, to those who can apply the advice I give them in their composition. Thus it is much less theoretical or aesthetical than technical-compositorial. Of course, musicologists might profit therefrom and add much of the knowledge I procure them to their tools of criticism. Besides, it will clarify many problems of this technique and prove how much inspiration must contribute in order to create a real work of art.

In case the B.B.C. would not like to broadcast and televise this lecture, I must know this at once, in order to conceive another idea and carry it out.

Please tell me as soon as possible, when about this lecture should be delivered. Perhaps B.B.C. suggests something herself where I can use my newly published records or some which have been privately made.

Looking forward to your response, I am with cordial greetings,

Yours,
Arnold Schoenberg

P.S. The review you sent me is very pleasant.

Schoenberg's death intervened.

Composing with Twelve Notes

By MATYAS SEIBER

This script, slightly edited for the present medium, was originally prepared for a 30 minutes' broadcast, and in such a short time the problems in question could obviously be only touched upon. The music examples given originally on the piano and on gramophone records are here reproduced in music type* though for reasons of space most of them have had to be shortened. The quotations from Schoenberg's 4th string Quartet are made by kind permission of G. Schirmer Inc., New York (Chappell & Co. Ltd., London).

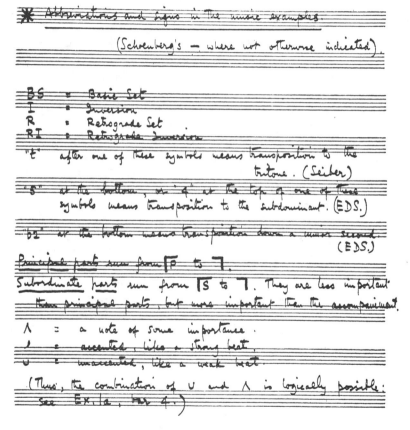

I'M afraid as soon as one starts talking about twelve-tone** composition one is apt to take up the attitude of an apologist, or a ' defender of the faith,' or something like that. But, let me assure the reader, this is not due to the crusading spirit of the followers of this method, but rather to the unreasonable attitude of so many musicians who spit blood and see red whenever the name ' twelve-note '** (or, Americanized : ' twelve-tone '**) music is mentioned. The most frequently heard objections are that this method is " arbitrary," " unnatural," " cerebral," and so on. Some years ago a friend of mine, a member of a famous string quartet, when he learned that one of my works was written according to the principles of this method, asked me rather condescendingly and sarcastically : " And now, tell me, what are the *rules of this game ?* " All right, I accept this : let's call it " rules of the game," but don't let us forget that the so-called " tonal " system of composition, with its harmony, counterpoint, etc., also has its " rules of the game " which must look just as arbitrary to the uninitiated. Here, at random, are just a few examples from standard textbooks :—

" Whenever 2 passing notes are used in succession *above* the Cantus Firmus, or whenever 2 passing notes and the 5th of the root are used in succession *below* the C.F., the melody must proceed in the same direction until an allowable harmony note is reached."

Or : " If resolved in the first of the 2 ways indicated, i.e. upon a Dominant discord, the 3rd of the super-tonic should fall a chromatic semitone to the 7th of the dominant and the 7th of the super-tonic should fall a minor 2nd to the 3rd of the dominant."

Or : " If the quaver and the unessential crotchet are in mutual dissonance, then the quaver must behave towards the latter as though it were an *essential* crotchet."

Or : " Rule 57 : The tritone progression might occur in a degree-progression if it appears as a constituent part of a sequence, or if one of its tones appears as neighbouring tone of a 5 or 4 progression."

I could continue this list for hours. And, I may add, I do not quote these rules to make fun of them ; because very good rules they are, codifications of common-sense practice evolved in the process of writing music. But anyone not conversant with the process of composition might well ask, quite bewildered : " How on earth can anybody write *music* with so many rules, regulations and restrictions in mind ? "

**Eric Blom and his forthcoming *Grove* are campaigning for the anglicized ' twelve-note.' After some hesitation as to which alternative to adopt, one of us (D.M.) has successfully suggested to the other that as an American citizen, Schoenberg had the right to have his own American technical term respected on this side of the Atlantic too. Resultant inconsistencies—obviously one has to speak of " the 12 notes of the chromatic scale " and indeed of " composing with twelve notes "—must needs be included in the bargain.—EDS.

The answer is, of course, that no one does ; one hasn't got to *think* consciously of these things all the time ; they become second nature to the composer through his training. In speaking we don't have to think consciously either whether we use a verb, a noun or an adjective and whether we connect them in the correct grammatical way ; these things become *automatic* through constant practice. But everybody who has had experience in teaching knows that the young student of composition has to be literally ' broken in ' until he can feel the necessity and justification of these rules and prohibitions.

At times, somebody who happens to like a twelve-tone composition will grudgingly admit that the composer succeeded in writing *real music* " in spite of the system." Very well then, but if this is true, we must also say that Bach " succeeded " in writing music in his *Art of Fugue* or *Musical Offering* " in spite of " all the contrapuntal and mathematical devices. And so had all the great composers of the contrapuntal era before him, whose works are full of the most complex contrapuntal ingenuities. Or again what about the ' Isorhythmic Motet ' of the Middle Ages ? The construction of this form shows an unparalleled rigidity, governed by strict numerical and geometrical principles ; and yet we find many works of great beauty written in this form. Compared with such practices, the method of twelve-tone composition seems very free and flexible, its regulations and restrictions not half as rigid as those of some earlier methods we accept by now as " natural." They would amount to something like this : don't repeat a note before the other eleven of our chromatic system have had their turn, in order to avoid the precedence of *one* note which might establish itself as a centre ; every particle of a piece, both melodically and harmonically, should have reference to a basic series of notes from which everything should stem.

The technique of " composing with twelve tones " was not suddenly ' invented ' by Schoenberg as an intellectual game ; on the contrary, it evolved slowly and organically from the actual creative process, just as did the rules of tonal composition. Twelve-tone technique is not a crossword-puzzle or acrostics ; it is not a 'system' either but a *method of working*. It is not theory, but *practice*.

Anybody who cares to examine the evolution of modern music will see how this idea gradually emerges and develops not only in Schoenberg's, but also in other composers' works.

I don't want to trace here the historical process of the gradual disintegration of tonality in the post-Wagnerian era. Through the increased use of all chromatic notes, through the incorporation of more and more remote key-relationships, the once so strong gravitational pull of a tonal centre became weaker and weaker, until it virtually ceased to exist. If a piece floats freely in the chromatic space and can be anywhere or nowhere at any given moment the composer does not make it more ' C major ' if he begins or ends with a C major chord. Schoenberg, as always, did not stop at half measures and thought his thoughts through to their logical end. He recognized the fundamental falsity of paying lip-service to an idea which, through historical collusion, lost its vital force and became an empty formula without inner meaning. He arrived at a point of complete freedom in the dimensions of melody and harmony, with only his instinct and his sense of balance as his guide.

But soon the necessity for a new order began to emerge. In a letter to Nicolas Slonimsky, Schoenberg described how he was groping his way for many years towards the realization of this new principle. As early as 1914 he sketched a movement with a theme consisting of all twelve notes of the chromatic scale, but, as he says, " I was still far away from the idea of using such a basic theme as a unifying means for a whole work. After that I was always occupied with the aim to base the structure of my music *consciously* on a unifying idea which produced not only all the ideas, but regulated also the accompaniment and the harmonies."

On the road towards a consistent twelve-tone technique the piano Pieces op. 23 and the *Serenade* op. 24 are important stations. In op. 23 we see Schoenberg working for the first time with tone-rows: the first piece, for instance, is based on 3 such rows, one of 21, the other of 20, the third of 13 notes. Another piece in this opus is based on a short series of 5 notes. The variation movement of the *Serenade* has a basic series of 14 notes which is used in a similar fashion as the later twelve-tone series. The first compositions " with twelve tones related only with one another," as Schoenberg called this method, were the last piano piece in op. 23, i.e. the *Waltz*, and the 4th movement of the *Serenade*, op. 24. " And here," Schoenberg writes (*ibid.*), " I became suddenly conscious of the real meaning of my aim : unity and regularity, which unconsciously led me this way."

Unity and regularity ! How is this achieved with the new method of composing with 12 notes ? In its classical formulation this method means that the basic idea of a piece should be presented in a series of notes, and that this series should contain the totality of our tonal resources, that is, all 12 semitones, in a characteristic order. The whole piece should be evolved from this basic set, by a process of continuous variation and development, so that every particle of the work can in some way be related to the basic idea. Both the horizontal and the vertical dimension of the musical ' space,' i.e. the melodic and harmonic aspects, are penetrated by the basic idea, so that not only the melodies but also the harmonies are regulated by the order of, and the relationships within, the series. To add greater variety to the resources, derivations of the basic set such as inversion, retrograde motion and transpositions are also used. For an example, take the main subject (Ex. 1: A+B+A^1) of Schoenberg's 4th string Quartet,

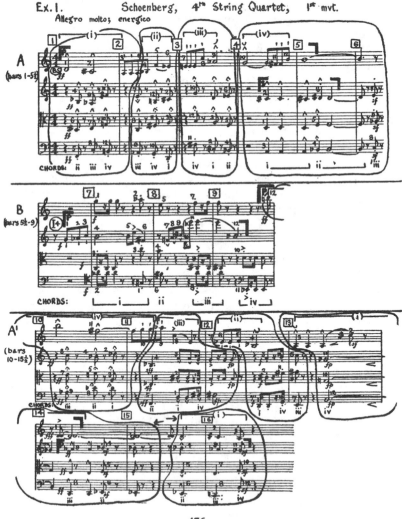

Ex. I.   Schoenberg, 4th String Quartet, 1st mvt.

where the basic set (Ex. 2a) is easily recognized, as it is contained in the energetic melody played by the 1st violin.

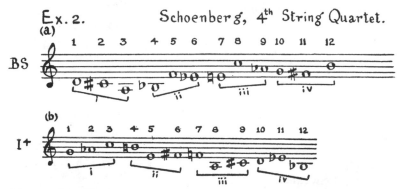

The melody is accompanied by marcato 3-note chords which, again, are built from the same series, so that notes 1-2-3 (D—C♯—A) form a chord (i); 4-5-6 (B♭—F—E♭) another (ii); 7-8-9 (E—C—A♭) a third one, (iii) ; and 10-11-12 (G—F♯—B) the fourth (iv). These chords appear in all sorts of positions and inversions, (i) for instance as Ex. 3, (ii) as Ex. 4 and so on. The chords are used in

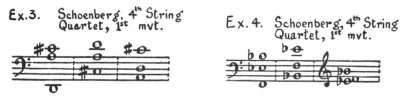

such a way that they complement the notes of the melody (see Ex. 1 : A). After the first statement (bars 1-5½) there is a shorter interim phrase or middle section of 3½ bars (bars 5½-9), based on the inversion of the basic series transposed to the subdominant, G (Ex. 2b). The accompaniment again consists of 4 three-note chords, built as before from neighbouring notes of this inverted series ; but a new rhythmic feature, Ex. 5, is introduced.

Ex. 5. Schoenberg, 4ᵗʰ String Quartet, 1ˢᵗ mvt.

After this there is a restatement (Ex. 1 : A¹) of the first, energetic part of the theme ; the melody, however, is now based on the retrograde form of the series, from the 12th note back to the 1st, and the accompaniment is enriched by imitations of the marcato quavers in bars 2 and 4 of Ex. 1:A (1st violin),*as well as by the dotted rhythm (Ex. 5) of the middle section.

*From Ex.1a.

As this article is only concerned with the purely *technical* aspects of twelve-tone composition, let me give some other instances from which, I hope, it will be gathered that this method is anything but mechanical. For instance, at the beginning (Ex. 6) of his 3rd string Quartet, Schoenberg employs

Ex.6. Schoenberg, 3rd String Quartet, 1st mvt.

quite a different method : the first 5 notes of the row (Ex. 7a) i.e.
G-E-D♯-A-C, are used as an ostinato in the middle parts,

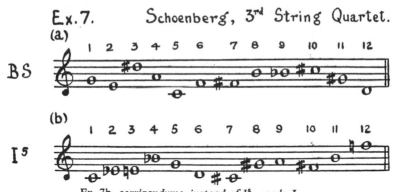

Ex. 7b, *corrigendum: instead of* I⁵, *read:* I₅.

while the remaining 7 notes, used with considerable freedom, group
themselves round them in the phrases of 1st violin and cello. In
the 2nd movement (Ex. 8), yet another method is employed.

The basic set (Ex. 7a) is distributed among the two violins in two-part harmony, while the viola plays a melody composed of the complete series : see Ex. 8. The consequent of the phrase (see Ex. 8) is based on the retrograde version of the inversion, again transposed to the subdominant (C): cf. Ex. 7b.

In the third movement, the lightish *Intermezzo* (see Ex. 9) the theme in the viola presents the basic set (Ex. 7a) while 2nd violin and cello play the accompaniment in 4-note groups, complementing the notes of the viola. The same arrangement is repeated with the retrograde version of the inversion transposed to C: cf. Ex. 7b. The theme is in recognizable ternary form, with the main statement of 6 bars, a middle section of 4 bars and a varied and extended recapitulation of 8 bars :

[Ex. 9 :—*Note the symmetrical arrangement of the accompaniment in bars 1 and 5, 2 and 4, and 3 and 6 respectively.*]

In the theme (Ex. 10) of the final Rondo movement, the notes are distributed with more freedom, in such a way that the minor ninth and major seventh intervals are emphasized. Like many classical rondo themes, this one has a symmetrical construction, falling distinctly into three sections of four bars each, according to the ABA pattern :

Ex. 10.   Schoenberg, 3rd String Quartet, 4th mvt.

[Ex. 10 :—*Note the 2-bar symmetry in the disposition of this theme. Bars 1 and 2 follow the same pattern of distribution, with 2nd violin and cello changing roles. In bars 3 and 4, 2nd violin and viola follow the same pattern. Bars 5 and 6 are entirely symmetrical, save for the inversion of intervals. As in many other works, Schoenberg uses, to start with, only 2 forms ; the basic series and its inversion transposed a fifth down (Ex. 7).*]

I have chosen on purpose examples from the same work, in order to show that the method is very flexible—that the number of characters, shapes, textures which can be drawn from the same series is practically limitless.

Another method, used by Schoenberg in his piano piece op. 33a, is to present the basic set in a number of chords. Luigi Dallapiccola

used this method in the striking opening (Ex. 11) of his opera
Il Prigioniero which made such a profound impression at last year's
ISCM Festival in Frankfurt :

Ex. 11.   Dallapiccola, opening of
"Il prigionero"

I used the same method in the fourth movement, the *Nocturne*,
of my *Ulysses* Cantata. I based this movement on a quotation, i.e.
the two chords from Schoenberg's op. 19, No. 6 (Ex. 12a). To these
two 3-note chords I added two supplementary ones (Ex. 12b).

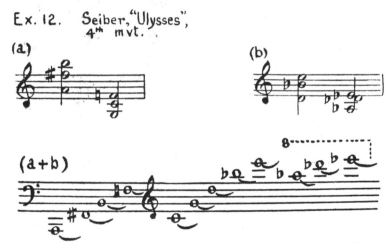

Ex. 12.   Seiber, "Ulysses",
4ᵗʰ mvt.

(a)

(b)

(a+b)

The four chords of Ex. 12a and 12b supply the material for the
whole movement. At one point all four chords are piled up on top
of each other, forming a twelve-tone chord containing all the notes
of our chromatic system (Ex. 12: a+b).

The methods of using the twelve-tone technique vary greatly with
different composers. There could hardly be a greater difference than
between Schoenberg's two principal pupils, Berg and Webern.
Berg had the tendency to include tonal elements, like triads, which
were at first rigorously excluded from dodecaphonic music. These

doubtless make his music the easiest to approach among the compositions of the Viennese school. A good example of this concession to 'tonal' listening habits is his last work, the violin Concerto. The basic set (Ex. 13) of this work consists of a succession of rising thirds, starting from G, and ends with three whole tones to complement the series :

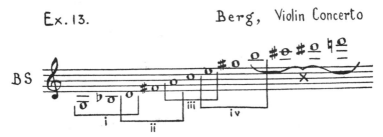

Ex. 13.   Berg, Violin Concerto

BS

Through this device, neighbouring notes of the series form G minor D major, A minor and E major chords (see Ex. 13 : i, ii, iii, and iv respectively), so that for instance the passage which introduces the first appearance of the complete series on the violin sounds entirely 'tonal', like tonic-dominant progressions in G minor and A minor (Ex. 14) :

Ex. 14.   Berg, Violin Concerto.

As the reader probably knows, Berg introduced the Bach Chorale " Es ist genug " in the last part of his Concerto. Here he was able to utilize the correspondence of that extraordinary ascending tritone at the beginning of the Chorale (Ex. 15)

Ex. 15.   Bach, Chorale "Es
                ist genug"

Es ist ge - nug!

with the last four notes of his series (the whole-tone sequence B—C♯—D♯—E♯; see Ex. 13: x). The Chorale melody is alternately

483

elaborated according to twelve-tone principles and shown in the original Bach harmonization.

Webern's method and style are the exact opposite of Berg's. Compared with Berg's lush harmonic idiom, Webern's will strike you as thin and ethereal. Against Berg's tendency to incorporate tonal elements, Webern's style is of the utmost strictness and logic. Here, indeed, one can speak of an almost 'astronomical' order which pervades every particle of this music, written with great economy and purity.

In his Songs op. 23 (cf. Ex. 18), Webern restricts himself to the straight and retrograde forms of the basic set (Ex. 16a), of *one* transposition to the tritone (Ex. 16b), and of their respective inversions (Exx. 16c and 16d):

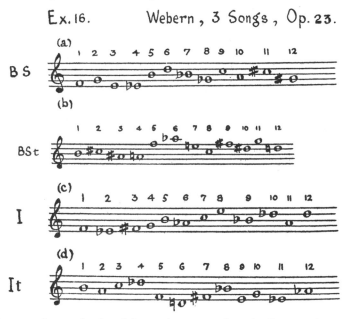

Ex. 16.   Webern, 3 Songs, Op. 23.

The row is manipulated in such a way that the harmonies are all derivations from Exx. 17a and 17b :

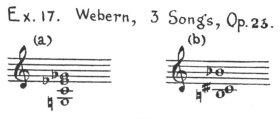

Ex. 17.   Webern, 3 Songs, Op. 23.

This method gives the songs a great unity and coherence, and an almost ascetic purity which is so typical of Webern's lyrical style (see Ex. 18) :

Ex. 18. Webern, first of the 3 Songs, Op. 23.

[Ex. 18 :—*Note how the pattern of the first 1½ bars is balanced by its inversion in the following 1½ bars. Throughout the piece Webern often lets the rows overlap, so that the last note becomes first of a new series (as in bars 3 and 6).*]

To those gloomy prophets who predict year after year that the method of twelve-tone composition has just been a "fashion" and is on the decline, I can only answer that as far as I can see, it is, on the contrary, increasing rapidly everywhere. In France, Italy, Switzerland, Germany, there are very strong groups of dodecaphonists, and the same is true for America and many South American states. Many composers adapt the method to their own particular needs and preferences ; others, while not actually employing the technique, have had their whole thinking strongly influenced by it. Composing of course, does not become easier by employing the twelve-tone method, and if a composer looks for an *easy formula*

485

for putting together a piece, he had better search elsewhere. It might suit some composers and might not at all suit others, just as employing a strict contrapuntal method might help some composers towards presenting their thoughts in a more comprehensive way, whilst it might cramp the style of others. But we still rightly insist that a young composer should have a good grounding in strict counterpoint, whether he is likely to employ it later in his compositions or not. I think Schoenberg is quite right when he says that " the time will come when the ability to draw thematic material from a basic set of twelve tones will be an unconditional requisite for obtaining admission into the composition class of a conservatory."

One of the strongest talents of my generation, Luigi Dallapiccola, has certainly improved immensely since he adopted the twelve-tone technique. Far from restricting his ideas or cramping his style, it seems to have liberated his colourful imagination. His song " La primavera ha venido " (see Ex. 20) on words by the Spanish poet Machado is built on a basic set of 6 rising notes (Ex. 19: a) answered by 6 falling ones (Ex. 19: b) which uses only major and minor seconds and minor thirds.

Ex. 19.   Dallapiccola, "La primavera ha venido."

BS♭2

Ex. 20.   Dallapiccola, "La primavera ha venido."

Voice

Piano

end of previous series

486

Curiously enough, quite independently, I availed myself of a similar principle a few years earlier, i.e. in the third movement of my *Ulysses*, the basis of which is a series of 6 ascending notes with regularly alternating minor thirds and minor seconds (Ex. 21: a) : answered by its inversion, (Ex. 21: b) :*

Ex. 21. Seiber, "Ulysses", 3rd mvt.

Dallapiccola, too, employs his rows with some freedom ; in the above-mentioned song (see Ex. 20), for example, he uses repeatedly a set of chords for which the order of the notes is slightly rearranged.

I have here written, as was my task in the original B.B.C. talk, mainly about the *technical* aspects of twelve-tone composition. I have done so somewhat reluctantly, because I know that to uncover the mechanics of a method might result in renewed assertions that the method is mechanical. But I think the reader has been offered enough examples to see that the possibility of writing music with this method are limitless. We must realize that the twelve-tone series only supplies the framework, a kind of ' pre-order,' as tonality has done before. But the tone-row certainly does not compose *itself !* The composer has to do that, now as before. And, as we have seen, the methods of composing still obey the same principles which evolved throughout centuries of European music, that is, the inven-

*Compare, moreover " the extremely close relation to, amounting to virtual identity with, Schoenberg's thematic thought in the *Ode to Napoleon* " which Hans Keller has shown in this journal's last issue, p. 434. By a strange coincidence, this relation first struck me when I listened to a recording of the *Ode* the night before I read Keller's article (which, incidentally, also draws attention to the recurrence of the thought in Malcolm Arnold's recent 1st string Quartet).

tion of some initial musical shapes, or themes, or motifs, and their development, variation, elaboration throughout the piece. In the examples tonight I showed you some of the *technique*, because it is technique alone which can be analysed. Anybody can learn the rules of fugue-writing and after a time construct a dry-as-dust textbook fugue without a spark of music in it. The same, I suppose, can be done by applying mechanically the rules of twelve-tone writing. But whether or not the result will be *music* depends entirely on the creative imagination, or *inspiration* of the composer. And nobody insisted more on the primacy—I could almost say "sanctity" —of inspiration than Schoenberg himself. How this born creator who just threw off his works in a white heat of inspiration, whose music teems with the most extraordinary ideas,—how this great composer can be dismissed as a kind of human calculating machine, is really beyond comprehension. *It is to the eternal shame of our time that it has let this great man die without the proper recognition of his genius.*

So now I would like to plead for a little more sanity in matters dodecaphonic. There is just as little reason to think that a work *must* be a masterpiece if it is written with the twelve-tone technique, as to reject it *ab ovo* as " no music at all." Those who like Berg's *Lyric Suite* will be scarcely disturbed because some of the movements are ' twelve-tone ' and others not. It does not make those movements either better or worse ; it's just that Berg chose this method of construction for certain movements while for others he preferred some other method. There never was, and never can be, any music without some sort of planning, construction, architecture. Those dark, germinating ideas which emerge from the depths of the unconscious have to be tamed, ordered, fashioned into an intelligible and coherent form. The twelve-tone technique is another way of achieving this.

I cannot see the twelve-tone method as an antithesis to tonality, but rather as an *extension* of it.* It brought about a re-orientation in musical thinking somewhat similar to the effect of the principle of relativity in the world of physics. In both cases, the new concept is the wider, more flexible, more comprehensive one ; it includes phenomena for which there was no room or explanation in the old system. Whilst in tonality—to use another simile—all lines converge towards a central note which can be likened to the vanishing point in perspectivic painting, in twelve-tone composition there is no such

*So did Schoenberg when he pointed the way from ' monotonality' over ' extended tonality ' to his own ' pantonality.' More about this in his forthcoming book on *Structural Functions of Harmony.*—EDS.

pull : the lines go from note to note, connecting the notes with *each other* in a certain way. Against the *centralized* character of classical tonality, I should call this a ' decentralized tonality,' but certainly not ' atonality,' which would mean a negation of all relationships between notes.

What Schoenberg strove for all his life is one of the eternal quests of musical composition : to develop a whole work from one germinal idea. The formulation of the twelve-tone principle showed a new way to achieve this end : *unity* and *coherence* within a musical work. Surely, this is not some diabolical, new-fangled invention, but a legitimate and noble aim, growing out of the tradition of European music of which Schoenberg was a very integral part.

Dodecaphony in Schoenberg's String Trio
By O. W. NEIGHBOUR

It is unfortunate that so many studies of Schoenberg's music concentrate on its dodecaphonic structure and ignore those aspects of form and style which give the works their character and value. My excuse for the present note is that the two essays on the same subject that I have seen are incomplete and therefore misleading. The first is in René Leibowitz's *Introduction à la musique de douze sons,* the second is William Hymanson's *Schönberg's** String Trio (1946)* in *The Music Review,* August, 1950. Both contain much that is valuable and my intention is to supplement, not to supersede them.

The following music example contains the material of the work :

There is no regular twelve-tone series.‡ Any group of six notes may be used with one of four other groups to make up the complete twelve. For instance, (I) finds its complement in its own inversion starting a fifth lower, in the corresponding inversion of (III), or in the original forms of (II) or (IV). The Trio is divided into three parts

*The Music Review persists in spelling " Schoenberg " as he spelt his name before he became an American.—Eds.
‡See footnote **p. 473.—Eds.

separated by two episodes. (I), (II), (III), and their inversions are introduced in the first four bars, and the first and second parts of the work are based entirely upon these groups with, of course, transpositions and retrograde forms. This idea was not new in Schoenberg, for he had made use of three groups of six notes bearing a similar relation to each other in the opera *Von heute auf morgen* (1929). The material of the two episodes is confined to groups (I) and (IV). The recapitulatory nature of the third part requires the use of all four forms, but (II) and (III) are still not used in conjunction with (IV).

Hymanson writes (p. 193) that " any group of six tones, taken from one of the half-rows, constitutes a unifying set of tones, regardless of the order." Such a statement, with certain qualifications, might not be out of place in a discussion of the *Ode to Napoleon* (1942),† but it does not fit the Trio. In the first place Hymanson has overlooked groups (III) and (IV) which explain some of the examples produced to support his view. Elsewhere he quotes minor irregularities such as those in bars 271 and 272 which are readily explained when they are seen in their context. For after using a certain pattern of serial distribution for a bar or so, Schoenberg will often introduce some variation which slightly disturbs the strict sequence of the series. Such cases are not peculiar to the Trio.

There is, however, one passage which does not derive from normal applications of the four groups. In the greater part of the second episode four new forms are used which are first built up from (I) and (IV). In bar 184, for example, the violin plays notes 1, 3 and 4 of (I) in counterpoint with notes 2, 5 and 6 on the viola in such a way that the series is heard in the slightly distorted order 132456. But immediately the cello plays the two phrases one after the other, producing the sequence 134256. By the same process the order of (IV) undergoes a parallel change, and the inversions of (IV) and (I) receive the form 643521. The four new forms are then subjected to the usual transformations during the course of the episode, though the normal forms of (I) and (IV) put in an occasional appearance. This is certainly an unusual piece of twelve-tone writing, but it remains serial and the constituent notes of the half-rows are not reshuffled haphazard.

†It is interesting to compare the varying linear arrangements of the six-note chord upon which much of the *Ode* is based with the serial versions (i.e. the two halves of the basic series and their inversions) in the *Suite* for seven instruments, op. 29.

Schoenberg: " George-Lieder," Op. 15
(DAS BUCH DER HÄNGENDEN GÄRTEN)
ESTHER SALAMAN AND PAUL HAMBURGER,
Third Programme, 10th January, 1952
by HUMPHREY SEARLE

So far as I know, this remarkable cycle of songs has not been given in England since Elisabeth Höngen's fine performance three or four years ago. All praise then to the present artists for learning it and to the B.B.C. for putting it on—it is a work that ought to be heard far more often, for it is one of Schoenberg's most beautiful and expressive creations, and being extremely " atmospheric," should not present much of a stumbling-block to the average intelligent listener. There were two drawbacks to the performance as I heard it, the first—an inevitable one with sound broadcasting—was that the words of the poems were read out immediately before each song, thus breaking up the continuity of the entire form. For the concert hall, one can print the words, and no doubt television could put them on a screen of some kind—but I don't see what else the Third Programme could have done. The other drawback (on my set at any rate) was that the studio or the recording (or both) made the tone sound extremely woolly and lacking in clarity and brilliance, and this did not help Miss Salaman's voice, which is on the low side for the part : Schoenberg had a soprano voice in mind.* The result, in spite of Mr. Hamburger's extremely sensitive and intelligent piano playing, tended to be monotonous and lacking in contrast. But a good deal of the curious atmosphere of these songs did succeed in getting across, and I hope we shall hear them again without so long to wait this time.

WE ARE ACCEDING TO THE I.S.C.M.'s REQUEST TO PUBLISH THE FOLLOWING NOTE UPON THE OCCASION OF THE 26TH I.S.C.M. FESTIVAL'S PERFORMANCE OF THE THEN 26-YEAR OLD ORAZIO BENEVOLI'S *MISSA SOLEMNIS* (1628) FOR 16 SOLOISTS, 4 CHOIRS, 6 ORHCESTRAS AND 2 ORGANS. THE 53-PART SCORE WAS COMPOSED FOR THE CONSECRATION OF THE SALZBURG CATHEDRAL WHERE IT IS TO BE PERFORMED ON JUNE 29TH.—EDs.

Zur Salzburger Auffuehrung von Orazio Benevolis Dom-Einweihungsmesse im Rahmen des 26. Internationalen Musikfestes.

ALS unter der Regierung des Erzbischofes Ernst Paris Graf Lodron (1619-1653) die Bauarbeiten am neuen Salzburger Dom endlich 1628 abgeschlossen waren,

*Few people, including musicians, are aware of this fact which I learnt from Erwin Stein, the greatest expert on these songs alive. (He coached them for the very first performance.) Thus Höngen was the wrong voice too (she recorded one of the songs with Mosco Carner), while the soprano Hilde Zadek recently expressed her regret to me that, not being a mezzo, she could not perform the " George-Lieder " (she had performed op. 6), and was completely surprised to hear from me that for that very reason she could. The Third Programme would not of course bother to find out about such things though they had Stein next door, with the result that Esther Salaman had to transpose several songs and—*pace* her achievement—neglect the work's harmonic structure—though it is true that the unavoidable reading of each poem before its song did so in any case.—ED.(H.K.).

491

wollte der Erzbischof die Einweihung des neuen Gotteshauses möglichst feierlich begehen und wandte sich an den römischen Komponisten Orazio Benevoli um Komposition einer den Verhältnissen des Salzburger Dome, eigens angepassten festlichen Messe, die alle Pracht der bis dahin bekannten Meisterwerke der römischen und venezianischen geistlichen Tonkunst übertreffen sollte.

Orazio Benevoli, damals erst 26 Jahre alt, aber als Meister der geistlichen Tonkunst schon in hohem Ansehen stehend, suchte in seinem Werk eine Synthese zwischen der von Palestrina auf den höchsten Gipfel geführten vokalen Satzkunst der römischen Schule und jener Eigentümlichkeit der venezianischen Schule, die die äussere Wirkung der gottesdienstlichen Musik noch durch den Einsatz mehrerer gegeneinandergestellter Chor- und Instrumental gruppen und durch die Verwendung solistischer Stimmen in Abwechslung mit den Chorgruppen zu steigern versuchte.

Gerade dieser letzteren Bestrebung Benevolis bot die Architektur des Salzburger Domes mit seinen zwei Orgeltribühnen an den Vierungspfeilern der Kuppel (die übrigens heute nicht mehr vorhanden sind) und den 12 von den Wänden in das Schiff hereinragenden " Marmor-Oratorien " ein reiches Feld, und dieser Architektur des Salzburger Domes ist auch das vielstimmige und vielchörige Konzept der berühmten Dom-Einweihungsmesse angepasst.   Die Partitur dieser einmaligen Messekomposition umfasst also folgende Klangkörper :

zwei 8-stimmige Chöre (die sich bisweilen in vier 4-stimmige auflösen),

zier solistische Vokal-Quartette,

zwei Streicher-Ensembles mit Violinen, Bratschen, Celli u. Bässen,

ein Chor von Holzbläsern (Flöten und Oboen), geführt von hohen Trompeten,

ein tragender Bläserchor von 2 Trompeten und 3 Posaunen, der als Zentrum mitten in der 53-linigen Partitur eingezeichnet ist.

Dazu kommen noch je 4 Blechbläser mit Pauken zum ersten und zweiten Vokalchor.   Beide Chorgruppen werden noch durch je eine Continuo-Orgel unterstützt.

Das stilistische Bild von Benevolis Komposition zeigt, dass der junge Meister schon damals den Geist der Renaissancemusik ziemlich überwunden hatte und weit in die barocke Sphäre vorstiess. Von der Imitationskunst, die in der römischen Kirchenmusikschule in hoher Blüte stand, wird in der Dom-Einweihungsmesse wenig Gebrauch gemacht, wahrscheinlich infolge der räumlichen Entfernung der einzelnen Chöre und Klanggruppen.   Hingegen ergehen sich namentlich die solistischen Gesangsstimmen in schwierigsten und virtuosen Koloraturen aller Art ; das erste und zweite Soloquartett hat die Exposition der Gedanken vorzutragen, während das dritte und vierte oft als eine Art Echowirkung verwendet wird.   Vielfach scheint der Stil des Werkes bereits die Tonsprache Händels vorauszuahnen.

Die Auffährung des gigantischen Werkes in den heutigen etwas beschränkten Raumverhältnissen des Salzburger Domes, stellt den Dirigenten Prof. Josef Messner vor verschiedene neue Aufgaben, die aber schon jetzt als befriedigend gelöst anzusehen sind.   Da die beiden Continuo-Orgeln stets alternierend verwendet erscheinen, ist es leicht möglich, beide Orgelparte auf der Hauptorgel zu spielen, zumal die Chororgel im Presbyterium ja nicht mehr existiert. Einzelne Klanggruppen werden hauptsächlich auf den Seitenemporen links und rechts im Kirchenschiff postiert werden, der Hauptbläserchor und die dominierenden Gruppen werden neben der Hauptorgel auf dem Orgelchor sitzen, von wo auch der Dirigent mit dem Rücken gegen die Orgel gewandt, einen Ueberblick über sämtliche Mitwirkende hat.

Die 53-stimmige Original-Partitur befindet sich als besondere Kostbarkeit im Besitz des Salzburger Städtischen Museums. Die Riesenpartitur ist von vorbildlicher Durchsichtigkeit und Uebersichtlichkeit, wie sie nicht einmal von Meistern der modernen Orchestrierungskunst erreicht werden konnte. Um die Rettung des kostbaren Autographs gebührt dem Domkapellmeister Innozenz Achleitner (er amtierte 1868-1881) besonderer Dank. Achleitner entdeckte die Partitur als Makulaturpapier bei einem Viktualienhändler, als gerade der Verkäufer ein Blatt herunterreissen und eine Ware darin einpacken wollte. Durch ein Trinkgeld konnte er sich in den Besitz des Autographs setzen und dieses dann dem Museum überantworten.

Correspondence

PRESS CLUB.

April, 1952.

DEAR DONALD MITCHELL,

You attack my *Evening Standard* article on Benjamin Britten. You do so as an extreme Britten devotee. My article ended with the assertion—sufficiently fulsome, I should have thought—that Mr. Britten is the finest thing that has happened to British music since Henry Purcell. But there is no satisfying extreme Brittenites. My offence is that I did not touch my forelock in every paragraph.

I do not propose to waste your space and my time in refuting your anxious strictures *seriatim*. But there is one rebuttal which must be made. Really you ought to think twice before accusing " the most expert of journalists " of using words sloppily or disingenuously. I never, in fact, wrote that Britten's dislike of Puccini was " childlike." This adjective crept into my article owing to an inadvertency which I had no opportunity of checking. The adjective of my choice was certainly severer.

You suggest that what I really meant to convey was " childish," " silly " or " puerile." I leave it to your readers to decide which epithet best suits a frame of mind (Mr. Britten's in December, 1945) which dismisses Puccini's music as mere " musical journalism."

Journalism is no mean craft. But it has not yet, so far as I am aware, produced either a *Trittico* or a *Turandot*. Nor has Mr. Britten.

Yours,

CHARLES REID.

Index

Compiled by Terence A. Miller

505

Martinon, Jean: *Sinfoniette*, 209 III
Martinu, Bohuslav:
  Double Concerto, 203 II, 275 II
  Sonata da Camera, 100 II
  Three Madrigals, **44** II
  Variations on a Theme of Rossini,
    44 II
  Violin Concerto, 204 III
Mary Barton (Cooke), 255 III
Maskarade Overture (Nielsen), 129 II
Mason, Ronald, on Britten's *Billy
  Budd*, 399 IV
Mathis der Maler (Hindemith), 11 II,
  80 II
Matrimonio Segreto, Il (Cimarosa),
  33-8 III
Max Reger (Haas), **194** II
May Day (Frankel), 276 II, 136 III,
  184 III
Mayer, Hans: 'Epic Theatre and
  Modern Music', 126 III
Mayfeld, Moriz v., 16 II
Mefistofele (Boito), **225** III
Meistersinger von Nürnberg, Die
  (Wagner), 239 III;
  at Bayreuth Festival, 417 IV,
    429-30 IV
  concert review (Stuart), **364-6** IV
  recordings, **129** II, **279** II, **215-20** II
Mellers, Wilfrid:
  on Blow's *Salvator Mundi*, **46** II
  on Britten's *The Beggar's Opera*,
    45-6 II, 233 II
  on Bush's English Suite, **184** III
  Carols, 73 II
  on Copland's *Danzon Cubano* and
    Hoe Down, **110** II
  Extravaganza, **267** II
  on Finzi's *Intimations of Mortality*,
    184 III
  Five Songs of Night, 74 II
  The Forgotten Garden, 74 II
  François Couperin..., **353-4** IV
  and Holst compared, 74 II
  Hutchings, A., on, **72-5** II
  list of works, 75-6 II
  on Milford's *Under the Greenwood
    Tree*, **259** II
  Motets in Diem Pacis, 55 II
  Music and Society, 73 II
  'News from Greece', 124 II
  on Orr's *Oedipus at Colonus*, **259** II
  on Orr's Sonata for Viola and Piano,
    110 II
  on Pitfield's Sonata for Flute and
    Piano, **260** II
  Prometheus, 73 II, 74 II, 75 II
  on Rawsthorne's Sonatina for Piano,
    110 II
  on Richardson's *French Suite*, **261** II
  on Rubbra's development, **187** III
  Ruth, 74-5 II, **202** II
  Shakespeare Songs, 74 II

String Trio, 74 II
Studies in Contemporary Music, 75 II
  on Vaughan Williams' Fantasia on
    the Old 104th, **191** III
  on Wellesz's *Essays in Opera*, **194** III
Melos (Mainz), 430-1 IV
Melville, Herman: *Billy Budd and
  other
  Stories*, 392-406 IV, 408 IV
Memories of Musick (North), 339 IV
Mendel, A. and H.T. David: *Bach
  Reader*, 129 III
Mendelssohn, Felix:
  Hussey, D., on, 13 III
  Violin Concerto in E minor, **281** II,
    78 III
Menuhin, Yehudi, 186 II, 66 III, 67 III
Mer, La (Debussy), 130 II
Mercury Record Company (U.S.A.),
  94 II
Messiah (Davie), 99 II
Messiah (Handel), 239 III
Messiah (Tobin), 362-3 IV
Messner, Joseph, 427 IV
Meyerstein, E.H.W.:
  on Bachauer, Gina, **273-4** II,
    379-81 IV
  on Bach's 'I call upon Thee, Lord,'
    103 II
  on Bach's *A Little Prelude*, **103** II
  on Balakirev, Mily, 66 III
  on Cecil Gray's *Autobiography*,
    39-41 II
  on Cherubini's C minor Requiem,
    59 II
  Mozart and Haydn compared, 201 II
  on Paganini, **59-60** II
  Richard Strauss, **90** II
  on Sceats' *Organ Works of
    Karg-Elert*, **265-6** II
  Schoenberg, obituary on, 314 IV
  on Schubert Songs, **108** II
  on *The Symphony* (ed. Hill), 13 III
  on Ujhelyi, Julius von, 59-60 II
  on Young's *Introduction
    to...Mendelssohn*, **264** II
Michaelides, Solon: *The Neohellenic
  Folk-Music*, **120** II
Mihalovici String Quartet No 3,
  189-90 II
Milan, La Scala Opera Company,
  126 III, **205** III
Miles, Maurice, 124 III
Milford, Robin: *Under the Greenwood
  Tree*, **259** II
Milhaud, Darius:
  Chansons de Ronsard, **105** II
  Ier Trio à Cordes, **190** II
  Le Pauvre Matelot, 125-6 III, 226 III
  Quatrains Valaisens, **190** II
  Scaramouche, 130 II
  Suite for Clarinet, Violin and Piano,
    273 II

520

527

530

533

535